or: The Spy Who Loved Travel

As Fodor's celebrates our 75th anniversary, we are honoring the colorful and adventurous life of Eugene Fodor, who revolutionized guidebook publishing in 1936 with his first book, *On the Continent, The Entertaining Travel Annual.*

Eugene Fodor's life seemed to leap off the pages of a great spy novel. Born in Hungary, he spoke six languages and graduated from the Sorbonne and the London School of Economics. During World War II he joined the Office of Strategic Services, the budding spy agency for the United States. He commanded the team that went behind enemy lines to liberate Prague, and recommended to Generals Eisenhower, Bradley, and Patton that Allied troops move to the capital city. After the war, Fodor worked as a spy in Austria, posing as a U.S. diplomat.

In 1949 Eugene Fodor—with the help of the CIA—established Fodor's Modern Guides. He was passionate about travel and wanted to bring his insider's knowledge of Europe to a new generation of sophisticated Americans who wanted to explore and seek out experiences beyond their borders. Among his innovations were annual updates, consulting local experts, and including cultural and historical perspectives and an emphasis on people—not just sites. As Fodor described it, "The main interest and enjoyment of foreign travel lies not only in 'the sites,' . . . but in contact with people whose customs, habits, and general outlook are different from your own."

Eugene Fodor died in 1991, but his legacy, Fodor's Travel, continues. It is now one of the world's largest and most trusted brands in travel information, covering more than 600 destinations worldwide in guidebooks, on Fodors.com, and in ebooks and iPhone apps. Technology and the accessibility of travel may be changing, but Eugene Fodor's unique storytelling skills and reporting style are behind every word of today's Fodor's guides.

Our editors and writers continue to embrace Eugene Fodor's vision of building personal relationships through travel. We invite you to join the Fodor's community at fodors.com/community and share your experiences with like-minded travelers. Tell us when we're right. Tell us when we're wrong. And share fantastic travel secrets that aren't yet in Fodor's. Together, we will continue to deepen our understanding of our world.

Happy 75th Anniversary, Fodor's! Here's to many more.

Tim Jarrell, Publisher

FODOR'S ITALY 2012

Editor: Matthew Lombardi
Editorial Contributors: Linda Cabasin, Robert Fisher
Writers: Nicole Arriaga, Martin Wilmot Bennett, Peter Blackman, Fergal Kavanagh, Bruce Leimsidor, Eric J. Lyman, Megan McCaffrey-Guerrera, Nan McElroy, Katie Parla, Sara Rosso, Patricia Rucidlo, Fiorella Squillante, Margaret Stenhouse, Mark Walters, Jonathan Willcocks

Production Editor: Carrie Parker
Maps & Illustrations: David Lindroth and Mark Stroud, *cartographers;* Bob Blake, Rebecca Baer, *map editors;* William Wu, *information graphics*
Design: Fabrizio La Rocca, *creative director*; Guido Caroti, *art director*; Jessica Walsh, Tina Malaney, Chie Ushio, *designers*; Melanie Marin, *associate director of photography*
Cover Photo: (Florence rooftops, viewed from the Duomo) Minerva Bloom, Fodors.com member
Production Manager: Angela L. McLean

COPYRIGHT

ISBN 978-0-679-00942-9

ISSN 0361–977X

SPECIAL SALES

This book is available at special discounts for bulk purchases for sales promotions or premiums. Special editions, including personalized covers, excerpts of existing books, and corporate imprints, can be created in large quantities for special needs. For more information, write to Special Markets/Premium Sales, 1745 Broadway, MD 3-2, New York, NY 10019, or e-mail specialmarkets@randomhouse.com.

AN IMPORTANT TIP & AN INVITATION

Although all prices, opening times, and other details in this book are based on information supplied to us at press time, changes occur all the time in the travel world, and Fodor's cannot accept responsibility for facts that become outdated or for inadvertent errors or omissions. So **always confirm information when it matters,** especially if you're making a detour to visit a specific place. Your experiences—positive and negative—matter to us. If we have missed or misstated something, **please write to us.** Share your opinion instantly through our online feedback center at fodors.com/contact-us.

PRINTED IN SINGAPORE

10 9 8 7 6 5 4 3 2 1

Fodor's 2012
ITALY
Fodor's Travel Publications New York, Toronto, London, Sydney, Auckland
www.fodors.com

CONTENTS

NORTHERN ITALY

CENTRAL ITALY

SOUTHERN ITALY

MAPS

ABOUT THIS BOOK

Our Ratings

At Fodor's, we spend considerable time choosing the best places in a destination so you don't have to. By default, anything we recommend in this book is worth visiting. But some sights, properties, and experiences are so great that we've recognized them with additional accolades. Orange **Fodor's Choice** stars indicate our top recommendations; black stars highlight places we deem **Highly Recommended**; and **Best Bets** call attention to top properties in various categories. Disagree with any of our choices? Care to nominate a new place? Visit our feedback center at www.fodors.com/feedback.

TripAdvisor

Fodor's partnership with TripAdvisor helps to ensure that our hotel selections are timely and relevant, taking into account the latest customer feedback about each property. Our team of expert writers selects what we believe will be the top choices for lodging in a destination. Then, those choices are reinforced by TripAdvisor reviews, so only the best properties make the cut.

For expanded hotel reviews, visit **Fodors.com**

Hotels

Hotels have private bath, phone, and TV, and do not offer meals unless we specify that in the review. We always list facilities but not whether you'll be charged an extra fee to use them.

Restaurants

Unless we state otherwise, restaurants are open for lunch and dinner daily. We mention dress only when there's a specific requirement and reservations only when they're essential or not accepted—it's always best to book ahead.

Credit Cards

We assume that restaurants and hotels accept credit cards. If not, we'll note it in the review.

Budget Well

Hotel and restaurant price categories from **¢** to **$$$$** are defined in the opening pages of the respective chapters. For attractions, we always give standard adult admission fees; reductions are usually available for children, students, and senior citizens.

Listings

- ★ Fodor's Choice
- ★ Highly recommended
- ✉ Physical address
- ✣ Directions or Map coordinates
- Mailing address
- ☎ Telephone
- Fax
- On the Web
- E-mail
- Admission fee
- Open/closed times
- Ⓜ Metro stations
- No credit cards

Hotels & Restaurants

- Hotel
- Number of rooms
- Facilities
- Meal plans
- ✕ Restaurant
- Reservations
- Dress code
- Smoking

Outdoors

- Golf
- Camping

Other

- Family-friendly
- ⇨ See also
- Branch address
- ☞ Take note

Experience Italy

WHAT'S NEW

Change comes slowly in the *Bel Paese*. There's a certain romance to the idea that the historical centers of Rome or Florence would be easily recognizable to residents 350 years ago.

Tiny cars and whining scooters in Italian cities and towns maneuver narrow cobblestone streets designed for horses and carriages; many restaurants rely on well-practiced classic dishes that haven't changed for decades; and some of the world's most magnificent classical architecture demands to be contemplated and studied rather than admired from the window of a passing vehicle.

But that timeless quality is matched by other aspects of Italian culture that are thoroughly modern. A proud G-8 nation and a founding member of the European Union, Italy is active on the international stage and modernizing its economy in an increasingly global marketplace. Status symbols like the newest car, most advanced smart phone, and latest designer threads abound. In numerous ways the country is indeed changing—but perhaps the change is slower than one might expect from a European country.

Train Upgrades

Some two decades after plans for a high-speed train network in Italy were first unveiled, and after more than €30 billion in expenditures, trains are moving faster.

Thanks to the new Alta Velocità lines, which can reach top speeds of more than 185 miles per hour, what was once a 4½-hour train ride between Rome and Milan can now be made in less than three hours. Rome to Florence now takes just over 90 minutes, Rome to Naples just over an hour, and Rome to Bari around four hours.

In 2011 new lines were set to open going farther south toward Reggio Calabria and eventually into Sicily. An east-west line is in the works linking Milan to Venice and Trieste.

The government is banking on the high-speed trains not only to link far-flung parts of the country more closely, but also to improve the environment by providing a more energy-efficient alternative to domestic air travel. For travelers from abroad, the faster service means it's easier to see more of Italy on a single trip.

Growing Immigration Conflicts

Over the past decades, as immigration to Italy from the Balkans, Eastern Europe, Africa, Asia, and the subcontinent have increased, so too has tension between Italy and its immigrant communities. Prominent political parties like the Lega Nord promote policies and expound rhetoric that are aimed at scapegoating Italy's foreign residents (both legal and illegal) for damaging the country's fragile economy and national character.

Further conflict seemed inevitable in 2011 as boatloads of immigrants arrived in southern Italy from war-torn North African nations. For years, Italy's deals with foreign governments kept immigrants out, but as these governments faltered and collapsed, the arrival of refugees skyrocketed, sparking protests and outrage in the cities of their arrival.

Old vs. New

For a country with a history and art tradition as rich and varied as Italy's, perhaps it shouldn't come as a surprise that when the present rubs up against the past, sparks can fly—often in a good way.

aThe most high-profile example of this phenomenon of modernity dates from 2010, when the MAXXI —the first

museum of twenty-first century art in Rome—opened north of the city center. The steel-and-concrete structure from Pritzker Prize–winning architect Zaha Hadid is a fascinating structure of volumes and curves that is perfectly integrated into its urban surroundings. Though immediately lauded for its beauty and innovation, it remains a rich topic for conversation and debate.

Film Festivals

At its peak, the Italian film industry was among the most respected in the world. Italy has still won more Oscars for foreign-language films than any other country, and the impact that renowned Italian maestros like Fellini, Rossellini, Antonioni, and De Sica have had on the film industry would be hard to overstate.

Notwithstanding occasional gems, Italy's present-day film industry falls short of its heyday. But when it comes to film festivals, Italy is moving stronger than ever.

The Venice Film Festival, started in 1932, is the oldest such festival in the world, and has long been known for its innovative lineup, as well as more than its fair share of glitz and glamour. Since its origin in 2006, the plucky Rome International Film Festival has made a place for itself, while more established events such as the Taormina Film Festival in Sicily and northern Italy's Turin Film Festival have grown in international importance.

All told, it's believed that Italy now has more film festivals than any other country.

Religion

Rome is still the spiritual home of the world's 1.1 billion Catholics, but church attendance in Italy has been eroding since the 1950s, and today fewer than one in five Italians attends church regularly. Nonetheless, religion maintains a powerful hold on Italian culture, with the Church regularly weighing in on political and social issues. Churches themselves remain a centerpiece of almost every Italian town, with the church on the main square the de facto meeting place for locals.

While church attendance slips, religion remains a hot topic in Italy as citizens react to increasing immigration from North Africa, Eastern Europe, Asia, the Middle East, and elsewhere. Today there are more different religions in Italy than at any point since Roman times—with Muslims, Protestants, Buddhists, Christian Orthodox, Jews, Scientologists, and Mormons all present. All told, slightly more than one in ten Italian residents is non-Catholic.

WHAT'S WHERE

1 Rome. Italy's capital is one of the great cities of Europe. It's a large, busy metropolis that lives in the here and now, yet there's no other place on earth where you'll encounter such powerful evocations of a long and spectacular past, from the Colosseum to the dome of St. Peter's.

2 Northern Italy. The prosperous north has Italy's most sophisticated culture and its most diverse landscape. **Venice** is a rare jewel of a city, while **Milan** and **Turin** are centers of commerce and style. Along the country's northern border, the mountain peaks of the **Dolomites** and **Valle d'Aosta** attract skiers in winter and hikers in summer, while the **Lake District** and the coastline of the **Riviera** are classic summertime playgrounds. Food here is also exceptional, from the French-influenced cuisine of **Piedmont** to Italian classics prepared with unrivaled skill in **Emilia-Romagna.**

3 Central Italy. No place better epitomizes the greatness of the Renaissance than **Florence,** where there's a masterpiece around every corner, from Michelangelo's *David* to Botticelli's *Venus.* Elsewhere, the central regions of **Tuscany** and **Umbria** are characterized by midsize cities and small hilltop towns, each with its own rich history and art treasures. Highlights include the walled city of **Lucca**; **Pisa** and its Leaning Tower; **Siena,** home of the Palio; and **Assisi,** the city of St. Francis. In between, the gorgeous countryside produces some of Italy's finest wine.

4 Southern Italy. The region of **Campania** is a popular place both to unwind—on the pint-size island of **Capri** or in the resort towns of the **Amalfi Coast**—and to explore the past—at the archaeological ruins of **Pompeii, Herculaneum,** and **Paestum**. In the middle of everything is the vibrant, chaotic city of **Naples**. Farther south, in the off-the-beaten-path regions of **Puglia, Basilicata,** and **Calabria,** you'll find attractive beaches, mysterious ancient dwellings, and the charming town of **Lecce.** Across a narrow strait from Calabria is **Sicily.** Baroque church-hopping could be a sport on the cacophonous streets of **Palermo** and **Siracusa,** while one of the world's best-preserved Greek ruins stand amid the almond groves of **Agrigento.**

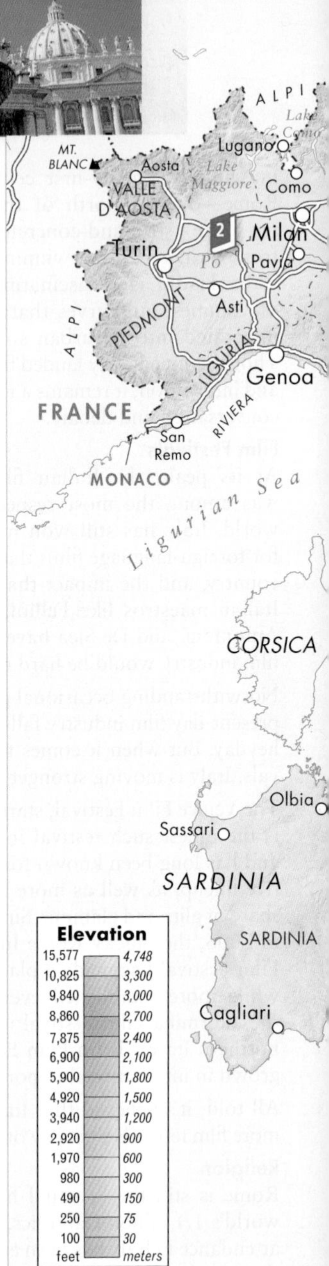

AUSTRIA
TRENTINO-ALTO ADIGE
Bolzano
FRIULI-VENEZIA GIULIA
Trento
THE DOLOMITES
Lake Garda
Udine
VENETO
SLOVENIA
Bergamo
Treviso
Trieste
Vicenza
Verona
Padua
Venice
CROATIA
LOMBARDY
Gulf of Venice
Parma
Modena
Ferrara
Bologna
EMILIA-ROMAGNA
Ravenna
Rimini
La Spezia
SAN MARINO
Pistoia
Lucca
Florence
SAN MARINO
Pisa
Arno
Livorno
TUSCANY
THE MARCHES
Ancona
Arezzo
Siena
Assisi
Perugia
ELBA
UMBRIA
Orvieto
Adriatic Sea
Terni
Pescara
MONTENEGRO
Tiber
ABRUZZO
ROME
Tivoli
LATIUM
MOLISE
Foggia
CAMPANIA
Bari
Naples
VESUVIUS
Potenza
PUGLIA
Brindisi
ISCHIA
Amalfi
CAPRI
Taranto
Lecce
BASILICATA
Paestum
Tyrrhenian Sea
Gulf of Taranto
Cosenza
Catanzaro
AEOLIAN ISLANDS
CALABRIA
EGADI ISLANDS
Palermo
Messina
Reggio
ETNA
SICILY
Mediterranean Sea
Catania
Agrigento
Siracusa
Ionian Sea
TUNIS
SICILY
TUNISIA
PANTELLERIA
0
100 miles
0
150 km
1
3
4

ITALY PLANNER

Getting Here

The major gateways to Italy are Rome's Aeroporto Leonardo da Vinci (FCO), better known as Fiumicino, and Milan's Aeroporto Malpensa (MAL). There are some direct flights to secondary airports, primarily Venice and Pisa, but to fly into most other Italian cities you need to make connections at Fiumicino, Malpensa, or another European hub. You can also take the FS airport train to Rome's Termini station or a bus to Milan's central train station (Centrale) and catch a train to any other location in Italy. It will take about one hour to get from either Fiumicino or Malpensa to the train station.

Italy's airports are not known for being new or efficient. They all have restaurants and snack bars, and there's Internet access. Each airport has at least one nearby hotel. Ramped-up security measures may include random baggage inspection and bomb-detection dogs. In the case of Florence and Pisa, the city centers are only a 15-minute taxi ride away—so if you encounter a long delay, spend it in town.

For further information about getting where you want to go, see "Getting Here" at the beginning of each section of this book.

What to Pack

In summer, stick with light clothing, as things can get steamy in June, July, and August. But throw in a sweater in case of cool evenings, especially if you're headed for the mountains and/or islands. Sunglasses, a hat, and sunblock are essential. Brief summer afternoon thunderstorms are common in inland cities, so an umbrella will come in handy. In winter, bring a coat, gloves, hats, scarves, and boots. In winter, weather is generally milder than in the northern and central United States, but central heating may not be up to your standards, and interiors can be cold and damp; take wools or flannel rather than sheer fabrics. Bring sturdy shoes for winter and comfortable walking shoes in any season.

As a rule, Italians dress exceptionally well. They don't usually wear shorts. Men aren't required to wear ties or jackets anywhere, except in some of the grander hotel dining rooms and top-level restaurants, but are expected to look reasonably sharp—and they do. Formal wear is the exception rather than the rule at the opera nowadays, though people in expensive seats usually do get dressed up.

A certain modesty of dress (no bare shoulders or knees) is expected in churches, and strictly enforced in many.

For sightseeing, **pack a pair of binoculars**; they'll help you get a good look at painted ceilings and domes. If you stay in budget hotels, **take your own soap.** Many such hotels do not provide it, or they give guests only one tiny bar per room. Washcloths, also, are rarely provided even in three- and four-star hotels.

Restaurants: The Basics

A full meal in Italy has traditionally consisted of five courses, and every menu you encounter will still be organized along some version of this five-course plan.

■ First up is the *antipasto* (appetizer), often consisting of cured meats or marinated vegetables. Next to appear is the *primo*, usually pasta or soup, and after that the secondo, a meat or fish course with, perhaps, a *contorno* (vegetable dish) on the side. A simple *dolce* (dessert) rounds out the meal.

■ This, you've probably noticed, is a lot of food. Italians have noticed as well—a full, five-course meal is an indulgence usually reserved for special occasions. Instead, restaurant meals are a mix-and-match affair: you might order a primo and a secondo, or an antipasto and a primo, or a secondo and a contorno.

■ The crucial rule of restaurant dining is that you should order at least two courses. It's a common mistake for tourists to order only a secondo, thinking they're getting a "main course" complete with side dishes. What they wind up with is one lonely piece of meat.

Hotels: The Basics

Hotels in Italy are usually well maintained (especially if they've earned our recommendation in this book), but in some respects they won't match what you find at comparably priced U.S. lodgings. Keep the following points in mind as you set your expectations, and you're likely to have a good experience:

■ First and foremost, rooms are usually smaller, particularly in cities. If you're truly cramped, ask for another room, but don't expect things to be spacious.

■ A "double bed" is commonly two singles pushed together.

■ In the bathroom, tubs are not a given—request one if it's essential. In budget places, showers sometimes use a drain in the middle of the bathroom floor. And washcloths are a rarity.

■ Most hotels have satellite TV, but there are fewer channels than in the United States, and only one or two will be in English.

■ Don't expect wall-to-wall carpeting. Particularly outside the cities, tile floors are the norm.

Speaking the Language

In most cities and many towns you won't have a hard time finding locals who speak at least rudimentary English. Odds are if the person you want to talk with doesn't know English, there will be someone within earshot who can help translate. The farther south you travel, the fewer English speakers you'll encounter, but if nothing else someone at your hotel will know a few words. No matter where in Italy you're going, if you learn some common phrases in Italian, your effort will be appreciated.

Italy from Behind the Wheel

Americans tend to be well schooled in defensive-driving techniques. Many Italians are not. When you hit the road, don't be surprised to encounter tailgating and high-risk passing. Your best response is to take the same safety-first approach you use at home. On the upside, Italy's roads are very well maintained. Note that wearing a seat belt and having your lights on at all times are required by law. Bear in mind that a vehicle in Italian cities is almost always a liability, but outside of the cities it's often crucial. An effective strategy is to start and end your Italian itinerary in major cities, car-free, and to pick up wheels for countryside touring in between.

ITALY TODAY

. . . is eating well

The old joke says that three-quarters of the food and wine served in Italy is good . . . and the rest is amazing. If that's true, the "good" 75% is getting even better.

Italy is home of one of the world's greatest cuisines, so it may seem disingenuous to claim that it's improving—but it clearly is. Ingredients that in the past were available only to the wealthy can now be found even in the remotest parts of the country at reasonable prices. Dishes originally conceived to make the most of inferior cuts of meat or the least flavorful part of vegetables are now made with the best.

The same is true of Italian wine. A generation ago, the omnipresent straw-basket Chianti was a mainstay of pizzerias around the world, but the wine inside was often watery and insipid. Today, through investment and experimentation, Italy's winemakers are figuring out how to get the most from their gorgeous vineyards. It's fair to say that Italy now produces more types of high-quality wine from more different grape varieties than any other country in the world.

Italian restaurateurs are keeping up with the changes. Though quaint family-run trattorias with checkered tablecloths, traditional dishes, and informal atmosphere are still common, there's no doubt that they're on the decline. And nearly every town has a newer eatery with matching flatware, a proper wine list, and an innovative menu.

. . . is passionate about soccer

Soccer stands without rival as the national sport of Italy, but recent years have seen some changes to the beautiful game. On the positive side, Italy won its fourth World Cup in 2006, giving the country more world titles than any other this side of Brazil. But since then, soccer lovers have digested a series of unwelcome developments involving alleged match fixing, backroom deals for television contracts, drug scandals among players, and a rising level of violence between rival fans.

Italian professional soccer leagues are trying to put those issues behind them and focus on on-the-field play, where the Italian leagues rank with England and Spain as the best in Europe. One emerging positive trend is geographic parity. After several years of the top *Serie A* league's being dominated by northern teams, along with a handful from the central part of the country, success recently has been spread more evenly around, much to the joy of soccer-mad fans from the south.

. . . endures ongoing political upheaval

The political landscape in Italy is less stable than in any other industrialized nation. The country has endured a new government an average of about once a year since the end of World War II, and hopes are slim that the situation will change much in the near future.

This virtual turnstile outside the prime minister's office takes its toll on Italy: economic growth is slow in part because businesses are continually adapting to new government policies, and polls show that rank-and-file Italians are increasingly cynical about their political institutions. As a result, they're much less likely to trust in or depend on the government than neighbors elsewhere in Europe do.

. . . is getting older

Italy's popultation is the oldest in Europe (worldwide, only Japan is older)—the result of its low birth rate, relatively strict immigration standards, and one of the highest life expectancy rates in the world.

As of 2010, the average Italian was 42.9 years old, and the number keeps rising.

The result is a remarkably stable population: the total number of Italian residents barely rises most years, and, according to the most recent estimates, is projected to start contracting by 2020. But the situation is putting a strain on the country's pension system and on families, since elderly family members are likely to live with their children or grandchildren in a country where nursing homes are rare.

The trend also has an impact on other areas, including politics (where older politicians are eager to promote policies aimed at older voters), the popular culture (where everything from fashion to television programming takes older consumers into consideration), and a kind of far-reaching nostalgia; thanks to a long collective memory, it's common to hear even younger Italians celebrate or rue something that happened 50 or 60 years earlier as if it had just taken place.

. . . lives with a black-market economy

Nobody knows how big Italy's black-market economy is, though experts all agree it's massive. Estimates place it at anywhere from a fourth to a half of the official, legal economy.

Put another way, if the highest estimates are correct, Italy's black market is about as large as the entire economy of Switzerland or Indonesia. If the estimated black-market figures were added to the official GDP, Italy would likely leapfrog France and the U.K. to become the world's fifth-largest economy.

The presence of the black market isn't obvious to the casual observer, but whenever a customer isn't given a printed receipt in a store or restaurant, tobacco without a tax seal is bought from a street seller, or a product or service is exchanged for another product or service, that means the transaction goes unrecorded, unreported, and untaxed.

. . . has a growing parks system

Italy boasts 25 national parks covering a total of around 1.5 million hectares (58,000 square mi), or about 5% of the entire surface area of the country—more than twice as much as 25 years ago. And a new park is added or an existing park is expanded every few months.

Part of the reason for the expansion has been a growing environmental movement in Italy, which has lobbied the government to annex undeveloped land for parks, thus protecting against development. But the trend is a boon for visitors and nature lovers, who can enjoy huge expanses of unspoiled territory.

. . . is staying home in August

Italy used to be the best example of Europe's famous August exodus—where city dwellers would spend most of the month at the seaside or in the mountains, leaving the cities nearly deserted. Today the phenomenon continues, but is much less prevalent, as economic pressures have forced companies to keep operating through August. As a result, vacations are more staggered and vacationers' plans are often more modest.

The loss of shared vacation time for Italian workers can be an advantage for visitors, both because in August there's more room at the seaside and in the mountains, and because cities have taken to promoting local events designed to appeal to residents who are staying put. These days, summers in Italy boast a plethora of outdoor concerts and plays; longer restaurant and museum hours; and food, wine, and culture fairs.

ITALY TOP ATTRACTIONS

The Vatican

(A) The home of the Catholic Church, a tiny independent state tucked within central Rome, holds some of the city's most spectacular sights, including St. Peter's Basilica, the Vatican Museums, and Michelangelo's Sistine Chapel ceiling. *(⇨ Chapter 1.)*

Ancient Rome

(B) The Colosseum and the Roman Forum are remarkable ruins from Rome's ancient past. Sitting above it all is the Campidoglio, with a piazza designed by Michelangelo and museums containing one of the world's finest collections of ancient art. *(⇨ Chapter 1.)*

Venice's Grand Canal

A trip down Venice's "Main Street," whether by water bus or gondola, is a signature Italian experience. *(⇨ Chapter 3.)*

Palladio's Villas and Palazzi

The 16th-century genius Andrea Palladio is one of the most influential figures in the history of architecture. You can visit his creations in his hometown of Vicenza, in and around Venice, and outside Treviso. *(⇨ Chapter 4.)*

Ravenna's Mosaics

This town off the Adriatic, once the capital of the Western Roman Empire and seat of the Byzantine Empire in the West. is home to 5th- and 6th-century mosaics that rank among the greatest art treasures in Italy. *(⇨ Chapter 9.)*

Galleria degli Uffizi, Florence

The Uffizi—Renaissance art's hall of fame—contains masterpieces by Leonardo, Michelangelo, Raphael, Botticelli, Caravaggio, and dozens of other luminaries. *(⇨ Chapter 10.)*

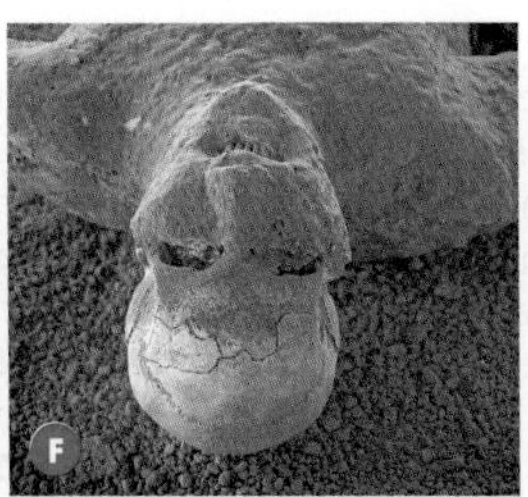

Duomo, Florence

(C) The massive dome of Florence's Cathedral of Santa Maria del Fiore (aka the Duomo) is one of the world's great feats of engineering. *(⇨ Chapter 10.)*

Piazza del Campo, Siena

(D) Siena is Tuscany's classic medieval hill town, and its heart is the Piazza del Campo, the beautiful, one-of-a-kind town square. *(⇨ Chapter 11.)*

Basilica di San Francesco, Assisi

(E) The giant basilica—made up of two churches, one built on top of the other—honors St. Francis with its remarkable fresco cycles. *(⇨ Chapter 12.)*

Palazzo Ducale, Urbino

No other building better exemplifies the principles and ideals of the Renaissance than this palace in the Marches region, east of Umbria. *(⇨ Chapter 12.)*

The Ruins of Pompeii

(F) When Vesuvius erupted in AD 79, its fallout froze the town of Pompeii in time. Walking its streets brings antiquity to life. *(⇨ Chapter 13.)*

Ravello, on the Amalfi Coast

(G) Nowhere else better captures the essence of the gorgeous Amalfi Coast than Ravello. Perched high above the Tyrrhenian Sea, it's the place to go for your blissful *la dolce vita* moment. *(⇨ Chapter 13.)*

Lecce, Puglia

With its lavish baroque architecture and engaging street life, Lecce takes the prize for the most appealing town in Italy's deep south. *(⇨ Chapter 14.)*

Valle dei Templi, Sicily

(H) The Greek influence in Sicily dates to ancient days, as is borne out by these well-preserved temple ruins. *(⇨ Chapter 15.)*

TOP EXPERIENCES

Church Going

Few images are more identifiable with Italy than the country's great churches, amazing works of architecture that often took centuries to build. The name Duomo (derived from the Latin for "house," *domus*, and the root of the English "dome") is used to refer to the principal church of a town or city. Generally speaking, the bigger the city, the more splendid its duomo. Still, impressive churches inhabit some unlikely places—in the Umbrian hill towns of **Assisi** and **Orvieto,** for example *(⇨ Chapter 12).*

In Venice the Byzantine-influenced **Basilica di San Marco** *(⇨ Chapter 3)* is a testament to the city's East-meets-West character. **Milan's Duomo** *(⇨ Chapter 6)* is the largest, most imposing Gothic cathedral in Italy. The spectacular dome of **Florence's Duomo** *(⇨ Chapter 10)* is a work of engineering genius. The **Basilica di San Pietro** in Rome *(⇨ Chapter 1)* has all the grandeur you'd expect from the seat of the Catholic Church. And Italy's classical past is on display at **Siracusa's Duomo** *(⇨ Chapter 15)*, which incorporates the columns of a 6th-century BC Greek temple.

Driving the Back Roads

If you associate Italian roads with unruly motorists and endless traffic snarls, you're only partly right. Along the rural back roads, things are more relaxed. You might stop on a lark to take a picture of a crumbling farmhouse, have a coffee in a time-frozen hill town, or enjoy an epic lunch at a rustic *agriturismo* inaccessible to public transportation. Driving, in short, is the best way to see Italy.

Among the countless beautiful drives, these are three of the most memorable: the legendary mountain ascent on **SS48, the Grande Strada delle Dolomiti** *(⇨ Chapter 5)*, takes you through the heart of the Dolomites, the famous Passo di Sella, and into the Val Gardena, passing unforgettable, craggy-peaked views. Every time the A1 autostrada tunnels through the mountains, the smaller **SS1, Via Aurelia** *(⇨ Chapter 8)*, stays out on the jagged coastline of the Italian Riviera, passing terraced vineyards, cliff-hanging villages, and shimmering seas. **SS222, the Strada Chiantigiana** *(⇨ Chapter 11)*, between Florence and Siena meanders through classic Tuscan landscapes. Be aware that Italian roads are often poorly marked. It helps to know a little geography, as many signs indicate the town the road leads to, but not what the road number is.

Hiking the Hills

Even if you don't fancy yourself a disciple of Reinhold Messner (the favorite son of the Dolomites and the first man to reach the peak of Everest without oxygen), you'll find great summer hiking aplenty all over Italy. The **Vie Ferrate (Iron Paths)** are reinforced trails through the mountains of Trentino–Alto Adige *(⇨ Chapter 5)*, once forged by the Italian and Austro-Hungarian armies; they're a great way to get off the beaten path in the Dolomites.

The **Cinque Terre**—five cliff-clinging villages along the Italian Riviera *(⇨ Chapter 8)*—are spectacular, and they're all connected by hiking trails with memorable views of the towns, the rocks, and the Ligurian Sea. In Umbria *(⇨ Chapter 12)* you can hike the **Paths of St. Francis** outside Assisi. An easy half-hour walk takes you from the town of Cannara to Pian d'Arca, site of St. Francis's sermon to the birds; with a bit more effort you can make the walk from Assisi to the Eremo delle Carceri, and from here to the summit of Monte Subasio, which has views for miles in every direction.

Tasting the Wine

When it comes to wine making, the Italian Renaissance is happening right now: from tip to toe, vintners are challenging themselves to produce wines of ever-higher quality. You can taste the fruits of their labor at wine bars and restaurants throughout the country, and in many areas you can visit the vineyards as well.

For touring guidance in the northeastern region of the Veneto, see **Traveling the Wine Roads** (⇨ *Chapter 4*). For the lowdown on Italy's "King of Wines," see **On the Trail of Barolo** (⇨ *Chapter 7*). And for a full primer on the wines of Tuscany, see **Grape Escapes** (⇨ *Chapter 11*).

Picking up Some Italian Style

"Made in Italy" is synonymous with style, quality, and craftsmanship, whether it refers to high fashion or Maserati automobiles.

Every region has its specialties: Venice is known for glassware, lace, and velvet; Milan and Como for silk; and the Dolomites and the mountains of Calabria and Sicily for hand-carved wooden objects. Bologna and Parma are the places for hams and cheeses; Modena for balsamic vinegar; Florence for straw goods, gold jewelry, leather, and paper products (including beautiful handmade notebooks); Assisi for embroidery; and Deruta, Gubbio, Vietri, and many towns in Puglia and Sicily for ceramics.

In Milan, Italy's fashion capital, the streets of the **Quadrilatero** district (⇨ *Chapter 6*) are where to go for serious shopping—or just for taking in the chic scene. Rome's **Piazza di Spagna** (⇨ *Chapter 1*) is another mecca for high-fashion shopping, and a few steps away is the Via del Corso, with more than a mile of stores of all varieties. To be overwhelmed by the aromas of Emilia-Romagna's legendary food, head to **Tamburini** in Bologna (⇨ *Chapter 9*), where you can get vacuum-packed delicacies to take home with you.

Il Dolce Far Niente

"The sweetness of doing nothing" has long been an art form in Italy. This is a country in which life's pleasures are warmly celebrated, not guiltily indulged.

Of course, doing "nothing" doesn't really mean nothing. It means doing things differently: lingering over a glass of wine for the better part of an evening as you watch the sun slowly set; savoring a slow and flirtatious evening *passeggiata* along the main street of a little town; and making a commitment—however temporary—to thinking that there's nowhere that you have to be next, and no other time than the magical present.

In the quiet, stunningly positioned hilltop village **Ravello** above the Amalfi Coast (⇨ *Chapter 13*), it's easy to achieve such a state of mind. The same holds true for **Bellagio**, on Lake Como (⇨ *Chapter 6*), where you can meander through stately gardens, dance on the wharf, or just watch the boats float by in the shadow of the Alps.

And there's still nothing more romantic than a **gondola ride** along Venice's canals (⇨ *Chapter 3*), your escorted trip to nowhere, watched over by Gothic palaces with delicately arched eyebrows.

QUINTESSENTIAL ITALY

Il Caffè (Coffee)

The Italian day begins and ends with coffee, and more cups of coffee punctuate the time in between. To live like the Italians do, drink as they drink, standing at the counter or sitting at an outdoor table of the corner bar. (In Italy, a "bar" is a coffee bar.) A primer: *caffè* means coffee, and Italian standard issue is what Americans call espresso—short, strong, and usually taken very sweet. *Cappuccino* is a foamy half-and-half of espresso and steamed milk; cocoa powder *(cacao)* on top is acceptable, cinnamon is not. If you're thinking of having a cappuccino for dessert, think again—Italians drink only caffè or caffè *macchiato* (with a spot of steamed milk) after lunchtime. Confused? Homesick? Order caffè *americano* for a reasonable facsimile of good-old filtered joe. Note that you usually pay for your coffee first, then take your receipt to the counter and tell the barista your order.

Il Calcio (Soccer)

Imagine the most rabid American football fans—the ones who paint their faces on game day and sleep in pajamas emblazoned with the logo of their favorite team. Throw in a dose of melodrama along the lines of a tear-jerking soap opera. Ratchet up the intensity by a factor of 10, and you'll start to get a sense of how Italians feel about their national game, soccer—known in the mother tongue as *calcio*. On Sunday afternoons throughout the long September-to-May season, stadiums are packed throughout Italy. Those who don't get to games in person tend to congregate around television sets in restaurants and bars, rooting for the home team with a passion that feels like a last vestige of the days when the country was a series of warring medieval city-states. How calcio mania affects your stay in Italy depends on how eager you are to get involved. At the very least, you may

If you want to get a sense of contemporary Italian culture and indulge in some of its pleasures, start by familiarizing yourself with the rituals of daily life. These are a few highlights—things you can take part in with relative ease.

notice an eerie Sunday-afternoon quiet on the city streets, or erratic restaurant service around the same time, accompanied by cheers and groans from a neighboring room. If you want a memorable, truly Italian experience, attend a game yourself. Availability of tickets may depend on the current fortunes of the local team, but they often can be acquired with help from your hotel concierge.

Il Gelato (Ice Cream)

During warmer months, gelato—the Italian equivalent of ice cream—is a national obsession. It's considered a snack rather than a dessert, bought at stands and shops in piazzas and on street corners, and consumed on foot, usually at a leisurely stroll *(see La Passeggiata, below)*. Gelato is softer, less creamy, and more intensely flavored than its American counterpart. It comes in simple flavors that capture the essence of the main ingredient. (You won't find Chunky Monkey or Cookies 'n' Cream.) Standard choices include pistachio, *nocciola* (hazelnut), caffè, and numerous fresh-fruit varieties. Quality varies; the surest sign that you've hit on a good spot is a line at the counter.

La Passeggiata (Strolling)

A favorite Italian pastime is the passeggiata (literally, the promenade). In the late afternoon and early evening, especially on weekends, couples, families, and packs of teenagers stroll the main streets and piazzas of Italy's towns. It's a ritual of exchanged news and gossip, window-shopping, flirting, and gelato-eating that adds up to a uniquely Italian experience. To join in, simply hit the streets for a bit of wandering. You may feel more like an observer than a participant, until you realize that observing is what la passeggiata is all about.

MAKING THE MOST OF YOUR EUROS

Below are suggestions for ways to save money on your trip, courtesy of the Travel Talk Forums at Fodors.com.

Transportation

"I take regional trains instead of the Eurostar trains. For example, Florence to Rome on Eurostar is 32.50 euro; the regional train is 15.80 euro. That's half the price; so what if it takes 15 minutes longer . . . big deal." —JoanneH

"Instead of taking the Leonardo Express from Fiumicino to Termini in Rome, take the FR1 to whichever station is most convenient for you. The FR1 departs every 15 minutes (instead of every 30 minutes for the Express), costs only €5.50 (instead of €10.50 for the Express), and avoids the hullabaloo of Termini." —Therese

Food and Drink

"Buy snacks and bottled water in bulk at a neighborhood supermarket at the beginning of your stay and keep them cool in your apartment or hotel fridge. Grab a bottle each when leaving in the AM and that way avoid buying expensive water or snacks near tourist attractions, where prices are much higher. Save your euros for espresso or gelato." —cruisinred

"Bars always have two different prices: If you have your coffee at the counter it's cheaper than when a waiter serves it at a table (*servizio al tavolo*)." —quokka

"Visit wine fill-up shops in Italy; get table wine from the cask for 2-3 euros a liter. In Rome we would get them filled at the Testaccio market . . . I will usually ask at the local bar where I go for my coffee." —susanna

"If you aren't hungry, skip to *secondo*—the 'second course.' Rarely do Italians eat a *primo e secondo* when they go out." —glittergirl

Sights

"The small cities can be less expensive but still fabulous. We were just in Assisi—all the sites were free, a delicious dinner for two with wine was 22 euros, and our hotel was reasonable at 65 euros per night." —rosetravels

"For the art lover on a budget: Most of the art I saw in Rome is free. Where else can you see countless Caravaggios, two Michelangelos, and even more Berninis for the cost of the wear and tear on the soles of your shoes?" —amyb

"One way to save on the expense of guided tours is to register online at Sound Guides (www.sound-guides.com/) and download the various free self-guided tours to your Ipod or MP3 player." —monicapileggi

Lodging

"Go off-season—March or November have better air prices and also accommodations, particularly if you stay in apartments, which you can rent for much less off-season (and plan some meals in-house—make the noon meal your biggest of the day, then have a small dinner in the apartment)." —bobthenavigator

"Everyone talks about going in the off season and mentions November or March. But in Florence at least, July is a shoulder season. I got a hotel room for half to a third the cost of the same room during the high season." —isabel

"We try to book apartments whenever we can and in Tuscany we rent farm houses. Especially if you are traveling with more than 2 persons these are usually much more reasonable." —caroltis

A GREAT ITINERARY

ROME, FLORENCE, VENICE, AND HIGHLIGHTS IN BETWEEN

This itinerary is designed for maximum impact—it will keep you moving. Think of it as rough draft for you to revise according to your own interests and time constraints.

Day 1: Venice

Arrive in Venice's Marco Polo Airport (there are a few direct flights from the United States), take the boat across the lagoon to Venice, check into your hotel, then get out, and get lost in the back canals for a couple of hours before dinner. If you enjoy fish, you should indulge yourself at a traditional Venetian restaurant. There's no better place for sweet, delicate Adriatic seafood.

Logistics: At the airport, follow signs for water transport and look for Alilaguna, which operates the soothing one-hour boat trip into Venice. The boats stop at the Lido and finally leave you near Piazza San Marco; from there you can get to your hotel on foot or by vaporetto. The water taxis are much more expensive and aren't really worth the cost, although they'll take you directly to your hotel.

Day 2: Venice

Begin by skipping the coffee at your hotel and have a real Italian coffee at a real Italian coffee shop. Spend the day at Venice's top few sights, including the Basilica di San Marco, Palazzo Ducale, and Galleria dell'Accademia. Stop for lunch, perhaps sampling Venice's traditional specialty, *sarde in saor* (grilled sardines in a mouth-watering sweet-and-sour preparation that includes onions and raisins), and be sure to check out the ancient fish market, Rialto Bridge, and sunset at the Zattere before dinner. Later, stop at one of the pubs around the Campo San Luca or Campo Santa Margarita, where you can toast to freedom from automobiles.

Logistics: Venice is best seen by wandering. The day's activities can be done on foot, with the occasional vaporetto ride.

Day 3: Ferrara/Bologna

Get an early start and head out of Venice on a Bologna-bound train. The ride to Ferrara—your first stop in Emilia-Romagna—is about an hour and a half. Visit the Castello Estense and Duomo before lunch; a panino and a beer at one of Ferrara's prim and proper cafés should fit the bill. Wander Ferrara's cobblestone streets before hopping on the train to Bologna (a ride of less than an hour). In Bologna, check into your hotel and take a walk around Piazza Maggiore before dinner. At night you can check out some of northern Italy's best nightlife.

Logistics: In Ferrara, the train station lies a bit outside the city center, so you'll want to take a taxi into town (check your luggage at the station). Going out, there's a taxi stand near the back of the castle, toward Corso Ercole I d'Este. In Bologna the walk into town from the station is more manageable, particularly if you're staying along Via dell'Indipendenza.

Day 4: Bologna/Florence

After breakfast, spend the morning checking out some of Bologna's churches and piazzas, including a climb up the leaning Torre degli Asinelli for a red rooftop–studded panorama. After lunch, head back to the train station, and take the short ride to Florence. You'll arrive in Florence in time for an afternoon siesta and an evening passeggiata.

Logistics: Florence's Santa Maria Novella train station is within easy access to some hotels, and farther from others. Florence's traffic is legendary, but taxis at the station are plentiful; make sure you get into a licensed, clearly marked car that's outside in line.

Day 5: Florence

This is your day to see the sights of Florence. Start with the Uffizi Gallery (reserve your tickets in advance), where you'll see Botticelli's *Primavera* and *Birth of Venus*. Next, walk to the Piazza del Duomo, the site of Brunelleschi's spectacular dome, which you can climb for an equally spectacular view. By the time you get down, you'll be more than ready for a simple lunch at a laid-back café. Depending on your preferences, either devote the afternoon to art (Michelangelo's *David* at the Galleria dell'Accademia, the magnificent Medici Chapels, and perhaps the church of Santa Croce) or hike up to Piazzale Michelangelo, overlooking the city. Either way, finish the evening in style with a traditional *bistecca alla fiorentina* (grilled T-bone steak with olive oil).

Day 6: Lucca/Pisa

After breakfast, board a train for Lucca. It's an easy 1½-hour trip on the way to Pisa to see this walled medieval city. Don't miss the Romanesque Duomo, or a walk in the park that lines the city's ramparts. Have lunch at a local trattoria before continuing on to Pisa, where you'll spend an afternoon seeing—what else—the Leaning Tower, along with the equally impressive Duomo and Battistero. Walk down to the banks of the Arno River, contemplate the majestic views at sunset, and have dinner at one of the many inexpensive local restaurants in the real city center—a bit away from the most touristy spots.

Logistics: Lucca's train station lies just outside the walled city, so hardier travelers may want to leave the station on foot; otherwise, take a taxi. Check your luggage at the station. Pisa's train station isn't far from the city center, although it's on the other side of town from the Campo dei Miracoli (site of the Leaning Tower).

Day 7: Orvieto/Rome

Three hours south of Pisa is Orvieto, one of the prettiest and most characteristic towns of the Umbria region, conveniently situated right on the Florence-Rome train line. Check out the memorable cathedral before a light lunch accompanied by one of Orvieto's famous white wines. Get back on a train bound for Rome, and in a little more than an hour you'll arrive in the Eternal City in time to make your way to your hotel and relax for a bit before you head out for the evening. When you do, check out Piazza Navona, Campo de' Fiori, and the Trevi Fountain—it's best in the evening—and take a stand-up *aperitivo* (Campari and soda is the classic) at an unpretentious local bar before dinner. It's finally pizza time; you can't go wrong at any of Rome's popular local pizzerias.

Logistics: To get from Pisa to Orvieto, you'll first catch a train to Florence and then get on a Rome-bound train from here. Be careful at Rome's Termini train station, which is a breeding ground for scam artists. Keep your possessions close at hand, and only get into a licensed taxi at the taxi stand.

Day 8: Rome

Rome took millennia to build, but unfortunately on this whirlwind trip you'll only have a day and a half to see it. In the morning, head to the Vatican Museums to see Michelangelo's glorious *Adam* at the Sistine Chapel. See St. Peter's Basilica and Square before heading back into Rome

proper for lunch around the Pantheon, followed by a coffee from one of Rome's famous coffee shops. Next, visit ancient Rome—first see the magnificent Pantheon, and then head across to the Colosseum, stopping along the way along Via dei Fori Imperiali to check out the Roman Forum from above. From the Colosseum, take a taxi to Piazza di Spagna, a good place to see the sunset and shop at stylish boutiques. Take another taxi to Piazza Trilussa at the entrance of Trastevere, a beautiful old working-class neighborhood where you'll have a relaxing dinner.

Day 9: Rome/Departure

Head by taxi to Termini station and catch the train ride to the Fiumicino airport. Savor your last cup of the world's richest coffee at one of the coffee bars in the airport before boarding.

Logistics: The train from Termini station to the airport is fast, inexpensive, and easy—for most people, it's preferable to an exorbitantly priced taxi ride that, in bad traffic, can take twice as long.

TIPS

- The itinerary can also be completed by car on the modern autostrade, although you'll run into dicey traffic in Florence and Rome. For obvious reasons, you're best off waiting to pick up your car on Day 3, when you leave Venice.
- Among trains, aim for the reservations-only Eurostar Italia—it's more comfortable and faster.
- The sights along this route are highly touristed; you'll have a better time if you make the trip outside the busy months of June, July, and August.

Rome and Environs

WHAT'S WHERE

1 Ancient Rome. Backstopped by the most stupendous monument of ancient Rome—the Colosseum—the Roman Forum and Palatine Hill were once the hub of western civilization.

2 The Vatican. The Vatican draws millions of pilgrims and art lovers to St. Peter's Basilica, the Vatican Museums, and the Sistine Chapel.

3 Navona and Campo. The *cuore*—heart—of the *centro storico* (historic quarter), this district revolves around the ancient Pantheon, bustling Campo de' Fiori, and spectacular Piazza Navona.

4 Corso. Rome's "Broadway" begins at Piazza Venezia and neatly divides the city center in two—an area graced by historic landmarks like the 17th-century Palazzo Doria-Pamphilj (famed for its Old Master collection) and the Column of Marcus Aurelius.

5 Spagna. Travel back to the days of the Grand Tour in this glamorous area. After some people-watching on Piazza di Spagna, shop like a true VIP along Via dei Condotti, then be sure to throw a coin in the Trevi Fountain.

6 Repubblica and Quirinale. A largely 19th-century district, Repubblica lets art lovers go for baroque with a bevy of Bernini works, including his St. Theresa in Ecstasy at Santa Maria della Vittoria. To the south looms the Palazzo Quirinale, Italy's presidential palace.

7 Villa Borghese and Piazza del Popolo. Rome's most famous park is home to playful fountains, sculptured gardens, and the treasure-packed Galleria Borghese. Piazza del Popolo—a beautiful place to watch the world go by—lies south.

8 Trastevere. Rome's left bank has kept its authentic roots thanks to mom-and-pop trattorias, medieval alleyways, and Santa Maria in Trastevere, stunningly spotlighted at night.

9 The Ghetto and Isola Tiberina. Once a Jewish quarter, the gentrified Ghetto still preserves the flavor of Old Rome. Alongside is moored Tiber Island, so picturesque it will click your camera for you.

10 The Catacombs and Appian Way. Follow in the footsteps of St. Peter to this district, home to the spirit-warm catacombs and the Tomb of Cecilia Metella.

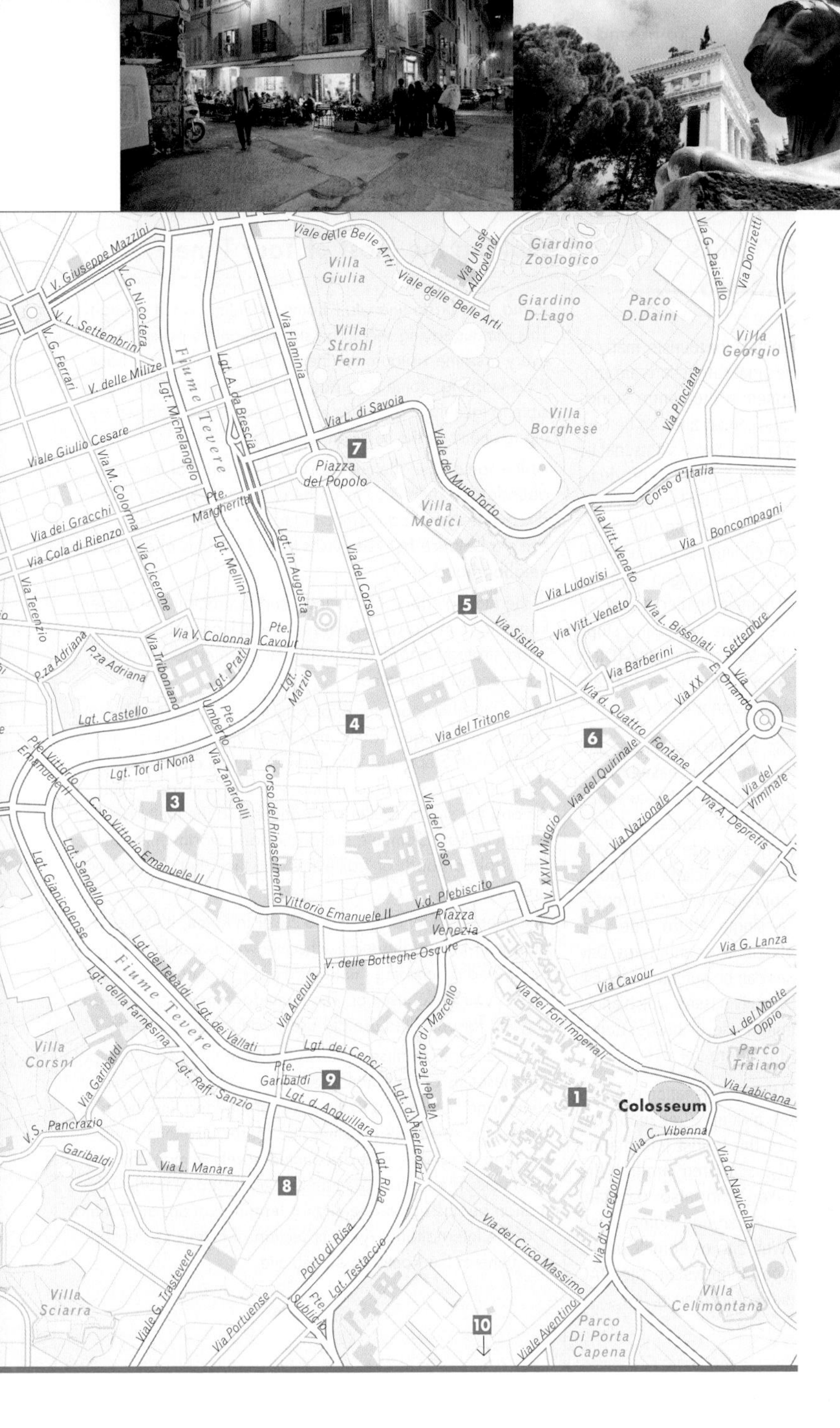
Viale delle Belle Arti
Via Ulisse Aldrovandi
Giardino Zoologico
Via G. Paisiello
Via Donizetti
Villa Giulia
Viale delle Belle Arti
Giardino D.Lago
Parco D.Daini
V. Giuseppe Mazzini
V. G. Nico-tera
V. L. Settembrini
Via Flaminia
Villa Strohl Fern
Villa Georgio
V. G. Ferrari
V. delle Milize
Fiume Tevere
Lgt. A. da Brescia
Lgt. Michelangelo
Via L. di Savoia
Villa Borghese
Via Pinciana
Viale Giulio Cesare
Via M. Colorma
7
Piazza del Popolo
Viale del Muro Torto
Corso d'Italia
Pte. Margherita
Villa Medici
Via dei Gracchi
Via Cola di Rienzo
Lgt. Mellini
Lgt. in Augusta
Via del Corso
Via Vitt. Veneto
Via Boncompagni
Via Cicerone
Via Terenzio
Via Ludovisi
5
Via V. Colonna
Pte. Cavour
Via Sistina
Via Vitt. Veneto
Via L. Bissolati
P.za Adriana
P.za Adriana
Via Triboniano
Lgt. Prati
Lgt. Marzio
Via Barberini
Via XX Settembre
E. Orlando
Lgt. Castello
Pte. Umberto
4
Via del Tritone
Via d. Quattro Fontane
6
Pte. Vittorio Emanuele II
Lgt. Tor di Nona
Via Zanardelli
Corso del Rinascimento
Via del Quirinale
Via del Viminale
3
C. so Vittorio Emanuele II
Via del Corso
V. XXIV Maggio
Via Nazionale
Via A. Depretis
Lgt. Sangallo
Lgt. Gianicolense
Vittorio Emanuele II
V.d. Plebiscito
Piazza Venezia
Via G. Lanza
Lgt. dei Tebaldi
V. delle Botteghe Oscure
Fiume Tevere
Lgt. della Farnesina
Lgt. dei Vallati
Via Arenula
Via del Teatro di Marcello
Via dei Fori Imperiali
Via Cavour
V. del Monte Oppio
Villa Corsni
Via Garibaldi
Lgt. dei Cenci
Parco Traiano
Lgt. Raff. Sanzio
Pte. Garibaldi
9
Lgt. d. Pierleoni
1
Colosseum
Via Labicana
V. S. Pancrazio
Lgt. d. Anguillara
Via C. Vibenna
Garibaldi
Via L. Manara
8
Lgt. Ripa
Via di S. Gregorio
Via d. Navicella
Via del Circo Massimo
Porto di Risa
Lgt. Testaccio
Viale G. Trastevere
Villa Sciarra
Via Portuense
Pte. Sublicio
Villa Celimontana
10
Viale Aventino
Parco Di Porta Capena

ROME AND ENVIRONS PLANNER

Don't Miss the Metro

Fortunately for tourists, many of Rome's main attractions are concentrated in the centro storico (historic center) and can be covered on foot. Some sights that lie nearer the border of this quarter can be reached via the Metro Line A, nicknamed the *linea rossa* (red line) and include: the Spanish Steps (Spagna stop), the Trevi Fountain (Barberini stop), St. Peter's Square (Ottaviano stop), and the Vatican Museums (Ottaviano or Cipro-Musei Vaticani stop), to name a few.

Tickets for the bus, tram, and Metro can be purchased for €1 at any *tabacchi* (tobacco shop), at some newsstands, and from machines inside Metro stations. These tickets are good for approximately 75 minutes for a single Metro ride and unlimited buses and trams. Day passes can be purchased for €4, and weekly passes, which allow unlimited use of buses, trams, and the Metro, for €16.

For a fuller explanation of Metro routes, pick up a free map from one of the tourist information booths scattered around the city. You can also navigate your way around Rome using the Web site of Rome's public transportation system, the ATAC (🌐 *www.atac.roma.it*).

Making the Most of Your Time

Roma, non basta una vita ("Rome, a lifetime is not enough"): This famous saying should be stamped on the passport of every first-time visitor to the Eternal City. On the other hand, it's a warning: Rome is so packed with sights that it's impossible to take them all in; it's easy to run yourself ragged trying to check off the items on your "bucket list".

At the same time, the saying is a celebration of the city's abundance. There's so much here, you're bound to make discoveries you hadn't anticipated. To conquer Rome, strike a balance between visits to major sights and leisurely neighborhood strolls.

In the first category, the Vatican and the remains of ancient Rome loom the largest. Both require at least half a day; a good strategy is to devote your first morning to one and your second to the other.

Leave the afternoons for exploring the neighborhoods that comprise "Baroque Rome" and the shopping district around the Spanish Steps and Via Condotti. If you have more days at your disposal, continue with the same approach. Among the sights, Galleria Borghese and the multilayered church of San Clemente are particularly worthwhile, and the neighborhoods of Trastevere and the Ghetto make for great roaming.

Since there's a lot of ground to cover in Rome, it's wise to plan your busy sightseeing schedule with possible savings in mind, and purchasing the Roma Pass (🌐 *www.romapass.it*) allows you to do just that. The three-day pass costs €25 and is good for unlimited use of buses, trams, and the metro.

It includes free admission to two of more than 40 participating museums or archaeological sites, including the Colosseum (and bumps you to the head of the long line there, to boot!), the Ara Pacis museum, the Musei Capitolini, and Galleria Borghese, plus discounted tickets to many other museums. The Roma Pass can be purchased at tourist information booths across the city, at Termini Station, at Terminal 3 of the International Arrivals section of Fiumicino Airport, or online at the Roma Pass Web site.

When to Go

Not surprisingly, spring and fall are the best times to visit, with mild temperatures and many sunny days; the famous Roman sunsets are also at their best. Summers are often sweltering. In July and August, learn to do as the Romans do—get up and out early, seek refuge from the afternoon heat, resume activities in early evening, and stay up late to enjoy the nighttime breeze. Come August, many shops and restaurants close as locals head out for vacation. Remember that air-conditioning, though increasingly prevalent, is still not ubiquitous in this city. Roman winters are relatively mild, with persistent rainy spells.

Hop-On, Hop-Off

Rome has its own "hop-on, hop-off" sightseeing buses. The Trambus 110 Open leaves every 15-minutes from Piazza dei Cinquecento (at the main Termini railway station), with a two-hour loop including the Quirinale, the Colosseum, Piazza Navona, St. Peter's, the Trevi Fountain, and Via Veneto. Tickets, valid for 24 hours, cost €16. The Archeobus departs every 30 minutes from the Piazza dei Cinquecento and heads to the Via Appia Antica, with stops at the Colosseum, Baths of Caracalla, and the catacombs. Tickets, valid for 24 hours, cost €10. A cumulative ticket covering both buses costs €20, is valid for 48 hours, and provides reduced admission to select city museums. The Web site for both is 🌐 *www.trambusopen.com.*

Roman Hours

Much of the city shuts down on Sundays, although museums and many restaurants are closed Mondays. Most stores in the centro storico area, the part of town that caters to tourists, remain open. Shop hours generally run from 10 am to 1 pm, then reopen around 3 pm until 7 or 7:30 pm. Unless advertised as having *orario continuato* (open all day), most businesses close from 1 to 3 pm. On Mondays, shops usually don't open until around 3 or 4 pm. Pharmacies tend to have the same hours of operation as stores unless they advertise *orario notturno* (night hours); two can be found on Corso Rinascimento and Piazza dei Cinquecento (near Termini Station). As for churches, most open at 8 or 9 in the morning, close from 12:30 to 3 or 4, then reopen until 6:30 or 7. St. Peter's, however, is open 7 am to 7 pm (6:30 pm October to March).

Information, Please

Rome's main Tourist Information Office is at Via Leopardi 24 (☎ *06/0608* 🌐 *www.romaturismo.it*), near Piazza Vittorio.

Green information kiosks with multilingual personnel are situated near the most important sights and squares, as well as at Termini Station and Leonardo da Vinci Airport. These kiosks, called Tourist Information Sites (Punti Informativi Turistici, or PIT) can be found at:

PIT Castel S. Angelo, Piazza Pia; open 9:30–7

PIT Navona, Piazza delle Cinque Lune (north end of Piazza Navona); open 9:30–7

PIT Fiumicino, Aeroporto Leonardo da Vinci, Arrivi Internazionali Terminal 3; open 9–6:30

PIT Ciampino, Aeroporto Ciampino, Arrivi Internazionali Baggae Claim; open 9–6:30

PIT Minghetti, Via Marco Minghetti (corner of Via del Corso); open 9:30–7

PIT Nazionale, Via Nazionale (Palazzo delle Esposizioni); open 9:30–7

PIT Santa Maria Maggiore, at Via dell'Olmata; open 9:30–7

PIT Termini, Stazione Termini, at Via Giovanni Giolitti 34; open 8–8

PIT Trastevere, on Piazza Sidney Sonnino; open 9:30–7

ROME TOP ATTRACTIONS

The Pantheon

Reputedly constructed to honor all pagan gods, this best-preserved building of ancient Rome was rebuilt in the 2nd century AD by Emperor Hadrian. The vast dome of perfect dimensions—142 feet high by 142 feet wide—was the largest freestanding dome until the 20th century.

The Vatican

Though its population numbers just shy of a thousand, the Vatican—home base for the Catholic Church and the pope—has millions of visitors each year. Savor Michelangelo's Sistine Ceiling, attend Papal Mass, and marvel at St. Peter's Basilica, embraced by the colonnades of St. Peter's Square.

The Colosseum

(A) Legend has it that as long as the Colosseum stands, Rome will stand; and when Rome falls, so will the world. One of the "new" seven wonders of the world, the mammoth amphitheater was begun by Emperor Vespasian and inaugurated by the next emperor, his son Titus, in the year 80. For "the grandeur that was Rome," this yardstick of eternity can't be topped.

Piazza Navona

(B) You couldn't concoct a more Roman street scene: cafés and crowded tables at street level, coral- and rust-colored houses above, most lined with wrought-iron balconies, and, at the center of this urban "living room" Bernini's spectacular Fountain of the Four Rivers and Borromini's super-theatrical Sant'Agnese.

Roman Forum

(C) Set between the Capitoline and Palatine hills, this fabled labyrinth of ruins variously served as a political playground, a commerce mart, and a place where justice was dispensed during the days of the Republic and Empire (509 BC to AD 476). Once adorned with stately buildings, triumphal arches, and impressive temples, the Forum today is a silent

ruin—*sic transit gloria mundi* ("so passes away the glory of the world").

The Campidoglio

(D) Catch an emperor's-eye view of the Roman Forum from beside Michelangelo's Palazzo Senatorio, situated atop one of the highest spots in Rome, the Capitoline Hill. Next door you'll find the Vittoriano, the Capitoline Museums, and beloved Santa Maria in Aracoeli.

Trevi Fountain

(E) One of the few fountains in Rome that's actually more absorbing than the people crowding around it, the Fontana di Trevi was designed by Nicola Salvi in 1732. Immortalized in *Three Coins in a Fountain* and *La Dolce Vita*, this fountain may be your ticket back to Rome—that is, if you throw a coin into it.

The Spanish Steps

(F) Byron, Shelley, and Keats all drew inspiration from this magnificent "Scalinata," constructed in 1723. Connecting the shops at the bottom with the hotels at the top, this is the place for prime people-watching. The steps face beautiful sunsets.

Galleria Borghese

(G) Only the best could satisfy the aesthetic taste of Cardinal Scipione Borghese, and that means famed Bernini sculptures, great paintings by Titian and Raphael, and the most spectacular 17th-century palace in Rome.

Trastevere

Located just across the Tiber River, this charming neighborhood is a maze of jumbled alleyways, cobblestone streets, and medieval houses. The area also boasts one of the oldest churches of Rome—Santa Maria in Trastevere.

TOP ROME EXPERIENCES

Say "Cheese," Spartacus

Taking a photo with one of those ersatz gladiators in front of the Colosseum will win some smiles—but maybe some frowns, too. Many of these costumed gladiators pounce on tourists who simply aim a camera at them and then proceed to shake them down for a "photo fee." Others have a craftier approach: before you know it, one may envelop your eight-year-old in his red cape and say *"Formaggio."* Indeed, this may turn out to be the greatest souvenir back home in fourth-grade class, so if interested, step right up, shake hands, and exchange some euros. But pick your Spartacus very carefully: some sloppy guys wear a helmet and cloak but have sweatsuits or sneakers on. Rumor has it that Rome's government is going to crack down on these "gladiators," but so far it's caveat emptor.

Life is a Piazza

For Italians young and old, la piazza serves as a *punto d'incontro*—a meeting place—for dinner plans, drinks, people-watching, catching up with friends, and, as Romans would say, exchanging *due chiacchiere* (two words). One of the most popular piazzas is Campo de' Fiori, right in the heart of the beautiful historic center. By day, the piazza is famous for its fresh food and flower market—no rival to Piazza Navona for picturesqueness, the market is nevertheless a favorite photo-op, due to the *ombrelloni* (canvas umbrella) food stands. By night, the piazza turns into a popular hangout for Romans and foreigners lured by its pubs and street cafés, so much so that it has been dubbed "the American college campus of Rome." As dinner approaches at 9, the big question is: Are you "in" or "out" (inside or outside table)? No matter: the people-watching is unrivaled anywhere you sit.

Truth or Dare

Long before the advent of lie-detector machines, and even before there were bibles to swear on, there was the Bocca della Verità—the Mouth of Truth, the famous gaping mouth that so successfully terrified Audrey Hepburn in *Roman Holiday*. Long-ago legends have it that people suspected of telling lies would be marched up to the Bocca and have their hand put inside the mouth of this massive stone relief (originally an ancient street drain cover). If the suspect told the truth, nothing to fear. But if lies were told, the grim unsmiling stone mouth would take its revenge.

This is a great spot for kids to get the truth out of their brother or sister, so have your camera—and your probing questions!—ready. Don't forget to take in the adjacent Santa Maria in Cosmedin church, one of Rome's most evocative and atmospheric churches.

Lights, Camera, Action!

The Festival Internazionale del Film di Roma (Rome International Film Festival; 🌐 *www.romacinemafest.it*), entering its sixth year, has hosted the likes of Martin Scorcese, Robert De Niro, and Meryl Streep. Though Rome is far from reclaiming its film prominence, lost decades ago, the festival draws important players in the world of film and sees its share of world premieres. The festival is held at the Auditorium Parco della Musica during a full week in the fall.

Two Coins in the Fountain

Rome has always been in love with *amore*. But romance is certainly nowhere more contagious than around its famous fountains. If a besotted couple can spare

the time, a trip up to Tivoli's Villa D'Este (an hour outside Rome via bus) is nirvana. Its seductive garden and endless array of fountains (about 500 of them) is the perfect setting to put anyone in the mood for love—it won't be long before you hear Frank Sinatra warble "Three Coins in the Fountain" in your head.

That's your cue to return to Rome and make a beeline for the luminous Trevi Fountain, even more enchanting at night than in the daytime. Make sure you and that special someone throw your coins into the fountain for good luck. Legend has it that those who do so are guaranteed a return trip back to Rome.

L'Aperitivo

Borrowed from *i Milanesi*, the trend of *l'aperitivo* has become *moda* in Rome. Not to be confused with happy hour, l'aperitivo is not about discounts or heavy drinking, but rather a time to meet up with friends and colleagues after work or on weekends—definitely an event to see and be seen. Aperitivo hours are usually from 7 to 9 pm.

Depending on where you go, the price of a drink often includes an all-you-can-eat appetizer buffet of finger foods, sandwiches, and pasta salads. Some aperitivo hotspots on the *trendissimo* list are Salotto Locarno (Via della Penna) near Piazza del Popolo; Bar del Fico (Piazza del Fico), and Salotto 42 (Piazza di Pietra) in the centro storico; Freni and Frizioni (Via del Politeama) in Trastevere; and Settembrini Caffe' (Via Settembrini) in Prati.

Trawling for Treasure

There are plenty of street markets scattered about Rome that specialize in clothing, fashion accessories, and every imaginable knickknack. The two largest are the one on Via Sannio in the San Giovanni district (Monday–Saturday), which deals mostly in new and used clothing and accessories, and the Porta Portese market in Trastevere (Sunday only), offering everything from antiques and bric-a-brac to clothing and souvenirs. Make sure to ask for a *sconto*—or a discount.

Don't Just Read *Angels & Demons,* Walk It!

What Dan Brown did for Paris in *The Da Vinci Code*, he does for Rome—big-time—in *Angels & Demons,* the 2000 "prequel." This time Brown's Robert Langdon does battle with the Illuminati, a secret society trying to unleash scientific terrorists against the Catholic Church. To find out if they succeed in incinerating the Vatican with an anti-matter bomb during a papal enclave, you'll have to read the book or see the Ron Howard movie (starring Tom Hanks and which opened in May 2009). Crowds still enjoy "Angels & Demons" walking tours in Rome, tracking down the "Path of Illumination" to such scenic stunners as Raphael's Chigi Chapel and Bernini's *Ecstasy of St. Theresa,* plus many other famous (and not-so-famous) Roman sights. Just a few of the tour companies offering this walk: 🌐 *www.*angelsdemonstour.*com*, 🌐 *www.througheternity.com*, and 🌐 *www.viator.com*.

GETTING HERE AND AROUND

Getting Here by Car

The main access routes from the north are A1 (Autostrada del Sole) from Milan and Florence. The principal route to or from points south, including Naples, is the A1, as well. All highways connect with the Grande Raccordo Anulare (GRA) Ring Road, which channels traffic into the city center. For driving directions, check out 🌐 *www.autostrade.it*. Note: Parking in Rome can be a nightmare—private cars are not allowed access to the entire historic center during the day (weekdays 6:30 am–8 pm; Saturday 2 pm–6 pm), except for residents.

Getting Here by Bus

Bus lines cover all of Rome's surrounding Lazio region and are operated by the Consorzio Trasporti Lazio, or COTRAL (☎ *06/72057205* 🌐 *www.cotralspa.it*). These bus routes terminate either near Tiburtina Station or at outlying Metro stops, such as Laurentina and Ponte Mammolo (Line B) and Anagnina (Line A). COTRAL buses are good options for taking short day trips from Rome, such as those that leave daily from Rome's Ponte Mammolo (Line B) Metro station for the town of Tivoli, where Hadrian's Villa and Villa D'Este are located.

Getting Here by Air

Rome's principal airport is Leonardo da Vinci Airport/Fiumicino (☎ *06/65951* 🌐 *www.adr.it*) commonly known by the name of its location, Fiumicino (FCO). It's 30 km (19 mi) southwest of the city but has a direct train link with downtown Rome. Rome's other airport, with no direct train link, is Ciampino (☎ *06/794941* 🌐 *www.adr.it*) or CIA, 15 km (9 mi) south of downtown and used mostly by low-cost airlines.

Two trains link downtown Rome with Fiumicino. Inquire at the PIT tourist information counter in the International Arrivals hall (Terminal 3) or train information counter near the tracks to determine which takes you closest to your destination in Rome. The 30-minute nonstop Airport-Termini express (called the Leonardo Express) goes direct to Termini Station, Rome's main train station; tickets cost €14. The FM1 train stops in Trastevere and Ostiense. Always stamp your tickets in the little machines near the track before you board. As for Ciampino, COTRAL buses connect to trains that go to the city and Terravision (☎ *06/97610632*; 🌐 *www.terravision.eu*) buses link the airport to Termini Station for €4 each way.

Taxi transport to and from Fiumicino carries a flat fee of €40; to and from Ciampino costs €30.

Getting Here by Train

State-owned Trenitalia (☎ *892/021 within Italy, 06/68475475 from abroad* 🌐 *www.trenitalia.it*) trains also serve some destinations on side trips outside Rome. The main Trenitalia stations in Rome are Termini, Tiburtina, Ostiense, and Trastevere. On long-distance routes (to Florence and Naples, for instance), you can either travel by the cheap, but slow regionali trains, or the fast but more expensive Intercity, Eurostar Alta Velocità. The state railways' Web site is user-friendly.

Getting Around by Public Transportation

Rome's integrated transportation system is ATAC (☎ *06/57003* 🌐 *www.atac.roma.it*), which includes the Metropolitana subway, city buses, and municipal trams. A ticket (BIT) valid for 75 minutes on any combination of buses and trams

and one entrance to the Metro costs €1. Day passes can be purchased for €4, and weekly passes for €16.

Tickets (singly or in quantity—it's a good idea to have a few tickets handy so you don't have to hunt for a vendor when you need one) are sold at tobacconists, newsstands, some coffee bars, automatic ticket machines in Metro stations, some bus stops, and ATAC ticket booths. A handful of buses also have ticket machines onboard. Time-stamp tickets at Metro turnstiles and in little yellow machines on buses and trams when boarding the first vehicle. The expiration date and time will be printed on the reverse side of the ticket.

Getting Around by Bus and Tram

ATAC city buses and trams are orange, gray-and-red, or blue-and-orange.

Remember to board at the front or rear and to exit at the middle; in most cases, you must buy your ticket before boarding, and always stamp it in a machine as soon as you enter. The ticket is good for a single Metro ride and unlimited buses and trams within the next 75 minutes.

Buses and trams run from 5:30 am to midnight, plus there's an extensive network of night (*notturno*) buses.

ATAC has a Web site (*www.atac.roma.it*) that will help you calculate the number of stops and bus routes needed.

There's also an iPhone app called Roma Bus (*itunes.apple.com/us/app/rome-bus/id317560714?mt=8*) that's useful for navigating the bus system.

Be aware that *festivi* buses are ones that run only on Sundays and holidays; regular buses will either say *feriali*, which means "daily," or won't have any special distinction.

Pick up a free Metro Routes map from one of the tourist info booths scattered through the city.

Getting Around by Metropolitana

The Metropolitana (or Metro) is the easiest and fastest way to get around Rome. The Metro A Line, known as the linea rossa, will take you to a chunk of the main attractions in Rome: Piazza di Spagna (Spagna stop), Piazza del Popolo (Flaminio), St. Peter's Square (Ottaviano–San Pietro), the Vatican Museums (both Ottaviano and Cipro–Musei Vaticani), and the Trevi Fountain (Barberini).

The B Line (linea blu) will take you to the Colosseum (Colosseo stop), Circus Maximus (Circo Massimo stop), the Pyramid (Piramide stop for Testaccio, Ostiense Station, and trains for Ostia Antica), and Basilica di San Paolo Fuori le Mura (San Paolo stop). The two lines intersect at Rome's main station, Termini.

Street entrances are marked with red and white "M" signs. The Metro opens at 5:30 am, and the last trains leave the last station at either end at 11:30 pm (on Friday and Saturday nights the last train leaves at 12:30 am).

Getting Around by Taxi

Taxis in Rome do not cruise, but if free they'll stop if you flag them down. They wait at stands but can also be called by phone (*06/5551, 06/6645, 06/3570, or 06/0609*).

Always ask for a receipt (*ricevuta*) to make sure the driver charges you the correct amount. Use only licensed cabs with a plaque next to the license plate reading "*Servizio Pubblico.*"

EATING AND DRINKING WELL IN ROME

In Rome traditional cuisine reigns supreme. Most chefs follow the mantra of freshness over fuss, and simplicity of flavor and preparation over complex cooking methods.

So when Romans continue ordering the standbys, it's easy to understand why. And we're talking about *very* old standbys: some restaurants re-create dishes that come from ancient recipes of Apicius, probably the first celebrity chef (to Emperor Tiberius) and cookbook author of the Western world. Today, Rome's cooks excel at what has taken hundreds, or thousands, of years to perfect.

Still, if you're hunting for newer-than-now developments, things are slowly changing. Talented young chefs are exploring new culinary frontiers, with results that tingle the taste buds: fresh pasta filled with carbonara sauce, cod "tiramisu," and mozzarella gelato with basil sorbet and semisweet tomatoes are just a few recent examples. Of course, there's grumbling about the number of chefs who, in a clumsy effort to be *nuovo*, end up with collision rather than fusion. That noted, Rome *is* the capital city, and the influx of residents from other regions of the country allows for many variations on the Italian theme.

FOODIE FINDS

Via Cola di Rienzo is home to two of Rome's best specialty shops: Franchi (✉ *Via Cola di Rienzo 200, Prati* ☎ *06/6874651*), pictured above, a gastroshop that sells high-quality cured meats, Italian cheeses, wines, pastas, and fresh truffles. Next door, Castroni (✉ *Via Cola di Rienzo 196/198, Prati* ☎ *06/6874383*) is well known among expats for its imported foreign foods from the United States, Great Britain, Japan, India, and Mexico, as well as its impressive selection of candies, preserves, olive oils, and balsamic vinegars. Castroni is a great place to stop in for *caffé* (coffee) and a *cornetto* (an Italian croissant).

ARTICHOKES

If there's one vegetable Rome is known for, it's the artichoke, or *carciofo*. The classic Roman preparation, *carciofo alla romana,* is a large, globe-shaped artichoke stripped of its outer leaves, stuffed with wild mint and garlic, then braised. It's available at restaurants throughout the city from February to May, when local artichokes are in season. For the excellent Roman-Jewish version, *carciofo alla giudia*— artichoke deep-fried until crisp and brown—head to any restaurant in the Ghetto.

BUCATINI ALL'AMATRICIANA

What may appear to the naked eye as spaghetti with red sauce is actually *bucatini all'amatriciana*—a spicy, rich, and complex dish that owes its flavor to an important ingredient: *guanciale,* or cured pork jowl. Once you taste a meaty, guanciale-flavor dish, you'll understand why Romans swear by it. Along with guanciale, the simple sauce features crushed tomatoes and red pepper flakes. It's served over *bucatini*, a hollow, spaghetti-like pasta, and topped with grated pecorino Romano cheese.

CODA ALLA VACCINARA

Rome's largest slaughterhouse in the 1800s was housed in the Testaccio neighborhood. That's where you'll find dishes like *coda alla vaccinara,* or "oxtail in the style of the cattle butcher." This dish is made from ox or veal tails stewed

with tomatoes, carrots, celery, and wine, and seasoned with cinnamon, pancetta, and myriad other flavorings. The stew cooks for hours then is finished with the sweet-and-sour element—often raisins and pine nuts or bittersweet chocolate.

GELATO

For many travelers, the first taste of gelato is one of the most memorable moments of their Italian trip. With a consistency that's a cross between regular American ice cream and soft serve, gelato's texture is dense but softer than hard ice cream because it's kept at a higher temperature. The best gelato is extremely flavorful, and made daily. In Rome, a few common flavors are caffè, pistacchio (pistachio), *nocciola* (hazelnut), *fragola* (strawberry), and *cioccolato* fondant (dark chocolate).

PIZZA

Roman pizza comes in two types: *pizza al taglio* (by the slice) and pizza tonda (round pizza). The former has a thicker focaccia-like crust and is cut into squares. These slices are sold by weight and available all day. In Rome, the typical pizza tonda has a very thin crust. It's cooked in wood-burning ovens that reach extremely high temperatures. Since they're so hot, the ovens are usually fired up in the evening, which is why Roman pizzerias are only open for dinner.

A GREAT ITINERARY

Rome wasn't built in a day, and even locals themselves will tell you that it takes a lifetime to discover all the treasures that the Eternal City has to offer. Jam-packed with monuments, museums, fountains, galleries, and picturesque neighborhoods, Mamma Roma makes it hard for visitors to decide which to tackle first during their adventurous Roman holiday. As Romans like to say, this one-day itinerary *basta e avanza* ("is more than enough") to get you started!

Rome 101

So you want to taste Rome, gaze at its beauty, and inhale its special flair, all in one breathtaking (literally) day? Think Rome 101, and get ready for a spectacular sunrise-to-sunset span. Begin at 9 by exploring Rome's most beautiful neighborhood—"Vecchia Roma" (the area around Piazza Navona, Campo de' Fiori, and the Pantheon) by starting out on the Corso (the big avenue which runs into Piazza Venezia, the traffic hub of the historic center).

A block away from each other are two opulently over-the-top monuments that show off Rome at its baroque best: the church of Sant'Ignazio and the princely Palazzo Doria-Pamphilj, aglitter with great Old Master paintings. By 10:30, head west a few blocks to find the granddaddy of monuments, the fabled Pantheon, still looking like Emperor Hadrian might arrive at any minute. A few blocks northwest is San Luigi dei Francesi, home to the greatest Caravaggio paintings in Rome. At 11:30 saunter a block or so westward into beyond-beautiful Piazza Navona, studded with Bernini fountains. Then take Via Cucagna (at the piazza's south end) and continue several blocks toward Campo de' Fiori's open-air food market for some lunch-on-the-run fixings. Two more blocks toward the Tiber brings you to fashionable Via Giulia, laid out by Pope Julius II in the early 16th century.

Walk past 10 blocks of Renaissance palaces and antiques shops to take a bus (from the stop near the Tiber) over to the Vatican. Arrive around 1 to gape at St. Peter's Basilica, then hit the treasure-filled Vatican Museums (Sistine Chapel) around 1:30—during lunch, the crowds diminish considerably. After two hours, head for the Ottaviano stop near the museum and Metro your way to the Colosseo stop.

Around 4 (earlier in winter, when last entrance to the archaeological zone is at 3:30), climb up into the Colosseum and picture it full of screaming toga-clad citizens enjoying the spectacle of gladiators in mortal combat. Striding past the massive Arch of Constantine, enter the Palatine Hill entrance at around 4:45, following signs for the Roman Forum. Photograph yourself giving a "Friends, Romans, Countrymen" oration (complete with upraised hand) among the marble fragments.

March down the Forum's Via Sacra toward the looming Vittorio Emanuele Monument (Il Vittoriano) and exit onto the Campidoglio.

Here, on the Capitoline Hill, tour the great ancient Roman art treasures of the Musei Capitolini (which are open most nights until 8, last entrance at 7), and snap the view from the terrace over the spotlighted Forum. After dinner, hail a cab—or take a long *passeggiata* (stroll) down *dolce vita* memory lane—to the Trevi Fountain, a gorgeously lit sight at night. Needless to say, toss that coin in to insure your return trip back to the Mother of Us All.

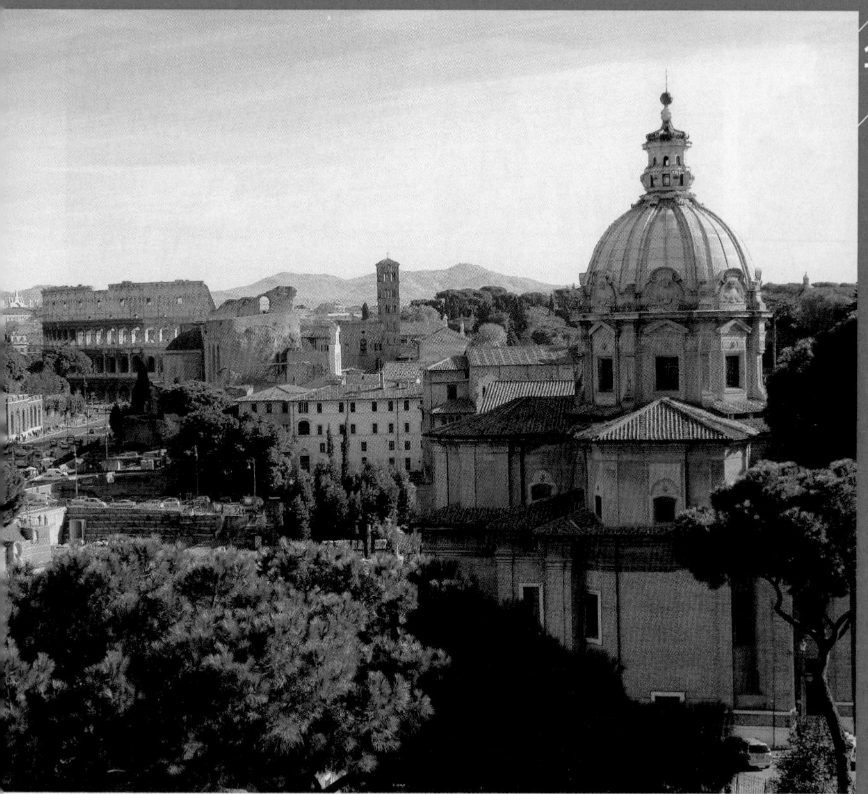

Rome

WORD OF MOUTH

"Once we got our 'Rome legs,' we loved the place. My philosophy is 'don't try to do Rome, let Rome do you.'"

—SallyJo

"Eat a lot of gelati. Eat more gelati. Have I mentioned gelati?"

—DWeller

Updated by Katie Parla and Nicole Arriaga

Coming off the Autostrada at Roma Nord or Roma Sud, you know by the convergence of heavily trafficked routes that you're entering a grand nexus: All roads lead to Rome.

And then the interminable suburbs, the railroad crossings, the intersections—no wonder they call it the Eternal City. As you forge on, features that match your expectations begin to appear: a bridge with heroic statues along its parapets; a towering slab of marble decorated with allegorical figures in extravagant poses; a piazza and an obelisk under an umbrella of pine trees. Then you spot what looks like a multistory parking lot; with a gasp, you realize it's the Colosseum.

You've arrived. You're in the city's heart. You step down from your excursion bus onto the broad girdle of tarmac that encircles the great stone arena of the Roman emperors, and scurry out of the way of the passing Fiats—the motorists behind the wheels seem to display the panache of so many Ben-Hurs. The excitement of arriving here jolts the senses and sharpens expectations.

The timeless city to which all roads lead, Mamma Roma, enthralls visitors today as she has since time immemorial. More than Florence, more than Venice, this is Italy's treasure storehouse. Here the ancient Romans made us heirs-in-law to what we call Western Civilization; where centuries later Michelangelo painted the Sistine Chapel; where Gian Lorenzo Bernini's baroque nymphs and naiads still dance in their marble fountains; and where, at Cinecittà Studios, Fellini filmed *La Dolce Vita* and *8½*. Today the city remains a veritable Grand Canyon of culture: Ancient Rome rubs shoulders with the medieval, the modern runs into the Renaissance, and the result is like nothing so much as an open-air museum.

But always remember: *Quando a Roma vai, fai come vedrai* ("When in Rome, do as the Romans do"). Don't feel intimidated by the press of art and culture. Instead, contemplate the grandeur from a table at a sun-drenched café on Piazza della Rotonda; let Rome's colorful life flow around you without feeling guilty because you haven't seen everything. It can't be done, anyway. There's just so much here that you'll have to come back again, so be sure to throw a coin in the Trevi Fountain.

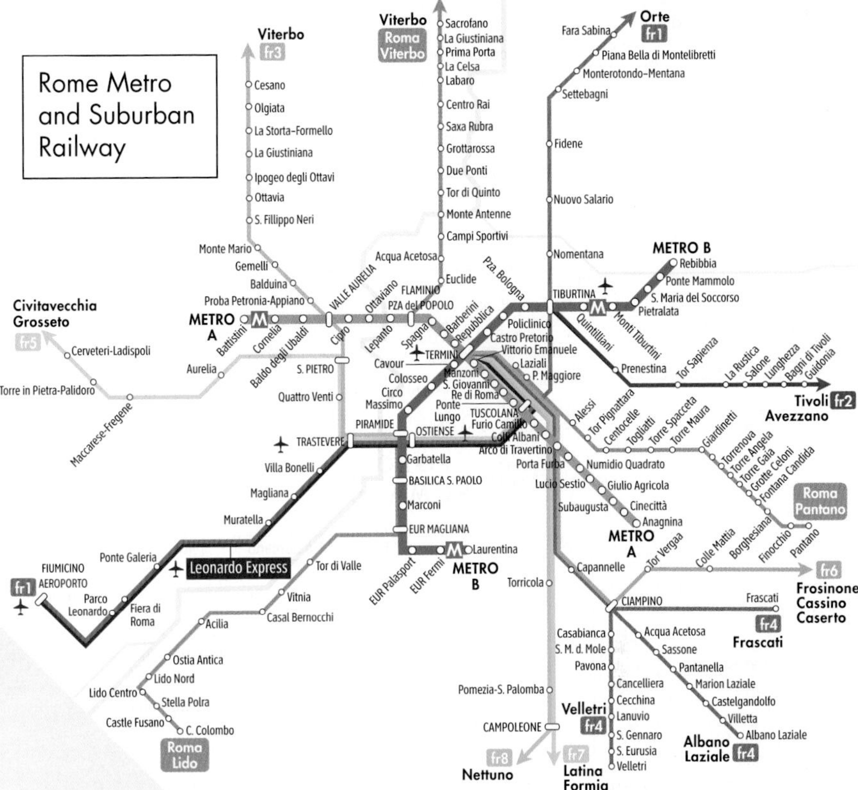

EXPLORING ROME

Updated by Katie Parla

Most everyone begins by discovering the grandeur that was Rome: the Colosseum, the Forum, and the Pantheon. Then many move on to the Vatican, the closest thing to heaven on Earth for some.

The historical pageant continues with the 1,001 splendors of the baroque era: glittering palaces, jewel-studded churches, and Caravaggio masterpieces. Arrive refreshed—with the help of a shot of espresso—at the foot of the Spanish Steps, where the picturesque world of the classic Grand Tour (peopled by such spirits as John Keats and Tosca) awaits you.

Thankfully, Rome provides delightful ways to catch your historic breath along the way: a walk through the cobblestone valleys of Trastevere or an hour stolen alongside a splashing Bernini fountain. Keep in mind that an uncharted ramble through the heart of the old city can be just as satisfying as the contemplation of a chapel or a trek through marbled museum corridors. No matter which aspect of Rome you end up enjoying the most, a visit to the Eternal City will live up to its name in memory.

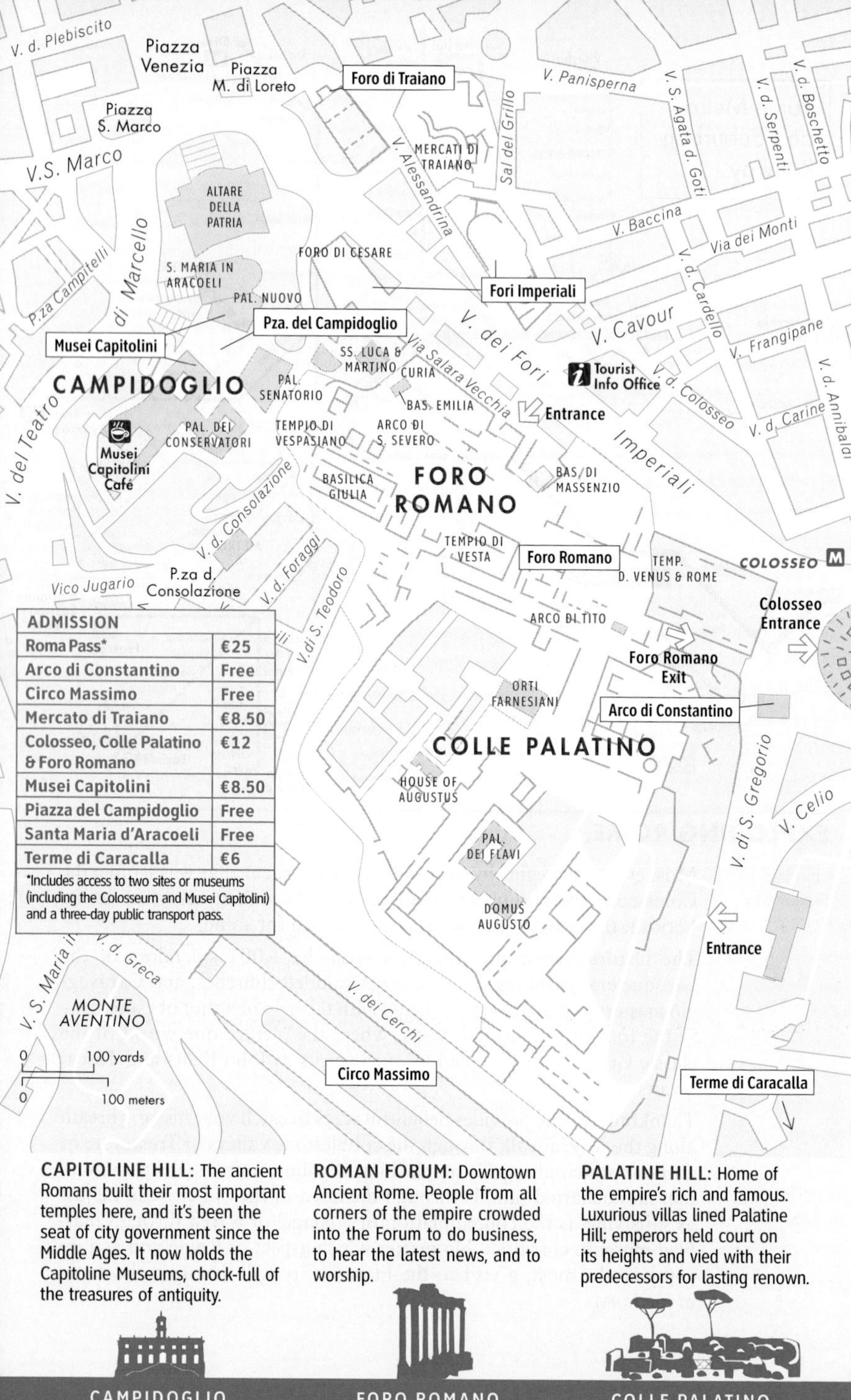

ADMISSION	
Roma Pass*	€25
Arco di Constantino	Free
Circo Massimo	Free
Mercato di Traiano	€8.50
Colosseo, Colle Palatino & Foro Romano	€12
Musei Capitolini	€8.50
Piazza del Campidoglio	Free
Santa Maria d'Aracoeli	Free
Terme di Caracalla	€6

*Includes access to two sites or museums (including the Colosseum and Musei Capitolini) and a three-day public transport pass.

CAPITOLINE HILL: The ancient Romans built their most important temples here, and it's been the seat of city government since the Middle Ages. It now holds the Capitoline Museums, chock-full of the treasures of antiquity.

ROMAN FORUM: Downtown Ancient Rome. People from all corners of the empire crowded into the Forum to do business, to hear the latest news, and to worship.

PALATINE HILL: Home of the empire's rich and famous. Luxurious villas lined Palatine Hill; emperors held court on its heights and vied with their predecessors for lasting renown.

CAMPIDOGLIO

FORO ROMANO

COLLE PALATINO

ANCIENT ROME
GLORIES OF THE CAESARS

Time has reduced ancient Rome to fields of silent ruins, but the powerful impact of what happened here, of the genius and power that made Rome the center of the Western world, echoes across the millennia.

In this one compact area of the city, you can step back into the Rome of Cicero, Julius Caesar, and Virgil. Walk along the streets they knew, cool off in the shade of the Colosseum that loomed over the city, and see the sculptures poised above their piazzas. At the end of a day of exploring, climb one of the famous hills and watch the sun set over what was once the heart of the civilized world.

Today, this part of Rome, more than any other, is a perfect example of that layering of historic eras, the overlapping of ages, of religions, of a past that is very much a part of the present. Christian churches rise from the foundations of ancient pagan temples. An immense marble monument to a 19th-century king shares a square with a Renaissance palace built by a pope. Still, the history and memory of ancient Rome dominate the area. It's fitting that in the aftermath of centuries of such pageantry Percy Bysshe Shelley and Edward Gibbon reflected here on the meaning of *sic transit gloria mundi* (so passes away the glory of the world).

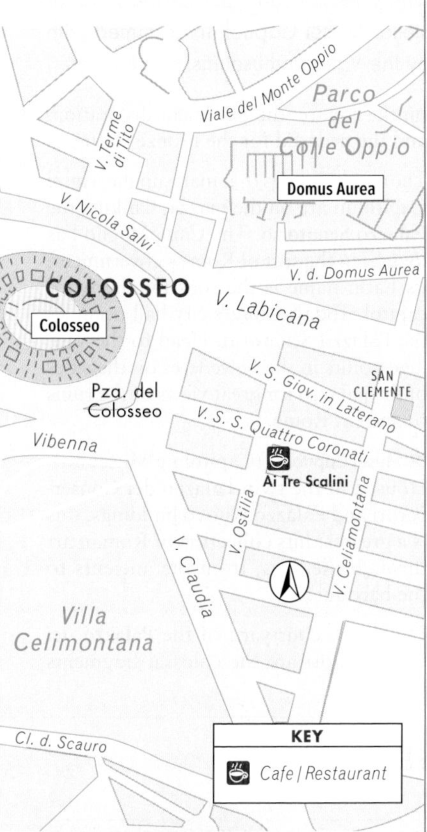

COLOSSEUM: Gladiators fought for the chance to live another day on the floor of the Colosseum, iconic symbol of ancient Rome.

CAMPIDOGLIO

TIMING TIPS

The Capitoline Museums are closed on Monday. Late evening is an option for this area. Though the Santa Maria d'Aracoeli church is closed, the museums are open until 8 PM, and the views of the city lights and the illuminated Altare della Patria (aka the Victor Emmanuel II monument) and the Foro Romano are striking.

CLIMB MICHELANGELO'S DRAMATIC RAMP TO THE SUMMIT of one of Rome's famous hills, the Campidoglio (also known as Capitoline Hill), for views across the rooftops of modern Rome in one direction and across the ruins of ancient Rome in the other. Check out the stellar Musei Capitolini, crammed with a collection of masterpieces rivaled only by the Vatican museums.

★ **Piazza del Campidoglio.** In Michelangelo's piazza at the top of the Campidoglio stands a bronze equestrian statue of Marcus Aurelius (AD 121–180). A legend foretells that some day the statue's original gold surface will return, heralding the end of the world. Pending the arrival of that day, the original 2nd century statue was moved inside the Musei Capitolini; a copy sits on the piazza. Stand with your back to it to survey central Rome.

The Campidoglio, the site of the Roman Republic's first and holiest temples, had fallen into ruin by the Middle Ages and was called *Monte Caprino* (Goat Hill). In 1536 Pope Paul III (1468–1549) decided to restore its grandeur for the triumphal entry into the city of Charles V (1500–1558), the Holy Roman Emperor. He called upon Michelangelo to create the staircase ramp, the buildings and facades on the square, the pavement decoration, and the pedestal for the bronze statue.

The two buildings that make up the **Musei Capitolini** are on the piazza, flanking the **Palazzo Senatorio**. The Campidoglio has long been the seat of Rome's government; its Latin name is the root for the word capitol. Today, Rome's city hall occupies the Palazzo Senatorio. Head to the vantage points in the belvederes on the sides of the palazzo for great views of the ruins of ancient Rome.

★ **Musei Capitolini** (Capitoline Museums). Housed in the twin Palazzo dei Conservatori and Palazzo Nuovo buildings, this is a greatest hits collection of Roman art through the ages, from the ancients to the baroque.

Lining the courtyard of the **Palazzo dei Conservatori** are the colossal fragments

AN EMPEROR CHEAT SHEET

OCTAVIAN/AUGUSTUS (27 BC–AD 14)

After the death of Julius Caesar, Octavian gained control of Rome following a decade-long civil war that ended with the defeat of Antony and Cleopatra at Actium. Later known as Caesar Augustus, he was Rome's first emperor. His rule began a 200-year period of peace known as the Pax Romana.

Colle Palatino

CALIGULA (AD 37–41)

Caligula was tremendously popular when he came to power at the age of 25, but he very soon became infamous for his excessive cruelty, immorality, and erratic behavior. His contemporaries universally considered him to be insane. He was murdered by his own guard within four years.

of a head, leg, foot, and hand—all that remains of the famous statue of the emperor Constantine. These immense effigies were much in vogue throughout the Roman Empire. The renowned symbol of Rome, the *Capitoline Wolf*, a medieval bronze (long thought to be Etruscan), holds a place of honor in the museum; the suckling twins were added during the Renaissance to adapt the statue to the legend of Romulus and Remus.

The Palazzo also contains some of baroque painting's great masterpieces, including Caravaggio's *La Buona Ventura* (1595) and *San Giovanni Battista* (1602), Peter Paul Rubens's *Romulus and Remus* (1615), and Pietro da Cortona's sumptuous portrait of Pope Urban VIII (1627). When museum fatigue sets in, enjoy the view and refreshments on a large open terrace in the Palazzo dei Conservatoria.

The **Palazzo Nuovo** contains hundreds of Roman busts of philosophers and emperors—a fascinating Who's Who of the ancient world. A dozen Roman emperors are represented. Unlike the Greeks, whose portraits are idealized, the Romans preferred a more realistic representation. Other notable sculptures include the poignant *Dying Gaul* and the regal *Capitoline Venus*. In the Capitolino courtyard is a gigantic, reclining sculpture of Oceanus, found in the Roman Forum and later dubbed *Marforio*. This was one of Rome's "talking statues" to which citizens from the 1500s to the 1900s affixed anonymous satirical verses and notes of political protest. ☎ *06/0608* 🌐 *www.museicapitolini.org* 🕙 *Tues.–Sun. 9–8.*

Santa Maria in Aracoeli. Seemingly endless, steep stairs climb from Piazza Venezia to the church of Santa Maria. There are 15th-century frescoes by Pinturicchio (1454–1513) in the first chapel on the right. ✉ *Scala dell'Arce Capitolina 14* 🕙 *May–Sept., daily, 9–12:30 and 3–6:30; Oct.–Apr., daily 9–12:30 and 3–5:30.*

NERO (AD 54–68)

Nero is infamous as a violent persecutor of Christians. He also murdered his wife, his mother, and countless others. Although it's certain he didn't actually fiddle as Rome burned in AD 64, he was well known as a singer and a composer of music.

Domus Aurea

DOMITIAN (AD 81–96)

The first emperor to declare himself "Dominus et Deus" (Lord and God), he stripped away power from the Senate. After his death, the Senate retaliated by declaring him "Damnatio Memoriae" (his name and image were erased from all public records).

Colle Palatino

FORO ROMANO

TIMING TIPS

It takes about an hour to explore the Roman Forum. There are entrances on the Via dei Fori Imperiali and from the Palatine Hill. A 30-minute walk will cover the Imperial Fora. You can reserve tickets online or by phone—operators speak English. If you are buying tickets in person, remember there are shorter lines here than at the Colosseum and the ticket is good for both sights.

EXPERIENCE THE ENDURING ROMANCE OF THE FORUM. Wander among its lonely columns and great, broken fragments of sculpted marble and stone—once temples, law courts, and shops crowded with people from all corners of the known world. This was the heart of ancient Rome and a symbol of the values that inspired Rome's conquest of an empire.

★ **Foro Romano** (Roman Forum). Built in a marshy valley between the Capitoline and Palatine hills, the Forum was the civic core of Republican Rome, the austere era that preceded the hedonism of the emperors. The Forum was the political, commercial, and religious center of Roman life. Hundreds of years of plunder and the tendency of later Romans to carry off what was left of the better building materials reduced it to the series of ruins you see today. Archaeological digs continue to uncover more about the sight; bear in mind that what you see are the ruins not of one period but of almost 900 years, from about 500 BC to AD 400.

The **Basilica Giulia**, which owes its name to Julius Caesar who had it built, was where the Centumviri, the hundred-or-so judges forming the civil court, met to hear cases. The open space before it was the core of the forum proper and prototype of Italy's famous piazzas. Let your imagination dwell on Mark Antony (circa 83 BC–30 BC), who delivered the funeral address in Julius Caesar's honor from the rostrum left of the **Arco di Settimio Severo**. This arch, one of the grandest of all antiquity, was built several hundred years later in AD 203 to celebrate the victory of the emperor Severus (AD 145–211) over the Parthians, and was topped by a bronze equestrian statuary group with four horses. You can explore the reconstruction of the large brick senate hall, the **Curia**; three Corinthian columns (a favorite of 19th-century poets) are all that remains of the **Tempio di Vespasiano el Tito**. In the **Tempio di Vesta**, six highly privileged vestal virgins kept the sacred fire, a tradition that dated back to the very earliest days of Rome. Their luxuious villa beside the temple was opened to the public in 2011. The cleaned and restored **Arco di Tito**, which stands in a slightly

AN EMPEROR CHEAT SHEET

TRAJAN (AD 98–117)

Trajan, from Southern Spain, was the first Roman emperor not born in Italy. He enlarged the empire's boundaries to include modern-day Romania, Armenia, and Upper Mesopotamia.

Colonna di Traiano, Foro di Traiano, Mercati di Traiano

HADRIAN (AD 117–138)

He expanded the empire in Asia and the Middle East. He's best known for rebuilding the Pantheon, constructing a majestic villa at Tivoli, and initiating myriad other constructions across the empire, including the famed wall across Britain.

elevated position on a spur of the Palatine Hill, was erected in AD 81 to honor the recently dead Emperor Titus. It depicts the sacking of Jerusalem 10 years earlier, after the great Jewish revolt. A famous relief shows the captured contents of Herod's Temple—including its huge seven-branched menorah—being carried in triumph down Rome's Via Sacra. The temple of Venus and Roma sits between the arch and the Colosseum. Making sense of the ruins isn't always easy; consider renting an audio guide (€4) or buying a booklet that superimposes an image of the Forum in its heyday over a picture of it today. ☎ *06/39967700* 🌐 *www.pierreci.it* ⏲ *Daily, Jan.–Feb. 15 and last Sun. in Oct.–Dec., 8:30–4:30; Feb. 16–Mar. 15, 8:30–5; Mar. 16–last Sat. in Mar., 8:30–5:30; last Sun. in Mar.–Aug., 8:30–7:15; Sept., 8:30–7; Oct.1–last Sat. in Oct., 8:30–6:30.*

THE OTHER FORA

Fori Imperiali (Imperial Fora). These five grandly conceived squares flanked with columnades and temples were built by Caesar, Augustus, Vespasian, Nerva, and Trajan. The original Roman Forum, built up over 500 years of Republican Rome, had grown crowded, and Julius Caesar was the first to attempt to rival it. He built the **Foro di Cesare** (Forum of Caesar), including a temple dedicated to the goddess Venus. Four emperors followed his lead, creating their own fora. The grandest was the **Foro di Traiano** (Forum of Trajan) a veritable city unto itself built by Trajan (AD 53–117). Here you find the 100-ft Colonna di Traiano (Trajan's Column, AD 110), carved with 2,600 figures in relief. In the 20th century, Benito Mussolini built the Via dei Fori Imperiali directly through the Imperial Fora area. Marble and limestone maps on the wall along the avenue portray the extent of the Roman Republic and Empire, and many of the remains of the Imperial Fora lay buried beneath its surface.

Mercati di Traiano (Trajan's Markets). This huge multilevel brick complex of 120 offices was one of the marvels of the ancient world. It provides a glimpse into Roman daily life and offers a stellar view from the belvedere at its top. ☎ *06/0608* 🌐 *www.mercatiditraiano.it* ⏲ *Tues.–Sun., 9–7.*

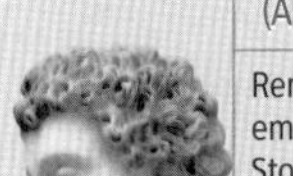

(AD 161–180)

Remembered as a humanitarian emperor, Marcus Aurelius was a Stoic philosopher and his *Meditations* are still read today. Nonetheless, he was an aggressive leader devoted to expanding the empire.

Piazza del Campidoglio

CONSTANTINE I (AD 306–337)

Constantine changed the course of history by legalizing Christianity. He legitimized the once-banned religion and paved the way for the papacy in Rome. Constantine also established Constantinople as an Imperial capital in the East.

Arco di Constantino

COLLE PALATINO

TIMING TIPS

A stroll on the Palatino, with a visit to the Museo Palatino, takes about two hours. The hill was once home to several major imperial palaces. Domitian's 1st-century AD palace is the best preserved. The Colle Palatino entrances are from the Roman Forum and at Via S. Gregorio 30.

IT ALL BEGAN HERE. ACCORDING TO LEGEND, ROMULUS, THE FOUNDER OF ROME, lived on the Colle Palatino (Palatine Hill). It was an exclusive address in ancient Rome, where emperors built palaces upon the slopes. Tour the Palatine's hidden corners and shady lanes, take a welcome break from the heat in its peaceful gardens, and enjoy a view of the Circo Massimo fit for an emperor.

★ **Colle Palatino** (Palatine Hill). A lane known as the Clivus Palatinus, paved with worn stones that were once trod by emperors and their slaves, climbs from the Forum area to a site that historians identify as one of Rome's earliest settlements. The legend goes that the infant twins Romulus and Remus were nursed by a she-wolf on the banks of the Tiber and adopted by a shepherd. Encouraged by the gods to build a city, Romulus chose this site in 753 BC. Remus preferred the Aventine. The argument that ensued left Remus dead and Romulus Rome's first king.

During the Republican era the hill was an important religious center, housing the Temple of Cybele and the Temple of Victory, as well as an exclusive residential area. Cicero, Catiline, Crassus, and Agrippa all had homes here. Augustus was born on the hill, and as he rose in power, he built libraries, halls, and temples here; the **House of Augustus,** opened in 2008, preserves exquisite 1st-century BC frescoes. Emperor Tiberius was the next to build a palace here; others followed. The structures most visible today date back to the late 1st century AD, when the Palatine experienced an extensive remodeling under Emperor Domitian. During the Renaissance, the powerful Farnese family built gardens in the area overlooking the ruins of the Forum. Known as the **Orti Farnesiani**, they were Europe's first botanical gardens. The **Museo Palatino** charts the history of the hill. Splendid sculptures, frescoes, and mosaic intarsia from various imperial buildings are on display. ☎ *06/39967700* 🌐 *www.pierreci.it* ⏱ *Daily, Jan.–Feb. 15 and last Sun. in Oct.–Dec., 8:30–4:30; Feb. 16–Mar. 15, 8:30–5; Mar. 16–last Sat. in Mar., 8:30–5:30; last Sun. in Mar.–Aug., 8:30–7:15; Sept., 8:30–7; Oct.1–last Sat. in Oct., 8:30–6:30.*

THE RISE AND FALL OF ANCIENT ROME

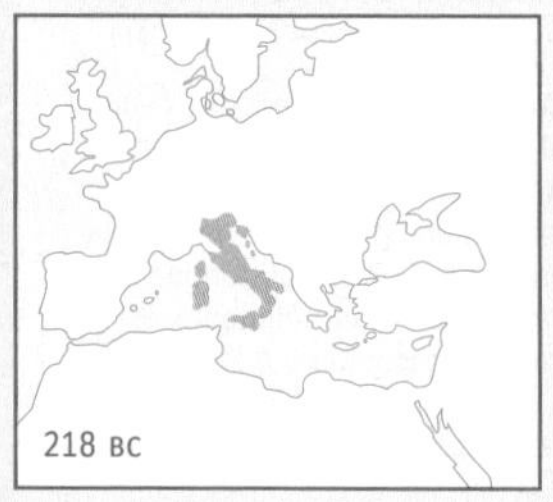

ca. 800 BC	Rise of Etruscan city-states.
509–510	Foundation of the Roman republic; expulsion of Etruscans from Roman territory.
343	Roman conquest of Greek colonies in Campania.
264–241	First Punic War (with Carthage): increased naval power helps Rome gain control of southern Italy and then Sicily.
212–202	Second Punic War: Hannibal's attempted conquest of Italy, using elephants, is eventually crushed.

NEAR THE COLLE PALATINO

Circo Massimo (Circus Maximus). Ancient Rome's oldest and largest racetrack lies in the natural hollow between the Palatine and Aventine hills. From the imperial box in the palace on Palatine Hill, emperors could look out over the oval course. Stretching about 660 yards from end to end, the Circus Maximus could hold more than 200,000 spectators. On certain occasions there were as many as 100 chariot races a day, and competitions could last for 15 days. The central ridge was framed by two Egyptian obelisks. Check out the panoramic views of the Circus Maximus from the Palatine Hill's Belvedere. You can also see the green slopes of the Aventine and Celian hills, as well as the bell tower of Santa Maria in Cosmedin.

Terme di Caracalla (Baths of Caracalla). For the Romans, public baths were much more than places to wash. The baths also had recital halls, art galleries, libraries, massage rooms, sports grounds, and gardens. Even the smallest public baths had at least some of these amenities, and in the capital of the Roman Empire, they were provided on a lavish scale. Ancient Rome's most beautiful and luxurious public baths were opened by the emperor Caracalla in AD 217 and were used until the 6th century.

Taking a bath was a long process, and a social activity first and foremost. You began by sweating in the *sudatoria*, small rooms resembling saunas. From these you moved on to the *calidarium* for the actual business of washing, using an olive-oil-and-sand exfoliant, then removing it with a *strigil* (scraper). Next was the *tepidarium*, where you gradually cooled down. Finally, you splashed around in the *frigidarium*, in essence a cold-water swimming pool. There was a nominal admission fee, often waived by officials and emperors wishing to curry favor with the plebeians. The baths' functioning depended on the slaves who cared for the clients and stoked the fires that heated the water. ☎ *06/39967700* 🌐 *www.pierreci.it* ⏲ *Tues.–Sun., Jan.–Feb. 15 and last Sun. in Oct.–Dec., 9–4:30; Feb. 16–Mar. 15, 9–5; Mar. 16–last Sat. in Mar., 9–5:30; last Sun. in Mar.–Aug., 9–7:15; Sept., 9–7; Oct. 1–last Sat. in Oct., 9–6:30. For all Mondays, 9–2.*

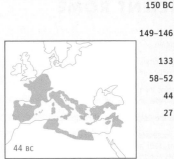

150 BC	Roman Forum begins to take shape as the principal civic center in Italy.
149–146	Third Punic War: Rome razes city of Carthage and emerges as the dominant Mediterranean force.
133	Rome rules entire Mediterranean Basin except Egypt.
58–52	Julius Caesar conquers Gaul.
44	Julius Caesar is assassinated.
27	Rome's Imperial Age begins; Octavian (now named Augustus) becomes the first emperor and is later deified. The Augustan Age is celebrated in the works of Virgil (70–19 BC), Ovid (43 BC–AD 17), Livy (59 BC–AD 17), and Horace (65–8 BC).

44 BC

COLOSSEO

TIMING TIPS

You can give the Colosseum a cursory look in about 30 minutes, but it deserves at least an hour. Make reservations by phone (there are English-speaking operators) or online at least a day in advance to avoid long lines. Or buy your ticket at the Roman Forum or Palatine Hill, where the lines are usually shorter.

LEGEND HAS IT THAT AS LONG AS THE COLOSSEUM STANDS, ROME WILL STAND; and when Rome falls, so will the world. No visit to Rome is complete without a trip to the obstinate oval that has been the iconic symbol of the city for centuries.

★ **Colosseo.** A program of games and shows lasting 100 days celebrated the opening of the massive and majestic Colosseum in AD 80. On the opening day Romans claimed that 5,000 wild beasts perished. More than 50,000 spectators could sit within the arena's 596-yard circumference, which had limestone facing, hundreds of statues for decoration, and a *velarium*—an ingenious system of sail-like awnings rigged on ropes manned by imperial sailors—to protect the audience from the sun and rain. Before the imperial box, gladiators would salute the emperor and cry, "*Ave, imperator, morituri te salutant*" ("Hail, emperor, men soon to die salute you"); it is said that when one day they heard the emperor Claudius respond, "Or maybe not," they were so offended that they called a strike.

Originally known as the Flavian Amphitheater, it took the name Colosseum after a truly colossal gilt bronze statue of Nero that stood nearby. Gladiator combat ended by the 5th century and staged animal hunts by the 6th. The arena later served as a quarry from which materials were looted to build Renaissance churches and palaces, including St. Peter's Basilica. Finally, it was declared sacred by the Vatican in memory of the many Christians believed martyred here. (Scholars now maintain that Christians met their death elsewhere.) During the 19th century, romantic poets lauded the glories of the ruins when viewed by moonlight. Now its arches glow at night with mellow golden spotlights.

Expect long lines at the entrance and actors dressed as gladiators who charge a hefty fee to pose for pictures. (Agree on a price in advance if you want a photo.) Once inside you can walk around about half of the outer ring of the structure and look down into the exposed passages under what was once the arena floor, now represented by a small stage at one end. Climb the steep stairs for panoramic views in the Colosseum and out to the Palatine and Arch of Constantine. A museum

THE RISE AND FALL OF ANCIENT ROME

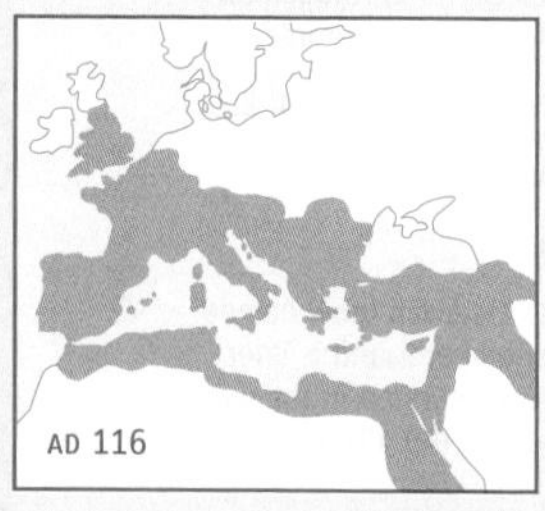

58 AD	Rome invades Britain.
50	Rome is the largest city in the world, with a population of possibly as much as a million.
64–68	Emperor Nero begins the persecution of Christians in the Empire; Saints Peter and Paul are executed.
72–80	Vespasian begins the Colosseum; Titus completes it.
98–117	Trajan's military successes are celebrated with his Baths (98), Forum (110), and Column (113); the Roman Empire reaches its apogee.

space on the second floor holds temporary archaeological exhibits. ☎ *06/39967700* 🌐 *www.pierreci.it* ⏲ *Daily, Jan.–Feb. 15 and last Sun. in Oct.–Dec., 8:30–4:30; Feb. 16–Mar. 15, 8:30–5; Mar. 16–last Sat. in Mar., 8:30–5:30; last Sun. in Mar.–Aug., 8:30–7:15; Sept., 8:30–7; Oct.1–last Sat. in Oct., 8:30–6:30.*

Arco di Costantino. The largest (69 feet high, 85 feet long, 23 feet wide) and the best preserved of Rome's triumphal arches was erected in AD 315 to celebrate the victory of the emperor Constantine (280–337) over co-emperor Maxentius (died 312). According to legend, it was just before this battle that Constantine, the emperor who legalized Christianity, had a vision of a cross in the heavens and heard the words "In this sign, thou shalt conquer."

NEAR THE COLOSSEO

Domus Aurea. At this writing, Nero's "Golden House"was closed, with the prospect of reopening uncertain. The site gives a good sense of the excesses of Imperial Rome. After fire destroyed much of the city in AD 64, Nero took advantage of the resulting open space to construct a lavish palace so large that it spread over a third of the city. It had a facade of marble, seawater piped into the baths, gilded vaults, decorations of mother-of-pearl, and vast gardens. Not much of this ornamentation has survived; a good portion of the building and grounds was buried under the public works with which subsequent emperors sought to make reparation to the Roman people for Nero's phenomenal greed. As a result, the site of the Domus Aurea itself remained unknown for many centuries. A few of Nero's original halls were discovered underground at the end of the 15th century. Raphael (1483–1520) was one of the artists who had themselves lowered into the rubble-filled rooms, which resembled grottoes. The artists copied the original painted Roman decorations, barely visible by torchlight, and scratched their names on the ceilings. Raphael later used these models—known as *grotesques* because they were found in the so-called grottoes—in his decorative motifs for the Loggia of Julius II in the Vatican. The palace remains impressive in scale, even if a lot of imagination is required to envision the original. ✉ *Via della Domus Aurea* ☎ *06/39967700* 🌐 *www.pierreci.it.*

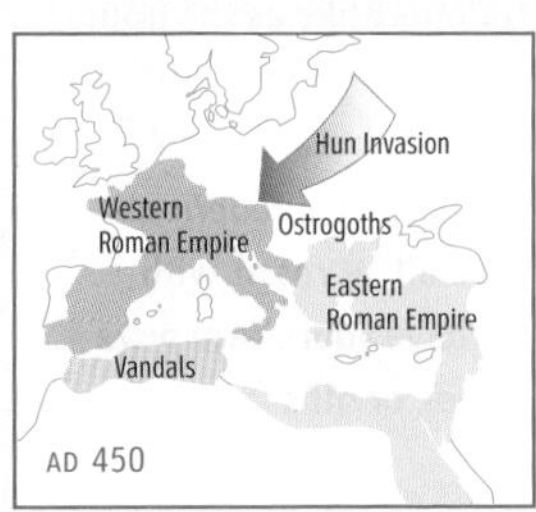

238 AD	The first wave of Germanic invasions penetrates Italy.
293	Diocletian reorganizes the Empire into West and East.
330	Constantine founds a new Imperial capital (Constantinople) in the East.
410	Rome is sacked by Visigoths.
476	The last Roman emperor, Romulus Augustus, is deposed. The western Roman Empire falls.

NAVONA AND CAMPO: BAROQUE ROME

Called the "Campo Marzio" (Field of Mars), this time-burnished district is the city's most beautiful neighborhood. Set between the Via del Corso and the Tiber bend, it's filled with narrow streets bearing curious names, airy piazzas, and half-hidden courtyards. Some of Rome's most coveted residential addresses are nestled here. So, too, are the ancient Pantheon and the Renaissance square of Campo de' Fiori, but the spectacular, over-the-top baroque monuments of the 16th and 17th centuries predominate.

The hub of the district is the queen of squares, Piazza Navona—a cityscape adorned with the most eye-knocking fountain by Gian Lorenzo Bernini, father of the baroque. Streets running off the square lead to many historic must-sees, including noble churches by Borromini and Caravaggio's greatest paintings at San Luigi dei Francesi. This district has been an integral part of the city since ancient times, and its position between the Vatican and Lateran palaces, both seats of papal rule, put it in the mainstream of Rome's development from the Middle Ages onward. Craftsmen, shopkeepers, and famed artists toiled in the shadow of the huge palaces built to consolidate the power of leading figures in the papal court. Artisans and artists still live here, but their numbers are diminishing as the district becomes increasingly posh and—so critics say—"Disneyfied." But three of the liveliest piazzas in Rome—Piazza Navona, Piazza della Rotonda (home to the Pantheon), and Campo de' Fiori—are lodestars in a constellation of some of Rome's most authentic cafés, stores, and wine bars.

GETTING HERE To bus it from Termini rail station or the Vatican, take the No. 40 Express or the No. 64 and get off at Corso Vittorio Emanuele II, a two-minute stroll to either Campo de' Fiori or Piazza Navona, or take little electric No. 116 from Via Veneto to Campo de' Fiori. Buses Nos. 87 and 571 link the area to the Forum and Colosseum. Tram No. 8 runs from Largo Argentina to Trastevere.

TOP ATTRACTIONS

★ **Campo de' Fiori.** Home to Rome's oldest (since 1869) outdoor produce market, open Monday through Saturday, this bustling square was originally used for public executions, making its name—"Field of Flowers"—a bit sardonic. In fact, the central statue commemorates the Dominican friar and philosopher Giordano Bruno, who was burned at the stake here in 1600 by the Inquisition. Today, he frowns down upon food vendors galore, who, by early afternoon, are all gone, giving way to the square's cafés and bars that attract throngs of Rome's hip, young professionals and American semester-abroad students alike as the hours wend their way into evening. ✉ *Campo de' Fiori, near Piazza Navona.*

QUICK BITES

Some of Rome's best pizza comes out of the ovens of Forno Campo de' Fiori (✉ *Campo de' Fiori 22* ☎ *06/68806662* 🌐 *www.fornocampodefiori.com*). Choose *pizza bianca*, topped with salt and olive oil, or *rossa*, with tomato sauce. Move to the annex across the alley to have your warm pizza filled with prosciutto and figs in August and September, or other mouthwatering combinations year-round.

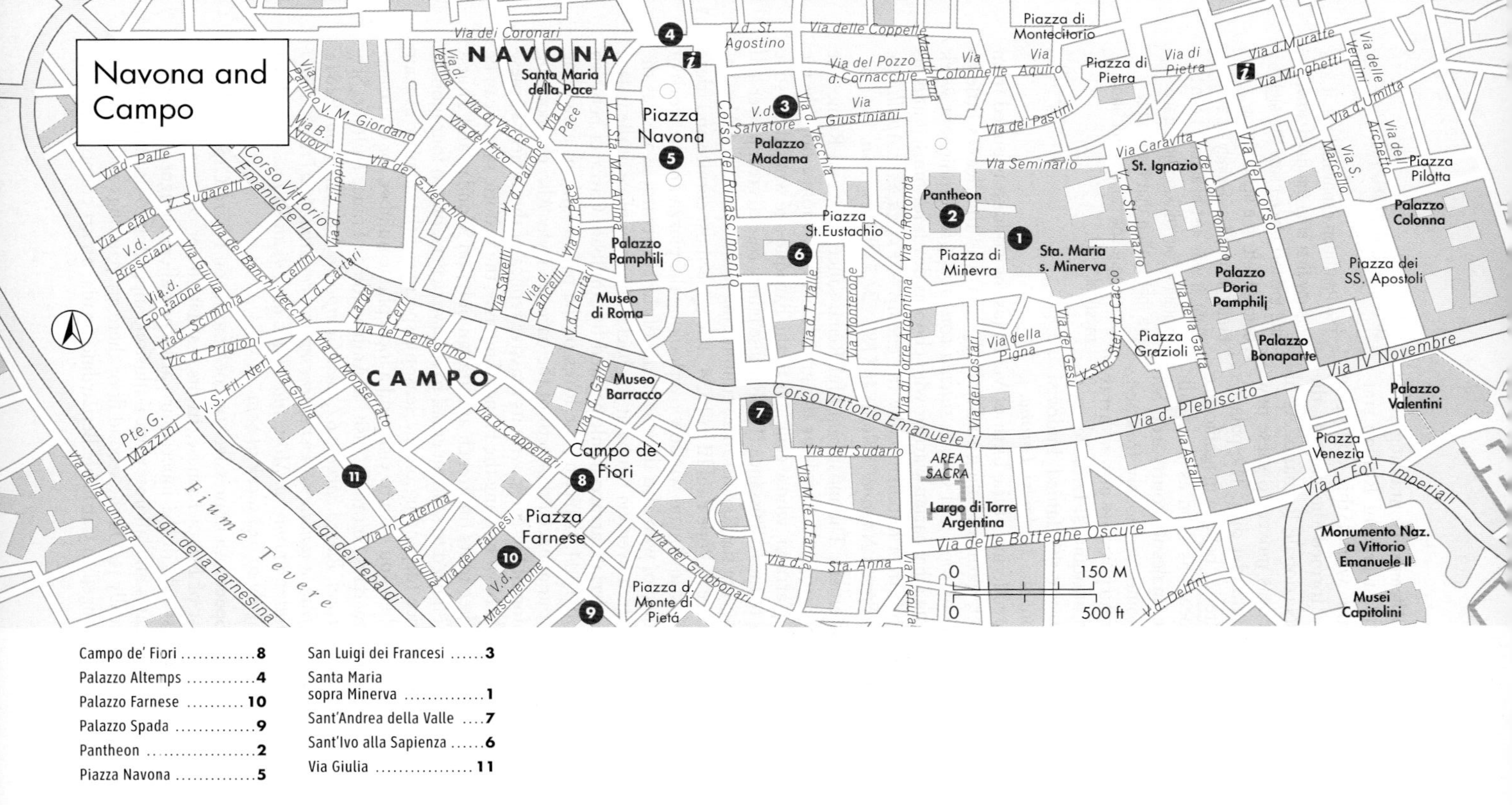
Navona and Campo
NAVONA
CAMPO
Santa Maria della Pace
Piazza Navona
Palazzo Madama
Piazza St.Eustachio
Pantheon
Piazza di Minevra
Sta. Maria s. Minerva
St. Ignazio
Palazzo Doria Pamphilj
Palazzo Bonaparte
Palazzo Colonna
Piazza dei SS. Apostoli
Palazzo Valentini
Piazza Venezia
Monumento Naz. a Vittorio Emanuele II
Musei Capitolini
Piazza di Montecitorio
Piazza di Pietra
Piazza Pilotta
Piazza Grazioli
Palazzo Pamphilj
Museo di Roma
Museo Barracco
Campo de' Fiori
Piazza Farnese
Piazza d. Monte di Pietá
AREA SACRA
Largo di Torre Argentina
Corso Vittorio Emanuele II
Corso del Rinascimento
Via del Corso
Via IV Novembre
Via d. Plebiscito
Via delle Botteghe Oscure
Via d. Fori Imperiali
Via dei Coronari
Via Giulia
Via del Pellegrino
Via di Monserrato
Via dei Giubbonari
Via Arenula
Lgt. dei Tebaldi
Lgt. della Farnesina
Via della Lungara
Fiume Tevere
Pte.G. Mazzini
0 150 M
0 500 ft

Palazzo Altemps. Containing some of the finest ancient Roman statues in the world, this collection formerly formed the core of the Museo Nazionale Romano. As of 1995, it was moved to these new, suitably grander digs. The palace's sober exterior belies a magnificence that appears as soon as you walk into the majestic courtyard. Set within some gorgeously frescoed, 16th-century rooms are an array of noted antiquities. Look for two works from the famed Ludovisi collection: the *Ludovisi Throne*, a sensual rendering of the birth of Venus (as the goddess is pulled from the water, garments cling to her body in a way that leaves little to the imagination), and *Galata suicida con la moglie*, a poignant work portraying a barbarian warrior who chooses death for himself and his wife rather than humiliation by the enemy. ✉ *Piazza Sant'Apollinare 46, near Piazza Navona* ☎ *06/68485182* 🎟 *€7* ⏲ *Tues.–Sun. 9–6:45.*

WORD OF MOUTH

"The Pantheon captivated me. It was my first stop the day I arrived and the last place I saw the night before I left. In a light mist, in bright sun and especially lit at night, it was just beautiful. I can't explain it, but looking at it gave me that feeling that I was truly somewhere special, ancient and mystical."

—amyb

Palazzo Farnese. The most beautiful Renaissance palace in Rome, the Palazzo Farnese is noted for the grandeur of its rooms, notably the Galleria Carracci, whose ceiling is to the baroque age what the Sistine ceiling is to the Renaissance. The Farnese family rose to great power and wealth during the Renaissance, culminating in the election of Alessandro Farnese as Pope Paul III in 1534. The uppermost cornice and frieze decorations and main window overlooking the piazza are the work of Michelangelo, who also designed part of the courtyard, as well as the graceful arch over Via Giulia at the back. The showpiece of the palace is the **Galleria Carracci** vault painted by Annibale Carracci between 1597 and 1604, depicting the loves of the pagan gods in a swirling style that announced the birth of the baroque style. Also eye-popping is the **Salon of Hercules,** with its massive replica of the ancient Farnese Hercules. Now housing the French Embassy, the historic salons can be seen on free tours (in French and Italian only) on Monday and Thursday. You'll need to send an email to reserve tickets, one to four months in advance (depending on the season), specifying the number in your party, when you wish to visit, and a local phone number, for confirmation a few days before the visit. ✉ Ambassade de France en Italie, Service Culturel, *Piazza Farnese 67, near Campo de' Fiori* ☎ *06/68892818* 🌐 *www.france-italia.it* ✉ *visitefarnese@france-italia.it* 🎟 *Free* ⏲ *Tours by appointment only on Mon. and Thurs. at 3, 4, and 5 pm. Closed last week in July to first week in Sept.*

Palazzo Spada. An impressive stuccoed facade on Piazza Capo di Ferro, southeast of Piazza Farnese, fronts a sedate inner courtyard. On the southeast side of the inner courtyard, the gallery designed by Borromini creates an elaborate optical illusion, appearing to be much longer than it really is. On the second floor there are paintings and sculptures that belonged to Cardinale Bernardino Spada, an art connoisseur who

CLOSE UP

Going Baroque

Flagrantly emotional, heavily expressive, and visually sensuous, the 17th-century artistic movement known as baroque was born in Rome. It was the creation of three geniuses: the sculptor and architect Gian Lorenzo Bernini (1598–1680), the painter and architect Pietro da Cortona (1596–1669), and the architect and sculptor Francesco Borromini (1599–1667). From the drama found in the artists' works to the jewel-laden, gold-on-gold detail of 17th-century Roman palaces, the baroque style was intended both to shock and delight by upsetting the placid, "correct" rules of proportion and scale of the Renaissance. If a building looks theatrical—like a stage or a theater, especially with curtains being drawn back—it's usually baroque. Look for over-the-top, curvaceous marble work, trompe l'oeils, allusions to other art, and high drama to identify the style. Baroque's appeal to the emotions made it a powerful weapon in the hands of the Counter-Reformation.

collected works by Italian and Flemish masters. ■ **TIP→ Note that the palazzo occasionally closes in the afternoon because of staff shortages.** ✉ *Piazza Capo di Ferro 13, near Campo de' Fiori* ☎ *06/6832409* 🌐 *www.galleriaborghese.it/spada/en/einfo.htm* 🎫 *€5* ⏲ *Tues.–Sun. 8:30–7:30.*

Fodor's Choice ★ **Pantheon.** One of Rome's most impressive and best-preserved ancient monuments, the Pantheon is particularly close to the hearts of Romans. The emperor Hadrian had it built around AD 120 on the site of an earlier temple that had been damaged by fire. Although the sheer size of the Pantheon is impressive (it's still the largest unreinforced concrete dome ever built), what's most striking is its tangible sense of harmony. In large part this feeling is the result of the building's symmetrical design: at 43.3 meters (142 feet), the height of the dome is equal to the diameter of the circular interior. The "eye of heaven" oculus, or hole in the dome, is open to the skies, illuminating the heavy stone dome. Originally, the dome was covered in bronze plates that would have reflected beams of sunlight, creating a celestial glow. Centuries of plunder by emperors and popes have stripped most of the bronze ornamentation, though the original bronze doors have survived more than 1,800 years. Art lovers can pay homage to the tomb of Raphael, who is buried in an ancient sarcophagus under the altar of Madonna del Sasso. ✉ *Piazza della Rotonda, Navona* ☎ *06/68300230* 🎫 *Free* ⏲ *Mon.–Sat. 8:30–7:30, Sun. 9–6.*

★ **Piazza Navona.** With its carefree air of the days when it was the scene of Roman circus games, medieval jousts, and 17th-century carnivals, the spectacularly beautiful Piazza Navona today often attracts fashion photographers on shoots and Romans out for their *passeggiata* (evening stroll). Bernini's splashing **Fontana dei Quattro Fiumi** (Fountain of the Four Rivers), with an enormous rock squared off by statues representing the four corners of the world, makes a fitting centerpiece. Behind the fountain is the church of **Sant'Agnese in Agone,** an outstanding example of baroque architecture built by the Pamphilj Pope Innocent X.

The facade—a wonderfully rich mélange of bell towers, concave spaces, and dovetailed stone and marble—is by Borromini, a contemporary and rival of Bernini, and by Carlo Rainaldi (1611–91). One story has it that the Bernini statue nearest the church, which represents the River Plate, has its hand up before its eye because it can't bear the sight of the Borromini facade. Though often repeated, the story is fiction: the facade was built after the fountain. From December 8 through January 6, a Christmas market fills the square with games, Nativity scenes (some well crafted, many not), and multiple versions of the Befana, the ugly but good witch who brings candy and toys to Italian children on Epiphany. (Her name is a corruption of the Italian word for "epiphany," *Epifania.*) ✉ *Junction of Via della Cuccagna, Corsia Agonale, Via di Sant'Agnese in Agone, and Via Agonale, Navona.*

★ **San Luigi dei Francesi.** The official church of Rome's French community and a pilgrimage spot for art lovers everywhere, San Luigi is home to the **Cappella Contarelli,** adorned with three stunningly dramatic works by Caravaggio (1571–1610). Set in the last chapel in the left aisle, they were commissioned by Cardinal Matthieu Cointrel (in Italian, Contarelli) and perfectly embody the baroque master's heightened approach to light and dark. The inevitable coin machine will light up his *Calling of St. Matthew, Matthew and the Angel,* and *Matthew's Martyrdom,* seen from left to right, and Caravaggio's mastery of light and shadow takes it from there. When painted, they caused considerable consternation to the clergy of San Luigi, who thought the artist's dramatically realistic approach was scandalously disrespectful. But these paintings did to 17th-century art what Picasso's *Demoiselles d'Avignon* did to the 20th century. ✉ *Piazza San Luigi dei Francesi 5, Navona* ☎ *06/688271* ⏲ *Fri.–Wed. 10–12:30 and 4–7.*

Santa Maria Sopra Minerva. Michelangelo's *Christ the Redeemer* and the tomb of the gentle 15th-century artist Fra Angelico are two noted sights in the only Gothic-style church in Rome. Have some coins handy to light up the **Cappella Carafa** in the right transept, where exquisite 15th-century frescoes by Filippino Lippi (circa 1457–1504) are well worth the small investment. Historians believe that Botticelli apprenticed under Lippi during this time. In front of the church is one of Rome's best photo ops, Bernini's charming elephant bearing an Egyptian obelisk; an inscription on the memorial's base states that it takes a strong mind to sustain solid wisdom. ✉ *Piazza della Minerva 42, Pantheon* ☎ *06/6793926* ⏲ *Mon.–Sat. 7–7, Sun. 8–noon and 4–7.*

★ **Via Giulia.** Named after Pope Julius II and serving for more than five centuries as the "salon of Rome," this street—running between Piazza Farnese and the Tiber—is still the address of choice for Roman aristocrats and rich foreigners. Built at the turn of the 16th century, the street is lined with elegant palaces, including the Palazzo Falconieri, old churches (one, Sant'Eligio, reputedly designed by Raphael himself), and, in springtime, glorious hanging wisteria. The area around Via Giulia is a wonderful place to wander in to get the feeling of daily life as carried on in a centuries-old setting—an experience enhanced by the dozens of antiques shops in the neighborhood. ✉ *1 block east of the Tiber River, Campo de' Fiori.*

WORTH NOTING

Sant'Andrea della Valle. Topped by the second-tallest dome in Rome (after St. Peter's), this huge 17th-century church looms mightily over a busy intersection. Puccini set the first act of his opera *Tosca* here; fans have been known to hire a horse-drawn carriage at night to trace the course of the opera from Sant'Andrea up Via Giulia to Palazzo Farnese—Scarpia's headquarters—to the locale of the opera's climax, Castel Sant'Angelo. Inside, above the apse, are striking frescoes depicting scenes from Saint Andrew's life by the Bolognese painter Domenichino (1581–1641). ✉ *Corso Vittorio Emanuele II, Navona* ☎ *06/6861339* ⏲ *Daily 7:30–12:30 and 4:30–7:30.*

Sant'Ivo alla Sapienza. Borromini's eccentric 17th-century church has what must surely be Rome's most unusual dome—topped by a softly molded spiral said to have been inspired by a beehive. Visit during the limited opening hours for a glimpse of Borromini's manic genius, an undulating white stucco interior bathed in gleaming daylight. ✉ *Corso Rinascimento 40, Navona* ☎ *06/3612562* ⏲ *Sun. 9–noon.*

CORSO AND SPAGNA: PIAZZA VENEZIA TO THE SPANISH STEPS

In spirit, and in fact, this section of the city is its most grandiose. The overblown Vittoriano monument, the labyrinthine treasure-chest palaces of Rome's surviving aristocracy, even the diamond-draped denizens of Via Condotti's shops—all embody the exuberant ego of a city at the center of its own universe. Here's where you'll see ladies in furs gobbling pastries at café tables, and walk through a thousand snapshots as you climb the famous Spanish Steps, admired by generations from Byron to Versace. Cultural treasures abound around here: gilded 17th-century churches, glittering palaces, and the greatest example of portraiture in Rome: Velázquez's incomparable *Innocent X* at the Galleria Doria Pamphilj. Have your camera ready—along with a coin or two—for that most beloved of Rome's landmarks, the Trevi Fountain.

GETTING HERE One of Rome's handiest subway stations, the Spagna Metro station is tucked just to the left of the Spanish Steps. Buses No. 117 (from the Colosseum area) and No. 119 (from Largo Argentina) hum through the neighborhood.

TOP ATTRACTIONS

Altare della Patria. Also known as the Monumento Vittorio Emanuele II or the Vittoriano, this vast marble monument was erected in the late 19th century to honor Italy's first king, Vittorio Emanuele II (1820–78), and the unification of Italy. Aesthetically minded Romans have derided the oversize structure, visible from many parts of the city, calling it "the typewriter" and "the wedding cake." Whatever you think of its design, the views from the top are memorable. Here also is the **Tomb of the Unknown Soldier** with its eternal flame. A side entrance in the monument leads to the rather somber **Museo del Risorgimento** (entrance to the right as you face the monument), which charts Italy's struggle for nationhood. For those not interested or able to climb the many stairs, there's now an elevator to the roof (use museum entrance). Before you head up, stop at the museum information kiosk to get a pamphlet identifying the sculpture groups on the monument itself and the landmarks you'll be able to see once at the top. ✉ *Piazza Venezia, Corso* ☎ *06/6991718* 🌐 *www.risorgimento.it* 🎫 *Monument free, museum free, elevator €7* ⏲ *Monument winter 9:30–4:30, summer 9:30–5:30; museum daily 9:30–6:30; elevator and panoramic terrace Mon.–Thurs. 9:30–6:30, Fri.–Sun. 9:30–7:30.*

WORD OF MOUTH

"Go up the Vittorio Emanuelle II monument at dusk and watch the sunset over the Colosseum and the rest of Rome. Awesome views—I got a real 'this is the life' feeling." —drjem

★ **Fontana di Trevi** *(Trevi Fountain)*. The huge fountain designed by Nicola Salvi (1697–1751) is a whimsical rendition of mythical sea creatures amid cascades of splashing water. The fountain is the world's most spectacular wishing well: legend has it that you can ensure your return to Rome by tossing a coin into the fountain. It was featured in the 1954 film *Three Coins in the Fountain* and was the scene of Anita Ekberg's aquatic frolic in Fellini's *La Dolce Vita.* By day this is one of the most crowded sites in town; at night the spotlighted piazza feels especially festive. ✉ *Piazza di Trevi, off Via del Tritone, Corso.*

Palazzetto Zuccari. The real treasure at the top of the Spanish Steps is not the somewhat dull church of Trinità dei Monti, but to the right on Via Gregoriana, the street that leads off to the right of the obelisk. Shaped to form a monster's face, this Mannerist-era house was designed in 1592 by noted painter Federico Zuccari (1540–1609). Typical of the outré style of the period, the entrance portal is through the monster's mouth (this is a great photo op—have someone photograph you standing in front of the door with your own mouth gaping wide). Via Gregoriana is a real charmer, and has long been one of Rome's most elegant addresses, with residents ranging from French 19th-century painters Ingres and David to famed couturier Valentino. Today the Palazzetto houses the Bibliotheca Hertziana, an important library for art historians. It's not open to the public. ✉ *Via Gregoriana 28, Spagna.*

Palazzo Colonna. Inside the fabulous, private Palazzo Colonna, the 17th-century **Sala Grande**—more than 300 feet long, with bedazzling chandeliers, colored marble, and enormous paintings—is best known as the site where Audrey Hepburn met the press in *Roman Holiday.* The entrance to the picture gallery, the **Galleria Colonna,** hides behind a plain, inconspicuous door. The private palace is open to the public Saturday only; reserve ahead to get a free guided tour in English. ✉ *Via della Pilotta 17, Corso, near Piazza di Trevi* ☎ *06/6784350* 🌐 *www.galleriacolonna.it* 🎫 *€7* ⏲ *Sept.–July, Sat. 9–1.*

★ **Palazzo Doria Pamphilj.** This bona fide patrician palace is still home to a princely family, which rents out many of its 1,000 rooms. You can visit the remarkably well-preserved **Galleria Doria Pamphilj** (pronounced pam-*fee*-lee), a picture-and-sculpture gallery that gives you a sense of the sumptuous living quarters. ■ **TIP→ Numbered paintings (the audio**

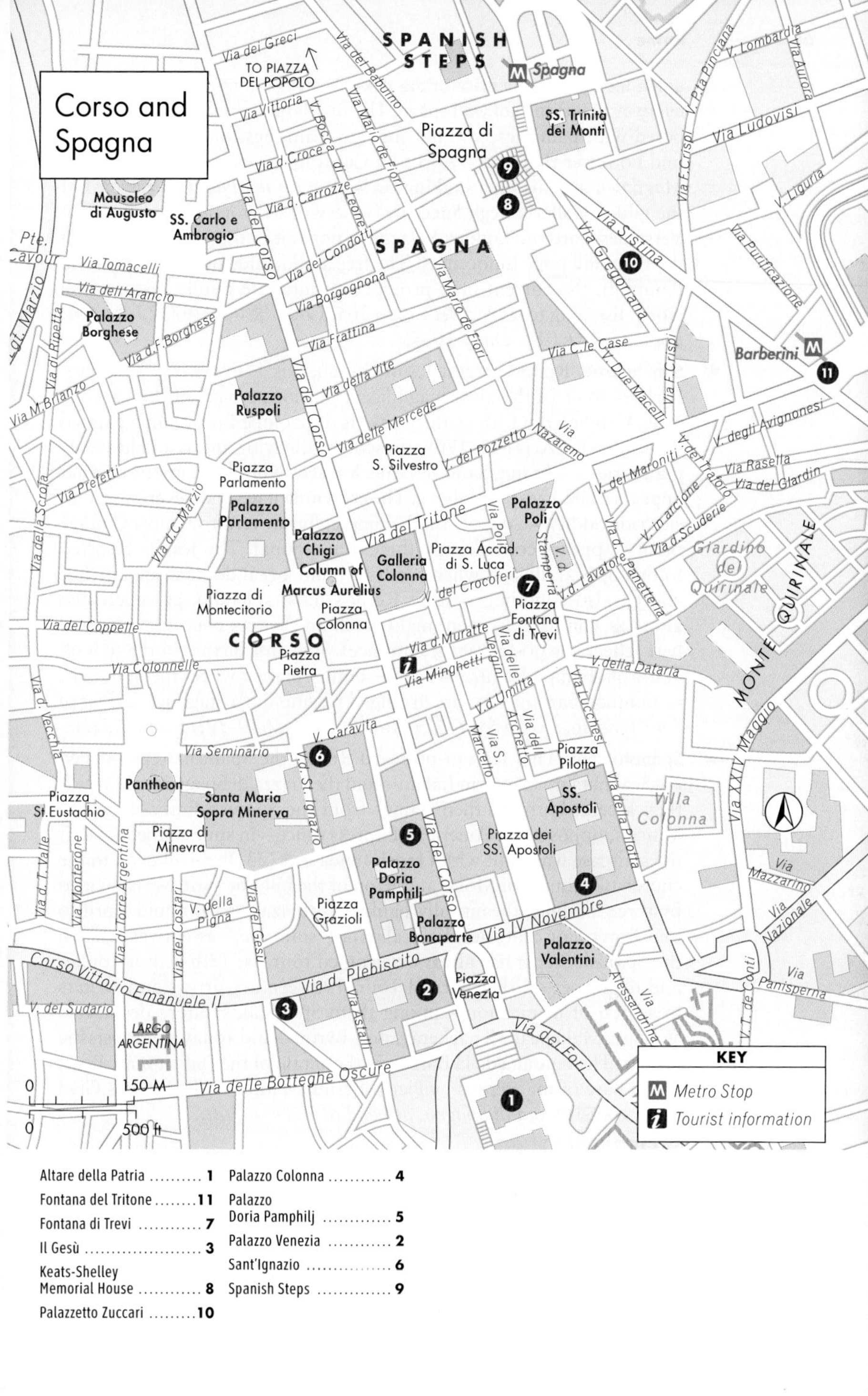

Altare della Patria 1
Fontana del Tritone 11
Fontana di Trevi 7
Il Gesù 3
Keats-Shelley Memorial House 8
Palazzetto Zuccari 10
Palazzo Colonna 4
Palazzo Doria Pamphilj 5
Palazzo Venezia 2
Sant'Ignazio 6
Spanish Steps 9

guide included in the price of the ticket comes in handy) are packed onto every available inch of wall space. The first large salon is nearly wallpapered with paintings, and not just any paintings: on one wall, you'll find no fewer than three works by Caravaggio, including his *Penitent Magdalen* and his breathtaking early *Rest on the Flight to Egypt*. Off the gilded **Galleria degli Specchi** (Gallery of Mirrors)—reminiscent of Versailles—are the famous Velázquez portrait and the Bernini bust of the Pamphilj pope Innocent X. The free audio guide by Jonathan Doria Pamphilj, the current heir, provides an intimate family history well worth listening to. ✉ *Via del Corso 305, Corso* ☎ *06/6797323* 🌐 *www.dopart.it* 🎟 *€10* ⏲ *Daily 10–5.*

★ **Sant'Ignazio.** Rome's largest Jesuit church, this 17th-century landmark harbors some of the most magnificent illusions typical of the baroque style. Capping the 17th-century nave is the trompe-l'oeil ceiling painted by Andrea Pozzo (1642–1709), frescoed with flying angels and heavenly dignitaries, including Saint Ignatius himself, who floats about in what appears to be a rosy sky above. The crowning jewel, however, is an illusionistic oddity—a cupola that's completely flat yet, from most vantage points, appears convincingly three-dimensional. The Jesuits resorted to this optical illusion when funds to build a real dome dried up. The church also contains some of Rome's most splendid, gilt-encrusted altars. If you're lucky, you might catch an evening concert performed here (check the posters at the entrance). Step outside the church to look at it from Filippo Raguzzini's 18th-century piazza, where the buildings, as in much baroque art, are arranged resembling a stage set. ✉ *Piazza Sant'Ignazio, Corso* ☎ *06/6794406* ⏲ *Daily 7:30–12:15 and 3–7:20.*

★ **Spanish Steps.** That icon of postcard Rome, the Spanish Steps—called the Scalinata di Spagna in Italian—and the Piazza di Spagna from which they ascend both get their names from the Spanish Embassy to the Vatican, opposite the American Express office—in spite of the fact that the staircase was built with French funds in 1723. In an allusion to the church of Trinità dei Monti at the top of the hill, the staircase is divided by three landings (beautifully banked with azaleas from mid-April to mid-May). For centuries, La Scalinata ("staircase," as natives refer to the Spanish Steps) has always welcomed tourists: 18th-century dukes and duchesses on their Grand Tour, 19th-century artists and writers in search of inspiration—among them Stendhal, Honoré de Balzac, William Makepeace Thackeray, and Byron—and today's enthusiastic hordes. The **Fontana della Barcaccia** (Fountain of the Unfortunate Boat) at the base of the steps is by Pietro Bernini, father of the famous Gian Lorenzo. ✉ *Piazza di Spagna, at head of Via Condotti.*

WORTH NOTING

Il Gesù. Grandmother of all baroque churches, this huge structure was designed by the architect Vignola (1507–73) to be the tangible symbol of the Jesuits, a major force in the Counter-Reformation in Europe. It remained unadorned for about 100 years, but when it finally was decorated, no expense was spared: the interior drips with lapis lazuli, precious marbles, gold, and more gold. A fantastically painted ceiling by Baciccia (1639–1709) seems to merge with the painted stucco figures at its base. Saint Ignatius's apartments, reached from the side entrance of the church, are also worth a visit (⏲ *Mon.–Sat. 4–6, Sun. 10–noon*) for the trompe-l'oeil frescoes and relics of the saint. ✉ *Piazza del Gesù, near Piazza Venezia, Corso* ☎ *06/697001* 🌐 *www.chiesadelgesu.org* ⏲ *Daily 7–12:30 and 4–7:45.*

Keats-Shelley Memorial House. English Romantic poet John Keats (1795–1821), famed for "Ode to a Nightingale" and "She Walks in Beauty," once lived in what is now a (very small) museum dedicated to him and his great contemporary and friend Percy Bysshe Shelley (1792–1822). You can visit his tiny rooms, at the foot of the Spanish Steps, preserved as they were when he died here. Just across the steps is Babington's Tea Room, a relic from the 19th-century Grand Tour era and still a favorite for Rome's grandes dames. ✉ *Piazza di Spagna 26* ☎ *06/6784235* 🌐 *www.keats-shelley-house.org* 🎟 *€4.50* ⏲ *Weekdays 10–1 and 2–6, Sat. 11–2 and 3–6.*

Palazzo Venezia. A Roman landmark on the city's busiest square, this palace is best known for the balcony over the main portal, from which Mussolini gave public addresses to crowds in Piazza Venezia during the dark days of fascism. Today it's home to a haphazard collection of mostly early-Renaissance weapons, ivories, and paintings in its grand salons; the palace also hosts touring art exhibits. ✉ *Via del Plebescito 118 Piazza Venezia, Corso* ☎ *06/699941* 🌐 *www.galleriaborghese.it/nuove/evenezia.htm* 🎟 *€4* ⏲ *Tues.–Sun. 8:30–7:30.*

PIAZZA DELLA REPUBBLICA AND THE QUIRINALE

This sector of Rome stretches down from the 19th-century district built up around the Piazza della Repubblica—originally laid out to serve as a monumental foyer between the Termini rail station and the rest of the city—and over the rest of the Quirinale. The highest of ancient Rome's famed seven hills, it's crowned by the massive Palazzo Quirinale, home to the popes until 1870 and now Italy's presidential palace. Along the way, you can see ancient Roman sculptures, Early Christian churches, and highlights from the 16th and 17th centuries, when Rome was conquered by the baroque—and by Bernini.

Although Bernini's work feels omnipresent in much of the city center, the Renaissance-man range of his work is particularly notable here. The artist as architect considered the church of Sant'Andrea al Quirinale one of his best; Bernini the urban designer and water worker is responsible for the muscle-bound sea god who blows his conch so provocatively in the fountain at the center of whirling Piazza Barberini. And Bernini the master gives religious passion a joltingly corporeal treatment in what is perhaps his greatest work, the *Ecstasy of St. Theresa,* in the church of Santa Maria della Vittoria.

GETTING HERE Bus No. 40 will get you from Termini station to Via Nazionale, an artery of the Quirinale in one stop; from the Vatican, take bus No. 64 or Line A to the very busy and convenient Repubblica Metro stop on the piazza of the same name. Bus No. 62 and the Metro also run from the Vatican to Piazza Barberini.

Fontana del Tritone 4
Il Quirinale 9
Palazzo Barberini 6
Palazzo Massimo alle Terme 1
Piazza della Repubblica 2
San Carlo alle Quattro Fontane 7
San Clemente 10
Santa Maria Immaculata Concezione 5
Santa Maria della Vittoria 3
Sant'Andrea al Quirinale 8

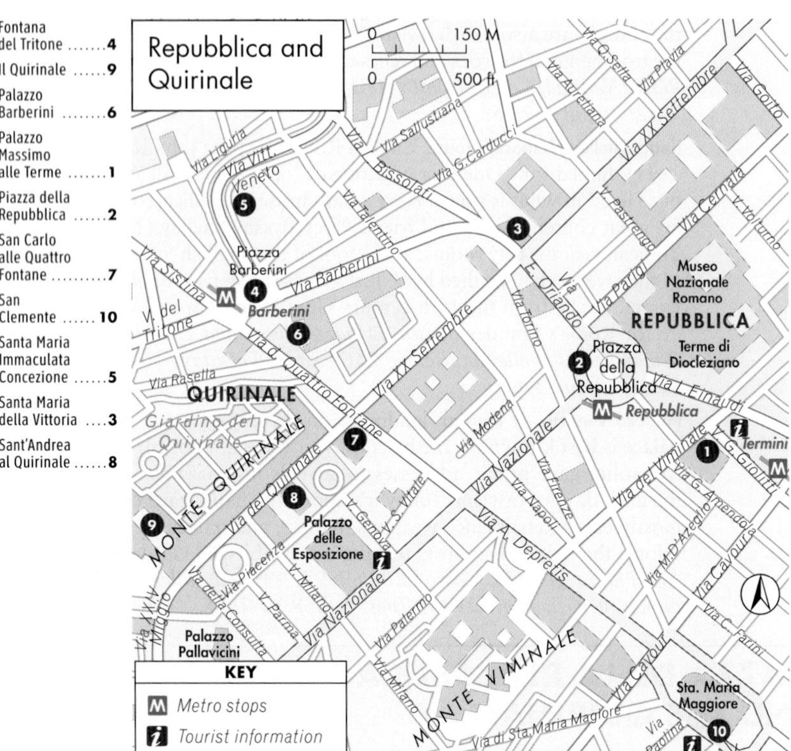

TOP ATTRACTIONS

Il Quirinale. The highest of ancient Rome's famed seven hills, this is where ancient senators, and later popes, built their residences in order to escape the deadly miasmas and malaria of the low-lying area around the Forum and Pantheon. Framing the hilltop vista, the fountain in the square has gigantic ancient statues of Castor and Pollux reining in their unruly steeds. The **Palazzo del Quirinale** passed from the popes to Italy's kings in the late 19th century; it's now the official residence of the nation's president. There's a daily ceremony of the changing of the guard at the portal, including a miniparade complete with band (June–September, daily 6 pm; October–May, Mon.–Sat. 3:15 pm and Sun. 4 pm). ✉ *Piazza del Quirinale, near Piazza di Trevi* ☎ *06/46991* 🌐 *www.quirinale.it.*

Directly opposite the main entrance of the Palazzo del Quirinale sits the **Scuderie del Quirinale**, the former papal stables. Built between 1722 and 1732, it was among the major achievements of post-baroque Rome. Now remodeled by eminent architect Gae Aulenti, they serve as a venue for blockbuster art exhibitions. ✉ *Via XXIV Maggio 16, Quirinale* ☎ *06/39967500* 🌐 *www.scuderiequirinale.it* 🎫 *€10* ⏲ *Sun.–Thurs. 10–8, Fri. and Sat. 10 am–10:30 pm.*

Palazzo Barberini. Along with architect Carlo Maderno (1556–1629), Borromini helped make the splendid 17th-century Palazzo Barberini a residence worthy of Rome's leading art patron, Pope Urban VIII, who acquired existing buildings in 1625 and had them transformed into a luxurious palace for his family. Inside, the **Galleria Nazionale d'Arte Antica** has some fine works by Caravaggio and Raphael, including the latter's portrait of his purported lover, *La Fornarina*. Rome's biggest ballroom is here; its ceiling, painted by Pietro da Cortona, depicts Immortality bestowing a crown upon Divine Providence escorted by a "bomber squadron"—to quote Sir Michael Levey—of mutant bees (bees adorn the family's heraldic crest). The museum expanded its exhibition space in late 2006, opening eight newly refurbished rooms. Restoration work inside the palace is ongoing. ✉ *Via delle Quattro Fontane 13, Quirinale* ☎ *06/4824184* 🌐 *www.galleriaborghese.it* 🎟 *€5* 🕒 *Tues.–Sun. 8:30–7:30.*

Palazzo Massimo alle Terme. This 19th-century palace in neobaroque style holds part of the collections of antiquities belonging to the Museo Nazionale Romano (the rest of the collection is exhibited in the Palazzo Altemps, Museo Nazionale delle Terme di Diocleziano, and the Crypta Balbi). Here you can see extraordinary examples of the fine mosaics and masterful frescoes that decorated ancient Rome's palaces and villas. Don't miss the fresco depicting a lush garden in bloom that came from the villa that Livia shared with her husband Emperor Augustus in Primaporta outside Rome. ✉ *Largo di Villa Peretti 1, Repubblica* ☎ *06/480201* 🎟 *€7 (includes admission to Palazzo Altemps, Terme di Diocleziano, and the Crypta Balbi* 🕒 *Tues.–Sun. 9–7:45.*

★ **San Clemente.** Worth the long detour, this extraordinary church–cum–archaeological site lies a good 20 blocks southeast of Piazza della Repubblica, nestled between the Celian Hill and the Colle Oppio park and just a few blocks east of the Colosseum. This ancient reference point is apropos because San Clemente is a 12th-century church built over a 4th-century church, which in turn was constructed over 1st- and 2nd-century Roman buildings, including a sanctuary dedicated to the Persian god Mithras. The upper church holds a beautiful early-12th-century mosaic showing a crucifixion on a gold background, surrounded by swirling green acanthus leaves teeming with little scenes of everyday life. From the right aisle, a door leads to the excavations ticket office. From there, there are stairs leading down to the remains of the 4th-century church—the former portico is decorated with marble fragments found during the excavations, and in the nave are colorful 11th-century frescoes of the life of Saint Clement and Saint Alexis. Another level down is the famous **Mithraeum,** a shrine dedicated to the god Mithras, whose cult spread from Persia to Rome in the 1st century BC and went on to gain a major hold in the 2nd and 3rd centuries. Farther up the Esquiline Hill are two other churches fabled for their Early Christian mosaics, Santa Prassede (Via di Santa Prassede 9/a) and Santa Pudenziana (Via Urbana 160). ✉ *Via San Giovanni in Laterano 108, Colosseo* ☎ *06/7740021* 🌐 *www.basilicasanclemente.com* 🎟 *€5 (archaeological area)* 🕒 *Mon.–Sat. 9–12:30 and 3–6, Sun. noon–6.*

Santa Maria Immacolata Concezione. In the crypt under the main Capuchin church, the bones of some 4,000 dead Capuchin monks are arranged in peculiar decorative designs around the skeletons of their kinsmen, a macabre reminder of the impermanence of earthly life. Signs declare: "What you are, we once were; what we are, you someday will be." Although not for the easily spooked, the crypt is oddly beautiful. ✉ *Via Veneto 27, Quirinale* ☎ *06/4871185* 🌐 *www.cappucciniviaveneto.it* 🎫 *Donation expected* ⏲ *Fri.–Wed. 9–noon and 3–6.*

Fodor's Choice ★ **Santa Maria della Vittoria.** The most famous feature here is Bernini's triumph of baroque decoration of the **Cappella Cornaro,** an exceptional fusion of architecture, relief, and sculpture. *The Ecstasy of St. Theresa,* an example of Counter-Reformation art at its most alluring, is the focal point. Bernini's audacious conceit was to model the chapel after a theater: members of the Cornaro family—seven cardinals and doges sculpted in white marble—watch from theater boxes as, center stage, Saint Theresa, in the throes of mystical rapture, is pierced by an angel's gilded arrow. To quote one 18th-century observer, President de Brosses: "If this is divine love, I know it well." ✉ *Via XX Settembre 17, Repubblica* ☎ *06/42740571* 🌐 *www.chiesamariavittoria.191.it* ⏲ *Mon.–Sat. 8–noon and 3:30–6.*

WORTH NOTING

Fontana del Tritone *(Triton Fountain).* The centerpiece of busy Piazza Barberini is Bernini's graceful fountain designed in 1642 for the sculptor's patron, Pope Urban VIII. The pope's Barberini family coat of arms, featuring bees, is at the base of the large shell. Close by, at the beginning of the Via Veneto, is the **Fontana delle Api** (Fountain of the Bees), the last fountain designed by Bernini. ✉ *Piazza Barberini, Repubblica.*

Piazza della Repubblica. Smog-blackened porticoes, a subway station, and a McDonald's can make this grand piazza feel a bit run-down. The racy **Fontana delle Naiadi** *(Fountain of the Naiads),* however, is anything but. An 1888–1901 addition to the square, the fountain depicts voluptuous bronze ladies wrestling happily with marine monsters. In ancient times, the Piazza della Repubblica served as the entrance to the immense Terme di Diocleziano *(Baths of Diocletian)*, an archaeological site today. Built in the early 4th century AD, these were among the largest and most impressive of the baths of ancient Rome, with vast halls, pools, and gardens that could accommodate up to 6,000 people at a time. Centerpiece of the **Museo delle Terme di Diocleziano** is the cloister designed by Michelangelo where a rich collection of ancient inscriptions is displayed. ✉ *Viale E. De Nicola 79, near Termini* ☎ *06/39967700* 🎫 *€7 (includes admission to Palazzo Altemps, Terme di Diocleziano, and the Crypta Balbi* ⏲ *Tues.–Sun. 9–7:45.*

The curving ancient Roman brick facade on one side of the Piazza della Repubblica marks the church of **Santa Maria degli Angeli e dei Martiri,** adapted by Michelangelo from the vast central chamber of the colossal baths. Look for the sundial inlaid in the floor. ✉ *Piazza della Repubblica* ☎ *064880812* 🌐 *www.santamariadegliangeliroma.it* ⏲ *Mon.–Sat. 7–6:30, Sun. 7 am–7:30 pm.*

San Carlo alle Quattro Fontane. In a church no larger than the base of one of the piers of St. Peter's, Borromini's so-called "San Carlino" approaches geometric architectural perfection. Characteristically, he chose a subdued white stucco for the interior decoration, so as not to distract from the form of the amazing honeycombed cupola. Don't miss the cloister, which you reach through the door to the right of the altar. The exterior of the church is Borromini at his bizarre best, all curves and rippling movement. (Keep an eye out for cars whipping around the corner as you're looking.) Outside, the *Quattro Fontane* (four fountains) frame views in four directions. ✉ *Via del Quirinale 23* ☎ *06/4883109* 🌐 *www.sancarlino.eu* ⏲ *Weekdays 10–1 and 3–6, Sat. 10–1, Sun. noon–1.*

Sant'Andrea al Quirinale. This small but imposing baroque church was designed and decorated by Bernini, Borromini's rival, who considered it one of his finest works. Notice the dome, which is an elongated play on the hemisphere of the Pantheon. ✉ *Via del Quirinale 29* ☎ *06/4740807* ⏲ *Daily 8:30–noon and 3:30–6.*

VILLA BORGHESE AND PIAZZA DEL POPOLO

Touring Rome's artistic masterpieces while staying clear of its hustle and bustle can be, quite literally, a walk in the park. Some of the city's finest sights are tucked away in or next to green lawns and pedestrian piazzas, offering a breath of fresh air for weary sightseers, especially in the Villa Borghese park. One of Rome's largest, this park can alleviate gallery gout by offering an oasis in which to cool off under the ilex, oak, and umbrella pine trees. If you feel like a picnic, have an *alimentari* (food shop) make you some panini before you go; food carts within the park are overpriced.

GETTING HERE Electric bus No. 119 does a loop that connects Largo Argentina, Piazza Venezia, Piazza di Spagna, and Piazza del Popolo. The No. 117 connects Piazza del Popolo to Piazza Venezia and the Colosseum. The No. 116 motors through the Villa Borghese to the museum and connects the area with Piazza Navona, Campo de' Fiori, and the Pantheon. Piazza del Popolo has a Metro stop called Flaminio.

TOP ATTRACTIONS

Ara Pacis *(Altar of Peace).* This magnificent classical monument, with an exquisitely detailed frieze, was erected in 13 BC to celebrate Emperor Augustus's triumphant return from military conflicts in Gaul and Spain. It's housed in one of Rome's newest landmarks, a glass-and-travertine structure designed by American architect Richard Meier. The building was opened in 2006 after 10 years of delays and heated controversy concerning the architect's appointment and design. Overlooking the Tiber on one side and the ruins of the dilapidated Mausoleo di Augusto (Mausoleum of Augustus) on the other, the result is a luminous oasis in the center of Rome. ✉ *Lungotevere in Augusta, near Piazza di Popolo* ☎ *06/0608* 🌐 *www.arapacis.it* 🎫 *€6.50* ⏲ *Tues.–Sun. 9–7.*

Fodor's Choice ★ **Galleria Borghese.** It's a real toss-up which is more magnificent—the villa built for Cardinal Scipione Borghese in 1615 or the collection of ancient and 17th- and 18th-century art that lies within. The luxury-loving cardinal built Rome's most splendiferous palace as a showcase for his antiquities collection. The interiors are a monument to 18th-century Roman interior decoration at its most luxurious, dripping with colored porphyry and alabaster, and they're a fitting showcase for the statues of various deities, including one officially known as *Venus Victrix*. There has never been any doubt, however, as to the statue's real subject: Pauline Bonaparte, Napoléon's sister, who married Prince Camillo Borghese in one of the storied matches of the 19th century. Sculpted by Canova (1757–1822), the princess reclines on a chaise, bare-breasted, her hips swathed in classical drapery, the very model of haughty detachment and sly come-hither. Pauline is known to have been shocked that her husband took pleasure in showing off the work to his guests. This coyness seems curious given the reply she is supposed to have made to a lady who asked her how she could have posed for the work: "Oh, but the studio was heated." Other rooms hold important sculptures by Bernini, including *David* and the breathtaking *Apollo and Daphne*. The picture collection has splendid works by Titian, Caravaggio, and Raphael, among others. ■ **TIP→ Entrance is every two hours, and reservations are required. Make sure to book online or by phone at least a few days in advance.** ✉ *Piazza Scipione Borghese 5, off Via Pinciana, Villa Borghese* ☎ *06/8413979 information, 06/32810 reservations* 🌐 *www.galleriaborghese.it* 🎫 *€10.50 (including €2 reservation fee), audio guide €5, English tour €6* ⏲ *Tues.–Sun. 9–7, with sessions on the hr every 2 hrs (9, 11, 1, 3, 5)* Ⓜ *Bus 910 from Piazza della Repubblica or Tram 19 or 3 from Policlinico (near Piazza del Popolo).*

> **WORD OF MOUTH**
>
> "Something about the Borghese reminded me of the Frick in New York; although the space is grand, it feels easily accessible to the visitor. . . . The interiors alone, even if the rooms had been empty, are worth the price of admission."
>
> —ekscrunchy

Piazza del Popolo. Designed by neoclassical architect Giuseppe Valadier (1762–1839) in the early 1800s, this piazza is one of the largest in Rome, and it has a 3,200-year-old obelisk in the middle. A favorite spot for café-sitting and people-watching, the pedestrians-only piazza is landmarked by its two bookend baroque churches, **Santa Maria dei Miracoli** and **Santa Maria in Montesanto.** On the piazza's eastern side, stairs lead uphill to Villa Borghese's **Pincio**, a formal garden that was highly fashionable in 19th-century Rome. Here you'll find the magnificent park pavilion restaurant known as the Casina **Valadier** (✉ *Piazza Bucarest, Pincio Gardens* ☎ *06/69922090* 🌐 *www.casinavaladier.it*). First designed in 1814, it has always attracted celebrities like King Farouk of Egypt, Richard Strauss, Gandhi, and Mussolini, all who came to see the lavish Empire-style salons and, of course, to be seen. At the north end of the piazza is the 400-year-old **Porta del Popolo,** Rome's northern city gate, and next to it the church of Santa Maria del Popolo. The city gate was designed by Bernini to welcome the Catholic convert Queen Christina of Sweden to Rome in 1655. ✉ *At head of the Corso, near Villa Borghese.*

Ara Pacis 4
Galleria Borghese 3
Piazza del Popolo 1
Santa Maria del Popolo 2

★ **Santa Maria del Popolo.** This church next to the Porta del Popolo goes almost unnoticed, but it has one of the richest art collections of any church in Rome. Here is Raphael's High Renaissance masterpiece the **Cappella Chigi** (which has found new fame as one of the "Altars of Science" in Dan Brown's *Angels & Demons* novel and the 2009 Tom Hanks film), as well as two stunning Caravaggios in the **Cappella Cerasi.** Each December an exhibit of Christmas Nativity scenes is held in the adjacent building. ✉ *Piazza del Popolo, near Villa Borghese* ☎ *06/3610836* ⏲ *Mon.–Sat. 7–noon and 4–7, Sun. 7:30–1:30 and 4:30–7:30* Ⓜ *Flaminio.*

WORTH NOTING

MAXXI—Museo Nazionale delle Arti del XXI Secolo (National Museum of 21st-Century Arts). Billed as a cultural space for the art of the 21st century, the museum—opened May 2010 and walkable from the Parco della Musica complex—contains 300 works from today and tomorrow's hottest artists. Arguably the most impressive exhibit of all is the hyper-dramatic building designed by architect Zaha Hadid. Get to this museum by taking Tram 2 from Piazzale Flaminia (near Piazza del Popolo). ✉ *Via Guido Reni 4A, near Villa Borghese* ☎ *06/39967350* 🌐 *www.fondazionemaxxi.it* 🎫 *€11* ⏲ *Tues., Wed., Fri., and Sun 11–7, Thurs. and Sat. 11–10* Ⓜ *Flaminio.*

THE VATICAN: ROME OF THE POPES

Capital of the Catholic Church, this tiny walled city-state is a place where some people go to find a work of art—Michelangelo's frescoes, rare ancient Roman marbles, or Bernini's statues. Others go to find their soul. Whatever the reason, thanks to being the seat of world Catholicism and also address to the most overwhelming architectural achievement of the 16th and 17th centuries—St. Peter's Basilica—the Vatican attracts millions of travelers every year. In addition, the Vatican Museums are famed for magnificent rooms decorated by Raphael, sculptures such as the *Apollo Belvedere* and the *Laocoön,* paintings by Giotto, frescoes by Raphael, and the celebrated ceiling of the Sistine Chapel. The Church power that emerged as the Rome of the emperors declined gave impetus to a profusion of artistic expression and shaped the destiny of the city for a thousand years. Allow yourself an hour to see St. Peter's Basilica, at least two hours for the museums, an hour for Castel Sant'Angelo, and an hour to climb to the top of the dome. Note that ushers at the entrance of St. Peter's Basilica and the Vatican Museums bar entry to people with "inappropriate" clothing—which means no bare knees or shoulders.

GETTING HERE From Termini station, hop on the No. 40 Express or the No. 64 to be delivered to Piazza San Pietro. Metro stops Cipro or Ottaviano will get you within about a 10-minute walk of the entrance to the Vatican Museums. Use Ottaviano for St. Peter's.

TOP ATTRACTIONS

★ **Basilica di San Pietro.** The largest church of Christendom, St. Peter's Basilica covers about 18,000 square feet, extends 208 yards in length, and carries a dome that rises 435 feet and measures 138 feet across its base. Its history is equally impressive: No fewer than five of Italy's greatest architects—Bramante, Raphael, Peruzzi, Antonio Sangallo the Younger, and Michelangelo—died while striving to erect this "new" St. Peter's. In fact, the church's history dates back to the year AD 320, when the emperor Constantine built a basilica over the site believed to be the tomb of Saint Peter (died circa AD 68). This early church stood for more than 1,000 years, undergoing a number of restorations, until it was on the verge of collapse.

In 1506 Pope Julius II (1443–1513) commissioned the architect Bramante to build a new and greater basilica, but construction would take more than 120 years. In 1546 Michelangelo was persuaded to take over the job, but the magnificent cupola he designed was finally completed after his death at age 89 by Giacomo della Porta (circa 1537–1602) and Domenico Fontana (1543–1607). The new church wasn't consecrated until 1626; by that time Renaissance had given way to baroque, and many of the plan's original elements had gone the way of their designers. Off the entry portico, architect and sculptor Gian Lorenzo Bernini's famous *Scala Regia,* the ceremonial entry to the Apostolic Palace—and originally the way to the Sistine Chapel—is one of the most magnificent staircases in the world and is graced with Bernini's dramatic statue of Constantine the Great.

Entering the sanctuary, take a moment to adjust to the enormity of the space stretching in front of you. The cherubs over the holy-water fonts have feet as long as the distance from your fingertips to your elbow. It's because the proportions are in such perfect harmony that the vastness may escape you at first. The megascale was inspired by the size of the ancient Roman ruins and propelled by the duty to celebrate Peter, Prince of the Apostles, and the first pope.

Over an altar in a side chapel to the right of the entrance is Michelangelo's *Pietà,* a sculpture of Mary holding her son Jesus' body after crucifixion—the star attraction here other than the basilica itself. Legend has it that the artist, only 24 at the time the work was completed, overheard other artists being given credit for his design. It's said that his offense at the implication was why he crept back that night and signed the piece on the sash that falls diagonally across the Virgin's chest.

At the crossing of the transept four massive piers support the dome, and the mighty Bernini **baldacchino** (canopy) rises high above the papal altar, where the pope celebrates mass. The bronze throne behind the main altar in the apse, the *Cathedra Petri* (Chair of Saint Peter), is Bernini's work (1657–1666), and it covers a wooden-and-ivory chair that Saint Peter himself is said to have used. However, scholars contend that this throne probably dates only from the Middle Ages. See how the adoration of a million caresses has completely worn down the bronze on the right foot of the statue of Saint Peter in front of the near-right pillar in the transept. St. Peter's is closed during ceremonies in the piazza. ✉ *Piazza San Pietro* ☎ *06/69883731* 🌐 *www.vatican.va* ⏲ *Apr.-Sept., daily 7–7 Oct.–Mar., daily 8–6:30* Ⓜ *Ottaviano-San Pietro.*

The **Grotte Vaticane** *(Vatican Grottoes)* directly beneath the basilica contain the tombs of many popes, including John Paul II. The entrance is beside the cupola entrance, outside the basilica. Often, the exit leads outside the church, so don't go down until you're finished elsewhere. 🎫 *Free* ⏲ *Apr.–Sept., daily 7–6; Oct.–Mar., daily 7–5 (1–5 on Wed. if the pope has audience in Piazza San Pietro).*

The **roof** of St. Peter's Basilica, reached by elevator or stairs, provides a view among a landscape of domes and towers. An interior staircase (170 steps) leads to the base of the dome for a dove's-eye look at the interior of St. Peter's. Only if you're stout of heart and sound of lung should you attempt the taxing and claustrophobic climb up the remaining 370 steps to the balcony of the lantern, where the view embraces the Vatican Gardens and all of Rome. The up and down staircases are one way; once you commit to climbing, there's no turning back. 🎫 *Elevator €7, stairs €5* ⏲ *Daily 8–5 (1–5 on Wed. if the pope has audience in Piazza San Pietro).*

Castel Sant'Angelo. For hundreds of years this fortress guarded the Vatican, to which it's linked by the **Passetto,** an arcaded passageway (the secret "lair of the Illuminati," according to Dan Brown's *Angels & Demons*, the Rome-based prequel to *The Da Vinci Code*). According to legend, Castel Sant'Angelo got its name during the plague of 590, when Pope Gregory the Great (circa 540–604), passing by in a religious procession, had a vision of an angel sheathing its sword atop the stone

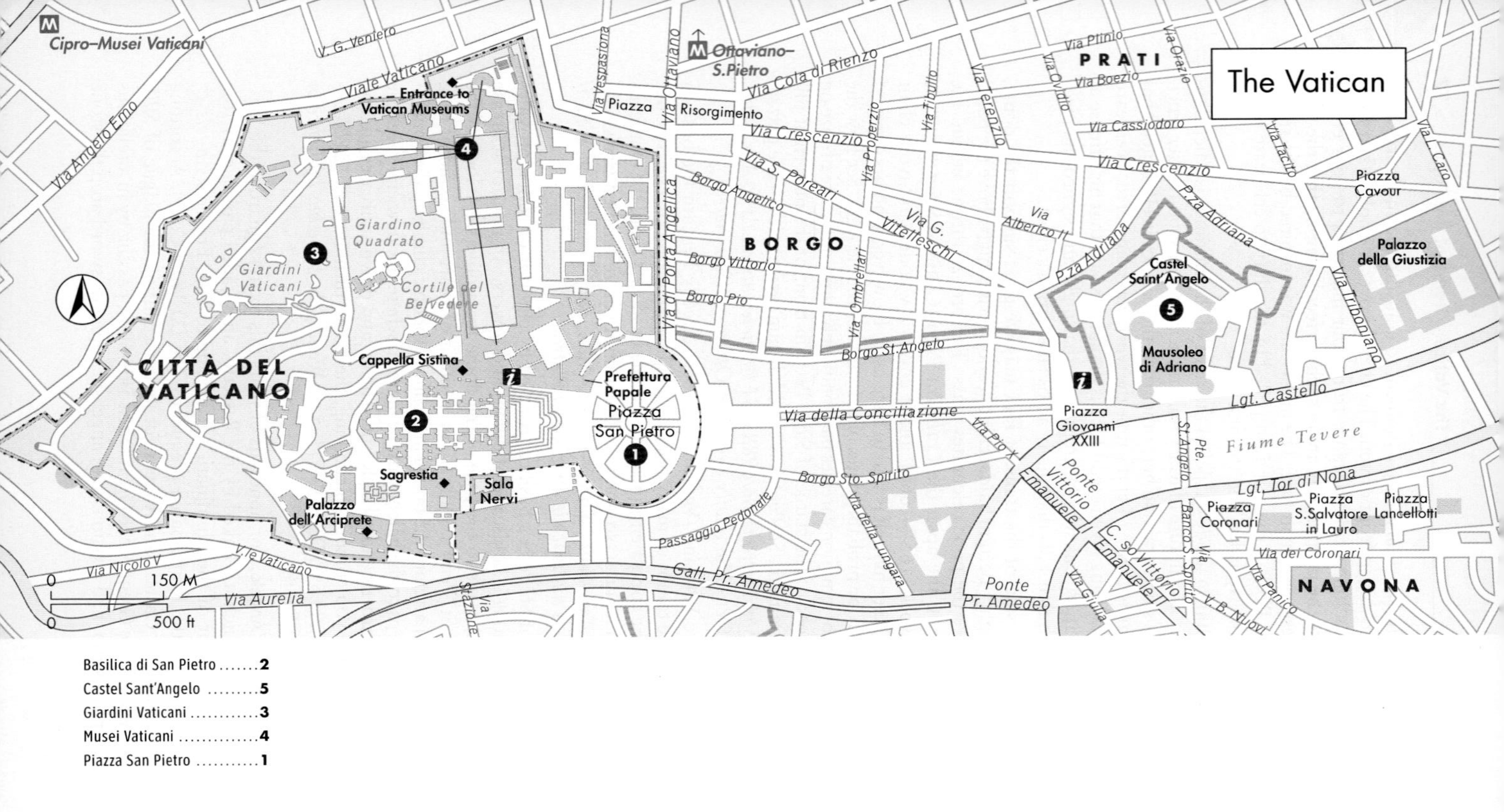

Basilica di San Pietro 2
Castel Sant'Angelo 5
Giardini Vaticani 3
Musei Vaticani 4
Piazza San Pietro 1

CLOSE UP

A Morning with the Pope

The pope holds audiences in St. Peter's Square (or a large, modern hall in inclement weather) on Wednesday morning at 10:30. To attend, you must get tickets; apply in writing by fax at least 10 days in advance to the **Papal Prefecture** (*Prefettura della Casa Pontificia* ✉ *Vatican City* ☎ *06/69884857* 🖷 *06/69885863* 🌐 *www.vatican.va*), indicating the full names of attendants, the date you prefer, your language, and your hotel's contact information. Pick up tickets through the Portone di Bronzo, the bronze door at the end of the colonnade on the right side of the piazza, from 3 to 7:30 the day before the audience or from 8 to 10:30 the day of.

You can also arrange to pick up free tickets on Tuesday from 5 to 6:30 at the **Santa Susanna American Church** (✉ *Via XX Settembre 15, near Piazza della Repubblica* ☎ *06/42014554* 🌐 *www.santasusanna.org*); call first. For a fee, travel agencies make arrangements that include transportation. Arrive early, as security is tight and the best places fill up fast.

ramparts. Though it may look like a stronghold, Castel Sant'Angelo was in fact built as a tomb for the emperor Hadrian (76–138) in AD 135. By the 6th century it had been transformed into a fortress, and it remained a refuge for the popes for almost 1,000 years. It has dungeons, battlements, cannon and cannonballs, and a collection of antique weaponry and armor. The lower levels formed the base of Hadrian's mausoleum; ancient ramps and narrow staircases climb through the castle's core to courtyards and frescoed halls, where temporary exhibits are held. Off the loggia is a café.

The upper terrace, with the massive angel statue commemorating Gregory's vision, evokes memories of Tosca, Puccini's poignant heroine in the opera of the same name, who threw herself off these ramparts with the cry, *"Scarpia, avanti a Dio!"* ("Scarpia, we meet before God!") On summer evenings exhibits and concerts are held inside the castle. One of Rome's most beautiful pedestrian bridges, **Ponte Sant'Angelo,** spans the Tiber in front of the fortress and is studded with graceful angels designed by Bernini. ✉ *Lungotevere Castello 50, near Vatican* ☎ *06/6819111* 🌐 *castelsantangelo.beneculturali.it* 🎫 *€5* ⏲ *Tues.–Sun. 9–7:30* Ⓜ *Ottaviano.*

Fodor's Choice ★ **Musei Vaticani** *(Vatican Museums)*. The building on your left as you exit St. Peter's Basilica is the Apostolic Palace, the papal residence since 1870, with an estimated 1,400 rooms, chapels, and galleries. Other than the pope and his court, the primary occupants are the galleries of the Musei Vaticani (Vatican Museums), containing some of art's greatest masterpieces. The Sistine Chapel is the headliner here, but in your haste to get there, don't overlook the Museo Egizio, with its fine Egyptian collection; the famed classical sculptures of the Chiaramonti and the Museo Pio Clementino; and the Stanze di Raffaello (Raphael Rooms), a suite of halls covered floor-to-ceiling in some of the master's greatest works.

Continued on page 88

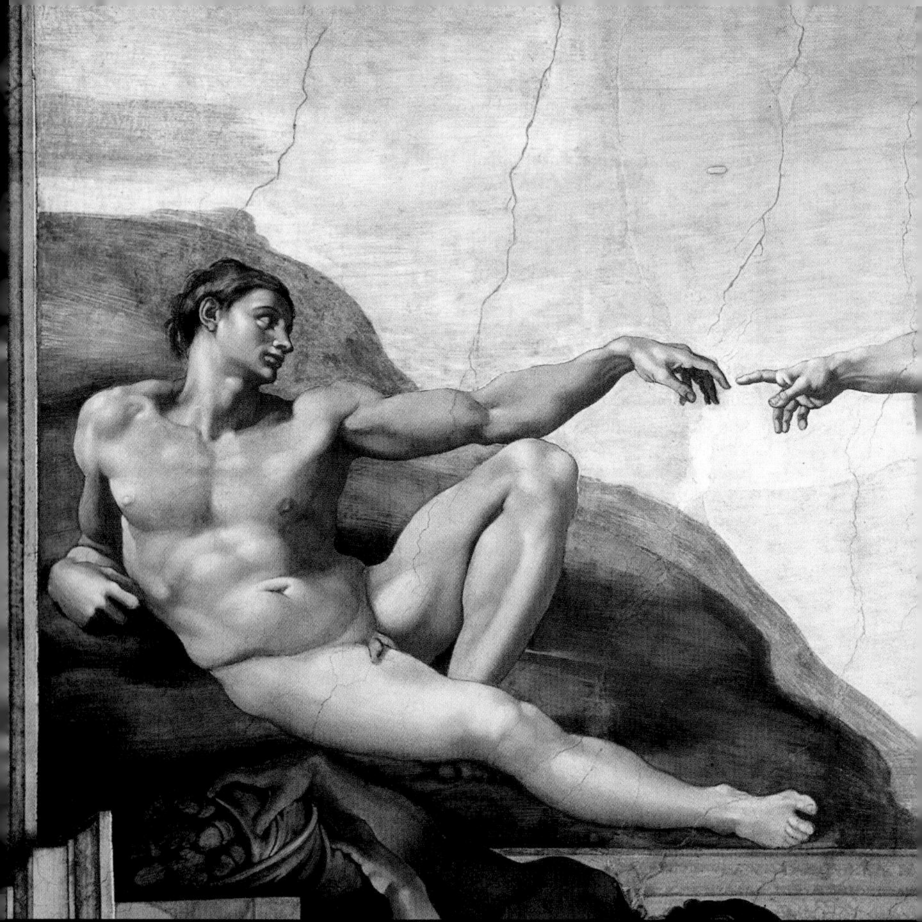

AGONY AND ECSTASY:
THE SISTINE CEILING

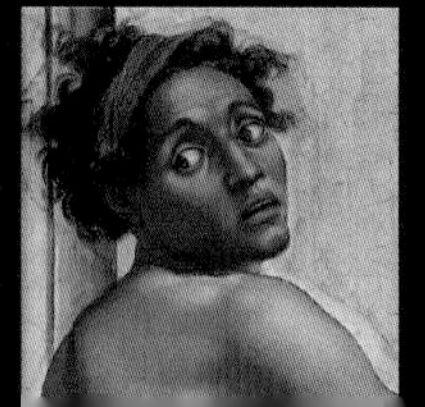

Forming lines that are probably longer than those waiting to pass through the Pearly Gates, hordes of visitors arrive at the Sistine Chapel daily to view what may be the world's most sublime example of artistry:

Michelangelo: *The Creation of Adam*, Sistine Chapel, The Vatican, circa 1511.

Michelangelo's Sistine Ceiling. To paint this 12,000-square-foot barrel vault, it took four years, 343 frescoed figures, and a titanic battle of wits between the artist and Pope Julius II. While in its typical fashion, Hollywood focused on the element of agony, not ecstasy, involved in the saga of creation, a recently completed restoration of the ceiling has revolutionized our appreciation of the masterpiece of masterpieces.

By Martin Wilmot Bennett

View of the Cappella Sistina

MICHELANGELO'S
MISSION IMPOSSIBLE

Designed to match the presumed proportions of Solomon's Temple described in the Old Testament, the Sistine Chapel is named after Pope Sixtus VI, who commissioned it as a place of worship for himself and as the venue where new popes could be elected. Before Michelangelo, the barrel-vaulted ceiling was an expanse of azure fretted with golden stars. Then, in 1504, an ugly crack appeared. Bramante, the architect, managed do some patchwork using iron rods, but when signs of a fissure remained, the new Pope Julius II summoned Michelangelo to cover it with a fresco 131 feet long and 43 feet wide.

Taking in the entire span of the ceiling, the theme connecting the various participants in this painted universe could be said to be mankind's anguished waiting. The majestic panel depicting the Creation of Adam leads, through the stages of the Fall and the expulsion from Eden, to the tragedy of Noah found naked and mocked by his own sons; throughout all runs the underlying need for man's redemption. Witnessing all from the side and end walls, a chorus of ancient Prophets and Sibyls peer anxiously forward, awaiting the Redeemer who will come to save the devoted followers of the Church.

THE WRATH OF GOD

The sweetness and pathos of his Pietà, carved by Michelangelo only ten years earlier, have been left behind. The new work foretells an apocalypse, its congregation of doomed sinners facing the wrath of heaven through hanging, beheading, crucifixion, flood, and plague. Michelangelo, by nature a misanthrope, was already filled with visions of doom thanks to the fiery orations of Savonarola, whose thunderous preachments he had heard before leaving his hometown of Florence. Vasari, the 16th-century art historian, coined the word "terrabilità" to describe Michelangelo's tension-ridden style, a rare case of a single word being worth a thousand pictures.

Michelangelo wound up using a *Reader's Digest* condensed version of the stories from Genesis, with the dramatis personae overseen by a punitive and terrifying God. In real life, poor Michelangelo answered to a flesh-and-blood taskmaster who was almost as vengeful: Pope Julius II. Less vicar of Christ than latter-day Caesar, he was intent on uniting Italy under the power of the Vatican, and was eager to do so by any means, including riding into pitched battle. Yet this "warrior pope" considered his most formidable adversary to be Michelangelo. Applying a form of blackmail, Julius threatened to wage war on Michelangelo's Florence, to which the artist had fled after Julius postponed a commission for a grand papal tomb, unless Michelangelo agreed to return to Rome and take up the task of painting the Sistine Chapel ceiling.

MICHELANGELO, SCULPTOR

A sculptor first and foremost, however, Michelangelo considered painting an inferior genre—"for rascals and sissies" as he put it. Second, there was the sheer scope of the task, leading Michelangelo to suspect he'd been set up by a rival, Bramante, chief architect of the new St. Peter's Basilica. As Michelangelo was also a master architect, he regarded this fresco commission as a Renaissance mission-impossible. Pope Julius's powerful will prevailed—and six years later the work of the Sistine Ceiling was complete. Irving Stone's famous novel *The Agony and the Ecstasy*—and the granitic 1965 film that followed—chart this epic battle between artist and pope.

THINGS ARE LOOKING UP

To enhance your viewing of the ceiling, bring along opera-glasses, binoculars, or just a mirror (to prevent your neck from becoming bent like Michelangelo's). Note that no photos are permitted. If you want to avoid crowds, the best time to visit is early in the morning—book an 8 am reservation. Failing that, get there late in the afternoon, when the crowds thin. Admission and entry to the Sistine Chapel is only through the Musei Vaticani (Vatican Museums).

SCHEMATIC OF THE SISTINE CEILING

HEAVEN'S ABOVE

The ceiling's biblical symbols were ideated by three Vatican theologians, Cardinal Alidosi, Egidio da Viterbo, and Giovanni Rafanelli, along with Michelangelo. As for the ceiling's painted "framework," this *quadratura* alludes to Roman triumphal arches because Pope Julius II was fond of mounting "triumphal entries" into his conquered cities (in imitation of Christ's procession into Jerusalem on Palm Sunday).

THE CENTER PANELS

Prophet turned art-critic or, perhaps doubling as ourselves, the ideal viewer, Jonah the prophet (painted at the altar end) gazes up at the

Creation, or Michelangelo's version of it.

1 The first of the ceiling's scenes, all taken from the Book of Genesis, God separates Light from Darkness.

2 God creates the sun and a craterless pre-Galilean moon while the panel's other half offers an unprecedented rear view of the Almighty creating the vegetable world.

3 In the panel showing God separating the Waters from the Heavens, the Creator tumbles towards us as in a self-made whirlwind.

4 Pausing for breath, next admire probably Western Art's most famous image—God giving life to Adam.

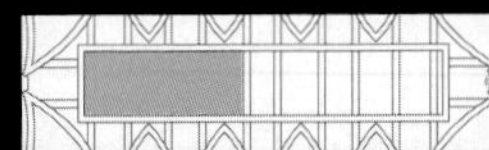

5 The Creation of Eve from Adam's rib leads to the sixth panel.

6 In a sort of diptych divided by the trunk of the Tree of Knowledge of Good and Evil, Michelangelo retells the Temptation and the Fall.

7 Illustrating Man's fallen nature, the last three panels narrate, in un-chronological order, the Flood. In the first Noah offers a post-Flood sacrifice of thanks.

8 Damaged by an explosion in 1797, next comes Michelangelo's version of Flood itself.

9 Finally, above the monumental Zachariah, you can just make out the small, wretched figure of Noah, lying drunk—in pose, the shrunken anti-type of the majestic Adam five panels down the wall.

THE CREATION OF ADAM

Michelangelo's Adam was partly inspired by the Creation scenes Michelangelo had studied in the sculpted doors of Jacopo della Quercia in Bologna and Lorenzo Ghiberti's Doors of Paradise in Florence. Yet in Michelangelo's version Adam's hand hangs limp, waiting God's touch to impart the spark of life. Facing his Creation, the Creator—looking a bit like the pagan god Jupiter—is for the first time ever depicted as horizontal, mirroring the Biblical "in his own likeness." Decades after its completion, a crack began to appear, amputating Adam's fingertips. Believe it or not, the most famous fingers in Western art are the handiwork, at least in part, of one Domenico Carnevale.

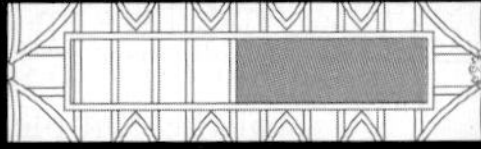

On a first visit to the Vatican Museums, you may just want to see the highlights—even that will take several hours and a good, long walk. ■ **TIP→ In peak tourist season, book reserved tickets through the Vatican Museums Web site to avoid long lines to enter the museums.** The best time to avoid lines and crowds is not first thing in the morning but during lunch hour and the Wednesday papal audiences. The collection is divided among different galleries, halls, and wings connected end to end. Pick up the blue Vatican guidebook at the main entrance to the museums to see the overall layout. The Sistine Chapel is at the far end of the complex, and the book charts several itineraries through other collections to reach it. An audio guide (€7, about 90 minutes) for the Sistine Chapel, the Stanze di Raffaello, and 350 other works and locations is worth the added expense. Book a guided tour (€31) online at the Vatican Museums Web site at least a week in advance (more during peak season). The main entrance to the museums, on Viale Vaticano, is a long walk from Piazza San Pietro along a busy thoroughfare. Some city buses stop near the main entrance: Bus 49 from Piazza Cavour stops right in front; bus 81 and Tram 19 stop at Piazza Risorgimento, halfway between St. Peter's and the museums. The Ottaviano–San Pietro and the Cipro–Musei Vaticani stops on Line A also are in the vicinity. Entry is free the last Sunday of the month, and the museum is closed on Catholic holidays, of which there are many. Last admission is two hours before closing. ■ **TIP→ Note: ushers at entrance of St. Peter's and Vatican Museums will bar entry to people with bare knees or bare shoulders.**

Besides the galleries mentioned here, there are many other wings along your way—full of maps, tapestries, classical sculpture, Egyptian mummies, Etruscan statues, and even Aztec treasures. From the main entrance of the Vatican Museums take the escalator up to the glass atrium. Follow the hall to the right to the **Pinacoteca** (Picture Gallery). This is a self-contained section, and it's worth visiting first for works by such artists as Giotto (circa 1266–1337), Melozzo da Forli (circa 1438–1494), and Leonardo (1452–1519), and the exceptional *Transfiguration, Coronation,* and *Foligno Madonna* by Raphael (1483–1520).

The **Cortile Ottagonale** (Octagonal Courtyard) of the Vatican Museums displays some of sculpture's most famous works, including the 1st century AD Roman copy of the 4th century BC Greek *Apollo Belvedere* (and Canova's 1801 *Perseus,* heavily influenced by it) and the 1st-century *Laocoön.*

The **Stanze di Raffaello** (Raphael Rooms) are second only to the Sistine Chapel in artistic interest—and draw crowds comparable. In 1508 Pope Julius II employed Raphael, on the recommendation of Bramante, to decorate the rooms with allegories, scenes of papal history, and biblical scenes. The result is a Renaissance tour de force. Of the four rooms, the second and third were decorated mainly by Raphael. The others were decorated by Giulio Romano (circa 1499–1546) and other assistants of Raphael, based on his designs.

The frescoed **Stanza della Segnatura** (Room of the Signature), where papal bulls were signed, is one of Raphael's finest works; indeed, they're thought by many to be some of the finest frescoes in the history of

Western art. This was Julius's private library, and the room's use is reflected in the frescoes' themes, philosophy, and enlightenment. A paradigm of High Renaissance painting, the works demonstrate the revolutionary ideals of naturalism (Raphael's figures lack the awkwardness of those painted only a few years earlier); humanism (the idea that human beings are the noblest and most admirable of God's creations); and a profound interest in the ancient world, the result of the 15th-century rediscovery of classical antiquity. The *School of Athens* glorifies some of philosophy's greats, including Plato (pointing to Heaven) and Aristotle (pointing to Earth) at the fresco's center. The pensive figure on the stairs is thought to be modeled after Michelangelo, who was painting the Sistine ceiling at the same time Raphael was working here. Look for a confident Raphael, dressed in a red cloak, on the far right, beside his white-clad friend Il Sodoma, the artist who frescoed the ceiling.

WORD OF MOUTH

"Free Sundays are usually packed at the Vatican Museums, be aware of that."

—daveesl

In 1508, just before Raphael started work on his rooms, the redoubtable Pope Julius II commissioned Michelangelo to paint single-handedly the more-than-10,000-square-foot ceiling of the **Cappella Sistina** (Sistine Chapel). For an in-depth look at Michelangelo's masterpiece, see our photo feature, "Agony and Ecstasy: The Sistine Ceiling." ✉ *Main museum entrance, Viale Vaticano 100* ☎ *06/69884947* 🌐 *www.vatican.va* 🎫 *€14* 🕒 *Mon.–Sat. 9–6 (last entrance at 4); closed Sun., except for last Sun. of month (9–2; last entrance at 12:30), when admission is free* Ⓜ *Cipro–Musei Vaticani or Ottaviano–San Pietro.*

QUICK BITES

You don't have to snack at the touristy joints outside the Vatican Museums; a short walk away are neighborhood restaurants catering to locals. Among them is Il Mozzicone (✉ *Borgo Pio 180, near San Pietro*), where you can fill up on solid Roman fare at moderate prices (closed Sunday). Pizzarium (✉ *Via della Meloria 43, beside the Cipro Metro stop, near the Musei Vaticani*) serves stellar pizza by the slice every day, except Sunday lunch. There are a few benches outside and it's a short walk to the museums' entrance.

Piazza San Pietro. As you enter St. Peter's Square you're officially entering Vatican territory. The piazza is one of Bernini's most spectacular masterpieces. It was completed in 1667 after 11 years' work, a relatively short time, considering the vastness of the task. The piazza can hold 250,000 people—as it did in the days following the death of Pope John Paul II. The piazza is surrounded by a curving pair of quadruple colonnades, topped by a balustrade and statues of 140 saints. Look for the two disks set into the pavement on either side of the obelisk at the center of the piazza. When you stand on either disk, a trick of perspective makes the colonnade closest to you seem to consist of a single row of columns. Remember to look for the Swiss Guards in their colorful uniforms; they've been standing at the Vatican entrances for more than 500 years. ✉ *At head of Via delle Conciliazione.*

WORTH NOTING

Giardini Vaticani *(Vatican Gardens).* Generations of popes have strolled in these beautifully manicured gardens, originally laid out in the 16th century. A two-hour guided tour, half by bus and half on foot, takes you through a haven of shady walkways, elaborate fountains, and exotic plants. Make reservations a week or more in advance on the Vatican Museums Web site. The cost of the tour includes admission to the Vatican Museums, as well. ✉ *Viale Vaticano 100* ☎ *06/69884947* 🌐 *www.vatican.va* 🎫 *€31* ⏲ *Mar.–Oct., Mon., Tues., Thurs.–Sat. 9 and 9:30; Nov.–Feb., Mon., Tues., Thurs.–Sat. 9:30* Ⓜ *Cipro–Musei Vaticani.*

THE GHETTO, TIBER ISLAND, AND TRASTEVERE

Each staunchly resisting the tides of change, these three areas are hard to beat for the authentic atmosphere of Old Rome. You begin in the old Ghetto, once a warren of twisting, narrow streets where Rome's Jewish community was at one time confined, now a combination of medieval, Renaissance, and modern structures. Ancient bridges, the Ponte Fabricio and Ponte Cestio, link the Ghetto to Tiber Island, the diminutive sandbar that's one of Rome's most picturesque sights. On the opposite side of the Tiber lies Trastevere—literally "across the Tiber"—long cherished as Rome's Greenwich Village and now subject to rampant gentrification. In spite of this, Trastevere remains about the most tightly knit community in the city, the Trasteverini proudly (and erroneously!) proclaiming their descent from the ancient Romans. This area is Rome's enchanting, medieval heart.

GETTING HERE From Termini station, nab the No. 40 Express or the No. 64 bus to Largo Torre Argentina, where you can get off to visit the Ghetto area. Switch to Tram No. 8 to get to Trastevere. The No. 75 bus departs from Termini, passes the Colosseum, passes through Trastevere, and later ascends the Janiculum Hill.

TOP ATTRACTIONS

Fontana delle Tartarughe. The 16th-century Fountain of the Tortoises in Piazza Mattei is one of Rome's loveliest. Designed by Giacomo della Porta (1539–1602) in 1581 and sculpted by Taddeo Landini (1550–96), the piece revolves around four bronze boys, each clutching a dolphin that jets water into marble shells. Several bronze tortoises, thought to have been added by Bernini, are held in each of the boys' hands and drink from the fountain's upper basin. The piazza is lined by a few interesting wine bars and shops. It was named for the Mattei family, who built several palaces in the area, including one on the square. Nearby at Via Michelangelo Caetani 32 is **Palazzo Mattei di Giove,** famed for its sculpture-rich, bust-adorned 17th-century courtyard—one of Rome's most photogenic. ✉ *Piazza Mattei, Ghetto.*

★ **Isola Tiberina.** Tiber Island is where a city hospital stands on a site that has been dedicated to healing ever since a temple to Aesculapius was erected here in 291 BC. Back then, the ancient Romans sheathed the entire island in travertine, sculpting it into a "boat" complete with obelisk "mast." Be sure to walk down the wide river embankment to

WALKING TOURS OF ROME

Context Travel: Rome, Enjoy Rome, Through Eternity, and Rome Walks are all reputable companies offering guided walking tours of the city.

Most walks focus on a theme—"Ancient Rome" and "The Vatican Museums" are perennial favorites, but there are other quirkier options as well, from "Rome at Twilight" to "The Architecture of Fascism." Here's how to contact the companies:

Context Travel (✉ *Via Santa Maria Maggiore 145, near the Basilica of Santa Maria Maggiore* ☎ *06/0697625204 or 1215/240–4347 in the U.S.* 🌐 *www.contextrome.com*). **Enjoy Rome** (✉ *Via Marghera 8A, near Termini* ☎ *06/4451843* 🌐 *www.enjoyrome.com*). **Rome Walks** (☎ *347/7955175* 🌐 *www.romewalks.com*). **Through Eternity** (☎ *06/7009336* 🌐 *www.througheternity.com*).

the southern tip to see one of the most astonishing remnants of ancient Rome: the island's sculpted marble "prow," meant to symbolize the ship of the Trojan hero Aeneas, father of the Italic people. Every summer, the city's Estate Romana hosts an open-air cinema on the island's paved shores. ✉ *Ponte Fabricio and Ponte Cestio, near Ghetto.*

Jewish Ghetto. Rome has had a Jewish community since the 2nd century BC, and from that time until the present its living conditions have varied widely according to its relations with the city's rulers. In 1555 Pope Paul IV Carafa established Rome's Ghetto Ebraico in the neighborhood marked off by the Portico d'Ottavia, the Tiber, and the Piazza dei Cenci. It measured only 200 yards by 250 yards. Jews were obligated to live there by law and the area quickly became Rome's most densely populated and least healthy. The laws were rescinded when Italy was unified in 1870 and the pope lost his political authority, but German troops tragically occupied Rome during World War II and in 1943 wrought havoc here. Today there are a few Judaica shops and kosher groceries, bakeries, and restaurants (especially on Via di Portico d'Ottavia), but the neighborhood mansions are now being renovated and much coveted by rich and stylish expats. The **Museo Ebraico** arranges tours of the Ghetto. The museum has exhibits detailing the millennial history of Rome's Jewish community. ✉ *Lungotevere Cenci, Ghetto* ☎ *06/68400661* 🌐 *www.museoebraico.roma.it* 🎫 *€10* ⏲ *Mid-Sept.–mid-Jun., Sun.–Thurs. 10–5, Fri. 9–2.; mid-Jun.–mid-Sept., Sun.–Thurs. 10–7, Fri. 10–4; closed Jewish holidays.*

Portico d'Ottavia. Along Via del Portico d'Ottavia in the heart of the Jewish Ghetto are buildings where medieval inscriptions, ancient friezes, and half-buried classical monuments attest to the venerable history of the neighborhood. The old **Chiesa di Sant'Angelo in Pescheria** was built right into the ruins of the ancient Roman Portico d'Ottavia, which was a monumental area enclosing a temple, library, and other buildings within colonnaded porticoes. ✉ *Via del Portico d'Ottavia 29, Ghetto.*

Fodor's Choice ★ **Santa Maria in Trastevere.** Shimmering at night thanks to its medieval facade mosaics, this is one of Rome's most magnificent and oldest churches, first built in the 3rd century and then greatly enlarged in the

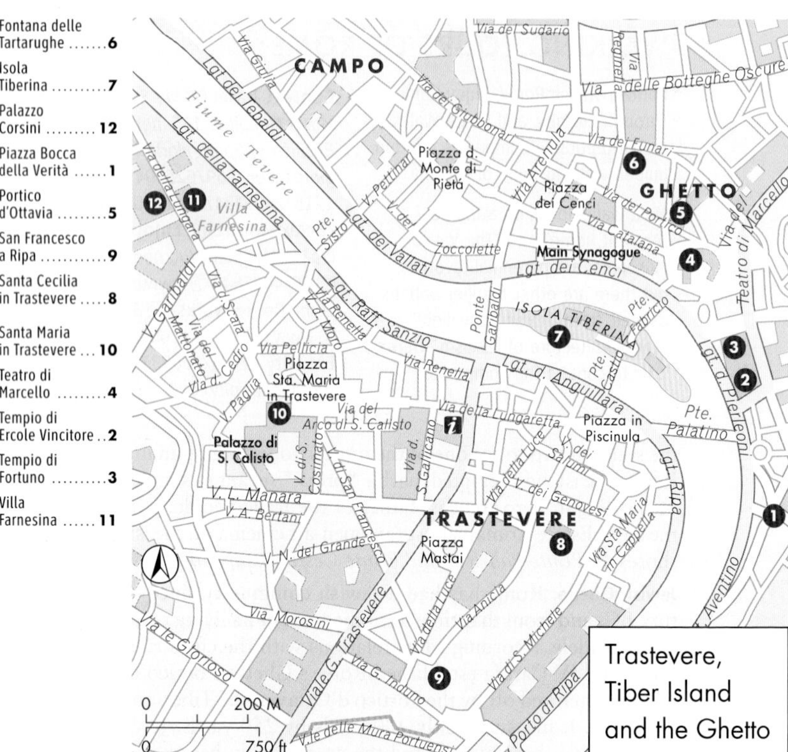

12th century. Inside, the nave, framed by a grand processional of two rows of columns taken from ancient Roman buildings, often produces involuntary gasps from unsuspecting visitors—this is probably as close as we can get to the imperial splendor of an ancient Roman basilica. A shining burst of Byzantine color and light is added by the celebrated 12th-century mosaics in the apse; also note the Cosmati work, a mosaic style from the 12th and 13th centuries in which tiny squares and triangles were laid with larger stones to form geometric patterns in the church floors. Outside, the **Piazza di Santa Maria in Trastevere** is a very popular spot for afternoon coffee and evening cocktails at its outdoor cafés. The 13th-century mosaics on Santa Maria's facade—which add light and color to the piazza, especially at night when they're in spotlight—are believed to represent the Wise and Foolish Virgins. In mid-July, processions honoring the Virgin Mary gather at the church as part of Trastevere's famous traditional feast, called *Festa de Noantri* ("Festival of We Others"). ✉ *Piazza di Santa Maria in Trastevere, Trastevere* ☎ *06/5819443* ⏲ *Daily 7:30 am–8 pm.*

Teatro di Marcello. The Teatro, hardly recognizable as a theater today, was originally designed to hold 20,500 spectators. It was begun by Julius Caesar and inaugurated by Augustus; today the 16th-century apartment building that sprouted out of its remains has become one of Rome's most prestigious residential addresses. The area west of the theater makes a grand stage for chamber music concerts in summer. ✉ *Via del Teatro di Marcello, Ghetto* ☎ *06/87131590 concert information* 🌐 *www.tempietto.it* ⏲ *Archeological site: spring and summer 9–7, fall and winter 9–6. Evening concerts: Jun.–early Oct.*

WORD OF MOUTH

"The Villa Farnesina is really lovely. . . . It's quite small and doesn't take too long to visit, especially because it's just inside Trastevere, very close to the Ponte Sisto pedestrian bridge. The entrance can be a bit tricky to find, so check your map closely!" —sacc

Trastevere. This area consists of a maze of narrow streets and is still, despite evident gentrification, one of the city's most authentically Roman neighborhoods. Literally translated, its name means "across the Tiber," and indeed the Trasteverini—the neighborhood's natives—are a breed apart. The area is hardly undiscovered, but among its self-consciously picturesque trattorias and trendy *enoteche* (wine bars) you can also find old shops and dusty artisans' workshops in alleys festooned with laundry hung out to dry. Stroll along Via dell'Arco dei Tolomei and Via dei Salumi, shadowy streets showing the patina of the ages. One of the least affected parts of Trastevere is a block in from the Tiber: on Piazza in Piscinula, north of Via dei Salumi and south of the Ponte Cestio. The smallest medieval church in the city, San Benedetto, stands opposite the restored medieval Casa dei Mattei. ✉ *Just west of the Tiber River, accessed by Ponte Sisto, Ponte Garibaldi, Ponte Cestio, Ponte Palatino, and Ponte Principe Amedeo, Trastevere.*

★ **Villa Farnesina.** Money was no object to extravagant patron Agostino Chigi, a Sienese banker who financed many a papal project. His munificence is evident in his elegant villa, completed in 1511. When Raphael could steal some precious time from his work on the Vatican Stanze and from wooing La Fornarina, he executed some of the frescoes, notably a luminous *Galatea* and the innovative loggia. Chigi delighted in impressing guests by having his servants cast precious dinnerware into the Tiber when it was time to clear the table. The guests didn't know of the nets he had stretched under the waterline to catch everything. The villa was eventually sold to the Farnese family after Agostino's death and renamed accordingly. ✉ *Via della Lungara 230, Trastevere* ☎ *06/68027397* 🌐 *www.lincei.it* 🎫 *€5* ⏲ *Mon.–Sat. 9–1.*

WORTH NOTING

Palazzo Corsini. This elegant palace across the street from the Villa Farnesina houses the collection of the **Galleria Nazionale d'Arte Antica,** including Roman sculptures, neoclassical statues, and 16th- and 17th-century paintings. Even if you're not interested in the artworks, stop in to climb the extraordinary 17th-century stone staircase, itself a drama of architectural shadows and sculptural voids. The adjacent Corsini gardens, now Rome's **Orto Botanico,** offer delightful tranquillity, with native and exotic plants and a marvelous view at the top. ✉ *Via della Lungara 10, Trastevere* ☎ *06/68802323* 🌐 *www.galleriaborghese.it* 🎫 *€4* ⏲ *Tues.–Sun. 8:30–7:30.*

Piazza Bocca della Verità. On the site of the Forum Boarium, ancient Rome's cattle market, this square was later used for public executions. Its name is derived from the marble **Bocca della Verità** (Mouth of Truth), a huge medieval drain cover in the form of an open-mouth face that's now set into the entry portico of the magically medieval 8th-century church of **Santa Maria in Cosmedin.** In the Middle Ages, legend had it that any person who told a lie with his hand in the mouth would have it chomped off. Today tour groups line up in this noisy, traffic-jammed piazza to give this ancient lie detector (which starred with Audrey Hepburn and Gregory Peck in *Roman Holiday*) a go. ✉ *Piazza Bocca della Verità, along the Tiber River beside Lungotevere dei Pierleoni, near Ghetto.*

San Francesco a Ripa. Ask the sacristan to show you the cell where Saint Francis slept when he came to seek the pope's approval for his new order. Also in this church is one of Bernini's most dramatic sculptures, the figure of the *Blessed Ludovica Albertoni,* ecstatic at the prospect of entering heaven. At this writing, the church was closed for restoration. ✉ *Piazza San Francesco d'Assisi 88, Trastevere* ☎ *06/5819020*

Santa Cecilia in Trastevere. Mothers and children love to dally in the delightful little courtyard in front of this church. Duck inside for a look at the 9th-century mosaics and the languid statue of Saint Cecilia under the altar. There are remains of Roman houses visible beneath the church. To see them, ask inside the church at the office to the left of the main entrance. Fragments of a *Last Judgment* fresco cycle by Pietro Cavallini (circa 1250–1330), dating from the late 13th century, remain one of his most important works. Though the Byzantine-influenced fragments are obscured by the structure, what's left reveals a rich luminosity in the seated apostles' drapery and a remarkable depth in their expressions. To view the frescoes, ring the bell at the convent to the left of the church's portico. ✉ *Piazza di Santa Cecilia 22, Trastevere* ☎ *06/5899289* *Excavations €2.50; frescoes €2.50* *Church and excavations Mon.–Sat. 9:30–12:30 and 4–6:30, Sun. 11:30–12:30 and 4–6:30. Frescoes Mon.–Sat. 10:15–12:15, Sun. 11:30–12:30.*

Tempio di Portuno. This rectangular temple devoted to Portunus, a river deity that protected this part of the Tiber shores, dates from the 2nd century BC and is built in the Greek style, as was the norm in the early years of Rome. For its age, its remains are remarkably well preserved, in part due to its subsequent consecration as a Christian church. ✉ *Piazza Bocca della Verità, near Ghetto.*

Tempio di Ercole Vincitore. All but one of the 20 original Corinthian columns in Rome's most evocative small ruin remain intact. It was built in the 2nd century BC. Long considered a shrine to Vesta, it's now believed the temple was devoted to Hercules by a successful olive merchant. ✉ *Piazza Bocca della Verità, near Ghetto.*

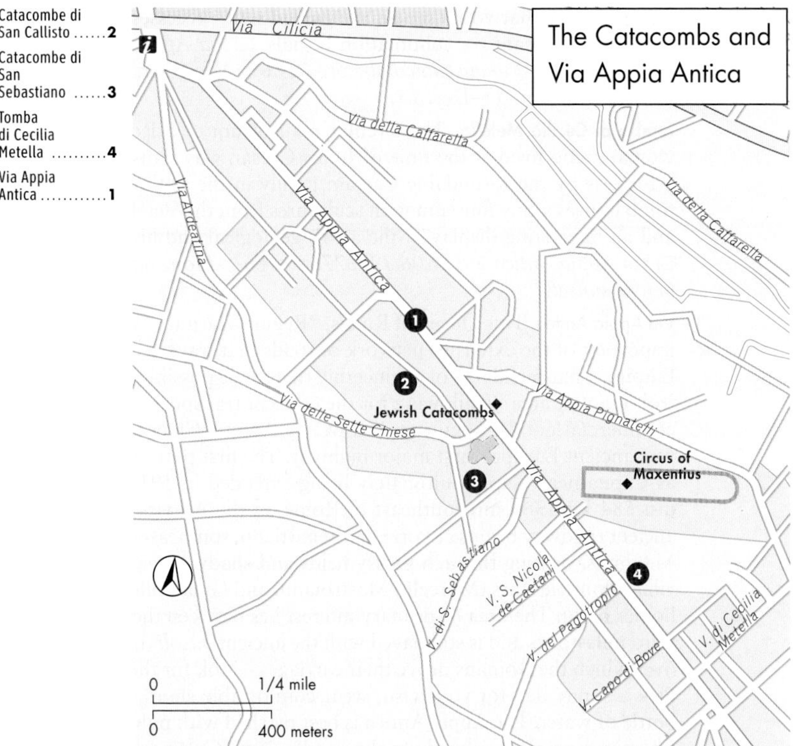

THE CATACOMBS AND VIA APPIA ANTICA

The Early Christian sites on the ancient Appian Way are some of the religion's oldest. Catacombs, where ancient pagans, Jews, and early Christians buried their dead, lie below the very road where tradition says Christ appeared to Saint Peter. The Via Appia Antica, built 400 years before, is a quiet, green place to walk and ponder the ancient world. There's a helpful office around the first milestone (at No. 58/60) that provides informative pamphlets and bicycle rentals.

GETTING HERE You can take Bus No. 118 from Circo Massimo, No. 218 from Piazza San Giovanni in Laterano, or No. 660 from the Colli Albani Metro station (Line A). There's also an Archeobus OpenTram bus from Termini (🌐 *www.trambusopen.com*).

TOP ATTRACTIONS

Catacombe di San Sebastiano (Catacombs of St. Sebastian). The 3rd-century Christian catacombs, named for the saint who was buried here, burrows underground on four levels. The only one of the catacombs to remain accessible during the Middle Ages, it's the origin of the term "catacomb," for it was in a spot where the road dips into a hollow, in Greek, *kata kymbe* ("down in the hollow"). The complex began as a pagan cemetery, then slowly transformed into a Christian one. It's this type of burial that you'll see on the guided visit—recesses carved into the galleries meant for inhumation burials. ✉ *Via Appia Antica 136* ☎ *06/7850350* 🌐 *www.catacombe.org* 🎫 *€6* ⏲ *Mon.–Sat. 9–noon and 2–5. Closed Nov. 15–Dec. 15.*

Tomba di Cecilia Metella. The circular mausoleum of a Roman noblewoman, who lived at the time of Julius Caesar, was transformed into a fortress by the formidable Caetani family in the 14th century. The tomb houses a tiny museum with sculptures from the Via Appia Antica and an interesting display of the area's geological and historical past. ✉ *Via Appia Antica 161* ☎ *06/39967700* 🎫 *€6* ⏲ *Mon.–Sat. 9 am–1 hr before sunset.*

★ **Via Appia Antica.** This Queen of Roads, "Regina Viarium," was the most important of the extensive network of roads that traversed the Roman Empire, a masterful feat of engineering that made possible Roman control of a vast area by allowing for the efficient transport of armies and commercial goods. Begun in 312 BC by Appius Claudius, the road was ancient Europe's first major highway. The first part reached as far as Capua near Naples, ultimately being extended in 191 BC to Brindisi 584 km (365 mi) southeast of Rome on the Adriatic Coast. The ancient roadway begins at Porta San Sebastiano, southeast of the Circus Maximus, passing through grassy fields and shady groves and by the villas of movie stars (Marcello Mastroianni and Gina Lollobrigida had homes here). The area of primary interest lies between the second and third milestones and is still paved with the ancient *basoli* (basalt stones) over which the Romans drove their carriages—look for the wheel ruts. Pick a sunny day for your visit, wear comfortable shoes, and bring a bottle of water. The Appia Antica is best reached with public transport (there are no sidewalks along the road); ⇨ *see Getting Here, above.* For more information, or bike rentals for exploring the Via Appia, visit the **Information Point** at (✉ *Via Appia Antica 58/60* ☎ *06/5135316* ⏲ *Daily 9:30–5:30 (4:30 in winter)* 🌐 *www.parcoappiaantica.it* ✉ *Exit Via Cristoforo Colombo at Circonvallazione Ardeatina, follow signs to Appia Antica parking lot.*

WORTH NOTING

Catacombe di San Callisto (Catacombs of St. Calixtus). A friar will guide you through the crypts and galleries of the well-preserved San Callisto catacombs. ✉ *Via Appia Antica 110* ☎ *06/51301580* 🌐 *www.catacombe.roma.it* 🎫 *€6* ⏲ *Mar.–Jan., Thurs.–Tues. 9–noon and 2–5.*

WHERE TO EAT

Updated by Katie Parla

Rome has been known since ancient times for its great feasts and banquets, and though the days of the triclinium and the Saturnalia are long past, dining out is still the Romans' favorite pastime. The city is distinguished more by its good attitude toward eating out than by a multitude of world-class restaurants. Simple, traditional cuisine reigns, although things are slowly changing as talented young chefs explore new culinary frontiers. Many of the city's restaurants cater to a clientele of regulars, and atmosphere and attitude are usually friendly and informal. The flip side is that in Rome the customer isn't always right—the chef and waiters are in charge, and no one will beg forgiveness if they refuse to serve you cappuccino after your meal. Be flexible and you're sure to *mangiar bene* (eat well). Lunch is served from approximately 12:30 to 2:30 and dinner from 7:30 or 8 until about 10:30, though some restaurants stay open later, especially in summer, when patrons linger at sidewalk tables to enjoy the parade of people and the *ponentino* (evening breeze).

Use the coordinate (⊕ B2) at the end of each listing to locate a site on the Where to Eat in Rome map.

WHAT IT COSTS IN EUROS

	¢	$	$$	$$$	$$$$
At dinner	under €20	€20–€30	€30–€45	€45–€65	over €65

Prices are for first course (primo), second course (secondo), and dessert (dolce).

PANTHEON AND NAVONA

PANTHEON

$$ MODERN ITALIAN

Il Bacaro. With a handful of choice tables set outside against an ivy-draped wall, this tiny candlelit spot not far from the Pantheon makes for an ideal evening, equally suited for a romantic twosome or close friends and convivial conversation. Pastas—like orecchiette (little ear-shaped pasta) with broccoli and sausage, a classic of Puglia—are star players. As a bonus, the kitchen keeps its diners from raiding each other's plates by offering side dishes of all the pastas ordered among those at the table. The choice main courses are mostly meat—the beef fillet with balsamic vinegar reduction and the sliced steak with cheese and wild mushrooms are winners. ✉ *Via degli Spagnoli 27, Pantheon* ☎ *06/6872554* 🌐 *www.ilbacaro.com* *Reservations essential* *Closed Sun. and 1 wk in Aug. No lunch Sat.* ⊕ *E3.*

$–$$ ITALIAN

La Sagrestia. This trattoria east of the Pantheon makes for a fun evening out, with a lively atmosphere and helpful servers accustomed to a foreign clientele. The decor is slightly kitsch, with loud frescoes painted on the walls and vaults. The menu consists of crispy, thin crust pizzas cooked in a wood burning oven, as well as an array of pastas, fish and meat dishes. The tonarelli al cartoccio (pasta and seafood cooked in parchment paper) is a house speciality. ✉ *Via del Seminario 89, Pantheon* ☎ *06/6797581* ⊕ *E4.*

NAVONA

$ WINE BAR Fodor's Choice ★

Cul de Sac. This popular wine bar near Piazza Navona is among the city's oldest enoteche and offers a book-length selection of wines from Italy, France, the Americas, and elsewhere. Food is eclectic, ranging from a huge assortment of Italian meats and cheeses (try the delicious *lonza,* cured pork loin, or *speck,* a northern Italian smoked prosciutto) to various Mediterranean dishes, including delicious baba ghanoush, a tasty Greek salad, and a spectacular wild boar pâté. Outside tables get crowded fast, so arrive early, or come late, as they serve until about

1 am. ✉ *Piazza Pasquino 73, Piazza Navona* ☎ *06/68801094* ⊙ *Closed 2 wks in Aug.* ✢ *D4.*

¢ PIZZA Fodor'sChoice ★ ✕ **Da Baffetto.** Down a cobblestone street not far from Piazza Navona, this is central Rome's most popular pizzeria and a summer favorite for street-side dining. The plain interior is mostly given over to the ovens, but there's another room with more paper-covered tables. Outdoor tables provide much-needed additional seating in the summertime. Turnover is fast, and lingering is not encouraged. ✉ *Via del Governo Vecchio 114, Navona* ☎ *06/6861617* ▭ *No credit cards* ⊙ *Closed Aug. No lunch* ✢ *D4.*

$$ MEDITERRANEAN ✕ **Etablì.** On a narrow *vicolo* off beloved Piazza del Fico, this multidimensional locale serves as a lounge-bar, and becomes a hot spot by aperitivo hour. Beautifully finished with vaulted wood-beam ceilings, wrought-iron touches, plush leather sofas, and chandeliers, it's all modern Italian farmhouse chic. In the restaurant section (the place is sprawling), it's minimalist Provençal hip (*etabli* is French for the regionally typical tables within), and the food is fresh and Mediterranean, with touches of Asia in the raw fish appetizers. Pastas are more traditional Italian, and the secondi run the gamut from land to sea. Arrive early, as the place fills up by dinnertime and it's a popular post-dining spot for sipping and posing. ✉ *Vicolo delle Vacche 9/a, Navona* ☎ *06/97616694* 🌐 *www.etabli.it* ⊙ *No dinner Sun.* ✢ *D3.*

$$$$ MODERN ITALIAN Fodor'sChoice ★ ✕ **Il Convivio Troiani.** In a tiny, nondescript vicolo north of Piazza Navona, the three Troiani brothers—Angelo in the kitchen, and brothers Giuseppe and Massimo presiding over the dining room and wine cellar—have quietly been redefining the experience of Italian eclectic alta cucina for many years. Antipasti include foie gras encrusted with dried figs and Sicilian pistachios, while a risotto with pumpkin, sheep's-milk cheese, and sea snails sates the appetites of those with dreams of fantasia. Main courses include four variations of a cold-weather pigeon, for which Il Convivio is famous. Service is attentive without being overbearing, and the wine list is exceptional. It's definitely a splurge spot. ✉ *Vicolo dei Soldati 31, Navona* ☎ *06/6869432* 🌐 *www.ilconviviotroiani.com* ✍ *Reservations essential* ⊙ *Closed Sun., 1 wk in Jan., and 2 wks in Aug. No lunch* ✢ *D3.*

¢ PIZZA Fodor'sChoice ★ ✕ **La Montecarlo.** Run by the niece of the owner of the pizzeria Da Baffetto, La Montecarlo has a similar pizza menu, but an added bonus of plentiful pasta dishes, second courses, and ample seating, both inside and out. Pizzas are super-thin and a little burned around the edges—the sign of a good wood-burning oven. It's one of the few pizzerias open for both lunch and dinner. ✉ *Vicolo Savelli 13, Navona* ☎ *06/6861877* 🌐 *www.lamontecarlo.it* ▭ *No credit cards* ⊙ *Closed Mon.* ✢ *E3.*

BEST BETS FOR ROME DINING

With hundreds of restaurants to choose from, how will you decide where to eat? Fodor's writers and editors have selected their favorite restaurants by price, cuisine, and experience in the Best Bets lists below. In the first column, Fodor's Choice properties represent the "best of the best" in every price category.

Fodor's Choice★

Agata e Romeo, $$$$, p. 105

Cul de Sac, $, p. 97

Da Baffetto, ¢, p. 98

Da Remo, ¢, p. 108

Glass Hostaria, $$$–$$$$, p. 107

Il Convivio Troiani, $$$$, p. 98

Il Sanlorenzo, $$$$, p. 103

La Montecarlo, ¢, p. 98

L'Angolo Divino $$, p. 102

La Pergola, $$$$, p. 107

L'Asino d'Oro, ¢, p. 105

Le Mani in Pasta, $$, p. 107

Palatium, $$, p. 105

Panattoni (Ai Marmi), ¢, p. 107

Trattoria Monti, $$, p. 105

BEST BY PRICE

¢

Da Remo, p. 108

L'Asino d'Oro, p. 105

Panattoni (Ai Marmi), p. 107

La Montecarlo, p. 98

$

Cul de Sac, p. 97

$$

L'Angolo Divino $$, p. 102

Le Mani in Pasta, $$, p. 107

Palatium, $$, p. 105

Trattoria Monti, p. 105

$$$

Checchino dal 1887, p. 108

Roscioli, p. 102

$$$$

Agata e Romeo, p. 105

Glass Hostaria, p. 107

La Pergola, p. 107

BEST BY CUISINE

MODERN ITALIAN

Agata e Romeo, $$$$, p. 105

Glass Hostaria, $$$–$$$$, p. 107

Il Convivio Troiani, $$$$, p. 98

L'Angolo Divino $$, p. 102

La Pergola, $$$$, p. 107

PIZZA

Da Remo, ¢, p. 108

La Montecarlo, ¢, p. 98

Panattoni (Ai Marmi), ¢, p. 107

ROMAN

Checchino dal 1887, $$$, p. 108

Perilli, $$, p. 108

WINE BAR

Cul de Sac, $, p. 97

L'Angolo Divino $$, p. 102

Roscioli, $$$, p. 102

BEST BY EXPERIENCE

OUTDOOR DINING

Il Palazzetto, $$$, p. 104

La Veranda dell'Hotel Columbus, $$$, p. 106

Osteria della Quercia, $$, p. 104

GORGEOUS SETTING

Il Convivio Troiani, $$$$, p. 98

Il Palazzetto, $$$, p. 104

La Pergola, $$$$, p. 107

La Veranda dell'Hotel Columbus, $$$, p. 106

LOTS OF LOCALS

Da Remo, ¢, p. 108

Perilli, $$ p. 108

Trattoria Monti, $$ p. 105

ROMANTIC

Glass Hostaria, $$$–$$$$, p. 107

Il Convivio Troiani, $$$$, p. 98

Il Sanlorenzo, $$$$, p. 103

La Pergola, $$$$, p. 107

GREAT WINE LIST

Glass Hostaria, $$$–$$$$, p. 107

Il Convivio Troiani, $$$$, p. 98

Palatium, $$, p. 105

GOOD FOR LUNCH

Cul de Sac, $, p. 97

L'Angolo Divino $$, p. 102

L'Asino d'Oro, ¢, p. 105

Osteria della Quercia, $$, p. 104

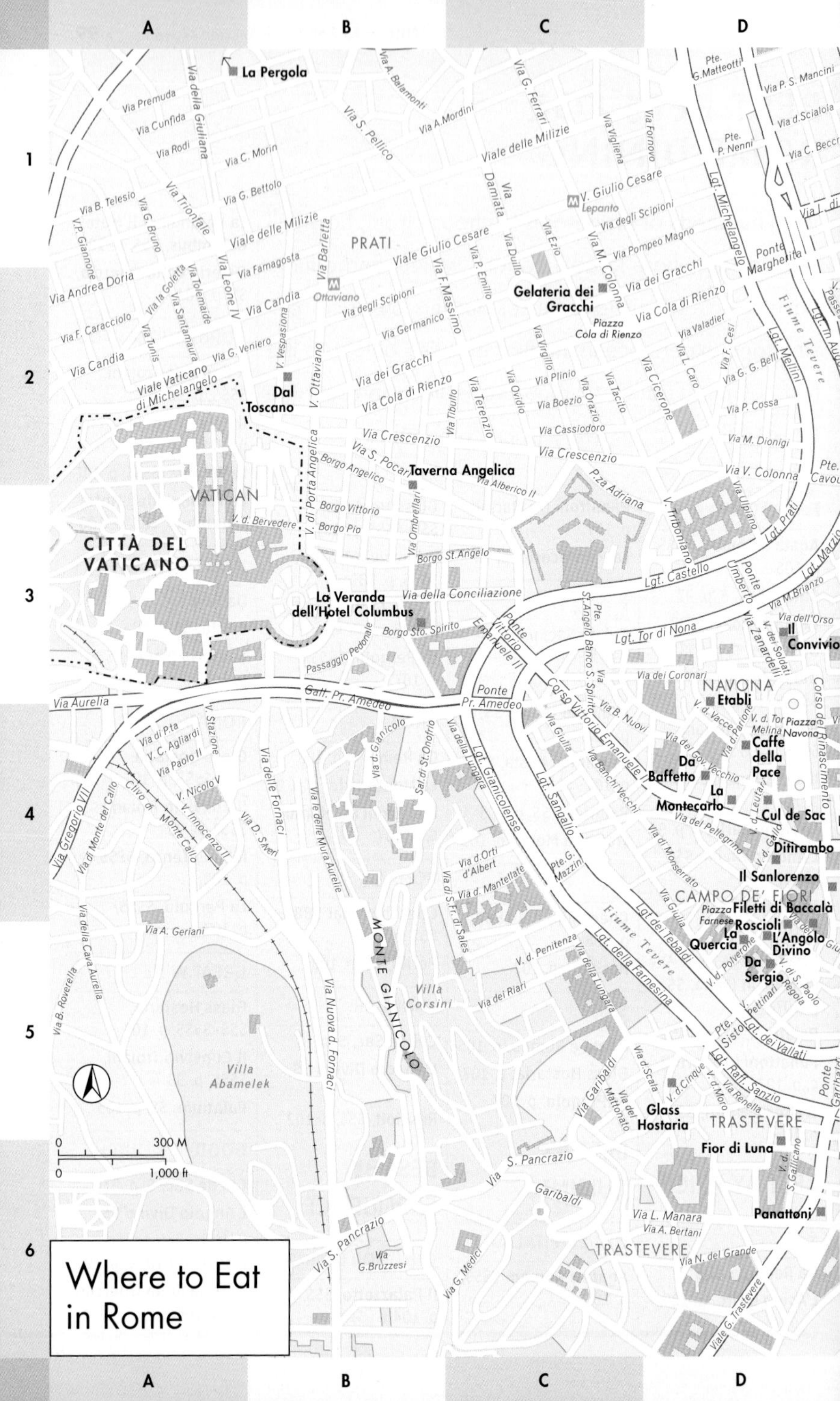
Where to Eat in Rome
A
B
C
D
1
2
3
4
5
6
La Pergola
Dal Toscano
Taverna Angelica
Gelateria dei Gracchi
La Veranda dell'Hotel Columbus
Il Convivio
Etabli
Caffe della Pace
Da Baffetto
La Montecarlo
Cul de Sac
Ditirambo
Il Sanlorenzo
Filetti di Baccalà
Roscioli
La Quercia
L'Angolo Divino
Da Sergio
Glass Hostaria
Fior di Luna
Panattoni
PRATI
VATICAN
CITTÀ DEL VATICANO
NAVONA
CAMPO DE' FIORI
TRASTEVERE
MONTE GIANICOLO
Villa Abamelek
Villa Corsini
Fiume Tevere
Ottaviano
Lepanto
0
300 M
1,000 ft

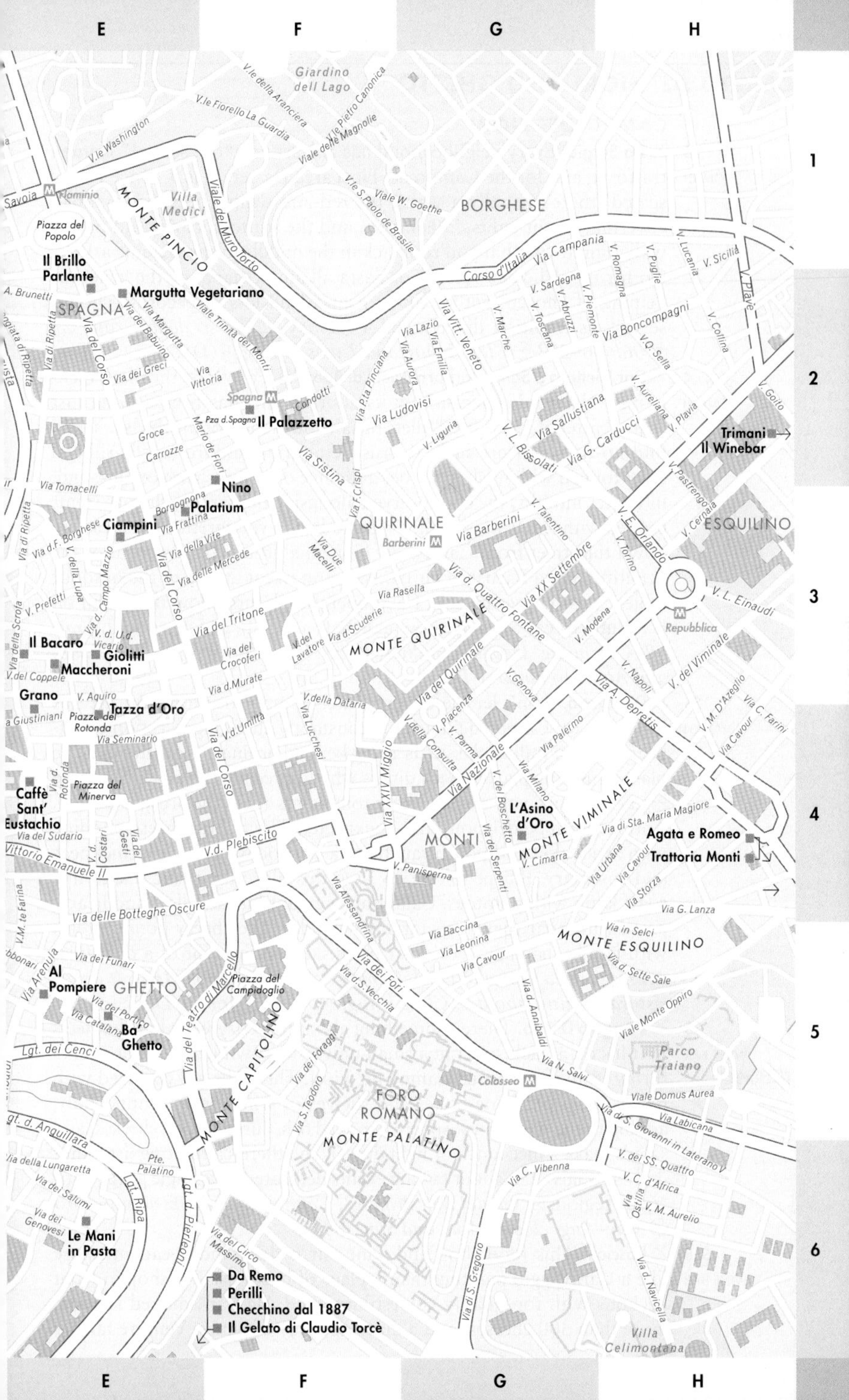

E
F
G
H
1
2
3
4
5
6
Giardino dell Lago
Villa Medici
MONTE PINCIO
BORGHESE
Piazza del Popolo
Flaminio
Il Brillo Parlante
Margutta Vegetariano
SPAGNA
Spagna
Pza d.Spagna
Il Palazzetto
Nino
Palatium
Ciampini
QUIRINALE
Barberini
ESQUILINO
Trimani Il Winebar
Repubblica
MONTE QUIRINALE
Il Bacaro
Giolitti
Maccheroni
Grano
Tazza d'Oro
Piazza del Rotonda
Piazza del Minerva
Caffè Sant' Eustachio
L'Asino d'Oro
MONTI
MONTE VIMINALE
Agata e Romeo
Trattoria Monti
MONTE ESQUILINO
Al Pompiere
GHETTO
Ba' Ghetto
Piazza del Campidoglio
MONTE CAPITOLINO
Colosseo
Parco Traiano
FORO ROMANO
MONTE PALATINO
Le Mani in Pasta
Da Remo
Perilli
Checchino dal 1887
Il Gelato di Claudio Torcè
Villa Celimontana
Via del Corso
Via Nazionale
Via XX Settembre
Via dei Fori
Via Cavour
Corso d'Italia
Via Vitt. Veneto
Vittorio Emanuele II
Via delle Botteghe Oscure
Via del Tritone
E
F
G
H

CAMPO DE' FIORI AND GHETTO

CAMPO DE' FIORI

$$ ROMAN ✕ **Da Sergio.** Every neighborhood has at least one "old-school" Roman trattoria, and for the Campo de' Fiori area Da Sergio is it. Once you're seated (there's usually a wait), the red-and-white-check paper table-covering, bright lights, '50s kitsch, and the stuffed boar's head on the wall remind you that you're smack in the middle of the genuine article. Go for the delicious version of pasta all'amatriciana, or the generous helping of gnocchi with a tomato sauce and lots of pecorino cheese, served, as tradition dictates, on Thursday. ✉ *Vicolo delle Grotte 27* ☎ *06/6864293* ⏲ *Closed Sun. and 2 wks in Aug.* ✣ *D5.*

¢ ITALIAN ✕ **Dar Filettaro a Santa Barbara (Filetti di Baccalà).** For years, the place nick-named "Filetti di Baccalà" by its adoring fans has been serving just that—battered, deep-fried fillets of salt cod—and not much else. You'll find no-frills starters such as bruschette al pomodoro (garlic-rubbed toast topped with fresh tomatoes and olive oil), beans with onions, and, in winter months, the cod is served alongside puntarelle, chicory stems topped with a delicious anchovy-garlic-lemon vinaigrette. The location, down the street from Campo de' Fiori in a little piazza in front of the beautiful Santa Barbara church, begs you to eat at one of the outdoor tables, weather permitting. Long operating hours allow those still on U.S. time to eat as early (how gauche!) as 6 pm. ✉ *Largo dei Librari 88, Campo de' Fiori* ☎ *06/6864018* ▭ *No credit cards* ⏲ *Closed Sun. and Aug. No lunch* ✣ *D5.*

$$ ITALIAN ✕ **Ditirambo.** Don't let the country-kitchen ambience fool you. At this little spot off Campo de' Fiori the constantly changing selection of off-beat takes on Italian classics is a step beyond ordinary Roman fare. The place is usually packed with diners who appreciate the adventuresome kitchen, though you may overhear complaints about the brusque service. Antipasti can be delicious and unexpected, like ricotta cheese pudding with artichokes and pomegranate, or a salt cod mousse with chickpeas and rosemary. But people really love this place for rustic dishes like roast lamb with potatoes, Calabrian eggplant "meatballs," and hearty pasta with boar ragù. Vegetarians will adore the cheesy potato gratin with truffle shavings. Desserts can be skipped in favor of a digestivo. ✉ *Piazza della Cancelleria 74, Campo de' Fiori* ☎ *06/6871626* 🌐 *www.ristoranteditirambo.it* ⏲ *Closed Aug. No lunch Mon.* ✣ *D4.*

$$ WINE BAR Fodor's Choice ★ ✕ **L'Angolo Divino.** There's something about this cozy wine bar that feels as if it's on a back street in a small university town instead of a stone's throw from the raucous Campo de' Fiori. The walls are veneered with panels from old wine boxes and shelves of wines from around Italy, adding to the warm atmosphere. Smoked fish, cured meats, cheeses, and salads make a nice lunch or light dinner, and there's a rotating list of hot daily specials. Ask about tasting events dedicated to a single grape variety or region. ✉ *Via dei Balestrari 12, Campo de' Fiori* ☎ *06/6864413* ⏲ *May–Aug. closed Mon. and Sun.* ✣ *D5.*

$$$ WINE BAR ✕ **Roscioli.** This food shop and wine bar is dark and decadent, more like a Caravaggio painting than a place of business. The shop in front beckons with top-quality comestibles: wild Alaskan smoked salmon, more than 300 cheeses, and a dizzying array of wines. Venture farther

inside to be seated in a wine cave–like room where you'll be served artisanal cheeses and *salumi*, as well as an extensive selection of unusual menu choices and straightforward takes on classics. Try the *burrata* with semi-sundried tomatoes, followed by carbonara, universally recognized as of the city's best. The menu is further divided among meats, seafood (including a nice selection of crudi—raw-fish preparations), and vegetarian-friendly items. ✉ *Via dei Giubbonari 21, Campo de' Fiori* ☎ *06/6875287* 🌐 *www.salumeriaroscioli.com* ✍ *Reservations essential* ⏲ *Closed Sun.* ✥ *D5.*

GHETTO

$$ ROMAN ✕ **Al Pompiere.** The entrance on a narrow side street leads you up a charming staircase and into the main dining room of this neighborhood favorite. Its Roman Jewish dishes, such as fried zucchini flowers, battered salt cod, and fried artichokes, all consistently good and served without fanfare on white dishes with a simple border. There are also some nice, historic touches like a beef-and-citron stew that comes from an ancient Roman recipe of Apicius. The menu is heavy on the *quinto quarto* (entrails) and their *trippa alla romana* (tripe in tomato sauce) is quite good. Save room for dessert. Their ricotta cake is divine. ✉ *Via Santa Maria dei Calderari 38, Ghetto* ☎ *06/6868377* 🌐 *www.alpompiereroma.com* ⏲ *Closed Sun. and Aug.* ✥ *E5.*

$$ ROMAN JEWISH ✕ **Ba' Ghetto.** The kitchen is kosher (many places featuring Roman Jewish fare are not), and not only do they feature an assortment of Roman Jewish dishes, they also offer a variety of Mediterranean–Middle Eastern Jewish fare. Enjoy starters like phyllo "cigars" stuffed with ground meat and spices, or the brik—egg and tomato wrapped in phyllo triangles and briefly fried. There's a nice assortment of pasta dishes, but we advise going for main plates like the assortment of couscous dishes (the spicy seafood is delicious) or *baccalà* with raisins and pine nuts. Interesting sides like chicory with bottarga (cured mullet roe) round out the meal. Kosher wines are on offer as well. Beware the strictly adhered-to hours: Saturday night, the restaurant posts post-Sabbath/sundown opening times to the minute on a blackboard out front. There's a second location near Piazza Bologna and a third in the Ghetto on Via del Portico d'Ottavia 2. ✉ *Via del Portico d'Ottavia 57, Ghetto* ☎ *06/68892868* 🌐 *www.kosherinrome.com* ⏲ *No dinner Fri. No lunch Sat.* ✥ *E5.*

$$$$ SEAFOOD Fodor's Choice ★ ✕ **Il Sanlorenzo.** This revamped, gorgeous space—think chandeliers and soaring original brickwork ceilings—houses one of the better seafood spots in the Eternal City. Tempting tasting menus are on offer, as well as à la carte items like a wonderful series of crudi, which can include a perfectly seasoned fish tartare trio, sweet scampi, and a wispy-thin carpaccio of red shrimp. The restaurant's version of spaghetti with lobster is an exquisite example of how this dish should look and taste (the secret is cooking the pasta in a lobster stock). Try a main course of a freshly caught seasonal fish prepared to order. Menu items often change based on the chef's whim and the catch of the day. A subterranean lounge and wine room offer refuge for those who seek private dining. ✉ *Via dei Chiavari 4/5, Campo de' Fiori* ☎ *06/6865097* 🌐 *www.ilsanlorenzo.it* ⏲ *No lunch Sat.–Mon.* ✥ *D4.*

$$ ITALIAN **Osteria della Quercia.** Diners can sit under the gorgeous looming oak tree that lends its name to beautiful Piazza della Quercia. The menu is simple—the usual suspects include fried starters like stuffed zucchini flowers and baccalà, as well as Roman pasta dishes like spaghetti carbonara and amatriciana. Main dishes include baby lamb chops, involtini (thinly sliced veal rolled around herbs and breadcrumbs), and meatballs in tomato sauce. The ubiquitous Roman sauteed cicoria (chicory) with olive oil and chili pepper is a good choice for a green side. Service is friendly and allows for lingering on balmy Roman afternoons and evenings—so close, and yet so seemingly far away from the chaos of nearby Campo de' Fiori. ✉ *Piazza dela Quercia 23, Ghetto* ☎ *06/68300932* 🌐 *www.laquerciaosteria.com* ✥ *D5.*

SPAGNA

$$ WINE BAR **Il Brillo Parlante.** Il Brillo Parlante's location near Piazza del Popolo makes it convenient for lunch or dinner after a bit of shopping in the Via del Corso area. Choose from 25 wines by the glass and more than 400 by the bottle. Have a drink at the bar or dinner downstairs in one of several wood-panel rooms. The menu goes beyond the basic enoteca fare. Choose from cured meats, crostini (toasted bread with various toppings such as pâté or prosciutto), homemade pastas, grilled meats, and even pizza. ✉ *Via della Fontanella 12, Spagna* ☎ *06/3243334* 🌐 *www.ilbrilloparlante.com* ⊙ *Closed Mon.* ✥ *E2.*

$$$ MODERN ITALIAN **Il Palazzetto.** This small restaurant near the Piazza di Spagna is part of the International Wine Academy of Rome. Chef Alessandro Stefoni creates seasonal menus using traditional Roman ingredients, which he gives a unique "twist" to in preparation and flavor pairings. Tagliatelle with marjoram and prawns hits all the right notes; fish soup with clementines and baby basil is a study in contrasting flavor and texture. In addition to à la carte selections, there are also two four-course tasting menus priced at €60 for a vegetarian meal and €65 for the classic menu. ✉ *Vicolo del Bottino 8, Spagna* ☎ *06/6993400* 🌐 *www.ilpalazzettoroma.com* ✥ *F2.*

$$ VEGETARIAN **Margutta Vegetariano.** Parallel to posh Via del Babuino, Via Margutta has long been known as the street where artists have their studios in Rome. How fitting, then, that the rare Italian vegetarian restaurant, with changing displays of modern art, sits on the far end of this gallery-lined street closest to Piazza del Popolo. Here it takes on a chic and cosmopolitan air, where you'll find meat-free versions of classic Mediterranean dishes as well as creative vegetable-based concoctions. Lunch (dubbed "brunch") is essentially a rich and varied buffet to which you help yourself, while dinner offers à la carte and prix-fixe options. ✉ *Via Margutta 118, Spagna* ☎ *06/32650577* 🌐 *www.ilmarguttavegetariano.it* ✥ *E2.*

$$ ITALIAN **Nino.** Tom Cruise and Katie Holmes had their celeb-studded rehearsal dinner here, a testament that this dressed-up trattoria has been a favorite among international journalists and the rich and famous for decades. Nino sticks to the classics, in food and decor, as well as in its waiters. Much of the menu consists of Roman staples with a Tuscan slant. To start, try a selection from the fine antipasto spread, or go for the cured meats or warm crostini spread with liver pâté. Move on to pappardelle

al lepre (a rich hare sauce) or the juicy grilled beef. One warning: if you're not Italian, or a regular, or a celebrity, the chance of brusque service multiplies. ✉ *Via Borgognona 11, Spagna* ☎ *06/6795676* 🌐 *www.ristorantenino.it* ⏲ *Closed Sun. and Aug.* ✣ *F2.*

$$ CENTRAL ITALIAN Fodor's Choice ★ ✕ **Palatium.** Palatium is a wine bar that serves the traditional dishes of Lazio, the region of Italy of which Rome is the capital. The menu, which is assembled exclusively from local products, changes regularly to reflect the season and market availability. Wintertime sees hearty soups like cicerchie (a legume similar to a chick pea whose cultivation in the region dates back to ancient times) with crispy *guanciale,* and in the spring artichokes and lamb reign. There's an extensive wine list drawing on the best Lazio has to offer. ✉ *Via Frattina 94, Spagna* ☎ *06/69202132* ⏲ *Closed Sun.* ✣ *E3.*

MONTI, ESQUILINO, AND SAN LORENZO

MONTI

¢ CENTRAL ITALIAN Fodor's Choice ★ ✕ **L'Asino d'Oro.** Umbrian chef Lucio Sforza has relocated his famed restaurant L'Asino d'Oro to the heart of the Monti district, a neighborhood that's just a few minutes walk from the Roman Forum. The menu draws its inspiration from the food of Umbria and northern Lazio, and relies heavily on homemade pastas, game, and offal. The menu changes frequently, but you might find *lombrichelli* (hand rolled noodles) with a delicate artichoke and lamb sauce or rabbit cooked with vinegar, tomatoes, and pine nuts. At lunch there's a set three-course menu for €12, and tapas-like portions are served for €3 from 5–7:30 pm. ✉ *Via del Boschetto 73, Monti* ☎ *06/48913832* 🌐 *www.lasinodororoma.it* ⏲ *Closed Mon. No dinner Sun.* ✣ *G4.*

ESQUILINO

$$$$ MODERN ITALIAN Fodor's Choice ★ ✕ **Agata e Romeo.** For the perfect marriage of fine dining, creative cuisine, and rustic Roman tradition, the husband-and-wife team of Agata Parisella and Romeo Caraccio is the top. Romeo presides over the dining room and delights in the selection of wine-food pairings. And Chef Agata was perhaps the first in the city to put a gourmet spin on Roman ingredients and preparations, elevating dishes of the common folk to new levels, wherein familiar staples like *cacio e pepe* are transformed with the addition of even richer Sicilian aged cheese and saffron. From antipasti (try the sweetbreads) to desserts, many dishes are the best versions of classics you can get. The prices here are steep, but for those who appreciate extremely high-quality ingredients, an incredible wine cellar, and warm service, dining here is a real treat. ✉ *Via Carlo Alberto 45, Esquilino* ☎ *06/4466115* ⏲ *Closed weekends and Aug.* ✣ *H4.*

$$ CENTRAL ITALIAN Fodor's Choice ★ ✕ **Trattoria Monti.** Not far from Santa Maria Maggiore, Trattoria Monti is one of the most dependable, moderately priced trattorias in the city, featuring the cuisine of the Marches, an area on Italy's Adriatic coast. The fare served up by the Camerucci family is hearty and simple, represented by various roasted meats and game, and a selection of generally vegetarian timbales and soufflés that change seasonally. The region's rabbit dishes are much loved, and here the *timballo di coniglio con patate* (rabbit casserole with potatoes) is no exception. ✉ *Via di San*

Vito 13, Esquilino ☎ *06/4466573* ⏲ *Closed Mon., Aug., 2 wks at Easter, and 10 days at Christmas. No dinner Sun.* ✥ *H4.*

REPUBBLICA

$$ WINE BAR ✕ **Trimani Il Winebar.** Trimani operates nonstop from 11 am to 12:30 am and serves hot food at lunch and dinner. Decor is minimalist, and the second floor provides a subdued, candlelit space to sip wine. There's always a choice of a soup and pasta plates, as well as second courses and torte salate (savory tarts). Around the corner is a wineshop, one of the oldest in Rome, of the same name. Call about wine tastings and classes (in Italian). ✉ *Via Cernaia 37/b, Repubblica* ☎ *06/4469630* 🌐 *www.trimani.com* ⏲ *Closed Sun. and 2 wks in Aug.* ✥ *H2.*

VATICAN, BORGO, PRATI, AND NORTHWEST ROME

BORGO

$$$ ROMAN ✕ **La Veranda dell'Hotel Columbus.** Deciding where to sit at La Veranda is not easy, since both the shady courtyard, torch-lit at night, and the frescoed dining room are among Rome's most spectacular settings. While La Veranda has classic Roman cuisine, the kitchen offers nice, refreshing twists on the familiar with an innovative use of flavor combinations. Try the unusual shrimp carpaccio with burrata and fried artichokes. Or go for the Iclandic cod with Nebbiolo sauce. Even the pastas are unexpected: Fassona oxtail ravioli with celery cream and tomato confit is subtle and elegant—much like the surroundings. Call ahead, especially on Saturday, because the hotel often hosts weddings, which close the restaurant, and you don't want to miss passing a few hours of your Roman holiday in these environs. ✉ *Borgo Santo Spirito 73, Borgo* ☎ *06/6872973* 🌐 *www.hotelcolumbus.net* ✍ *Reservations essential* ✥ *B3.*

$$ MODERN ITALIAN ✕ **Taverna Angelica.** The area surrounding St. Peter's Basilica isn't known for culinary excellence, but Taverna Angelica is an exception. Its tiny size allows the chef to concentrate on each individual dish, and the menu is creative without being pretentious. Dishes such as marinated zucchini with feta and black olives, and risotto with shrimp, asparagus, and lemon are more about taste than presentation. It may be difficult to find, on a section of the street that's set back and almost subterranean, but it's worth searching out. ✉ *Piazza A. Capponi 6, Borgo* ☎ *06/6874514* 🌐 *www.tavernaangelica.it* ✍ *Reservations essential* ✥ *B3.*

PRATI

$$ TUSCAN ✕ **Dal Toscano.** An open wood-fired grill and classic dishes such as ribollita (a thick bread and vegetable soup) and pici (fresh, thick pasta) with wild hare sauce, are the draw at this great family-run Tuscan trattoria near the Vatican. The cuts of beef visible at the entrance tell you right away that the house special is the prized bistecca alla fiorentina—a thick grilled steak left rare in the middle and seared on the outside, with its rub of gutsy Tuscan olive oil and sea salt forming a delicious crust to keep in the natural juices of the beef. Seating outside on the sidewalk in warm weather is a nice touch. ✉ *Via Germanico 58/60,*

Prati ☎ 06/39723373 🌐 www.ristorantedaltoscano.it ⊙ Closed Mon., 3 wks in Aug., and 1 wk in Jan. ✥ B2.

NORTHWEST ROME

$$$$ MODERN ITALIAN Fodor's Choice ★

✕ **La Pergola.** La Pergola's rooftop location offers a commanding view of the city, and as you're seated in your plush chair, you know you're in for a luxe experience. First, your waiter will present you with menus—food, wine, and water (you read correctly). Then you must choose between the German wunderchef Heinz Beck's alta cucina specialties, though most everything will prove to be the best version of the dish you've ever tasted. Mediterranean lobster is oh-so-lightly poached, and melt-in-your-mouth lamb with artichokes is deceptively simple but earthy and perfect. Each course comes with a flourish of sauces or extra touches that makes it an event in its own right, while the cheese cart is well explained by knowledgeable servers. The dessert course is extravagant, including tiny petits fours and treats tucked away in small drawers that make up the serving "cabinet." The wine list is as thrilling as one might expect of a restaurant of this caliber, with 53,000 bottles and 3,000 labels making it one of the top wine cellars in Italy. *✉ Cavalieri Hilton, Via Cadlolo 101, Monte Mario, Northwest Rome ☎ 06/35092152 🌐 www.romecavalieri.com/lapergola.php ✍ Reservations essential. Jacket and tie ⊙ Closed Sun. and Mon., 2 wks in Aug. and 3 wks in Jan. No lunch ✥ A1.*

TRASTEVERE

$$$–$$$$ MODERN ITALIAN Fodor's Choice ★

✕ **Glass Hostaria.** After 14 years in Austin, Texas, Glass chef Cristina Bowerman returned to Rome to reconnect with her Italian roots. Her cooking is as innovative as the building she works in—which has received numerous recognitions for its architecture and design—but Bowerman still abides by some cardinal Italian kitchen rules, such as the use of fresh, local, seasonal ingredients. With an impassioned sense for detail, taste, and presentation, she serves a delicious Parmesan-cheese stuffed ravioli with asparagus, Isigny butter, and black truffles. Another favorite dish is coffee-encrusted lamb served with asparagus and pumpkin. And for dessert: hazelnut dacquoise with coriander ice cream. *✉ Vicolo del Cinque 58, Trastevere ☎ 06/58335903 🌐 www.glass-restaurant.it ⊙ Closed Mon. No lunch ✥ D5.*

$$ ROMAN Fodor's Choice ★

✕ **Le Mani in Pasta.** Here you can find fish-based trattoria fare with a few Roman staples thrown in. Start with crudi, then move onto the house specialty, linguini *all'astice* (with lobster in a light tomato sauce) or *paccheri* (tube shaped pasta) with langoustines and zucchini. These seafood dishes share the menu with the likes of *abbacchio scottadito* (grilled lamb) and *saltimbocca*, both classic Roman dishes. The tables are tight and the service is brisk, but that's part of the fun. *✉ Via dei Genovesi 37, Trastevere ☎ 06/5816017 🌐 www.lemaniinpasta.com ✍ Reservations essential ⊙ Closed Mon. ✥ E6*

¢ PIZZA Fodor's Choice ★

✕ **Panattoni** (Ai Marmi). Romans queue up on the pavement on Viale di Trastevere hoping to score a table at this popular neighborhood institution. Panattoni goes by several other names—Ai Marmi and L'Obitorio (the mortuary)—but all its monikers are synonymous with tasty thin-crust Roman-style pizza served in a hectic setting. Be sure to begin with the signature starter, *supplì al telefono*, fried rice balls stuffed with bits of melted mozzarella that dangle in long strands between bites. ✉ *Viale Trastevere 53/59, Trastevere* ☎ *06/5800919* ▭ *No credit cards* ⏲ *Closed Wed. and 3 wks in mid-Aug. No lunch* ✣ *D6.*

TESTACCIO

$$$ ROMAN ✕ **Checchino dal 1887.** Literally carved out of a hill of ancient shards of amphorae, Checchino remains an example of a classic, family-run Roman restaurant, but with the added benefit of an impressive wine cellar. Though the slaughterhouses of Testaccio are long gone, an echo of their past existence lives on in the restaurant's soul food—mostly offal and other less appealing cuts like trippa (tripe), pajata (lamb intestine with the mother's milk still inside), and coratella (heart, lungs, and liver of a lamb) are all still on the menu for die-hard Roman purists. For the less adventuresome, house specialties include braised milk-fed lamb with seasonal vegetables. ✉ *Via di Monte Testaccio 30* ☎ *06/5746318* 🌐 *www.checchino-dal-1887.com* ⏲ *Closed Sun., Mon., Aug., and 1 wk at Christmas* ✣ *F6.*

¢ PIZZA Fodor's Choice ★ ✕ **Da Remo.** Expect a wait at this perennial favorite in Testaccio frequented by students and locals. You won't find tablecloths or other nonessentials, just classic Roman pizza and boisterous conversation. Pies are crispy, thin-crusted, and lightly sauced. Begin with *fritti* (fried starters) and wrap up with *torta di ricotta* (ricotta cake), a local favorite. ✉ *Piazza Santa Maria Liberatrice 44, Testaccio* ☎ *06/5746270* ▭ *No credit cards* ⏲ *Closed Sun., Aug., and Christmas wk. No lunch* ✣ *F6.*

$$ ITALIAN ✕ **Perilli.** In this restaurant dating from 1911, the old Testaccio remains, and it has the decor to prove it. A seasonal antipasto table starts things off, offering Roman specialties like braised Roman artichokes and puntarelle (curled chicory stems in a garlicky vinaigrette based on lots of lemon and anchovy). The waiters wear crooked bow ties and are just a little bit too hurried—until, that is, you order classics like pasta all'amatriciana and carbonara, which they relish tossing in a big bowl tableside. This is also the place to try rigatoni alla pajata (with milk-fed lambs intestines)—if you're into that sort of thing. Secondi plates are for carnivores only, and the house wine is a golden enamel-remover from the Castelli Romani. ✉ *Via Marmorata 39, Testaccio* ☎ *06/5742415* ⏲ *Closed Wed. and Aug.* ✣ *F6.*

CAFÉS

Café-sitting is a popular leisure-time activity in Rome, practiced by all and involving nothing more strenuous than gesturing to catch the waiter's eye. Part of the pleasure is resting your tired feet; you won't be rushed, even when the cafés are most crowded, just before lunch and dinner. (Be aware, though, that you pay for your seat—prices are higher at tables than at the counter.) Nearly every corner in Rome holds a faster-paced coffee bar, where locals stop for a quick caffeine hit at the counter. You can get coffee drinks, fruit juices, pastries, sandwiches, liquor, and beer there, too.

With its sidewalk tables taking in Santa Maria della Pace's adorable piazza, **Caffè della Pace** (✉ *Via della Pace 3/7, Navona* ☎ *06/6861216* ✣ *D4*) has long been the haunt of Rome's *beau monde*. Set on a quiet street near Piazza Navona, it also has two rooms filled with old-world personality.

Fodor's Choice ★ **Caffè Sant'Eustachio** (✉ *P. Sant'Eustachio 82, Pantheon* ☎ *06/68802048* 🌐 *www.santeustachioilcaffe.it* ✣ *E4*), traditionally frequented by Rome's literati, has what is generally considered Rome's best cup of coffee. Servers are hidden behind a huge espresso machine, vigorously mixing the sugar and coffee to protect their "secret method" for the perfectly prepared cup. (If you want your *caffè* without sugar here, ask for it *amaro.)*

Tazza d'Oro (✉ *Via degli Orfani, Pantheon* ☎ *06/6789792* ✣ *E3*) has many admirers who flock here for one of the city's best cups of coffee. The hot chocolate in winter, all thick and gooey goodness, is a treat. And in warm weather the coffee granita is the perfect cooling alternative to a regular espresso.

GELATO

Along with the listings here, you can find a number of gelaterias in Via di Tor Millina, a street off the west side of Piazza Navona.

At **Ciampini** (✉ *Piazza San Lorenzo in Lucina, Corso* ☎ *06/6876606* 🌐 *www.caffeciampini.com* ✣ *E3*), creamy classic flavors are scooped from stainless steel containers. The marron glacè, made from candied chestnuts, is without parallel. **Fior di Luna** (✉ *Via della Lungaretta 96, Trastevere* ☎ *No phone* ✣ *D6*) offers artisanal gelato made from local, seasonal fruit, organic ingredients, and fair-trade chocolate. In the winter, they also make their own chocolate bars. **Gelateria dei Gracchi** (✉ *Via dei Gracchi 272, Prati* ☎ *06/3216668* ✣ *C2*), in Prati, gets rave reviews for both classic flavors and newfangled inventions such as cardamom and chestnut, which draw gelato fans from all over Rome. For years **Giolitti** (✉ *Via degli Uffici del Vicario 40, Pantheon* ☎ *06/6991243* 🌐 *www.giolitti.it* ✣ *E3*) was considered the best gelateria in Rome, and it's still worth a stop if you're near the Pantheon.

Fodor's Choice ★ **Il Gelato di Claudio Torcè** (✉ *Viale Aventino 59, Aventino* ☎ *No phone* ✣ *F6*) makes perhaps the most celebrated gelato in all of Rome, without artificial colors, flavors, or additives. It's worth crossing town for. There's another outlet in EUR at Viale dell'Aeronautica 105.

WHERE TO STAY

Updated by Nicole Arriaga

Lodging options in Rome are abundant. Over the past decade or so there's been an upswing in the number of bed-and-breakfasts, stylish boutique hotels, and lodgings with over-the-top opulence. At the same time, there continue to be many modest, budget hotels and pensioni (small family-run accomodations).

If swanky is what you're after, the best place to look is in the Spanish Steps and Via Veneto areas. On the flip side, many of the city's lower-cost accommodations are scattered near the Stazione Termini. But for the most authentic Roman experience, stay in or near the *centro storico* (the historic center), where you'll be able to cover most of the main attractions on foot.

Hotel reviews have been condensed for this book. Please go to Fodors.com for expanded reviews of each property.

Use the coordinate (✣ B2) at the end of each listing to locate a site on the Where to Stay in Rome map.

WHAT IT COSTS IN EUROS					
	¢	$	$$	$$$	$$$$
For two people	under €75	€75–€125	€125–€200	€200–€300	over €300

Prices are for a standard double room in high season.

PANTHEON, NAVONA, AND TREVI

PANTHEON

$$$ Fodor's Choice ★ **Albergo Santa Chiara.** For over 70 years, the Corteggiani family has made this well-appointed midrange hotel a home away from home for its guests. **Pros:** great location in the historic center behind the Pantheon; most of the rooms are spacious; the staff is polite and helpful. **Cons:** layout is mazelike (you must take two elevators to some of the rooms); the furnishings in some rooms are a little outdated; not a lot of natural light in most rooms. **TripAdvisor:** "a block away from the Pantheon," "on a quiet piazza," "wonderful chocolate croissants." ✉ *Via Santa Chiara 21, Pantheon* ☎ *06/6872979* 🌐 *www.albergosantachiara.com* *96 rooms, 3 suites, 3 apartments* *In-room: kitchen (some). In-hotel: room service, bar* *Breakfast* ✣ *E4.*

$$$–$$$$ **Pantheon.** Tucked away on a side street from the monument that holds its name, the Pantheon is a superb place to stay. **Pros:** proximity to the Pantheon; big, clean bathrooms; friendly staff. **Cons:** the lighting is low and the carpets are worn; the breakfast lacks variety. **TripAdvisor:** "perfect location for sightseeing," "Pantheon right across square," "staff were very welcoming." ✉ *Via dei Pastini 131, Pantheon* ☎ *06/6787746* 🌐 *www.hotelpantheon.com* *13 rooms, 1 suite* *In-room: Wi-Fi. In-hotel: room service, bar* *Breakfast* ✣ *E4.*

NAVONA

$$$ **Genio.** The proximity to Piazza Navona and a rooftop terrace with citywide views make this medium-size hotel a favorite for many travelers. **Pros:** rooms are a decent size for a Roman hotel; the bathrooms have been designed especially well. **Cons:** on a busy street next to a bus stop, so there's often traffic noise; you might hear your neighbors through the walls. **TripAdvisor:** "cannot beat the location," "very welcoming and helpful," "beds are a bit hard." ✉ *Via G. Zanardelli 28, Navona* ☎ *06/6832191* 🌐 *www.hotelgenioroma.it* *60 rooms* *In-hotel: room service, bar, business center, parking* *Breakfast* ✣ *D3.*

TREVI

$$$ **Trevi.** Location, location, location: This delightful place is tucked away down one of Old Rome's quaintest alleys near the Trevi Fountain. **Pros:** comfortable rooms; roof garden. **Cons:** staff is a bit uptight; some rooms on small side. **TripAdvisor:** "30 seconds to the Trevi Fountain," "utterly charming room," "outstanding concierge." ✉ *Vicolo del Babbuccio 20/21, Piazza di Trevi* ☎ *06/6789563* 🌐 *www.hoteltrevirome.com* *29 rooms* *In-room: Internet. In-hotel: room service, parking, pets allowed (some)* *Breakfast* ✣ *F3.*

CAMPO DE' FIORI AND GHETTO

CAMPO DE' FIORI

$$ Fodor's Choice ★ **Casa di Santa Brigida.** One of the nicest convents to stay in is run by the friendly sisters of Santa Brigida. **Pros:** no curfew; source for papal-audience tickets; location in the Piazza Farnese. **Cons:** weak air-conditioning; no TVs in the rooms (though there's a common TV room); breakfast is nothing special. **TripAdvisor:** "beautiful convent," "these nuns are so nice," "relief from the hustle and bustle." ✉ *Piazza Farnese 96, Campo de' Fiori* ☎ *06/68892497* 🌐 *www.brigidine.org* *20 rooms* *In-room: no TV, Internet. In-hotel: no-smoking rooms* *Breakfast* ✣ *D4.*

$$$ **Hotel Campo de' Fiori.** At this ivy-draped boutique hotel each room has its own color scheme and furniture design, but they all share a refined feel. **Pros:** superb location; cozy fireplace in lobby; rooftop terrace. **Cons:** some of the rooms are very small; the staff can be a bit rude and don't necessarily go out of their way to help you settle in. **TripAdvisor:** "great central location," "amazing roof terrace," "rooms were beautifully decorated." ✉ *Via del Biscione 6, Campo de' Fiori* ☎ *06/68806865* 🌐 *www.hotelcampodefiori.it* *23 rooms* *In-room: Internet, Wi-Fi.* *Breakfast* ✣ *D4.*

$$$ **Hotel Ponte Sisto.** With its central location, Hotel Ponte Sisto is ideal for travelers who want a little peace and quiet without being away from it all. **Pros:** staff is friendly; rooms with views (and some with balconies and terraces); luxury bathrooms; beautiful courtyard garden. **Cons:** street-side rooms can be a bit noisy; some rooms are on the small side. **TripAdvisor:** "breakfast was fantastic," "lovely inner courtyard," "amenities were tops." ✉ *Via dei Pettinari 64, Campo de' Fiori* ☎ *06/686310* 🌐 *www.hotelpontesisto.it* *103 rooms, 4 suites* *In-room: Internet. In-hotel: restaurant, room service, bar, business center, parking, some pets allowed* *Breakfast* ✣ *D5.*

BEST BETS FOR ROME LODGING

Fodor's offers a selective listing of quality lodgings at every price range, from the city's best budget motel to its most sophisticated luxury hotel. Here, we've compiled our top picks by price and experience. The best properties—those that provide a particularly remarkable experience in their price range—are designated in the listings with the Fodor's Choice logo.

Fodor's Choice★

Albergo Santa Chiara, $$$, p. 110
Aleph, $$$$, p. 113
The Beehive, ¢-$, p. 117
Casa di Santa Brigida, $$, p. 111
Daphne Veneto, $$, p. 113
Eden, $$$$, p. 113
Hassler, $$$$, p. 113
Hotel San Pietrino, ¢-$, p. 118
Relais Le Clarisse, $$$, p. 119
Scalinata di Spagna, $$$-$$$$, p. 116
Yes Hotel, $$, p. 118

By Price

¢

The Beehive, p. 117
Hotel San Pietrino, p. 118

$

Hotel Trastevere, p. 119
Italia, p. 116
Panda, p. 116

$$

Casa di Santa Brigida, p. 111
Daphne Veneto, p. 113
Hotel Campo de' Fiori, p. 111
Hotel Santa Maria, p. 119
Yes Hotel, p. 118

$$$

Albergo Santa Chiara, p. 110
Hotel Ponte Sisto, p. 111
Pantheon, p. 110
Relais Le Clarisse, p. 119
Scalinata di Spagna, p. 116

$$$$

Aleph, p. 113
Eden, p. 113
Hassler, p. 113
Hotel de Russie, p. 116

Best by Experience

B&BS

Daphne Veneto, $$, p. 113
Relais Le Clarisse, $$$, p. 119

BUSINESS TRAVEL

Cavalieri Hilton, $$$$, p. 118
Exedra, $$$$, p. 117

CONCIERGE

The Beehive, ¢-$, p. 117
Daphne Veneto, $$, p. 113
Hotel Lancelot, $$–$$$, p. 120
Scalinata di Spagna, $$$–$$$$, p. 116

DESIGN

Capo d'Africa, $$$$, p. 120
Cavalieri Hilton, $$$$, p. 118
Exedra, $$$$, p. 117

CHILD-FRIENDLY

Cavalieri Hilton, $$$$, p. 118
Hassler, $$$$, p. 113
Hotel Lancelot, $$–$$$, p. 120
Hotel Ponte Sisto, $$$, p. 111
Hotel de Russie, $$$$, p. 116
Mascagni, $$$$, p. 117

GREAT VIEWS

Cavalieri Hilton, $$$$, p. 118
Eden, $$$$, p. 113
Genio, $$$, p. 111
Hassler, $$$$, p. 113
Hotel Campo de' Fiori, $$, p. 111

HIDDEN OASES

Capo d'Africa, $$$$, p. 120
Domus Aventina, $$$, p. 119
Hotel Lancelot, $$–$$$, p. 120
Hotel Santa Maria, $$, p. 119

MOST ROMANTIC

Daphne Veneto, $$, p. 113
Relais Le Clarisse, $$$, p. 119

GHETTO

$$ **Arenula.** A bargain rate (at the low end of this price category) and great location are the draws at this pleasant, no-frills hotel. **Pros:** genuine bargain; close to Campo de' Fiori and Trastevere; spotlessly clean. **Cons:** four floors and no elevator; traffic and tram noise can be heard throughout the night despite the double-glazing. **TripAdvisor:** "in central historical Rome," "stairs are a bit of an effort," "unfriendly clerks at the reception desk." ✉ *Via Santa Maria dei Calderari 47, off Via Arenula, Ghetto* ☎ *06/6879454* 🌐 *www.hotelarenula.com* *50 rooms* *In-room: Wi-Fi. In-hotel: business center* *Breakfast* ✣ *E5.*

VENETO AND SPAGNA

VENETO

$$$$ Fodor's Choice ★ **Aleph.** The uber-sleek interior of the Aleph makes it one of Rome's most unfalteringly fashionable hotels. **Pros:** award-winning design; spa with sauna, Turkish baths, and thermal swimming pool. **Cons:** rooms are small for the price; cocktails are expensive; Internet is costly, too. **TripAdvisor:** "well-designed funky hotel," "door staff were always pleasant," "walking distance of many tourist sites." ✉ *Via San Basilio 15, Veneto* ☎ *06/422901* 🌐 *96 rooms, 6 suites* *In-room: Internet. In-hotel: restaurant, room service, bars, gym, spa, business center, parking* *No meals* ✣ *G2.*

$$ Fodor's Choice ★ **Daphne Veneto.** Inspired by baroque artist Gian Lorenzo Bernini's exquisite *Apollo and Daphne* sculpture at the Borghese Gallery, the Daphne Inn at Via Veneto is an "urban B&B" run by people who love Rome and who will do their best to make sure you love it, too. **Pros:** personalized service; comfortable beds. **Cons:** no TVs; some bathrooms are shared. **TripAdvisor:** "one block from Piazza Barberini," "clean, modern, and comfortable," "staff was very helpful." ✉ *Via di San Basilio 55, Veneto* ☎ *06/87450087* 🌐 *www.daphne-rome.com* *7 rooms, 2 suites* *In-room: no TV, Wi-Fi. In-hotel: business center, parking* *Breakfast* ✣ *G3.*

$$$$ Fodor's Choice ★ **Eden.** Once the preferred haunt of Hemingway, Ingrid Bergman, and Fellini, this superlative hotel combines dashing luxury with stunning vistas of Rome. **Pros:** gorgeous panoramic view from roof terrace; the cache of celebrity guests; 24-hour room service. **Cons:** expensive; a bit out of the historic center; some say the staff can be hit-or-miss. **TripAdvisor:** "old-school class and elegance," "close to the Spanish Steps," "truly unique service." ✉ *Via Ludovisi 49, Veneto* ☎ *06/478121* 🌐 *www.edenroma.com* *121 rooms, 13 suites* *In-room: Internet. In-hotel: restaurant, room service, bars, gym, business center, parking, some pets allowed* *No meals* ✣ *G2.*

SPAGNA

$$$$ Fodor's Choice ★ **Hassler.** When it comes to million-dollar views, this exclusive hotel has the best seats in the house. **Pros:** charming old-world feel; prime location and panoramic views at the top of the Spanish Steps; just steps away from some of the best shopping in the world. **Cons:** VIP prices; many think the staff is too standoffish; cuisine at the rooftop restaurant doesn't merit the gourmet price tag. **TripAdvisor:** "five-star service," "rooms luxuriously comfortable," "great view of the Vatican." ✉ *Piazza Trinità dei Monti 6, Spagna* ☎ *06/699340* 🌐 *www.hotelhasslerroma.*

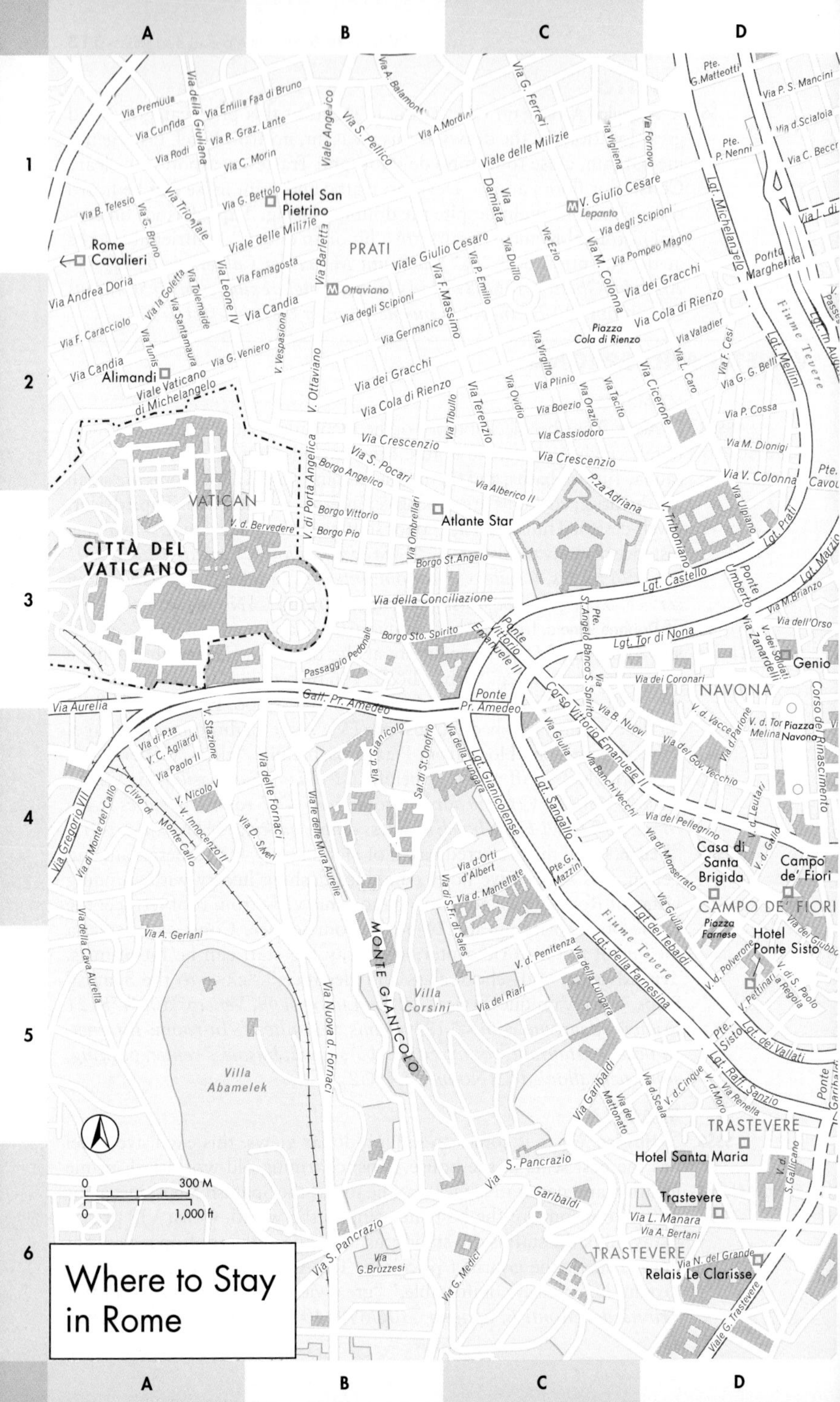
Where to Stay in Rome
A
B
C
D
1
2
3
4
5
6
Hotel San Pietrino
Rome Cavalieri
Alimandi
Atlante Star
Genio
Casa di Santa Brigida
Campo de' Fiori
Hotel Ponte Sisto
Hotel Santa Maria
Trastevere
Relais Le Clarisse
PRATI
VATICAN
CITTÀ DEL VATICANO
NAVONA
CAMPO DE' FIORI
TRASTEVERE
MONTE GIANICOLO
Villa Corsini
Villa Abamelek
Piazza Cola di Rienzo
Piazza Navona
Piazza Farnese
Fiume Tevere
Ottaviano
Lepanto
Viale delle Milizie
Viale Giulio Cesare
Via Cola di Rienzo
Via dei Gracchi
Via Crescenzio
Via della Conciliazione
Borgo Sto. Spirito
Borgo St.Angelo
Borgo Pio
Borgo Vittorio
Borgo Angelico
Via di Porta Angelica
Via Candia
Via Andrea Doria
Viale Vaticano
Via Aurelia
Gall. Pr. Amedeo
Ponte Pr. Amedeo
Ponte Vittorio Emanuele II
Corso Vittorio Emanuele II
Lgt. Castello
Lgt. Tor di Nona
Lgt. Gianicolense
Lgt. Sangallo
Lgt. dei Tebaldi
Lgt. della Farnesina
Lgt. dei Vallati
Lgt. Raff. Sanzio
Lgt. Prati
Lgt. Michelangelo
Ponte Umberto
Pte. Cavour
Pte. Margherita
Pte. Sisto
Pte. G. Mazzini
Pte. S. Angelo
Pte. G. Matteotti
Pte. P. Nenni
Via Giulia
Via della Lungara
Via dei Coronari
Via del Pellegrino
Via di Monserrato
Via Garibaldi
Via S. Pancrazio
Via Nuova d. Fornaci
Via delle Fornaci
Via delle Mura Aurelie
Via Gregorio VII
Viale di Trastevere
Via Urbano
Via dei Riari
Corso del Rinascimento
0
300 M
0
1,000 ft

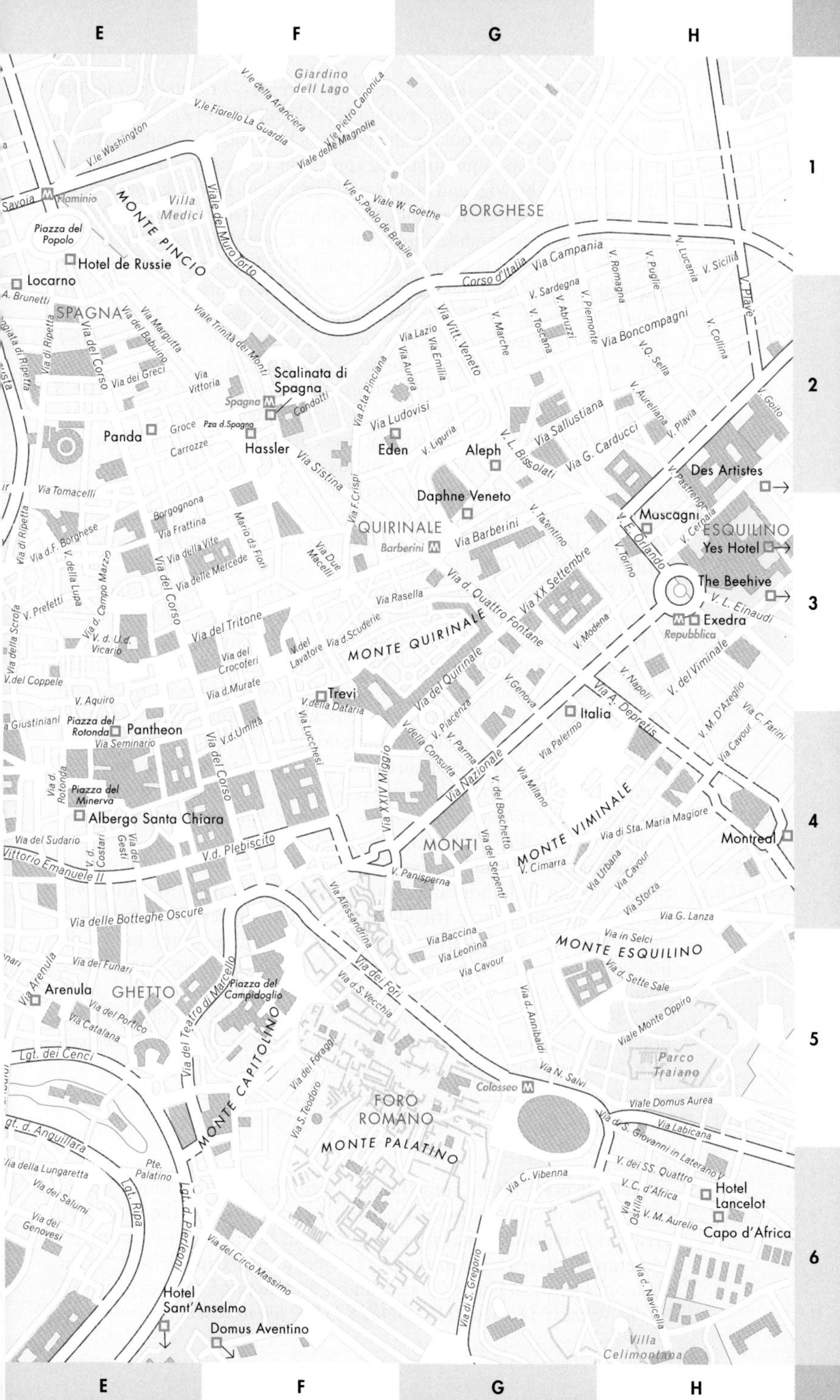
E
F
G
H
1
2
3
4
5
6
Giardino dell Lago
BORGHESE
Villa Medici
MONTE PINCIO
Piazza del Popolo
Flaminio
Hotel de Russie
Locarno
SPAGNA
Scalinata di Spagna
Spagna
Pza d.Spagna
Panda
Hassler
Eden
Aleph
Daphne Veneto
Des Artistes
Muscagni
ESQUILINO
Yes Hotel
The Beehive
Exedra
Repubblica
QUIRINALE
Barberini
MONTE QUIRINALE
Trevi
Italia
Piazza del Rotonda
Pantheon
Piazza del Minerva
Albergo Santa Chiara
MONTI
MONTE VIMINALE
Montreal
MONTE ESQUILINO
Arenula
GHETTO
Piazza del Campidoglio
MONTE CAPITOLINO
Parco Traiano
Colosseo
FORO ROMANO
MONTE PALATINO
Hotel Lancelot
Capo d'Africa
Hotel Sant'Anselmo
Domus Aventino
Villa Celimontana
Via del Corso
Via del Tritone
Via Sistina
Via Vitt. Veneto
Via XX Settembre
Via Nazionale
Via Cavour
Via dei Fori
Vittorio Emanuele II
Via delle Botteghe Oscure
Via del Circo Massimo
Corso d'Italia
E
F
G
H

com 85 *rooms, 13 suites* *In-room: Internet. In-hotel: restaurant, room service, bar, gym, spa, parking* *No meals* ✢ *F2.*

$$$$ Hotel de Russie. Overlooking the Piazza del Popolo on Via del Babuino (a street fit for a boutique shopping spree), the de Russie is a ritzy retreat for government bigwigs and Hollywood highrollers. **Pros:** big potential for celebrity sightings; special activities for children; extensive gardens (including a butterfly reserve); first-rate luxury spa. **Cons:** decor is a little generic given the price; breakfast is nothing special. **TripAdvisor:** "renovated with exquisite taste," "glorious gardens," "service was amazing." ✉ *Via del Babuino 9, Spagna* ☎ *06/328881* 🌐 *www.hotelderussie.it* *122 rooms, 34 suites* *In-room: Internet. In-hotel: restaurant, room service, bar, pool, gym, spa, children's programs, parking* *Breakfast* ✢ *E1.*

$$$–$$$$ **Locarno.** The sort of place that inspired a movie (Bernard Weber's 1978 *Hotel Locarno,* to be exact), this has been a longtime choice for art aficionados and people in the cinema. **Pros:** luxurious feel; free Wi-fi; spacious rooms (even by American standards); free bicycles for exploring Rome. **Cons:** some of the rooms are dark; the annex doesn't compare to the main hotel; the regular staff probably won't go out of their way to help you. **TripAdvisor:** "excellent location for all the sights," "very nice rooftop terrace," "older, but so charming." ✉ *Via della Penna 22, Spagna* ☎ *06/3610841* 🌐 *www.hotellocarno.com* *64 rooms, 2 suites* *In-room: Wi-Fi. In-hotel: restaurant, bar, business center* *Breakfast* ✢ *E2.*

$ **Panda.** Given its prime location, just a hop, skip, and a jump from the Spanish Steps, you couldn't find a better deal in Rome than at the Panda. **Pros:** discount if you pay cash; free Wi-Fi; located on a quiet street but still close to the Spanish Steps. **Cons:** rooms on the small side; not all rooms have private bathrooms; no elevator; no TVs in the rooms. **TripAdvisor:** "just off the Spanish Steps," "clean and well-maintained," "staff is very friendly." ✉ *Via della Croce 35, Spagna* ☎ *06/6780179* 🌐 *www.hotelpanda.it* *20 rooms, 14 with bath* *In-room: no a/c (some), no TV, Wi-Fi* *Breakfast* ✢ *E2.*

$$$–$$$$ Fodor's Choice ★ **Scalinata di Spagna.** A longtime favorite of hopeless romantics, this charming little boutique hotel is often booked up months, even years, in advance. **Pros:** friendly and helpful concierge; fresh fruit in the rooms; free Wi-Fi throughout. **Cons:** it's a hike up the hill to the hotel; no porter and no elevator; service can be hit-or-miss. **TripAdvisor:** "warm and very cozy," "beautiful terrace," "hot-from-the-oven cornettos." ✉ *Piazza Trinità dei Monti 17, Spagna* ☎ *06/6793006* 🌐 *www.hotelscalinata.com* *16 rooms* *In-room: Wi-Fi. In-hotel: room service, business center, parking* *Breakfast* ✢ *F2.*

MONTI, REPUBBLICA, AND SAN LORENZO

MONTI

$ **Italia.** It may not be something to write home to Momma about, but for the price, this budget pensione certainly does the job. **Pros:** great price; individual attention and personal care; free Wi-Fi. **Cons:** it's sometimes noisy; air-conditioning is an extra €10. **TripAdvisor:** "in the center of historical Rome," "very simple and quaint," "not expensive." ✉ *Via Venezia 18, Monti* ☎ *06/4828355* 🌐 *www.hotelitaliaroma.com*

31 rooms, 1 apartment In-room: Wi-Fi. In-hotel: bar, business center, parking Breakfast G3.

$ **Montreal.** A good choice for budget travelers, this hotel is on a central avenue across the square from Santa Maria Maggiore, three blocks from Stazione Termini, Rome's main transportation hub. **Pros:** informative staff provides maps and good recommendations; plenty of reasonably priced restaurants in the area. **Cons:** location can be noisy at night; it's either a bus, metro, or long walk to most historic sights. **TripAdvisor:** "room was lovely in all ways," "very helpful desk staff," "reasonable price." *Via Carlo Alberto 4, Monti 06/4457797 www.hotelmontrealroma.com 27 rooms In-room: In-hotel: room service, bar, business center, parking Breakfast H4.*

REPUBBLICA

¢–$ Fodor's Choice ★ **The Beehive.** You won't feel like you're in Rome once you step foot into this hip alternative budget hotel, which could be taken for a holistic center or a yoga studio. **Pros:** yoga, massage, and other therapies offered on-site; vegetarian café with "name your own price" policy. **Cons:** no TV, air-conditioning, baggage storage, or private bathrooms; breakfast isn't included in the room rate. **TripAdvisor:** "nicely appointed rooms," "funky modern furniture," "very inexpensive option." *Via Marghera 8, Repubblica 06/44704553 www.the-beehive.com 8 rooms, 1 dormitory, 3 apartments In-room: no a/c, kitchen (some), no TV, Wi-Fi No meals H3.*

$$$$ **Exedra.** High rollers love to host splashy parties here and magazines love to rave about them. **Pros:** spacious and attractive rooms; great spa and pool; terrace with cocktail service; close to Termini station. **Cons:** food and beverages are expensive; beyond the immediate vicinity; parts of the neighborhood seems unsavory. **TripAdvisor:** "five-star all the way," "location is very nice," "very exclusive feel." *Piazza della Repubblica 47, Repubblica 06/489381 www.boscolohotels.com 240 rooms, 18 suites In-room: Wi-Fi. In-hotel: restaurants, room service, bars, pool, gym, spa, business center, parking, some pets allowed Breakfast H3.*

$$$$ **Mascagni.** Situated on one of Rome's busiest streets and close to one of Rome's most impressive piazzas (*Piazza della Repubblica*), sits the hotel Mascagni. **ros:** staff is friendly and attentive with good advice; bathrooms are spacious and come with nice toiletries; great for families with kids. **Cons:** small lobby; weak air-conditioning. **TripAdvisor:** "in a 19th-century palace," "romantic ambiance," "very considerate staff." *Via Vittorio Emanuele Orlando 90, Repubblica 06/48904040 www.hotelmascagni.com 40 rooms In-room: Internet. In-hotel: bar, business center, parking Breakfast H3.*

SAN LORENZO

$ **Des Artistes.** The three personable Riccioni brothers have transformed their hotel into the best in the neighborhood in its price range. **Pros:** good value; decent-size rooms; relaxing roof garden terrace. **Cons:** breakfast area is overcrowded. **TripAdvisor:** "hotel is beyond expectations," "clean and nicely furnished room," "rooftop terrace was a real treat." *Via Villafranca 20 San Lorenzo 06/4454365 www.*

hoteldesartistes.com ⇨ *40 rooms, 27 with bath* *In-room: no a/c (some), Wi-Fi. In-hotel: bar, parking* *Breakfast* ⊕ *H2.*

$$ Fodor's Choice ★ **Yes Hotel.** This is a budget hotel, but with a contemporary style that makes it feel like something more. **Pros:** satellite TV; discount if you pay cash; great value. **Cons:** rooms are small; no individual climate control or refrigerators in the rooms. **TripAdvisor:** "rooms were ample and comfortable," "on a very quiet street," "close to the train station." ✉ *Via Magenta 15, San Lorenzo* ☎ *06/44363836* 🌐 *www.yeshotelrome.com* ⇨ *29 rooms, 1 suite* *In-room: Wi-Fi. In-hotel: parking* *Breakfast* ⊕ *H3.*

VATICAN, BORGO, PRATI, AND NORTHWEST ROME

VATICAN

$$ **Alimandi.** Just behind the Vatican Museums, this family-run hotel is a real bargain considering the location and service. **Pros:** nice family-owned hotel with a friendly staff; reasonably priced restaurants and shops in the area. **Cons:** breakfast is a good spread but it goes quickly; rooms are small; not close to much of interest other than the Vatican. **TripAdvisor:** "steps from the Vatican," "a great value for Rome," "breakfast is the best we had." ✉ *Via Tunisi 8, Vatican* ☎ *06/39723948* 🌐 *www.alimandi.it* ⇨ *35 rooms* *In-room: Wi-Fi. In-hotel: bar, gym, business center, parking* *Breakfast* ⊕ *A2.*

BORGO

$$$–$$$$ **Atlante Star.** The lush rooftop-terrace garden café with probably the best views of St. Peter's is one of the prime reasons to stay here. **Pros:** close to St. Peter's; impressive view from the restaurant and some of the rooms. **Cons:** some rooms are nicer than others (and some aren't as pretty as the ones on the Web site); the area can be overrun with tourists; it's not close to Rome's other attractions. **TripAdvisor:** "basic style but brilliant value," "beautiful breakfast room," "nice and friendly service." ✉ *Via Vitelleschi 34, Borgo* ☎ *06/6873233* 🌐 *www.atlantestarhotel.com* ⇨ *70 rooms, 15 suites* *In-room: Internet. In-hotel: restaurant, room service, bar, business center, parking* *Breakfast* ⊕ *B3.*

PRATI

¢–$ Fodor's Choice ★ **Hotel San Pietrino.** How this simple but cute hotel close to the Vatican manages to keep its bargain prices is a mystery. **Pros:** heavenly prices near the Vatican; TVs with DVD players; high-speed Internet; close to Rome's famous farmers' market, Mercato Trionfale. **Cons:** a couple of Metro stops away from the center of Rome; no breakfast; no bar. **TripAdvisor:** "easy walk to Vatican," "vintage elevator," "reasonably priced." ✉ *Via Giovanni Bettolo 43, Prati* ☎ *06/3700132* 🌐 *www.sanpietrino.it* ⇨ *12 rooms* *In-room: Internet, Wi-Fi. In-hotel: business center* *No meals* ⊕ *B1.*

NORTHWEST ROME

$$$$ **Cavalieri Hilton.** Though the Cavalieri is outside the city center, distance has its advantages, one of them being the magnificent view over Rome (ask for a room facing the city), and another, that elusive element of more central Roman hotels: space. **Pros:** beautiful bird's-eye view of Rome;

shuttle to the city center; world-class dining. **Cons:** you pay for the luxury of staying here—everything is expensive; outside the city center; not all rooms have the view. **TripAdvisor:** "breathtaking view of St. Peter's," "balcony with a fantastic view," "a ways from things you want to see." ✉ *Via Cadlolo 101, Monte Mario* ☎ *06/35091* 🌐 *www.cavalieri-hilton.com* *357 rooms, 17 suites* *In-room: Internet. In-hotel: restaurants, bars, tennis court, pools, gym, spa, business center* *Breakfast* ✣ *A1.*

TRASTEVERE

$$ **Hotel Santa Maria.** This ivy-covered, mansard-roofed, rosy-brick-red, erstwhile Renaissance-era convent has been transformed by Paolo and Valentina Vetere into a true charmer. **Pros:** a quaint and pretty oasis in a chaotic city; relaxing courtyard; free bicycles. **Cons:** can be tricky to find. **TripAdvisor:** "garden cloister filled with orange trees," "near vibrant neighborhood," "breakfast is generous and delicious." ✉ *Vicolo del Piede 2, Trastevere* ☎ *06/5894626* 🌐 *www.htlsantamaria.com* *18 rooms, 2 suites* *In-hotel: bar, business center* *Breakfast* ✣ *D6.*

$ **Hotel Trastevere.** This tiny hotel captures the village-like charm of the Trastevere district. **Pros:** cheap with a good location; convenient to transportation; friendly staff. **Cons:** no frills; few amenities. **TripAdvisor:** "in a lovely part of Rome," "good view over piazza," "rooms are small." ✉ *Via Luciano Manara 24–25, Trastevere* ☎ *06/5814713* 🌐 *www.hoteltrastevere.net* *20 rooms, 3 apartments* *In-room: Wi-Fi* *Breakfast* ✣ *D6.*

$$$ Fodor's Choice ★ **Relais Le Clarisse.** In one of Rome's most popular neighborhoods, this charming little oasis features five simple, but classically styled accommodations (two doubles and three suites) with terra-cotta-tiled floors, wrought-iron bed frames, and oak furnishings. **Pros:** spacious rooms with comfy beds; high-tech showers/tubs with good water pressure; staff is multilingual, friendly, and at your service. **Cons:** this part of Trastevere can be noisy at night; the rooms here fill up quickly; they serve only American coffee. **TripAdvisor:** "simple, elegant hotel," "clean, well maintained, well managed," "lemon trees in the courtyard." ✉ *Via Cardinale Merry del Val 20, Trastevere* ☎ *06/58334437* 🌐 *www.leclarisse.com* *5 rooms, 3 suites* *In-room: Internet. In-hotel: room service, business center, parking* *Breakfast* ✣ *D6.*

AVENTINO

$$$ **Domus Aventina.** The best part of this quaint, friendly hotel is that it's situated between two of Rome's loveliest gardens: a municipal rose garden and Rome's famous Orange Garden, where you can often catch a glimpse of brides and grooms taking their wedding pictures. **Pros:** quiet location; walking distance to tourist attractions; complimentary Wi-Fi in rooms and public spaces. **Cons:** no elevator in the hotel; small showers; no tubs. **TripAdvisor:** "in a beautiful old building," "quiet, mainly residential location," "beautiful patio with orange trees." ✉ *Via di Santa Prisca 11/b, Aventino* ☎ *06/5746135* 🌐 *www.domus-aventina.com* *26 rooms* *In-room: Wi-Fi. In-hotel: bar, business center, parking* *Breakfast* ✣ *F6.*

$$$ Hotel San Anselmo. For those looking for a little peace and quiet away from the hustle and bustle of the city center, the Hotel San Anselmo is the perfect romantic retreat. **Pros:** historic building with artful decor; great showers with jets; a garden where you can enjoy your breakfast. **Cons:** a bit of a hike to sights; limited public transportation; the Wi-Fi is pricey. **TripAdvisor:** "elegant yet hip vibe," "away from the noise and chaos," "breakfast spread was delicious." ✉ *Piazza San Anselmo 2, Aventino* ☎ *06/570057* 🌐 *www.aventinohotels.com* *45 rooms* *In-room: Internet. In-hotel: room service, bar, parking* *Breakfast* ✣ *E6.*

COLOSSEO AREA

$$$$ **Capo d'Africa.** Many find the modern look and feel of Capo d'Africa—not to mention its plush beds and deep bathtubs—refreshing after a long day's journey through ancient Rome. **Pros:** quiet, comfortable rooms; fitness center. **Cons:** far from the other Roman sites and the rest of the city scene; not a lot of restaurants in the immediate neighborhood. **TripAdvisor:** "very romantic," "views of the Colosseum," "breakfast on the roof terrace." ✉ *Via Capo d'Africa 54, Colosseo* ☎ *06/772801* 🌐 *www.hotelcapodafrica.com* *64 rooms, 1 suite* *In-room: Wi-Fi. In-hotel: room service, bar, gym, parking* *Breakfast* ✣ *H6.*

$$–$$$ **Hotel Lancelot.** For old-world charm near the Colosseum, check out Hotel Lancelot, a family affair in operation since 1970. **Pros:** hospitable staff; secluded and quiet; very family-friendly. **Cons:** some of the bathrooms are on the small side; no refrigerators in the rooms; room walls are a bit thin, which means you can sometimes hear your neighbors next door. **TripAdvisor:** "walk to all the main attractions," "staff was very friendly," "a fab place to stay." ✉ *Via Capo d'Africa 47, Colosseo* ☎ *06/70450615* 🌐 *www.lancelothotel.com* *60 rooms* *In-room: Wi-Fi. In-hotel: restaurant, room service, bar, business center, parking* *Breakfast* ✣ *H6.*

NIGHTLIFE AND THE ARTS

THE ARTS

Updated by Nicole Arriaga

Rome has a good range of publications with timely information regarding events and happenings in the city. Begin with the city's official Web site (🌐 *www.comune.roma.it*). Likewise, events listings can be found in the *Cronaca* and *Cultura* section of Italian newspapers, as well as in *Metro* (the free newspaper). The most comprehensive listings are in the weekly *roma c'è* booklet, which comes out every Wednesday. Flip to the back for the brief yet detailed English-language section. Check out the events site 🌐 *inromenow.com and* 🌐 *www.romeing.it, in English,* as well as the monthly-updated *Time Out: Rome* (🌐 *www.timeout.com/travel/rome*) and *The American* (🌐 *www.theamericanmag.com*). In addition, consult the monthly English-language periodical (with accompanying Web site), *Wanted in Rome* (🌐 *www.wantedinrome.com*), available at many newsstands.

VENUES

★ Rome used to be a performing arts backwater until 2002, when it opened its state-of-the-art **Auditorium-Parco della Musica** (✉ *Via de Coubertin 15, Flaminio* ☎ *06/80241; 06/68801044 information and tickets* 🌐 *www.auditorium.com*), a 10-minute tram ride (north) from Piazza del Popolo. Three futuristic concert halls designed by famed architect Renzo Piano have excellent acoustics and a large courtyard used for concerts and other events—everything from chamber music to jazz to big-name pop, even film screenings, art exhibits, fashion shows, and "philosophy festivals." On Sunday the restaurant RED, located at the Auditorium, is packed with people there for its sumptuous aperitivo buffet spread. To get to the Auditorium from Rome's Termini train station, take Bus No. 910, which drops you off directly in front of the complex. Just behind Piazza del Popolo in Piazzale Flaminio, hop on the No. 2 tram for six stops to the Auditorium area. Using the Metro, take Line A to Flaminio, then switch to No. 2 tram for six stops to the Auditorium.

Teatro Argentina (✉ *Largo di Torre Argentina 52* ☎ *06/6840001* 🌐 *www.teatrodiroma.net*), built in 1732 by the architect Theoldi, has been the home of the Teatro Sabile theater company since 1994. The theater is a beautiful, ornate structure, with velvet seats and chandeliers, and plays host to many plays, classical music performances, operas, and dance performances. Both the city's ballet and opera companies, as well as visiting international performers, appear at the **Teatro dell'Opera** (✉ *Piazza Beniamino Gigli 7, Repubblica* ☎ *06/481601, 06/48160255 tickets* 🌐 *www.operaroma.it*). **Teatro Olimpico** (✉ *Piazza Gentile da Fabriano 17, Flaminio* ☎ *06/3265991* 🌐 *www.teatroolimpico.it*) hosts both concerts and dance performances.

Teatro Valle (✉ *Via del Teatro Valle 21, Navona* ☎ *06/68803794* 🌐 *www.teatrovalle.it*) hosts dramatic performances of the same caliber as its neighbor, Teatro Argentina, but often with a more experimental bent, particularly in fall. Dance and classical music are also presented here. The ancient **Terme di Caracalla** (✉ *Via delle Terme di Caracalla 52, Aventino* ☎ *06/48160255* 🌐 *www.operaroma.it*) has one of the most spectacular and enchanting outdoor stages in the world, often hosting performances presented by Rome's opera company ranging from *Aida* (with elephants) to avant-garde.

TICKETS

Tickets for major events can be bought online at **Ticket One** (🌐 *www.ticketone.it*). Tickets for larger musical performances as well as many cultural events can usually be found at **Hello Ticket** (🌐 *www.helloticket.it*), which lists all cultural events and the many *punta di vendita,* ticket sellers, in Rome. You can buy tickets in person at **Orbis** (✉ *Piazza Esquilino 37, Repubblica* ☎ *06/4744776*). **Mondadori** (✉ *Via del Corso 472, Spagna* ☎ *06/684401*) is a huge, central store that sells music, DVDs, books, and concert tickets. **Feltrinelli** (✉ *Largo Torre Argentina 11, Pantheon* ☎ *06/68663001)* is another major store where you can buy tickets.

Sometimes waiting can pay off. An underutilized project sponsored by the city of Rome gives last-minute buyers a chance to attend theater performances at half price. Information on which shows are discounted can be found at **Il Botteghino Last Minute Teatro** (🌐 *www.spettacoloromano.it*).

CONCERTS

Christmas time is an especially busy classical concert season in Rome. Many small classical concert groups perform in cultural centers and churches year-round; most performances in Catholic churches are religious music and are free. Look for posters outside the churches. Pop, jazz, and world music concerts are frequent, especially in summer, although they may not be well advertised. Many of the bigger-name acts perform outside the center, so it's worth asking about transportation *before* you buy your tickets (about €10–€40).

CLASSICAL

A year-round classical concert series, often showcasing the famed Orchestra dell'Accademia di Santa Cecilia, is organized by the **Accademia di Santa Cecilia** (*Concert hall and box office* ✉ *Via Pietro de Coubertin 34, Flaminio* ☎ *06/8082058* 🌐 *www.santacecilia.it*). The **Accademia Filarmonica Romana** (✉ *Via Flaminia 118, Flaminio* ☎ *06/3201752, 06/3265991 tickets* 🌐 *www.filarmonicaromana.org*) has concerts at the Teatro Olimpico. The Renaissance-era **Chiostro del Bramante** (✉ *Arco della Pace 5, Navona* ☎ *06/68809098* 🌐 *www.chiostrodelbramante.it*) has a summer concert series. **Il Tempietto** (☎ *06/87131590* 🌐 *www.tempietto.it*) organizes classical music concerts indoors in winter and in otherwise inaccessible sites (such as Teatro Marcello) in summer. The internationally respected **Oratorio del Gonfalone series** (✉ *Via del Gonfalone 32/a, Campo de' Fiori* ☎ *06/6875952*) focuses on baroque music. The **Orto Botanico** (✉ *Largo Cristina di Svezia 24, Trastevere* ☎ *06/6864193*), off Via della Lungara in Trastevere, has a summer concert series with a beautiful, verdant backdrop. The church of **Sant'Ignazio** (✉ *Piazza Sant'Ignazio, near Pantheon* ☎ *06/6889951*) often hosts classical concerts in its spectacularly frescoed setting.

DANCE

Modern dance and classical ballet companies from Russia, the United States, and Europe sporadically visit Rome; performances are at the Teatro dell'Opera, Teatro Olimpico, or one of the open-air venues in summer. Small dance companies from Italy and abroad perform in numerous venues.

The **Rome Opera Ballet** (☎ *06/481601, 06/48160255 tickets* 🌐 *www.operaroma.it*) performs at the Teatro dell'Opera, often with international guest stars.

FILM

Movie tickets range in price from €4.50 for matinees and some weeknights up to €10 for reserved seats on weekend evenings; all films, unless noted "V.O." in the listing, which means *versione originale* (original version or original language), are shown in Italian. Certain movie theaters offer special discounts to women on Tuesday, with tickets for as little as €4.50. Check listings in *roma c'è* or 🌐 *www.inromenow.com* for reviews of all English-language films currently playing, or visit 🌐 *www.mymovies.it* for a list of current features. The five-screen **Space Cinema Moderno** (✉ *Piazza della Repubblica 45–46* ☎ *06/47779202* 🌐 *www.*

CLOSE UP

Entertainment Alfresco

Roman nightlife moves outdoors in summertime, and that goes not only for pubs and discos but for higher culture as well. Open-air opera in particular is a venerable Italian tradition; competing companies commandeer church courtyards, ancient villas, and soccer stadiums for performances that range from student-run mom-and-poperas to full-scale extravaganzas. The same goes for dance and for concerts covering the spectrum of pop, classical, and jazz. Look for performances at the Baths of Caracalla, site of the famous televised "Three Tenors" concert; regardless of the production quality, it's a breathtaking setting. In general, though, you can count on performances being quite good, even if small productions often resort to school-play scenery and folding chairs to cut costs. An outdoor theater is also set up in Villa Borghese; Shakespeare productions are popular. Tickets run about €15–€50. The more-sophisticated productions may be listed in newspapers and magazines such as *roma c'è*, but your best sources for information are old-fashioned posters plastered all over the city, advertising classics such as *Tosca* and *La Traviata*.

thespacecinema.it), close to the train station, usually has one theater with an English-language film.

OPERA

The season for the **Opera Theater of Rome** (☎ *06/481601, 06/48160255 tickets* 🌐 *www.operaroma.it*) runs from November or December to May. Main performances are staged at the Teatro dell'Opera, on Piazza Beniamino Gigli, in cooler weather, and at outdoor locations, such as Piazza del Popolo and the spectacular Terme di Caracalla (Baths of Caracalla), in summer.

NIGHTLIFE

Rome's nightlife is decidedly more happening for locals and insiders who know whose palms to grease and when to go where. The "flavor of the month" factor is at work here, and many places fade into oblivion after their 15 minutes of fame. Smoking has been banned in all public areas in Italy (that's right, it actually happened); Roman aversion to clean air has meant a decrease in crowds at bars and clubs. The best sources for an up-to-date list of nightspots are the *roma c'è, Romeing,* and *Time Out Roma* magazines. Trastevere and the area around Piazza Navona are both filled with bars, restaurants, and, after dark, people. In summer, discos and many bars close to beat the heat (although some simply relocate to the beach, where many Romans spend their summer nights). The city-sponsored *Estate Romana* (Rome Summer) festival takes over, lighting up hot city nights with open-air concerts, bars, and discos. Pick up the event guide at newsstands.

CAFÉS AND WINE BARS

Ai Tre Scalini (✉ *Via Panisperna 251, Monti* ☎ *06/48907495* 🌐 *www.aitrescalini.org*) is a rustic local hangout with a wooden bar in Monti, one of the new boho sections of Rome. It serves delicious antipasti and light entrées.

★ Celebrities and literati hang out at the coveted outdoor tables of **Antico Caffè della Pace** (✉ *Via della Pace 5, Navona* ☎ *06/6861216*), set on the enchanting *piazzatina* (tiny piazza) of Santa Maria della Pace. The only drawbacks: overpriced table service and distracted waiters. After being closed for a year, the historic **Bar del Fico** (✉ *Piazza del Fico 26, Navona* ☎ *06/68808413*) has returned to the Roman nightlife scene. By day old-timers play chess in the piazza under the fig trees. By night, it's a completely different scene. For everyone from curious tourists to bohemian hipsters, the bar is back to being the *punto d'incontro* (place to meet).

Enoteca Antica (✉ *Via della Croce 76/b, Spagna* ☎ *06/6790896* 🌐 *www.anticaenoteca.com*) is Piazza di Spagna's most celebrated wine bar, occupying a prime people-watching corner just below the piazza. In addition to a vast selection of wine (also available for takeout), Enoteca Antica has delectable antipasti, perfect for a snack or a light lunch. **Fluid** (✉ *Via del Governo Vecchio 46/47, Navona* ☎ *06/6832361* 🌐 *www.fluideventi.com*), with its slick design and Zen waterfall, is all about the scene, especially with its looking-glass front window and ice cube–shaped chairs that often draw in tourists. For the cocktail crowd, Fluid's many variations on the traditional martini are quite laudable. **Freni e Frizioni** (✉ *Via de Politeama 4–6, Trastevere* ☎ *06/58334210* 🌐 *www.freniefrizioni.com*) is one of Rome's latest artsy hangouts—it spills out onto its Trastevere piazza and down the stairs, filling the area around Piazza Trilussa with an attractive crowd of local mojito-sippers. The wood-paneled walls of **L'Angolo Divino** (✉ *Via dei Balestrari 12, Campo de' Fiori* ☎ *06/6864413*) are racked with more than 700 bottles of wine. A quiet enoteca in a back alley behind Campo, L'Angolo Divino allows you to sidestep the crowds while enjoying homemade pastas with a vintage bottle.

Fodor's Choice ★ **Shaki** (✉ *Via Mario de Fiori 29a, Spagna* ☎ *06/6791694*), Piazza di Spagna's mod wine bar and restaurant (think Los Angeles meets Rome) is perfect for aperitivi, after-dinner drinks, and just being seen. **Vineria Reggio** (✉ *Campo de' Fiori 15, Campo* ☎ *06/68803268*), or "Vineria" as those in-the-know call it, is the quintessential local Roma wine bar where the crowd ranges from grandfathers to glitterati.

ROOFTOP TERRACES AND UPSCALE BARS

★ For a dip into La Dolce Vita, the **Jardin de Hotel de Russie** (✉ *Via del Babuino 9, Popolo* ☎ *06/328881* 🌐 *www.hotelderussie.it*) is the location for every Hollywood VIP, as well as up-and-coming starlets. Mixed drinks are well above par, as are the prices.

Fodor's Choice ★ **Rosé Terrazzo at the St. George Hotel** (✉ *Via Giulia 62, Campo de' Fiori* ☎ *06/686611* 🌐 *www.stgeorgehotel.it*) is the latest front-runner in Rome's ever-growing list of rooftop sweet spots. With a delicious oyster selection headlining its seafood-only menu, the Rosé Terrazzo's dizzying drink selection includes cocktails, wine, and many rosés—from pink champagnes to Italian *rosati*. This option, on Rome's classiest street, is open only in the summer months.

Sitting in front of a 2nd-century temple, **Salotto 42** (⊠ *Piazza di Pietra 42, Pantheon* ☎ *06/6785804* 🌐 *www.salotto42.it*) holds court from morning until late in the evening. The cozy-sleek room (high-back velvet chairs, zebra-print rugs, chandeliers) is a smorgasbord of the owners' Roman–New York–Swedish pedigree. The den, complete with art books, local sophisticates, and models moonlighting as waitresses, is the fashionista's favorite choice for late-night drinks.

★ **Tazio** (⊠ *Hotel Exedra, Piazza della Repubblica 47* ☎ *06/489381*), named after the original Italian paparazzo (celebrity photographer), is an Adam Tihany–designed champagne bar. The red, black, and white lacquered interior, with crystal chandeliers, has a distinct '80s feel (think Robert Palmer, *Addicted to Love*). In summer, the hotel's rooftop bar **Sensus** is the place to be, with its infinity pool and terrace view overlooking downtown. Decadence with a capital D.

Terrace Bar of the Hotel Raphael (⊠ *Largo Febo 2, Navona* ☎ *06/682831* 🌐 *www.raphaelhotel.com*) is noted for its bird's-eye view of the campaniles and palazzi of the Piazza Navona. High up in the moonlit sky, the Terrace Bar is a perfect place for a quiet evening.

NIGHTCLUBS AND DISCOS

Most dance clubs open about 10:30 pm and charge an entrance fee of about €20, which may include the first drink (subsequent drinks cost about €10). Clubs are usually closed Monday, and all those listed here close in summer, when the city's nightlife scene goes seaside to the beaches of Ostia and Fregene. The liveliest areas for clubs with a younger clientele are the grittier working-class districts of Testaccio, Ostiense, and San Lorenzo. Any of the clubs lining Via Galvani, leading up to Monte Testaccio, are fair game for a trendy, crowded dance-floor experience—names and ownership of clubs change frequently, but the overall scene has shown exciting staying power, growing into a DJ "Disneyland."

Behind the Vatican Museums, **Alexanderplatz** (⊠ *Via Ostia 9, Vaticano* ☎ *06/39742171* 🌐 *www.alexanderplatz.it*), Rome's most famous jazz and blues club, has a bar and a restaurant. Local and internationally known musicians play nightly. **Brancaleone** (⊠ *Via Levana 11, Montesacro* ☎ *06/82004382*) is a bit out of the way, but it's widely popular among the university crowd and grungy hipsters with an itch for house and underground music. In trendy Testaccio, **Caffè Latino** (⊠ *Via Monte Testaccio 96* ☎ *06/57288556* 🌐 *www.caffelatinodiroma.com*) is a vibrant Roman locale that has live music (mainly Latin) almost every night, followed by recorded soul, funk, and '70s and '80s revival; it's closed Monday. **Gilda** (⊠ *Via Mario de' Fiori 97, Spagna* ☎ *06/6784838* 🌐 *www.gildabar.it*) used to be the place to spot famous Italian actors and politicians. Now it's host to B-actors and leftover politniks. This nightspot near the Spanish Steps has a piano bar as well as a restaurant and dance floors with live and disco music. Jackets are required. **Hulala** (⊠ *Via dei Conciatori 7, Ostiense* ☎ *06/57300429*) is home to Rome's fashionistas. Mod films are projected on the walls, and champagne is drunk through straws.

★ Housed in a medieval palazzo is **La Cabala** (✉ *Via dei Soldati 23, Navona* ☎ *06/68301192* 🌐 *www.hdo.it*), Rome's version of a supper club. This three-level space has a piano bar, restaurant, and club, and often has a very dressy crowd vying to get past the velvet rope.

★ Lounge fever is all over Rome, with **La Maison** (✉ *Vicolo dei Granari 4, Navona* ☎ *06/6833312* 🌐 *www.lamaisonroma.it*) being one of the best. Bedecked in purple velvet and crystal chandeliers, the club has two distinct spaces, a VIP area and a dance floor, with a DJ dishing up the latest dance tunes. Head straight to the back room and grab a couch. **Qube** (✉ *Via di Portonaccio 212, San Lorenzo* ☎ *06/4385445*), open only Thursday through Saturday, is Rome's biggest underground disco, where bodies mix and mingle like a rugby game. Friday night hosts the **Muccassassina** (🌐 *www.muccassassina.com*), Rome's most popular gay event. It has paid a price for its fame, and is now more straight than gay.

SHOPPING

Updated by Nicole Arriaga

They say when in Rome to do as the Romans do—and the Romans love to shop. After all, this is the city that gave us the Gucci "moccasin" loafer, the Fendi bag, and the Valentino dress that Jackie O wore when she became Mrs. Onassis. Stores are generally open from 10 to 1 and from 3:30 or 4 to 7 or 7:30 (with the exception of Monday, when most are closed in the morning). There's a tendency for shops in central districts to stay open all day, and hours are becoming more flexible throughout the city. Many places close all day Sunday, though this is changing, too, especially in the city center. Some stores also close Saturday afternoon from mid-June through August.

You can stretch your euros by taking advantage of the Tax-Free for Tourists V.A.T. tax refunds, available at most large stores for purchases over €155. Or hit Rome in January and early February or in late July and August, when stores clean house with the justly famous biannual sales. There are so many hole-in-the-wall boutiques selling top-quality merchandise in Rome's center that even just wandering you're sure to find something that catches your eye.

SHOPPING DISTRICTS

The city's most famous shopping district, **Piazza di Spagna,** is conveniently compact, fanning out at the foot of the Spanish Steps in a galaxy of boutiques selling gorgeous wares with glamorous labels. Here you can prance back and forth from Gucci to Prada to Valentino to Versace with less effort than it takes to pull out your credit card. If your budget is designed for lower altitudes, you also can find great clothes and accessories at less-extravagant prices. But here buying is not necessarily the point—window displays can be works of art, and dreaming may be satisfaction enough. Via dei Condotti is the neighborhood's central axis, but there are shops on every street in the area bordered by Piazza di Spagna on the east, Via del Corso on the west, between Piazza San Silvestro and Via della Croce, and extending along Via del Babuino to

Piazza del Popolo. **Via Margutta,** a few blocks north of the Spanish Steps, is a haven for contemporary art galleries.

Shops along **Via Campo Marzio,** and adjoining Piazza San Lorenzo in Lucina, stock eclectic, high-quality clothes and accessories—by both big names (Bottega Veneta, Louis Vuitton) and smaller European designers—at slightly lower prices. Running from Piazza Venezia to Piazza del Popolo lies **Via del Corso,** a main shopping avenue that has more than a mile of clothing, shoes, leather goods, and home furnishings from classic to cutting-edge. Running west from Piazza Navona, **Via del Governo Vecchio** has numerous women's boutiques and secondhand-clothing stores.

Via Cola di Rienzo, across the Tiber from Piazza del Popolo and extending to the Vatican, is block after block of boutiques, shoe stores, department stores, and mid-level chain shops, as well as street stalls and upscale food shops. **Via dei Coronari,** across the Tiber from Castel Sant'Angelo, has quirky antiques and home furnishings. **Via Giulia** and other surrounding streets are good bets for decorative arts. Should your gift list include religious souvenirs, look for everything from rosaries to Vatican golf balls at the shops between Piazza San Pietro and **Borgo Pio.** Liturgical vestments and statues of saints make for good window-shopping on **Via dei Cestari,** near the Pantheon.

Via Nazionale is a good bet for affordable stores along the lines of Benetton, and for shoes, bags, and gloves. The **Termini** train station has become a good one-stop place for many shopping needs. Its 60-plus shops are open until 10 pm and include a Nike store, the Body Shop, Sephora, Mango (women's clothes), a UPIM department store, a grocery store, and a three-story bookstore with selections in English. Local designers and smaller designer boutiques also pepper the trendy shopping districts of **Monti** near the Forum and **Trastevere** across the Tiber from the historic center.

MARKETS

Outdoor markets are open Monday–Saturday from 7:30 am till about 1 pm (a bit later on Saturday), but get there early for the best selection. Remember to keep an eye on your wallet—the money changing hands draws Rome's most skillful pickpockets. And don't go if you can't stand crowds. Rome's most central outdoor food market is at **Campo de' Fiori,** south of Piazza Navona, though for a more authentic feel head to **Testaccio,** where the covered market is far less touristy. There's room for bargaining at the Sunday-morning flea market at **Porta Portese** (⊠ *Piazza Ippolito Nievo, Trastevere*). You can find it all here: in the maze of stalls there's secondhand clothing, bric-a-brac, antique furniture, bootleg CDs, electronics to be wary of, lots of junk, and a few treasures. The renovated **Trionfale market** (⊠ *Via Andrea Doria, near Vatican*) has the largest selection of fresh produce, and is a stone's throw from the Vatican Museums; you can reach it from Via Tunisi and Via Santamaura. New and used clothes and accessories can be found at any number of stalls at the **Via Sannio flea market** (⊠ *Via Sannio, San Giovanni*).

SPECIALTY STORES

DESIGNER CLOTHING

All of Italy's top fashion houses and many international designers have stores near Piazza di Spagna. Buying clothes can be a bit tricky for American women, as sizes tend to be cut for a petite Italian frame. A size 12 (European 46) is not always easy to find, but the more-expensive stores should carry it. Target less expensive stores for accessories if this is an issue.

D&G (✉ *Piazza di Spagna 94* ☎ *06/69924999*), a spin-off of the top-of-the-line Dolce&Gabbana, sells trendy casual wear and accessories for men and women. The flagship store for **Fendi** (✉ *Largo Carlo Goldoni 419-421, near Piazza di Spagna* ☎ *06/334501*) is in the former Palazzo Boncompagni, renamed "Palazzo Fendi." It overlooks the famed intersection of Via dei Condotti and Via del Corso, and it's the quintessential Roman fashion house, presided over by the Fendi sisters. Their signature baguette bags, furs, accessories, and sexy separates are all found here. The **Giorgio Armani** (✉ *Via dei Condotti 77, near Piazza di Spagna* ☎ *06/6991460*) shop is as understated and elegant as its designs. **Gucci** (✉ *Via dei Condotti 8, near Piazza di Spagna* ☎ *06/6790405*) often has lines out the door of its two-story shop, testament to the continuing popularity of its colorful bags, wallets, and shoes in rich leathers. Edgy clothes designs are also available. There's another Gucci boutique nearby on Via Borgognona. Sleek, vaguely futuristic **Prada** (✉ *Via dei Condotti 92-95, near Piazza di Spagna* ☎ *06/6790897*) has two entrances: the one for the men's boutique is to the left of the women's. Rome's immortal fashion superstar, **Valentino** (*Valentino Donna* ✉ *Via dei Condotti 15, near Piazza di Spagna* ☎ *06/6739420 Valentino Uomo* ✉ *Via Bocca di Leone 15, near Piazza di Spagna* ☎ *06/36001906*), is recognized the world over by the "V" logo. The now-retired couturier has new designers manning his shops for the *donna* (woman) and the *uomo* (man) not far from his headquarters in Piazza Mignanelli beside the Spanish Steps. **Versace** (✉ *Via Bocca di Leone 26-27, near Piazza di Spagna* ☎ *06/6780521*) sells the rock-star styles that made the house's name.

MEN'S CLOTHING

Brioni (✉ *Via dei Condotti 21, near Piazza di Spagna* ☎ *06/6783428* ✉ *Via Barberini 79, near Piazza Barberini* ☎ *06/485855*) has a well-deserved reputation as one of Italy's top tailors. There are ready-to-wear garments in addition to impeccable custom-made apparel. **Davide Cenci** (✉ *Via Campo Marzio 1-7, near Piazza della Rotonda [Pantheon]* ☎ *06/6990681*), Rome's answer to a high-end department store, is famed for conservative clothing of exquisite craftsmanship. **Ermenegildo Zegna** (✉ *Via Borgognona 7/e, near Piazza di Spagna* ☎ *06/6789143*) has the finest in men's elegant styles and accessories. **Il Portone** (✉ *Via delle Carrozze 73, near Piazza di Spagna* ☎ *06/6793355*) embodies a tradition in custom shirt-making.

WOMEN'S CLOTHING

38 Leopardo (✉ *Vicolo del Leopardo 38, Trastevere* ☎ *06/45435476*), American designer Jessica Harris's shop in Trastevere, evokes the image of a large-scale dollhouse where her one-of-a-kind collections are displayed alongside dresses, separates, and accessories by other local designers. Her clothes are delicately constructed by hand from the finest materials. She has a second shop, Leopardessa, on Via Panisperna in the Monti district.

Fodor's Choice ★ **L'Anatra all'Arancia** (✉ *Via Tiburtina 105, San Lorenzo* ☎ *06/4456293*) has the locals in this bustling working-class district agog at its window displays of flowing innovative designer clothes, teeny-weeny bikinis, and zany underwear. Owner Donatella Baroni believes in fashion being fun. The men's shop is across the road at No. 130, where style-conscious hipsters can find pure linen shirts and trousers in unusual colors. The clientele includes Italian TV and stage personalities who live in the trendy area.

★ **Maga Morgana** (✉ *Via del Governo Vecchio 27, near Piazza Navona* ☎ *06/6879995* ✉ *Via del Governo Vecchio 98, Navona* ☎ *06/6878085*) is a family-run little boutique near Piazza Navona. Two brothers turn out shabby-chic clothes and accessories with an attitude for all walks of life.

Save the Queen (✉ *Via del Babuino 49, Spagna* ☎ *06/36003039*) is a hot Florentine design house with pieces with artistic frills, cut-outs, and textures. The silhouettes are youthful-chic and not the least bit discreet.

Victory (✉ *Via S. Francesco a Ripa 19, Trastevere* ☎ *06/5812437*) spotlights youthful, lighthearted styles created by lesser-known stylists, such as Rose D, Nina, Alessandrini, and Marithé et François Girbaud. Victory's clothing is made for flaunting. A menswear version of the store is located at Piazza San Calisto 10 in Trastevere.

JEWELRY

Fodor's Choice ★ **Gioielli in Movimento** (✉ *Via della Stelletta 23, near Piazza Navona* ☎ *06/6867431*) draws celebrity customers hooked on Carlo Cardena's ingenious designs. Carlo's "Twice as Nice" earrings, which can be transformed from fan-shape clips into elegant drops, were Uno Erre's best-selling earrings between 1990 and 1998, and his "Up and Down" pendant, which can be worn two different ways, is another hit. **Quattrocolo** (✉ *Via della Scrofa 54, near Piazza Navona* ☎ *06/68801367*) has been specializing in antique micro-mosaic jewelry and baubles from centuries past since 1938.

SHOES AND LEATHER ACCESSORIES

Bruno Magli (✉ *Via dei Condotti 6, near Piazza di Spagna* ☎ *06/69292121*) has classy shoes with simple, elegant lines—for men and women—that have character without compromising comfort. For shoes worn by the likes of Audrey Heburn and Ava Gardner during the Dolce Vita days, head to **Dal Co'** (✉ *Via Vittoria 65, near Piazza di Spagna* ☎ *06/6786536*). **Di Cori** (✉ *Piazza di Spagna 53* ☎ *06/6784439*) has gloves in every color of the spectrum.

Fausto Santini (✉ *Via Frattina 120, near Piazza di Spagna* ☎ *06/6784114*) gives a hint of extravagance in minimally decorated, all-white show windows displaying surprising shoes that fashion mavens love. Santini's footwear for men and women is bright, colorful, and trendy, sporting unusual forms, especially in heels. Coordinated bags and wallets add to the fun. **Furla** (✉ *Piazza di Spagna 22* ☎ *06/69200363*) has 14 franchises in Rome alone. At its flagship store, to the left of the Spanish

Steps, be prepared for crowds of passionate shoppers, all anxious to possess one of the delectable bags, wallets, or watch straps in ice-cream colors. **Salvatore Ferragamo** (✉ *Via dei Condotti 65, near Piazza di Spagna* ☎ *06/6781130* ✉ *Via dei Condotti 73/74, near Piazza di Spagna* ☎ *06/6791565*) is one of the top-10 most-wanted men's footwear brands in the world and for years has been providing Hollywood glitterati and discerning clients with unique handmade designs. The Florentine design house also specializes in handbags, small leather goods, men's and women's ready-to-wear, and scarves and ties. Men's styles are found at Via dei Condotti 64, women's at 73/74. For gloves as pretty as Holly Golightly's, shop at **Sermoneta** (✉ *Piazza di Spagna 61* ☎ *06/6791960*). Any color or style one might desire, from elbow-length black leather to scallop-edged lace-cut lilac suede, is available at this glove institution.

Fodor's Choice ★ **Tod's** (✉ *Via Fontanella di Borghese 56a, near Via del Corso* ☎ *06/68210066*) has become hyperfashionable again due in large part to owner Diego Della Valle's ownership of Florence's soccer team. The brand is known for its sporty flats and comfortable, casual styling. Tod's occupies the ground floor in the celebrated 16th-century Palazzo Ruspoli. There's another location on Via Condotti, Rome's version of Rodeo Drive

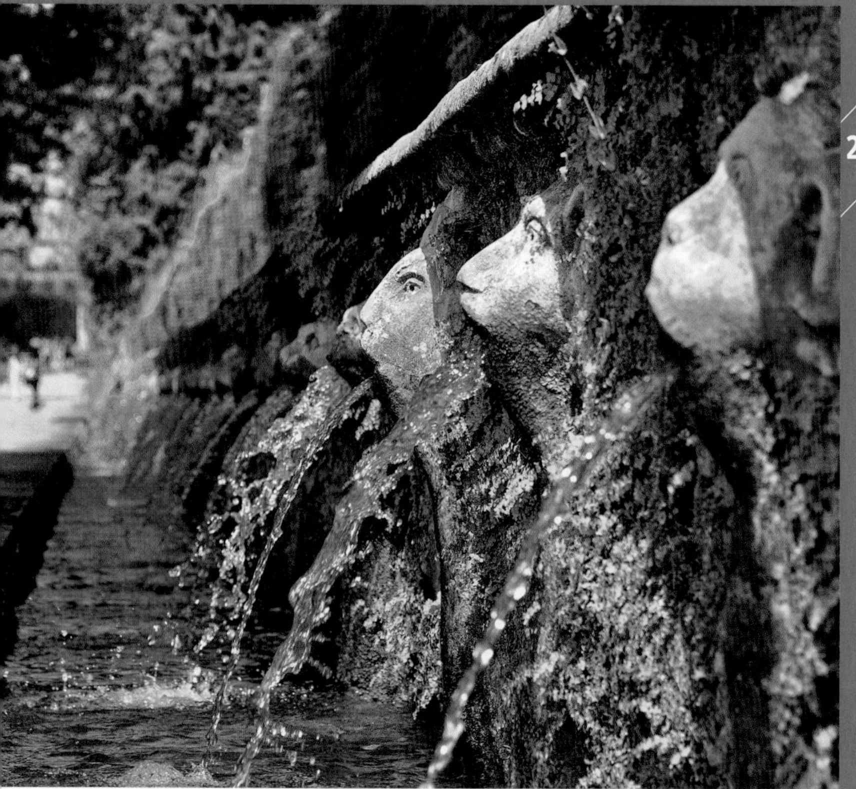

2

Side Trips from Rome

WORD OF MOUTH

"In my book Villa Adriana should not be considered a villa, not even an estate, this place must have been categorized as a mid-sized town! It is amazing. I could not help but marvel at the sheer power the emperor must have yielded in order to gather the resources necessary to build an estate of this magnitude."

—marigross

WELCOME TO LAZIO

TOP REASONS TO GO

★ **Ostia Antica:** Perhaps even more than Pompeii, the excavated port city of ancient Rome conveys a picture of everyday life in the days of the Empire.

★ **Tivoli's Villa d'Este:** Hundreds of fountains cascading and shooting skyward (one even plays music on organ pipes) will delight you at this spectacular garden.

★ **Castelli Romani:** Be a Roman for a day and enjoy the pleasures of the ancient hilltop wine towns on the city's doorstep.

★ **Get "Middle-Aged" in Viterbo:** This town may be modern, but it has a Gothic papal palace, a Romanesque cathedral, and the magical medieval quarter of San Pellegrino.

★ **Gardens Bizarre and Beautiful:** Just a few miles from each other, the 16th-century proto-Disneyland Parco dei Mostri (Monster Park) is famed for its fantastic sculptures, while the Villa Lante remains the stateliest Renaissance garden of them all.

1 Tuscia. The San Pellegrino district of **Viterbo** is a 13th-century time capsule, while at the gardens and palaces of nearby **Bagnaia**, **Caprarola**, and **Bomarzo** you can time-travel back to the Renaissance.

2 Ostia Antica. This ancient Roman port is now a parklike archaeological site.

3 East of Rome. Rising above the heat of Rome is cool, green **Tivoli**, a fitting setting for the regal Villa Adriana and Villa d'Este. A few miles to the south, **Palestrina**'s majestic hillside once protected a great Roman temple and now shelters the Palazzo Barberini museum.

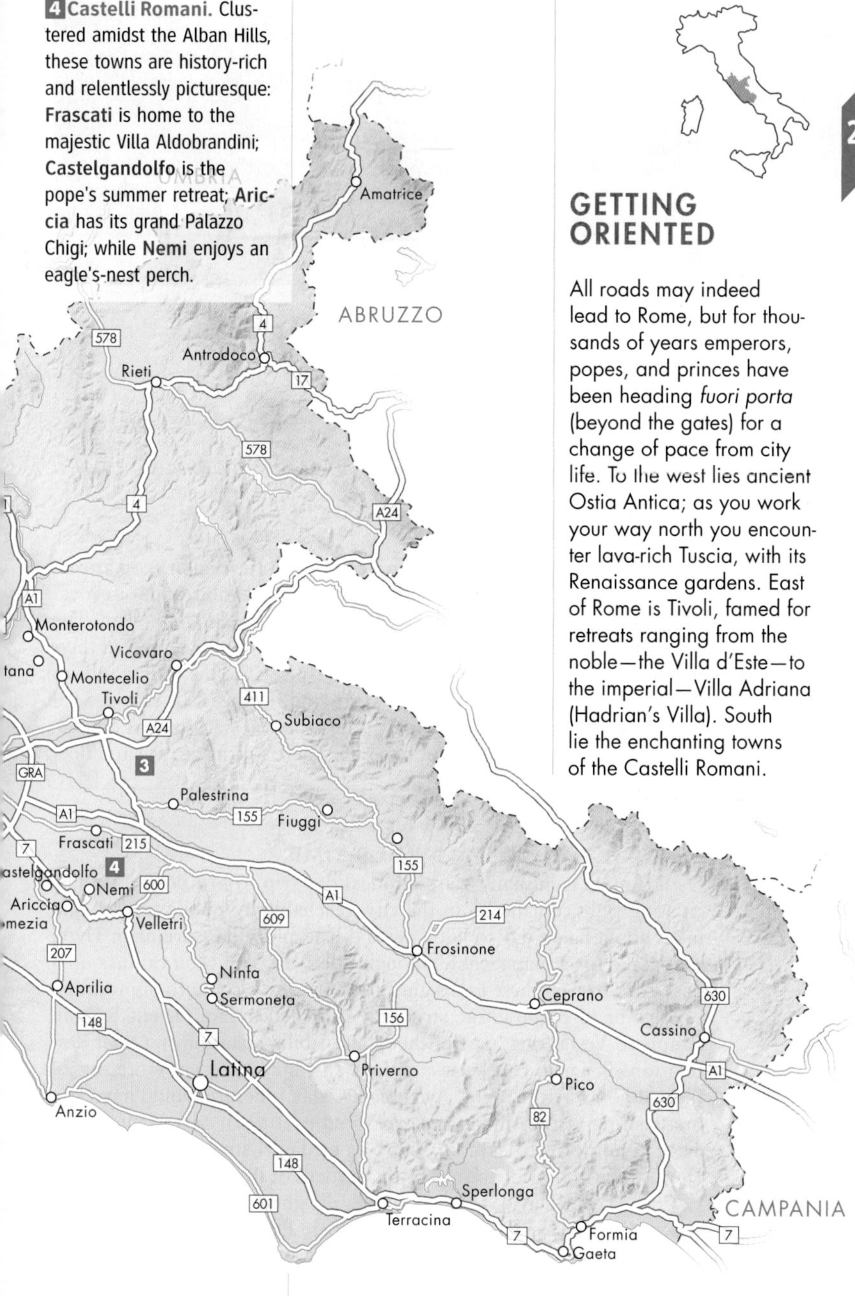

4 Castelli Romani. Clustered amidst the Alban Hills, these towns are history-rich and relentlessly picturesque: **Frascati** is home to the majestic Villa Aldobrandini; **Castelgandolfo** is the pope's summer retreat; **Ariccia** has its grand Palazzo Chigi; while **Nemi** enjoys an eagle's-nest perch.

GETTING ORIENTED

All roads may indeed lead to Rome, but for thousands of years emperors, popes, and princes have been heading *fuori porta* (beyond the gates) for a change of pace from city life. To the west lies ancient Ostia Antica; as you work your way north you encounter lava-rich Tuscia, with its Renaissance gardens. East of Rome is Tivoli, famed for retreats ranging from the noble—the Villa d'Este—to the imperial—Villa Adriana (Hadrian's Villa). South lie the enchanting towns of the Castelli Romani.

Updated by Margaret Stenhouse

A trip out of Rome introduces you to a different kind of Italy: people are friendlier (but speak less English), schedules are looser, and it feels as though you've stepped a few years back in time. You'll find fewer lines, lower prices, and a more relaxed style of tourism.

Ostia Antica, ancient Rome's seaport, is one of the region's top attractions—it rivals Pompeii in the quality of its preservation, and for evocativeness and natural beauty, it easily outshines the Roman Forum. The pre-Roman inhabitants of the area were wiped out in the city, but their remains—and some say, their bloodlines—persist in the rolling hills of Tuscia and the Etruscan seaboard north and northeast of Rome. So if the screeching traffic and long lines at the Colosseo start to wear on you, do as the Romans do—get out of town. There's plenty to see and do.

PLANNING

MAKING THE MOST OF YOUR TIME

Ostia Antica is in many ways an ideal day trip from Rome: it's a fascinating sight, not far from the city, reachable by public transit, and takes about half a day to "do." Villa d'Este and Villa Adriana in Tivoli also make for a manageable, though fuller, day trip. You can use up a flash card just on these two sights alone but leave room to photograph Tivoli's picturesque gorge strikingly crowned by an ancient Roman temple to Vesta (now part of the famed Sibilla restaurant). Other destinations in Lazio can be visited in a day, but you'll get more out of them if you stay the night. A classic five-day itinerary would have you first visiting Ostia Antica, the excavated port town of ancient Rome. Then head north to explore Viterbo's medieval streets on Day 2. On Day 3, take in the hot springs or the gardens of Bomarzo, Bagnaia, and Caprarola. For Day 4, head to Tivoli's delights. Then on Day 5 take a relaxing trip to the Castelli Romani, where Frascati wine is produced. Admire the monumental gardens of the aristocrats of yore and explore the narrow streets of these small hill towns. Grand villas, ancient ruins, pretty villages—what more could any vacationer want?

GETTING HERE AND AROUND

There's reliable public transit from Rome to Ostia Antica, Tivoli, and Viterbo. For other destinations in the region, a car is a big advantage—going by train or bus can add hours to your trip, and routes and schedules are often puzzling. For train information, check with **Ferrovie dello Stato** (☎ *892021* 🌐 *www.ferroviedellostato.it*), the national rail service. Buses in the region are handled by **COTRAL** (☎ *800/1744711* 🌐 *www.cotralspa.it*).

VISITOR INFORMATION

Tourist information kiosks in Rome can give you information about the Castelli Romani, Ostia Antica, and Tivoli. For information about Viterbo, Bomarzo, Bagnaia, and Caprarola, contact either the local tourist offices or the central **APT Provincia di Roma tourist office** (✉ *Via XX Settembre 26, Viterbo* ☎ *06/421381* 🌐 *www.aptprovroma.it or www.viterboonline.com*) in Viterbo.

ABOUT THE HOTELS

With relatively few exceptions (spas, beaches, and hill resorts such as Viterbo), accommodations in Lazio cater more to commercial travelers than to tourists. Rooms tend to be short on character, but they'll do the trick for an overnight.

Hotel reviews have been condensed for this book. Please go to Fodors.com for full reviews of each property.

WHAT IT COSTS IN EUROS

	¢	$	$$	$$$	$$$$
Restaurants	under €20	€20–€30	€30–€45	€45–€65	over €65
Hotels	under €75	€75–€125	€125–€200	€200–€300	over €300

Restaurant prices are for a first course (primo), second course (secondo), and dessert (dolce). Hotel prices are for two people in a standard double room in high season, including tax and service.

OSTIA ANTICA

30 km (19 mi) southwest of Rome.

GETTING HERE

The best way to get to Ostia Antica is by train. The Ostia Lido train leaves every half hour from the station adjacent to Rome's Piramide Metro B subway station, stopping off at Ostia Antica en route. The trip takes 35 minutes. By car, take the Via del Mare that leads off from Rome's EUR district. Be prepared for heavy traffic, especially at peak hours, on weekends, and in summer.

EXPLORING

Founded around the 4th century BC, Ostia served as Rome's port city for several centuries until the Tiber changed course, leaving the town high and dry. What has been excavated here is a remarkably intact Roman town in a pretty, parklike setting. Fair weather and good walking shoes are essential. On hot days, be here when the gates open or go

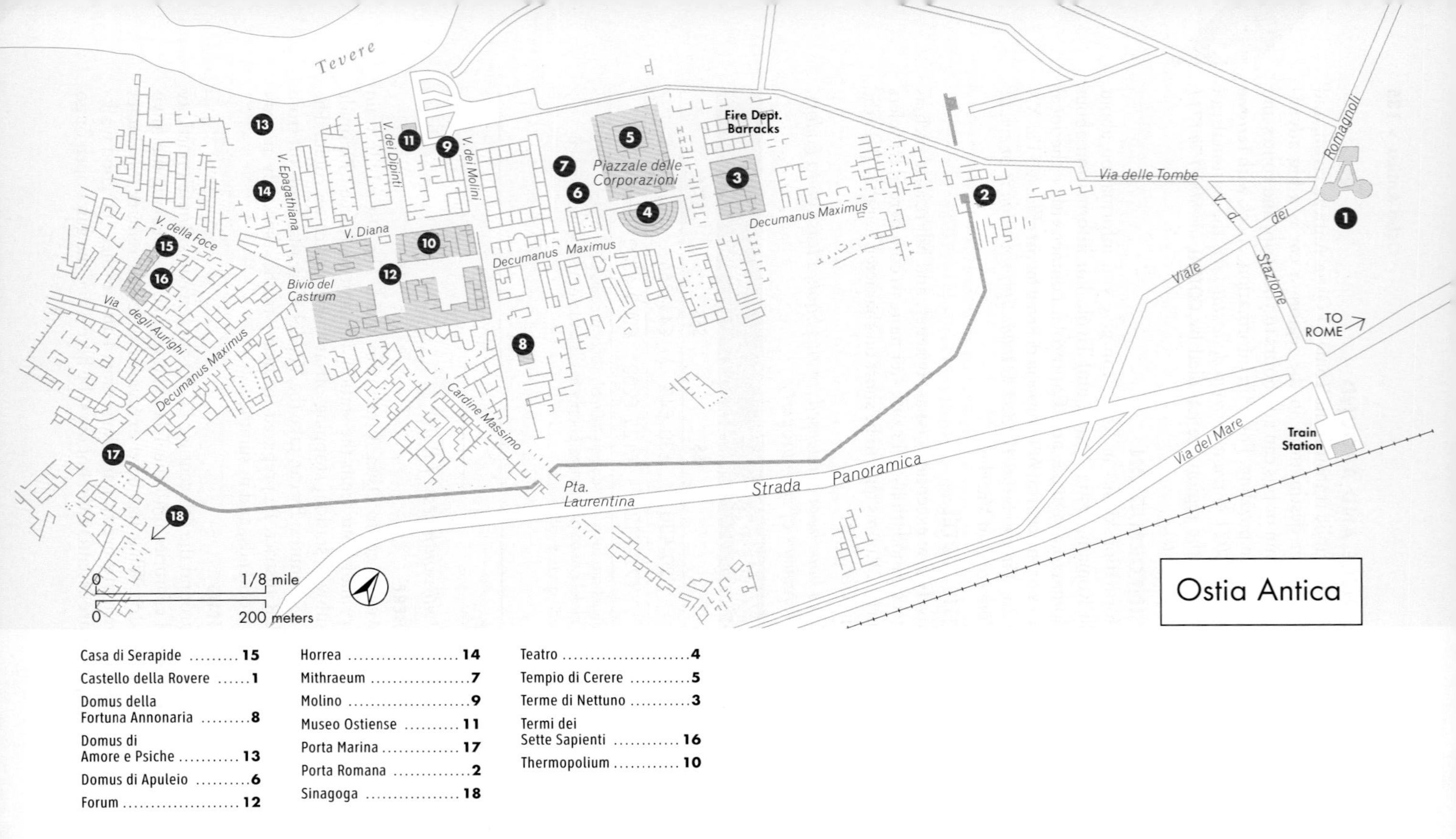
Ostia Antica
Tevere
Romagnoli
Via delle Tombe
V. d. del Stazione
Viale
Via del Mare
TO ROME
Train Station
Fire Dept. Barracks
Piazzale delle Corporazioni
Decumanus Maximus
V. dei Molini
V. dei Dipinti
V. Epagathiana
V. Diana
V. della Foce
Bivio del Castrum
Via degli Aurighi
Cardine Massimo
Pta. Laurentina
Strada Panoramica
0 1/8 mile
0 200 meters
Casa di Serapide 15
Castello della Rovere 1
Domus della Fortuna Annonaria 8
Domus di Amore e Psiche 13
Domus di Apuleio 6
Forum 12
Horrea 14
Mithraeum 7
Molino 9
Museo Ostiense 11
Porta Marina 17
Porta Romana 2
Sinagoga 18
Teatro 4
Tempio di Cerere 5
Terme di Nettuno 3
Termi dei Sette Sapienti 16
Thermopolium 10

A GOOD WALK: OSTIA ANTICA

The **Porta Romana** ❷, one of the city's three gates, is where you enter the Ostia Antica excavations. It opens onto the Decumanus Maximus, the main thoroughfare crossing the city from end to end. To your right, a staircase leads to a platform—the remains of the upper floor of the **Terme di Nettuno** ❸ (Baths of Neptune)—from which you get a good view of the mosaic pavements showing a marine scene with Neptune and the sea goddess Amphitrite. Behind the baths are the barracks of the fire department. On the north side of the Decumanus Maximus is the beautiful **Teatro** ❹ (Theater), built by Agrippa, remodeled by Septimius Severus in the 2nd century AD, and restored by the Rome City Council in the 20th century. In the vast Piazzale delle Corporazioni, where trade organizations had their offices, is the **Tempio di Cerere** ❺ (Temple of Ceres)—only appropriate for a town dealing in grain imports, Ceres being the goddess of agriculture. From there you can visit the **Domus di Apuleio** ❻ (House of Apuleius), built in Pompeian style, lower to the ground and with fewer windows than was characteristic of Ostia. Next door, the **Mithraeum** ❼ has balconies and a hall decorated with symbols of the cult of Mithras, a male-only religion imported from Persia.

On Via Semita dei Cippi, just off Via dei Molini, the **Domus della Fortuna Annonaria** ❽ (House of Fortuna Annonaria) is the richly decorated residence of a wealthy Ostian; one of the rooms opens onto a secluded garden. On Via dei Molini you can see a **molino** ❾ (mill), where grain was ground with stones that are still here. Along Via di Diana you come upon a **thermopolium** ❿ (bar) with a marble counter and a fresco depicting the foods sold here.

At the end of Via dei Dipinti is the **Museo Ostiense** ⓫ (Ostia Museum), which displays sarcophagi, massive marble columns, and large statuary. (The last entry to the museum is a half hour before the Scavi closes.) The **Forum** ⓬, on the south side of Decumanus Maximus, holds the monumental remains of the city's most important temple, dedicated to Jupiter, Juno, and Minerva. It's also the site of other ruins of baths, a basilica (which in Roman times was a hall of justice), and smaller temples.

Via Epagathiana leads toward the Tiber, where there are large **horrea** ⓮ (warehouses) erected during the 2nd century AD for the enormous amounts of grain imported into Rome during the height of the Empire. West of Via Epagathiana, the **Domus di Amore e Psiche** ⓭ (House of Cupid and Psyche), a residence, was named for a statue found here (now on display in the museum); the house's enclosed garden is decorated with marble and mosaic motifs and has the remains of a large pool. The **Casa di Serapide** ⓯ (House of Serapis) on Via della Foce is a 2nd-century multilevel dwelling; another apartment building stands a street over on Via degli Aurighi. Nearby, the **Termi dei Sette Sapienti** ⓰ (Baths of the Seven Wise Men) are named for a group of bawdy frescoes. The **Porta Marina** ⓱ leads to what used to be the seashore and the **sinagoga** ⓲, dating from the 4th century AD.

late in the afternoon. A visit to the excavations takes two to three hours, including 20 minutes for the museum. Inside the site, there's a snack bar and a bookshop. Ostia Antica is 30 km (19 mi) southwest of Rome.

Before exploring Ostia Antica's ruins, it's worthwhile to take a tour through the medieval *borgo* (town). The distinctive **Castello della Rovere**, easily spotted as you come off the footbridge from the train station, was built by Pope Julius II when he was the cardinal bishop of Ostia in 1483. Its triangular form is unusual for military architecture. Inside are (badly faded) frescoes by Baldassare Peruzzi. ✉ *Piazza della Rocca* ☎ *06/56358013* 🌐 *www.ostiaantica.net* 🎫 *Free* ⏲ *Tues.–Sun. tours at 10 and noon; Tues. and Thurs. additional tour at 3.*

Fodor's Choice ★ Tidal mud and windblown sand covered the ancient port town, which lay buried until the beginning of the 20th century when it was extensively excavated. The **Scavi di Ostia Antica** *(Ostia Antica excavations)* continue to be well maintained today. A cosmopolitan population of rich businessmen, wily merchants, sailors, slaves, and their respective families once populated the city. The great warehouses were built in the 2nd century AD to handle huge shipments of grain from Africa; the *insulae* (forerunners of the modern apartment building) provided housing for the city's growing population. Under the combined assaults of the barbarians and the malaria-carrying mosquito, and after the Tiber changed course, the port was eventually abandoned. ✉ *Viale dei Romagnoli 717* ☎ *06/56350215* 🌐 *www.ostia-antica.org* 🎫 *€6.50 includes Museo Ostiense* ⏲ *Tues.–Sun. 8:30–1 hr before sunset.*

WHERE TO EAT

$ ITALIAN ✕ **Cipriani.** Tucked away in the little medieval town under the shadow of the castle, this cozy trattoria is decorated with reproductions of fresco fragments from a Roman palace. The kitchen offers a varied menu of Roman specialties and seasonal fare. Owner Fabrizio Cipriani speaks English and will be happy to guide you in your choice of dishes and wine from his comprehensive wine list. ✉ *Via del Forno 11* ☎ *06/563529560* 🌐 *www.ristorantecipriani.com* ⏲ *Closed Wed.*

TUSCIA

Tuscia (the modern name for the Etruscan domain of Etruria) is a region of dramatic beauty punctuated by deep, rocky gorges and thickly forested hills, with dappled light falling on wooded paths. This has long been a preferred locale for the retreats of wealthy Romans, a place where they could build grand villas and indulge their sometimes eccentric gardening tastes. The provincial capital, Viterbo, which overshadowed Rome as a center of papal power for a time during the Middle Ages, lies in the heart of Tuscia. The farmland east of Viterbo conceals small quarries of the dark, volcanic *peperino* stone, which shows up in the walls of many buildings here. Lake Bolsena is an extinct volcano, and the sulfur springs still bubbling up in the spas were used by the ancient Romans. Bagnaia and Caprarola are home to palaces and gardens; the garden statuary at Bomarzo is in a league of its own—somewhere between the beautiful and the bizarre.

The ideal way to explore this region is by car. By train from Rome you can reach Viterbo and then get to Bagnaia by local bus. If you're traveling by train or bus, check schedules carefully; you may have to allow for an overnight if you want to see all four locations.

VITERBO

25 km (16 mi) east of Tuscania, 104 km (64 mi) northwest of Rome.

GETTING HERE

Viterbo is well served by public transport from Rome. A direct train service takes an hour and 40 minutes. Try to avoid peak hours, as many commuters live in towns along the line. By road, take the A1 toll highway to Attigliano. The trip can take a couple of hours, depending on traffic.

VISITOR INFORMATION

Viterbo tourism office (✉ *Via Ascenzi 4* ☎ *0761/325992* 🌐 *www.viterboonline.com*).

EXPLORING

Viterbo's moment of glory was in the 13th century, when it became the seat of the papal court. The medieval core of the city still sits within 12th-century walls. Its old buildings, with windows bright with geraniums, are made of dark peperino, the local stone that colors the medieval part of Viterbo a dark gray, contrasted here and there with the golden tufa rock of walls and towers. Peperino is also used in the characteristic and typically medieval exterior staircases that you see throughout the old town.

Viterbo has blossomed into a regional commercial center, and much of the modern city is loud and industrial. However, Viterbo's San Pellegrino district is a place to get the feel of the Middle Ages, seeing how daily life is carried on in a setting that has remained practically unchanged over the centuries. The Palazzo Papale and the cathedral enhance the effect. The city has remained a renowned spa center for its natural hot springs just outside town, frequented by popes—and the laity—since medieval times.

The Gothic **Palazzo Papale** *(Papal Palace)* was built in the 13th century as a residence for popes looking to get away from the city. At that time Rome was a notoriously unhealthful place, ridden with malaria and plague and rampaging factions of rival barons. In 1271 the palace was the scene of a novel type of rebellion. A conclave held here to elect a new pope had dragged on for months. The people of Viterbo were exasperated by the delay, especially as custom decreed that they had to provide for the cardinals' board and lodging for the duration of the conclave. So they tore the roof off the great hall where the cardinals were meeting, and put them on bread and water. Sure enough, a new pope—Gregory X—was elected in short order. ✉ *Piazza San Lorenzo* ☎ *338/1336529* 🌐 *www.museocolledelduomo.com* 🎫 *€5, includes Museo del Colle del Duomo* ⏲ *Tues.–Sun.; arrange for visit at nearby Museo del Colle del Duomo.*

Viterbo's Romanesque Duomo, **Chiesa di San Lorenzo**, was built over the ruins of the ancient Roman Temple of Hercules. During World War II the roof and the vault of the central nave were destroyed by a bomb. Subsequently, the church was rebuilt to its original medieval design.

Side Trips from Rome
Spoleto
Orvieto
S. Lorenzo Nuovo
Lago di Corbara
UMBRIA
Bolsena
Lago di Bolsena
Montefiascone
Terni
Bomarzo
Orte
Tuscania
Viterbo
Bagnaia
Rieti
Antrodoco
Norchia
Vetralla
Lago di Vico
Caprarola
Civita Castellana
Tevere
Lago di Salto
Tarquinia
Monterosi
Lago di Bracciano
Lago di Turano
Tolfa
Civitavecchia
Bracciano
Carsoli
Monterotondo
Mentana
Vicovaro
Montecelio
Santa Marinella
Cerveteri
Bagni di Tivoli
Tivoli
Villa Adriana
Subiaco
Ladispoli
ROME
GRA
Palestrina
Ciampino
Frascati
Lago di Albano
Castelgandolfo
Fiumicino
Lido di Ostia
Ariccia
Nemi
Velletri
Ostia Antica see detail map
Pomezia
Aprilia
Ninfa
Tor Vaianica
Sermoneta
Mare Tirreno
Lido di Pini
Latina
Nettuno
Anzio
TO SPERLONGA
A1
448
E45
74
209
3
71
E45
4
2
578
204
674
578
674
2
4
495
1
A1
3
A1
4
493
2
1
A12
A24
411
A12
155
A1
A91
215
296
7
A1
600
148
609
207
601
148
7
148
601
0 15 mi
0 15 km

Three popes are buried here, including Pope Alexander IV (1254–61), whose body was hidden so well by the canons, who feared it would be desecrated by heretics, that it has never been found. The small adjoining **Museo del Colle del Duomo** has a collection of 18th-century reliquaries, Etruscan sarcophagi, and a crucifixion painting attributed to Michelangelo. ✉ *Piazza San Lorenzo* ☎ *338/1336529* 🌐 *www.museocolledelduomo.com* 🎟 *Museum €5, includes Palazzo Papale* ⏲ *Church: daily 10–1 and 3–6. Museum: Tues.–Sun. 10–1 and 3–6.*

The medieval district of **San Pellegrino** is one of the best preserved of such neighborhoods in Italy. It has charming vistas of arches, vaults, towers, exterior staircases, worn wooden doors on great iron hinges, and tiny hanging gardens. You pass many antiques shops and craft workshops as you explore the little squares and byways. The **Fontana Grande** in the piazza of the same name is the largest and most extravagant of Viterbo's authentic Gothic fountains. ✉ *Via San Pellegrino.*

Viterbo has been a spa town for centuries, and the **Terme dei Papi** continues the tradition. This excellent spa has the usual health and beauty treatments with an Etruscan twist: try a facial with local volcanic mud, or a steam bath in an ancient cave, where scalding hot mineral water direct from the spring splashes down a waterfall to a pool beneath your feet. The Terme dei Papi's main draw, however, is the *terme* (baths) themselves: a 21,000-square-foot outdoor limestone pool, into the shallow end of which Viterbo's famous hot water pours at 59°C (138°F)—and intoxicates with its sulfurous odor. Floats and deck chairs are for rent, but bring your own bathrobe and towel unless you're staying at the hotel. ✉ *Strada Bagni 12, 5 km (3 mi) west of town center* ☎ *0761/3501* 🌐 *www.termedeipapi.it* 🎟 *Weekdays €12, Sat. €20, Sun. €25* ⏲ *Pool: Wed.–Mon. 9–7. Spa: daily 9–7.*

WHERE TO EAT

$$$ CENTRAL ITALIAN

✕ **Enoteca La Torre.** One of the best wine cellars in Italy takes center stage at the elegant Enoteca La Torre. It's also a temple to good eating: in addition to an ever-changing menu there are lists for cheeses, mineral waters, oils, and vinegars. Seasonal risottos and rabbit served in four different ways are recommended specialties, but whatever you choose will be local, traditional, and of the highest quality. ✉ *Via della Torre 5* ☎ *0761/226467* 🌐 *www.enotecalatorrevt.com* ⏲ *No dinner Sun.*

$ CENTRAL ITALIAN

✕ **Osteria dell' Enoteca La Torre.** Enjoy impeccably executed classics for pocket change at this casual eatery, which shares a kitchen with the more upscale Enoteca La Torre, and is set in the heart of town. Try whatever is listed as the daily rotating special, such as pappardelle (fresh, wide-cut pasta) or chickpea and chestnut soup. You can select a glass or bottle from the Enoteca's epic wine list, which includes a complex matrix of ratings from Italy's foremost wine reviewers. ✉ *Via della Torre 1* ☎ *0761/226467* 🌐 *www.enotecalatorrevt.com* ⏲ *No dinner Sun.*

$ CENTRAL ITALIAN

✕ **Tre Re.** Viterbo's oldest restaurant—and one of the most ancient in Italy—has been operating in the *centro storico* (historic center) since 1622. The kitchen focuses on traditional local dishes, such as *acquacotta viterbese* (literally, "cooked water"), a hearty vegetable-and-hot-pepper soup. The wine list offers the best of Italian wines. The small, wood-paneled dining room was a favorite haunt of movie director

Federico Fellini and, before that, of Anglo-American soldiers during World War II. Local diners make a point of touching the old inn sign of the "Three Kings," hanging on the wall inside, as this is supposed to bring good luck. ✉ *Via Macel Gattesco 3* ☎ *0761/304619* 🌐 *www.ristorantetrere.com* ⏲ *Closed Thurs.*

WHERE TO STAY

$$$ **Hotel Niccolò V.** This upscale hotel is connected to Viterbo's mineral baths and spa at Terme dei Papi. **Pros:** friendly staff; comfortable rooms; relaxing atmosphere. **Cons:** guests lounge in the lobby in bathrobes; several miles out of town. **TripAdvisor:** "great facilities for recreation," "swim in the hot springs," "distinctive sulfur smell." ✉ *Strada Bagni 12, 5 km (3 mi) west of center* ☎ *0761/350555* 🌐 *www.termedeipapi.it* *20 rooms, 3 suites* *In-room: Wi-Fi. In-hotel: restaurant, bar, pool, spa* *Breakfast.*

$ **La Terrazza Medioevale.** Right in the heart of old Viterbo's San Pellegrino district, this stylish B&B is situated on the first floor of the historic Palazzo Perotti. **Pros:** elegant furnishings at bargain price. **Cons:** no credit cards accepted; hotel Web site has history of malfunctioning. **TripAdvisor:** "splendid accommodation," "exquisite hospitality," "owners were welcoming and helpful." ✉ *Via S. Pellegrino 1* ☎ *0761/307034* 🌐 *www.laterrazzamedioevale.com* *3 rooms* *No credit cards.*

BAGNAIA

5 km (3 mi) east of Viterbo.

GETTING HERE

Just outside Viterbo, Bagnaia can be reached by local buses. By local train, it's 10 minutes beyond the Viterbo stop . . . if your train stops here (very few local trains actually do, so be sure to check).

EXPLORING

The village of Bagnaia is the site of 16th-century cardinal Alessandro Montalo's summer retreat. The hillside garden and park that surround the two small, identical residences are the real draw, designed by virtuoso architect Giacomo Barozzi (circa 1507–73), known as Vignola, who later worked with Michelangelo on St. Peter's.

Villa Lante is a terraced extravaganza. On the lowest terrace a delightful Italian garden has a centerpiece fountain fed by water channeled down the hillside. On another terrace, a stream of water runs through a groove carved in a long stone table where the cardinal entertained his friends alfresco, chilling wine in the running water. That's only one of the most evident of the whimsical water games that were devised for the cardinal. The symmetry of the formal gardens contrasts with the wild, untamed park adjacent to it, reflecting the paradoxes of nature and artifice that are the theme of this pleasure garden. ✉ *Via G. Baroni 71* ☎ *0761/288008* 🌐 *www.villalante.it* *€5* ⏲ *Tues.–Sun. 8:30–1 hr before sunset.*

CAPRAROLA

21 km (16 mi) southeast of Bagnaia, 19 km (12 mi) southeast of Viterbo.

GETTING HERE

Caprarola is served by COTRAL bus, leaving from the Saxa Rubra station on the Roma Nord line.

EXPLORING

The wealthy and powerful Farnese family took over this sleepy village in the 1500s and had the architect Vignola design a huge palace and gardens to rival the great residences of Rome. He also rearranged the little town of Caprarola to enhance the palazzo's setting.

The huge and splendid 400-year-old **Palazzo Farnese**, built on an unusual pentagonal plan, has an ingenious system of ramps and terraces that leads right up to the main portal. This nicety allowed carriages and mounts to arrive directly in front of the door. Though the salons are unfurnished, the palace's grandeur is still evident. An artificial grotto decorates one wall, the ceilings are covered with frescoes glorifying the Farnese family, and an entire room is frescoed with maps of the world as it was known to 16th-century cartographers. The palace is surrounded by a magnificent formal garden. ✉ *Piazza Farnese 1* ☎ *0761/646052* 🎟 *€5* ⏲ *Palazzo: Tues.–Sun. 8:30–1 hr before sunset. Garden: Tues.–Sun. 10–1 hr before sunset.*

BOMARZO

15 km (9 mi) northeast of Viterbo.

GETTING HERE

Bomarzo is 6 km (4 mi) from the A1 autostrada Attigliano exit, so if you are coming to Viterbo by car, it's easy to stop off on the way. Alternatively, you can get a public bus from Viterbo.

EXPLORING

The eerie 16th-century **Parco dei Mostri** *(Monster Park)* was originally known as the Village of Marvels, or the Sacred Wood. Created in 1552 by Prince Vicino Orsini, it's a kind of Disneyland forerunner, populated with weird and fantastic sculptures of mythical creatures, intended to astonish illustrious guests. The sculptures, carved in outcroppings of mossy stone in shady groves and woodland, include giant tortoises and griffins and an ogre's head with an enormous gaping mouth. Children love it, and there are photo ops galore. The park has a self-service café and a souvenir shop. ✉ *1½ km (1 mi) west of Bomarzo* ☎ *0761/924029* 🌐 *www.parcodeimostri.com* 🎟 *€9* ⏲ *Daily 8–sunset.*

TIVOLI AND PALESTRINA

Tivoli is a five-star draw, its attractions being its two villas—an ancient one in which Hadrian reproduced the most beautiful monuments in the then-known world, and a Renaissance one, in which cardinal Ippolito d'Este put a river to work for his delight. Unfortunately, the road from Rome to Tivoli passes through miles of uninspiring industrial areas with chaotic traffic. Grit your teeth and persevere. It'll be worth it. In the heart of this gritty shell lie two pearls that are rightly world famous. You'll know you're close to Tivoli when you see vast quarries of travertine marble and smell the sulfurous vapors of the little spa, Bagni di Tivoli. Both sites in Tivoli are outdoors and entail walking. With a car, you can continue your loop through the mountains east of Rome, taking the ancient pagan sanctuary at Palestrina, spectacularly set on the slopes of Mount Ginestro.

TIVOLI

36 km (22 mi) northeast of Rome.

GETTING HERE

Unless you have nerves of steel, it's best not to drive to Tivoli. Hundreds of industries line the Via Tiburtina from Rome and bottleneck traffic is nearly constant. You can avoid some, but not all, of the congestion by taking the Roma–L'Aquila toll road. Luckily, there's abundant public transport. Buses leave every 15 minutes from the Ponte Mammolo stop on the Metro A line. The ride takes an hour. Regional Trenitalia trains connect from both Termini and Tiburtina stations and will have you there in under an hour. Villa d'Este is in the town center, and a frequent bus service from Tivoli's main square goes to Hadrian's Villa.

VISITOR INFORMATION

Tivoli tourism office (✉ *Piazzale Nazioni Unite* ☎ *0774/313536* 🌐 *www.comune.tivoli.rm.it*).

EXPLORING

In ancient times, just about anybody who was anybody had a villa in Tivoli, including Crassius, Trajan, Hadrian, Horace, and Catullus. Tivoli fell into obscurity in the medieval era until the Renaissance, when popes and cardinals came back to the town and built villas showy enough to rival those of their extravagant predecessors.

Nowadays Tivoli is small but vibrant, with winding streets and views over the surrounding countryside, including the deep Aniene River gorge, which runs right through the center of town, and comes replete with a romantically sited bridge, cascading waterfalls, and two jewels of ancient Roman architecture that crown its cliffs—the round Temple of Vesta and the ruins of the rectangular Sanctuary of the Sibyl, probably built earlier. These can be picturesquely viewed across the gorge from the Villa Gregoriana park, named for Pope Gregory XVI, who saved Tivoli from chronic river damage by diverting the river through a tunnel, weakening its flow. An unexpected (but not unappreciated) side effect was the creation of the Grande Cascata (Grand Cascade), which shoots a huge jet of water into the valley below. The Villa Gregoriana is at Largo Sant'Angelo (from the Largo Garibaldi bus stop, follow Via Pacifici—it changes name six times—and veer left on Via Roma to the Largo). There's a small admission charge to the park, which affords a sweaty, steep hike down to the river, so you may prefer to repair to the Antico Ristorante Sibilla, set right by the Temple of Vesta. From its dining terrace, you can drink in one of the most memorably romantic landscape views in Italy, one especially prized by 19th-century painters.

★ The astonishingly grand 2nd-century **Villa Adriana** *(Hadrian's Villa)*, 6 km (4 mi) south of Tivoli, was an emperor's theme park: an exclusive retreat below the ancient settlement of Tibur where the marvels of the classical world were reproduced for a ruler's pleasure. Hadrian, who succeeded Trajan as emperor in AD 117, was a man of genius and intellectual curiosity, fascinated by the accomplishments of the Hellenistic world. From AD 125 to 134, architects, laborers, and artists worked on the villa, periodically spurred on by the emperor himself when he returned from another voyage full of ideas for even more daring constructions (he also gets credit for Rome's Pantheon). After his death in AD 138 the fortunes of his villa declined as it was sacked by barbarians and Romans alike. Many of his statues and decorations ended up in the Vatican Museums, but the expansive ruins are nonetheless compelling. It's not the single elements but the delightful effect of the whole that makes Hadrian's Villa a treat. Oleanders, pines, and cypresses growing among the ruins heighten the visual impact. To help you get your bearings, maps are issued free with the audio guides (€4). A visit here takes about two hours, more if you like to savor antiquity slowly. In summer visit early to take advantage of cool mornings. ✉ *Bivio di Villa Adriana off Via Tiburtina, 6 km (4 mi) southwest of Tivoli* ☎ *0774/382733 reservations* 🎫 *€6.50* ⏲ *Daily 9–1 hr before sunset.*

★ In the center of Tivoli, **Villa d'Este**, created by Cardinal Ippolito d'Este in the 16th century, was the most amazing pleasure garden of its day and still stuns visitors with its beauty. Este (1509–72), a devotee of the Renaissance celebration of human ingenuity over nature, was inspired by the excavation of Villa Adriana and paid architect Pirro Ligorrio an astronomical sum to create a mythical garden with water as its artistic centerpiece. To console himself for his seesawing fortunes in the political intrigues of his time (he happened to be cousin to Pope Alexander VI), he had his builders tear down part of a Franciscan monastery to clear the site, then divert the Aniene River to water the garden and feed the fountains—and what fountains: big, small, noisy, quiet, rushing, running, and combining to create a late-Renaissance, proto–Busby Berkeley masterpiece in which sunlight, shade, water, gardens, and carved stone create an unforgettable experience. To this day, several hundred fountains cascade, shoot skyward, imitate birdsongs, and simulate rain. The musical **Fontana dell'Organo** has been restored to working order: the organ plays a watery tune every two hours from 10:30 to 6:30 (until 2:30 in winter). Romantics will love the night tour of the gardens and floodlit fountains, available on Friday and Saturday from June until September. Allow at least an hour for the visit, and bear in mind that there are a lot of stairs to climb. There's also a café on the upper terrace leading from the palace entrance, where you can sit and admire the view. ✉ *Piazza Trento 1* ☎ *0774/312070* 🌐 *www.villadestetivoli.info* 🎫 *€8* ⏲ *Tues.–Sun. 8:30–1 hr before sunset.*

WHERE TO EAT AND STAY

$$$ ITALIAN Fodor's Choice ★ **Antico Ristorante Sibilla.** This famed restaurant should be included among the most beautiful sights of Tivoli. Built in 1730 beside the circular Roman Temple of Vesta and the Sanctuary of the Sibyl, the terrace garden has a spectacular view over the deep gorge of the Aniene River, with the thundering waters of the waterfall in the background. Marble plaques on the walls list the royals who have come here to dine over 2½ centuries. In decades gone by, the tour buses arrived and the food suffered. Today, however, food, wine, and service standards are high, as befits the sublime setting. ✉ *Via della Sibilla 50* ☎ *0774/335281* 🌐 *www.ristorantesibilla.com.*

$ **Adriano.** At the entrance to Hadrian's Villa, this small inn is a modest but comfortable place to overnight and handy spot to have lunch before or after your trip around the ruins. **Pros:** wonderful location; peaceful garden; attentive service. **Cons:** busloads of tourists disembark under the windows; restaurant can be crowded. **TripAdvisor:** "looks and feels like the 1920s," "staff was friendly and accommodating," "needs a good work over." ✉ *Via di Villa Adriana 194* ☎ *0774/382235* 🌐 *www.hoteladriano.it* *10 rooms* *In-hotel: restaurant, tennis court, bar* ⏲ *No dinner Sun. Nov.–Mar.* *Breakfast.*

$$ **Hotel Torre Sant'Angelo.** This deluxe hotel 1 km (½ mi) outside Tivoli has a magnificent view of the old town, the Aniene Falls, and the Temple of the Sybil. **Pros:** 21st-century comfort in a historic mansion house. **Cons:** isolated location two miles out of town. **TripAdvisor:** "rooms are small but pleasant," "very romantic," "great for the view." ✉ *Via Quintilio Varo* ☎ *0774/332533* 🌐 *www.hoteltorresangelo.it* *25 rooms, 10 suites* *Breakfast.*

PALESTRINA

27 km (17 mi) southeast of Tivoli, 37 km (23 mi) east of Rome.

GETTING HERE

COTRAL buses leave from the Anagnina terminal on Rome's Metro A line and from the Tiburtina railway station. Alternatively, you can take a train to Zagarolo, where a COTRAL bus takes you on to Palestrina. The total trip takes 40 minutes. By car, take the A2 Autostrada del Sole to the San Cesareo exit and follow the signs to Palestrina. Expect it to take about an hour.

VISITOR INFORMATION

Palestrina tourism office (✉ *Piazza della Cortina 1* ☎ *06/9573176* 🌐 *www.comune.palestrina.rm.it*).

EXPLORING

Except to students of ancient history and music lovers, Palestrina is surprisingly little known outside Italy. Its most famous native son, Giovanni Pierluigi da Palestrina, born here in 1525, is considered the master of counterpoint and polyphony. He composed 105 masses, as well as madrigals, magnificats, and motets. But the town was celebrated long before the composer's lifetime.

Ancient Praeneste (modern Palestrina) flourished much earlier than Rome. It was the site of the Temple of Fortuna Primigenia, which dates from the 2nd century BC. This was one of the largest, richest, most frequented temple complexes in all antiquity—people came from far and wide to consult its famous oracle. In modern times no one had any idea of the extent of the complex until World War II bombings exposed ancient foundations occupying huge artificial terraces stretching from the upper part of the town as far downhill as its central Duomo.

Large arches and terraces scale the hillside up to the imposing **Palazzo Barberini**, which crowns a flight of steep, stone stairs. The palace was built in the 17th century along the semicircular lines of the original temple. It now contains the **Museo Nazionale Archeologico di Palestrina,** with material found on the site that dates from throughout the classical period. This well-labeled collection of Etruscan bronzes, pottery, and terra-cotta statuary as well as Roman artifacts takes second place to the chief attraction, a first-century BC mosaic representing the Nile in flood. This delightful work—a large-scale composition in which form, color, and innumerable details captivate the eye—is alone worth the trip to Palestrina. But there's more: a model of the temple as it was in ancient times helps you appreciate the immensity of the original construction. ✉ *Piazza della Cortina 1* ☎ *06/9538100* 🎟 *€5* ⏲ *Museum: daily 9–8. Archaeological zone: daily 9–1 hr before sunset.*

WHERE TO EAT

$$ ITALIAN ✕ **Il Piscarello.** Tucked away at the bottom of a steep side road, this elegant restaurant comes as a bit of a surprise. The yellow damask table linen and the deep gold curtains give the spacious dining room a warm and sunny look. There's a trim patio overlooking the garden for alfresco dining in good weather. Specialties on the menu include seafood and dishes anointed with black and white truffles. ✉ *Via del Piscarello 2* ☎ *06/9574326* 🌐 *www.ristoranteilpiscarello.it* ⏲ *Closed Mon.*

THE CASTELLI ROMANI

The "castelli" aren't really castles, as their name would seem to imply. They're little towns that are scattered on the slopes of the Alban Hills near Rome. And the Alban Hills aren't really hills, but extinct volcanoes. There were castles here in the Middle Ages, however, when each of these towns, fiefs of rival Roman lords, had its own fortress to defend it. Some centuries later, the area became given over to villas and retreats, notably the pope's summer residence at Castelgandolfo, and the 17th- and 18th-century villas that transformed Frascati into the Beverly Hills of Rome. Arrayed around the rim of an extinct volcano that encloses two crater lakes, the string of picturesque towns of the Castelli Romani are today surrounded by vineyards, olive groves, and chestnut woods—no wonder overheated Romans have always loved to escape here.

Ever since Roman times, the Castelli towns have been renowned for their wine. In the narrow, medieval alleyways of the oldest parts, you can still find old-fashioned hostelries where the locals sit on wooden benches, quaffing the golden nectar straight from the barrel. Following the mapped-out **Castelli Wine Route** (🌐 *www.stradadeivinideicastelliromani.it*) around the numerous vineyards and wine cellars is a more sophisticated alternative. Exclusive local gastronomic specialties include the bread of Genzano, baked in traditional wood-fire ovens, the *porchetta* (roast suckling pig) of Ariccia, and the *pupi* biscuits of Frascati, shaped like women or mermaids with three or more breasts (an allusion to ancient fertility goddesses). Each town has its own feasts and saints' days, celebrated with costumed processions and colorful events. Some are quite spectacular, like Marino's annual Wine Festival in October, where the town's fountains flow with wine, or the Flower Festival of Genzano in June, when an entire street is carpeted with millions of flower petals, arranged in elaborate patterns.

FRASCATI

20 km (12 mi) south of Rome.

GETTING HERE

An hourly train service along a single-track line through vineyards and olive groves takes you to Frascati from Termini station. The trip takes 45 minutes. By car, take the Via Tuscolano, which branches off the Appia Nuova road just after St. John Lateran in Rome, and drive straight up.

VISITOR INFORMATION

Frascati Point (tourism office) (✉ *Piazza G. Marconi 5* ☎ *06/94015378* ✉ *frascatipoint@libero.it*).

EXPLORING

It's worth taking a stroll through Frascati's lively old center. Via Battisti, leading from the Belvedere, takes you into Piazza San Pietro with its imposing gray-and-white cathedral. Inside is the cenotaph of Prince Charles Edward, last of the Scottish Stuart dynasty, who tried unsuccessfully to regain the British Crown, and died an exile in Rome in 1788. A little arcade beside the monumental fountain at the back of the piazza leads into Market Square, where the smell of fresh baking will entice you into the Purificato family bakery to see the traditional pupi biscuits, modeled on old pagan fertility symbols.

Take your pick from the cafés and trattorias fronting the central Piazzale Marconi, or do as the locals do—buy fruit from the market gallery at Piazza del Mercato, then get a huge slice of porchetta from one of the stalls, a hunk of *casareccio* bread, and a few *ciambelline frascatane* (ring-shaped cookies made with wine), and take your picnic to any one of the numerous *cantine* (homey wine bars), and settle in for some sips of tasty, inexpensive vino.

Frascati was the chosen sylvan retreat of prelates and princes, who built magnificent villas on the sun-drenched slopes overlooking the

Roman plain. The most spectacular of these is **Villa Aldobrandini**, which dominates Frascati's main square from the top of its steeply sloped park.

Built in the late 16th century and adorned with frescoes by the Zuccari brothers and the Cavalier d'Arpino, the hulking villa is still privately owned by the Princes Aldobrandini. However, its park is a marvel of baroque fountains and majestic box-shaded avenues, and you can go and see the magnificent Water Theater that Cardinal Pietro Aldobrandini, Pope Clement VIII's favorite nephew, built to impress his guests, thinking nothing of diverting the water supply that served the entire area in order to make his fountains play. The gigantic central figure of Atlas holding up the world is believed to represent the pope. You can also see another Water Theater in the grounds of nearby Villa Torlonia, which is now a public park. ✉ *Via Cardinale Massaia* ☎ *06/9426887* 🎟 *Free* ⏲ *Weekdays 9–2 and 3–6.*

★ **Grottaferrata** is only a couple of miles from Frascati, but it's quite different in character. The original village has expanded enormously to accommodate a vast army of commuters, and traffic can be very congested at peak hours. In compensation, the town has excellent restaurants and an interesting weekly market. Its main attraction, however, is the **Abbey of San Nilo,** a walled citadel founded by the 90-year-old St. Nilo, who brought his group of Basilian monks here in 1004. The order is unique in that it's Roman Catholic but observes Greek Orthodox rites.

The fortified abbey, considered a masterpiece of martial architecture, was restructured in the 15th century by Antonio da Sangallo for the future Pope Julius II. The abbey church, inside the second courtyard, is a jewel of oriental opulence, with glittering Byzantine mosaics and a revered icon set into a marble tabernacle designed by Bernini. The Farnese chapel, leading from the right nave, contains a series of frescoes by Domenichino. There are free guided tours of the abbey on Saturday and Sunday at 4.

If you make arrangements in advance you can visit the library, which is one of the oldest in Italy. The abbey also has a famous laboratory for the restoration of antique books and manuscripts, where Leonardo's *Atlantic Code* was restored in 1962 and more than a thousand precious volumes were saved after the disastrous Florence flood in 1966. ✉ *Corso del Popolo 128* ☎ *06/9459309* 🌐 *www.abbaziagreca.it* 🎟 *Free* ⏲ *8:30–12:30 and 4–6.*

WHERE TO EAT AND STAY

$$$ CENTRAL ITALIAN ★ ✕ **Al Fico Vecchio.** This historic coaching inn, dating to the 16th century, is situated on an old Roman road a couple of miles outside Frascati. It has a charming garden shaded by the old fig tree that gave the place its name. The dining room has been tastefully renovated, preserving many of the characteristic antique features. The menu offers a wide choice of local dishes, such as gnocchi with cheese and truffles. ✉ *Via Anagnini 257* ☎ *06/9459261.*

$$$ ★ 🏨 **Park Hotel Villa Grazioli.** One of the region's most famous residences, this elegant patrician villa halfway between Frascati and Grottaferrata is now a first-class hotel. **Pros:** wonderful views of the countryside;

elegant atmosphere; professional staff. **Cons:** difficult to find. **TripAdvisor:** "sunset from the terrace was stunning," "grand Italian villa," "a virtual art museum." ✉ *Via Umberto Pavoni 19, Grottaferrata* ☎ *06/9454001* 🌐 *www.villagrazioli.com* *56 rooms, 2 suites* *In-hotel: restaurant, bar, pool* *Breakfast.*

CASTELGANDOLFO

8 km (5 mi) southwest of Frascati, 25 km (15 mi) south of Rome.

GETTING HERE

There's an hourly train service for Castelgandolfo from Termini station (Rome-Albano line). Otherwise, buses leave frequently from the Anagnina terminal of the Metro A subway. The trip takes about 30 minutes. By car, take the Appian Way from San Giovanni in Rome and follow it straight to Albano, where you branch off for Castelgandolfo (about an hour, depending on traffic).

EXPLORING

This little town is well known as the pope's summer retreat. It was the Barberini Pope Urban VIII who first headed here, eager to escape the malarial miasmas that afflicted summertime Rome; before long, the city's princely families also set up country estates around here.

The 17th-century **Villa Pontificia** has a superb position overlooking Lake Albano and is set in one of the most gorgeous gardens in Italy; unfortunately, neither the house nor the park is open to the public (although crowds are admitted into the inner courtyard for papal audiences). On the little square in front of the palace there's a fountain by Bernini, who also designed the nearby Church of San Tommaso da Villanova, which has works by Pietro da Cortona.

The village has a number of interesting craft workshops and food purveyors, in addition to the souvenir shops on the square. On the horizon, the silver astronomical dome belonging to the Specola Vaticana observatory—one of the first in Europe—where the scientific Pope Gregory XIII indulged his interest in stargazing, is visible for miles around.

The **lakeside lido** is lined with restaurants, ice-cream parlors, and cafés and is a favorite spot with Roman families. No motorized craft are allowed on the lake, but you can rent paddleboats and kayaks. The waters are full of seafowl, such as swans and herons, and nature trails are mapped out along both ends of the shore. All along the central part there are bathing establishments where you can rent deck chairs, or stop to eat a plate of freshly prepared pasta or a gigantic Roman sandwich at one of the little snack bars under the oak and alder trees. There's also a small, permanent fairground for children.

WHERE TO EAT

$$$ CENTRAL ITALIAN ★ ✕ **Antico Ristorante Pagnanelli.** One of most refined restaurants in the Castelli Romani, this has been in the same family since 1882. The present generation—Aurelio Pagnanelli, his Australian wife, Jane, and their four sons—have lovingly restored this old railway inn perched high above Lake Albano. The dining-room windows open onto a breathtaking view across the lake to the conical peak of Monte Cavo. In winter a log fire

blazes in a corner; in summer dine out on the flower-filled terrace. Many of the dishes are prepared with produce from the family's own farm. The wine cellar, carved out of the living tufa rock, boasts more than 3,000 labels. ✉ *Via Gramsci 4* ☎ *06/9360004* 🌐 *www.pagnanelli.it.*

ARICCIA

8 km (5 mi) southwest of Castelgandolfo, 26 km (17 mi) south of Rome.

GETTING HERE

For Ariccia, take the COTRAL bus from the Anagnina terminal of the Metro A underground line. All buses on the Albano-Genzano-Velletri line go through Ariccia. If you take a train to Albano, you can proceed by bus to Ariccia or go on foot (it's just under 3 km [2 mi]). If you are driving, follow the Appian road to Albano and carry on to Ariccia.

EXPLORING

Ariccia is a gem of baroque town planning. When millionaire banker Agostino Chigi became Pope Alexander VII, he commissioned Gian Lorenzo Bernini to redesign his country estate to make it worthy of his new station. Bernini consequently restructured not only the existing 16th-century palace, but also the town gates, the main square with its loggias and graceful twin fountains, and the round church of **Santa Maria dell'Assunzione** (the dome is said to be modeled on the Pantheon). The rest of the village coiled around the apse of the church down into the valley below.

Strangely, Ariccia's splendid heritage has been largely forgotten in the 20th century, and yet it was once one of the highlights of every artist's and writer's Grand Tour. Corot, Ibsen, Turner, Longfellow, and Hans Christian Andersen all came to stay here.

★ **Palazzo Chigi** is a rare example of a baroque residence whose original furniture, paintings, drapes, and decorations are still mostly intact. Italian film director Lucchino Visconti used the villa for most of the interior scenes in the film *The Leopard*. The rooms contain intricately carved pieces of 17th-century furniture, as well as textiles and costumes from the 16th to the 20th century. See the Room of Beauties, lined with paintings of the loveliest ladies of the day, and the Nuns' Room, with portraits of 10 Chigi sisters, all of whom took the veil. The park stretching behind the palace is a wild wood, the last remnant of the ancient Latium forest, where herds of deer still graze under the trees. Book ahead for tours in English. ✉ *Piazza di Corte 14* ☎ *06/9330053* 🌐 *www.palazzochigiariccia.it* 🎫 *€7* 🕐 *Tours Tues.–Fri. at 11, 4, and 5:30; weekends every hr 10:30–12:30 and 4–7.*

WHERE TO EAT

A visit to Ariccia is not complete without tasting the local gastronomic specialty: porchetta, a delicious roast whole pig stuffed with herbs. The shops on the Piazza di Corte will make up a sandwich for you, or you can do what the Romans do: take a seat at one of the *fraschette* wine cellars that serve cheese, cold cuts, pickles, olives, and sometimes a plate of pasta. Conditions are rather rough and ready—you sit on a wooden bench at a trestle table covered with simple white paper—but there's no better place to make friends and maybe join in a sing-along.

¢ CENTRAL ITALIAN ✕ **La Locanda del Brigante Gasparone**. The first of the string of informal lodgings you find clustered under the Galloro bridge, on the right-hand side of Palazzo Chigi, this *locanda* (inn) has seats either inside or outside under an awning—a fine place to enjoy simple, robust pasta dishes. ✉ *Via Borgo San Rocco 7* ☎ *06/9333100* ▭ *No credit cards* ⊙ *Closed Tues. No dinner Sun.*

$ CENTRAL ITALIAN ✕ **L'Ariccíarola**. Tucked in a corner under the Galloro bridge, this is a great place for people-watching while you enjoy the local porchetta (whole roast pig stuffed with herbs), washed down with a carafe of local Castelli wine. ✉ *Via Borgo S. Rocco 9* ☎ *06/9334103* ▭ *No credit cards* ⊙ *Closed Mon.*

NEMI

8 km (5 mi) west of Ariccia, 34 km (21 mi) south of Rome.

GETTING HERE

Nemi is a bit difficult to get to unless you come by car. Buses from the Anagnina Metro A station go to the town of Genzano, where a local bus travels to Nemi every two hours. If the times aren't convenient, you can take a taxi or walk the 5 km (3 mi) around Lake Nemi. By car, take the panoramic route known as the Via dei Laghi (Road of the Lakes). Follow the Appia Nuova from St. John Lateran and branch off on the well-signposted route after Ciampino airport. Follow the Via dei Laghi toward Velletri until you see signs for Nemi.

EXPLORING

Nemi is the smallest and prettiest village of the Castelli Romani. Perched on a spur of rock 600 feet above the small crater lake of the same name, it has an eagle's-nest view over the rolling Roman countryside as far as the coast some 18 km (11 mi) away. The one main street, Corso Vittorio Emanuele, takes you to the (now privately owned) baronial Castello Ruspoli, with its 11th-century watchtower, and the quaint little Piazza Umberto 1, lined with outdoor cafés serving the tiny wood-strawberries harvested from the crater bowl.

If you continue on through the arch that joins the castle to the former stables, you come to the entrance of the dramatically landscaped public gardens, which curve steeply down to the panoramic **Belvedere** terrace. If you enjoy walking, you can follow the road past the garden entrance and go all the way down to the bottom of the crater.

Nemi may be small, but it has a long and fascinating history. In Roman times it was an important sanctuary dedicated to the goddess Diana and drew thousands of pilgrims from all over the Roman Empire. In the 1930s the Italian government drained the lake in order to recover two magnificent ceremonial ships, loaded with sculptures, bronzes, and art treasures, that were submerged for 2,000 years.

Unfortunately, the ships were burned during World War II. The state-of-the-art **Museo delle Navi Romani** *(Roman Ship Museum)* on the lakeshore, which was built to house them, has scale models and photographs of the complex recovery operation, as well as some finds from the sanctuary. ✉ *Via del Tempio di Diana 9* ☎ *06/9398040* 🎫 *€3* 🕐 *Daily 9–6.30.*

WHERE TO EAT

$$ ITALIAN ✕ **Specchio di Diana**. Halfway down the main street is the town's most historic inn—Byron reputedly stayed here when visiting the area. A wine bar and café are on street level, while the restaurant proper on the second floor offers marvelous views, especially at sunset. Pizzas are popular, but don't neglect Nemi's regional specialties: *fettucine al sugo di lepre* (fettucine with hare sauce), roasted porcini mushrooms, and the little wood-strawberries with whipped cream. ✉ *Corso Vittorio Emanuele 13* ☎ *06/9368805* 🌐 *www.specchiodidiana.it* 🕐 *Closed Mon.*

Northern Italy

WHAT'S WHERE

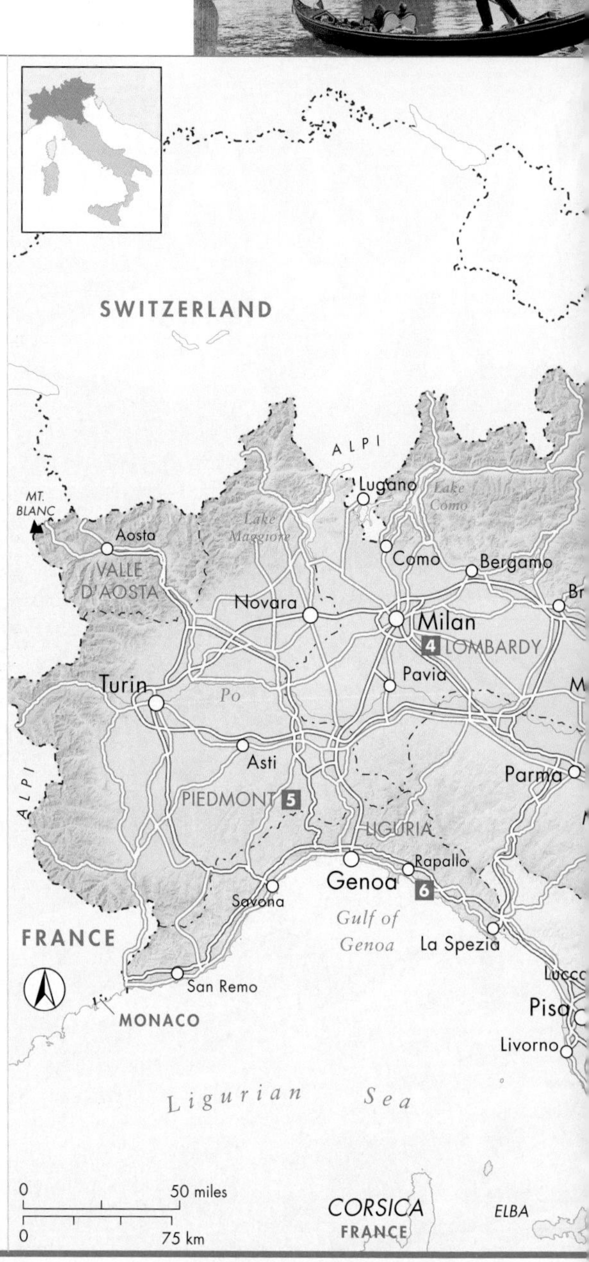

1 Venice. One of the world's most unusual cities—and one of the most beautiful—Venice has canals where the streets should be and an atmosphere of faded splendor that practically defines the word *decadent.*

2 The Veneto and Friuli-Venezia Giulia. The green plains stretching west of Venice hold three of northern Italy's most artistically significant midsize cities: Padua, Vicenza, and Verona. Farther north and east, Alpine foothills are dotted with small, welcoming towns and some of Italy's most distinguished vineyards.

3 The Dolomites. Along Italy's northeast border, the Dolomites are the country's finest mountain playground, with gorgeous cliffs, curiously shaped peaks, lush meadows, and crystal-clear lakes. The skiing is good, and the scenery is different from what you find in the Austrian, Swiss, or French Alps.

4 Milan, Lombardy, and the Lakes. The deep-blue lakes of the Lombardy region—Como, Garda, and Maggiore—have been attracting vacationers since the days of ancient Rome. At the center of Lombardy is Milan, Italy's second-largest city and its business capital. It holds

Italy's most renowned opera house, and as the epicenter of Italian fashion and design, it's a shopper's paradise.

5 Piedmont and Valle d'Aosta. A step off the usual tourist circuit, these regions in Italy's northwest corner have attractions that are well worth a visit. You'll find here great Alpine peaks along the French and Swiss borders, a highly esteemed food-and-wine culture, and an elegant regional capital in Turin.

6 The Italian Riviera. Northern Italy's most attractive coastline runs along the Italian Riviera in the region of Liguria. The best beaches are west of Genoa, but the main appeal lies to the east, where fishing villages are interspersed aong beautiful seaside cliffs and coves.

7 Emilia-Romagna. Many of Italy's signature foods come from here—including Parmigiano-Reggiano cheese, prosciutto di Parma, and balsamic vinegar—and the pasta is considered Italy's finest. But there's more than food to draw you here. Bologna has important museums, elegant piazzas, and arcaded streets; the mosaics of Ravenna are glittering Byzantine treasures; and Ferrara, Parma, and Modena all have artistic jewels.

NORTHERN ITALY PLANNER

Speaking the Language

People who interact regularly with tourists—such as hotel, restaurant, museum, and transportation personnel—generally speak some English. However, even in the cosmopolitan north, although knowledge of foreign languages is increasing, often highly educated Italians speak only Italian. Many are slightly offended if a foreigner assumes they speak English without first asking politely, "*Parla Lei inglese?*" If you do ask, most Italians, even those with no English, will try to be helpful. Perhaps because of their own linguistic limitations, Italians are very tolerant of foreigners who try to speak their language and do wonders in understanding fractured Italian.

Even if you speak Italian, don't be surprised if you can't understand conversations going on around you, which may be in local dialect. Because of television and mass education, now almost everyone speaks standard Italian, and in cities such as Milan dialect has almost died out, but it still thrives in the Veneto and in areas that have not had a large influx of residents from other parts of Italy. Among friends, at home, and in moments of high emotion, standard Italian gives way to the local language.

Getting Here

Aeroporto Malpensa, 50 km (31 mi) northwest of Milan, is the major northern Italian hub for intercontinental flights and also sees substantial European and domestic traffic. Venice's **Aeroporto Marco Polo** also serves international destinations.

There are regional airports in Turin, Genoa, Bologna, Verona, Trieste, Treviso, Bolzano, and Parma, and Milan has a secondary airport, Linate. You can reach all of these on connecting flights from within Italy and from other European cities. If you fly into Malpensa, but Milan isn't your final destination, you can also get where you're going by train, using the Italian national rail system, **Ferrovie dello Stato** (☎ *892021 toll-free within Italy* 🌐 *www.trenitalia.com*). Shuttle buses run three times an hour (less often after 10 pm) between Malpensa and Milan's main train station, Stazione Centrale; the trip takes about 75 minutes, depending on traffic. The Malpensa Express Train, which leaves twice an hour, takes 40 minutes and delivers you to Cadorna station in central Milan.

Typical Travel Times

	Hours by Car	Hours by Train
Milan–Venice	3:30	2:35
Milan–Turin	2:00	2:00
Milan–Genoa	2:00	1:45
Milan–Bologna	2:30	1:00
Venice–Bologna	2:15	1:25
Venice–Turin	5:00	4:20
Venice–Genoa	4:45	4:30
Bologna–Genoa	3:15	3:00
Bologna–Turin	3:30	2:00
Genoa–Turin	2:00	2:00

When to Go

Spring: Late April, May, and early June are ideal times to tour northern Italy: the weather is mild, and the volume of tourists isn't as large as in summer. Although there's some rain, springtime is generally drier in northern Italy than it is in northern Europe or the east coast of North America. By May the coastal towns of Liguria are beginning to come to life. Meanwhile, in the mountains hiking trails can remain icy well into June.

Summer: Anywhere away from the mountains, summers are warm and humid. Bring sunscreen, since it seldom rains, and when it does, it's mainly in the late afternoon and at night. Summer is prime hiking season in the Alps, and the lakes and the Riviera are in full swing (meaning lodging reservations are a must).

Note that a large portion, maybe even the majority, of tourists in northern Italy are not foreigners; they're Italians seeing their own country, and they come in summer, when the kids are out of school and families can travel together.

Fall: Much like spring, autumn, with its mild weather, is an ideal time for touring most of the region. Much of Northern Italy enjoys pleasant, sunny weather through September and well into October. Most years it doesn't really begin to get cold until mid-November, though in the mountains, temperatures drop sharply in September. Many of the mountain tourist facilities close down entirely until the ski season kicks in.

Winter: In the Dolomites most ski resorts are open from mid-December through April, but snowfall in early winter is unreliable, and the best conditions often aren't seen until late February. Likewise, in Piedmont and Valle d'Aosta snow conditions vary drastically year to year—some years there's good snow beginning in November, while others don't see much more than a flake or two until February.

In Venice winters are relatively mild, with fewer tourists, but there are frequent rainy spells, and at the beginning and end of the season there's the threat of *acqua alta*, when tides roll in and flood low-lying parts of the city. (The floods last at most three hours.) The larger cities are active year-round, but the resort towns of the Lake District and the Riviera are all but shut down.

On the Calendar

Taking part in seasonal events can give your trip an added dose of local culture. Here are a few of the north's best:

From December through June, the **opera season** is in full swing, most notably in Milan, Venice, Turin, Parma, and Genoa. In Milan the **Festa di Sant'Ambrogio** in early December officially launches the season at La Scala; it's celebrated by a huge street fair around the Castello Sforzesco.

Venice's **Carnevale**, during the 10 days preceding Lent (usually falling in February), includes concerts, plays, masked balls, fireworks, and indoor and outdoor happenings of every sort. It's probably Italy's most famous festival, attracting hundreds of thousands.

The **Festa del Redentore** (Feast of the Redeemer) in Venice on the third Sunday in July commemorates the end of the plague of 1575. Venetians eat a traditional dinner in boats on San Marco Basin or along the water and then watch the spectacular fireworks.

Venice's **Mostra del Cinema**, the oldest of the international film festivals, takes place in late August and early September.

L'Arena di Verona Stagione Lirica (Arena of Verona Outdoor Opera Season), from early July to late August, is known for its grand productions, performed in Verona's 22,000-seat Roman amphitheater.

NORTHERN ITALY TOP ATTRACTIONS

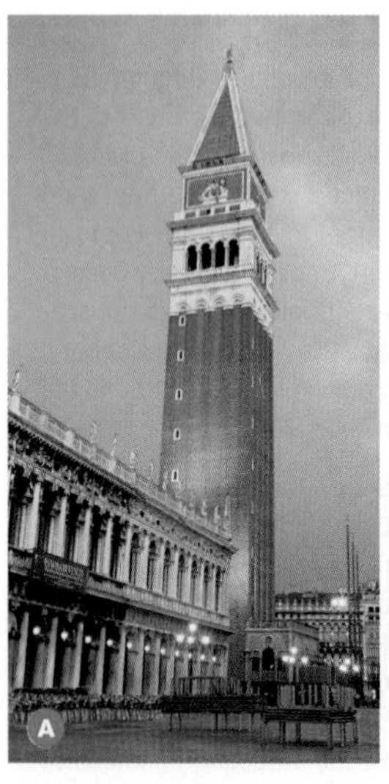

Venice's Piazza San Marco

(A) Perhaps nowhere else in the world gathers together so many of man's noblest artistic creations. The centerpiece of the piazza is the Basilica di San Marco, arguably the most beautiful Byzantine church in the West, with not only its shimmering Byzantine Romanesque facade, but also its jewel-like mosaic-encrusted interior. Right next door is the Venetian Gothic Palazzo Ducale, which was so beloved by the Venetians that when it burned down in the 16th century they rejected projects by the greatest architects of the Renaissance and had their palace rebuilt *come era, dove era*—exactly how and where it was. *(⇨ Chapter 3.)*

Venice's Grand Canal

(B) No one ever forgets a first trip down the Grand Canal. The sight of its magnificent palaces, with the light reflected from the canal's waters shimmering across their facades, is one of Italy's great experiences. *(⇨ Chapter 3.)*

Ravenna's Mosaics

(C) This small, out-of-the-way city houses perhaps the world's greatest treasure trove of early Christian art. After the decline of Rome, Ravenna was the capital of the Western Roman Empire and, a bit later, the seat of the Byzantine Empire in the West. The exquisite and surprisingly moving 5th- and 6th-century mosaics decorating several churches and other religious buildings still retain their startling brilliance. *(⇨ Chapter 9.)*

Palladio's Villas and Palazzi

(D) The great 16th-century architect Palladio created harmoniously beautiful buildings that were influential in spreading the neoclassical style to northern Europe, England, and, later, America. He did most of his work in and around his native city of Vicenza. If a visit to Vicenza simply whets your appetite for Palladio, you can see

another wonderful Palladian villa outside Venice (La Malcontenta) and his famous collaboration with Veronese outside Treviso (Villa Barbaro). (⇨ *Chapter 4.*)

Lake Como

(E) Just a short drive or train ride north of Milan, Lake Como combines spectacular mountain scenery with the elegance of baroque and neoclassical villas and gardens and the charm of picturesque villages. It's great any time of year, but best in the spring, when the azaleas are in bloom in the gardens of Villa Carlotta. (⇨ *Chapter 6.*)

Giotto's Frescoes in the Scrovegni Chapel, Padua

(F) Dante's contemporary Giotto decorated this chapel with an eloquent and beautiful fresco cycle. Its convincing human dimension helped to change the course of Western art. (⇨ *Chapter 4.*)

Mantua

(G) This charming town, slightly off the beaten track in Lombardy, contains a highpoint of 15th-century painting: Mantegna's frescoes in the wedding chamber of the Palazzo Ducale, a masterpiece of spatial illusion. On the outskirts of town, Giulio Romano's Palazzo Te is an elegant pleasure palace, frescoed with illusionistic painting carrying the tradition established by Mantegna several steps further. (⇨ *Chapter 6.*)

Leonardo's *Last Supper*

(H) On the refectory wall of Santa Maria della Grazia in Milan one of the world's most famous paintings still evokes wonder, not at all trivialized by millions of reproductions or dulled by its poor state of conservation. (⇨ *Chapter 6.*)

TOP EXPERIENCES

Discovering the Cinque Terre

Along the Italian Riviera east of Genoa are five tiny, remote fishing villages known collectively as the Cinque Terre. The beauty of the landscape—with steep, vine-covered hills pushing smack-dab against an azure sea—and the charm of the villages have turned the area into one of Italy's top destinations. The number-one activity is hiking the trails that run between the villages—the views are once-in-a-lifetime gorgeous—but if hiking isn't your thing, you can still have fun lounging about in cafés, admiring the water, and wandering through the medieval streets of the villages.

Taking Part in Venice's Festivals

Few people love a good party as much as the Venetians. The biggest is, of course, **Carnevale,** culminating on Fat Tuesday, the day before Lent, but with revelry beginning about 10 days earlier. Visitors from the world over join the Venetians in a period of institutionalized fantasy, dressing in sometimes exquisitely elaborate costumes. The program changes each year and includes public, mostly free cultural events in all districts of the city.

The **Redentore,** on the third weekend in July, is a festival essentially for Venetians, but guests are always welcome. The Venetians pack a picnic dinner and eat in boats decorated with paper lanterns in the Bacino di San Marco. Just before midnight, there's a magnificent fireworks display. The next day (Sunday), everyone crosses a temporary bridge spanning the Canale della Giudecca to Palladio's Redentore church to light a candle.

Venice Biennale is a cutting-edge international art exposition held in odd numbered years from June to November in special exhibition halls in the Venice Public Gardens (Giardini) and in the 14th-century industrial complex (Le Corderie) in the Arsenale. It's the most important exhibition of contemporary art in Italy and one of the three most important in Europe.

Eating in Bologna

Italians recognize Emilia as the star of its culinary culture and Bologna as its epicenter. Many dishes native to Bologna, such as the slow-cooked meat-and-tomato sauce *sugo alla Bolognese*, have become so famous that they're widely available in all regions of Italy and abroad. But you owe it to yourself to try them in the city where they were born and are a subject of local pride. Take note, however: in Bologna a *sugo* is never served with spaghetti, but rather with an egg pasta in the form of tagliatelle, lasagne, or tortellini.

Fashion and Style in Milan

Italian clothing and furniture design are world famous, and the center of the Italian design industry is Milan. The best way to see what's happening in the world of fashion is to browse the designer showrooms and boutiques of the fabled *quadrilatero della moda*, along and around Via Montenapoleone. The central event in the world of furniture design is Milan's annual Salone Internazionale del Mobile, held at the Milan fairgrounds for a week in April. Admission is generally restricted to the trade, but the Salone is open to the general public for one day, generally on a Sunday, during the week of the show.

NORTHERN ITALY TODAY

. . . feels the influence of immigration
The population of northern Italy, especially the western regions, has undergone a substantial transformation due to immigration. Beginning during the economic boom of the 1960s and continuing to the 1980s, Italians from the south moved to the great industrial centers of Turin and Milan, changing the face of those cities. The southerners, or at least their children, adopted most northern customs—few now go home for a nap at midday—but their presence has had a clear influence on the culture of the north. Especially in the cities, local dialects died out, and at the dinner table the traditional polenta and risotto now share the scene with spaghetti and other pastas, and southern dishes often appear on menus.

Prosperity, and immigration, came later to the northeast. Venetians still enjoy the 18th-century dialect comedies of Goldoni, and it's not uncommon to hear dialect spoken by elegant opera-goers at La Fenice. Emilia-Romagna, an essentially agricultural region that attracted few Italian immigrants, has kept its great culinary culture intact.

Northern Italy, like the rest of the country, has recently experienced an influx of foreign immigrants, although their numbers are smaller relative to the local population than in many other European countries. Their welcome has varied widely: proudly cosmopolitan Venice is fairly open to the newcomers, while in cities where the government is controlled by the overtly xenophobic Northern League, integration has been contentious. But despite fears stemming from cultural differences, and perhaps because labor is sorely needed by local industry, northern Italians tend to accept new arrivals.

. . . struggles with the global economy
Parts of northern Italy are among the most prosperous areas in Europe. But recently even these economic powerhouses have run into trouble. The industrial base consists mainly of small and midsize businesses, many of which have had to either close or outsource to Eastern Europe or Central Asia because of a lack of unskilled and semiskilled labor at home. And many of those businesses, such as those in the textile sector, have had difficulty dealing with competition from China.

. . . remains influenced by the Church
Despite Italy's being officially a secular state, most Italians, whether pious or pagan, would agree that it's difficult to separate Italian politics from the Roman Catholic Church. The Church's influence is greatest when it acts in support of the political right and conservative social policies. So, divorce is complicated, and gays and lesbians enjoy fewer rights than in most other European countries. The Church's power is more limited if it tries to espouse liberal causes: it treads lightly when condemning corruption and scandalous behavior on the part of powerful politicians, and recent attempts to foster the rights of immigrants and ethnic minorities have fallen on deaf ears.

The Veneto has been the stronghold of the socially conservative successors to the Church-oriented Christian Democratic Party. Emilia-Romagna, on the other hand, has had a strong socialist, and even communist, tradition, but the Church still is a powerful force there also. The dichotomy has been raised to the level of a folk legend by the novels and films featuring disputes between Don Camillo and Peppone, a priest and the communist mayor of Brescello, a town in Emilia.

A GREAT ITINERARY

Day 1: Bellagio

If you're flying to northern Italy from overseas, there's no better way to rest up after a long flight than a day on Lake Como, combining some of Italy's most beautiful scenery with elegant historic villas and gardens. At the center of it all is Bellagio, a pretty village with world-class restaurants and hotels, as well as more economical options. From Bellagio you can ferry to other points along the lake, take walking tours, go hiking, or just sit on a terrace watching the light play on the sapphire water and the snow-capped mountains in the distance.

Logistics: There are inexpensive bus-train combinations from Milan's Malpensa airport. A limousine service, Fly to Lake (☎ *0341/286887* 🌐 *www.flytolake.com*), leaves Malpensa four times per day (€35–€70 per person depending on the number of travelers; no service Sunday, late fall, or winter). The trip takes a little over two hours. In Bellagio you won't need a car, since most of your touring will be on foot, by ferry, or by bus.

Day 2: Milan

After a leisurely breakfast in Bellagio, take the ferry to Varenna (15 min) and then the train (1.25 hrs) to Milan's Central Station. Milan is a leading center of fashion and design, and many visitors keep to the area of elegant shops around Via Montenapoleone. But the city also houses some of Europe's great art treasures in the Brera Gallery and has two churches by Bramante, perhaps the most refined of the Italian High Renaissance architects. And then, of course, there's Leonardo's *Last Supper*. You may want to spend your evening taking in an opera at Italy's most illustrious opera house, La Scala.

Logistics: Central Milan is compact, with excellent public transportation. Milan does have its share of crime; keep an eye on your possessions around the train station and avoid hotels in that area.

Days 3 to 5: Verona/Mantua/Vicenza

Take an early express train to Verona (1.5 hrs from Milan) and settle into your hotel, where you'll stay for three nights; you'll be using this stately medieval city as your base to see three of the most important art cities in northern Italy. Verona, with its ancient Roman arena, theater, and city gates, its brooding medieval palaces and castle, and its graceful bridge spanning the Adige, is probably the most immediately impressive of the three, and you'll want to spend the first day exploring its attractions. But the real artistic treasures are in the two smaller cities you'll see on day trips out of Verona.

The next day, take a short train trip to Mantua (30–45 min). Be sure to arrive in time for lunch, because Mantua has one of the most interesting local cuisines in northern Italy. The great local specialty is *tortelli di zucca* (pumpkin, cheese, and almond-paste filled ravioli), served with sage butter and Parmesan cheese. The top artistic attractions are the Mantegna frescoes in the Palazzo Ducale, and you should also pay a visit to Giulio Romano's Palazzo Te, a 16th-century pleasure palace, on the outskirts of town. Take the train back to Verona in time for dinner, and perhaps catch an opera performance in Verona's Roman amphitheater.

The day after, take a short train trip to Vicenza (30 min) to see the palaces, villas, and public buildings of the lion of late 16th-century architecture, Andrea Palladio. Don't miss his Teatro Olimpico and his most famous villa, La Rotonda,

slightly out of town. For lunch, try the *baccalà alla vicentina*, the local version of dried salt cod, which is surprisingly good. Also be sure to see the frescoes by Gianbattista and Giandomenico Tiepolo in the Villa dei Nani, near the Rotonda. In the spring and summer there are musical performances in the Teatro Olimpico; if you want to attend, you'll have to book a hotel in Vicenza for the night, since you'll miss the last train back to Verona.

Day 6: Padua

Most people visit this important art and university center on a day trip out of Venice, but then they miss one of Padua's main attractions, the night life that goes on in the city's wine bars and cafés from evening until quite late. Most cities in northern Italy, even Venice and Milan, have surprisingly little to offer after dinner or the theater, but in Padua going out for a nightcap or coffee with friends is a tradition, not only for students but also for older folks, too. Arrive early enough to see at least the Giotto frescoes in the Cappella degli Scrovegni and the Basilica di San Antonio before lunch, then spend a relaxing afternoon at the Villa Pisani, enjoying its gardens and important Tiepolo fresco.

Logistics: Trains are frequent to Padua from Verona (1 hr) and Vicenza (30 min); you don't really have to schedule ahead.

Day 7: Venice

Three days are hardly enough to see one of the world's most beautiful cities and one of the cradles of modern Western civilization. But running from museum to museum, church to church would be a mistake, since Venice is a wonderful place to stroll or "hang out," taking in some of the atmosphere that inspired such great art.

The first things you'll probably want to do in Venice are to take a vaporetto ride down the Grand Canal and see the Piazza San Marco. These are best done in the morning: before 8:30 you'll avoid rush hour on the vaporetto, and while there's likely to be a line at San Marco when it opens, it'll be shorter than later in the day. Afterwards, move on to the adjacent Palazzo Ducale and Sansovino's Biblioteca Marciana, facing it in the Piazzetta.

For lunch, take vaporetto #1 to the Ca' Rezzonico stop and have a sandwich and a *spritz* in the Campo Santa Margherita, where you can mingle with the university students in one of Venice's most lively squares. From there, make your way to the Galleria dell'Accademia and spend a few hours taking in its wonderful

collection of Venetian paintings. In the evening, take a walk up the Zattere and have a drink at one of the cafés overlooking the Canale della Giudecca.

Logistics: Be careful selecting your early train from Padua to Venice; some can be very slow. The 7:38 is one of the fastest (34 min), and will get you into Venice in time to beat rush hour on the Grand Canal vaporetto. To get an early start, unless your hotel is very near San Marco, deposit your luggage at the station, and pick it up later, after you've seen the Piazza. Seeing the Grand Canal and Piazza San Marco in relative tranquillity will be your reward for getting up at the crack of dawn and doing a little extra planning.

Day 8: Venice

If the Accademia has just whet your appetite for Venetian painting, start out the day by visiting churches and institutions where you can see more of it. For Titian, go to Santa Maria Glorioa dei Frari church and Santa Maria della Salute; for Tintoretto, Scuola Grande di San Rocco; for Bellini, the Frari and San Giovanni e Paolo; for Tiepolo, Ca' Rezzonico, Scuola Grande dei Carmini, and the Gesuati; for Carpaccio, Scuola di San Giorgio; and for Veronese, San Sebastiano. If your taste runs to more modern art, there are the Guggenheim Collection and, down the street from it, the Pinault Collection in the refashioned Punta della Dogana.

In the afternoon, head for the Fondamenta Nuova station to catch a vaporetto to one or more of the outer islands: Murano, where you can shop for Venetian glass and visit a glass museum and workshops; Burano, known for lacemaking and colorful houses; and Torcello, Venice's first inhabited island and home to a beautiful cathedral.

Day 9: Venice

Venice is more than a museum—it's a lively city. The best way to see that aspect of La Serenissima is to pay a visit to the Rialto Market, where the Venetians buy their fruits and vegetables and, most important, their fish, at one of Europe's largest and most varied fish markets. Have lunch in one of the excellent restaurants in the market area.

On your last afternoon in Venice, allow time to sit and enjoy a coffee or spritz in one of the city's lively squares or in a café along the Fondamenta della Misericordia in Cannaregio, simply watching the Venetians go about their daily lives. There's certainly a good deal more art and architecture to see in the city, and if you can't resist squeezing in another few churches, you may want to see Palladio's masterpiece of ecclesiastical architecture, the Redentore church on the Giudecca, or Tullio Lombardo's lyrical Miracoli, a short walk from the San Marco end of the Rialto Bridge.

Day 10: Venice/Departure

Take one last vaporetto trip up the Grand Canal to Piazzale Roma and, after saying good-bye to Venice, catch city bus #5 to the airport.

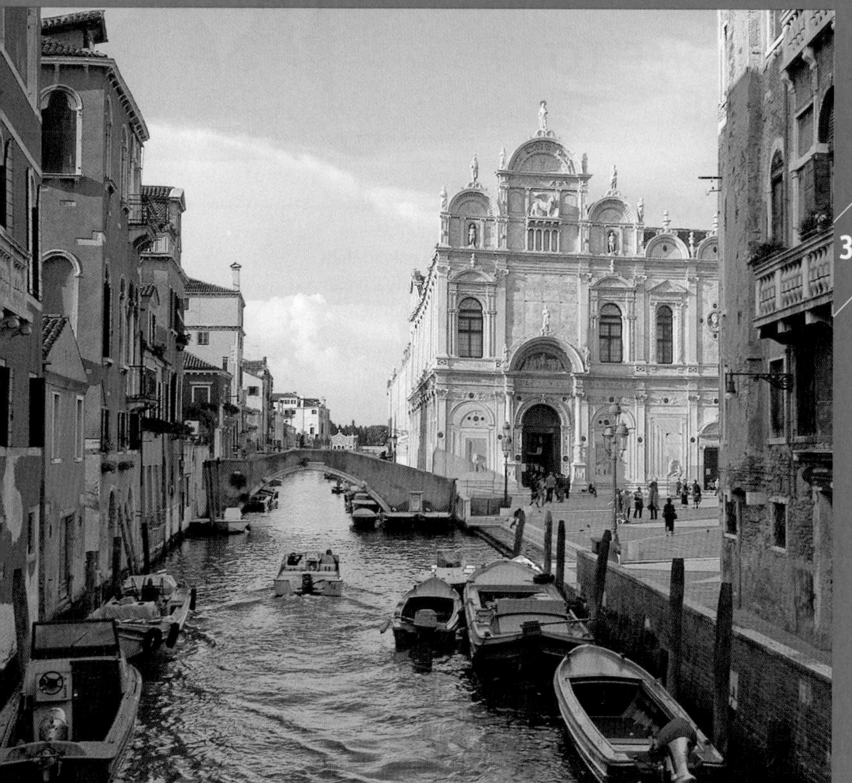

3

Venice

WORD OF MOUTH

"My favorite memory of Venice is just walking the little alleyways in the evening. . . . We happened upon a little bar, ordered a couple glasses of wine and sat outside on the steps of the bridge nearby. As the evening went on, the bar became pretty full of locals, all joining us on the bridge to relax."

—sherhatfield

WELCOME TO VENICE

TOP REASONS TO GO

★ **Basilica di San Marco:** Don't miss the gorgeous mosaics inside. They're worth standing on line for.

★ **Santa Maria Gloriosa dei Frari:** Its austere, cavernous interior houses some of the most beautiful and significant art works in Venice.

★ **Gallerie dell'Accademia:** The world's most extensive collection of Venetian painting is on display at this world-class museum.

★ **Cruising the Grand Canal:** The beauty of its palaces, enhanced by plays of light on the water, make a trip down Venice's main street unforgettable.

★ **Snacking at a bacaro:** For a sample of tasty local cuisine in a uniquely Venetian setting, head for one the city's many wine bars.

1 The Grand Canal. Venice's major thoroughfare is lined with grand palazzi that once housed the city's most prosperous and prominent families.

2 San Marco. The neighborhood at the center of Venice streets is filled with fashion boutiques, art galleries, and grand hotels. Its Piazza San Marco—which Napoléon is said to have called "the drawing room of Europe"—is one of the world most beautiful and elegant urban spaces.

3 Dorsoduro. This elegant residential area is home to the Santa Maria della Salute, the Gallerie dell'Accademia, and the Peggy Guggenheim Collection. The Zattere promenade is one of the best spots to stroll with a gelato or linger at an outdoor café.

4 Santa Croce and San Polo. These bustling *sestieri* (districts) are both residential and commercial, with all sorts of shops and artisan studios, several major sights, and the Rialto fish and produce markets.

5 Cannaregio. Brimming with residential Venetian life, this sestiere provides some of the sunniest open-air canal-side walks in town. The Fondamenta della Misericordia is a hub of restaurants and cafés, and the Jewish Ghetto has a fascinating history and tradition all its own.

6 Castello. Along with Cannaregio, this area is home to most of the locals. With its gardens, park, and narrow, winding walkways, it's the sestiere least influenced by Venice's tourist culture—except when the Biennale art festival is on.

GETTING ORIENTED

Venice proper is divided into six *sestieri*, or districts (the word *sestiere* means, appropriately, "sixth"): Cannaregio, Santa Croce, San Polo, Dorsoduro, San Marco, and Castello. More-sedate outer islands float around them—San Giorgio Maggiore and the Giudecca just to the south, beyond them the Lido, the barrier island; to the north, Murano, Burano, and Torcello.

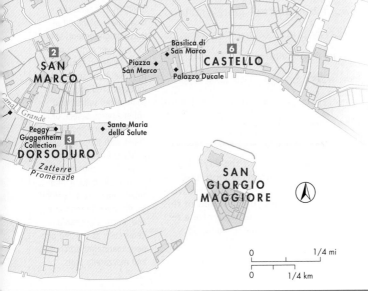

1
Canal Grande
Ca' d'Oro
4
SAN POLO
2
SAN MARCO
Basilica di San Marco
6
Piazza San Marco
CASTELLO
Palazzo Ducale
Canal Grande
Peggy Guggenheim Collection
3
Santa Maria della Salute
DORSODURO
Zatterre Promenade
SAN GIORGIO MAGGIORE

0 1/4 mi
0 1/4 km

EATING AND DRINKING WELL IN VENICE

The catchword in Venetian restaurants is fish, often at its tastiest when it looks like nothing you've seen before. Even if you're not normally a fish fan, it's worth trying here—there's nothing quite like an expertly prepared fish that was, as the vendors like to say, swimming with its brothers only a few hours before. The best restaurants won't even give you a lemon, believing that it masks the pure, fresh flavor.

How do you learn about the catch of the day? A visit to the Rialto's *pescheria* (fish market) is more instructive than any book. And when you're dining at a well-regarded restaurant (such as one you've found in this chapter), don't be reluctant to ask your waiter for a recommendation, either: that's what a local would do.

GOING BACARO

You can sample regional wines and scrumptious *cicchetti* (bite-size snacks) in *bacari* (traditional wine bars), a great Venetian tradition. For centuries, locals have gathered at these neighborhood spots to chat over a glass of *sfuso* (wine on tap) or the ubiquitous spritz: an iridescent red cocktail of white wine, seltzer, and either Aperol, Select, or Bitter liqueur. *Crostini* (toast with toppings) and *polpette* (meat, fish, or vegetable croquettes) are popular cicchetti, as are small sandwiches, seafood salads, baccalà mantecato, and toothpick-speared items such as roasted peppers, marinated artichokes, and mozzarella balls.

3

SEAFOOD

Granseola (crab), *moeche* (soft-shell crab), sweet *canoce* (mantis shrimp), *capelunghe* (razor clams), calamari, and *seppie* or *seppioline* (cuttlefish) are all prominently featured, as well as *rombo* (turbot), *branzino* (sea bass), *San Pietro* (John Dory), *sogliola* (sole), *orate* (gilthead), *triglia* (mullet)—to name but a few of the options. Trademark dishes include *sarde in saor* (panfried sardines with olive oil, vinegar, onions, pine nuts, and raisins), *la frittura mista* (tempura-like fried fish and vegetables), and *baccalà mantecato* (creamed cod with olive oil). When prepared whole, fish is usually priced by the *etto* (100 grams, about 4 ounces) and can be expensive; but once you try it that way, you'll never want filleted fish again.

RISOTTO, PASTA, POLENTA

As a first course, Venetians favor the creamy rice dish risotto *al onda* ("undulating," as opposed to firm), prepared with vegetables or shellfish. Pasta is accompanied by seafood sauces, too: *pasticcio di pesce* is lasagna-type pasta baked with fish, usually *baccalà* (salt cod), and *bigoli* is a strictly local pasta shaped like short, thick spaghetti, usually served *in salsa* (an anchovy sauce), or with *nero di seppia* (squid-ink sauce).

A classic first course is pasta *e fagioli* (bean soup with pasta). Polenta (creamy cornmeal) is another staple;

it's often served with *fegato alla veneziana* (calves' liver and onions) or *schie* (lagoon shrimp).

VEGETABLES

The larger islands of the lagoon are legendary for fine vegetables, such as the Sant'Erasmo *castraure* artichokes that herald spring. Just a few stalls at the Rialto Market sell local crops, but most feature high-quality produce from the surrounding regions. Spring treats are fat white asparagus, and artichoke bottoms (*fondi*), usually sautéed with olive oil, parsley, and garlic. From December to March the prized *radicchio di Treviso* is grilled and used in salads and risottos. Fall brings small wild mushrooms called *chiodini,* and *zucca barucca,* a bumpy squash used in soups and to stuff ravioli.

SWEETS

Tiramisu lovers will have ample opportunity to sample this creamy concoction made from ladyfingers soaked in espresso and covered with sweetened mascarpone cheese—a dessert invented in the Veneto. In addition to sorbets and *semifreddi* (ice cream and cake desserts), other sweets frequently seen on Venetian menus are almond cakes and strudels, as well as dry cookies served with dessert wine. Gelato (ice cream) is sold all over; the best is homemade, labeled *produzione propria* or *fatto in casa.*

Updated by Bruce Leimsidor and Nan McElroy

It's called La Serenissima, "the most serene," a reference to the majesty, wisdom, and impressive power of this city that was for centuries the unrivaled leader in trade between Europe and the Orient, and a major center of European culture. Built entirely on water by a people who saw the sea as a defense and ally, Venice is unlike any other town.

No matter how often you've seen it in photos and films, the real thing is more dreamlike than you could ever imagine. Its landmarks, the Basilica di San Marco and the Palazzo Ducale, are hardly what we normally think of as Italian: fascinatingly idiosyncratic, they are exotic mixes of Byzantine, Romanesque, Gothic, and Renaissance styles. Shimmering sunlight and silvery mist soften every perspective here; it's easy to understand how the city became renowned in the Renaissance for its artists' use of color. It's full of secrets, inexpressibly romantic, and at times given over to sensuous enjoyment.

You'll see Venetians going about their daily affairs in *vaporetti* (water buses), aboard the *traghetti* (gondola ferries) that carry them across the Grand Canal, in the *campi* (squares), and along the *calli* (narrow streets). They are nothing if not skilled—and remarkably tolerant—in dealing with the veritable armies of tourists from all over the world who fill the city's streets.

PLANNING

MAKING THE MOST OF YOUR TIME

The hoards of tourists visiting Venice are legendary, especially in spring and fall, but during other seasons, too—there is really no "off-season" in Venice. Unfortunately, tales of impassible, tourist-packed streets and endless queues to get into the Basilica di San Marco are not exaggerated. A little bit of planning, however, will help you avoid the worst of the crowds.

The majority of tourists do little more than take the *vaporetto* (water bus) down the Grand Canal to Piazza San Marco, see the piazza and the basilica, and walk up to the Rialto and back to the station. You will want to visit these areas, too, but do so in the early morning, before most tourists have finished their breakfast cappuccinos. You can further decrease your competition with other tourists for Venice's pleasures by choosing weekdays, instead of weekends, to visit the city.

Away from San Marco and the Rialto, the streets and quays of Venice's beautiful medieval and Renaissance residential districts receive only a moderate amount of traffic. Besides the Grand Canal and the Piazza San Marco, and perhaps Torcello, the other historically and artistically important sites are seldom overcrowded. Even on weekends you probably won't have to queue up to get into the Accademia museum.

Venice proper is quite compact, and you should be able to walk across it in a couple of hours, counting even a few minutes for getting lost. The water buses will save wear and tear on tired feet, but won't always save you much time.

PASSES AND DISCOUNTS

Avoid lines and save money by booking services and venue entry online with **Venice Connected** (🌐 *veniceconnected.com*). The service was introduced in 2009 and continues to evolve. Currently, you must book at least seven days in advance; discounts depend on arrival dates. For example, during the "medium/low" season, a weeklong vaporetto transit pass is €37.50 instead of €50. Venice Connected guarantees the lowest prices on parking, public transit passes, toilet service, museum passes, Wi-Fi access, and airport transfers. Venice Connected may replace the **VENICEcard** (☎ *041/2424* 🌐 *www.hellovenezia.com*), a pass that provides more comprehensive discounted access to sights and transportation.

Sixteen of Venice's most significant churches are part of the **Chorus Foundation** (☎ *041/2750462* 🌐 *www.chorusvenezia.org*) umbrella group, which coordinates their administration, hours, and admission fees. Churches in the group are open to visitors all day except Sunday morning. Single church entry costs €3; you have a year to visit all 16 with the €10 Chorus Pass. Family and student discounts are also available. Get a pass at any church or online.

The **Museum Pass** (€18) from **Musei Civici** (☎ *041/2715911* 🌐 *www.museicivicivenezianі.it*) includes one-time entry to 12 Venice museums. The **Museums of San Marco Pass Plus** (€13; April–October) is good for the museums on the piazza, plus another civic museum of your choice. The **Museums of San Marco Pass** (€12; November–March) is good only for the piazza's museums. All these passes are discounted at 🌐 *VeniceConnected.com*.

GETTING HERE AND AROUND

AIR TRAVEL

Venice's **Aeroporto Marco Polo** (☎ *041/2609260* 🌐 *www.veniceairport.it*) is 10 km (6 mi) north of the city on the mainland. It's served by domestic and international flights, including connections from 21 European cities, plus direct flights from New York's JFK.

WATER TRANSFERS From Marco Polo terminal it's a mostly covered seven-minute walk to the dock where boats depart for Venice's historic center. **Alilaguna** (☎ *041/2401701* 🌐 *www.alilaguna.it*) has regular ferry service from predawn until nearly midnight. The charge is €13, including bags, and it takes about 1½ hours to reach the landing near Piazza San Marco; some ferries also stop at Fondamente Nove, Murano, Lido, the Cannaregio Canal, and the Rialto. For €25 you can take the one-hour Oro line direct to San Marco. A *motoscafo* (water taxi) carries up to four people and four bags to the city center in a powerboat—with a base cost of €95 for the 25-minute trip. Each additional person, bag, and stop costs extra; it's essential to agree on a fare before boarding.

LAND TRANSFERS Buses run by **ATVO** (☎ *0421/383672* 🌐 *www.atvo.it*) make a quick (20-minute) and cheap (€3) trip from the airport to Piazzale Roma, from where you can get a vaporetto to the stop nearest your hotel. Tickets are sold from machines and at the airport booth in Ground Transportation (open daily 9–7:30), and on the bus when tickets are otherwise unavailable. The public ACTV Bus 5 also runs to the Piazzale Roma in about the same time. Tickets (€ 2.50) are available at the airport ground transportation booth. A taxi to Piazzale Roma costs about €35.

CAR TRAVEL

Venice is at the end of SR11, just off the east–west A4 autostrada. There are no cars in Venice; if possible, return your rental when you arrive.

A warning: don't be waylaid by illegal touts, often wearing fake uniforms, who try to flag you down and offer to arrange parking and hotels; use one of the established garages. Consider reserving a space in advance. The **Autorimessa Comunale** (☎ *041/2727211* 🌐 *www.asmvenezia.it*) costs €24 for 24 hours, less if you book with Venice Connected (🌐 *www.veniceconnected.com*). The **Garage San Marco** (☎ *041/5232213* 🌐 *www.garagesanmarco.it*) costs €24 for up to 12 hours and €30 for 12 to 24 hours with online reservations. On its own island, **Tronchetto** (☎ *041/5207555*) charges €21 for 6 to 24 hours. Watch for signs coming over the bridge—you turn right just before Piazzale Roma. Many hotels and the casino have guest discounts with San Marco or Tronchetto garages. A cheaper alternative is to park in Mestre, on the mainland, and take a train (10 minutes, €1) or bus into Venice. The garage across from the station and the Bus 2 stop costs €8–€10 for 24 hours.

TRAIN TRAVEL

Venice has rail connections with many major cities in Italy and Europe. Note that Venice's train station is **Venezia Santa Lucia,** not to be confused with Venezia-Mestre, which is the mainland stop prior to arriving in the historic center. Some trains do not continue beyond the Mestre station; in such cases you can catch the next Venice-bound train. Get a €1 ticket from the newsstand on the platform and validate it (in the yellow time-stamp machine) to avoid a fine.

VISITOR INFORMATION

The multilingual staff of the **Venice tourism office** (☎ *041/5298711* 🌐 *www.turismovenezia.it*) can provide directions and up-to-the-minute information. Its free, quarterly *Show and Events Calendar* lists current happenings and venue hours. Tourist office branches are at Marco Polo Airport; the Venezia Santa Lucia train station; Garage Comunale, on Piazzale Roma; at Piazza San Marco near Museo Correr at the southwest corner; the Venice Pavilion (including a Venice-centered

PUBLIC TRANSPORTATION IN VENICE

WATER BUSES

Venice's primary public transportation is the *vaporetto* (water bus). The **ACTV** (☎ *041/2424* 🌐 *www.hellovenezia.com*) operates *vaporetti* on routes throughout the city. Beginning at about 11:30 pm there is limited, but fairly frequent, night service. Although most landings are well marked, the system takes some getting used to; check before boarding to make sure the boat is going in your desired direction. Line 1 is the Grand Canal local, making all stops and continuing via San Marco to the Lido. The trip takes about 35 minutes from Ferrovia to San Marco. Line 2 travels up the Grand Canal (with fewer stops), down the Giudecca Canal to San Zaccaria, and back again (continuing to Lido in summer).

A single ticket for all lines costs €6.50, and is good for 60 minutes one-way. A better option is a Travel Pass: €16 for 12 hours, €18 for 24 hours, €33 for 72 hours, and €50 for a week of unlimited travel. Travelers ages 14–29 can opt for the €4 Rolling Venice card (available from the HelloVenezia booth at principal vaporetto stops), which allows 72 hours of travel for €18. A ticket to take the vaporetto one stop across the Grand Canal is €2. ■ **TIP→ The best discounts are available in advance through** 🌐 *VeniceConnected.com.*

Line information is posted at each landing, and complete timetables are available at ACTV ticket booths and at most major stops, and are free for download at 🌐 *HelloVenezia.com.* ■ **TIP→ If you board without a valid ticket, ask immediately to buy one on board to avoid a €35 fine.** The law says you must buy tickets for bags more than 28 inches long (the charge is waived if you have a Travel Pass), but this is generally enforced only for very bulky bags. If you are sitting in the open-air front seats, do not stand up while in transit, as this blocks the driver's view.

WATER TAXIS

A *motoscafo* (water taxi) isn't cheap: you'll spend about €60 for a short trip in town, €75 to the Lido, and €90 per hour to visit the outer islands. The fare system is convoluted, with luggage handling, waiting time, early or late hours, and even ordering a taxi from your hotel adding expense. However, a water taxi can carry up to 14 passengers, so if you're traveling in a group, it may not that much more expensive than a vaporetto. Always agree on the price before departing.

TRAGHETTI

Many tourists are unaware of these two-man gondola ferries that cross the Grand Canal at or near many gondola stations. At €0.50, they're the cheapest and shortest gondola ride in Venice—and can also save a lot of walking. Look for "Traghetto" signs and hand your fare to the gondolier when you board; they're marked on many maps. Stand up in these gondolas, straddling the width to keep your balance, unless the gondolier tells you otherwise. Most traghetti operate only in the morning.

bookstore), on the *riva (canal-front street)* between the San Marco vaporetto stop and the Royal Gardens; and on the Lido at the main vaporetto stop. The train-station branch is open daily 8–6:30; other branches generally open at 9:30.

PIAZZA SAN MARCO

One of the world's most beautiful squares, Piazza San Marco (Saint Mark's Square) is the spiritual and artistic heart of Venice, a vast open space bordered by an orderly procession of arcades marching toward the fairy-tale cupolas and marble lacework of the Basilica di San Marco. From mid-morning on it is generally packed with tourists. (If Venetians have business in the piazza, they try to conduct it in the early morning, before the crowds swell.) At night it can be magical, especially in winter, when mists swirl around the lampposts and the campanile.

If you face the basilica from in front of the Correr Museum, you'll notice that rather than being a strict rectangle, the square is wider at the basilica end, creating the illusion that it's even larger than it is. On your left, the long, arcaded building is the Procuratie Vecchie, renovated to their present form in 1514 as offices and residences for the powerful procurators (magistrates). On your right is the Procuratie Nuove, built half a century later in a more imposing, classical style. It was originally planned by Venice's great Renaissance architect, Jacopo Sansovino (1486–1570), to carry on the look of his Libreria Sansoviniana (Sansovinian Library), but he died before construction on the Nuove had begun. Vincenzo Scamozzi (circa 1552–1616), a pupil of Andrea Palladio (1508–80), completed the design and construction. Still later, the Procuratie Nuove was modified by architect Baldassare Longhena (1598–1682), one of Venice's baroque masters.

When Napoléon (1769–1821) entered Venice with his troops in 1797, he called Piazza San Marco "the drawing room of Europe"—and promptly gave orders to alter it. His architects demolished a church with a Sansovino facade in order to build the Ala Napoleonica (Napoleonic Wing), or Fabbrica Nuova (New Building), which linked the two 16th-century *procuratie* (procurators' offices) and effectively enclosed the piazza.

Piazzetta San Marco is the "little square" leading from Piazza San Marco to the waters of Bacino San Marco (Saint Mark's Basin); its *molo* (landing) once served as the grand entrance to the Republic. Two imposing columns tower above the waterfront. One is topped by the winged lion, a traditional emblem of Saint Mark that became the symbol of Venice itself; the other supports Saint Theodore, the city's first patron, along with his dragon. (A third column fell off its barge and ended up in the bacino before it could be placed alongside the others.) Though the columns are a glorious vision today, the Republic traditionally executed convicts between them. Even today, some superstitious Venetians avoid walking between the two columns.

Continued on page 184

CRUISING THE GRAND CANAL

THE BEST INTRODUCTION TO VENICE IS A TRIP DOWN MAIN STREET

Venice's Grand Canal is one of the world's great thoroughfares. It winds its way in the shape of a backward "S" from Ferrovia (the train station) to Piazza San Marco, passing 200 palazzos born of a culture obsessed with opulence and fantasy. There's a theatrical quality to a boat ride on the canal: it's as if each pink- or gold-tinted facade is trying to steal your attention from its rival across the way.

The palaces were built from the 12th to 18th centuries by the city's richest families. A handful are still private residences, but many have been converted to other uses, including museums, hotels, government offices, university buildings, a post office, a casino, and even a television station.

It's romantic to see the canal from a gondola, but the next best thing, at a fraction of the cost, is to take the Line 1 *vaporetto* (water bus) from Ferrovia to San Marco. The ride costs €6 and takes about 35 minutes. Invest in a Travel Card (€15 buys 24 hours of unlimited passage) and you can spend the better part of a day hopping on and off at the vaporetto's 16 stops, visiting the sights along the banks.

Either way, keep your eyes open for the highlights listed here; the major sites also have fuller descriptions later in this chapter.

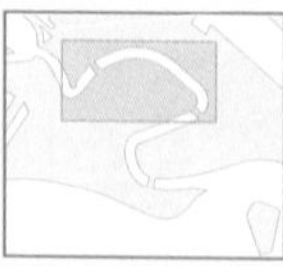

FROM FERROVIA TO RIALTO

Palazzo Labia
On September 3, 1951, during the Venice Film Festival, the Palazzo Labia hosted what's been dubbed "the party of the century." The Aga Khan, Winston Churchill, Orson Welles, and Salvador Dalì were among those who donned 18th-century costume and danced in the Tiepolo-frescoed ballroom.

Santa Maria di Nazareth

Ponte di Scalzi

R. Di BIASIO

FERROVIA

Stazione Ferrovia Santa Lucia

SANTA CROCE

As you head out from Ferrovia, the baroque church immediately to your left is . Its shoeless friars earned it the nickname Chiesa degli Scalzi (Church of the Barefoot).

One of the four bridges over the Grand Canal is the . The original version was built of iron in 1858; the existing stone bridge dates from 1934.

After passing beneath the Ponte di Scalzi, ahead to the left you'll spy , one of the most imposing buildings in Venice, looming over the bell tower of the church of San Geremia.

A hundred yards or so further along on the left bank, the uncompleted façade of the church of gives you an idea of what's behind the marble decorations of similar 18th-century churches in Venice. Across the canal, flanked by two *torricelle* (side wings in the shape of small towers) and a triangular *merlatura* (crenellation), is the one of the oldest Byzantine palaces in Venice; it's now a natural history museum. Next comes the plain brick , a 15th-century granary—note the lion marking it as Serenissima property—and beyond it the obelisk-topped . Both are upstaged by the on the opposite bank: this Renaissance gem was built in the 1480s, at a time when late-Gothic was still the prevailing style. A gilded banner identifies the palazzo as site of Venice's casino.

The white, whimsically baroque church of on the right bank is distinguished by a host of

Palazzo Vendramin-Calergi
The German composer Richard Wagner died in Palazzo Vendramin-Calergi in 1883, soon after the success of his opera Parsifal. His room has been preserved—you can visit it on Saturday mornings by appointment.

CANNAREGGIO

Church of San Marcuola

GHETTO

S. MARCUOLA

Ca' Belloni-Battagia

S. STAE

Ca' Pesaro

Ca' d'Oro
Ca' d'Oro means "house of gold," but the gold is long gone—the gilding that once accentuated the marble carvings of the facade has worn away over time.

Fondaco dei Turchi

Depositi del Megio

San Stae Church

CA' D'ORO

SAN POLO

Ca' Corner della Regina

Pescheria
The pescheria has been in operation for over 1,000 years. Stop by in the morning to see the exotic fish for sale—one of which may wind up on your dinner plate. Produce stalls fill the adjacent *fondamenta*, and butchers and cheesemongers occupy the surrounding shops.

Rialto Mercato

Fondaco dei Tedeschi

Ca' dei Camerlenghi

RIALTO

SAN MARCO

marble saints on its facade. Further along the bank is another baroque showpiece, , followed by the tall, balconied . Next up on the left is the flamboyant pink-and-white , arguably the finest example of Venetian Gothic design.

Across from Ca' d'Oro is the loggia-like, neo-Gothic , Venice's fish market, where boats dock in the morning to deliver their catch.

The canal narrows as you approach the impressive Rialto Bridge. To the left, just before the bridge, is the i. This was once the busiest trading center of the republic—German, Austrian, and Hungarian merchants kept warehouses and offices here; today it's the city's main post office. Across the canal stands the curiously angled . Built in 1525 to accommodate the State Treasury, it had a jail for tax evaders on the ground floor.

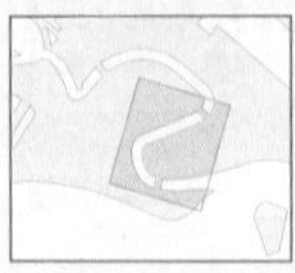

FROM RIALTO TO THE PONTE DELL' ACCADEMIA

SAN POLO

Ponte di Rialto

RIALTO

Ca' Foscari

Positioned at one of the busiest junctures along the Grand Canal, Ca' Foscari was recently restored after suffering severe foundation damage as a result of the relentless wake from passing boats.

Palazzo Barzizza

Ca' Loredan

S. SILVESTRO

Ca' Farsetti

Palazzo Pisani Moretta

Ca' Grimani

S. ANGELO

TOMA

Ca' Garzoni

Ca' Corner-Spinelli

If Ca' Corner-Spinelli has a familiar look, that's because it became a prototype for later Grand Canal buildings—and because its architect, Mauro Codussi, himself copied the windows from Palazzo Vendramin-Calergi.

Palazzo Grassi

Palazzo Falier

Palazzo Falier is said to have been the home of Doge Martin Fallier, who was beheaded for treason in 1355.

Ca' Rezzonico

REZZONICO

SAN MARCO

ACCADEMIA

Gallerie dell'Accademia

DORSODURO

Until the 19th century, the shop-lined **Ponte di Rialto** was the only bridge across the Grand Canal.

Rialto is the only point along the Grand Canal where buildings don't have their primary entrances directly on the water, a consequence of the two spacious *rive* (waterside paths) once used for unloading two Venetian staples: coal and wine. On your left along Riva del Carbon stand **Ca' Loredan** and **Ca' Farsetti**, 13th-century Byzantine palaces that today make up Venice's city hall. Just past the San Silvestro vaporetto landing on Riva del Vin is the 12th- and 13th-century facade of **Palazzo Barzizza**, an elegant example of Veneto-Byzantine architecture that managed to survive a complete renovation in the 17th century. Across the water, the sternly Renaissance **Ca' Grimani** has an intimidating presence that seems appropriate for today's Court of Appeals. At the Sant'Angelo landing, the vaporetto passes close to another massive Renaissance palazzo, **Ca' Corner-Spinelli**.

Back on the right bank, in a salmon color that seems to vary with the time of day, is elegant **Palazzo Pisani Moretta**, with twin water entrances. To your left, four-storied **Ca' Garzoni**, part of the Universita di Venezia Ca' Foscari, stands beside the San Toma *traghetto* (gondola ferry), which has operated since 1354. The boat makes a sharp turn and, on the right, passes one of the city's tallest Gothic palaces, **Ca' Foscari**.

The vaporetto passes baroque **Ca' Rezzonico** so closely that you get to look inside one of the most fabulous entrances along the canal. Opposite stands the Grand Canal's youngest palace, **Palazzo Grassi**, commissioned in 1749. Just beyond Grassi and Campo San Samuele, the first house past the garden was once Titian's studio. It's followed by **Palazzo Falier**, identifiable by its twin loggias (windowed porches).

Approaching the canal's fourth and final bridge, the vaporetto stops at a former church and monastery complex that houses the world-renowned **Gallerie dell'Accademia**.

The wooden pilings on which Venice was built (you can see them at the bases of the buildings along the Grand Canal) have gradually hardened into mineral form.

ARCHITECTURAL STYLES ALONG THE GRAND CANAL

BYZANTINE: 12th and 13th centuries. **Distinguishing characteristics:** high, rounded arches, relief panels, multicolored marble. **Examples:** Fondaco dei Turchi, Ca' Loredan, Ca' Farsetti, Palazzo Barzizza (and, off the canal, Basilica di San Marco).

GOTHIC: 14th and 15th centuries. **Distinguishing characteristics:** Pointed arches, high ceilings, and many windows. **Examples:** Ca' d'Oro, Ca' Foscari, Ca' Franchetti, Palazzo Falier (and, off the canal, Palazzo Ducale).

RENAISSANCE: 16th century. **Distinguishing characteristics:** classically influenced emphasis on order, achieved through symmetry and balanced proportions. **Examples:** Palazzo Vendramin-Calergi, Ca' Grimani, Ca' Corner-Spinelli, Ca' dei Camerlenghi (and, off the canal, Libreria Sansoviniana on Piazza San Marco and the church of San Giorgio Maggiore).

BAROQUE: 17th century. **Distinguishing characteristics:** Renaissance order wedded with a more dynamic style, achieved through curving lines and complex decoration. **Examples:** churches of Santa Maria di Nazareth and San Stae, Ca' Pesaro, Ca' Rezzonico (and, off the canal, the church of Santa Maria della Salute).

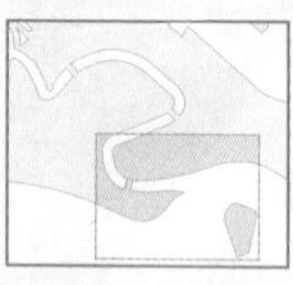

FROM THE PONTE DELL'ACCADEMIA TO SAN ZACCARIA

Ca' Franchetti
Until the late 19th century, Ca' Franchetti was a *squero* (gondola workshop). A few active *squeri* remain, though none are on the Grand Canal. The most easily spotted is Squero di San Trovaso, in Dorsoduro on a small canal near the Zattere boat landing.

Ca' Barbaro
Monet, Henry James, and Cole Porter are among the guests who have stayed at Ca' Barbaro. Porter later lived aboard a boat in Giudecca Canal.

SAN MARCO

Ponte dell' Accademia

Casetta Rossa

Ca' Pisani-Gritti

ACCADEMIA

S. M. DEL GIGLIO

DORSODURO

Ca' Barbarigo

SALUTE

Palazzo Salviati

S. Maria della Salute

Palazzo Venier dei Leoni
When she was in residence at Palazzo Venier dei Leoni, Peggy Guggenheim kept her private gondola parked at the door and left her dogs standing guard (in place of Venetian lions).

Ca' Dario
However tilted Dario might be, it has outlasted its many owners, who seem plagued by misfortune. They include the Italian industrialist Raul Gardini, whose 1992 suicide followed charges of corruption and an unsuccessful bid to win the America's Cup.

The wooden **Ponte dell' Accademia**, like the Eiffel Tower (with which it shares a certain structural grace), wasn't intended to be permanent. Erected in 1933 as a quick replacement for a rusting iron bridge built by the Austrian military in 1854, it was so well liked by Venetians that they kept it. (A perfect replica, with steel bracing, was installed 1986.)

You're only three stops from the end of the Grand Canal, but this last stretch is packed with sights. The lovely **Ca' Franchetti**, with a central balcony made in the style of Palazzo Ducale's loggia, dates from the late Gothic period, but its gardens are no older than the cedar tree standing at their center.

Ca' Barbaro, next door to Ca' Franchetti, was the residence of the illustrious family who rebuilt the church of Santa Maria del Giglio.

Farther along on the left bank, a garden, vibrant with flowers in summer, surrounds **Casetta Rossa** (small red house) as if it were the centerpiece of its bouquet. Across the canal, bright 19th-century mosaics on **Ca' Barbarigo** give you some idea how the frescoed facades of many Venetian palaces must have looked in their heyday. A few doors down are the lush gardens within the walls of the unfinished **Palazzo Venier dei Leoni**, which holds the **Peggy Guggenheim Collection** of contemporary art.

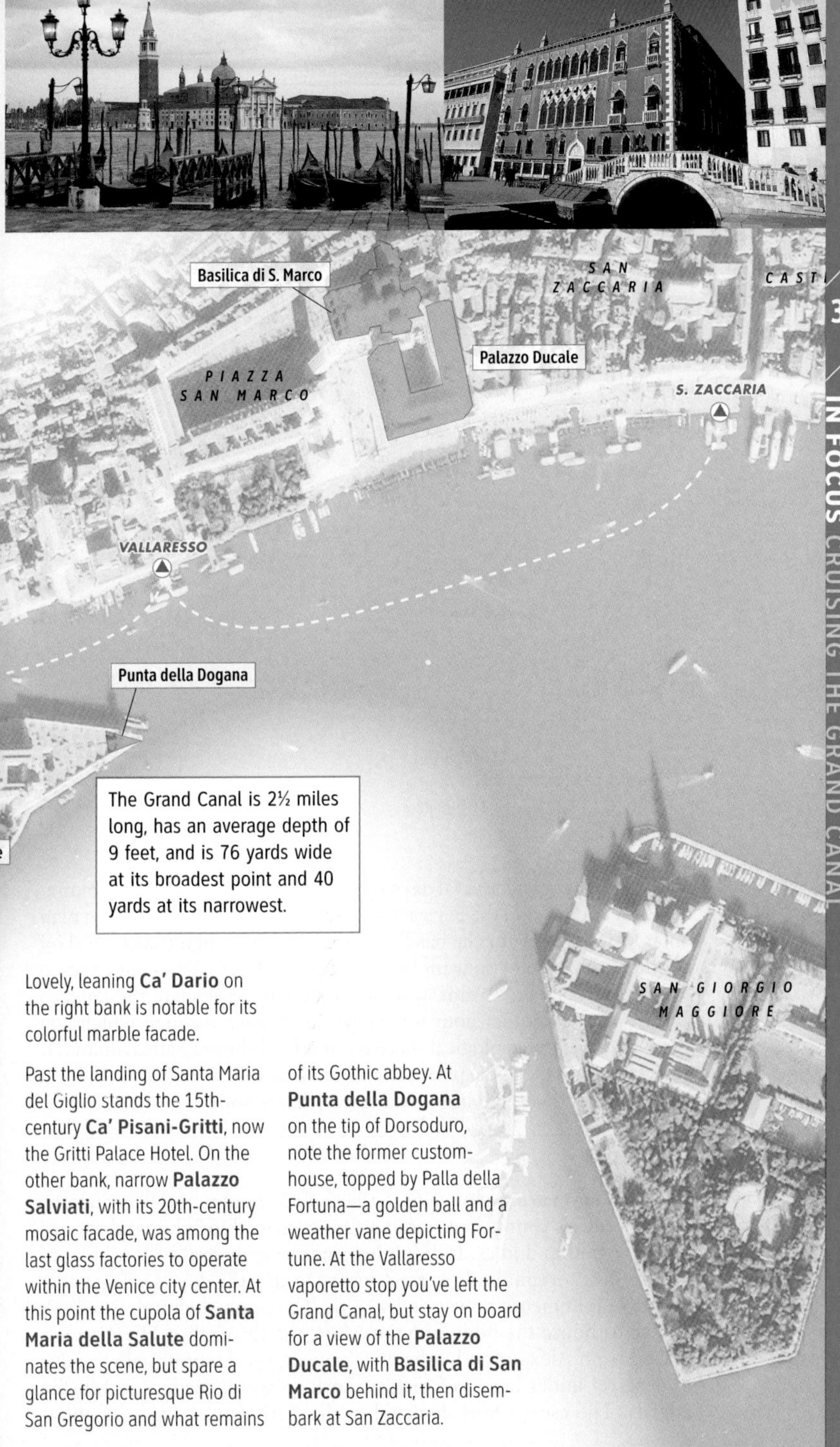

The Grand Canal is 2½ miles long, has an average depth of 9 feet, and is 76 yards wide at its broadest point and 40 yards at its narrowest.

Lovely, leaning **Ca' Dario** on the right bank is notable for its colorful marble facade.

Past the landing of Santa Maria del Giglio stands the 15th-century **Ca' Pisani-Gritti**, now the Gritti Palace Hotel. On the other bank, narrow **Palazzo Salviati**, with its 20th-century mosaic facade, was among the last glass factories to operate within the Venice city center. At this point the cupola of **Santa Maria della Salute** dominates the scene, but spare a glance for picturesque Rio di San Gregorio and what remains of its Gothic abbey. At **Punta della Dogana** on the tip of Dorsoduro, note the former customhouse, topped by Palla della Fortuna—a golden ball and a weather vane depicting Fortune. At the Vallaresso vaporetto stop you've left the Grand Canal, but stay on board for a view of the **Palazzo Ducale**, with **Basilica di San Marco** behind it, then disembark at San Zaccaria.

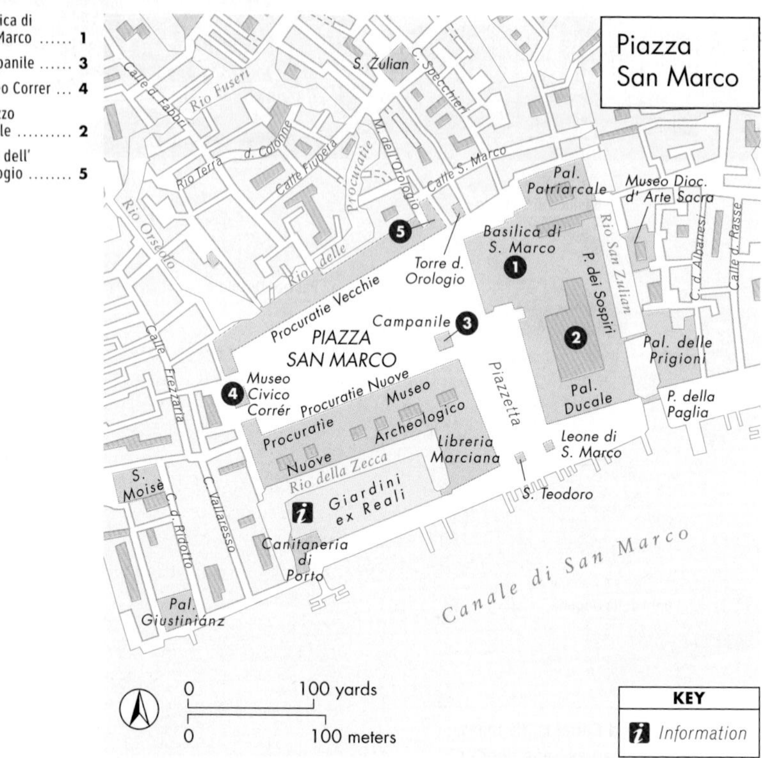

TIMING

You can easily spend several days seeing the historical and artistic monuments in and around the Piazza San Marco, but at a bare minimum plan on at least an hour for the basilica, with its wonderful mosaics. Add on another half hour if you want to see its Pala d'Oro, Galleria, and Museo di San Marco. You'll want at least an hour to appreciate the Palazzo Ducale. Leave another hour for the Museo Correr, through which you enter also the archaeological museum and the Libreria Sansoviniana. If you choose to take in the piazza itself from a café table with an orchestra, keep in mind there will be an additional charge for the music.

TOP ATTRACTIONS

Fodor's Choice ★ **Basilica di San Marco.** An opulent synthesis of Byzantine and Romanesque styles, Venice's gem is laid out in a Greek-cross floor plan and topped with five plump domes. It didn't become the cathedral of Venice until 1807, but its original role as the *Chiesa Ducale* (the doge's private chapel) gave it immense power and wealth. The original church was built in 828 to house the body of Saint Mark the Evangelist. His remains, filched from Alexandria by the doge's agents, were supposedly hidden in a barrel under layers of pickled pork to sneak them past Muslim guards. The escapade is depicted in the 13th-century mosaic above the door farthest left of the front entrance, one of the earliest mosaics on the heavily decorated facade; look closely to see the church as it appeared at that time.

A 976 fire destroyed most of the original church. It was rebuilt and reopened in 1094, and for centuries it would serve as a symbol of Venetian wealth and power, endowed with all the riches admirals and merchants could carry off from the Orient, to the point where it earned the nickname "Chiesa d'Oro" (Golden Church). The four bronze horses that prance and snort over the doorway are copies of sculptures that victorious Venetians took from Constantinople in 1204 after the fourth crusade (the originals are upstairs in the Museo di San Marco). The rich, colorful exterior decorations, including the numerous different marble columns, all came from the same source. Look for a medallion of red porphyry in the floor of the porch inside the main door. It marks the spot where, in 1177, Doge Sebastiano Ziani orchestrated the reconciliation between Barbarossa—the Holy Roman emperor—and Pope Alexander III. Dim lighting, galleries high above the naves—they served as the *matroneum* (women's gallery)—the *iconostasis* (altar screen), and the single massive Byzantine chandelier all seem to wed Christianity with the Orient, giving San Marco its exotic blend of majesty and mystery.

The basilica is famous for its 43,055 square feet of mosaics, which run from floor to ceiling thanks to an innovative roof of brick vaulting. Many of the original windows were filled in to make room for even more artwork. At midday, when the interior is fully illuminated, the mosaics truly come alive, the shimmer of their tiny gold tiles becoming nothing short of magical. The earliest mosaics are from the 11th and 12th centuries, and the last were added in the early 1700s. One of the most recent is the *Last Judgment,* believed to have been designed by Tintoretto (1518–94), on the arch between the porch and the nave. Inside the main entrance, turn right on the porch to see the Book of Genesis depicted on the ceiling. Ahead through a glass door, 13th-century mosaics depict Saint Mark's life in the **Cappella Zen** (Zen Chapel). The **Cappella della Madonna di Nicopeia,** in the left transept, holds the altar icon that many consider Venice's most powerful protector. In nearby **Cappella della Madonna dei Mascoli,** the life of the Virgin Mary is depicted in fine 15th-century mosaics that are believed to be based on drawings by Jacopo Bellini (1400–71) and Andrea Mantegna (1431–1506).

In the **Santuario** (Sanctuary), the main altar is built over the tomb of Saint Mark, its green marble canopy lifted high on carved alabaster columns. Perhaps even more impressive is the **Pala d'Oro,** a dazzling gilt silver screen encrusted with 1,927 precious gems and 255 enameled panels. Originally commissioned (976–978) in Constantinople by Doge Orseolo I, it was enlarged and embellished over four centuries by master craftsmen and wealthy merchants. The bronze door leading from the sanctuary into the sacristy is by Jacopo Sansovino. In the top left corner the artist included a self-portrait, and above that, he pictured friend and fellow artist Titian (1485–1576). The **Tesoro** (Treasury), entered from the right transept, contains many treasures carried home from conquests abroad.

Climb the steep stairway to the **Galleria** and the **Museo di San Marco** for the best overview of the basilica's interior. From here you can step outdoors for a sweeping panorama of Piazza San Marco and out over the lagoon to San Giorgio. The displays focus mainly on the types of mosaic and how they have been restored over the years. But the highlight is a close-up view of the original gilt bronze horses that were once on the outer gallery. The four were most probably cast in Rome and taken to Constantinople, where the Venetians pillaged them after sacking that city. When Napoléon sacked Venice in 1797, he took them to Paris. They were returned after the fall of the French Empire, but came home "blind"—their big ruby eyes had been sold.

Be aware that guards at the basilica door turn away anyone with bare shoulders, midriff, or knees: no shorts, short skirts, or tank tops are allowed. Volunteers offer free, guided tours in English from April to October—look for the calendar to the right of the center entrance, or get more info by calling the phone number below. ■ **TIP→ To skip the line at the Basilica entrance, reserve your arrival—at no extra cost—on the Basilica Web site** ✉ *Piazza San Marco, San Marco 328* ☎ *041/2708311 basilica, 041/2413817 (10–noon weekdays) tour info* 🌐 *www.basilicasanmarco.it* 🎫 *Basilica free, Tesoro €2, Santuario and Pala d'Oro €1.50, Galleria and Museo di San Marco €3* ⏲ *May–Sept., Mon.–Sat. 9:45–5, Sun. 2–5; Oct.–Apr., Mon.–Sat. 9:45–5, Sun. 2–4. Last entry 1 hr before closing; interior illuminated Mon.–Sat. 11:30–12:30, Sun. 2–5* Ⓥ *Vallaresso/San Zaccaria.*

Fodor's Choice ★ **Palazzo Ducale** *(Doge's Palace)*. Rising above the Piazzetta San Marco, this Gothic fantasia of pink-and-white marble is a majestic expression of Venetian prosperity and power. While the site was the doge's residence from the 10th century, the building began to take its present form around 1340; what you seen now is essentially a product of the first half of the 15th century. It served not only as the doge's residence, it was also the central administrative center of the Venetian Republic.

The Palazzo Ducale took so long to finish that by the time it was completed, around 1450, it was already a bit out of fashion. It barely predates the main gate of the Arsenale, built in 1460 in fully conceived Renaissance classical style. The Venetians, however, even later on, were not disturbed by their palazzo's dated look. In the 1570s the upper floors were destroyed by fire and Palladio submitted an up-to-date design for its reconstruction, but the Venetians refused his offer and insisted on reconstruction "*come era, dove era*" (as it was, where it was).

Unlike other medieval seats of authority, the Palazzo Ducale is free of any military defenses—a sign of the Republic's self-confidence. The position of the loggias below instead of above the retaining wall, and the use of pink marble to emphasize the decorative function of that wall, gave the palazzo a light and airy aspect, one that could impress visitors—and even intimidate them, though through opulence and grace rather than fortresslike bulk. Near the basilica you'll see Giovanni and Bartolomeo Bon's Gothic **Porta della Carta** (Gate of the Paper), built between 1438 and 1442, where official decrees were traditionally posted, but you enter the palazzo under the portico facing the water. You'll find yourself in an immense courtyard that holds some of the first evidence of Renaissance architecture in Venice, Antonio Rizzo's **Scala dei Giganti** (Stairway of the Giants), erected between 1483 and 1491, directly ahead, guarded by Sansovino's huge statues of Mars and Neptune, added in 1567. Though ordinary mortals must use the central interior staircase, its upper flight is the lavishly gilded **Scala d'Oro** (Golden Staircase), designed also by Sansovino in 1555. The palace's sumptuous chambers have walls and ceilings covered with works by Venice's greatest artists. Visit the **Anticollegio,** a waiting room outside the Collegio's chamber, where you can see the *Rape of Europa* by Veronese and Tintoretto's *Bacchus and Ariadne Crowned by Venus.* Veronese also painted the ceiling of the adjacent **Sala del Collegio.** The ceiling of the **Sala del Senato** (Senate Chamber), featuring *The Triumph of Venice* by Tintoretto, is magnificent, but it's dwarfed by his masterpiece *Paradise* in the **Sala del Maggiore Consiglio** (Great Council Hall). A vast work commissioned for a vast hall, this dark, dynamic piece is the world's largest oil painting (23 by 75 feet). The room's carved gilt ceiling is breathtaking, especially with Veronese's majestic *Apotheosis of Venice* filling one of the center panels. Around the upper walls, study the portraits of the first 76 doges, and you'll notice one picture is missing near the left corner of the wall opposite *Paradise.* A black painted curtain, rather than a portrait, marks Doge Marin Falier's fall from grace; he was beheaded for treason in 1355, which the Latin inscription bluntly explains.

A narrow canal separates the palace's east side from the cramped cell blocks of the **Prigioni Nuove** (New Prisons). High above the water arches the enclosed marble **Ponte dei Sospiri** (Bridge of Sighs), which earned its name in the 19th century, from Lord Byron's *Childe Harold's Pilgrimage.*" **■TIP→ Reserve your spot for the palazzo's popular Secret Itineraries tour well in advance.** You'll visit the doge's private apartments, through hidden passageways to the interrogation (torture) chambers, and into the rooftop *piombi* (lead) prison, named for its lead roofing. Venetian-born writer and libertine Giacomo Casanova (1725–98), along with an accomplice, managed to escape from the piombi in 1756; they were the only men ever to do so. ✉ *Piazzetta San Marco* ☎ *041/2715911, 041/5209070 Secret Itineraries tour* 🌐 *www.museicivicivenezianі.it* 🎫 *Museums of San Marco Pass €12 (Nov.–Mar.) or €13 (Apr.–Oct.), Musei Civici Pass €18, Secret Itineraries tour €18* ⏲ *Apr.–Oct., daily 9–7; Nov.–Mar., daily 9–5. Last entry 1 hr before closing* Ⓥ *San Zaccaria, Vallaresso.*

QUICK BITES

Caffè Florian (☎ *041/5205641*), in the piazza's Procuratie Nuove, has served coffee to the likes Goldoni, Wagner, Casanova, Charles Dickens, and Marcel Proust. It's Venice's oldest café, continuously in business since 1720 (though you'll find it closed Wednesday in winter). Counter seating is less expensive than taking a table, especially when there's live music. In the Procuratie Vecchie, Caffè Quadri (☎ *041/5289299*) exudes almost as much history as Florian across the way, and is similarly pricey. It was shunned by 19th-century Venetians when the occupying Austrians made it their gathering place. In winter it closes on Monday.

WORTH NOTING

Campanile. Venice's famous brick bell tower (325 feet tall, plus the angel) had been standing nearly 1,000 years when in 1902, practically without warning, it collapsed, taking with it Jacopo Sansovino's 16th-century marble loggia at the base (the largest original bell, called the *marangona*, remains). The crushed loggia was promptly restored, and the new tower, rebuilt to the old plan, reopened in 1912. In the 15th century, clerics found guilty of immoral behavior were suspended in wooden cages from the tower, some forced to subsist on bread and water for as long as a year, others left to starve. The stunning view from the tower on a clear day includes the Lido, the lagoon, and the mainland as far as the Alps, but, strangely enough, none of the myriad canals that snake through the city. ✉ *Piazza San Marco* ☎ *041/5224064* *€8* *Easter–June, Oct., and Nov., daily 9–7; July–Sept., daily 9–9; Nov.–Easter, daily 9–3:45. Last entry 1 hr before closing* V *Vallaresso, San Zaccaria.*

Museo Correr. Exhibits in this museum of Venetian art and history range from the absurdly high-sole shoes worn by 16th-century Venetian ladies (who walked with the aid of a servant) to the huge *Grande Pianta Prospettica* by Jacopo de' Barbari (circa 1440–1515), which details in carved wood every nook and cranny of 16th-century Venice. The city's proud naval history is evoked in several rooms through highly descriptive paintings and numerous maritime objects, including ships' cannons and some surprisingly large iron mast-top navigation lights. The Correr has a room devoted entirely to antique games, and its second-floor **Quadreria** (Picture Gallery) has works by Venetian, Greek, and Flemish painters. The Correr exhibition rooms lead directly into the **Museo Archeologico** and the **Stanza del Sansovino,** the only part of the **Biblioteca Nazionale Marciana** open to visitors. ✉ *Piazza San Marco, Ala Napoleonica (opposite the basilica)* ☎ *041/2405211* *www.museiciviciveneziani.it* *Museums of San Marco Pass €12 (Nov.–Mar.) or €13 (Apr.–Oct.), Musei Civici Pass €18* *Apr.–Oct., daily 9–7; Nov.–Mar., daily 9–5. Last entry 1 hr before closing* V *Vallaresso, San Zaccaria.*

Torre dell'Orologio. Five hundred years ago, when this enameled clock was built, twin Moor figures would strike the hour, and three wise men with an angel would walk out and bow to the Virgin Mary on Epiphany (January 6) and during Ascension Week (40 days after Easter). An inscription on the tower reads "Horas non numero nisi serenas" ("I only count happy hours"). After years of painstaking work, the clock tower has been reassembled and returned to its former glory. Visits in English are offered daily and must be booked in advance at the Museo Correr or online. ✉ *North side of Piazza San Marco at the Merceria* ☎ *041/5209070* *www.museiciviciveneziani.it* *€12* *Tours in English Mon.–Wed. at 10 and 11; Thurs.–Sun. at 2 and 3* V *Vallaresso, San Zaccaria.*

VENICE THROUGH THE AGES

BEGINNINGS

Venice was founded in the 5th century when the Veneti, inhabitants of the mainland region roughly corresponding to today's lower Veneto, fled their homes to escape invading Lombards. The unlikely city, built on islands in the lagoon and atop wooden posts driven into the marshes, would evolve into a maritime republic lasting over a thousand years.

After liberating the Adriatic from marauding pirates, its early fortunes grew as a result of its active role in the Crusades, beginning in 1095 and culminating in the Venetian-led sacking of Constantinople in 1204. The defeat of rival Genoa in the Battle of Chioggia (1380) established Venice as the dominant sea power in Europe.

EARLY DEMOCRACY

As early as the 7th century, Venice was governed by a participatory democracy, with a ruler, the doge, elected to a lifetime term. Beginning in the 12th century, the doge's power was increasingly subsumed by a growing number of councils, commissions, and magistrates. In 1268 a complicated procedure for the doge's election was established to prevent nepotism, but by that point power rested foremost with the Great Council, which at times numbered as many as 2,000 members.

Laws were passed by the Senate, a group of 200 elected from the Great Council; executive powers belonged to the College, a committee of 25. In 1310 the Council of Ten was formed to protect state security. When circumstances dictated, the doge could expedite decision making by consulting only the Council of Ten. To avoid too great a concentration of power, these 10 served only one year and belonged to different families.

A LONG DECLINE

Venice reached the height of its wealth and territorial expansion in the early 15th century, during which time its domain included all of the Veneto region and part of Lombardy, but the seeds of its decline were soon to be sown, with the fall of Constantinople to the Turks in 1453.

By the beginning of the 16th century, the pope, threatened by Venice's mainland expansion, organized the League of Cambrai, defeated Venice in 1505, and effectively put a stop to the Republic's mainland territorial designs. The Ottoman Empire blocked Venice's Mediterranean trade routes, and newly emerging sea powers such as Britain and the Netherlands ended Venice's monopoly by opening oceanic trading routes.

When Napoléon arrived in 1797, he took the city without a fight, gave it briefly to the Austrians, and then got it back in 1805. With his defeat Venice was ceded again to the Austrians at the Council of Vienna in 1815, and they ruled until 1848. In that tumultuous year throughout Europe, the Venetians rebelled, but the rebellion was defeated the following year. Venice remained in Austrian hands until the formation of the Italian Republic in 1866.

SAN MARCO AND DORSODURO

The sestiere Dorsoduro (named for its "hard back" solid clay foundation) is across the Grand Canal to the south of San Marco. It is a place of monumental churches, meandering canals, modern art galleries, the city's finest art museums, and a promenade called the Zattere, where on sunny days you'll swear half the city is out for a *passeggiata,* or stroll. The eastern tip of the peninsula, the Punta della Dogana, was once the city's customs point; it became accessible to the public in 2009 when the old customs house was reopened as a contemporary art museum. At the western end of the sestiere is the Stazione Marittima, where in summer cruise ships line the dock. Midway between these two points, just off the Zattere, is the Squero di San Trovaso, one of the three remaining workshops where gondolas have been built and repaired for centuries. It is not open to the public.

Dorsoduro is also home to the Gallerie dell'Accademia, which has an unparalleled collection of Venetian painting, and gloriously restored Ca' Rezzonico, which houses the Museo del Settecento Veneziano. Another of its landmark sites, the Peggy Guggenheim Collection, has a fine selection of 20th-century art.

TIMING

The Gallerie dell'Accademia demands a few hours, but if time is short an audio guide can help you cover the highlights in about an hour. Ca' Rezzonico deserves at least an hour.

TOP ATTRACTIONS

★ **Ca' Rezzonico.** Designed by Baldassare Longhena in the 17th century, this palace was completed nearly 100 years later by Giorgio Massari and became the last home of English poet Robert Browning (1812–89). Stand on the bridge by the Grand Canal entrance to spot the plaque with Browning's poetic excerpt, "*Open my heart and you will see graved inside of it, Italy . . .*" on the left side of the palace. Today Ca' Rezzonico is the home of the **Museo del Settecento** (Museum of Venice in the 1700s). Its main floor successfully retains the appearance of a magnificent Venetian palazzo, decorated with period furniture and tapestries in gilded salons, as well as Tiepolo ceiling frescoes and oil paintings. Upper floors contain a fine collection of paintings by 18th-century Venetian artists, including the famous genre and Pucinella frescoes by Giabattista Tiepolo's son, Giandomenico, moved here from the Villa di Zianigo. There's even a restored apothecary, complete with powders and potions. ✉ *Fondamenta Rezzonico, Dorsoduro 3136* ☎ *041/2410100* 🌐 *www.museicivicivenezani.it* 🎫 *€6.50, Musei Civici Pass €18* ⏲ *Apr.–Oct., Wed.–Mon. 10–6; Nov.–Mar., Wed.–Mon. 10–5. Last entry 1 hr before closing* Ⓥ *Ca' Rezzonico.*

Fodor's Choice ★ **Gallerie dell'Accademia.** Napoléon founded these galleries in 1807 on the site of a religious complex he had suppressed. They were carefully and subtly restructured between 1945 and 1959 by the renowned architect Carlo Scarpa. In them you'll find the world's most extensive collection of Venetian paintings.

CLOSE UP

Wading Through the Acqua Alta

There are two ways to get anywhere in Venice: walking and by water. Occasionally you walk *through* water, when falling barometers, southeasterly winds, and even a full moon may exacerbate normally higher fall and spring tides. The result is *acqua alta*—flooding in the lowest parts of town, especially Piazza San Marco. It generally occurs in late fall and, to a lesser extent, in spring, and lasts a few hours until the tide recedes.

Venetians handle the high waters with aplomb, donning waders and erecting temporary walkways, but they're well aware of the damage caused by the flooding and the threat it poses to their city. The Moses Project, underwater gates that would close off the lagoon when high tides threaten, is still in progress. The expensive works have altered the lagoon-scape, and still represent a much-debated response to an emotionally charged problem, particularly after the historic tide in December 2008. How to protect Venice from high tides—aggravated by the deep channels dug to accommodate oil tankers and cruise ships, as well as the lagoon-altering wave action caused by powerboats—is among the city's most contentious issues.

Jacopo Bellini is considered the father of the Venetian Renaissance, and in Room 2 you can compare his *Madonna and Child with Saints* with such later works as *Madonna of the Orange Tree* by Cima da Conegliano (circa 1459–1517) and *Ten Thousand Martyrs of Mt. Ararat* by Vittore Carpaccio (circa 1455–1525). Jacopo's more-accomplished son Giovanni (circa 1430–1516) attracts your eye not only with his subjects but also with his rich color. Rooms 4 and 5 have a good selection of his Madonnas. Room 5 contains *Tempest* by Giorgione (1477–1510), a revolutionary work that has continued to intrigue viewers and critics over the centuries. It is unified not only by physical design elements, as was usual, but more importantly by a mysterious, somewhat threatening atmosphere. In Room 10, *Feast in the House of Levi,* commissioned as a Last Supper, got Veronese summoned to the Inquisition over its depiction of dogs, jesters, and other extraneous figures. The artist responded with the famous retort, "*Noi pittori ci prendiamo le stesse libertà dei poeti e dei pazzi.*" ("We painters permit ourselves the same liberties that poets and madmen do." He resolved the problem by simply changing the title, so that the painting represented a different, less-solemn biblical feast.

Room 10 also houses several of Tintoretto's finest works, including three paintings from the life of St. Mark. Titian's *Presentation of the Virgin* (Room 24) is the collection's only work originally created for the building in which it hangs. Don't miss rooms 20 and 21, with views of 15th- and 16th-century Venice by Carpaccio and Gentile Bellini (1429–1507), Giovanni's brother—you'll see how little the city has changed.

Booking tickets in advance isn't essential, but helps during busy seasons and costs only an additional €1. Booking is necessary to see the **Quadreria,** where additional works cover every inch of a wide hallway. A free map names art and artists, and the bookshop sells a more

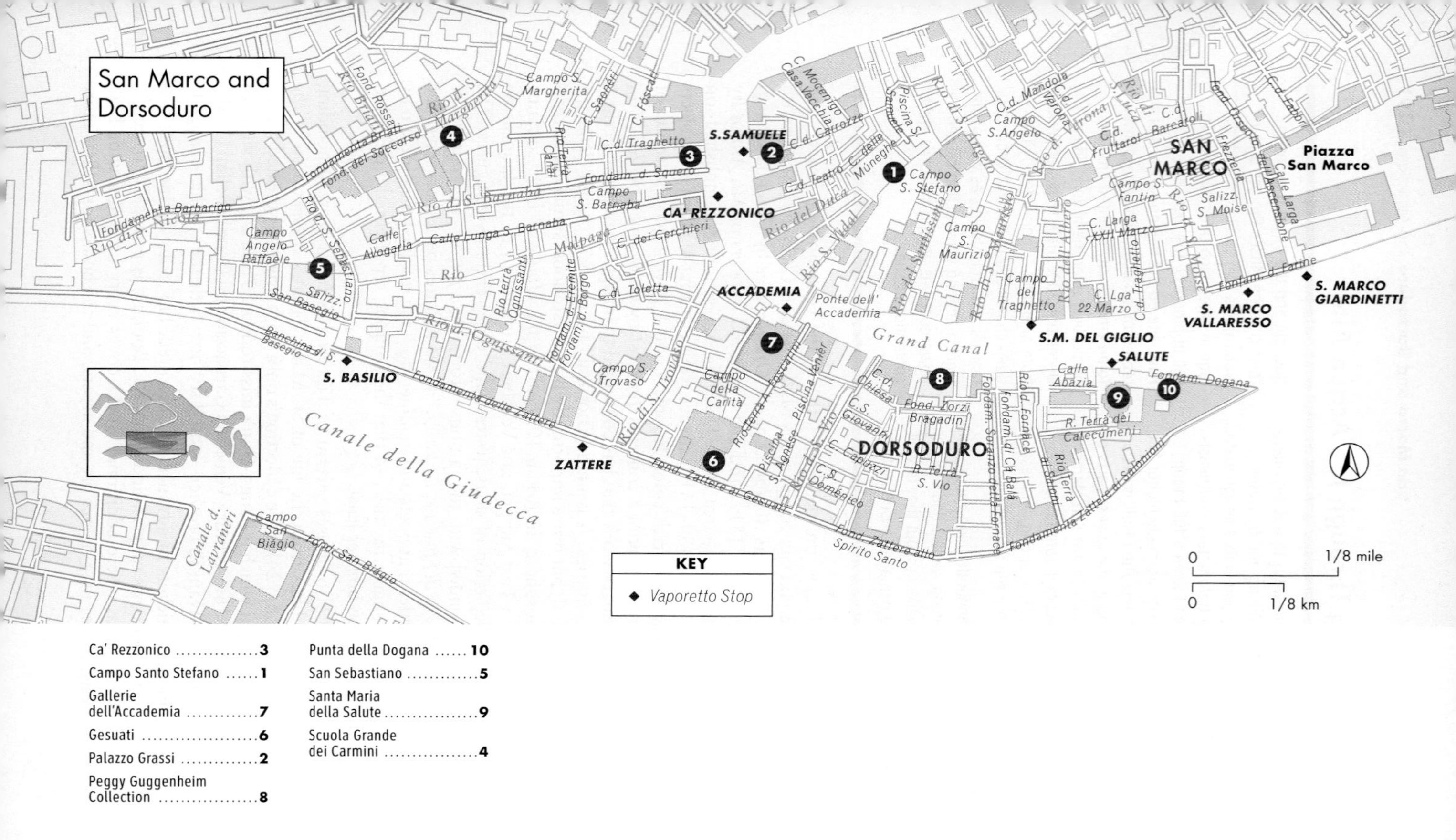

Ca' Rezzonico **3**
Campo Santo Stefano **1**
Gallerie dell'Accademia **7**
Gesuati **6**
Palazzo Grassi **2**
Peggy Guggenheim Collection **8**
Punta della Dogana **10**
San Sebastiano **5**
Santa Maria della Salute **9**
Scuola Grande dei Carmini **4**

informative English-language booklet. In the main galleries a €4 audio guide saves reading but adds little to each room's excellent annotation. ✉ *Campo della Carità just off the Accademia Bridge, Dorsoduro 1050* ☎ *041/5222247, 041/5200345 reservations* 🌐 *www.gallerieaccademia.org* 🎫 *€6.50, €11 includes Ca' d'Oro and Museo Orientale* ⏲ *Galleria: Tues.–Sun. 8:15 am –7:15 pm, Mon. 8:15–2. Quadreria: Fri. 11 am–1 pm, Sat. 11–noon* Ⓥ *Accademia.*

QUICK BITES

There's no sunnier spot in Venice than Fondamenta delle Zattere, along the southern edge of Dorsoduro. It's the city's gigantic public terrace, with bustling bars and gelato shops; come here to stroll, read in the open air, and play hooky from sightseeing. Enjoy the Zattere's most decadent treat at Gelateria Nico (✉ *Dorsoduro 922* ☎ *041/5225293*) —their famous *gianduiotto*, a slab of chocolate-hazelnut ice cream floating on a cloud of whipped cream—and relax on the big, welcoming deck. Saunter up to El Chioschetto (✉ *Dorsoduro 1406* ☎ *041/5225293*) for a fine sandwich or *bibita* (soft drink).

3

Peggy Guggenheim Collection. A small selection of 20th-century painting and sculpture is on display at this gallery in the late heiress Peggy Guggenheim's Grand Canal home. The collection represents the eccentric lady's generally excellent taste. Through wealth and social connections, Guggenheim (1898–1979) became an important art dealer and collector from the 1930s through the 1950s, and her personal collection here in Palazzo Venier dei Leoni includes works by Picasso, Kandinsky, Pollock, Motherwell, and Ernst (at one time her husband). The museum serves beverages, snacks, and light meals in its refreshingly shady, artistically sophisticated garden. On Sunday at 3 pm the museum offers a free tour and art workshop for children 12 and under. ✉ *Fondamenta Venier dei Leoni, Dorsoduro 701* ☎ *041/2405411* 🌐 *www.guggenheim-venice.it* 🎫 *€10* ⏲ *Wed.–Mon. 10–6* Ⓥ *Accademia.*

★ **Santa Maria della Salute.** The view of La Salute (as this church is commonly called) from the Riva degli Schiavoni at sunset or from the Accademia Bridge by moonlight is unforgettable. Baldassare Longhena was 32 years old when he won a competition in 1631 to design a shrine honoring the Virgin Mary for saving Venice from a plague that in the space of two years (1629–30) killed 47,000 residents, or one-third the population of the city. Outside, this ornate white Istrian stone octagon is topped by a colossal cupola with snail-like ornamental buttresses and a baroque facade; inside are a polychrome marble floor and six chapels. The Byzantine icon above the main altar has been venerated as the Madonna della Salute (Madonna of Health) since 1670, when Francesco Morosini brought it here from Crete. Above it is a sculpture showing Venice on her knees to the Madonna as she drives the wretched plague from the city.

Do not leave the church without a visit to the **Sacrestia Maggiore,** which contains a dozen works by Titian, including his *San Marco Enthroned with Saints* altarpiece. You'll also see Tintoretto's *The Wedding at Cana*. For the Festa della Salute, held November 21, a votive bridge is constructed across the Grand Canal, and Venetians make pilgrimages here to light candles in prayer for another year's health. ✉ *Punta della Dogana, Dorsoduro* ☎ *041/2743928* 🎫 *Church free, sacristy €2* ⏲ *Apr.–Sept., daily 9–noon and 3–6:30; Oct.–Mar., daily 9–noon and 3–5:30* Ⓥ *Salute.*

QUICK BITES

Lined with cafés and restaurants generally filled with university students, Campo Santa Margherita also has produce vendors, pizza by the slice, and benches where you can sit and take in the bustling local life of the campo. For more than a portable munch, bask in the sunshine at popular Il Caffè (✉ *Dorsoduro 2963* ☎ *041/5287998*), commonly called Bar Rosso for its bright red exterior. It's open past midnight, serving drinks and light refreshment every day except Sunday.

WORTH NOTING

Campo Santo Stefano. In Venice's most prestigious residential neighborhood you'll find one of the city's busiest crossroads just over the Accademia Bridge; it's hard to believe this square once hosted bullfights, with bulls or oxen tied to a stake and baited by dogs. For centuries the *campo* was grass except for a stone avenue called the *liston.* It was so popular for strolling that in Venetian dialect "*andare al liston*" still means "to go for a walk." A sunny meeting spot popular with Venetians and visitors alike, the campo also hosts outdoor fairs during Christmas and Carnevale seasons. Check out the 14th-century **Chiesa di Santo Stefano.** The pride of the church is its very fine Gothic portal, created in 1442 by Bartomomeo Bon. Inside, you'll see works by Tintoretto. ✉ *Campo Santo Stefano, San Marco* ☎ *041/2750462 Chorus Foundation* 🌐 *www.chorusvenezia.org* 🎫 *€3, Chorus Pass €10* ⏲ *Mon.–Sat. 10–5, Sun. 1–5* Ⓥ *Accademia.*

Gesuati. When the Dominicans took over the church of Santa Maria della Visitazione from the suppressed order of Gesuati laymen in 1668, Giorgio Massari was commissioned to build this structure. It has an important Tiepolo illusionistic ceiling and several other works by Giambattista Tiepolo (1696–1770), Giambattista Piazzetta (1683–1754), and Sebastiano Ricci (1659–1734). ✉ *Zattere, Dorsoduro* ☎ *041/2750462* 🌐 *www.chorusvenezia.org* 🎫 *€3, Chorus Pass €10* ⏲ *Mon.–Sat. 10–5, Sun. 1–5* Ⓥ *Zattere.*

Palazzo Grassi. Built between 1748 and 1772 by Giorgio Massari for a Bolognese family, this palace is one of the last of the great noble residences on the Grand Canal. Once owned by auto magnate Giovanni Agnelli, it was bought by French businessman François Pinaut in 2005 to house his very important collection of modern and contemporary art. Pinaut brought in Japanese architect Tadao Ando to remodel the interior. Check online for a schedule of temporary exhibitions. ✉ *Campo San Samuele, San Marco* ☎ *041/5231680* 🌐 *www.palazzograssi.it* 🎫 *€15, €20 includes the Punta della Dogana* ⏲ *Daily 9–6* Ⓥ *San Samuele.*

Punta della Dogana. The François Pinault Foundation had Japanese architect Tadao Ando redesign this former customs house, now home to works from Pinault's collection of contemporary art. The streaming light, polished

CLOSE UP

Speaking Venetian

Venice is one of the few Italian cities where the local dialect is still alive and well. Much of the language you will hear in Venice is not Italian, but rather Venetian, or Italian heavily laced with Venetian. Venetian has its own rich and widely respected literature. The Venetian-dialect comedies of Goldoni, the great 18th-century playwright, are regularly performed in the city.

Even when speaking Italian, Venetians will use dialect terms to refer to certain common objects. Sometimes the term means something totally different in standard Italian.

Here are a few frequently used words:

sestiere: One of six neighborhoods in central Venice.

rio: A canal. Only the Grand Canal and a few other major waterways are called "canali." Everything else is a "rio."

fondamenta: A quay, a street running along a canal or a "rio."

calle: A street, what is elsewhere in Italy called a "via." "Via" is used in Venice, but it means "boulevard."

campo: A square—what is elsewhere in Italy called a piazza. (The only piazza in Venice is Piazza San Marco.)

bacaro: A traditional wine bar.

cicheto (pronounced chee-*kay*-toh)*:* An hors d'oeuvre —roughly the Venetian equivalent of tapas, Generally served at a bacaro and in many cafés.

ombra: A small glass of wine.

focaccia: A traditional Venetian raised sweet cake, similar to a panettone, but much lighter and without candied fruit or raisins. (Very different from the better-known Genoese focaccia, a dense slightly raised bread sometimes flavored with herbs or cheese.)

Venetians tend to use the informal second person form, "tu," much more readily than people do in other parts of Italy. Venetians also frequently address each other with the term *amore* (love), as is done sometimes in England. But in Venice it is used even between members of the same sex, without any romantic connotation.

3

surfaces, and clean lines of Ando's design contrast beautifully with the brick, massive columns, and sturdy beams of the original Dogana. Even if you don't visit the museum, walk down to the *punta* (point) for a maginficent view of the Venetian basin. Check online for a schedule of temporary exhibitions. ✉ *Punta della Dogana, Dorsoduro* ☎ *041/5231680* 🌐 *www.palazzograssi.it* 🎫 *€15, €20 includes the Palazzo Grassi* ⏲ *Wed.–Mon. 10–7. Last entry 1 hr before closing. Closed Dec. 24–Jan. 1* Ⓥ *Salute.*

San Sebastiano. Paolo Veronese (1528–88), although still in his twenties, was already the official painter of the Republic when he began the oil panels and frescoes at this, his parish church, in 1555. For decades he continued to embellish the church with very beautiful illusionistic scenes. The cycles of panels in San Sebastiano are considered to be his supreme accomplishment. Veronese is buried beneath his bust near the organ. ✉ *Campo San Sebastiano, Dorsoduro* ☎ *041/2750462* 🌐 *www.chorusvenezia.org* 🎫 *€3, Chorus Pass €10* ⏲ *Mon.–Sat. 10–5, Sun. 1–5* Ⓥ *San Basilio.*

CLOSE UP

Touring Venice

If you want some expert guidance around Venice, you may opt for private tours, semiprivate tours, or large group tours. Any may include a boat tour as a portion of a longer walking tour. For private tours, make sure to choose an authorized guide.

PRIVATE TOURS

Walks Inside Venice (🌐 *www.walksinsidevenice.com*) offers a host of particularly creative private tours from historic to artistic to gastronomic. Luisella Romeo of **See Venice** (🌐 *www.seevenice.it*) is a delightful guide capable of bringing to life even the most convoluted aspects of Venice's art and history. **A Guide in Venice** (🌐 *www.aguideinvenice.com*) offers a wide variety of innovative, entertaining, and informative themed tours for groups of up to 10 people. **Venice Events** (✉ *Frezzaria, San Marco 1827* ☎ *041/5239979* 🌐 *www.tours-venice-italy.com*) offers a daily, 10-person-max canal tour, along with many other group and private tour options.

SEMIPRIVATE TOURS

Venice Cultural Tours (🌐 *venice-cultural-tours.com*) is group of collaborating guides who offer regularly scheduled, semiprivate group tours with a maximum of only eight participants, making a nice alternative to more costly private tours.

LARGE GROUP TOURS

Visit any **Venice tourism office** (☎ *041/5298711* 🌐 *www.turismovenezia.it*) to book walking tours of the San Marco area (€38), which ends with a glassblowing demonstration daily (no Sunday tour in winter). From April to October there's also an afternoon walking tour that ends with a gondola ride (€40), and a daily serenaded gondola ride (€40). Other options can be purchased at local travel agencies. Check the tourist office or Web site for scheduled offerings. The **Cooperativa Guide Turistiche Autorizzate** (✉ *San Marco 750, near San Zulian* ☎ *041/5209038* 🌐 *www.guidevenezia.it*) has a list of more than 100 licensed guides. Two-hour tours with an English-speaking guide start at €133 for up to 30 people. Agree on a total price before you begin, as there can be additional administrative and pickup fees. Guides are of varying quality.

Scuola Grande dei Carmini. When the order of Santa Maria del Carmelo commissioned Baldassare Longhena to build Scuola Grande dei Carmini in the late 1600s, their brotherhood of 75,000 members was the largest in Venice and one of the wealthiest. Little expense was spared in the decorating of stuccoed ceilings and carved ebony paneling, and the artwork was choice, even before 1739, when Tiepolo painted the **Sala Capitolare.** In what many consider his best work, Tiepolo's nine great canvases vividly transform some rather conventional religious themes into dynamic displays of color and movement. ✉ *Campo dei Carmini, Dorsoduro 2617* ☎ *041/5289420* 🎫 *€5* ⏲ *Daily 10–5* Ⓥ *Ca' Rezzonico.*

SAN POLO AND SANTA CROCE

The two smallest of Venice's six *sestieri* (districts), San Polo and Santa Croce, were named after their main churches, though the Chiesa di Santa Croce was demolished in 1810. The city's most famous bridge, the Ponte di Rialto, unites sestiere San Marco (east) with San Polo (west). The Rialto takes its name from Rivoaltus, the high ground on which it was built.

San Polo has two other major sites, Santa Maria Gloriosa dei Frari and the Scuola Grande di San Rocco, as well as some worthwhile but lesser-known churches.

Shops abound in the area surrounding the Rialto Bridge. On the San Marco side you'll find fashions, on the San Polo side, food. Chiesa di San Giacometto, where you see the first fruit vendors as you come off the bridge on the San Polo side, was probably built in the 11th and 12th centuries, about the time the surrounding market came into being. Public announcements were traditionally read in the church's campo; its 24-hour clock, though lovely, has rarely worked.

TIMING

To do the area justice requires at least half a day. If you want to take part in the food shopping, come early to beat the crowds. Campo San Giacomo dell'Orio, west of the main thoroughfare that takes you from the Ponte di Rialto to Santa Maria Gloriosa dei Frari, is a peaceful place for a drink and a rest. The museums of Ca' Pesaro are a time commitment—you'll want at least two hours to see them both.

TOP ATTRACTIONS

Ponte di Rialto *(Rialto Bridge)*. The competition to design a stone bridge across the Grand Canal (replacing earlier wooden versions) attracted the late-16th-century's best architects, including Michelangelo, Palladio, and Sansovino, but the job went to the less famous but appropriately named Antonio da Ponte (1512–95). His pragmatic design featured shop space and was high enough for galleys to pass beneath; it kept decoration and cost to a minimum at a time when the Republic's coffers were low due to continual wars against the Turks and the competition brought about by the Spanish and Portuguese opening of oceanic trade routes. Along the railing you'll enjoy one of the city's most famous views: the Grand Canal vibrant with boat traffic. Ⓥ *Rialto*.

Fodor's Choice ★ **Santa Maria Gloriosa dei Frari.** This immense Gothic church of russet-color brick was completed in the 1400s after more than a century of work. *I Frari* (as it's known locally) contains some of the most brilliant paintings in any Venetian church. Visit the sacristy first, to see Giovanni Bellini's 1488 triptych *Madonna and Child with Saints* in all its mellow luminosity, painted for precisely this spot. The Corner Chapel on the other side of the chancel is graced by Bartolomeo Vivarini's (1415–84) 1474 altarpiece *St. Mark Enthroned and Saints John the Baptist, Jerome, Peter, and Nicholas,* which is much more conservative, displaying attention to detail generally associated with late medieval painting. In the first south chapel of the chorus, there is a fine sculpture

Campo San Polo **6**
Ca' Pesaro **3**
Ponte di Rialto **1**
San Giacomo dell'Orio **5**
San Giovanni Elemosinario ... **2**
San Stae **4**
Santa Maria Gloriosa dei Frari......... **7**
Scuola Grande di San Rocco **8**

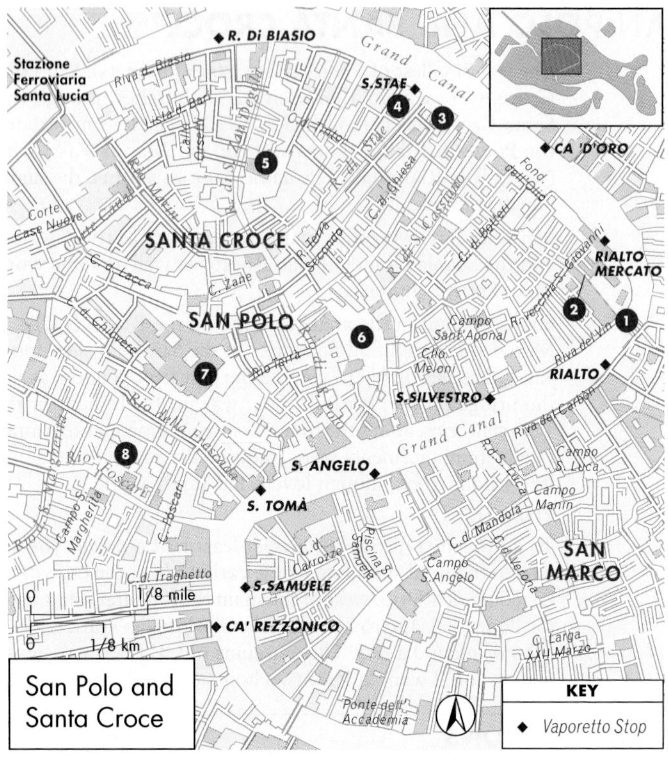

San Polo and Santa Croce

of Saint John the Baptist by Donatello, done in the 1450s and displaying a psychological intensity rare for early Renaissance sculpture. You can see the rapid development of Venetian Renaissance painting by contrasting Bellini with the heroic energy of Titian's *Assumption,* over the main altar, painted only 30 years later. Unveiled in 1518, it was the artist's first public commission and did much to establish his reputation.

Titian's beautiful *Madonna di Ca' Pesaro* is in the left aisle. The painting took almost 10 years to complete, and in it Titian disregarded the conventions of his time by moving the Virgin out of center and making the saints active participants. The composition, built on diagonals, anticipates structural principals of the baroque painting of the following century. ✉ *Campo dei Frari, San Polo* ☎ *041/2728618, 041/2750462 Chorus Foundation* 🌐 *www.chorusvenezia.org* 💰 *€3, Chorus Pass €10* ⏲ *Mon.–Sat. 9–6, Sun. 1–6* 🅥 *San Tomà.*

★ **Scuola Grande di San Rocco.** Saint Rocco's popularity stemmed from his miraculous recovery from the plague and his care for fellow sufferers. Throughout the plague-filled Middle Ages, followers and donations abounded, and this elegant example of Venetian Renaissance architecture, built between 1517 and 1560 and including the work of at least four architects, was the result. Although it is bold and dramatic outside, its contents are even more stunning—a series of more than 60 paintings

CLOSE UP

Venice's Scuola Days

An institution you'll inevitably encounter from Venice's glory days is the *scuola*. These weren't schools, as the word today translates, but important fraternal institutions. The smaller ones (*scuole piccole*) were established by different social groups—enclaves of foreigners, tradesmen, followers of a particular saint, and parishioners. The *scuole grandi*, however, were open to all citizens and included people of different occupations and ethnicities. They formed a more democratic power base than the Venetian governmental Grand Council, which was limited to nobles.

For the most part secular, despite their devotional activities, the scuole concentrated on charitable work, either helping their own membership or assisting the city's neediest citizens. The tradesmen's and servants' scuole formed social security nets for elderly and disabled members. Wealthier scuole assisted orphans or provided dowries so poor girls could marry. By 1500 there were more than 200 minor scuole in Venice, but only six scuole grandi, some of which contributed substantially to the arts. The Republic encouraged their existence—the scuole kept strict records of the names and professions of contributors to the brotherhood, which helped when it came time to collect taxes.

by Tintoretto. In 1564 Tintoretto edged out competition for a commission to decorate a ceiling by submitting not a sketch, but a finished work, which he moreover offered free of charge. *Moses Striking Water from the Rock, The Brazen Serpent,* and *The Fall of Manna* represent three afflictions—thirst, disease, and hunger—that San Rocco and later his brotherhood sought to relieve. ✉ *Campo San Rocco, San Polo 3052* ☎ *041/5234864* 🌐 *www.scuolagrandesanrocco.it* 🎫 *€7 (includes audio guide)* 🕓 *Daily 9:30–5:30. Last entry ½ hr before closing* Ⓥ *San Tomà.*

QUICK BITES

Just over the bridge in front of the Frari church is Caffè dei Frari (✉ *Fondamenta dei Frari, San Polo* ☎ *041/5241877*), where you'll find a delightful assortment of sandwiches and snacks. Established in 1870, it's one of the last Venetian tearooms with its original decor. Pasticceria Tonolo (✉ *Calle Crosera, Dorsoduro 3764* ☎ *041/5237209*), in operation since 1886, is widely considered among Venice's premier confectionaries. During Carnevale it's still the best place in town for *fritelle,* fried doughnuts (traditional raisin or cream-filled), and before Christmas and Easter, Venetians order their *focaccia,* the traditional raised cake eaten especially at holidays, from here well in advance. Closed Monday, and there's no seating any time.

WORTH NOTING

Campo San Polo. Only Piazza San Marco is larger than this square, and the echo of children's voices bouncing off the surrounding palaces makes the space seem even bigger. Campo San Polo once hosted bull races, fairs, military parades, and packed markets, and now comes especially alive on summer nights, when it's home to the city's outdoor cinema. The **Chiesa di San Polo** has been restored so many times that little remains of the original 9th-century church, and sadly, 19th-century alterations were so costly that the friars sold off many great paintings to pay bills. Though Giambattista Tiepolo is represented here, his work is outdone by 16 paintings by his son Giandomenico (1727–1804), including the *Stations of the Cross* in the oratory to the left of the entrance. The younger Tiepolo also created a series of expressive and theatrical renderings of the saints. Look for altarpieces by Tintoretto and Veronese that managed to escape auction. San Polo's bell tower remained unchanged through the centuries—don't miss the two lions guarding it, playing with a disembodied human head and a serpent. ✉ *Campo San Polo* ☎ *041/2750462 Chorus Foundation* 🌐 *www.chorusvenezia.org* 🎫 *€3, Chorus Pass €10* 🕑 *Mon.–Sat. 10–5, Sun. 1–5* Ⓥ *San Silvestro, San Tomà.*

Ca' Pesaro. Baldassare Longhena's grand baroque palace is the beautifully restored home of two impressive collections. The **Galleria Internazionale d'Arte Moderna** has works by 19th- and 20th-century artists such as Klimt, Kandinsky, Matisse, and Miró. It also has a collection of representative works from Venice's Biennale art show that amounts to a panorama of 20th-century art. The pride of the **Museo Orientale** is its collection of Japanese art, and especially armor and weapons, of the Edo period (1603–1868). It also has a small but striking collection of Chinese and Indonesian porcelains and musical instruments. ✉ *San Stae, Santa Croce 2076* ☎ *041/721127 Galleria, 041/5241173 Museo Orientale* 🌐 *www.museiciviciveneziani.it* 🎫 *€7 includes both museums, Museums of San Marco Plus Pass €13 (Apr.–Oct.), Musei Civici Pass €18* 🕑 *Apr.–Oct., daily 10–6; Nov.–Mar., daily 10–5. Last entry 1 hr before closing* Ⓥ *San Stae.*

San Giacomo dell'Orio. It was named after a laurel tree *(orio)*, and today trees give character to this square. Add benches and a fountain (with a drinking bowl for dogs), and the pleasant, oddly shaped campo becomes a welcoming place for friendly conversation and neighborhood kids at play. Legend has it the **Chiesa di San Giacomo dell'Orio** was founded in the 9th century on an island still populated by wolves. The current church dates from 1225; its short unmatched Byzantine columns survived renovation during the Renaissance, and the church never lost the feel of an ancient temple sheltering beneath its 15th-century ship's-keel roof. In the sanctuary, large marble crosses are surrounded by a group of small medieval Madonnas. The altarpiece is *Madonna with Child and Saints* (1546) by Lorenzo Lotto (1480–1556), and the sacristies contain works by Palma il Giovane (circa 1544–1628). ✉ *Campo San Giacomo dell'Orio, Santa Croce* ☎ *041/2750462 Chorus Foundation* 🌐 *www.chorusvenezia.org* 🎫 *€3, Chorus Pass €10* 🕑 *Mon.–Sat. 10–5, Sun. 1–5* Ⓥ *San Stae.*

San Giovanni Elemosinario. Storefronts make up the facade, and the altars were built by market guilds—poulterers, messengers, and fodder merchants—at this church intimately bound to the Rialto Market. The original church was completely destroyed by a fire in 1514 and rebuilt in 1531 by Antonio Abbondi, who had also worked on the Scuola di san Rocco. During a recent restoration workers stumbled upon a frescoed cupola by Pordenone (1484–1539) that had been painted over centuries earlier. Don't miss Titian's *St. John the Almsgiver* and Pordenone's *Sts. Catherine, Sebastian, and Roch,* which in 2002 were returned after 30 years by the Gallerie dell'Accademia. ✉ *Rialto Ruga Vecchia San Giovanni, Santa Croce* ☎ *041/2750462 Chorus Foundation* 🌐 *www.chorusvenezia.org* 🎫 *€3, Chorus Pass €10* ⏲ *Mon.–Sat. 10–5. Last entry ¼ hr before closing* Ⓥ *San Silvestro, Rialto.*

San Stae. The most renowned Venetian painters and sculptors of the early 18th century decorated this church around 1717 with the legacy left by Doge Alvise Mocenigo II, who's buried in the center aisle. Stae affords a good opportunity to see the early works of Tiepolo, Ricci, and Piazzetta, as well as those of the previous generation of Venetian painters. ✉ *Campo San Stae, Santa Croce* ☎ *041/2750462 Chorus Foundation* 🌐 *www.chorusvenezia.org* 🎫 *€3, Chorus Pass €10* ⏲ *Mon.–Sat. 9–5* Ⓥ *San Stae.*

CANNAREGIO

Seen from above, this part of town seems like a wide field plowed by several long, straight canals that are linked by intersecting straight streets—not typical of Venice, where the shape of the islands usually defines the shape of the canals. Cannaregio's main drag, the Strada Nova (literally, "New Street," as it was opened in 1871), is the longest street in Venice. It runs parallel to the Grand Canal, and was once a canal itself. Today it's lined with fruit and vegetable stalls (near Ponte delle Guglie), quiet shops, gelaterias, and bakeries, and serves as a pedestrian expressway from the train station to Ca' d'Oro.

Though Cannaregio has noble palaces built along the Grand Canal, the northern part of the sestiere was, and still is, a typical working-class neighborhood, where many *bacari* (wine bars) fill up with old card players every afternoon. Highlights include the Jewish Ghetto, with its rooftop synagogues, and the Ca' d'Oro and the churches of Madonna dell'Orto and the Miracoli, which are among the most beautiful and interesting buildings in the city.

TOP ATTRACTIONS

★ **Ca' d'Oro.** This exquisite Venetian Gothic palace was once literally a "Golden House," when its marble traceries and ornaments were embellished with gold. It was created by Giovanni and Bartolomeo Bon between 1428 and 1430 for the patrician Marino Contarini as a present to his wife. The last proprietor, Baron Giorgio Franchetti, left Ca' d'Oro to the city, after having had it carefully restored and furnished with antiquities, sculptures, and paintings that today make up the **Galleria Franchetti.** Besides Andrea Mantegna's *St. Sebastian* and

Ca' d'Oro 3
Gesuiti 5
Jewish Ghetto 1
Madonna dell'Onto 6
Palazzo Vendramin-Calergi 2
Santa Maria dei Miracoli 4

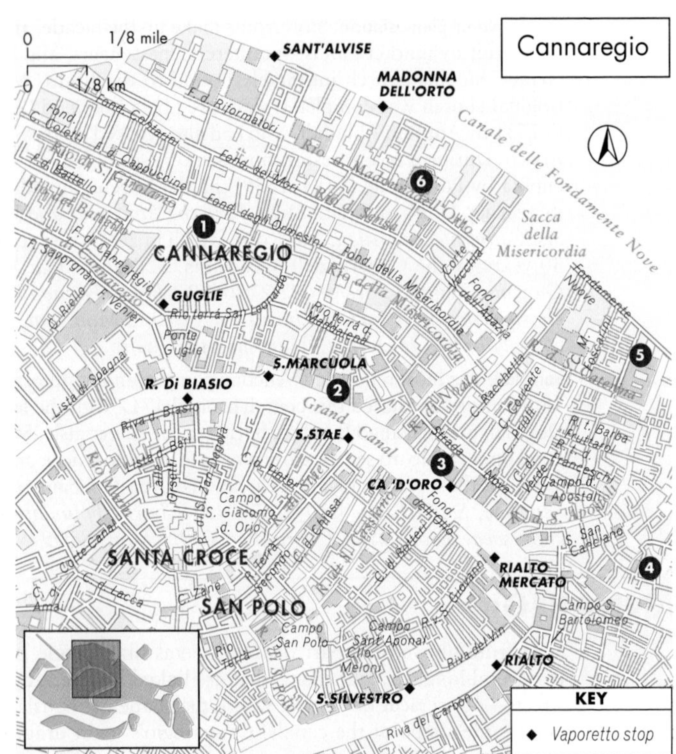

other Venetian works, the Galleria Franchetti contains the type of fresco that once adorned the exteriors of Venetian buildings (commissioned by those who could not afford a marble facade). One such detached fresco displayed here was made by the young Titian for the facade of the Fondaco dei Tedeschi, now the main post office near the Rialto. ✉ *Calle Ca' d'Oro, Cannaregio 3933* ☎ *041/5238790* 🌐 *www.cadoro.org* 🎟 *€5, plus €1 to reserve; €11 includes Gallerie dell'Accademia and Museo Orientale* 🕒 *Tues.–Sun. 8:15–7, Mon. 8:15–2. Last entry ½ hr before closing* Ⓥ *Ca' d'Oro*.

★ **Jewish Ghetto.** The neighborhood that gave the world the word *ghetto* is today a quiet neighborhood surrounding a large campo. It is home to Jewish institutions, two kosher restaurants, a rabbinical school, and five synagogues. Present-day Venetian Jews live all over the city, and the contemporary Jewish life of the ghetto, with the exception of the Jewish museum and the synagogues, is an enterprise conducted almost exclusively by American Hassidic Jews of Eastern European descent and tradition.

Though Jews may have arrived earlier, the first synagogues weren't built and a cemetery (on the Lido) wasn't founded until the Askenazim, or Northern European Jews, came in the late 1300s. Dwindling coffers may have prompted the Republic to sell temporary visas to Jews, who were over the centuries alternately tolerated and expelled. The Rialto commercial district, as mentioned in Shakespeare's *The Merchant of Venice,* depended on Jewish moneylenders for trade, and to help cover ever-increasing war expenses.

In 1516 relentless local opposition forced the Senate to confine Jews to an island in Cannaregio, then on the outer reaches of the city, named for its *geto* (foundry). The term "ghetto" also may come from the Hebrew "ghet" meaning separation or divorce. Gates at the entrance were locked at night, and boats patrolled the surrounding canals. Jews were allowed only to lend money at low interest, operate pawnshops controlled by the government, trade in textiles, or practice medicine. Jewish doctors were highly respected and could leave the ghetto at any hour when on duty. Though ostracized, Jews were nonetheless safe in Venice, and in the 16th century the community grew considerably, primarily with refugees from the Inquisition, which persecuted Jews in southern and central Italy, Spain, and Portugal. The ghetto was allowed to expand twice, but it still had the city's densest population and consequently ended up with the city's tallest buildings. Although the gates were pulled down after Napoléon's 1797 arrival, during the Austrian occupation the ghetto was reinstated. The Jews realized full freedom only in 1866 with the founding of the Italian state. Many Jews fled Italy as a result of Mussolini's 1938 racial laws, and on the eve of World War II there were about 1,500 Jews left in the ghetto. Jews continued to flee, and the remaining 247 were deported by the Nazis; 8 returned.

The area has Europe's highest density of Renaissance-era synagogues, and visiting them is interesting not only culturally, but also aesthetically. Though each is marked by the tastes of its individual builders, Venetian influence is evident throughout. Women's galleries resemble those of theaters from the same era, and some synagogues were decorated by artists who were simultaneously active in local churches; Longhena, the architect of Santa Maria della Salute, renovated the Spanish synagogue in 1635.

The small but well-arranged **Museo Ebraico** highlights centuries of Jewish culture with splendid silver Hanukkah lamps and Torahs, and handwritten, beautifully decorated wedding contracts in Hebrew. Hourly tours (on the half hour) of the ghetto in Italian and English leave from the museum. ✉ *Campo del Ghetto Nuovo, Cannaregio 2902/B* ☎ *041/715359* 🌐 *www.museoebraico.it* 🎫 *Museum €3; guided tour, museum, and synagogues €8.50* ⏲ *June–Sept., Sun.–Fri. 10–7; Oct.–May, Sun.–Fri. 10–6. Tours hourly starting at 10:30* Ⓥ *San Marcuola, Guglie.*

You might complete your circuit of Jewish Venice with a visit to the **Antico Cimitero Ebraico** *(Ancient Jewish Cemetery)* on the Lido, full of fascinating old tombstones half hidden by ivy and grass. The earliest grave dates from 1389; the cemetery remained in use until the late 18th century. ✉ *Via Cipro at San Nicolo, Lido* ☎ *041/715359* 🎫 *€8.50* ⏲ *Tours Apr.–Oct., Sun. at 2:30, by appointment other days; call to reserve* Ⓥ *Lido, San Nicolo.*

Madonna dell'Orto. Though built toward the middle of the 14th century, this church takes its character from its beautiful late Gothic facade, added between 1460 and 1464; it's one of the most beautiful

Gothic churches in Venice. Tintoretto lived nearby, and this, his parish church, contains some of his most powerful work. Lining the chancel are two huge (45 feet by 20 feet) canvases, *Adoration of the Golden Calf* and *Last Judgment*. In glowing contrast to this awesome spectacle is Tintoretto's *Presentation of the Virgin at the Temple* and the simple chapel where Tintoretto and his children, Marietta and Domenico, are buried. Paintings by Domenico, Cima da Conegliano, Palma il Giovane, Palma il Vecchio, and Tiziano also hang in the church. A chapel displays a photographic reproduction of a precious *Madonna with Child* by Giovanni Bellini. The original was stolen one night in 1993. ✉ *Campo della Madonna dell'Orto, Cannaregio* ☎ *041/2750462 Chorus Foundation* 🌐 *www.chorusvenezia.org* 🎟 *€3, Chorus Pass €10* ⏲ *Mon.–Sat. 10–5, Sun. 1–5* Ⓥ *Orto.*

★ **Santa Maria dei Miracoli.** Tiny yet harmoniously proportioned, this early-Renaissance gem built between 1481 and 1489 is sheathed in marble and decorated inside with exquisite marble reliefs. Architect Pietro Lombardo (circa 1435–1515) miraculously compressed the building into its confined space, then created the illusion of greater size by varying the color of the exterior, adding extra pilasters on the building's canal side, and offsetting the arcade windows to make the arches appear deeper. The church was built in the 1480s to house *I Miracoli*, an image of the Virgin Mary that is said to perform miracles—look for it on the high altar. ✉ *Campo Santa Maria Nova, Cannaregio* ☎ *041/2750462 Chorus Foundation* 🌐 *www.chorusvenezia.org* 🎟 *€3, Chorus Pass €10* ⏲ *Mon.–Sat. 10–5* Ⓥ *Rialto.*

WORTH NOTING

Gesuiti. Extravagantly baroque, this 18th-century church completely abandons classical Renaissance straight lines in favor of flowing, twisting forms. Its interior walls resemble brocade drapery, and only touching them will convince skeptics that rather than paint, the green-and-white walls are inlaid marble. Over the first altar on the left, the *Martyrdom of St. Lawrence* is a dramatic example of Titian's feeling for light and movement. ✉ *Campo dei Gesuiti, Cannaregio* ☎ *041/5286579* ⏲ *Daily 10–noon and 4–6* Ⓥ *Fondamente Nove.*

Palazzo Vendramin-Calergi. This Renaissance classic on the Grand Canal is the work of Mauro Codussi (1440–1504). You can see some of its interior by dropping into the **Casinò di Venezia.** Fans of Richard Wagner (1813–83) might enjoy visiting the **Sala di Wagner,** the room (separate from the casino) in which the composer died. Though rather plain, it's loaded with music memorabilia. To visit the Sala, call the dedicated tour line by noon the day before a scheduled tour, or book a private tour. ✉ *Cannaregio 2040* ☎ *041/5297111, 338/4164174 Sala di Wagner tours* 🌐 *www.casinovenezia.it* 🎟 *Casinò €10, Sala di Wagner tour €5 suggested donation* ⏲ *Casinò Sun.–Thurs. 3:30 pm–2:30 am, Fri. and Sat. 3:30 pm–3 am; slot machines open daily at 3 pm. Sala di Wagner tours Tues. and Sat. at 10:30, Thurs. at 2:30 (call until noon the day before to reserve)* Ⓥ *San Marcuola.*

CASTELLO

Castello, Venice's largest sestiere, includes all of the land from east of Piazza San Marco to the city's easternmost tip. Its name probably comes from a fortress that once stood on one of the eastern islands.

WORD OF MOUTH

"Be sure to wander off the beaten path and get yourself lost in the endless mazes of canals, streets, alleys. Every turn will reveal a new discovery for the intrepid photographer."

—bg_collier

Not every well-off Venetian family could afford to build a palazzo on the Grand Canal. Many that couldn't instead settled in western Castello, taking advantage of its proximity to the Rialto and San Marco, and built the noble palazzos that today distinguish this area from the fishermen's enclave in the more easterly streets of the sestiere.

There is a lot to see here. The church of Santi Giovanni e Paolo is a major attraction, and Carpaccio's paintings at the Scuola di San Giorgio degli Schiavoni are worth a long look. San Francesco della Vigna, with a Palladio facade and Sansovino interior, certainly deserves a stop, as do the church San Zaccaria and the Querini-Stampalia museum.

TOP ATTRACTIONS

Arsenale. Visible from the street, the Arsenale's impressive Renaissance gateway, the **Porta Magna** (1460), was the first classical revival structure to be built in Venice. It is guarded by four lions, war booty of Francesco Morosini, who took the Peloponnese from the Turks in 1687. The 10-foot-tall lion on the left stood sentinel more than 2,000 years ago near Athens, and experts say its mysterious inscription is runic "graffiti" left by Viking mercenaries hired to suppress 11th-century revolts in Piraeus. If you look at the winged lion above the doorway, you'll notice that the Gospel at his paws is open but lacks the customary *Pax* inscription; praying for peace perhaps seemed inappropriate above a factory that manufactured weapons. The interior is not regularly open to the public, since it belongs to the Italian Navy, but it opens for the Biennale and for Venice's festival of traditional boats, **Mare Maggio** (🌐 *www.maremaggio.it*), held every May. If you're here during those times, don't miss the chance for a look inside, even entering from the back via a northern-side walkway leading from the Ospedale vaporetto stop.

The Arsenale is said to have been founded in 1104 on twin islands. The immense facility that evolved—it was the largest industrial complex in Europe built prior to the Industrial Revolution—was given the old Venetian dialect name *arzanà,* borrowed from the Arabic *darsina'a,* meaning "workshop." At times it employed as many as 16,000 *arsenalotti,* workers who were among the most respected shipbuilders in the world. (Dante immortalized these sweating men armed with pitch and boiling tar in his *Inferno.*) Their diligence was confirmed time and again—whether building 100 ships in 60 days to battle the Turks in Cyprus (1597) or completing one perfectly armed warship—start to

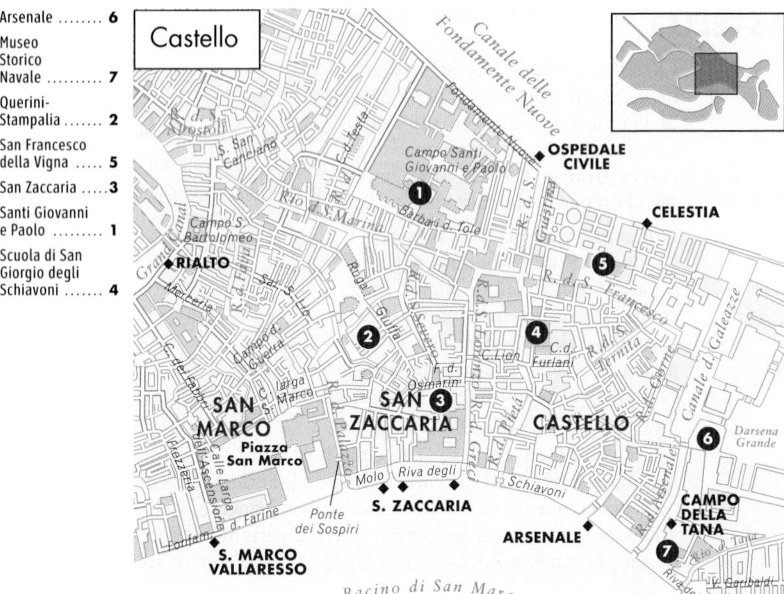

finish—while King Henry III of France attended a banquet. ✉ *Campo dell'Arsenale, Castello* Ⓥ *Arsenale.*

Fodor's Choice ★ **Santi Giovanni e Paolo.** This massive Dominican church, commonly called San Zanipolo, contains a wealth of art. The 15th-century stained-glass window near the side entrance is breathtaking for its brilliant colors and beautiful figures, made from drawings by Bartolomeo Vivarini and Gerolamo Mocetto (circa 1458–1531). The second official church of the Republic after San Marco, San Zanipolo is the Venetian equivalent of London's Westminster Abbey, with a great number of important people, including 25 doges, buried here. Artistic highlights include an outstanding polyptych by Giovanni Bellini (right aisle, second altar), Alvise Vivarini's *Christ Carrying the Cross* (sacristy), and Lorenzo Lotto's *Charity of St. Antonino* (right transept). Don't miss the Cappella del Rosario (Rosary Chapel), off the left transept, built in the 16th century to commemorate the 1571 victory of Lepanto, in western Greece, when Venice led a combined European fleet to defeat the Turkish Navy. The chapel was devastated by a fire in 1867 and restored in the early years of the 20th century with works from other churches, among them the sumptuous Veronese ceiling paintings. However quick your visit, don't miss the Pietro Mocenigo tomb to the right of the main entrance, by Pietro Lombardo and his sons. ✉ *Campo dei Santi Giovanni e Paolo,*

Castello ☎ *041/5235913* 🎫 *€2.50* ⏲ *Mon.–Sat. 9–6, Sun. noon–6* Ⓥ *Fondamente Nove, Rialto.*

QUICK BITES

To satisfy your sweet tooth, head for Campo Santa Marina and the family-owned and -operated Didovich Pastry Shop (✉ *Campo Santa Marina, Castello* ☎ *041/5230017*). It's a local favorite, especially for Carnevale-time *fritelle* (fried doughnuts). There is limited seating inside, but in the warmer months you can sit outside. Un Mondo di Vino (✉ *Salizzada San Cancian, Cannaregio* ☎ *041/5211093*), below Campo Santa Maria Nova on Calle San Canciano, is a friendly place to recharge with a *cicchetto* (snack) or two and some wine. It's closed Sunday.

3

WORTH NOTING

Museo Storico Navale *(Museum of Naval History).* The boat collection here includes scale models such as the doges' ceremonial *Bucintoro*, and full-size boats such as Peggy Guggenheim's private gondola complete with romantic *felze* (cabin). There's a range of old galley and military pieces, and also a large collection of seashells. ✉ *Campo San Biagio, Castello 2148* ☎ *041/2441399* 🌐 *www.marina.difesa.it/venezia/museo.asp* 🎫 *€1.55* ⏲ *Weekdays 8:45–1:30, Sat. 8:45–1* Ⓥ *Arsenale.*

Querini-Stampalia. The art collection at this Renaissance palace includes Giovanni Bellini's *Presentation in the Temple* and Sebastiano Ricci's triptych *Dawn, Afternoon, and Evening.* Portraits of newlyweds Francesco Querini and Paola Priuli were left unfinished on the death of Giacomo Palma il Vecchio (1480–1528); note the groom's hand and the bride's dress. Original 18th-century furniture and stuccowork are a fitting background for Pietro Longhi's portraits. Nearly 70 works by Gabriele Bella (1730–99) capture scenes of Venetian street life; downstairs is a café. ✉ *Campo Santa Maria Formosa, Castello 5252* ☎ *041/2711411* 🌐 *www.querinistampalia.it* 🎫 *€8* ⏲ *Tues.–Sat. 10–8, Sun. 10–7. Last entry 1 hr before closing* Ⓥ *San Zaccaria.*

San Francesco della Vigna. Although this church contains some interesting and beautiful painting, it's the architecture that makes it worth the hike through a lively middle-class Venetian residential neighborhood to get here. The Franciscan church was enlarged and rebuilt by Sansovino in 1534, and its facade was added in 1562 by Palladio. It represents, therefore, a unique collaboration of the two great stars of Veneto 16th-century architecture. Antonio Vivarini's (circa 1415–84) triptych of Saints Girolamo, Bernardino da Siena, and Ludovico hangs to your right as you enter the main door. Giovanni Bellini's *Madonna with Saints* is down some steps to the left, inside the Cappella Santa. ✉ *Campo di San Francesco della Vigna, Castello* ☎ *041/5206102* 🎫 *Free* ⏲ *Daily 8–12:30 and 3–7* Ⓥ *Celestia.*

San Zaccaria. A striking Renaissance facade, with central and upper portions representing some of Mauro Codussi's best work, is attached to this 14th-century Gothic church. The facade was completed in 1515, some years after Codussi's death in 1504, and retains the proportions of the rest of the essentially Gothic structure. Giovanni Bellini's celebrated

CLOSE UP

Let's Get Lost

Getting around Venice presents some unusual problems: the city's layout has few straight lines; house numbering seems nonsensical; and the six sestieri of San Marco, Cannaregio, Castello, Dorsoduro, Santa Croce, and San Polo all duplicate each other's street names. The numerous vaporetto lines can be bewildering, and often the only option for getting where you want to go is to walk. Yellow signs, posted on many busy corners, point toward the major landmarks—San Marco, Rialto, Accademia, and so forth—but don't count on finding such markers once you're deep into residential neighborhoods. Even buying a good map at a newsstand—the kind showing all street names and vaporetto routes—won't necessarily keep you from getting lost.

Fortunately, as long as you maintain your patience, getting lost in Venice can be a pleasure. For one thing, being lost is a sign that you've escaped the tourist throngs. And although you might not find the Titian masterpiece you'd set out to see, instead you could wind up coming across an ageless bacaro or a quirky shop that turns out to be the highlight of your afternoon. Opportunities for such serendipity abound. Keep in mind that the city is nothing if not self-contained: sooner or later, perhaps with the help of a patient native, you can rest assured you'll regain your bearings.

altarpiece, *La Sacra Conversazione*, is easily recognizable in the left nave. Completed in 1505, when the artist was 75, it shows Bellini's ability to incorporate the esthetics of the High Renaissance into his work. It bears a closer resemblance to the contemporary works of Leonardo (it dates from approximately the same time as the *Mona Lisa*) than it does to much of Bellini's early work. The **Cappella di San Tarasio** displays frescoes by Tuscan Renaissance artists Andrea del Castagno (1423–57) and Francesco da Faenza (circa 1400–1451). Castagno's frescoes (1442) are considered the earliest examples of Renaissance painting in Venice. The three outstanding Gothic polyptychs attributed to Antonio Vivarini earned it the nickname "Golden Chapel." ✉ *Campo San Zaccaria, 4693 Castello* ☎ *041/5221257* 🎟 *Church free, chapels and crypt €1* ⏲ *Mon.–Sat. 10–noon and 4–6, Sun. 4–6* Ⓥ *San Zaccaria.*

Scuola di San Giorgio degli Schiavoni. Founded in 1451 by the Dalmatian community, this small scuola was, and still is, a social and cultural center for migrants from what is now Croatia. It's dominated by one of Italy's most beautiful rooms, lavishly yet harmoniously decorated with the *teleri* (large canvases) of Vittore Carpaccio. A lifelong Venice resident, Carpaccio painted legendary and religious figures against backgrounds of Venetian architecture. Here he focused on saints especially venerated in Dalmatia: Saints George, Tryphone, and Jerome. He combined keen empirical observation with fantasy, a sense of warm color, and late medieval realism. (Note the priests fleeing Saint Jerome's lion, or the body parts in the dragon's lair.) ✉ *Calle dei Furlani, Castello 3259/A* ☎ *041/5228828* 🎟 *€4* ⏲ *Tues.–Sat. 9:15–1 and 2:45–6, Sun. 10–12:30. Last entry 1 hr before closing* Ⓥ *Arsenale, San Zaccaria.*

SAN GIORGIO MAGGIORE AND THE GIUDECCA

Beckoning travelers across Saint Mark's Basin, sparkling white through the mist, is the island of San Giorgio Maggiore, separated by a small channel from the Giudecca. A tall brick campanile on that distant bank perfectly complements the Campanile of San Marco. Beneath it looms the stately dome of one of Venice's greatest churches, San Giorgio Maggiore, the creation of Andrea Palladio.

You can reach San Giorgio Maggiore via vaporetto Line 2 from San Zaccaria. The next three stops on the line take you to the Giudecca. The island's past may be shrouded in mystery, but today it's about as down to earth as you can get and one of the city's few remaining neighborhoods that feels truly Venetian.

TIMING

A half day should be plenty of time to visit the area. Allow about a half hour to see each of the churches and an hour or two to look around the Giudecca.

TOP ATTRACTIONS

San Giorgio Maggiore. There's been a church on this island since the 8th century, with a Benedictine monastery added in the 10th century (closed to the public). Today's refreshingly airy and simply decorated church of brick and white marble was begun in 1566 by Palladio and displays his architectural hallmarks of mathematical harmony and classical influence. *The Last Supper* and the *Gathering of Manna,* two of Tintoretto's later works, line the chancel. To the right of the entrance hangs *The Adoration of the Shepherds* by Jacopo Bassano (1517–92); his affection for his foothills home, Bassano del Grappa, is evident in the bucolic subjects and terra-firma colors he chooses. The monks are happy to show Carpaccio's *St. George and the Dragon,* hanging in a private room, if they have time. The campanile dates from 1791, the previous structures having collapsed twice. ✉ *Isola di San Giorgio Maggiore* ☎ *041/5227827* 🎟 *Church free, campanile €3* ⏲ *Daily 9–12:30 and 2:30–6* Ⓥ *San Giorgio.*

Santissimo Redentore. After a 16th-century plague claimed some 50,000 people, nearly one-third of the city's population, Andrea Palladio was asked to design a commemorative church. Giudecca's Capucin friars offered land and their services, provided the building was in keeping with the simplicity of their hermitage. Consecrated in 1592, Palladio's creation, which is considered his supreme achievement in ecclesiastical design, is dominated by a dome and a pair of slim, almost minaret-like bell towers. Its deceptively simple, stately facade leads to a bright, airy interior.

For hundreds of years, on the third weekend in July the doge would make a pilgrimage here to give thanks to the Redeemer for ending a 16th-century plague. The event has become the Festa del Redentore, a favorite Venetian festival featuring boats, fireworks, and outdoor feasting. It's the one time of year you can walk to Giudecca—across a temporary pontoon bridge connecting Redentore with the Zattere. ✉ *Fondamenta San Giacomo, Giudecca* ☎ *041/5231415, 041/2750462 Chorus Foundation* 🎫 *€3, Chorus Pass €10* ⏲ *Mon.–Sat. 10–5, Sun. 1–5* Ⓥ *Redentore.*

WORTH NOTING

Giudecca. The island's name is something of a mystery. It may come from a possible 14th-century Jewish settlement, or because 9th-century nobles condemned to *giudicato* (exile) were sent here. It became a pleasure garden for wealthy Venetians during the Republic's long and luxurious decline, but today, like Cannaregio, it's largely working class. The Giudecca provides spectacular views of Venice and is becoming increasingly gentrified. Thanks to several bridges, you can walk the entire length of the Giudecca's promenade, relaxing at one of several restaurants or just taking in the lively atmosphere. Accommodations run the gamut from youth hostels to the city's most exclusive hotel, Cipriani. ✉ *Fondamenta San Giacomo, Giudecca* ☎ *041/2750462 Chorus Foundation* 🌐 *www.chorusvenezia.org* 🎫 *€3, Chorus Pass €10* ⏲ *Mon.–Sat. 10–5* Ⓥ *Redentore.*

ISLANDS OF THE LAGOON

The perfect vacation from your Venetian vacation is an escape to Murano, Burano, and sleepy Torcello, the islands of the northern lagoon. Torcello offers ancient mosaics, greenery, breathing space, and picnic opportunities (remember to pack lunch). Burano is an island of fishing traditions and houses painted in a riot of colors—blue, yellow, pink, ocher, and dark red. Visitors still love to shop here for "Venetian" lace, even though the vast majority of it is machine-made in Taiwan; visit the island's Museo del Merletto (Lace Museum) to discover the undeniable difference between the two.

Murano is renowned for its glass, plenty of which you can find in Venice itself. It's also notorious for high-pressure sales on factory tours, even those organized by top hotels. Vaporetto connections to Murano aren't difficult, and for the price of a boat ticket (included in any vaporetto pass), you'll buy your freedom and more time to explore. The Murano "guides" herding new arrivals follow a rotation so that factories take turns giving tours, but you can avoid the hustle by just walking away. **■ TIP→ Don't take a "free" taxi to Murano: it only means that should you choose to buy (and you will be strongly encouraged), your taxi fare and commission will be included in the price you pay.**

TIMING

Hitting all the sights on all the islands takes a busy, full day. If you limit yourself to Murano and San Michele, you can easily explore for an ample half day; the same goes for Burano and Torcello. In summer, the express vaporetto Line 5 will take you to Murano from San Zaccaria (the Jolanda landing) in 25 minutes; otherwise, local Line 41 makes a 45-minute trip from San Zaccaria every 20 minutes, circling the east end of Venice, stopping at Fondamente Nove and San Michele

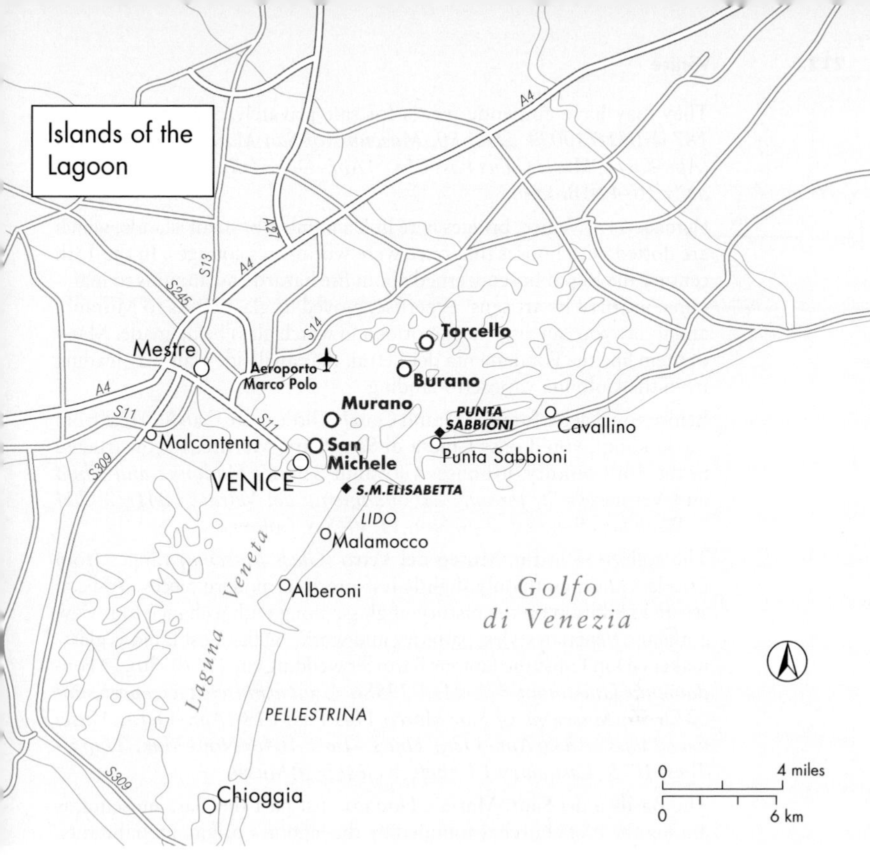

island cemetery on the way. To see glassblowing, get off at Colonna; the Museo stop will put you near the Museo del Vetro.

Line LN goes from Fondamente Nove direct to Murano and Burano every 30 minutes (Torcello is a 5-minute ferry from there); the full trip takes 45 minutes each way. To get to Burano and Torcello from Murano, pick up Line LN at the Faro stop (Murano's lighthouse).

TOP ATTRACTIONS

★ **Burano.** Cheerfully painted houses line the canals of this quiet village where lace making rescued a faltering fishing-based economy centuries ago. As you walk the 100 yards from the dock to Piazza Galuppi, the main square, you pass stall after stall of lace vendors. These good-natured ladies won't press you with a hard sell, but don't expect precise product information or great bargains—authentic, handmade Burano lace costs $1,000 to $2,000 for a 10-inch doily.

The **Museo del Merletto** (Lace Museum) lets you marvel at the intricacies of Burano's lace making. At this writing, the museum is closed for renovations, with plans to reopen in 2011. The museum will likely continue to host a "sewing circle" of sorts, where on most weekdays you can watch local women carrying on the lace-making tradition.

They may have authentic pieces for sale privately. ✉ *Piazza Galuppi 187* ☎ *041/730034* 🎟 *€4.50, Museums of San Marco Plus Pass €13 (Apr.–Oct.), Musei Civici Pass €18* ⏲ *Apr.–Oct., daily 10–5; Nov.–Mar., daily 10–4* Ⓥ *Burano.*

Murano. As in Venice, bridges here link a number of small islands, which are dotted with houses that once were workmen's cottages. In the 13th century the Republic, concerned about fire hazard and anxious to maintain control of its artisans' expertise, moved its glassworks to Murano, and today you can visit the factories and watch glass being made. Many of them line the Fondamenta dei Vetrai, the canal-side walkway leading from the Colonna vaporetto landing.

Before you reach Murano's Grand Canal (a little more than 800 feet from the landing), you'll pass **Chiesa di San Pietro Martire.** Reconstructed in the 16th century, it houses Giovanni Bellini's *Madonna and Child* and Veronese's *St. Jerome.* ✉ *Fondamenta dei Vetrai* ☎ *041/739704* ⏲ *Weekdays 9–6, Sat. 2–6, Sun. 11:30–5* Ⓥ *Colonna.*

The collection at the **Museo del Vetro** *(Glass Museum)* ranges from priceless antiques to only slightly less-precious modern pieces. You can see an exhibition on the history of glass, along with a chance to review authentic Venetian styles, patterns, and works by the most famous glassmakers. Don't miss the famous Barovier wedding cup (1470–80). ✉ *Fondamenta Giustinian 8* ☎ *041/739586* 🌐 *www.museiciviciveneziani.it* 🎟 *€6.50, Museums of San Marco Plus Pass €13 (Apr.–Oct.), Musei Civici Pass €18* ⏲ *Apr.–Oct., Thurs.–Tues. 10–6; Nov.–Mar., Thurs.–Tues. 10–5. Last entry 1 hr before closing* Ⓥ *Museo.*

The **Basilica dei Santi Maria e Donato,** just past the glass museum, is among the first churches founded by the lagoon's original inhabitants. The elaborate mosaic pavement includes the date 1140; its ship's-keel roof and Veneto-Byzantine columns add to the semblance of an ancient temple. ✉ *Fondamenta Giustinian* ☎ *041/739056* ⏲ *Mon.–Sat. 8–6, Sun. 2–6* Ⓥ *Museo.*

★ **Torcello.** In their flight from barbarians 1,500 years ago, the first Venetians landed here, prospering even after many left to found the city of Venice. By the 10th century, Torcello had a population of 10,000 and was more powerful than Venice. From the 12th century on, the lagoon around the island began silting up, and a malarial swamp developed. As malaria took its toll, Torcello was gradually abandoned and its palaces and houses were dismantled, their stones used for building materials in Venice. **Santa Maria Assunta** was built in the 11th century, and Torcello's wealth at the time is evident in the church's high-quality mosaics. The mosaics show the gradually increasing cultural independence of Venice from Byzantium. The magnificent late-12th-century mosaic of the Last Judgment shows the transition from the stiffer Byzantine style on the left to the more-fluid Venetian style on the right. The virgin in the main apse dates possibly from about 1185, and is of a distinctly Byzantine type, with her right hand pointing to the Christ child held with her left arm. The 12 apostles below her are possibly the oldest mosaics in the church and date from the early 12th century. The adjacent **Santa Fosca** church, built when the body of the saint arrived in 1011, is still used for religious services. The bell tower is undergoing renovation (completion date is unknown at this writing). It is not accessible to visitors. ✉ *Isola di Torcello* ☎ *041/2960630* 🎫 *Santa Maria Assunta €5, audio guide €1* ⏲ *Basilica: Mar.–Oct., daily 10:30–6; Nov.–Feb., daily 10–5. Campanile: Mar.–Oct., daily 10:30–5:30; Nov.–Feb., daily 10–4:30. Last entry ½ hr before closing* Ⓥ *Torcello.*

QUICK BITES

Locanda Cipriani (✉ *Piazza Santa Fosca 29, Isola di Torcello* ☎ *041/730150*), closed Tuesday and January, is famous for good food and its connection to Ernest Hemingway, who often came to Torcello seeking solitude. Today the restaurant (still in the Cipriani family, along with Harry's Bar in Venice) is busy with well-heeled customers speeding in for lunch (dinner also on weekends). Dining is pricey, but you can relax in the garden with just a glass of prosecco.

WORTH NOTING

San Michele. Tiny, cypress-lined San Michele is home to the pretty **San Michele in Isola** Renaissance church—and to some of Venice's most illustrious deceased—and nothing else. The church was designed by Codussi; the graves include those of poet Ezra Pound (1885–1972), impresario and art critic Sergey Diaghilev (1872–1929), and composer Igor Stravinsky (1882–1971). Surrounded by the living sounds of Venice's lagoon, this would seem the perfect final resting place. However, these days newcomers are exhumed after 10 years and transferred to a less-grandiose location. ✉ *Isola di San Michele* ☎ *041/7292811* ⏲ *Apr.–Sept., daily 7:30–6; Oct.–Mar., daily 7:30–4* Ⓥ *Cimitero.*

WHERE TO EAT

Dining options in Venice range from the ultra high-end, where jackets and ties are a must, to the very casual. Once staunchly traditional, many restaurants have renovated their menus along with their dining rooms, creating dishes that blend classic Venetian elements with ingredients less common to the lagoon environs.

Mid-range restaurants are often more willing to make the break, offering innovative options while keeping dishes like *sarde in saor* and *fegato alla veneziana* available as mainstays. Restaurants are often quite small with limited seating, so make sure to reserve ahead. It's not uncommon for restaurants to have two seatings a night, one at 7 and one at 9.

There's no getting around the fact that Venice has more than its share of overpriced, mediocre eateries that prey on tourists. Avoid places with cajoling waiters standing outside, and beware of restaurants that don't display their prices. At the other end of the spectrum, showy *menu turistico* (tourist menu) boards make offerings clear in a dozen languages, but for the same €15–€20 you'd spend at such places you could do better at a *bacaro* making a meal of *cichetti* (savory snacks).

Use the coordinate (⊕ B2) at the end of each listing to locate a site on the Where to Eat and Stay in Venice map.

3

WHAT IT COSTS IN EUROS					
	¢	$	$$	$$$	$$$$
At dinner	under €20	€20–€30	€30–€45	€45–€65	over €65

Prices are for a first course (primo), second course (secondo), and dessert (dolce).

CANNAREGIO

$$$ VENETIAN ✕ **Al Fontego dei Pescatori.** Having had a stall at the Rialto fish market for more than 25 years, and being the president of the area fishmongers association for 10, proprietor "Lolo" knows his fish. The seafood served here might just be the freshest in Venice. Antipasti include Orologio, a "clock" of raw selections; Poker, four different *tartars* of seafood and fresh fruit; and succulent grilled *capelunghe* (razor clams). The pasta is served al dente, the risotto *al onda* (undulating, as opposed to firm). Chef Massimo prepares entrées simply but always with a twist, such as *branzino* (sea bass) topped with its own crispy skin or a frizzle of zucchini. The wine list includes excellent regional choices that pair well with fish. There's meat for non–fish eaters, too. The dining rooms are spacious and the garden is enchanting in temperate weather. ✉ *Calle Priuli, Cannaregio 3711* ☎ *041/5200538* ⊙ *Closed Mon., 3 wks in Jan., 2 wks in Aug. No lunch in July and Aug.* Ⓥ *Ca' d'Oro* ✥ *D2.*

$$ ITALIAN ✕ **Algiubagiò.** A waterfront table is still relatively affordable at lunchtime here on Venice's northern Fondamente Nove, where you can gaze out toward San Michele and Murano—on a clear day you can even see the Dolomites. Algiubagiò has a dual personality: pizzas and big salads at lunch; at dinner, creative *primi* (first courses) like ravioli stuffed with *pecorino di fossa* (a hard sheep's-milk cheese) are followed by elegant *secondi* (second courses) such as Angus fillets with vodka and Gorgonzola. The young, friendly staff also serves ice cream, drinks, and sandwiches all day. A lunch table here is worth the walk for the view; the price rises considerably at dinner. ✉ *Fondamente Nove, Cannaregio 5039* ☎ *041/5236084* 🌐 *www.algiubagio.net* ✍ *Reservations essentialfor dinner* Ⓥ *Fondamente Nove* ✥ *E2.*

$–$$ VENETIAN ✕ **Anice Stellato.** Off the main concourse, on one of the most romantic *fondamente* (canal-side streets) of Cannaregio, this family-run bacaro-trattoria is the place to stop for fairly priced, satisfying fare, though service can feel indifferent. The space has plenty of character: narrow columns rise from the colorful tile floor, dividing the room into cozy sections. Venetian classics are enriched with such offerings as *carpacci di pesce* (thin slices of raw tuna, swordfish, or salmon dressed with olive oil and fragrant herbs), tagliatelle with king prawns and zucchini flowers, and several tasty fish stews. They also serve several meat dishes, including a tender beef fillet stewed in Barolo wine with potatoes. Book early to grab one of the outdoor waterside tables on summer evenings. ✉ *Fondamenta de la Sensa, Cannaregio 3272* ☎ *041/720744* ⊙ *Closed Mon. and Tues., 1 wk in Feb., and 3 wks in Aug.* Ⓥ *San Alvise or San Marcuola* ✥ *C1.*

$–$$ ITALIAN ★ **Botteghe di Promessi Sposi.** The former Promessi Sposi eatery was rejuvenated when three *fioi* (guys) with decades of restaurant experience joined forces to open this restaurant. Claudio mans the kitchen, while Nicola and Cristiano will serve you either an *ombra* (small glass of wine) and cicchetto at the *banco* (counter), or a delightful meal in the dining room or the intimate courtyard. A season-centered menu includes standards like Venetian calves' liver and grilled *canestrelli* (tiny Venetian scallops) along with more adventurous creations, like homemade ravioli stuffed with *rapi rossi* (red turnip) and topped with the Sardinian ricotta *salata* (a firm, medium-aged ricotta), or a steak tartar served with bean sprouts and spoonfuls of capers, paprika, mustard, and minced red onions. It's the best of many worlds: a comfy trattoria where there's something for everyone. ✉ *Calle de l'Oca (just off Campo Santi Apostoli), Cannaregio 4367* ☎ *041/2412747* ✍ *Reservations essential* ▭ *No credit cards* ⏲ *Closed Wed.* V *Ca' d'Oro* ✥ *E2.*

$$$$ ITALIAN **Fiaschetteria Toscana.** Contrary to what the name suggests, there's nothing Tuscan about this restaurant's menu. It was formerly a Tuscan wine-and-oil storehouse, and it's worth a visit for its cheerful and courteous service, fine *cucina* (cooking), and noteworthy cellar. The owners, Albino and Mariuccia Busatto, make their presence felt as they walk among the well-appointed tables, opening special bottles of wine and discussing the menu. Gastronomic highlights include a light *tagliolini neri al ragù di astice* (thin spaghetti served with squid ink and mixed with a delicate lobster sauce), and zabaglione. ✉ *Campo San Giovanni Crisostomo, Cannaregio 5719* ☎ *041/5285281* 🌐 *www.fiaschetteriatoscana.it* ✍ *Reservations essential* ⏲ *Closed Tues. and 4 wks in July and Aug. No lunch Wed.* V *Rialto* ✥ *E3.*

$ CONTEMPORARY **La Cantina.** With its understated facade, you'd never guess that La Cantina offered anything more than a nice sandwich and an acceptable pinot grigio. Perhaps if you spotted the fresh raw oysters, a whole tuna patiently waiting to be filleted, or the sign for today's *zuppa di lenticchie* (lentil soup), you might begin to understand how satisfying a meal here can be. Co-owner and chef Francesco chooses from only the choicest meats and cheeses, the freshest vegetables, seasonings, and fish to create his inspired meals. There's effectively no menu: tell co-owner Andrea or wine expert Giovanni your preferences and your budget, then sit back and wait to be satisfied. One caveat: Service can be slow on busier evenings, especially after 8 pm. ✉ *Campo San Felice, Cannaregio 3689* ☎ *041/5228258* ✍ *Reservations essential* ⏲ *Closed Sun. and Mon.* V *Ca' d'Oro* ✥ *D2.*

$$ ITALIAN Fodor's Choice ★ **Osteria Orto dei Mori.** "Pure pleasure" might be the best way to describe the dining experience here: from the fanciful, tasteful interior decor, to romantic candlelit tables dotting the Campo dei Mori, to the inspired cucina. The attentive expertise of chef and co-owner Lorenzo is evident in every dish: try the *fagotti* (bundles of beef marinated in Chianti with goat cheese) or a seafood version with prawns, zucchini, and ricotta. Risotto with scampi and savory *fenferli* mushrooms won't disappoint, nor will the signature parchment-baked monkfish. Co-owner Micael has artfully constructed the wine list—ask about periodic tastings. The osteria is just under the nose of the campo's corner statue. ✉ *Campo*

dei Mori, Fondamenta dei Mori, Cannaregio 3386 ☎ 041/5235544 ⊗ Closed Tues. V Orto, Ca d'Oro, or San Marcuola ✣ D1.*

¢ CAFÉ ✕ **Tiziano.** A staggering array of *tramezzini* (sandwiches) lines the display cases at this *tavola calda* (roughly the Italian equivalent of a cafeteria) on the main drag from the Rialto to Santi Apostoli; inexpensive salad plates and daily pasta specials are also served. Whether you choose to sit or stand, it's a handy—and popular—spot for a quick meal or a snack at very modest prices. Vegetarians delight in Tiziano's version of the classic Italian toast, in this case a grilled-cheese sandwich with eggplant slices and roasted zucchini. ✉ *Salizzada San Giovanni Crisostomo, Cannaregio 5747* ☎ *041/5235544* ▭ *No credit cards* V *Rialto* ✣ *E3.*

$$ VENETIAN Fodor's Choice ★ ✕ **Vini da Gigio.** Paolo and Laura, a brother-sister team, run this refined trattoria as if they've invited you to dinner in their home, while keeping the service professional. Deservedly popular with Venetians and visitors alike, it's one of the best values in the city. Indulge in homemade pastas such as rigatoni with duck sauce and arugula-stuffed ravioli. Fish is well represented—try the sesame-encrusted tuna—but the meat dishes steal the show. The *anatra* (duck) is a flavorful fricassee; the steak with red-pepper sauce and the *tagliata di agnello* (sautéed lamb fillet with a light, crusty coating) are both superb, and you'll never enjoy a better *fegato alla veneziana* (Venetian-style liver with onions). It's a shame to order the house wine here: just let Paolo know your budget and he'll choose for you from his more than 3,000 labels. ✉ *Fondamenta San Felice, Cannaregio 3628/A* ☎ *041/5285140* ⊕ *www.vinidagigio.com* ✍ *Reservations essential* ⊗ *Closed Mon. and Tues., 2 wks in Jan., and 3 wks in Aug.* V *Ca' d'Oro* ✣ *D2.*

CASTELLO

$ WINE BAR ★ ✕ **El Rèfolo.** This hip hangout is named after a play by turn-of-the-20th-century emancipated lady Amalia Rosselli—look for the framed title page inside. El Rèfolo (The Breeze, in Venetian) is a contemporary cantina in a very Venetian neighborhood, and is more for lunch, *un aperitivo* (an aperitif), or supper than formal dinner. Owner Massimiliano pairs great wines with select meats, savory cheese, and seasonal vegetable combos. In temperate weather this niche-size *enoteca*'s exuberance effervesces out onto the city's broadest street. It's open every day but Sunday from 9:30 am to 12:30 am. ✉ *Via Garibaldi 1580, Castello* ☎ *No phone* ⊗ *Closed Sun., hrs limited in winter* V *Arsenale* ✣ *H5.*

$$$$ VENETIAN ✕ **Il Ridotto.** Longtime restaurateur Gianni Bonaccorsi of nearby Acigheta fame has succeeded in opening a locale that is the pure expression of the best he has to offer. Ridotto, "reduced" in Italian, may refer to the size of this tiny, gracious restaurant. The dimensions allow Gianni to spoil you, should you manage to snag one of the five tables (easier at lunch). The artful menu is revised daily, a luxury only such a personalized restaurant can afford; you may find fettuccine with Piedmont Fassona beef ragout or scampi with crustacean sauce, and, for dessert, pistachio flan. The tasting menu never fails to impress. Have Gianni choose a wine for you from his excellent cantina. ✉ *Campo SS Filippo e Giacomo, Castello 4509* ☎ *041/5208280* ⊕ *www.ilridotto.com* ✍ *Reservations essential* ⊗ *Closed Wed. No lunch Thurs.* V *San Zaccaria* ✣ *F4.*

3

BEST BETS FOR VENICE DINING

With hundreds of restaurants to choose from, how will you decide where to eat? Fodor's writers and editors have selected their favorite restaurants by price and experience in the Best Bets lists below. In the first column, Fodor's Choice properties represent the "best of the best."

Fodor's Choice ★

Al Paradiso, $$$, p. 219
Antiche Carampane, $$$, p. 222
La Zucca, $, p. 223
Osteria Orto dei Mori, $$, p. 215
Vini da Gigio, $$, p. 216

By Price

¢

Cantinone già Schiavi, p. 224

$

Al Prosecco, p. 223
Antico Panificio, p. 222
Botteghe di Promessi Sposi, p. 215
La Cantina, p. 215
La Zucca, p. 223
Muro Pizzeria con Cucina, p. 223
Ostaria al Garanghelo, p. 222

$$

Anice Stellato, p. 214
La Bitta, p. 218
Osteria Orto dei Mori, p. 215
Vini da Gigio, p. 216

$$$

Al Fontego dei Pescatori, p. 214
Al Paradiso, p. 219
Antiche Carampane, p. 222

$$$$

De Pisis, p. 219
Fiaschetteria Toscana, p. 215
Il Ridotto, p. 216

Best by Experience

OUTDOOR DINING

Al Fontego dei Pescatori, $$$, p. 214
Algiubagiò, $$, p. 214
La Cantina, $, p. 215
Muro Pizzeria con Cucina, $, p. 223
Osteria Orto dei Mori, $$, p. 215
Ristorante Riviera, $$$, p. 219

ROMANTIC

Al Fontego dei Pescatori, $$$, p. 214
Al Paradiso, $$$, p. 219
Anice Stellato, $$, p. 214
De Pisis, $$$$, p. 219
Osteria Orto dei Mori, $$, p. 215
Ristorante Riviera, $$$, p. 219

GOOD FOR KIDS

Antico Panificio, $, p. 222
La Trattoria ai Tosi, $, p. 218
Ostaria al Garanghelo, $, p. 222

IF YOU DON'T WANT FISH

La Bitta, $$, p. 218
La Zucca, $, p. 223
Muro Pizzeria con Cucina (Frari location), $, p. 223
Vini da Gigio, $$, p. 216

GREAT VIEWS

Algiubagiò, $$, p. 214
De Pisis, $$$$, p. 219
Ristorante Riviera, $$$, p. 219

EXCEPTIONAL WINE LIST

Antiche Carampane, $$$, p. 222
La Cantina, $, p. 215
Osteria Orto dei Mori, $$, p. 215
Ristoteca Oniga, $$, p. 219
Vini da Gigio, $$, p. 216

GOOD FOR LUNCH

Al Prosecco, $, p. 223
El Rèfolo, $, p. 216
La Cantina, $, p. 215
La Zucca, $, p. 223
Muro Pizzeria con Cucina, $, p. 223
Ostaria al Garanghelo, $, p. 222

CUCINA ALTA (SOPHISTICATED CUISINE)

De Pisis, $$$$, p. 219
Il Ridotto, $$$$, p. 216

CASALINGA (HOME COOKING)

Antico Panificio, $, p. 222
La Trattoria ai Tosi, $, p. 218
Ostaria al Garanghelo, $, p. 222

$ ✕ **La Trattoria ai Tosi.** Getting off the beaten track to find good, basic local
ITALIAN cuisine isn't easy in Venice, but La Trattoria ai Tosi (aka Ai Tosi Piccoli) fills the bill with its remote (but not too), tranquil location, homey atmosphere, and variety of fine traditional fare at prices that make it worth the walk from anywhere in the city. The baccalà mantecato "sanwicini" are excellent, as are the classic frittura mista and the spaghetti with scallops and zucchini (a bargain at €10). You'll also find a grilled steak and ribs platter that should fulfill any meat cravings. The fixed-price lunch menu, created for local workers with limited time, is another good deal, and there's even decemt pizza. (Note: make sure you end up at this smaller, locally owned Tosi, rather than the Tosi Grande across the way that's no longer family owned.) ✉ *Seco Marina 738, Castello* ☎ *041/5237102* ⏲ *Closed Mon.* Ⓥ *Giardini* ✣ *H5.*

DORSODURO

$$ ✕ **Ai 4 Feri.** The paper tablecloths and cozy, laid-back ambience are part
VENETIAN of this small restaurant's charm. The menu varies according to what's fresh that day; imaginative combinations of ingredients in the primi—herring and sweet peppers, salmon and radicchio, giant shrimp and broccoli with pumpkin gnocchi—are the norm. A meal here followed by after-dinner gelato at Il Doge or drinks in Campo Santa Margherita, a five-minute walk away, makes for a lovely evening. The kitchen is open until 10:30 pm. ✉ *Calle Lunga San Barnaba, Dorsoduro 2754/A* ☎ *041/5206978* ▭ *No credit cards* ⏲ *Closed Sun. and 2 wks in June* Ⓥ *Ca' Rezzonico* ✣ *B4.*

$$ ✕ **La Bitta.** The decor is more discreet, the dining hours longer, and
ITALIAN the service friendlier and more efficient here than in many small restaurants in Venice—and the creative non-fish menu is a temptation at every course. You can start with a light salad of Treviso radicchio and crispy bacon, followed by smoked-beef carpaccio or *gnocchetti ubriachi al Montasio* (small, marinated gnocchi with Montasio cheese). Then choose a secondo such as lamb chops with thyme, *anatra in pevarada* (duck in a pepper sauce), or Irish Angus fillet steak. Secondi are served with vegetables, which helps bring down the price. The restaurant is open only for dinner, but serves much earlier and later than most, continuously from 6:30 to 11. ✉ *Calle Lunga San Barnaba, Dorsoduro 2753/A* ☎ *041/5230531* ✍ *Reservations essential* ▭ *No credit cards* ⏲ *Closed Sun. and July. No lunch* Ⓥ *Ca' Rezzonico* ✣ *B4.*

$ ✕ **L'Incontro.** This trattoria between San Barnaba and Campo Santa Mar-
ITALIAN gherita has a faithful clientele of Venetians and visitors, attracted by
★ flavorful Sardinian food, sociable service, and reasonable prices. Starters include Sardinian sausages, but you might skip to the delicious traditional primi, such as *culingiones* (large ravioli filled with pecorino, saffron, and orange peel). The selection of secondi is heavy on herb-crusted meat dishes such as *coniglio al mirto* (rabbit baked on a bed of myrtle sprigs) and the *costine d'agnello con rosmarino e mentuccia* (baby lamb ribs with rosemary and wild mint). ✉ *Rio Terà Canal (just off Campo Santa Margherita), Dorsoduro 3062/A* ☎ *041/5222404* ⏲ *Closed Mon., Jan., and 2 wks in Aug. No lunch Tues.* Ⓥ *Ca' Rezzonico* ✣ *B4.*

$$$ NORTHERN ITALIAN ✕ **Ristorante Riviera.** Two lovely dining rooms and a canal-side terrace with an exquisite view, combined with truly inspired cuisine, make a visit to Riviera one to remember. Chef Monica Scarpa brings her creative touch to both traditional and contemporary dishes. Fish lovers will enjoy the tuna tartare, seafood risotto, or a mixed-fish platter, while carnivores can dig into prosciutto with figs and pecorino cheese followed by a plate of succulent lamb chops with blueberry sauce. Host Luca excels at selecting the perfect wine for any combination of foods. A simple but appealing children's menu is offered. ✉ *Zattere, Dorsoduro 1473* ☎ *041/5227621* 🌐 *www.ristoranteriviera.it* *Reservations essential* *Closed Mon. and 4 wks in Jan. and Feb. No lunch Wed.* Ⓥ *San Basilio* ✥ *B5.*

$$ VENETIAN ✕ **Ristoteca Oniga.** Marino Oniga and his wife, Annika, successfully combine classic Venetian elements in an out-of-the-ordinary way, adding a touch of personality and imagination to both creation and presentation. Delectably roasted duck is one of several meat alternatives to the fresh fish; the wine list is ample, and Annika's desserts are all *fatto in casa* (homemade). The outdoor seating in Campo San Barnaba makes a charming setting for a delightful meal. ✉ *Campo San Barnaba, Dorsoduro 2852* ☎ *041/0997534* 🌐 *www.oniga.it* *Reservations essential* *Closed Tues.* Ⓥ *Ca' Rezzonico* ✥ *B4.*

SAN MARCO

$$$$ MODERN ITALIAN ✕ **De Pisis.** Romance and elegance pervade the interior and luminous terrace here, which has a Grand Canal panorama that includes the radiant Santa Maria della Salute. The service is impeccable, as is Chef Giovanni Ciresa's cuisine, where you'll find Venetian, Asian, and Mediterranean influences synthesized to create inspired, delectable works of art. If you're feeling adventurous, do try one of the chef's experimental dishes for which he is quite famous and let your sommelier suggest a wine from their masterful list. This formal restaurant attracts well-dressed clientele and is a fine choice for a splurge. ✉ *Calle San Moise, San Marco 1459* ☎ *041/5207022* *Reservations essential* Ⓥ *Valaresso or Santa Maria del Giglio* ✥ *E5.*

SAN POLO

$$$ MODERN ITALIAN Fodor's Choice ★ ✕ **Al Paradiso.** In a small dining room made warm and cozy by its pleasing and unpretentious decor, proprietor Giordano makes all diners feel like honored guests. Pappardelle "al Paradiso" takes pasta with seafood sauce to new heights, while risotto with shrimp, champagne, and grapefruit puts a delectable twist on a traditional dish. The inspired and original array of entrées includes meat and fish selections such as a salmon with honey and balsamic vinegar in a stunning presentation. Desserts include a perfect panna cotta. ✉ *Calle del Paradiso, San Polo 767* ☎ *041/5234910* *Reservations essential* *Closed Mon. and 3 wks in Jan. and Feb.* Ⓥ *San Silvestro* ✥ *D3.*

$$$ VENETIAN ✕ **Alla Madonna.** Locals relax at Alla Madonna, which prides itself on the freshness, abundance, and quality of their fish. In business since 1954 (Rado Fluvio still runs the place), it is a classic in service, atmosphere, and cuisine. The *materia prima* (the principal ingredients) are

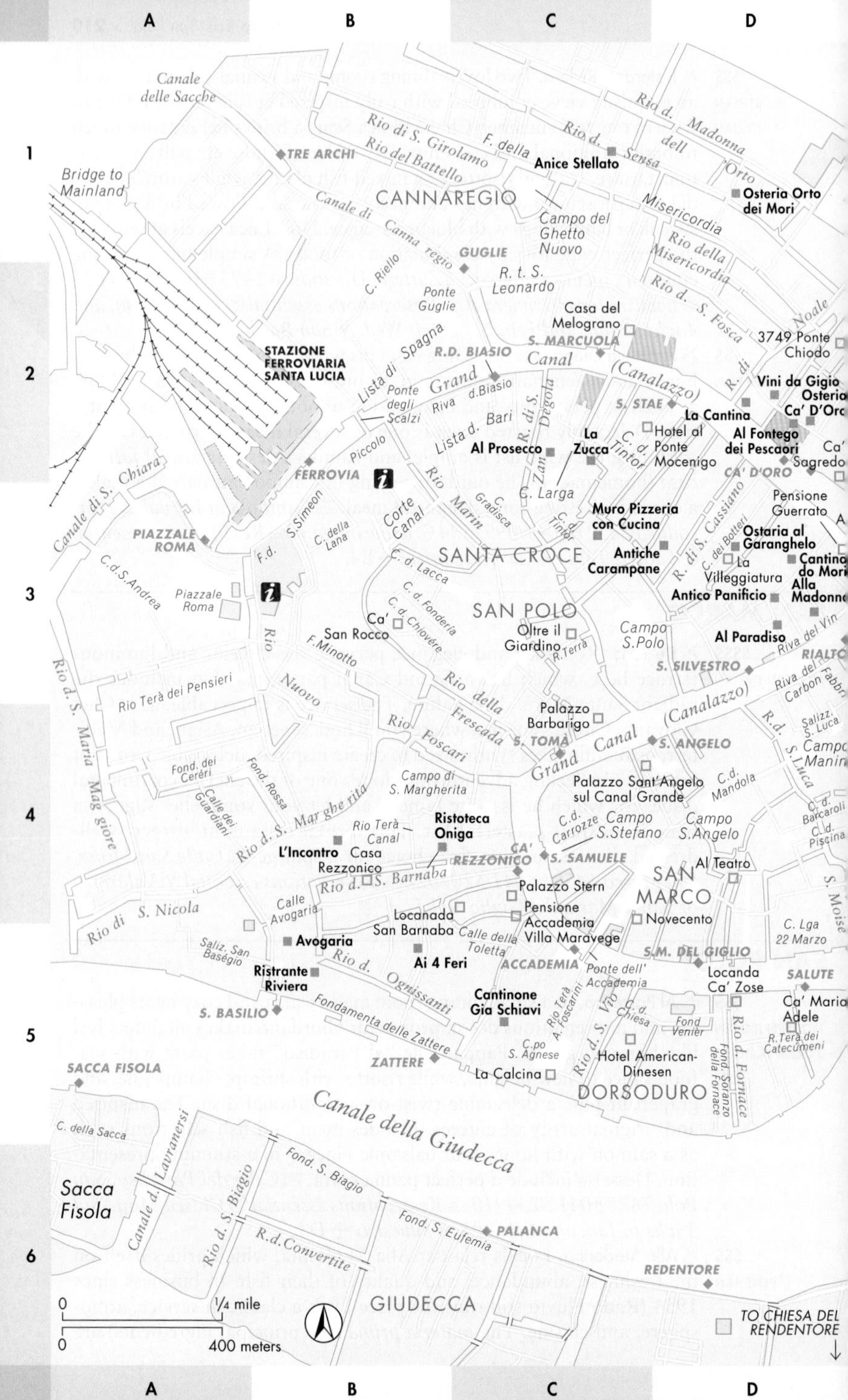

A
B
C
D
1
2
3
4
5
6
Canale delle Sacche
TRE ARCHI
Bridge to Mainland
Rio di S. Girolamo
Rio del Battello
F. della
Rio d. Sensa
Anice Stellato
Rio d. Madonna dell 'Orto
Osteria Orto dei Mori
CANNAREGIO
Canale di Canna regio
Campo del Ghetto Nuovo
Misericordia
Rio della Misericordia
GUGLIE
C. Riello
R. t. S. Leonardo
Ponte Guglie
Rio d. S. Fosca
Casa del Melograno
Noale
3749 Ponte Chiodo
STAZIONE FERROVIARIA SANTA LUCIA
Lista di Spagna
R.D. BIASIO
S. MARCUOLA
Grand Canal (Canalazzo)
Riva d.Biasio
Ponte degli Scalzi
S. STAE
R. di S. Zan Degola
R. di
Vini da Gigio
Osteria Ca' D'Oro
La Cantina
Lista d. Bari
Al Prosecco
La Zucca
C. d. Tintor
Hotel al Ponte Mocenigo
Al Fontego dei Pescaori
Ca' Sagredo
Piccolo
FERROVIA
Rio Marin
C. Larga
CA' D'ORO
Pensione Guerrato
Canale di S. Chiara
S.Simeon
C. della Lana
Corte Canal
C. Gradisca
C. d. Tintor
Muro Pizzeria con Cucina
R. di S. Cassiano
C. del Botteri
Ostaria al Garanghelo
PIAZZALE ROMA
F.d.
SANTA CROCE
Antiche Carampane
La Villeggiatura
Cantina do Mori
C.d.S.Andrea
Piazzale Roma
C. d. Lacca
Antico Panificio
Alla Madonna
C. d. Fonderia
C. d. Chiovere
SAN POLO
Ca'
San Rocco
Oltre il Giardino
R.Terà
Campo S.Polo
Al Paradiso
Riva del Vin
Rio
F.Minotto
S. SILVESTRO
RIALTO
Rio d. S. Maria Mag giore
Rio Terà dei Pensieri
Nuovo
Rio della Frescada
Riva del Carbon Fabbri
Palazzo Barbarigo
Grand Canal (Canalazzo)
Rio Foscari
S. TOMÀ
S. ANGELO
R.d. S. Luca
Salizz. S. Luca
Campo Manin
Fond. dei Cerèri
Fond. Rossa
Calle dei Guardiani
Campo di S. Margherita
Palazzo Sant'Angelo sul Canal Grande
C.d. Mandola
Rio d. S. Mar ghe rita
Rio Terà Canal
Ristoteca Oniga
C.d. Carrozze
Campo S.Stefano
Campo S.Angelo
C. d. Barcaroli
C. d. Piscina
L'Incontro
Casa Rezzonico
CA' REZZONICO
S. SAMUELE
Al Teatro
Rio d. S. Barnaba
Palazzo Stern
SAN MARCO
S. Moise
Rio di S. Nicola
Calle Avogaria
Locanda San Barnaba
Pensione Accademia Villa Maravege
Novecento
C. Lga 22 Marzo
Avogaria
Calle della Toletta
S.M. DEL GIGLIO
Saliz. San Basègio
Ai 4 Feri
ACCADEMIA
Ristrante Riviera
Rio d. Ognissanti
Ponte dell' Accademia
Locanda Ca' Zose
SALUTE
Cantinone Gia Schiavi
Rio Terà A. Foscarini
C. d. Chiesa
Fond Venier
Ca' Maria Adele
S. BASILIO
Fondamenta delle Zattere
Rio d. S. Vio
Rio d. Fornace
R.Terà dei Catecùmeni
C.po S. Agnese
Hotel American-Dinesen
Fond. Soranzo della Fornace
ZATTERE
SACCA FISOLA
La Calcina
DORSODURO
Canale della Giudecca
C. della Sacca
Canale d. Lavranersi
Fond. S. Biagio
Sacca Fisola
Rio d. S. Biagio
Fond. S. Eufemia
PALANCA
R.d.Convertite
REDENTORE
0
1/4 mile
0
400 meters
GIUDECCA
TO CHIESA DEL RENDENTORE
A
B
C
D

E
F
G
H
Where to Eat and Stay in Venice
1
2
3
4
5
6
CIMITERO
Cimitero San Michele
Sacca della sericordia
Canale delle Fondamente Nuove
FOND. NUOVE
Algiubagiò
Fondamente Nuove
Al Palazzetlo
Hotel UNA Venezia
El Sbarlefo
Botteghe di Promessi Sposi
Hotel Antico Doge
Fiaschetteria Toscana
Tiziano
Enoteca al Volto
Campo S. Marina
C.S. Maria Formosa
Ruzzini Palace
Acqua Plaace
Locanda Orseolo
SAN ZACCARIA
Il Ridotto
Ca' dei Dogi
Santa Maria della Pietá
CASTELLO
Metropole
PIAZZA SAN MARCO
OSPEDALE CIVILE
CELESTIA
Darsena Grande
Riva degli Schiavoni
S. ZACCARIA
S. ZACCARIA JOLANDA
S. ZACCARIA DANIELI
ARSENALE
SAN MARCO GIARDINETTI
VALLARESSO
Bauer Il Palazzo
Hotel Bucintoro
El Rèfolo
La Trattoria Ai Tosi
V. Garibaldi
Riva dei Sette Martiri
Bacino San Marco
S. GIORGIO
S. Giorgio Maggiore
GIARDINI
ZITELLE
Fond. delle Zitelle
Calle Michelangelo
KEY
Hotels
Restaurants
Tourist information
Vaporetto stop

of paramount importance here, and impeccable preparation ensures its characteristics are always accentuated, never overwhelmed. Get your server's recommendation for the day. There are a variety of meat dishes, a fine wine list, and space for groups. It's a popular spot, so expect a lively and bustling atmosphere. ✉ *Calle della Madonna, San Polo 594* ☎ *041/5223824* 🌐 *www.ristoranteallamadonna.com* ✍ *Reservations essential* ⏲ *Closed Sun., Jan., and 2 wks in Aug.* V *San Silvestro* ✣ *D3.*

WORD OF MOUTH

"It is very easy to spend a lot of money for very bad food in Venice, but we have found some gems over the years. Probably my first recommendation would be Alla Madonna near the Rialto bridge. Nothing but seafood, nothing fancy, really terrific."

—tejana

$$$ VENETIAN Fodor's Choice ★ ✕ **Antiche Carampane.** Since its appearance in the first of Donna Leon's *Inspector Brunetti* mysteries, Piera Bortoluzzi Librai's trattoria has lost none of its charm but gained considerably in elegance. You'll find all the classic Venetian fish dishes ranging from a mixed seafood antipasto to fish soups, pasta, and perfectly grilled fish. Updated plates such as seafood and fruit salads for starters and entrées like turbot with citrus sauce also delight diners. Chocolate mousse, panna cotta, and sweet wine with biscotti make delectable desserts. Francesco, the son of Franco and Piera, whose family recipes elevate many of the classics, is responsible for some of the new presentations. ✉ *Rio Terà della Carampane, San Polo 1911* ☎ *041/5240165* 🌐 *www.antichecarampane.com* ✍ *Reservations essential* ⏲ *Closed Sun. and Mon., 10 days in Jan., and 3 wks in July and Aug.* V *San Silvestro* ✣ *D3.*

$ ITALIAN ✕ **Antico Panificio.** Tasty, economical fare in a friendly atmosphere *senza pretesa* (without pretense) can be a tall order in Venice, but the Antico Panificio succeeds in offering just that: traditional, satisfying dishes, from pizza in every form conceivable to pasta with meat sauce, to a grilled pork chop or fillet of sole—all at a handy location just down from the Rialto. It's apparent from the mix of locals and travelers chattering away that the Panificio is no secret, so arrive on the early side for lunch, and be sure to reserve in the evening. Service can be a bit slow when the place is full, so it's best not to come here in a rush. ✉ *Campiello del Sole, San Polo 945/A–B* ☎ *041/2770967* ⏲ *Closed Tues.* V *San Silvestro* ✣ *D3.*

$ ITALIAN ★ ✕ **Ostaria al Garanghelo.** Superior quality, competitive prices, and great ambience mean this place is often packed with Venetians, especially for lunch and an after-work ombra (glass of wine) and cicchetti (snack). Chef Renato takes full advantage of the fresh ingredients from the Rialto Market, a few steps away, bakes his own bread daily, and prefers cooking many dishes *al vapore* (steamed). The spicy *fagioli al uciletto* (literally "bird-style beans," prepared with a light marinara sauce) has an unusual name and Tuscan origins; it's a perfect companion to a plate of fresh pasta. Don't confuse this restaurant with one of the same name in Via Garibaldi. ✉ *Calle dei Boteri, San Polo 1570* ☎ *041/721721* ⏲ *Closed Sun.* V *Rialto* ✣ *D3.*

SANTA CROCE

$ WINE BAR **Al Prosecco.** Locals stream into this friendly wine bar, down a "spritz" (a combination of white wine, Campari or Aperol, and seltzer water), and continue on their way. Al Prosecco is the perfect place to explore wines from the region—or from anywhere in the county for that matter. They accompany a carefully chosen selection of meats, cheeses, and other food from small, artisanal producers, used in tasty panini like the *porchetta romane verdure* (roast pork with greens). Proprietors Davide and Stefano preside over a young and friendly staff who reel off the day's specials with ease. There are a few tables in the intimate back room, and when the weather cooperates you can sit outdoors on the lively campo, watching the Venetian world go by. It's open 9 to 9, and later if the mood strikes. ✉ *Campo San Giacomo dell'Orio, Santa Croce 1503* ☎ *041/5240222* 🌐 *www.alprosecco.com* 💳 *No credit cards* ⏲ *Closed Sun.* Ⓥ *San Stae* ✣ *C2.*

$ ITALIAN Fodor's Choice ★ **La Zucca.** The simple place settings, lattice-wood walls, canal window, and mélange of languages make La Zucca (the pumpkin) feel as much like a typical vegetarian restaurant as you could expect to find in Venice. Though the menu does have superb meat dishes such as the *piccata di pollo ai caperi e limone con riso* (sliced chicken with capers and lemon served with rice), more attention is paid to dishes from the garden: try the radicchio *di Treviso con funghi e scaglie di Montasio* (with mushrooms and shavings of Montasio cheese) or the *finocchi piccanti con olive* (fennel in a spicy tomato-olive sauce). In good weather, dining at outdoor table couldn't be more pleasant. Reserve several days in advance to book one of two dinner seatings, at 7–7:30 or 9–9:30. ✉ *Calle del Tintor (at Ponte de Megio), Santa Croce 1762* ☎ *041/5241570* 🌐 *www.lazucca.it* ✍ *Reservations essential* ⏲ *Closed Sun. and 1 wk in Dec.* Ⓥ *San Stae* ✣ *C2.*

$ ITALIAN **Muro Pizzeria con Cucina.** Don't let the moniker *pizzeria con cucina* fool you: Muro offers a varied menu and uses high-quality ingredients, taking its cue from its more refined sister restaurant, Muro Rialto. Select from excellent Venetian fare and pizza in classic and innovative forms—try the *arrotolata amoretesoro* (a rolled pizza) with *bresaola* (thinly sliced salt-cured beef), *scamorza* (mozzarella-like cow's-milk cheese), and radicchio. Chef Francesco adds dimension to the menu with classic Italian selections, along with the *piatti unici*, a single course fancifully combining elements of first and second courses. A wide selection of beer is on tap. ✉ *Campiello dello Spezier, Santa Croce 2048* ☎ *041/5241628* 🌐 *www.murovenezia.com* ✍ *Reservations essential* ⏲ *Closed Tues.* Ⓥ *San Stae* ✣ *C2.*

BACARI (WINE BARS)

While the list below covers a few of the best of Venice's bacari, it's by no means exhaustive. Venetians themselves don't know how many bacari thrive in their hometown, and often the perfect one is the one you happen upon when hunger strikes.

¢ Fodor's Choice ★ **Cantina Do Mori.** This bacaro par excellence—cramped but warm and cozy under hanging antique copper pots—has been catering to the workers of the Rialto Market since before Columbus discovered America. In addition to young, local whites and reds, the well-stocked cellar offers about 600 more refined labels, many available by the glass. Between sips you can munch on crunchy *grissini* (breadsticks) draped with prosciutto or a few well-stuffed, tiny tramezzini, appropriately called *francobolli* (postage stamps). Don't leave without tasting the delicious baccalà mantecato. Come here a second time and you'll be received like an old friend. *Calle dei Do Mori, San Polo 429* *041/5225401* *No credit cards* *Closed Sun., 3 wks in Aug., and 1 wk in Jan.* *Rialto Mercato* *D3.*

¢ Fodor's Choice ★ **Cantinone già Schiavi.** This beautiful 19th-century bacaro opposite the *squero* (gondola repair shop) of San Trovaso has original furnishings and one of the best wine cellars in town—the walls are covered floor to ceiling by bottles for purchase. Cicchetti here are some of the most inventive in Venice—try the crostini-style layers of bread, smoked swordfish, and slivers of raw zucchini, or pungent slices of *parmeggiano* (Parmesan cheese), fig, and toast. They also have a creamy version of baccalà mantecato spiced with herbs, and there are nearly a dozen open bottles of wine for experimenting at the bar. *Fondamenta Nani, Dorsoduro 992* *041/5230034* *No credit cards* *Closed 2 wks in Aug. and most Sun. after 2 pm* *Zattere, Accademia* *C5.*

¢ **El Sbarlefo.** This odd name is Venetian for "smirk," although you'd be hard pressed to find one of those around here. A recent entry onto the bacaro scene, Sbarlefo has arrived with aplomb. Making the most of their limited space, owners Alessandro and Andrea have installed counters and stools inside, tables outside, and external banco-access for ordering a second round. And order you will, selecting from a spread of delectable cicchetti to suit every taste. They've paid equal attention to their wine list—ask for to recommendation and you're likely to make a new discovery. *Salizzada del Pistor (off Campo Santi Apostoli), Cannaregio 4556/C* *041/5233084* *No credit cards* *Ca d'Oro* *E2.*

$–$$ **Enoteca al Volto.** A short walk from the Rialto Bridge, this bar has been around since 1936; the fine cicchetti and primi have a lot to do with its staying power. Two small, dark rooms with a ceiling plastered with wine labels provide a classic backdrop for simple fare. The place prides itself on its considerable wine list of both Italian and foreign vintages, as you might reckon from the decoration. If you stick to panini (sandwiches) and a cicchetto or two, you'll eat well for relatively little. If you opt for one of the primi of the day, the price category goes up a notch. *Calle Cavalli, San Marco 4081* *041/5228945* *www.alvoltoenoteca.it* *Reservations essential* *No credit cards* *Closed Sun.* *Rialto* *E3.*

¢ ✕ **Osteria Ca' D'Oro (alla Vedova).** "The best *polpette* in town," you'll hear fans of the venerable Vedova say, and that explains why it's an obligatory stop on any *giro d'ombra* (bacaro tour). The Vedova is a full-fledged restaurant as well, but it's appreciated far more for its cicchetti than for its sit-down meals. It's one of the few places that still serve house wine in tiny, traditional *palline* glasses. ✉ *Calle del Pistor (off the Strada Nova), Cannaregio 3912* ☎ *041/5285324* ▭ *No credit cards* ⏲ *Closed Aug.* Ⓥ *Ca d'Oro* ✣ *D2.*

WHERE TO STAY

Many of Venice's hotels are in renovated palaces, but space is at a premium—and comes for a price—and rooms may feel cramped by American standards. The most exclusive hotels are indeed palatial, although they may well have some small, dowdy rooms, so it's best to verify ahead of time that yours isn't one of them. Smaller hotels may not have lounge areas, and because of preservation laws, some are not permitted to install elevators, so if these features are essential, ask ahead of time. Although the city has no cars, it does have boats plying the canals and pedestrians chattering in the streets sometimes late into the night (most likely along principal thoroughfares, in San Marco and near the Rialto), so ask for a quiet room if you're concerned about noise.

Many travelers assume a hotel near Piazza San Marco will give them the most convenient location, but keep in mind that Venice is scaled to humans (on foot) rather than automobiles; it's difficult to find a location that's *not* convenient to most of the city. Areas away from San Marco may also offer the benefit of being less overrun by day-trippers.

It is essential to have detailed directions to your hotel when you arrive. Arm yourself with not only a clear map and postal address (e.g., Dorsoduro 825), but the actual street name (e.g., Fondamenta San Trovaso) and the nearest campo.

You can compare Venice hotels from A to Z at **Venezia.net** (🌐 *www.venezia.net*); it furnishes links to hotels' official Web sites. The Web site of **Venezia Sì** (☎ *199/173309 in Italy, 39/0415222264 from abroad* ⏲ *Mon.–Sat. 9 am–11 pm* 🌐 *www.veneziasi.it*) lists most hotels in town (with some photographs), and they offer a free reservation service over the phone. It's the public relations arm of AVA (Venetian Hoteliers Association) and has booths where you can make same-day reservations at Piazzale Roma (☎ *041/5231397* ⏲ *Daily 9 am–10 pm*), Santa Lucia train station (☎ *041/715288 or 041/715016* ⏲ *Daily 8 am–9 pm*), and Marco Polo Airport (☎ *041/5415133* ⏲ *Daily 9 am–10 pm*). Be aware that if you arrive in the afternoon without a reservation, pickings will be slim and you may be unable to find a room at all.

Hotel reviews have been condensed for this book. Please go to Fodors.com for full reviews of each property.

Use the coordinate (✣ B2) at the end of each listing to locate a site on the Where to Eat and Stay in Venice map.

PRICES

Venetian hotels cater to all tastes and come in a variety of price ranges. Rates are about 20% higher than in Rome and Milan but can be reduced by as much as half off-season, from November to March (excluding Christmas, New Year's, and Carnevale), and likely in August as well.

WHAT IT COSTS IN EUROS

	¢	$	$$	$$$	$$$$
HOTELS	under €75	€75–€125	€125–€200	€200–€300	over €300

Prices are for a standard double room in high season.

CANNAREGIO

$–$$ **3749 Ponte Chiodo.** This cheery, homey bed-and-breakfast takes its name from the bridge leading to its entrance (one of only two left in the lagoon without hand railings). **Pros:** highly attentive service; warm, relaxed atmosphere; private garden; canal or garden views. **Cons:** no elevator could be a problem for some. **TripAdvisor:** "nice view of the canal," "touch of luxury," "super affordable." ✉ *Calle Racchetta, Cannaregio 3749* ☎ *041/2413935* 🌐 *www.pontechiodo.it* *6 rooms* *In-room: no phone, safe, refrigerator, Wi-Fi. In-hotel: room service, bar, Wi-Fi hotspot, Internet terminal* *Breakfast* Ⓥ *Ca' d'Oro* ✣ *D2.*

$–$$ ★ **Al Palazzetto.** Understated yet gracious Venetian decor, original open-beam ceilings and terrazzo flooring, spotless marble baths, and friendly, attentive service are the hallmarks of this intimate, family-owned *locanda* (inn). **Pros:** standout service; owner on-site; quiet, side canal views from some rooms; free Wi-Fi. **Cons:** not for amenity-seekers or lovers of ultramodern decor. **TripAdvisor:** "classic Venetian style," "on quiet back canal," "room was quite cozy." ✉ *Calle delle Vele, Cannaregio 4057* ☎ *041/2750897* 🌐 *www.guesthouse.it* *6 rooms, 1 suite* *In-room: safe, refrigerator, Internet, Wi-Fi. In-hotel: Wi-Fi hotspot, laundry facilities* *Breakfast* Ⓥ *Ca' d'Oro* ✣ *E2.*

$$$–$$$$ Fodor's Choice ★ **Al Ponte Antico.** The Peruch family, proprietors of this 16th-century palace inn (as well as Locanda Orseolo), has lined its Gothic windows with tiny white lights, creating an inviting glow that's emblematic of the hospitality and sumptuous surroundings that await you inside. **Pros:** upper-level terrace overlooks Grand Canal; family run; superior service; Internet is free. **Cons:** in one of the busiest areas of the city. **TripAdvisor:** "beautiful small palazzo," "on the Grand Canal," "staff unfailingly friendly." ✉ *Calle dell'Aseo, Cannaregio 5768* ☎ *041/2411944* 🌐 *www.alponteantico.com* *12 rooms, 1 junior suite* *In-room: safe, refrigerator, Internet, Wi-Fi. In-hotel: room service, bar, laundry service, Internet terminal, Wi-Fi hotspot* *Breakfast* Ⓥ *Rialto* ✣ *E3.*

$$$–$$$$ ★ **Hotel Antico Doge.** Once the home of Doge Marino Falier, this palazzo has been attentively modernized in elegant Venetian style, with some fine, original furnishings—quite rare in many newer hotels. **Pros:** meticulous renovation in true Venetian style, convenient to the Rialto and beyond. **Cons:** on a busy thoroughfare; no outdoor garden or terrace; no elevator. **TripAdvisor:** "each room was lovely," "staff were first-rate,"

BEST BETS FOR VENICE LODGING

Fodor's provides a selective listing of hotels in every price range, from comfortable, well-maintained bargain finds to luxury pleasure palaces. Here's we've compiled our top recommendations, by price category and type of experience. The best of the best earn our Fodor's Choice logo.

Fodor's Choice★

Al Ponte Antico, $$$–$$$$, p. 226

Bauer Il Palazzo, $$$$, p. 232

Ca' dei Dogi, $$, p. 232

Hotel al Ponte Mocenigo, $$, p. 234

Hotel American-Dinesen, $$$–$$$$, p. 230

Hotel Bucintoro, $$$–$$$$, p. 229

La Calcina, $$–$$$, p. 230

Locanda Orseolo, $$$, p. 232

Oltre il Giardino-Casaifrari, $$–$$$, p. 233

Pensione Accademia Villa Maravege, $$–$$$, p. 231

Ruzzini Palace Hotel, $$$–$$$$, p. 229

$

Casa del Melograno, p. 228

Santa Maria della Pietà, p. 230

$$

Al Palazzetto, p. 226

Hotel UNA Venezia, p. 228

La Villegiatura, p. 233

Locanda San Barnaba, p. 231

Pensione Guerrato, p. 233

$$$

Acqua Palace, p. 229

Ca' Sagredo Hotel, p. 228

Hotel Antico Doge, p. 226

Novecento, p. 232

$$$$

Metropole, p. 229

Palazzo Abadessa, p. 228

Palazzo Barbarigo, p. 233

Palazzo Stern, p. 231

Best by Experience

CANAL VIEWS

3749 Ponte Chiodo, $–$$, p. 226

Hotel American-Dinesen, $$$–$$$$, p. 230

La Calcina, $$–$$$, p. 230

Palazzo Sant'Angelo, $$$$, p. 232

ROMANTIC

Ca' dei Dogi, $$, p. 232

La Calcina, $$–$$$, p. 230

Oltre il Giardino-Casaifrari, $$–$$$, p. 233

Palazzo Barbarigo, $$$$, p. 233

Ruzzini Palace Hotel, $$$–$$$$, p. 229

GOOD FOR FAMILIES

Al Palazzetto, $–$$, p. 226

Al Teatro, $$, p. 231

Casa Rezzonico, $$, p. 230

Locanda Ca' Zose, $$, p. 231

Pensione Guerrato, $$, p. 233

AWAY FROM THE CROWDS

3749 Ponte Chiodo, $–$$, p. 226

Ca' Maria Adele, $$$$, p. 230

Ca' San Rocco, $$, p. 233

Casa Rezzonico, $$, p. 230

Hotel al Ponte Mocenigo, $$, p. 234

PERSONAL SERVICE

Al Ponte Antico, $$$–$$$$, p. 226

Al Teatro, $$, p. 231

Ca' dei Dogi, $$, p. 232

Hotel American-Dinesen, $$$–$$$$, p. 230

Locanda Orseolo, $$$, p. 232

CLASSIC VENETIAN DESIGN

Al Ponte Antico, $$$–$$$$, p. 226

Ca' Sagredo Hotel, $$$–$$$$, p. 228

Palazzo Abadessa, $$$–$$$$, p. 228

CONTEMPORARY DESIGN

Acqua Palace, $$$, p. 229

Hotel UNA Venezia, $$–$$$, p. 228

"away from the frantic pace." ✉ *Campo Santi Apostoli, Cannaregio 5643* ☎ *041/2411570* 🌐 *www.anticodoge.com* *19 rooms, 1 suite* *In-room: safe, Wi-Fi, In-hotel: bar, laundry service, Wi-Fi hotspot, Internet terminal* 🍽 *Breakfast* Ⓥ *Ca' d'Oro or Rialto* ✥ *E3.*

$–$$ **Casa del Melograno.** This renovated classic Venetian residence is modestly appointed, but you'll still find features like Venetian terrazzo flooring, frescoed ceilings, and tiled baths. **Pros:** simple; pristine; gracious; handy to vaporetto stop and the train station for day trips. **Cons:** not opulent; may be too far from San Marco for some. **TripAdvisor:** "old Venetian style," "charmed by the hospitality," "overlooking the lovely garden." ✉ *Fondamenta del Ponte Storto, Cannaregio 2023* ☎ *041/5208807* 🌐 *www.locandadelmelograno.it* *6 rooms* *In-room: safe, refrigerator, Internet, Wi-Fi. In-hotel: Internet terminal, Wi-Fi hotspot, some pets allowed* 🍽 *Breakfast* Ⓥ *San Marcuola* ✥ *C2.*

$$$–$$$$ ★ **Ca' Sagredo Hotel.** This expansive palace, the Sagredo family residence since the mid-1600s, is a study in Venetian opulence: the massive staircase has Longhi frescoes soaring above it; the large common areas are adorned with original art by Tiepolo, Longhi, and Ricci, among others. **Pros:** excellent location; authentic yet comfortable renovation of Venice's patrician past. **Cons:** more opulent than intimate. **TripAdvisor:** "historic but with modern facilities," "view of the marketplace," "greeted with champagne." ✉ *Campo San Sofia, Cannaregio 4198/99* ☎ *041/2413111* 🌐 *www.casagredohotel.com* *42 rooms, 2 junior suites, 3 suites* *In-room: safe, refrigerator, Internet, Wi-Fi. In-hotel: bar* 🍽 *Breakfast* Ⓥ *Ca' d'Oro* ✥ *D2.*

$$–$$$ ★ **Hotel UNA Venezia.** Up a narrow calle and across the bridge from the bustling Strada Nova, this 15th-century palazzo lingers silently over a tranquil canal and an evocative corner campo named for its two cisterns, or *pozzi.* **Pros:** an intimate, boutique hideaway still handy for exploring the city. **Cons:** classic rooms are on the smallish side; no Internet in the attic room. **TripAdvisor:** "short walk from main attractions," "beautifully clean and quiet," "elegantly decorated." ✉ *Ruga Do Pozzi, Cannaregio 4173* ☎ *041/2442711* 🌐 *www.unahotels.com* *28 rooms, 3 junior suites, 3 suites* *In-room: safe, refrigerator, Internet, Wi-Fi. In-hotel: room service, bar, laundry facilities, laundry service, Internet terminal, Wi-Fi hotspot, some pets allowed* 🍽 *Breakfast* Ⓥ *Ca' d'Oro* ✥ *E2.*

$$$–$$$$ ★ **Palazzo Abadessa.** At this elegant late-16th-century palazzo, you can experience gracious hospitality and a luxurious atmosphere in keeping with Venice's patrician heritage. **Pros:** a unique, historic lodging; spacious rooms and garden; superb guest service. **Cons:** not best for families with young children, who may have difficulty dodging the antique accessories. **TripAdvisor:** "authentic Venetian palace," "fantastic decor and traditional," "charm and serenity." ✉ *Calle Priuli off Strada Nova, Cannaregio 4011* ☎ *041/2413784* 🌐 *www.abadessa.com* *10 rooms, 5 suites* *In-room: safe, refrigerator, Wi-Fi. In-hotel: room service, bar, Wi-Fi hotspot, laundry service, some pets allowed* 🍽 *Breakfast* Ⓥ *Ca' d'Oro* ✥ *E2.*

CASTELLO

> **WORD OF MOUTH**
>
> "I don't think you can select a 'wrong place' to stay in Venice. Each district or sestiere is unique. All are safe and delightful to be in."
> —Mormor

$$$ ★ **Acqua Palace.** The Caputo family wanted to name its accommodation to recall Venice's perpetual relationship with water, particularly since the five-story former Scalfarotto residence hovers over one of the most gondola-traversed canals in the city. **Pros:** family-run; thoughtful renovation; lots of canal views; Wi-Fi is free. **Cons:** no outdoor breakfast area or bar. **TripAdvisor:** "18th-century style," "bathrooms positively palatial," "immaculate and tasteful." ✉ *Calle della Malvasia, Castello 1083* ☎ *041/2960442* 🌐 *www.aquapalace.it* *12 rooms, 5 junior suites, 6 suites* *In-room: safe, refrigerator, Internet, Wi-Fi. In-hotel: room service, laundry service, Internet terminal, Wi-Fi hotspot, some pets allowed* ⏲ *Closed Jan.* *Breakfast* *Rialto* *E3.*

$$$–$$$$ Fodor's Choice ★ **Hotel Bucintoro.** "All rooms with a view" touts this pensione-turned-four-star-hotel. **Pros:** recent renovation; lagoon views from all rooms, waterfront without the San Marco crowds. **Cons:** yachts sometimes dock outside the hotel, partially blocking lagoon views on lower floors. **TripAdvisor:** "best view in Venice," "peace and quiet," "breakfast of champions." ✉ *Riva degli Schiavoni, Castello 2135/A* ☎ *041/5209909* 🌐 *www.hotelbucintoro.com* *20 rooms, 6 junior suites* *In-room: safe, refrigerator, Wi-Fi. In-hotel: bar, laundry service, Internet terminal, Wi-Fi hotspot, some pets allowed* *Breakfast* *Arsenale* *G5.*

$$$$ ★ **Metropole.** Eccentrics, eclectics, and fans of Antonio Vivaldi (who taught music here) love the Metropole, a labyrinth of intimate, opulent spaces featuring exotic Eastern influences and jammed with cabinets displaying collections of ivory-adorned cigarette cases, antique corkscrews, beaded bags, and more. **Pros:** owner has exquisite taste and collections; hotel harkens back to a gracious Venice of times past. **Cons:** one of the most densely touristed locations in the city. **TripAdvisor:** "very grand," "museum-like display," "breakfast in the garden." ✉ *Riva degli Schiavoni, Castello 4149* ☎ *041/5205044* 🌐 *www.hotelmetropole.com* *67 rooms, 13 junior suites, 9 suites* *In-room: safe, refrigerator, Internet. In-hotel: restaurant, room service, bar, laundry service, Wi-Fi hotspot, some pets allowed* *Breakfast* *San Zaccaria* *F4.*

$$$–$$$$ Fodor's Choice ★ **Ruzzini Palace Hotel.** After a painstaking renovation, the historic Ruzzini Palace once again graces the northern end of the lively Campo Santa Maria Formosa. **Pros:** excellent service; a luminous, pristine, aristocratic ambience. **Cons:** the walk from San Zaccaria or Rialto includes two bridges and can be cumbersome for those with mobility issues or significant amounts of luggage. **TripAdvisor:** "nicely converted palace," "mixing the modern and old," "greeted us by name." ✉ *Campo Santa Maria Formosa, Castello 5866* ☎ *041/2410447* 🌐 *www.ruzzinipalace.com* *19 rooms, 6 junior suites, 3 suites.* *In-room: safe, refrigerator, Wi-Fi (free), DVD (some). In-hotel: room service, bar, laundry service, Wi-Fi hotspot* *Breakfast* *San Zaccaria or Rialto* *F3.*

$ Santa Maria della Pietà. Though this *casa per ferie* (vacation house) is more spartan than sumptuous, there's more light and space here than in many of Venice's four-star lodgings. **Pros:** space, light, and views at a bargain price. **Cons:** not luxurious; few amenities. **TripAdvisor:** "spectacular views," "clean, spacious," "affordable accommodations." ✉ *Calle della Pietà, Castello 3701* ☎ *041/2443639* 🌐 *www.pietavenezia.org/casaferie.htm* *15 rooms with shared bath* *In-room: no phone, no TV. In-hotel: bar* *No credit cards* *Breakfast* Ⓥ *Arsenale or San Zaccaria* ✥ *F4.*

DORSODURO

$$$$ Ca' Maria Adele. One of Venice's most elegant small hotels is a mix of classic style—terrazzo floors, dramatic Murano chandeliers, antique furnishings—and touches of the contemporary, found in the African-wood reception area and breakfast room. **Pros:** quiet and romantic; imaginative contemporary decor; free Wi-Fi. **Cons:** moreformal atmosphere may not suit young children. **TripAdvisor:** "decor is truly beautiful," "small staff was cordial," "glamour of a private house." ✉ *Campo Santa Maria della Salute, Dorsoduro 111* ☎ *041/5203078* 🌐 *www.camariaadele.it* *12 rooms, 4 suites* *In-room: safe, refrigerator, Wi-Fi. In-hotel: room service, bar, laundry service, Wi-Fi hotspot, some pets allowed* *Breakfast* Ⓥ *Salute* ✥ *D5.*

$$ ★ Casa Rezzonico. Rooms here are the rarest occurrence in Venice: an excellent value. **Pros:** spacious garden for relaxing; canal views at a reasonable rate; two lively squares nearby; great for families. **Cons:** must reserve well in advance. **TripAdvisor:** "old-world charm," "spacious and quiet," "overlooking the garden." ✉ *Fondamenta Gherardini, Dorsoduro 2813* ☎ *041/2770653* 🌐 *www.casarezzonico.it* *6 rooms* *In-room: safe, Internet, Wi-Fi. In-hotel: Wi-Fi hotspot* *Breakfast* Ⓥ *Ca' Rezzonico* ✥ *B4.*

$$$–$$$$ Fodor's Choice ★ Hotel American–Dinesen. This quiet, family-run hotel has a yellow stucco facade typical of Venetian houses. **Pros:** high degree of personal service; on a bright, quiet, exceptionally picturesque canal; free Wi-Fi. **Cons:** no elevator. **TripAdvisor:** "just off the Grand Canal," "ideal location for sightseeing," "staff is super-friendly." ✉ *San Vio, Dorsoduro 628* ☎ *041/5204733* 🌐 *www.hotelamerican.com* *28 rooms, 2 suites* *In-room: safe, refrigerator, Wi-Fi. In-hotel: room service, bar, laundry service, Wi-Fi hotspot, some pets allowed* *Breakfast* Ⓥ *Accademia or Salute* ✥ *C5.*

$$–$$$ Fodor's Choice ★ La Calcina. The elegant, eclectic Calcina sits in an enviable position along the sunny Zattere, with front rooms offering heady vistas across the expansive Giudecca Canal. **Pros:** rooftop altana; panoramic views from some rooms; elegant, historic atmosphere. **Cons:** quite eclectic; not for travelers who prefer ultramodern surroundings; no elevator. **TripAdvisor:** "simple and elegant," "really rather atmospheric," "lovely furnishings." ✉ *Dorsoduro 780* ☎ *041/5206466* 🌐 *www.lacalcina.com* *27 rooms, 26 with bath; 5 suites* *In-room: safe, refrigerator, Internet, Wi-Fi. In-hotel: restaurant, room service, bar, laundry service, Wi-Fi hotspot* *Breakfast* Ⓥ *Zattere* ✥ *C5.*

$$ **Locanda Ca' Zose.** The idea that the Campanati sisters named the 15 rooms in their locanda after the stars and constellations of the highest magnitude in the northern hemisphere says something about how personally this place is run. **Pros:** quiet but convenient location; efficient, personal service. **Cons:** no outdoor garden or terrace; no Wi-Fi in rooms (at this writing). **TripAdvisor:** "romantic and happening area," "just off the beaten track," "good value for money." ✉ *Calle del Bastion, Dorsoduro 193/B* ☎ *041/5226635* 🌐 *www.hotelcazose.com* *10 rooms, 1 junior suite, 1 suite* *In-room: safe, refrigerator. In-hotel: Wi-Fi hotspot, Internet terminal, some pets allowed* *Breakfast* Ⓥ *Salute* ✣ *D5.*

3

$$ ★ **Locanda San Barnaba.** This family-run establishment, housed in a 16th-century palazzo, is handily located just off the Ca' Rezzonico vaporetto stop. **Pros:** garden and terrace; close to vaporetto stop. **Cons:** no elevator, minibar, or Internet access. **TripAdvisor:** "over a quiet canal," "magnificent hall upstairs," "great family hotel." ✉ *Calle del Traghetto, Dorsoduro 2785–2786* ☎ *041/2411233* 🌐 *www.locanda-sanbarnaba.com* *11 rooms, 2 junior suites* *In-room: safe. In-hotel: room service, bar, some pets allowed* *Breakfast* Ⓥ *Ca' Rezzonico* ✣ *C4.*

$$$–$$$$ ★ **Palazzo Stern.** The gracious terrace that eases onto the Grand Canal is almost reason alone to stay here. **Pros:** excellent service; lovely views from many rooms; modern renovation retains historic ambience; steps from vaporetto stop. **Cons:** multiple renovations over centuries may turn off some Venetian architectural purists. **TripAdvisor:** "overlooking the Grand Canal," "breakfast on the terrace," "room was plush." ✉ *Calle del Traghetto, Dorsoduro 2792* ☎ *041/2770869* 🌐 *www.palazzostern.com* *18 rooms, 5 junior suites, 1 suite* *In-room: safe, refrigerator, Internet, Wi-Fi. In-hotel: room service, bar, laundry service, Wi-Fi hotspot, some pets allowed* *Breakfast* Ⓥ *Ca' Rezzonico* ✣ *C4.*

$$–$$$ Fodor'sChoice ★ **Pensione Accademia Villa Maravege.** Though the Salmaso family is not originally Venetian, they have created and maintained one of the most quintessentially Venetian accommodations in the city for over 40 years. **Pros:** a historic, classic Venetian property. **Cons:** formal setting with antiques not well suited to children; standard rooms are on the small side. **TripAdvisor:** "so quaint and cozy," "away from the crowds," "wood-burning fireplace." ✉ *Fondamenta Bollani, Dorsoduro 1058* ☎ *041/5210188* 🌐 *www.pensioneaccademia.it* *27 rooms, 2 suites* *In-room: safe, Internet, Wi-Fi. In-hotel: bar, laundry service, Wi-Fi hotspot* *Breakfast* Ⓥ *Accademia* ✣ *C4.*

SAN MARCO

$$ **Al Teatro.** Behind the Fenice Theater, just off the Maria Callas Bridge, this small B&B is the renovated home of owners Fabio and Eleonora—in fact, it's where Eleanora was born. **Pros:** airy rooms; convenient San Marco location; good for families. **Cons:** the intimacy of a family B&B is not for everyone. **TripAdvisor:** "end of a quiet little street," "beautiful old ceiling fresco," "a great hostess." ✉ *Fondamenta della Fenice, San Marco 2554* ☎ *041/5204271* 🌐 *www.bedandbreakfastalteatro.com* *3 rooms* *In-room: safe, refrigerator, Wi-Fi. In-hotel: room service, Internet terminal, Wi-Fi hotspot* *Breakfast* Ⓥ *Santa Maria del Giglio* ✣ *D4.*

$$$$ Fodor's Choice ★ **Bauer Il Palazzo.** This is the ultimate word in luxury, Venetian-style. **Pros:** pampering service; high-end luxury. **Cons:** in one of the busiest areas of the city. **TripAdvisor:** "spectacular arrival," "beautiful rooftop terrace," "like royalty in your own palace." *Campo San Moisè, San Marco 1413/D 041/5207022 www.ilpalazzovenezia.com 44 rooms, 38 suites In-room: safe, refrigerator, DVD, Wi-Fi. In-hotel: restaurant, room service, bars, gym, laundry service, Internet terminal, some pets allowed EP San Marco or Vallaresso E4.*

$$ Fodor's Choice ★ **Ca' dei Dogi.** Amid the crush of mediocre hotels around Piazza San Marco, this delightful choice, in a 15th-century palace and in a quiet courtyard secluded from the melee, stands out. **Pros:** offers respite from San Marco crowds; terraces with views of the Doge's Palace. **Cons:** rooms are not expansive; nearby dining selection is limited. **TripAdvisor:** "great boutique hotel," "down a romantic narrow alley," "downright luxurious." *Corte Santa Scolastica, Castello 4242 041/2413751 www.cadeidogi.it 6 rooms In-room: safe, refrigerator. In-hotel: room service, Internet terminal, some pets allowed Breakfast San Zaccaria F4.*

$$$ Fodor's Choice ★ **Locanda Orseolo.** This cozy, elegant hotel offers a welcome respite from the throngs churning around Piazza San Marco. **Pros:** intimate and romantic; friendly staff; Wi-Fi is free. **Cons:** in the one of the busiest and most commercial areas of the city. **TripAdvisor:** "magical experience," "service from the heart," "good value for our money." *Corte Zorzi off Campo San Gallo, San Marco 1083 041/5204827 www.locandaorseolo.com 12 rooms In-room: safe, refrigerator, Wi-Fi. In-hotel: room service, laundry facilities, laundry service, Internet terminal, Wi-Fi hotspot Closed Jan. Breakfast Rialto or Vallaresso E4.*

$$$ ★ **Novecento.** This small, family-run hotel is on a quiet street a 10-minute walk from the Piazza San Marco. **Pros:** intimate, romantic atmosphere; free Wi-Fi. **Cons:** a bit of a walk to vaporetto stop. **TripAdvisor:** "off the beaten track," "hard to beat this quiet place," "beautifully decorated." *Calle del Dose, Campo San Maurizio, San Marco 2683/84 041/2413765 www.novecento.biz 9 rooms In-room: safe, refrigerator, Internet, Wi-Fi. In-hotel: bar, laundry service, Internet terminal, Wi-Fi hotspot, some pets allowed Breakfast Santa Maria del Giglio C4.*

$$$$ **Palazzo Sant'Angelo sul Canal Grande.** There's a distinguished yet comfortable feel to this elegant palazzo, which is large enough to deliver expected facilities and services but small enough to pamper its guests. **Pros:** convenient to vaporetto stop. **Cons:** some rooms have no special view; fee for Wi-Fi. **TripAdvisor:** "sumptuously Venetian," "chocolate on your pillow," "rate was very affordable." *Campo Sant'Angelo, San Marco 3488 041/2411452 www.palazzosantangelo.com 14 rooms In-room: safe, refrigerator, Internet, Wi-Fi. In-hotel: bar, laundry service, Wi-Fi hotspot, some pets allowed EP Sant'Angelo D4.*

SAN POLO

$$ **Ca' San Rocco.** Through an iron gate on a calle just off the main thoroughfare from Piazzale Roma to the San Tomà vaporetto stop, you'll spy the small, inviting garden terrace of the Ca' San Rocco. **Pros:** lots of greenery and outdoors areas; extraordinarily quiet. **Cons:** a bit of a walk from the vaporetto stops. **TripAdvisor:** "everything was immaculate," "on a lightly traveled street," "lovely balcony and view." *Ramo Cimesin, San Polo 3078 041/716744 www.casanrocco.it 6 rooms In-room: safe, refrigerator, Wi-Fi. In-hotel: Wi-Fi hotspot Breakfast Piazzale Roma or San Tomà B3.*

3

$$–$$$ ★ **La Villeggiatura.** If eclectic Venetian charm is what you seek, don't be dismayed by La Villegiatura's unprepossessing entrance or the number of stairs (36) you'll climb to reach this lofty attic lodging. **Pros:** relaxed atmosphere; meticulously maintained; well located. **Cons:** positioned high over a popular and busy thoroughfare; no elevator; modest breakfast. **TripAdvisor:** "lovely, authentic rooms," "convenient area of Venice," "a modern delight." *Calle dei Botteri, San Polo 1569 041/5244673 www.lavilleggiatura.it 6 rooms In-room: safe, refrigerator, Wi-Fi (free). In-hotel: Wi-Fi hotspot (free) Breakfast Rialto Mercato D3.*

$$–$$$ Fodor's Choice ★ **Oltre il Giardino–Casaifrari.** It's easy to overlook—and it can be a challenge to find—this secluded palazzo, sheltered behind a brick wall just over the bridge from the Frari church. **Pros:** a peaceful, gracious, and convenient setting; walled garden. **Cons:** no Grand Canal views. **TripAdvisor:** "very elegant place," "decorated with great style," "charming garden." *San Polo 2542 041/2750015 www.oltreilgiardino-venezia.com 4 rooms, 4 suites In-room: safe, refrigerator, Internet, Wi-Fi. In-hotel: room service, bar, Internet terminal, some pets allowed Breakfast San Tomà C3.*

$$$$ ★ **Palazzo Barbarigo.** It is not unusual to find an opulent hotel along the Grand Canal; it is unusual to discover black marble, matte lacquer, indirect lighting, and decidedly art deco contours ensconced in a 16th-century Venetian palace. **Pros:** small; lavish; an uncommon ambience. **Cons:** no outdoor terrace. **TripAdvisor:** "nice details and cool furnishings," "bedrooms are a delight," "bar is absolutely beautiful." *San Polo 3765 041/74072 www.palazzobarbarigo.it 8 rooms, 6 junior suites In-room: safe, refrigerator, Internet, Wi-Fi. In-hotel: bar, laundry service Breakfast San Tomà C4.*

$$ **Pensione Guerrato.** This welcoming, rambling pensione is housed in one of oldest palaces in one of the oldest parts of the city. **Pros:** economic lodging; friendly, efficient service; spacious accommodations. **Cons:** no elevator; reception is one flight up; rooms are on upper floors. **TripAdvisor:** "decorated with glass chandeliers," "beautiful regional decor," "good value." *Campiello Calle Drio le Scimia, San Polo 240/A 041/5285927 www.pensioneguerrato.it 14 rooms In-room: safe, a/c (some), Wi-Fi (some). In-hotel: no elevator, Wi-Fi hotspot (free) Breakfast Rialto Mercato D3.*

SANTA CROCE

$$ Fodor's Choice ★ **Hotel al Ponte Mocenigo.** A columned courtyard welcomes you to this elegant, charming palazzo, former home of the Santa Croce branch of the Mocenigo family (which has a few doges in its past). **Pros:** enchanting courtyard; water access; friendly staff; free Wi-Fi. **Cons:** rooms do not overlook a canal (although the courtyard and foyer do). **TripAdvisor:** "17th-century Venetian style," "loved the Murano glass," "picturesque courtyard." ✉ *Fondamento de Rimpeto a Ca' Mocenigo, Santa Croce 2063* ☎ *041/5244797* 🌐 *www.alpontemocenigo.com* *10 rooms, 1 junior suite* *In-room: safe, refrigerator, Wi-Fi. In-hotel: room service, bar, Internet terminal, Wi-Fi hotspot* *Breakfast* Ⓥ *San Stae* ✣ *D2.*

NIGHTLIFE AND THE ARTS

THE ARTS

A Guest in Venice, an online portal and a monthly bilingual booklet free at most hotels, is an up-to-date guide to Venice happenings. It also includes information about pharmacies, vaporetto and bus lines, and the main trains and flights. Visit 🌐 *www.aguestinvenice.com* for a preview of musical, artistic, and sporting events. *Venezia News* (VENews), available at newsstands, has similar information but also includes in-depth articles about noteworthy events. The tourist office publishes a handy, free quarterly *Calendar* in Italian and English, listing daily events and current museum and venue hours. *Venezia da Vivere* is a seasonal guide listing nightspots and live music. Several Venice Web sites allow you to scan the cultural horizon before you arrive; try 🌐 *www.turismovenezia.it, www.veneziasi.it, www.veniceonline.it,* and *www.venicebanana.com.* And don't ignore the posters you'll see plastered on the walls as you walk—they're often the most up-to-date information you can find.

CARNEVALE

The first historical evidence of *Carnevale* (Carnival) in Venice dates from 1097, and for centuries the city marked the days preceding *quaresima* (Lent) with abundant feasting and wild celebrations. The word *carnevale* is derived from the words for meat (*carne*) and to remove (*levare*), as eating meat was prohibited during Lent. Venice earned its international reputation as the "city of Carnevale" in the 18th century, when partying would begin right after Epiphany (January 6) and the city seemed to be one continuous decadent masquerade. With the Republic's fall in 1797, the city lost a great deal of its vitality, and the tradition of Carnevale celebrations was abandoned.

It was revived in the 1970s when residents began taking to the calli and campi in their own impromptu celebrations. It didn't take long for the tourist industry to embrace the revival as a means to stimulate business during low season. The efforts were successful. Each year over the 10- to 12-day Carnevale period (ending on the Tuesday before

Ash Wednesday) more than a half million people attend concerts, theater and street performances, masquerade balls, historical processions, fashion shows, and contests. Since 2008 Carnevale has been organized by **Venezia Marketing & Eventi** (*www.carnevale.venezia.it*). *A Guest in Venice* is also a complete guide to public and private Carnevale festivities. Stop by the **tourist office** (*041/5298711* *www.turismovenezia.it*) or Venice Pavilion for information, but be aware they can be mobbed. If you're not planning on joining in the revelry, you'd be wise to choose another time to visit Venice. Crowds clog the streets (which become one-way, with police directing foot traffic), bridges are designated "no-stopping" zones to avoid gridlock, and prices skyrocket.

FESTIVALS

The **Biennale** (*www.labiennale.org*) cultural institution organizes events year-round, including the **Venice Film Festival,** which begins the last week of August. **La Biennale di Venezia,** an international exhibition of contemporary art, is held in odd-numbered years, usually from mid-June to early November, at the Giardini della Biennale, and in the impressive Arsenale. On the third weekend of July the **Festa del Redentore** *(Feast of the Redeemer)* commemorates the end of a 16th-century plague that killed about 47,000 city residents. Just as doges have done annually for centuries, you, too, can make a pilgrimage across the temporary bridge connecting the Zattere to the Giudecca. Venetians take to the water to watch fireworks at midnight, but if you can't find a boat, the Giudecca is the best place to be. Young people traditionally greet sunrise on the Lido beach while their elders attend church.

MUSIC

The vast majority of music you'll hear is classical, with Venice's famed composer, Vivaldi, frequently featured. Churches, palazzi, and scuole *grandi* host a broad variety of concerts and even opera, as do the Ca' Rezzonico and Querini-Stampalia museums. To find out what's on, stop by the tourist pavilion, or look in the tourist office's *Shows and Events Calendar* and in *A Guest in Venice* (*www.aguestinvenice.com*). You can book at the tourist office, any travel agency, the venue itself, or online with Music in Venice (*musicinvenice.com*).

HelloVenezia (*Isola nova del Tronchetto 21* *041/2424* *www.hellovenezia.it* *Piazzale Roma*) has information about events at the Fenice, the Malibran, and a variety of other venues. Check their online calendar and purchase your tickets on the Web site or through any booking service. Scan the posters and notices on the streets to spot free concerts offered by local choral groups and music schools.

OPERA

Teatro La Fenice (*Campo San Fantin, San Marco* *041/786511* *www.teatrolafenice.it*), one of Italy's oldest opera houses, has witnessed many memorable premieres, including the 1853 first-night flop of Verdi's *La Traviata.* It's also had its share of disasters, including not one but two fires, the most recent being deliberately set in January 1996. It was impeccably and luxuriously restored, and reopened to great fanfare in 2004. Visit the HelloVenezia Web site (⇨ *above)* for a schedule of performances and to buy tickets. HelloVenezia also handles tickets for the smaller, enchanting **Teatro Malibran** (✉ *Campo San Fantin, Cannaregio* ☎ *041/786511* 🌐 *www.teatrolafenice.it*).

NIGHTLIFE

Piazza San Marco is a popular meeting place in nice weather, when the cafés stay open late and all seem to be competing to offer the best live music. The younger crowd, Venetians and visitors alike, tends to gravitate toward the area around Rialto Bridge, with Campi San Bartolomeo and San Luca on one side and Campo Rialto Nuovo on the other. Especially popular with university students are the bars along Cannaregio's Fondamenta della Misericordia and around Campo Santa Margherita and San Pantalon. Pick up a booklet of *2Night* or visit 🌐 *www.2night.it* for nightlife listings and reviews.

BARS AND CLUBS

Al Chioschetto is among Venice's "nonbars," consisting only of a kiosk set up to serve some outdoor tables. Located on the Zattere, it's popular in nice weather for late-night *panini* (sandwiches) or a sunny breakfast. Live funk, reggae, jazz, or soul is on tap once a week in summer, usually Friday or Saturday. ✉ *Near Ponte Lungo, Dorsoduro 1406/A* ☎ *338/1174077* 🅥 *Zattere*.

Bácaro Jazz has hot jazz on the sound system and hot meals until 2 am. It also has a very interactive owner and staff, so you're not likely to feel lonely even if you arrive alone. ✉ *Across from Rialto Post Office, San Marco 5546/A* ☎ *041/5285249* 🌐 *www.bacarojazz.com*.

Comfortably warm **Bagolo,** with its contemporary Murano glass sconces that are never too bright, welcomes clientele of all ages and all lifestyles. It's open daily, except Monday, from 7 am until midnight or later. ✉ *Campo San Giacomo dell'Orio, Santa Croce 1584* ☎ *041/717584* 🅥 *San Stae*.

Caffè Blue is a very popular bar for students from nearby Ca' Foscari, with a top-shelf whiskey selection, absinthe for the adventurous, and free Internet. Sandwiches are available from noon until 2 am. There are frequent art openings and occasional live music performances. ✉ *Calle dei Preti near San Pantalon, Dorsoduro 3778* ☎ *041/710227* 🅥 *San Tomà*.

★ It's tiny dimensions notwithstanding, **El Refolo** is inviting to anyone on their way up or down Via Garibaldi, owing to its savory snacks, wine selection, and live music on most Friday nights when the weather's fine. There's no set closing hour—they'll tell you when it's time to leave. ✉ *Via Garibaldi, Castello 1580* 🅥 *Arsenale*.

Il Caffè, commonly called "Bar Rosso" for its bright-red exterior, hosts occasional summer jazz concerts and has far more tables outside than in. A favorite with students, it's famous for strong *spritz,* the preferred Venetian aperitif, of white wine, Campari or Aperol, soda water, and a twist of lemon. ✉ *Campo Santa Margherita, Dorsoduro 2963* ☎ *041/5287998*.

Modern, hip, and complemented by a nice internal garden, **Orange** anchors the south end of Campo Santa Margherita, the liveliest campo in Venice. You can have *piadine* sandwiches and drinks while watching soccer games on a massive screen inside, or sit at the tables in the campo. ✉ *Campo Santa Margherita, Dorsoduro 3054/A* ☎ *041/5234740.*

Paradiso Perduto has been catering to night owls since the '70s with drinks, wine, and slightly overpriced fish dishes (a better option is the *cicchetti*). It often serves up live music on weekends, mainly jazz and ethnic music. With closely placed tables, this huge room is full of conviviality; in temperate weather patrons fill the fondamenta until they're shooed away. It's open Thursday through Monday. ✉ *Fondamenta della Misericordia, Cannaregio 2540* ☎ *041/720581.*

3

★ At **Teamo** (*te amo* is Italian for "I love you"), owner Gianni has brought a passion for his native region of Friuli and a contemporary aesthetic sense to a San Marco locale. This is today's Venice: young (but not too), sophisticated, and friendly. You can indulge in inventive cicchetti here until 10 pm daily—and even get breakfast starting at 8 am. Teamo is closed all of August. ✉ *Rio Terà de la Mandola, San Marco 3795* ☎ *347/3665016* 🌐 *www.teaamo.it* Ⓥ *Sant'Angelo.*

Nothing special by day, **Torino@notte** is a lively nightspot, often spilling out into the campo in summer. Cocktails, served until 2 am, include the popular *cubino* (rum and Coke). Snacks are available until 7 pm. ✉ *Campo San Luca, San Marco 459* ☎ *041/5223914* Ⓥ *Rialto.*

★ **Venice Jazz Club** hosts the only live jazz concerts in town; €20 gets you a concert, a table, and your first drink. They also serve cold cuts and sandwiches before the music begins at 9 pm. It's best to reserve a table—you can book through the Web site. The club is closed in August. ✉ *Near Ponte dei Pugni, Dorsoduro 3102* ☎ *041/5232056 or 340/1504985* 🌐 *www.venicejazzclub.com* Ⓥ *Ca' Rezzonico.*

Zanzibar is a kiosk bar that's very popular on warm summer evenings, especially Friday, when there's live music. Food available is limited to sandwiches and ice cream, but the location along the canal near Chiesa di Santa Maria Formosa makes it a pleasant place to sip a drink. ✉ *Campo Santa Maria Formosa, Castello 5840* ☎ *347/1460107* Ⓥ *San Zaccaria.*

SHOPPING

Alluring shops abound in Venice. You'll find countless vendors of trademark Venetian wares such as glass and lace; the authenticity of some goods can be suspect, but they're often pleasing to the eye regardless of their place of origin. For more sophisticated tastes (and deeper pockets), there are jewelers, antiques dealers, and high-fashion boutiques on a par with those in Italy's larger cities but often maintaining a uniquely Venetian flair. There are also some interesting craft and art studios, where you can find high-quality one-of-a-kind articles, from handmade shoes to decorative lamps and mirrors.

If you pass a shop that interests you, make sure to mark your map or collect their business card so you'll be sure to find it again in the maze of tiny streets. Regular store hours are usually 9 to 12:30 and 3:30 or 4 to 7:30; some stores close Saturday afternoons or Monday mornings. Food shops are open 8 to 1 and 5 to 7:30, and may close Wednesday afternoon and all day Sunday. Many tourist-oriented shops are open all day, every day. Some shops close for both a summer and a winter vacation.

FOOD MARKETS

Smaller fresh markets dot the city, but the morning open-air fruit-and-vegetable market at **Rialto** offers animated local color and commerce. On Tuesday through Saturday mornings the **fish market** (adjacent to the Rialto produce market) will amaze you with an impressive lesson in ichthyology; it's fun to count the number of species you've never seen before. You can also find a lively food market weekday mornings on **Via Garibaldi** in the Castello district, in the San Leonardo area in Cannaregio, and in Campo San Margherita in Dorsoduro.

SHOPPING DISTRICTS

The **San Marco** area is full of shops and couture boutiques such as Armani, Missoni, Valentino, Fendi, and Versace. **Le Mercerie**, the Frezzeria, Calle dei Fabbri, and Calle Larga XXII Marzo, all leading from Piazza San Marco, are some of Venice's busiest shopping streets. Other good shopping areas surround Calle del Teatro and Campi San Salvador, Manin, San Fantin, and San Bartolomeo. You can find somewhat less expensive, more varied and imaginative shops between the Rialto Bridge and San Polo and in Santa Croce, and art galleries in Dorsoduro from the Salute to the Accademia.

SPECIALTY STORES

ART GLASS

The glass of Murano is Venice's number-one product, and you'll be confronted by mind-boggling displays of traditional and contemporary glassware, too much of it kitsch. Traditional Venetian glass is hot, blown glass, not lead crystal; it comes in myriad forms including the classic ornate goblets and chandeliers, to beads, vases, sculpture, and more. To make a smart purchase, take your time and be selective. You can learn a great deal without sales pressure at the Museo del Vetro on Murano; unfortunately you'll likely find the least-attractive glass where public demonstrations are offered. Although prices in Venice and on Murano are comparable, shops in Venice with wares from various glassworks may charge slightly less. ■ **TIP→ A "free" taxi to Murano always comes with sales pressure. Take the vaporetto that's included in your transit pass, and if you prefer, a private guide who specializes in the subject but has no affinity to any specific furnace.**

At **Angolo del Passato,** Giordana Naccari collects 20th-century glassware and produces her own intriguing cups, plates, and pitchers at prices that are quite accessible. ✉ *Campiello dei Squelini, Dorsoduro 3276* ☎ *041/5287896.*

Ma.Re sells Salviati glass, as well as other blown and solid glass. It also sells one-of-a-kind objects by leading glass artists. ✉ *Via XXII Marzo, San Marco 2088* ☎ *041/5231191* 📠 *041/5285745* 🌐 *www.mareglass.com* Ⓥ *San Marco.*

Marina and Susanna Sent have had their glass jewelry featured in *Vogue.* Vases and design pieces are also exceptional. ✉ *Campo San Vio, Dorsoduro 669* ☎ *041/5208136* Ⓥ *Accademia.*

3

Pauly & C, established in 1866, features a truly impressive selection of authentic Murano art glass (both traditional and contemporary styles) by the most accomplished masters—and at better prices than on the island. The showroom at No. 73 houses the more traditional collection; at No. 77 you can find works by artists and designers. ✉ *Piazza San Marco 73 and 77, San Marco* ☎ *041/5235484 or 041/2770279* 🌐 *www.pauly.it.*

LACE AND FABRICS

Bevilacqua has kept the weaving tradition alive in Venice since 1875, using 18th-century hand looms for its most precious creations. Its repertoire of 3,500 different patterns and designs yields a ready-to-sell selection of hundreds of brocades, Gobelins, damasks, velvets, taffetas, and satins. You'll also find tapestry, cushions, and braiding. Fabrics made by this prestigious firm have been used to decorate the Vatican, the Royal Palace of Stockholm, and the White House. ✉ *Campo di Santa Maria del Giglio, San Marco 2520* ☎ *041/2410662* Ⓥ *Giglio* ✉ *Fondamenta della Canonica, San Marco 337/B* ☎ *041/5287581* 🌐 *www.luigi-bevilacqua.com* Ⓥ *San Marco* ✉ *Factory: Campiello della Comare, Santa Croce 1320* ☎ *041/721576* ⏲ *Visits by appointment only* Ⓥ *Riva di Biasio.*

Capricci e Vanità, a small shop near the Church of San Pantalon, is where owner and lace-lover Signora Giovanna Gamba sells her wonderful authentic Burano lace. She specializes in tablecloths and lingerie made on the bobbin as well as rarer and more precious pieces made with a needle in the extra-light Burano stitch. ✉ *Calle San Pantalon, Dorsoduro 3744* ☎ *041/5231504* Ⓥ *San Tomà.*

La Bottega di Cenerentola, or "Cinderella's Workshop," creates unique handmade lamp shades out of silk, old lace, and real parchment, embroidered and decorated with gold braids and cotton or silk trim. The pieces on display are a perfect match for country- and antique-style furniture. The owner, Lidiana Vallongo, and her daughter will be happy to discuss special orders. ✉ *Calle dei Saoneri, San Polo 2718/A* ☎ *041/5232006* 🌐 *www.cenerentola.eu* Ⓥ *San Tomà.*

Venetia Studium creates exclusive velvet fabrics in a splendid array of colors and turns them into scarves, bags, stoles, and pillows of various sizes. They also make the famous pleated Fortuny dress and Fortuny lamps. ✉ *Calle Larga XXII Marzo, San Marco 2403* ☎ *041/5229281* ✉ *Calle Larga XXII Marzo, San Marco 723* ☎ *041/5229859* 🌐 *www.venetiastudium.com.*

MASKS

Mondonovo is the "new world" of master craftsman Guerrino Lovato. His masks have appeared in films by Stanley Kubrick, Kenneth Branagh, and Franco Zeffirelli. You can also admire his papier-mâché ceiling figures in the restored Fenice theater. ✉ *Rio Terà Canal, Dorsoduro 3063* ☎ *041/5287344* 🌐 *www.mondonovomaschere.it*.

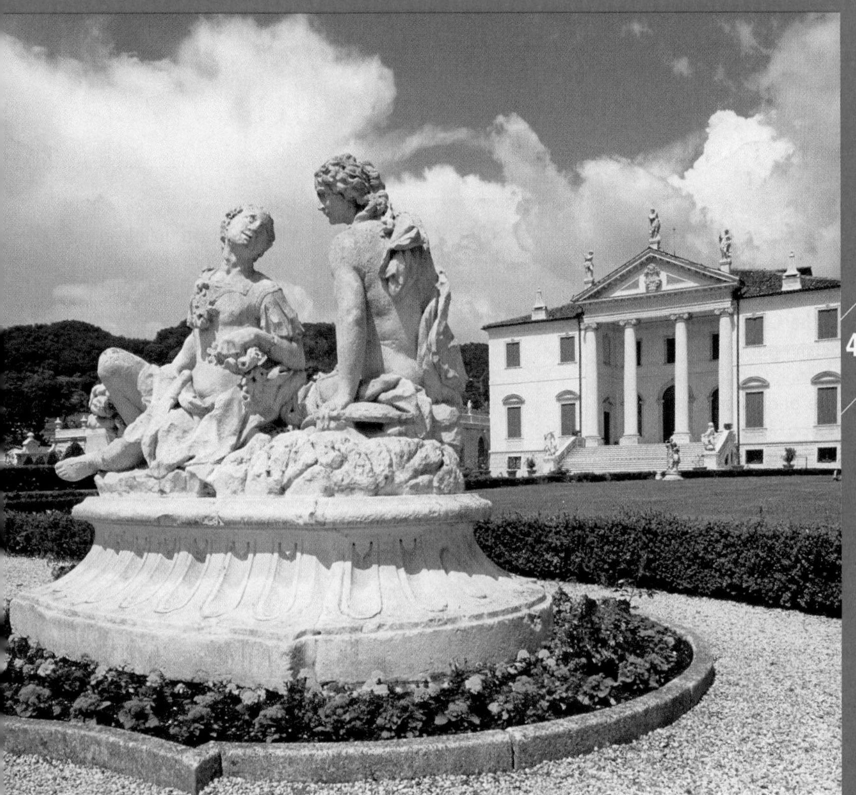

4

The Veneto and Friuli–Venezia Giulia

WORD OF MOUTH

"Verona is a wonderful walking town. We took the first of what were many walks down the upscale Via Mazzini to the Piazza Erbe. Piazza Erbe appears to be the heart of the city and is filled with stalls selling all sorts of things, from foodstuffs to tacky things for tourists. We shared a cone of hot chestnuts as we walked."

—basingstoke2

WELCOME TO THE VENETO AND FRIULI–VENEZIA GIULIA

TOP REASONS TO GO

★ **Giotto's frescoes in the Cappella degli Scrovegni:** In this Padua chapel, Giotto's expressive and innovative frescos foreshadowed the painting techniques of the Renaissance.

★ **Villa Barbaro in Maser:** Master architect Palladio's graceful creation meets Veronese's splendid paintings in a one-time-only collaboration.

★ **Opera in Verona's ancient arena:** The performances may not be top-notch, but even serious opera fans can't resist the almost campy spectacle of these shows.

★ **Roman and early Christian ruins at Aquileia:** Aquileia's ruins offer an image of the transition from pagan to Christian Rome, and are almost entirely free of tourists.

★ **The wine roads north of Treviso:** A series of routes takes you through beautiful hillsides to some of Italy's finest wines.

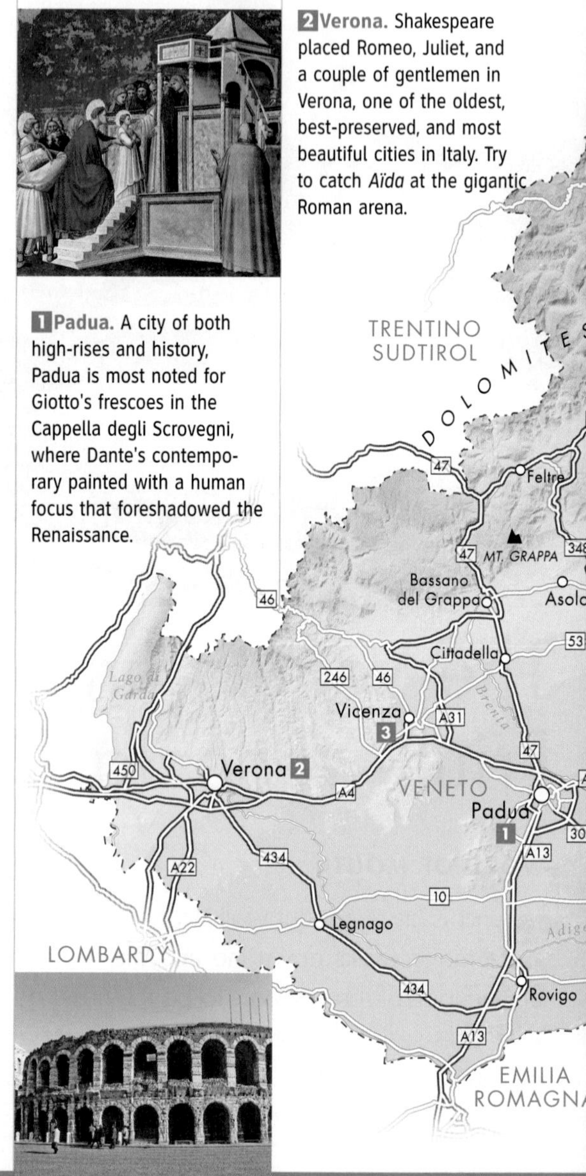

1 Padua. A city of both high-rises and history, Padua is most noted for Giotto's frescoes in the Cappella degli Scrovegni, where Dante's contemporary painted with a human focus that foreshadowed the Renaissance.

2 Verona. Shakespeare placed Romeo, Juliet, and a couple of gentlemen in Verona, one of the oldest, best-preserved, and most beautiful cities in Italy. Try to catch *Aïda* at the gigantic Roman arena.

3 Vicenza. This elegant art city, on the green plain reaching inland from Venice's lagoon, bears the signature of the great 16th-century architect Andrea Palladio, including several palazzi and other important buildings.

4 Treviso and the Hillside Towns. Treviso is a busy town with a touch of Venetian style. Asolo (the City of a Hundred Horizons) is the most popular destination in a series of charming towns that dot the wine-producing hills north of Treviso.

GETTING ORIENTED

The Venetian Arc is the sweep of land curving north and east from the River Adige to the Slovenian border. It's made up of two Italian regions—the Veneto and Friuli–Venezia Giulia—that were once controlled by Venice, and the culture is a mix of Venetian, Alpine, and central European sensibilities.

5 Friuli–Venezia Giulia. Set between the Adriatic Sea and Slovenia in the eastern corner of Italy, this is a region where menus run the gamut from gnocchi to goulash. The port city of Trieste has a mixed Venetian-Austrian heritage. It contains several belle-epoque cafés and palaces built for Habsburg nobility.

EATING AND DRINKING WELL IN THE VENETO AND FRIULI–VENEZIA GIULIA

With the decisive seasonal changes of the Venetian Arc, it's little wonder that many restaurants shun printed menus. Elements from field and forest define much of the region's cuisine, including white asparagus, wild herbs, chestnuts, radicchio, and mushrooms.

Restaurants of the Venetian Arc tend to cling to tradition, not only in the food they serve but how they serve it. This means that from 3 in the afternoon until 8 in the evening most places are closed tight (though you can pick up a snack at a bar during these hours), and on Sunday afternoon restaurants are packed with Italian families and friends indulging in a weekly ritual of lunching out. Meals are still a sacred ritual for most Italians, so don't be surprised if you get disapproving looks when you gobble down a sandwich or a slice of pizza while seated on the church steps or a park bench. In many places it is actually illegal to do so. If you want to fit in with the locals, eat while standing at the bar and they may not even notice that you are a tourist.

THE BEST IN BEANS

Pasta e fagioli, a thick bean soup with pasta, served slightly warm or at room temperature, is made all over Italy. Folks in Veneto, though, take a special pride in their version. It features particularly fine beans that are grown around the village of Lamon, near Belluno.

Even when bought in the Veneto, the beans from Lamon cost more than double the next most expensive variety, but their rich and delicate taste is considered to be well worth the added expense. You never knew bean soup could taste so good.

PASTA, RISOTTO, POLENTA

For *primi* (first courses), the Veneto dines on *bigoli* (thick whole-wheat pasta) generally served with an anchovy-onion sauce, and risotto—saturated with red wine in Verona and prosecco in Conegliano. Polenta is everywhere, varying from a stiff porridge topped with Gorgonzola or stew, to a patty grilled alongside meat or fish, as in the photo below.

FISH

The catch of the day is always a good bet, whether sweet and succulent Adriatic shellfish, sea bream, bass, or John Dory, or freshwater fish from Lake Garda near Verona. But be sure to note whether the fish is wild or farmed—the taste, texture, and price difference are considerable.

A staple in the Veneto is *baccalà,* dried salt cod, soaked in water or milk, and then prepared in a different way in each city. In Vicenza, *baccalà alla vicentina,* pictured at left, is cooked with onions, milk, and cheese, and is generally served with polenta. Locals consider it as central to their city's identity as Palladio.

MEAT

Inland, meat prevails: pork and veal are standards, while goose, duck, and guinea fowl are common poultry options. Lamb is best in spring, when it's young and delicate. In Friuli–Venezia Giulia, menus show the influences of Austria-Hungary: you may find venison and hare on the menu, as well as Eastern European–style goulash. Throughout the Veneto an unusual treat is *nervetti*—cubes of gelatin from a cow's knee with onions, parsley, olive oil, and lemon.

RADICCHIO DI TREVISO

In fall and winter be sure to try the radicchio di Treviso, pictured above, a red endive grown near that town but popular all over the region. It's best in a stew with chicken or veal, in a risotto, or just grilled or baked with a drizzle of olive oil and perhaps a bit of taleggio cheese from neighboring Lombardy.

WINE

Wine is excellent here: the Veneto produces more D.O.C. (Denominazione di Origine Controllata) wines than any other region in Italy. Amarone, the region's crowning achievement, is a robust and powerful red with an alcohol content as high as 16%. Valpolicella and Bardolino are other notable appellations.

The best of the whites are Soave, sparkling prosecco, and pinot bianco (pinot blanc). In Friuli–Venezia Giulia, the local wines par excellence are Tocai Friulano, a dry, lively white made from Tocai grapes that has attained international stature, and piccolit, perhaps Italy's most highly prized dessert wine.

4

Updated by Bruce Leimsidor

The arc around Venice—stretching from Verona to Trieste, encompassing the Veneto and Friuli–Venezia Giulia regions—has, in recent centuries, fallen under the cultural influence of its namesake city. Whether coastal or inland, the emblem of Venice, Saint Mark's winged lion, is emblazoned on palazzi or poised on pedestals, and the art, architecture, and way of life all reflect, since the 16th century, Venetian splendor.

But in the Middle Ages Padua and Verona were independent cities that developed substantial cultural traditions of their own, leaving behind many artistic treasures. And 16th-century Vicenza, even while under Venetian political domination, contributed more to the cultural heritage of La Serenissima than it took from her.

The area is primarily flat green farmland. As you move inland, though, you encounter low hills, which swell and rise in a succession of plateaus and high meadows, culminating in the snowcapped Dolomite Alps. Much of the pleasure of exploring here comes from discovering the variations on the Venetian theme that give a unique character to each of the towns. Some, such as Verona, Treviso, and Udine, have a solid medieval look; Asolo, dubbed "the town of a hundred horizons," has an idyllic setting; Bassano del Grappa combines a bit of both of these qualities. Padua, with its narrow arcaded streets, is romantic. Vicenza, ennobled by the architecture of Palladio, is elegant. In Friuli–Venezia Giulia, Udine is a genteel, intricately sculpted city that's home to the first important frescoes by Giambattista Tiepolo. In Trieste, its past as a port of the Austro-Hungarian Empire is still alive in its Viennese-inspired coffeehouses.

PLANNING

MAKING THE MOST OF YOUR TIME

Lined up in a row west of Venice are Padua, Vicenza, and Verona—three prosperous small cities, each worth at least a day on a northern Italy itinerary. Verona has the greatest charm, and it's probably the best choice for a base in the area (though Verona also draws the most tourists). The hills north of Venice make for good drives, with appealing villages set in a visitor-friendly wine country.

East of the Veneto, the region of Friuli–Venezia Giulia is off the main tourist circuit. You probably won't go here on a first trip to Italy, but by your second or third visit you may be drawn by its caves and castles, its battle-worn hills, and its mix of Italian and central European culture. The port city of Trieste, famous for its elegant cafés, has quiet character that some people find dull and others find alluring. (Famed travel writer Jan Morris's book in praise of the city is tellingly titled *Trieste and the Meaning of Nowhere.*)

Three of the top sights in the region demand advance planning:

Reservations are required to see the Giotto frescoes in Padua's Cappella degli Scrovegni—though if there's space, you can "reserve" on the spot.

On the outskirts of Vicenza, Villa della Rotonda, one of star architect Palladio's masterpieces, is open to the public only on Wednesday from mid-March through October. (Hours for visiting the grounds are less restrictive.)

Another important Palladian villa, Villa Barbaro near Maser, is open weekends and several days during the week March to October. From November to February it's open only on weekends. *For details about Cappella degli Scrovegni, look in this chapter under "Top Attractions" in Padua. For the villas, see "Top Attractions" in Vicenza and Palladio Country.*

GETTING HERE AND AROUND

BUS TRAVEL

There are interurban and interregional connections throughout the Veneto and Friuli, handled by nearly a dozen private bus lines. To figure out which line will get you where, the best strategy is to get assistance from local tourist offices *(listed throughout this chapter)*.

CAR TRAVEL

Padua, Vicenza, and Verona are on the highway and train line between Venice and Milan. Seeing them without a car isn't a problem; in fact, having a car can complicate matters. The cities sometimes limit access, permitting only cars with plates ending in an even number on even days, odd on odd, or prohibiting cars altogether on weekends. There's no central source for information about these sporadic traffic restrictions; the best strategy is to check with your hotel before arrival for an update. On the other hand, you'll need a car to get the most out of the hill country that makes up much of the Venetian Arc.

The two main access roads to the Venetian Arc from southern Italy are both linked to the A1 (Autostrada del Sole), which connects Bologna, Florence, and Rome. They are the A13, which culminates in Padua, and the A22, which passes through Verona running north–south. Linking the region from east to west is the A4, the primary route from Milan to Trieste, skirting Verona, Padua, and Venice along the way. The distance from Verona to Trieste via A4 is 263 km (163 mi, 2½ hours), with one break in the autostrada near Venice/Mestre. Branches link the A4 with Treviso (A27), Pordenone (A28), and Udine (A23).

TRAIN TRAVEL

Trains on the main routes from the south stop almost hourly in Verona, Padua, and Venice. From northern Italy and the rest of Europe, trains usually enter via Milan or through Porta Nuova station in Verona. Treviso and Udine both lie on the main line from Venice to Tarvisio. Unfortunately, there are no daytime express trains between Venice and Tarvisio, only the slower interregional and regional service.

To the west of Venice, the main line running across the north of Italy stops at Padua (30 minutes from Venice), Vicenza (1 hour), and Verona (1½ hours); to the east is Trieste (2 hours). Local trains link Venice to Bassano del Grappa (1 hour), Padua to Bassano del Grappa (1 hour), Vicenza to Treviso (1 hour), and Udine to Trieste (1 hour).

Be sure to take express trains whenever possible—a local "milk run" that stops in every village along the way can take considerably longer. The fastest trains are the Eurostars, but reservations are obligatory and fares are higher than on regular express trains. You can check schedules at the Web site of the Italian national railway, **FS** (☎ *892021* 🌐 *www.trenitalia.com*).

ABOUT THE HOTELS

There's a full range of accommodations throughout the region. Hotels often renovate and raise their prices, but good low-cost options can still be found. Ask about weekend discounts, often available at hotels catering to business clients. Rates tend to be higher in Padua and Verona; in Verona especially, seasonal rates vary widely and soar during trade fairs and the opera season. There are fewer good lodging choices in Vicenza, perhaps because more overnighters are drawn to the better restaurant scene in Verona and Padua. *Agriturismo* (farm stay) information is available at tourist offices and sometimes on their Web sites.

Hotel reviews have been condensed for this book. Please go to Fodors.com for full reviews of each property.

WHAT IT COSTS IN EUROS

	¢	$	$$	$$$	$$$$
Restaurants	under €20	€20–€30	€30–€45	€45–€65	over €65
Hotels	under €75	€75–€125	€125–€200	€200–€300	over €300

Restaurant prices are for a first course (primo), second course (secondo), and dessert (dolce). Hotel prices are for two people in a standard double room in high season, including tax and service.

PADUA

A romantic warren of arcaded streets, Padua has long been one of the major cultural centers of northern Italy. It's home to Italy's second-oldest university, founded in 1222, which attracted such cultural icons as Dante (1265–1321), Petrarch (1304–74), and Galileo Galilei (1564–1642), thus earning the city the sobriquet *La Dotta* (The Learned). Padua's Basilica di Sant'Antonio, begun around 1238, is dedicated to Saint Anthony, and it attracts droves of pilgrims, especially on his feast day, June 13. Three great artists—Giotto (1266–1337), Donatello (circa 1386–1466), and Mantegna (1431–1506)—left significant works in Padua, with Giotto's Scrovegni Chapel one of the best-known, and most meticulously preserved, works of art in the country. Today a cycle-happy student body—some 50,000 strong—flavors every aspect of local culture. Don't be surprised if you spot a *laurea* (graduation) ceremony marked by laurel leaves, mocking lullabies, and X-rated caricatures.

4

GETTING HERE

Many people visit Padua from Venice: the train trip between the cities is short, and regular bus service originates from Venice's Piazzale Roma. By car from Milan or Venice, Padua is on the Autostrada Torino–Trieste A4/E70. Take the San Carlo exit and follow Via Guido Reni to Via Tiziano Aspetti into town. From the south, take the Autostrada Bologna Padova A13 to its Padua terminus at Via Ballaglia. Regular bus service connects Venice's Marco Polo airport with downtown Padua.

Padua is a pedestrian's city. If you arrive by car, leave your vehicle in one of the parking lots on the outskirts, or at your hotel. Unlimited bus service is included with the Padova Card (€15 or €20, valid for 48 or 72 hours), which allows entry to all the city's principal sights. It is available at tourist information offices and at some museums and hotels.

VISITOR INFORMATION

Padua tourism office (✉ *Padova Railway Station* ☎ *049/8752077* ✉ *Galleria Pedrocchi* ☎ *049/8767927* 🌐 *www.turismopadova.it*).

EXPLORING PADUA

TOP ATTRACTIONS

★ **Basilica di Sant'Antonio** *(Basilica del Santo)*. Thousands of faithful make the pilgrimage here each year to pray at the tomb of Saint Anthony. The huge church, which combines elements of Byzantine, Romanesque, and Gothic styles, was probably begun around 1238, seven years after the death of the Portuguese-born saint. It was completed in 1310, with structural modifications added from the end of the 14th century into the mid-15th century. The imposing interior contains works by the 15th-century Florentine master Donatello. He sculpted the series of bronze reliefs illustrating the miracles of Saint Anthony, as well as the bronze statues of the Madonna and saints on the high altar. But because of the site's popularity with pilgrims, Masses are held in the basilica almost constantly, which makes it difficult to see these works. More accessible is the recently restored **Cappella del Santo**, housing the tomb of the saint, which dates from the 16th century. Its walls are covered with

Basilica di Sant'-Antonio **6**
Cappella degli Scrovegni **1**
Chiesa degli Eremitani **2**
Museo Civici degli Eremitani . **2**
Orto Botanico **7**
Palazzo del Bo' . **3**
Palazzo della Ragione **4**
Piazza dei Signori **5**
Villa Pisani **8**

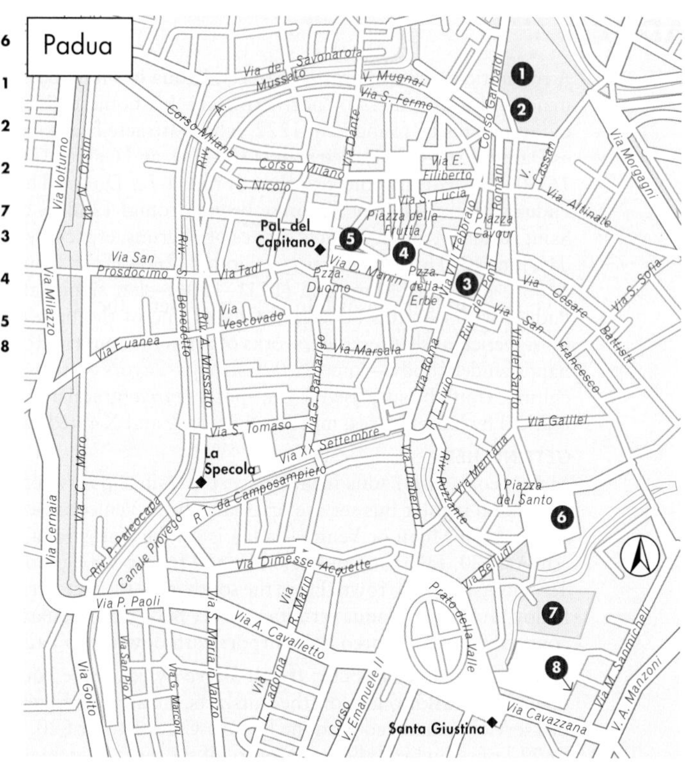

impressive reliefs by various important Renaissance sculptors, including Jacopo Sansovino (1486–1570), the architect of the library in Venice's Piazza San Marco, and Tullio Lombardo (1455–1532), the greatest in a family of sculptors who decorated many churches in the area, among them Venice's Santa Maria dei Miracoli. In front of the church is an undisputed masterpiece of Italian Renaissance sculpture, Donatello's equestrian statue (1453) of the *condottiere* (mercenary general) Erasmo da Narni, known as Gattamelata. Inspired by the ancient statue of Marcus Aurelius in Rome's Campidoglio, it is the first in a series of Italian Renaissance monumental equestrian statues. ✉ *Piazza del Santo* ☎ *049/8789722* 🌐 *www.santantonio.org* ⏲ *Oct.–Apr., daily 6:20 am–7 pm; May–Sept., daily 6:20 am–7:45 pm.*

Fodor's Choice ★ **Cappella degli Scrovegni** *(The Arena Chapel)*. This world-famous chapel and its frescoes were commissioned by Enrico Scrovegno to atone for the sins of his deceased father, Reginaldo, the usurer encountered by Dante in the Seventh Circle of the Inferno in his *Divine Comedy.* Giotto and his assistants decorated the interior from 1303 to 1305 with a universally acclaimed fresco cycle illustrating the lives of Mary and Jesus. The 38 panels are arranged in tiers and are to be read from left to right. The spatial depth, emotional intensity, and naturalism of these frescoes—note the use of blue sky instead of the conventional, depth-destroying gold background of medieval painting—broke new ground in Western art. Opposite the altar is a *Last Judgment,* most likely designed and painted by Giotto's assistants, where Enrico offers his chapel to the Virgin, celebrating her role in human salvation—particularly appropriate, given the penitential purpose of the chapel.

Mandatory reservations are for a specific time and are nonrefundable. They can be made well in advance at the ticket office, online, or by phone. Payments online or by phone by credit card must be made one day in advance; payments by bank transfer (possible by phone only) should be made four days in advance. Reservations are necessary even if you have a Padova Card. In order to preserve the artwork, doors are opened only every 15 minutes. A maximum of 25 visitors at a time must spend 15 minutes in an acclimatization room before making a 15-minute (20-minute in winter, late June, and July) chapel visit. Punctuality is essential; tickets should be picked up at least one hour before your reservation time. If you don't have a reservation, it's sometimes possible to buy your chapel admission on the spot—but you might have to wait a while until there's a group with an opening. You can see fresco details as part of a virtual tour at Musei Civici degli Eremitani. A good place to get some background before visiting the chapel is the multimedia room, which offers films and interactive computer presentations. ✉ *Piazza Eremitani 8* ☎ *049/2010020 for reservations* 🌐 *www.cappelladegliscrovegni.it* 🎫 *€13 includes Musei Civici, or €1 with Padova Card* 🕓 *Early Nov.–early Mar. and mid-June–early Aug., daily 9–7; early Mar.–mid-June and early Aug.–early Nov., Mon. 9–7, Tues.–Sun. 9 am–10 pm; entry by reservation only.*

★ **Palazzo della Ragione.** Also known as Il Salone, this spectacular arcaded reception hall, which divides the Piazza delle Frutta from the Piazza delle Erbe, was built between 1303 and 1309, with later 15th-century additions. Giotto painted the original frescoes, which were destroyed in a fire in 1420. In the Middle Ages, as its name implies, the building housed Padua's law courts; today its street-level arcades shelter shops and cafés. Art shows are often held upstairs in the frescoed **Salone,** at 85 feet high one of the largest and most architecturally pleasing halls in Italy. In the Salone there's an enormous wooden horse, crafted for a 15th-century public tournament, with a head and tail later remodeled to replicate the steed from Donatello's *Gattamelata*. In the piazza surrounding the building are Padua's colorful open-air fruit and vegetable markets. ✉ *Piazza della Ragione* ☎ *049/8205006* 🎫 *Salone €4, free with Padova Card* 🕓 *Feb.–Oct., Tues.–Sun. 9–7; Nov.–Jan., Tues.–Sun. 9–6.*

Piazza dei Signori. Some fine examples of 15th- and 16th-century buildings line this square. On the west side, the **Palazzo del Capitanio** (facade constructed 1598–1605) has an impressive **Torre dell'Orologio,** with an astronomical clock dating from 1344 and a portal made by Falconetto in 1532 in the form of a Roman triumphal arch. The 12th-century **Battistero del Duomo** (Cathedral Baptistry), with frescoes by Giusto de Menabuoi (1374–78), is just a few steps away. ✉ *Piazza del Duomo* ☎ *049/656914* 🎫 *€2.80, free with Padova Card* 🕓 *Daily 10–6.*

Villa Pisani. Extensive grounds with rare trees, ornamental fountains, and garden follies surround this extraordinary palace built in 1721 for the Venetian doge Alvise Pisani in Stra, 13 km (8 mi) southeast of Padua. Recalling Versailles more than a Veneto villa, it was one of the last and grandest of many stately residences constructed along the Brenta River from the 16th to 18th century by wealthy Venetians for their *villeggiatura*—vacation and escape from the midsummer humidity. Gianbattista Tiepolo's (1696–1770) spectacular frescoes on the ballroom ceiling alone are worth the visit. For a relaxing afternoon, explore the gorgeous park and maze. To get here from Venice, take Bus 53 from Piazzale Roma. The villa is a five-minute walk from the bus stop in Stra. ✉ *Via Doge Pisani 7, Stra* ☎ *049/502074* 🌐 *www.villapisani.beniculturali.it* *Villa, maze, and park €10; maze and park only €7.50* ⏲ *Villa and park: Apr. and May, Tues.–Sun. 9–8; June–Sept., Tues.–Sun. 8:30–8; Oct.–Mar., Tues.–Sun. 9–5. Last entry 1 hr before closing. Maze: Apr.–Sept. 9–1:30 and 2:15–7:15.*

WORD OF MOUTH

"Scrovegni Chapel was one of the highlights of our whole trip. I booked a double length slot of 40 minutes actually in the chapel—only available in the evening—as opposed to the usual 20, and we were so glad of that. It really was quite overwhelming."
—Caroline_Edinburgh

WORTH NOTING

Chiesa degli Eremitani. This 13th-century church houses substantial fragments of Andrea Mantegna's frescoes (1448–50), damaged by Allied bombing in World War II. Despite their fragmentary condition, Mantegna's still beautiful and historically important frescoes depicting the martyrdom of Saint James and Saint Christopher show the young artist's mastery of extremely complex problems of perspective. ✉ *Piazza degli Eremitani* ☎ *049/8756410* ⏲ *Nov.–Mar., weekdays 7:30–12:30 and 3:30–7, weekends 9–12:30 and 3:30–7; Apr.–Oct., weekdays 8–12:30 and 4–7, weekends 9–12:30 and 4–7.*

Musei Civici degli Eremitani *(Civic Museum).* What was formerly a monastery now houses works of Venetian masters, as well as fine collections of archaeological pieces and ancient coins. Notable are the Giotto Crucifix, which once hung in the Scrovegni Chapel, and the *Portrait of a Young Senator* by Giovanni Bellini (1430–1516). ✉ *Piazza Eremitani 10* ☎ *049/8204551* *€10, €12 with Scrovegni Chapel, free with Padova Card* ⏲ *Tues.–Sun. 9–7.*

Orto Botanico *(Botanical Garden).* The Venetian Republic ordered the creation of Padua's botanical garden in 1545 to supply the university with medicinal plants. You can stroll the arboretum and wander through hothouses and beds of plants that were first introduced to Italy in this late-Renaissance garden, which still maintains its original layout. A St. Peter's palm, planted in 1585, inspired Goethe to write his 1790 essay called "The Metamorphosis of Plants." ✉ *Via Orto Botanico 15* ☎ *049/8272119* 🌐 *www.ortobotanico.unipd.it* *€4, free with Padova Card* ⏲ *Apr.–Oct., daily 9–1 and 3–7; Nov.–Mar., Mon.–Sat. 9–1.*

Palazzo del Bo'. The University of Padua, founded in 1222, centers around this 16th-century palazzo with an 18th-century facade. It's named after the Osteria del Bo' (*bo'* means "ox"), an inn that once stood on the site. It's worth a visit to see the exquisite and perfectly proportioned anatomy theater (1594), the beautiful "Old Courtyard," and a hall with a lectern used by Galileo. You can enter only as part of a guided tour. Most guides speak English, but it is worth checking ahead by phone. ✉ *Via VIII Febbraio* ☎ *049/8273044* 🌐 *www.unipd.it* *€5* ⏲ *Nov.–Feb., Mon., Wed., and Fri. at 3:15 and 4:15, Tues., Thurs., and Sat. at 10:15 and 11:15; Mar.–Oct., Mon., Wed., and Fri. at 3:15, 4:15, and 5:15, Tues., Thurs., and Sat. at 9:15, 10:15, and 11:15.*

4

WHERE TO EAT

$$$ MODERN ITALIAN ✕ **La Finestra.** Perhaps the trendiest restaurant in Padua, cozy yet elegant La Finestra richly deserves its reputation. The carefully prepared and creatively presented dishes may not always stick to the traditional recipes, but no one can contest that owners Carlo Vidali and Hélène Dao know what they're doing in the kitchen. Their version of the regional classic *pasta e fagioli,* for example, uses the most exquisite beans in the region, leaves out the pasta, and substitutes croutons and a dollop of foie gras. This is not grandma's bean soup, but it's heavenly. ✉ *Via dei Tadi 15* ☎ *049/650313* 🌐 *www.ristorantefinestra.it* ⏲ *Closed Mon. and 3 wks in Aug. No lunch Tues.–Thurs., no dinner Sun.*

$ WINE BAR ★ ✕ **L'Anfora.** This mix between a traditional *bacaro* (wine bar) and an *osteria* (tavernlike restaurant) is a local institution. Stand at the bar shoulder to shoulder with a cross section of Padovano society, from construction workers to professors, and let the friendly and knowledgeable proprietors help you choose a wine. The reasonably priced menu offers simple *casalinga* (home-cooked dishes), plus salads and a selection of cheeses. Portions are ample, and no one will look askance if you don't order the full meal. The place is packed with loyal regulars at lunchtime, so come early or expect a wait; if you come alone, you'll probably end up with a table of friends before you leave. ✉ *Via Soncin 13* ☎ *049/656629* ⏲ *Closed Sun. (except in Dec.), 1 wk in Jan., and 1 wk in Aug.*

$$$$ MODERN ITALIAN ✕ **Le Calandre.** If you are willing to shell out €400 to €500 for a dinner for two, Le Calandre should definitely be on your itinerary. The quietly elegant restaurant is consistently judged by major critics as one of the two or three best restaurants in the country. The food, based on traditional Veneto recipes, is given a highly sophisticated and creative treatment. The traditional squid in its ink, for example, is served as a "cappuccino," in a glass with a crust of potato foam. The menu changes seasonally, with owner-chef Massimiliano Alajmo's creative impulses. Alajmo considers food to be an art form, not nourishment, so be prepared for minuscule portions. Make reservations well in advance. Le Calandre is in the village of Sarmeola di Rubano, a few kilometers west of Padua and easily reached by taxi. ✉ *Via Liguria 1, Sarmeola di Rubano* ☎ *049/630303* 🌐 *www.calandre.com* ✍ *Reservations essential* ⏲ *Closed Sun. and Mon., late Dec.–early Jan., and mid-Aug.–early Sept.*

THE VENETIAN ARC, PAST AND PRESENT

Long before Venetians made their presence felt on the mainland in the 15th century, Ezzelino III da Romano (1194–1259), a larger-than-life scourge who was excommunicated by Pope Innocent IV, laid claim to Verona, Padua, and the surrounding lands and towns. After he was ousted, powerful families such as Padua's Carrara and Verona's della Scala (Scaligeri) vied throughout the 14th century to dominate these territories. With the rise of Venetian rule came a time of relative peace, when noble families from the lagoon and the mainland commissioned Palladio and other accomplished architects to design their palazzi and villas. This rich classical legacy, superimposed upon medieval castles and fortifications, is central to the identities of present-day Padua, Vicenza, and Verona. The region remained under Venetian control until the Napoleonic invasion and the fall of the Venetian Republic in 1797. The Council of Vienna ceded it, along with Lombardy, to Austria in 1815. The region revolted against Austrian rule and joined the Italian Republic in 1866.

Friuli–Venezia Giulia has a diverse cultural history that's reflected in its architecture, language, and cuisine. It's been marched through, fought over, hymned by patriots, and romanticized by writers James Joyce, Rainer Maria Rilke, and Jan Morris. Trieste was also vividly depicted in the novels of the towering figure of early-20th-century Italian letters, Italo Svevo. The region has seen Fascists and Communists, Romans, Habsburgs, and Huns. It survived by forging sheltering alliances—Udine beneath the wings of San Marco (1420), Trieste choosing Duke Leopold of Austria (1382) over Venetian domination.

Some of World War I's fiercest fighting took place in Friuli–Venezia Giulia, where memorials and cemeteries commemorate hundreds of thousands who died before the arrival of Italian troops in 1918 finally liberated Trieste from Austrian rule. Trieste, along with the whole of Venezia Giulia, was annexed to Italy in 1920. During World War II the Germans occupied the area and placed Trieste in an administrative zone along with parts of Slovenia. One of Italy's two concentration camps was near Trieste. After the war, during a period of Cold War dispute, Trieste was governed by an allied military administration; it was officially reannexed to Italy in 1954, when Italy ceded the Istrian peninsula to the south to Yugoslavia. These arrangements, long de facto in effect, were ratified by Italy and Yugoslavia in 1975.

$$$ ITALIAN ✕ **Nerodiseppia.** Behind the Basilica di San Antonio, Nerodiseppia has a cool atmosphere and unadorned decor. Don't be put off, as this is one of the finest fish restaurants in a region noted for its seafood. Patrizia and Eugenia Rubin, its friendly Padovane owners, serve up simply but carefully prepared dishes using the freshest fish from the catch of the day. The reasonably priced menu varies according to the season and what local fishermen brought in that day. In fall, locals flock here to try the *moeche*, baby soft-shell crabs dipped in eggs and flour and fried to a crispy, golden brown. The weekday set lunch, ranging from €16.50 to €18, is one of the city's gastronomic bargains. ✉ *Via San Francesco*

161 ☎ 049/8364049 ⊕ www.ristorantenerodiseppia.it ⊗ Closed Sun. and Mon., Dec. 26–Jan. 7, and Aug.

$$ VENETIAN ★ ✕ **Osteria Dal Capo.** A friendly trattoria in the heart of what used to be Padua's Jewish ghetto, Osteria Dal Capo serves almost exclusively traditional Veneto dishes and does so with refinement and care. The liver and onions is extraordinarily tender. Even the accompanying polenta is grilled to perfection—slightly crisp on the outside and moist on the inside. And the desserts are nothing to scoff at, either. Word is out among locals about this hidden gem, and the tiny place fills up quickly, so reservations are necessary. ✉ *Via degli Oblizzi 2 ☎ 049/663105 Reservations essential ⊗ Closed Sun., 2 wks in early Jan., and 3 wks in Aug. No lunch Mon.*

4

WHERE TO STAY

$ **Al Fagiano.** This delightfully funky budget hotel sits near Basilica di Sant'Antonio, and some rooms have views of the church's spires and cupolas. **Pros:** large rooms; relaxed atmosphere; convenient location. **Cons:** no room service or help with baggage; some find the eccentric decor a bit much. **TripAdvisor:** "large rooms for reasonable prices," "nice view into a cute courtyard," "artwork is bizarre." ✉ *Via Locatelli 45 ☎ 049/8750073 ⊕ www.alfagiano.com 40 rooms In room: a/c, Wi-Fi (some). In-hotel: room service, bar, Wi-Fi hotspot, some pets allowed, parking (paid) No meals.*

$ ★ **Albergo Verdi.** Located close to the Piazza dei Signori, this is one of the best-situated hotels in the city. **Pros:** excellent location; attentive staff; pleasant and warm atmosphere; quiet. **Cons:** rooms, while ample, are not large; few views; charge for Wi-Fi access; hefty parking fee (€15). **TripAdvisor:** "rooms are small and clean," "great little breakfast room," "delightful and inexpensive." ✉ *Via Dondi dell'Orlogio 7 ☎ 049/8364163 ⊕ www.albergoverdipadova.it 14 rooms In-room: safe, Wi-Fi. In-hotel: bar, Internet terminal, parking (paid), some pets allowed Breakfast.*

$ ★ **Methis.** The strikingly modern Methis takes its name from the Greek word for style and spirit. **Pros:** attractive rooms; helpful and attentive staff; pleasant little extras like umbrellas. **Cons:** a 15-minute walk from major sights and restaurants; public spaces are cold and uninviting. **TripAdvisor:** "across from a 10th-century castle," "balconies overlooking the canal," "modern urban style." ✉ *Riviera Paleocapa 70 ☎ 049/8725555 ⊕ www.methishotel.com 52 rooms, 7 suites In-room: safe, refrigerator, Wi-Fi. In-hotel: bar, gym, Internet terminal, parking (free) Breakfast.*

CAFÉS AND WINE BARS

No visit to Padua is complete without a trip to **Caffè Pedrocchi** (✉ *Piazzetta Pedrocchi ☎ 049/8781231 ⊕ www.caffepedrocchi.it*). You can still sit here, as the French writer Stendhal did shortly after the café was established in 1831, and observe a good slice of Veneto life, especially, as he noted, the elegant ladies sipping their coffee. The massive café, built in a style reflecting the fashion set by Napoléon's expeditions in Egypt, has long been central to the city's social life. It also serves lunch and dinner, and is proud of its innovative menu. Open 9 am to midnight daily from mid-June to mid-September; hours for the rest of the year are Sunday to Wednesday 9 to 9, Thursday to Saturday 9 am to midnight.

Hostaria Ai Do Archi (✉ *Via Nazario Sauro 23* ☎ *049/652335*) is the most popular Padovano version of the bacari that are so typical of the Veneto: wine bars where people sip wine, sample local treats, and talk politics. The Ai Do Archi is as famous for its impressive platters of sliced meats as it is for its selections of wine. Besides attracting students and locals, it is also a meeting place for many of Padova's reggae fans.

COCKTAIL HOUR ON PADUA'S PIAZZAS

One of Padua's greatest traditions is the outdoor en-masse consumption of aperitifs: *spritz* (a mix of Aperol or Campari, soda water, and wine), prosecco (sparkling wine), or wine. It all happens in the Piazza delle Erbe and Piazza delle Frutta. Several bars there provide drinks in plastic cups, so you can take them outside and mingle among the crowds. The ritual, practiced primarily by students, begins at 6 pm or so, at which hour you can also pick up a snack from one of the outdoor vendors. On weekends the open-air revelry continues into the wee hours.

VICENZA

Vicenza bears the distinctive signature of the 16th-century architect Andrea Palladio, whose name has been given to the "Palladian" style of architecture. He effectively emphasized the principles of order and harmony in the classical style of architecture established by Renaissance architects such as Brunelleschi, Alberti, and Sansovino. He used these principles and classical motifs not only for public buildings but also for private dwellings. His elegant villas and palaces were influential in propagating classical architecture in Europe, especially Britain, and later in America—most notably at Thomas Jefferson's Monticello.

In the mid-16th century Palladio was commissioned to rebuild much of Vicenza, which had been greatly damaged during wars waged against Venice by the League of Cambrai, an alliance of the papacy, France, the Holy Roman Empire, and several neighboring city-states. He made his name with the basilica, begun in 1549 in the heart of Vicenza, and then embarked on a series of lordly buildings, all of which adhere to the same classicism and principles of harmony.

GETTING HERE

Vicenza is midway between Padua and Verona, and several trains leave from both cities every hour. By car, take the Autostrada Brescia–Padova/Torino–Trieste A4/E70 to SP247 North directly into Vicenza.

VISITOR INFORMATION

Vicenza tourism office (✉ *Piazza Giacomo Matteotti 12* ☎ *0444/320854* 🌐 *www.vicenzae.org*).

EXPLORING VICENZA

Many of Palladio's works are interspersed among the Venetian Gothic and baroque palaces that line Corso Palladio, an elegant shopping thoroughfare where Vicenza's status as one of Italy's wealthiest cities is evident. Part of this wealth stems from Vicenza's being a world center for gold jewelry.

TOP ATTRACTIONS

Fodor's Choice ★ **Teatro Olimpico.** Palladio's last, and perhaps most spectacular work, was completed after his death by Vincenzo Scamozzi (1552–1616). Based closely on the model of ancient Roman theaters, it represents an important development in theater and stage design and is noteworthy for its acoustics and the cunning use of perspective in Scamozzi's permanent backdrop. The anterooms are frescoed with images of important figures in Venetian history. ✉ *Piazza Matteotti* ☎ *0444/222800* 🎫 *€8 includes admission to Palazzo Chiericati* ⏲ *Sept.–June, Tues.–Sun. 9–5; July and Aug., Tues.–Sun. 9–7; times may vary depending on performance schedule.*

Villa della Rotonda (Villa Almerico Capra). This beautiful Palladian villa, commissioned in 1556 as a suburban residence for Paolo Almerico, is undoubtedly the purest expression of Palladio's architectural theory and aesthetic. Although it seems more of a pavilion showplace, it was in fact commissioned as a residence, and as such demonstrates the priority Palladio gave to architectural symbolism of celestial harmony over practical considerations. It's more a villa-temple than a house to live in, and in this respect, it goes beyond the rational utilitarianism of Renaissance architecture. Although a visit to the interior of the building may be difficult to schedule (it's still privately owned), it is well worth the effort in order to get an idea of how the people who commissioned the residence actually lived. Viewing the exterior and the grounds is a must for any visit to Vicenza. The villa is a 20-minute walk from town or a short ride on Bus 8 from Piazza Roma. ✉ *Via della Rotonda* ☎ *0444/321793* 🎫 *Grounds and interior €10, grounds €5* ⏲ *Mar. 15–Nov. 10: grounds Tues.–Sun. 10–noon and 3–6; interior Wed. and Sat. 10–noon and 3–6.*

Villa Valmarana ai Nani. Inside this 17th- to 18th-century country house, named for the statues of dwarfs adorning the garden, is a series of frescoes executed in 1757 by Gianbattista Tiepolo depicting scenes from classical mythology, *The Illiad,* Tasso's *Gerusalemme Liberata,* and Ariosto's *Orlando Furioso.* They include his *Sacrifice of Iphigenia,* unanimously acclaimed by critics as a major masterpiece of 18th-century painting. The neighboring *foresteria* (guest house) is also part of the museum; it contains frescoes showing 18th-century life at its most charming, and scenes of chinoiserie popular in the 18th century, by Tiepolo's son Giandomenico (1727–1804). The garden dwarves are probably taken from designs by Giandomenico. You can reach the villa on foot by following the same path that leads to Palladio's Villa della Rotonda. ✉ *Via dei Nani 2/8* ☎ *0444/321803* 🎫 *€8* ⏲ *Mid-Mar.–Oct., Tues.–Sun. 10–noon and 3–6; Nov.–mid-Mar., weekends 10–noon and 2–4.*

WORTH NOTING

Palazzo Chiericati. This imposing Palladian palazzo (1550) would be worthy of a visit even if it didn't house Vicenza's **Museo Civico.** Because of the ample space surrounding the building site, Palladio combined here

4

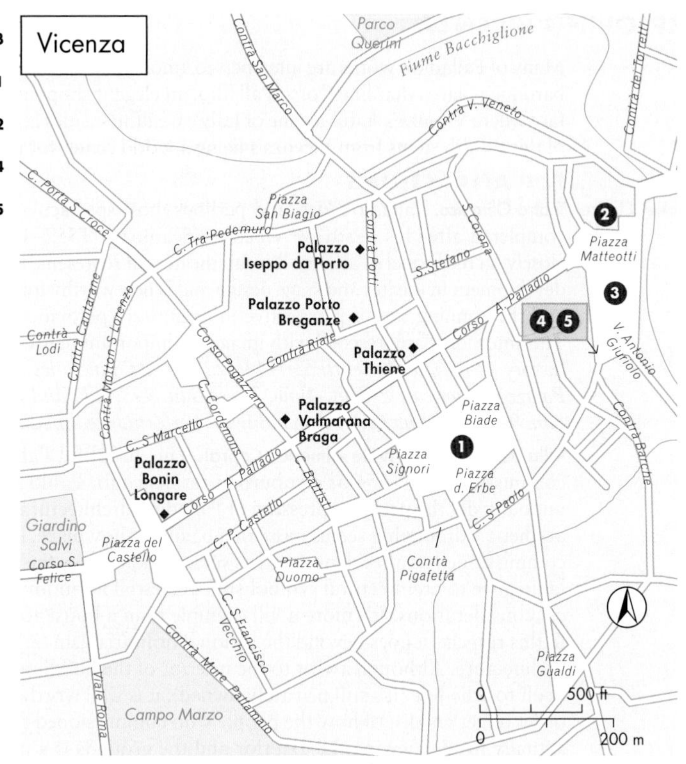

elements of an urban palazzo with those he used in his country villas. The museum's important Venetian collection includes significant paintings by Cima, Tiepolo, Piazetta, and Tintoretto, but its main attraction is an extensive collection of highly interesting and rarely found painters from the Vicenza area, such as Jacopo Bassano (1515–92) and the eccentric and innovative Francesco Maffei (1605–60), whose work foreshadowed important currents of Venetian painting of subsequent generations. ✉ *Piazza Matteotti* ☎ *0444/325071* 💳 *€8 includes admission to Teatro Olimpico* ⏲ *Sept.–June, Tues.–Sun. 9–5; July and Aug., Tues.–Sun. 9–5.*

Piazza dei Signori. At the heart of Vicenza sits this square, which contains the **Palazzo della Ragione** (1549), commonly known as Palladio's basilica, a courthouse, and public meeting hall (the original Roman meaning of the term "basilica"). The previously almost-unknown Palladio made his name by successfully modernizing the medieval building, grafting a graceful two-story exterior loggia onto the existing Gothic structure. Take a look also at the **Loggia del Capitaniato,** opposite, which Palladio designed but never completed. The palazzo and the loggia are open to the public only when there's an exhibition; ask at the tourist office. The interior of the basilica is closed for restorations projected to continue into 2012.

WHERE TO EAT

$$ NORTHERN ITALIAN **Antico Ristorante agli Schioppi.** When they want to eat well, Vicenza's natives generally travel to the neighboring countryside—Antico Ristorante agli Schioppi is one of the few in the city frequented by Vicentino families and businessmen. Veneto country-style decor, with enormous murals, matches simple, well-prepared regional cuisine at this family-run restaurant. The risotto, delicately flavored with wild mushrooms and zucchini flowers, is creamy and—a rarity in restaurant risottos—beautifully textured. This is also an excellent place to try baccalà, a cod dish that is a Vicenza specialty. *Contrà Piazza del Castello 26 0444/543701 www.ristoranteaglischioppi.com Closed Sun., last wk of July–late Aug., and Jan. 1–6. No lunch Mon.*

¢ PIZZERIA **Da Vittorio.** It has little in the way of atmosphere or decor, but Vicentini flock to this small eatery for what is perhaps the best pizza north of Naples. There's an incredible array of toppings, from the traditional to the exotic (mangoes), but the pies are all so authentic that they will make you think you are sitting by the Bay of Naples. The service is friendly and efficient. This is a great place to stop for lunch if you're walking to Palladio's Rotonda or the Villa Valmarana. *Borgo Berga 52 0444/525059 No credit cards Closed Tues. and 2 wks in July.*

$ NORTHERN ITALIAN ★ **Ponte delle Bele.** Vicenza lies at the foot of the Alps, and many residents spend at least a part of summer in the mountains to escape the heat. Alpine cuisine has been incorporated into the local culture and can be enjoyed at this popular and friendly Veneto trattoria. The house specialty, *stinco di maiale al forno* (roast port shank), is wonderfully fragrant with herbs and aromatic vegetables. Also try such game as venison with blueberries or guinea fowl roasted with white grapes. The rather kitschy decor doesn't detract from the good, hearty food. *Contrà Ponte delle Bele 5 0444/320647 www.pontedellebele.it Closed Sun. and 2 wks in mid-Aug.*

¢ ITALIAN **Righetti.** For a city of its size, Vicenza has few distinguished restaurants. That's why many people gravitate to this popular cafeteria, which serves classic dishes without putting a dent in your wallet. There's frequently a hearty soup such as *orzo e fagioli* (barley and bean) on the menu. The classic *baccalà alla vicentina*, a cod dish, is a great reason to stop by on Friday. *Piazza Duomo 3 0444/543135 No credit cards Closed weekends, 1st wk in Jan., and Aug.*

WHERE TO STAY

During annual gold fairs in January, May, and September, it may be quite difficult to find lodging. Be sure to reserve well in advance and expect to pay higher rates.

$$ **Campo Marzio.** A five-minute walk from the railway station, this comfortable hotel is right in front of the city walls. **Pros:** central location; more amenities than its competitors; set back from the street, so it's quiet and bright. **Cons:** public spaces are uninspiring; incredibly expensive during fairs. **TripAdvisor:** "close to old town," "concierge was friendly and helpful," "rooms are actually quite nice." *Viale Roma 21 0444/5457000 www.hotelcampomarzio.com 36 rooms*

In-room: safe, refrigerator, Internet, Wi-Fi. In-hotel: bar, parking (free), some pets allowed *Breakfast.*

$ ★ **Due Mori.** Authentic turn-of-the-20th-century antiques fill the rooms at this 1883 hotel, one of the oldest in the city. **Pros:** tastefully furnished rooms; friendly staff; central location. **Cons:** no air-conditioning (although ceiling fans minimize the need for it); no one to help with baggage. **TripAdvisor:** "location is great for sightseeing," "one-of-a-kind antique furniture," "very good value." *Contrà Do Rode 24* *0444/321886* *www.hotelduemori.com* *53 rooms* *In-room: no a/c, no TV, Wi-Fi (some). In-hotel: bar, parking (free), some pets allowed* *Closed 1st 2 wks of Aug. and 2 wks in late Dec.* *No meals.*

VERONA

On the banks of the fast-flowing River Adige, 60 km (37 mi) west of Vicenza, enchanting Verona has timeless monuments, a picturesque town center, and a romantic reputation as the setting (in fiction only) of Shakespeare's *Romeo and Juliet.* With its lively Venetian air and proximity to Lake Garda, it attracts hordes of tourists, especially Germans and Austrians. Tourism peaks during summer's renowned season of open-air opera in the arena and during spring's **Vinitaly** (*Fiera di Verona, Viale del Lavoro 8* *045/8298170* *www.vinitaly.com*), one of the world's most important wine expos. For five days you can sample the wines of more than 3,000 wineries from dozens of countries.

Verona grew to power and prosperity within the Roman Empire as a result of its key commercial and military position in northern Italy. With its Roman arena, theater, and city gates, it has the most significant monuments of Roman antiquity north of Rome. After the fall of the empire, the city continued to flourish under the guidance of barbarian kings such as Theodoric, Alboin, Pepin, and Berenger I, reaching its cultural and artistic peak in the 13th and 14th centuries under the della Scala (Scaligero) dynasty. (Look for the *scala,* or ladder, emblem all over town.) In 1404 Verona traded its independence for security and placed itself under the control of Venice. (The other recurring architectural motif is the lion of Saint Mark, a symbol of Venetian rule.)

GETTING HERE

Verona is midway between Venice and Milan. It is served by a small airport, Aeroporto Valerio Catullo, which accommodates domestic and European flights; however, many travelers still prefer to fly into Venice or Milan and drive or take the train to Verona. Several trains per hour depart from any point on the Milan–Venice line. By car, from the east or west, take the Autostrada Trieste–Torino A4/E70 to the SS12 and follow it north into town. From the north or south, take the Autostrada del Brennero A22/E45 to the SR11 East (initially, called the Strada Bresciana) directly into town.

VISITOR INFORMATION

Verona tourism office (*Piazza Brà* *045/8068680* *Porta Nuova railway station* *045/8000861* *www.tourism.verona.it*).

Continued on page 266

PALLADIO COUNTRY

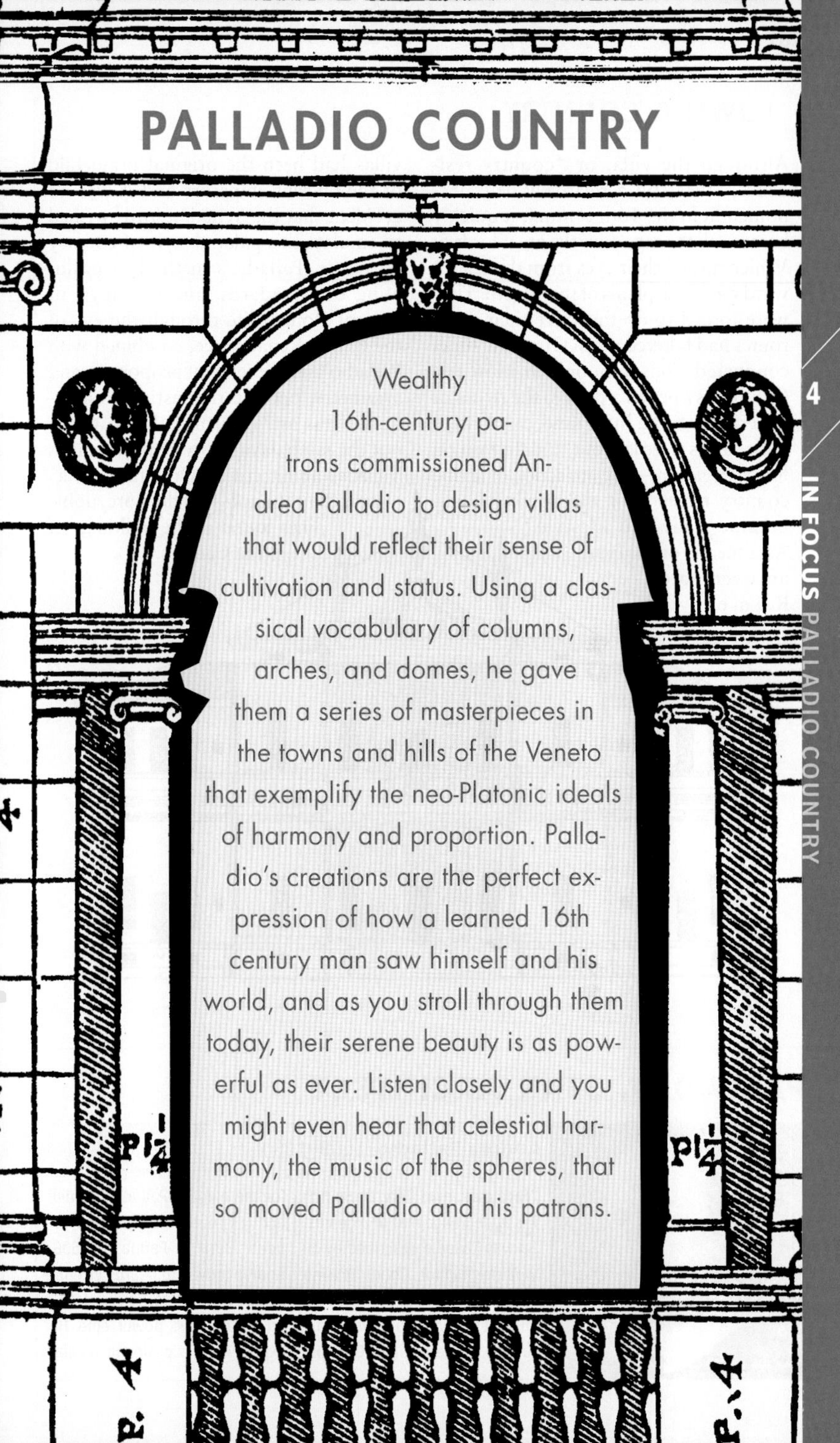

Wealthy 16th-century patrons commissioned Andrea Palladio to design villas that would reflect their sense of cultivation and status. Using a classical vocabulary of columns, arches, and domes, he gave them a series of masterpieces in the towns and hills of the Veneto that exemplify the neo-Platonic ideals of harmony and proportion. Palladio's creations are the perfect expression of how a learned 16th century man saw himself and his world, and as you stroll through them today, their serene beauty is as powerful as ever. Listen closely and you might even hear that celestial harmony, the music of the spheres, that so moved Palladio and his patrons.

TOWN & COUNTRY

Although the villa, or "country residence," was still a relatively new phenomenon in the 16th century, it quickly became all the rage once the great lords of Venice turned their eyes from the sea toward the fertile plains of the Veneto. They were forced to do this once their trade routes had faltered when Ottoman Turks conquered Constantinople in 1456 and Columbus opened a path to the riches of America in 1492. In no time, canals were built, farms were laid out, and the fashion for *villeggiatura*—the attraction of idyllic country retreats for the nobility—became a favored lifestyle. As a means of escaping an overheated Rome, villas had been the original brainchild of the ancient emperors and it was no accident that the Venetian lords wished to emulate this palatial style of country residence. Palladio's method of evaluating the standards, and standbys, of ancient Roman life through the eye of the Italian Renaissance, combined with Palladio's innate sense of proportion and symmetry, became the lasting foundation of his art. In turn, Palladio threw out the jambalaya of styles prevalent in Venetian architecture—Oriental, Gothic, and Renaissance—for the pure, noble lines found in the buildings of the Caesars.

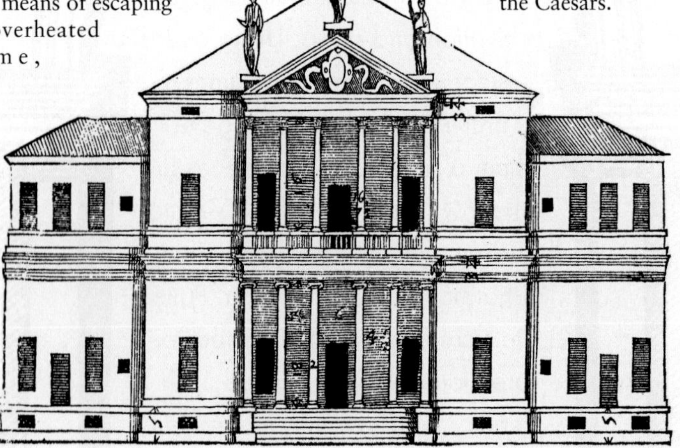

PALLADIO, STAR ARCHITECT

Andrea Palladio (1508–1580)

"Face dark, eyes fiery. Dress rich. His appearance that of a genius." So was Palladio described by his wealthy mentor, Count Trissino. Trissino encouraged the young student to trade in his birth name, Andrea di Pietro della Gondola, for the elegant Palladio. He did, and it proved a wise move indeed. Born in Padua in 1508, Andrea moved to nearby Vicenza in 1524 and was quickly taken up by the city's power elite. He experienced a profound revela-

THE OLD BECOMES NEW

La Malcontenta

Studying ancient Rome with the eyes of an explorer, Palladio employed a style that linked old with new—but often did so in unexpected ways. Just take a look at Villa Foscari, nicknamed **"La Malcontenta"** (Mira, 041/5470012, www.lamalcontenta.com €8. Open May–Oct., Tues. and Sat. 9–noon; from Venice, take an ACTV bus from Piazzale Roma to Mira or opt for a boat ride up on the Burchiello). Shaded by weeping willows and mirrored by the Brenta Canal, "The Sad Lady" was built for Nicolò and Alvise Foscari and is the quintessence of Palladian poetry. Inspired by the grandeur of Roman public buildings, Palladio applied the ancient motif of a temple facade to a domestic dwelling, topped off by a pediment, a construct most associated with religious structures. Inside, he used the technique of vaulting seen in ancient Roman baths, with giant windows and immense white walls ready-made for the colorful frescoes painted by Zelotti. No one knows for certain the origin of the villa's nickname—some say it came from a Venetian owner's wife who was exiled there due to her scandalous behavior. Regardless of the name, it's hard today to associate such a beautiful, graceful villa with anything but harmony and contentment.

tion on his first trip, in 1541, to Rome, where he sensed the harmony of the ancient ruins and saw the elements of classicism that were working their way into contemporary architecture. This experience led to his spectacular conversion of the Vicenza's Palazzo della Ragione (1545) into a basilica recalling the great meeting halls of antiquity. In years to come, after relocating to Venice, he created some memorable churches, such as S. Giorgio Maggiore (1564). Despite these varied projects, Palladio's unassailable position as one of the world's greatest architects is tied to the countryside villas, which he spread across the Veneto plains like a firmament of stars. Nothing else in the Veneto illuminates more clearly the idyllic beauty of the region than these elegant residences, their stonework now nicely mellowed and suntanned after five centuries.

VICENZA, CITY OF PALLADIO

Palazzo della Ragione

La Rotonda

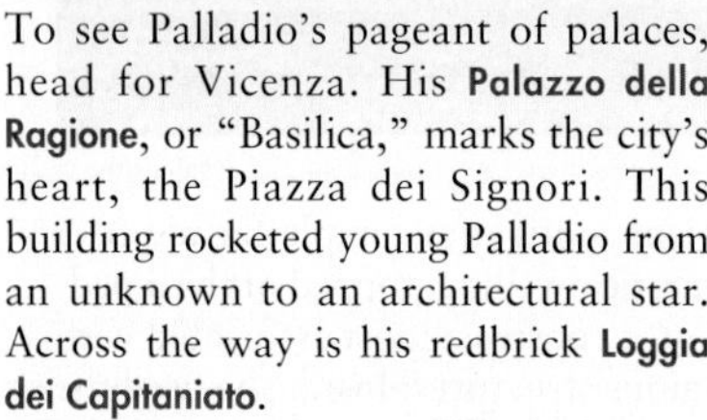

To see Palladio's pageant of palaces, head for Vicenza. His **Palazzo della Ragione**, or "Basilica," marks the city's heart, the Piazza dei Signori. This building rocketed young Palladio from an unknown to an architectural star. Across the way is his redbrick **Loggia dei Capitaniato.**

One block past the Loggia is Vicenza's main street, appropriately named Corso Andrea Palladio. Just off this street is the Contrà Porti, where you'll find the **Palazzo Barbaran da Porto** (1570) at No. 11, with its fabulously rich facade erupting with Ionic and Corinthian pillars. Today, this is the Centro Internazionale di Studi di Architettura Andrea Palladio (0444/323014, www.cisapalladio.org), a study center which mounts impressive temporary exhibitions. A few steps away, on the Contrà San Gaetano Thiene, is the Palazzo Thiene (1542-58), designed by Giulio Romano and completed by Palladio.

Doubling back to Contrà Porti 21, you find the **Palazzo Iseppo da Porto** (1544), the first palazzo where you can see the neoclassical effects of young Palladio's trip to Rome. Following the Contrà Reale, you come to Corso Fogazzaro 16 and the **Palazzo Valmarana Braga** (1565). Its gigantic pilasters were a first for domestic architecture.

Returning to the Corso Palladio, head left to the opposite end of the Corso, about five blocks, to the Piazza Mattoti and **Palazzo Chiericati** (1550). This was practically a suburban area in the 16th century, and for the palazzo Palladio combined elements of urban and rural design. The pedestal raising the building and the steps leading to the entrance—unknown in urban palaces—were to protect from floods and to keep cows from wandering in the front door. (For opening times and details, see the main text).

Across the Corso Palladio is Palladio's last and one of his most spectacular works, the **Teatro Olimpico** (1580). By careful study of ancient ruins and architectural texts, he reconstructed a Roman theater with archaeological precision. Palladio died before it was completed, but he left clear plans for the project. (For opening times and details, see the main text.)

Although it's on the outskirts of town, the **Villa Almerico Capra**, better known as **La Rotonda** (1566), is an indispensable part of any visit to Vicenza. It's the iconic Palladian building, the purest expression of his aesthetic. (For opening times, details, and a discussion of the villa, see the main text.)

A MAGNIFICENT COLLABORATION

Villa Barbaro

At the **Villa Barbaro** (1554) near the town of Maser in the province of Treviso, 48 km (30 miles) northeast of Vicenza, you can see the results of a one-time collaboration between two of the greatest artists of their age.

Palladio was the architect, and Paolo Veronese decorated the interior with an amazing cycle of trompe l'oeil frescoes—walls dissolve into landscapes, and illusions of courtiers and servants enter rooms and smile down from balustrades.

Legend has it a feud developed between Palladio and Veronese, with Palladio feeling the illusionistic frescoes detracted from his architecture; but there is practically nothing to support the idea of such a rift.

It's also noteworthy that Palladio for the first time connected the two lateral granaries to the main villa. This was a working farm, and Palladio thus created an architectural unity by connecting with graceful arcades the working parts of the estate to the living quarters, bringing together the Renaissance dichotomy of the active and the contemplative life. *Via Cornuda 7, Maser, 0432/923004 www.villadimaser.it , €5 Open April- October Tues. and weekends 3-6; Nov.- March, weekends 2:30- 5, or by reservation; Closed 24 Dec.- 6 Jan.*

ALONG THE BRENTA CANAL

During the 16th century the Brenta was transformed into a landlocked version of Venice's Grand Canal with the building of nearly 50 waterside villas. Back then, boating parties viewed them in *"burchielli"*—beautiful boats. Today, the Burchiello excursion boat (Via Orlandini 3, Padua, 049/8206910, www.ilburchiello.it) makes full- and half-day tours along the Brenta, from March to November, departing from Padua on Wednesday, Friday, and Sunday and from Venice on Tuesday, Thursday, and Saturday; tickets are €40–€71 and can also be bought at American Express at Salizzada San Moisè in Venice. You visit three houses, including the Villas Pisani and Foscari, with a lunchtime break in Oriago. Another canal excursion is run by the Battelli del Brenta (www.battellidel brenta.it). Note that most houses are on the left side coming from Venice, or the right from Padua.

EXPLORING VERONA

If you're going to visit more than one or two sights, it's worthwhile to purchase a VeronaCard, available at museums, churches, and tobacconists for €10 (one day) or €15 (three days). It buys a single admission to most of the city's significant museums and churches, plus you can ride free on city buses. If you are mostly interested in churches, a €5 Chiese Vive Card is sold at Verona's major houses of worship and gains you entry to the Duomo, San Fermo Maggiore, San Zeno Maggiore, Sant'Anastasia, and San Lorenzo. Do note that Verona's churches strictly enforce their dress code: no sleeveless shirts, shorts, or short skirts.

TOP ATTRACTIONS

Fodor's Choice ★ **Ancient City Gates/Triumphal Arch.** In addition to its famous arena and Roman theater, two of ancient Verona's city gates and a beautiful triumphal arch have survived from antiquity. These graceful and elegant portals give us an idea of the high aesthetic standards of ancient Verona. The oldest, the Porta dei Leoni (on Via Leoni, just a few steps from Piazza delle Erbe), dates from the 1st century BC, but its original earth-and-brick structure was sheathed in local marble during early Imperial times. The Porta dei Borsari (at the beginning of Corso Porta Borsari, just a few steps from the opposite side of Piazza della Erbe), as its elegant decoration suggests, was the main entrance to ancient Verona, and, in its present state, dates from the 1st century AD. Continuing down Corso Cavour, which starts on the other (front) side of Porta dei Borsari, you can find the beautiful Arco dei Gavi, which is simpler and less imposing, but certainly more graceful, than the triumphal arches in Rome. It was built in the 1st century AD by the architect Lucius Vitruvius Cerdo to celebrate the accomplishments of the patrician Gavia family. It was highly esteemed by several Renaissance architects, including Palladio.

Fodor's Choice ★ **Arena di Verona.** Only Rome's Colosseum and Capua's arena would dwarf this amphitheater. Though four arches are all that remain of the arena's outer arcade, the main structure is complete. It dates from the early Imperial age, and was used for gymnastic competitions, choreographed sacrificial rites, and games involving hunts, fights, battles, and wild animals. Unlike at Rome's Colosseum, there is no evidence that Christians were ever put to death here. Today you can visit the arena year-round; in summer, you can join up to 16,000 people packing the stands for one of Verona's spectacular opera productions. Even those who aren't crazy about opera can sit in the stands and enjoy Italians enjoying themselves—including, at times, singing along with their favorite hits. ✉ *Arena di Verona, Piazza Brà 5* ☎ *045/8003204* 🌐 *www.arena.it* 🎫 *€6, free with Chiese Vive and VeronaCard* ⏲ *Mon. 1:30–7:30, Tues.–Sun. 8:30–7:30 (8–4:30 on performance days). Last entry 45 mins before closing.*

Castelvecchio *(Old Castle)*. This crenellated, russet brick building with massive walls, towers, turrets, and a vast courtyard was built for Cangrande II della Scala in 1354. It presides over a street lined with attractive old buildings and palaces of the nobility. Only by going inside the **Museo di Castelvecchio** can you really appreciate this massive castle complex with its vaulted halls. You also get a look at a significant

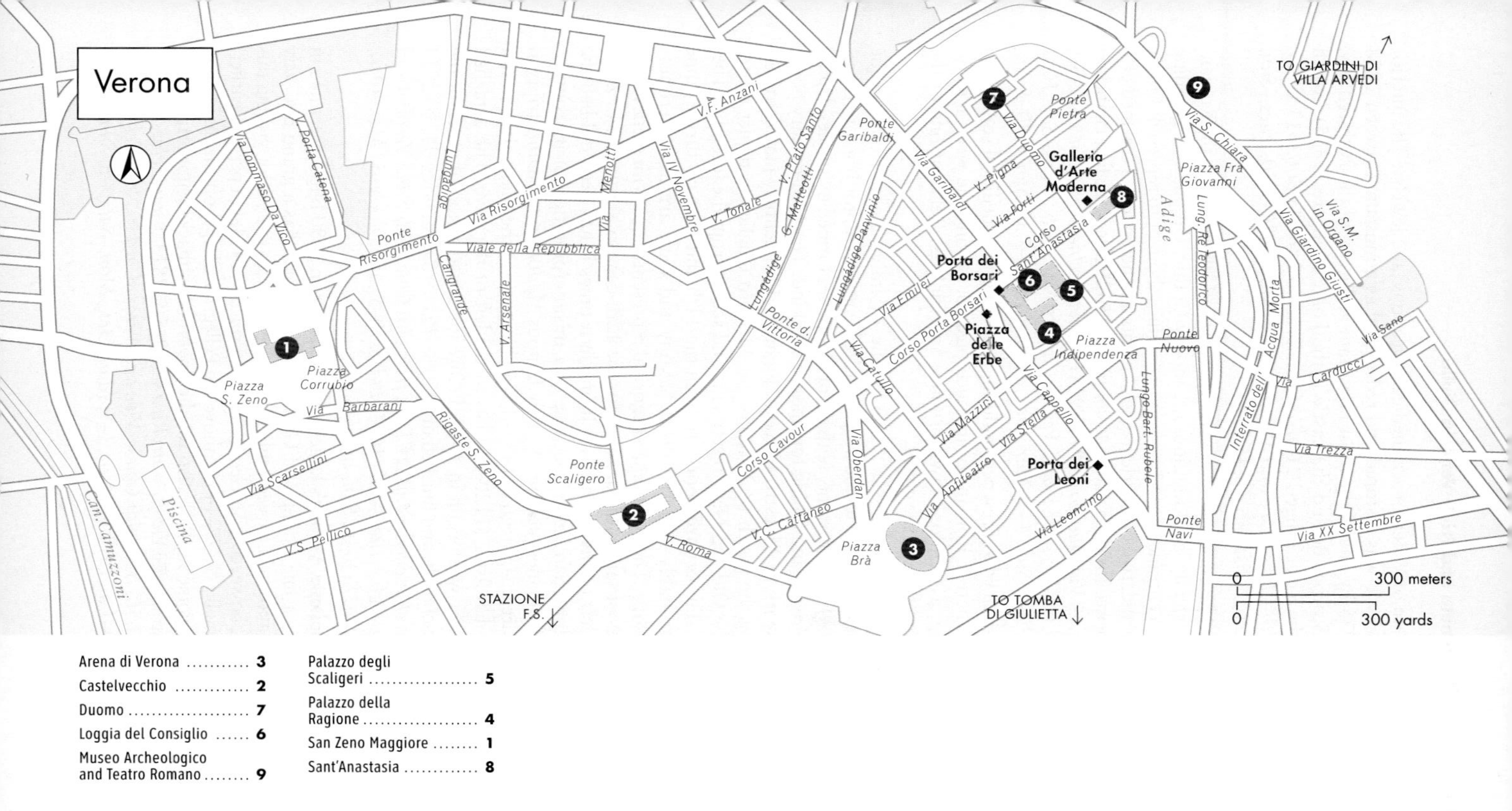

Verona
TO GIARDINI DI VILLA ARVEDI
Via Tommaso Da Vico
V. Porta Catena
Piazza S. Zeno
Piazza Corrubio
Via Barbarani
Via Scarsellini
V.S. Pellico
Piscina
Can. Camuzzoni
Ponte Risorgimento
Via Risorgimento
Lungadige
Cangrande
Viale della Repubblica
V. Arsenale
Via Menotti
Rigaste S. Zeno
Ponte Scaligero
V.F. Anzani
Via IV Novembre
V. Tonale
V. Prato Santo
G. Matteotti
Lungadige
Ponte d. Vittoria
Ponte Garibaldi
Lungadige Panvinio
Corso Cavour
V. Roma
V.C. Cattaneo
Via Oberdan
Piazza Brà
STAZIONE F.S.
TO TOMBA DI GIULIETTA
Via Catullo
Via Emilei
Corso Porta Borsari
Porta dei Borsari
Piazza delle Erbe
Via Garibaldi
Via Duomo
V. Pigna
Via Forti
Corso Sant'Anastasia
Galleria d'Arte Moderna
Ponte Pietra
Piazza Indipendenza
Via Mazzini
Via Cappello
Via Stella
Via Anfiteatro
Porta dei Leoni
Via Leoncino
Adige
Lung. Re Teodorico
Piazza Fra Giovanni
Via S. Chiara
Via S.M. in Organo
Via Giardino Giusti
Ponte Nuovo
Lungo Bart. Rubele
Ponte Navi
Acqua Morta
Interrato dell'
Via Carducci
Via Sano
Via Trezza
Via XX Settembre
0 300 meters
0 300 yards
Arena di Verona 3
Castelvecchio 2
Duomo 7
Loggia del Consiglio 6
Museo Archeologico and Teatro Romano 9
Palazzo degli Scaligeri 5
Palazzo della Ragione 4
San Zeno Maggiore 1
Sant'Anastasia 8

collection of Venetian art, medieval weapons, and jewelry. The interior of the castle was restored and redesigned as a museum between 1958 and 1975 by one of the most important architects of the 20th century, Carlo Scarpa. Behind the castle is the Ponte Scaligero (1355), which spans the River Adige. ✉ *Corso Castelvecchio 2* ☎ *045/8062611* 🎫 *€6, free with Chiese Vive and VeronaCard* ⏲ *Mon. 1:30–7:30, Tues.–Sun. 8:30–7:30. Last entry 6:45.*

Duomo. The present church was begun in the 12th century in the Romanesque style; its later additions are mostly Gothic. On pilasters guarding the main entrance are 12th-century carvings thought to represent Oliver and Roland, two of Charlemagne's knights and heroes of several medieval epic poems. Inside, Titian's *Assumption* (1532) graces the first chapel on the left. ✉ *Via Duomo* ☎ *045/592813* 🌐 *www.chieseverona.it* 🎫 *€2.50, free with Chiese Vive and VeronaCard* ⏲ *Nov.–Feb., Tues.–Sat. 10–1 and 1:30–5, Sun. 1–5; Mar.–Oct., Mon.–Sat. 10–5:30, Sun. 1:30–5:30.*

Piazza delle Erbe. Frescoed buildings surround this medieval square, on a site where a Roman forum once bustled. During the week it's still bustling, as vendors hawk produce and trinkets. Relax at one of the cafés and take in the chaos.

★ **San Zeno Maggiore.** San Zeno is one of Italy's finest Romanesque churches. The rose window by the 13th-century sculptor Brioloto represents a wheel of fortune, with six of the spokes formed by statues depicting the rising and falling fortunes of mankind. The 12th-century porch is the work of Maestro Niccolò. Eighteen 12th-century marble reliefs flanking the porch by Niccolò and Maestro Guglielmo depict scenes from the Old and New Testaments and scenes from the legend of Theodoric. The bronze doors are from the 11th and 12th centuries; some were probably imported from Saxony and some are from Veronese workshops. They combine allegorical representations with scenes from the lives of saints. Inside, look for the 12th-century statue of San Zeno to the left of the main altar. In modern times it has been dubbed the "Laughing San Zeno" because of a misinterpretation of its conventional Romanesque grin. A justly famous *Madonna and Saints* triptych by Andrea Mantegna (1431–1506) hangs over the main altar, and a peaceful cloister (1120–38) lies to the left of the nave. The detached bell tower was begun in 1045, before the construction of much of the present church, and finished in 1173. ✉ *Piazza San Zeno* ☎ *045/592813* 🌐 *www.chieseverona.it* 🎫 *€2.50, free with Chiese Vive and VeronaCard* ⏲ *Nov.–Feb., Tues.–Sat. 10–1 and 1:30–5, Sun. noon–5; Mar.–Oct., Mon.–Sat. 8:30–6, Sun. noon–6.*

Sant'Anastasia. Verona's largest church, begun in 1290 but consecrated in 1471, is a fine example of Gothic brickwork and has a grand doorway with elaborately carved biblical scenes. The main reason for visiting this church, however, is *St. George and the Princess* (1434, but perhaps earlier) by Pisanello (1377–1455) above the Pellegrini Chapel off the main altar. As you come in, look also for the *gobbi* (hunchbacks) supporting holy-water stoups. ✉ *Vicolo Sotto Riva 4* ☎ *045/592813* 🌐 *www.chieseverona.it* 🎫 *€2.50, free with Chiese Vive and VeronaCard* ⏲ *Nov.–Feb., Tues.–Sat. 10–1 and 1:30–5, Sun. 1–5; Mar.–Oct., Mon.–Sat. 9–6, Sun. 1–6.*

WORTH NOTING

Arche Scaligere. On a little square adjacent to the Piazza dei Signori are the fantastically sculpted Gothic tombs of the della Scalas, who ruled Verona during the late Middle Ages. The 19th-century English traveler and critic John Ruskin described the tombs as graceful places where people who have fallen asleep live. The tomb of Cangrande I hangs over the portal of the adjacent church and is the work of the Maestro di Sant'Anastasia. The tomb of Mastino II, begun in 1345, has an elaborate baldachin, originally painted and gilded, and is surrounded by an iron grillwork fence and topped by an equestrian statue. The latest and most elaborate tomb is that of Cansignorio (1375), the work principally of Bonino di Campione. The major tombs are all visible from the street.

4

Loggia del Consiglio. This graceful structure on the north flank of the Piazza dei Signori was finished in 1492 and built to house city council meetings. Although the city was already under Venetian rule, Verona still had a certain degree of autonomy, which was expressed by the splendor of the loggia. Very strangely for a Renaissance building of this quality, its architect remains unknown, but it is undoubtedly the finest surviving example of late-15th-century architecture in Verona. ✉ *Piazza dei Signori* ⏲ *Closed to the public.*

Museo Archeologico and Teatro Romano. Housed in what was a 15th-century monastery, the museum's collections were formed largely out of the donated collections of Veronese citizens proud of their city's classical past. Though there are few blockbusters here, there are some very noteworthy pieces (especially among the bronzes), and it is interesting to see what cultured Veronese from the 17th to 19th centuries collected. The museum sits high above the Teatro Romano, ancient Verona's theater, dating from the 1st century AD. ✉ *Rigaste del Redentore 2* ☎ *045/8000360* 🎫 *€4.50, free with Chiese Vive and VeronaCard* ⏲ *Mon. 1:30–7:30, Tues.–Sun. 8:30–7:30. Last entry 6:45.*

Palazzo degli Scaligeri (Palazzo di Cangrande). The della Scalas ruled Verona from this stronghold built at the end of the 13th century by Cangrande I. At that time Verona controlled the mainland Veneto as far as Treviso and Lombardy to Mantua and Brescia. The portal facing the Piazza dei Signori was added in 1533 by the accomplished Renaissance architect Michele Sanmicheli. You have to admire the palazzo from the outside, as it's not open to the public. ✉ *Piazza dei Signori* ⏲ *Closed to the public.*

Palazzo della Ragione. An elegant pink marble staircase leads up from the *mercato vecchio* (old market) courtyard to the magistrates' chambers in the 12th-century palace, built at the intersection of the main streets of the ancient Roman city. The building is now used for art exhibitions. You can get the highest view in town from atop the attached 270-foot-tall **Torre dei Lamberti,** which attained its present height through a modification in 1452. ✉ *Piazza dei Signori* ☎ *045/8032726* 🎫 *€6, free with Chiese Vive and VeronaCard* ⏲ *Daily 8:30–7:30. Last entry 6:45.*

WHERE TO EAT

> **WORD OF MOUTH**
>
> "I was fortunate enough to see Aïda in the amphitheatre in Verona. It was spectacular, particularly, of course, the triumphant march. Aïda makes full use of the incredible surroundings. The stone terrace seats can be very, very hot, even in the evening." —Cathinjoetown

$ NORTHERN ITALIAN ★ ✕ **Antica Osteria al Duomo.** This friendly side-street eatery, lined with old wood paneling and decked out with musical instruments, serves Veronese food to a Veronese crowd; they come to quaff the local wine (€1 to €3 per glass) to savor excellent versions of local dishes like *bigoli con sugo di asino* (thick whole-wheat spaghetti with sauce made from donkey meat) and *pastissada con polenta* (horsemeat stew with polenta). Don't be put off by the dishes featuring unconventional meats; they're tender and delicious, and this is probably the best place in town to sample them. First-rate Veronese home cooking comes at very reasonable prices here and is served by helpful, efficient staff. This is a popular place, so arrive early. Reservations are not possible on weekends. ✉ *Via Duomo 7/A* ☎ *045/8007333* ⏲ *Closed Sun. (except in Dec. and during wine fair).*

$$$$ NORTHERN ITALIAN ✕ **Dodici Apostoli.** In a city where many high-end restaurants tend toward nouvelle cuisine, this highly esteemed restaurant is an exceptional place to enjoy classic dishes made with elegant variations on traditional recipes. Near Piazza delle Erbe, it stands on the foundations of a Roman temple. Specialties include gnocchi *di zucca e ricotta* (with squash and ricotta cheese) and *vitello alla Lessinia* (veal with mushrooms, cheese, and truffles). ✉ *Vicolo Corticella San Marco 3* ☎ *045/596999* 🌐 *www.12apostoli.it* ⏲ *Closed Mon., Jan. 1–10, and June 15–30. No dinner Sun.*

$$$$ MODERN ITALIAN ✕ **Il Desco.** *Cucina dell'anima*, meaning food of the soul, is how Chef Elia Rizzo describes his cuisine. True to Italian culinary traditions, his technique preserves natural flavors through quick cooking and limiting the number of ingredients. But there is little tradition in the inventive and even daring way in which he combines those few ingredients in dishes such as duck breast with grappa, grapes, and eggplant puree, or beef cheeks with goose liver and caramelized pears. For a gastronomic adventure, order the tasting menu (€130), which includes appetizers, two first courses, two second courses, and dessert. The decor is elegant, if overdone, with tapestries, paintings, and an impressive 16th-century lacunar ceiling. The service is efficient, if not exactly friendly. ✉ *Via Dietro San Sebastiano 7* ☎ *045/595358* ✍ *Reservations essential* ⏲ *Closed Sun. and Mon. (open for dinner Mon. in July, Aug., and Dec.), Dec. 25–Jan. 10, and 1st 2 wks in June.*

$$$$ MODERN ITALIAN ★ ✕ **Ostaria La Fontanina.** Veronese go to La Fontanina to enjoy a sumptuous meal under vine-covered balconies on a quiet street in one of the oldest sections of town. The Tapparini family takes great pride in the kitchen's modern versions of traditional dishes. Particularly successful is the risotto made with Verona's famed sweet wine, riciotto di Soave, accompanied with a slice of foie gras. There are also such standards as *risotto al Amarone* made with Verona's treasured red wine, *pastissada*

(horse-meat stew) with polenta, and, of course, an excellent version of assorted baccalà preparations. There are several reasonably priced set menus. ✉ *Portichiette fontanelle S. Stefano 3* ☎ *045/913305* 🌐 *www.ristorantelafontanina.com* ✍ *Reservations essential* ⏲ *Closed Sun., 1 wk in Jan., and 2 wks in Aug. No lunch Mon.*

WHERE TO STAY

Book hotels months in advance for spring's Vinitaly, usually the second week in April, and for opera season. Verona hotels are also very busy during the January, May, and September gold fairs in neighboring Vicenza. Hotels jack up prices considerably during trade fairs and the opera season.

4

$$–$$$ ★ **Hotel Accademia.** The columns and arches of Hotel Accademia's stately facade are a good indication of what you can discover inside: an elegant, full-service historic hotel in the center of old Verona. **Pros:** central location; Old World charm; up-to-date services. **Cons:** expensive parking; few standard rooms. **TripAdvisor:** "walk to most of the sites," "sophisticated decor," "breakfast was outstanding." ✉ *Via Scala 12* ☎ *045/596222* 🌐 *www.accademiavr.it* *93 rooms* *In-room: safe, refrigerator, Wi-Fi. In-hotel: restaurant, bars, parking (paid)* *Breakfast.*

$$$ **Hotel Victoria.** Busy business executives and tourists demanding a bit of pampering frequent this full-service hotel located near the Piazza delle Erbe. **Pros:** quiet and tasteful rooms; central location; good business center. **Cons:** no views; expensive parking; staff not particularly helpful. **TripAdvisor:** "in the historic section of Verona," "original frescoes," "charging for extras was annoying." ✉ *Via Adua 8* ☎ *045/5905664* 🌐 *www.hotelvictoria.it* *66 rooms* *In-room: safe, refrigerator, Wi-Fi. In-hotel: bar, gym, laundry service, parking (paid)* *No meals.*

$ **Torcolo.** At this budget hotel you can count on a warm welcome from the owners and courteous, helpful service; pleasant rooms decorated tastefully with late-19th-century furniture; and a central location close to Piazza Brà. **Pros:** tastefully decorated rooms; staff gives reliable advice. **Cons:** some street noise; no help with baggage; pricey parking. **TripAdvisor:** "loved the atmosphere," "staff were absolutely brilliant," "block away from the main piazza." ✉ *Vicolo Listone 3* ☎ *045/8007512* 🌐 *www.hoteltorcolo.it* *19 rooms* *In-room: safe, refrigerator. In-hotel: bar, parking (paid), some pets allowed* ⏲ *Closed Dec. 21–27 and 2 wks in Jan. and Feb.* *No meals.*

OPERA

Fodor'sChoice ★ Milan's La Scala, Venice's La Fenice, and Parma's Teatro Regio offer performances more likely to satisfy serious opera fans, but none offers a greater spectacle than the **Arena di Verona** (*Box office* ✉ *Via Dietro Anfiteatro 6/b* ☎ *045/8005151* 🌐 *www.arena.it* *Tickets start at €22* ⏲ *Box office Sept.–June 20, weekdays 9–noon and 3:15–5:45, Sat. 9–noon; June 21–Aug., daily noon–9*). Many Italian opera lovers claim that their enthusiasm was initiated when they were taken as children to a production at the arena. During its summer season (July–September) audiences of as many as 16,000 sit on the original stone terraces or in modern cushioned stalls. Most of the operas presented are the big, splashy ones, like *Aïda* or *Turandot,* which demand huge choruses, lots of color and movement, and, if possible, camels, horses, or elephants. Order tickets by phone or online: if you book a spot on the cheaper terraces, be sure to take or rent a cushion—four hours on a 2,000-year-old stone bench can be an ordeal.

TREVISO AND THE HILLSIDE TOWNS

North of Venice, the Dolomites spawn rivers and streams that flow through market towns dotting the foothills. Villa Barbaro, one of Palladio's most graceful country villas (*see the "Palladio Country" feature*), is nearby, as are the arcaded streets and romantic canals of undiscovered Treviso and the graceful Venetian Gothic structures of smaller hill towns.

MAROSTICA

26 km (16 mi) northeast of Vicenza, 93 km (58 mi) northwest of Venice.

GETTING HERE

There is no train station in Marostica. The closest rail connection is Bassano del Grappa, about 8 km (5 mi) away. There are regular bus connections from Vicenza's main station on FTV Bus 5; the trip takes about 45 minutes. By car, take SP248 northeast from Vicenza, or southwest from Bassano.

VISITOR INFORMATION

Marostica tourism office (✉ *Piazza Castello 1* ☎ *0424/72127* 🌐 *www.marosticaschacci.it*).

EXPLORING

From the 14th-century Castello Inferiore, where the town council still meets, an ancient stone wall snakes up the hill to enclose the Castello Superiore, with its commanding views. Marostica's most celebrated feature is the checkerboard-like square made with colored stone, Piazza Castello.

A human-scale chess game known as **Partita a Scacchi** is acted out in Piazza Castello by players in medieval costume on the second weekend in September in even-number years. The game dates from 1454 and originated as a peaceful way of settling a love dispute for the hand of the daughter of the Lord of Marostica Castle. The orders are still given in the local Veneto dialect. There's a game presented Friday–Sunday evenings and there are Sunday-afternoon shows. If you book an evening show and do not have a hotel reservation in Marostica, be sure you have a way of reaching your lodgings afterward. Buses do not run late in the evening, and taxis, if you can find one, may hike up their prices. Tickets (€10 to €80) go on sale in February; the tourist office can help with bookings.

WHERE TO STAY

$$ **Due Mori.** Although this inn dates from the 18th century, the decor is severely minimalist. **Pros:** one of very few hotels in town; central location; train station transfers available; great views of castle from some rooms. **Cons:** parking fee (unheard of for rural hotels); only one hour

free Wi-Fi; rather bland decor. **TripAdvisor:** "wonderful view of the castle," "hospitality at its finest," "short walk to the town square." ✉ *Corso Mazzini 73* ☎ *0424/471777* 🌐 *www.duemori.com* *10 rooms* *In-room: refrigerator, Wi-Fi. In-hotel: restaurant, Internet terminal, parking (paid), some pets allowed* ⏲ *Some yrs closed 1st wk in Jan. and 2 wks in mid-Aug.* 🍽 *Breakfast.*

BASSANO DEL GRAPPA

7 km (4½ mi) east of Marostica, 37 km (23 mi) northwest of Venice by local roads, 85 km (53 mi) by highway.

4

GETTING HERE

Several trains leave every hour from Venice's Santa Lucia station. The trip takes a little over an hour. By car, take the A13 from Venice, via Padua, to Bassano (1 hour, 20 minutes).

VISITOR INFORMATION

Bassano del Grappa tourism office (✉ *Largo Corona d'Italia 35* ☎ *0424/524351* 🌐 *www.vicenzae.org*).

EXPLORING

Nestled at the base of the Mt. Grappa massif (5,880 feet), with the mountain-fresh Brenta River sluicing through, this town seems to be higher in the mountains than it actually is. Bassano has old streets lined with low-slung buildings adorned with wooden balconies and colorful flowerpots. Bright ceramic wares produced in the area are displayed in shops along byways that curve uphill toward a centuries-old square and, even higher, to a belvedere with a good view of Mt. Grappa and the beginning of the Val Sugana.

★ Bassano's most famous landmark is the **Ponte degli Alpini**, a covered bridge named for Italy's Alpine soldiers. There's been a bridge across the Brenta here since 1209, but floods and wars have necessitated repeated rebuilding. Following World War II, soldiers constructed the present version using a variation on Andrea Palladio's 16th-century design. (At the insistence of the town fathers, they went against Palladio's plan to build a classical stone bridge, essentially reproducing the original 13th-century structure with some technical changes.)

Almost as famous as Bassano's bridge is the adjacent **Grapperia Nardini** (✉ *Ponte Vecchio 2* ☎ *0424/527741*). The Nardini family was one of the first to distill grappa on a commercial scale. The site of this family's first grappa distillery, opened in 1779, and its original still is open to the public. Grappa Nardini continues to be a major producer of a standard, commercial-grade grappa; visit for the history, not the middling brandy. You can schedule a visit to the current distillery, 2 km (1 mi) out of town, and take in *Le Bolle,* striking architectural "Bubbles" (futuristic constructions housing a research center and reception halls designed by Massimilliano Fuksas), as well.

Grappa, once a working man's drink, has developed into a drink of considerable delicacy and refinement, with great care given to selection of ingredients and distillation techniques. A few steps uphill from Ponte degli Alpini, high-quality grappa producer Poli has set up the **Poli Grappa**

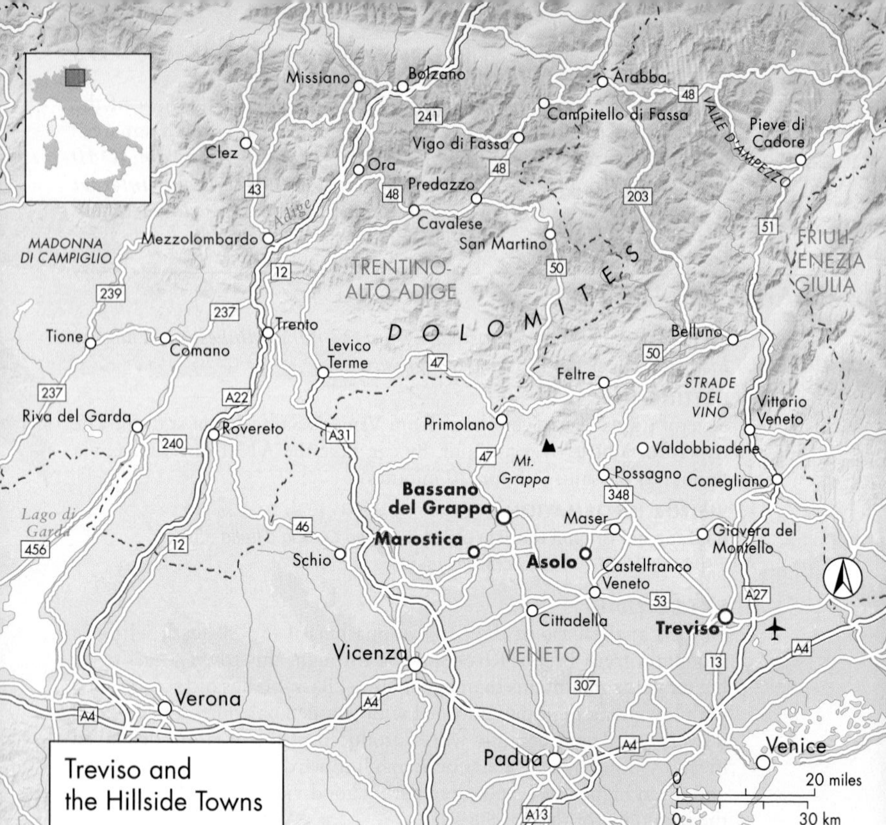

Museum (✉ *Ponte Vecchio* ☎ *0424/524426* 🎫 *Free* ⏲ *Daily 9 am–7:30 pm*). Most interesting are the old grappa stills, their glass tubes twisting into improbably shaped coils. You can taste many of Poli's numerous grappas (for free) and purchase a bottle or two.

★ The most significant cultural monument in the area is the **Museo Canova (Gypsoteca)**, dedicated to the work of the Italian neoclassical sculptor Antonio Canova (1757–1822). Set up shortly after the sculptor's death in his hometown, the village of Possagno, a short ride from Bassano, the gypsoteca houses most of the original plaster casts, models, and drawings made by the artist in preparation for his marble sculptures. In 1957 the museum was extended by the world famous Italian architect Carlo Scarpa. Buses leave regularly for Possagno from the Bassano railroad station. By car follow SP26 out to Bassano to Possagno. Allow 40 minutes for the 17½-km (11-mi) drive. ✉ *Via Canova 74, Possagno* ☎ *0423544323* 🌐 *www.museocanova.it* 🎫 *€7* ⏲ *Tues.–Sun. 9:30–6.*

In Possagno is also the Tempio Canoviano, a church designed by Canova in 1819 and finished in 1830, which combines motifs from the rotunda of the Roman Pantheon and the *pronaos* (inner portico) of the Parthenon. It contains several works by Canova, including his tomb, along with paintings by Luca Giordano, Palma il Giovane, and il Pordenone. ✉ *Piazza Canova, Possagno* ☎ *0423544323* ⏲ *Winter, Tues.–Sun. 9–oon and 2–5; summer, Tues.–Sun. 9–noon and 3–6.*

WHERE TO EAT AND STAY

$$ NORTHERN ITALIAN ✕ **Trattoria del Borgo.** This well-established trattoria a few steps from the center of town features regional dishes prepared with the freshest seasonal ingredients. This is the place to try Bassano's famous white asparagus in spring or hearty bean and chickpea soup in winter. There's also always a good selection of homemade pastas. For a main dish, try the braised veal cheeks or baccalà *alla vicentina* (cooked with onions, milk, and cheese). There is also a good selection of wines and, of course, grappas. ✉ *Via Margnan 7* ☎ *0424/522155* ⏲ *Closed 2 wks in Jan., Wed. in winter, and Sun. in summer. No lunch Sat.*

$ **Al Castello.** In a restored town house at the foot of the medieval Torre Civica, the Cattapan family's Castello is a reasonably priced, attractive choice. **Pros:** central location; some rooms have views; attentive and helpful staff. **Cons:** pricey breakfast. **TripAdvisor:** "plenty of character," "overlooking one of the small squares," "neat and clean at all times." ✉ *Piazza Terraglio 19* ☎ *0424/228665* 🌐 *www.hotelalcastello.it* *11 rooms* *In-room: Wi-Fi (some). In-hotel: bar, parking (free), some pets allowed* ⏲ *Closed 1 wk in Aug, 1st wk in Feb.* *No meals.*

$$ ★ **Ca' Sette.** The main building is in an 18th-century villa that has been tastefully modernized; there are also rooms available in the former granary, which dates from the 16th century and has rustic beamed ceilings. **Pros:** very atmospheric; great restaurant; helpful staff. **Cons:** outside city's historic center; a 20-minute scenic walk to town. **TripAdvisor:** "traditional country cottage," "beautifully furnished," "romantic getaway." ✉ *Via Cunizza da Romano 4* ☎ *0424/383350* 🌐 *www.ca-sette.it* *17 rooms, 2 suites* *In-room: safe, refrigerator, Wi-Fi. In-hotel: restaurant, bicycles, parking (free), some pets allowed* ⏲ *Restaurant closed Mon., 1st wk in Jan., and 3 wks in mid-Aug. No dinner Sun.* *Breakfast.*

ASOLO

16 km (10 mi) east of Bassano del Grappa, 33 km (20½ mi) northwest of Treviso.

GETTING HERE

There is no train station in Asolo; the closest one is in Montebelluna, 12 km (7½ mi) away. Bus connections are infrequent and buses are not coordinated with trains, making it about a 2½-hour trip from Venice via public transportation. Therefore, it is recommended that you drive.

By car from Treviso, take Via Feltrina and continue onto Via Padre Agostino Gemelli (SR348). Follow SR348 about 16 km (10 mi), then turn left on SP667, which you follow for almost 4 km (2½ mi). At the roundabout, take the first exit, Via Monte Grappa (SP284) and follow it for 6½ km (4 mi) to Via Loredan, where you turn right and then left onto Via Bordo Vecchio. Asolo is less than 7 km (4½ mi) away from the Palladian Villa Barbaro at Maser.

VISITOR INFORMATION

Asolo tourism office (✉ *Piazza Garibaldi* ☎ *0423/529046* 🌐 *www.asolo.it*).

4

EXPLORING

A pleasant place to stop for lunch on a visit to the Palladian villa of Maser, or to use as a base for touring the surrounding countryside, the visually striking hillside hamlet of Asolo was the consolation prize of an exiled queen. At the end of the 15th century, Venetian-born Caterina Cornaro was sent here by Venice's doge to keep her from interfering with Venetian administration of her former kingdom of Cyprus, which she had inherited from her husband. To soothe the pain of exile she established a lively and brilliant court in Asolo. It was in this court that the Renaissance poet-essayist Pietro Bembo set his famous *Gli asolani* (1505), in which six Venetian courtiers discuss the pros and cons of love. Through the centuries, Veneto aristocrats continued to build elegant villas on the hillside, and in the 19th-century Asolo once again became the idyllic haunt of musicians, poets, and painters. And it's no wonder why—this is one of Italy's most strikingly situated villages, with views across miles of hilly countryside. Here, you can stroll past villas once inhabited by Robert Browning and actress Eleonora Duse, the mistress of the poet Gabriele D'Annunzio. Be warned that the town's charm vaporizes on holiday weekends when the crowds pour in. Even on weekdays, the village, given over to tourism and vacation residences, has almost no local population. Asolo hosts a modest antiques market on the second Sunday of every month except July and August.

One of the major monuments of contemporary Italian architecture, the **Brion family tomb** (✉ *SP6, Via Castellan, about 7 km [4½ mi] south of Asolo, near village of San Vito* ☎ *No phone* 🎫 *Free* ⏲ *Apr.–Sept., daily 8–7; Oct.–Mar., daily 9–3:30*) was designed and built by the highly celebrated architect Carlo Scarpa (1906–78) between 1970 and 1972. Combining Western rationalism with Eastern spirituality, Scarpa avoids the gloom and bombast of conventional commemorative monuments, creating, in his words, a secluded Eden.

Renaissance palaces and antique cafés grace **Piazza Maggiore**, Asolo's town center. In the piazza, the frescoed 15th-century Loggia del Capitano contains the Museo Civico, which displays memorabilia—Eleonora Duse's correspondence, Robert Browning's spinet, and portraits of Caterina Cornaro. ✉ *Piazza Maggiore* ☎ *0423/952313* 🎫 *€4* ⏲ *Weekends 10–noon and 3–7 and by reservation.*

QUICK BITES

While away some idle moments at Caffè Centrale (✉ *Via Roma 72* ☎ *0423/952141* 🌐 *www.caffecentrale.com* ⏲ *Closed Tues.*), which has overlooked the fountain in Piazza Maggiore and the Duomo since about 1700. Now half café and half tourist shop, it's open until 1 am.

WHERE TO EAT

$ NORTHERN ITALIAN ✕ **Al Bacaro.** This family-style restaurant offers affordable home-style food. Take the leap and try a dish with stewed game, tripe, or snails. Less-adventurous diners can go for goulash, polenta with cheese and mushrooms, or one of Bacaro's open-face sandwiches generously topped with fresh salami, speck, or other cold cuts. ✉ *Via Browning 165* ☎ *0423/55150* ⏲ *Closed Wed.*

$$$ NORTHERN ITALIAN ★ **Locanda Baggio.** Here you can choose between the formality of the Locanda's white-lace tablecloths or the rustic tables (with simpler dishes and lower prices) of its adjacent enoteca. Chef Nino Baggio specializes in elegant versions of traditional cuisine—the rabbit stuffed with sausage, for example, is deboned and served with a crust of grana cheese—and takes pride in his homemade pasta, bread, and desserts. This is one of the best restaurants in Asolo, and the €35 prix-fixe menu is one of the best values in the region. *Via Bassane 1* *0423/529648* *www.caderton.com* *Closed 2 wks in Aug. No dinner Sun. or Mon. No lunch Mon. in summer.*

WHERE TO STAY

$$–$$$ ★ **Al Sole.** This elegant pink-washed hotel in a 16th-century building overlooks the main square. **Pros:** central location; beautiful views; attentive service. **Cons:** restaurant open only in summer; substantial difference between low- and high-season rates. **TripAdvisor:** "all of the comforts one would want," "lovely room overlooking the square," "very charming with amazing views." *Via Collegio 33* *0423/951332* *www.albergoalsole.com* *22 rooms, 1 suite* *In-room: safe, refrigerator, Wi-Fi. In-hotel: restaurant, bar, gym, parking (free), some pets allowed* *Breakfast.*

$$ **Duse.** A spiral staircase winds its way up this narrow, centrally located building to rooms with a view of the main square. **Pros:** simple but tasteful rooms; central location. **Cons:** some street noise; not as much of a bargain when you add fees for breakfast and parking. **TripAdvisor:** "staff could not have been nicer," "smack on the main square," "a bit worn." *Via Browning 190* *0423/55241* *www.hotelduse.com* *14 rooms* *In-room: refrigerator, Wi-Fi. In-hotel: bar, parking (paid)* *Closed 3 wks in Jan. and Feb.* *No meals.*

$$$$ **Villa Cipriani.** A romantic garden surrounded by gracious country homes is the setting for this 16th-century villa, which once belonged to the famous Venice restaurateur and hotelier Harry Cipriani. **Pros:** incomparable views; truly elegant grounds; good spa services. **Cons:** small bathrooms; furnishings are old but not always tasteful; restaurant is pricey. **TripAdvisor:** "oasis of beauty, relaxation and peace," "room was elegant and spacious," "attentive to our every need." *Via Canova 298* *0423/523411* *www.villaciprianiasolo.com* *31 rooms* *In-room: safe, refrigerator, Wi-Fi. In-hotel: restaurant, bar, spa, parking (paid), some pets allowed* *Breakfast.*

TREVISO

35 km (22 mi) southeast of Maser, 30 km (19 mi) north of Venice.

GETTING HERE

Treviso is only 30 minutes by train from Venice; there are frequent daily departures. By car from Venice, pick up the SS13 in Mestre (Via Terraglio) and follow it all the way to Treviso; the trip takes about 45 minutes.

VISITOR INFORMATION

Treviso tourism office (*Piazza Monte di Pietà 8* *0422/547632* *turismo.provincia.treviso.it*).

EXPLORING

Treviso has been dubbed "Little Venice" because of its meandering, moss-banked canals. They can't really compare with Venice's spectacular waterways, but on the whole, Treviso's historic center, with its medieval arcaded streets, has a great deal of charm. It's a fine place to stop for a few hours on the way from Venice to the wine country to the north or to the Palladian villas in the hinterland.

Treviso is one of the wealthiest small cities in the country, with fashionable shops and boutiques at every turn in the busy city center. Though a World War II Allied bombing on Good Friday 1944 destroyed half the city, Treviso meticulously preserved what remained of its old town's narrow streets while simultaneously introducing modernity far more gently than in many other parts of Italy.

Inside Treviso's **Duomo**, which was modified during the 19th century, the Malchiostro Chapel contains an *Annunciation* by Titian and frescoes by Pordenone (1484–1539), including an *Adoration of the Magi*. The crypt has 12th-century columns. Bring a handful of 10- and 20-cent coins for the coin-operated lights that illuminate the artwork. To the left of the Duomo is the Romanesque Battistero di San Giovanni (11th to 12th century), which is probably quite similar in style to the medieval Duomo. It's open only for special exhibitions. ✉ *Piazza del Duomo* ☎ *0422/545720* ⊙ *Mon.–Sat. 8–noon and 3:30–6, Sun. 8–1 and 3:30–6.*

The **Piazza dei Signori** is the center of medieval Treviso and still the town's social hub, with outdoor cafés and some impressive public buildings. The most important of these, the Palazzo dei Trecento (1185–1268), was the seat of the city government, composed of the Council of 300, during the Middle Ages. Behind it is a small alley that leads to the *pescheria* (fish market), on an island in one of the small canals that flow through town.

While strolling the city, take in the restored **Quartiere Latino**, an area between Riviera Garibaldi and Piazza Santa Maria Battuti. It's the site of university buildings, upscale apartments, and a number of bustling restaurants and shops. If you walk along the northern part of the historic city wall, you'll look down on the island home of a number of ducks, geese, and goats. Their little farm occupies some of the city's prettiest real estate.

The most important church in Treviso is **San Nicolò**, a huge Venetian Gothic structure of the early 14th century, with an ornate vaulted ceiling and frescoes (circa 1350) of saints by Tommaso da Modena (circa 1325–79) on the columns; the depiction of *St. Agnes* on the north side is particularly interesting. Also worth examining are Tommaso's realistic portraits of 40 Dominican friars, found in the seminary next door. They include the earliest-known painting of a subject wearing glasses, an Italian invention (circa 1280–1300). ✉ *Seminario Vescovile, Via San Nicolò* ☎ *0422/3247* ⊙ *Daily 8–noon and 3:30–6.*

OFF THE BEATEN PATH

Conegliano. The town of Conegliano, 23 km (14 mi) north of Treviso, is in wine-producing country. The town itself is attractive, with Venetian-style villas, arcaded streets, and an elegant 14th-century Duomo, housing an altarpiece (1492) by Gianbattista Cima (called Cima di

Conegliano). Along with prosecco, Cima's work is the town's main claim to fame. Alongside Giovanni Bellini, Cima is one of the greatest painters of the early Venetian Renaissance. The front of the Duomo is formed by the frescoed late medieval facade and Gothic arcade of the Scuola dei Battuti. If you stop in town, be sure to taste the prosecco, sold in local wine bars and shops.

WHERE TO EAT

$$$ NORTHERN ITALIAN ★ **Beccherie.** The name means butcher shop, and in fact this area behind Treviso's Palazzo Trecento is where people bought and sold meat for centuries. It is only fitting that Beccherie should specialize in *bollito*, a celebrated dish of assorted boiled meats and sauces, which originated in Piedmont but is now so much a part of Veneto cooking that most Veneti regard it as their own. The varied menu, based on the local cuisine, changes according to the season, offering hearty fare in winter and lighter choices in summer. The owner's mother, Depillo Alba Campeol, invented the famous dessert tiramisu in the 1960s, and the Beccharie still serves it according to the original, featherlight recipe. Locals have been keeping this family-owned restaurant busy since 1939. Reservations are recommended for dinner. ✉ *Piazza Ancilotto 10* ☎ *0422/540871* ⏲ *Closed Mon. and last 2 wks in July. No dinner Sun.*

$$ NORTHERN ITALIAN **Toni del Spin.** Wood-paneled and styled with 1930s decor, this friendly, bustling place oozes old-fashioned character. The reasonably priced, wholesome menu, chalked on a hanging wooden board, is based on local Veneto cooking. The "Spin" in the restaurant's name is the spine of the baccalà, one of the restaurant's specialties. In autumn and winter, don't miss trying Treviso's hallmark product, radicchio, in risotto or pasta. The chef-owner, Alfredo Sturlese, is also justly proud of his *sopa coada* (pigeon-and-bread soup). ✉ *Via Inferiore 7* ☎ *0422/543829* 🌐 *www.ristorantetonidelspin.com* ✍ *Reservations essential* ⏲ *Closed Sun. and 3 wks in July and Aug. No lunch Mon.*

$$ NORTHERN ITALIAN **Vineria.** One of the first tenants in Treviso's restored Quartiere Latino, Vineria specializes in food with local ingredients and has a €30 three-course prix-fixe meal with ingredients strictly from the province. Chef Alberto Toè follows a cardinal rule of classic Italian cooking: use the best, freshest ingredients and prepare them simply, seasoning just enough to enhance their flavor. ✉ *Largo Umanesimo Latino 2* ☎ *0422/419787.*

WHERE TO STAY

$$ **Carlton Hotel.** Pass the river flowing outside, walk through the lobby, and seek out the huge terrace right on top of the old city wall. **Pros:** central location. **Cons:** decor is not always tasteful. **TripAdvisor:** "conveniently located," "service-minded staff," "a bit tired." ✉ *Largo di Porta Altinia 15* ☎ *0422/411661* 🌐 *www.hotelcarlton.it* *93 rooms* *In-room: safe, refrigerator, Wi-Fi. In-hotel: restaurant, bar, bicycles, parking (paid), some pets allowed* *Breakfast.*

CLOSE UP

Traveling the Wine Roads

You'd be hard-pressed to find a more stimulating and varied wine region than northeastern Italy. From the Valpolicella, Bardolino, and Soave produced near Verona to the superlative whites of the Collio region, wines from the Veneto and Friuli–Venezia Giulia earn more Denominazione di Origine Controllata seals for uniqueness and quality than those of any other area of Italy.

You can travel on foot, by car, or by bicycle over hillsides covered with vineyards, each field nurturing subtly different grape varieties. On a casual trip through the countryside you're likely to come across wineries that will welcome you for a visit; for a more organized tour, check local tourist information offices, which have maps of roads, wineries, and vendors. Be advised that Italy has become more stringent about its driving regulations; seat belts and designated drivers can save fines, embarrassment, or worse.

One of the most hospitable areas in the Veneto for wine enthusiasts is the stretch of country north of Treviso, where you can follow designated wine roads—tours that blend a beautiful rural setting with the delights of the grape. Authorized wineshops where you can stop and sample are marked with a sign showing a triangular arrangement of red and yellow grapes. There are three routes to choose from, and they're manageable enough that you can do them all comfortably over the course of a day or two.

MONTELLO AND ASOLO HILLS

This route provides a good balance of vineyards and nonwine sights. It winds from Nervesa della Battaglia, 18 km (10 mi) north of Treviso, past two prime destinations in the area, the lovely village of Asolo and the Villa Barbaro at Maser. Asolo produces good prosecco, whereas Montello favors merlot and cabernet. Both areas also yield pinot and chardonnay.

PIAVE RIVER

The circular route follows the Piave River and runs through orchards, woods, and hills. Among the area's gems are the Torchiato di Fregona and Refrontolo Passito, both made according to traditional methods.

Raboso del Piave, renowned since Roman times, ages well and complements local dishes such as beans and pasta or goose stuffed with chestnuts. Other reds are cabernet, merlot, and cabernet sauvignon. As an accompaniment to fish, try a Verduzzo del Piave or, for an aperitif, the warm-yellow Pinot Grigio del Piave.

PROSECCO

This route runs for 47 km (29 mi) between Valdobbiadene and Conegliano, home of Italy's first wine institute, winding between knobby hills covered in grapevines. These hang in festoons on row after row of pergolas to create a thick mantle of green.

Turn off the main route to explore the narrower country lanes, most of which eventually join up. They meander through tiny hamlets and past numerous family wineries where you can taste and purchase the wines. Spring is an excellent time to visit, with no fewer than 15 local wine festivals held between March and early June.

FRIULI–VENEZIA GIULIA

The peripheral location of the Friuli–Venezia Giulia region in Italy's northeastern corner makes it easy to overlook, but with its mix of Italian, Slavic, and central European cultures, along with a legendary wine tradition, it's a fascinating area to explore. Venetian culture crept northward until it merged with northern European into the Veneto-Byzantine style evident in places like the medieval city of Udine. The Cividale del Friuli and the Collio wine regions are a short hop away from Udine, and the old Austrian port of Trieste was, in the late 19th and early 20th centuries, an important center of Italian literature.

UDINE

94 km (58 mi) northeast of Treviso, 127 km (79 mi) northeast of Venice.

GETTING HERE

There is frequent train service from both Venice and Trieste; the trip takes about two hours from Venice, and a little over an hour from Trieste. By car from Venice, take the SR11 to the E55 and head east. Take the E55 (it eventually becomes the Autostrada Alpe Adria) to SS13 (Viale Venezia) east into Udine. Driving from Trieste, take the SS202 to the E70, which becomes the A4. Turn off onto the E55 north, which is the same road you would take coming from Venice. Driving times are 1½ hours from Venice and 1 hour from Trieste.

VISITOR INFORMATION

Udine tourism office (✉ *Piazza I Maggio 7* ☎ *0432/295972* 🌐 *www.turismo.fvg.it*).

EXPLORING

Udine, the largest city on the Friuli side of the region, has a provincial, genteel atmosphere and lots of charm. The city sometimes seems completely unaffected by tourism, and things are still done the way they were decades ago. In the medieval and Renaissance historic center of town, you'll find unevenly spaced streets with appealing little wine bars and open-air cafés. Friulani are proud of their local culture, with many restaurants featuring Friulano cuisine, and street signs and announcements written in both Italian and Friulano dialect. But the main reason for devoting some time to Udine is to see the largest assembly outside Venice of works by the last of the great Italian painters, Gianbattista Tiepolo (1696–1770), distributed in several palaces and churches around town. Udine calls itself, in fact, *la città di Tiepolo*.

Commanding a view from the Alpine foothills to the Adriatic Sea, Udine stands on a mound that, according to legend, was erected so Attila the Hun could watch the burning of Aquileia, an important Roman center to the south. Although the legend is a bit dubious (Attila burned Aquileia about 500 years before the first historical mention of Udine), the view from Udine's castle across the alluvial plane down to the sea is impressive. In the Middle Ages Udine flourished, thanks to its favorable trade location and the right granted by the local patriarch to hold regular markets.

Udine was conquered by the Venetians in 1420, so there is a distinctly Venetian stamp on the architecture of the historic center, most noticeably in the large main square, the **Piazza della Libertà**. The Loggia del Leonello, begun in 1428, dominates the square and houses the municipal government. Its similarity to the facade of Venice's Palazzo Ducale (finished in 1424) is clear, but there is no evidence that it is an imitation of that palace. It's more likely a product of the same architectural fashion. Opposite stands the Renaissance Porticato di San Giovanni (1533–35) and the Torre dell'Orologio, a 1527 clock tower complete with naked *mori* (the Moors who strike the hours) on the top.

★ The **Palazzo Arcivescovile** (also known as Palazzo Patriarcale) contains several rooms of frescoes by the young Gianbattista Tiepolo, painted from 1726 to 1732. They comprise the most important collection of early works by Italy's most brilliant 18th-century painter. The Galleria del Tiepolo (1727) contains superlative Tiepolo frescoes depicting the stories of Abraham, Isaac, and Jacob. The *Judgment of Solomon* (1729) graces the Pink Room. There are also beautiful and important Tiepolo frescoes in the staircase, throne room, and palatine chapel of this palazzo. Even in these early works we can see the Venetian master's skill in creating an illusion of depth, not only through linear perspective, but also through subtle gradations in the intensity of the colors, with the stronger colors coming forward and the paler ones receding into space. Tiepolo was one of the first artists to use this method of representing space and depth, which reflected the scientific discoveries of perception and optics in the 17th century. In the same building, the **Museo Diocesano** features a collection of sculptures from Friuli churches from the 13th through the 18th century. ✉ *Piazza Patriarcato 1* ☎ *0432/25003* 🌐 *www.museiprovinciaud.it* 🎫 *€5, includes Museo Diocesano* ⏲ *Wed.–Sun. 10–noon and 3:30–6:30.*

From the hilltop **Castello** (construction began 1517) panoramic views extend to Monte Nero (7,360 feet) in neighboring Slovenia. Here Udine's civic museums of art and archaeology are centralized under one roof. Particularly worth seeing is the national and regional art collection in the **Galleria d'Arte Antica,** which has canvases by Venetians Vittore Carpaccio (circa 1460–1525) and Giambattista Tiepolo, an excellent Caravaggio, and a carefully selected collection of works by lesser known but still interesting Veneto and Friuli artists. The museum also has a small but wonderful collection of drawings, containing several by Tiepolo; some find his drawings even more moving than his paintings. ✉ *Castello di Udine* ☎ *0432/271591* 🌐 *www.comune.udine.it* 🎫 *€5 (€8 during special exhibits)* ⏲ *Tues.–Sun. 10:30–7.*

Just a few steps from the Piazza della Libertà is Udine's 1335 **Duomo**. Its Cappella del Santissimo has important early frescoes by Tiepolo, and the Cappella della Trinità has a Tiepolo altarpiece. There is also a beautiful late Tiepolo *Resurrection* (1751) in an altar by the sculptor Giuseppi Toretti. Ask the Duomo's attendant to let you into the adjacent **Chiesa della Purita** to see more important late paintings by Tiepolo. ✉ *Piazza del Duomo 1* ☎ *0432/506830* ⏲ *Mon.–Sat. 9–noon and 4–6, Sun. 4–6.*

WHERE TO EAT

$$ FRIULIAN ✕ **Hostaria alla Tavernetta.** One of Udine's most trusted food addresses since 1954, this restaurant has rustic fireside dining downstairs and smaller, more elegantly decorated rooms upstairs, where there's even a small terrace. Steps from the Piazza Duomo, it serves regional specialties such as *orzotto* (barley prepared like risotto), delicious *cjalzòns* (ravioli stuffed with ricotta, apples, raisins, and spices and topped with smoked ricotta, butter, and cinnamon), and perhaps the tenderest suckling pig you have ever eaten. The restaurant offers a reasonably priced prix-fixe menu. The service is pleasant and attentive, and there's a fine selection of Friuli's celebrated wines and grappas. ✉ *Via di Prampero 2* ☎ *0432/501066* ⏲ *Closed Sun. and Mon., 1 wk in June, 2 wks in mid-Aug., and 2nd wk in Jan.*

$ FRIULIAN ★ ✕ **Osteria Al Vecchio Stallo.** This former stable bursts with character, its beautiful courtyard shaded by grape arbors. The menu includes a wide choice of traditional Friuli home cooking. As an appetizer, try the prized prosciutto from the neighboring village of San Daniele, which some regard even more highly than the famous prosciutto from Parma. For the first course try cjalzòns (the region's answer to ravioli), or the excellent *mignàculis con luagne* (pasta with local sausage). Friuli classics such as *frico con patate* (hash-brown potatoes with Montasio cheese) or goulash with polenta are good second courses. On Friday there are also fish dishes. There's a great selection of wines by the glass, and the gregarious chef-owner is a gracious host. ✉ *Via Viola 7* ☎ *0432/21296* ▭ *No credit cards* ⊙ *Closed Wed. Sept.–June, Sun. in July and Aug., 3 wks in Aug., and Dec. 25–Jan. 7.*

WHERE TO STAY

$$ **Hostaria Hotel Allegria.** In this 15th-century building a humble osteria has grown into a modern, comfortable family-run hotel. **Pros:** well-appointed rooms; great staff; discounted weekend rates. **Cons:** rooms may be too minimalist for some; fee for parking. **TripAdvisor:** "smart, comfortable hotel," "room was large and well appointed," "beautifully styled and elegantly appointed." ✉ *Via Grazzano 18* ☎ *0432/201116* ⊕ *www.hotelallegria.it* *20 rooms* *In-room: safe, refrigerator, Internet. In-hotel: restaurant, bar, parking (paid), Wi-Fi hotspot* ⊙ *No dinner Sun. No lunch Mon.* *Breakfast.*

$$ ★ **Hotel Clocchiatti.** You have two choices here: stay in the restored 19th-century villa, where large double doors open onto canopy beds and Alpine-style wood ceilings and paneling, or opt for the rich colors and spare furnishings of the starkly angular rooms in the ultramodern (and slightly more expensive) "Next" wing. **Pros:** individually decorated rooms; quiet surroundings; swimming pool. **Cons:** 10-minute drive from town center; small bathrooms. **TripAdvisor:** "felt very much at home," "staff are very friendly and helpful," "location is wonderful." ✉ *Via Cividale 29* ☎ *0432/505047* ⊕ *www.hotelclocchiatti.it* *27 rooms* *In-room: safe, refrigerator, Wi-Fi. In-hotel: bar, pool, bicycles, laundry service, parking (free), some pets allowed* *Breakfast.*

CIVIDALE DEL FRIULI

17 km (11 mi) east of Udine, 144 km (89 mi) northeast of Venice.

GETTING HERE

There is hourly train service from Udine. Since the Udine-Cividale train line is not part of the Italian national rail system, you have to buy the tickets from the tobacconist or other retailers within the Udine station. You cannot buy a ticket through to Cividale from another city.

By car from Udine, take Via Cividale, which turns into SS54; follow SS54 into Cividale.

VISITOR INFORMATION

Cividale tourism office (✉ *Corso Poalino d'Aquileria 10* ☎ *0432/731398*).

EXPLORING

Cividale is the best place to see the art of the Lombards, a Germanic people who entered Italy in 568 and ruled until the late 8th century. The city was founded in AD 53 by Julius Caesar, then commander of Roman legions in the area. Here you can also find Celtic, Roman, and medieval Jewish ruins alongside Venetian Gothic buildings, including the Palazzo Comunale. Strolling through the part of the city that now occupies the former gastaldia, the Lombard ducal palace, affords spectacular views of the medieval city and the river.

Cividale's Renaissance **Duomo** is largely the work of Pietro Lombardo, principal architect of Venice's justly famous Santa Maria dei Miracoli.

It contains a magnificent 12th-century silver gilt altarpiece. ✉ *Piazza Duomo* ☎ *0432/731144* ⏲ *Daily 7:30–7:30.*

The **Museo Cristiano e Tesoro del Duomo,** which you enter in a courtyard off to the right of the Duomo, contains two interesting and important monuments of Lombard art: the Altar of Duke Ratchis (737–744) and the Baptistry of Patriarch Callisto (731–776). Both were found under the floor of the present Duomo in the early 20th century. The museum also has two fine paintings by Veronese, one by Pordenone, and a small but fine collection of medieval and Renaissance vestments. ✉ *Via Candotti 1* ☎ *0432/730403* 🎫 *Combined ticket with Tempietto Longobardo €4* ⏲ *Wed.–Sun. 10–1 and 3–6.*

★ Seeing the beautiful and historically important **Tempietto Longobardo** *(Lombard church)* from the 8th century is more than sufficient reason to visit Cividale. Now within the Monastery of Santa Maria in Valle (16th century), the Tempietto was originally the chapel of the ducal palace, or the gastaldia. The west wall is the best-preserved example of the art and architecture of the Lombards, a Germanic people who entered Italy in 568. It has an archway with an exquisitely rendered vine motif, guarded by an 8th-century procession of female figures, showing the Lombard interpretation of classical forms that resembles the style of the much earlier Byzantine mosaics in Ravenna, which had passed briefly to Lombard rule in 737. This procession of female figures had originally extended to the side walls of the Tempietto, but was destroyed by the earthquake of 1222. The post-Lombard frescoes decorating the vaults and the east wall date from the 13th and 14th centuries, and the fine carved wooden stalls also date from the 14th century. The Tempietto has been nominated to be a UNESCO World Heritage site. ✉ *Via Monastero Maggiore* ☎ *0432/700867* 🌐 *www.museiprovinciaud.it* 🎫 *€3; combined ticket with Tempietto Longobardo €4* ⏲ *Apr.–Sept., Mon.–Sat. 9:30–12:30 and 3–6:30, Sun. 9:30–1 and 3–7:30; Oct.–Mar., Mon.–Sat. 9:30–12:30 and 3–5, Sun. 9:30–12:30 and 2:30–6.*

WHERE TO STAY

$$ **Locanda Al Castello.** Set on a peaceful hillside a few minutes' drive out of town, this creeper-covered hotel was once a monastery. **Pros:** quiet area; discounts possible, depending on availability. **Cons:** need a car to get around. **TripAdvisor:** "nice view of the Friulian Plain," "small but well-made spa," "service was grumpy but efficient." ✉ *Via del Castello 12* ☎ *0432/733242* 🌐 *www.alcastello.net* *25 rooms, 2 suites* *In-room: a/c, safe, refrigerator, Wi-Fi. In-hotel: restaurant, bar, tennis courts, spa, parking (free), some pets allowed* 🍽 *Breakfast.*

AQUILEIA

77 km (48 mi) west of Trieste, 163 km (101 mi) east of Venice.

GETTING HERE

Getting to Aquileia by public transport is difficult, but not impossible. There is frequent train service from Venice and Trieste to Cervignano di Friuli, which is 8 km (5 mi) away by taxi (about €20) or infrequent bus service. (Ask the newsstand attendant or the railroad ticket teller for assistance.) By car from Venice or Trieste, take Autostrada A4 (Venezia–Trieste) to the Palmanova exit and continue 17 km (11 mi) to Aquileia. From Udine, take Autostrada A23 to the Palmanova exit.

VISITOR INFORMATION

Aquileia tourism office (✉ *Piazza Capitolo* ☎ *0431/919491*).

EXPLORING

This sleepy little town was, in the time of Emperor Augustus, Italy's fourth most important city (after Rome, Milan, and Capua). It was the principal northern Adriatic port of Italy and the beginning of Roman routes north. Its prominence continued into the Christian era. The patriarchate (bishopric) of Aquileia was founded here around 314, just after the Edict of Milan halted the persecution of Christians and about the time that the Emperor Constantine officially declared his conversion. After several centuries of decline and frequent pillaging, including a sacking by Attila the Hun in 452, the town regained its stature in the 11th century, which it held onto until the end of the 14th century. Aquileia's Roman and early Christian remains offer an image of the transition from pagan to Christian Rome. Aquileia is also refreshingly free of the mass tourism that you might expect at such a culturally historic place.

★ Aquileia's **Basilica** was founded by Theodore, its first patriarch, who built two parallel basilicas, now the north and the south halls, on the site of a 3rd-century Gnostic chapel. These were joined by a third hall, forming a U, with the baptismal font in the middle. The complex was rebuilt between 1021 and 1031, and later accumulated different elements including the Romanesque portico and the Gothic bell tower, producing the church you see today. The highlight of this monument is the spectacular 3rd- to 4th-century mosaic covering the entire floor of the basilica and the adjacent crypt, comprising one of the most beautiful and important early Christian monuments. The mosaic floor of the present-day basilica is essentially the remains of the floor of Theodore's south hall, while those of the Cripta degli Scavi are those of his north hall, along with the remains of the mosaic floor of a pre-Christian Roman house and warehouse.

The mosaics of the basilica are important not only because of their beauty, but also because they provide a window into Gnostic symbolism and the conflict between Gnosticism and the early Christian church. In his north hall, Theodore retained much of the floor of the earlier Gnostic chapel, whose mosaics, done largely in the 3rd century, represent the ascent of the soul, through the realm of the planets and constellations, to God, who is represented as a ram. (The ram, at the head of the zodiac, is the Gnostic generative force.) Libra is not the scales, but rather a battle between good (the rooster) and evil (the tortoise); the constellation Cancer is represented as a shrimp on a tree. The basis for the representation in Aquileia is the Pistis Sophia, a 2nd-century Gnostic tract written in Alexandria.

This integration of Gnosticism into a Christian church is particularly interesting, since Gnosticism had already been branded a heresy by influential early Church fathers. In retaining these mosaics, Theodore may have been making a rather daring political gesture, publicly expressing a leaning toward Gnosticism. Alternatively, the area of the north hall may have been Theodore's private residence, where the retention of Gnostic symbolism may have been more acceptable.

The 4th-century mosaics of the south hall (the present-day nave of the basilica) are somewhat more doctrinally conventional, and represent the story of Jonah as prefiguring the salvation offered by the Church.

Down a flight of steps, the **Cripta degli Affreschi** contains beautiful 12th-century frescoes, among them Saint Peter sending Saint Mark to Aquileia and the beheading of Saints Hermagoras and Fortunatus, to whom the basilica is dedicated. ✉ *Piazza Capitolo* ☎ *0431/91067* 🎫 *Basilica free, both crypts €3, campanile €1.20* ⏲ *Apr.–Oct., daily 9–7; Nov.–Mar., weekdays 9–4:30, weekends 9–5.*

Beyond the basilica and across the road, the **archaeological site** among the cypresses reveals Roman remains of the forum, houses, cemetery, and port. The little stream was once an important waterway extending to Grado. The area is well signposted. Unfortunately, many of the excavations of Roman Aquileia could not be left exposed because of the extremely high water table under the site. Much of Roman Aquileia had to be reburied after archaeological studies had been conducted; nevertheless, what remains aboveground, along with the monuments in the archaeological museum, is sufficient to give an idea of the grandeur of this ancient city. 🌐 *www.museoarcheo-aquileia.it* 🎫 *Free* ⏲ *Daily 8:15–7.*

The **Museo Archeologico** is rewarding, containing a wealth of material from the Roman era. Notable are the portrait busts from Republican times, semiprecious gems, amber and gold work—including preserved flies—a fine glass collection, and beautiful pre-Christian mosaics from the floors of Roman houses and palaces. ✉ *Via Roma 1* ☎ *0431/91096* 🌐 *www.museoarcheo-aquileia.it* 🎫 *€4* ⏲ *Tues.–Sun. 8:30–7:30.*

The **Museo Paleocristiano** is not simply a museum, it is rather an early-Christian 4th-century suburban basilica that was transformed in the 9th century into a monastery and then, lastly, into a farmhouse. Some of the fragments of 4th-century mosaics preserved here are even more delicate than those in the main basilica. ✉ *Località Monastero* ☎ *0431/91035* 🌐 *www.museoarcheo-aquileia.it* 🎫 *Free* ⏲ *Tues.–Sun. 8:30–1:45.*

TRIESTE

77 km (48 mi) east of Aquileia, 163 km (101 mi) east of Venice.

GETTING HERE

Trains to Trieste depart regularly from Venice, Udine, and other major Italian cities. By car, it is the eastern terminus of the Autostrada Torino–Trieste (E70). Trieste is served by Ronchi dei Ligioneri Airport, which receives flights from major Italian airports and some European cities. The airport is 33 km (20½ mi) from the city; transportation into Trieste is by taxi or Bus 51.

VISITOR INFORMATION

Trieste tourism office (✉ *Piazza dell'Unità d'Italia 4/b* ☎ *040/3478312* 🌐 *www.triesteturismo.com*).

EXPLORING

Trieste is built along a fringe of coastline where a rugged karst plateau tumbles abruptly into the beautiful Adriatic. It was, up until the end of World War I, the only port of the Austro-Hungarian Empire and therefore a major industrial and financial center. In the early years of the 20th century Trieste and its surroundings also became famous for their association with some of the most important names of Italian literature, such as Italo Svevo, and English and German letters. James Joyce drew inspiration from the city's multiethnic population, and Rainer Maria Rilke was inspired by the seacoast west of the city.

Trieste has lost its importance as a port and a center of finance, but perhaps because of its multicultural nature at the juncture of Latin, Slavic, and Germanic Europe, it has never fully lost its role as an intellectual center. In recent years the city has become a center for science and the computer industry. The streets hold a mix of monumental, neoclassical, and art nouveau architecture built by the Austrians during Trieste's days of glory, granting an air of melancholy stateliness to a city that lives as much in the past as the present.

Italian revolutionaries of the 1800s rallied their battle cry around Trieste, because of what they believed was foreign occupation of their motherland. After World War II the sliver of land including Trieste and a small part of Istria became an independent, neutral state that was officially recognized in a 1947 peace treaty. Although it was actually occupied by British and American troops for its nine years of existence, the Free Territory of Trieste issued its own currency and stamps. In 1954 a Memorandum of Understanding was signed in London, giving civil administration of Trieste to Italy.

★ The sidewalk cafés on the vast seaside **Piazza dell'Unità d'Italia** are popular meeting places in the summer months. The imposing square, ringed by grandiose facades, was set out as a plaza open to the sea, like Venice's Piazza San Marco, in the late Middle Ages. It underwent countless changes through the centuries and its present size and architecture are essentially products of late-19th- and early-20th-century Austria. The huge square was named and renamed, according to the political fortunes of the city; it was given its current name in 1955, when Trieste was finally given to Italy. On the inland side of the piazza note the facade of the **Palazzo Comunale** (Town Hall) designed by the Triestino architect Giuseppi Bruni in 1875. Sadly, it was from this building's balcony in 1938 that Mussolini proclaimed the infamous racial laws, depriving Italian Jews of most of their rights.

A statue of Habsburg emperor Leopold I looks out over **Piazza della Borsa**, which contains Trieste's original stock exchange, the **Borsa Vecchia** (1805), an attractive neoclassical building now serving as the chamber of commerce. It sits at the end of the Canal Grande, a canal dug in the 18th century by the Austrian empress Maria Theresia as a first step in the expansion of what was then a small fishing village of 7,000 into the port of her empire.

The ruins of a 1st century AD amphitheater, **Teatro Romano**, near the Via Giuseppi Mazzini opposite the city's *questura* (police station), were

CLOSE UP

Trieste's Caffè Culture

Trieste is justly famous for its coffee. The elegant civility of Trieste plays out beautifully in a *caffè* culture combining the refinement of Vienna with the passion of Italy. In Trieste, as elsewhere in Italy, ask for a caffè and you'll get a thimbleful of high-octane espresso. Your cappuccino here will also come in an espresso cup, with only half as much frothy milk as you'll find elsewhere and, in the Viennese fashion, a dollop of whipped cream. Many cafés are part of a *torrefazione* (roasting shop), so you can sample a cup and then buy beans to take with you.

Few cafés in Italy can rival **Antico Caffè San Marco** (✉ *Via Battisti 18* ☎ *040/363538* ⏲ *Closed Mon.*) for its bohemian atmosphere. After being destroyed in World War I, it was rebuilt in the 1920s, and then restored several more times, but some of the original art nouveau decor remains. It became a meeting place for local intellectuals and was the haunt of the Triestino writers Italo Svevo and Umberto Saba. For a great view of the great piazza, you couldn't do better than **Caffè Degli Specchi** (✉ *Piazza dell'Unità d'Italia 7* ☎ *040/365777*), where the many mirrors heighten the opportunities for people-watching. Originally opened in 1839, it was taken over by the British Navy after World War II, and Triestini were not allowed in unless accompanied by an Englishman. Because of its location, it is the café most frequented by tourists; it's open daily until midnight. Founded in 1830, classic **Caffè Tommaseo** (✉ *Piazza Tommaseo 4/C* ☎ *040/362666*) is a comfortable place to linger, especially on weekend evenings and Sunday morning (11–1:30), when there's live music. It's open daily until 12:30 am. **Cremcaffè** (✉ *Piazza Carlo Goldoni 10* ☎ *040/636555* ⏲ *Closed Sun.*) isn't the ideal place to sit and read the paper, but its downtown location and selection of 20 coffee blends make it one of the busiest cafés in town. The atmosphere is more modern than Old World at **I Paesi del Caffè** (✉ *Via Einaudi 1* ☎ *040/633897* ⏲ *Closed Sun.*), which brews coffee and sells beans of most of the top varieties, including Jamaica Blue Mountain.

discovered during 1938 demolition work. Its statues are now displayed at the Museo Civico, and the space is used for summer plays and concerts. ✉ *Via del Teatro Romano.*

The 14th-century **Cattedrale di San Giusto**, built on the site of an ancient Roman forum, contains remnants of at least three previous buildings built on the same ground, the earliest a hall dating from the 5th century. A section of the original floor mosaic still remains, incorporated into the floor of the present church. In the 9th and 11th centuries two adjacent churches were built on the same site, the Church of the Assumption and the Church of San Giusto. The beautiful apse mosaics of these churches, done in the 12th and 13th centuries by a Venetian artist, still remain in the apses of the side aisles of the present church. In the 14th century the two churches were joined and a Romanesque-Gothic facade was attached, ornamented with fragments of Roman monuments taken from the forum. The jambs of the main doorway are the most conspicuous Roman element. ✉ *Piazza della Cattedrale 2* ☎ *040/309666* ⏲ *Apr.–Oct., Mon.–Sun. 7:30–7:30; Nov.–Mar., Mon.–Sat. 7:30–noon and 3–6:30, Sun. 7:30–1 and 3:30–7.*

The hilltop **Castello di San Giusto** (built 1470–1630) was constructed on the ruins of the Roman town of Tergeste. Given the excellent view, it's no surprise that 15th-century Venetians turned the castle into a shipping observation point; the structure was further enlarged by Trieste's subsequent rulers, the Habsburgs. ✉ *Piazza della Cattedrale 3* ☎ *040/309362* 🎟 *€4* ⏲ *Nov.–Mar., daily 9–5; Apr.–Oct., daily 9–7.*

On the hill near the Castello is the **Civico Museo di Storia ed Arte**, an eclectic history and art museum with statues from the Roman theater and artifacts from Egypt, Greece, and Rome. There's also an assortment of glass and manuscripts. The **Orto Lapidario** (Lapidary Garden) has classical statuary, pottery, and a small Corinthian temple. ✉ *Via Cattedrale 15* ☎ *040/310500* 🎟 *€4* ⏲ *Tues.–Sun. 9–1.*

The **Civico Museo Revoltella e Galleria d'Arte Moderna** was founded in 1872, when the city inherited the palazzo, library, and art collection of shipping magnate Baron Pasquale Revoltella. The collection holds almost exclusively 19th- and 20th-century Italian art, much of which was collected by Revoltella himself. Along with the palace, the museum presents a good picture of the tastes of a Triestino captain of industry during the city's days of glory. Call for hours during special exhibits. The museum's rooftop café, where the view rivals the artwork, is open some evenings in summer. ✉ *Via Armando Diaz 27* ☎ *040/6754350* 🎟 *€6.50* ⏲ *Wed.–Mon. 10–7.*

OFF THE BEATEN PATH

Castello Di Duino. The 14th-century Castle of Duino, where in 1912 Rainer Maria Rilke was inspired to write his masterpiece, the *Duino Elegies*, is just 12 km (7½ mi) from Trieste. Take Bus 44 or 51 from the Trieste railway station. The easy path along the seacoast from the castle toward Trieste has gorgeous views that rival the Amalfi Coast and the Cinque Terre. The castle itself, still the property of the Princes of Thurn and Taxis, is open to the public; it contains a fine collection of antique furnishings and an amazing Palladian circular staircase. ✉ *Frazione Duino 32, Duino-Ausina* ☎ *040/208120* 🌐 *www.castellodiduino.it* 🎟 *€7* ⏲ *Apr.–Sept., Wed.–Mon. 9:30–5:30; Oct.–Mar., weekends and holidays 9:30–4.*

WHERE TO EAT

¢ SEAFOOD ★

✕ **Antipastoteca di Mare.** Hidden halfway up the hill to the Castello di San Giusto, in what the Triestini call the old city, this little informal restaurant specializes in traditional preparations from the *cucina povera*. The inexpensive fish—bluefish, sardines, mackerel, mussels, and squid—are accompanied by salad, potatoes, polenta, and house wine. The consistently tasty and fresh dishes, especially the fish soup and the *sardoni in savor* (large sardines with raisins, pine nuts, and caramelized onions; "savor" is the Triestino-dialect equivalent of the Venetian "saor"), show what a talented chef can do on a limited budget. ✉ *Via della Fornace 1* ☎ *040/309606* ▭ *No credit cards* ⏲ *Closed Mon. No dinner Sun.*

¢ NORTHERN ITALIAN

✕ **Da Pepi.** A Triestino institution, Da Pepi is the oldest and most esteemed of the many "buffet" restaurants around town. It specializes in *bollito di maiale*, a dish of boiled pork and pork sausages accompanied by delicately flavored sauerkraut, mustard, and grated horseradish. This hole-in-the-wall eatery with few tables and simple decor, and others like it, are as much a part of the Triestino scene as the cafés. Unlike other Italian restaurants, buffets don't close between lunch and dinner, and tap beer is the drink of choice. ✉ *Via Cassa di Risparmio 3* ☎ *040/366858* ⊙ *Closed Sun. and last 2 wks in July.*

$$ NORTHERN ITALIAN ✕ **Suban.** An easy trip slightly outside town, this landmark trattoria operated by the hospitable Suban family has been in business since 1865. Sit by the dining room fire or relax on a huge terrace and watch the sunset. This is Italian food with a Slovene, Hungarian, and Austrian accent. Start with *jota carsolina* (a rich soup of cabbage, potatoes, and beans), and then you might order a steak grilled and sliced at your table. Lighter fare includes *insalatine tiepide* (warm salads with smoked pork or duck) and a smoked beef that is truly special. To get here you can take Bus 35 from Piazza Oberdan. ✉ *Via Comici 2* ☎ *040/54368* ⊙ *Closed Tues., 1st 3 wks in Aug., and 2 wks in early Jan. No lunch weekdays.*

WHERE TO STAY

$ **Filoxenia.** The location on the city waterfront, and the reasonable prices, make this small hotel a good choice for travelers on a tight budget. **Pros:** central location; friendly staff; budget price. **Cons:** some very small, spartan rooms; some street noise; showers are cramped. **TripAdvisor:** "very satisfied with the location," "nice and very central," "budget prices." ✉ *Via Mazzini 3* ☎ *040/3481644* 🌐 *www.filoxenia.it* *20 rooms* *In-room: Wi-Fi. In-hotel: restaurant, bar, parking (paid), some pets allowed* *Breakfast.*

$$ ★ **L'Albero Nascosto Hotel Residence.** Though hardly noticeable on its busy, narrow street, this hotel residence is one of the best values in Trieste. **Pros:** very central location; clean and spacious rooms. **Cons:** steps to climb; no staff on-site after 8 pm (though late arrivals can be arranged). **TripAdvisor:** "great taste in the decor," "amazing restoration of an ancient building," "staff is extremely kind and careful." ✉ *Via Felice Venezian 18* ☎ *040/300188* 🌐 *www.alberonascosto.it* *10 rooms* *In-room: no phone, kitchen, Wi-Fi. In-hotel: bar, parking (paid), some pets allowed* *Breakfast.*

$$ ★ **Riviera & Maximilian's.** Seven kilometers (4½ mi) north of Trieste, this lovely hotel commands views across the Golfo di Trieste, including nearby Castello di Miramare; dining areas, the bar, and all guest rooms enjoy this stunning panorama. **Pros:** great views; gorgeous grounds. **Cons:** far from town; some rooms are cramped. **TripAdvisor:** "hillside has incredible views," "nice place to enjoy the sun," "superb views over the bay." ✉ *Strada Costiera 22* ☎ *040/224551* 🌐 *www.hotelrivieraemaximilian.com* *56 rooms, 2 suites, 9 apartments* *In-room: safe, refrigerator, Wi-Fi. In-hotel: restaurant, bar, pool, beachfront, Internet terminal, parking (free), some pets allowed* *Breakfast.*

4

CASTELLO DI MIRAMARE

7 km (4½ mi) northwest of Trieste.

GETTING HERE

Bus 36 from Piazza Oberdan in Trieste runs here every half hour.

EXPLORING

★ Archduke Maximilian of Habsburg, brother of Emperor Franz Josef and retired commander of the Austrian Navy, built this seafront extravaganza from 1856 to 1860. The throne room has a ship's-keel wooden ceiling; in accordance with late 19th-century taste, the rooms are generally furnished with very elaborate somewhat ponderous versions of medieval, Renaissance, and French period furniture, and the walls are covered in red damask. Maximilian's retirement was interrupted in 1864, when he became emperor of Mexico at the initiative of Napoléon III. He was executed three years later by a Mexican firing squad. His wife, Charlotte of Belgium, went mad and returned to Miramar, and later to her native country. During the last years of the Habsburg reign, Miramar became one of the favorite residences of the wife of Franz Josef, the Empress Elizabeth (Sissi). The castle was later owned by Duke Amadeo of Aosta, who renovated some rooms in the rationalist style and installed modern plumbing in his art deco bathroom. Tours in English are available by reservation. Surrounding the castle is a 54-acre park, partly wooded and partly sculpted into attractive gardens. ✉ *Viale Miramare off SS14, Trieste* ☎ *040/224143* 🌐 *www.castello-miramare.it* 🎫 *Castle €4 (€6 during some special exhibits), guided tour €4, park free* ⏲ *Castle: daily 9–7. Last entry ½ hr before closing. Park: Apr.–Sept., daily 8–7; Nov.–Feb., daily 8–5; Mar. and Oct., daily 8–6.*

5

The Dolomites

TRENTINO–ALTO ADIGE

WORD OF MOUTH

". . . an unearthly experience. Bare rock towers, boulders the size of cars strewn all about . . . quite bleak, quite surreal and quite amazing . . . The Dolomites truly need to be seen to be appreciated, as pictures don't do them justice."

—pjal

WELCOME TO THE DOLOMITES

TOP REASONS TO GO

★ **Museo Archeologico dell'Alto Adige, Bolzano:** The impossibly well-preserved body of the iceman Ötzi, the star attraction here, provokes countless questions about the meaning of life 5,000 years ago.

★ **Hiking:** No matter your fitness level, there's an unforgettable walk in store for you here.

★ **Trento:** A graceful fusion of Austrian and Italian styles, this breezy, frescoed town is famed for its imposing castle.

★ **Grande Strada delle Dolomiti (Great Dolomites Road):** Your rental Fiat will think it's a Ferrari as it wends its way along this gorgeous drive through the Heart of the Dolomites.

1 Trentino. This butterfly-shaped province is Italy with a German accent. Its principal city, history-rich Trento, is at the center. To the northwest are Madonna di Campiglio, one of Italy's most fashionable ski resorts, and Bormio, another notable skiing destination that doubles as a gateway to the Parco Nazionale dello Stelvio.

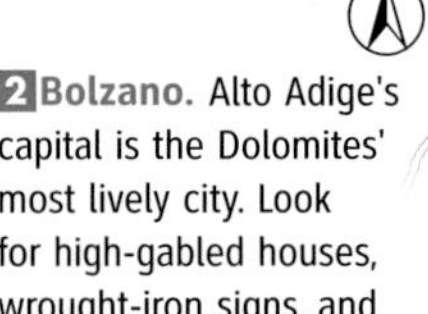

2 Bolzano. Alto Adige's capital is the Dolomites' most lively city. Look for high-gabled houses, wrought-iron signs, and centuries-old wine cellars.

3 Alto Adige. This region was a part of Austria until the end of World War I, and Austrian sensibilities still predominate over Italian. At the spa town of Merano you can soak in hot springs, take the "grape cure," and stroll along lovely walkways. To the southwest, Caldaro has an appealing wine-growing region.

4 Heart of the Dolomites. The spectacular Sella mountain range and the surrounding Val di Fassa and Val Gardena make up this region. It's distinguished by great views and great mountain sports, both summer and winter. At the town of Canazei, the cable car 3,000 feet up to the Col Rodella lookout packages the vast panorama perfectly.

GETTING ORIENTED

Shadowed by the Dolomite Mountains—whose other-worldly pinnacles Leonardo depicted in the background of his *Mona Lisa*—the northeast Italian provinces of Trentino and Alto Adige are centered around the valleys of the Adige and Isarco rivers, which course from the Brenner Pass south to Bolzano.

5 Cortina d'Ampezzo. A former hangout of the ultrahip, Cortina has aged gracefully into the grande dame of Italian ski resorts. But it's arguably at its best in summer, when there are countless options for hiking and mountain activities.

EATING AND DRINKING WELL IN THE DOLOMITES

Everything in Alto Adige (and, to a lesser extent, Trentino) has more than a tinge of the Teutonic—and the food is no exception. The rich and creamy food here, including fondues, polentas, and barley soups, reflects the Alpine climate and Austrian and Swiss influence.

The quintessential restaurant here is the wood-panel Tirolean *Stube* (pub) serving hearty meat-and-dumpling fare, and there's also a profusion of pastry shops and lively beer halls.

Although the early dining schedule you'll find in Germany or Austria is somewhat tempered here, your options for late-night meals are more limited than in southern Italy, where *la dolce vita* has a firmer grip.

Thankfully, the coffee is every bit as good as in parts south—just expect to hear "*danke, grazie*" when paying for your cappuccino.

BEST OF THE WURST

Not to be missed are the outdoor wurst carts, even (or perhaps especially) in colder weather. After placing your order you'll get a sheet of wax paper, followed by a dollop of mustard, a Kaiser roll, and your chosen sausage.

You can sometimes make your selection by pointing to whatever picture is most appealing; if not, pass on the familiar-sounding *Frankfurter* and try the local *Meraner.* Carts can reliably be found in Bolzano (try Piazza delle Erbe, or in front of the archaeological museum) and Merano (Piazza del Grano, or along the river).

POLENTA AND DUMPLINGS

Polenta is a staple in the region, in both its creamy and firm varieties, often topped with cheese or mushrooms (or both). Dumplings also appear on many menus; the most distinctive to the region are *canederli* (also known as *Knoedel*), pictured at right, made from seasoned bread in many variations, and served either in broth or with a sauce.

Other dumplings to look for are the dense *strangolapreti* (literally "priest-chokers") and *gnocchi di ricotta alla zucca* (ricotta and pumpkin dumplings).

CHEESE

Cheese from the Alpine dairy cows of Trentino–Alto Adige is a specialty, with each isolated mountain valley seeming to make its own variety, to be found nowhere else—it's often simply called *nostrano* (ours).

The best known of the cheeses are the mild Asiago and *fontal* and the more-pungent *puzzone di Moena* (literally, "stinkpot"). If your doctor permits it, try the *schiz:* fresh cheese that is sliced and fried in butter, sometimes with cream added.

PASTRIES AND BAKED GOODS

Bakeries turn out a wide selection of crusty dark rolls and caraway-studded rye breads—maybe not typical Italian bread, but full of flavor. Pastries are reminiscent of what you'd expect to find in Vienna. Apple strudel, pictured below, is everywhere, and for good reason: the best apples in Italy are grown here. There's other exceptional fruit as well, including pears, plums, and grapes, that makes its way into baked goods.

5

ALIMENTARI

If you're planning a picnic or getting provisions for a hike, you'll be well served by the fine *alimentari* (food shops) of Trentino and Alto Adige. They stock a bounty of regional specialties, including cheeses, pickles, salami, and smoked meats. These are good places to pick up a sample of *speck tirolese*, the salt-cured, cold-smoked, deboned ham hock usually cut in paper-thin slices, like prosciutto (though proud speck producers often bristle at the comparison). Don't discard the fat of the speck—it's considered the best part.

WINE

Though Trentino and Alto Adige aren't as esteemed for their wines as many other Italian regions, they produce a wide variety of crisp, dry, and aromatic whites—Kerner, Müller Thurgau, and Traminer, to name a few—not surprisingly, more like what you'd expect from German vineyards than Italian. Among the reds, look for Lagrein and the native Teroldego, a fruity, spicy variety produced only in the tiny valley north of Trento. The Trento D.O.C. is a marvelous sparkling wine in a class with Champagne.

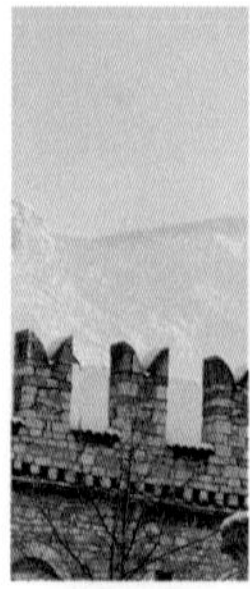

Updated by Nan McElroy

The vast, mountainous domain of northeastern Italy, unlike other celebrated Alpine regions, has remained relatively undeveloped. Strange, rocky pinnacles jut straight up like chimneys, looming over scattered, pristine mountain lakes. Below, rivers meander through valleys dotted with peaceful villages and protected by picture-book castles. In the most secluded Dolomite vales, unique cultures have flourished: the Ladin language, an offshoot of Latin still spoken in the Val Gardena and Val di Fassa, owes its unlikely survival to centuries of topographic isolation.

The more-accessible parts of Trentino–Alto Adige, on the other hand, have a history of near-constant intermingling of cultures. The region's Adige and Isarco valleys make up the main access route between Italy and central Europe, and as a result, the language, cuisine, and architecture are a blend of north and south. Whereas the province of Trentino is largely Italian-speaking, Alto Adige is predominantly Germanic: until World War I the area was Austria's South Tirol. As you move north toward the famed Brenner Pass—through the prosperous valley towns of Rovereto, Trento, and Bolzano—the Teutonic influence is increasingly dominant; by the time you reach Bressanone, it's hard to believe you're in Italy at all.

PLANNING

MAKING THE MOST OF YOUR TIME

For a brief stay, your best choice for a base is vibrant Bolzano, where you can get a sense of the region's contrasts—Italian and German, medieval and ultramodern. After a day or two in town, venture an hour south to history-laden Trento, north to the lovely spa town of Merano, or southwest to Caldaro and its Strada di Vino; all are viable day trips from Bolzano, and Trento and Merano make good places to spend the night as well.

If you have more time, you'll want to get up into the mountains, which are the region's main attraction. The trip on the Grande Strada delle Dolomiti (Great Dolomites Road) through the Heart of the Dolomites to Cortina d'Ampezzo is one of Italy's most spectacular drives. Summer or winter, this is a great destination for mountain sports, with scores of trails for world-class hiking and skiing.

SKIING VACATIONS

The Dolomites have some of the most spectacular downhill skiing in Europe, with the facilities to match. The most comprehensive centers are the upscale resorts of the massive Cortina d'Ampezzo and Madonna di Campiglio, which draw an international clientele with impressive terrain, expansive lift systems, and lively après-ski. For traditional Tirolean *Gemütlichkeit* (congeniality), try one of the more rustic resorts: in the Val di Fassa or Val Gardena your lift mate is more likely to be from a neighboring town than from Milan. Both major resorts and out-of-the-way villages have well-marked trails for *sci di fondo* (cross-country skiing). With the exception of the main bargain period known as *settimane bianche* (white weeks) in January and February, the slopes are seldom overcrowded.

GETTING HERE AND AROUND

BUS TRAVEL

Regular bus service connects larger cities to the south (Verona, Venice, and Milan) with valley towns in Trentino–Alto Adige (Rovereto, Trento, Bolzano, and Merano). You'll need to change to less frequent local buses to reach resorts and smaller villages in the mountains beyond.

If you're equipped with current schedules and don't mind adapting your schedules to theirs, it's possible to visit even the remotest villages by bus. For information, contact **Trentino Trasporti** (☎ *0461/821000* 🌐 *www.ttesercizio.it*) or Alto Adige's **SIT** (*Servizio Integrato di Trasporto* ☎ *0471/415480 or 800/846047* 🌐 *www.sii.bz.it*).

Winter service with **CortinaExpress** (☎ *0436/867350* 🌐 *www.cortinaexpress.it*) connects the resort with Venice airport and nearby Mestre train station. **ATVO** (☎ *0421/383671* 🌐 *www.atvo.it*) provides year-round service to Cortina from Venice's Piazzale Roma bus park. **DolomitiBus** (☎ *0437/217111* 🌐 *www.dolomitibus.it*) covers the eastern Dolomites, including a number of small towns.

CAR TRAVEL

Driving is easily the most convenient way to travel in the Dolomites; it can be difficult to reach the ski areas (or any town outside of Rovereto, Trento, Bolzano, and Merano) without a car. Driving is also the most exhilarating way to get around, as you rise from broad valleys into mountains with narrow, winding roads straight out of a sports-car ad. Caution is essential (tap your horn in advance of hairpin turns), as are chains in winter, when roads are often covered in snow. Sudden closures are common, especially on high mountain passes, and can occur as early as November and as late as May. Even under the best conditions, expect to negotiate mountain roads at speeds no greater than 50 kph (30 mph).

The most important route in the region is the A22, the main north–south highway linking Italy with central Europe by way of the Brenner Pass. It connects Innsbruck with Bressanone, Bolzano, Trento, and

Rovereto, and near Verona joins autostrada A4 (which runs east–west across northern Italy, from Trieste to Turin). By car, Trento is 3 hours from Milan and 2½ hours from Venice. Bolzano is another hour's drive to the north, with Munich four hours farther on.

If you're planning a driving tour of the Dolomites, consider flying into Munich. Car rentals are less expensive in Germany, and it's easier to get automatic transmission (though manual is better suited to challenging mountain roads).

TRAIN TRAVEL

The rail line following the course of the Isarco and Adige valleys—from Munich and Innsbruck, through the Brenner Pass, and southward past Bressanone, Bolzano, Trento, and Rovereto en route to Verona—is well trafficked, making trains a viable option for travel between these towns. Eurocity trains on the Dortmund–Venice and Munich–Innsbruck–Rome routes stop at these stations, and you can connect with other Italian lines at Verona. Although branch lines from Trento and Bolzano do extend into some of the smaller valleys (including hourly service between Bolzano and Merano), most of the mountain attractions are beyond the reach of trains. Check **Trenitalia** (☎ *892021 within Italy* 🌐 *www.trenitalia.com*) for more information.

ABOUT THE HOTELS

Classic Dolomite lodging options range from restored castles to chalets to stately 19th-century hotels. The small villages that pepper the Dolomites often have scores of flower-bedecked, Alpine-shuttered inns, many of them inexpensive. Hotel information offices at train stations and tourist offices can help if you've arrived without reservations. The Bolzano train station has a 24-hour hotel service, and tourist offices will give you a list of all the hotels in the area, arranged by location, stars, and price. Hotels at ski resorts cater to longer stays at full or half board: you should book ski vacations as packages well in advance. Most rural accommodations close from early November to mid- or late December, as well as for a month or two after Easter.

Hotel reviews have been condensed for this book. Please go to Fodors.com for full reviews of each property.

WHAT IT COSTS (IN EUROS)

	¢	$	$$	$$$	$$$$
Restaurants	under €20	€20–€30	€30–€45	€45–€65	over €65
Hotels	under €75	€75–€125	€125–€200	€200–€300	over €300

Restaurant prices are for a first course (primo), second course (secondo), and dessert (dolce). Hotel prices are for two people in a standard double room in high season, including tax and service.

TRENTINO

Until the end of World War I, Trentino was Italy's frontier with the Austro-Hungarian Empire, and although this province remains unmistakably Italian, Germanic influences are tangible in all aspects of life here, including architecture, cuisine, culture, and language. Visitors are drawn by historic sights reflecting a strategic position at the intersection of southern and central Europe: Trento was the headquarters of the Catholic Counter-Reformation; Rovereto the site of an emblematically bloody battle during the Great War. Numerous year-round mountain resorts, including fashionable Madonna di Campiglio, are in the wings of the butterfly-shaped region.

TRENTO

5

51 km (32 mi) south of Bolzano, 24 km (15 mi) north of Rovereto.

VISITOR INFORMATION

Trento tourism office (✉ *Via Manci 2* ☎ *0461/216000* 🌐 *www.apt.trento.it*).

EXPLORING

Trento is a prosperous, cosmopolitan university town that retains an architectural charm befitting its historical importance. It was here, from 1545 to 1563, that the structure of the Catholic Church was redefined at the Council of Trent. This was the starting point of the Counter-Reformation, which brought half of Europe back to Catholicism. The word *consiglio* (council) appears everywhere in Trento—in hotel, restaurant, and street names, and even on wine labels.

Today the Piazza del Duomo remains splendid, and its enormous medieval palazzo dominates the city landscape in virtually its original form. The 24-hour Trento Card (€10) grants admission to all major town sights and can be purchased at the tourist office or any museum. A 48-hour card (€15) is also available, and includes entrance to the modern art museum in Rovereto. Both cards provide a number of other perks, including tours, free public transportation, wine tastings, and the cable car ride to Belvedere di Sardagna.

Guided tours of Trento depart Saturday from the **Trento tourism office**. You can meet at 10 am for a visit to the Castello del Buonconsiglio (€6, including admission to the castle), or at 3 pm for a tour of the city center (€3). Reservations are not required; these tours and others are included in the Trento Card. ✉ *Via Manci 2* ☎ *0461/216000* 🌐 *www.apt.trento.it*.

The massive Romanesque **Duomo**, also known as the Cathedral of San Vigilio, forms the southern edge of the Piazza del Duomo. Locals refer to this square as the city's *salotto* (sitting room), as in fine weather it's always filled with students and residents drinking coffee, sipping an aperitif, or reading the newspaper. The baroque **Fontana del Nettuno** presides over it all. When skies are clear, pause here to savor the view of the mountaintops enveloping the city.

Within the Duomo, unusual arcaded stone stairways border the austere nave. Ahead is the *baldacchino* (altar canopy), a copy of Bernini's masterpiece in St. Peter's in Rome. To the left of the altar is a mournful

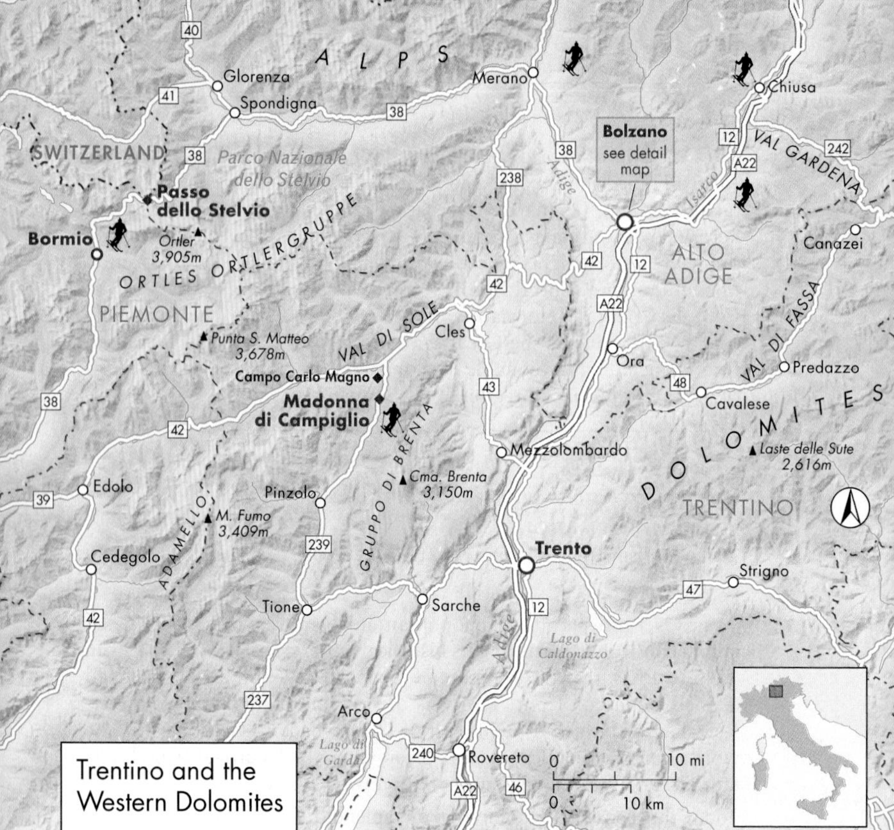

16th-century crucifixion, flanked by the Virgin Mary and John the Apostle. This crucifix, by German artist Sisto Frey, was a focal point of the Council of Trent: each decree agreed on during the two decades of deliberations was solemnly read out in front of it. Stairs on the left side of the altar lead down to the 4th-century Paleo-Christian burial vault. Outside, walk around to the back of the cathedral to see an exquisite display of 14th-century stonemason's art, from the small porch to the intriguing knotted columns on the graceful apse. ✉ *Piazza del Duomo* ☎ *0461/980132* ⏲ *Daily 6:30–noon and 2–8.*

The crenellated **Palazzo Pretorio**, situated so as to seem like a wing of the Duomo, was built in the 13th century as the fortified residence of the prince-bishops, who enjoyed considerable power and autonomy within the medieval hierarchy. The remarkable palazzo has lost none of its original splendor. The crenellations are not merely decorative: the square pattern represents ancient allegiance to the Guelphs (the triangular crenellations seen elsewhere in town represent Ghibelline loyalty). The palazzo now houses the **Museo Diocesano Tridentino,** where you can see paintings showing the seating plan of the prelates during the Council of Trent; early-16th-century tapestries by Pieter van Aelst (1502–56), the Belgian artist who carried out Raphael's 15th-century designs for the Vatican tapestries; carved wood altars and statues; and an 11th-century sacramentary, or book of services. These and other precious objects all come from the cathedral's treasury. Accessible through the museum, a subterranean archaeological area reveals the 1st-century Roman Porta Veronensis, which marked the road to Verona. ✉ *Piazza del Duomo 18* ☎ *0461/234419* 🌐 *www.museodiocesanotridentino.it* 🎟 *€4 includes archaeological area* ⏲ *June–Sept., Wed.–Mon. 9:30–12:30 and 2:30–6; Oct.–May, Wed.–Mon. 9:30–12:30 and 2–5:30.*

★ The ancient Roman city of **Tridentum** lies beneath much of Trento's city center. Centuries of Adige River flooding buried ruins that only recently have been unearthed on public and private land. Beneath this piazza lies the largest of the archaeological sites, revealing some marvels of Roman technology, such as under-floor home heating and under-street sewers complete with manhole covers. The Romans even used lead pipes for four centuries before recognizing it was hazardous to health. Other excavations you can visit lie beneath the Palazzo Pretoria and the Scrigno del Duomo restaurant. ✉ *Piazza Cesare Battisti* ☎ *0461/230171* 🎟 *€2* ⏲ *June–Sept., Tues.–Sun. 9:30–1 and 2–6; Oct.–May, Tues.–Sun. 9–1 and 2–5:30.*

5

QUICK BITES

Scrigno del Duomo. Upstairs, the Scrigno ("casket" in Italian) serves more than 30 wines by the glass, with an excellent selection of local cheeses to match, in a building with some of the oldest frescoes in town. Salads and regional specialties are also available; the *canederli* (seasoned bread dumplings) are especially flavorful here. In the upscale restaurant downstairs, Roman-era walls—this was the level of the ancient square that became Piazza del Duomo—now protect 750 different wines. ✉ *Piazza del Duomo 30* 🌐 *www.scrignodelduomo.com* ☎ *0461/220030*).

Many sessions of the Council of Trent met at the Renaissance church **Santa Maria Maggiore**. Limited light enters through the simple rose window over the main door, so you have to strain to see the magnificent ceiling, an intricate combination of stucco and frescoes. The church is off the northwest side of the Piazza del Duomo, about 200 yards down Via Cavour. Note that at this writing, the church was closed for renovation, with reopening expected toward the end of 2011. ✉ *Vicolo Orsoline 1* ☎ *0461/230037* ⏲ *Daily 8–noon and 2:30–6.*

Locals refer to **Via Belenzani** as Trento's outdoor gallery because of the frescoed facades of the hallmark Renaissance palazzi. It's an easy 50-yard walk up the lane behind the church of Santa Maria Maggiore.

The **Torre Vanga** is a 13th-century tower near the Adige River and one of the bridges that crosses it, the Ponte San Lorenzo.

You can take the Funivia Trento–Sardagna cable car up to the **Belvedere di Sardagna**, a lookout point 1,200 feet above medieval Trento. *Cable car* ✉ *Ponte San Lorenzo* ☎ *0461/983627* 🎟 *€2 round-trip; free with Trento Card* ⏲ *Daily 7–5.*

★ The **Castello del Buonconsiglio** *(Castle of Good Counsel)* was once the stronghold of the prince-bishops; its position and size made it easier to defend than the Palazzo Pretorio. Look for the evolution of architectural styles: the medieval fortifications of the Castelvecchio section (on the far left) were built in the 13th century; the fancier Renaissance Magno

Palazzo section (on the far right) wasn't completed until 300 years later. Part of the Castello now houses the **Museo Provinciale d'Arte,** where permanent and visiting exhibits of art and archaeology hang in frescoed medieval halls or under Renaissance coffered ceilings. The 13th-century **Torre dell'Aquila** (Eagle's Tower) is home to the castle's artistic highlight, a 15th-century *ciclo dei mesi* (cycle of the months). The four-wall fresco is full of charming and detailed scenes of medieval life in both court and countryside. Reservations are required visit the tower; check schedule at the ticket office. ✉ *Via Bernardo Clesio 5* ☎ *0461/233770* 🌐 *www.buonconsiglio.it* 🎫 *Museo €7, Torre dell'Aquila €1 extra* ⏲ *Apr.–mid-July, Tues.–Sun. 10–6; July–Mar., Tues.–Sun. 9:30–5.*

The **Torre Verde** (*Green Tower*) is part of Trento's 13th-century fortifications, standing alongside other fragments of the city walls. You can't go inside, but the exterior is worth a look. ✉ *Piazza Raffaello Sanzio near castle.*

The **Museo d'Arte Moderna e Contemporanea di Trento e Rovereto** is installed in the Palazzo delle Albere, a Renaissance villa on the Adige River. Works in the permanent collection date from the 19th and 20th centuries, but the real focus here is the rotating exhibitions of contemporary artists. A €10 ticket allows you to visit this museum plus the two sister installations in the town of Rovereto, 24 km (15 mi) south of Trento. ✉ *Via Roberto da Sanseverino 45* ☎ *800/397760 or* 0424/600435 🌐 *www.mart.trento.it* 🎫 *€6* ⏲ *Tues.–Sun. 10–6.*

WHERE TO EAT

$ NORTHERN ITALIAN ✕ **Al Vò.** Trento's oldest trattoria (it's the descendant of a 14th-century tavern) remains one of its most popular lunch spots. Locals crowd into a simple, modern dining room to enjoy regional specialites like *crema di zucca e castagne* (squash and chestnut soup) and grilled meats served in copper skillets, such as the reliable *filetto di maialino* (pork fillet). An impressive (and inexpensive) selection of local wines is available; try the food-friendly red Teroldego, made in the valley north of Trento. ✉ *Vicolo del Vò 11* ☎ *0461/985374* 🌐 *www.ristorantealvo.it* ⏲ *Closed Sun. No dinner Sat. or Mon.–Wed.*

¢ NORTHERN ITALIAN ✕ **Antica Birreria Pedavena.** Come here for the beer—a half dozen varieties are brewed in-house (as evidence by the big vats looming in front of you) and served up in a cavernous old-fashioned-but-newly-renovated beer hall. Meals include wursts, meat and cheese platters, pizzas, and huge salads. It's open continuously from 9 am to midnight (until 1 am on Friday and Saturday). Smaller wood-paneled dining rooms and a summer terrace allow for more peaceful dining. ✉ *Piazza Fiera 13* ☎ *0461/986255* 🌐 *www.birreriapedavena.com* ⏲ *Closed Tues.*

$–$$ NORTHERN ITALIAN ✕ **Chiesa.** Near the castle, a 15th-century building conceals a bright, modern restaurant that attracts romancing couples and power lunchers alike. Ubiquitous apple imagery and excellent risotto *alle mele* (with apples) celebrate the local produce—there's even a set meal featuring apples in every course. Otherwise, the food is traditional: specialties are *maccheroncini con salsiccia e verze* (short, narrow pasta tubes with sausage and cabbage) and *tonco de Pontesel* (a stew of mixed meat made according to a 15th-century recipe). ✉ *Via San Marco 64* ☎ *0461/238766* 🌐 *www.ristorantechiesa.it* ⏲ *Closed Sun. and Jan.*

$$$ NORTHERN ITALIAN ★ **Le Due Spade.** This intimate restaurant, around the corner from the Duomo, started out as a Tirolean tavern around the time of the Council of Trent. Able servers deliver superb cuisine, both traditional and more innovative, amid the coziness of wood paneling and an antique stove. You can sample *maialino* (suckling pig) wrapped in a crust of speck, or be more adventurous with *agnello in manto alle fave di cacao* (lamb coated with cocoa beans) served with foie-gras sauce. Given the restaurant's deserved popularity with locals and the limited seating, reservations are a must. ✉ *Via Rizzi 11* ☎ *0461/234343* 🌐 *www.leduespade.com* *Reservations essential* ⏲ *Closed Sun. No lunch Mon.*

$$ NORTHERN ITALIAN **Trattoria Orso Grigio.** The family-run "gray bear," just off the main piazza, serves tasty fare in a congenial atmosphere. Choose from typical regional dishes—look for *rufioi* (homemade ravioli stuffed with savoy cabbage)—served in a bright garden courtyard when the weather it fine. The wine list is mostly regional and pairs well with the menu. ✉ *Via degli Orti 19* ☎ *0461/984400* ⏲ *Closed Sun.*

5

WHERE TO STAY

$$ **Accademia.** This friendly hotel occupies an ancient, character-filled house in the historic center of Trento, close to Piazza del Duomo. **Pros:** central location; charming outdoor restaurant. **Cons:** some rooms are small; stark decor; basic breakfast. **TripAdvisor:** "no two rooms are the same," "beautiful terrace," "right at city center." ✉ *Vicolo Colico 4* ☎ *0461/233600* 🌐 *www.accademiahotel.it* *35 rooms, 5 suites* *In-room: safe, refrigerator, Internet, Wi-Fi. In-hotel: bar, some pets allowed* ⏲ *Closed late Dec.–early Jan.* *Breakfast.*

$–$$ **Castel Pergine.** A 13th-century castle, appropriated by Trento's prince-bishops in the 16th century, is now skillfully managed by Theo Schneider, an architect, and his charming wife, Verena Neff (a former translator), both from Switzerland. **Pros:** romantic setting; great restaurant. **Cons:** simple accommodations; need a car to get around. **TripAdvisor:** "gardens within the castle walls," "hilltop with stunning views," "intelligent, attentive service." ✉ *Via al Castello 10, Pergine Val Sugana* ✥ *12 km (7½ mi) east of Trento* ☎ *0461/531158* 🌐 *www.castelpergine.it* *21 rooms, 14 with bath* *In-room: no a/c, no TV. In-hotel: restaurant, bar, parking (free)* ⏲ *Closed Nov.–Mar. No lunch Mon.* *Breakfast.*

$$ **Grand Hotel Trento.** Its contemporary rounded facade amid ancient palaces makes this hotel on Piazza Dante an anomaly. **Pros:** near train station; professional service; great breakfast. **Cons:** not a quaint hotel; busy neighborhood. **TripAdvisor:** "elegant, comfortable and well-located," "bar is a happening place," "rooms are silent and spacious." ✉ *Via Alfieri 1* ☎ *0461/271000* 🌐 *www.grandhoteltrento.com* *126 rooms, 10 suites* *In-room: safe, refrigerator, Internet. In-hotel: restaurant, bar, spa, laundry service, Internet terminal, parking (paid)* *No meals.*

$$ **Hotel Garni Aquila d'Oro.** A prime location near Piazza del Duomo is a main selling point for the Aquila d'Oro. **Pros:** excellent location; friendly service. **Cons:** common areas rather cramped. **TripAdvisor:** "heart of the historic center," "small yet sophisticated hotel," "romantic experience." ✉ *Via Belenzani 76* ☎ *0461/986282* 🌐 *www.aquiladoro.it* *16 rooms* *In-room: safe, refrigerator, Wi-Fi. In-hotel: bar* ⏲ *Closed late Dec.–mid-Feb.* *Breakfast.*

¢ **Hotel Garni Venezia.** For reasonably priced accommodations, it's hard to beat this *garni* (bed-and-breakfast) right on Piazza Duomo. **Pros:** location; no TVs. **Cons:** piazza can be noisy; no TVs. **TripAdvisor:** "beautiful view," "basic but clean," "unbeatable location." ✉ *Piazza Duomo 45* ☎ *0461/234114* 🌐 *www.hotelveneziatn.it* *50 rooms* *In-room: no TV, Wi-Fi. In-hotel: parking (paid), some pets allowed* *Breakfast.*

$$$ **Imperial Grand Hotel Terme.** If you're in the mood for some pampering, choose the graciously restored, golden yellow palace in the nearby spa town of Levico Terme. **Pros:** beautiful park setting; pleasant indoor pool. **Cons:** standard rooms are small; use of thermal baths not included in rates. **TripAdvisor:** "fabulous former summer palace," "great garden," "just above the old village." ✉ *Via Silva Domini 1, Levico Terme* ✣ *20 km (12 mi) east of Trento* ☎ *0461/706104* 🌐 *www.imperialhotel.it* *69 rooms, 12 suites* *In-room: safe, refrigerator, Wi-Fi. In-hotel: 4 restaurants, bars, pools, gym, spa, bicycles, laundry service, parking (paid), some pets allowed* ⏲ *Closed Nov.–Mar.* *Some meals.*

SHOPPING

You can pick up meats, cheeses, produce, local truffles, and porcini mushrooms at the small morning market in **Piazza Alessandro Vittoria**. **Enoteca di Corso** (✉ *Corso 3 Novembre 64* ☎ *0461/916424*), a bit outside the town center, is a delightful shop laden with local products, including wine and sweets. A picnic can be handily assembled with local salamis and cheeses from **La Salumeria Mattei** (✉ *Via Mazzini 46* ☎ *0461/238053*). Whole-grain breads and delicate pastries can be purchased at fragrant **Panificio Pulin** (✉ *Via Cavour 23* ☎ *0461/234544*).

EN ROUTE

Traveling west and then north from Trento to Madonna di Campiglio, you zigzag through lovely mountain valleys, past small farming communities such as Tione. Outside the small mountain village of Pinzolo (on SS239), stop at the church of **San Vigilio** to see the remarkable 16th-century fresco on the exterior south wall. Painted in 1539 by the artist Simone Baschenis, the painting describes the Dance of Death: a macabre parade of 40 sinners from all walks of life (in roughly descending order of worldly importance), each guided to his end by a ghoulish escort. Unfortunately, the church's interior is closed to the public.

MADONNA DI CAMPIGLIO

80 km (50 mi) northwest of Trento, 100 km (62 mi) southwest of Bolzano.

VISITOR INFORMATION

Madonna di Campiglio tourism office (✉ *Via Pradalago 4* ☎ *0465/447501* 🌐 *www.campiglio.it*).

EXPLORING

The chichi winter resort of Madonna di Campiglio vies with Cortina d'Ampezzo as the most fashionable place for young Italians to ski and be seen in the Dolomites. Madonna's popularity is well deserved, with 39 lifts connecting more than 120 km (75 mi) of well-groomed ski runs. The resort itself is a modest 5,000 feet above sea level, but the downhill runs, summer hiking paths, and mountain-biking trails venture high up into the surrounding peaks (including Pietra Grande at

9,700 feet). Madonna's cachet is evident in its well-organized lodging, skiing, and trekking facilities.

The stunning pass at **Campo Carlo Magno** (5,500 feet) is 3 km (2 mi) north of Madonna di Campiglio. This is where Charlemagne is said to have stopped in AD 800 on his way to Rome to be crowned emperor. Stop here to glance over the whole of northern Italy. If you continue north, take the descent with caution—in the space of a mile or so, hairpin turns and switchbacks deliver you down more than 2,000 feet.

WHERE TO EAT AND STAY

$$ NORTHERN ITALIAN ★ **Cascina Zeledria.** This remote, rustic mountain restaurant near Campo Carlo Magno is not accessible by car; in winter you'll be collected on a motorized Sno-Cat and ferried up the slopes. After the 10-minute ride, sit down to grill your own meats and vegetables over stone griddles; the kitchen-prepared mushrooms and polenta are house specialties. Although the majority of meals in Madonna are taken in resort hotels, Italians consider an on-mountain dinner to be an indispensable part of a proper ski week. Call in advance to reserve a table—and arrange for transportation. ✉ *Località Zeledria* ☎ *0465/440303* 🌐 *www.zeledria.it* *Reservations essential* ⊗ *Closed May, June, Oct., and Nov.*

$$$–$$$$ **Golf Hotel.** You need to make your way north to the Campo Carlo Magno Pass to reach this grand hotel, the former summer residence of Habsburg emperor Franz Josef. **Pros:** attractive indoor pool; elegant rooms. **Cons:** long walk into town; popular with business groups. **TripAdvisor:** "nice views of the slopes," "high-level spa," "very professional and pleasant." ✉ *Via Cima Tosa 3* ☎ *0465/441003* 🌐 *www.atahotels.it* *109 rooms, 13 suites* *In-room: no a/c, safe, refrigerator, Internet, Wi-Fi. In-hotel: restaurant, room service, bar, golf course, pool, gym, spa, laundry service, parking (free), some pets allowed (paid)* ⊗ *Closed mid-Apr.–June and Sept.–Nov.* *Some meals.*

$$$ **Grifone.** A comfortable lodge sits catching the sun with a distinctive wood facade and flower-bedecked balconies. **Pros:** convenient location; charming decor. **Cons:** half board is mandatory; lacks air-conditioning. **TripAdvisor:** "contemporary and clean," "staff are incredibly friendly," "large lounge area." ✉ *Via Vallesinella 7* ☎ *0465/442002* 🌐 *www.hotelgrifone.it* *38 rooms, 2 suites* *In-room: no a/c, safe. In-hotel: restaurant, bar, spa, Internet terminal, Wi-Fi hotspot, parking (free)* ⊗ *Closed mid-Apr.–June and Sept.–Nov.* *Some meals.*

SPORTS AND THE OUTDOORS

HIKING AND CLIMBING

The Madonna di Campiglio tourism office has maps of a dozen trails leading to waterfalls, lakes, and stupefying views. The cable car to 6,900-foot **Punta Spinale** (*Spinale Peak* ✉ *Off Via Monte Spinale* ☎ *0465/447744* *Cable car €9 round-trip*) offers skiers magnificent views of the Brenta Dolomites in winter. It also runs during peak summer season.

SKIING

Miles of interconnecting ski runs—some of the best in the Dolomites—are linked by the cable cars and lifts of **Funivie Madonna di Campiglio** (✉ *Via Presanella 12* ☎ *0465/447744* 🌐 *www.funiviecampiglio.it*). Advanced skiers will delight in the extremely difficult terrain found on certain mountain faces, but there are also many intermediate and beginner runs, all accessible from town. There are also plenty of off-piste opportunities. Ski passes (€35–€38 per day, discounts for multiple days) can be purchased at the main *funivia* (cable car) in town.

EN ROUTE

The route between Madonna di Campiglio and Bormio (2½ hours) takes you through a series of high mountain passes. After Campo Carlo Magno, turn left at Dimaro and continue 37 km (23 mi) west through Passo del Tonale (6,200 feet). At Ponte di Legno, turn north on SS300. You pass the *Lago Nero* (Black Lake) on your left just before the summit. Continue on to Bormio through the Passo di Gavia (8,600 feet).

THE WESTERN DOLOMITES

The Parco Nazionale dello Stelvio extends through western Trentino and the Altoaltesino area of Alto Adige, and even into eastern Lombardia. It's named for the famed Stelvio, Europe's highest road pass and the site of the highest battle fought during World War I. The town of Bormio is well preserved and merits a visit for its history and character, even if you don't want to ski or indulge in spa treatments, both of which it's renowned for.

BORMIO

97 km (60 mi) northwest of Madonna di Campiglio, 100 km (62 mi) southwest of Merano.

VISITOR INFORMATION

Bormio tourism office (✉ *Via Roma 131/B* ☎ *0342/903300* 🖷 *0342/904696* 🌐 *www.bookbormio.com or www.valtellina.it*).

EXPLORING

At the foot of Stelvio Pass, Bormio is the most famous ski resort on the western side of the Dolomites, with 38 km (24 mi) of long pistes and a 5,000-plus-foot vertical drop. In summer its cool temperatures and clean air entice Italians away from cities in the humid Lombard plain. This dual-season popularity supports the plentiful shops, restaurants, and hotels in town. Bormio has been known for the therapeutic qualities of its waters since the Roman era, and there are numerous spas.

Ancient Roman baths predate the wonderland of thermal springs, caves, and waterfalls now known as the **Bagni Vecchi** *(Old Baths)*; Leonardo da Vinci soaked here in 1493. ✉ *Strada Statale Stelvio* ☎ *0342/910131* 🌐 *www.bagnidibormio.it* 🎫 *Weekdays €41, weekends €45* ⏲ *Daily 11–8, weekends 11–11.*

Modern facilities and comprehensive spa treatments are available at **Bormio Terme.** ✉ *Via Stelvio 14* ☎ *0342/901325* 🌐 *www.bormioterme.it* 🎫 *Weekdays €19, weekends €23* ⏲ *Sat.–Tues., Thurs. 9–9; Wed., Fri. 9 am–10:30 pm; closed 20 days in May.*

Bormio makes a good base for exploring the Alps' biggest national park, the **Parco Nazionale dello Stelvio** spread over 1,350 square km (520 square mi) and four provinces. Opened in 1935 to preserve flora and protect fauna, today it has more than 1,200 types of plants, 600 different mushrooms, and more than 160 species of animals, including the chamois, ibex, and roe deer. There are many entrances to the park, and a dozen visitor centers; the closest entrance to Bormio is the year-round gateway at Torre Alberti. ✉ *Via Roma 26* ☎ *0342/901654* 🌐 *www.parks.it/parco.nazionale.stelvio* *Free.*

WHERE TO EAT AND STAY

$ NORTHERN ITALIAN ✕ **Caffe Kuerc.** This building was for centuries where justice was publicly served to accused witches, among others. These days, things at the restaurant are rather more refined: enjoy local specialties like *bresaola* (salted, air-dried beef) with lemon and olive oil, or *pizzoccheri* (buckwheat pasta) with garlic and winter vegetables. ✉ *Piazza Cavour 8* ☎ *0342/910787* ⏲ *Closed Tues.*

$–$$ ★ **La Genzianella.** Here you get Alpine chic without expense or pretense. **Pros:** great for bikers; handy to slopes and town. **Cons:** no pool. **TripAdvisor:** "you really feel at home," "right level of informal comfort," "short walk off the slope." ✉ *Via Zandilla 6* ☎ *0342/904485* 🌐 *www.genzianella.com* *40 rooms* *In-room: no a/c, safe, Wi-Fi. In-hotel: restaurant, bar, gym, sauna, Wi-Fi hotspot, parking (free)* ⏲ *Closed May and Sept.–Dec.* *Breakfast.*

$$ **Nazionale.** Bordering Stelvio National Park, the Nazionale caters to both the winter and summer crowds. **Pros:** great location; winter and summer activities; family-friendly environment. **Cons:** no air-conditioning; may require a 20% supplement for stays of fewer than three nights. **TripAdvisor:** "excellent food," "plenty of hot water," "Internet access too expensive." ✉ *Via al Forte 28* ☎ *0342/903361* 🌐 *www.nazionalebormio.it* *48 rooms* *In-room: no a/c, safe, refrigerator, Wi-Fi. In-hotel: 2 restaurants, bar, gym, pool, parking (free), Wi-Fi hotspot* *Some meals.*

SKIING

You can buy a ski pass (€34–€38 per day) and pick up a trail map at the base **funivia** (*Cable car* ✉ *Via Battaglion Morbegno 25* ☎ *0342/902770* 🌐 *www.skipassaltavaltellina.it*) in the center of town to connect to the Bormio 2000 station (6,600 feet) on Vallecetta, the main resort mountain. From there, you can ski down intermediate trails (which comprise the majority of Bormio's runs), use the extensive lift network to explore secondary ski areas, or get another funivia up to the Bormio 3000 station at Cima Bianca (9,800 feet) for more challenging terrain. The cable car also runs July to mid-September, when it is used by mountain bikers to reach long trails through breathtaking Alpine terrain; less ambitious visitors can wander around and then ride the cable car back down.

PASSO DELLO STELVIO

20 km (12 mi) north of Bormio, 80 km (48 mi) west of Merano.

★ At more than 9,000 feet, the Passo dello Stelvio is the second-highest pass in Europe, connecting the Valtellina in Lombardy with the Val Venosta in Alto Adige. The view from the top is well worth the drive; looking north you can see Switzerland. The pass is open from May or June to October, depending on weather conditions. Stelvio itself is a year-round skiing center, with many of its runs open in summer.

EN ROUTE Between the Stelvio Pass and the town of Spondigna, 30 km (19 mi) of road wind down 48 hair-raising hairpin turns. The views are spectacular, but this descent is not for the faint of heart. In Spondigna, keep to the right for the road to Naturno.

BOLZANO (BOZEN)

32 km (19 mi) south of Merano, 50 km (31 mi) north of Trento.

Bolzano (Bozen), capital of the autonomous province of Alto Adige, is tucked among craggy peaks in a Dolomite valley 77 km (48 mi) from the Brenner Pass and Austria. Tirolean culture dominates Bolzano's language, food, architecture, and people. It may be hard to remember that you're in Italy when walking the city's colorful cobblestone streets and visiting its lantern-lighted cafés, where you may enjoy sauerkraut and a beer among a lively crowd of blue-eyed German speakers. However, fine Italian espresso, fashionable boutiques, and reasonable prices will help remind you where you are. With castles and steeples topping the landscape, this quiet city at the confluence of the Isarco (Eisack) and Talvera rivers has retained a provincial appeal. Proximity to fabulous skiing and mountain climbing—not to mention the world's oldest preserved mummy—make it a worthwhile, and still undiscovered, tourist destination. And its streets are immaculate: with the highest per capita earnings of any city in Italy, Bolzano's residents enjoy a standard of living that is second to none.

VISITOR INFORMATION

Bolzano tourism office (✉ *Piazza Walther 8* ☎ *0471/307000* 📠 *0471/980128* 🌐 *www.bolzano-bozen.it*).

EXPLORING BOLZANO

TOP ATTRACTIONS

Chiesa dei Domenicani. The 13th-century Dominican Church is renowned as Bolzano's main repository for paintings, especially frescoes. In the adjoining **Cappella di San Giovanni** you can see works from the Giotto school that show the birth of a pre-Renaissance sense of depth and individuality; come prepared with 50-cent coins for the lights. The church and chapel are closed to the public during religious ceremonies. ✉ *Piazza Domenicani* ☎ *0471/973133* ⏲ *Mon.–Sat. 9:30–5, Sun. noon–6.*

Duomo. A lacy spire looks down on the mosaic-like roof tiles of the city's Gothic cathedral, built between the 12th and 14th centuries. Inside are 14th- and 15th-century frescoes and an intricately carved stone pulpit dating from 1514. Outside, don't miss the **Porta del Vino** (Wine Gate) on the northeast side; decorative carvings of grapes and harvest workers attest to the long-standing importance of wine to this region. The church is closed to the public during religious ceremonies. ✉ *Piazza Walther* ☎ *0471/978676* ⏲ *Mon.–Sat. 10–noon and 2–5.*

Fodor's Choice ★ **Museo Archeologico dell'Alto Adige.** This museum has gained international fame for Ötzi, its 5,300-year-old iceman, discovered in 1991 and the world's oldest naturally preserved body. In 1998 Italy acquired it from

Chiesa dei Domenicani **3**
Duomo **2**
Museo Archeologico dell'Alto Adige **5**
Piazza delle Erbe **4**
Piazza Walther **1**

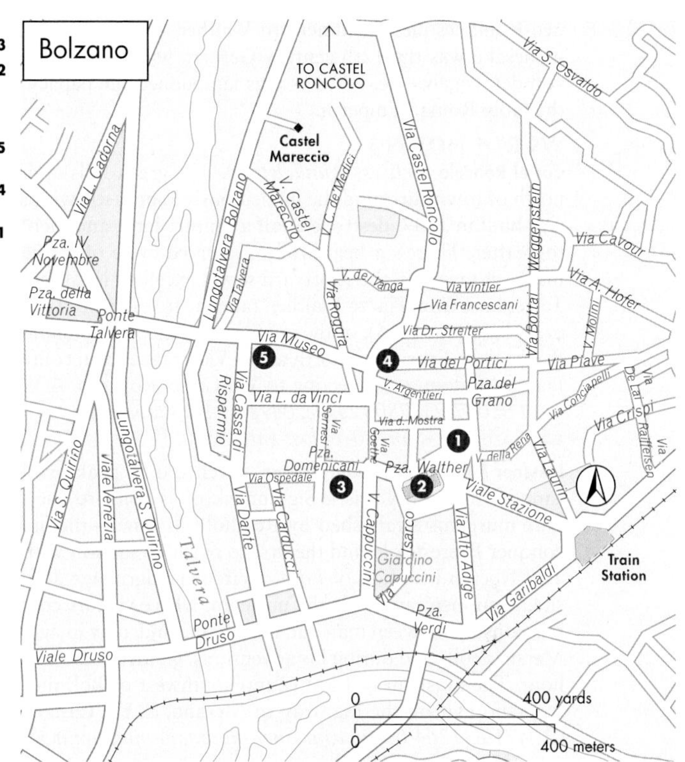

Austria after it was determined that the body lay 100 yards inside Italy. The iceman's leathery remains are displayed in a freezer vault, preserved along with his longbow, ax, and clothing. The rest of the museum relies on models and artifacts from nearby archaeological sites (an eloquent English audio guide is €2) to lead you not only through Ötzi's Copper Age, but also into the preceding Mesolithic and Neolithic eras, and the Bronze and Iron ages that followed. In July and August, the museum's supervised play area keeps young children entertained while adults experience the museum. ✉ *Via Museo 43* ☎ *0471/320120* 🌐 *www.iceman.it* 🎫 *€9* ⏲ *July, Aug., and Dec., daily 10–6; Jan.–June and Sept.–Nov., Tues.–Sun. 10–6; last entry 5:30.*

Piazza delle Erbe. A bronze statue of Neptune, which dates to 1745, presides over a bountiful fruit-and-vegetable market in this square. The stalls spill over with colorful displays of local produce; bakeries and grocery stores showcase hot breads, pastries, cheeses, and delicatessen meats—a complete picnic. Try the *speck tirolese* (a thinly sliced smoked ham) and the apple strudel.

Piazza Walther. This pedestrians-only square is Bolzano's heart; in warmer weather it serves as an open-air living room where locals and tourists alike can be found at all hours sipping a drink (such as a glass of chilled Riesling). In the center stands Heinrich Natter's white-marble,

5

neo-Romanesque **Monument to Walther,** built in 1889. The piazza's namesake was the 12th-century German wandering minstrel Walther von der Vogelweide, whose songs lampooned the papacy and praised the Holy Roman Emperor.

WORTH NOTING

Castel Roncolo *(Schloss Runkelstein)*. The green hills and farmhouses north of town surround the meticulously kept castle with a red roof. It was built in 1237, destroyed half a century later, and then rebuilt soon thereafter. There's a beautifully preserved cycle of medieval frescoes inside. A tavern in the courtyard serves excellent local food and wines. To get here from Piazza Walther, take the free shuttle (Tuesday–Sunday every half hour 10–5), or the number 12 bus. It's a 20-minute walk from Piazza delle Erbe: head north along Via Francescani, continue through Piazza Madonna, connecting to Via Castel Roncolo. ✉ *Via San Antonio 1* ☎ *0471/329808 castle, 0471/324073 tavern* 🌐 *www.roncolo.info* 🎟 *€8* 🕓 *Tues.–Sun. 10–6; last entry 5:30.*

Messner Mountain Museum Firmian. Perched on a peak overlooking Bolzano, 10th-century Castle Sigmundskron is home to one of five Dolomite museums established by Reinhold Messner—the first climber to conquer Everest solo and the first to reach its summit without oxygen. The Tibetan tradition of *kora,* a circular pilgrimage around a sacred site, is an inspiration for the museum, where visitors contemplate the relationship between man and mountain, guided by images and objects Messner collected during his adventures. Guided tours begin every half hour. The museum is 3 km (2 mi) southwest of Bolzano, just off the Appiano exit on the highway to Merano. ✉ *Via Castel Firmiano 53* ☎ *0471/631264* 🌐 *www.messner-mountain-museum.it* 🎟 *€8* 🕓 *Mar.–late-Nov., Tues.–Sun. 10–6.*

Passeggiata del Guncina. An 8-km (5-mi) botanical promenade dating from 1892 ends with a panoramic view of Bolzano. ✉ *Entrance near Vecchia Parrocchiale, in Gries, across river and up Corso Libertà.*

Vecchia Parrocchiale *(Old Parish Church)*. Visit this church, said to have been built in 1141, to see its two medieval treasures: an 11th-century Romanesque crucifix and an elaborately carved 15th-century wooden altar by Michael Pacher—a true masterpiece of the Gothic style. ✉ *Via Martin Knoller, in Gries, across river and up Corso Libertà* ☎ *0471/283089* 🕓 *Apr.–Oct., weekdays 10:30–noon and 2:30–4.*

WHERE TO EAT

$–$$ NORTHERN ITALIAN

✕ **Alexander.** Typical Tirolean dishes are served at this convivial restaurant. The venison ham and the lamb cutlets *al timo con salsa all'aglio* (with thyme and garlic sauce) are particularly good, but make sure to leave room for the rich chocolate cake. ✉ *Via Aosta 37* ☎ *0471/918608* 🕓 *Closed Sat.*

$ WINE BAR ★

✕ **Batzenhausl.** Locals hold animated conversations over glasses of regional wine in a modern take on the traditional Weinstube (wine tavern, often abbreviated to "stube"). Tasty south Tirolean specialties include speck tirolese and *mezzelune casarecce ripiene* (house-made stuffed half-moons of pasta). If you're seeking a quiet meal, ask for a table on the second floor, near the handsome stained-glass windows. This is a good spot for a late bite, as food is served until midnight. ✉ *Via Andreas Hofer 30* ☎ *0471/050950* 🌐 *www.batzen.it.*

$ NORTHERN ITALIAN ✕ **Cavallino Bianco.** This restaurant near Via dei Portici is a dependable favorite with residents and visitors alike. A wide selection of Italian and German dishes is served in a spacious, comfortable dining room, where there are usually many extended families enjoying their meals together. ✉ *Via Bottai 6* ☎ *0471/973267* ⏲ *Closed Sun. No dinner Sat.*

$ NORTHERN ITALIAN ✕ **Hopfen & Co.** Fried white *Würstel* (sausage), sauerkraut, and grilled ribs complement the excellent home-brewed Austrian-style pilsner and wheat beer at this lively pub-restaurant. There's live music on Thursday night, attracting Bolzano's students and young professionals. ✉ *Piazza delle Erbe, Obstplatz 17* ☎ *0471/300788* 🌐 *www.boznerbier.it.*

$$ NORTHERN ITALIAN ✕ **Wirthaus Vögele.** Ask residents of Bolzano where they like to dine out, and odds are good they'll tell you Vögele, one of the area's oldest inns. The classic wood-panel dining room on the ground level is often packed with diners, but don't despair, as the restaurant has two additional floors. The menu features Sud Tyrol standards, including canederli with speck and venison. ✉ *Goethestr 3* ☎ *0471/973938* 🌐 *www.voegele.it* ⏲ *Closed Sun.*

5

WHERE TO STAY

$$$ Fodor's Choice ★ **Hotel Greif.** Even in a hospitable region, the Greif is a rare gem. **Pros:** elegant decor; helpful staff; central location. **Cons:** rooms vary in size; sometimes filled with tour groups. **TripAdvisor:** "right on the main town square," "room was clearly lovingly designed," "Bulgari toiletries were a classy touch." ✉ *Piazza Walther 1* ☎ *0471/318000* 🌐 *www.greif.it* *27 rooms, 6 suites* *In-room: safe, refrigerator, Internet. In-hotel: laundry service, parking (paid)* *Breakfast.*

$$ **Luna-Mondschein.** This central yet secluded hotel in a tranquil garden dates from 1798. **Pros:** central location; great buffet breakfast. **Cons:** rooms vary in size; rooms facing garage noisy. **TripAdvisor:** "location was great," "small balcony overlooking the park," "staff were courteous and helpful." ✉ *Via Piave 15* ☎ *0471/975642* 🌐 *www.hotel-luna.it* *80 rooms* *In-room: a/c (some), Wi-Fi (some). In-hotel: 3 restaurants, room service, bar, laundry service, parking (paid), some pets allowed* *Breakfast.*

$$–$$$ ★ **Parkhotel Laurin.** An exercise in art nouveau opulence, Parkhotel Laurin ranks among the finest lodging in all of Alto Adige, with art-filled modern guest rooms and handsome public spaces. **Pros:** convenient location; excellent restaurant. **Cons:** rooms facing park can be noisy; packed with business groups. **TripAdvisor:** "large, old-fashioned hotel," "room was very large and bright," "amazing garden area." ✉ *Via Laurin 4* ☎ *0471/311000* 🌐 *www.laurin.it* *93 rooms, 7 suites* *In-room: safe, refrigerator, Internet. In-hotel: Internet terminal, restaurant, bar, pool, laundry service, parking (paid)* *Breakfast.*

$$–$$$ ★ **Schloss Korb.** This romantic 13th-century castle with crenellations and a massive tower is perched in a park amid vine-covered hills. **Pros:** romantic setting; charming traditional furnishings. **Cons:** not all rooms are in the castle; need a car to get around. **TripAdvisor:** "feeling you

CLOSE UP

Enrosadira and the Dwarf King

The Dolomites, the inimitable craggy peaks Le Corbusier called "the most beautiful work of architecture ever seen," are never so arresting as at dusk, when the last rays of sun create a pink hue that languishes into purple. In the Ladin language, spoken only in the isolated valleys below, this magnificent transformation has its own word—the *enrosadira*. You can certainly enjoy this phenomenon from a distance, but one of the things that makes the Dolomites such an appealing year-round destination is the multitude of options for getting onto the mountains themselves. Whether you come for a pleasant stroll or a technical ascent in summer, to plunge down sheer faces or glide across peaceful valleys in winter, or to brave narrow switchbacks in a rented Fiat, your perspective, like the peaks around you, can only become more rose colored.

The enrosadira is so striking that it has prompted speculation about its origins. The French nobleman and geologist Déodat Guy Silvain Tancrède Gratet de Dolomieu (1750–1801) took the scientific approach: he got his name applied to the range after demonstrating that the peaks have a particular composition of stratified calcium magnesium carbonate that generates the evening glow. For those unconvinced that such a phenomenon can be explained by geology alone, Ladin legend offers a compelling alternative.

Laurin, King of the Dwarfs, became infatuated with the daughter of a neighboring (human) king, and captured her with the aid of a magic hood that made him invisible. As he spirited her back to the mountains, the dwarf king was pursued by many knights who were able to track the kidnapper after spotting his beloved rose garden. Laurin was captured and imprisoned, and when he finally managed to escape and return home, he cast a spell turning the betraying roses into rocks—so they could be seen neither by day nor by night. But Laurin forgot to include dusk in his spell, which is why the Dolomites take on a rosy glow just before nightfall. (This story is the subject of frescoes in the bar of Bolzano's Parkhotel Laurin.)

are staying with royalty," "perfect hideaway in the mountains," "ideal for a romantic holiday." ✉ *Via Castel d'Appiano 5, Missiano/Appiano* ☎ *0471/636000* 🌐 *www.schlosskorb.com* *35 rooms, 10 suites* *In-room: Internet, no a/c. In-hotel: restaurant, bar, tennis courts, pools, gym, laundry service, Internet terminal, parking (paid)* ⊗ *Closed Nov.–Mar.* 🍽 *Some meals.*

ALTO ADIGE

Prosperous valley towns (such as the famed spa center Merano) and mountain resorts entice those seeking both relaxation and adventure. Alto Adige (Südtirol) was for centuries part of the Austro-Hungarian Empire, only ceded to Italy at the end of World War I. Ethnic differences led to inevitable tensions in the 1960s and again in the '80s, though a large measure of provincial autonomy has, for the most part, kept the lid on nationalist ambitions. Today Germanic and Italian balance harmoniously, as do medieval and modern influences, with ancient castles regularly playing host to contemporary art exhibitions.

MERANO (MERAN)

★ *24 km (15 mi) north of Bolzano, 16 km (10 mi) east of Naturno.*

VISITOR INFORMATION

Merano tourism office (✉ *Corso Libertà 45* ☎ *0473/272000* 🌐 *www.meran.eu*).

EXPLORING

The second-largest town in Alto Adige, Merano (Meran) was once the capital of the Austrian region of Tirol. When the town and surrounding area were ceded to Italy as part of the 1919 Treaty of Versailles, Innsbruck became the capital. Merano, however, continued to be known as a spa town, attracting European nobility for its therapeutic waters and its grape cure, which consists simply of eating the grapes grown on the surrounding hillsides. Sheltered by mountains, Merano has an unusually mild climate, with summer temperatures rarely exceeding 80°F (27°C) and winters that usually stay above freezing, despite the skiing that is within easy reach. Along the narrow streets of Merano's old town, houses have little towers and huge wooden doors, and the pointed arches of the Gothic cathedral sit next to neoclassical and art nouveau buildings. Merano serves as a good respite from mountain adventures, or from the bustle of nearby Trento and Bolzano.

The 14th-century Gothic **Duomo**, with a crenellated facade and an ornate campanile, sits in the heart of the old town. The Capella di Santa Barbara, just behind the cathedral, is an octagonal church containing a 15th-century pietà. ✉ *Piazza del Duomo* ☎ *0473/230174* ⏲ *Easter–Sept., daily 8–noon and 2:30–8; Oct.–Easter, daily 8–noon and 2:30–7.*

★ The **Terme di Merano** is a sprawling spa complex with 25 pools (including a brine pool with underwater music) and eight saunas (with an indoor "snow room" available for cooling down). Along with the family-friendly options for bathing, personalized services for grown-ups include traditional cures using local products, such as grape-based applications and whey baths. An admission charge of €11 gets you two hours in thermal baths; €23 is for a full day's use of all baths and saunas. ✉ *Piazza Terme 9* ☎ *0473/252000* 🌐 *www.termemerano.it* ⏲ *Daily 9 am–10 pm.*

Castel Trauttmansdorff, a Gothic castle 2 km (1 mi) southeast of town, was restored in the 19th century, and now serves as a museum, celebrating 200 years of tourism in south Tirol. Outside, a sprawling garden has

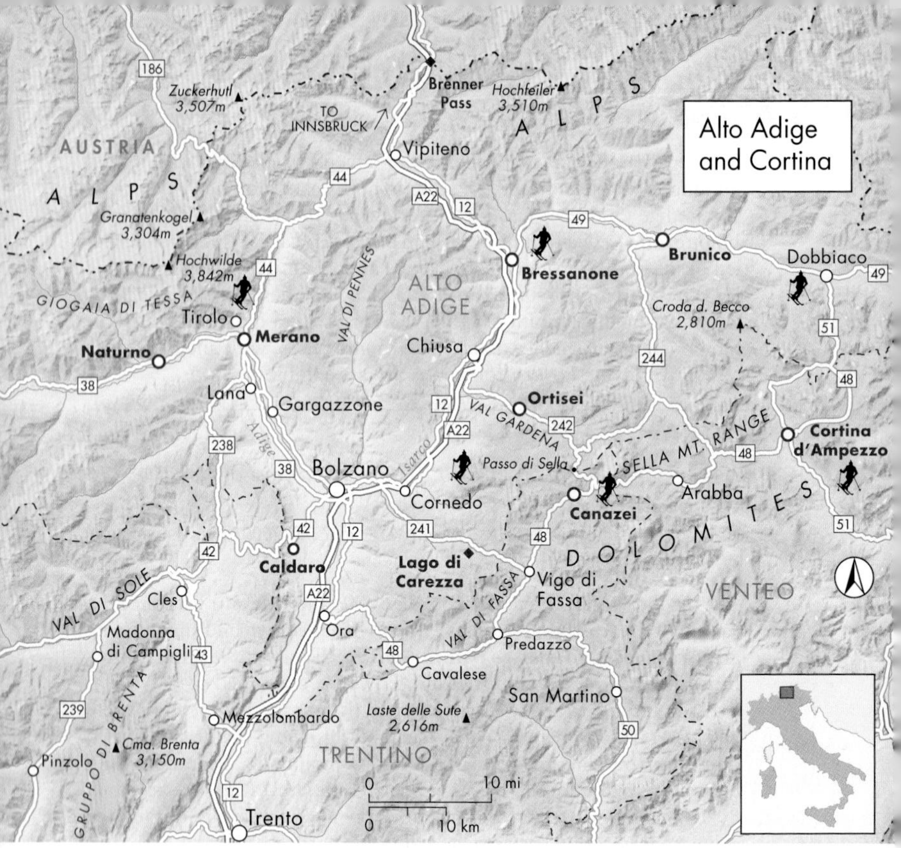

an extensive display of exotic flora organized by country of origin. An English-language audio guide is available for €2.50. ✉ *Via Valentino 51a* ☎ *0473/235730* 🌐 *www.trauttmansdorff.it* 🎫 *€10.20* ⏲ *Apr.–May 14 and Sept. 16–Nov. 15, daily 9–6; May 15–Sept. 15, daily 9–9.*

Overlooking the town atop Mt. Tappeinerweg is Castel Fontana, which was the home of poet Ezra Pound from 1958 to 1964. Still in the Pound family, the castle now houses the **Museo Agricolo di Brunnenburg**, devoted to Tirolean country life. Among its exhibits are a blacksmith's shop and, not surprisingly, a room with Pound memorabilia. To get here, take Bus 3, which departs every hour on the hour, from Merano to Dorf Tirol (20 minutes). ✉ *Via Castello 17, Brunnenburg* ☎ *0473/923533* 🎫 *€3* ⏲ *Apr.–Oct., Sun.–Thurs. 10–5.*

Fodor's Choice ★ A stroll along one of Merano's well-marked, impossibly pleasant **promenades** may yield even better relaxation than a spa treatment. **Passeggiata Tappeiner** (Tappeiner's Promenade) is a 3-km (2-mi) path with panoramic views from the hills north of the Duomo and diverse botanical pleasures along the way. **Passeggiata d'Estate** (Summer Promenade) runs along the shaded south bank of the Passirio River, and the **Passeggiata d'Inverno** (Winter Promenade), on the exposed north bank, provides more warmth and the Wandelhalle—a sunny area decorated with idyllic paintings of surrounding villages. The popular Austrian empress Sissi (Elisabeth of Wittelsbach, 1837–98) put Merano on the map as a spa destination; a trail named in her honor, the **Sentiero di Sissi** (Sissi's Walk), follows a path from Castel Trauttmansdorff to the heart of Merano.

QUICK BITES

Cafe Saxifraga (✉ *Passeggiata Tappeiner* ☎ *0473/239249* 🌐 *www.saxifraga.it*) occupies an enviable position overlooking Merano and the peaks enveloping the town; an extensive selection of teas and other beverages can be enjoyed on the patio, which has panoramic views.

WHERE TO EAT

$ NORTHERN ITALIAN — ✕ **Haisrainer.** Among the rustic wine taverns lining Via dei Portici, this one is most popular with locals and tourists alike; a menu in English is available for the latter. Warm wooden walls provide a comfortable setting for Tirolean and Italian standards: try the *zuppa al vino bianco* (stew with white wine) or the seasonal risottos (with asparagus in spring, or Barolo wine in chillier months). ✉ *Via dei Portici 100* ☎ *0473/237944* ⏲ *Closed Sun.*

$$ ITALIAN — ✕ **Sieben.** Young Meraners crowd the hip bar on the ground floor of this modern bistro, in the town's central arcade. Upstairs, a more mature crowd enjoys the contemporary cooking and attentive service in the jazz-themed dining room. Sieben occasionally hosts jazz concerts in summer. ✉ *Via dei Portici 232* ☎ *0473/210636* 🌐 *www.bistrosieben.it* ⏲ *Closed Tues. Nov.–Mar.*

$$$ NORTHERN ITALIAN ★ — ✕ **Sissi.** In this relaxed, light-filled restaurant just off Via dei Portici, rustic regional dishes are prepared with the precision of haute Italian cooking. Menu choices may include gnocchi *di formaggio con salsa all' erba cipollina* (with cheese and chives) and *vitello alle castagne e tartufo nero* (veal with chestnuts and black truffles); a set menu (€60–€65) provides a complete four-course dinner. ✉ *Via Galilei 44* ☎ *0473/231062* 🌐 *www.andreafenoglio.com* ✍ *Reservations essential* ⏲ *Closed Mon. and last 2 wks Feb.*

$$ NORTHERN ITALIAN — ✕ **Vinoteca-Pizzeria Relax.** If you have difficulty choosing from the long list of appetizing pizzas here, ask the friendly English-speaking staff for help with the menu. You're unlikely to find a better selection of wine, or a more pleasant environment for sampling. You can also buy bottles of the locally produced vintage to take home. ✉ *Via Cavour 31, opposite Palace Hotel* ☎ *0473/236735* 🌐 *www.weine-relax.it* ⏲ *Closed Sun. and 2 wks in late Feb.*

WHERE TO STAY

$$$–$$$$ — 🏨 **Castello Labers.** The red-tile gables, towers, and turrets give this castle its unmistakably Tirolean style, as it sits on a hilltop amid forested slopes. **Pros:** romantic setting; spectacular views. **Cons:** long walk into town; some bathrooms are small. **TripAdvisor:** "full of antiques," "lovely views over the vineyards," "basic and lacking a finesse." ✉ *Via Labers 25* ☎ *0473/234484* 🌐 *www.labers.it* 🛏 *32 rooms, 1 suite* 👍 *In-room: no a/c, safe, Wi-Fi (some). In-hotel: restaurant, tennis court, pool, Internet terminal* ⏲ *Closed early-Nov.–late-Apr.* 🍽 *Breakfast.*

$ — 🏨 **Conte di Merano.** If you don't feel like paying for one of Merano's resorts, this simple central hotel is a good alternative. **Pros:** excellent base for exploring Merano; reasonable rates. **Cons:** basic decor; some street noise. ✉ *Via delle Corse 78* ☎ *0473/490260* 🌐 *www.grafvonmeran.com* *20 rooms* *In-room: safe, refrigerator. In-hotel: restaurant, bar* *Breakfast.*

NATURNO (NATURNS)

44 km (27 mi) northwest of Bolzano, 61 km (38 mi) east of Passo dello Stelvio.

VISITOR INFORMATION

Naturno tourism office (✉ *Piazza Municipio 1* ☎ *0473/666077* 📠 *0473/666369* 🌐 *www.naturns.it*).

EXPLORING

Colorful houses covered with murals line the streets of Naturno (Naturns), a sunny horticultural center.

Art lovers will appreciate the church of **San Procolo** *(Prokolus)*. The frescoes inside are some of the oldest in the German-speaking world, dating from the 8th century. A small, modern museum offers multimedia installations (in Italian or German only) presenting four epochs in the region's history: ancient, medieval, Gothic, and the era of the Great Plague of 1636 (which claimed a quarter of Naturno's population, some of whom are buried in the church's cemetery). ✉ *Via San Procolo* ☎ *0473/667312* 🌐 *www.procolo.org* *€5 church and museum* *2 wks before Easter–Oct., Tues.–Sun. 9:30–noon and 2:30–5:30; Nov.–2 wks before Easter, Tues.–Sun. 9:30–noon and 2:30–5.*

The 13th-century **Castel Juval** is in the hills above the hamlet of Stava, a five-minute shuttle ride from Naturno (there is no parking at the castle), or an hour's hike on many local trails. Since 1983 it's been the home of the South Tirolese climber and polar adventurer Reinhold Messner—the first climber to conquer Everest solo. Part of the castle has been turned into one of five in Messner's chain of Dolomite museums, giving guided tours of his collection of Tibetan art and masks from around the world. ✉ *Viale Europa 2* ☎ *0473/631264, 0473/668058 shuttle* 🌐 *www.messner-mountain-museum.it* *€7* *Apr.–mid-Nov., Tues.–Sun. 10–6.*

WHERE TO EAT

$–$$ NORTHERN ITALIAN **Schlosswirt Juval.** Below Castel Juval, Reinhold Messner's restored farmhouse is home to an old-style restaurant serving Mediterranean standards and traditional local dishes. Not to be missed are the smoked hams and flavorful cheeses provisioned from the farm outside; they are well paired with the estate's Castel Juval wine. Dinner is often accompanied by live jazz. ✉ *Juval 2* ☎ *0473/668056* 🌐 *www.schlosswirtjuval.it* *No credit cards* *Closed Wed. and mid-Dec.–mid-Mar.*

CALDARO (KALTERN)

15 km (9 mi) south of Bolzano.

VISITOR INFORMATION

Caldaro tourism office (✉ *Piazza Mercato 8* ☎ *0471/963169* 🌐 *www.kaltern.com or www.suedtiroler-weinstrasse.it*).

EXPLORING

A vineyard village with clear views of castles high up on the surrounding mountains represents the centuries of division that forged the unique character of the area. Caldaro architecture is famous for the way it blends Italian Renaissance elements of balance and harmony with the soaring windows and peaked arches of the Germanic Gothic tradition. The church of Santa Caterina, on the main square, is a good example.

Close to Caldaro's main square is the **South Tyrolean Wine Museum**, with exhibits on how local wine has historically been made, stored, served, and worshipped. You can board the bus in front of the tourist office at 10 each Thursday for a museum tour and wine tasting in the cellar, or call ahead to reserve. ✉ *Via dell'Oro 1* ☎ *0471/963168* 🌐 *www.weinmuseum.it* 🎫 *€3, wine tasting €4.60* ⏲ *Easter–Oct., Tues.–Sat. 10–5, Sun. 10–noon.*

5

BRESSANONE (BRIXEN)

40 km (25 mi) northeast of Bolzano.

VISITOR INFORMATION

Bressanone tourism office (✉ *Via Stazione 9* ☎ *0472/836401* 🌐 *www.brixen.org*).

EXPLORING

Bressanone (Brixen) is an important artistic center and was the seat of prince-bishops for centuries. Like their counterparts in Trento, these medieval administrators had the delicate task of serving two masters—the pope (the ultimate spiritual authority) and the Holy Roman Emperor (the civil and military power), who were virtually at war throughout the Middle Ages. Bressanone's prince-bishops became experts at tact and diplomacy.

The imposing **Duomo** was built in the 13th century but acquired a baroque facade 500 years later; its 14th-century cloister is decorated with medieval frescoes. Free guided tours (in German or Italian) are available April–October, Monday–Saturday at 10:30 and 3. ✉ *Piazza Duomo* ⏲ *Daily 6–noon and 3–6.*

The Bishop's Palace houses the **Museo Diocesano** *(Diocesan Museum)* and its abundance of local medieval art, particularly Gothic wood carvings. The wooden statues and liturgical objects were all collected from the cathedral treasury. During the Christmas season, curators arrange the museum's large collection of antique Nativity scenes; look for the shepherds wearing Tirolean hats. ✉ *Palazzo Vescovile 2* ☎ *0472/830505* 🌐 *www.dioezesanmuseum.bz.it* 🎫 *€7* ⏲ *Museum: mid-Mar.–Oct. and Nov. 27–Jan. 6, Tues.–Sun. 10–5; closed Dec. 24 and 25.*

At **Abbazia di Novacella,** an Augustinian abbey founded in 1142, they've been making wine for at least nine centuries. In the tasting room you can sample varietals produced in the Isarco Valley; Novacella is most famous for the delicate stone-fruit character of its dry white Sylvaner. You can also wander the delightful grounds; note the progression of Romanesque, Gothic, and baroque building styles. Guided tours of the abbey (in Italian and German) depart daily at 10, 11, 2, 3, and 4, as well as at noon and 1 in summer; from January through March, tours are by reservation only. ✉ *Località Novacella 1, Varna* ✣ *3 km (2 mi) north of Bressanone* ☎ *0472/836189* 🌐 *www.kloster-neustift.it* 🎫 *Grounds and tasting room free, guided tours €5.50* ⏲ *Grounds: Mon.–Sat. 10–7. Tasting room: Mon.–Sat. 9:15–noon and 2–6.*

WHERE TO EAT AND STAY

$$ NORTHERN ITALIAN ✕ **Fink.** The rustic wood-paneled dining room is upstairs in this restaurant under the arcades of the pedestrians-only town center. Try the *carré di maiale gratinato* (pork chops roasted with cheese and served with cabbage and potatoes) or the *castrato alla paesana,* a substantial lamb stew. In addition to hearty Tirolean specialties, there's an affordable daily set menu, as well as homemade pastries. ✉ *Via Portici Minori 4* ☎ *0472/834883* 🌐 *www.restaurant-fink.it* ⏲ *Closed Wed., 1 wk in Feb., 2 wks in May. No dinner Tues.*

$$$ ★ 🏨 **Elephant.** This cozy inn, 550 years old and still one of the region's best, takes its name from the 1551 visit of King John III of Portugal, who stopped here while leading an elephant (a present for Austria's Emperor Ferdinand) over the Alps. **Pros:** central location; good restaurant. **Cons:** rooms vary in size; often filled with groups. **TripAdvisor:** "generous and airy rooms," "authentically old inn," "beautiful mountain passes nearby." ✉ *Via Rio Bianco 4* ☎ *0472/832750* 🌐 *www.hotelelephant.com* *44 rooms* *In-room: refrigerator, Internet. In-hotel: restaurant, bar, tennis courts, pool, gym, parking (paid)* ⏲ *Closed early Jan.–late Mar.* 🍽 *Breakfast.*

BRUNICO (BRUNECK)

★ *33 km (20 mi) east of Bressanone, 65 km (40 mi) northwest of Cortina d'Ampezzo.*

VISITOR INFORMATION

Brunico tourism office (✉ *Piazza Municipio 7* ☎ *0474/555722* 🌐 *www.bruneck.com*).

EXPLORING

With its medieval quarter nestling below the 13th-century bishop's castle, Brunico (Bruneck) is in the heart of the Val Pusteria. This quiet and quaint town is divided by the Rienza River, with the old quarter on one side and the modern town on the other.

The open-air **Museo Etnografico dell'Alto Adige** *(Alto Adige Ethnographic Museum)* recreates a Middle Ages farming village, built around a 300-year-old mansion. The wood-carving displays are most interesting. The museum is in the district of Teodone, northeast of the center. ✉ *Herzog-Diet-Straße 24* ☎ *0474/552087* 🌐 *www.volkskundemuseum.*

it *€5* *Tues.–Sat. 9:30–5:30, Sun. 2–6 (in Aug.: Tues.–Sat. 9:30–6:30, Sun. 2–7).*

WHERE TO STAY

$$–$$$ **Hotel Post.** The Von Grebmer family runs a homey hotel in a building dating from the 1880s. **Pros:** family-run friendliness; central location. **Cons:** no air-conditioning; deposit required to confirm reservations. **TripAdvisor:** "spacious, clean and comfortable," "convenient logistically," "all around are miles of walks." *Via Bastioni 9* *0474/555127* *www.hotelpost-bruneck.com* *33 rooms, 6 suites* *In-room: no a/c, safe, refrigerator, Internet. In-hotel: restaurant, spa, laundry service, parking (free), some pets allowed* *Breakfast.*

SKIING

The **Alta Badia** (*0471/836366 Corvara* *www.altabadia.org*) ski area, which includes 52 ski lifts and 130 km (80 mi) of slopes, can be reached by heading 30 km (19 mi) south on SS244 from Brunico. It's less expensive (€30–€36)—and more Austrian in character—than other, more famous ski destinations in this region. Groomed trails for cross-country skiing (usually loops marked off by the kilometer) accommodate differing degrees of ability. Inquire at the local tourist office.

5

THE HEART OF THE DOLOMITES

The area between Bolzano and the mountain resort Cortina d'Ampezzo is dominated by two major valleys, Val di Fassa and Val Gardena. Both share the spectacular panorama of the Sella mountain range, known as the Heart of the Dolomites. Val di Fassa cradles the beginning of the Grande Strada delle Dolomiti (Great Dolomites Road—SS48 and SS241), which runs from Bolzano as far as Cortina. This route, opened in 1909, comprises 110 km (68 mi) of relatively easy grades and smooth driving between the two towns—a slower, more scenic alternative to traveling by way of Brunico and Dobbiaco along SS49.

In both Val di Fassa and Val Gardena, recreational options are less expensive, though less comprehensive, than in better-known resorts like Cortina. The culture here is firmly Germanic. Val Gardena is freckled with well-equipped, photo-friendly towns with great views overlooked by the oblong *Sasso Lungo* (Long Rock), which is more than 10,000 feet above sea level. It's also home to the Ladins, descendants of soldiers sent by the Roman emperor Tiberius to conquer the Celtic population of the area in the 1st century AD. Forgotten in the narrow cul-de-sacs of isolated mountain valleys, the Ladins have developed their own folk traditions and speak an ancient dialect that is derived from Latin and similar to the Romansch spoken in some high valleys in Switzerland.

CANAZEI

60 km (37 mi) west of Cortina d'Ampezzo, 52 km (32 mi) east of Bolzano.

VISITOR INFORMATION

Canazei tourism office (*Stréda de Pareda 63* *0462/608811* *www.canazei.org*).

CLOSE UP

Hiking the Dolomites

For many overseas visitors the Dolomites conjure images of downhill skiing at Cortina d'Ampezzo and Madonna di Campiglio. But summer, not winter, is high season here; Italians, German-speaking Europeans, and in-the-know travelers from farther afield come here for clear mountain air and world-class hiking. In 2009 UNESCO (the United Nations Educational, Scientific and Cultural Organization) named the Dolomites to its exclusive list of natural heritage sites. The dramatic terrain, inspiring vistas, an impossibly pleasant climate have are complemented by excellent facilities for enjoying the mountains.

PICKING A TRAIL

The Dolomites boast a well-maintained network of trails for hiking and rock climbing. As long as you're in reasonably good shape, the number of appealing hiking options can be overwhelming.

Trails are well marked and designated by grades of difficulty: T for tourist path, H for hiking path, EE for expert hikers, and EEA for equipped expert hikers. On any of these paths you're likely to see carpets of mountain flowers between clutches of dense evergreens, with chamois and roe deer mulling about.

If you're just out for a day in the mountains, you can leave the particulars of your walk open until you're actually on the spot; local tourist offices (especially those in Cortina, Madonna, and the Heart of the Dolomites) can help you choose the right route based on trail conditions, weather, and desired exertion level. **Club Alpino Italiano**, the world's oldest organization of its kind, is an excellent resource for more ambitious

adventures. Serious mountaineers might consider joining the group; their annual dues of €42 give you half-price rates when you reserve some mountain refuges and include insurance for air rescue. (Helicopters run €70 per minute!) It has offices in Bolzano and Trento. ✉ *Piazza delle Erbe 46, Bolzano* ☎ *0471/978172* 🌐 *www.cai.it* ✉ *Via Manci 57, Trento* ☎ *0461/982804.*

TRAVELING THE VIE FERRATE

If you're looking for an adventure somewhere between hiking and climbing, consider a guided trip along the Vie Ferrate (Iron Paths). These routes offer fixed climbing aids (steps, ladders, bridges, safety cables) left by Alpine divisions of the Italian and Austro-Hungarian armies and later converted for recreational use. Previous experience is generally not required, but vertigo-inducing heights do demand a strong stomach.

Detailed information about Vie Ferrate in the eastern Dolomites can be found at 🌐 *www.dolomiti.org.* Capable tour organizers include **Scuola di Alpinismo** (Mountaineering School) in Madonna di Campiglio (☎ *0465/442634* 🌐 *www.*

guidealpinecampiglio.it) and Cortina d'Ampezzo (☎ *0436/868505* 🌐 *www.guidecortina.com*).

BEDDING DOWN

One of the pleasures of an overnight adventure in the Dolomites is staying at a *rifugio*, one of the refuges that dot the mountainsides. There are hundreds of them, often in remote locations and ranging from spartan shelters to posh retreats. Most fall somewhere in between—they're cozy mountain lodges with dormitory-style accommodations. Pillows and blankets are provided (so there's no need to carry a sleeping bag), but you have to supply your own sheet. Bathrooms are usually shared, as is the experience of a cold shower in the morning.

The majority of rifugi are operated by the **Club Alpino Italiano** (🌐 *www.cai.it*). Contact information for both CAI-run and private rifugi is available from local tourist offices; most useful are those in Madonna di Campiglio (🌐 *www.campiglio.to*), Cortina d'Ampezzo (🌐 *www.dolomiti.org*), Val di Fassa (🌐 *www.fassa.com*), and Val Gardena (🌐 *www.val-gardena.net*). Reservations are a must, especially in August, although Italian law requires rifugi to accept travelers for the night if there is insufficient time to reach other accommodations before dark.

EATING WELL

Food is as much a draw at rifugi as location. Although the dishes served are the sort of the rustic cuisine you might expect (salami, dumplings, hearty stews), the quality is uniformly excellent—an impressive feat, made all the more remarkable when you consider that supplies often have to arrive by helicopter. Your dinner may cost as much as your bed for the night—about €20 per person—and it's difficult to determine which is the better bargain.

Snacks and packed lunches are available for purchase, but many opt to sit down for the midday meal. Serving as both holiday hiking destination and base camp for difficult ascents, the rifugi welcome walkers and climbers of all stripes from intersecting trails and nearby faces. Multilingual stories are swapped, food and wine shared, and new adventures launched.

5

STUMBLING ON ÖTZI

It was at the Similaun rifugio in September 1991 that a German couple arrived talking of a dead body they'd discovered near a "curious pickax." This was to be the world's introduction to Ötzi, the oldest mummy ever found.

The couple, underestimating the age of the corpse by about 5,300 years, thought it was a matter for the police. World-famous mountaineers Reinhold Messner and Hans Kammerlander happened to be passing through the same rifugio during a climbing tour, and a few days later they were on the scene, freeing the iceman from the ice. Ötzi's remarkable story was under way. You can see him on display, along with his longbow, ax, and clothes, at Bolzano's Museo Archeologico dell'Alto Adige, where he continues to be preserved at freezing temperatures.

EXPLORING

Of the year-round resort towns in the Val di Fassa, Canazei is the most popular. The mountains around this small town are threaded with hiking trails and ski slopes, surrounded by large clutches of conifers.

About 4 km (2½ mi) west of Canazei, an excursion from Campitello di Fassa to the vantage point at **Col Rodella** is a must. A cable car (€13.50 round-trip) rises some 3,000 feet to a full-circle vista of the Heart of the Dolomites, including the Sasso Lungo and the rest of the Sella range.

> WORD OF MOUTH
>
> "We love Ortisei . . . It makes the perfect base location for the Val Gardena and has a wealth of good hotel and food options."
> —bobthenavigator

WHERE TO STAY

$–$$ **Alla Rosa.** The view of the imposing Dolomites is the real attraction at this central hotel, so ask for a room with a balcony. **Pros:** in the center of town; great views. **Cons:** half board mandatory in winter high season; busy neighborhood. ✉ *Strèda del Faure 18* ☎ *0462/601107* 🌐 *www.hotelallarosa.com* *49 rooms* *In-room: Wi-Fi, no a/c, refrigerator. In-hotel: restaurant, bar, gym, Internet terminal, parking (paid), Wi-Fi hotspot* *Breakfast.*

LAGO DI CAREZZA

22 km (14 mi) west of Canazei, 29 km (18 mi) east of Bolzano.

Glacial Lake Carezza is some 5,000 feet above sea level. The crystal, almost florescent azure blue of the waters can at times change to magical greens and purples, reflections of the dense surrounding forest and rosy peaks of the Dolomites. You can hike down to this quintessential mountain lake from the nearby village of the same name; there's a fountain with two marmots in the center of town. If you're just driving by, there's free roadside parking before and after the lake; otherwise, look for the paid parking lot across from it.

EN ROUTE

The **Passo di Sella** *(Sella Pass)* can be approached from SS48, affording some of the most spectacular mountain vistas in Europe before it descends into the Val Gardena. The road continues to Ortisei, passing the smaller resorts of Selva Gardena and Santa Cristina.

ORTISEI (ST. ULRICH)

28 km (17 mi) north of Canazei, 35 km (22 mi) northeast of Bolzano.

VISITOR INFORMATION

Ortisei (✉ *Via Rezia 1* ☎ *0471/777600* 🌐 *www.valgardena.it*).

EXPLORING

Ortisei (St. Ulrich), the jewel in the crown of Val Gardena's resorts, is a hub of activity in both summer and winter; there are hundreds of miles of hiking trails and accessible ski slopes. Hotels and facilities are abundant—swimming pools, ice rinks, health spas, tennis courts, and bowling alleys. Most impressive of all is the location, a valley surrounded by formidable views in all directions.

For centuries Ortisei has also been famous for the expertise of its wood-carvers, and there are still numerous workshops. Apart from making religious sculptures—particularly the wayside calvaries you come upon everywhere in the Dolomites—Ortisei's carvers were long known for producing wooden dolls, horses, and other toys. As itinerant peddlers they traveled every spring on foot with their loaded packs as far as Paris, London, and St. Petersburg. Shops in town still sell woodcrafts.

WORD OF MOUTH

"The drive from Cortina to Bolzano is spectacular—its only about 76 km but will take a full day. We also like the hiking and lakes around Cortina. The funicular takes you up the mountain where you can either hike or just enjoy the views."

—cmeyer54

Fine historic and contemporary examples of local woodworking can be seen at the **Museo della Val Gardena.** ✉ *Via Rezia 83* ☎ *0471/797554* 🌐 *www.museumgherdeina.it* 🎫 *€5* ⏲ *Jan. 12–Mar., Thurs. and Fri. 10–noon and 2–5; May 15–Oct., weekdays 10–noon and 2–6 (July and Aug., also Sun. 3–6, Thurs. 8 am–10 pm); Dec. 27–Jan. 9, daily 10–noon and 2–5.*

WHERE TO STAY

$$$–$$$$ ★ **Adler.** This hotel has been under the same family management since 1810. **Pros:** breathtaking views; superb staff; lots of family activities. **Cons:** standard rooms need redecorating; long walk to town center. **TripAdvisor:** "fantastic food and fantastic location," "like staying in a luxurious mansion," "pools are simply heavenly." ✉ *Via Rezia 7* ☎ *0471/775000, 0471/775001 reservations* 🌐 *www.adler-dolomiti.com* *123 rooms* *In-room: safe, refrigerator, Internet, Wi-Fi. In-hotel: restaurant, bar, pool, gym, spa, children's programs (ages 4–12), Internet terminal, parking (free)* ⏲ *Closed mid-Apr.–mid-May* *Some meals.*

$$$–$$$$ **Cavallino Bianco.** With delicate wooden balconies and an eye-catching wooden gable, the pink Cavallino Bianco (the Little White Horse) looks like a gigantic dollhouse, and it is in fact marketed especially toward families with children. **Pros:** family-friendly atmosphere; cheerful rooms. **Cons:** in the busy town center; a bit impersonal. **TripAdvisor:** "services were at the highest level," "hotel ski guides are fantastic," "children loved the kids club." ✉ *Via Rezia 22* ☎ *0471/783333* 🌐 *www.cavallino-bianco.com* *184 rooms* *In-room: safe, refrigerator, Internet. In-hotel: 2 restaurants, bar, pool, spa, bicycles, children's programs (ages 2–12), parking (paid)* *All meals.*

SKIING

With almost 600 km (370 mi) of accessible downhill slopes and more than 90 km (56 mi) of cross-country skiing trails, Ortisei is one of the most popular ski resorts in the Dolomites. Prices are good, and facilities are among the most modern in the region. In warmer weather the slopes surrounding Ortisei are a popular hiking destination, as well as a playground for vehicular mountain adventures: biking, rafting, even paragliding.

An immensely popular ski route, the **Sella Ronda** relies on well-placed chairlifts to connect 26 km (16 mi) of downhill skiing around the colossal Sella massif, passing through several towns along the way. You can ski the loop, which requires intermediate ability and a full day's effort, either clockwise or counterclockwise. Going with a guide is recommended. Chairlifts here, as elsewhere in the Dolomites, are covered by the **Dolomiti Superski pass** (🌐 *www.dolomitisuperski.com*), available for varying prices and durations. The **Val Gardena tourism office** (✉ *Via Dursan 81, Santa Cristina* ☎ *0471/777777* 🌐 *www.valgardena.it*) can provide detailed information about sport-equipment rental outfits and guided-tour operators. **Val Gardena Active** (☎ *335/6849031* 🌐 *www.selva-active.com*) outfits a particularly large choice of year-round mountain sport activities.

CORTINA D'AMPEZZO

The archetypal Dolimite resort, Cortina d'Ampezzo entices those seeking both relaxation and adventure. The town is the western gateway to the Strade Grande delle Dolomiti, and actually crowns the northern Veneto region and an area known as Cadore in the northernmost part of the province of Belluno. Like Alto Adige to the west, Cadore (birthplace to the Venetian Rennaisance painter Titian) was on the Alpine front during the First World War, and the scene of many battles commemorated in refuges and museums.

VISITOR INFORMATION

Cortina d'Ampezzo tourism office (✉ *Piazzetta San Francesco 8* ☎ *0436/3231* 🌐 *www.infodolomiti.it*).

EXPLORING

Cortina d'Ampezzo has been the Dolomites' mountain resort of choice for more than 100 years; half a century before Turin, the Winter Olympics were held here in 1956. Although its glamorous appeal to younger Italians may have been eclipsed by steeper, sleeker Madonna di Campiglio, Cortina remains, for many, Italy's most idyllic incarnation of an Alpine ski town.

Surrounded by mountains and dense forests, the "Queen of the Dolomites" is in a lush meadow 4,000 feet above sea level. The town hugs the slopes beside a fast-moving stream, and a public park extends along one bank. Higher in the valley, luxury hotels and the villas of the rich are identifiable by their attempts to hide behind stands of firs and spruces. The bustling center of Cortina d'Ampezzo has little nostalgia, despite its Alpine appearance. The tone is set by smart shops and cafés as chic as their well-dressed patrons, whose corduroy knickerbockers may well have been tailored by Armani. Unlike neighboring resorts that have a strong Germanic flavor, Cortina d'Ampezzo is unapologetically Italian and distinctly fashionable.

On Via Cantore, a winding road heading up out of town to the northeast (becoming SS48), you can stop and see the **Pista Olimpica di Bob** *(Olympic Bobsled Course)* used in the 1956 Winter Games.

WHERE TO EAT

$$ NORTHERN ITALIAN ✕ **Tavernetta.** Near the Olympic ice-skating rink, this popular restaurant has Tirolean-style wood-paneled dining rooms. Join the local clientele in sampling Cortina specialties such as pasta with *ragu bianco tartuffato* (white truffle sauce), and wild game. ✉ *Via Castello 53* ☎ *0436/868102* ⊙ *Closed May, June, Nov., and Tues.*

WHERE TO STAY

$$ **Corona.** Noted ski instructor Luciano Rimoldi, who has coached such luminaries as Alberto Tomba, runs a cozy Alpine lodge. **Pros:** cozy atmosphere; friendly staff; quiet location. **Cons:** small rooms; outside the town center. **TripAdvisor:** "very short walk to town," "common areas authentic and charming," "home away from home." ✉ *Via Val di Sotto 12* ☎ *0436/3251* ⊕ *www.hotelcoronacortina.it* *44 rooms* *In-room: Wi-Fi, no a/c. In-hotel: restaurant, bar, Internet terminal, parking (free)* ⊙ *Closed Apr., May, and mid-Sept.–Nov.* *Breakfast.*

$$$–$$$$ ★ **De la Poste.** Loyal skiers return year after year to this classic old-school hotel; its main terrace bar is one of Cortina's social centers. **Pros:** professional service; romantic atmosphere. **Cons:** a bit stuffy; in a busy neighborhood. **TripAdvisor:** "icon that has been here for years," "room was in excellent shape," "staff was friendly and very helpful." ✉ *Piazza Roma 14* ☎ *0436/4271* ⊕ *www.delaposte.it* *83 rooms* *In-room: no a/c, Wi-Fi, safe, refrigerator. In-hotel: 2 restaurants, bar, parking (free)* ⊙ *Closed Apr.–mid-June and Oct.–mid-Dec.* *Breakfast.*

$$$$ **Miramonti Majestic.** This imposing and luxe hotel, more than a century old, has a magnificent mountain-valley position about 1 km (½ mi) south of town. **Pros:** magnificent location; old-world charm; splendid views. **Cons:** outside town center; minimum stay in high season. **TripAdvisor:** "beautiful, old fashioned hotel," "large and lavish," "view spectacular." ✉ *Località Peziè 103* ☎ *0436/4201* ⊕ *www.miramontimajestic.it* *122 rooms* *In-room: no a/c, refrigerator. In-hotel: restaurant, bar, golf course, tennis courts, pool, gym, laundry service, Internet terminal, parking (free)* ⊙ *Closed Apr.–June and Sept.–mid-Dec.* *Breakfast.*

SPORTS AND THE OUTDOORS

HIKING AND CLIMBING

Hiking information is available at the excellent local **tourism office** (✉ *Piazzetta San Francesco 8* ☎ *0436/3231* ⊕ *www.infodolomiti.it*). The **Gruppo Guide Alpine Cortina Scuola di Alpinismo** (*Mountaineering School* ✉ *Corso Italia 69* ☎ *0436/868505* ⊕ *www.guidecortina.com*) organizes climbing trips and trekking adventures.

5

SKIING

Cortina's long and picturesque ski runs will delight intermediates, but advanced skiers might lust for steeper terrain, which can be found only off-piste. Efficient ski bus service connects the town with the high-speed chairlifts and gondolas that ascend in all directions from the valley.

The **Dolomiti Superski pass** (✉ *Via Marconi 15* ☎ *0471/795397* 🌐 *www.dolomitisuperski.com*) provides access to the surrounding Dolomites (€40–€45 per day)—with 450 lifts and gondolas serving 1,200 km (750 mi) of trails. Buy one at the ticket office next to the bus station. The **Faloria gondola** (✉ *Via Ria de Zeta 10* ☎ *0436/2517*) runs from the center of town. From its top you can get up to most of the central mountains. Some of the most impressive views (and steepest slopes) are on **Monte Cristallo**, based at Misurina, 15 km (9 mi) northeast of Cortina by car or bus. The topography of the **Passo Falzarego** ski area, 16 km (10 mi) east of town, is quite dramatic.

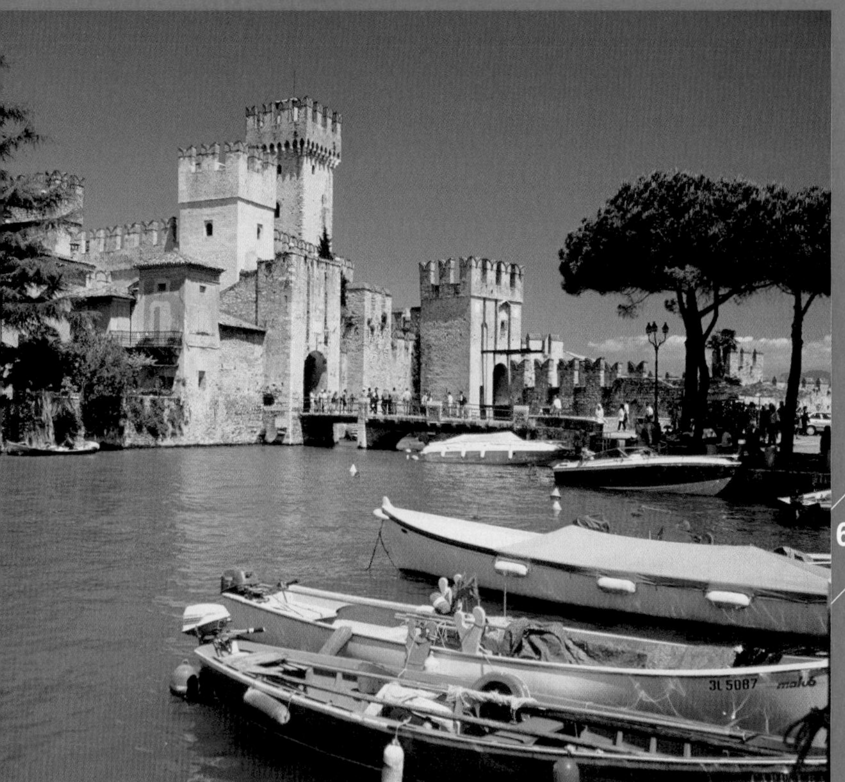

Milan, Lombardy, and the Lakes

WORD OF MOUTH

"The towns around Lake Maggiore are beautiful, Isola Bella with its palace and garden is unique. Also the gardens of Villa Taranto are like a dream, full of floral arrangements, there are splendid views of the lake."

—Valtor

WELCOME TO MILAN, LOMBARDY, AND THE LAKES

TOP REASONS TO GO

★ **Lake Como:** Ferries crisscross the waters, taking you from stately villas to tiny towns.

★ **Leonardo Da Vinci's** *The Last Supper*: Behold one of the world's most famous works of art.

★ **Bergamo Alta:** A funicular ride takes you up to the magnificent medieval city.

★ **Window-shopping in Milan:** Italians' refined fashion sense is on full display in the famed Quadrilatero shopping district.

★ **La Scala:** There's no better place to spend a night at the opera.

1 Milan. Italy lives in the present tense here. The country's leading city of commerce is also one of the world's fashion capitals, and there are cultural treasures here that rival those of Florence and Rome.

2 Pavia, Cremona, and Mantua. South of Milan are the walled cities where Renaissance dukes built towering palaces and intricate churches. They sit on the Po Plain, one of Italy's wealthiest regions.

3 Lake Garda. Italy's largest lake measures 16 km (10 mi) across at its widest point and 50 km (31 mi) from end to end. There are more tourists here than at the other lakes, but that means you can also find more opportunities for outdoor activities.

4 Lake Como. This relatively narrow lake is probably the country's best-known body of water. You can almost always see across to the other side, which lends a great sense of intimacy. Lake Lecco, to the southeast, is actually a branch of Lake Como.

5 Lake Maggiore. It may be smaller than Lake Garda and less famous than Lake Como, but Lake Maggiore is impressively picturesque with the Alps as a backdrop. One of the greatest pleasures here is exploring the lake's islands.

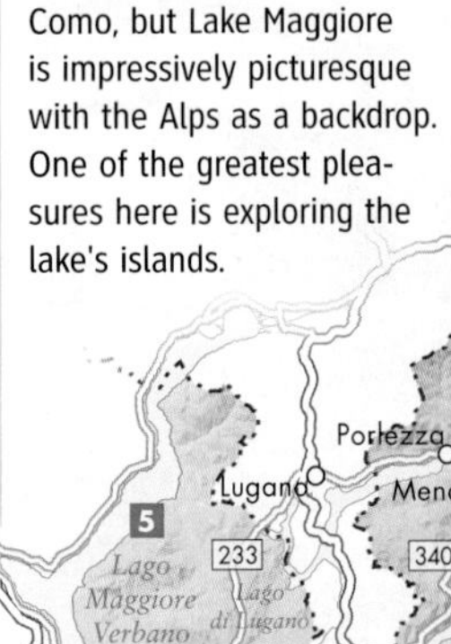

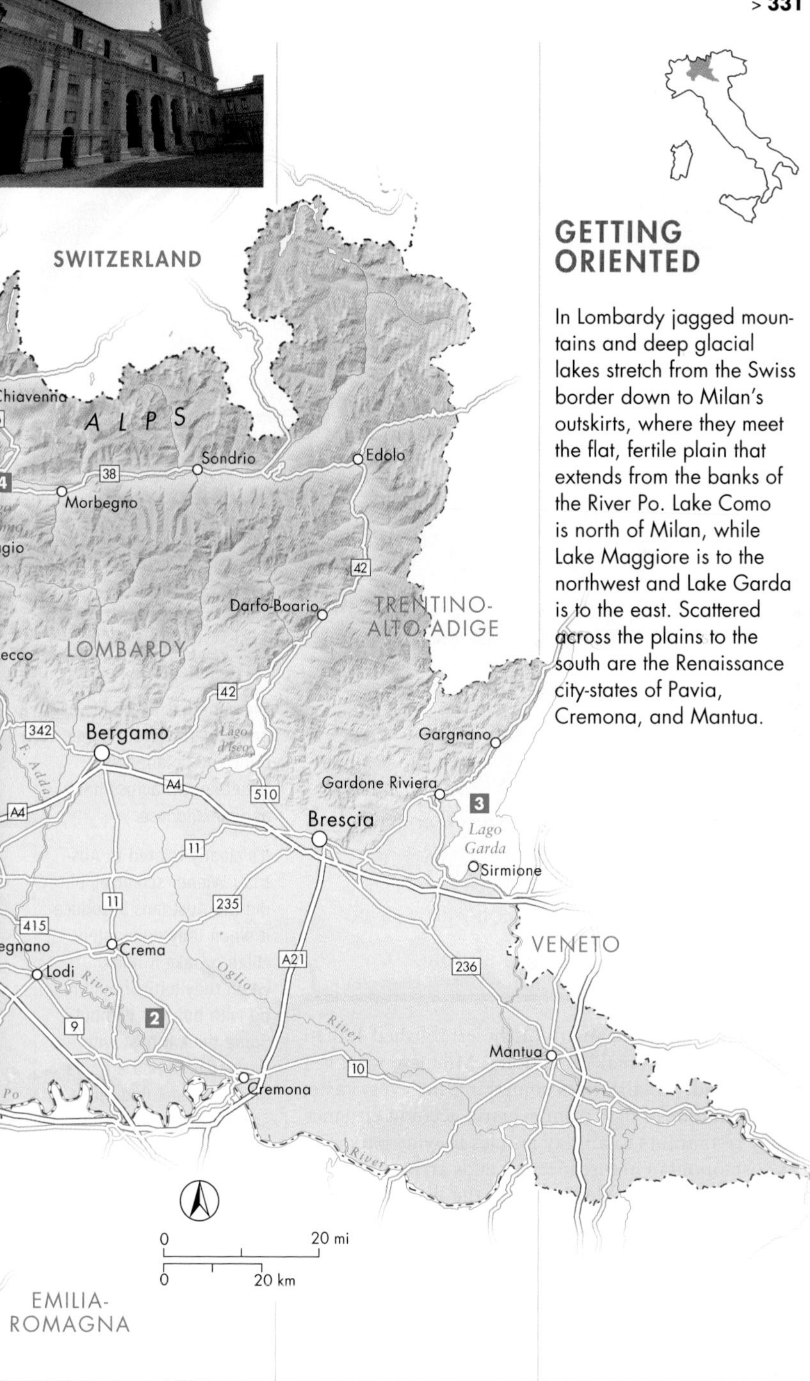

GETTING ORIENTED

In Lombardy jagged mountains and deep glacial lakes stretch from the Swiss border down to Milan's outskirts, where they meet the flat, fertile plain that extends from the banks of the River Po. Lake Como is north of Milan, while Lake Maggiore is to the northwest and Lake Garda is to the east. Scattered across the plains to the south are the Renaissance city-states of Pavia, Cremona, and Mantua.

6

EATING WELL IN MILAN, LOMBARDY, AND THE LAKES

Lombardy may well offer Italy's most varied cuisine. Local cooking is influenced by the neighboring regions of the north; foreign conquerors have left their mark; and today well-traveled Milanese, business visitors, and industrious immigrants all appreciate exotic flavors not so eagerly embraced elsewhere in Italy.

Milan runs counter to many of the established Italian dining customs. A "real" traditional Milanese meal is a rarity; instead, Milan offers something for every taste, budget, and time of day, from expense-account elegance in fancy restaurants to all-day nibbles in wine bars. The city's cosmopolitan nature means trends arrive here first, and things move fast. Meals are not the drawn-out pastime they tend to be elsewhere in Italy. But food is still consistently good—competition among restaurants is fierce, and the local clientele is demanding, which means you can be reasonably certain that if a place looks promising, it won't disappoint.

THE COTOLETTA QUESTION

Everyone has an opinion on *cotoletta*, photo upper right, the breaded veal cutlet known across Italy as *una Milanese.*

It's clearly related to Austria's Wiener schnitzel, but did the Austrians introduce it when they dominated Milan or take it home when they left? Should it be with bone or without? Some think it best with fresh tomato and arugula on top; others find this a sacrilege.

Two things unite all camps: the meat must be well beaten until it is thin, and it must never leave a grease spot after it is fried.

REGIONAL SPECIALTIES

Ask an Italian what Lombards eat, and you're likely to hear *cotoletta, càsoeûla,* and *risotto giallo*—all dishes that reinforce Lombardy's status as the crossroads of Italy. *Cotoletta alla Milanese* has likely Austrian influences. *Càsoeûla* is a cabbage-and-pork stew that resembles French cassoulet, though some say it has Spanish origins. *Risotto giallo* (also known as *Milanese*), pictured at left, is colorful and perfumed with exotic saffron. With no tomatoes, olive oil, or pasta, these dishes hardly sound Italian.

BUTTER AND CHEESE

Agricultural traditions and geography mean that animal products are more common here than in southern Italy—and that means butter and cream take olive oil's place. A rare point of agreement about cotoletta is that it's cooked in butter. The first and last steps of risotto making—toasting the rice and letting it "repose" before serving—use ample amounts of butter. And the second-most-famous name in Italian cheese (after Parmesan) is likely Gorgonzola, named for a town near Milan. The best now comes from Novara.

RISOTTO

Novara is the center of Italian (and European) rice production. Introduced from the Orient and grown here since the 15th century, rice is Lombardy's answer to pasta. From Milan's risotto giallo with

its costly saffron tint to Mantua's risotto with pumpkin or sausage, there's no end to the variety of rice dishes. Canonic risotto should be *all'onda,* or flow off the spoon like a wave. Keeping with the Italian tradition of nothing wasted, yesterday's risotto is flattened in a pan and fried in butter to produce *riso al salto,* which at its best has a crispy crust and a tender middle.

PANETTONE

Panettone, a sweet yeast bread with raisins and citron, pictured below left, is a national Christmastime treat invented in Milan. It's now so ubiquitous that its price is used as an economic indicator: is it up or down, compared to last year? Consumption begins on December 7, Milan's patron saint's day, and goes until supplies run out at January's end.

WINE

Lombardy is not one of Italy's most heralded wine regions, but its reputation is growing. Production is scattered throughout the province. The Valtellina area to the northeast of Milan produces two notable red DOCGs from the nebbiolo grape: Valtellina Superiore and the intense dessert wine Sforzato di Valtellina. The Franciacorta region around Brescia makes highly regarded sparkling wines. Lake breezes bring crisp, smooth whites from the shores around Lake Garda.

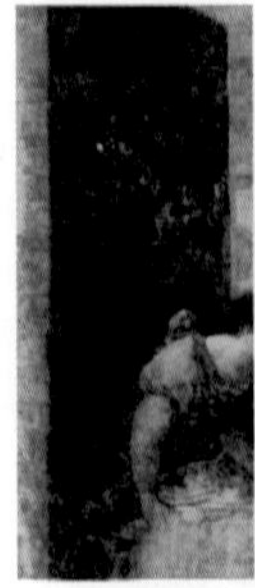

Updated by Sara Rosso

It's tempting to describe Lombardy as a region that offers something for everyone. Milan is the country's business capital and the center for everything that's up to the minute. The great Renaissance cities of the Po Plain—Pavia, Cremona, and Mantua—are stately and serene, embracing their past with nostalgia while ever keeping an eye on the present. Topping any list of the region's attractions are the lakes—glacial waters stretching out below the Alps—which have been praised as the closest thing to paradise by writers throughout the ages, from Virgil to Hemingway.

Millions of travelers have concurred: for sheer beauty, the lakes of northern Italy—Como, Maggiore, Garda, and Orta—have few equals. Along their shores are 18th- and 19th-century villas, exotic formal gardens, sleepy villages, and dozens of resorts that were once Europe's most fashionable, and still retain a powerful allure.

Milan can be disappointingly modern—a little too much like the place you've come to Italy to escape—but its historic buildings and art collections in many ways rival those of Florence and Rome. And if you love to shop, Milan is a mecca. It truly offers a fashion experience for every taste, from Corso Buenos Aires, which has a higher ratio of stores per square foot than anywhere else in Europe, to upscale but affordable Corso Vercelli and elegant Via Montenapoleone, where there is no limit on what you can spend. Milan is home to global fashion giants such as Armani, Prada, and Trussardi; behind them stands a host of less famous designers who help fill all those fabulous shops.

PLANNING

MAKING THE MOST OF YOUR TIME

Italy's capital of commerce isn't a top priority for most leisure travelers, but the city has a sophisticated urban appeal: its fashionable shops rival tose of New York and Paris, its soccer teams are Italy's answer to the Yankees and the Mets, its opera performances set the standard for the world, and its art treasures are considerable.

The biggest draw in the region, though, is the lake district. Lakes Como, Garda, Maggiore, and Orta all have long histories as travel destinations, and each has its own distinct character. If you have limited time, visit the lake you think best suits your style, but if you have more time, make the rounds to two or three to get a sense of their contrasts.

Note that reservations are required to see Leonardo da Vinci's *The Last Supper,* housed in the refectory of Milan's Santa Maria delle Grazie church. You should call as far in advance as possible to make them, particularly if you're planning to go on a weekend. *For details, see the Santa Maria delle Grazie listing in this chapter.*

GETTING HERE AND AROUND

BUS TRAVEL

Bus service isn't a good option for travel between cities here—it's not faster, cheaper, or more convenient than the train. For those determined to travel by bus, **Autostradale** (☎ *02/33910794* 🌐 *www.autostradale.it*) goes to Turin, Bergamo, and Brescia from its hub at Lampugnano (metro line 1), northwest of Milan's city center. Reservations are required.

CAR TRAVEL

Outside Milan, driving is the best way to see the region. Getting almost anywhere is a snap, as several major highways intersect at Milan, all connected by the *tangenziale*, the road that rings the city. The A4 runs west to Turin and east to Venice; A1 leads south to Bologna, Florence, and Rome; A7 angles southwest down to Genoa. A8 goes northwest toward Lake Maggiore, and A9 north runs past Lake Como and over the St. Gotthard Pass into Switzerland.

Your car-rental company should be your first resource if you have a problem while driving in Italy, but it's also good to know that the **ACI** (☎ *803/116* 🌐 *www.aci.it*), the Italian auto club, offers 24-hour roadside assistance (free for members, for a fee for nonmembers). Regularly spaced roadside service phones are available on the autostrade.

TRAIN TRAVEL

Milan's massive Central Station (Milano Centrale), 3 km (2 mi) northwest of the Duomo, is one of Italy's major passenger-train hubs, with frequent direct service within the region to Como, Bergamo, Brescia, Sirmione, Pavia, Cremona, and Mantua. Soaring domed glass ceilings and plenty of signage have significantly improved the renovated station's navigability, but its sheer size requires considerable walking and patience, so allow for some extra time here. For general information on trains and schedules, as well as online ticket purchase, visit the Web site of the Italian national railway, **FS** (🌐 *www.trenitalia.com*).

Tickets bought without a reservation need to be validated by stamping them in yellow machines on the train platforms. Tickets with reservations do not require validation. When in doubt, validate: it can't hurt.

ABOUT THE HOTELS

The hotels in Italy's wealthiest region generally cater to a clientele willing to pay for extra comfort. Outside Milan, many are converted villas with well-landscaped grounds. Most of the famous lake resorts are expensive; more reasonable rates can be found in the smaller towns. Local tourism offices can be an excellent source of information about affordable lodging.

Prices in almost all hotels can go up dramatically during Milan's big trade fairs, especially during the Furniture Fair in early April. Fashion, travel, and tech fairs also draw big crowds throughout the year, raising prices. In contrast to other cities in Italy, however, you can often find discounts on weekends and higher prices during the week. The three lake districts—Maggiore, Garda, and Como—have little to offer except quiet from November to March, when most gardens, hotels, and restaurants are closed.

Hotel reviews have been condensed for this book. Please go to Fodors.com for full reviews of each property.

WHAT IT COSTS (IN EUROS)

	¢	$	$$	$$$	$$$$
Restaurants	under €20	€20–€30	€30–€45	€45–€65	over €65
Hotels	under €75	€75–€125	€125–€200	€200–€300	over €300

Restaurant prices are for a first course (primo), second course (secondo), and dessert (dolce). Hotel prices are for two people in a standard double room in high season, including tax and service.

MILAN

Milan is Italy's business hub and crucible of chic. Between the Po's rich farms and the industrious mountain valleys, it has long been the country's capital of commerce, finance, fashion, and media. Rome may be bigger and have the political power, but Milan and the affluent north are what really make the country go. It's also Italy's transport hub, with the biggest international airport, the most rail connections, and the best subway system. Leonardo da Vinci's *The Last Supper* and other great works of art are here, as well as a spectacular Gothic Duomo, the finest of its kind. Milan even reigns supreme where it really counts (in the minds of many Italians), routinely trouncing the rest of the nation with its two premier soccer teams.

And yet, Milan hasn't won the battle for hearts and minds. Most tourists prefer Tuscany's hills and Venice's canals to Milan's hectic efficiency and wealthy indifference, and it's no surprise that in a country of medieval hilltop villages and skilled artisans, a city of grand boulevards and global corporations leaves visitors asking the real Italy to please stand up. They're right, of course. Milan is more European than Italian, a new buckle on an old boot, and although its old city can stand cobblestone for cobblestone against the best of them, seekers of Roman ruins and fairy-tale towns may pass. But Milan's secrets reveal themselves slowly to those who look. A side street conceals a garden complete with flamingos (Via dei Cappuccini, just off Corso Venezia), and a renowned 20th-century art collection hides modestly behind an unspectacular facade a block from Corso Buenos Aires (the Casa Museo Boschi-di Stefano). Visitors lured by the world-class shopping will appreciate Milan's European sophistication while discovering unexpected facets of a country they may have thought they knew.

Virtually every invader in European history—Gaul, Roman, Goth, Longobard, and Frank—as well as a long series of rulers from France, Spain, and Austria, took a turn at ruling the city. After being completely sacked by the Goths in AD 539 and by the Holy Roman Empire under Frederick Barbarossa in 1157, Milan became one of the first independent city-states of the Renaissance. Its heyday of self-rule proved comparatively brief. From 1277 until 1500 it was ruled by the Visconti and subsequently the Sforza dynasties. These families were known, justly or not, for a peculiarly aristocratic mixture of refinement, classical learning, and cruelty, and much of the surviving grandeur of Gothic and Renaissance art and architecture is their doing. Be on the lookout in your wanderings for the Visconti family emblem—a viper, its jaws straining wide, devouring a child.

VISITOR INFORMATION

The **tourism office** (✉ *Piazza Duomo 19/A, Piazza Duomo* ☎ *02/77404343* 🌐 *www.visitamilano.it* ⏲ *Mon.–Sat. 8:45–1 and 2–6, Sun. 9–1 and 2–5*) in Piazza Duomo is the perfect place to begin your visit. It's accessible by elevator and down a deco stairway under the arches on the north side of Piazza Duomo; you can also enter from the Galleria in front of the Park Hyatt hotel. There are excellent maps, booklets with museum descriptions and itineraries on a variety of themes, and a selection of brochures about smaller museums and cultural initiatives. Pick up a copy of the English-language *Hello Milano* (ask, if it is not on display, or see 🌐 *www.hellomilano.it*), a monthly publication with a day-to-day schedule of events of interest to visitors and a comprehensive map. The Autostradale bus operator, sightseeing companies, and a few theaters have desks in the tourism office where you can buy tickets.

LOMBARDY THROUGH THE AGES

Lombardy has had a tumultuous history. Control by outsiders dates back more than 3,000 years, to when the Etruscans of central Italy first wandered north of the River Po. They dominated the region for centuries, to be followed by the Cenomani Gauls, then the Romans in the later days of the Republic. The region was known as Cisalpine Gaul ("Gaul this side of the Alps"), and under the rule of Augustus became a Roman province.

The decline of the Roman Empire was followed by invasion by Attila of the Huns and Theodoric of the Goths. These conquerors gave way to the Lombards, who then ceded to Charlemagne their iron crown, which became the emblem of his vast, unstable empire. Even before the bonds of the empire had begun to snap, the cities of Lombardy were erecting walls in defense against the Hungarians, and against each other.

These city-states formed the Lombard League, which in the 12th century finally defeated the German ruler Frederick Barbarossa. With the northern invaders gone, new and even bloodier strife began. In each city the Guelphs (bourgeois supporters of the popes) and the Ghibellines (noblemen loyal to the Holy Roman Empire) clashed. The city-states declined, falling under the yoke of a few powerful regional rulers. The Republic of Venice dominated Brescia and Bergamo. Mantua was ruled by the Gonzaga family, and the Visconti and Sforza families took over Como, Cremona, Milan, and Pavia.

The Battle of Pavia in 1525, in which the generals of Holy Roman Emperor Charles V defeated the French, brought on 200 years of occupation by the Spanish—who proved generally less cruel than the local tyrants. The War of the Spanish Succession in the early years of the 18th century brought in the Austrians.

Napoléon and his generals defeated the Austrians at the turn of the 19th century. The Treaty of Campoformio resulted in the proclamation of the Cisalpine Republic, which soon became the Republic of Italy and then the Kingdom of Italy—which lasted only until Napoléon's defeat brought back the Austrians. In March of 1848, demonstrations in Milan took on surprising force: the Austrians were driven out of the city, and a provisional government of Milan soon became a provisional government of Lombardy. In June of the same year, Lombardy united with Sardinia—the first step toward Italian unification in 1870.

The spirit of 1848 was rekindled in 1943. Discontent with fascism provoked workers to strike in Turin and Milan, marking the beginning of the end of fascist dominance. The Lombardy-based partisan insurrection against Mussolini and the German regime was better organized and more successful than in many other parts of the country. Indeed, Milan was liberated from the Germans by its own partisan organization before the Allied troops entered the city.

Dissatisfaction with the federal government is practically a given among Lombardy residents, and the prevailing attitude has been to ignore Rome and get on with business. It's an approach that's proven successful: Lombardy accounts for one-fifth of Italy's economy.

THE DUOMO AND POINTS NORTH

Milan's main streets radiate out from the massive Duomo, a late-Gothic cathedral that was started in 1386. Leading north is the handsome Galleria Vittorio Emanuele, an enclosed walkway that takes you to the world-famous opera house known as La Scala. Beyond are the winding streets of the elegant Brera neighborhood, once the city's bohemian quarter. Here you'll find many art galleries, as well as the academy of fine arts. Heading northeast from La Scala is Via Manzoni, which leads to the *Quadrilatero della moda,* or fashion district. Its streets are lined with elegant window displays from the world's most celebrated designers—the Italians taking the lead, of course.

Leading northeast from the Duomo is Corso Vittorio Emanuele. Locals and visitors stroll along this pedestrians-only street, looking at the shop windows, buying ice cream, or stopping for a coffee at one of the sidewalk cafés. Northwest of the Duomo is Via Dante, at the top of which is the imposing outline of the Castello Sforzesco.

TOP ATTRACTIONS

6

★ **Castello Sforzesco.** For the serious student of Renaissance military engineering, the Castello must be something of a travesty, so often has it been remodeled or rebuilt since it was begun in 1450 by the *condottiere* (hired mercenary) who founded the city's second dynastic family, Francesco Sforza, fourth duke of Milan. Though today "mercenary" has a pejorative ring, during the Renaissance all Italy's great soldier-heroes were professionals hired by the cities and principalities that they served. Of them—and there were thousands—Francesco Sforza (1401–66) is considered one of the greatest, most honest, and most organized. It is said he could remember the names not only of all his men but of their horses as well. His rule signaled the enlightened age of the Renaissance but preceded the next foreign rule by a scant 50 years. The castle's crypts and battlements, including a tunnel that emerges well into the Parco Sempione behind, can be visited with privately reserved guides from **Ad Artem** (☎ *02/6596937* 🌐 *www.adartem.it*) or **Opera d'Arte** (☎ *02/45487400* 🌐 *www.operadartemilano.it/turismo-eng.html*). Since the turn of the 20th century, the Castello has been the depository of several city-owned collections of Egyptian and other antiquities, musical instruments, arms and armor, decorative arts and textiles, prints and photographs (on consultation), paintings, and sculpture. Highlights include the **Sala delle Asse,** a frescoed room still sometimes attributed to Leonardo da Vinci (1452–1519), which, at the time of writing, is closed for restoration (scheduled to reopen sometime before 2015). Michelangelo's unfinished *Rondanini Pietà* is believed to be his last work—an astounding achievement for a man nearly 90, and a moving coda to his life. The *pinacoteca* (picture gallery) features paintings from medieval times to the 18th century, including 230 works by Antonello da Messina, Canaletto, Andrea Mantegna, and Bernardo Bellotto. The **Museo dei Mobili** (furniture museum), which illustrates the development of Italian furniture from the Middle Ages to current design, includes a delightful collection of Renaissance treasure chests of exotic woods with tiny drawers and miniature architectural details. A single

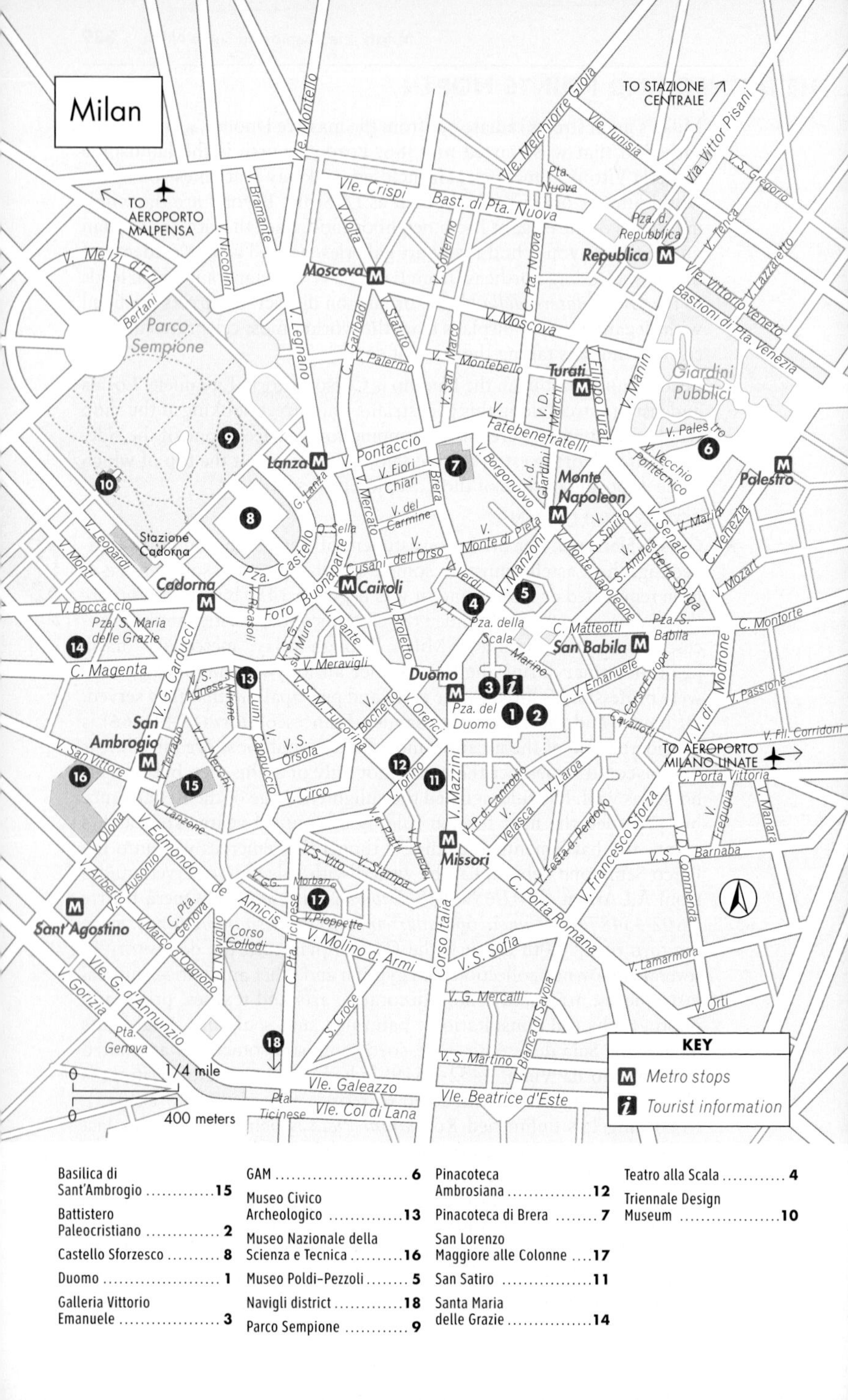
Milan
TO AEROPORTO MALPENSA
TO STAZIONE CENTRALE
TO AEROPORTO MILANO LINATE
Parco Sempione
Giardini Pubblici
Stazione Cadorna
Moscova
Republica
Turati
Lanza
Cadorna
Cairoli
Duomo
Monte Napoleon
San Babila
Palestro
San Ambrogio
Missori
Sant'Agostino
Vle. Crispi
Bast. di Pta. Nuova
Vle. Melchiorre Gioia
Vle. Tunisia
Pta. Nuova
Via. Vittor Pisani
V. S. Gregorio
Pza. d. Repubblica
V. Tenca
V. Lazzaretto
Vle. Vittorio Veneto
Bastioni di Pta. Venezia
V. Montello
V. Bramante
V. Niccolini
V. Melzi d'Eril
V. Bertani
V. Volta
V. Solferino
C. Pta. Nuova
V. Legnano
C. Garibaldi
V. Statuto
V. Palermo
V. San Marco
V. Moscova
Montebello
V. D. Marchi
V. Filippo Turati
V. Manin
V. Fatebenefratelli
V. Palestro
V. Vecchio Politecnico
V. Pontaccio
V. Fiori Chiari
V. Brera
V. Borgonuovo
V. d. Giardini
V. Mercato
V. del Carmine
G. Lanza
Q. Sella
Pza. Castello
Foro Buonaparte
V. Cusani
V. dell'Orso
V. Monte di Pietà
V. Manzoni
V. Verdi
V. S. Spirito
V. S. Andrea
V. Monte Napoleone
V. Senato
V. della Spiga
V. Maria
C. Venezia
V. Mozart
C. Monforte
V. Leopardi
V. Monti
V. Boccaccio
Pza. S. Maria delle Grazie
C. Magenta
V. G. Carducci
V. Ricasoli
V. S. G. sul Muro
V. Dante
V. Broletto
Pza. della Scala
Marino
C. Matteotti
Pza. S. Babila
C. V. Emanuele
C. Europa
Cavallotti
V. Meravigli
V. S. M. Fulcorina
V. Bocchetto
V. Orefici
Pza. del Duomo
V. S. Agnese
V. Nirone
V. Luini
V. Cappuccio
V. S. Orsola
V. Terraggio
V. L. Necchi
V. San Vittore
V. Lanzone
V. Circo
V. Torino
V. Mazzini
V. P. d. Cannobio
V. Velasca
V. Larga
V. Festa d. Perdono
V. V. di Modrone
V. Passione
V. Fil. Corridoni
C. Porta Vittoria
V. Freguglia
V. Manara
V. S. Barnaba
V. D. Commenda
V. Francesco Sforza
C. Porta Romana
V. Olona
V. Edmondo de Amicis
V. Ausonio
V. Ariberto
V. Marco d'Oggiono
C. Pta. Genova
D. Naviglio
Corso Collodi
V. G.G. Morbano
V. S. Vito
V. Stampa
V. Pioppette
C. Pta. Ticinese
V. Molino d. Armi
Corso Italia
V. S. Sofia
V. Lamarmora
V. Orti
V. Amedei
V. e Prato
Vle. G. d'Annunzio
V. Gorizia
Pta. Genova
S. Croce
V. G. Mercalli
V. Bianca di Savoia
V. S. Martino
Vle. Galeazzo
Vle. Beatrice d'Este
Pta. Ticinese
Vle. Col di Lana
0
1/4 mile
0
400 meters
KEY
Metro stops
Tourist information
Basilica di Sant'Ambrogio 15
Battistero Paleocristiano 2
Castello Sforzesco 8
Duomo 1
Galleria Vittorio Emanuele 3
GAM 6
Museo Civico Archeologico 13
Museo Nazionale della Scienza e Tecnica 16
Museo Poldi-Pezzoli 5
Navigli district 18
Parco Sempione 9
Pinacoteca Ambrosiana 12
Pinacoteca di Brera 7
San Lorenzo Maggiore alle Colonne 17
San Satiro 11
Santa Maria delle Grazie 14
Teatro alla Scala 4
Triennale Design Museum 10

GETTING AROUND MILAN

The city center is compact and walkable; trolleys and trams make it even more accessible, and the efficient Metropolitana (subway) and buses provide access to locations farther afield. Driving in Milan is difficult and parking miserable, so a car is a liability. In addition, drivers within the second ring of streets (the *bastioni*) must hold an Ecopass. (Ask your hotel about getting a pass.)

BY PUBLIC TRANSIT

A standard public transit ticket costs €1 and is valid for a 75-minute trip on a subway, bus, or tram. An all-inclusive subway, bus, and tram pass costs €3 for 24 hours or €5.50 for 48 hours. Individual tickets and passes can be purchased from news vendors and tobacconists, and at ticket counters and ticket machines at larger stops. Another option is a carnet (€9.20), good for 10 tram or subway rides. Once you have your ticket or pass, either stamp it or insert it into slots in station turnstiles or on poles inside trolleys and buses. (The electronic tickets will not function if bent or demagnetized. If you have a problem, contact a station manager, who can usually issue a new ticket.) Trains run from 6 am to 12:20 am (1:30 am on Saturday). From 8 pm to 2 am **Radiobus** (☎ *02/48034803* 🌐 *www.atm-mi.it/en*) will pick you up and drop you off anywhere in Milan for a €1.50 supplement to a transit pass. Advance booking is required. For more information, check the Web site of **ATM** (*Azienda Trasporti Milanesi* 🌐 *www.atm-mi.it/en*) or visit information offices at the Duomo, Stazione Cadorna, Stazione Centrale, Garibaldi, and Loreto stops.

BY TAXI

Taxi fares in Milan are higher than in American cities. A short ride will run about €15. Taxis wait at stands marked by an orange "Taxi" sign, or you can call one of the city's taxi companies—**Amicotaxi** (☎ *02/4000*), **Autoradiotaxi** (☎ *02/8585*), **Radiotaxi–Yellow Taxi** (☎ *02/6969*), or **Taxiblu** (☎ *02/4040*). Dispatchers may speak some English; they'll ask for the phone number you're calling from, and they'll tell you the number of your taxi and how long it will take to arrive. If you're in a restaurant or bar, ask the staff to call a cab for you. For car service, contact **Autonoleggio Pini** (☎ *02/29400555* 🌐 *www.limousinepini.eu*). English-speaking drivers are available.

BY BICYCLE

The innovative BikeMI (🌐 *www.bikemi.com*) makes hop-on, drop-off bicycles available at designated spots around the city. There are more than 100 stations, and more than 300 stations are planned. Weekly and daily rates for tourists are available. Buy your subscription online; the site has a map showing stations and availability.

TOURS

A refurbished 1920s tramcar operates a hop-on/hop-off **Tram Turistico** (☎ *800/808181*) tour of the city. Tickets (€20) are valid all day and can be purchased on board. Departures are at 11 and 1 (also at 3, April–October) from Piazza Castello. **City Sightseeing Milano** (🌐 *www.milano.city-sightseeing.it*) has open-top double-decker buses running hop-on/hop-off tours on two routes departing from Piazza Castello. An all-inclusive day pass costs €20.

ticket purchased in the office in an inner courtyard admits visitors to these separate installations, which are dispersed around the castle's two immense courtyards. ✉ *Piazza Castello, Brera* ☎ *02/88463700* 🌐 *www.milanocastello.it* ⏲ *Castle: Apr.–Oct, daily 7–7; Nov.–Mar., daily 7–6. Museums: Tues.–Sun. 9–5:30; last entry at 5* 💵 *Museums: €3, free Fri. after 2 and daily after 4:30* Ⓜ *Cairoli; Tram 1, 3, 4, 7, 12, 14, or 27.*

★ **Duomo.** This intricate Gothic structure has been fascinating and exasperating visitors and conquerors alike since it was begun by Galeazzo Visconti III (1351–1402), first duke of Milan, in 1386. Consecrated in the 15th or 16th century, it was not completed until just before the coronation of Napoléon as king of Italy in 1809. Whether you concur with travel writer H.V. Morton's 1964 assessment that the cathedral is "one of the mightiest Gothic buildings ever created," there is no denying that for sheer size and complexity it is unrivaled. It is the second-largest church in the world—the largest being St. Peter's in Rome. The capacity is reckoned to be 40,000. Usually it is empty, a sanctuary from the frenetic pace of life outside and the perfect place for solitary contemplation.

The building is adorned with 135 marble spires and 2,245 marble statues. The oldest part is the apse. Its three colossal bays of curving and counter-curved tracery, especially the bay adorning the exterior of the stained-glass windows, should not be missed. At the end of the southern transept down the right aisle lies the **tomb of Gian Giacomo Medici**. The tomb owes some of its design to Michelangelo but was executed by Leone Leoni (1509–90), and is generally considered to be his masterpiece; it dates from the 1560s. Directly ahead is the Duomo's most famous sculpture, the gruesome but anatomically instructive figure of San Bartolomeo (St. Bartholomew), whose glorious martyrdom consisted of being flayed alive. It is usually said the saint stands "holding" his skin, but this is not quite accurate. It would appear more that he is luxuriating in it, much as a 1950s matron might have shown off a new fur stole.

As you enter the apse to admire those splendid windows, glance at the sacristy doors to the right and left of the altar. The lunette on the right dates from 1393 and was decorated by Hans von Fernach. The one on the left also dates from the 14th century and is ascribed jointly to Giacomo da Campione and Giovanni dei Grassi. Don't miss the view from the Duomo's roof; walk out the left (north) transept to the stairs and elevator. Sadly, air pollution drastically reduces the view on all but the rarest days. As you stand among the forest of marble pinnacles, remember that virtually every inch of this gargantuan edifice, including the roof itself, is decorated with precious white marble dragged from quarries near Lake Maggiore by Duke Visconti's team along road laid fresh for the purpose and through the newly dredged canals. Audio guides can be rented inside the Duomo from March to December and at Duomo Point in Piazza Duomo (just behind the cathedral) all year long. Exhibits at the **Museo del Duomo** shed light on the cathedral's history and include some of the treasures removed from the exterior for preservation purposes. At this writing, the museum is closed for restoration with no estimated date for completion. ✉ *Piazza del Duomo*

☏ *02/72023375* 🌐 *www.duomomilano.it* 🎟 *Stairs to roof €5, elevator €8* ⏲ *Cathedral daily 8:30–6:45. Roof Nov.–Mar., daily 9–4:45; Apr.–Oct., daily 9–9. Museum closed for restoration* Ⓜ *Duomo.*

★ **Galleria Vittorio Emanuele.** This spectacular, late-19th-century glass-topped, belle epoque, barrel-vaulted tunnel is essentially one of the planet's earliest and most select shopping malls. Like its suburban American cousins, the Galleria Vittorio Emanuele fulfills numerous social functions. This is the city's heart, midway between the Duomo and La Scala. It teems with life, inviting people-watching from the tables that spill from the bars and restaurants, where you can enjoy an overpriced coffee. Books, records, clothing, food, pens, pipes, hats, and jewelry are all for sale. Known as Milan's "parlor," the Galleria is often viewed as a barometer of the city's well-being. By the 1990s the quality of the stores (with the exception of the Prada flagship) and restaurants was uninspired. The city government, which owns the Galleria, and merchants' groups evicted some longtime tenants who had enjoyed anomalously low rents, in favor of Gucci, Tod's, and Louis Vuitton. The historic, if somewhat overpriced and inconsistent, Savini restaurant hosts the beautiful and powerful of the city, just across from McDonald's. Like the cathedral, the Galleria is cruciform in shape. Even in poor weather the great glass dome above the octagonal center is a splendid sight. Look up! The paintings at the base of the dome represent Europe, Asia, Africa, and America. Those at the entrance arch are devoted to science, industry, art, and agriculture. And the floor mosaics are a vastly underrated source of pleasure, even if they are not to be taken too seriously. Be sure to follow tradition and spin your heels once or twice on the more-"delicate" parts of the bull beneath your feet in the northern apse; the Milanese believe it brings good luck. ✉ *Piazza del Duomo* Ⓜ *Duomo.*

QUICK BITES

One thing has remained constant in the Galleria: the Caffè Zucca (🌐 *www.caffemiani.it*), known by the Milanese as Camparino. Its inlaid counter, mosaics, and wrought-iron fixtures have been welcoming tired shoppers since 1867. Enjoy a Campari or Zucca *aperitivo* (aperitif) as well as the entire range of Italian coffees, served either in the Galleria or in an elegant upstairs room where lunch is also served.

Museo Poldi-Pezzoli. This exceptional museum, opened in 1881, was once a private residence and collection, and contains not only pedigreed paintings but also porcelain, textiles, and a cabinet with scenes from Dante's life. The gem is undoubtedly the *Portrait of a Lady* by Antonio Pollaiuolo (1431–98), one of the city's most prized treasures and the source of the museum's logo. The collection also includes masterpieces by Botticelli (1445–1510), Andrea Mantegna (1431–1506), Giovanni Bellini (1430–1516), and Fra Filippo Lippi (1406–69). Private guided tours are available by reservation. ✉ *Via Manzoni 12, Quadrilatero* ☏ *02/794889* 🌐 *www.museopoldipezzoli.it* 🎟 *€8* ⏲ *Wed.–Mon. 10–6* Ⓜ *Montenapoleone.*

6

Parco Sempione. Originally the gardens and parade ground of the Castello Sforzesco, this open space was reorganized during the Napoleonic era, when the arena on its northeast side was constructed, and then turned into a park during the building boom at the end of the 19th century. It is still the lungs of the city's fashionable western neighborhoods, and the **Aquarium** (✉ *Viale Gadio 2* ☎ *02/884957* 🌐 *www.acquariocivicomilano.eu* 🎟 *Free* ⏲ *Tues.–Sun. 9–1 and 2–5:30*) still attracts Milan's schoolchildren. The park became a bit of a design showcase in 1933 with the construction of the Triennale *(see below)*. The Fiat café offers outdoor dining in summer along with a view of De Chirico's sculpture-filled fountain *Bagni Misteriosi* (*Mysterious Baths*).

WORD OF MOUTH

"La Scala: Wow! We paid admission to the museum to gain access to the various boxes in the theater. Like nothing we've seen before."
—dina4

Even if a walk in the park is not appealing, it is worth visiting to see the **Torre Branca** (✉ *Parco Sempione* ☎ *02/3314120* 🎟 *€4* ⏲ *Irregular, seasonal hrs; check at* 🌐 *www.branca.it/torre/dati.asp*). Designed by architect Gio Ponti, who was behind so many of the projects that made Milan the design capital that it is, this steel tower rises 330 feet over the Triennale. Take the elevator up to get a nice view of the city, then have a drink at the glitzy Just Cavalli Café (Monday–Saturday, 8 pm–2 am) at its base. *Parco Sempione:* ✉ *Piazza Castello, Sempione-Castello* ⏲ *Nov.–Feb., daily 6:30–8; Mar. and Apr., daily 6:30–9; May and Oct., daily 6:30–10; June–Sept., daily 6:30–11:30* Ⓜ *Cadorna; Bus 61.*

★ **Pinacoteca di Brera** *(Brera Gallery)*. The collection here is star-studded even by Italian standards. The entrance hall (Room I) displays 20th-century sculpture and painting, including Carlo Carrà's (1881–1966) confident, stylish response to the schools of cubism and surrealism. The museum has nearly 40 other rooms, arranged in chronological order—pace yourself.

The somber, moving *Cristo Morto* (*Dead Christ*) by Mantegna dominates Room VI, with its sparse palette of umber and its foreshortened perspective. Mantegna's shocking, almost surgical precision—in the rendering of Christ's wounds, the face propped up on a pillow, the day's growth of beard—tells of an all-too-human agony. It is one of Renaissance painting's most quietly wondrous achievements, finding an unsuspected middle ground between the excesses of conventional gore and beauty in representing the Passion's saddest moment.

Room XXIV offers two additional highlights of the gallery. Raphael's (1483–1520) *Sposalizio della Vergine* (*Marriage of the Virgin*), with its mathematical composition and precise, alternating colors, portrays the betrothal of Mary and Joseph (who, though older than the other men gathered, wins her hand when the rod he is holding miraculously blossoms). *La Vergine con il Bambino e Santi* (*Madonna with Child and Saints*), by Piero della Francesca (1420–92), is an altarpiece commissioned by Federico da Montefeltro (shown kneeling, in full armor, before the Virgin); it was intended for a church to house the duke's tomb. The ostrich egg hanging from the apse, depending on whom you ask, either commemorates the miracle of his fertility—Federico's wife died months after giving birth to a long-awaited male heir—or alludes to his appeal for posthumous mercy, the egg symbolizing the saving power of grace. ✉ *Via Brera 28, Brera* ☎ *02/92800361* 🌐 *www.brera.beniculturali.it* 🎫 *€11, higher during special exhibitions* ⏲ *Tues.–Sun. 8:30–7:15; last admission 45 mins before closing* Ⓜ *Montenapoleone or Lanza.*

Teatro alla Scala. You need know nothing of opera to sense that, like Carnegie Hall, La Scala is closer to a cathedral than an auditorium. Here Verdi established his reputation and Maria Callas sang her way into opera lore. It looms as a symbol—both for the performer who dreams of singing here and for the opera buff who knows every note of *Rigoletto* by heart. Audiences are notoriously demanding and are apt to jeer performers who do not measure up. The opera house was closed after destruction by Allied bombs in 1943, and reopened at a performance led by Arturo Toscanini in 1946.

If you are lucky enough to be here during the opera season, which runs from December to June, do whatever is necessary to attend. Tickets go on sale two months before the first performance and are usually sold out the same day. Hearing opera sung in the magical setting of La Scala is an unparalleled experience.

6

At **Museo Teatrale alla Scala** you can admire an extensive collection of librettos, paintings of the famous names of Italian opera, posters, costumes, antique instruments, and design sketches for the theater. It is also possible to take a look at the theater, which was completely restored in 2004. Special exhibitions reflect current productions. ✉ *Piazza della Scala; museum Largo Ghiringhelli 1, Duomo* ☎ *02/72003744 theater, 02/88797473 museum* 🌐 *www.teatroallascala.org* 🎫 *Museum €5* ⏲ *Museum daily 9–12:30 and 1:30–5:30; last entry ½ hr prior to closing* Ⓜ *Duomo.*

Triennale Design Museum. After decades of false starts and controversy, Milan's Triennale is a museum that honors Italy's design talent, as well as offering a regular series of exhibitions on design from around the world. Originally the home of triennial decorative arts shows, a spectacular bridge entrance leads to a permanent collection, an exhibition space, and a stylish café (whose seating is an encyclopedia of design icons). The Triennale also manages the museum-studio of designer Achille Castiglione in nearby Piazza Castello. ✉ *Via Alemagna 6, Parco Sempione* ☎ *02/724341* 🌐 *www.triennaledesignmuseum.com* 🎫 *€8* ⏲ *Tues., Wed., and Fri.– Sun. 10:30–8:30, Thurs. 10:30 am–11 pm; last entrance 1 hr before closing* Ⓜ *Cadorna.*

WORTH NOTING

Battistero Paleocristiano. Beneath the Duomo's piazza lies this baptistery ruin dating from the 4th century. Although opinion remains divided, it is widely believed to be where Ambrose, Milan's first bishop and patron saint, baptized Augustine. Tickets are available at the kiosk inside the cathedral. ✉ *Piazza del Duomo, enter through Duomo* ☎ *02/72022656* 🎫 *€4* ⏲ *Daily 9:30–5:30* Ⓜ *Duomo.*

Casa-Museo Boschi di Stefano *(Boschi di Stefano House and Museum)*. To most people Italian art means Renaissance art. But the 20th century in Italy was a productive—if less well-known—era. Just a block behind the Corso Buenos Aires shopping area, the Casa-Museo Boschi di Stefano is a tribute to the enlightened private collectors who replaced popes and nobles as Italian patrons. An apartment on the second floor of a stunning art deco building designed by Milan architect Portaluppi houses this private collection, which was donated to the city of Milan in 2003. Its walls are lined with the works of postwar greats, such as Fontana, De Chirico, and Morandi. Along with the art, the museum holds distinctive postwar furniture and stunning Murano glass chandeliers. ✉ *Via Jan 15, Corso Buenos Aires* ☎ *02/20240568* 🌐 *www.fondazioneboschidistefano.it* 🎫 *Free* 🕑 *Tues.–Sun. 10–6; last entry at 5:30* Ⓜ *Lima; Tram 33; Bus 60.*

★ **GAM: Galleria d'Arte Moderna/Villa Reale.** One of the city's most beautiful buildings, this museum is an outstanding example of neoclassical architecture. It was built between 1790 and 1796 as a residence for a member of the Belgioioso family. It later became known as the Villa Reale (royal) when it was donated to Napoléon, who lived here briefly with Empress Josephine. Its origins as residence are reflected in the elegance of its proportions and its private garden behind.

Likewise, the collection of paintings is domestic rather than monumental. There are many portraits, as well as collections of miniatures on porcelain. Unusual for an Italian museum, this collection derives from private donations from Milan's hereditary and commercial aristocracies. On display are the collection left by prominent painter and sculptor Marino Marini and the immense *Quarto Stato* (*Fourth Estate*), which is at the top of the grand staircase. Completed in 1901 by Pellizza da Volpedo, this painting of striking workers is an icon of 20th-century Italian art and labor history, and as such it has been satirized almost as much as the *Mona Lisa*. This museum is a unique glimpse of the splendors hiding behind Milan's discreet and often stern facades. ✉ *Via Palestro 16* ☎ *02/88445947* 🌐 *www.gam-milano.com* 🎫 *Free* 🕑 *Tues.–Sun. 9–1 and 2–5:30; last entry 15 mins before closing* Ⓜ *Palestro or Turati.*

The **Giardini Pubblici** *(Public Gardens)*, across Via Palestro from the Villa Reale, were laid out by Giuseppe Piermarini, architect of La Scala, in 1770. They were designed as public pleasure gardens, and today they still are popular with families who live in the city center. Generations of Milanese have taken pony rides and gone on the miniature train and merry-go-round. The park also contains a small planetarium and the **Museo Civico di Storia Naturale** (*Municipal Natural History Museum)*. ✉ *Corso Venezia 55* ☎ *02/88463337* 🌐 *www.assodidatticamuseale.it* 🎫 *€5* 🕑 *Weekdays 9:30–1 and 2–4:30, weekends 9:30–1 and 2–5:30* Ⓜ *Palestro.*

SOUTH AND WEST OF THE DUOMO

If the part of the city to the north of the Duomo is dominated by its shops, the section to the south is famous for its works of art. The most famous is *Il Cenacolo*—known in English as *The Last Supper.* If you have time for nothing else, make sure you see this masterwork, which has now been definitively restored, after many, many years of work. Reservations will be needed to see this fresco, housed in the refectory of Santa Maria delle Grazie. Make these at least three weeks before you depart for Italy, so you can plan the rest of your time in Milan.

There are other gems as well. Via Torino, the ancient road for Turin, leads to a half-hidden treasure: Bramante's Renaissance masterpiece, the church of San Satiro. At the intersection of Via San Vittore and Via Carducci is the medieval Basilica di Sant'Ambrogio, named for Milan's patron saint. Another lovely church southeast of Sant'Ambrogio along Via de Amicis is San Lorenzo Maggiore. It's also known as San Lorenzo alle Colonne because of the 16 columns running across the facade.

6

TOP ATTRACTIONS

Basilica di Sant'Ambrogio *(Basilica of Saint Ambrose).* Noted for its medieval architecture, the church was consecrated by Milan's bishop, Saint Ambrose (one of the original Doctors of the Catholic Church), in AD 387. Saint Ambroeus, as he is known in Milanese dialect, is the city's patron saint, and his remains—dressed in elegant religious robes, a miter, and gloves—can be viewed inside a glass case in the crypt below the altar. Until the construction of the more imposing Duomo, this was Milan's most important church. Much restored and reworked over the centuries (the gold-and-gem-encrusted altar dates from the 9th century), Sant'Ambrogio still preserves its Romanesque characteristics (5th-century mosaics may be seen for €2). The church is often closed for weddings on Saturday. ✉ *Piazza Sant'Ambrogio 15, Corso Magenta* ☎ *02/86450895* 🌐 *www.santambrogio-basilica.it* ⏲ *Mon.–Sat. 9:30–12:30 and 2:30–5:15; Sun. 3–5:15* Ⓜ *Sant'Ambrogio.*

QUICK BITES

A bit overcrowded at night, when teenagers virtually block the sidewalk and traffic, the Bar Magenta (✉ *Via Carducci 13, at Corso Magenta, Sant'Ambrogio* ☎ *02/8053808* Ⓜ *Sant'Ambrogio or Cadorna*) can be a good stop en route during the day. Beyond coffee at all hours, lunch, and beer, the real attraction is its mix of old and new, trendy and aristocratic—a quintessentially Milanese ambience. It celebrated its 100th birthday in 2007 and is open weekdays 8 am–2 am and weekends 9 am–2 am. There's free Wi-Fi.

Pinacoteca Ambrosiana. Cardinal Federico Borromeo, one of Milan's native saints, founded this picture gallery in 1618 with the addition of his personal art collection to a bequest of books to Italy's first public library. More recent renovations have reunited the core works of the collection, including such treasures as Caravaggio's *Basket of Fruit*; Raphael's monumental preparatory drawing (known as a "cartoon") for *The School of Athens,* which hangs in the Vatican; and the *Codice Atlantico,* the largest collection of designs by Leonardo da Vinci (on display through 2015). Heavy on Lombard artists, there are also paintings by

Leonardo, Botticelli, Luini, Titian, and Jan Brueghel. Previous renovations done in the 1930s with their mosaics and stained-glass windows are worth a look, as are other odd items, including 18th-century scientific instruments and gloves worn by Napoléon at Waterloo. Access to the library, the Biblioteca Ambrosiana, is limited to researchers who apply for entrance tickets. ✉ *Piazza Pio XI 2, near Duomo* ☎ *02/806921* 🌐 *www.ambrosiana.it* 🎫 *€15* ⏲ *Tues.–Sun. 9–7* Ⓜ *Duomo.*

San Lorenzo Maggiore alle Colonne. Sixteen ancient Roman columns line the front of this sanctuary; 4th-century paleo-Christian mosaics survive in the Cappella di Sant'Aquilino (Chapel of Saint Aquilinus). ✉ *Corso di Porta Ticinese 39* ☎ *02/89404129* 🌐 *www.sanlorenzomaggiore.com* 🎫 *Mosaics €2* ⏲ *Weekdays 7:30–12:30 and 2:30–6:30; weekends 7:30–6:30.*

★ **San Satiro.** Just a few steps from the Duomo, this architectural gem was first built in 876 and later perfected by Bramante (1444–1514), demonstrating his command of proportion and perspective, keynotes of Renaissance architecture. Bramante tricks the eye with a famous optical illusion that makes a small interior seem extraordinarily spacious and airy, while accommodating a beloved 13th-century fresco. ✉ *Via Speronari 3, near Duomo* ☎ *02/874683* ⏲ *Weekdays 7:30–11:30 and 3:30–6:30, Sat. 3:30–7, Sun. 9:30–noon and 3:30–7* Ⓜ *Duomo.*

★ **Santa Maria delle Grazie.** Leonardo da Vinci's *The Last Supper,* housed in the church and former Dominican monastery of Santa Maria delle Grazie, has had an almost unbelievable history of bad luck and neglect—its near destruction in an American bombing raid in August 1943 was only the latest chapter in a series of misadventures, including, if one 19th-century source is to be believed, being whitewashed over by monks. Well-meant but disastrous attempts at restoration have done little to rectify the problem of the work's placement: it was executed on a wall unusually vulnerable to climatic dampness. Yet Leonardo chose to work slowly and patiently in oil pigments—which demand dry plaster—instead of proceeding hastily on wet plaster according to the conventional fresco technique. Novelist Aldous Huxley (1894–1963) called it "the saddest work of art in the world." After years of restorers' patiently shifting from one square centimeter to another, Leonardo's masterpiece is free of the shroud of scaffolding—and centuries of retouching, grime, and dust. Astonishing clarity and luminosity have been regained.

Despite Leonardo's carefully preserved preparatory sketches in which the apostles are clearly labeled by name, there still remains some small debate about a few identities in the final arrangement. But there can be no mistaking Judas, small and dark, his hand calmly reaching forward to the bread, isolated from the terrible confusion that has taken the hearts of the others. One critic, Frederick Hartt, offers an elegantly terse explanation for why the composition works: it combines "dramatic confusion" with "mathematical order." Certainly, the amazingly skillful and unobtrusive repetition of threes—in the windows, in the grouping of the figures, and in their placement—adds a mystical aspect to what at first seems simply the perfect observation of spontaneous human gesture.

Reservations are required to view the work. Viewings are in 15-minute, timed slots, and visitors must arrive 15 minutes before their assigned time in order not to lose their slot. Reservations can be made via phone (☎ *02/92800360*) or online (🌐 *www.cenacolovinciano.net*); it is worthwhile to make a call, because tickets are set aside for phone reservations. Call at least three weeks ahead if you want a Saturday slot, two weeks for a weekday slot. The telephone reservation office is open 9 am to 6 pm weekdays and 9 am to 2 pm on Saturday. Operators do speak English, though not fluently, and to reach one you must wait for the Italian introduction to finish and then press "2." However, you can sometimes get tickets from one day to the next. Some city bus tours include a visit in their regular circuit, which may be a good option. Guided tours in English are available for €3.50 and require a reservation.

The painting was executed in what was the order's refectory, which is now referred to as the **Cenacolo Vinciano.** Take a moment to visit Santa Maria delle Grazie itself. It's a handsome, completely restored church, with a fine dome, which Bramante added along with a cloister about the time that Leonardo was commissioned to paint *The Last Supper.* If you're wondering how two such giants came to be employed decorating and remodeling the refectory and church of a comparatively modest religious order, and not, say, the Duomo, the answer lies in the ambitious but largely unrealized plan to turn Santa Maria delle Grazie into a magnificent Sforza family mausoleum. Though Ludovico il Moro Sforza (1452–1508), seventh duke of Milan, was but one generation away from the founding of the Sforza dynasty, he was its last ruler. Two years after Leonardo finished *The Last Supper,* Ludovico was defeated by Louis XII and spent the remaining eight years of his life in a French dungeon. ✉ *Piazza Santa Maria delle Grazie 2, off Corso Magenta, Sant'Ambrogio* ☎ *02/4987588 Last Supper; 02/4676111 church* 🌐 *www.cenacolovinciano.net* 🎫 *Last Supper €6.50 plus €1.50 reservation fee; church free* ⏲ *Last Supper: Tues.–Sun. 8:15–6:45; church: weekdays 10–noon and 3–5:30, Sun. 3:30–5:30* Ⓜ *Cadorna; Tram 16.*

6

WORTH NOTING

Museo Civico Archeologico *(Municipal Archaeological Museum).* Appropriately situated in the heart of Roman Milan, this museum's garden encloses the polygonal Ansperto Tower, which was once part of the Roman walls. Housed in a former monastery, this museum has some everyday utensils, jewelry, an important silver plate from the last days of paganism, and several fine examples of mosaic pavement. Part of the early Middle Ages section is closed for restructuring. ✉ *Corso Magenta 15, Sant'Ambrogio* ☎ *02/86450011* 🎫 *€2* ⏲ *Tues.–Sun. 9–1 and 2–5:30; last entry at 5* Ⓜ *Cadorna.*

Museo Nazionale della Scienza e Tecnica *(National Museum of Science and Technology).* This converted cloister is best known for the collection of models based on Leonardo da Vinci's sketches (although these are not captioned in English, the labeling in many other exhibits is bilingual). On the ground level—in the hallway between the courtyards—is a room featuring interactive, moving models of the famous *vita aerea* (aerial screw) and *ala battente* (beating wing), thought to be forerunners of the modern helicopter and airplane, respectively. The museum also houses a varied collection of industrial artifacts including trains, a celebrated Italian-built submarine, and several reconstructed workshops including a watchmaker's, a lute maker's, and an antique pharmacy. Displays also illustrate papermaking and metal founding, which were fundamental to Milan's—and the world's—economic growth. There's a bookshop and a bar. The 16th-century church in the same piazza is **San Vittore al Corpo** (*Sat.–Tues. and Thurs. 3–5:45*), which has one of the most beautiful interiors in Milan. *Via San Vittore 21, Sant'Ambrogio 02/485551 www.museoscienza.org €8 Wed.–Fri. 9:30–5, weekends 9:30–6:30 Sant'Ambrogio; Bus 50, 58, or 94.*

Navigli District. In medieval times a network of *navigli,* or canals, crisscrossed the city. Almost all have been covered over, but two—Naviglio Grande and Naviglio Pavese—are still navigable. Once a down-at-the-heels neighborhood, the Navigli district has undergone some gentrification over the last 20 years. Humble workshops have been replaced by boutiques, art galleries, cafés, bars, and restaurants. The Navigli at night is about as close as you will get to more southern-style Italian street life in Milan. On weekend nights it is difficult to walk (and impossible to park, although an underground parking area has been under construction for years) among the youthful crowds thronging the narrow streets along the canals. Check out the antiques fair on the last Sunday of the month. *South of Corso Porta Ticinese, Porta Genova Porta Genova; Tram 2, 3, 9, 14, 15, 29, or 30.*

WHERE TO EAT

BRERA

$–$$ NORTHERN ITALIAN

La Libera. Although this establishment in the heart of Brera calls itself a *birreria con cucina* (beer cellar with kitchen), locals come here for excellent evening meals in relaxed surroundings. A soft current of jazz and sylvan decor soothe the ripple of conversation. The creative cooking varies with the season, but could include linguine *al pescato* (with a fish sauce); *fritto di gamberi, zucchine e totanetti* (fried shrimp, zucchini, and baby squid); or *rognone alla senape* (veal kidneys cooked in mustard). *Via Palermo 21, Brera 02/8053603 or 02/86462773 www.ristorantelaliberamilano.com AE, DC, MC, V No lunch Moscova.*

CINQUE GIORNATE

$$$ ITALIAN

Da Giacomo. The fashion and publishing crowd, as well as international bankers and businessmen, favor this Tuscan/Ligurian restaurant. The emphasis is on fish; even the warm slice of pizza served while you study the menu has seafood in it. The specialty, *gnocchi Da Giacomo,* has a savory seafood-and-tomato sauce. Service is friendly and efficient; the wine list broad; and the dessert cart, with tarte tatin and Sicilian *cassata* (a concoction of sponge cake, ricotta, and candied fruit), rich and varied. With its tile floor and bank of fresh seafood, it has a refined neighborhood-bistro style. *Via P. Sottocorno 6, entrance in Via Cellini, Cinque Giornate 02/76023313 www.giacomomilano.com Reservations essential Closed Christmas wk and last 2 wks of Aug. Tram 9, 12, 27, 29, or 30; Bus 54 or 60.*

DUOMO

$$$$ MODERN ITALIAN ★ **Cracco.** To international epicures, Carlo Cracco is on a similar plane as innovators Heston Blumenthal and Ferran Adrià. The tasting menus are a good way to savor many of the delicate inventions of Cracco's creative talent, though an à la carte menu is available. Delightful appetizers and desserts vary seasonally, but may include the scampi cream with freshwater shrimp, the disk of "caramelized Russian salad," and the mango cream with mint gelatin. Specialties include Milanese classics revisited—Cracco's take on saffron risotto and cotoletta (breaded veal cutlet) should not be missed. The elegant dining room favors cool earth tones and clean lines. *Via Victor Hugo 4, Duomo 02/876774 www.ristorantecracco.it Reservations essential Closed 3 wks in Aug. and last wk in Dec.; Sept.–June, closed Sun., no lunch Sat. and Mon. M Duomo.*

$$$ MODERN ITALIAN ★ **Don Carlos.** One of the few restaurants open after La Scala lets out, Don Carlos, in the Grand Hotel et de Milan, is nothing like its indecisive operatic namesake (whose betrothed was stolen by his father). Flavors are bold, presentation is precise and full of flair, and service is attentive. The walls are blanketed with sketches of the theater, and the low-key opera recordings are every bit as well chosen as the wine list, setting the perfect stage for discreet business negotiation or, better yet, refined romance. A gourmet menu costs €85 for six courses (two-person minimum), excluding wine. *Grand Hotel et de Milan, Via Manzoni 29, Duomo 02/7234640 www.ristorantedoncarlos.it Reservations essential No lunch M Montenapoleone; Tram 1 or 2.*

$–$$ ECLECTIC **Rinascente Food & Restaurants.** The seventh floor of this famous Italian department store is a gourmet food market surrounded by several small restaurants that can be a good option for lunch, aperitivo, or dinner if you've been shopping or touring the Duomo. There are several places to eat, including the popular mozzarella bar Obika, My Sushi, De Santis for "slow food" sandwiches, and the sophisticated Maio restaurant. A terrace overlooking the Duomo is shared by three locations. It's best to get here early—it's popular, and there are often lines at mealtimes. *Piazza Duomo 02/8852471 www.rinascente.it M Duomo.*

GARIBALDI

$–$$ NORTHERN ITALIAN **Osteria Vecchi Sapori.** Simple but savory fare and a menu that varies weekly characterize one osteria with two locations run by two brothers, Paolo and Roberto. Specialties include their truffle tagliolini, and primi of stuffed pasta like Gorgonzola-filled fiocchetti, or pear and parmigiano-filled ravioli with a saffron butter sauce. Their extensive, meat-rich second-course dishes are paired with creamy polenta *taragna* (made with cornmeal and buckwheat flour) or their hand-cut fried potatoes. The dessert menu changes daily with in-house cakes, tiramisu, and *crostate* (fruit tarts) reflecting traditional tastes and seasonal availability. *Via Carmagnola 3, Garbaldi 02/6686148 www.vecchisapori.it Reservations essential Closed Sun. No lunch M Garibaldi or Zara; Tram 3, 4, 7, or 31; Bus 82, 86, 90, or 91.*

$–$$ PIZZA **Pizzeria La Fabbrica.** This lively pizzeria has two wood-burning ovens going full-steam every day of the week. Skip the appetizers and go straight to the pizza. Pizzas vary from traditional (*quattro stagioni*) to vegetable-based (with leeks and Gorgonzola) to in-house specialties

6

like the *tartufona* (with truffles). The menu also offers pasta like *pici* with Tuscan sausage and main *secondi* dishes. Save room for a worthy dessert like the *torta caprese al cioccolato* or tiramisu—though after pizza, you might want to share. The Fabbrica is spacious enough to handle groups; seek out a seat in the spacious garden area when the weather's fine. ✉ *Viale Pasubio 2, Garbaldi* ☎ *02/6552771* 🌐 *www.lafabbricapizzeria.it* ⏲ *No lunch Sun.* Ⓜ *Garibaldi.*

LORETO

$–$$ MILANESE ★ ✕ **Da Abele.** If you love risotto, then make a beeline for this neighborhood trattoria. The superb risotto dishes change with the season, and there may be just two or three on the menu at any time. It is tempting to try them all. The setting is relaxed, the service informal, the prices strikingly reasonable. Outside the touristy center of town but quite convenient by subway, this trattoria is invariably packed with locals. ✉ *Via Temperanza 5, Loreto* ☎ *02/2613855* ⏲ *Closed Mon., Aug., and Dec. 22–Jan. 7. No lunch* Ⓜ *Pasteur.*

PORTA VENEZIA

$$$$ VEGETARIAN ✕ **Joia.** At this haute-cuisine vegetarian restaurant near Piazza della Repubblica, delicious dishes are artistically prepared by chef Pietro Leemann. Vegetarians, who often get short shrift in Italy, will marvel at the variety of culinary traditions—Asian and European—and artistry offered here. The ever-changing menu offers dishes in unusual formats: tiny glasses of creamed cabbage with ginger, spheres of crunchy vegetables that roll across the plate. Fish also makes an appearance. Joia's restful dining room has been refurbished, another room added, and its kitchen enlarged. The fixed-price lunch "box" is a good value (€17 and €35), but be sure to reserve ahead. Multicourse menus in the evening range from €50 to €100, excluding wine. ✉ *Via Panfilo Castaldi 18, Porta Venezia* ☎ *02/29522124* 🌐 *www.joia.it* ✍ *Reservations essential* ⏲ *Closed Sun., 3 wks in Aug., and Dec. 24–Jan. 7. No lunch Sat.* Ⓜ *Repubblica; Tram 1, 5, 11, 29, or 30.*

¢ PIZZA ✕ **Pizza OK.** Pizza is almost the only item on the menu at this family-run pizzeria with three locations, the oldest near Corso Buenos Aires in the Porta Venezia area. The pizza is extra thin and large, and possibilities for toppings seem endless. A good choice for families, this dining experience will be easy on your pocketbook. Other locations are on Via San Siro 9 in Corso Vercelli, and Piazza Sempione 8. ✉ *Via Lambro 15, Porta Venezia* ☎ *02/29401272* ⏲ *Closed Aug. 7–20 and Dec. 24–Jan. 7* Ⓜ *Porta Venezia.*

PROCACCINI

$$ MILANESE Fodor's Choice ★ ✕ **Trattoria Montina.** Twin brothers Maurizio and Roberto Montina have turned this restaurant into a local favorite. Don't be fooled by the "trattoria" name. The sage-green paneling makes it airy and cozy on a gray Milan day. Chef Roberto creates exquisite modern Italian dishes such as warmed risotto with merlot and taleggio cheese, while Maurizio chats with guests, regulars, and local families. Milan's famous cotoletta (breaded veal cutlet) is light and tasty. Try fish or the *frittura impazzita,* a wild-and-crazy mix of delicately fried seafood. There's a fine selection of sweets on the dessert cart. ✉ *Via Procaccini 54, Procaccini*

☎ *02/3490498* ⊙ *Closed Sun., Aug., and Dec. 25–Jan. 7. No lunch Mon.* Ⓜ *Tram/Bus 1, 7, 29, 43, or 57.*

QUADRILATERO

$$ ITALIAN **Paper Moon.** Hidden behind Via Montenapoleone and thus handy to the restaurant-scarce Quadrilatero, Paper Moon is a cross between a neighborhood restaurant and a celebrity hangout. Clients include families from this well-heeled area, professionals, football players, and television stars. What the menu lacks in originality it makes up for in reliable consistency—pizza and cotoletta, to name just two. Like any Italian restaurant, it's not child-friendly in an American sense—no high chairs or children's menu—but children will find food they like. It's open until 12:30 am. ✉ *Via Bagutta 1, Quadrilatero* ☎ *02/76022297* ⊙ *Closed Sun. and 2 wks in Aug.* Ⓜ *San Babila.*

SANT'AMBROGIO

$ WINE BAR **Taverna Moriggi.** This dusky, wood-panel wine bar near the stock exchange, built in 1910, is the perfect spot to enjoy a glass of wine with cheese and cold cuts. Pasta dishes and more-robust secondi like cotoletta alla Milanese are available at both lunch and dinner; if you're coming for a meal, a reservation is a good idea. ✉ *Via Morigi 8, Duomo* ☎ *02/80582007* 🌐 *www.tavernamoriggi.it* ⊙ *Closed Sun., Dec. 25–Jan. 7, and Aug. No lunch Sat.* Ⓜ *Cairoli.*

6

BEYOND CITY CENTER

$$$$ ITALIAN Fodor's Choice ★ **Antica Osteria del Ponte.** Rich, imaginative seasonal cuisine composed according to the inspired whims of chef Ezio Santin is reason enough to make your way 20 km (12 mi) southwest of Milan to one of Italy's finest restaurants. The setting is a traditional country inn, where a wood fire warms the rustic interior in winter. The menu changes regularly; in fall, wild porcini mushrooms are among the favored ingredients. Various fixed menus (€55 at lunch and €85 at dinner) offer broad samplings of antipasti, primi, and meat or fish; some include appropriate wine selections, too. ✉ *Piazza G. Negri 9, Beyond City Center, Cassinetta di Lugagnano* ⇔ *3 km (2 mi) north of Abbiategrasso* ☎ *02/9420034* 🌐 *www.anticaosteriadelponte.it* ✍ *Reservations essential* ⊙ *Closed Sun. and Mon., Dec. 24–Jan. 10, and Aug.*

WHERE TO STAY

DUOMO

$$–$$$ **Ariston.** This hotel claims it is designed around "bio-architectural" principles. **Pros:** good location; parking available. **Cons:** plain rooms. **TripAdvisor:** "five-minute walk from the Duomo," "very pleasant neighborhood," "tram noise can be loud." ✉ *Largo Carrobbio 2, Duomo* ☎ *02/72000556* 🌐 *www.aristonhotel.com* ⇆ *52 rooms* ♢ *In-room: Wi-Fi. In-hotel: room service, bar, bicycles, laundry service, Internet terminal, Wi-Fi hotspot, parking (paid), some pets allowed* 🍽 *Breakfast* Ⓜ *Duomo; Tram 2 or 14.*

$$–$$$ **Hotel Gran Duca di York.** This small hotel has spare but classically elegant and efficient rooms—four with private terraces. **Pros:** central; airy; well priced. **Cons:** rooms are simple. **TripAdvisor:** "lovely

reception area," "excellent hotel given its price," "great bar in the foyer." ✉ *Via Moneta 1/a, Duomo* ☎ *02/874863* 🌐 *www.ducadiyork.com* *33 rooms* *In-room: a/c, safe (some), Wi-Fi. In-hotel: room service, bar, laundry service, Internet terminal, Wi-Fi hotspot, parking (paid)* *Closed Aug.* *No meals* Ⓜ *Cordusio.*

$$$–$$$$ **Hotel Spadari al Duomo.** That this hotel is owned by an architect's family shows in the details, including architect-designed furniture and a fine collection of contemporary art. **Pros:** good breakfast; good location; attentive staff. **Cons:** some rooms on the small side. **TripAdvisor:** "little gem of a hotel," "walking distance to cultural icons," "free Wi-Fi." ✉ *Via Spadari 11, Duomo* ☎ *02/72002371* 🌐 *www.spadarihotel.com* *40 rooms, 3 suites* *In-room: a/c, safe, Internet. In-hotel: bar, Internet terminal, Wi-Fi hotspot (free), parking (paid), laundry service, room service (limited), some pets allowed* *Breakfast* Ⓜ *Duomo.*

$$$$ Fodor's Choice ★ **Park Hyatt Milan.** Extensive use of warm travertine stone creates a sophisticated, yet inviting and tranquil backdrop for the Park Hyatt. **Pros:** central; contemporary; refined. **Cons:** not particularly intimate. **TripAdvisor:** "contemporary luxury," "have never had better service," "miles of travertine marble." ✉ *Via Tommaso Grossi 1, Duomo* ☎ *02/88211234* 🌐 *milan.park.hyatt.com* *83 rooms, 29 suites* *In-room: Wi-Fi, Internet, safe. In-hotel: restaurant, room service, bar, gym, spa, laundry service, bicycles, parking (paid), some pets allowed* *No meals* Ⓜ *Montenapoleone.*

$$$ **UNA Maison Milano.** An understated entrance leads the visitor into what seems more like a sophisticated, upscale residence than a hotel—which is precisely the feeling the designers of Maison were striving for. **Pros:** the warmth of a residence and luxury of a design hotel. **Cons:** breakfast not included. **TripAdvisor:** "stone's throw from the Duomo," "feels more like a private residence," "young staff is very friendly." ✉ *Via Mazzini 4, Duomo* ☎ *02/85605* 🌐 *www.unamaisonmilano.it* *13 rooms, 6 junior suites, 5 suites, penthouse* *In-room: safe, Internet. In-hotel: restaurant, bar, Internet terminal, Wi-Fi hotspot, laundry service, some pets allowed* *No meals* Ⓜ *Duomo.*

PIAZZA REPUBBLICA

$–$$ **Hotel Casa Mia Milan.** Easy to reach from the central train station (a few blocks away) and easy on the budget, this tiny hotel, up a flight of stairs, is family-run. **Pros:** clean; good value; free Wi-Fi for guests. **Cons:** not the nicest neighborhood in Milan. **TripAdvisor:** "rooms are small, but comfortable," "prices are reasonable," "steep set of stairs in climb." ✉ *Viale Vittorio Veneto 30, Piazza Repubblica* ☎ *02/6575249* 🌐 *www.hotelcasamiamilano.it* *15 rooms* *In-hotel: room service, bar, laundry service, Internet terminal, Wi-Fi hotspot, parking (paid)* *Breakfast* Ⓜ *Repubblica.*

$$$$ ★ **Principe di Savoia.** Milan's grande dame has all the trappings of an exquisite traditional hotel: lavish mirrors, drapes, and carpets, and Milan's largest guest rooms, outfitted with eclectic fin de siècle furnishings. **Pros:** substantial spa/health club (considered chic by Milanese) in town; close to Central Station. **Cons:** overblown luxury in a not-very-central or attractive neighborhood. **TripAdvisor:** "atmosphere is always wonderful," "high level of customer service," "palatial feel." ✉ *Piazza della Repubblica*

17, Piazza Repubblica ☎ *02/62301* 🌐 *www.hotelprincipedisavoia.com* ⇨ *269 rooms, 132 suites* ♿ *In-room: safe, DVD, Wi-Fi. In-hotel: restaurant, room service, bar, pool, gym, spa, laundry service, Internet terminal, parking (paid), some pets allowed* 🍴 *No meals* Ⓜ *Repubblica.*

$$$$ **Westin Palace.** Milan's premier business hotel offers comfort and connectivity, with high-speed Internet access in every room. **Cons:** not much local character. **TripAdvisor:** "lobby is very grand indeed," "very nice, spacious room," "not much close by." ✉ *Piazza della Repubblica 20, Porta Nuova* ☎ *02/63361* 📠 *02/63366337* 🌐 *www.westinpalacemilan.it* ⇨ *228 rooms, 29 suites* ♿ *In-room: a/c, safe, Wi-Fi. In-hotel: 2 restaurants, room service, bar, laundry service, gym, spa, Wi-Fi hotspot, Internet terminal, parking (paid), some pets allowed* 🍴 *No meals* Ⓜ *Repubblica.*

"LET'S GO TO THE COLUMNS"

Andiamo al Le Colonne in Milanese youthspeak means to meet up at the sober Roman columns in front of the Basilica San Lorenzo Maggiore. Attracted by the bars and shops along Corso di Porta Ticinese, the young spill out on the street to chat and drink. Neighbors may complain about the noise and confusion, but students and nighthawks find it indispensable for socializing at all hours. It's a street—no closing time.

QUADRILATERO

$$$$ **Four Seasons.** The Four Seasons has been cited more than once by the Italian press as the country's best city hotel—perhaps because once you're inside, the feeling is anything but urban. **Pros:** beautiful setting that feels like Tuscany rather than central Milan. **Cons:** expensive. **TripAdvisor:** "very modern and contemporary," "staff were courteous, polite, prompt," "bathroom with La Prairie toiletries." ✉ *Via Gesù 6–8, Quadrilatero* ☎ *02/7708167* 🌐 *www.fourseasons.com* ⇨ *77 rooms, 41 suites* ♿ *In-room: safe, DVD, Internet, Wi-Fi. In-hotel: 2 restaurants, room service, bar, Wi-Fi hotspot, Internet terminal, laundry service, parking (paid)* 🍴 *No meals* Ⓜ *Montenapoleone.*

SANT'AMBROGIO

$$$ **Antica Locanda Leonardo.** Only a block from the church that houses *The Last Supper* and in one of Milan's most desired and historic neighborhoods with elegant shops and bars, this hotel has been family-run for more than 100 years. **Pros:** very quiet and homey; breakfast is ample. **Cons:** more like a bed-and-breakfast than a hotel. **TripAdvisor:** "this little hotel was perfect," "amazingly friendly and helpful staff," "still miss the chocolate croissants." ✉ *Corso Magenta 78, Sant'Ambrogio* ☎ *02/463317* 🌐 *www.anticalocandaleonardo.com* ⇨ *20 rooms* ♿ *In-room: safe, Wi-Fi. In-hotel: bar, Wi-Fi hotspot, laundry service, room service, parking (paid)* ⊙ *Closed Dec. 31–Jan. 7 and 3 wks in Aug.* 🍴 *Breakfast* Ⓜ *Sant'Ambrogio.*

SCALA

$$$$ **Grand Hotel et de Milan.** Only blocks from La Scala, this hotel, which opened in 1863, is sometimes called the Hotel Verdi because the composer lived here for 27 years. **Pros:** traditional and elegant; great location. **Cons:** gilt decor may not suit those who like more modern design.

CLOSE UP

'Appy Hour

The *aperitivo*, or prelunch or predinner drink, is part of life everywhere in Italy, and each town has its own rites and favorite drinks, but the Milanese aperitivo culture is particularly noteworthy—it's a must-try. Milan bar owners have enriched the usual nibbles of olives, nuts, and chips with full finger (and often fork) buffets serving cubes of pizza and cheese, fried vegetables, rice salad, sushi, and even pasta, and they baptized it 'Appy Hour—with the first "h" dropped and the second one pronounced. For the price of a drink (around €8), you can make a meal of hors d'oeuvres (though don't be a glutton; remember Italians value the quality of the food, not the quantity).

There are 'Appy Hours and *aperitivi* for all tastes and in all neighborhoods; you'll find the most options in Corso Sempione, Corso Como, and the Navigli areas. Changes happen fast, but these are reliable: **Arthé** (✉ *Via Pisacane 57* ☎ *02/29528353*) is a chic *enoteca* (wine bar) with fresh and fried vegetables and pasta. The **Capo Verde** (✉ *Via Leoncavallo 16* ☎ *02/26820430* 🌐 *www.capoverde.com*) is in a greenhouse/nursery and is especially popular for after-dinner drinks. **G Lounge** (✉ *Via Larga 8* ☎ *02/8053042* 🌐 *www.glounge.it*) has rotating DJs and quality music. The elegant **Hotel Sheraton Diana Majestic** (✉ *Viale Piave 42* ☎ *02/20581* 🌐 *www.sheratondianamajestic.com*) attracts a young professional crowd in good weather to its beautiful garden, which gets yearly thematic transformations. In the Brera neighborhood, the highly rated enoteca **'N Ombra de Vin** (✉ *Via S. Marco 2* ☎ *02/6599650* 🌐 *www.nombradevin.it*) serves wine by the glass and, in addition to the plates of sausage and cheese nibbles, has light food and not-so-light desserts. Check out the impressive vaulted basement where the bottled wine and spirits are sold. **Peck** (✉ *Via Cesare Cantù 3* ☎ *02/8023161* 🌐 *www.peck.it*), the Milan gastronomical shrine near the Duomo, also has a bar that serves up traditional—and excellent—pizza pieces, olives, and toasted nuts in a refined setting.

TripAdvisor: "plush old-world hotel," "price was very reasonable," "appealing to an opera fan." ✉ *Via Manzoni 29, Scala* ☎ *02/723141* 🌐 *www.grandhoteletdemilan.it* *72 rooms, 23 suites* *In-room: Wi-Fi, safe. In-hotel: restaurant, room service, bar, gym, laundry service, Internet terminal, parking (paid), some pets allowed* *No meals* Ⓜ *Montenapoleone.*

VIA SANTA SOFIA

$–$$ **Hotel Canada.** In pricey Milan, the Hotel Canada is a relative bargain. **Pros:** services and decor make it a good value. **Cons:** although trams and buses are handy, it's a short walk to the nearest metro stop. **TripAdvisor:** "small and intimate," "good-sized modern rooms," "old-fashioned lobby." ✉ *Via San Sofia 16, Via San Sofia* ☎ *02/58304844* 🌐 *www. canadahotel.it* *37 rooms* *In-room: safe, Wi-Fi. In-hotel: room service, bar, Internet terminal, Wi-Fi hotspot, laundry service, parking (paid), some pets allowed* *Breakfast* Ⓜ *Repubblica.*

NIGHTLIFE AND THE ARTS

THE ARTS

For events likely to be of interest to non–Italian speakers, see *Hello Milano* (🌐 *www.hellomilano.it*), a monthly magazine available at the tourist office in Piazza Duomo, or *The American* (🌐 *www.theamericanmag.com*), which is available at international bookstores and newsstands, and which has a thorough cultural calendar. The tourist office publishes the monthly *Milano Mese,* which also includes some listings in English.

MUSIC

The modern **Auditorium di Milano** (✉ *Largo Gustav Mahler [Corso San Gottardo, 39 at Via Torricelli], Conchetta, Navigli* ☎ *02/83389401 [also 402 and 403]* 🌐 *www.laverdi.org*), known for its excellent acoustics, is home to the **Orchestra Verdi,** founded by Milan-born conductor Richard Chailly. The season, which runs from September to June, includes many top international performers and rotating guest conductors.

The two halls belonging to the **Conservatorio** (✉ *Via del Conservatorio 12, Duomo* ☎ *02/762110* 🌐 *www.consmilano.it* Ⓜ *San Babila*) host some of the leading names in classical music. Series are organized by several organizations, including the venerable chamber music society, the **Società del Quartetto** (☎ *02/76005500* 🌐 *www.quartettomilano.it*).

6

The **Teatro Dal Verme** (✉ *Via San Giovanni sul Muro 2, Castello* ☎ *02/87905* 🌐 *www.dalverme.org* Ⓜ *Cairoli*) stages frequent classical music concerts from October to May.

OPERA

Milan's hallowed **Teatro alla Scala** (✉ *Piazza della Scala* ☎ *02/72003744* 🌐 *www.teatroallascala.org* ⏲ *Daily 9–noon* Ⓜ *Duomo*) underwent a complete renovation from 2002 to 2004, with everything refreshed, refurbished, or replaced except the building's exterior walls. Special attention was paid to the acoustics, which have always been excellent. The season runs from December 7, the feast day of Milan patron Saint Ambrose, through June. Plan well in advance, as tickets sell out quickly. For tickets, visit the **Biglietteria Centrale** (✉ *Galleria del Sagrato, Piazza Del Duomo* ⏲ *Daily noon–6* Ⓜ *Duomo*), which is in the Duomo subway station. To pick up tickets for performances from two hours prior until 15 minutes after the start of a performance, go to the box office at the theater, which is around the corner in Via Filodrammatici 2. Although you might not get seats for the more popular operas with big stars, it is worth trying; ballets are easier. The theater is closed from the end of July through August and on national and local holidays.

NIGHTLIFE

BARS

Milan has a bar somewhere to suit any style; those in the better hotels are respectably chic and popular meeting places for Milanese as well as tourists. **Blue Note** (✉ *Via Borsieri 37, Garibaldi* ☎ *02/69016888* 🌐 *www.bluenotemilano.com*), the first European branch of the famous New York nightclub, features regular performances by some of the most famous names in jazz, as well as blues and rock concerts. Dinner is available, and there's a popular jazz brunch on Sunday. It's closed

Continued on page 362

THE FASHIONISTA'S MILAN

Opera buffs and lovers of Leonardo's *Last Supper,* skip ahead to the next section. No one else should be dismayed to learn that clothing is Milan's greatest cultural achievement. The city is one of the fashion capitals of the world and home base for practically every top Italian designer. The same way art aficionados walk the streets of Florence in a state of bliss, the style-conscious come here to be enraptured.

It all happens in the *quadrilatero della moda,* Milan's toniest shopping district, located just north of the Duomo. Along the cobblestone streets, Armani, Prada, and their fellow *stilisti* sell the latest designs from flagship stores that are as much museums of chic as retail establishments. Any purchase here qualifies as a splurge, but you can have fun without spending a euro—just browse, window-shop, and people-watch. Not into fashion? Think of the experience as art, design, and theater all rolled into one. If you wouldn't visit Florence without seeing the Uffizi, you shouldn't visit Milan without seeing the quadrilatero.

FLORENCE HAS THE *DAVID.* ROME HAS THE PANTHEON. MILAN HAS THE CLOTHES.

On these pages we give a selective, street-by-street list of stores in the area. Hours are from around 10 in the morning until 7 at night, Monday through Saturday.

VIA DELLA SPIGA
(east to west)

Dolce & Gabbana (No. 2)
☎ 02/795747
www.dolcegabbana.it
women's accessories

Gio Moretti (No. 4)
☎ 02/76003186
women's and men's clothes: many labels, as well as books, CDs, flowers, and an art gallery

Bulgari Italia (No. 6)
☎ 02/777001
www.bulgari.com
jewelry, fragrances, accessories

Boutique Ferré (No. 6)
☎ 02/783050
www.gianfrancoferre.com
women's, men's, and children's sportswear

Malo (No. 7)
☎ 02/76016109
www.malo.it
everything cashmere

cross Via Sant'Andrea

Fay (No. 15)
☎ 02/76017597
www.fay.it
women's and men's clothes, accessories: a flagship store, designed by Philip Johnson

Prada (No. 18)
☎ 02/76394336
www.prada.com
accessories

Giorgio Armani (No. 19)
☎ 02/783511
www.giorgioarmani.com
accessories

Tod's (No. 22)
☎ 02/76002423
www.tods.com
shoes and handbags: the Tod's flagship store

Dolce & Gabbana (No. 26)
☎ 02 76001155
www.dolcegabbana.it
women's clothes, in a baroque setting

Moschino (No. 30)
☎ 02/76004320
www.moschino.it
women's, men's, and children's clothes: Chic and Cheap, so they say

✔ **Just Cavalli** (No. 30)
☎ 02/76390893
www.robertocavalli.net
women's and men's clothes, plus a café serving big salads and carpaccio. It's the offspring of the Just Cavalli Café in Parco Sempione, one of the hottest places in town for drinks (with or without dinner).

Roberto Cavalli (No. 42)
☎ 02/76020900
www.robertocavalli.net
women's and men's clothes, accessories: 3,200 square feet of Roberto Cavalli

I Pinco Pallino (No. 42) ☎ 02/781931
www.ipincopallino.it
extravagant children's clothing

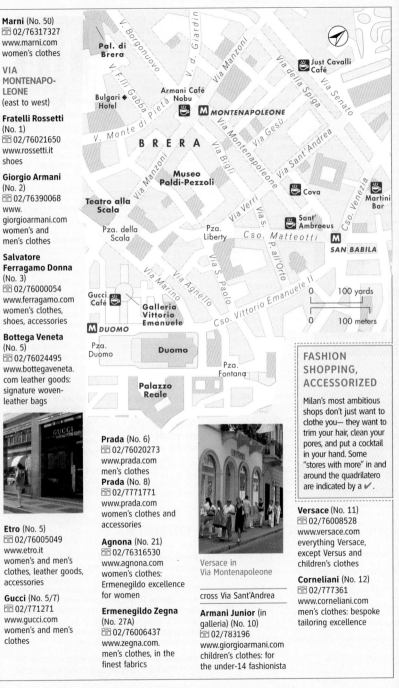

Marni (No. 50)
☎ 02/76317327
www.marni.com
women's clothes

VIA MONTENAPOLEONE
(east to west)

Fratelli Rossetti (No. 1)
☎ 02/76021650
www.rossetti.it
shoes

Giorgio Armani (No. 2)
☎ 02/76390068
www.giorgioarmani.com
women's and men's clothes

Salvatore Ferragamo Donna (No. 3)
☎ 02/76000054
www.ferragamo.com
women's clothes, shoes, accessories

Bottega Veneta (No. 5)
☎ 02/76024495
www.bottegaveneta.com leather goods: signature woven-leather bags

Etro (No. 5)
☎ 02/76005049
www.etro.it
women's and men's clothes, leather goods, accessories

Gucci (No. 5/7)
☎ 02/771271
www.gucci.com
women's and men's clothes

Prada (No. 6)
☎ 02/76020273
www.prada.com
men's clothes

Prada (No. 8)
☎ 02/7771771
www.prada.com
women's clothes and accessories

Agnona (No. 21)
☎ 02/76316530
www.agnona.com
women's clothes: Ermenegildo excellence for women

Ermenegildo Zegna (No. 27A)
☎ 02/76006437
www.zegna.com.
men's clothes, in the finest fabrics

Versace in Via Montenapoleone

---

cross Via Sant'Andrea

Armani Junior (in galleria) (No. 10)
☎ 02/783196
www.giorgioarmani.com
children's clothes: for the under-14 fashionista

FASHION SHOPPING, ACCESSORIZED

Milan's most ambitious shops don't just want to clothe you— they want to trim your hair, clean your pores, and put a cocktail in your hand. Some "stores with more" in and around the quadrilatero are indicated by a ✔.

Versace (No. 11)
☎ 02/76008528
www.versace.com
everything Versace, except Versus and children's clothes

Corneliani (No. 12)
☎ 02/777361
www.corneliani.com
men's clothes: bespoke tailoring excellence

REFUELING

If you want refreshments and aren't charmed by the quadrilatero's in-store cafés, try traditional **Cova** (Via Montenapoleone 8, ☎ 02/76000578) or more mod **Sant'Ambroeus** (Corso Matteotti 7, ☎ 02/76000540). Both serve coffee, aperitifs, and snacks in an ambience of starched tablecloths and chandeliers.

Cova's courtyard café

When the hurly-burly's done, head for the **Bulgari Hotel** (Via Fratelli Gabba 7b, ☎ 02/8058051), west of Via Manzoni, for a quiet (if pricey) drink. In summer, the bar extends into a beautiful, mature garden over an acre in size.

Aspesi (No. 13)
☎ 02/76022478
www.aspesi.it
low-key local design genius

Lorenzi (No. 9)
☎ 02/76022848
www.glorenzi.com
unique Milan—cutlery, razors, gifts

Valentino (No. 20)
corner Via Santo Spirito
☎ 02/76020285
www.valentino.it
women's clothes: elegant designs for special occasions

Salvatore Ferragamo Uomo (No. 20/4)
☎ 02/76006660
www.ferragamo.com
men's clothing and accessories

Loro Piana (No. 27c)
☎ 02/7772901
www.loropiana.it
women's and men's clothes, accessories: cashmere everything

VIA SAN PIETRO ALL'ORTO
(east to west)

Belfe-Postcard (No. 7)
☎ 02/781023
www.belfe.it
chic sport and skiwear

Pomellato (No. 17)
☎ 02/76006086
www.pomellato.it
classic Milan—style jewelry

Jimmy Choo (No. 17)
☎ 02/45481770
www.jimmychoo.com
women's and men's shoes

CORSO VENEZIA
(south to north)

Prada Linea Rossa (No. 3)
☎ 02/76001426
www.prada.com
Prada's sports line for men and women

D&G (No. 7)
☎ 02/76004095
www.dolcegabbana.it
swimwear, underwear, accessories: Dolce & Gabbana's younger line

Armani Collezioni (No. 9)
☎ 02/76390068
men's and women's clothing and accessories

✔ **Dolce & Gabbana** (No. 15)
☎ 02/76028485
www.dolcegabbana.it
Men's clothes, sold in a four-story, early 19th-century patrician home. An added feature is the Martini Bar, which also serves light lunches.

VIA VERRI
(south to north)

cross Via Bigli

D&G in Via della Spiga

Etro Profumi
corner Via Bigli
☎ 02/76005450
www.etro.it
fragrances

VIA SANT'ANDREA
(south to north)

✔ **Trussardi** (No. 5)
☎ 02/76020380
www.trussardi.com
Women's and men's clothes. The nearby flagship store (Piazza della Scala 5) includes the Trussardi Marino alla Scala Café (☎ 02/80688242), a fashion-forward bar done in stone, steel, slate, and glass. For a more substantial lunch, and views of Teatro alla Scala, head upstairs to the Marino alla Scala Ristorante (☎ 02/80688201), which serves creative Mediterranean cuisine.

Missoni (angolo via Bagutta)
☎ 02/76003555

BARGAIN-HUNTING AT THE OUTLETS

Milan may be Italy's richest city, but that doesn't mean all its well-dressed residents can afford to shop at the boutiques of the quadrilatero. Many pick up their designer clothes at outlet stores, where prices can be reduced by 50 percent or more.

Salvagente (Via Bronzetti 16 ☎ 02/76110328, www.salvagentemilano.it) is the top outlet for designer apparel and accessories from both large are small houses. There's a small men's department. To get there, take the 60 bus, which runs from the Duomo to the Stazione Centrale, to the intersection of Bronzetti and Archimede. Look for the green iron gate with the bronze sign, between the hairdressers and an apartment building. No credit cards.

DMagazine Outlet (Via Montenapoleone 26 ☎ 02/76006027, www.dmagazine.it) has bargains in the women's and men's clothing

Banner (No. 8/A)
☎ 02/76004609
women's and men's clothes: a multibrand boutique

Moschino (No. 12)
☎ 02/76000832
www.moschino.it
women's clothes: world-renowned window displays

✔ **Gianfranco Ferré** (No. 15)
☎ 02/794864
www.gianfrancoferre.com
Everything Ferré, plus a spa providing facials, Jacuzzis, steam baths, and mud treatments. Reservations are essential (☎ 02/76017526), preferably a week in advance.

Miu Miu (No. 21)
☎ 02/76001799
www.prada.com
Prada's younger line

Armani in Via Manzoni

VIA MANZONI
(south to north)

Valextra (No. 3)
☎ 02/99786000
www.valextra.it
glamorous bags and luggage

✔ **Armani Megastore** (No. 31)
☎ 02/72318600
www.giorgioarmani.com
The quadrilatero's most conspicuous shopping complex. Along with many Armani fashions, you'll find a florist, a bookstore, a chocolate shop (offering Armani pralines), the Armani

Prada store in the Galleria

Caffè, and Nobu (of the upscale Japanese restaurant chain). The Armani Casa furniture collection is next door at number 37.

CORSO COMO

✔ **10 Corso Como**
☎ 02/29000727
www.10corsocomo.com
Outside the quadrilatero, but it's a must see for fashion addicts. The bazaar-like 13,000-square-foot complex includes women's and men's boutiques, a bar and restaurant, a bookstore, a record shop, and an art gallery specializing in photography. You can even spend the night (if you can manage to get a reservation) at Milan's most exclusive B&B, Three Rooms (☎ 02/626163). The furnishings are a modern design-lover's dream.

GALLERIA VITTORIO EMANUELE

(not technically part of the quadrilatero, but nearby)

✔ **Gucci**
☎ 02/8597991
www.gucci.com
Gucci accessories, plus the world's first Gucci café. Sit outside behind the elegant boxwood hedge and watch the world go by.

Prada (No. 63-65)
☎ 02/876979
www.prada.com
the original store: look for the murals downstairs.

Louis Vuitton
☎ 02/72147011
www.vuitton.com
accessories, women's and men's shoes, watches

Tod's
☎ 02/877997
www.tods.com
women's and men's shoes, leather goods, accessories

Borsalino (No. 92
☎ 02/804337
www.borsalino.com
hats

Galleria Vittorio Emanuele

midst of the quadrilatero. Names on sale include Armani, Cavalli, Gucci, and Prada.

(Galleria San Carlo 6 ☎ 02/76000829) sells last year's Max Mara, Max & Co, Sportmax, Marella, Penny Black, and Marina Rinaldi. It's just 300 meters from the Max Mara store located on Corso Vittorio Emanuele at the corner of Galleria de Cristoforis.

At the outlet (Via Tazzoli 3 ☎ 02/29015130, www.10corsocomo.com) you can find clothes, shoes, bags, and accessories. It's open Fri.–Sun. 11–7.

Fans of who have a little time on their hands will want to check out the outlet (Via Tajani 1 ☎ 02/70009735 or 02/71040332, www.marni.com). Take the 61 bus to the terminus at Largo Murani, from which it's about 200 meters on foot. has an outlet, but it's way out of town—off the A3, most of the way to Como. The address is Strada Provinciale per Bregnano 13, in the town of Vertemate (☎ 031 887373, www.giorgioarmani.com).

Monday. **Brellin Café** (✉ *Vicolo Lavandai at Alzaia Naviglio Grande* ☎ *02/58101351* 🌐 *www.brellin.com*) in the arty Navigli district has live music and serves late-night snacks. **Café Trussardi** (✉ *Piazza della Scala 5, Duomo* ☎ *02/80688295* 🌐 *www.trussardi.it*) has an enormous plasma screen that keeps hip barflies entertained with video art. Open throughout the day, it's a great place for coffee. In Brera, check out the **Giamaica** (✉ *Via Brera 32* ☎ *02/876723* 🌐 *www.jamaicabar.it*), a traditional hangout for students from the nearby Brera art school. On summer nights this neighborhood pulses with life; street vendors and fortune-tellers jostle for space alongside the outdoor tables. For an evening of live music—predominantly rock to jazz—head to perennial favorite **Le Scimmie** (✉ *Via Ascanio Sforza 49, Navigli* ☎ *02/89402874* 🌐 *www.scimmie.it*). It features international stars, some of whom jet in to play here, while others, including Ronnie Jones, are longtime residents in Milan. Dinner is an option. The bar of the **Sheraton Diana Majestic** (✉ *Viale Piave 42* ☎ *02/20581*), which has a splendid garden, is a prime meeting place for young professionals and the fashion people from the showrooms of the Porta Venezia neighborhood. For a break from the traditional, check out ultratrendy **SHU** (✉ *Via Molino delle Armi, Ticinese* ☎ *02/58315720*), whose gleaming interior looks like a cross between *Star Trek* and Cocteau's *Beauty and the Beast.*

NIGHTCLUBS

For nightclubs, note that the cover charges can change depending on the day of the week. **Magazzini Generali** (✉ *Via Pietrasanta 14, Porta Vigentina* ☎ *02/5393948* 🌐 *www.magazzinigenerali.it*), in what was an abandoned warehouse, is a fun, futuristic venue for dancing and concerts. The €20 cover charge includes a drink. Its venerable age notwithstanding, **Plastic** (✉ *Viale Umbria 120* ☎ *02/733996* 🌐 *www.thisisplastic.com*), closed Monday through Wednesday and some Thursdays, is still considered Milan's most transgressive, avant-garde, and fun club, complete with drag-queen shows. The action starts late, even by Italian standards—don't bother going before midnight. Cover is €15 to €20. To its regular discotheque fare, **Tocqueville** (✉ *Via Alexis de Tocqueville, Corso Como* ☎ *02/29002973* 🌐 *www.tocqueville13.it* ⏲ *Closed Mon.*) has added two nights per week of live music, featuring young and emerging talent. The cover at this ever-popular Milan club is €10–€13.

SPORTS

SOCCER

AC Milan and Inter Milan, two of the oldest and most successful teams in Europe, vie for the heart of soccer-mad Lombardy. For residents, the city is *Milano* but the teams are *Milan,* a vestige of their common founding as the Milan Cricket and Football Club in 1899. When an Italian-led faction broke off in 1908, the new club was dubbed F.C. Internazionale (or "Inter") to distinguish it from the bastion of English exclusivity that would become AC Milan (or simply "Milan"). Since then, the picture has become more clouded: although Milan prides itself as the true team of the city and of its working class, Inter can more persuasively claim pan-Italian support.

CLOSE UP

Milan's Furniture Fair

During the Salone del Mobile, Milan's furniture fair, in early April, the city is a scene—there are showroom openings, cocktail parties, and product launches, and design types dressed in black and wearing funny glasses fill the sidewalks and bars.

Except for a few free days, the Salone del Mobile is for professionals only, but you can still participate. Newspapers such as *Corriere della Sera* usually run an English supplement, and special design-week freebies list public events around Milan called "Fuorisalone" (🌐 *www.fuorisalone.it*). Major players such as bathroom and kitchen specialist Boffi (Via Solferino 11) and Capellini (Via Santa Cecilia 4) launch new products in their stores. Warning: Do not visit if you have not planned ahead. Hotel rooms and restaurant seating are impossible to find. See 🌐 *www.fieramilano.it* for dates.

AC Milan and Inter Milan share the use of **San Siro Stadium (Stadio Meazza)** (✉ *Via Piccolomini*) during their August through May season. With more than 60,000 of the 85,000 seats appropriated by season-ticket holders and another couple thousand allocated to visiting fans, tickets to Sunday games can be difficult to come by. You can purchase advance **AC Milan** (🌐 *www.acmilan.com*) tickets at Cariplo bank branches, including one at Via Verdi 8, or at the club's Web site. **Inter** (🌐 *www.inter.it*) tickets are available at Banca Popolare di Milano branches, including one at Piazza Meda 4, or at the club's Web site. To reach San Siro, take subway Line 1 (red) toward Molino Dorino, exit at the Lotto station, and board a bus for the stadium.

If you're a soccer fan but can't get in to see a game, you might settle for a **stadium tour** (☎ *02/4042432* 🌐 *www.sansirotour.com*), which includes a visit to the Milan-Inter museum. Tours are available every half hour from Gate 21 from 10 am to 5 pm, except on game Sundays. Museum costs €7, stadium €12.50. Call for reservations a few days before your visit.

6

SHOPPING

The heart of Milan's shopping reputation is the **Quadrilatero della moda** district north of the Duomo. Here the world's leading designers compete for shoppers' attention, showing off their ultrastylish clothes in stores that are works of high style themselves. You won't find any bargains, but regardless of whether you're making a purchase, the area is a great place for window-shopping and people-watching. But fashion is not limited to one neighborhood, and there is a huge and exciting selection of clothing that is affordable, well made, and often more interesting than what is offered by the international luxury brands with shops in the Quadrilatero.

Wander around the **Brera** to find smaller shops with some appealing offerings from lesser-known names that cater to the well-schooled taste of this upscale neighborhood. The densest concentration is along Via

Brera, Via Solferino, and Corso Garibaldi. For inexpensive and trendy clothes—for the under-25 set—stroll **Via Torino**, which begins in Piazza Duomo. Stay away on Saturday afternoon if you don't like crowds. Milan has several shopping streets that serve nearby residential concentrations. In the Porta Venezia area, visit **Corso Buenos Aires**, which runs northeast from the Giardini Pubblici. The wide and busy street is lined with affordable shops. It has the highest concentration of clothing stores in Europe, so be prepared to give up halfway. Avoid Saturday after 3 pm, when it seems the entire city is here looking for bargains. Near the Corso Magenta area, walk a few blocks beyond *The Last Supper* to **Corso Vercelli**, where you will find everything from a branch of the Coin department store to the quintessentially Milanese **Gemelli** (✉ *Corso Vercelli 16* ☎ *02/48004689* 🌐 *www.gemelli.it*).

QUICK BITES

Pasticceria Biffi (✉ *Corso Magenta 87* ☎ *02/48006702* 🌐 *www.biffipasticceria.it*) is a Milan institution and the official pastry shop of this traditionally wealthy neighborhood. Have a coffee or a rich hot chocolate in its paneled room before facing the crowds in Corso Vercelli.

MARKETS

Weekly open markets selling fruits and vegetables—and a great deal more—are still a regular sight in Milan. Many also sell clothing and shoes. Monday- and Thursday-morning markets in **Mercato di Via S. Marco** (✉ *Brera*) cater to the wealthy residents of this central neighborhood. In addition to food stands where you can get cheese, roast chicken, and dried beans and fruits, there are several clothing and shoe stalls that are important stops for some of Milan's most elegant women. Check out the knitwear at Valentino, about midway down on the street side. Muscle in on the students from the prestigious high school nearby who rush here for the french fries and potato croquettes at the chicken stand at the Via Montebello end.

Bargains in designer apparel can be found at the huge **Mercato Papiniano** (✉ *Porta Genova*) on Saturday all day and Tuesday from about 9 to 1. The stalls to look for are at the Piazza Sant'Agostino end of the market. It's very crowded and demanding—watch out for pickpockets.

PAVIA, CREMONA, AND MANTUA

Once proud medieval fortress towns rivaling Milan in power, these centers of industry and commerce on the Po Plain still play a key role in Italy's wealthiest, most populous region. Pavia is celebrated for its extraordinarily detailed Carthusian monastery, Cremona for its incomparable violin-making tradition. Mantua—the most picturesque of the three—was the home of the fantastically wealthy Gonzaga dynasty for almost 300 years.

PAVIA

41 km (25 mi) south of Milan.

GETTING HERE

By car from Milan, start out on the A7 autostrada and exit onto A53 as you near Pavia; the drive is 40 km (25 mi) and takes about 45 minutes. Pavia is 30 to 40 minutes by train from Milan and 1½ hours (by slower regional service) from Cremona. The Certosa is 30 minutes by train from several Milan stations.

VISITOR INFORMATION

Pavia tourism office (✉ *Palazzo del Broletto, Piazza della Vittoria* ☎ *0382/597001* 🌐 *www.turismo.provincia.pv.it*).

EXPLORING

Pavia was once Milan's chief regional rival. The city dates from at least the Roman era and was the capital of the Lombard kings for two centuries (572–774). It was at one time known as "the city of a hundred towers," but only a handful have survived the passing of time. Its prestigious university was founded in 1361 on the site of a 10th-century law school, but it has roots that can be traced to antiquity.

6

The 14th-century **Castello Visconteo** now houses the local **Museo Civico** (Municipal Museum), with a Romanesque and Renaissance sculpture gallery, an archaeological collection, and a large picture gallery featuring works by Correggio, Bellini, Tiepolo, Hayez, Pelizza da Volpedo, and La Foppa, among others. ✉ *Viale* XI *Febbraio* 35, *near Piazza Castello* ☎ *0382/33853* 🌐 *www.museicivici.pavia.it* 🎫 *€6* ⏲ *Feb.–June and Sept.–Nov., Tues.–Sun. 10–6; July, Aug., Dec., and Jan., Tues.–Sun. 9–1:30. Last entry 45 mins before closing.*

The main draw in Pavia is the **Certosa** *(Carthusian monastery)*, 9 km (5½ mi) north of the city center. Its elaborate facade shows the same relish for ornamentation as the Duomo in Milan. The Certosa's extravagant grandeur was due in part to the plan to have it house the tombs of the family of the first duke of Milan, Galeazzo Visconti III (who died during a plague, at age 49, in 1402). The best marble was used, taken undoubtedly by barge from the quarries of Carrara, roughly 240 km (150 mi) away. Though the floor plan may be Gothic—a cross shape divided into a series of squares—the gorgeous fabric that rises above it is triumphantly Renaissance. On the facade, in the lower frieze, are medallions of Roman emperors and Eastern monarchs; above them are low reliefs of scenes from the life of Christ and from the career of Galeazzo Visconti III.

The first duke was the only Visconti to be interred here, and not until some 75 years after his death, in a tomb designed by Gian Cristoforo Romano. Look for it in the right transept. In the left transept is a more appealing tomb—that of a rather stern middle-aged man and a beautiful young woman. The man is Ludovico il Moro Sforza, seventh duke of Milan, who commissioned Leonardo to paint *The Last Supper.* The woman is Ludovico's wife, Beatrice d'Este (1475–97), one of the most celebrated women of her day, the embodiment of brains, culture, birth, and beauty. Married when he was 40 and she was 16, they had enjoyed six years together when she died while delivering a stillborn child. Ludovico commissioned the sculptor Cristoforo Solari to design a joint tomb for the high altar of Santa Maria delle Grazie in Milan. Originally much larger, the tomb for some years occupied the honored place as planned. Then, for reasons that are still mysterious, the Dominican monks sold the tomb to their Carthusian brothers to the south. Sadly, part of the tomb and its remains were lost. ✉ *Certosa, Località Monumento 4, 9 km (5½ mi) north of Pavia* ☎ *0382/925613* 🌐 *www.comune.pv.it/certosadipavia* 🎫 *Donations accepted* ⏲ *May–Aug., Tues.–Sun. 9–11:30 and 2:30–6; Apr. and Sept., Tues.–Sun. 9–11:30 and 2:30–5:30; Mar. and Oct., Tues.–Sun. 9–11:30 and 2:30–5; Nov.–Feb., Tues.–Sun. 9–11 and 2:30–4:30.*

In the Romanesque church of **San Pietro in Ciel d'Oro** you can visit the tomb of Christianity's most celebrated convert, Saint Augustine, housed in an intricately carved, Gothic, white marble ark on the high altar. ✉ *San Pietro in Ciel d'Oro 2* ☎ *0382/303036* 🌐 *santagostinopavia.it* ⏲ *Daily 7–noon and 3–7:30. Mass: Mon.–Sat. 9 and 6:30, Sun. 9, 11, and 6:30.*

WHERE TO EAT

$$$ NORTHERN ITALIAN ✕ **Locanda Vecchia Pavia al Mulino.** At this sophisticated art nouveau restaurant 150 yards from the Certosa you can find creative versions of traditional regional cuisine, including *risotto alla certosina* (with sturgeon eggs, frogs' legs, and river shrimp). *Casoncelli* (stuffed pasta), *petto d'anatra* (duck breast), and veal cutlet alla Milanese are done with style, as are the imaginative seafood dishes. There's a veranda open in summer with a view of the Certosa. ✉ *Via al Monumento 5, Certosa* ☎ *0382/925894* 🌐 *www.vecchiapaviaalmulino.it* ✍ *Reservations essential* ⏲ *Apr.–Oct., no lunch Mon. and Tues.; Nov.–Mar., no lunch Mon., closed Sun.*

CREMONA

104 km (65 mi) east of Pavia, 106 km (66 mi) southeast of Milan.

GETTING HERE

By car from Milan, start out on the A1 autostrada and switch to A21 at Piacenza; the drive is 100 km (62 mi) and lasts about 1½ hours. From Pavia, take SS617 to A21; the trip is 70 km (44 mi) and lasts about 1¼ hours. By train, Cremona is about an hour from Milan and 1½ hours from Desenzano, near Sirmione on Lake Garda.

VISITOR INFORMATION

Cremona tourism office (✉ *Piazza del Comune 5* ☎ *0372/23233* 🌐 *turismo.provincia.cremona.it* ⏲ *Daily 9–1 and 2–5; July and Aug., closed Sun. afternoon*).

EXPLORING

Cremona is where the world's best violins are made. Andrea Amati (1510–80) invented the modern instrument here in the 16th century. Though cognoscenti continue to revere the Amati name, it was an apprentice of Amati's nephew for whom the fates had reserved wide and lasting fame. In a career that spanned an incredible 68 years, Antonio Stradivari (1644–1737) made more than 1,200 instruments—including violas, cellos, harps, guitars, and mandolins, in addition to his fabled violins. Labeled simply with a small printed slip reading "antonius stradivarius cremonensis. faciebat anno," followed by the date inserted in a neat italic hand, they remain the most coveted, most expensive stringed instruments in the world.

Strolling about this quiet, medium-size city, you cannot help noting that violin making continues to flourish. There are, in fact, more than 50 *liutai,* many of them graduates of the Scuola Internazionale di Liuteria (International School of Violin Making). You are usually welcome to these ateliers, where traditional craftsmanship reigns supreme, especially if you are contemplating the acquisition of your own instrument; the tourist office can provide addresses.

Cremona's other claim to fame is *torrone* (nougat), which is said to have been created here in honor of the marriage of Bianca Maria Visconti and Francesco Sforza, which took place in October 1441. The new confection, originally prepared by heating almonds, egg whites, and honey over low heat and shaped and named after the city's tower, was created in symbolic celebration. The annual Festa del Torrone is held in the main piazza on the third Sunday in October.

QUICK BITES

Prepare to visit the sites of Cremona or wait for the next train at the Pasticceria Dondeo (✉ *Via Alghieri Dante 38* ☎ *0372/21224*), visible from and just to the right of the station. Dating back to 1912, this is one of Cremona's oldest and most beautiful art nouveau café and pastry shops. The fresh zabaglione and beignets are heaven.

The **Piazza del Comune**, surrounded by the Duomo, tower, baptistery, and city hall, is distinctive and harmonious: the combination of old brick, rose- and cream-color marble, terra-cotta, and old copper roofs brings Romanesque, Gothic, and Renaissance together with unusual success. The city's collection of stringed treasures is on display: a viola and five violins, including the golden-orange "Il Cremonese 1715" Stradivarius. ✉ *Piazza del Comune 5* ☎ *0372/803618* 🌐 *www.musei.comune.cremona.it* 🎫 *Violin collection €6* ⏲ *Tues.–Sat. 9–6, Sun. 10–6.*

Dominating Piazza del Comune is the **Torrazzo** *(Big Tower)*, the city's symbol and perhaps the tallest campanile in Italy, visible for a considerable distance across the Po Plain. It's open to visitors, but in winter hours fluctuate depending on the weather. The tower's astronomical clock is the 1583 original. ✉ *Piazza del Comune* ☎ *0372/495029* 🎫 *€6.50* ⏲ *Tues.–Sun. 10–1 and 2:30–6.*

Cremona's Romanesque **Duomo** was consecrated in 1190. Here you can find the beautiful *Story of the Virgin Mary and the Passion of Christ,* the central fresco of an extraordinary cycle commissioned in 1514 and featuring the work of local artists, including Boccacio Boccancino, Giovan Francesco Bembo, and Altobello Melone. ✉ *Piazza del Comune* ☎ *0372/495011* ⏲ *Weekdays 8–noon and 3:30–7.*

Legendary violin maker Antonio Stradivari lived, worked, and died near the verdant square at **No. 1 Piazza Roma**. According to local lore, Stradivari kept each instrument in his bedroom for a month before varnishing it, imparting part of his soul before sealing and sending it out

The Po Plain
and Lake Garda
Lago Maggiore Verbano
Lago di Como
Aeroporto Malpensa
Legnano
Lainate
Rho
Como
Lecco
Giussano
Monza
Milan
Buccinasco
Rozzano
Melegnano
Mortara
Ticino
Pavia
River
Fiume Po
Lodi
River
Crema
Casalpusterlengo
TO PARMA
Treviglio
F. Adda
LOMBARDY
Bergamo
Lago d'Iseo
Darfo-Boario
Brescia
Oglio
River
Cremona
TRENTINO-ALTO ADIGE
Riva del Garda
Malcesine
Gargnano
Gardone Riviera
Salò
Punta di San Vigilio
Bardolino
Lago Garda
Sirmione
TO VERONA
TO VENICE
Mantua
0
10 mi
0
10 km
36
639
342
583
342
42
42
A9
233
35
36
527
A8
A4
A4
11
11
11
11
A50
494
415
A1
9
A7
35
211
235
9
591
591
415
235
234
A1
A21
A21
A21
10
10
420
62
62
236
236
12
A22
249
Biz. 45
Biz. 45
572
510

into the world. In the center of the park is **Stradivari's grave,** marked by a simple tombstone.

The **Museo Stradivariano** *(Stradivarius Museum)* in Palazzo Affaitati houses a collection of antique and modern instruments and informative exhibits of Stradivari's paper patterns, wooden models, and various tools. ✉ *Via Ugolani Dati 4* ☎ *0372/803622* 🎫 *€7* ⏲ *Tues.–Sat. 9–6, Sun. 10–6.*

WHERE TO EAT

$ NORTHERN ITALIAN ★ ✕ **Centrale.** Close to the cathedral, this old-style trattoria is a favorite among locals for traditional regional fare, such as succulent *cotechino* (pork sausage) and *tortelli di zucca* (a small pasta with pumpkin filling), at moderate prices. ✉ *Vicolo Pertusio 4* ☎ *0372/28701* ⏲ *Closed Thurs. and July.*

$ NORTHERN ITALIAN ✕ **La Sosta.** This traditional restaurant looks to the 16th century for culinary inspiration, following a time-tested recipe for a favored first course, gnocchi *Vecchia Cremona.* The homemade salami is also excellent. To finish off the evening, try the *semifreddo al torroncino* (chilled almond cake) and a dessert wine. ✉ *Via Sicardo 9* ☎ *0372/456656* 🌐 *www.osterialasosta.it* 💳 *AE, DC, MC, V* ⏲ *Closed Mon. and 3 wks in Aug. No dinner Sun.*

WHERE TO STAY

$$ 🏨 **Delle Arti Design Hotel.** The name fits at this central hotel with elegant modern interiors and eclectic designer furniture. **Pros:** ultramodern, industrial design; friendly staff; lots of amenities. **Cons:** probably too contemporary for those seeking more traditional Italy. **TripAdvisor:** "fairytale-like ambiance," "sleek design hotel," "impressive all-black facade." ✉ *Via Bonomelli 8* ☎ *0372/23131* 🌐 *www.dellearti.com* 🛏 *33 rooms, 3 suites* 👍 *In-room: Internet, Wi-Fi. In-hotel: room service, bar, gym, Wi-Fi hotspot, parking (paid)* ⏲ *Closed Aug. 5–29 and late Dec.* 🍽 *Breakfast.*

$ 🏨 **Hotel Impero.** This comfortable, modern hotel is well equipped to satisfy both leisure and business travelers. **Pros:** highly professional staff; quiet rooms. **Cons:** rooms may seem a little out of style for some. **TripAdvisor:** "peaceful and elegant," "tastefully furnished," "below is a lively piazza." ✉ *Piazza della Pace 21* ☎ *0372/413013* 🌐 *www.hotelimpero.cr.it* 🛏 *53 rooms* 👍 *In-room: refrigerator, Wi-Fi. In-hotel: bar, Wi-Fi hotspot, parking (paid)* 🍽 *Breakfast.*

SHOPPING

For Cremona's specialty nougat, visit famed **Sperlari** (✉ *Via Solferino 25* ☎ *0372/22346* 🌐 *www.fieschi1867.com*). In addition to nougat, Cremona's best *mostarda* (a condiment made from preserved fruit served with meat and cheese) has been sold from this handsome shop since 1836; Sperlari and parent company Fieschi have grown into a confectionary empire. Look for the historical product display in the back.

MANTUA

192 km (119 mi) southeast of Milan.

GETTING HERE

Mantua is 5 km (3 mi) west of the A22 autostrada. The drive from Milan, following A4 to A22, takes a little more than two hours. The drive from Cremona, along SS10, is 1¼ hours. Most trains arrive in just under 2 hours from Milan, depending on the type of service, and about 1½ hours from Desenzano, near Sirmione on Lake Garda, via Verona.

VISITOR INFORMATION

Mantua tourism office (✉ *Piazza A. Mantegna 6* ☎ *0376/432432* 🌐 *www.turismo.mantova.it* 🕙 *Daily 9–5*). Ask about the museum pass, which entitles you to reduced entrance fees at participating museums (not including the Palazzo Ducale or the Palazzo Te).

EXPLORING

Mantua stands tallest among the ancient walled cities of the Po Plain. Its fortifications are circled on three sides by the passing Mincio River, which long provided Mantua with protection, fish, and a steady stream of river tolls as it meandered from Lake Garda to join the Po. It may not be flashy or dramatic, but Mantua's beauty is subtle and deep, hiding a rich trove of artistic, architectural, and cultural gems beneath its slightly somber facade.

Although Mantua first came to prominence in Roman times as the home of Virgil, its grand monuments date from the glory years of the Gonzaga dynasty. From 1328 until the Austrian Habsburgs sacked the city in 1708, the dukes and marquesses of the Gonzaga clan reigned over a wealthy independent commune, and the arts thrived in the relative peace of that period. Raphael's star pupil Andrea Mantegna, who served as court painter for 50 years, was the best known of a succession of artists and architects who served Mantua through the years, and some of his finest work, including his only surviving fresco cycle, can be seen here. Giulio Romano (circa 1499–1546), Mantegna's apprentice, built his masterpiece, Palazzo Te, on an island in the river. Leon Battista Alberti (1404–72), who designed two impressive churches in Mantua, was widely emulated later in the Renaissance.

★ The 500-room **Palazzo Ducale**, the palace that dominates the skyline, was built for the Gonzaga family. Unfortunately, as the Gonzaga dynasty waned in power and prestige, much of the art within the castle was sold or stolen. The highlight is the Camera Degli Sposi—literally, the "Chamber of the Wedded Couple"—where Duke Ludovico and his wife held court. Mantegna painted it over a nine-year period at the height of his power, finishing at age 44. He made a startling advance in painting by organizing the picture plane in a way that systematically mimics the experience of human vision. Even now, more than five centuries later, you can sense the excitement of a mature artist, fully aware of the great importance of his painting, expressing his vision with a masterly, joyous confidence. The circular trompe l'oeil around the vaulted ceiling is famous for the many details that attest to Mantegna's greatness: the three-dimensional quality of the seven Caesars (the Gonzagas saw themselves as successors to the Roman emperors and paid homage to classical culture throughout the palazzo); the self-portrait of Mantegna (in purple, on the right side of the western fresco); and the dwarf peering out from behind the dress of Ludovico's wife (on the northern fresco). Only 20 people at a time are allowed in the Camera Degli Sposi, and only for 10 minutes at a time. Read about the room before you enter, so that you can spend your time looking up.

WORD OF MOUTH

"Mantua! A small city, midway between Venice and Milan, surrounded on three sides by lagoons which are covered by flowering lotus in the summer, a funny sort of place where they eat donkey ragù and pumpkin ravioli and drink fizzy wine. Italians go there for the art and the lakes, but tourists from other countries haven't discovered it yet. Oh, and the art! Astonishing, amazing Renaissance art!"

—Julia1

6

Walk-up visitors to Mantua's Palazzo Ducale may take a fast-paced guided tour conducted in Italian; signs in each room provide explanations in English. Audio guides are available for €4. Alternatively, call the **tourism office** (☎ *0376/432432*) to arrange for English-language tours. ✉ *Piazza Sordello 40* ☎ *0376/224832* 🎟 *€6.50, additional €1 for reservation to see Camera Degli Sposi* ⏲ *Tues.–Sun. 8:30–7; last entry at 6:30.*

Serious Mantegna aficionados will want to visit the **Casa di Andrea Mantegna**, designed by the artist himself and built around an intriguing circular courtyard, which is usually open to view. The exterior is interesting for its unusual design, and the interior, with its hidden frescoes, can be seen by appointment or during occasional art exhibitions. Prices vary depending on the exhibition. ✉ *Via Acerbi 47* ☎ *0376/360506* 🌐 *www.casadelmantegna.it* ⏲ *Tues.–Fri. 10–1, weekends 10–1 and 3–6.*

Mantegna's tomb is in the first chapel to the left in the basilica of **Sant'Andrea**, most of which was built in 1472. The current structure, a masterwork by the architect Alberti, is the third built on this spot to house the relic of the Precious Blood. The crypt holds two reliquaries containing earth believed to be soaked in the blood of Christ, brought to Mantua by Longinus, the soldier who pierced his side. They are displayed only on Good Friday. ✉ *Piazza di Mantegna* ☎ *0376/328504* 🎟 *Free, €1 to visit the crypt* ⏲ *Weekdays 8–noon and 3–7; Sat. 10:30–noon and 3–6; Sun. 11:45–12:15 and 3–6.*

★ **Palazzo Te** is one of the greatest of all Renaissance palaces, built between 1525 and 1535 by Federigo II Gonzaga. It is the mannerist masterpiece of artist-architect Giulio Romano, who created a pavilion where the strict rules of courtly behavior could be relaxed for libertine pastimes. Romano's purposeful breaks with classical tradition are lighthearted and unprecedented. For example, note the "slipping" triglyphs along the upper edge of the inside courtyard. Two highlights are the *Camera di Amore e Psiche* (Room of Cupid and Psyche) that depicts a wedding set among lounging nymphs, frolicking satyrs, and even a camel and an elephant; and the gasp-producing *Camera dei Giganti* (Room of the Giants) that shows Jupiter expelling the Titans from Mount Olympus.

The scale of the work is overwhelming; the floor-to-ceiling work completely envelops the viewer. The room's rounded corners, and the river rock covering the original floor, were meant to give it a cavelike feeling. It is a "whisper chamber" in which words softly uttered in one corner can be heard in the opposite one. For fun, note the graffiti from as far back as the 17th century. ✉ *Viale Te 13* ☎ *0376/323266* 🌐 *www.centropalazzote.it* 🎫 *€8* ⏲ *Tues.–Sun. 9–6; Mon. 1–6; last entry at 5:30.*

WHERE TO EAT

$$$$ NORTHERN ITALIAN ★ ✕ **Ambasciata.** Heralded by food critics the world over as one of Italy's finest restaurants, Ambasciata (Italian for "embassy") takes elegance and service to new levels. Chef Romano Tamani, who is co-owner with his brother Francesco, makes frequent appearances abroad but is at home in tiny Quistello, 20 km (12 mi) southeast of Mantua. He offers those willing to make the trek (and pay the bill) an ever-changing array of superlative creations such as *timballo di lasagne verdi con petto di piccione sauté alla crème de Cassis* (green lasagna with breast of pigeon and red currant). ✉ *Via Martiri di Belfiore 33, Quistello* ☎ *0376/619169* 🌐 *www.ristoranteambasciata.com* ✍ *Reservations essential* ⏲ *Closed Mon., Jan. 1–15, and Aug. No dinner Sun.*

¢ ITALIAN ✕ **Ristorante Pavesi.** Locals have been coming to this central restaurant for delicious food at reasonable prices since 1918. The menu changes every other month; homemade pasta is always a good bet. In warmer months you can dine on Mantua's handsome main square. ✉ *Piazza delle Erbe 13* ☎ *0376/323627* 🌐 *www.ristorantepavesi.com* ⏲ *Closed Tues. and from Jan. 6 to 14.*

WHERE TO STAY

$$ **Casa Poli.** Refreshing, minimalist influences, creative touches (like the room number projected onto the hall floor) and attention to detail create a welcoming ambience in this contemporary hotel. **Pros:** attentive staff; tasteful, unusual decor; families welcome. **Cons:** although convenient, not in the absolute center of the city. **TripAdvisor:** "modern hotel in an old palazzo," "polite and very helpful stuff," "garage is a huge plus." ✉ *Corso Garibaldi 32* ☎ *0376/288170* 🌐 *www.hotelcasapoli.it* *27 rooms* *In-room: a/c, safe, Wi-Fi. In-hotel: bar, elevator, laundry service, bicycles, Internet terminal, Wi-Fi hotspot, parking (paid)* *Breakfast.*

$$ **Hotel Rechigi.** With its white marble lobby and silver-and-taupe lounge, this modern hotel and its collection of contemporary art offer quiet refuge from the busy streets in the center of Mantua, only a block away. **Pros:** quiet and central with friendly service. **Cons:** spare design might leave some guests cold. **TripAdvisor:** "entrance is impressive," "modern design," "beds are concrete." ✉ *Via Pier Fortunato Calvi 30* ☎ *059/283600* 🌐 *www.rechigi.com* *50 rooms, 7 suites* *In-room: safe, Wi-Fi. In-hotel: bar, laundry service, Internet terminal, Wi-Fi hotspot, parking (paid), some pets allowed* *No meals.*

LAKE GARDA

Lake Garda has had a perennial attraction for travelers and writers alike; even essayist Michel de Montaigne (1533–92), whose 15 months of travel journals contain not a single other reference to nature, paused to admire the view down the lake from Torbole, which he called "boundless."

Lake Garda is 50 km (31 mi) long, ranges roughly 1 km to 16 km (½ mi to 10 mi) wide, and is as much as 1,135 feet deep. The terrain is flat at the lake's southern base and mountainous at its northern tip. As a consequence, its character varies from stormy inland sea to crystalline Nordic-style fjord. It's the biggest lake in the region and by most accounts the cleanest. Drivers should take care on the hazardous hairpin turns on the lake road.

GETTING HERE

The town of Sirmione, at the south end of the lake, is 10 km (6 mi) from Desenzano, which has regular train service; it's about an hour and 20 minutes by train from Milan and 25 minutes from Verona. The A4 autostrada passes to the south of the lake, and A22 runs north–south about 10 km (6 mi) from the eastern shore.

BERGAMO

52 km (32 mi) northeast of Milan.

GETTING HERE

Bergamo is along the A4 autostrada. By car from Milan, take A51 out of the city to pick up A4; the drive is 52 km (32 mi) and takes about 45 minutes. By train, Bergamo is about 1 hour from Milan and 1½ hours from Sirmione.

VISITOR INFORMATION

Bergamo tourism office (✉ Torre del Gombito, *Via Gombito 13, Bergamo Alta* ☎ *035/242226* ⏲ *Daily 9–12:30 and 2–5:30* ✉ *Piazzale Marconi, Bergamo Bassa* ☎ *035/210204* ⏲ *Closed holidays and winter weekends* 🌐 *www.comune.bergamo.it; summer events:* 🌐 *www.bergamoestate.com*).

EXPLORING

If you're driving from Milan to Lake Garda, the perfect deviation from your autostrada journey is the lovely medieval town of Bergamo. Bergamo is also a wonderful side trip by train from Milan. In less than an hour, you will be whisked from the restless pace of city life to the medieval grandeur of Bergamo Alta, where the pace is a tranquil remnant of the past.

From behind a set of battered Venetian walls high on an Alpine hilltop, Bergamo majestically surveys the countryside. Behind are the snowcapped Bergamese Alps, and two funiculars connect the modern **Bergamo Bassa** (Lower Bergamo) to the ancient **Bergamo Alta** (Upper Bergamo). Bergamo Bassa's long arteries and ornate piazze speak to its centuries of prosperity, but it's nonetheless overshadowed by Bergamo Alta's magnificence.

The massive **Torre Civica** offers a great view of the two cities. ✉ *Piazza Vecchia* ☎ *035/247116* 🎫 *€3, minimum 5 people* ⏲ *Mar.–Oct., Tues.–Fri. 9:30–7, weekends 9:30–9:30; Nov.–Feb., Tues.–Fri. by appointment, weekends 9:30–4:30.*

> **WORD OF MOUTH**
>
> "You definitively need a car at Lake Garda. The landscape is so fantastic. Nowhere else on earth you will see such a dramatic meeting of mountain and lake as in the northern section of Lake Garda. And the only way to see it is driving by car."
>
> —traveller1959

Bergamo's **Duomo** and **Battistero** are the most substantial buildings in Piazza Duomo. But the most impressive structure is the **Cappella Colleoni**, with stunning marble decoration. ✉ *Piazza Duomo* ☎ *Duomo 035/210223; cappella 035/210061* ⏲ *Duomo, daily 7:30–11:45 and 3–5:30; cappella Mar.–Oct., daily 9–12:30 and 2:30–6; Nov.–Feb., Tues.–Sun. 9–12:30 and 2–4:30.*

In the **Accademia Carrara** you will find an art collection that is surprisingly rewarding given its size and remote location. Many of the Venetian masters are represented—Mantegna, Bellini, Carpaccio (circa 1460–1525/26), Tiepolo (1727–1804), Francesco Guardi (1712–93), Canaletto (1697–1768)—as well as Botticelli (1445–1510). At this writing the museum is undergoing remodeling, but a selection of works can be seen at Palazzo della Regione in Piazza Vecchia, Bergamo Alta. ✉ *Bergamo Bassa, Piazza Carrara 82* ☎ *035/270413* 🌐 *www.accademiacarrara.bergamo.it* 🎫 *€5* ⏲ *Palazzo della Regione: June–Sept., Sun. and Tues.–Fri. 10–9, Sat. 10 am–11 pm; Oct.–May, Sun. and Tues.–Fri. 9:30–5:30, Sat. 10–6.*

WHERE TO EAT

$ NORTHERN ITALIAN ✕ **Agnello d'Oro.** A 17th-century tavern on the main street in Upper Bergamo, with wooden booths and walls hung with copper utensils and ceramic plates, Agnello d'Oro is a good place to imbibe the atmosphere as well as the good local wine. Specialties are Bergamo-style risotto and varieties of polenta served with game and mushrooms. ✉ *Via Gombito 22, Bergamo Alta* ☎ *035/249883* ⏲ *Closed Mon. and Jan. 7–Feb. 5. No dinner Sun.*

$ WINE BAR Fodor's Choice ★ ✕ **Al Donizetti.** Find a table in the back of this central, cheerful enoteca before choosing local hams and cheeses to accompany your wine (more than 800 bottles are available, many by the glass). Heartier meals are also available, such as eggplant stuffed with cheese and salami, but save room for the desserts, which are well paired with dessert wines. ✉ *Via Gombito 17/a, Bergamo Alta* ☎ *035/242661* 🌐 *www.donizetti.it.*

$–$$ NORTHERN ITALIAN ✕ **Da Ornella.** The vaulted ceilings of this popular trattoria on the main street in the upper town are marked with ancient graffiti, created by (patiently) holding candles to the stone overhead. Ornella herself is in the kitchen, turning out casoncelli in butter and sage and platters of assorted roast meats. Ask her to suggest the perfect wine pairing for your meal. Three prix-fixe menus are available during the week, two on the weekend. ✉ *Via Gombito 15, Bergamo Alta* ☎ *035/232736* ⏲ *Closed Thurs.*

$$$ ITALIAN ★ **Taverna Colleoni dell'Angelo.** Angelo Cornaro is the name behind the Taverna Colleoni, on the Piazza Vecchia right behind the Duomo. He serves imaginative fish and meat dishes, both regional and international, all expertly prepared. *Piazza Vecchia 7, Bergamo Alta 035/232596 www.colleonidellangelo.com Closed Mon.*

WHERE TO STAY

$$–$$$ **Excelsior San Marco.** The most comfortable hotel in Lower Bergamo, the Excelsior San Marco is only a short walk from the walls of the upper town. **Pros:** modern, plush, spectacular surroundings; lots of rooms means it's good for late reservations and groups. **Cons:** not for those seeking an intimate environment. **TripAdvisor:** "overlooking the mountains," "well worth the money," "greeted courteously." *Piazza della Repubblica 6 035/366111 www.hotelsanmarco.com 155 rooms In-room: safe (some), Wi-Fi. In-hotel: restaurant, bar, laundry service, Internet terminal, Wi-Fi hotspot, parking (paid) Breakfast.*

$–$$ **Mercure Bergamo Palazzo Dolci.** Opened in 2004, the hotel offers modern comfort in a restructured 19th-century palazzo in Lower Bergamo. **Pros:** convenient to train station and some shopping. **Cons:** few luxury amenities; caters to business travelers. **TripAdvisor:** "clean, contemporary style," "good view of the Old Town," "soundproofing is great." *Viale Papa Giovanni XXIII 100 035/227411 www.mercure.com 88 rooms In-room: safe, Wi-Fi, Internet. In-hotel: bar, room service, Internet terminal, Wi-Fi hotspot, parking (paid) No meals.*

6

SIRMIONE

★ *138 km (86 mi) east of Milan.*

VISITOR INFORMATION

Sirmione tourism office (*Viale Marconi 2 030/916114 www.sirmione.com*).

EXPLORING

Dramatically rising out of Lake Garda is the enchanting town of Sirmione. *"Paene insularum, Sirmio, insularumque ocelle,"* sang Catullus in a homecoming poem: "It is the jewel of peninsulas and islands, both." The forbidding Castello Scaligero stands guard behind the small bridge connecting Sirmione to the mainland; beyond, cobbled streets wind their way through medieval arches past lush gardens, stunning lake views, and gawking crowds. Originally a Roman resort town, Sirmione served under the dukes of Verona and later Venice as Garda's main point of defense. It has now reclaimed its original function, bustling with visitors in summer. Cars aren't allowed into town; parking is available by the tourist office at the entrance.

Locals will almost certainly tell you that the so-called **Grotte di Catullo** *(Grottoes of Catullus)* was once the site of the villa of Catullus (87–54 BC), one of the greatest pleasure-seeking poets of all time. Present archaeological wisdom, however, does not concur, and there is some consensus that this was the site of two villas of slightly different periods, dating from about the 1st century AD. But never mind—the view through the cypresses and olive trees is lovely, and even if Catullus didn't have a villa here, he is closely associated with the area and undoubtedly did have a villa nearby. The ruins are at the top of the isthmus and are poorly signposted: walk through the historic center and past the various villas to the top of the spit; the entrance is on the right. A small museum offers a brief overview of the ruins (on the far wall); for guided group tours in English, call ☎ *02/20421469.* ✉ *Piazzale Orti Manara* ☎ *030/916157* €4 ⊙ *Apr.–Oct., Tues.–Sat. 8:30–7, Sun. 8:30–6; Nov.–Feb., Tues.–Sat. 8:30–5, Sun. 8:30–1:30; Mar., Tues.–Sat. 8:30–7, Sun. 8:30–1:30.*

The **Castello Scaligero** was built, along with almost all the other castles on the lake, by the Della Scala family. As hereditary rulers of Verona for more than a century before control of the city was seized by the Visconti in 1402, they counted Garda among their possessions. You can go inside to take in the nice view of the lake from the tower, or you can swim at the nearby beach. ✉ *Piazza Castello* ☎ *030/916468* €4 ⊙ *Tues.–Sun. 8:30–7.*

WHERE TO EAT

$$$ ITALIAN **La Rucola.** Next to Sirmione's castle, this elegant, intimate restaurant has a creative menu, with seafood and meat dishes accompanied by a good choice of wines. Three fixed-price menus are available. ✉ *Via Strentelle 3* ☎ *030/916326* 🌐 *www.ristorantelarucola.it* ⊙ *Closed Thurs. and Jan.–mid-Feb. No lunch Fri.*

$ SEAFOOD **Ristorante Al Pescatore.** Lake fish is the specialty at this simple, popular restaurant in Sirmione's historic center. Try grilled trout with a bottle of local white wine and settle your meal with a walk in the nearby public park. ✉ *Via Piana 20* ☎ *030/916216* 🌐 *ristorantealpescatore.com* ⊙ *Closed Wed. and Dec. 10–25.*

WHERE TO STAY

$$$$ **Hotel Sirmione.** Just inside the city walls, near the Castello, this hotel and spa sits amid lakeside gardens and terraces. **ripAdvisor:** "beautiful views of harbor and lake," "staff were attentive and cheerful," "room was cleaned immaculately." ✉ *Piazza Castello 19* ☎ *030/916331* 🌐 *www.termedisirmione.com* *101 rooms* *In-room: Internet. In-hotel: restaurant, bars, pool, spa, Wi-Fi hotspot, room service, laundry service, parking (paid), some pets allowed* *Breakfast.*

$$$$ ★ **Villa Cortine.** This former private villa in a secluded park risks being just plain ostentatious, but it's saved by the sheer luxury of its setting and the extraordinary professionalism of its staff. **Pros:** an opulent experience. **Cons:** in summer a three-night minimum stay and half board are required. **TripAdvisor:** "nobleman's private villa," "beautiful ornamental garden," "impressive entrance gate." ✉ *Via Grotte 6* ☎ *030/9905890* 🌐 *www.palacehotelvillacortine.com* *40 rooms, 2 suites* *In-room: safe. In-hotel: 3 restaurants, bar, laundry service, room service, Wi-Fi hotspot, tennis court, pool, beachfront, parking (free)* ⊙ *Closed mid-Oct.–Mar.* *Breakfast.*

GETTING AROUND THE LAKES

Frequent daily ferry and hydrofoil services link the lakeside towns and villages. Residents take them to get to work and school, while visitors use them for exploring the area. There are also special round-trip excursions, some with (optional) dining service on board. Schedules and ticket price are available on the Web site of **Navigazione Laghi** (✉ *Via Ariosto 21, Milan* ☎ *02/4676101, 03/9149511 Lake Garda* 🌐 *www.navigazionelaghi.it*) and are posted at the landing docks.

To get around the lakes by car, you have to follow secondary roads—often of great beauty. S572 follows the southern and western shores of Lake Garda, SS45b edges the northernmost section of the western shore, and S249 runs along the eastern shore. Around Lake Como, follow S340 along the western shore, S36 on the eastern shore, and S583 on the lower arms. S33 and S34 trace the western shore of Lake Maggiore. Although the roads around the lake can be beautiful, they're full of harrowing twists and turns, making for a slow, challenging drive.

There's regular bus service between the small towns on the lakes. It's less convenient than going by boat or by car, and it's used primarily by locals (particularly schoolchildren), but sightseers can use it as well. The bus service around Lake Garda serves mostly towns on the western shore. Call the bus operator **SIA** (☎ *030/44061* 🌐 *www.sia-autoservizi.it*) for information.

6

TOWNS ALONG LAKE GARDA'S EASTERN SHORE

VISITOR INFORMATION

Malcesine tourism office (✉ *Via Capitanato 6/8* ☎ *0457/400044* 🌐 *www.malcesineweb.it*).

Bardolino (🌐 *www.bardolinoweb.it*), famous for its red wine, hosts the Cura dell'Uva (Grape Cure Festival) in late September–early October. It's a great excuse to indulge in the local vino, which is light, dry, and often slightly sparkling. (Bring aspirin, just in case the cura turns out to be worse than the disease.) Bardolino is one of the most popular summer resorts on the lake. It stands on the eastern shore at the wider end of the lake. Here there are two handsome Romanesque churches: **San Severo,** from the 11th century, and **San Zeno,** from the 9th. Both are in the center of the small town.

Just about everyone agrees that **Punta San Vigilio** is the prettiest spot on Garda's eastern shore. The highlight is the cypress-filled gardens of the 15th-century **Villa Guarienti di Brenzone** (✉ *Frazione Punta San Vigilio 1*). The villa is closed to the public, but the nearby Locanda San Vigilio hotel ($$$$) is picturesque and has a private beach and restaurant.

Malcesine, about 30 km (20 mi) north of Punta San Vigilio, is one of the loveliest areas along the upper eastern shore of Lake Garda. It's principally known as a summer resort, with sailing and windsurfing schools. It tends to be crowded in season, but there are nice walks from the town toward the mountains. Six ski lifts and more than 11 km (7 mi) of runs of varying degrees of difficulty serve skiers. Dominating the town is the 12th-century **Castello Scaligero** (☎ *045/6570333* 🎫 *€6* ⏲ *Apr.–Oct., daily 9:30–7; Nov.–Mar., Sun. 11–4*), built by Verona's dynastic Della Scala family.

The futuristic *funivia* (cable car) zipping visitors to the top of **Monte Baldo** (5,791 feet) is unique because it rotates. After a 10-minute ride you're high in the Veneto, where you can stroll while enjoying spectacular views of the lake. You can ride the cable car down or bring along a mountain bike (or hang glider) for the descent. ✉ *Via Navene Vecchia 12* ☎ *045/7400206* 🌐 *www.funiviamalcesine.com* 🎫 *Round-trip €18* ⏲ *Daily 8–7. Closed Nov.–mid-Dec.*

RIVA DEL GARDA

18 km (11 mi) north of Malcesine, 180 km (112 mi) east of Milan.

VISITOR INFORMATION

Riva del Garda tourism office (✉ *Largo Medaglie d'Oro al Valor Militare 5* ☎ *0464/554444* 🌐 *www.gardatrentino.it*).

EXPLORING

Set on the northern tip of Lake Garda against a dramatic backdrop of jagged cliffs and miles of beaches, Riva del Garda is the lake's quintessential resort town. The old city, set around a pretty harbor, was built up during the 15th century, when it was a strategic outpost of the Venetian Republic.

The heart of Riva del Garda, the lakeside **Piazza 3 Novembre,** is surrounded by medieval palazzi. Standing in the piazza and looking out onto the lake you can understand why Riva del Garda has become a windsurfing mecca: air currents ensure good breezes on even the most sultry midsummer days.

The **Torre Apponale**, predating the Venetian period by three centuries, looms above the medieval residences of the main square; its crenellations recall its defensive purpose. Thanks to a complete restoration in 2002, visitors can climb the 165 steps to see the view from the top. ☎ *0464/573869* 🎫 *€1* ⏲ *Late Mar.–June and Oct., Tues.–Sun. 10–12:30 and 1:30–6; July–Sept., daily 10–12:30 and 1:30–6.*

WHERE TO EAT

$$ NORTHERN ITALIAN ✕ **Castel Toblino.** A lovely stop for a lakeside drink or a romantic dinner, this castle is right on a lake in Sarche, about 20 km (12 mi) north of Riva toward Trento. The compound is said to have been a prehistoric, then Roman, village, and was later associated with the Church of Trento. Bernardo Clesio had it rebuilt in the 16th century in the Renaissance style. It's now a sanctuary of fine food, serving such local specialties as lake fish and guinea fowl. ✉ *Via Caffaro 1, Sarche* ☎ *0461/864036* 🌐 *www.casteltoblino.com* ⏲ *Closed Tues. and Jan. and Feb.*

WHERE TO STAY

$$$ 🏨 **Hotel du Lac et du Parc.** Riva's most splendid hotel has elegance befitting its cosmopolitan name, with personalized service rarely found on Lake Garda since its aristocratic heyday. **Pros:** expansive and lush surroundings offering myriad lodging options; a pampering and indulgent staff. **Cons:**

not a cozy atmosphere. **TripAdvisor:** "stunning location, superb rooms," "beautiful tropical grounds," "cost was excellent." ✉ *Viale Rovereto 44* ☎ *0464/566600* 🌐 *www.dulacetduparc.com* *164 rooms, 5 suites* *In-room: a/c. In-hotel: 2 restaurants, bars, tennis courts, pools, spa, gym, beachfront, parking (free), some pets allowed* *Closed Nov.–Mar.* *Breakfast.*

WORD OF MOUTH

"Because you're most likely to get around among the main towns on Lake Como by steamer or ferry, you'll be best off scheduling dinners in your own town and doing lunches in others, since transport is quite frequent during the day and less so, even ending early, in the evening."

—JulieVikmanis

$$ **Hotel Sole.** Within a lakeside 15th-century palazzo in the center of town, this lovely, understated hotel offers comfortable, affordable rooms. **Pros:** a classic lake resort updated with modern hotel conveniences. **Cons:** not for those looking for ultracontemporary design. **TripAdvisor:** "splendid location right on the lake," "overlooking the old town," "rooftop sun terrace." ✉ *Piazza 3 Novembre 35* ☎ *0464/552686* 🌐 *www.hotelsole.net* *52 rooms* *In-room: safe, refrigerator, Wi-Fi. In-room: safe. In-hotel: 2 restaurants, room service, bars, laundry service, bicycles, Wi-Fi hotspot, parking (free)* *Closed Nov.–Dec. 19 and mid-Jan.–mid-Mar.* *Breakfast.*

$$ **Luise.** This cozy, reasonably priced hotel has great amenities, including a big garden, a large swimming pool, and a welcome bowl of fresh fruit on arrival. **Pros:** pleasant, reasonably priced option; great for kids. **Cons:** because it's popular with families, may not be the best choice if you want to avoid kids. **TripAdvisor:** "impeccable in every aspect," "pool and gardens are lovely," "children's playroom was a godsend." ✉ *Viale Rovereto 9* ☎ *0464/550858* 🌐 *www.feelinghotelluise.com* *68 rooms* *In-room: refrigerator, safe, no a/c (some), Wi-Fi. In-hotel: restaurant, room service, tennis court, pool, laundry facilities, bicycles, Internet terminal, parking (free), some pets allowed* *Breakfast.*

EN ROUTE

After passing the town of Limone—where it is said the first lemon trees in Europe were planted—take the fork to the right about 5 km (3 mi) north of Gargnano and head to Tignale. The view from the Madonna di Monte Castello church, some 2,000 feet above the lake, is spectacular. Adventurous travelers will want to follow this pretty inland mountain road to Tremosine; be warned that the road winds its way up the mountain through hairpin turns and blind corners that can test even the most experienced drivers.

GARGNANO

30 km (19 mi) south of Riva del Garda, 144 km (89 mi) east of Milan.

VISITOR INFORMATION

Gargnano tourism office (✉ *Piazza Boldini 2* ☎ *0365/791243* 🌐 *www.gargnanosulgarda.it*).

EXPLORING

This small port town was an important Franciscan center in the 13th century, and now comes alive in the summer months when German tourists, many of whom have villas here, crowd the small pebble beach. An Austrian flotilla bombarded the town in 1866, and some of the houses still bear marks of cannon fire. Mussolini owned two houses in Gargnano: one is now a language school and the other, Villa Feltrinelli, has been restored and reopened as a luxury hotel.

WHERE TO EAT AND STAY

$$$ NORTHERN ITALIAN ✕ **La Tortuga.** This rustic trattoria is more sophisticated than it first appears, with an extensive wine cellar and nouvelle-style twists on local dishes. Specialties include *agnello con rosmarino e timo* (lamb with rosemary and thyme), *persico con rosmarino* (perch with rosemary), and *carpaccio d'anatra all'aceto balsamico* (duck carpaccio with balsamic vinegar). ✉ *Via XXIV Maggio at small harbor* ☎ *0365/71251* ⏲ *Closed Tues. and Dec.–Feb. No lunch.*

$ **Garni Bartabel.** **Pros:** adorable; a bargain for this in area. **Cons:** not luxurious. **TripAdvisor:** "very friendly but also professional," "book a room with a view," "enchanting little terrace." ✉ *Via Roma 35* ☎ *0365/71300* 🌐 *www.hotelbartabel.it* *10 rooms* *In-room: no a/c, Wi-Fi. In-hotel: bar, room service, Wi-Fi hotspot, some pets allowed* ⏲ *Closed Nov.–mid-Mar.* *No meals.*

$$$$ **Villa Feltrinelli.** This 1892 art nouveau villa hotel, named for the Italian publishing family that used to vacation here, is immersed in private gardens and overlooks the lake. **Pros:** first-class luxury hotel; like stepping into a bygone era. **Cons:** one of the most expensive hotels on the lake. **TripAdvisor:** "truly magnificent place," "service is impossible to fault," "amazing luxury." ✉ *Via Rimembranza 38/40* ☎ *0365/798000* 🌐 *www.villafeltrinelli.com* *21 rooms* *In-room: safe, refrigerator, Wi-Fi. In-hotel: restaurant, room service, bar, pool, laundry service, parking (free)* ⏲ *Closed mid-Oct.–mid-Apr.* *Breakfast.*

SPORTS AND THE OUTDOORS

The **Upper Brescian Garda Park** stretches over nine municipalities on the western side of the lake, from Salò to Limone, covering 380 square km (147 square mi). Call the **Limone Hotel Owners Association** (✉ *Via Quattro Novembre 2/c* ☎ *0365/954720*) for trail and bicycle-rental information. They're also the people to contact if you'd like to take part in one of the free treks led by the Gruppo Alpini Limone every Sunday from June to September.

GARDONE RIVIERA

12 km (7 mi) south of Gargnano, 139 km (86 mi) east of Milan.

EXPLORING

Gardone Riviera, a once-fashionable 19th-century resort now pleasantly faded, is the former home of the flamboyant Gabriele d'Annunzio (1863–1938), one of Italy's greatest modern poets. D'Annunzio's estate, **Il Vittoriale**, perched on the hills above the town, is an elaborate memorial to himself, filled with the trappings of conquests in art, love, and war (of which the largest is a ship's prow in the garden), and complete with an imposing mausoleum. ✉ *Via Vittoriale 12* ☎ *0365/296511* 🌐 *www.vittoriale.it* 🎫 *€11 for house or museum, €16 for both* ⏲ *Grounds: Apr.–Sept., daily 8:30–8; Oct.–Mar., daily 9–5. House and museum: Apr.–Sept., Tues.–Sun. 9:30–7; Oct.–Mar., Tues.–Sun. 9–1 and 2–5.*

More than 2,000 Alpine, subtropical, and Mediterranean species thrive at the **Giardino Botanico Hruska.** ✉ *Via Roma* ☎ *0366/410877* 🌐 *www.hellergarden.com* 🎫 *€9* ⏲ *Mar.–Oct., daily 9–7.*

OFF THE BEATEN PATH

Salò Market. Four kilometers (2½ mi) south of Gardone Riviera is the enchanting lakeside town of Salò, which history buffs may recognize as the capital of the ill-fated Social Republic set up in 1943 by the Germans after they liberated Mussolini from the Gran Sasso. Every Saturday morning an enormous market is held in the Piazza dei Martiri della Libertà, with great bargains on everything from household goods to clothing to foodstuffs. In August or September a lone vendor often sells locally unearthed *tartufi neri* (black truffles) at affordable prices.

WHERE TO STAY

$$$ ★ **Gran Hotel Gardone.** Directly facing the lake, this majestic 1800s palace is surrounded by an attractive landscaped garden. **Pros:** well-appointed; expansive gardens; lauded service. **Cons:** as of this writing, no Internet in the rooms. **TripAdvisor:** "style of a bygone age," "polished and attentive service," "wonderful views over the lake." ✉ *Via Zanardelli 84* ☎ *0365/20261* 🌐 *www.grangardone.it* *143 rooms, 25 suites* *In-room: safe. In-hotel: 2 restaurants, bar, Wi-Fi hotspot, Internet terminal, pool, spa, room service, laundry service, parking (paid), some pets allowed* ⏲ *Closed mid-Oct.–Mar.* *Breakfast.*

$$$ **Grand Hotel Fasano.** A former 19th-century hunting lodge between Gardone and Maderno, the Fasano has matured into a seasonal hotel of a high standard. **Pros:** every room has a view of the lake. **Cons:** not all rooms have Wi-Fi; no credit cards accepted. **TripAdvisor:** "fairytale experience," "view is just overwhelming," "very nice spa facility." ✉ *Corso Zanardelli 190* ☎ *0365/290220* 🌐 *www.ghf.it* *68 rooms* *In-room: a/c, safe, refrigerator, Wi-Fi (some), Internet. In-hotel: 2 restaurants, bar, tennis court, pool, room service, laundry service, beachfront, gym, Wi-Fi hotspot, Internet terminal, parking (free), some pets allowed* *No credit cards* ⏲ *Closed mid-Oct.–Mar.* *Breakfast.*

$$$$ ★ **Villa del Sogno.** A narrow winding road takes you from town to this imposing villa, which surveys the valley and the lake below it. **Pros:** endless amenities; individually decorated rooms; expansive terrace overlooking the lake. **Cons:** per-person prices can be confusing. **TripAdvisor:** "enviable location, attractive grounds," "staff very approachable

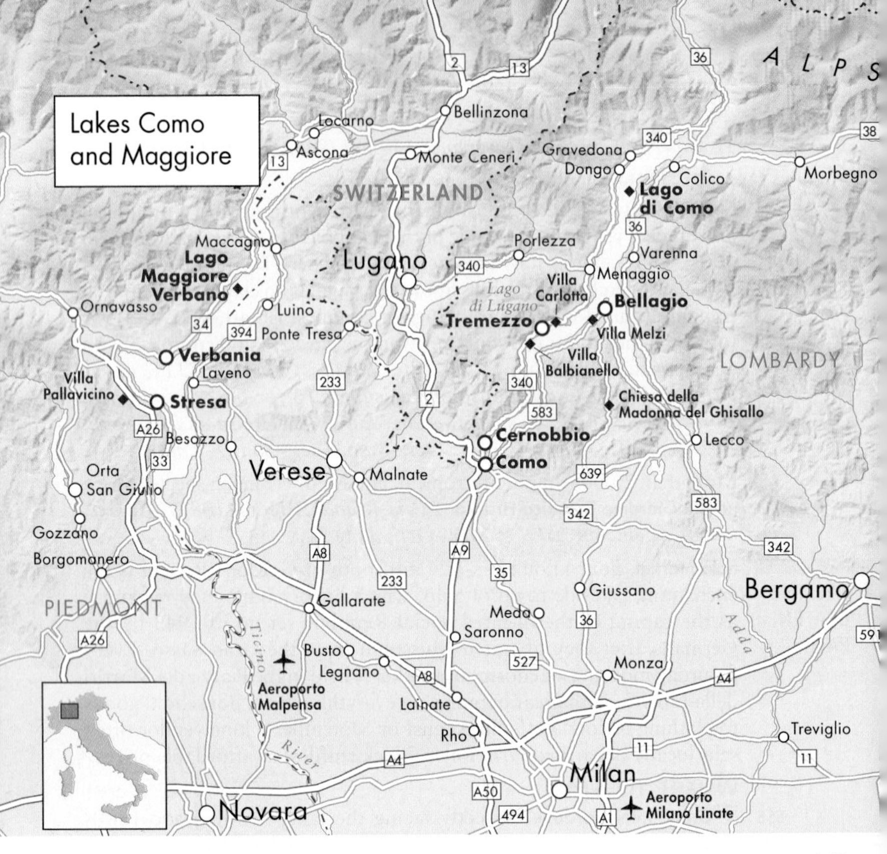

and friendly," "breakfast on the main terrace." ✉ *Corso Zanardelli 107* ☎ *0365/290181* 🌐 *www.villadelsogno.it* *35 rooms, 5 suites* *In-room: safe. In-hotel: 2 restaurants, bar, tennis court, pool, spa, room service, laundry service, parking (free)* *Closed Nov.–Mar.* *Breakfast.*

$$$$ ★ **Villa Fiordaliso.** The pink-and-white lakeside Villa Fiordaliso—once home to Claretta Petacci, given to her by Benito Mussolini—is a high-quality restaurant, but it also has seven tastefully furnished rooms, some overlooking the lake. **Pros:** has the charm of an intimate B&B. **Cons:** short on amenities given the price category. **TripAdvisor:** "sweeping views of the lake," "service was thoroughly professional," "beautifully historic." ✉ *Corso Zanardelli 132* ☎ *0365/20158* 🌐 *www.villafiordaliso.it* *6 rooms, 1 suite* *In-room: safe, refrigerator, Wi-Fi. In-hotel: 2 restaurants, Internet, Wi-Fi hotspot, room service, laundry service, parking (free)* *Closed Nov.–mid-Mar.* *Breakfast.*

¢ **Villa Maria Elisabetta.** Many of the rooms in this charming hotel run by a group of hospitable nuns have views of Lago di Garda. **Pros:** a great bargain for a laid-back stay. **Cons:** no Internet; no a/c; some rooms have no TV. ✉ *Corso Zanardelli 180* ☎ *0365/20206* 🌐 *www.monasterystays.com* *42 rooms* *In-room: no a/c; TV (some). In-hotel: restaurant, bar, parking (free)* *Closed Oct. 15–Dec. 15* *Breakfast.*

LAKE COMO

If your idea of nirvana is palatial villas, rose-laden belvederes, hanging wisteria and bougainvillea, lanterns casting a glow over lakeshore restaurants, and majestic Alpine vistas, heaven is Lake Como. In his *Charterhouse of Parma,* Stendhal described it as an "enchanting spot, unequaled on earth in its loveliness." Virgil called it simply "our greatest" lake. Though summer crowds threaten to diminish the lake's dreamy mystery and slightly faded old-money gentility, the allure of this spectacular place endures. Como remains a consummate pairing of natural and man-made beauty. The villa gardens, like so many in Italy, are a union of two landscape traditions: that of Renaissance Italy, which values order, and that of Victorian England, which strives to create the illusion of natural wildness. Such gardens are often framed by vast areas of picturesque farmland—fruit trees, olive groves, and vineyards.

Lake Como is some 47 km (30 mi) long north to south and is Europe's deepest lake (almost 1,350 feet). Como itself is a leading textile center famous for its silks. Many travelers hasten to the vaporetti waiting to take them to Bellagio and the *centro di lago,* the center region of the lake's three branches, and its most beautiful section. The 2,000-year-old walled city of Como should not be missed, however. Car ferries traverse the lake in season, making it easy to get to the other main towns, Cernobbio, Tremezzo, and Varenna. Remember that Como is extremely seasonal: if you go to Bellagio, for example, from November through February, you will find nothing open—not a bar, restaurant, or shop.

GETTING HERE

Trains run regularly from Milan to the town of Como; the trip takes half an hour from the Central Station and an hour from the Cardorna Station. There's also service to the tiny town of Varenna, just across the lake from Bellagio; the trip from Milan takes 1¼ hours. Como is off the A9 autostrada. To get to the town from Milan, take A8 to A9; the drive takes about an hour. Ferries (mainly pedestrian) run regularly from Como and Varenna to different spots around the lake. Schedules can be consulted online at *www.navigazionelaghi.it.*

BELLAGIO

Fodor's Choice ★ *30 km (19 mi) northeast of Como, 56 km (35 mi) northwest of Bergamo.*

VISITOR INFORMATION

Bellagio tourism office (*Piazza Mazzini [Pontile Imbarcadero]* *031/950204* *www.bellagiolakecomo.com*).

EXPLORING

Sometimes called the prettiest town in Europe, Bellagio always seems to be flag-bedecked, with geraniums ablaze in every window and bougainvillea veiling the staircases, or *montées,* that thread through the town. At dusk Bellagio's nightspots—including the wharf, where an orchestra serenades dancers under the stars—beckon you to come and make merry. It's an impossibly enchanting location, one that inspired

French composer Gabriel Fauré to call Bellagio "a diamond contrasting brilliantly with the sapphires of the three lakes in which it is set."

Boats ply the lake to Tremezzo, where Napoléon's worst Italian enemy, Count Sommariva, resided at Villa Carlotta; and a bit farther south of Tremezzo, to Villa Balbianello. Check with the tourist office for the hours of the launch to Tremezzo.

★ **Villa Serbelloni**, a property of the Rockefeller Foundation, has celebrated gardens on the site of Pliny the Elder's villa overlooking Bellagio. There are only two 1½-hour-long guided visits per day, restricted to 30 people each, and in May these tend to be commandeered by group bookings. It's wise to arrive early to sign up. ✉ *Near Palazza della Chiesa* ☎ *031/951555* 🎫 *€8.50* ⏲ *Guided visits Apr.–early Nov., Tues.–Sun. at 11 and 3:30; tours gather 15 mins before start.*

The famous gardens of the **Villa Melzi** were once a favorite picnic spot for Franz Lizst, who advised author Louis de Ronchaud in 1837: "When you write the story of two happy lovers, place them on the shores of Lake Como. I do not know of any land so conspicuously blessed by heaven." The gardens are open to the public, and though you can't get into the 19th-century villa, don't miss the lavish Empire-style family chapel. The Melzi were Napoléon's greatest allies in Italy (the family has passed down the name "Josephine" to the present day). ✉ *Via Melzi d'Eril 8* ☎ *3394573838* 🌐 *www.giardinidivillamelzi.it* 🎫 *€6* ⏲ *Late Mar.–early Nov., daily 9:30–6:30.*

By ferry from Bellagio it's a quick trip across the lake to Varenna. The principal sight here is the spellbinding garden of the **Villa Monastero**, which, as its name suggests, was originally a monastery. Now it's an international science and convention center. Guided tours can be booked. ✉ *Viale Polvani 2, Varenna* ☎ *0341/295450* 🌐 *www.villamonastero.eu* 🎫 *Garden €5, house and garden €8* ⏲ *Garden: mid-Mar.–Apr., weekdays 10–5, weekends 10–1 and 2–5; May–Sept., weekdays 9–7, weekends 10–7; Oct. 1–10, weekdays 10–6, weekends 10–1 and 2–6. House museum: mid-Mar.–Apr., weekends 10–1 and 2–5; May–Sept., Fri. 2–7, weekends 10–7; Oct. 1–10, weekends 10–1 and 2–6.*

WHERE TO EAT

$–$$ NORTHERN ITALIAN ✕ **La Pergola**. Try to reserve a table on the terrace at this popular lakeside restaurant a short walk (with many steps) from central Bellagio on the east side of the peninsula. The food is average, with the best option being the freshly caught fish; the view and the tranquility of the terrace are the main draws. You can also stay in one of the inn's 11 rooms ($$), all of which have baths. ✉ *Piazza del Porto 4, Pescallo* ☎ *031/950263* 🌐 *www.lapergolabellagio.it* ⏲ *Closed Tues. Mar.–Nov.*

$ NORTHERN ITALIAN ✕ **Silvio**. At the edge of town, this family-owned trattoria with a lakeshore terrace specializes in fresh fish. Served cooked or marinated, with risotto or as a ravioli stuffing, the lake's bounty is caught by Silvio's family—it's local cooking at its best. There are also 17 modestly priced ($) guest rooms with balconies and lake views. ✉ *Lòppia di Bellagio, Via Carcano 12* ☎ *031/950322* 🌐 *www.bellagiosilvio.com* ⏲ *Closed Jan. and Feb.*

WHERE TO STAY

$$–$$$ **Du Lac.** In the center of Bellagio, by the landing dock, this comfortable, medium-size hotel owned by an Anglo-Italian family has a relaxed and congenial feel. **Pros:** complimentary shuttle bus service. **Cons:** some decor a little worn at the edges. **TripAdvisor:** "stunning views over Lake Como," "can only be described as magical," "happy, smiling chambermaids." *Piazza Mazzini 32 031/950320 www.bellagiohoteldulac.com 42 rooms In-room: safe. In-hotel: 2 restaurants, bar, Wi-Fi hotspot, parking (paid), some pets allowed Closed Nov.–Mar. Breakfast.*

$$$$ **Grand Hotel Villa Serbelloni.** Designed to cradle nobility in high style, this hotel is a refined haven for the discreetly wealthy, set within a pretty park down the road from the Punta di Bellagio. **Pros:** historic lake hotel; great pool. **Cons:** high rates for yesteryear ambience but limited deluxe amenities. **TripAdvisor:** "more beautiful than the photographs," "wonderful details everywhere," "a real grand hotel." *Via Roma 1 031/950216 www.villaserbelloni.com 95 rooms In-room: safe, Internet. In-hotel: 2 restaurants, room service, tennis court, pools, gym, spa, laundry service, Internet terminal, Wi-Fi hotspot, parking (free) Closed early Nov.–early Apr. Breakfast.*

6

$$$–$$$$ ★ **Hotel Belvedere.** In Italian, belvedere means "beautiful view," and it's an apt name for this enchanting spot. **Pros:** attention to detail; great views. **Cons:** breakfast is only so-so; a climb from the waterfront. **TripAdvisor:** "charmingly quaint," "nothing short of spectacular," "lovely sparkling pool." *Via Valassina 31 031/950410 www.belvederebellagio.com 59 rooms, 5 suites In-room: safe, Internet. In-hotel: restaurant, bar, pool, spa, parking (free), some pets allowed Closed Nov.–Mar. Breakfast.*

$$ **Hotel Florence.** This villa dating from the 1880s has an impressive lobby with vaulted ceiling and an imposing Florentine fireplace. **Pros:** central location; appealing public spaces. **Cons:** location may feel too central if you're looking to get away from it all. **TripAdvisor:** "old-world atmosphere," "wonderful guest service," "quiet and very restful." *Piazza Mazzini 46 031/950342 www.hotelflorencebellagio.it 30 rooms In-room: safe, Internet, no a/c (some). In-hotel: restaurant, room service, bar, spa, Wi-Fi hotspot Closed Nov.–Mar. Some meals.*

TREMEZZO

34 km (21 mi) north of Cernobbio, 78 km (48 mi) north of Milan.

VISITOR INFORMATION

Tremezzo tourism office (Via Regina 3 *0344/40493 Daily 9–noon and 3:30–6*).

EXPLORING

If you're lucky enough to visit the small lakeside town of Tremezzo in late spring or early summer, you will find the magnificent **Villa Carlotta** a riot of color, with more than 14 acres of azaleas and dozens of varieties of rhododendrons in full bloom. The height of the blossoms is late April to early May. The villa was built between 1690 and 1743 for the luxury-loving marquis Giorgio Clerici. The garden's collection is remarkable, particularly considering the difficulties of transporting delicate plants before the age of aircraft. Palms, banana trees, cacti, eucalyptus, a sequoia, orchids, and camellias are counted among the more than 500 species.

The villa's interior is worth a visit, particularly if you have a taste for the romantic sculptures of Antonio Canova (1757–1822). The best known is his *Cupid and Psyche,* which depicts the lovers locked in an odd but graceful embrace, with the young god above and behind, his wings extended, while Psyche awaits a kiss that will never come. The villa can be reached by boats from Bellagio and Como. ✉ *Via Regina 2, Tremezzo* ☎ *0344/40405* 🌐 *www.villacarlotta.it* 🎫 *€8.50* ⏲ *Mar. and Nov., daily 10–4; Apr.–Oct., daily 9–6.*

★ **Villa Balbianello** may be the most magical house in all of Italy. It sits on its own little promontory, Il Dosso d'Avedo—separating the bays of Venus and Diana—around the bend from the tiny fishing village of Ossuccio. Relentlessly picturesque, the villa is composed of loggias, terraces, and *palazzini* (tiny palaces), all spilling down verdant slopes to the lakeshore, where you'll find an old Franciscan church, a magnificent stone staircase, and a statue of San Carlo Borromeo blessing the waters. The villa is most frequently reached by launch from Como and Bellagio. Check with the **Como tourism office** (☎ *031/3300128* 🌐 *www.lakecomo.it*) for hours. Visits are usually restricted to the gardens, but if you plan in advance it's also possible to tour the villa itself. You pay €30 for a guide—regardless of how many are in your party—and an additional €5 entrance fee. ✉ *Il Dosso d'Avedo; ferry stop Lenno* ☎ *0344/56110* 🎫 *Gardens €5* ⏲ *Mid-Mar.–mid-Nov., Tues. and Thurs.–Sun. 10–6; last entry to gardens 5:30. Nov. 4–mid-Nov., pedestrian entrance is open Tues. and Thurs.–Sun., otherwise access is only by boat.*

WHERE TO STAY

$$$$ **Grand Hotel Tremezzo.** One hundred windows of this turn-of-the-20th-century building face the lake. **Pros:** lakeside location; beautiful views. **Cons:** not well situated if you're looking for shopping or nightlife. **TripAdvisor:** "magic view of Lake Como," "full of old Italian charm," "a sublime spot." ✉ *Via Regina 8* ☎ *0344/42491* 🌐 *www.grandhoteltremezzo.com* *98 rooms, 2 suites* *In-room: safe, Wi-Fi, DVD. In-hotel: 2 restaurants, room service, bars, tennis court, pools, gym, spa, beachfront, Internet terminal, Wi-Fi hotspot, parking (free), some pets allowed* ⏲ *Closed mid-Nov.–Feb.* 🍽 *Breakfast.*

$ **Rusall.** On the hillside above Tremezzo in the midst of a large garden, this small, reasonably priced hotel offers quiet and privacy. **Pros:** lovely walks into town and in the countryside; more intimate than grander lake hotels. **Cons:** no pool; takes some effort to reach the hillside location. **TripAdvisor:** "this place is splendid," "terrace was a lovely place to sit," "stunning setting on a hilltop." ✉ *Via San Martino 2* ☎ *0344/40408* 🌐 *www.rusallhotel.com* *23 rooms* *In-room: some a/c, Wi-Fi. In-hotel: Wi-Fi hotspot, Internet terminal, restaurant, bar, tennis court* 🍽 *No meals.*

CERNOBBIO

5 km (3 mi) north of Como, 53 km (34 mi) north of Milan.

VISITOR INFORMATION

Cernobbio tourism office (✉ *Via Regina* 23 ☎ *031*/349341).

EXPLORING

The legendary resort of Villa d'Este is reason enough to visit this jewel on the lake, but the town itself is worth a stroll. Despite the fact that George Clooney lunches here regularly, the place still has a neighborhood feel to it, especially on summer evenings and weekends when the piazza is full of families and couples taking their *passeggiata* (stroll).

Built on the site of a former nunnery, Cardinal Tolomeo Gallio's summer residence, **Villa d'Este**, has had a colorful and somewhat checkered history since its completion in 1568, swinging wildly between extremes of grandeur and dereliction. Its tenants have included the Jesuits, two generals, a ballerina, Caroline of Brunswick—the disgraced and estranged wife of the future king of England, George IV—a family of ordinary Italian nobles, and, finally, a czarina of Russia. Its life as a private summer residence ended in 1873, when it was turned into the fashionable hotel it has remained ever since.

6

WHERE TO EAT AND STAY

$–$$ NORTHERN ITALIAN ✕ **Il Gatto Nero.** This restaurant in the hills above Cernobbio has a splendid view of the lake. Specialties include *filetto con aceto balsamico* (filet mignon with balsamic vinegar), *pappardelle al ragù di selvaggini* (pasta with wild game sauce), and lake fish. Save room for the warm chocolate torte with its delicious liquid chocolate center. Reservations are encouraged as this is a regular haunt of Italian soccer stars as well as the jet set. ✉ *Via Monte Santo 69, Rovenna* ☎ *031/512042* 🌐 *www.il-gatto-nero.it* ⊗ *Closed Mon. No lunch Tues.*

$–$$ NORTHERN ITALIAN, PIZZA ✕ **Il Giardino.** Aptly named "The Garden," this restaurant has an expansive shaded patio that's a welcome respite from the summer sun. With an extensive menu balanced between fish, meat, pizza, and salads, there's something for everyone. You can also stay the night in one of Il Giardino's 12 basic rooms ($). ✉ *Via Regina 73* ☎ *031/511154* 🌐 *www.giardinocernobbio.com* ⊗ *Closed some days in Nov.*

¢–$ PIZZA ✕ **Pizzeria L'Ancora.** For the best pies in Como, and perhaps in the region, you won't want to miss this local haunt, run by a Neapolitan family that has been making pizza for three generations. Even Italians from out of town rave about the pizza here. Three sisters—Barbara, Grazie, and Linda—dish out hospitality as fine as the food. ✉ *Via Conciliazione 11, Tavernola* ☎ *031/340769* ▭ *No credit cards* ⊗ *Closed Wed.*

$$$$ Fodor's Choice ★ **Villa d'Este.** One of the grandest hotels in Italy, the 16th-century Villa d'Este has long welcomed Europe's rich and famous, from Napoléon to the Duchess of Windsor. **Pros:** fine service; world-renowned clientele. **Cons:** may seem too formal to some. **TripAdvisor:** "experience of a lifetime," "treated very specially," "gardens are a joy." ✉ *Via Regina 40* ☎ *031/3481* 🌐 *www.villadeste.it* *152 rooms 7 suites, 2 private villas* *In-room: safe, Internet. In-hotel: 2 restaurants, bar, room service,*

tennis courts, pools, laundry service, Wi-Fi hotspot, parking (free), some pets allowed ⏲ Closed mid-Nov.–Feb. 🍴 All meals.

COMO

5 km (3 mi) south of Cernobbio, 30 km (19 mi) southwest of Bellagio, 49 km (30 mi) north of Milan.

VISITOR INFORMATION

Como tourism office (✉ *Piazza Cavour 17* ☎ *031/269712* 🌐 www.lakecomo.com ⏲ *Mon.–Sat. 9–1 and 2:30–6* ✉ *Via Maestri Cumacini* ☎ *031/264215* ⏲ *Tues.–Fri. 10:30–12:30 and 2:30–6, weekends 10–8* ✉ *Piazza Matteotti* ☎ 0313/300128 ⏲ *Feb.–Dec., weekdays 10:30–12:30 and 2:30–6, weekends 10–6*).

EXPLORING

Como, on the south shore of the lake, is only part elegant resort, where cobbled pedestrian streets wind their way past parks and bustling cafés. The other part is an industrial town renowned for its fine silks. If you're traveling by car, leave it at the edge of the town center in the clean, well-lighted underground parking facility right on the lake.

The splendid 15th-century Renaissance-Gothic **Duomo** was begun in 1396. The facade was added in 1455, and the transepts were completed in the mid-18th century. The dome was designed by Filippo Juvara (1678–1736), chief architect of many of the sumptuous palaces of the royal house of Savoy. The facade has statues of two of Como's most famous sons, Pliny the Elder and Pliny the Younger, whose writings are among the most important documents from antiquity. Inside, the works of art include Luini's *Holy Conversation,* a fresco cycle by Morazzone, and the *Marriage of the Virgin Mary* by Ferrari. ✉ *Piazza del Duomo* ☎ *031/265244* ⏲ *Daily 8–noon and 3–7.*

At the heart of Como's medieval quarter, the city's first cathedral, **San Fedele**, is worth a peek, if only because it is one of the oldest churches in the region. The apse walls and ceiling are completely frescoed as are the ceilings above the altar. ✉ *Piazza San Fedele* ☎ *031/272334* ⏲ *Daily 7–noon and 3–7.*

If you brave Como's industrial quarter, you will find the beautiful church of **Sant'Abbondio**, a gem of Romanesque architecture begun by Benedictine monks in 1013 and consecrated by Pope Urban II in 1095. Inside, the five aisles of the church converge on a presbytery with a semicircular apse decorated with a cycle of 14th-century frescoes—now restored to their original magnificence—by Lombard artists heavily influenced by the Sienese school. To see them, turn right as you enter and put €0.50 in the mechanical box for a few minutes of lighting. In the nave, the cubical capitals are the earliest example of this style in Italy. ✉ *Via Sant'Abbondio* ⏲ *Daily 8–5.*

Exhibiting the path of production from silkworm litters to moire-finishing machinery, the **Museo Didattico della Seta** *(Silk Museum)* is small but complete. The museum preserves the history of a manufacturing region that continues to supply almost three-fourths of Europe's silk. The friendly staffers will give you an overview of the museum; they are also happy to provide brochures and information about local retail shops. The museum's location isn't well marked: follow the textile school's driveway around to the low-rise concrete building on the left, and follow the shallow ramp down to the entrance. ✉ *Via Castelnuovo 9* ☎ *031/303180* 🌐 *www.museosetacomo.com* *€8* *Tues.–Fri. 9–noon and 3–6. Guided tours, booked in advance, Mon. and weekends.*

WHERE TO STAY

$$–$$$ **Terminus.** Commanding a panoramic view over Lake Como, this early-20th-century art nouveau building is the city's best hotel. **Pros:** old-world charm; right on the lake. **Cons:** limited number of rooms with lake views; decor in some rooms seems dated. **TripAdvisor:** "best hotel we had in Italy," "very good candlelit dinner," "staff were helpful and very attentive." ✉ *Lungolario Trieste 14* ☎ *031/329111* 🌐 *www.albergoterminus.com* *50 rooms* *In-room: safe, Internet, Wi-Fi. In-hotel: restaurant, room service, bar, gym, bicycles, laundry service, Wi-Fi hotspot, parking (paid), some pets allowed* *Breakfast.*

$–$$ **Tre Re.** This clean, spacious, welcoming hotel is a few steps west of the cathedral and convenient to the lake. **Pros:** friendly staff; homey atmosphere. **Cons:** rooms are functional, not elegant—decor is spartan. **TripAdvisor:** "wonderful, quiet getaway," "great location for the price," "breakfast totally rocked." ✉ *Via Boldoni 20* ☎ *031/265374* 🌐 *www.hoteltrere.com* *48 rooms* *In-room: Wi-Fi (some). In-hotel: Wi-Fi hotspot, Internet terminal, restaurant, bar, parking (free)* *Closed mid-Dec.–mid-Jan.* *Breakfast.*

6

SPORTS AND THE OUTDOORS

Lake Como has many opportunities for sports enthusiasts, from windsurfing at the lake's northern end to boating, sailing, and jet skiing at Como and Cernobbio. The lake is also quite swimmable in the summer months. For hikers there are lovely paths all around the lake. For an easy trek, take the funicular up to Brunate, and walk along the mountain to the lighthouse for a stunning view of the lake.

LAKE MAGGIORE

Magnificently scenic, Lake Maggiore has a unique geographical position: its mountainous western shore is in Piedmont, its lower eastern shore is in Lombardy, and its northern tip is in Switzerland. The lake stretches nearly 50 km (30 mi) and is up to 5 km (3 mi) wide. The better-known resorts are on the western shore.

GETTING HERE

Trains run regularly from Milan to the town of Stresa on Lake Maggiore; the trip takes from 1 to 1½ hours, depending on the type of train. By car from Milan to Stresa, take the A8 autostrada to A8dir, and from A8dir take A26; the drive is about 1¼ hours.

STRESA AND THE ISOLE BORROMEE

80 km (50 mi) northwest of Milan.

VISITOR INFORMATION

Stresa tourism office (✉ *Piazza Marconi 16* ☎ *0323/30150* 🌐 *www.distrettolaghi.it or www.stresaturismo.it* ⏲ *Weekdays 10–12:30 and 3–6:30, weekends 10–12:30.*

EXPLORING

One of the better-known resorts on the western shore, Stresa is a tourist town that provided one of the settings for Hemingway's *A Farewell to Arms*. It has capitalized on its central lakeside position and has to some extent become a victim of its own success. The luxurious elegance that distinguished its heyday has faded; the grand hotels are still grand, but traffic now encroaches upon their parks and gardens. Even the undeniable loveliness of the lakeshore drive has been threatened by the roar of diesel trucks and BMW traffic. The best way to escape is to head for the Isole Borromee (Borromean Islands) in Lake Maggiore. For amazing views, take the Funivia (🌐 *www.stresa-mottarone.it*), a cable car that takes you to heights from which you can see all seven lakes.

As you wander around the palms and semitropical shrubs of **Villa Pallavicino**, don't be surprised if you're followed by a peacock or even an ostrich: they're part of the zoological garden and are allowed to roam almost at will. From the top of the hill on which the villa stands you can see the gentle hills of the Lombardy shore of Lake Maggiore and, nearer and to the left, the jewel-like Borromean Islands. In addition to a bar and restaurant, the grounds also have picnic spots. ✉ *Via Sempione 8* ☎ *0323/31533* 🌐 *www.parcozoopallavicino.it* 🎟 *€9* ⏲ *Early Mar.–Oct., daily 9–6.*

Boats to the **Isole Borromee** (🌐 *www.borromeoturismo.it*) depart every 15 to 30 minutes from the dock at Stresa's Piazza Marconi, as well as from Piazzale Lido at the northern end of the promenade. There is also a boat from Verbania; check locally for the seasonal schedule. Although you can hire a private boatman, it's cheaper and just as convenient to use the regular service. Make sure you buy a ticket allowing you to visit all the islands—Bella, Dei Pescatori, and Madre. The islands take their name from the Borromeo family, which has owned them since the 12th century.

Isola Bella *(Beautiful Island)* is the most famous of the three, and the first that you'll visit. It is named after Isabella, whose husband, Carlo III Borromeo (1538–84), built the palace and terraced gardens for her as a wedding present. Before Count Carlo began his project, the island was rocky and almost devoid of vegetation; the soil for the garden had to be transported from the mainland. Wander up the 10 terraces of the gardens, where peacocks roam among the scented shrubs, statues, and fountains, for a splendid view of the lake. Visit the palazzo to see the rooms where famous guests—including Napoléon and Mussolini—stayed in 18th-century splendor. Those three interlocked rings on walls and even streets represent the powerful Borromeo, Visconti, and Sforza families. ☎ *0323/30556* 🎟 *Garden and palazzo €12* ⏲ *Mid-Mar.–mid-Oct., daily 9–5:30. Painting gallery: daily 9–1 and 1:30–5.*

Stop for a while at the tiny **Isola dei Pescatori** (*Island of the Fishermen*, also known as Isola Superiore), less than 100 yards wide and only about ½ km (¼ mi) long. It's the perfect place for a seafood lunch before, after, or in between your visit to the other two islands. Of the 10 or so restaurants on this tiny island, the three worth visiting are **Ristorante Unione** (☎ *0323/933798*), **Ristorante Verbano** (☎ *0323/30408*), and **Ristorante Belvedere** (☎ *0323/32292*). The island's little lanes strung with fishing nets and dotted with shrines to the Madonna are the definition of picturesque; little wonder that in high season the village is crowded with postcard stands.

Isola Madre *(Mother Island)* is nicknamed the "Botanical Island." The entire island is a botanical garden, whose season stretches from late March to late October due to the climatic protection of the mighty Alps and the tepid waters of Lago Maggiore. The vision of cacti and palm trees on Isola Madre, its position so far north and so near the border of Switzerland, is a beautiful and unexpected surprise. Take time to see the profusion of exotic trees and shrubs running down to the shore in every direction. Two special times to visit are April (for the camellias) and May (for azaleas and rhododendrons). Also on the island is a 16th-century palazzo, where the Borromeo family still resides at different times throughout the year and where an antique puppet theater is on display, complete with string puppets, prompt books, and elaborate scenery designed by Alessandro Sanquirico, who was a scenographer at La Scala in Milan. ☎ *0323/31261* *€10* *Late Mar.–Oct., daily 9–5:30.*

6

For more information about the islands, contact the tourism office or ask at the docks (look for Navigazione Lago Maggiore signs).

WHERE TO EAT AND STAY

$ PIEDMONTESE ✕ **Da Cesare.** Off Piazza Cadorna and close to the embarcadero, this restaurant serves tasty risotto *con filetti di persico* (with perch fillets) and typical Piedmontese meat dishes, such as beef braised in Barolo wine. Da Cesare also has hotel rooms ($). ✉ *Via Mazzini 14* ☎ *0323/31386* 🌐 *www.dacesare.com.*

$$$–$$$$ **Grand Hotel des Iles Borromees.** This palatial, Liberty-style establishment has catered to a demanding European clientele since 1863. **Pros:** the grace and style of a bygone era, with modern amenities. **Cons:** some might consider it isolated. **TripAdvisor:** "the absolute best location," "staff was great and awesome," "wonderful mix of colorful flowers beds." ✉ *Corso Umberto I 67* ☎ *0323/938938* 🌐 *www.borromees.it* *179 rooms, 11 suites* *In-room: a/c, safe, Internet. In-hotel: restaurant, room service, bar, tennis court, pools, spa, laundry service, Wi-Fi hotspot, parking (free)* *Breakfast.*

$ **Primavera.** A few blocks up from the lake, Primavera has compact, simply furnished rooms in a 1950s building hung with flower boxes. **Pros:** good value; convenient location. **Cons:** no lake views; small, plainly furnished rooms. **TripAdvisor:** "room was spacious," "lots of storage," "very basic hotel." ✉ *Via Cavour 39* ☎ *0323/31286* 🌐 *www.hotelprimaverastresa.com* *37 rooms* *In-room: Wi-Fi, safe, refrigerator. In-hotel: bar, Internet terminal, parking (paid)* *AE, DC, MC, V* *Closed mid-Nov.–mid-Mar.* *Breakfast.*

VERBANIA

16 km (10 mi) north of Stresa, 95 km (59 mi) northwest of Milan.

EXPLORING

Quaint Verbania is across the Gulf of Pallanza from its touristy neighbor Stresa. It is known for the **Villa Taranto**, which has magnificent botanical gardens. The villa was acquired in 1931 by Scottish captain Neil McEachern, who expanded the gardens considerably, adding terraces, waterfalls, more than 3,000 plant species from all over the world, and broad meadows sloping gently to the lake. In 1938 McEachern donated the entire complex to the Italian people. ✉ *Via Vittorio Veneto 111* ☎ *0323/404555* 🌐 *www.villataranto.it* *€9* ⏲ *Late Mar.–Oct., daily 8:30–6:30; last entry 1 hr before closing.*

WHERE TO STAY

$ **Il Chiostro.** Originally a 17th-century convent, this hotel expanded into the adjoining 19th-century textile factory, adding some conference facilities. **Pros:** friendly and efficient staff. **Cons:** rooms are fairly plain. **TripAdvisor:** "treated like old friends," "very quiet," "food is simple but very good." ✉ *Via Fratelli Cervi 14* ☎ *0323/404077* 🌐 *www.chiostrovb.it* *100 rooms* *In-room: Internet, Wi-Fi. In-hotel: restaurant, bar, Internet terminal, Wi-Fi hotspot* *Breakfast.*

$$$ Fodor's Choice ★ **Il Sole di Ranco.** The same family has run this elegant lakeside inn, perched high on the banks of the lake opposite and below Stresa, for more than 150 years. **Pros:** classic lake setting; tranquil grounds, meticulously maintained. **Cons:** a bit distant from lake's tourist center (although hotel offers excursions with private driver). **TripAdvisor:** "surrounded by lovely gardens," "private, intimate feel," "period charm but modern fittings." ✉ *Piazza Venezia 5, Ranco* ✣ *near Angera* ☎ *0331/976507* 🌐 *www.ilsolediranco.it* *2 rooms, 10 suites* *In-room: safe, a/c, Wi-Fi. In-hotel: restaurant, pool, laundry service, parking (free)* ⏲ *Closed Nov. 15–Jan. 21. Restaurant closed Tues. No lunch Mon.* *Breakfast.*

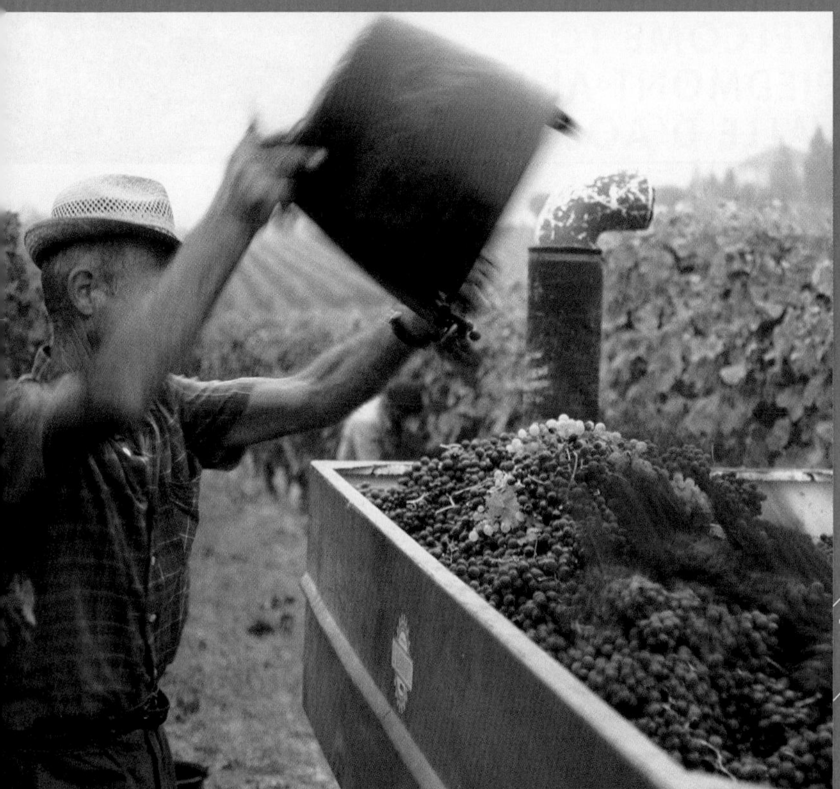

7

Piedmont and Valle d'Aosta

WORD OF MOUTH

"Piemonte is an absolutely gorgeous area, and each town is cuter than the next. The food is fantastic, has a bit of a French influence (while still being Italian) and it's very easy to go over the top in terms of consumption!"

—Lexma90

WELCOME TO PIEDMONT AND VALLE D'AOSTA

TOP REASONS TO GO

★ **Sacra di San Michele:** Explore one of the country's most spectacularly situated religious buildings.

★ **Castello Fénis:** This castle transports you back in time to the Middle Ages.

★ **Monte Bianco:** The cable car ride over the snowcapped mountain will take your breath away.

★ **Turin's Museo Egizio:** A surprising treasure—one of the world's richest collections of Egyptian art outside Cairo.

★ **Regal wines:** Some of Italy's most revered reds—led by Barolo, dubbed "the king wines"—come from the hills of southern Piedmont.

1 Turin. The region's main city isn't just the car capital of Italy and home to the Holy Shroud. Neoclassical piazzas, shops filled with chocolates and chic fashions, and elegant baroque palazzos have been restored in grand style.

2 The Colline. Gracing the "little hills" west of Turin are some opulent monuments of the 17th-century Piedmontese style, including the palace at Venaria Reale, designed by for the Savoy kings in the 16th and 17th centuries. Less worldly is the mesmerizingly medieval hilltop monastery of Sacra di San Michele.

3 Monferrato and the Langhe. These hills are famous among food and wine connoisseurs. Asti gave the world Asti Spumante, Alba is known for its truffles and mushrooms, and the Langhe hills produce some of Italy's finest wines.

4 Valle d'Aosta. The mountains and valleys of this region fairly cry out to be strolled, climbed, and skied. Here, the highest Alpine peaks—including Monte Bianco (aka Mont Blanc) and the Matterhorn—shelter resorts such as Breuil-Cervinia and Courmayeur and the great nature preserve known as the Gran Paradiso.

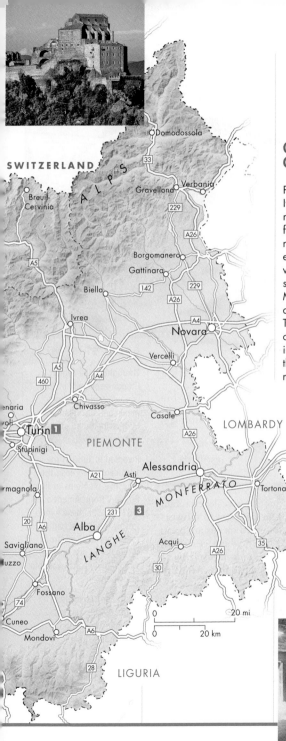

GETTING ORIENTED

Piedmont (Piemonte in Italian) means "foot of the mountains," and the name fits: Turin, the region's major city, sits on the western end of the Po Plain, with the Maritime Alps due south and the hills of the Monferrato and Langhe districts to the southeast. To the north is mountainous Valle d'Aosta, where imposing castles sit in the shadow of Europe's most impressive peaks.

7

EATING AND DRINKING WELL IN PIEDMONT AND VALLE D'AOSTA

In Piedmont and Valle d'Aosta you can find rustic specialties from farmhouse hearths, fine cuisine with a French accent, and everything in between. The Piedmontese take their food and wine very seriously.

There is a significant concentration of upscale restaurants in Piedmont, with refined cuisine designed to showcase the region's fine wines. Wine-oriented menus are prevalent both in cities and in the country, where even simply named trattorias may offer a *menu di degustazione* (a multicourse tasting menu) accompanied by wines paired to each dish.

In Turin the ritual of the *aperitivo* (aperitif) has been finely tuned, and most cafés from the early evening onward provide lavish buffets that are included in the price of a cocktail—a respectable substitute for dinner if you are traveling on a limited budget. As a result, restaurants in Turin tend to fill only after 9 pm.

GREAT GRISSINI

Throughout the region, though especially in Turin, you will find that most meals are accompanied by *grissini* (bread sticks), pictured above.

Invented in Turin in the 17th century to ease the digestive problems of little Prince Vittorio Amedeo II (1675–1730), these, when freshly made and hand-rolled, are a far cry from the thin and dry, plastic-wrapped versions available elsewhere.

Napoléon called them *petits batons* and was, according to legend, addicted to them.

TRUFFLES

The truffle (*tartufo* in Italian) is a peculiar delicacy—a gnarly clump of fungus that grows wild in forests a few inches underground. It's hunted down using truffle-sniffing dogs and can sell for a small fortune. The payoff is a powerful, perfume flavor that makes gourmets swoon. Though truffles are more abundant farther south in Umbria, the most coveted ones are the *tartufi bianchi* (white truffles), pictured at right, from Alba in Piedmont. A thin shaving of truffle often tops pasta dishes; they're also used to flavor soups and other dishes.

POLENTA AND PASTA

The area's best-known dish is probably polenta, creamy cornmeal served with *carbonada* (a meat stew), melted cheese, or wild mushrooms. *Agnolotti*—crescent-shaped pasta stuffed with meat filling, pictured below—is another specialty, often served with the pan juices of roast veal. *Agnolotti del Plin* is a smaller version topped with melted butter and shaved truffles.

CHEESE

In keeping with their northern character, a regional specialty in both Piedmont and Valle d'Aosta is *fonduta,* a version of fondue made with melted cheese, eggs, and sometimes grated truffles. Fontina and ham also often deck out

the ubiquitous French-style crepes *alla valdostana,* served casserole style.

MEAT

The locally raised beef of Piedmont is some of Italy's most highly prized; it's often braised or stewed with the region's hearty red wine. In winter, *bollito misto* (various meats, boiled and served with a rich sauce) shows up on many menus, and *fritto misto,* a combination of fried meats and vegetables, is another specialty.

DESSERTS AND SWEETS

Though desserts here are less sweet than in some other Italian regions, treats like *panna cotta* (a cooked milk custard), *torta di nocciole* (hazelnut torte), and *bonet* (a pudding made with hazelnuts, cocoa, milk, and macaroons) are delights. Turin is renowned for its delicate pastries and fine chocolates, especially for *gianduiotti,* made with hazelnuts.

WINE

Piedmont is one of Italy's most important wine regions, producing full-bodied reds, such as Barolo, Barbaresco, Freisa, Barbera, and the lighter Dolcetto. Asti Spumante, a sweet sparkling wine, comes from the region, while Valle d'Aosta is famous for schnappslike brandies made from fruits or herbs.

Updated by Peter Blackman

A pair of contrasting characteristics define the appeal of northwest Italy's Piedmont and Valle d'Aosta regions: mountain splendor and bourgeois refinement. Two of Europe's most famous peaks—Monte Bianco (aka Mont Blanc) and Monte Cervino (the Matterhorn)—straddle Valle d'Aosta's borders with France and Switzerland, and the entire region is a magnet for skiers and hikers.

To the south, the mist-shrouded lowlands skirting the Po River are home to Turin, a city that may not have the artistic treasures of Rome or the cutting-edge style of Milan, but has developed a sense of urban sophistication that makes it a pleasure to visit. You also taste a mountain/city contrast in the cuisine: the hearty peasant cooking served in tiny stone villages and the French-accented delicacies found in the plain are both eminently satisfying. Meals are accompanied by Piedmontese wines commonly held to be Italy's finest.

Napoléon's regime controlled Piedmont and Valle d'Aosta in the 19th century, and French influence remains evident in everything from traditional recipes redolent of mountain cheeses, truffles, and cream to Versailles-style gardens and wide, tree-lined boulevards. Well-dressed women in the cafés of Turin are addressed more often as *madama* than *signora,* and French is often spoken in the more-remote mountain hamlets.

PLANNING

MAKING THE MOST OF YOUR TIME

Turin, the first capital of unified Italy and the fourth largest city in the country, is a commercial center once overlooked on tourist itineraries. But after hosting the Winter in Olympics in 2006, and getting a further polish for the 2011 celebration of the 150th anniversary of Italian unification, Turin is on the radar. There is good cause: the museum system is second to none, gourmet restaurants abound, the nightlife is hopping, and there are an unusual number of attractions for children. If you also like the idea of an Italian city with touches of Parisian sophistication, Turin will strike your fancy.

In the mountains that surround Turin the hiking, climbing, and skiing are exceptional. On the Piedmont–Valle d'Aosta border, the Gran Paradiso National Park has beautiful trails. Farther north is Monte Bianco, which should be a priority; you can ascend by cable car, or, if you're an experienced climber, make a go of it with professional guides. You'll find extensive ski slopes in Sestriere in Piedmont and in Breuil-Cervinia on the Matterhorn. Food and wine lovers should head for the hills of the Langhe, just south of Turin, home to world-class wines and the redolent white truffles.

GETTING HERE AND AROUND

BUS TRAVEL

Turin's main bus station is on the corner of Corso Inghilterra and Corso Vittorio Emanuele. Urban buses, trams, and the subway are operated by the agency **GTT** (☎ *800/019152* 🌐 *www.comune.torino.it/gtt*). Turin-based bus line **SADEM** (☎ *800/801600* 🌐 *www.sadem.it*) provides service throughout Piedmont and Valle d'Aosta. Aosta-based **SAVDA** (☎ *0165/262027* 🌐 *www.savda.it*) specializes in mountain service, providing frequent links between Aosta, Turin, and Courmayeur as well as Milan. There's also a major bus station at Aosta, across the street from the train station.

7

CAR TRAVEL

Like any rugged, mountainous region, the Italian Alps can be tricky to navigate by car. Roads that look like superhighways on the map can be narrow and twisting, with steep slopes and cliff-side drops. Generally, roads are well maintained, but the sheer distance covered by all of those curves tends to take longer than you might expect, so it's best to figure in extra time for getting around. This is especially true in winter, when weather conditions can cause slow traffic and road closings. Check with local tourist offices or, in a pinch, with the police, to make sure roads are passable and safe, and to find out whether you may need tire chains for snowy and icy roads.

For travel across the French, Swiss, and Italian borders in Piedmont and Valle d'Aosta, only a few routes are usable year-round: the 12-km (7-mi) Mont Blanc tunnel connecting Chamonix with Courmayeur; the Colle del Gran San Bernardo/Col du Grand St. Bernard (connecting Martigny with Aosta on Swiss highway E27 and Italian highway SS27, with 6 km [4 mi] of tunnel); and the Traforo del Fréjus (between Modane and Susa, with 13 km [8 mi] of tunnel). There are other passes, but they become increasingly unreliable between November and April.

TRAIN TRAVEL

Turin is on the main Paris–Rome TGV express line and is also connected with Milan, only 90 minutes away on the fast train. The fastest (Frecciarossa) trains cover the 667-km (414-mi) trip to Rome in just over four hours; other trains take between five and seven hours.

Services to the larger cities east of Turin are part of the extensive and reliable train network of the Lombard Plain. West of the region's capital, however, the train services soon peter out in the mountains.

Continuing connections by bus serve these valleys; information about train-bus mountain services can be obtained from train stations and tourist information offices, or by contacting **FS–Trenitalia** (☎ *892021* 🌐 *www.trenitalia.com*), the Italian national train service.

ABOUT THE HOTELS

High standards and opulence are characteristic of Turin's better hotels, and the same is true, translated into the Alpine idiom, at the top mountain resorts. Hotels in Turin and other major towns are generally geared to business travelers; make sure to ask whether lower weekend rates or special deals for two- or three-night stays are available.

Summer vacationers and winter skiers keep occupancy rates and prices high at the resorts during peak seasons. Many mountain hotels accept half- or full-board guests only and require that you stay for several nights; some have off-season rates that can reduce the cost by a full price category. If you're planning to ski, ask about package deals that give you a discount on lift tickets.

Hotel reviews have been condensed for this book. Please go to Fodors.com for full reviews of each property.

WHAT IT COSTS (IN EUROS)

	¢	$	$$	$$$	$$$$
Restaurants	under €20	€20–€30	€30–€45	€45–€65	over €65
Hotels	under €75	€75–€125	€125–€200	€200–€300	over €300

Restaurant prices are for a first course (primo), second course (secondo), and dessert (dolce). Hotel prices are for two people in a standard double room in high season, including tax and service.

TURIN

Turin—Torino, in Italian—is roughly in the center of Piedmont/Valle d'Aosta and 128 km (80 mi) west of Milan; it's on the Po River, on the edge of the Po Plain, which stretches eastward all the way to the Adriatic. Turin's flatness and wide, angular, tree-lined boulevards are a far cry from Italian *metropoli* to the south; the region's decidedly northern European bent is quite evident in its nerve center. Apart from its role as northwest Italy's major industrial, cultural, intellectual, and administrative hub, Turin also has a reputation as Italy's capital of black magic and the supernatural. This distinction is enhanced by the presence of Turin's most famous, and controversial, relic, the Sacra Sindone (Holy Shroud), still believed by many Catholics to be the cloth in which Christ's body was wrapped when he was taken down from the cross.

GETTING HERE

Turin is well served by the Italian highway system and can be reached easily by car from all directions: from Milan on the A4 highway (two hours); from Bologna (four hours) and Florence (five hours) on the A1 and A21 highways; from Genoa on the A6 highway (two hours).

Bus service to and from other major Italian cities is also plentiful, and Turin can be reached by fast train service from Paris in less than six hours. Fast train service also connects the city with Milan, Genova, Bologna, Florence, and Rome.

VISITOR INFORMATION

Turin's group and personally guided tours are organized by the city's tourist office. They also provide maps and details about a wide range of thematic self-guided walks through town. The Torino+Piemonte card, which provides discounts on transportation and museum entrances for two-, three-, five-, or seven-day visits can be purchased here, as well as Turin's unique Chocopass, which allows you to indulge in 10 tastings in as many chocolate shops.

Turin tourism office (✉ *Piazza Castello* ☎ *011/535181* 🌐 *www.turismotorino.org*).

DOWNTOWN TURIN

Many of Turin's major sights are clustered around Piazza Castello, and others are on or just off the portico-lined Via Roma, one of the city's main thoroughfares, which leads 1 km (½ mi) from Piazza Castello south to Piazza Carlo Felice, a landscaped park in front of the train station. First opened in 1615, Via Roma was largely rebuilt in the 1930s, during the Mussolini era.

7

TOP ATTRACTIONS

Duomo di San Giovanni. The most impressive part of Turin's 15th-century cathedral is the shadowy black marble–walled **Cappella della Sacra Sindone** (Chapel of the Holy Shroud), where the famous relic was housed before a fire in 1997. The chapel was designed by the priest and architect Guarino Guarini (1604–83), a genius of the baroque style who was official engineer and mathematician to the court of Duke Carlo Emanuele II of Savoy. The fire caused severe structural damage, and the chapel is closed indefinitely while restoration work proceeds.

The Sacra Sindone is a 4-yard-long sheet of linen, thought by millions to be the burial shroud of Christ, bearing the light imprint of his crucified body. The shroud first made an appearance around the middle of the 15th century, when it was presented to Ludovico of Savoy in Chambéry. In 1578 it was brought to Turin by another member of the Savoy royal family, Duke Emanuele Filiberto. It was only in the 1990s that the Catholic Church began allowing rigorous scientific study of the shroud. Not surprisingly, results have bolstered both sides of the argument. On the one hand, three separate university teams—in Switzerland, Britain, and the United States—have concluded, as a result of carbon 14 dating, that the cloth is a forgery dating from between 1260 and 1390. On the other hand, they are unable to explain how medieval forgers could have created the shroud's image, which resembles a photographic negative, and how they could have had the knowledge or means to incorporate traces of Roman coins covering the eyelids and endemic Middle Eastern pollen woven into the cloth. Either way, the shroud continues to be revered as a holy relic, exhibited to the public on very rare occasions—the next official display is planned for 2025.

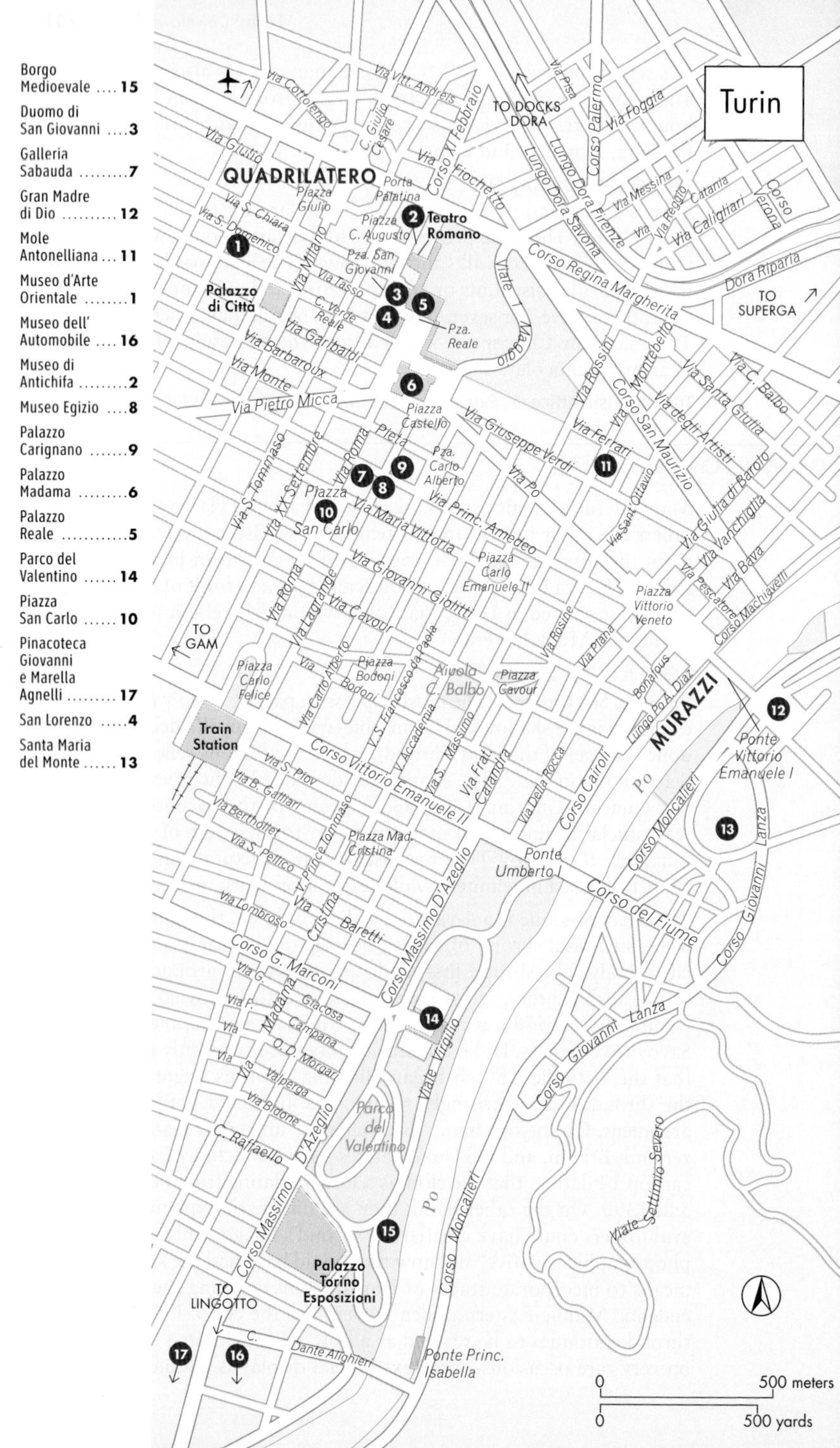

Turin
Borgo Medioevale 15
Duomo di San Giovanni 3
Galleria Sabauda 7
Gran Madre di Dio 12
Mole Antonelliana ... 11
Museo d'Arte Orientale 1
Museo dell' Automobile 16
Museo di Antichifa 2
Museo Egizio 8
Palazzo Carignano 9
Palazzo Madama 6
Palazzo Reale 5
Parco del Valentino 14
Piazza San Carlo 10
Pinacoteca Giovanni e Marella Agnelli 17
San Lorenzo 4
Santa Maria del Monte 13
QUADRILATERO
MURAZZI
Teatro Romano
Palazzo di Città
Porta Palatina
Piazza Giulio
Piazza C. Augusto
Pza. San Giovanni
Pza. Reale
Piazza Castello
Pza. Carlo Alberto
Piazza San Carlo
Piazza Carlo Emanuele II
Piazza Vittorio Veneto
Piazza Carlo Felice
Piazza Bodoni
Aiuola C. Balbo
Piazza Cavour
Piazza Mad. Cristina
Train Station
Parco del Valentino
Palazzo Torino Esposizioni
Ponte Umberto I
Ponte Vittorio Emanuele I
Ponte Princ. Isabella
TO DOCKS DORA
TO SUPERGA
TO GAM
TO LINGOTTO
Dora Riparia
Po
Via Cottolengo
Via Vitt. Andreis
C. Giulio Cesare
Corso XI Febbraio
Via Fiochetto
Via Giulio
Via S. Chiara
Via S. Domenico
Via Milano
Via Tasso
C. Verde Reale
Via Garibaldi
Via Barbaroux
Via Monte
Via Pietro Micca
Viale I Maggio
Corso Regina Margherita
Lungo Dora Savona
Lungo Dora Firenze
Corso Palermo
Via Prisa
Via Foggia
Via Messina
Via Reggio
Catania
Via Caligliari
Corso Verona
Via Rossini
Via Montebello
Corso San Maurizio
Via Santa Giulia
Via C. Balbo
Via degli Artisti
Via Giuseppe Verdi
Via Ferrari
Via Po
Via Sant'Ottavio
Via Giulia di Barolo
Via Vanchiglia
Via Pescatore
Via Bava
Corso Machiavelli
Via S. Tommaso
Via XX Settembre
Via Roma
Pietà
Via Maria Vittoria
Via Princ. Amedeo
Via Giovanni Giolitti
Via Lagrange
Via Cavour
Via Carlo Alberto
Via Bodoni
V. S. Francesco da Paola
V. Accademia
Via S. Massimo
Via Frat. Calandra
Via Rosine
Via Plana
Via Della Rocca
Corso Cairoli
Bonafous
Lungo Po A. Diaz
Corso Moncalieri
Corso Vittorio Emanuele II
Via S. Pio V
Via B. Galliari
Via Berthollet
Via S. Pellico
Via Lombroso
V. Prince Tommaso
Via Cristina
Via Baretti
Corso Massimo D'Azeglio
Corso del Fiume
Corso Giovanni Lanza
Corso G. Marconi
Via G. Giacosa
Via F. Campana
Via Madama
Via O. D. Morgari
Via Valperga
Via Bidone
C. Raffaello
Viale Virgilio
Viale Settimio Severo
Corso Massimo D'Azeglio
C. Dante Alighieri
0
500 meters
0
500 yards

NORTHWEST ITALY, PAST AND PRESENT

Ancient history. Piedmont and Valle d'Aosta were originally inhabited by Celtic tribes, who over time were absorbed by the conquering Romans. As allies of Rome, the Celts held off Hannibal when he came down through the Alpine passes with his elephants, but they were eventually defeated, and their capital—Taurasia, the present Turin—was destroyed. The Romans rebuilt the city, giving its streets the grid pattern that survives today. (Roman ruins can be found throughout both regions and are particularly conspicuous in the town of Aosta.)

The Middle Ages and the Savoy. With the fall of the Roman Empire, the region suffered the fate of the rest of Italy and was successively occupied and ravaged by barbarians from the east and the north. In the 11th century, the feudal French Savoy family ruled Turin briefly; toward the end of the 13th century it returned to the area, where it would remain, almost continuously, for 500 years. In 1798 the French republican armies invaded Italy, but when Napoléon's empire fell, the house of Savoy returned to power.

Risorgimento. Beginning in 1848, Piedmont was one of the principal centers of the Risorgimento, the movement for Italian unity. In 1861 the Chamber of Deputies of Turin declared Italy a united kingdom, with Turin as the new nation's capital. The capital moved to Florence in 1865, and then to Rome in 1870, effectively marking the end of Piedmont's prominence in national politics.

Industry and affluence. Piedmont became one of the first industrialized regions in Italy, and the automotive giant FIAT—the Fabbrica Italiana Automobili Torino—was established here in 1899. Today the region is the center of Italy's automobile, metalworking, chemical, and candy industries, having attracted thousands of workers from Italy's south. The FIAT company, led by the Agnelli family—roughly Italy's equivalent of the Kennedys—has been arguably the most important factor in the region's rise to affluence.

7

In lieu of the real thing, a photocopy is on permanent display near the altar of the Duomo. ✉ *Piazza San Giovanni, Centro* ☎ *011/4361540* ⏲ *Mon.–Sat. 6:30–noon and 3–7, Sun. 8–noon and 3–7.*

Galleria Sabauda. Some of the most important paintings from the vast collections of the house of Savoy are displayed here. The collection is particularly rich in 16th- and 17th-century Dutch and Flemish paintings: note the *Stigmate di San Francesco* (*St. Francis Receiving Stigmata*) by Jan Van Eyck (1395–1441), in which the saint receives the marks of Christ's wounds while a companion cringes beside him. Other Dutch masterpieces include paintings by Anthony Van Dyck (1599–1641) and Rembrandt (1606–69). *L'arcangelo Raffaele e Tobiolo (Tobias and the Angel)* by Piero del Pollaiuolo (circa 1443–96) is showcased, and other featured Italian artists include Fra Angelico (circa 1400–55), Andrea Mantegna (1431–1506), and Paolo Veronese (1528–88). Along with the Egyptian Museum, the gallery is housed in the **Palazzo dell'Accademia delle Scienze,** a baroque tour de force designed by priest-architect Guarino Guarini. At this writing, there are plans to move the entire collection of paintings permanently to the Palazzo Reale in 2011. ✉ *Via Accademia delle Scienze 6, Centro* ☎ *011/547440* 🌐 *www.museitorino.it* 🎫 *€7.50* ⏲ *Fri.–Sun. and Tues. 8:30–2, Wed. 2–7:30 and Thurs. 10–7:30.*

★ **Mole Antonelliana.** You can't miss the unusual square dome and thin, elaborate spire of this Turin landmark above the city's rooftops. This odd structure, built between 1863 and 1889, was originally intended to be a synagogue, but costs escalated and eventually it was bought by the city of Turin. In its time it was the tallest brick building in the world, and it is still the tallest building in Italy. You can take the crystal elevator to reach the terrace at the top of the dome for an excellent view of the city, the plain, and the Alps beyond. Also worth a visit is the Mole Antonelliana's **Museo Nazionale del Cinema** (National Cinema Museum), which covers more than 34,000 square feet and houses many items of film memorabilia as well as a film library with some 7,000 titles. ✉ *Via Montebello 20, Centro* ☎ *011/8138560 museum* 🌐 *www.museocinema.it(museum)* 🎫 *Museum €7, elevator €5, combination ticket €9* ⏲ *Museum: Tues.–Fri. and Sun. 9–8, Sat. 9 am–11 pm; ticket sales end 45 mins before closing. Elevator: Tues.–Fri. and Sun. 10–8, Sat. 10 am–11 pm.*

★ **Museo d'Arte Orientale.** Housed in the magnificently renovated 17th-century Palazzo Mazzonis, this beautifully displayed collection of Southeast Asian, Chinese, Japanese, Himalayan, and Islamic art is a must-see for anyone interested in oriental sculpture, painting, and ceramics. Highlights include a towering 13th-century wooden statue of the Japanese temple guardian Kongo Rikishi and a sumptuous assortment of Islamic manuscripts. ✉ *Via San Domenico 9/11, Centro* ☎ *011/4436927* 🌐 *www.maotorino.it* 🎫 *€7.50* ⏲ *Tues.–Sun. 10–6; ticket sales end 1 hr before closing.*

Fodor's Choice ★ **Museo Egizio.** The Egyptian Museum's superb collection includes statues of pharaohs and mummies and entire frescoes taken from royal tombs—all in all, it's one of the world's finest and largest museums of its kind. Designed by Oscar-winner Dante Ferretti, the striking sculpture gallery is a veritable who's who of ancient Egypt. Look for the magnificent 13th-century BC statue of Ramses II and the fascinating Tomb of Kha. The latter was found intact with furniture, supplies of food and clothing, writing instruments, and a complete set of personal cosmetics and toiletries. Unfortunately, the museum's objects are not always displayed according to modern standards. Along with carefully constructed exhibits with detailed information in English and Italian you will also find rooms that resemble warehouses filled with objects, with little or no information provided. ✉ *Via Accademia delle Scienze 6, Centro* ☎ *011/5617776* 🌐 *www.museoegizio.it* 🎫 *€7.50* ⏲ *Tues.–Sun. 8:30–7:30; ticket sales end 1 hr before closing.*

Palazzo Madama. In the center of Piazza Castello, this castle was named for the Savoy queen Maria Cristina, who made it her home in the 17th century. The building incorporates the remains of a Roman gate with later-medieval and Renaissance additions. The castle's monumental baroque facade and grand entrance staircase were designed by Filippo Juvarra (1678–1736). The palace now houses the **Museo Civico d'Arte Antica,** whose collections comprise more than 30,000 items dating from the Middle Ages to the baroque era. The paintings, sculptures, illuminated manuscripts, and various decorative objects on display illustrate almost 10 centuries of Italian and European artistic production. Works by Jan van Eyck, Antonella da Messina (circa 1430–79), and Orazio Gentileschi (1563–1639) highlight the collection. ✉ *Piazza Castello, Centro* ☎ *011/4433501* 🌐 *www.palazzomadamatorino.it* *Grand staircase and medieval courtyard free, museum €7.50* ⏲ *Grand staircase and medieval courtyard: Tues.–Sat. 9–6, Sun. 10–8. Museum: Tues.–Fri. 10–6, Sun. 10–8. Ticket sales end 1 hr before closing.*

Palazzo Reale. This 17th-century palace, a former Savoy royal residence, is an imposing work of brick, stone, and marble that stands on the site of one of Turin's ancient Roman city gates. In contrast to its sober exterior, the palace's interior is swathed in luxurious, mostly rococo trappings, including tapestries, gilt ceilings, and sumptuous 17th- to 19th-century furniture. You can head down to the basement and the old kitchens to see where food for the last kings of Italy was once dished up, and behind the palace you can relax in the royal gardens. At this writing, extensive restoration work is underway to allow the opening of all floors of the palace and for the permanent transfer here of the painting collection of the Galleria Sabauda in 2011.

The **Armeria Reale** *(Royal Armory)* ✉ *Entrance at Piazza Castello 191, Centro* ☎ *011/543889* *€4* ⏲ *Tues.–Fri. 9–2, weekends 1–7)*, in a wing of the Royal Palace, holds one of Europe's most extensive collections of arms and armor. It's a must-see for connoisseurs. ✉ *Piazzetta Reale, Centro* ☎ *011/4361455* *Gardens free, palace €6.50* ⏲ *Palace: Tues.–Sun. 8:30–7:30; guided visits depart every 40 mins. Gardens: daily 9 am–1 hr before sunset.*

7

Piazza San Carlo. Surrounded by shops, arcades, fashionable cafés, and elegant baroque palaces, this is one of the most beautiful squares in Turin. In the center stands a statue of Duke Emanuele Filiberto of Savoy, victor at the battle of San Quintino in 1557. The melee heralded the peaceful resurgence of Turin under the Savoy after years of bloody dynastic fighting. The fine bronze statue erected in the 19th century is one of Turin's symbols. At the southern end of the square, framing the continuation of Via Roma, are the twin baroque churches of San Carlo and Santa Cristina.

QUICK BITES

A chocolate lover's pilgrimage to Turin inevitably leads to **Al Bicerin** (✉ *Piazza della Consolata 5, Centro* ☎ *011/4369325* 🌐 *www.bicerin.it* ⏲ *Closed Wed. and Aug.*), which first opened its doors in 1763. Cavour, Nietzsche, Puccini, and Dumas have all sipped here, and if you order the house specialty, the *bicerin* (a hot drink with layers of chocolate, coffee, and cream), you'll understand why. Don't be surprised if the friendly and energetic owner, Marité Costa, also tries to tempt you with one of her flavored *zabajoni* (warm eggnogs). Chocolate goodies, including chocolate-flavor pasta, are on sale in the café store. The historic **Caffè San Carlo** (✉ *Piazza San Carlo 156, Centro* ☎ *011/532586*) is usually lively with locals gathered at the marble-top tables under the huge crystal chandelier. Breakfast and lunch, afternoon snacks, and evening aperitifs are all served in this particularly elegant neoclassical setting.

★ **San Lorenzo.** Architect Guarino Guarini was in his mid-sixties when he began this church in 1668. The masterful use of geometric forms and the theatrical control of light and shadow show him working at his mature and confident best. Stand in the center of the church and look up into the cupola to enjoy the full effect. ✉ *Via Palazzo di Città 4, Centro* ☎ *011/4361527* 🌐 *www.sanlorenzo.torino.it* 🕓 *Weekdays 7:30–noon and 4:30–7; weekends 9–1 and 3–7:30.*

WORD OF MOUTH

"Torino is elegant, people in Torino are also elegant, it has a special flavor. I really loved it."
—Graziella5b

QUICK BITES

Baratti e Milano (✉ *Piazza Castello 27, Centro* ☎ *011/4407138* 🌐 *www.barattiemilano.it* 🕓 *Closed Mon.*), in the glass-roofed Galleria Subalpina near Via Po, is one of Turin's charming old cafés. It's famous for its exquisite chocolates—indulge your sweet tooth or buy some *gianduiotti* (hazelnut chocolates) or candied chestnuts to take home to friends. Light lunches are served at the tables to the rear of the café. The tiny café **Mulassano** (✉ *Piazza Castello 15, Centro* ☎ *011/547990*), decorated with marble and finely carved wood panels, is famous for its *tramezzini* (small triangular sandwiches made with white bread), invented here in the 1920s. Popular with the pre- and post-theater crowd, the café also offers a unique roulette system for clients trying to decide on who pays the bill—ask the cashier for an explanation.

WORTH NOTING

Museo di Antichità. A small but fascinating collection of artifacts found at archaeological sites in and around Turin is on display here. A spiral ramp winds through the subterranean museum, and like in a real archaeological site, the deeper you go the older the objects displayed. A life-size silver bust of the Roman Emperor Lucio Vero (AD 161–169) is one of the masterpieces of the collection. ✉ *Via XX Settembre 88c, Centro* ☎ *011/5212251* 🌐 *www.museoantichita.it* 🎫 *€4* 🕓 *Tues.–Sun. 8:30–7:30.*

Palazzo Carignano. A baroque triumph by Guarino Guarini (the priest who designed several of Turin's most noteworthy structures), this red-brick palace was built between 1679 and 1685 and played an important role in the 19th-century unification of Italy. Vittorio Emanuele II of Savoy (1820–78), united Italy's first king, was born within these walls, and Italy's first parliament met here from 1860 to 1865. The palace now houses the **Museo del Risorgimento,** a museum honoring the 19th-century movement for Italian unity. ✉ *Via Accademia delle Scienze 5, Centro* ☎ *011/5621147* 🌐 *www.regione.piemonte.it/cultura/risorgimento* 🎫 *€7* 🕓 *Tues.–Sun. 9–7; ticket sales end 1 hr before closing.*

OFF THE BEATEN PATH

Galleria Civica d'Arte Moderna e Contemporanea (GAM). In 1863 Turin was the first Italian city to begin a public collection devoted to contemporary art. Housed in a modern building on the edge of downtown, a permanent display of more than 600 paintings, sculptures, and installation pieces provides an exceptional glimpse of how Italian contemporary art has evolved since the late 1800s. The futurist, pop, neo-Dada, and *arte povera* movements are particularly well represented, and the gallery has a fine video and art film collection. ✉ *Via Magenta 31, Centro* ☎ *011/4429518* 🌐 *www.gamtorino.it* 🎟 *€7.50* 🕒 *Tues.–Sun. 10–6.*

ALONG THE PO

The Po River is narrow and unprepossessing here in Turin, only a hint of the broad waterway that it becomes as it flows eastward toward the Adriatic. It's flanked, however, by formidable edifices, a park, and a lovely pedestrian path. Public boats, operated by Turin's **public transport system** (☎ *800/019152 or 011/5764733* 🌐 *www.comune.torino.it/gtt*) make for a pleasant way to reach the Borgo Medioevale from the Murazzi dock at the northern end of the Parco del Valentino.

TOP ATTRACTIONS

Borgo Medioevale. Along the banks of the Po, this complex, built for a General Exhibition in 1884, is a faithful reproduction of a typical Piedmont village in the Middle Ages: crafts shops, houses, a church, and stores cluster the narrow lanes, and in the center of the village the **Rocca Medioevale,** a medieval castle, provides the town's main attraction. ✉ *Southern end of Parco del Valentino, San Salvario* ☎ *011/4431701* 🌐 *www.borgomedioevaletorino.it* 🎟 *Village free, Rocca Medioevale €5* 🕒 *Village: Apr.–Oct., daily 9–8; Nov.–Mar., daily 9–7. Rocca Medioevale: Apr.–Oct., daily 9–7; Nov.–Mar., Tues.–Sun. 9–6; groups of no more than 25 enter castle every ½ hr. Ticket counter closes at 6:15.*

★ **Museo dell'Automobile.** No visit to car-manufacturing Turin would be complete without a pilgrimage to see perfectly conserved Bugattis, Ferraris, and Isotta Fraschinis. Here you can get an idea of the importance of FIAT—and automobiles in general—to Turin's economy. There's a collection of antique cars from as early as 1896, and displays show how the city has changed over the years as a result of its premier industry. For the true automobile fan, there's even a section devoted to the history of car tires. ✉ *Corso Unità d'Italia 40, Millefonti* ☎ *011/677666* 🌐 *www.museoauto.it* 🎟 *€7* 🕒 *Tues.–Sun. 10–6:30.*

Parco del Valentino. This pleasant riverside park is a great place to stroll, bike, or jog. Originally the grounds of a relatively simple hunting lodge, the park owes its present arrangement to Madama Maria Cristina of France, who received the land and lodge as a wedding present after her marriage to Vittorio Amedeo I of Savoy. With memories of 16th-century French châteaus in mind, she began work in 1620 and converted the lodge into a magnificent palace, the **Castello del Valentino.** The building, now home to the University of Turin's Faculty of Architecture, is not open to the general public. Next to the palace are botanical gardens, established in 1729, where local and exotic flora can be seen in a hothouse, herbarium, and arboretum. ✉ *Parco del Valentino, San Salvario* ☎ *011/6612447 botanical gardens* 🎟 *Gardens €3* 🕒 *Gardens Apr.–Sept., weekends 9–1 and 3–7.*

Fodor's Choice ★ **Pinacoteca Giovanni e Marella Agnelli.** This gallery was opened in 2002 by Gianni Agnelli (1921–2003), the head of FIAT and patriarch of one of Italy's most powerful families, just four months before his death. The emphasis here is on quality rather than quantity: 25 works of art from the Agnelli private collection are on permanent display, along with temporary exhibitions. There are four magnificent scenes of Venice by Canaletto (1697–1768); two splendid views of Dresden by Canaletto's nephew, Bernardo Bellotto (1720–80); several works by Manet (1832–83), Renoir (1841–1919), Matisse (1869–1954), and Picasso (1881–1973); and fine examples of the work of Italian futurist painters Balla (1871–1958) and Severini (1883–1966). The gallery is on the top floor of the **Lingotto,** a former FIAT factory that was completely transformed between 1982 and 2002 by architect Renzo Piano. The multilevel complex is now home to a shopping mall, several movie theaters, restaurants, two hotels, and an auditorium. ✉ *Via Nizza 230, Lingotto* ☎ *011/0062713* 🌐 *www.pinacoteca-agnelli.it* 🎫 *€4* ⏲ *Tues.–Sun. 10–7; last entrance at 6:15.*

WORTH NOTING

Gran Madre di Dio. On the east bank of the Po, this neoclassical church is modeled after the Pantheon in Rome. It was built between 1827 and 1831 to commemorate the return of the house of Savoy to Turin after the fall of Napoléon's empire. ✉ *Piazza Gran Madre di Dio, Borgo Po* ☎ *011/8193572* ⏲ *Mon.–Sat. 7:30–noon and 3:30–7, Sun. 7:30–1 and 3:30–7.*

Santa Maria del Monte. The church and convent standing on top of 150-foot Monte dei Cappuccini date from 1583. Don't be surprised if you find yourself in the middle of a wedding party, as couples often come here to be photographed. Next to the church is the tiny **Museo Nazionale della Montagna,** dedicated to mountains and mountaineers. ✉ *Piazzale Monte dei Cappuccini above Corso Moncalieri, Borgo Po* ☎ *011/6604414 church, 011/6604104 museum* 🌐 *www.museomontagna.org* 🎫 *Church free, museum €6* ⏲ *Church: daily 9–noon and 2:30–6. Museum: Tues.–Sun. 9–7; last entrance 6:30.*

OFF THE BEATEN PATH

Basilica di Superga. Since 1731, the Basilica di Superga has been the burial place of kings. Visible from miles around, the thoroughly baroque church was designed by Juvarra in the early 18th century, and no fewer than 58 members of the Savoy family are memorialized in the crypt. ✉ *Strada della Basilica di Superga 73, Sassi* ☎ *011/8997456* 🌐 *www.basilicadisuperga.com* 🎫 *Basilica free, crypt €4* ⏲ *Basilica: weekdays 9–noon and 3–5, weekends 9–noon and 3–6. Crypt: Mar.–Oct., daily 9–7:30; Nov.–Feb., weekends 9:30–6:30.*

Sassi–Superga Cog Train. The 18-minute ride from Sassi up the Superga hill is an absolute treat on a clear day. The view of the Alps is magnificent at the hilltop **Parco Naturale Collina Torinese,** a tranquil retreat from the bustle of the city. If you feel like a little exercise, you can walk back down to Sassi (about two hours) on one of the well-marked wooded trails that start from the upper station. Other circular trails lead through the park and back to Superga. ✉ *Piazza G. Modena, Sassi* ☎ *011/5764733* 🌐 *www.comune.torino.it/gtt* 🎫 *Weekdays €2 one-way, weekends €3.50 one-way* ⏲ *Hourly service Mon. and Wed.–Fri. 9–noon and 2–5, hourly service weekends 9–8; bus service replaces train on Tues.*

WHERE TO EAT

$$$ PIEDMONTESE Fodor's Choice ★ ✕ **Al Garamond.** The ocher-color walls and the ancient brick vaulting in this small, bright space set the stage for traditional meat and seafood dishes served with creative flair. Try the tantalizing *rombo in crosta di patate al barbera* (turbot wrapped in sliced potatoes and baked with Barbera wine). For dessert, the mousse *di liquirizia e salsa di cioccolato bianco* (licorice mousse with white-chocolate sauce) is a must, even if you don't usually like licorice. The level of service here is high, even by demanding Turin standards. ✉ *Via G. Pomba 14, Centro* ☎ *011/8122781* ⊗ *Closed Sun., Jan. 1–6, and 3 wks in Aug. No lunch Sat.*

$$$$ PIEDMONTESE ✕ **Del Cambio.** Set in a palace dating from 1757, this is one of Europe's most beautiful and historic restaurants, with decorative moldings, mirrors, and hanging lamps that look just as they did when Italian national hero Cavour dined here more than a century ago. The cuisine draws heavily on Piedmontese tradition and is paired with fine wines of the region. Agnolotti pasta with *sugo d'arrosto* (roast veal sauce) is a recommended first course. ✉ *Piazza Carignano 2, Centro* ☎ *011/546690* ✍ *Reservations essential* ⊗ *Closed Sun., Jan. 1–6, and 3 wks in Aug.*

$$ PIEDMONTESE ✕ **L'Agrifoglio.** This intimate local favorite has just 10 tables. Specialties change with the seasons, but you might find such delicacies as risotto *al Barbaresco* (with Barbaresco wine) and agnolotti *farciti di brasato* (crescent-shaped stuffed pasta) on the menu. L'Agrifoglio stays open late for the after-theater and after-cinema crowds. ✉ *Via Andrea Provana 7/E, Centro* ☎ *011/8136837* ⊗ *Closed Sun. and Mon.*

$$ PIEDMONTESE ✕ **Micamale.** The enthusiasm of chef and owner Mario Ferrero permeates three small rooms decorated with a few choice pictures and antique furniture. His kitchen turns out creative takes on Piedmontese specialties that change with the seasons. The bread and pasta are homemade, and the wine cellar is tended with equal care. ✉ *Via Corte d'Appello 13, Centro* ☎ *011/4362288* ⊗ *Closed Sun. No lunch Sat.*

$$ PIEDMONTESE ✕ **Porta di Po.** They're vigilant about sticking to Piedmontese specialties at this elegant restaurant with minimalist decor. All the seasonal favorites are here: the *guanciale di vitello brasato* (braised veal cheek) melts in your mouth, and the fritto misto (mixed fried meats), which you must order in advance, is a treat. Desserts are all traditional, and the wine list, though limited, presents a reasonable collection of regional wines. ✉ *Piazza Vittorio Veneto 1, Centro* ☎ *011/8127642* ⊗ *Closed Sun. and 2 wks in Sept. No lunch Mon.*

$$ SEAFOOD ✕ **Trattoria Anna.** If you are hankering for something different from the usual meat-based Piedmontese cuisine, give this simple, extremely popular, family-run spot a try. They serve only seafood, and they do it well. The *tagliatelle Walter* (pasta with shellfish) and the *grigliata di pesce* (mixed grilled fish) are both excellent. ✉ *Via Bellezia 20, Centro* ☎ *011/4362134* ✍ *Reservations essential* ⊗ *Closed Sun. and 2 wks in Aug. No lunch.*

$$$ NORTHERN ITALIAN ★ ✕ **Vintage 1997.** The first floor of an elegant town house in the center of Turin makes a fitting location for this sophisticated restaurant. You might try such specialties as *vitello tonnato alla nostra maniera* (roast veal with a light tuna sauce) or *filetto di pesce con asparagi purè dell'orto e foie gras* (fish filet with asparagus puree and foie gras). For the especially hungry gourmet there's the *menu del Vintage*, a 13-course

feast that covers the full range of the restaurant's cuisine. There's an excellent wine list, with regional, national, and international vintages well represented. ✉ *Piazza Solferino 16/H, Centro* ☎ *011/535948* ⊗ *Closed Sun. and 3 wks in Aug. No lunch Sat.*

WHERE TO STAY

The **Turin Tourist Board** (✉ *Via Bogino 8, Centro* ☎ *011/535181* 🌐 *www.turismotorino.org*) provides a booking service for hotels and bed-and-breakfast-style accommodations in the city and throughout the region. In order to use the service, you must book hotels 48 hours in advance and B&Bs seven days in advance.

$$ **Genio**. Though steps away from the main train station, spacious and tastefully decorated rooms provide a quiet haven from the bustle of the city. **Pros:** recently refurbished property; close to the central train station; very friendly service. **Cons:** 15-minute walk to the center of town; area around the hotel is a little seedy. **TripAdvisor:** "price is absolutely great," "staff is very friendly and helpful," "set up well for business travel." ✉ *Corso Vittorio Emanuele II 47, Centro* ☎ *011/6505771* 🌐 *www.hotelgenio.it* *125 rooms, 3 suites* *In-room: safe, Wi-Fi. In-hotel: laundry service, Wi-Fi hotspot, parking (paid), some pets allowed* *Breakfast.*

$$$ ★ **Grand Hotel Sitea**. One of the city's finest hotels, the Sitea is in the historic center. **Pros:** central location; well-appointed rooms; large bathrooms. **Cons:** some find the air-conditioning noisy; carpets are a little worn. **TripAdvisor:** "classical decor," "first-class reception staff," "large and very comfortable bed." ✉ *Via Carlo Alberto 35, Centro* ☎ *011/5170171* 🌐 *www.sitea.thi-hotels.com* *118 rooms, 4 suites* *In-room: safe, Internet. In-hotel: restaurant, bar, spa, Wi-Fi hotspot, parking (paid), some pets allowed* *Breakfast.*

$$$$ **Le Meridien Turin Art+Tech**. Designed by architect Renzo Piano, this luxury hotel is part of the former Lingotto FIAT factory. **Pros:** interesting design and location; good ($$) weekend rates. **Cons:** outside the city center; some signs of wear and tear; services are a little limited for the price. **TripAdvisor:** "public spaces were vast and tasteful," "wonderful, stylish and creative," "a bit far from the city center." ✉ *Via Nizza 230, Lingotto* ☎ *011/6642000* 🌐 *www.lemeridien.com* *141 rooms, 1 suite* *In-room: safe. In-hotel: restaurant, bar, gym, Internet terminal, Wi-Fi hotspot* *Breakfast.*

$$$ Fodor's Choice ★ **Victoria**. Rare style, attention to detail, and comfort are the hallmarks of this boutique hotel furnished and managed to create the feeling of a refined English town house. **Pros:** tranquil location in the center of town; excellent spa facilities; wonderful breakfast. **Cons:** entrance is a little run-down; hotel parking lot is a couple of blocks away and finding a spot on the street is difficult. **TripAdvisor:** "clean, comfortable, classy," "wonderful spa," "breakfast garden is charming." ✉ *Via Nino Costa 4, Centro* ☎ *011/5611909* 🌐 *www.hotelvictoria-torino.com* *97 rooms, 9 suites* *In-room: safe, Wi-Fi. In-hotel: bar, pool, spa, bicycles, Wi-Fi hotspot, parking (paid)* *Breakfast.*

NIGHTLIFE AND THE ARTS

THE ARTS

MUSIC

Classical music concerts are held in the **Giovanni Agnelli Auditorium** (✉ *Via Nizza 280, Lingotto* ☎ *011/6677415*), a space designed by Renzo Piano in the Lingotto district; internationally famous conductors and orchestras are frequent guests.

The **MITO Settembre Musica Festival** (☎ *011/4424703*), held for three weeks in September, highlights classical works. Traditional sacred music and some modern religious pieces are performed in the **Duomo** (✉ *Via Montebello 20, Centro* ☎ *011/8154230*) on Sunday evening; performances are usually advertised in the vestibule or in the local edition of Turin's nationally distributed newspaper, *La Stampa*. The Friday edition comes with a supplement on music and other entertainment possibilities.

OPERA

The **Teatro Regio** (✉ *Piazza Castello 215, Centro* ☎ *011/8815557* 🌐 *www.teatroregio.torino.it*), one of Italy's leading opera houses, has its season from October to June. You can buy tickets for most performances (premieres sell out well in advance) at the box office or on the Web site, where discounts are offered on the day of the show.

NIGHTLIFE

Two areas of Turin are enormously popular nightlife destinations: the Quadrilatero, to the north of the city center, and the Murazzi embankment, near the Ponte Vittorio Emanuele I.

On the Murazzi, near the Ponte Vittorio Emanuele I, is **Jammin's** (✉ *Murazzi del Po 17, Centro* ☎ *011/882869* ⏲ *May–Sept., Mon.–Sat. 9 pm–4 am*), a popular disco with a varied crowd; there's live music on Friday. The center of town is also popular, especially earlier in the evening. A trendy meeting place for an aperitif or a predisco drink in the piazza at the end of Via Po is the wine bar **Caffè Elena** (✉ *Piazza Vittorio Veneto 5, Centro* ☎ *011/8123341*). South of the main train station is **Rockcity** (✉ *Via Bertini 2, San Salvario* ☎ *011/3184737*), where you'll find a smart crowd in their mid-twenties to mid-thirties listening to rock, techno, and commercial music. The Quadrilatero Romano, which roughly corresponds to the grid pattern of Roman Turin and lies to the south of Piazza della Reppublica, is a hopping area filled with nightclubs and ethnic restaurants. Places open and close with startling frequency in the Quadrilateral, but **Pastis** (✉ *Piazza Emanuele Filiberto 9b, Centro* ☎ *011/5211085*) has shown considerable staying power—several cultural groups hold their meetings in the bar.

SPORTS

BIKE RENTALS

Turin has about 160 km (100 mi) of bike paths running through the city and its parks. From April to October the **Ufficio Iniziative Ambientali** (✉ *Via Padova 29, Madonna di Campagna* ☎ *011/4020177* 🌐 *www.comune.torino.it/ambiente/bici/index.shtml*) provides bicycles for daily rental. Their Web site provides a detailed map of the bike paths and rental locations.

SHOPPING

CHOCOLATE

The tradition of making chocolate began in Turin in the early 17th century. Chocolate at that time was an aristocratic drink, but in the 19th century a Piedmontese invention made it possible to further refine cocoa, which could then be used to create solid bars and candies.

★ The most famous of all Turin chocolates is the *gianduiotto* (with cocoa, sugar, and hazelnuts), first concocted in 1867. The tradition of making these delicious treats has been continued at the small, family-run **Peyrano** (✉ *Corso Moncalieri 47, Centro* ☎ *011/6602202* 🌐 *www.peyrano.it*), where more than 80 types of chocolates are concocted. **Stratta** (✉ *Piazza San Carlo 191, Centro* ☎ *011/547920*), one of Turin's most famous chocolate shops, has been in business since 1836 and sells confections of all kinds—not just the chocolates in the lavish window displays but also fancy cookies, rum-laced fudges, and magnificent cakes.

MARKETS

Go to the famous **Balon Flea Market** (✉ *Piazza Repubblica, Centro*) on Saturday morning for excellent bargains on secondhand books and clothing and good browsing among stalls selling local specialties such as gianduiotti. (Be aware, however, that the market is also famous for its pickpockets.) The second Sunday of every month a special antiques market, appropriately called the **Gran Balon**, sets up shop in Piazza Repubblica.

SPECIALTY STORES

Most people know that Turin produces more than 75% of Italy's cars, but they are often unaware that it's also a hub for clothing manufacturing. Top-quality boutiques stocking local, national, and international lines are clustered along Via Roma and Via Garibaldi. Piazza San Carlo, Via Po, and Via Maria Vittoria are lined with antiques shops, some—but not all—specializing in 18th-century furniture and domestic items.

★ With branches in Milan, Bologna, and New York, **Eataly** (✉ *Via Nizza 230, Lingotto* ☎ *011/19506801* 🌐 *www.eatalytorino.it*) is perhaps Turin's most famous food emporium. As well as a food market, food-related bookstore, and wine bar, there are several different food counters and restaurants offering everything from hamburgers to haute cuisine.

Specialty food stores and delicatessens abound in central Turin. For a truly spectacular array of cheeses and other delicacies, try Turin's famous **Borgiattino** (✉ *Via Accademia Albertina 38/A, Centro* ☎ *011/8394686*).

THE COLLINE AND SAVOY PALACES

As you head west from Turin into the Colline ("little hills"), castles and medieval fortifications begin to pepper the former dominion of the house of Savoy, and the Alps come into better and better view. In the region lie the storybook medieval town of Rivoli; 12th-century abbeys; and, farther west in the mountains, the ski resort of Sestriere, one of the venues used during the 2006 Winter Olympics.

VENARIA REALE

10 km (6 mi) northwest of Turin.

GETTING HERE

Starting in Turin, from the north side of Piazza della Reppublica, take Bus 11 to reach Venaria; the trip takes approximately 40 minutes. By car, follow Corso Regina Margherita to the A55 highway. Head north and leave the highway at the Venaria exit, following signs for the Venaria Reale.

EXPLORING

★ The **Reggia di Venaria Reale** was built in the mid-16th century as a sumptuous hunting lodge for Carlo Emanuele II of Savoy. Extensive Italianate gardens surround the palace, and the Great Gallery inside is worthy of Versailles. The basements now house a historical exhibition that relates the story of the Savoy. The upper floors are given over to changing exhibitions. A sound-and-light show by Peter Greenaway enlivens rooms throughout the palace, and a permanent installation of works by arte povera artist Giuseppe Penone can be found in the Lower Park outside. ✉ *Piazza della Reppublica 4* ☎ *011/992333* 🎫 *€12; €4 gardens only* ⏲ *Reggia: Tues.–Fri. 9–5; Sat. 9 am–9:30 pm; Sun. 9–8; last entrance 1 hr before closing. Gardens: Tues.–Sun. 9–1 hr before sunset.*

7

RIVOLI

16 km (10 mi) west of Venaria, 13 km (8 mi) west of Turin.

GETTING HERE

GTT buses and trams regularly link central Turin with Rivoli. The journey takes just over one hour.

By car, follow Corso Francia from central Turin all the way to Rivoli. Unless there's a lot of traffic, the trip should take a half hour.

EXPLORING

The Savoy court was based in Rivoli in the Middle Ages. The 14th- to 15th-century **Casa del Conte Verde** *(House of the Green Count)* sits right in the center of town, and the richness of its decorations hints at the wealth and importance of its owner, Amedeo VI of Savoy, during the period. Inside, a small gallery hosts temporary exhibitions. ✉ *Via Fratelli Piol 8* ☎ *011/9563020* 🎫 *Admission varies with exhibits* ⏲ *Varies with exhibits.*

Fodor's Choice ★ The castle of Rivoli now houses the **Museo d'Arte Contemporanea** *(Museum of Contemporary Art)*. The building was begun in the 17th century and then redesigned but never finished by Juvarra in the 18th century; it was finally completed in the late 20th century by minimalist Turin architect Andrea Bruno. On display are changing international exhibitions and a permanent collection of 20th-century Italian art. To get to Rivoli from downtown Turin, take Metro line 1 to Fermi and then the shuttle bus service to the museum. The schedule and cost of the shuttle bus can be found on the museum's Web site. ✉ *Piazzale Mafalda di Savoia* ☎ *011/9565222* 🌐 *www.castellodirivoli.org* 🎟 *€6.50* ⏲ *Tues.–Thurs. 10–5, Fri.–Sun. 10–9.*

ABBAZIA DI SANT'ANTONIO DI RANVERSO

6 km (4 mi) west of Rivoli, 23 km (14 mi) west of Turin.

GETTING HERE

GTT offers twice-daily bus service to the abbey from Turin. By car, the abbey is 10 minutes from Rivoli on SS25.

EXPLORING

Abbazia di Sant'Antonio di Ranverso. This abbey was originally a hospital, founded in the 12th century by the Hospitallers of St. Anthony to care for victims of St. Anthony's Fire, a painful medical condition brought on by consuming contaminated rye. Pilgrims came here over the centuries for cures and to offer thanks for a miraculous recovery. The 15th-century frescoes with their lifelike depictions of pilgrims and saints retain their original colors. ✉ *Buttigliera Alta west of Rivoli, off SS25* ☎ *011/9367450* 🎟 *€2.60* ⏲ *Wed.–Sun. 9–12:30 and 3–5:30; last entrance ½ hr before closing.*

SACRA DI SAN MICHELE

20 km (13 mi) west of Abbazia di Sant'Antonio di Ranverso, 43 km (27 mi) west of Turin.

GETTING HERE

Unless you want to do a 14-km (9-mi) uphill hike from the town of Avigliana, a car is essential for an excursion to the Abbey of Saint Michael—take the Avigliana Est exit from the Torino–Bardonecchia highway (A32).

EXPLORING

★ Perhaps best known as inspiration for the setting of Umberto Eco's novel *The Name of the Rose*, **Sacra di San Michele** was built on Monte Pirchiriano in the 11th century so it would stand out: it occupies the most prominent location for miles around, hanging over a 3,280-foot bluff. When monks came to enlarge the abbey they had to build part of the structure on supports more than 90 feet high—an engineering feat that was famous in medieval Europe and is still impressive today. By the 12th century this important abbey controlled 176 churches in Italy, France, and Spain; one of the abbeys under its influence was Mont-Saint-Michel in France. Because of its strategic position the Abbey of Saint Michael came under frequent attacks over the next five centuries and was eventually abandoned in 1622. It was restored, somewhat heavy-handedly, in the late 19th and early 20th centuries.

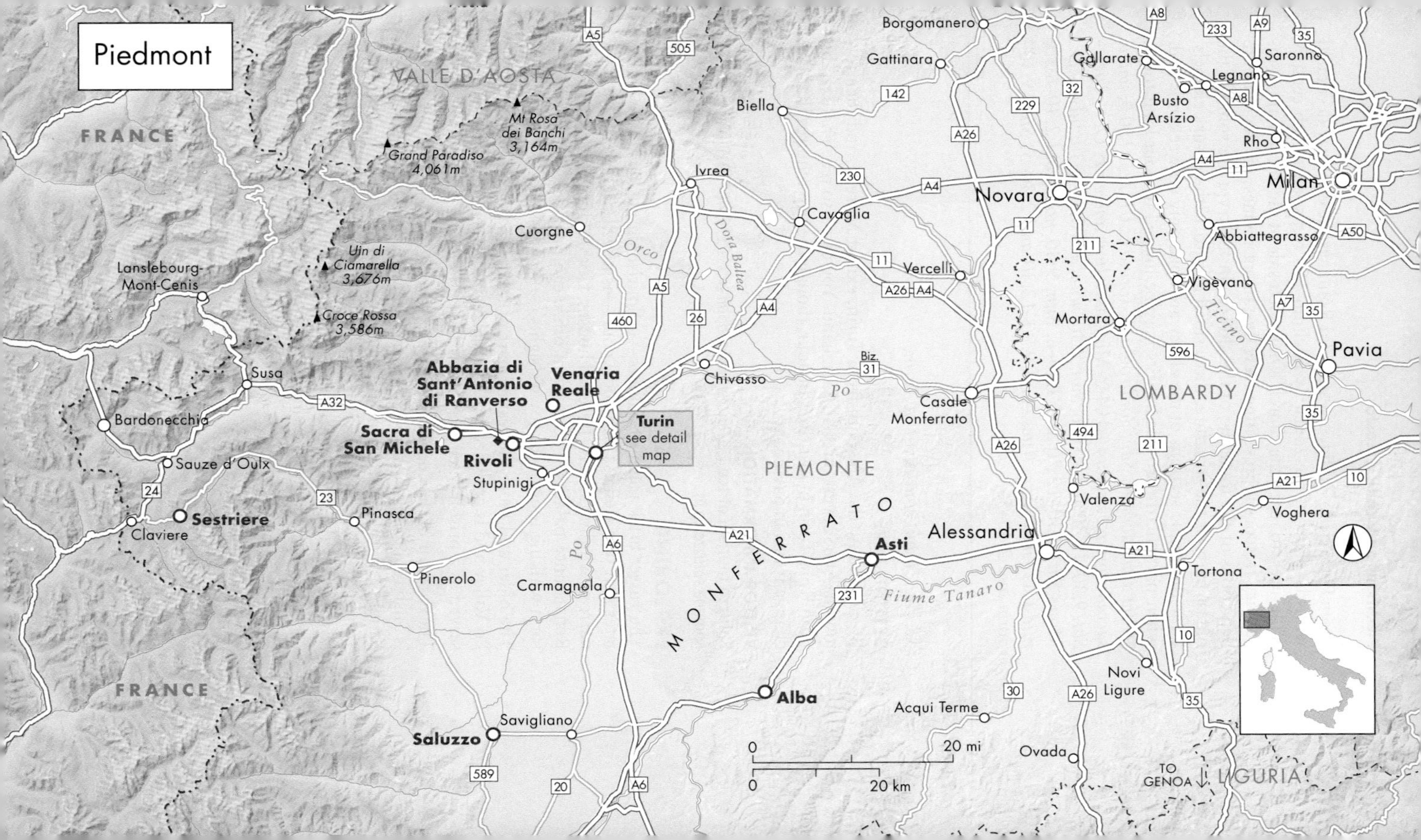
Piedmont
FRANCE
VALLE D'AOSTA
Mt Rosa dei Banchi 3,164m
Grand Paradiso 4,061m
Uin di Ciamarella 3,676m
Croce Rossa 3,586m
Lanslebourg-Mont-Cenis
Susa
Bardonecchia
Sauze d'Oulx
Claviere
Sestriere
Pinasca
Pinerolo
Cuorgne
Ivrea
Biella
Cavaglia
Abbazia di Sant'Antonio di Ranverso
Sacra di San Michele
Rivoli
Venaria Reale
Turin see detail map
Stupinigi
Carmagnola
Chivasso
Orco
Dora Baltea
Po
PIEMONTE
MONFERRATO
Asti
Alba
Saluzzo
Savigliano
Borgomanero
Gattinara
Vercelli
Casale Monferrato
Biz.
Novara
Mortara
Valenza
Alessandria
Fiume Tanaro
Acqui Terme
Ovada
Novi Ligure
Tortona
Voghera
Gallarate
Busto Arsízio
Legnano
Saronno
Rho
Milan
Abbiattegrasso
Vigèvano
Ticino
Pavia
LOMBARDY
TO GENOA
LIGURIA
0 20 mi
0 20 km
A5
505
142
229
32
A8
233
A9
35
A26
230
A4
11
211
A50
A26
460
26
A7
31
596
A32
35
494
24
23
A21
10
A6
231
30
589
20

From **Porta dello Zodiaco,** a splendid Romanesque doorway decorated with the signs of the zodiac, you climb 150 steps, past 12th-century sculptures, to reach the church. On the left side of the interior are 16th-century frescoes representing New Testament themes; on the right are depictions of the founding of the church. In the crypt are some of the oldest parts of the structure, three small 9th- to 12th-century chapels. Note that some sections of the abbey are open only on weekends and, when particularly crowded, visits may be limited to hour-long tours. ✉ *Via alla Sacra 4 , Sant'Ambrogio di Torino* ☎ *011/939130* 🌐 *www.sacradisanmichele.com* 🎫 *€4* ⏲ *Mid-Mar.–June and early Oct., Tues.–Sat. 9:30–12:30 and 4:30–6, Sun. 9:30–noon and 2:40–6:30; July–Sept., Mon.–Sat. 9:30–12:30 and 4:30–6, Sun. 9:30–noon and 2:40–6:30; mid-Oct.–mid-Mar., Tues.–Sat. 9:30–12:30 and 2:30–5, Sun. 9:30–noon and 2:40–5.*

SALUZZO

58 km (36 mi) southwest of Turin.

GETTING HERE

By car, follow the A6 south from Turin, exit at Marene, and then follow the SP662 west through Savigliano. You can also reach Saluzzo by train from Turin in just over an hour, though the trip requires that you change trains in Savigliano.

VISITOR INFORMATION

Saluzzo tourism office (✉ *Piazzetta Mondagli 5* ☎ *0175/46710* 🌐 *www.comune.saluzzo.cn.it*).

EXPLORING

The russet-brick town of Saluzzo—a flourishing medieval center and later seat of a Renaissance ducal court—is a well-preserved gem with narrow, winding streets, frescoed houses, Gothic churches, and elegant Renaissance palaces. The tourism office can provide you with a map for a walking tour of the town's sights.

The older and more interesting part of the town hugs a hilltop in the Po Valley and is crowned by **La Castiglia**, a 13th-century castle that has served as a prison since the 1820s.

The exterior of the **Castello della Manta**, 4 km (2½ mi) south of Saluzzo, is austere, but inside are frescoes and other decorations of the period. Knights and damsels from an allegorical poem written by Marquis Tommaso III of Saluzzo, humanist lord of the castle, parade in full costume in the 15th-century frescoes of the **Sala del Barone.** The castle sometimes hosts exhibits, at which time higher admission is charged. ✉ *Via al Castello 14, Manta* ☎ *0175/87822* 🎫 *€5* ⏲ *Mar.–Sept., Tues.–Sun. 10–6.*

SESTRIERE

32 km (20 mi) east of Briançon, 93 km (58 mi) west of Turin.

GETTING HERE

By car, follow the A32 west from Turin, exit at Oulx, and follow the SS24 to Sestriere. Train service is available from Turin as far as Oulx—regularly running SAPAV buses complete the journey to Sestriere.

VISITOR INFORMATION

Sestriere tourism office (✉ *Via Louset 14* ☎ *0122/755444* 🌐 *www.comune.sestriere.to.it*).

EXPLORING

In the early 1930s, before skiing became a more egalitarian sport, the patriarch of the FIAT automobile dynasty had this resort built to cater to the elite. The resort has two distinctive tower hotels and ski facilities that have been developed into some of the best in the Alps. It lacks the charm of older Alpine centers, overdevelopment has added some eyesores, and the mountains don't have the striking beauty of those in Valle d'Aosta, but skiers have an excellent choice of trails, some of which cross the border into France.

WHERE TO STAY

$$$ **Hotel Cristallo.** Half the rooms at this hotel face the slopes of Sestriere, and the ski-lift station is just across the road. **Pros:** excellent location in the center of town; professional and helpful staff; good restaurant; pleasant decor. **Cons:** half-board and week stays may be required, not all rooms have views and terraces; standard rooms are small. **TripAdvisor:** "food is sensational," "rooms were quite small," "a stone's throw from the slopes." ✉ *Via Pinerolo 5* ☎ *0122/750707* 🌐 *www.newlinehotels.com* *46 rooms* *In-room: safe, Internet. In-hotel: restaurant, bar, gym, Internet terminal, parking (paid)* *Breakfast.*

$$$ **Roseo.** Large and elegant, this luxurious hotel sits on the slopes above the town, near the lifts and the town's golf course. **Pros:** secluded location; great service; outstanding views. **Cons:** outside the town center; pool area and rooms are a little run-down; half board is mandatory. ✉ *Via Sauze 3/B* ☎ *0122/7941* 🌐 *www.roseohotelsestriere.com* *96 rooms, 4 suites* *In-room: safe. In-hotel: restaurant, bar, pool, spa, Wi-Fi hotspot, some pets allowed* *Closed early Apr.–June and Sept.–Nov.* *Some meals.*

SPORTS AND THE OUTDOORS

SKIING

At 6,670 feet, the ski resort of **Sestriere** (☎ *0122/799411 for conditions* 🌐 *www.vialattea.it*) was built in the late 1920s under the auspices of Turin's Agnelli family. The slopes get good snow some years from November through May, other years from February through May. The **tourist office** (✉ *Via Louset 14* ☎ *0122/755444* 🌐 *www.comune.sestriere.to.it*) in Sestriere provides complete information about lift tickets, ski runs, mountain guides, and equipment rentals, here and in neighboring towns such as Bardonecchia and Claviere. Its excellent Web site is also navigable in English. A quaint village with slate-roof houses, **Claviere** (✉ *17 km [11 mi] west of Sestrie*) is one of Italy's oldest ski resorts. Its slopes overlap with those of the French resort of Montgenèvre.

CLOSE UP

Skiing in Piedmont and Valle d'Aosta

Skiing is the major sport in both Piedmont and Valle d'Aosta. Excellent facilities abound at resort towns such as Courmayeur and Breuil-Cervinia. The so-called Via Lattea (Milky Way)—five skiing areas near Sestriere with 400 km (almost 250 mi) of linked runs and 90 ski lifts—provides practically unlimited skiing. Lift tickets, running around €35 for a day's pass, are significantly less expensive than at major U.S. resorts.

To Italian skiers, a weeklong holiday on the slopes is known as a *settimana bianca* (white week). Ski resort hotels in Piedmont and Valle d'Aosta encourage these getaways by offering six- and seven-day packages, and though they're designed with the domestic market in mind, you can get a bargain by taking advantage of the offers. The packages usually, though not always, include half or full board.

You should have your passport with you if you plan a day trip into France or Switzerland—though odds are you won't be asked to show it.

THE MONFERRATO AND THE LANGHE

Southeast of Turin, in the hilly wooded area around Asti known as the Monferrato and farther south in a similar area around Alba known as the Langhe, the rolling landscape is a patchwork of vineyards and dark woods dotted with hill towns and castles. This is wine country, producing some of Italy's most famous reds and sparkling whites. And hidden away in the woods are the secret places where hunters and their dogs unearth the precious, aromatic truffles worth their weight in gold at Alba's truffle fair.

ASTI

60 km (37 mi) southeast of Turin.

GETTING HERE

Asti is less than an hour away from Turin by car on the A21. GTT bus service connects the two towns, but is not direct. Train service to Asti, on the other hand, is frequent and fast.

VISITOR INFORMATION

Asti tourism office (✉ *Piazza Alfieri 29* ☎ *0141/530357* 🌐 *www.astiturismo.it*).

EXPLORING

Asti is best known outside Italy for its wines—excellent reds as well as the famous sparkling white spumante—but its strategic position on trade routes at Turin, Milan, and Genoa has given it a broad economic base. In the 12th century Asti began to develop as a republic, at a time when other Italian cities were also flexing their economic and military muscles. It flourished in the following century, when the inhabitants began erecting lofty **towers** (✉ *West end of Corso Vittorio Alfieri*) for its defense, giving rise to the medieval nickname "city of 100 towers." In the center of Asti some of these remain, among them the 13th-century **Torre**

Continued on page 422

ON THE TRAIL OF BAROLO

Picture yourself in the background of a grand medieval mural, and you won't be far off from what you experience driving through the idyllic wooded landscape south of Turin, in Piedmont's Langhe district.

The crests of the graceful hills are dotted with villages, each lorded over by an ancient castle. The gentle slopes of the valleys below are lined with row upon row of Nebbiolo grapes, the choicest of which are used to make Barolo wine. Dubbed "the king of wines and wine of kings" in the 19th century after finding favor with King Carlo Alberto, Barolo still wears the crown, despite stiff competition from all corners of Italy.

Above, Serralunga's castle
Right, bottles of old vintage Barolo

The Langhe district is smaller and surprisingly less visited by food-and-wine enthusiasts than Chianti and the surrounding areas of Tuscany, but it yields similar rewards. The best way to tour the Barolo-producing region is on day trips from the delightful truffle town of Alba—getting around is easy, the country roads are gorgeous, and the wine is fit for a king.

ALL ABOUT BAROLO

The Nebbiolo grapes that go into this famous wine come not just from Barolo proper (the area surrounding the tiny town of Barolo), but also from a small zone that encompasses the hill towns of Novello, Monforte d'Alba, Serralunga d'Alba, Castiglione Falletto, La Morra, and Verduno. All are connected by small but easy-to-navigate roads.

When wine lovers talk about Barolo, they talk about tannins—the quality that makes red wine dry out your mouth. Tannins come from the grape skins; red wine—which gets its color from the skins—has them, white wine doesn't. Tannins can be balanced out by acidity (the quality that makes your mouth water), but they also soften over time. As a good red wine matures, flavors emerge more clearly, achieving a harmonious balance of taste and texture.

A bottle of Barolo is often born so overwhelmingly tannic that many aficionados won't touch the stuff until it has aged 10 or 15 years. But a good Barolo ages beautifully, eventually spawning complex, intermingled tastes of tobacco, roses, and earth. It's not uncommon to see bottles for sale from the 1960s, 1950s, or even the 1930s.

WHERE TO DRINK IT

The word *enoteca* in Italian can mean a wine store, or a wine bar, or both. The words "wine bar," on the other hand—which are becoming increasingly trendy—mean just that. Either way, these are great places to sample and buy the wines of the Langhe.

An excellent enoteca in Alba is **Vincafé** (Via V. Emanuele, 12, Alba, 0173/364603). It specializes in tastes of Langhe wines, accompanied by *salumi* (cured meats), cheeses, and other regional products. More than 350 wines, as well as grappas and liqueurs, grace Vincafé's distinguished list. It's open from noon to midnight, and there's food until 9 pm.

In the fortfied hill town of Barolo, visit the **Castello di Barolo** (Piazza Falletti, 0173/56277, www.baroloworld.it) which has a little wine bar and a museum dedicated to Barolo.

HOW MUCH DOES IT COST?

The most reasonably priced, but still enjoyable Barolos will cost you €20 to €30. A very good but not top-of-the-line bottle will cost €40 to €60. For a top-of-the-line bottle you may spend anywhere from €80 to €200.

LABELS TO LOOK FOR

Barolo is a strictly controlled denomination, but that doesn't mean all Barolos are equal. Legendary producers include Prunotto, Aldo Conterno, Giacomo Conterno, Bruno Giacosa, Famiglia Anselma, Mascarello, Pio Cesare, and Michele Chiarlo.

WINE ESTATES TO VISIT

Right in the town of Barolo, an easy, if touristy, option for a visit is **Marchesi di Barolo** (Via Alba 12, Barolo, 0173/564400, www.marchesibarolo.com). In the estate's user-friendly enoteca you can taste wine, buy thousands of different bottles from vintages going way back, and look at display bottles, including an 1859 Barolo. Marchesi di Barolo's *cantine* (wine cellars, Via Roma 1, Barolo) are open daily 10:30–5:30. The staff here is used to catering to visitors, so you won't have to worry too much about endearing yourself to them.

From there you might want to graduate to **Famiglia Anselma** (Loc. Castello della Volta, Barolo, 0173/787217, www.anselma.it). Winemaker Maurizio Anselma, in his mid-20s, is something of a prodigy in the Barolo world, and he's quite open to visitors. He is known for his steadfast commitment to produce only Barolo—nothing else—and for his policy of holding his wines for several years before release.

A good, accessible example of the new school of Barolo winemaking is **Podere Rocche dei Manzoni** (3, Loc. Manzini Soprano, Monforte d'Alba, 0173/78421, www.barolobig.com). The facade of the cantina is like a Roman temple of brick, complete with imposing columns. Rocche dei Manzoni's reds include four Barolos, one Dolcetto, one Langhe Rosso, two Langhe DOCs, and two Barbera d'Albas.

WINE TOUR TIPS

Keep in mind that visiting wineries in Italy is different from what you might have experienced in the Napa Valley or in France. Wherever you go, reservations are most definitely required, and you'll usually be the only person or group on the tour—so be sure to show up when you say you will, and keep in mind that it's impolite not to buy something in the end.

Wine buyers and wine professionals are the expected audience for tours. While this attitude is slowly changing and many winemakers are beginning to welcome interested outsiders, it's important to be humble and enthusiastic. You'll be treated best if you come in with an open mind, respect that the winemaker probably knows more about wine than you do, and make it clear that you aren't just looking to drink for free. It helps to speak Italian, but if you don't, the international language of effusive compliments can still go a long way.

BEYOND BAROLO

Neive, in the Barbaresco region

By no means do the fruits of the Langhe end with Barolo. The region boasts Italy's highest concentration of DOC (denominazione di origine controllata) and DOCG (denominazione di origine controllata e garantita) wines, the two most prestigious categories of appellation in Italy. The other DOCG in the Langhe is Barbaresco, which, like Barolo, is made from the Nebbiolo grape. Barbaresco is not quite as tannic as Barolo, however, and can be drunk younger.

Comentina and the well-preserved **Torre Troyana,** a tall, slender tower attached to the **Palazzo Troya.** The 18th-century church of **Santa Caterina** has incorporated one of Asti's medieval towers, the **Torre Romana** (itself built on an ancient Roman base), as its bell tower. Corso Vittorio Alfieri is Asti's main thoroughfare, running west–east across the city. This road, known in medieval times as Contrada Maestra, was built by the Romans.

> **WORD OF MOUTH**
>
> "We went to Piedmont in early May and the weather was awesome. The red poppies were blooming everywhere and the vines were just starting to leaf. One of the best parts was the clear view of the Alps with the snow on them and the vineyards and towns in the foreground."
>
> —montysc

The **Duomo** is an object lesson in the evolution of Gothic architecture. Built in the early 14th century, it's decorated so as to emphasize geometry and verticality: pointed arches and narrow vaults contrast with the earlier, Romanesque attention to balance and symmetry. The porch on the south side of the cathedral facing the square was built in 1470 and represents Gothic at its most florid and excessive. ✉ *Piazza Cattedrale* ☎ *0141/592924* ⏲ *Daily 8:30–noon and 3:30–5:30.*

The Gothic church of **San Secondo** is dedicated to Asti's patron saint, reputedly decapitated on the spot where the church now stands. Secondo is also the patron of the city's favorite folklore and sporting event, the annual Palio di Asti, the colorful medieval-style horse race (similar to Siena's) held each year on the third Sunday of September in the vast Campo del Palio to the south of the church. ✉ *Piazza San Secondo, south of Corso Vittorio Alfieri* ☎ *0141/530066* ⏲ *Mon.–Sat. 10:45–noon and 3:30–5:30, Sun. 3:30–5:30.*

WHERE TO EAT

$$$$ PIEDMONTESE Fodor's Choice ★ ✕ **Gener Neuv.** One of Italy's finest restaurants, the family-run Gener Neuv is known for its rustic elegance. The setting on the bank of the Tanaro River is splendid. The menu of regional specialties may include agnolotti *ai tre stufati* (with a filling of ground rabbit, veal, and pork), and to finish, *zabaione caldo al vino Vecchio Samperi* (warm eggnog flavored with a dessert wine). Fixed-price menus are available with or without the wine included. As you might expect, the wine list is first-rate. ✉ *Lungo Tanaro 4* ☎ *0141/557270* 🌐 *www.generneuv.it* ✍ *Reservations essential* ⏲ *Closed Aug. and Mon. No dinner Sun.*

$$$ PIEDMONTESE ✕ **L'Angolo del Beato.** Regional specialties such as *bagna cauda* (literally "hot bath," a dip for vegetables made with anchovies, garlic, butter, and olive oil) and *tagliolini al ragu di anatra* (pasta with a duck sauce) are the main attractions at this central Asti restaurant, housed in a building that dates to the 12th century. There's also a good wine list. ✉ *Via Guttuari 12* ☎ *0141/531668* 🌐 *www.angolodelbeato.it* ⏲ *Closed Sun., last wk of Dec., 1st wk of Jan., and 3 wks in Aug.*

WHERE TO STAY

$ **Reale.** This hotel in a 19th-century building is on Asti's main square. **Pros:** spacious rooms; central location. **Cons:** lobby area looking a little worn; rooms facing the main square can be noisy. **TripAdvisor:** "grand old inn," "in the middle of town," "singing barista." *Piazza Alfieri 6 0141/530240 www.hotelristorantereale.it 24 rooms In-room: Internet. In-hotel: parking (paid), Wi-Fi hotspot, some pets allowed Breakfast.*

FESTIVALS

September is a month of fairs and celebrations in Asti, and the **Palio di Asti**, a horse race run through the streets of town, highlights the festivities. First mentioned in 1275, this annual event has been going strong ever since. After an elaborate procession in period costumes, nine horses and jockeys representing different sections of town vie for the honor of claiming the *palio*, a symbolic flag of victory. For 10 days in early September Asti is host to the **Douja d'Or National Wine Festival**—an opportunity to see Asti and celebrate the product that made it famous. During the course of the festival a competition is held to award "Oscars" to the best wine producers, and stands for wine tastings allow visitors to judge the winners for themselves. Musical events and other activities accompany the festival. Contact the **tourist office** (*0141/530357 www.astiturismo.it*) for the schedule of events.

SHOPPING

Tuit, a branch of Turin's Eataly food emporium, is a shop and café on a quiet street just off Piazza Alfieri. Open Tuesday-Saturday 10 am–10 pm, it's a great place to shop for local and regional food specialties and have a light meal ($). *Via Carlo Grandi 3 0141/095813 Closed Mon.*

7

ALBA

30 km (18 mi) southwest of Asti.

GETTING HERE

By car from Turin follow the A6 south to Marene and then take the A33 east. GTT offers frequent bus service between Alba and Turin—the journey takes approximately 1½ hours. There is no direct train service, but you can get to Alba from Turin by making one transfer in Asti, Bra, or Cavallermaggiore; the entire trip takes about 1½ hours.

VISITOR INFORMATION

Alba tourism office (*Piazza Risorgimento 2 0173/35833 www.langheroero.it*).

EXPLORING

This small town has a gracious atmosphere and a compact core studded with medieval towers and Gothic buildings. In addition to being a wine center of the region, Alba is known as the "City of the White Truffle" for the dirty little tubers that command a higher price per ounce than diamonds. For picking out your truffle and having a few wisps shaved on top of your food, expect to shell out an extra €16—which is well worth it.

WORD OF MOUTH

"I would recommend the area around Asti and Alba as the best and most central location to stay in Piedmont for visiting the wine country and sampling the fabulous cuisine (also, November is the best season for truffles). You really should rent a car as the best wineries and restaurants are located in little hilltop villages and there are the wonderful panaramic drives."

—Sampaguita

WHERE TO EAT

$$$ PIEDMONTESE ★ **Locanda del Pilone.** The elegant, formal dining room of the Locanda del Pilone hotel is one of the best restaurants in the region, serving refined variations of traditional dishes. The *carnaroli allo zafferano mantecato al Castelmagno con riduzione di Barbera d'Asti* (cheese and saffron risotto with wine sauce) is as delicious as it is unusual. ✉ *Località Madonna di Como 34* ☎ *0173/366616* 🌐 *www.locandadelpilone.com.*

$ PIEDMONTESE ★ **Vigin Mudest.** Delicious regional specialties are served at this lively, family-run restaurant in the center of Alba. There's a sumptuous buffet spread of hot and cold antipasti, and their version of *carne cruda albese* (beef carpaccio in the style of Alba) is a favorite with the locals who flock here. All of the pasta (including the thin egg-yolk rich *tajarin* traditional to the region) is homemade, and the risotto *al Barolo* is particularly tasty. Outdoor seating is available in summer. ✉ *Via Vernazza 11* ☎ *0173/441701* *Reservations essential* *Closed Mon.*

WHERE TO STAY

$ **La Meridiana.** If Alba strikes your fancy, consider a night at this reasonably priced belle epoque–style B&B, on a hill overlooking the historic center and surrounded by Dolcetto and Nebbiolo grapevines. **Pros:** friendly, family atmosphere; in a secluded setting convenient for exploring the Langhe. **Cons:** long walk to nearest restaurants; no air-conditioning in some rooms. **TripAdvisor:** "lovely place in a lovely setting," "staff was friendly and helpful," "working farm with vineyards and orchards." ✉ *Località Altavilla 9* ☎ *0173/440112* 🌐 *www.villalameridiana.it* *9 rooms, 1 suite* *In-room: no a/c (some), no phone. In-hotel: pool, gym* *No credit cards* *Breakfast.*

$$ ★ **Locanda del Pilone.** It would be hard to imagine a more commanding position for this hotel above Alba. **Pros:** spectacular location with 360-degree views; excellent restaurant. **Cons:** isolation makes own transportation a must; no air-conditioning. **TripAdvisor:** "on a hilltop amongst the vineyards," "charming details in the decor," "room was very nice and cozy." ✉ *Località Madonna di Como 34* ☎ *0173/366616* 🌐 *www.locandadelpilone.it* *7 rooms, 1 suite* *In-room: no a/c* *Breakfast.*

$$ **Palazzo Finati.** This small boutique hotel in a carefully restored 19th-century town house has charm and character that set it apart from the other more business-oriented hotels in Alba. **Pros:** quiet location in the center of town; rooms facing the courtyard have terraces. **Cons:** staff coverage is limited at night; breakfast room is a bit gloomy. **TripAdvisor:** "beautifully decorated and furnished," "impeccably clean rooms," "incredibly charming and affordable." ✉ *Via Vernazza 8* ☎ *0173/366324* 🌐 *www.palazzofinati.it* *4 rooms, 5 suites* *In-room:*

Wi-Fi. In-hotel: Wi-Fi hotspot, parking (paid) ⏲ Closed 2 wks in Aug., and Christmas–mid-Jan. 🍽 Breakfast.

FESTIVALS

Alba's hilarious **Palio degli Asini** (donkey race), a lampoon of Asti's eminently serious horse race, is held on the first Sunday of October. Tickets to watch this competition between Alba's districts, with riders dressed in medieval garb astride their stubborn beasts, can be difficult to obtain; they go on sale at the beginning of July each year. Contact Alba's **tourist information office** (☎ *0173/35833* 🌐 *www.langheroero.it*) for details.

On weekends every fall from the second Saturday in October to the second Sunday in November, Alba hosts the **Fiera Internazionale del Tartufo Bianco** (International White Truffle Fair) (✉ *Cortile della Madalena* ☎ *0173/361051* 🌐 *www.fieradeltartufo.org*). Merchants, chefs, and other aficionados of this pungent, yet delicious, fungus come from all over the world to buy and to taste white truffles at the height of their season. Though the affair has become increasingly commercialized, it still makes Alba a great place to visit in fall. Note that hotel and restaurant reservations for October and November should be made well in advance.

VALLE D'AOSTA

The unspoiled beauty of the highest peaks in the Alps, the Matterhorn and Monte Bianco, competes with the magnificent scenery of Italy's oldest national park in Valle d'Aosta, a semiautonomous, bilingual region tucked away at the border with France and Switzerland. Luckily, you don't have to choose—the region is small, so you can fit skiing, après-ski, and wild ibex into one memorable trip. The main Aosta Valley, largely on an east–west axis, is hemmed in by high mountains where glaciers have gouged out 14 tributary valleys, 6 to the north and 8 to the south. A car is helpful here, but take care: though distances are relatively short as the crow flies, steep slopes and winding roads add to your mileage and travel time.

Coming up from Turin, beyond Ivrea the road takes you through countryside that becomes hillier and hillier, passing through steep ravines guarded by brooding, romantic castles. Pont St. Martin, about 18 km (11 mi) north of Ivrea, is the beginning of bilingual (Italian and French) territory.

BARD

65 km (40 mi) north of Turin.

GETTING HERE

Bard is just off the A5 highway that runs north from Turin into the Valle d'Aosta—by car the trip takes about an hour. Train service from Turin is infrequent, but Aosta has regular service. Traveling to Bard by bus is not a viable option.

EXPLORING

★ A few minutes beyond the French-speaking village of Pont St. Martin, you pass through the narrow Gorge de Bard and reach the **Forte di Bard,** a 19th-century reconstruction of a fort that stood for eight centuries, serving the Savoys for six of them. In 1800 Napoléon entered Italy through this valley and used the cover of darkness to get his artillery units past the castle unnoticed. Ten years later he remembered this inconvenience and had the fortress destroyed.

The rebuilt fort houses the high-tech and lavishly multimedia **Museo degli Alpi,** dedicated to the history and culture of the Alps and the Valle d'Aosta region. *Forte di Bard 0125/833811 www.fortedibard.it €8 Tues.–Fri. 10–6, weekends 10–7; last entrance 1 hr before closing.*

EN ROUTE

Between Bard and the town of Donnas, 5 km (3 mi) south along the S26, you can walk on a short but fascinating section of a 1st-century Roman consular road that passed here on its way to France. Still showing the deeply worn tracks left by the passage of cart and chariot wheels, this section of road includes an archway carved through solid rock (used during the Middle Ages as the city gate of Donnas) and a milestone (XXXVI, to indicate 36 Roman miles from Aosta).

BREUIL-CERVINIA/THE MATTERHORN

50 km (30 mi) north of Bard, 116 km (72 mi) north of Turin.

GETTING HERE

From Aosta take the A5 and then the SR46 (one hour); from Turin take the A5 and then the SR46 (90 minutes). SADEM has regular bus service from Turin; SAVDA buses travel here from Milan. Breuil-Cervinia is not on a train line.

VISITOR INFORMATION

Breuil-Cervinia tourism office (*Piazzale Funivie 0166/944311 www.cervinia.it*).

EXPLORING

Breuil-Cervinia is a village at the base of the **Matterhorn** *(Monte Cervino in Italian; Mont Cervin in French).* Like the village, the famous peak straddles the border between Italy and Switzerland, and all sightseeing and skiing facilities are operated jointly. Splendid views of the peak can be seen from **Plateau Rosa** and the **Cresta del Furggen,** both of which can be reached by cable car from the center of Breuil-Cervinia. Although many locals complain that the tourist facilities and condominiums have changed the face of their beloved village, most would agree that the cable car has given them access to climbing and off-trail skiing in ridges that were once inaccessible.

WHERE TO STAY

$$ **Cime Bianche.** This calm, quiet mountain lodge offers commanding views of the Matterhorn and surrounding peaks from the balconies of its guest rooms. **Pros:** next to the ski slopes; great restaurant; lovely views. **Cons:** lobby is showing wear; busy during the ski season; location is far from everything but slopes. **TripAdvisor:** "fantastic location," "nice and cozy," "good food." *Località La Vieille 44, near ski lift 0166/949046 www.hotelcimebianche.com 13 rooms*

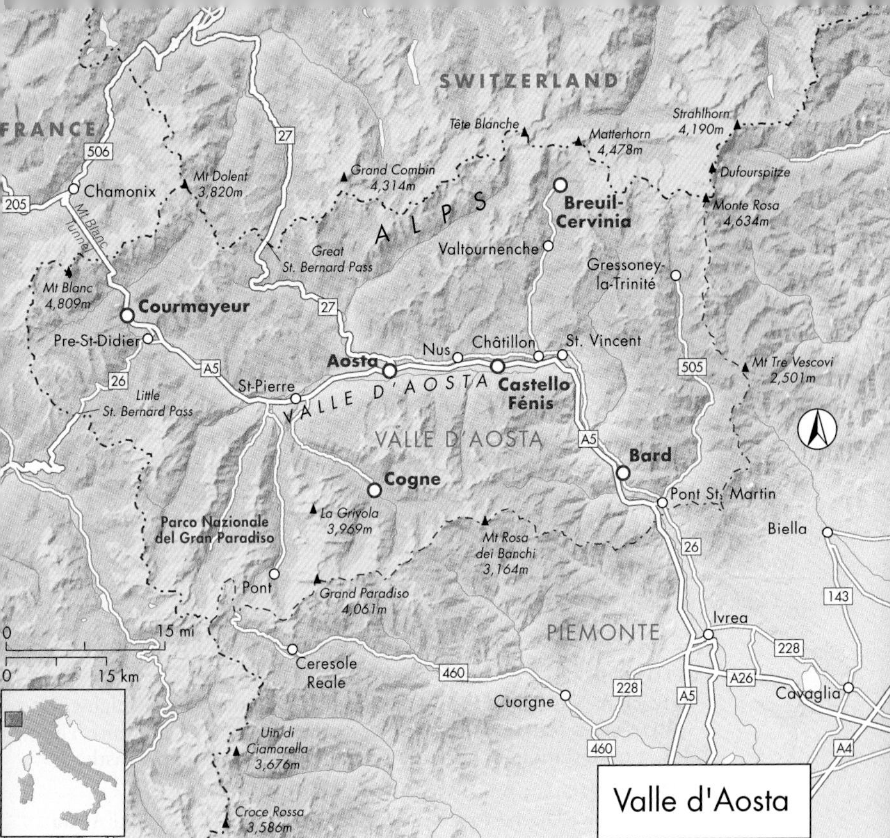

In-room: no a/c. In-hotel: restaurant, bar, Wi-Fi hotspot Closed Mon., and May, June, and Oct. Some meals.

$$$$ **Hermitage.** The entryway's marble relief of Saint Theodolus reminds you that this was the site of a hermitage, but asceticism has given way to comfort and elegance at what is now one of the most exclusive hotels in the region. **Pros:** superlative staff; refined atmosphere; frequent shuttle service into town and to ski lifts. **Cons:** located 2 km (1 mi) from the town center; half board is mandatory during the winter season. **TripAdvisor:** "great spa facility," "extraordinary service," "skiing is fantastic." *Via Piolet 1, Località Chapellette 0166/948998 www.hotelhermitage.com 30 rooms, 6 suites In-room: safe, Wi-Fi. In-hotel: restaurant, bar, pool, gym, Wi-Fi hotspot Closed May, June, Sept., and Nov. Some meals.*

$$$ ★ **Les Neiges d'Antan.** In an evergreen forest at Perrères, just outside Cervinia, this family-run inn is quiet and cozy, with three big fireplaces and a nice view of the Matterhorn. **Pros:** secluded and beautiful setting; excellent restaurant; well-designed spa facilities. **Cons:** 5 km (3 mi) outside Breuil-Cervinia (a car is essential); entrance and lobby areas are showing some wear. **TripAdvisor:** "view from the sauna is spectacular," "set in the pine forests," "interior design is cool and funky." *Località Perrères 0166/948775 www.lesneigesdantan.it 21 rooms, 3 suites In-room: no a/c, safe, DVD, Wi-Fi. In-hotel: restaurant, bar, spa, Wi-Fi hotspot, Internet terminal Closed May and June Breakfast.*

SPORTS AND THE OUTDOORS

CLIMBING

Serious climbers can make the ascent of the Matterhorn from Breuil-Cervinia after registering with the local mountaineering officials at the tourist office. This climb is for experienced climbers only. Before embarking on an excursion, contact the representative of the **Club Alpino Italiano** (✉ *Piazza E. Chanoux 8, Aosta* ☎ *0165/40194* 🌐 *www.cai.it*) for information about hikes and the risks. Guides from the **Società delle Guide Alpine** (✉ *Strada Villair 2, Courmayeur* ☎ *0165/842064* 🌐 *www.guidecourmayeur.com*) can accompany you on treks and also lead skiing, canyoning, and ice-climbing excursions. Less-demanding hikes follow the lower slopes of the valley of the River Marmore, to the south of town.

SKIING

Because its slopes border the Cervino glacier, this resort at the foot of the Matterhorn offers year-round skiing. Sixty lifts and a few hundred miles of ski runs ranging from beginner to expert make the area one of the best and most popular in Italy. Contact the tourist office for information.

CASTELLO FÉNIS

34 km (22 mi) northwest of Bard, 104 km (65 mi) north of Turin.

GETTING HERE

To reach the castle by car, take the Nus exit from the main A5 highway. SAVDA buses provide infrequent service between Aosta and Fénis. The closest train station, in Nus, is a 5-km (3-mi) walk from the castle.

EXPLORING

Fodor's Choice ★

Castello Fénis. The best-preserved medieval fortress in Valle d'Aosta, the many-turreted Castello Fénis was built in the mid-14th century by Aimone di Challant, a member of a prolific family related to the Savoys. The castle, which used a double ring of walls for its defense, is the sort imagined by schoolchildren, with pointed towers, portcullises, and spiral staircases. The 15th-century courtyard surrounded by wooden balconies is elegantly decorated with well-preserved frescoes. Inside you can see the kitchen, with an enormous fireplace that provided central heat in winter; the armory; and the spacious, well-lighted rooms used by the lord and lady of the manor. If you have time to visit only one castle in Valle d'Aosta, this should be it. ✉ *Frazione Chez Croiset 22* ☎ *0165/764263* 🎫 *€5* ⏲ *Mar.–June and Sept., daily 9–6:30; July and Aug., daily 9–7:30; Oct.–Feb., Mon. and Wed.–Sat. 10–noon and 1:30–4:30; Sun. 10–noon and 1:30–5:30. Maximum of 25 people allowed to enter every ½ hr.*

EN ROUTE

The highway continues climbing through Valle d'Aosta to the town of Aosta itself. The road at this point is heading almost due west, with rivulets from the wilderness reserve Parco Nazionale del Gran Paradiso streaming down from the left to join the Dora Baltea River, one of the major tributaries of the Po and an increasingly popular spot for rafting. Be careful driving here in late spring, when melting snow can turn some of these streams into torrents.

AOSTA

12 km (7 mi) west of Castello Fénis, 113 km (70 mi) north of Turin.

GETTING HERE

Aosta can easily be reached by car or bus from Milan and Turin. The town is off the main A5 highway. SAVDA buses regularly travel to and from Milan, Turin, and Chamonix in France. Direct train service (two hours) is also available from Turin, but a change of trains is required if traveling here from Milan (three hours).

VISITOR INFORMATION

Aosta tourism office (✉ *Piazza E. Chanoux 2* ☎ *0165/236627* 🌐 *www.lovevda.it*).

EXPLORING

Aosta stands at the junction of two of the important trade routes that connect France and Italy—the valleys of the Rhône and the Isère. Its significance as a trading post was recognized by the Romans, who built a garrison here in the 1st century BC. At the eastern entrance to town, in the Piazza Arco d'Augusto and commanding a fine view over Aosta and the mountains, is the **Arco di Augusto** *(Arch of Augustus)*, built in 25 BC to mark Rome's victory over the Celtic Salassi tribe. (The sloping roof was added in 1716 in an attempt to keep rain from seeping between the stones.) The present-day layout of streets in this small city tucked away in the Alps more than 644 km (400 mi) from Rome is the clearest example of Roman urban planning in Italy. Well-preserved Roman walls form a perfect rectangle around the center of Aosta, and the regular pattern of streets reflects its role as a military stronghold. Saint Anselm, born in Aosta, later became archbishop of Canterbury in England.

7

The **Collegiata di Sant'Orso** is the sort of church that has layers of history in its architecture. Originally there was a 6th-century chapel on this site founded by the Archdeacon Orso, a local saint. Most of this structure was destroyed or hidden when an 11th-century church was erected over it. This church, in turn, was encrusted with Gothic, and later baroque, features, resulting in a jigsaw puzzle of styles, but, surprisingly, not a chaotic jumble. The 11th-century features are almost untouched in the crypt, and if you go up the stairs on the left from the main church you can see the 11th-century frescoes (ask the sacristan who let you in). These restored frescoes depict the life of Christ and the apostles. Although only the tops are visible, you can see the expressions on the faces of the disciples. Take the outside doorway to the right of the main entrance to see the church's crowning glory, its 12th-century cloister. Next to the church, it's enclosed by some 40 stone columns with masterfully carved capitals depicting scenes from the Old and New Testaments and the life of Saint Orso. The turrets and spires of Aosta peek out above. ✉ *Via Sant'Orso* ☎ *0165/40614* ⏲ *Apr.–Sept., daily 9–5; Oct.–Mar., daily 10–5.*

The huge **Roman Porta Pretoria**, regally guarding the city, is a remarkable relic from the Roman era. The area between the massive inner and outer gates was used as a small parade ground for the changing of the guard. ✉ *West end of Via Sant'Anselmo.*

The 72-foot-high ruin of the facade of the **Teatro Romano** guards the remains of the 1st-century BC amphitheater, which once held 20,000 spectators. Only a bit of the outside wall and seven of the amphitheater's original 60 arches remain. The latter, once incorporated into medieval buildings, are being brought to light by ongoing archaeological excavations. ✉ *Via Anfiteatro 4.*

Aosta's **Duomo** dates from the 10th century, but all that remains from that period are the bell towers. The decoration inside is primarily Gothic, but the main attraction of the cathedral predates that era by 1,000 years: a carved ivory diptych portraying the Roman Emperor Honorius and dating from AD 406 is among the many ornate objects housed in the treasury. ✉ *Via Monsignor de Sales* ☎ *0165/40251* ⏲ *Duomo: Easter–Sept. 7, Mon.–Sat. 6:30 pm–8 pm, Sun. 7 am–8 pm; Sept. 8–Easter, Mon.–Sat. 6:30–noon and 3–7, Sun. 7–noon and 3–7. Treasury: Apr.–Sept., Tues.–Sun. 9–11:30 and 3–5:30; Oct.–Mar., Sun. 3–5:30.*

WHERE TO EAT

$$ ITALIAN — ✕ **La Brasserie du Commerce.** In the heart of Aosta, this small and lively eatery specializing in grilled meat dishes sits near the Piazza Emile Chanoux. On a sunny summer day try to snag a table in the restaurant's courtyard garden. Typical valley dishes such as fonduta are on the menu, as well as many vegetable dishes and chef's salads. Pizza is also served, but only on the ground floor. ✉ *Via de Tillier 10* ☎ *0165/35613* 🌐 *www.brasserieducommerce.com* ⏲ *Closed Sun.*

$–$$ NORTHERN ITALIAN — ✕ **Praetoria.** Just outside the Porta Pretoria, this simple and unpretentious restaurant serves hearty local dishes such as *crespelle alla valdostana* (crepes with cheese and ham). The pasta is made on the premises, and all of the menu offerings are prepared from traditional recipes. ✉ *Via Sant'Anselmo 9* ☎ *0165/44356* ⏲ *Closed Thurs. No dinner Wed.*

$$$ NORTHERN ITALIAN — ✕ **Vecchio Ristoro.** Housed in a converted mill, the intimate spaces of this elegant restaurant are furnished with antiques, and a traditional ceramic stove provides additional warmth in cool weather. The chef-proprietor takes pride in creative versions of regional recipes, including *gnocchetti di castagnesu crema di zucca* (chestnut gnocchi with pumpkin cream) and *quaglietto disossata farcita alle castagne fatta al forno* (roast quail with chestnut stuffing). ✉ *Via Tourneuve 4* ☎ *0165/33238* 🌐 *www.ristorantevecchioristoro.it* ⏲ *Closed Sun., June, and 1 wk in Nov. No lunch Mon.*

WHERE TO STAY

$ — **Casa Ospitaliera del Gran San Bernardo.** Here's your chance to sleep in a 12th-century castle without emptying your wallet. **Pros:** good base for budget-conscious skiers and hikers; secluded atmosphere. **Cons:** isolated location (no towns or restaurants nearby); extremely simple accommodations. ✉ *Rue de Flassin 3, Saint-Oyen* ☎ *0165/78247* 🌐 *www.gsbernard.net* *15 rooms* *In-room: no a/c, no phone, no TV* *No credit cards* ⏲ *Closed May* 🍽 *All meals.*

$$$ ★ — **Le Miramonti.** On the road leading up to the Little Saint Bernard Pass and only 20 minutes by car from the French border, this delightful Alpine inn is perfectly situated for those who wish to participate in the area's enormous variety of year-round outdoor activities. **Pros:**

Friendly, efficient service; excellent location for outdoor sports. **Cons:** isolated location in a small village; rooms facing the mountain river can be noisy. **TripAdvisor:** "traditional-style painted ceilings," "view over the river," "staff were very pleasant and helpful." ✉ *Via Piccolo San Bernardo 3, La Thuile* ☎ *0165/883084* 🌐 *www.lemiramonti.it* *35 rooms, 5 suites* *In-room: no a/c, safe, Wi-Fi. In-hotel: restaurant, spa, Wi-Fi hotspot, parking (free), bicycles* *Closed May, Oct., and Nov.* *Breakfast.*

$$ **Milleluci.** This small and inviting family-run hotel sits in an enviable position overlooking Aosta, 1 km (½ mi) north of town. **Pros:** panoramic views; great spa facilities; cozy and traditionally decorated rooms. **Cons:** need a car to get around; no air-conditioning. **TripAdvisor:** "fun-to-explore converted farmhouse," "fabulous swimming pool," "huge spa." ✉ *Località Porossan Roppoz 15* ☎ *0165/235278* 🌐 *www.hotelmilleluci.com* *31 rooms* *In-room: no a/c, safe, Wi-Fi. In-hotel: bar, pool, spa, Wi-Fi hotspot* *Breakfast.*

Fodor's Choice ★

FESTIVALS

The streets of Aosta are brightened each year on the last weekend of January by the **Sant'Orso Fair**, an arts-and-crafts market that brings artisans from all over the Valle d'Aosta to display and sell their work. All the traditional techniques are featured: wood carving and sculpture, soapstone work, wrought iron, leather, wool, lace, and household items of all kinds. Food and wine are sold at outdoor stands and wandering minstrels enliven the whole event. Contact the tourist office (☎ *0165/236627* 🌐 *www.lovevda.it*) for details.

7

COURMAYEUR/MONTE BIANCO

★ *35 km (21 mi) northwest of Aosta, 150 km (93 mi) northwest of Turin.*

GETTING HERE

Courmayeur is on the main A5 highway and can easily be reached by car from both Turin and Milan via Aosta. SAVDA buses run regularly from both Turin and Milan. Train service is not available.

VISITOR INFORMATION

Courmayeur tourism office (✉ *Piazzale Monte Bianco 13* ☎ *0165/842060* 🌐 *www.aiat-monte-bianco.com*).

EXPLORING

The main attraction of Courmayeur is a knock-'em-dead view of Europe's tallest peak, **Monte Bianco** *(Mont Blanc)*. Jet-set celebrities flock here, following a tradition that dates from the late 17th century, when Courmayeur's natural springs first began to draw visitors. The spectacle of the Alps gradually surpassed the springs as the biggest draw (the Alpine letters of the English poet Percy Bysshe Shelley were almost advertisements for the region), but the biggest change came in 1965 with the opening of the Mont Blanc tunnel. Since then, ever-increasing numbers of travelers have passed through the area.

Luckily, planners have managed to keep some restrictions on wholesale development within the town, and its angled rooftops and immaculate cobblestone streets maintain a cozy (if prepackaged) feeling.

From La Palud, a small town 4 km (2½ mi) north of Courmayeur, you can catch the cable car up to the top of Monte Bianco. In summer, if you get the inclination, you can then switch cable cars and descend into Chamonix, in France. In winter you can ski parts of the route off-piste. The Funivie La Palud whisks you up first to the Pavillon du Mont Fréty—a starting point for many beautiful hikes—and then to the Rifugio di Torino, before arriving at the viewing platform at **Punta Helbronner** (more than 11,000 feet), which is also the border post with France. Monte Bianco's attraction is not so much its shape (much less distinctive than that of the Matterhorn) as its expanse and the vistas from the top.

The next stage up—only in summer—is on the **Télépherique de L'Aiguille du Midi,** as you pass into French territory. The trip is particularly impressive: you dangle over a huge glacial snowfield (more than 2,000 feet below) and make your way slowly to the viewing station above Chamonix. It's one of the most dramatic rides in Europe. From this point you're looking down into France, and if you change cable cars at the Aiguille du Midi station you can make your way down to Chamonix itself. The return trip, through the Monte Bianco tunnel, is made by bus. Schedules are unpredictable, depending on weather conditions and demand; contact the **Funivie Monte Bianco** for information. ✉ *Frazione La Palud 22* ☎ *0165/89925 Italian side, 0450/532275 French side* 🌐 *www.montebianco.com* 🎫 *€16 round-trip to Pavillon du Mont Fréty, €38 round-trip to Helbronner, €62 round-trip to Aiguille du Midi, €96 round-trip to Chamonix with return by bus* ⏲ *Call for hrs. Closed mid-Oct.–mid-Dec., depending on demand and weather.*

WHERE TO EAT

$$ NORTHERN ITALIAN ★ ✕ **Cadran Solaire.** The Garin family made over the oldest tavern in Courmayeur to create a warm and inviting restaurant that has a 17th-century stone vault, old wooden floor, and huge stone fireplace. The menu offers seasonal specialties and innovative interpretations of regional dishes: when available, the ravioli maison (filled with ricotta cheese flavored with walnuts and bathed with butter and sage) are particularly delicious. The cozy bar is a popular place for a before-dinner drink. ✉ *Via Roma 122* ☎ *0165/844609* ✍ *Reservations essential* ⏲ *Closed Tues., May, and Oct.*

$$ NORTHERN ITALIAN ★ ✕ **Maison de Filippo.** Here you'll find country-style home cooking in a mountain house with lots of atmosphere, furnished with antiques, farm tools, and bric-a-brac of all kinds. There's a set menu only, which includes an abundance of antipasti, a tempting choice of local soups and pasta dishes, and an equally impressive array of traditional second courses, including fonduta *valdostana* (cheese fondue), and an equally hearty *carbonada* (beef stew and polenta). Cheese, dessert, and fresh fruit complete the meal. Don't head here if you are looking for something light to eat, and make sure to reserve in advance—it's one of the most popular restaurants in Valle d'Aosta. ✉ *Via Passerin d'Entrèves 8* ☎ *0165/869797* 🌐 *www.lamaison.com* ✍ *Reservations essential* ⏲ *Closed Tues., mid-May–June, Oct., and Nov.*

WHERE TO STAY

$$–$$$ **Auberge de la Maison.** This modern hotel's stone-and-wood construction, typical of this region, gives it the feeling of a country inn. **Pros:** secluded location in the center of Entrèves; nice spa; charming decor. **Cons:** isolated location (a car is essential); not all standard rooms have views of Monte Bianco. **TripAdvisor:** "rooms are delightful," "low-key but high-class," "relaxing common areas." ✉ *Via Passerin d'Entrèves 16* ☎ *0165/869811* 🌐 *www.aubergemaison.it* *30 rooms, 3 suites* *In-room: no a/c, safe, Wi-Fi. In-hotel: restaurant, spa, Wi-Fi hotspot, parking (free)* *Closed May and 15 days in Nov.* *Breakfast.*

$$ **Croux.** This bright, comfortable hotel is near the town center on the road leading to Monte Bianco. **Pros:** central location; great views; B&B rates are available. **Cons:** only half the rooms have views; on a busy road in the town center. **TripAdvisor:** "hard to beat for location," "staff are very helpful and attentive," "towels very thin." ✉ *Via Croux 8* ☎ *0165/846735* 🌐 *www.hotelcroux.it* *31 rooms* *In-room: no a/c. In-hotel: bar, Wi-Fi hotspot* *Closed mid-Apr.–mid-June, Oct., and Nov.* *Breakfast.*

$$$$ **Royal e Golf.** A longtime landmark in the center of Courmayeur, the Royal rises high above the surrounding town. **Pros:** central location on Courmayeur's main pedestrian street; panoramic views; heated outdoor pool. **Cons:** standard rooms can be small; meal plan required; town center can be busy. **TripAdvisor:** "fabulous view of Mont Blanc," "spa area was really nice," "short walk to the ski lift." ✉ *Via Roma 87* ☎ *0165/831611* 🌐 *www.hotelroyalegolf.com* *80 rooms, 6 suites* *In-room: no a/c, safe, Internet. In-hotel: restaurant, bar, pool, gym, some pets allowed, Wi-Fi hotspot* *Closed wk after Easter–mid-June and mid-Sept.–Nov.* *Some meals.*

$$$–$$$$ Fodor's Choice ★ **Villa Novecento.** Run with the friendly charm and efficiency of Franco Cavaliere and his son Stefano, the Novecento is a peaceful haven near Courmayeur's otherwise busy center. **Pros:** charming and cozy accommodations; good restaurant; close to town center but away from the hubbub. **Cons:** parking is limited; no air-conditioning. **TripAdvisor:** "great view of the mountains," "in a quiet part of the town," "romantic, charming, well-decorated." ✉ *Viale Monte Bianco 64* ☎ *0165/843000* 🌐 *www.villanovecento.it* *26 rooms* *In-room: no a/c, safe, Wi-Fi. In-hotel: restaurant, bar, gym, some pets allowed, Wi-Fi hotspot* *Breakfast.*

SKIING

Courmayeur pales in comparison to its French neighbor, Chamonix, in both the number (it has only 24) and the quality of its trails. But with good natural snow cover, the trails and vistas are spectacular. A huge gondola leads from the center of Courmayeur to Plan Checrouit, where gondolas and lifts lead to the slopes. The skiing around Monte Bianco is particularly good, and the off-piste options are among the best in Europe. The off-piste routes from Cresta d'Arp (the local peak) to Dolonne, and from La Palud area into France, should be done with a guide. Contact the **Funivie Courmayeur/Mont Blanc** (☎ *0165/89925* 🌐 *www.montebianco.com*) for complete information about lift tickets,

7

ski runs, and weather conditions. For Alpine guide services contact the **Società delle Guide Alpine** (✉ *Strada Villair 2* ☎ *0165/842064* 🌐 *www.guidecourmayeur.com*).

COGNE AND THE PARCO NAZIONALE DEL GRAN PARADISO

52 km (32 mi) southeast of Courmayeur, 134 km (83 mi) northwest of Turin.

GETTING HERE

Cogne is easily reached by car from the A5—take the Aosta Ovest–St. Pierre exit and follow the SR47 for 20 km (12 mi). SAVDA buses arrive here frequently from Aosta, but no train service is available.

VISITOR INFORMATION

Cogne tourism office (✉ *Via Bourgeois 34* ☎ *0165/74040* 🌐 *www.cogne.org*).

EXPLORING

Cogne is the gateway to the **Parco Nazionale del Gran Paradiso.** This huge park, once the domain of King Vittorio Emanuele II (1820–78) and bequeathed to the nation after World War I, is one of Europe's most rugged and unspoiled wilderness areas, with wildlife and many plant species protected by law. This is one of the few places in Europe where you can see the ibex (a mountain goat with horns up to 3 feet long) and the chamois (a small antelope). The park is open free of charge throughout the year and is managed by a park board, the **Ente Parco Nazionale Gran Paradiso** (✉ *Via della Rocca 47, Turin* ☎ *011/8606211 park board, 0165/749264 visitor information center* 🌐 *www.grand-paradis.it*). Try to visit in May, when spring flowers are in bloom and most of the meadows are clear of snow.

HIKING

There's wonderful hiking to be done here, both on daylong excursions and longer journeys with overnight stops in the park's mountain refuges. The **Cogne tourism office** (✉ *Via Bourgeois 34* ☎ *0165/74040* 🌐 *www.cogne.org*) has a wealth of information and trail maps to help.

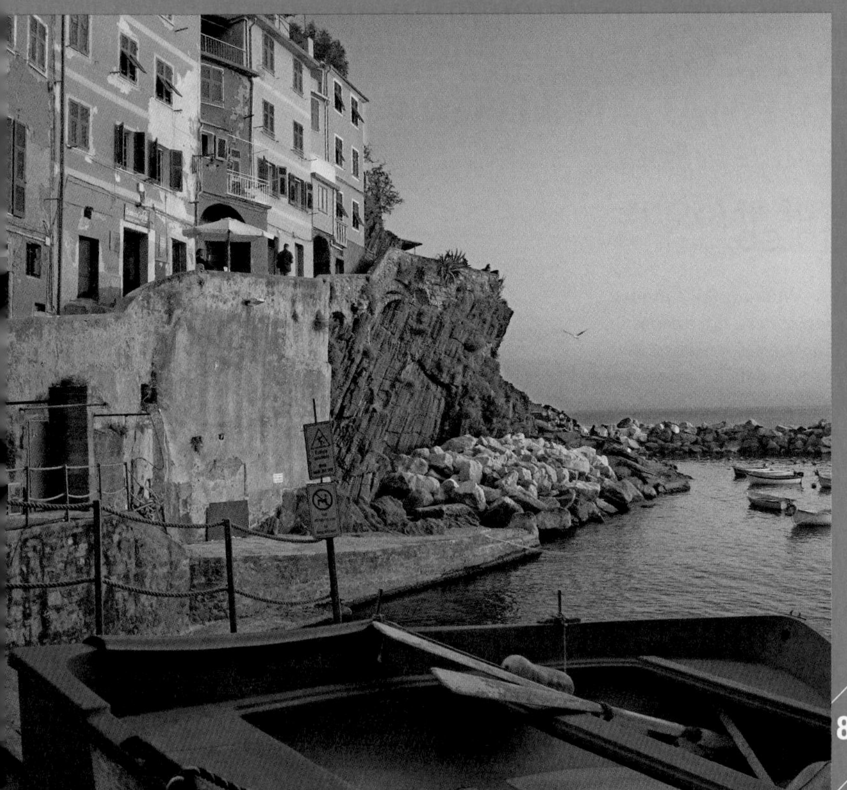

The Italian Riviera

WORD OF MOUTH

"Somewhat against my will, I stumbled into the Riviera the first time, picking a town almost by accident, didn't do ANYTHING for 3 days despite my plans to be a good tourist, and ended up living here. It's just BELLA, so come enjoy, no worries."

—zeppole

WELCOME TO THE ITALIAN RIVIERA

TOP REASONS TO GO

★ **Walking the Cinque Terre:** Hike the famous Cinque Terre trails past gravity-defying vineyards, rock-perched villages, and the deep blue sea.

★ **Portofino:** See the world through rose-tinted sunglasses at this glamorous little harbor village.

★ **Genoa's historic center and port:** From the palaces of Via Garibaldi to the labyrinthine backstreets of the old city to the world-class aquarium, the city is full of surprising delights.

★ **Giardini Botanici Hanbury:** A spectacular natural setting harbors one of Italy's largest, most exotic botanical gardens.

★ **Pesto:** The basil-rich sauce was invented in Liguria, and it's never been equaled elsewhere.

1 Riviera di Levante. East of Genoa, the Riviera of the Rising Sun has tiny bays and inlets set among dramatic cliffs, making for some of the most beautiful coastline in Italy. The pastel-hue town of Portofino has charmed generations of the rich and famous.

2 Cinque Terre. Five isolated seaside villages seem removed from the modern world—despite the many hikers who populate the trails between them.

3 Genoa. Birthplace of Christopher Columbus, this city is an urban anomaly among Liguria's charming villages. At its heart is Italy's largest historic district, filled with beautiful architecture.

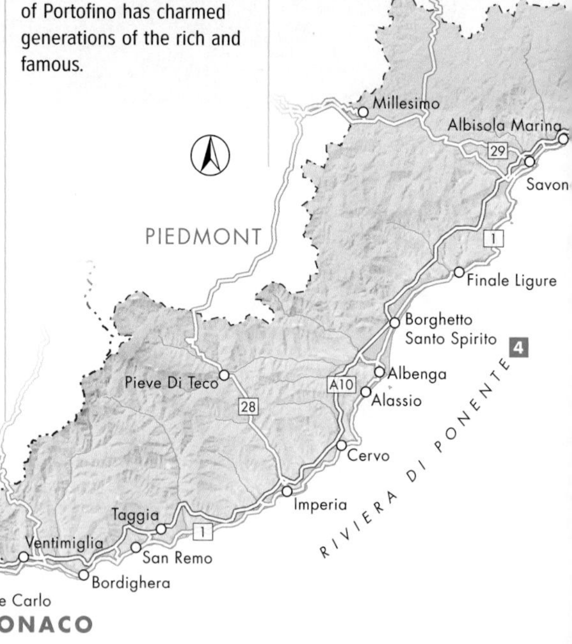

4 Riviera di Ponente. The Riviera of the Setting Sun, reaching from the French border to Genoa, has protected bays and sandy beaches. The seaside resorts of Bordighera and San Remo share some of the glitter of their French cousins to the west.

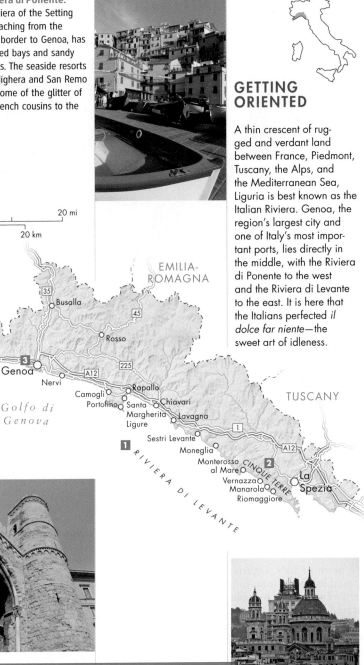

GETTING ORIENTED

A thin crescent of rugged and verdant land between France, Piedmont, Tuscany, the Alps, and the Mediterranean Sea, Liguria is best known as the Italian Riviera. Genoa, the region's largest city and one of Italy's most important ports, lies directly in the middle, with the Riviera di Ponente to the west and the Riviera di Levante to the east. It is here that the Italians perfected *il dolce far niente*—the sweet art of idleness.

EATING AND DRINKING WELL IN THE ITALIAN RIVIERA

Ligurian cuisine might surprise you. As you'd expect given the long coastline, it employs all sorts of seafood, but the real claim to fame is the exemplary use of vegetables and herbs.

Basil is practically revered in Genoa (the word is derived from the Greek *basileus*, meaning "king"), and the city is considered the birthplace of pesto, the basil-rich pasta sauce. This and other herbs—laurel, fennel, and marjoram—are cultivated but also grow wild on the sun-kissed hillsides. Seafood also plays a prominent role on the menu, appearing in soups, salads, and pasta dishes. Especially bountiful are anchovies, sea bass, squid, and octopus. Vegetables—particularly artichokes, eggplant, and zucchini—are abundant, usually prepared with liberal amounts of olive oil and garlic.

Like much of Italy, Liguria has a full range of eating establishments from cafeteria-like *tavole calde* to family-run trattorias to sophisticated *ristoranti*. Lunch is served between 12:30 and 2:30 and dinner between 7:30 and 11. Also popular, especially in Genoa, are *enoteche* (wine bars), which serve simply prepared light meals late into the night.

FABULOUS FOCACCIA

When you're hankering for a snack, turn to bakeries and small eateries serving focaccia *(pictured above)*. The flat bread here is more dense and flavorful than what's sold as focaccia in American restaurants; it's the region's answer to pizza, usually eaten on the go.

It comes simply salted and dribbled with olive oil; flavored with rosemary and olives; covered with cheese or anchovies; and even *ripiena* (filled), usually with cheese or vegetables and herbs. Another local delicacy is *farinata*, a chickpea pancake baked like a pizza.

ANTIPASTI

Seafood antipasti are served in abundance at most Ligurian restaurants. These usually include marinated anchovies from Monterosso, *cozze ripiene* (mussel shells stuffed with minced mussel meat, prosciutto, Parmesan, herbs, and bread crumbs), and *sopressato di polpo* (flattened octopus in olive oil and lemon sauce).

PASTA

Liguria's classic pasta sauce is pesto, made from basil, garlic, olive oil, pine nuts, and hard cheese. It's usually served with *trenette* (similar to spaghetti) or the slightly sweet *testaroli* (a flat pasta made from chestnut flour).

You can also find *pansotti* (triangular pockets of pasta filled with a cheese mixture (*pictured below*), and *trofie* (doughy, short pasta twists) with *salsa di noci,* a rich sauce of garlic, walnuts, and cream that, as with pesto, is ideally pounded with a mortar and pestle.

Spaghetti *allo scoglio* is an olive oil, tomato, and white wine–based sauce containing an assortment of local *frutti di mare* (seafood) including shrimp, clams, mussels, and cuttlefish.

FISH AND MEAT

Fish is the best bet for a second course: the classic preparation is a whole grilled or baked whitefish—*branzino* (sea bass) and *orata* (dorado) are good choices—served with olives, potatoes, Ligurian

spices, and a drizzle of olive oil. A popular meat dish is *cima alla Genovese,* a veal roll stuffed with a mixture of eggs and vegetables, served as a cold cut.

PANIGACCI

One of the real treats of the region is *panigacci* from the Lunigiana area, the valley extending inland along the border between Liguria and Tuscany.

Balls of dough are laid in a small, terra-cotta dishes known as *testine* and stacked one on top of the other in order to flatten the dough. Then they are placed over hot coals (or in a pizza oven), and what emerges is flat, firm, almost pitalike bread.

Panigacci are usually served with *stracchino* cheese (similar to cream cheese), pesto, or nut sauce and cold cuts—a delicious, hearty meal.

WINE

Local vineyards produce mostly light and refreshing whites such as Pigato, Vermentino, and Cinque Terre. Rossese di Dolceacqua, from near the French border, is the best red wine the region has to offer, but for a more robust accompaniment to meats opt for the more full-bodied reds of the neighboring Piedmont region.

Updated by Megan McCaffrey-Guerrera

Like the family jewels that bedeck its habitual visitors, the Italian Riviera is glamorous, but in the old-fashioned way. The resort towns and coastal villages that stake intermittent claim on the rocky shores of the Ligurian Sea are the long-lost cousins of newer seaside paradises found elsewhere.

Here the grandest palazzi share space with frescoed, angular, late-19th-century apartment buildings. The rustic and elegant, the provincial and chic, the small-town and cosmopolitan all collide here in a sun-drenched blend that defines the Italian side of the Riviera. There is the glamour of its chic resorts such as San Remo and Portofino, the tranquil beauty and outdoor adventures of the Cinque Terre, plus the history and architectural charm of Genoa. Mellowed by the balmy breezes blowing off the sea, travelers bask in the sun, explore the picturesque fishing villages, and pamper themselves at the resorts that dot this ruggedly beautiful landscape.

PLANNING

MAKING THE MOST OF YOUR TIME

Your first decision, particularly with limited time, is between the two Rivieras. The Riviera di Levante, east of Genoa, is quieter and has a more distinct personality with the rustic Cinque Terre, ritzy Portofino, and the panoramic Gulf of Poets. The Riviera di Ponente, west of Genoa, is a classic European resort experience with many white-sand beaches and more nightlife—similar to, but not as glamorous as, the French Riviera across the border.

In either case, your second choice is whether to visit Genoa. Despite its rough exterior and (diminishing) reputation as a seamy port town, Genoa's artistic and cultural treasures are significant—you won't find anything remotely comparable elsewhere in the region. Unless your goal is to avoid urban life entirely, consider a night or two in the city.

Season is everything. Shops, cafés, clubs, and restaurants stay open late in resorts during high season (at Easter and from June through August), but during the rest of the year they close early, if they're open at all.

HIKING

Walking Liguria's extensive network of trails, and taking in the gorgeous views, is a major outdoor activity. The mild climate and laid-back state of mind can lull you into underestimating just how strenuous such walks can be. Wear good shoes, use sunscreen, and carry water—you'll be glad you did. Trail maps are available from tourist information offices, or upon entry to the Cinque Terre National Park.

Other walks to consider: On Portofino promontory, the relatively easy walk to the Abbazia di San Fruttuoso is popular, and there's a more challenging hike from Ruta to the top of Monte Portofino. From Genoa, you can take the Zecca–Righi funicular up to Righi and walk along the ring of fortresses that used to defend the city, or ride the Genova–Casella railroad to one of the trailheads near the station stops.

Walking tours can introduce you to lesser-known aspects of the region. For the Cinque Terre and the rest of the Province of La Spezia, the **Cooperativa Arte e Natura** (✉ *Viale Amendola 172, La Spezia* ☎ *0187/739410* ✉ *coop.arte@tin.it*) is a good source for English-speaking guides. A half day costs around €150.

GETTING HERE AND AROUND

BOAT TRAVEL

With so much coastline—350 km (217 mi)—and so many pretty little harbors, Liguria is a great place to get around by boat. A busy network of local ferry lines, such as **Servizio Marittimo del Tigullio** (☎ *0185/284670* 🌐 *www.traghettiportofino.it*) and **Alimar** (☎ *010/256775*), connects many of the resorts. **Golfo Paradiso** (☎ *0185/772091* 🌐 *www.golfoparadiso.it*) lines run between Camogli, San Fruttuoso (on the Portofino promontory), and Recco, and in summer from the port of Genoa and Nervi to Portofino, the Cinque Terre, and Portovenere, stopping in Recco and Camogli. **Navigazione Golfo dei Poeti** (☎ *0187/732987* 🌐 *www.navigazionegolfodeipoeti.it*) runs regular ferry services between Lerici, Portovenere, the Cinque Terre, Santa Margherita, and Genoa.

But you can have as much fun (or more) negotiating a price with a boat owner at one of the smaller ports such as Camogli, Portovenere, and Lerici. You're likely to deal with someone who has a rudimentary command of English at best, but that's all you need to discuss price, time, and destination. For smaller groups (eight or fewer) interested in seeing the Cinque Terre by sea, local fisherman **Angelo Benvenuto** (✉ *Monterosso* ☎ *333/3182967* ✉ *angelosboattours@yahoo.com*) offers a variety of boating excursions. A private half day costs approximately €300.

BUS TRAVEL

Generally speaking, buses are a difficult way to come and go in Liguria. **Diana Tours** (☎ *800/651931*) provides service from the airport in Nice, but there's no bus service between Genoa and other major Italian cities. There's no regular service connecting Genoa with the towns along the Riviera di Ponente. Things are somewhat easier along the Riviera di Levante where **Tigullio Trasporti** (☎ *0185/373234* 🌐 *www.tigulliotrasporti.it*) runs regular service.

8

CAR TRAVEL

With the freedom of a car you could drive from one end of the Riviera to the other on the autostrada in less than three hours. Two good roads run parallel to each other along the coast of Liguria. Closer to shore and passing through all the towns and villages is SS1, the Via Aurelia, which was laid out by the ancient Romans and has excellent views at almost every turn but gets crowded in July and August.

More direct and higher up than SS1 are the autostrade, A10 west of Genoa and A12 to the south—engineering wonders with literally hundreds of long tunnels and towering viaducts. These routes save time on weekends, in summer, and on days when festivals slow traffic in some resorts to a standstill.

TRAIN TRAVEL

Train travel is convenient throughout the region. It takes three hours for an express train to cover the entire Liguria coast. Local trains take upward of five hours to get from one end of the coast to the other, stopping in or near all the towns along the way. For schedules, check the Web site of the national railway, **FS** (☎ *892021* 🌐 *www.trenitalia.com*).

ABOUT THE HOTELS

Liguria's lodging options may be a step behind such resort areas as Positano and Taormina, so reservations for its better accommodations, and limited ones in the Cinque Terre, should be made far in advance. Lodging tends to be pricey in high season, particularly June to August. At other times of year, ask for a *sconto bassa stagione* (low-season discount).

Hotel reviews have been condensed for this book. Please go to Fodors.com for full reviews of each property.

WHAT IT COSTS IN EUROS

	¢	$	$$	$$$	$$$$
Restaurants	under €20	€20–€30	€30–€45	€45–€65	over €65
Hotels	under €75	€75–€125	€125–€200	€200–€300	over €300

Restaurant prices are for a first course (primo), second course (secondo), and dessert (dolce). Hotel prices are for two people in a standard double room in high season, including tax and service.

RIVIERA DI LEVANTE

East of Genoa lies the Riviera di Levante (Riviera of the Rising Sun). It has a more raw, unpolished side to it than the Riviera di Ponente, and its stretches of rugged coastline are dotted with fishing villages. Around every turn of this area's twisting roads the hills plummet sharply to the sea, forming deep, hidden bays and coves. Beaches on this coast tend to be rocky, backed by spectacular sheer cliffs. (Yet there are some rather lovely sandy beaches in Lerici, Monterosso, Levanto, and Paraggi.) It is also home to one of Europe's well-known playgrounds for the rich and famous, the inlet of Portofino.

LERICI

106 km (66 mi) southeast of Genoa, 65 km (40 mi) west of Lucca.

GETTING HERE

By car, Lerici is less than a 10-minute drive west from the A12 with plenty of blue signs indicating the way. There is a large pay-parking lot about a 10-minute walk along the seaside promenade from the center. By train, the closest station is either Sarzana (10-minute drive) or La Spezia Centrale (20-minute drive) on the main north–south line between Genoa and Pisa.

VISITOR INFORMATION

Lerici tourism office (✉ *Via Biaggini 6* ☎ *0187/967346* 🌐 *www.aptcinqueterre.sp.it*).

EXPLORING

Near Liguria's border with Tuscany, this colorful village dates to the 1200s. It is set on a magnificent coastline of gray cliffs and surrounded by a national park of pine forests and olive trees. The waterfront piazza is filled with deceiving trompe-l'oeil frescoes, and seaside cafés line its charming little harbor that holds boats of all sizes.

There are several white beaches and bathing establishments dotting the 2-km (1-mi) walk along the bay from the village center to nearby San Terenzo. It was here that the writer and poet Percy Shelley spent some of his happiest days. After his death in 1822 the bay was renamed the *Golfo dei Poeti* (Gulf of Poets) in his and Lord Byron's honor.

With its proximity to the autostrada, Lerici makes a great base for exploring not only the more famous attractions of the area but also the tiny hill towns and walled villages that dot the hinterlands.

8

Its promontory is dominated by the 13th-century **Castello di Lerici.** The Pisan castle now houses a museum of paleontology. ✉ *Piazza S. Giorgio 1* ☎ *0187/969042* 🌐 *www.castellodilerici.it* 🎫 *€5* 🕐 *Mar. 16–June, Sept.–Oct. 19, and Dec. 26–Jan. 6, Tues.–Sun. 10:30–12:30 and 2:30–5:30; July and Aug., daily 10:30–12:30 and 6:30–midnight; Oct. 20–Dec. 23 and Jan. 7–Mar. 15, Tues.–Fri. 10:30–12:30, weekends 10:30–12:30 and 2:30–5:30.*

WHERE TO EAT

$ PIZZA ✕ **Bonta Nascoste.** In the local dialect, *bonta nascoste* means "hidden goodness," a reference to this restaurant's side-street location and consistently good food. Some of the best pizza and farinata in the Gulf of Poets is served here, but the pasta, fish, and meat dishes are also all noteworthy. There are only eight tables (and a couple more outside in summer), so reserve ahead. ✉ *Via Cavour 52* ☎ *0187/965500* 🌐 *www.bontanascoste.it* ✍ *Reservations essential* 🕐 *Closed Wed. and 2 wks in Nov. and June.*

$$ LIGURIAN ✕ **Golfo dei Poeti.** Owners Claudio and Annalisa have taken this grotto-like space on the waterfront and created a fun restaurant specializing in delicious homemade pasta dishes and seafood. Their tagliatelle with *gamberi* (shrimp) and zucchini in an olive oil and white wine sauce is mouthwateringly good. Very good pizza is served in the evening. ✉ *Calata Mazzini 52* ☎ *0187/966414* 🕐 *Closed Tues. and 2 wks in Nov. No lunch Mon. and Wed.*

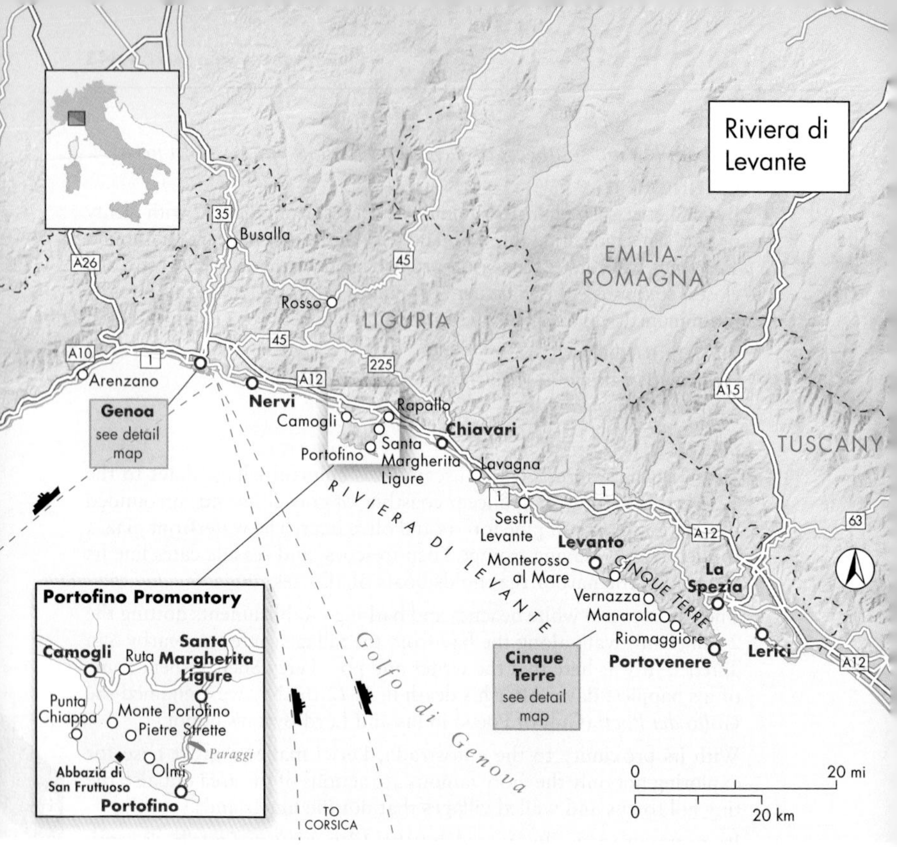

$$$ LIGURIAN **Miranda.** Perched amid the clustered old houses in seaside Tellaro, 4 km (2½ mi) southeast of Lerici, this small family-run restaurant has become a gourmet's destination because of chef Angelo Cabani's imaginative Ligurian cooking. His seafood menu changes daily, but might include shrimp and lobster salad with fennel, or risotto with asparagus and shrimp. This pretty building is also a small inn with seven charming and comfortable rooms ($$). ✉ *Via Fiascherino 92, Tellaro* ☎ *0187/964012* 🌐 *www.miranda1959.com* ⏲ *Closed Mon. and Nov. and Jan.*

$$–$$$ LIGURIAN **Osteria di Redarca.** Within the pine forest of the Montemarcello National Park, this *osteria* (a simple, informal restaurant) serves some of the best homemade pastas in the area. It also offers a "surf-and-turf"–type menu, with abundant cooked-to-perfection fish platters and succulent meat dishes. The location may not be seaside, but the setting and the food are both a treat. ✉ *Rocchetta Località Redarca 6, Lerici* ☎ *0187/966140* ⏲ *Closed Wed. and 2 wks in Jan.*

WHERE TO STAY

$$–$$$ **Doria Park.** Nestled between olive-tree hills and the village center, with views over the harbor and bay beyond, the Doria has the best location in Lerici. **Pros:** sea views; comfortable beds; not far from the main piazza and harbor. **Cons:** many stairs, including several sets that can be challenging for people with weak knees or heavy bags.

TripAdvisor: "overlooking the sea," "good central location," "room is small but comfortable." ✉ *Via Doria 2* ☎ *0187/967124* 🌐 *www.doriaparkhotel.it* *48 rooms, 5 suites* *In-room: safe, Wi-Fi. In-hotel: restaurant, bar, laundry service, Wi-Fi hotspot, parking (free), some pets allowed* *Breakfast.*

$$ **Florida.** This seafront, family-run establishment has a sunny, welcoming facade and a friendly staff inside. **Pros:** beachfront location; bay views. **Cons:** small rooms; beach across the street can be noisy, especially on Thursday and Saturday nights in summer. **TripAdvisor:** "in the heart of tiny Lerici," "views of the beach were breathtaking," "room was fine, a little spartan." ✉ *Lungomare Biaggini 35* ☎ *0187/967332* 🌐 *www.hotelflorida.it* *40 rooms* *In-room: safe, refrigerator. In-hotel: bar, beachfront, Wi-Fi hotspot* *Closed approximately Dec.–Feb.* *Breakfast.*

$$$ **Piccolo Hotel del Lido.** Although the 12 waterfront rooms at this boutique hotel are not large, they are well equipped and tastefully decorated. **Pros:** beachfront; great views; large bathrooms. **Cons:** limited parking; adjacent beach club can get noisy by day during high season. **TripAdvisor:** "superb location right on the beach," "decor clean and minimalist," "very quiet and private." ✉ *Lungomare Biaggini 24* ☎ *0187/968159* 🌐 *www.locandadellido.it* *12 rooms* *In-room: safe, refrigerator* *Closed late Oct.–Easter* *Breakfast.*

EN ROUTE

Ten minutes inland from Lerici is the medieval village of **Sarzana**, designed by the military leader Castruccio Castracani, who also designed Lucca. Here you will find some of the most authentic and well-restored palazzos in Liguria. Its pedestrians-only cobblestone streets bustling with people, fine boutiques, and packed cafés are perfect for a *passeggiata* (late-afternoon stroll).

8

LA SPEZIA

11 km (7 mi) northwest of Lerici, 103 km (64 mi) southeast of Genoa.

GETTING HERE

By car, take the La Spezia exit off the A12. La Spezia Centrale train station is on the main north–south railway line between Genoa and Pisa.

VISITOR INFORMATION

La Spezia tourism office (✉ *Via Mazzini 45* ☎ *0187/770900* 🌐 *www.aptcinqueterre.sp.it*).

EXPLORING

La Spezia is sometimes thought of as nothing but a large, industrialized naval port en route to the Cinque Terre and Portovenere, but it does possess some charm, and it gives you a look at a less tourist-focused part of the Riviera. Its palm-lined promenade, fertile citrus parks, renovated Liberty-style palazzos, and colorful balcony-lined streets make parts of La Spezia surprisingly beautiful. On mornings Monday through Saturday, you can stroll through the fresh fish, produce, and local-cheese stalls at the outdoor market on Piazza Cavour, and on Friday take part in the lively flea market on Via Garibaldi.

The remains of the massive 13th-century **Castel San Giorgio** now house a small museum dedicated to local archaeology. ✉ *Via XX Settembre* ☎ *0187/751142* 🎟 *€5* ⏲ *June–Aug., Wed.–Mon. 9:30–12:30 and 5–8; Apr., May, and Sept., Wed.–Mon. 9:30–12:30 and 3–8; Oct.–Mar., Wed.–Mon. 9:30–12:30 and 2–5.*

WHERE TO EAT

¢ ✕ **La Pia.** Considered an institution in La Spezia, this *farinateria* and pizzeria dates back to 1887. During the lunch hour you will find a line out the door, while inside—and on the patio in summer—locals munch on *farinata,* a chickpea pancake that's a Ligurian delicacy, and on thick-crust pizzas served hot out of the wood-burning oven. ✉ *Via Magenta 12* ☎ *0187/739999* ⏲ *Closed Wed. and 2 wks in Nov. and Aug.*

PORTOVENERE

★ *12 km (7 mi) south of La Spezia, 114 km (70 mi) southeast of Genoa.*

GETTING HERE

By car from the port city of La Spezia, follow the blue signs for Portovenere. It is about a 20-minute winding drive along the sea through small fishing villages. From the La Spezia train station you can hire a taxi for about €30. By bus from Via Garibaldi in La Spezia (a 10-minute walk from the train station) it takes 20 minutes.

VISITOR INFORMATION

Portovenere doesn't have a tourist office; you get information at the Commune (Town Hall) or at the tourist office in La Spezia Centrale train station.

EXPLORING

The colorful facades and pedestrians-only *calata* (promenade) make Portovenere a quintessential Ligurian seaside village. Its tall, thin *terratetto* (houses) date from as far back as the 11th century and are connected in a wall-like formation to protect against attacks by the Pisans and local pirates. At the tip of the peninsula, with a dramatic position over the sea, stands the commanding San Pietro church. The *caruggi* (alleylike passageways) lead to an array of charming shops, homes, and gardens.

Lord Byron (1788–1824) is said to have written *Childe Harold's Pilgrimage* in Portovenere. Near the entrance to the huge, strange **Grotto Arpaia,** at the base of the sea-swept cliff, is a plaque recounting the poet's strength and courage as he swam across the gulf to the village of San Terenzo, near Lerici, to visit his friend Shelley (1792–1822).

San Pietro, a 13th-century Gothic church, is built on the site of an ancient pagan shrine, on a formidable solid mass of rock above the Grotto Arpaia. With its black-and-white-striped exterior, it is a landmark recognizable from far out at sea. There's a spectacular view of the Cinque Terre coastline from the front porch of the church. ✉ *Waterfront promenade* ☎ *No phone* ⏲ *Apr.–Oct., daily 7 am–8 pm; Nov.–Mar., daily 7 am–6 pm.*

WHERE TO EAT

¢ WINE BAR **Bacicio.** Tucked away on Portovenere's main caruggio, this *enoteca* (wine bar) and antipasto bar is popular with locals and slowly being discovered by tourists looking for good, local dishes. The owner whips up some wonderful finger food—including *crostini* (grilled bread) with fresh anchovies, and smoked herring with spicy orange salsa—and offers a robust list of local wines. He also designed the entire place, right down to the tables and chairs made from anchors and pieces of old boats. *Via Cappellini 17* *0187/792054* *Reservations not accepted* *No credit cards* *Closed Wed., Nov., and Jan.*

$$–$$$ LIGURIAN **Da Iseo.** Try to get one of the tables outside at this waterfront restaurant with bistro accents and paintings of Portovenere. Seafood here is fresh and plentiful, and the pasta courses are inventive. Try spaghetti *alla Giuseppe* (with shellfish and fresh tomato) or *alla Iseo* (with a seafood curry sauce). *Calata Doria 9* *0187/790610* *Closed Wed., Dec. 1–15, and Jan. 15–Feb. 1.*

$$$$ LIGURIAN **Le Bocche.** At the end of the Portovenere promontory in the shadow of San Pietro, this is the village's most exclusive and possibly most delicious restaurant. The menu consists of only the freshest in-season fish, prepared with a creative touch, such as marinated tuna encrusted with pistachios or asparagus soup with small fillets of sole. The setting is romantic and unique, as you feel almost immersed in the Mediterranean. The dinner menu is quite expensive (as is the lengthy wine list), but you can get a real deal at lunch with a limited but equally good menu at lower prices. *Calata Doria 102* *0187/790622* *www.lebocche.it* *Closed Nov.–Feb.*

$$–$$$ LIGURIAN **Locanda Lorena.** Across the small bay of Portovenere lies the rugged island of Palmaria. There is only one restaurant on the island, the sister establishment to Da Iseo, and here Iseo (aka Giuseppe), an accomplished chef, actually still does the cooking. Fresh pasta and local fish such as *branzino* (sea bass) are headliners at this fun dining spot with lovely views looking back toward Portovenere. To get here, take the restaurant's free speedboat from the dock just outside Da Iseo. *Palmaria Island* *0187/792370* *www.locandalorena.com* *Closed Nov.*

8

WHERE TO STAY

$$–$$$ **Grand Hotel Portovenere.** Built in the 13th century as a Franciscan convent, this pale pink building with arches and frescoes is now the best hotel in the village. **Pros:** nice location; many extra amenities such as the spa; cooking lessons. **Cons:** lobby and rooms could use a revamping. **TripAdvisor:** "overlooking the harbor and the town," "room was spacious," "best place in town." *Via Garibaldi 5* *0187/792610* *www.portovenerehotel.it* *44 rooms, 10 suites* *In-room: refrigerator. In-hotel: restaurant, bar, spa, Internet terminal* *Breakfast.*

$$ **Hotel Belvedere.** This sunny Liberty-style building has simply furnished guest rooms that don't break the bank in what can be an expensive destination. **Pros:** reasonably priced rooms with water views. **Cons:** parts of the hotel could use a makeover; limited parking. **TripAdvisor:** "tremendous views," "quick stroll to the ferries," "rooms were pretty basic." *Via G. Garibaldi 26* *0187/790608* *www.belvedereportovenere.it* *19 rooms* *In-room: safe. In-hotel: beachfront, Internet terminal, parking (free), some pets allowed* *Closed Nov.–mid-Mar.* *Breakfast.*

LEVANTO

8 km (5 mi) northwest of Monterosso al Mare, 60 km (36 mi) southeast of Genoa.

GETTING HERE

By car, take the Carodanno/Levanto exit off the A12 for 25 minutes to the town center. By train, Levanto is on the main north–south railway, one stop north of Monterosso.

VISITOR INFORMATION

Levanto tourism office (✉ *Piazza Mazzini 1* ☎ *0187/808125* 🌐 *www.aptcinqueterre.sp.it*).

EXPLORING

Tucked nicely between two promontories, Levanto offers an alternative and usually less-expensive base to explore the Cinque Terre and the Riviera di Levante. This town retains much of the typical Ligurian character with trompe-l'oeil frescoed villas and the olive tree–covered hills of the national park. Monterosso, one of the Cinque Terre villages, is a four-minute train ride away.

WHERE TO STAY

$$ **La Giada del Mesco.** On Punto Mesco headland, this stone bed-and-breakfast has unobstructed vistas of the Mediterranean and Riviera coastline. **Pros:** great position; nice pool and sunning area. **Cons:** shuttle service is not always available; the 3½ km (1½ mi) into town is quite a walk, so you'll want a car. **TripAdvisor:** "outstanding view of the sea," "shuttle service to town," "very expensive." ✉ *Via Doria 2* ☎ *0187/967124* 🌐 *www.lagiadadelmesco.it* *12 rooms* *In-room: safe, refrigerator. In-hotel: pool, Wi-Fi hotspot, parking (free)* *Closed mid-Nov.–Feb.* *Breakfast.*

CHIAVARI

46 km (29 mi) northwest of Levanto, 38 km (23 mi) southeast of Genoa.

GETTING HERE

By car, take the Chiavari exit off the A12. The Chiavari train station is on the main north–south train line between Genoa and Pisa.

VISITOR INFORMATION

Chiavari tourism office (✉ *Via Remolari 9* ☎ *0185/365216* 🌐 *www.apttigullio.liguria.it*).

EXPLORING

Chiavari is a fishing town (rather than village) of considerable character, with narrow, twisting streets and a good harbor. Chiavari's citizens were intrepid explorers, and many emigrated to South America in the 19th century. The town boomed, thanks to the wealth of the returning voyagers, but Chiavari retains many medieval traces in its buildings.

In the town center, the **Museo Archeologico** displays objects from an 8th-century BC necropolis, or ancient cemetery, excavated nearby. The museum closes the first and third Sunday of the month. ✉ *Palazzo Costaguta, Via Costaguta 4, Piazza Matteotti* ☎ *0185/320829* *Free* *Tues.–Sat. and 2nd and 4th Sun. of month 9–1:30.*

Continued on page 458

THE CINQUE TERRE

FIVE REMOTE VILLAGES MAKE ONE MUST-SEE DESTINATION

"Charming" and "breathtaking" are adjectives that get a workout when you're traveling in Italy, but it's rare that both apply to a single location. The Cinque Terre is such a place, and this combination of characteristics goes a long way toward explaining its tremendous appeal.

The area is made up of five tiny villages (Cinque Terre literally means "Five Lands") clinging to the cliffs along a gorgeous stretch of the Ligurian coast. The terrain is so steep that for centuries footpaths were the only way to get from place to place. It just so happens that these paths provide beautiful views of the rocky coast tumbling into the sea, as well as access to secluded beaches and grottoes.

Backpackers "discovered" the Cinque Terre in the 1970s, and its popularity has been growing ever since. Despite summer crowds, much of the original appeal is intact. Each town has maintained its own distinct charm, and views from the trails in between are as breathtaking as ever.

Monterosso Corniglia Terracing around Cornig

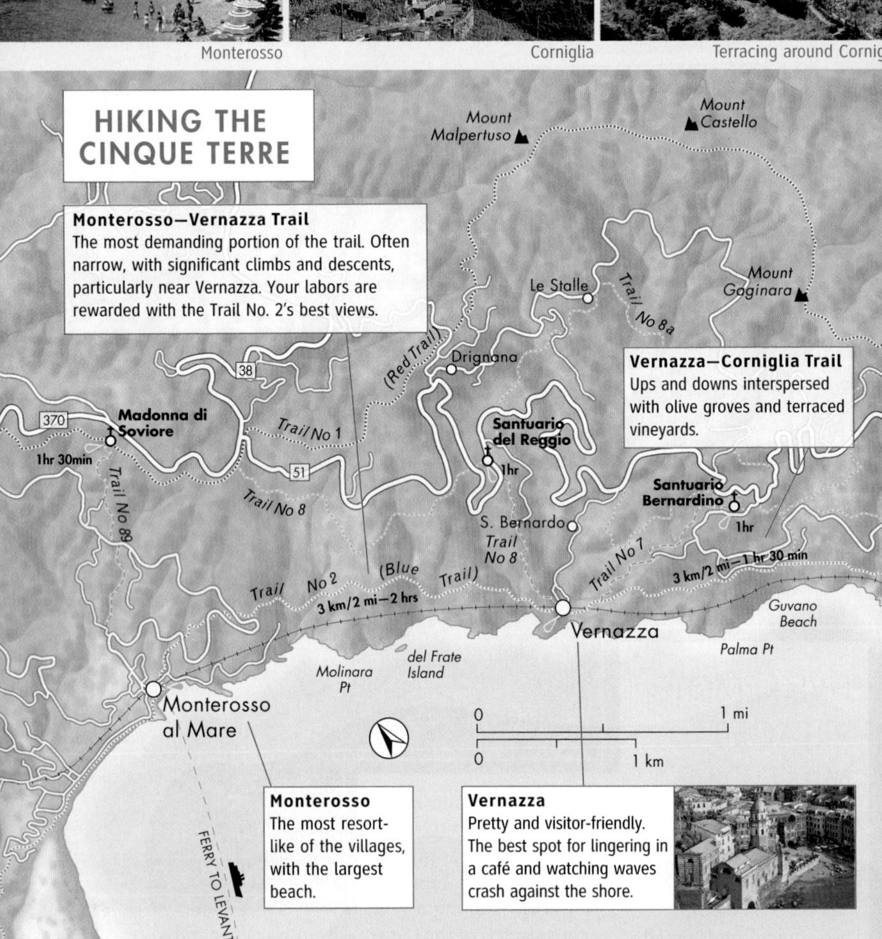

THE CLASSIC HIKE

Hiking is the most popular way to experience the Cinque Terre, and Trail No. 2, the Sentiero Azzurro (Blue Trail), is the most traveled path. To cover the entire trail is a full day: it's approximately 13 km (8 mi) in length, takes you to all five villages, and requires about five hours, not including stops, to complete. The best approach is to start at the easternmost town of Riomaggiore and warm up your legs on the easiest segment of the trail. As you work your way west, the hike gets progressively more demanding. For a less strenuous experience, you can choose to skip a leg or two and take the ferry (which provides its own beautiful views) or the inland train running between the towns instead.

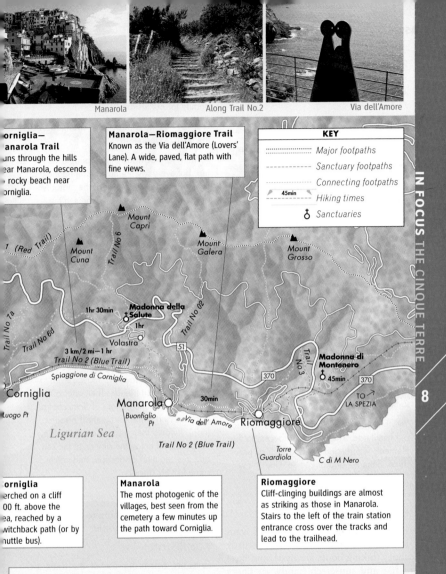

Manarola

Along Trail No.2

Via dell'Amore

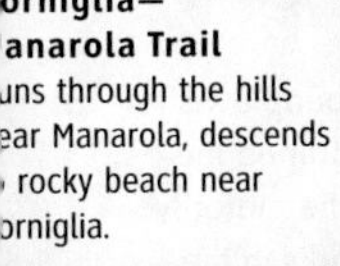

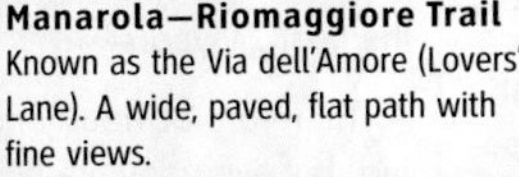

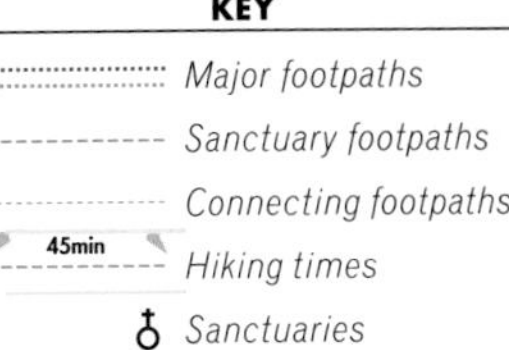

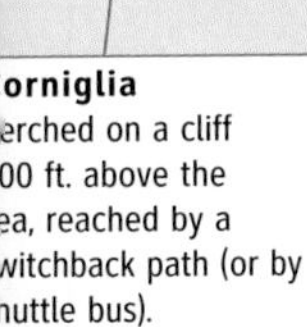

BEYOND TRAIL NO.2

Trail No. 2 is just one of a network of trails crisscrossing the hills. If you're a dedicated hiker, spend a few nights and try some of the other routes. Trail No. 1, the Sentiero Rosso (Red Trail), climbs from Portovenere (east of Riomaggiore) and returns to the sea at Levanto (west of Monterosso al Mare). To hike its length takes from 9 to 12 hours; the ridge-top trail provides spectacular views from high above the villages, each of which can be reached via a steep path. Other shorter trails go from the villages up into the hills, some leading to religious sanctuaries. Trail No. 9, for example, starts from the old section of Monterosso and ends at the Madonna di Soviore Sanctuary.

FODOR'S FIRST PERSON

Angelo Benvenuto
Fisherman,
Monterosso al Mare

Angelo Benvenuto is a 10th-generation fisherman from Monterosso who organizes special boating excursions along the Cinque Terre in his *lampara* (wooden anchovy fishing boat).

Q: Although hiking the Cinque Terre has become a favorite with travelers, you and others maintain that the "way of life" in the Cinque Terre is really that of the sea. . . .

A: For nearly one thousand years Monterosso has been a fishing village. We eat, live, and breathe the sea. In fact, when the barbarians invaded Italy during the middle ages, they did not come down to Monterosso because they were afraid of the sea. Because of this Monterosso as well as the other villages were protected and untouched. Everyday life is always connected to the sea.

Yet, the *sentiri* (trails) were also essential to our livelihood. They provided access to the elements we needed on land such as produce, animals, and of course wine! Now they are a source of entertainment and beauty for our visitors.

Q: How has the Cinque Terre changed over the past 20 years?

A: There are obviously more people visiting, but everyday life has remained the same. I still go out to fish for the majority of our meals, and my wife works in the garden to provide us with fresh vegetables, fruit, even eggs. It is this way for most of the Cinque Terre.

Of course, many of us have gone into the tourism business—hotels, restaurants, cafes. The tourists have brought us opportunity and some financial stability which is very good for us, for all of the villages.

Q: What is your perfect day in the Cinque Terre?

A: Take a hike up to the garden (located on the slopes above town) or maybe even to Vernazza to visit friends. Then after a nice fresh seafood lunch, glass of *Sciacchetra'* (local dessert wine) and a short *pisolino* (nap), I would then head out to sea on my lampara and enjoy the silence of the sea and the beautiful landscape, and catch some fish for dinner!

PRECAUTIONS

If you're hitting the trails, you'll want to carry water with you, wear sturdy shoes (hiking boots are best), and have a hat and sunscreen handy. ⚠ **Check weather reports before you start out; especially in late fall and winter, thunderstorms can send townspeople running for cover and make the shelterless trails slippery and dangerous. Rain in October and November can cause landslides and close the trails.** Note that the lesser-used trails aren't as well maintained as Trail No. 2. If you're undertaking the full Trail No. 1 hike, bring something to snack on as well as your water bottle.

ADMISSION

Entrance tickets for use of the trails are available at ticket booths located at the start of each section of Trail No. 2, and at information offices in the Levanto, Monterosso, Vernazza, Corniglia, Manarola, Riomaggiore, and La Spezia train stations.

A one-day pass costs €5, which includes a trail map and a general information leaflet. Information about local train and boat schedules is also available from the information offices.

Working Cinque Terre's vertical vineyards

GETTING HERE AND AROUND

The local train on the Genoa–La Spezia line stops at each of the Cinque Terre, and runs approximately every 30 minutes. Tickets for each leg of the journey (€1.30) are available at the five train stations. In Corniglia, the only one of the Cinque Terre that isn't at sea level, a shuttle service (€1) is provided for those who don't wish to climb (or descend) the hundred-or-so steps that link the train station with the cliff-top town.

Along the Cinque Terre coast two ferry lines operate. From June to September, Golfo Paradiso runs from Genoa and Camogli to Monterosso al Mare and Vernazza. The smaller, but more frequent, Golfo dei Poeti stops at each village from Lerici (east of Riomaggiore) to Monterosso, with the exception of Corniglia, four times a day. A one-day ticket costs €22.

WHEN TO GO

The ideal times to see the Cinque Terre are September and May, when the weather is mild and the summer tourist season isn't in full swing.

SWIMMING & BEACHES

Each town has something that passes for a beach, but there are only two options where you'll find both sand and decent swimming. The more accessible is in Monterosso, opposite the train station; it's equipped with chairs, umbrellas, and snack bars. The other is the secluded, swimwear-optional Guvano Beach, between Corniglia and Vernazza. To reach it from the Corniglia train station, bypass the steps leading up to the village, instead following signs to an abandoned train tunnel. Ring a bell at the tunnel's entrance, and the gate will automatically open; after a dimly lit 10-minute walk, you'll emerge at the beach. Both beaches have a nominal admission fee.

Monterosso al Mare

THE TOWNS

Riomaggiore

At the eastern end of the Cinque Terre, Riomaggiore is built into a river gorge (thus the name, which means "river major") and is easily accessible from La Spezia by train or car. It has a tiny harbor protected by large slabs of alabaster and marble, which serve as as tanning beds for sunbathers, as well as being the site of several outdoor cafes with fine views. According to legend, settlement of Riomaggiore dates far back to the 8th century, when Greek religious refugees came here to escape persecution by the Byzantine emperor.

Manarola

The enchanting pastel houses of Manarola spill down a steep hill overlooking a spectacular turquoise swimming cove and a bustling harbor. The whole town is built on black rock. Above the town, ancient terraces still protect abundant vineyards and olive trees. This village is the center of the wine and olive oil production of the region, and its streets are lined with shops selling local products.

Corniglia

The buildings, narrow lanes, and stairways of Corniglia are strung together amid vineyards high on the cliffs; on a clear day views of the entire coastal strip are excellent. The high perch and lack of harbor make this farming community the most remote of the Cinque Terre. On a pretty pastel square sits the 14th-century church of **San Pietro.** The rose window of marble imported from Carrara is impressive, particularly considering the work required to get it here. ✉ *Main Sq.* ☎ *0187/3235582* ⏲ *Wed. 4–6, Sun. 10–noon.*

Vernazza

With its narrow streets and small squares, Vernazza is arguably the most charming of the five towns. Because it has the best access to the sea, it became wealthier than its neighbors—as evidenced by the elaborate arcades, loggias, and marblework. The village's pink, slate-roof houses and colorful squares contrast with the remains of the medieval fort and castle, including two towers, in the old town. The Romans first inhabited this rocky spit of land in the 1st century.

Today Vernazza has a fairly lively social scene. It's a great place to refuel with a hearty seafood lunch or linger in a café between links of the hike on Trail No. 2.

Monterosso al Mare

Beautiful beaches, rugged cliffs, crystal-clear turquoise waters, and plentiful small hotels and restaurants make Monterosso al Mare, the largest of the Cinque Terre villages (population 1,730), the busiest in midsummer. The village center bustles high on a hillside. Below, connected by stone steps, are the port and seaside promenade, where there are boats for hire. The medieval tower, Aurora, on the hills of the Cappuccini, separates the ancient part of the village from the more modern part. The village is encircled by hills covered with vineyards and olive groves, and by a forest of scrubby bushes and small trees.

Monterosso has the most festivals of the five villages, starting with the Lemon Feast on the Saturday preceding Ascension Sunday, followed by the Flower Festival of Corpus Christi, celebrated yearly on the second Sunday after Pentecost. During the afternoon, the streets and alleyways of the *centro storico* (historic center) are decorated with thousands of colorful flower petals set in beautiful designs that the evening procession passes over. Finally, the Salted Anchovy and Olive Oil Festival takes place each year during the second weekend of September.

Thursday, the **market** attracts mingled crowds of tourists and villagers from along the coast to shop for everything from pots and pans and underwear to fruits, vegetables, and fish. Often a few stands sell local art and crafts as well as olive oil and wine. ✉ *Old town center* ⏲ *Thurs. 8–1.*

The **Chiesa di San Francesco,** was built in the 12th century in the Ligurian Gothic style. Its distinctive black stripes and marble rose window make it one of the most photographed sites in the Cinque Terre. ✉ *Piazza Garibaldi* ☎ *No phone* 🎫 *Free* ⏲ *Daily 9–1 and 4–7.*

Main Square, Vernazza

WHERE TO EAT AND STAY

From June through September, reservations are essential if you plan to stay in a hotel or B&B here. *Affitacamere* (rooms for rent in private homes) are a more modest alternative, often indicated by a simple sign on the front door. At agencies in Riomaggiore and Monterosso you can book officially licensed affitacamere. Rooms run the gamut; arrive early for a good selection.

Riomaggiore

$$–$$$ ✕ La Lanterna. Chalkboards in front of this small trattoria by the harbor list the day's selection of fresh fish; the set-up seems modest, but this is arguably the finest restaurant in the Cinque Terre. In winter, Chef Massimo teaches at the Culinary Academy in Switzerland; he always returns with new ideas for his menu. When available, *cozze ripiene* (stuffed mussels) shouldn't be missed. Other offerings may be a touch exotic, such sting ray with ligurian herbs. ✉ *Via San Giacomo* 10 ☎ 0187/920589 ⊙ *Closed Jan and 2 wks in Nov.*

Manarola

$$$ 🏨 La Torretta. A welcome retreat after a day of exploring, this boutique accommodation has well-appointed rooms, most with sea views. The hotel has many nice touches such as a free aperitivo (aperitif) at sunset, a solarium, and iPod docking stations. **Pros:** head and shoulders above most accommodations in the area; lovely views. **Cons:** five- to ten-minute walk to the reception. ✉ *Via Volto 20, 19017* ☎ *0187/920327* 🖷 *0187/920678* 🌐 *www.torrettas.com* *4 rooms, 5 suites* *In-room: a/c (some), Wi-Fi. In-hotel: bar* ⊙ *Closed Nov.–mid-Mar.* 🍽 *Breakfast.*

Corniglia

$–$$ 🏨 Cecio. On the outskirts of Corniglia, many of the spotless rooms at the family-run Cecio have spectacular views of the town. The same memorable vista can be enjoyed from the hotel's restaurant, which serves inexpensive and well-prepared local seafood dishes. Try the delicious lasagna with pesto sauce as a first course. ✉ *Via Serra 58, 19010, toward Vernazza* ☎ *0187/812043* 🖷 *0187/812138* *12 rooms* *In-room: no a/c, no TV (some). In-hotel: restaurant* 🍽 *Breakfast.*

Vernazza

$$$ ✕ Bel Forte. High above the sea in one of Vernazza's remaining stone towers is this unique restaurant serving typical Cinque Terre dishes. The prices are high, but it's worth it. People come from all over Liguria for Bel Forte's famous stuffed mussels and insalata di polpo (octopus salad). The setting is magnificent. ✉ *Via Guidoni 42* ☎ *0187/812222* ⊙ *Closed Tues. and Nov.–Easter.*

$$–$$$ ✕ Gambero Rosso. Relax on Vernazza's main square at this fine trattoria looking out at a church. Enjoy such delectable dishes as shrimp salad, vegetable torte, and squid-ink risotto. The creamy pesto, served atop spaghetti, is some of the best in the area. End your meal with Cinque Terre's own *sciacchetrà,* a dessert wine served with semisweet biscotti. Don't drink it out of the glass—dip the biscotti in the wine instead. ✉ *Piazza Marconi 7* ☎ *0187/812265* ⏲ *Closed Mon. Jan. and Feb.*

$$$ La Malà. A cut above other lodging options in the Cinque Terre, this family-run B&B has only four rooms, and they fill up quickly. The rooms are small but well equipped, with flat screen TVs, a/c, marble showers, and comfortable bedding. Two of the rooms have sea views; the other two face the port of Vernazza. There's a shared terrace literally suspended over the Mediterranean. Book early! ✉ *Giovanni Battista 29, 19018* ☎ *334/2875718* 🌐 *www.lamala.it* *4 rooms* *In-room: a/c* ⏲ *Closed Jan. 10–Mar.* *Breakfast.*

Monterosso al Mare

★ $$$ ✕ Miky. Specialties here are anything involving seafood. The *insalata di mare* (seafood salad), with squid and fish, is more than tasty; so are the grilled fish and any pasta with seafood. Miky has a beautiful little garden in the back, perfect for lunch on a sunny day. ✉ *Via Fegina 104* ☎ *0187/817608* ⏲ *Closed Nov. and Dec., and Tues. Sept.–July.*

$ ✕ Enoteca Internazionale. Located on the main street in centro, this wine bar offers a large variety of vintages, both local from further afield, plus delicious light fare; its umbrella-covered patio is a perfect spot to recuperate after a day of hiking. The owner, Susanna, is a certified sommelier who's always forthcoming with helpful suggestions on local wines. ✉ *Via Roma 62* ☎ *0187/817278* ⏲ *Closed Tues., Jan–Mar.*

$$ Il Giardino Incantato. This small B&B in the historic center of Monterosso oozes comfort and old-world charm. The building dates back to the 16th century and still maintains its wood beam ceiling and stone walls. Each room has been impeccably restored with modern amenities. Breakfast is served either in your room on request or in their lovely private garden under the lemon trees. The owner, Maria Pia, goes out of her way to make you feel at home and whips up a fabulous frittata for breakfast. ✉ *Via Mazzini 18, 19016* ☎ *0185/818315* 🌐 *www.ilgiardinoincantato.net* *3 rooms, 1 junior suite* *Breakfast.*

$$$ Porto Roca. The Cinque Terre's only "high-end" hotel is perched on the famous terraced cliffs, hovering over the magnificent sea below, and thankfully removed from the crowds. The hotel has an old-fashioned feel but the large balconies and panoramic views make it all worth it. There is also a nice restaurant serving very good Ligurian cuisine. Avoid the back rooms as they are dark and have no view. Pros: unobstructed sea views; tranquil position. Cons: some of the rooms could use updating; back-facing rooms can be a bit dark. ✉ *Via Carrone 1, 19016* ☎ *0187/817502* 🌐 *www.portoroca.it* *40 rooms* *In-room: a/c (some). In-hotel: restaurant, bar, spa* *Breakfast.*

SANTA MARGHERITA LIGURE

60 km (37 mi) northwest of Levanto, 31 km (19 mi) southeast of Genoa.

GETTING HERE

By car, take the Rapallo exit off the A12 and follow the blue signs, about a 10-minute drive. The Santa Margherita Ligure train station is on the main north–south line between Genoa and Pisa.

VISITOR INFORMATION

Santa Margherita Ligure tourism office (✉ *Via XXV Aprile 2/B* ☎ *0185/287485* 🌐 *www.apttigullio.liguria.it*).

EXPLORING

A beautiful old resort town favored by well-to-do Italians, Santa Margherita Ligure has everything a Riviera playground should have—plenty of palm trees and attractive hotels, cafés, and a marina packed with yachts. Some of the older buildings here are still decorated on the outside with the trompe-l'oeil frescoes typical of this part of the Riviera. This is a pleasant, convenient base, which for many represents a perfect balance on the Italian Riviera: more spacious than the Cinque Terre; less glitzy than San Remo; more relaxing than Genoa and environs; and ideally situated for day trips, such as an excursion to Portofino.

WHERE TO EAT

$$–$$$ LIGURIAN

✕ **La Paranza.** From the piles of tiny *bianchetti* (young sardines) in oil and lemon that are part of the antipasto *di mare* (of the sea) to the simple, perfectly grilled whole sole, fresh seafood in every shape and form is the specialty here. Mussels, clams, octopus, salmon, or whatever else is fresh that day is what's on the menu. Locals say this is the town's best restaurant, but if you're looking for a stylish evening out, look elsewhere—La Paranza is about food, not fashion. It's just off Santa Margherita's port. ✉ *Via Jacopo Ruffini 46* ☎ *0185/283686* ✍ *Reservations essential* ⊗ *Closed Mon. and Nov.*

$$$ LIGURIAN Fodor's Choice ★

✕ **La Stalla dei Frati.** The breathtaking hilltop views of Santa Margherita from this villa-turned-restaurant are worth the harrowing 3-km (2-mi) drive northwest to get here from Santa Margherita's port. Cesare Frati, your congenial host, is likely to tempt you with his homemade fettuccine *ai frutti di mare* (with seafood) followed by the *pescato del giorno alla moda ligure* (catch of the day baked Ligurian style, with potatoes, olives, and pine nuts) and a delightfully fresh lemon sorbet to complete the feast. ✉ *Via G. Pino 27, Nozarego* ☎ *0185/289447* ⊗ *Closed Mon. and Nov.*

$$$–$$$$ INTERNATIONAL ★

✕ **Oca Bianca.** The menu at this small, excellent restaurant breaks away from the local norm—there is no seafood on offer. Meat dishes are the specialty, and choices may include mouthwatering preparations of lamb from France or New Zealand, steak from Ireland or Brazil, South African ostrich, and Italian pork. Delicious antipasti, an extensive wine list, and the attentive service add to the experience. Dinner is served until 1 am. ✉ *Via XXV Aprile 21* ☎ *0185/288411* ✍ *Reservations essential* ⊗ *Closed Mon. and Jan.–mid-Feb. No lunch Tues.–Thurs. Sept.–Dec.*

$$–$$$ LIGURIAN Fodor's Choice ★ ✕ **U' Giancu.** Owner Fausto Oneto is a man of many hats. Though original cartoons cover the walls of his restaurant and a playground is the main feature of the outdoor seating area, Fausto is completely serious about his cooking. Lamb dishes are particularly delicious, his own garden provides the freshest possible vegetables, and the wine list (ask to visit the cantina) is excellent. For those who want to learn the secrets of Ligurian cuisine, Fausto provides lively morning cooking lessons. U' Giancu is 8 km (5 mi) northwest of Santa Margherita Ligure. ✉ *Via San Massimo 78, Località San Massimo, Rapallo* ☎ *0185/261212* 🌐 *www.ugiancu.it* ⊗ *Closed Wed. and mid-Dec.–early Jan. No lunch.*

WORD OF MOUTH

"Portofino is a beautiful site. I wouldn't miss a hike to Castello Brown or the scenic path to the lighthouse at Punta da Capo. Both offer lovely and very photogenic views."

—waggis

WHERE TO STAY

$$–$$$ **Continental.** Built in the early 1900s, this stately seaside mansion with a columned portico stands in a lush garden shaded by tall palms and pine trees. **Pros:** lovely location; private beach. **Cons:** rooms in the annex are not as nice as those in the main building; breakfast is unimaginative. **TripAdvisor:** "nicest place in town," "wonderful panoramic view," "gym was excellent." ✉ *Via Pagana 8* ☎ *0185/286512* 🌐 *www.hotel-continental.it* *70 rooms, 4 suites* *In-room: safe, refrigerator, Wi-Fi. In-hotel: restaurant, bar, Wi-Fi hotspot, parking (paid), some pets allowed* *Breakfast.*

$$$$ ★ **Grand Hotel Miramare.** Classic Riviera elegance prevails at this palatial hotel overlooking the bay south of the town center. **Pros:** top-notch service; private beach; well-maintained rooms. **Cons:** unfinished parking structure can be an eyesore from some rooms and create some noise in low- and mid-season (construction stops May to September); traffic in summer from the road in front of the hotel. **TripAdvisor:** "charm, charm and more charm," "swimming pool is divine," "quite formal and old-fashioned." ✉ *Via Milite Ignoto 30* ☎ *0185/287013* 🌐 *www.grandhotelmiramare.it* *75 rooms, 9 suites* *In-room: safe, refrigerator, Internet. In-hotel: 2 restaurants, bars, pool, beachfront, Internet terminal, some pets allowed* *Breakfast.*

$$ **Hotel Jolanda.** It may not have a sea view, but the Jolanda is stylish and comfortable. **Pros:** reasonable rates in a high-price area. **Cons:** no sea view; parking is limited and expensive. **TripAdvisor:** "strolling distance of the waterfront," "astounded at the level of service," "new spa and fitness area." ✉ *Via Luisito Costa 6* ☎ *0185/287512* 🌐 *www.hoteljolanda.it* *47 rooms, 3 suites* *In-room: safe, refrigerator, Wi-Fi. In-hotel: restaurant, bar, gym, Wi-Fi hotspot, parking (paid)* *Breakfast.*

8

PORTOFINO

★ *5 km (3 mi) south of Santa Margherita Ligure, 36 km (22 mi) east of Genoa.*

GETTING HERE

By car, exit at Rapallo off the A12 and follow the blue signs (about a 20-minute drive mostly along the coast). The nearest train station is Santa Margherita Ligure.

Trying to reach Portofino by bus or car on the single narrow road can be a nightmare in summer and on holiday weekends. No trains go directly to Portofino: you must stop at Santa Margherita and take the Number 82 public bus from there (€1). An alternative is to take a boat from Santa Margherita.

Portofino can also be reached from Santa Margherita on foot: it's about a 40-minute (very nice) walk along the sea.

VISITOR INFORMATION

Portofino tourism office (✉ *Via Roma 35* ☎ *0185/269024* 🌐 *www.apttigullio.liguria.it*).

EXPLORING

One of the most photographed villages along the coast, with a decidedly romantic and affluent aura, Portofino has long been a popular destination for the rich and famous. Once an ancient Roman colony and taken by the Republic of Genoa in 1229, it has also been ruled by the French, English, Spanish, and Austrians, as well as by marauding bands of 16th-century pirates. Elite British tourists first flocked to the lush harbor in the mid-1800s. Some of Europe's wealthiest lay anchor in Portofino in summer, but they stay out of sight by day, appearing in the evening after buses and boats have carried off the day-trippers.

There's not actually much to *do* in Portofino other than stroll around the wee harbor, see the castle, walk to Punta del Capo, browse at the pricey boutiques, and sip a coffee while people-watching. However, weaving through picture-perfect cliff-side gardens and gazing at yachts framed by the turquoise Ligurian Sea and the cliffs of Santa Margherita can make for quite a relaxing afternoon. There are also several tame, photo-friendly hikes into the hills to nearby villages.

Unless you're traveling on a deluxe budget, you may want to stay in Camogli or Santa Margherita Ligure rather than at one of Portofino's few very expensive hotels. Restaurants and cafés are good but also pricey (don't expect to have a beer here for much under €10).

From the harbor, follow the signs for the climb to the **Castello di San Giorgio**, the most worthwhile sight in Portofino, with its medieval relics, impeccable gardens, and sweeping views. The castle was founded in the Middle Ages but restored in the 16th through 18th centuries. In true Portofino form, it was owned by Genoa's English consul from 1870 until it opened to the public in 1961. ✉ *Above harbor* ☎ *0185/269046* 🎫 *€3* 🕙 *Apr.–Sept., Wed.–Mon. 10–6; Oct.–Mar., Wed.–Mon. 10–5.*

The small church **San Giorgio**, sitting on a ridge, was rebuilt four times during World War II. It is said to contain the relics of its namesake, brought back from the Holy Land by the Crusaders. Portofino enthusiastically celebrates Saint George's Day every April 23. ✉ *Above harbor* ☎ *0185/269337* ⏲ *Daily 7–6.*

Pristine views can be had from the deteriorating *faro* (lighthouse) at **Punta Portofino**, a 15-minute walk along the point that begins at the southern end of the port. Along the seaside path you can see numerous impressive, sprawling private residences behind high iron gates.

The only sand beach near Portofino is at **Paraggi**, a cove on the road between Santa Margherita and Portofino. The bus will stop here on request.

On the sea at the foot of Monte Portofino, the medieval **Abbazia di San Fruttuoso** *(Abbey of San Fruttuoso)*, built by the Benedictines of Monte Cassino, protects a minuscule fishing village that can be reached only on foot or by water—a 20-minute boat ride from Portofino and also reachable from Camogli, Santa Margherita Ligure, and Rapallo. The restored abbey is now the property of a national conservation fund (FAI) and occasionally hosts temporary exhibitions. The church contains the tombs of some illustrious members of the Doria family. The old abbey and its grounds are delightful places to spend a few hours, perhaps lunching at one of the modest beachfront trattorias nearby (open only in summer). Boatloads of visitors can make it very crowded very fast; you might appreciate it most off-season. ✉ *15-min boat ride or 2-hr walk northwest of Portofino* ☎ *0185/772703* *€7 Apr.–Sept., €5 Oct.–Mar.* ⏲ *Mar., Apr., and Oct., Tues.–Sun. 10–3:45; May–Sept., daily 10:45–6; Nov.–Feb., Tues.–Sun. 10–3:45. Last entry 45 mins before closing.*

WHERE TO EAT

¢ BAKERY **Canale.** If the staggering prices of virtually all of Portofino's restaurants put you off, the long line outside this family-run bakery indicates that you're not alone and that something special is in store. Here all the focaccia is baked on the spot and served fresh from the oven, along with all kinds of sandwiches, pastries, and other refreshments. The only problem is there's nowhere to sit—time for a picnic! ✉ *Via Roma 30* ☎ *0185/269248* *No credit cards* ⏲ *Closed Nov.–Feb.*

$$$ LIGURIAN **Ristorante Puny.** A table at this tiny restaurant is difficult to come by in summer, as the manager caters mostly to friends and regulars. If you are lucky enough to get in, however, the food will not disappoint you, nor will the cozy but elegant yellow interior. The unforgettable *pappardelle* (large, flat noodles) *al portofino* delicately blends two of Liguria's tastes: tomato and pesto. Ligurian seafood specialties include baked fish with bay leaves, potatoes, and olives as well as the inventive *moscardini al forno* (baked mini-octopus with lemon and rosemary in tomato sauce). ✉ *Piazza Martiri dell'Olivetta 4–5, on harbor* ☎ *0185/269037* *Reservations essential* ⏲ *Closed Thurs. and Jan. and Feb.*

WHERE TO STAY

$$$$ **San Giorgio.** If you decide to stay in Portofino, this is perhaps your best choice. **Pros:** luxurious accommodations in the middle of the village; secluded garden at the back. **Cons:** some of the lower-level rooms do not receive much light. **TripAdvisor:** "room was lovely - very modern," "accept that everything is expensive," "walking distance to the port."

8

✉ *Via Del Fondaco 11* ☎ *0185/26991* 🌐 *www.portofinohsg.it* *17 rooms, 1 suite* *In-room: safe, refrigerator, Internet. In-hotel: bar, Internet terminal, some pets allowed* *Closed Dec.–Feb.* *Breakfast.*

$$$$ **Splendido.** Arriving at this 1920s luxury hotel is so much like entering a Jazz Age film set that you'd almost expect to see a Bugatti or Daimler roll up the winding drive from the seaside below. **Pros:** gorgeous rooms; caring staff; lovely views. **Cons:** be prepared to spend upward of €100 for a simple lunch for two (it's not just the rooms that are pricey). **TripAdvisor:** "old-world elegance," "genuine caring for the guests," "manicured lawns and gardens." ✉ *Salita Baratta 16* ☎ *0185/267801* 🌐 *www.hotelsplendido.com* *31 rooms, 34 suites* *In-room: safe, refrigerator, Wi-Fi. In-hotel: restaurant, bars, tennis court, pool, gym, Wi-Fi hotspot, parking (paid), some pets allowed* *Closed mid-Nov.–late Mar.* *MAP.*

SPORTS AND THE OUTDOORS

HIKING

If you have the stamina, you can hike to the Abbazia di San Fruttuoso from Portofino. It's a steep climb at first, and the walk takes about 2½ hours one-way. If you're extremely ambitious and want to make a day of it, you can hike another 2½ hours all the way to Camogli. Much more modest hikes from Portofino include a 1-hour uphill walk to Cappella delle Gave, a bit inland in the hills, from where you can continue downhill to Santa Margherita Ligure (another 1½ hours) and a gently undulating paved trail leading to the beach at Paraggi (½ hour). Finally, there's a 2½-hour hike from Portofino that heads farther inland to Ruta, through Olmi and Pietre Strette. The trails are well marked and maps are available at the tourist information offices in Rapallo, Santa Margherita, Portofino, and Camogli.

CAMOGLI

★ *15 km (9 mi) northwest of Portofino, 20 km (12 mi) east of Genoa.*

GETTING HERE

By car, exit the A12 at Recco and follow the blue signs. There are several pay-parking lots near the village center. Camogli is on the main north–south railway line between Genoa and La Spezia.

VISITOR INFORMATION

Camogli tourism office (✉ *Via XX Settembre 33/R* ☎ *0185/771066* 🌐 *www.camogli.it*).

EXPLORING

Camogli, at the edge of the large promontory and nature reserve known as the Portofino Peninsula, has always been a town of sailors. By the 19th century it was leasing its ships throughout the continent. Today multicolor houses, remarkably deceptive trompe-l'oeil frescoes, and a massive 17th-century seawall mark this appealing harbor community, perhaps as beautiful as Portofino but without the glamour. When exploring on foot, don't miss the boat-filled second harbor, which is reached by ducking under a narrow archway at the northern end of the first one.

The Castello Dragone, built onto the sheer rock face near the harbor, is home to the **Acquario** *(Aquarium)*, which has tanks filled with local marine life built into the ramparts. ✉ *Via Isola* ☎ *0185/773375* 🎟 *€3* ⏲ *May–Sept., daily 10–noon and 3–7; Oct.–Apr., Fri.–Sun. 10–noon and 2:30–6, Tues.–Thurs. 10–noon.*

OFF THE BEATEN PATH

Ruta. The footpaths that leave from Ruta, 4 km (2½ mi) east of Camogli, thread through rugged terrain and contain a multitude of plant species. Weary hikers are sustained by stunning views of the Riviera di Levante from the various vantage points along the way.

WHERE TO EAT AND STAY

$$ LIGURIAN

✕ **Vento Ariel.** This small, friendly restaurant serves some of the best seafood in town. Dine on the shaded terrace in summer months and watch the bustling activity in the nearby port. Only the freshest of seafood is served; try the spaghetti *alle vongole* (with clams) or the mixed grilled fish. ✉ *Calata Porto* ☎ *0185/771080* ⏲ *Closed Wed., 1st half of Dec., and Jan.*

$$$–$$$$ ★

Cenobio dei Dogi. Perched majestically a step above Camogli, overlooking harbor, peninsula, and sea, this is indisputably the best address in town. **Pros:** location and setting are wonderful. **Cons:** crowds make it seem overbooked in summer; decor is a bit old-fashioned. **TripAdvisor:** "dramatic, beautiful, romantic," "pool with a beautiful view," "service people are not friendly." ✉ *Via Cuneo 34* ☎ *0185/7241* 🌐 *www.cenobio.it* *102 rooms, 4 suites* *In-room: safe, refrigerator, Wi-Fi. In-hotel: restaurant, bar, tennis court, pool, gym, beachfront, Wi-Fi hotspot* 🍴 *Breakfast.*

$$–$$$

Villa Rosmarino. This small boutique hotel is a recent addition to the beautiful Camogliese hillside. **Pros:** large beds; well-equipped bathrooms; total sense of relaxation. **Cons:** rooms are small and may not have enough amenities for everyone's taste. **TripAdvisor:** "modern Italian design," "views of the Mediterranean," "pool was beautiful." ✉ *Via Figari 38* ☎ *0185/771580* 🌐 *www.villarosmarino.com* *6 rooms* *In-room: no a/c, no TV, Wi-Fi. In-hotel: Wi-Fi hotspot, parking (free), no kids under 8* 🍴 *Breakfast.*

NIGHTLIFE AND THE ARTS

★ **Sagra del Pesce,** the highlight of the festival of San Fortunato, is held on the second Sunday of May each year. It's a crowded, festive, and free-to-the-public feast of freshly caught fish, cooked outside at the port in a frying pan 12 feet wide.

8

GENOA

GETTING HERE

By car, take the Genoa Ovest exit off the A12 and take the upper bridge (*sopralevata*) to the second exit, Genova Centro–Piazza Corvetto. But be forewarned: driving in Genoa is harrowing and is best avoided whenever possible—if you want to see the city on a day trip, go by train; if you're staying in the city, park in a garage or by valet and go by foot and by taxi throughout your stay.

Regular train service operates from Genoa's two stations. Departures from **Stazione Principe** (✉ *Piazza del Principe, San Teodoro*) travel to points west. Departures from **Stazione Brignole** (✉ *Piazza Giuseppe Verdi, Foce* ☎ *892021*) go to points east and south. All the coastal resorts are on this line.

VISITOR INFORMATION

The Terminal Crociere tourist office is closed October–April.

Genoa tourism offices (✉ *Palazzo delle Torrette, Via Garibaldi 12r, Maddalena* ☎ *010/5572903* ✉ *Aeroporto Internazionale Cristoforo Colombo, Ponente* ☎ *010/6015247* ✉ *Via Roma 11* ☎ *010/576791* ✉ *Terminale Crociere, Ponte dei Mille* ☎ *No phone* 🌐 *www.apt.genova.it*).

EXPLORING

Genoa (Genova in Italian) was the birthplace of Christopher Columbus, but the city's proud history predates that explorer by hundreds of years. Genoa was already an important trading station by the 3rd century BC, when the Romans conquered Liguria. The Middle Ages and the Renaissance saw it rise into a jumping-off place for the Crusaders, a commercial center of tremendous wealth and prestige, and a strategic bone of international contention. A network of fortresses defending the city connected by a wall second only in length to the Great Wall of China was constructed in the hills above, and Genoa's bankers, merchants, and princes adorned the city with palaces, churches, and impressive art collections.

Known as *La Superba* (The Proud), Genoa was a great maritime power in the 13th century, rivaling Venice and Pisa in strength and splendor. But its luster eventually diminished, and it was outshone by these and other formidable cities. By the 17th century it was no longer a great sea power. It has, however, continued to be a profitable port. Modern container ships now unload at docks that centuries ago served galleons and vessels bound for the spice routes. Genoa is now a busy, sprawling, and cosmopolitan city, apt to break the spell of the coastal towns in a hurry.

Crammed into a thin crescent of land between sea and mountains, Genoa expanded up rather than out, taking on the form of a multilayer wedding cake, with churches, streets, and entire residential neighborhoods built on others' rooftops. Public elevators and funiculars are as common as buses and trains.

But with its impressive palaces and museums, the largest medieval city center in Europe, and an elaborate network of ancient hilltop fortresses, Genoa may be just the dose of culture you are looking for. Europe's biggest boat show, the annual Salone Nautico Internazionale, is held here. Fine restaurants are abundant, and classical dance and music are richly represented; the Teatro Carlo Felice is the local opera venue, and where the internationally renowned annual Niccolò Paganini Violin Contest takes place.

GETTING AROUND GENOA

The best way by far to get around Genoa is on foot, with the occasional assistance of public transportation. Many of the more interesting districts are either entirely closed to traffic, have roads so narrow that no car could fit, or are, even at the best of times, blocked by gridlock. Although it might seem a daunting task, exploring the city is made simple by its geography. The historic center of Genoa occupies a relatively narrow strip of land running between the mountains and the sea. You can easily visit the most important monuments in one or two days.

The main bus station in Genoa is at Piazza Principe. Local buses, operated by the municipal transport company **AMT** (✉ *Piazza Acquaverde* ☎ *010/5582414* 🌐 *www.amt.genova.it*), serve the steep valleys that run to some of the towns along the western coast. Tickets may be bought at local bus stations or at newsstands. (You must have a ticket before you board.) AMT also operates the funicular railways and the elevators that service the steeper sections of the city.

THE MEDIEVAL CORE AND POINTS ABOVE

The medieval center of Genoa, threaded with tiny streets flanked by 11th-century portals, is roughly the area between the port and Piazza de Ferrari. This mazelike pedestrian zone is officially called the Caruggi District, but the Genovese, in their matter-of-fact way, simply refer to the area as the place of the *vicoli* (alleys). In this warren of narrow, cobbled streets extending north from Piazza Caricamento, the city's oldest churches sit among tiny shops selling antique furniture, coffee, cheese, rifles, wine, gilt picture frames, camping gear, and even live fish. The 500-year-old apartment buildings lean so precariously that penthouse balconies nearly touch those across the street, blocking what little sunlight would have shone down onto the cobblestones. Wealthy Genovese built their homes in this quarter in the 16th century, and prosperous guilds, such as the goldsmiths for whom Vico degli Indoratori and Via degli Orefici were named, set up shop here.

8

TOP ATTRACTIONS

★ **Cimitero Monumentale di Staglieno.** One of the most famous of Genovese landmarks is this bizarrely beautiful cemetery; its fanciful marble and bronze sculptures sprawl haphazardly across a hillside on the outskirts of town. A pantheon holds indoor tombs and some remarkable works like an 1878 *Eve* by Villa. Don't miss Rovelli's 1896 **Tomba Raggio,** which shoots Gothic spires out of the hillside forest. The cemetery began operation in 1851 and has been lauded by such visitors as Mark Twain and Evelyn Waugh. It covers a good deal of ground; allow at least half a day to explore. It's difficult to locate; reach it via Bus 480 or 482 from the Stazione Genova Brignole, Bus 34 from Stazione Principe, or a taxi. ✉ *Piazzale Resasco, Piazza Manin* ☎ *010/870184* 🎟 *Free* ⏲ *Daily 7:30–5; last entry at 4:30.*

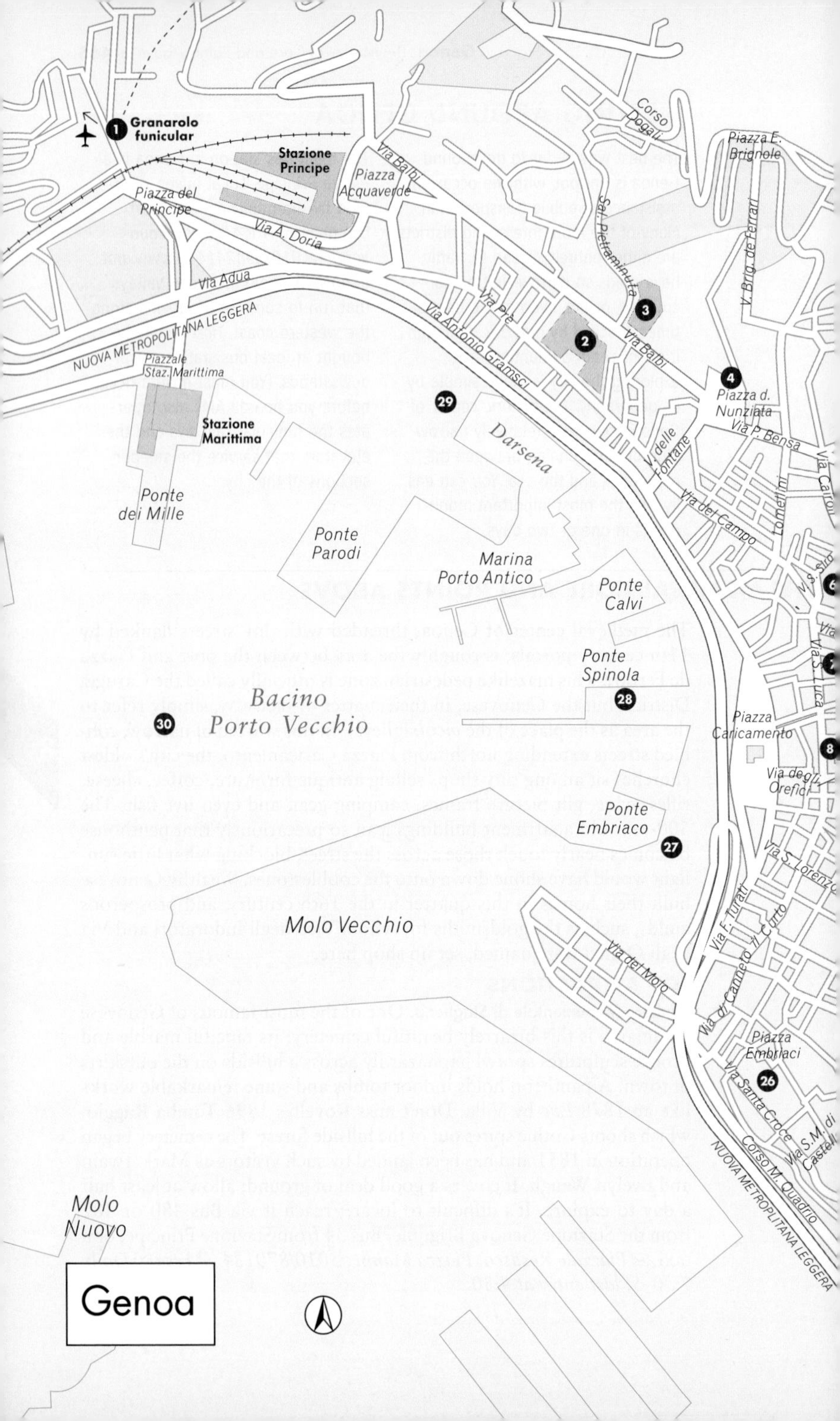

Granarolo funicular
Stazione Principe
Piazza Acquaverde
Piazza del Principe
Via A. Doria
Via Balbi
Corso Dogali
Piazza E. Brignole
Sal. Pietraminuta
V. Brig. de Ferrari
Via Adua
NUOVA METROPOLITANA LEGGERA
Via Prè
Via Antonio Gramsci
Via Balbi
Piazzale Staz. Marittima
Stazione Marittima
Piazza d. Nunziata
Via P. Bensa
Darsena
V. delle Fontane
Via Cairoli
Lomellini
Via del Campo
Ponte dei Mille
Ponte Parodi
Marina Porto Antico
Ponte Calvi
Ponte Spinola
Bacino Porto Vecchio
Piazza Caricamento
Via S. Luca
Via degli Orefici
Ponte Embriaco
Via S. Lorenzo
Molo Vecchio
Via F. Turati
Via del Molo
Via di Canneto il Corto
Piazza Embriaci
Via Santa Croce
Via S.M. di Castello
Corso M. Quadrio
NUOVA METROPLITANA LEGGERA
Molo Nuovo
Genoa
1
2
3
4
8
26
27
28
29
30

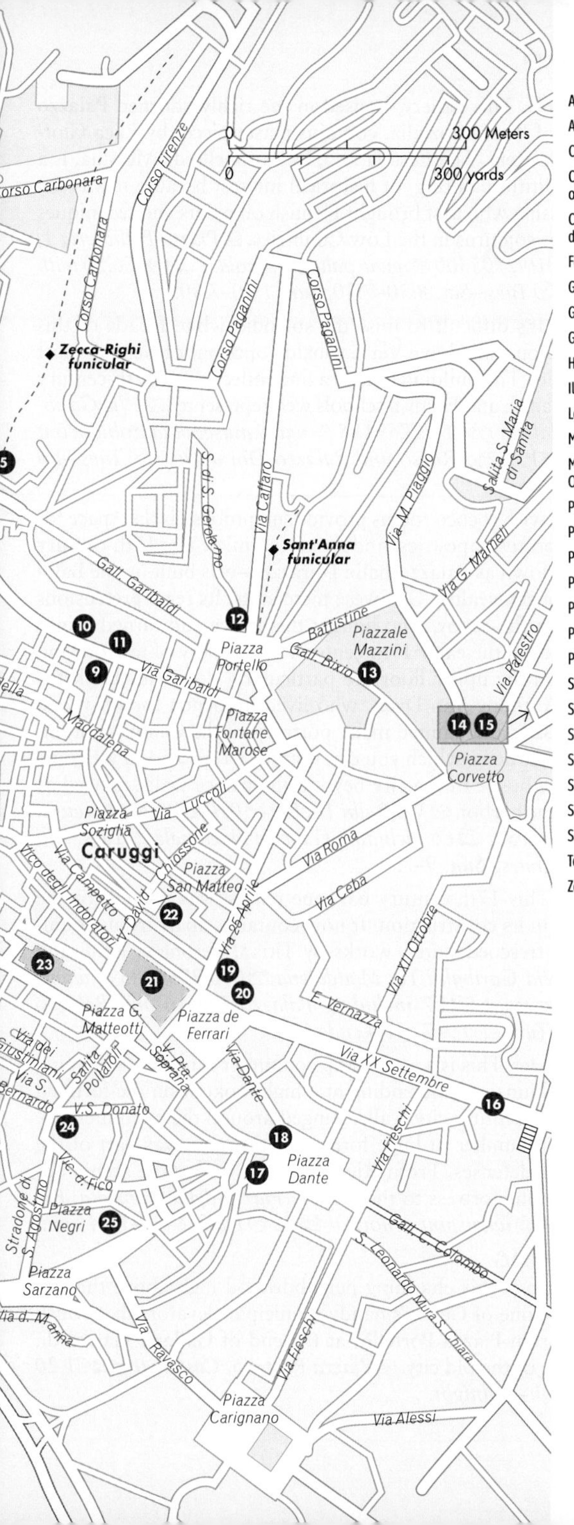

Accademia delle Belle Arti **20**
Acquario di Genova **28**
Castelletto **12**
Childhood home of Christopher Columbus **18**
Cimitero Monumentale di Staglieno **14**
Ferrovia Genova–Casella **15**
Galata Museo del Mare **29**
Galleria Nazionale **7**
Granarolo funicular **1**
Harbor **30**
Il Bigo **27**
Loggia dei Mercanti **8**
Mercato Orientale **16**
Museo d'Arte Orientale Chiossone **13**
Palazzo Bianco **10**
Palazzo dell'Università **3**
Palazzo Doria Tursi **11**
Palazzo Ducale **21**
Palazzo Reale **2**
Palazzo Rosso **9**
Porta Soprana **17**
San Donato **24**
San Lorenzo **23**
San Matteo **22**
San Siro **6**
Sant'Agostino **25**
Santa Maria di Castello **26**
Santissima Annunziata **4**
Teatro Carlo Felice **19**
Zecca-Righi funicular **5**

Galleria Nazionale. This gallery, housed in the richly adorned **Palazzo Spinola** north of Piazza Soziglia, contains masterpieces by Luca Giordano and Guido Reni. The *Ecce Homo,* by Antonello da Messina, is a hauntingly beautiful painting, of historical interest because it was the Sicilian da Messina who first brought Flemish oil paints and techniques to Italy from his sojourns in the Low Countries. ✉ *Piazza Pellicceria 1, Maddalena* ☎ *010/2705300* 🌐 *www.palazzospinola.it* 🎫 *€4, €6.50 with Palazzo Reale* ⏲ *Tues.–Sat. 8:30–7:30, Sun. 1:30–7:30.*

Palazzo Bianco. It's difficult to miss the splendid white facade of this town palace as you walk down Via Garibaldi, once one of Genoa's most important streets. The building houses a fine collection of 17th-century art, with the Spanish and Flemish schools well represented. ✉ *Via Garibaldi 11, Maddalena* ☎ *010/2759185* 🌐 *www.museopalazzobianco.it* 🎫 *€7, includes Palazzo Rosso and Palazzo Doria Tursi* ⏲ *Tues.–Fri 9–7, weekends 10–7.*

Fodor's Choice ★ **Palazzo Reale.** Lavish rococo rooms provide sumptuous display space for paintings, sculptures, tapestries, and Asian ceramics. The 17th-century palace—also known as Palazzo Balbi Durazzo—was built by the Balbi family, enormously wealthy Genovese merchants. Its regal pretensions were not lost on the Savoy, who bought the palace and turned it into a royal residence in the early 19th century. The gallery of mirrors and the ballroom on the upper floor are particularly decadent. Look for works by Sir Anthony Van Dyck, who lived in Genoa for six years, beginning in 1621, and painted many portraits of the Genovese nobility. The formal gardens, which you can visit for €1, provide a welcome respite from the bustle of the city beyond the palace walls, as well as great views of the harbor. ✉ *Via Balbi 10, Pré* ☎ *010/2710236* 🌐 *www.palazzorealegenova.it* 🎫 *€6 including Galleria Nazionale* ⏲ *Tues. and Wed. 9–1:30, Thurs.–Sun. 9–7.*

Palazzo Rosso. This 17th-century baroque palace was named for the red stone used in its construction. It now contains, apart from a number of lavishly frescoed suites, works by Titian, Veronese, Reni, and Van Dyck. ✉ *Via Garibaldi 18, Maddalena* ☎ *010/2759185* 🌐 *www.museopalazzorosso.it* 🎫 *€7 including Palazzo Bianco and Palazzo Doria Tursi* ⏲ *Tues.–Fri 9–7, weekends 10–7.*

Zecca-Righi funicular. This is a seven-stop commuter funicular beginning at Piazza della Nunziata and ending at a high lookout on the fortified gates in the 17th-century city walls. Ringed around the circumference of the city are a number of huge fortresses; this gate was part of the city's system of defenses. From Righi you can undertake scenic all-day hikes from one fortress to the next. ✉ *Piazza della Nunziata, Pré* ☎ *010/5582414* 🌐 *www.amt.genova.it* 🎫 *€2* ⏲ *Daily 6 am–11:45 pm.*

WORTH NOTING

Castelletto. To reach this charming neighborhood high above the city center, you take one of Genoa's handy municipal elevators that whisk you skyward from Piazza Portello, at the end of Galleria Garibaldi, for a good view of the old city. ✉ *Piazza Portello, Castelletto* 🎫 *€1.20* ⏲ *Daily 6:40 am–midnight.*

Ferrovia Genova–Casella. In continuous operation since 1929, the Genova–Casella Railroad runs from Piazza Manin in Genoa (follow Via Montaldo from the center of town, or take Bus 33 or 34 to Piazza Manin) through the beautiful countryside above the city, finally arriving in the rural hill town of Casella. On the way, the tiny train traverses a series of precarious switchbacks that afford sweeping views of the forested Ligurian hills. In Casella Paese (the last stop) you can hike, eat lunch, or just check out the view and ride back. There are two restaurants and two pizzerias near the Casella station; try local cuisine at Trattoria Teresin in Località Avosso. **Canova** (two stops from the end of the line) is the start of two possible hikes through the hills: one a two-hour, one-way trek to a small sanctuary, **Santuario della Vittoria,** and the other a more grueling four-hour hike to the hill town of **Creto.** Another worthwhile stop along the rail line is **Sant'Olcese Tullo,** where you can take a half-hour (one-way) walk along a river and through the **Sentiero Botanico di Ciaé,** a botanical garden and forest refuge with labeled specimens of Ligurian flora and a tiny medieval castle. For Canova and Sant'Olcese, inform your conductor that you want him to stop. The Genova–Casella Railroad is a good way to get a sense of the rugged landscape around Genoa, and you may have it to yourself. The train departs about every hour. ✉ *Piazza Manin* ☎ *010/837321* 🌐 *www.ferroviagenovacasella.it* 🎫 *€3.20 round-trip* 🕑 *Mon.–Sat. 7:30–7:30, Sun. 9–8:15.*

WORD OF MOUTH

"Be sure to wander around the maze of narrow lanes in the ancient part of (Genoa) by the port—all scrubbed up recently—this warren of tiny lanes is the epitome of old-world charm—once a dicey area now all gussied up for tourists."

—PalenQ

8

Granarolo funicular. Take a cog railway up the steeply rising terrain to another part of the city's fortified walls. It takes 15 minutes to hoist you from Stazione Principe, on Piazza Acquaverde, to **Porta Granarolo,** 1,000 feet above, where the sweeping view gives you a sense of Genoa's size. The funicular departs about every half hour. ✉ *Piazza del Principe, San Teodoro* ☎ *010/5582414* 🌐 *www.amt.genova.it* 🎫 *€2* 🕑 *Daily 6 am–11:45 pm.*

Loggia dei Mercanti. This merchants' row dating from the 16th century is lined with shops selling local foods and gifts as well as raincoats, rubber boots, and fishing line. ✉ *Piazza Banchi, Maddalena.*

Museo d'Arte Orientale Chiossone. In the Villetta di Negro park on the hillside above Piazza Portello, the Chiossone Oriental Art Museum has one of Europe's most noteworthy collections of Japanese, Chinese, and Thai objects. There's a fine view of the city from the museum's terrace. ✉ *Piazzale Mazzini 4, Maddalena* ☎ *010/542285* 🌐 *www.museochiossonegenova.it* 🎫 *€4* 🕑 *Tues.–Fri. 9–7, weekends 10–7.*

Palazzo dell'Università. Built in the 1630s as a Jesuit college, this has been Genoa's university since 1803. The exterior is unassuming, but climb the stairway flanked by lions to visit the handsome courtyard, with its portico of double Doric columns. ✉ *Via Balbi 5, Pré* ☎ *01020991* 🌐 *www.unige.it.*

Palazzo Doria Tursi. In the 16th century, wealthy resident Nicolò Grimaldi had a palace built of pink stone quarried in the region. It's been reincarnated as Genoa's Palazzo Municipale (Municipal Building), and so most of the goings-on inside are the stuff of local politics and quickie weddings. You can visit the richly decorated **Sala Paganini,** where the famous Guarnerius violin that belonged to Niccolò Paganini (1782–1840) is displayed, along with the gardens that connect the palace with the neighboring Palazzo Bianco. ✉ *Via Garibaldi 9, Maddalena* ☎ *010/2759185* 🌐 *www.stradanuova.it* 🎫 *€7, includes Palazzo Bianco and Palazzo Rosso* ⏲ *Tues.–Fri. 9–7, weekends 10–7.*

San Siro. Genoa's oldest church was the city's cathedral from the 4th to the 9th century. Rebuilt in the 16th and 17th centuries, it now feels a bit like a haunted house—imposing frescoes line dank hallways, and chandeliers hold crooked candles flickering in the darkness. ✉ *Via San Luca, Maddalena* ☎ *010/22461468* ⏲ *Daily 7:30–noon and 4–7.*

Santissima Annunziata. Exuberantly frescoed vaults decorate the 16th- to 17th-century church, which is an excellent example of Genovese baroque architecture. ✉ *Piazza della Nunziata, Pré* ☎ *010/297662* ⏲ *Daily 9–noon and 3–7.*

SOUTHERN DISTRICTS AND THE AQUARIUM

Inhabited since the 6th century BC, the oldest section of Genoa lies on a hill to the southwest of the Caruggi District. Today, apart from a section of 9th-century wall near Porta Soprana, there is little to show that an imposing castle once stood here. Though the neighborhood is considerably run-down, some of Genoa's oldest churches make it a worthwhile excursion. No visit to Genoa is complete, however, without at least a stroll along the harbor front. Once a squalid and unsafe neighborhood, the port was given a complete overhaul during Genoa's preparations for the Columbus quincentennial celebrations of 1992, and additional restorations in 2003 and 2004 have done much to revitalize the waterfront. You can easily reach the port on foot by following Via San Lorenzo downhill from Genoa's cathedral, Via delle Fontane from Piazza della Nunziata, or any of the narrow vicoli that lead down from Via Balbi and Via Pré.

TOP ATTRACTIONS

★ **Acquario di Genova.** Europe's biggest aquarium, second in the world only to Osaka's in Japan, is the third-most-visited museum in Italy and a must for children. Fifty tanks of marine species, including sea turtles, dolphins, seals, eels, penguins, and sharks, share space with educational displays and re-creations of marine ecosystems, including a tank of coral from the Red Sea. If arriving by car, take the Genova Ovest exit from the autostrada. ✉ *Ponte Spinola, Porto Vecchio* ☎ *0101/23451* 🌐 *www.acquario.ge.it* 🎫 *€14* ⏲ *Mar.–June, weekdays 9–7:30, weekends 8:45–8:30; July and Aug., daily 8:30 am–10 pm; Nov.–Feb., weekdays 9:30–7:30, weekends 9:30–8:30. Entry permitted every ½ hr; last entry 1½ hrs before closing.*

Galata Museo del Mare. Devoted entirely to the city's seafaring history, this museum is probably the best way, at least on dry land, to get an idea of the changing shape of Genoa's busy port. Highlighting the displays is a full-size replica of a 17th-century Genovese galleon. ✉ *Calata de Mari 1, Ponte dei Mille* ☎ *010/2345655* 🌐 *www.galatamuseodelmare.it* 🎫 *€10* ⏲ *Mar.–Oct., daily 10–7:30; Nov.–Feb., Tues.–Fri. 10–6, weekends 10–7:30. Last entry 1½ hrs before closing.*

The Harbor. A boat tour gives you a good perspective on the layout of the harbor, which dates to Roman times. The Genoa inlet, the largest along the Italian Riviera, was also used by the Phoenicians and Greeks as a harbor and a staging area from which they could penetrate inland to form settlements and to trade. The port is guarded by the Diga Foranea, a striking wall 5 km (3 mi) long built into the ocean. The **Lanterna,** a lighthouse more than 360 feet high, was built in 1544; it's one of Italy's oldest lighthouses and a traditional emblem of Genoa. Boat tours of the harbor, operated by the **Consorzio Liguria Viamare** (✉ *Via Sottoripa 7/8, Porto Vecchio* ☎ *010/265712* 🌐 *www.liguriaviamare.it* 🎫 *€10* ⏲ *Daily; departure times vary*), launch from the aquarium pier and run about an hour. The tour includes a visit to the breakwater outside the harbor, the Bacino delle Grazie, and the Molo Vecchio (Old Port). Reservations aren't necessary.

Palazzo Ducale. This palace was built in the 16th century over a medieval hall, and its facade was rebuilt in the late 18th century and later restored. It now houses temporary exhibitions and a restaurant-bar serving fusion cuisine. Reservations are necessary to visit the dungeons and tower. Guided tours (€4) of the palace and its exhibitions are sometimes available. ✉ *Piazza Matteotti 9, Portoria* ☎ *010/5574004* 🌐 *www.palazzoducale.genova.it* 🎫 *Free* ⏲ *Tues.–Sun. 9–9.*

8

San Lorenzo. Contrasting black slate and white marble, so common in Liguria, embellishes the cathedral at the heart of medieval Genoa—inside and out. Consecrated in 1118, the church honors Saint Lawrence, who passed through the city on his way to Rome in the 3rd century. For hundreds of years the building was used for religious and state purposes such as civic elections. Note the 13th-century Gothic portal, the fascinating twisted barbershop columns, and the 15th- to 17th-century frescoes inside. The last campanile dates from the early 16th century. The **Museo del Tesoro di San Lorenzo** (San Lorenzo Treasury Museum) housed inside has some stunning pieces from medieval goldsmiths and silversmiths, for which medieval Genoa was renowned. ✉ *Piazza San Lorenzo, Molo* ☎ *010/2471831* 🎫 *Cathedral free, museum €5.50* ⏲ *Cathedral daily 8–11:45 and 3–6:45. Museum Mon.–Sat. 9–11:30 and 3–5:30.*

Sant'Agostino. This 13th-century Gothic church was damaged during World War II, but it still has a fine campanile and two well-preserved cloisters that house an excellent museum displaying pieces of medieval architecture and fresco paintings. Highlighting the collection are the enigmatic fragments of a tomb sculpture by Giovanni Pisano (circa 1250–1315). ✉ *Piazza Sarzano 35/R, Molo* ☎ *010/2511263* 🌐 *www.museosantagostino.it* 🎫 *€4* ⏲ *Tues.–Fri. 9–7, weekends 10–7.*

CLOSE UP

The Art of the Pesto Pestle

You may have known Genoa primarily for its salami or its brash explorer, but the city's most direct effect on your life away from Italy may be through its cultivation of one of the world's best pasta sauces. The sublime blend of basil, extra-virgin olive oil, garlic, pine nuts, and grated pecorino and Parmigiano Reggiano cheeses that forms *pesto alla Genovese* is one of Italy's crowning culinary achievements, a concoction that Italian food guru Marcella Hazan has called "the most seductive of all sauces for pasta." Ligurian pesto is served only over spaghetti, gnocchi, lasagna, or—most authentically—*trenette* (a flat, spaghetti-like pasta) or *trofie* (short, doughy pasta twists), and then typically mixed with boiled potatoes and green beans. Pesto is also occasionally used to flavor minestrone. The small-leaf basil grown in the region's sunny seaside hills is considered by many to be the best in the world, and pesto sauce was invented primarily as a showcase for that singular flavor. The simplicity and rawness of pesto is one of its virtues, as cooking (or even heating) basil ruins its delicate flavor. In fact, pesto aficionados refuse even to subject the basil leaves to an electric blender; Genovese (and other) foodies insist that true pesto can be made only with mortar and pestle.

Santa Maria di Castello. One of Genoa's most significant religious buildings, an early Christian church, was rebuilt in the 12th century and finally completed in 1513. You can visit the adjacent cloisters and see the fine artwork contained in the museum. Museum hours vary during religious services. ✉ *Salita di Santa Maria di Castello 15, Molo* ☎ *010/2549511* 🎫 *Free* ⏲ *Daily 9–noon and 3:30–6.*

WORTH NOTING

Accademia delle Belle Arti. Founded in 1751, the Academy of Fine Arts, as well as being a school, houses a collection of paintings from the 16th to the 19th century. Genovese artists of the baroque period are particularly well represented. ✉ *Largo Pertini 4, Portoria* ☎ *010/581957* 🌐 *www.accademialigustica.it* 🎫 *Free* ⏲ *Mon.–Sat. 9–1.*

Childhood home of Christopher Columbus. The ivy-covered remains of this fabled medieval house stand in the gardens below the Porta Soprana. A small and rather disappointing collection of objects and reproductions relating to the life and travels of Columbus is on display inside. ✉ *Piazza Dante, Molo* ☎ *010/2465346* 🎫 *€4* ⏲ *Tues.–Sun. 9–5.*

Il Bigo. This spiderlike white structure, designed by world-renowned architect Renzo Piano, was erected in 1992 to celebrate the Columbus quincentenary. You can take its **Ascensore Panoramico Bigo** (Bigo Panoramic Elevator) up 650 feet for a 360-degree view of the harbor, city, and sea. In winter there's an ice-skating rink next to the elevator, in an area covered by sail-like awnings. ✉ *Ponte Spinola, Porto Vecchio* ☎ *010/2345278 skating rink* 🎫 *Elevator €4, skating rink €8* ⏲ *Elevator: Jan. 7–Feb. and Nov.–Dec. 25, weekends 10–5; Mar.–May, Sept., and Oct., Mon. 2–6, Tues.–Sun. 10–6; June–Aug., Mon. 4–11 pm, Tues.–Sun. 10 am–11 pm; Dec. 26–Jan. 6, daily 10–5. Skating rink: Nov. or Dec.–Mar., weekdays*

8 am–9:30 pm, Sat. 10 am–2 am, Sun. 10 am–midnight.

Mercato Orientale. In the old cloister of a church along Via XX Settembre, this bustling produce, fish, and meat market is a wonderful sensory overload. Get a glimpse of colorful everyday Genovese life watching the merchants and buyers banter over prices. ✉ *Via XX Settembre, Portoria* ⏲ *Weekdays 7–1.*

WORD OF MOUTH

"If you stay in Nervi, don't miss a meal of foccacia al formaggio at the restaurant Marinella on the beautiful seaside promenade." —stepsbeyond

Porta Soprana. A striking 12th-century twin-tower structure, this medieval gateway stands on the spot where a road from ancient Rome entered the city. It is just steps uphill from Columbus's boyhood home, and legend has it that the explorer's father was employed here as a gatekeeper. ✉ *Piazza Dante, Molo.*

San Donato. Although somewhat marred by 19th- and 20th-century restorations, the 12th-century San Donato—with its original portal and octagonal campanile—is a fine example of Genovese Romanesque architecture. Inside, an altarpiece by the Flemish artist Joos Van Cleve (circa 1485–1540) depicts the Adoration of the Magi. ✉ *Piazza San Donato, Portoria* ☎ *010/2468869* ⏲ *Mon.–Sat. 8–noon and 3–7, Sun. 9–12:30 and 3–7.*

San Matteo. This typically Genovese black-and-white-striped church dates from the 12th century; its crypt contains the tomb of Andrea Doria (1466–1560), the Genovese admiral who maintained the independence of his native city. The well-preserved Piazza San Matteo was, for 500 years, the seat of the Doria family, which ruled Genoa and much of Liguria from the 16th to the 18th centuries. The square is bounded by 13th- to 15th-century houses decorated with portals and loggias. ✉ *Piazza San Matteo, Maddalena* ☎ *010/2474361* ⏲ *Mon.–Sat. 8–noon and 4–7, Sun. 9:30–10:30 and 4–5.*

Teatro Carlo Felice. The World War II–ravaged opera house in Genoa's modern center, Piazza de Ferrari, was rebuilt and reopened in 1991 to host the fine Genovese opera company; its massive tower has been the subject of much criticism. ✉ *Passo Eugenio Montale 4, Piazza de Ferrari, Portoria* ☎ *010/53811* 🌐 *www.carlofelice.it.*

8

WHERE TO EAT

$$$–$$$$ LIGURIAN ✕ **Antica Osteria del Bai.** Look out from a large dark wood–paneled room over the Ligurian Sea from this romantic upscale restaurant perched high on a cliff. A seaside theme pervades the art and menu, which might include black gnocchi with lobster sauce or ravioli ai frutti di mare. The restaurant's traditional elegance is reflected in its white tablecloths, dress code, and prices. ✉ *Via Quarto 16, Quarto* ☎ *010/387478* 🌐 *www.osteriadelbai.it* 👔 *Jacket and tie* ⏲ *Closed Mon., Jan. 10–20, and Aug. 1–20.*

$ LIGURIAN ✕ **Bakari.** Hip styling and ambient lighting hint at this eatery's creative, even daring, takes on Ligurian classics. Sure bets are the spinach-and-cheese gnocchi, any of several carpaccios, and the delicate beef dishes.

Reserve ahead, requesting a table on the more imaginative ground floor or just stop by for an aperitivo and people-watching. ✉ *Vico del Fieno 16/R, northwest of Piazza San Matteo, Maddalena* ☎ *010/291936* ⏲ *No lunch weekends.*

$–$$ LIGURIAN ✕ **Da Domenico.** Don't be dismayed by the labyrinth of rooms and wood passages that lead to your table at this restaurant in a quiet square near Piazza Dante—you've found one of those hidden corners that only the Genovese know. Traditional seafood and meat dishes make up most of the menu. ✉ *Piazza Leonardo 3, Molo* ☎ *010/540289* ✍ *Reservations essential* ⏲ *Closed Mon.*

$$ WINE BAR ✕ **Enoteca Sola.** Menus are chosen specifically to complement wines at Pino Sola's airy, casually elegant enoteca in the heart of the modern town. The short menu emphasizes seafood and varies daily, but might include stuffed artichokes or baked stockfish. The real draw, though, is the wine list, which includes some of the winners of the prestigious Italian Tre Bicchieri (Three Glasses) Award, denoting only the very best. ✉ *Via C. Barabino 120/R, Foce* ☎ *010/594513* ⏲ *Closed Sun. and Aug.*

$ LIGURIAN ✕ **Exultate.** When the weather permits, umbrella-shaded tables spread out from this tiny eatery into the nearby square. Popular with locals, the restaurant's inexpensive daily menu is presented on a chalkboard for all to see; excellent pizza, meal-size salads, and homemade delicious desserts highlight the list. ✉ *Piazza Lavagna 15/R, Maddalena* ☎ *010/2512605* ⏲ *Closed Sun.*

$$ LIGURIAN ✕ **Le Rune.** The intimate setting, creative Ligurian dishes, and fine service make this a favorite with local businessmen and the after-opera crowd from nearby Teatro Carlo Felice. Standouts from the menu include the *tagliata di tonno* served with fresh fennel and a grapefruit sauce, and for an antipasto, the wonderful *timballo di robiola,* which is similar to a cheese soufflé served with a pear and cinnamon sauce. It's so good you could almost have it again for dessert. ✉ *Vico Domoculta 14/R, just off Via XXV Aprile, Portoria* ☎ *010/594951* ⏲ *No lunch weekends.*

$$ ITALIAN ✕ **Maxela.** Beef is king at this upscale but casual trattoria. The building dates to a restaurant started in 1790. The owners have retained most of its original design, including wood benches and slabs of marble for tables. Daily specials are listed on chalkboards, or you can just walk up to the butcher counter and pick your cut of choice. ✉ *Vico Inferiore del Ferro 9/R, Maddalena* ☎ *010/2474209* 🌐 *www.maxela.it* ⏲ *Closed Sun.*

$$$$ LIGURIAN ✕ **Zeffirino.** The five Belloni brothers share chef duties at this well-known restaurant full of odd combinations, including decor that has both rustic wood and modern metallic pieces. Try the *passutelli* (ravioli stuffed with ricotta cheese, herbs, and fruit) or any of the homemade pasta dishes. With a Zeffirino restaurant in Las Vegas and another in Hong Kong, the enterprising Bellonis have gone international, yet their Ligurian location remains an institution among the Genovese. ✉ *Via XX Settembre 20, Portoria* ☎ *010/591990* 🌐 *www.zeffirino.com* ✍ *Reservations essential* 🧥 *Jacket required.*

WHERE TO STAY

¢–$ **Agnello d'Oro.** The friendly owner at Agnello d'Oro does double duty as a travel agent: he's happy to help you with plane reservations and travel plans. **Pros:** 100 yards from Stazione Principe; near the Palazzo Reale. **Cons:** few amenities. **TripAdvisor:** "overlooking the harbor," "good cheap place," "caretakers are friendly." *Vico delle Monachette 6, Pré 010/2462084 www.hotelagnellodoro.it 25 rooms In-room: no a/c (some). In-hotel: restaurant, bar, parking (paid), some pets allowed Breakfast.*

$$$$ **The Bentley Hotel.** Glamour has returned to Genoa with this luxury hotel on the wide, tree-lined road leading down to the port. **Pros:** for top-of-the-line style and amenities, this is Genoa's best bet. **Cons:** it's a bit of a walk to the port and centro. **TripAdvisor:** "best hotel in Genoa," "fabulous bar and lounge," "gorgeous design." *Via Corsica 4, Carignano 010/5315111 www.bentley.thi.it 85 rooms, 14 suites In-room: safe, Internet. In-hotel: restaurant, bar, gym, spa, laundry service, Wi-Fi hotspot, parking (paid) Breakfast.*

$$ **Best Western City.** In the heart of the city, near Via Roma, the grand shopping street, and one block from Piazza de Ferrari, which divides new Genoa from old Genoa, a bland apartment-building exterior gives way to a polished lobby and light, modern rooms. **Pros:** location can't be beat. **Cons:** regular rooms are small. **TripAdvisor:** "easy walking distance to the port," "modern and spotlessly clean," "personnel is quite skilled." *Via San Sebastiano 6, Portoria 010/584707 010/586301 www.bwcityhotel-ge.it 63 rooms, 3 suites In-room: safe, Internet, Wi-Fi. In-hotel: restaurant, bar, Wi-Fi hotspot, parking (paid) Breakfast.*

$ **Best Western Metropoli.** This welcoming hotel is on the border of the historic district and Via Garibaldi. **Pros:** guest rooms and bathrooms are large. **Cons:** parking lot is a bit of a hike; can be confusing to find if you are driving. **TripAdvisor:** "elegant, clean and well-furnished," "great value for money," "pretty quiet." *Piazza Fontane Marose, Portoria 010/2468888 www.bestwestern.it 48 rooms In-room: refrigerator, Wi-Fi. In-hotel: bar, laundry service, Wi-Fi hotspot, parking (paid), some pets allowed Breakfast.*

$$$–$$$$ ★ **Bristol Palace.** The 19th-century grand hotel carefully guards its reputation for courtesy and service. **Pros:** in the heart of the shopping district. **Cons:** busy street outside can sometimes be noisy. **TripAdvisor:** "beautifully furnished with antiques," "very friendly and helpful," "wonderful golden staircase." *Via XX Settembre 35, Portoria 010/592541 www.hotelbristolpalace.com 128 rooms, 5 suites In-room: safe, refrigerator. In-hotel: restaurant, bar, Wi-Fi hotspot, parking (paid), some pets allowed Breakfast.*

8

NERVI: A SIDE TRIP FROM GENOA

★ *11 km (7 mi) east of Genoa.*

GETTING HERE

By car, exit the A12 at Genova Nervi and follow the "Centro" signs. The Nervi train station is on the main north–south line, and you can also take the local commuter trains from Genova Principe and Brignole. It can also be reached on Bus 15 from Genoa's Piazza Cavour.

EXPLORING

The identity of this stately late-19th-century resort, famous for its 1½-km-long (1-mi-long) seaside promenade—the **Passeggiata Anita Garibaldi**—its palm-lined roads, and its 300 acres of parks rich in orange trees, is given away only by the sign on the sleepy train station. Although Nervi is technically part of the city, its peace and quiet are as different from Genoa's hustle and bustle as its clear blue water is from Genoa's crowded port. From the centrally located train station, walk east along the seaside promenade to reach the beaches, a cliff-hanging restaurant, and the 2,000 varieties of roses in the public **Parco Villa Grimaldi,** all the while enjoying one of the most breathtaking views on the Riviera. Nervi, and the road between it and Genoa, is known for its nightlife in summer.

WHERE TO EAT AND STAY

$$ LIGURIAN **Marinella.** Here you can have a casual but sophisticated dining experience while overlooking the Ligurian Sea. Try the *zuppa di pesce* (fish soup) and freshly baked focaccia; main dishes change according to the day's catch. The restaurant perches on seaside shoals: be sure to ask for one of the tables on the terrace, where you are suspended above the sea. There's a nice, inexpensive hotel on-site as well. ✉ *Passeggiata Anita Garibaldi 18/R, Nervi* ☎ *010/3728343* ⏲ *Closed Mon. and Nov.*

$$$ Fodor's Choice ★ **Romantik Hotel Villa Pagoda.** In a 19th-century merchant's mansion modeled after a Chinese temple, this luxury hotel has a private park, access to the famed cliff-top walk, and magnificent ocean views. **Pros:** lovely guest and common rooms; everything has a touch of class. **Cons:** nearby train can be softly heard. **TripAdvisor:** "villa and park are very nice," "in a residential area," "staff was super-friendly." ✉ *Via Capolungo 15, Nervi* ☎ *010/3726161* 🌐 *www.villapagoda.it* *13 rooms, 4 suites* *In-room: safe, refrigerator. In-hotel: restaurant, bar, tennis court, pool, some pets allowed* *Breakfast* ⏲ *Closed Nov.–Mar.*

RIVIERA DI PONENTE

The Riviera di Ponente (Riviera of the Setting Sun) covers the narrow strip of northwest Liguria from Genoa to the French border. The sapphire-color Mediterranean Sea to one side and the verdant foothills of the Alps on the other allow for temperate weather and a long growing season—hence its nickname Riviera dei Fiori (Riviera of the Flowers). Once filled with charming seaside villages, elegant structures, and sophisticated visitors, this area now struggles to maintain a balance between its natural beauty and development. Highly populated resort areas and some overly industrialized areas are jammed into the thin stretch of white-sand and pebble beaches. Yet, while its sister Riviera (di Levante) may retain more of its natural beauty, the Ponente remains a popular and well-organized retreat for visitors looking for sunshine, nightlife, and relaxation.

ALBISOLA MARINA

43 km (27 mi) west of Genoa.

GETTING HERE

By car, take the Albisola exit off the A10 and follow the signs for the Albisola marina center. Albisola is on the main railway line between Genoa and France.

EXPLORING

Albisola Marina has a centuries-old tradition of ceramics making. Numerous shops here sell the distinctive wares, and a whole sidewalk, **Lungomare degli Artisti**, which runs along the beachfront, has been transformed by the colorful ceramic works of well-known artists.

The 18th-century **Villa Faraggiana**, near the parish church, has exhibits on the history of pottery and hosts an array of events from concerts to weddings. ✉ *Via dell'Oratorio* ☎ *019/480622* 🎫 *Free* 🕑 *Apr.–Sept., Wed.–Mon. 3–7.*

SHOPPING

Ceramiche San Giorgio (✉ *Corso Matteotti 5* ☎ *019/482747*) has been producing ceramics since the 17th century, and is known for both classic and modern designs. **Ernan** (✉ *Corso Mazzini 77, Albisola Superiore* ☎ *019/489916*) sells blue-and-white-patterned ceramics typical of the 18th century. **Mazzotti** (✉ *Corso Matteotti 25* ☎ *019/481626*) has an exclusive ceramics selection and a small museum.

8

FINALE LIGURE

30 km (19 mi) southwest of Albisola Marina, 72 km (44 mi) southwest of Genoa.

GETTING HERE

By car, take the Finale Ligure exit off the A10 and follow the "Centro" signs. Finale Ligure is on the main train line between Genoa and France.

VISITOR INFORMATION

Finale Ligure tourism office (✉ *Via San Pietro 13* ☎ *019/681019* 🌐 *www.inforiviera.it*).

EXPLORING

Finale Ligure is actually made up of three small villages: Finalmarina, Finalpia, and Finalborgo. The former two have fine sandy beaches and modern resort amenities. The most attractive of the villages is Finalborgo, less than 1 km (½ mi) inland. It's a hauntingly preserved medieval settlement, planned to a rigid blueprint, with 15th-century walls. The surrounding countryside is pierced by deep, narrow valleys and caves; the limestone outcroppings provide the warm pinkish stone found in many buildings in Genoa. Rare reptiles lurk among the exotic flora.

OFF THE BEATEN PATH

Noli. Just 9 km (5½ mi) northeast of Finale Ligure, the ruins of a castle loom benevolently over the tiny medieval gem of Noli. It's hard to imagine that this charming seaside village was—like Genoa, Venice, Pisa, and Amalfi—a prosperous maritime republic in the Middle Ages. If you don't have a car, get a bus for Noli at Spotorno, where local trains stop.

WHERE TO EAT AND STAY

$$$–$$$$ LIGURIAN

✕ **Ai Torchi.** You could easily become a homemade-pesto snob at this Finalborgo eatery. The high prices are justified by excellent inventive seafood and meat dishes and by the setting—a restored 5th-century olive-oil refinery. ✉ *Via dell'Annunziata 12, Finalborgo* ☎ *019/690531* ⏲ *Closed Jan. 7–Feb. 10 and Tues. Sept.–July.*

$$$

Punta Est. This lovely small resort hotel is perched above the white-sand beaches of Finale Ligure. **Pros:** nice pool and garden areas. **Cons:** rooms are a bit outdated. **TripAdvisor:** "breakfast on the wonderful terrace," "spa was brilliant," "a touch of dolce vita." ✉ *Via Aurelia 1* ☎ *39/019600611* 🌐 *www.puntaest.com* *40 rooms* *In-room: safe, refrigerator, Wi-Fi. In-hotel: restaurant, bars, pool, gym, beachfront, laundry service, Internet terminal, Wi-Fi hotspot, parking (free)* ⏲ *Closed Nov.–Apr.* *Breakfast.*

ALBENGA

20 km (12 mi) southwest of Finale Ligure, 90 km (55 mi) southwest of Genoa.

GETTING HERE

By car, take the Albenga exit off the A10 and follow the "Centro" signs. Albenga is on the main train line between Genoa and France.

VISITOR INFORMATION

Albenga tourism office (✉ *Lungocento Croce Bianca 12* ☎ *0182/558444* 🌐 *www.inforiviera.it*).

EXPLORING

Albenga has a medieval core, with narrow streets laid out by the ancient Romans. A network of alleys is punctuated by centuries-old towers surrounding the 18th-century Romanesque cathedral, with a late-14th-century campanile and a baptistery dating to the 5th century. It's a nice place to take an afternoon stroll and explore the many quaint shops and cafés.

OFF THE BEATEN PATH

Bardineto. For a look at some of the Riviera's mountain scenery, make an excursion by car to this attractive village in the middle of an area rich in mushrooms, chestnuts, and raspberries, as well as local cheeses. A ruined castle stands above the village. From Borghetto Santo Spirito (between Albenga and Finale Ligure), drive inland 25 km (15 mi).

WHERE TO STAY

$$$ **La Meridiana.** An oasis of hospitality and refinement occupies a handsome farmhouse compound surrounded by a garden. **Pros:** nice in-house restaurant. **Cons:** high cost for amenities available on-site. **TripAdvisor:** "in the gently rolling hills," "pretty swimming pool," "uniquely Italian treat." ✉ *Via ai Castelli (off A10), Garlenda* ✣ *8 km (5 mi) north of Albenga* ☎ *0182/580271* 🌐 *www.lameridianaresort.com* *10 rooms, 18 suites* *In-room: safe, refrigerator, Internet. In-hotel: 3 restaurants, bar, pool, bicycles, Internet terminal, some pets allowed* ⊗ *Closed Nov.–Mar.* *Breakfast.*

ALASSIO

100 km (62 mi) southwest of Genoa.

GETTING HERE

By car, take the Albenga exit off the A10 and follow the blue signs for Alassio. Alassio is on the main train line between Genoa and France.

8

VISITOR INFORMATION

Alassio tourism office (✉ *Palazzo Commune, Piazza della Libertà* ☎ *0182/6021* 🌐 *www.comune.alassio.sv.it*).

EXPLORING

Although Alassio is no longer a sleepy fishing village, the centro still possesses some Old World charm, colorful buildings, a great beachfront promenade, and white-sand beaches. Spend the day soaking up some sun, grab a seafood lunch or pizza along the boardwalk, and then finish off with a passeggiata and shopping on its caruggi.

CERVO

23 km (14 mi) southwest of Albenga, 106 km (65 mi) southwest of Genoa.

GETTING HERE

By car, take the Diano Marina exit off the A10 and follow the signs for Cervo located just east of Diano Marina. Diano Marina is on the main train line between Genoa and France.

EXPLORING

Cervo is the quintessential sleepy Ligurian coastal village, nicely polished for the tourists who come to explore its narrow byways and street staircases. It's a remarkably well-preserved medieval town, crowned with a big baroque church. In July and August the square in front of the church is the site of chamber music concerts.

IMPERIA

12 km (7 mi) west of Cervo, 116 km (71 mi) southwest of Genoa.

GETTING HERE

By car, take the Imperia Est exit off the A10 and follow the signs for "Centro" or "Porto Maurizio." Both Imperia and Porto Maurizio are on the main rail line between Genoa and France.

VISITOR INFORMATION

Imperia tourism office (✉ *Viale Matteotti 37* ☎ *0183/660140* 🌐 *www.rivieradeifiori.org*).

EXPLORING

Imperia actually consists of two towns: Porto Maurizio, a medieval town built on a promontory, and Oneglia, now an industrial center for oil refining and pharmaceuticals. Porto Maurizio has a virtually intact medieval center, an intricate spiral of narrow streets and stone portals, and some imposing 17th- and 18th-century palaces. There's little of interest in modern Oneglia, except for a visit to the olive-oil museum.

Imperia is king when it comes to olive oil, and the story of the olive is the theme of the small **Museo dell'Olivo**. Displays of the history of the olive tree, farm implements, presses, and utensils show how olive oil has been made in many countries throughout history. ✉ *Via Garessio 11, Oneglia* ☎ *0183/720000* 🌐 *www.museodellolivo.com* 🎫 *Free* ⏲ *Wed.–Mon. 9–12:30 and 3–6:30.*

WHERE TO STAY

$$ **Relais San Damian.** At this charming bed-and-breakfast, set among the olive trees high above Porto Maurizio, all the rooms are suites, and you can take in the views from an inviting infinity pool. **Pros:** large suites and plenty of outdoor space; gorgeous pool area. **Cons:** limited amenities (no TVs or phones). **TripAdvisor:** "calm and peaceful haven," "owners were very welcoming," "aroma of lemon blossoms." *Strada Vasia 47 0183/280309 www.san-damian.com 9 suites In-room: no phone, no TV, safe, kitchenettes, refrigerator. In-hotel: pool, laundry service, Wi-Fi hotspot, parking (free), some pets allowed, no kids under 14 Closed Nov.–Mar. Breakfast.*

TAGGIA

20 km (12 mi) west of Imperia, 135 km (84 mi) southwest of Genoa.

GETTING HERE

By car, take the Arma di Taggia exit off the A10 and follow the signs for "Centro." The closest train station is in San Remo. From the train station it is a 20-minute taxi ride.

EXPLORING

The town of Taggia has a medieval core and one of the most imposing medieval bridges in the area.

The church of **San Domenico,** with a small museum, was once part of a monastery founded in the 15th century that remained a beacon of faith and learning in Liguria for 300 years. An antiques market is held here, just south of Taggia, on the fourth weekend of the month. *Piazzale San Domenico, Arma di Taggia No phone Free Fri.–Wed. 9–5.*

8

SAN REMO

50 km (31 mi) southwest of Cervo, 146 km (90 mi) southwest of Genoa.

GETTING HERE

By car, take the San Remo exit off the A10 and follow the "Centro" signs. San Remo is on the main train line between Genoa and France.

VISITOR INFORMATION

San Remo tourism office (*Palazzo Riviera, Largo Nuvoloni 1 0184/59059 www.sanremonet.com*).

EXPLORING

Once the crown jewel of the Riviera di Ponente, San Remo is still the area's largest resort, lined with polished hotels, exotic gardens, and seaside promenades. Renowned for its VIPs, glittering casino, and romantic setting, San Remo maintains remnants of its glamorous past from the late 19th century to World War II, but it also suffers from the same epidemic of overbuilding that has changed so much of the western Riviera for the worse. Still, it continues to be a lively town, even in the off-season.

The Mercato dei Fiori, Italy's most important wholesale flower market, is held here in a market hall between Piazza Colombo and Corso Garibaldi and open to dealers only. More than 20,000 tons of carnations, roses, mimosa flowers, and innumerable other cut flowers are dispatched from here each year. As the center of northern Italy's flower-growing industry, the town is surrounded by hills where verdant terraces are now blanketed with plastic to form immense greenhouses.

Explore the warren of alleyways in the old part of San Remo, **La Pigna** *(The Pinecone)*, which climbs upward to Piazza Castello and offers a splendid view of the town.

In addition to gaming, the art nouveau **San Remo Casinò** has a restaurant, a nightclub, and a theater that hosts concerts and the annual San Remo Music Festival. If you want to try your luck at the gaming tables, there's a €7.50 cover charge on weekends. Dress is elegant, with jacket and tie requested at the French gaming tables. ✉ *Corso Inglesi 18* ☎ *0184/5951* ⏲ *Slot machines: Sun.–Fri. 10 am–2:30 am, Sat. 10 am–3:30 am. Tables: Sun.–Fri. 2:30 pm–2:30 am, Sat. 2:30 pm–3:30 am.*

The onion-dome Russian Orthodox church of **Cristo Salvatore, Santa Caterina d'Alessandria, e San Serafino di Sarov** testifies to a long Russian presence on the Italian Riviera. Russian empress Maria Alexandrovna, wife of Czar Alexander I, built a summer house here, and in winter San Remo was a popular destination for other royal Romanovs. The church was consecrated in 1913. ✉ *Via Nuvoloni 2* ☎ *0184/531807* *€1 donation* ⏲ *Daily 9:30–noon and 3–6.*

OFF THE BEATEN PATH

Bussana Vecchia. In the hills where flowers are cultivated for export sits Bussana Vecchia, a self-consciously picturesque former ghost town largely destroyed by an earthquake in 1877. The inhabitants packed up and left en masse after the quake, and for almost a century the houses, church, and crumbling bell tower were empty shells, overgrown by weeds and wildflowers. Since the 1960s an artists' colony has evolved among the ruins. Painters, sculptors, artisans, and bric-a-brac dealers have restored dwellings. ✉ *8 km (5 mi) east of San Remo.*

WHERE TO EAT AND STAY

$ LIGURIAN

✕ **Nuovo Piccolo Mondo.** Old wooden chairs dating from the 1920s, when the place opened, evoke the homey charm of this small, family-run trattoria. The place has a faithful clientele, so get here early to grab a table and order such Ligurian specialties as *sciancui* (a roughly cut flat pasta with a mixture of beans, tomatoes, zucchini, and pesto) and *polpo e patate* (stewed octopus with potatoes). ✉ *Via Piave 7* ☎ *0184/509012* ▭ *No credit cards* ⏲ *Closed Mon. No dinner Sun.*

$$–$$$

Paradiso. A quiet palm-fringed garden gives the Paradiso an air of seclusion in this sometimes hectic resort city. **Pros:** friendly service; comfortable accommodations. **Cons:** a steep walk up some stairs and a hill from town. **TripAdvisor:** "San Remo's little gem," "staff cared for us," "quiet and priced reasonably." ✉ *Via Roccasterone 12* ☎ *0184/571211* 🌐 *www.paradisohotel.it* *41 rooms* *In-room: safe, refrigerator. In-hotel: restaurant, bar, pool, Wi-Fi hotspot* *Breakfast.*

$$$–$$$$

Royal. This is arguably Liguria's second-most-luxurious resort after the Splendido in Portofino. **Pros:** the glamour of yesteryear with all the expected high-end amenities. **Cons:** some of the property seems outdated (though at this writing renovations are planned); on-site meals and beverages are expensive. **TripAdvisor:** "spacious grounds with broad sea views," "style of the 19th century," "very grand public lounges." ✉ *Corso Imperatrice 80* ☎ *0184/5391* 🌐 *www.royalhotelsanremo.com* *114 rooms, 13 suites* *In-room: safe, Wi-Fi. In-hotel: 3 restaurants, room service, bars, tennis court, pool, gym, spa, beachfront, laundry service* ⏲ *Closed Nov.–mid-Feb.* *Breakfast.*

BORDIGHERA

12 km (7 mi) west of San Remo, 155 km (96 mi) southwest of Genoa.

GETTING HERE

By car, take the Bordighera exit off the A10 and follow the signs for "Centro," about a 10-minute drive. Bordighera is on the main railway line between Genoa and France.

VISITOR INFORMATION

Bordighera tourism office (✉ *Via Vittorio Emanuele II 172* ☎ *0184/262322* 🌐 *www.rivieradeifiori.org*).

EXPLORING

On a lush promontory, Bordighera sits as a charming seaside resort with panoramas from Genoa (on a clear day) to Monte Carlo. A large English colony, attracted by the mild climate, settled here in the second half of the 19th century and is still very much in evidence today; you regularly find people taking afternoon tea in the cafés, and streets are named after Queen Victoria and Shakespeare. This garden spot was the first town in Europe to grow date palms, and its citizens still have the exclusive right to provide the Vatican with palm fronds for Easter celebrations.

Thanks partly to its many year-round English residents, Bordighera does not close down entirely in the off-season like some Riviera resorts but rather serves as a quiet winter haven for all ages. With plenty of hotels and restaurants, Bordighera makes a good base for exploring the region and is quieter and less commercial than San Remo.

Running parallel to the ocean, **Lungomare Argentina** is a pleasant promenade, 1½ km (1 mi) long, which begins at the western end of the town and provides good views westward to the French Côte d'Azur.

WHERE TO EAT AND STAY

$ LIGURIAN ✕ **Bagni Sant'Ampeglio.** This combination beach club and seafront restaurant has wonderful choices for both lunch and dinner. Try the house-specialty *branzino in carciofi* (sea bass with artichokes) and homemade desserts. ✉ *Lungomare Argentina 3* ☎ *0184/262106* ⏲ *Closed Wed. in Sept.–Nov., 1st half of Jan., and Feb.–May.*

$ WINE BAR ✕ **Il Tempo Ritrovato.** A small wine bar and restaurant combine forces here on Bordighera's seaside promenade. Simple pasta dishes and a spectacular wine list make this a great choice. ✉ *Bagni Amarea on Lungomare Argentina* ☎ *0184/261207* ⏲ *Closed Sun. and Mon.*

$$$ LIGURIAN Fodor's Choice ★ ✕ **Magiargè.** A mix of great charm and great food make this small osteria in the historic center an absolute dining delight. Dishes are Ligurian with a creative twist, such as the *stoccafisso sopra panizza* (salt cod served over a chickpea polenta) and *fritteline di bianchetti* (small frittatas made with tiny white fish). The selection of local wines is

excellent. ✉ *Via della Loggia 6* ☎ *0184/262946* 🌐 *www.magiarge.it* ⏲ *Closed 2 wks in Feb. and Oct. No lunch June–Aug.*

$$ **Hotel Piccolo Lido.** This quaint hotel along the promenade provides clean and simple rooms at reasonable prices year-round. **Pros:** a good value. **Cons:** few amenities. **TripAdvisor:** "on a fine beach," "absolutely magnificent sun terrace," "truly genuine hospitality." ✉ *Lungomare Argentina 2* ☎ *0184/261297* 🌐 *www.hotelpiccololido.it* *33 rooms* *In-room: safe, refrigerator. In-hotel: restaurant, beachfront, parking (paid)* *Breakfast.*

$$ **Hotel Villa Elisa.** On a street filled with beautiful old villas, this Victorian-style hotel has a relaxed and friendly atmosphere, beautiful gardens, and well-equipped rooms at reasonable prices. **Pros:** helpful staff; a good value. **Cons:** only partial views in sea-view rooms; limited parking; covered parking costs extra. **TripAdvisor:** "rooms are comfortable and pleasant," "view over the town rooftops," "surrounded by large, exotic gardens." ✉ *Via Romana 70* ☎ *0184/261313* 🌐 *www.villaelisa.com* *33 rooms, 2 suites, 1 apartment for up to 6 people* *In-room: safe, refrigerator. In-hotel: restaurant, bar, pools, laundry service, Wi-Fi hotspot, parking (free), some pets allowed* *Breakfast.*

EN ROUTE

From Ventimiglia, 2 mi west of Bordighera, a provincial road swings 10 km (6 mi) up the Nervi River valley to a lovely sounding medieval town, **Dolceacqua** (its name translates as Sweetwater), with a ruined castle. Liguria's best-known red wine is the local Rossese di Dolceacqua. A further 6 km (4 mi) along the road lies Pigna, a fascinating medieval village built in concentric circles on its hilltop.

GIARDINI BOTANICI HANBURY

6 km (4 mi) west of Ventimiglia, 10 km (6 mi) west of Bordighera.

GETTING HERE

Take the S1 along the coast west from Bordighera, through the town of Ventimiglia, and toward the French border. The gardens are about 1 km (½ mi) beyond the tunnel.

Fodor's Choice ★

Giardini Botanici Hanbury. Mortola Inferiore, only 2 km (1 mi) from the French border, is the site of the world-famous Giardini Botanici Hanbury (Hanbury Botanical Gardens), one of the largest and most beautiful in Italy. Planned and planted in 1867 by a wealthy English merchant, Sir Thomas Hanbury, and his botanist brother Daniel, the terraced gardens contain species from five continents, including many palms and succulents. There are panoramic views of the sea from the gardens. ✉ *Corso Montecarlo 43, Località Mortola Inferiore* ☎ *0184/229507* *€7.50 July–Mar. 19, €9 Mar. 20–June* ⏲ *Mar.–June 15, daily 9:30–6; June 16–Sept. 15, daily 9:30–7; Sept. 16–last Sat. in Oct., daily 9:30–6; last Sun. in Oct.–Feb., Tues.–Sun. 10–6. Last entry 1 hr before closing.*

9

Emilia–Romagna

WORD OF MOUTH

"I completely understand wanting to visit Bologna for the food. We loved it and had fabulous meals, inspiring us to return. Remember though, that the entire Emilia-Romagna region is known for its food."

—BlueSwimmer

WELCOME TO EMILIA-ROMAGNA

TOP REASONS TO GO

★ **The signature food of Emilia:** This region's food—prosciutto *crudo,* Parmigiano-Reggiano, balsamic vinegar, and above all, pasta—makes the trip to Italy worthwhile.

★ **Mosaics that take your breath away:** The intricate tiles in Ravenna's Mausoleo di Galla Placidia, in brilliantly well-preserved colors, depict vivid portraits and pastoral scenes.

★ **Europe's oldest wine bar:** Nicholas Copernicus tippled here while studying at Ferrara's university in the early 1500s; Osteria al Brindisi, in the *centro storico* (historic center), has been pouring wine since 1435.

★ **The nightlife of Bologna:** This red-roofed, leftist-leaning city has had a lively student culture since the university—Europe's oldest—was founded in the late 11th century.

★ **The medieval castles of San Marino:** Its three castles dramatically perch on a rock more than 3,000 feet above the flat landscape of Romagna.

1 Emilia. A landscape of medieval castles and crumbling farmhouses begins just east of Milan, in the western half of Emilia-Romagna. You'll find here the delicious delights of **Parma**, with its buttery prosciutto, famous cheese, and crenellated palaces. Next along the road, continuing east, comes **Reggio Emilia**, of Parmigiano-Reggiano cheese fame, then **Modena**, the city of balsamic vinegar.

2 Bologna. Emilia's principal cultural and intellectual center is famed for its arcaded sidewalks, grandiose medieval towers, and fabulous restaurants.

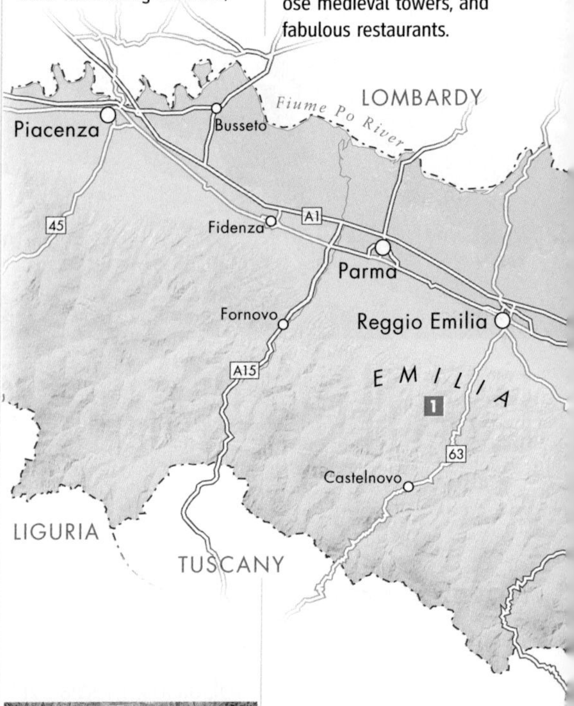

LOMBARDY
Fiume Po River
Piacenza
Busseto
A1
45
Fidenza
Parma
Fornovo
Reggio Emilia
A15
EMILIA
1
63
Castelnovo
LIGURIA
TUSCANY

3 Ferrara. This prosperous, tidy city to the north of Bologna has a rich medieval past, with its own distinctive cuisine.

4 Romagna. The eastern half of Emilia-Romagna begins east of Bologna, where spa towns span to the north and south of the Via Emilia and the A1 autostrada, and extends to the Adriatic. **San Marino**, south of Rimini, is an anomaly in every way—it's its own tiny republic, hanging implausibly on a cliff above the Romagna plain.

5 Ravenna. The main attractions of this well-preserved Romagna city are its memorable mosaics—glittering treasures left from Byzantine rule.

GETTING ORIENTED

Emilia-Romagna owes its beginnings to the Romans, who built the Via Emilia in 187 BC. Today the road bisects the flat, foggy region, paralleling the Autostrada del Sole (A1), making it easy to drive straight through. Bologna is in the middle of everything, with Piacenza, Parma, and Modena to the west, and the Adriatic to the east. Ferrara and Ravenna are the only detours—they're to the north of Via Emilia.

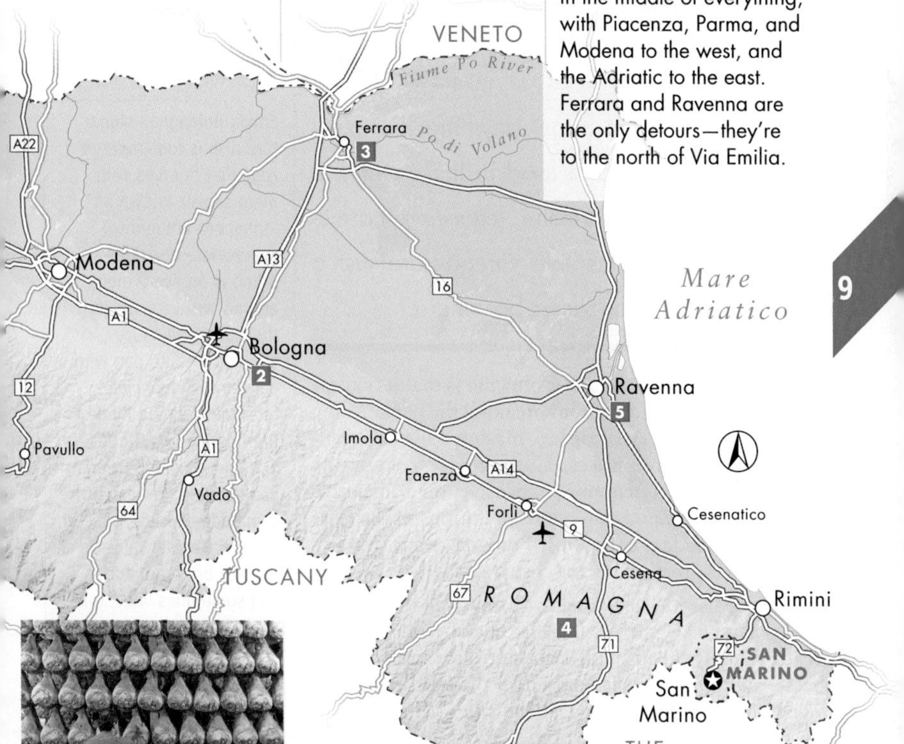

VENETO
Fiume Po River
Ferrara
3
Po di Volano
A22
A13
Modena
16
Mare Adriatico
A1
Bologna
2
12
Ravenna
5
Imola
Pavullo
A1
Faenza
A14
Vado
64
Forli
9
Cesenatico
Cesena
TUSCANY
67
ROMAGNA
Rimini
4
71
72
SAN MARINO
San Marino
THE MARCHES

EATING AND DRINKING WELL IN EMILIA-ROMAGNA

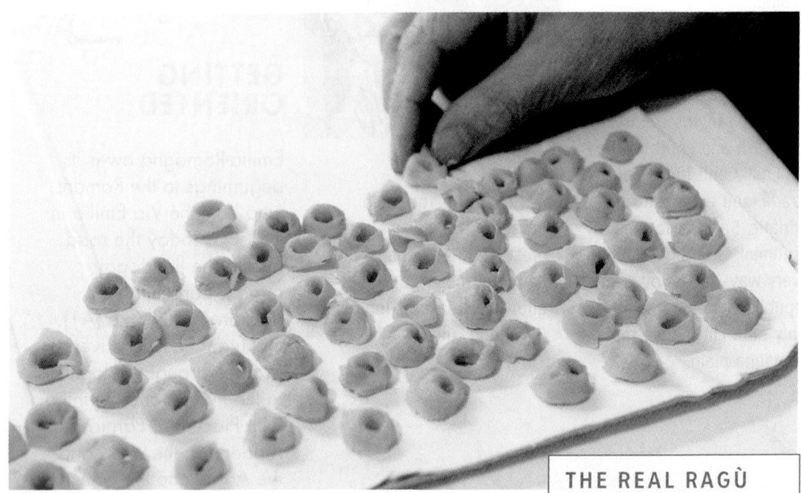

Italians rarely agree about anything, but most would say that the best food in the country is in Emilia-Romagna. Tortellini, fettuccine, Parmesan cheese, and balsamic vinegar are just a few of the Italian delicacies born here.

One of the beauties of Emilia-Romagna is that its exceptional food can be had without breaking the bank. Many trattorias serve up classic dishes, mastered over the centuries, at reasonable prices. Cutting-edge restaurants and wine bars are often more expensive; their inventive menus are full of *fantasia*—reinterpretations of the classics. For the budget-conscious, Bologna is a university town and has great places for cheap eats.

Between meals, you can sustain yourself with the region's famous sandwich, the *piadina*. It's made with pita-thin bread, usually filled with prosciutto or mortadella, cheese, and vegetables. It's put under the grill and served hot, with the cheese oozing at the sides. These addictive sandwiches can be savored at sit-down places or ordered to go.

THE REAL RAGÙ

Emilia-Romagna's signature dish is *tagliatelle al ragù* (flat noodles with meat sauce), known as "spaghetti Bolognese" everywhere else. This primo is on every menu, and no two versions are the same. The sauce starts in a sauté pan with pancetta or *guanciale* (unsmoked bacon made from pork jowls), butter, and minced onions. Purists use nothing but beef, but some add sausage, veal, or chicken. Regular ministrations of broth are added, and sometimes wine, milk, or cream. After a couple of hours of cooking, the ragù is ready to be joined with pasta and Parmesan and brought to the table.

PORK PRODUCTS

It's not just mortadella and cured pork products like prosciutto and *culatello* that Emilia-Romagnans go crazy for—they're wild about the whole hog.

You'll frequently find *cotechino* and *zampone,* both secondi (second courses), on menus; cotechino, photo below, is a savory, thick, fresh sausage served with lentils on New Year's Day (the combination is said to augur well for the new year) and with mashed potatoes year-round. Zampone, a stuffed pig's foot, is redolent of garlic, and is deliciously fatty.

BOLLITO MISTO

The name means "mixed boil," and they do it exceptionally well in this part of Italy. According to Emilia-Romagnans, it was invented here (its true origins are up for grabs, as other northern Italians, especially from Milan and the Piedmont, would argue this point). Chicken, beef, tongue, and zampone are tossed into a stockpot and boiled; they're then removed from the broth and served with a fragrant *salsa verde* (green sauce), made green by parsley and spiced with anchovies, garlic, and capers. This simple yet rich dish is usually served with mashed potatoes on the side, and savvy diners will mix some of the piquant salsa verde into the potatoes as well.

STUFFED PASTA

Among the many Emilian variations on stuffed pasta, tortellini (pictured at left), are the smallest. *Tortelli* (photo upper right), and *cappellacci* are larger pasta "pillows," about the size of a brussels sprout, but with the same basic form as tortellini; they're often filled with pumpkin or spinach and cheese.

Tortelloni are, in theory, even bigger, although their sizes vary. Stuffed pastas are generally served simply, with melted butter, sage, and (what else?) Parmigiano-Reggiano cheese, or (in the case of tortellini) *in brodo* (in beef or chicken broth), which brings out the subtle richness of the filling.

WINES

Emilia-Romagna's wines accompany the region's fine food rather than vying with it for accolades. The best known is Lambrusco, a sparkling red produced on the Po Plain that has some admirers and many detractors. It's praised for its tartness and condemned for the same quality. The region's best wines include Sangiovese di Romagna, somewhat similar to Chianti, from the Romagnan hills, and Barbera, from the Colli Piacetini and Apennine foothills. Castelluccio, Bonzara, Zerbina, Leone Conti, and Tre Monti are among the region's top producers—keep an eye out for their bottles.

Updated by Patricia Rucidlo

Gourmets the world over claim that Emilia-Romagna's greatest contribution to humankind has been gastronomic. Birthplace of fettuccine, tortellini, lasagna, prosciutto, and Parmesan cheese, the region has a spectacular culinary tradition. But there are many reasons to come here aside from the desire to be well fed: Parma's Correggio paintings, Giuseppe Verdi's villa at Sant'Agata, the medieval splendor of Bologna's palaces and Ferrara's alleyways, the rolling hills of the Romagna countryside, and, perhaps foremost, the Byzantine beauty of mosaic-rich Ravenna—glittering as brightly today as it did 1,500 years ago.

As you travel through Emilia, the western half of the region, you'll encounter sprawling plants of the industrial food giants of Italy, such as Barilla and Fini, standing side by side with fading villas and farmhouses that have long punctuated the flat, fertile land of the Po Plain. Bologna, the principal city of Emilia, is a busy cultural and, increasingly, business center, less visited but in many ways just as engaging as Italy's more famous tourist destinations—particularly given its acknowledged position as the leading city of Italian cuisine. The rest of the region follows suit: eating is an essential part of any Emilian experience.

The area's history is replete with culinary legends, such as how the original *tortellino* (singular of tortellini) was modeled on the shape of Venus's navel and the original *tagliolini* (long, thin egg pasta) was served at the wedding banquet of Annibale Bentivoglio and Lucrezia d'Este—a marriage uniting two of the noblest families in the region. You'll need to stay focused even just to make sure you try all the basics: Parma's famed prosciutto and Parmigiano-Reggiano cheese; Modena's balsamic vinegar; the ragù—slow-simmered meat sauce—whose poor imitations are known elsewhere in the world as "Bolognese"; and, of course, the best pasta in the world.

The historic border between Emilia to the west and Romagna to the east lies near the fortified town of Dozza. Emilia is flat; but just east of the Romagnan border the landscape gets hillier and more sparsely settled, in places covered with evergreen forests and steaming natural springs. Finally, it flattens again into the low-lying marshland of the Po Delta, which meets the Adriatic Sea. Each fall, in both Romagna and Emilia, the trademark fog rolls in off the Adriatic to hang over the flatlands in winter, coloring the region with a spooky, gray glow.

PLANNING

MAKING THE MOST OF YOUR TIME

Plan on spending at least two days or nights in Bologna, the region's cultural and historical capital. You shouldn't miss Parma, with its stunning food and graceful public spaces. Also plan on visiting Ferrara, a misty, mysterious medieval city. If you have time, go to Ravenna for its memorable Byzantine mosaics and Modena for its harmonious architecture and famous balsamic vinegar.

If you have only a few days in the region, it's virtually impossible to do all five of those cities justice. If you're a dedicated gourmand (or *buona forchetta*, as Italians say), move from Bologna west along the Via Emilia (SS9) to Modena and Parma. If you're more interested in architecture, art, and history, choose the eastern route, heading north on the A13 to Ferrara and then southeast on the SS16 to Ravenna.

If you have more time, you won't have to make such tough choices. You can start in Milan, go east, and finish on the Adriatic—or vice versa.

GETTING HERE AND AROUND

CAR TRAVEL

Driving is the best way to get around Emilia-Romagna. Roads are wide, flat, and well marked; distances are short, and beautiful farmhouses and small villages make for easily accessible detours. A car is particularly useful for visiting the spa towns of Romagna, which aren't well connected by train. Historic centers are off-limits to cars, but they're also quite walkable, so you may just want to park your car and get around on foot once you arrive at your hotel.

Entering Emilia-Romagna by car is as easy as it gets. Coming in from the west on the Autostrada del Sole (A1), Piacenza will be the first city you'll hit. It's a mere 45 minutes southeast of Milan. On the other side of the region, Venice is about an hour from Ferrara by car on the A13.

Bologna is on the autostrada, so driving between cities is a breeze, though do take special care if you're coming from Florence, as the road is winding and drivers speed. The Via Emilia (SS9), one of the oldest roads in the world, runs through the heart of the region. It's a straight, low-lying modern road, the length of which can be traveled in a few hours. Although less scenic, the A1 toll highway, which runs parallel to the Via Emilia from Bologna, can get you where you're going about twice as fast. From Bologna, the A13 runs north to Ferrara, and the A14 takes you east to Ravenna. Note that much of the historic center of Bologna is closed off to cars daily from 7 am to 8 pm.

TRAIN TRAVEL

When it comes to public transportation in the region, trains are better than buses—they're fairly efficient and quite frequent, and most stations aren't too far from the center of town. The railway line follows the Via Emilia (SS9). In Emilia, it's generally 30 to 45 minutes from one major city to the next. To reach Ferrara or Ravenna, you usually have to change to a local train at the Bologna station. Trains run frequently, and connections are easy. Ferrara is a half hour north of Bologna on the train, and Ravenna is just over an hour.

Bologna is an important rail hub for northern Italy and has frequent, fast service to Milan, Florence, Rome, and Venice. The routes from Bologna to the south usually go through Florence, which is an hour away. The high-speed train service Alta Velocità cuts the time from Milan to Bologna to just one hour. On the northeastern edge of the region, Venice is 1½ hours east of Ferrara by train. Check the Web site of the state railway, the **Ferrovie dello Stato** (☎ *892021 toll-free within Italy* 🌐 *www.trenitalia.com*), for information, or stop in a travel agency, as many sell train tickets (without a markup) and agents often speak English.

ABOUT THE HOTELS

Emilia-Romagna has a reputation for demonstrating a level of efficiency uncommon in most of Italy. Even the smallest hotels are usually well run, with high standards of quality and service. Bologna is very much a businessperson's city, and many hotels here cater to the business traveler, but there are smaller, more intimate hotels as well. It's smart to book in advance—the region hosts many fairs and conventions that can fill up hotels even during low season.

Though prices are sometimes high, you can expect an experience delightfully free of the condescending attitude that sometimes mars Italy's tourist meccas.

Hotel reviews have been condensed for this book. Please go to Fodors.com for full reviews of each property.

WHAT IT COSTS (IN EUROS)

	¢	$	$$	$$$	$$$$
Restaurants	under €20	€20–€30	€30–€45	€45–€65	over €65
Hotels	under €75	€75–€125	€125–€200	€200–€300	over €300

Restaurant prices are for a first course (primo), second course (secondo), and dessert (dolce). Hotel prices are for two people in a standard double room in high season, including tax and service.

EMILIA

The Via Emilia runs through Emilia's heart in a straight shot from medieval Piacenza, 67 km (42 mi) southeast of Milan, through Bologna, and ultimately to Romagna and the Adriatic Coast. On the way you encounter many of Italy's cultural riches—from the culinary and artistic treasures of Parma to the birthplace and home of Giuseppe Verdi. Take time to detour into the countryside, with its ramshackle farmhouses and 800-year-old abbeys; to stop for a taste of prosciutto; and to detour north to the mist-shrouded tangle of streets that make up Ferrara's old Jewish ghetto.

PIACENZA

67 km (42 mi) southeast of Milan, 150 km (93 mi) northwest of Bologna.

GETTING HERE

Regional trains run often from Milan to Piacenza and take a little more than an hour; Eurostar service cuts the travel time in half, and the new Alta Velocità trains make it from Milan to Bologna in an hour. The Intercity from Bologna to Piacenza takes about 1½ hours and closer to two hours on regional trains. Both have frequent service. Piacenza is easily accessible by car via the A1, either from Milan or from Bologna. If you're coming from Milan, take the Piacenza Nord exit; from Bologna, the Piacenza Est exit.

VISITOR INFORMATION

Piacenza tourism office (⊠ *Piazza Cavalli 7* ☎ *0523/329324* 🌐 *www.provincia.piacenza.it*).

EXPLORING

Piacenza has always been associated with industry and commerce. Its position on the Po River has made it an important inland port since the earliest times; the Etruscans, and then the Romans, had thriving settlements here. As you approach the city today you could be forgiven for thinking that it holds little of interest. Piacenza is surrounded by ugly industrial suburbs (with particularly unlovely concrete factories and a power station), but if you forge ahead you'll discover a delightfully preserved medieval downtown and an unusually clean city. The city's prosperity is evident in the great shopping along Corso Vittorio Emanuele II.

Attached like a sinister balcony to the bell tower of Piacenza's 12th-century **Duomo** is a *gabbia* (iron cage), where miscreants were incarcerated naked and subjected to the scorn of the crowd in the marketplace below. Inside the cathedral, less evocative but equally impressive medieval stonework decorates the pillars and the crypt, and there are extravagant frescoes in the dome of the cupola begun by Morazzone (1573–1626); Guercino (1591–1666) completed them upon Morazzone's death. The Duomo can be reached by following Via XX Settembre from Piazza dei Cavalli. ⊠ *Piazza Duomo* ☎ *0523/335154* ⏲ *Daily 7:30–noon and 4–7.*

The **Musei di Palazzo Farnese**, the city-owned museum of Piacenzan art and antiquities, is housed in the vast **Palazzo Farnese.** The ruling family had commissioned a monumental palace, but construction, begun in

9

EMILIA-ROMAGNA THROUGH THE AGES

Ancient History. Emilia-Romagna owes its beginnings to a road. In 187 BC the Romans built the Via Aemilia, a long road running northwest from the Adriatic port of Rimini to the central garrison town of Piacenza, and it was along this central spine that the primary towns of the region developed.

Despite the unifying factor of what came to be known as the Via Emilia, the region has had a fragmented history. Its eastern part, roughly the area from Faenza to the coast, known as Romagna, first looked to the Byzantine east and then to Rome for art, political power, and, some say, national character. The western part, Emilia, from Bologna to Piacenza, looked more to the north with its practice of self-government and dissent.

Bologna was founded by the Etruscans and eventually came under the influence of the Roman Empire. The Romans established a garrison here, renaming the old Etruscan settlement Bononia. It was after the fall of Rome that the region began its fragmentation. Romagna, centered in Ravenna, was ruled from Constantinople. Ravenna eventually became the capital of the empire in the west in the 5th century, passing to papal control in the 8th century. Even today, the city is still filled with reminders of two centuries of Byzantine rule.

Family Ties. The other cities of the region, from the Middle Ages on, became the fiefdoms of important noble families—the Este in Ferrara and Modena, the Pallavicini in Piacenza, and the Bentivoglio in Bologna. Today all these cities bear the marks of their noble patrons. When in the 16th century the papacy managed to exert its power over the entire region, some of these cities were divided among the papal families—hence the stamp of the Farnese family on Parma, Piacenza, and Ferrara.

A Leftward Tilt. Bologna and Emilia-Romagna have established a robust tradition of rebellion and dissent. The Italian socialist movement was born in the region, as was Benito Mussolini. In keeping with the political climate of his home state, he was a firebrand socialist during the early part of his career. Despite having Mussolini as a native son, Emilia-Romagna didn't take to fascism: it was here that the antifascist resistance was born, and during World War II the region suffered terribly at the hands of the fascists and the Nazis.

1558, was never completed as planned. The highlight of the museum's rather eclectic collection is the tiny 2nd-century BC Etruscan *Fegato di Piacenza,* a bronze tablet shaped like a *fegato* (liver), with the symbols of the gods of good and ill fortune marked on it. By comparing this master "liver" with one taken from the body of a freshly slaughtered sacrifice, priests predicted the future. The collection also contains Botticelli's recently restored *Madonna and Child with St. John the Baptist.* Because it's under glass, you have the rare opportunity of getting very close to the piece to admire the artist's brushwork. Reserve ahead for free 1½-hour guided tours. ✉ *Piazza Cittadella 29* ☎ *0523/492661* 🌐 *www.musei.piacenza.it* 🎫 €6 ⏲ *Museum: Tues.–Thurs. 9–1, Fri.–Sun. 9–1 and 3–6. Free tours (in Italian): Tues.–Thurs. at 10, Fri. at 10 and 3:30, weekends at 9:30, 11, 3, and 4:30.*

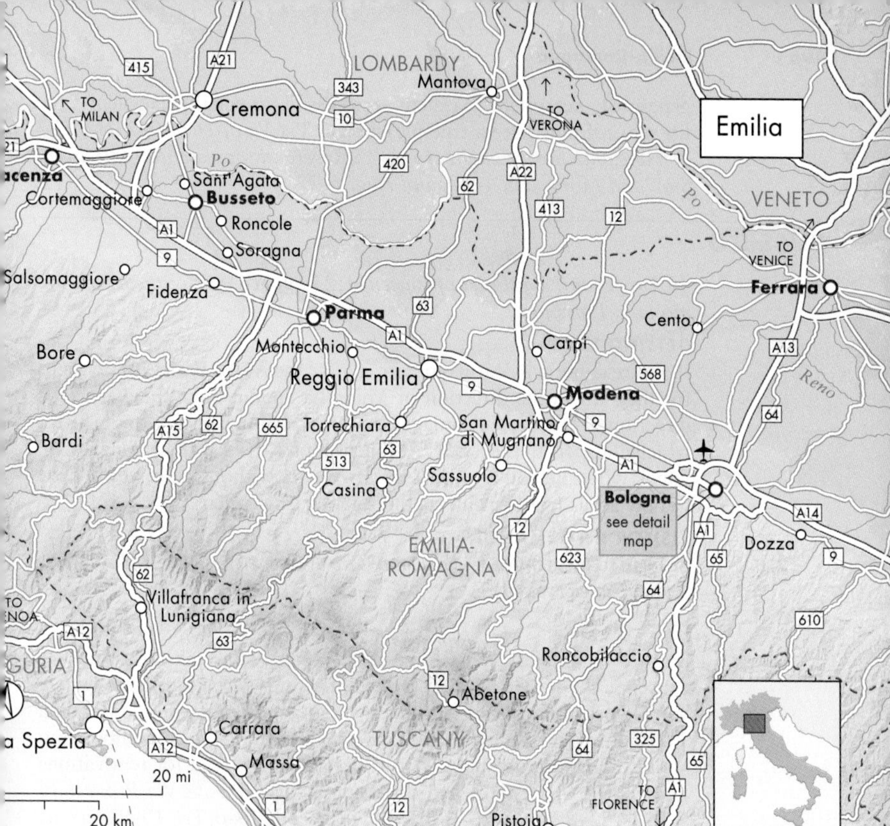

The heart of the city is the **Piazza dei Cavalli** *(Square of the Horses)*. The flamboyant equestrian statues from which the piazza takes its name are depictions of Ranuccio Farnese (1569–1622) and, on the left, his father, Alessandro (1545–92). Alessandro was a beloved ruler, enlightened and fair; Ranuccio, his successor, less so. Both statues are the work of Francesco Mochi, a master baroque sculptor. Dominating the square is the massive 13th-century **Palazzo Pubblico,** also known as il Gotico. This two-tone, marble-and-brick, turreted and crenellated building was the seat of town government before Piacenza fell under the iron fists of the ruling Pallavicini and Farnese families.

WHERE TO EAT

$$$$ MODERN ITALIAN ★

✕ **Antica Osteria del Teatro.** A simple 15th-century palazzo on a lovely little square in the center of town gives no hint to what awaits inside. Warm ochre-sponged walls adorned with contemporary prints provide the backdrop for some serious food. Chef Filippo Chiappini Dattilo has combined his love of Italian food with French influences, and has created a marvelous menu. The local specialty, culatello, is served with exquisite *porcini sott'olio (mushrooms in olive oil)*; another traditional dish, *pisarei e faso* (Piacentinian for pasta fagioli), is livened up with shrimp and squid. The colorful *risotto mantecato con granchio reale* (risotto with crab) arrives redolent of mandarin, with which it has been generously seasoned. Excellent service and an equally excellent wine list make dining here a true pleasure. ✉ *Via Verdi 16* ☎ *0523/323777* 🌐 *www.anticaosteriadelteatro.it* ✍ *Reservations essential* ⏲ *Closed Sun. and Mon., Jan. 1–10, and Aug. 1–25.*

BUSSETO

30 km (19 mi) southeast of Piacenza, 25 km (16 mi) southeast of Cremona in Lombardy.

GETTING HERE

If you're coming by car from Parma, take the A1/E35, and follow signs for the A15 in the direction of Milan/La Spezia. Take the exit in the direction of Fidenza/Salsomaggiore Terme, following signs to the SP12, which connects to the SS9W. At Fidenza, take the SS588 heading north, which will take you into Busseto. If you are without a car, you'll have to take a bus from Parma, as there's no train service.

VISITOR INFORMATION

Busseto tourism office (✉ *Comune, Piazza G. Verdi 10* ☎ *0524/92487* 🌐 *www.bussetolive.com*).

EXPLORING

Busseto's main claim to fame is its native son, master composer Giuseppe Verdi (1813–1901). The 15th-century **Villa Pallavicino** is where Verdi worked and lived with his mistress (and later wife) Giuseppina Strepponi. On display are the maestro's piano, scores, composition books, and walking sticks. The villa had been closed for renovations since 2001, but it reopened to the public in 2009. ✉ *Via Provesi 36* ☎ *0524/92487* ⏲ *Tues.–Thurs. and weekends 10–6, Fri. 10–9* 🌐 *www.bussetolive.com.*

In the center of Busseto is the lovely **Teatro Verdi**, dedicated, as you might expect, to the works of the hamlet's famous son. Guided tours of the well-preserved, ornate 19th-century-style theater are offered every half hour. Check with the Busseto tourist office for the performance schedule. ✉ *Piazza G. Verdi 10* ☎ *0524/92487* 🎫 *Tours €4* ⏲ *Tours: Nov.–Feb. 9:30–1 and 2:30–5:30; Mar.–Oct. Tues.–Sun. 9:30–1 and 3–6:30.*

For Verdi lovers, **Villa Sant'Agata** (also known as Villa Verdi) is a veritable shrine. It's the grand country home Verdi built for himself in 1849, the place where some of his greatest works were composed. Visits are by tour only, and you have to reserve a few days in advance by phone or online. ✉ *Via Verdi 22, Sant'Agata Villanova sull'Arda* ✥ *4 km (2½ mi) north of Busseto on SS588, toward Cremona* ☎ *0523/1885208* 🌐 *www.villaverdi.org* 🎫 *Tours €8* ⏲ *Tours: Weekdays 10–3:45, weekends 9:30–5.*

PARMA

40 km (25 mi) southeast of Busseto, 97 km (60 mi) northwest of Bologna.

GETTING HERE

Train service, via Eurostar, Intercity, and Regionale trains, runs frequently from Milan and Bologna. It takes a little over an hour from Milan, and just under an hour from Bologna. By car, Parma is just off the A1 autostrada, halfway between Bologna and Piacenza.

VISITOR INFORMATION

Parma tourism office (✉ *Via Melloni 1/a* ☎ *0521/218889* 🌐 *www.turismo.comune.parma.it*).

EXPLORING

Parma stands on the banks of a tributary of the Po River. Despite damage during World War II, much of the stately historic center seems untouched by modern times. Parma is a prosperous town, and it shows in its well-dressed residents, clean streets, and immaculate piazzas.

Bursting with gustatory delights, Parma draws crowds for its sublime cured ham, prosciutto *crudo di Parma* (known locally simply as "prosciutto crudo"). The pale-yellow Parmigiano-Reggiano cheese produced here and in nearby Reggio Emilia is the original—and best—of a class known around the world as Parmesan.

Almost every major European power has had a hand in ruling Parma at one time or another. The Romans founded the city—then little more than a garrison on the Via Emilia—after which a succession of feudal lords held sway. In the 16th century came the ever-conniving Farnese family, which died out in 1731 upon the death of Antonio Farnese. It then went to the Spanish, and fell into French hands in 1796. In 1805 Marie-Louise (better known to the parmigiani as Maria Luigia), the wife of Napoléon, took command of the city. She was a much-beloved figure in her adopted town until her death in 1847.

9

★ **Piazza Garibaldi** is the heart of Parma. Here's where people gather to pass the time of day, start their *passeggiata* (evening stroll), or simply hang out. Strada Cavour, leading off the piazza, is Parma's prime shopping street, and is crammed with wine bars teeming with locals. This square and nearby Piazza del Duomo make up one of the loveliest historic centers in Italy.

The delightful, 16th-century church of **Santa Maria della Steccata** has one of Parma's most recognizable domes, as well as a wonderful decorative fresco in the dome's large arch by Francesco Mazzola, better known as Parmigianino (1503–40). He took so long to complete it that his patrons briefly imprisoned him for breach of contract. ✉ *Piazza Steccata 9, off Via Dante near Piazza Garibaldi* ☎ *0521/234937* 🌐 *www.santuari.it/steccata* ⏲ *Daily 9–noon and 3–6.*

The spacious **Piazza del Duomo** contains the cathedral and the Battistero, as well as the Palazzo del Vescovado (Bishop's Palace). Behind the Duomo is the baroque church of San Giovanni.

The magnificent 12th-century **Duomo** has two vigilant stone lions standing guard beside the main door. The arch of the entrance is decorated with a delicate frieze of figures representing the months of the year, a motif repeated inside the baptistery. Some of the church's original artwork still survives, notably the simple yet evocative *Descent from the Cross,* a carving in the right transept by Benedetto Antelami (active 1178–1230), a sculptor and architect whose masterwork is this cathedral's baptistery. It's an odd juxtaposition to turn from this austere work to the exuberant fresco in the dome, the *Assumption of the Virgin* by Antonio Allegri, better known to us as Correggio (1494–1534). The fresco was not well received when it was unveiled in 1530. "A mess of frogs' legs," the bishop of Parma is said to have called it. Today Correggio is acclaimed as one of the leading masters of mannerist painting. It's best viewed when the sun's strong, as this building is not particularly well lit. ✉ *Piazza del Duomo* ☎ *0521/235886* ⏲ *Daily 7:30–12:30 and 3–7.*

WORD OF MOUTH

"One of the highlights of our trip was going to Parmesan cheese and Parma ham factory tour. We saw manufacturing process, quality control, etc. It was so much fun!"
—Mochi

The impressive **Battistero** *(Baptistery)* has a simple pink-stone Romanesque exterior and an uplifting Gothic interior. The doors are richly decorated with figures, animals, and flowers, and the interior is adorned with stucco figures—probably carved by Antelami—showing the months and seasons. Early 14th-century frescoes depicting scenes from the life of Christ adorn the walls. ✉ *Piazza del Duomo* ☎ *No phone* 🎫 *€5* ⏲ *Daily 9–12:30 and 3–6:30.*

Once beyond the elaborate baroque facade of **San Giovanni Evangelista,** the Renaissance interior reveals several works by Correggio; his *St. John the Evangelist* (left transept) is considered the finest. Also in this church (in the second and fourth chapels on the left) are works by Parmigianino, a contemporary of Correggio's. Once seen, Parmigianino's long-necked Madonnas are never forgotten. ✉ *Piazzale San Giovanni 1, Piazza del Duomo* ☎ *0521/235311* ⏲ *Daily 8–noon and 3–5:45.*

★ The **Camera di San Paolo** was the reception room for the erudite abbess Giovanna da Piacenza; in 1519 she hired Correggio to provide its decoration. Its mythological scenes depict the *Triumphs of the Goddess Diana,* the *Three Graces,* and the *Three Fates.* ✉ *Via Melloni 15, off Strada Garibaldi, near Piazza Pilotta* ☎ *0521/233309* 🎫 *€2* ⏲ *Tues.–Sun. 8:30–2.*

Three museums outside Parma showcase the city and the region's most famous foods. The **Musei del Cibo** *(Food Museums)*, as they're collectively known, offer tastings, a bit of history, and a tour through the process of making these specialties. None is more than a 20-minute drive or taxi ride from the city. It's a good idea to call before making the trek, as opening hours are limited. The **Museo del Prosciutto di Parma** (✉ *Via Bocchialini, Langhirano* ☎ *0521/858347* 🎫 *€3, plus €3 for tasting* ⏲ *weekends 10–6 by reservation only*) gives you an in-depth look at Italy's most famous ham. The **Museo del Parmigiano Reggiano** (✉ *Soragna* ☎ *0521/355009* 🎫 *€5* ⏲ *Mar.–Oct., Fri.–Sun. 9–12:30 and 3–6, Tues.–Thurs. by reservation only*) focuses on the trademark crumbly cheese. The **Museo del Salame** ✉ *Castello di Felino* ☎ *0521/596129* 🎫 *€5* ⏲ *weekends 10–12:30 and 3–6, Wed.–Fri. by reservation only*) is all about cured meats.

WHERE TO EAT

¢ WINE BAR ★ **Enoteca Antica Osteria Fontana.** Gregarious locals flock to this old-school *enoteca* (wine bar). Decor is minimal (yellow walls, wooden tables, and chairs), but the wine list and sandwich offerings are substantial. Low prices make this a real draw for Parma's twentysomethings—the two rooms are crammed with people, who manage to spill out into the streets, wine glasses in hand. The grilled panini are ample and good, and include such standards as *coppa* (a cured pork product) and pancetta and Gorgonzola. The enoteca has an enormous collection of wine bottles to go—you can avoid the madding crowd with takeout. *Strada Farini 24/a, near Piazza Garibaldi 0521/286037 Reservations not accepted Closed Sun. and Mon.*

$$ EMILIAN **La Filoma.** If you want to try Parmesan specialties without breaking the bank, this is the place to go. The dining room evokes the turn of two centuries ago with its high ceilings and damask drapes, though an element of kitsch prevails. The food shines, from the classic *anolini in brodo di manzo e cappone* (a local variation of tortellini in brodo) to the exquisite guinea fowl stuffed with prosciutto and Parmesan. Vegetarian options include a fragrant and tasty *tortina di zucca con porcini fritti* (pumpkin flan with fried porcini mushrooms). Friendly staff and a terrific wine list add to the enjoyment. *Borgo XX Marzo 15 0521/2061811 Reservations essential Closed Tues. No lunch Wed. Closed weekends July and Aug.*

$$ EMILIAN **La Greppia.** The most talked-about restaurant in the city serves up the innovative treats of well-known chef Paola Cavazzini, like *anelli con cavolo nero e mostarda della Paola* (small ring-shaped pasta with Tuscan kale and caramelized fruits) and *faraona al tartufo nero di Fragno* (guinea hen with black truffle and chestnut puree). Service is personal and friendly, in part thanks to the place's tiny size, and the unpretentious surroundings keep the focus on the food. Signora Cavazzini and her all-female crew adhere to a seasonal menu. *Via Garibaldi 39/a 0521/233686 Reservations essential Closed Mon. and Tues., July, and Dec. 23–Jan. 5.*

9

$$$ EMILIAN ★ **Parizzi Ristorante.** Chef-owner Marco Parizzi is the third generation cook in this elegant restaurant. His grandfather's *salumeria* (delicatessen) evolved over the years into a restaurant serving Parmesan classics. The Piatti Tipici offers an *anolini in brodo di gallina e manzo* (stuffed pasta in meat broth), redolent with hints of nutmeg, that shouldn't be missed. The more contemporary side of the menu allows the chef to indulge in tasty flights of fancy: the *petto di anatra caramellato* allows the most decidedly non-Italian Jerusalem artichoke to pair beautifully with caramelized duck breast served with a very Italian type of chicory. The well-priced wine list, culled by Marco's wife Cristina, has a section of "Rarità" collected by the two elder Parizzi, as well as a lengthy selection of contemporary wines. *Strada Repubblica 71 0521/285952 Reservations essential Closed Mon., Aug., and Jan. 8–15.*

WHERE TO STAY

$$$ **Hotel Palace Maria Luigia.** Top quality and convenient to the historic center of Parma and to the train station, this hotel is popular with business travelers. **Pros:** high-quality business hotel. **Cons:** short on

intimacy. **TripAdvisor:** "friendly service," "close to everything," "nothing like the pictures online." ✉ *Viale Mentana 140* ☎ *0521/281032* 🌐 *www.sinahotels.com* *90 rooms, 11 suites* *In-room: Wi-Fi. In-hotel: restaurant, bar, gym* *No meals.*

$$ Fodor's Choice ★ **Palazzo dalla Rosa Prati.** Vittorio dalla Rosa Prati has converted seven rooms of his family's 15th-century palace into luxurious, self-catering accommodations in Piazza del Duomo. **Pros:** unbeatable location; the hotel has an opera box at Teatro Regio that guests may reserve; Penhaligon's bath products. **Cons:** staff leaves at 10 pm. **TripAdvisor:** "lots of character," "high level of service," "spacious, clean and elegant." ✉ *Strada al Duomo 7* ☎ *0521/386429* 🌐 *www.palazzodallarosaprati.it* *7 rooms* *In-room: kitchen, Wi-Fi. In-hotel: bar, some pets allowed* *No meals.*

MODENA

56 km (35 mi) southeast of Parma, 38 km (24 mi) northwest of Bologna.

GETTING HERE

Modena is easily accessible by train, as it's on the Bologna-Milan line. Trains run frequently, and it's an easy walk from the train station to the centro storico. There's an Intercity connection from Florence that takes about an hour and a half. By car, Modena is just off the A1 autostrada, between Bologna and Parma.

VISITOR INFORMATION

Modena tourism office (✉ *Piazza Grande 14* ☎ *059/2032660* 🌐 *turismo.comune.modena.it*).

EXPLORING

Modena is famous for local products: Maserati, Ferrari, and opera star Luciano Pavarotti, who was born near here and was buried in his family plot in Montale Rangone in September 2007. However, it's Modena's heavenly scented balsamic vinegar, aged up to 40 years, that's probably its greatest achievement. The town has become another Emilian food mecca, with terrific restaurants and *salumerie* (delicatessens) at every turn. Though extensive modern industrial sprawl surrounds the center, the small historic center is filled with narrow medieval streets, pleasant piazzas, and typical Emilian architecture.

The 12th-century Romanesque **Duomo** was begun by the architect Lanfredo in 1099 and consecrated in 1184. Medieval sculptures depicting scenes from Genesis adorn the facade; do walk around to the Piazza Grande side to see the building's marvelous arcading. It's a rare example of a cathedral having more than one principal view. The interior, completely clad in brick, imparts a sober and beautiful feel. An elaborate gallery has scenes of the Passion of Christ carved by Anselmo da Campione and his assistants circa 1160–80. The tomb of San Geminiano is in the crypt. At this writing, both the Duomo facade and the tower are undergoing a restoration; work may be completed in 2012. The white-marble bell tower is known as **La Torre Ghirlandina** (the Little Garland Tower) because of its distinctive weather vane. ✉ *Piazza Grande* ☎ *059/216078* 🌐 *www.duomodimodena.it* ⏲ *Daily 6:30–12:30 and 3:30–7.*

Continued on page 506

EMILIA
ONE TASTE AT A TIME

4 towns, dozens of foods, and a mouthful of flavors you'll never forget

Imagine biting into the silkiest prosciutto in the world or the most delectable homemade tortellini you've ever tasted. In Emilia, Italy's most famous food region, you'll discover simple tastes that exceed all expectations. Beginning in Parma and moving eastward to Bologna, you'll find the epicenters of such world-renowned culinary treats as *prosciutto crudo*, Parmigiano-Reggiano, *aceto balsamico*, and tortellini. The secret to this region is not the discovery of new and exotic delicacies, but rather the rediscovery of foods you thought you already knew—in much better versions than you've ever tasted before.

TASTE 1 | PROSCIUTTO CRUDO

From Piacenza to the Adriatic, ham is the king of meats in Emilia-Romagna, but nowhere is this truer than in **Parma**.

Parma is the world's capital of *prosciutto crudo*, raw cured ham (*crudo* for short). Ask for *crudo di Parma* to signal its local provenance; many other regions also make their own crudo.

CRUDO LANGUAGE

It's easy to get confused with the terminology. Crudo is the product that Americans simply call "prosciutto" or the Brits might call "Parma ham." *Prosciutto* in Italian, however, is a more general term that means any kind of ham, including *prosciutto cotto*, or simply *cotto*, which means "cooked ham." Cotto is an excellent product and frequent pizza topping that's closer to (but much better than) what Americans would put in a deli sandwich.

Crudo is traditionally eaten in one of three ways: in a dry sandwich (*panino*); by itself as an appetizer, often with shaved butter on top; or as part of an appetizer or snack platter of assorted *salumi* (cured meats).

WHAT TO LOOK FOR

For the best crudo di Parma, look for slices, always cut to order, that are razor thin and have a light, rosy red color (not dark red). Don't be shy about going into a simple *salumeria* (a purveyor of cured meats) and ordering crudo by the pound. You can enjoy it straight out of the package on a park bench—and why not?

BEST SPOT FOR A SAMPLE

You can't go wrong with any of Parma's famed salumerie, but **Salumeria Garibaldi** (Via Farini 9) is one of the town's oldest and most reliable. You'll find not only spectacular prosciutto crudo, but also delectable cheeses, wines, porcini mushrooms, and more.

LEARN MORE

For more information on crudo di Parma, contact the **Consorzio del Prosciutto di Parma** (Via Marco dell'Arpa 8/b, 0521/246211, www.prosciuttodiparma.com/eng).

Quality testing

Greasing the ham

Fire branding

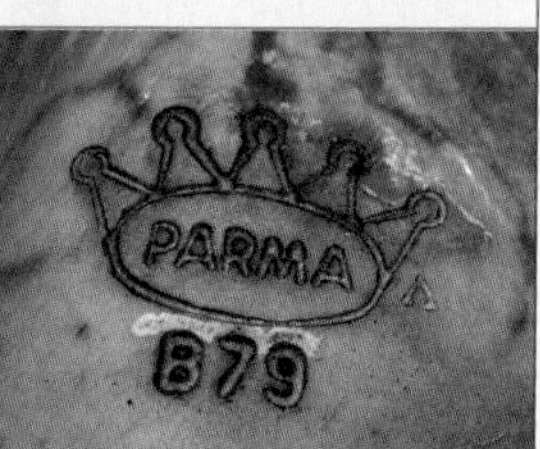

Quality trademark

TASTE 2 PARMIGIANO-REGGIANO

From Parma, it's only a half-hour trip east to **Reggio Emilia**, the birthplace of the crumbly and renowned Parmigiano-Reggiano cheese. Reggio (not to be confused with Reggio di Calabria in the south) is a charming little Emilian town that has been the center of production for this legendary cheese for more than 70 years.

SAY CHEESE

Grana is the generic Italian term for hard, aged, full-flavored cheese that can be grated. Certain varieties of Pecorino Romano, for example, or Grana Padano, also fall under this term, but Parmigiano-Reggiano, aged for as long as four years, is the foremost example.

NOT JUST FOR GRATING

In Italy, Parmigiano-Reggiano is not only grated onto pasta, but also often served by itself in chunks, either as an appetizer—perhaps accompanied by local salumi (cured meats)—or even for dessert, when it might be drizzled with honey or Modena's balsamic vinegar.

MEET THE MAKERS

If you're a cheese enthusiast, you shouldn't miss the chance to take a free two-hour guided tour of a Parmigiano-Reggiano–producing farm. You'll witness the entire process and get to meet the cheesemakers. Tours can be arranged by contacting the **Consorzio del Formaggio Parmigiano-Reggiano** in Reggio Emilia (0522/307741, staff@parmigiano-reggiano.it, www.parmigiano-reggiano.it) at least 20 days in advance. (Ask specifically for an English-language tour if that's what you want.)

BEST SPOT FOR A SAMPLE

The production of Parmigiano-Reggiano is heavily controlled by the Consorzio del Formaggio, so you can buy the cheese at any store or supermarket in the region and be virtually guaranteed equal quality and price. For a more distinctive shopping experience, however, try buying Parmigiano-Reggiano at the street market on Reggio's central square. The market takes place on Tuesday and Friday from 8 AM to 1 PM year-round.

Warming milk in copper cauldrons

Breaking up the curds

Placing cheese in molds

Aging cheese wheels

Parmigiano-Reggiano

TASTE 3 ACETO BALSAMICO DI MODENA

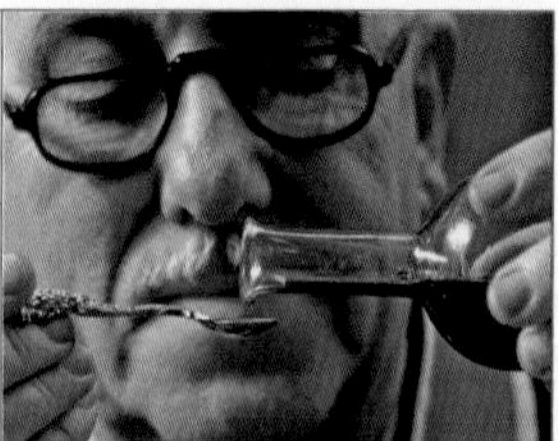
Tasting tradizionale vinegar

Wooden casks for fermenting

Modena is home to *Aceto Balsamico Tradizionale di Modena*, a kind of balsamic vinegar unparalleled anywhere else on Earth. The balsamic vinegar you've probably tried—even the pricier versions sold at specialty stores—may be good on salads, but it bears only a fleeting resemblance to the real thing.

HOW IS IT MADE?

The *tradizionale* vinegar that passes strict government standards is made with Trebbiano grape must, which is cooked over an open fire, reduced, and fermented from 12 to 25 or more years in a series of specially made wooden casks. As the vinegar becomes more concentrated, so much liquid evaporates that it takes more than 6 gallons of must to produce one quart of vinegar 12 years later. The result is an intense and syrupy concoction best enjoyed sparingly on grilled meats, strawberries, or Parmigiano-Reggiano cheese. The vinegar has such a complexity of flavor that some even drink it as an after-dinner liqueur.

BEST SPOT FOR A SAMPLE

The **Consorzio Produttori Aceto Balsamico Tradizionale di Modena** (Strada Vacigho 1085/1, 059/395633, www.balsamico.it) offers tours and tastings by reservation only. The main objective of the consortium is to monitor the quality of the authentic balsamic vinegar, made by only a few licensed restaurants and small producers.

The consortium also limits production, keeping prices sky high. Expect to pay €60 for a 100-ml (3.4 oz) bottle of tradizionale, which is generally aged 12 to 15 years, or €90 and up for the older tradizionale extra vecchio variety, which is aged 25 years.

WHERE TO EAT

In Modena, it's hard to find a bad meal. Local trattorie do great versions of tortellini and other stuffed pasta. If you can find *zampone* (a sausage made from stuffed pig's trotter), don't miss it—it's an adventurous Modena specialty. **Hosteria Giusti** (Vicolo Squallore 46, 059/222533, www.giusti1605.com) is a particularly good place to try local specialties; the adjacent **Salumeria Giusti** is reputedly the world's oldest deli, founded in 1605.

OTHER TASTES OF EMILIA

❑ **Cotechino**: a sausage made from pork and lard, a specialty of Modena

❑ **Culatello de Zibello**: raw cured ham produced along the banks of the Po River, and cured and aged for more than 11 months

❑ **Mortadella**: soft, smoked sausage made with beef, pork, cubes of pork fat, and seasonings, a specialty of Bologna

❑ **Ragù**: a sauce made from minced pork and beef, simmered in milk, onions, carrots, and tomatoes

❑ **Salama da sugo**: salty, oily sausage aged and then cooked, a specialty of Ferrara

❑ **Tortelli and cappellacci**: pasta pillows with the same basic form as tortellini, but stuffed with cheese and vegetables

TASTE 4 | TORTELLINI

The venerable city of **Bologna** is called "the Fat" for a reason: this is the birthplace of tortellini, not to mention other specialties such as mortadella and ragù. Despite the city's new reputation for chic nightclubs and flashy boutiques, much of the food remains as it ever was.

You'll find the many Emilian variations on stuffed pasta all over the region, but they're perhaps at their best in Bologna, especially the native tortellini.

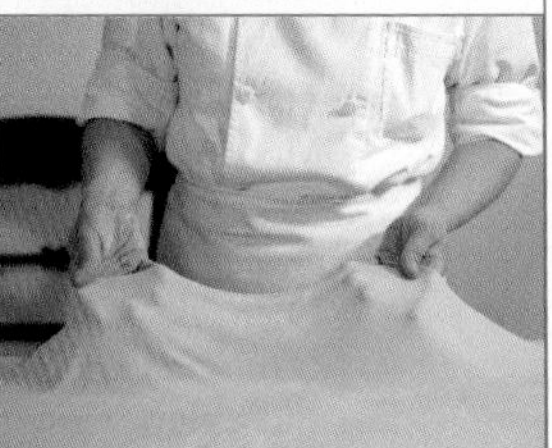

Stretching the dough

INSPIRED BY THE GODS

According to one legend, tortellini was inspired by the bellybutton of Venus, goddess of love. As the story goes, Venus and some other gods stopped at a local inn for the night. A nosy chef went to their room to catch a glimpse of Venus. Peering through the keyhole, he saw her lying only partially covered on the bed. He was so inspired after seeing her perfect navel that he created a stuffed pasta, tortellini, in its image.

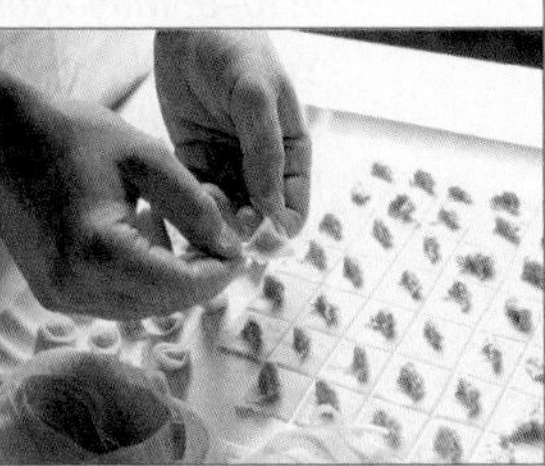

Adding the filling

ON THE MENU

Tortellini is usually filled with beef (sometimes cheese), and is served two ways: *asciutta* is "dry," meaning it is served with a sauce such as ragù, or perhaps just with butter and Parmigiano. *Tortellini in brodo* is immersed in a lovely, savory beef broth.

BEST SPOT TO BUY

Don't miss **Tamburini** (Via Drapperie 1, 051/234726), Bologna's best specialty food shop, where smells of Emilia-Romagna's famous specialties waft out through the room and into the streets.

Shaping each piece

WHERE TO EAT

The classic art deco restaurant **Rosteria Luciano** (Via Nazario Sauro 19, 051/231249, www.rosterialuciano.it) is a great place to try tortellini in brodo, one of the best choices on their fixed menu. A changing list of daily specials augments the menu. For a meat course it's usually best to order whatever special the kitchen has that day. The selection of local cheeses is also good. Please note that the restaurant is closed on Wednesday, the whole month of August, and Sunday from June through September.

Tortellini di Bologna

Modena's principal museum is housed in the **Palazzo dei Musei**, a short walk from the Duomo. The collection was assembled in the mid-17th century by Francesco d'Este (1610–58), Duke of Modena, and the **Galleria Estense** is named in his honor. The gallery also houses the **Biblioteca Estense**, a huge collection of illuminated manuscripts, of which the best known is the beautifully illustrated *Bible of Borso d'Este* (1455–61). A map dated 1501 was one of the first in the world to show that Columbus had discovered America. To get here, follow Via Emilia, the old Roman road that runs through the heart of the town, to Via di Sant'Agostino. ✉ *Piazza Sant'Agostino 337* ☎ *059/4395711* 🎫 *€4* ⏲ *Museum: Tues.–Sun. 8:30–7:30. Gallery: Tues.–Sat. 8:30—7.*

★ The **Galleria Ferrari**, in the suburb of Maranello 17 km (11 mi) south of Modena, has become a pilgrimage site for auto enthusiasts. The museum takes you through the illustrious history of Ferrari, from the early 1951 models to the present, such as the legendary F50, to the cars driven by Michael Schumacher in Formula One victories. You can also take a look at the glamorous life of Enzo Ferrari, including a re-creation of his office and a glance into the production process. ✉ *Via Dino Ferrari, Maranello* ☎ *0536/943204* 🌐 *www.galleria.ferrari.com* 🎫 *€13* ⏲ *Oct.–Apr., daily 9:30–6; May–Nov., daily 9:30–7.*

You can do a tasting with the **Consorzio Produttori Aceto Balsamico Tradizionale di Modena**. They'll arrange for you to visit one of their local producers. The best way to arrange a tour is to contact the Consorzio through their Web site. ✉ *Strada Vaciglio Sud 1085/1* ☎ *059/395633* 🌐 *www.balsamico.it* 🎫 *Free* ⏲ *By appointment.*

WHERE TO EAT

¢ EMILIAN ★ ✕ **Aldina**. On the second floor of a building across from the covered market, steps from the Piazza Grande, this simple, typical trattoria is in the very nerve center of the city. Here you'll find exemplary preparations of the region's crown jewels: tortellini in brodo, tagliatelle al ragù, and roast meats. Wash it down with Lambrusco, as locals have for ages, and save room for the *zuppa inglese* (layered sponge cake with custard), which is terrific here. The kitchen also turns out dishes with *fantasia*, putting a contemporary twist on classics. ✉ *Via Albinelli 40* ☎ *059/236106* 💳 *No credit cards* ⏲ *Closed Sun., and July and Aug. No dinner Mon.–Thurs.*

$ EMILIAN ✕ **Da Enzo**. The Nora-Tassi family has been running this cheerful and crowded no-frills trattoria since 1950. Enzo and son Giovanni run the front, and Argia, Enzo's wife, makes all the tasty desserts. It's packed with Modenesi eager to eat terrific food at relatively inexpensive prices. The tortellini in brodo makes an excellent starter, as does *maccheroncini di Enzo* (macaroni in a minced veal-prosciutto ragù). The bollito misto comes with the usual salsa verde and *mostarda* (a fruit condiment) made in house. Many meats are served *al balsamico*, and since you're in the town that gave the world this precious commodity, why not indulge? Wash it down with the local wine, which happens to be a frizzy Lambrusco served slightly chilled. Note that the trattoria is up two flights of stairs. ✉ *Via Coltellini 17* ☎ *059/225177* ⏲ *Closed Mon. and Aug. No dinner Sun.*

¢ EMILIAN **Ermes.** Ebullient host Ermes greets you as you walk in, and seats you wherever he happens to have room—no matter that you might be seated with people you don't know. It's part of the fun, as this quasi-communal style of lunching encourages conviviality. The wine is local, simple, and cheap; in the kitchen, Bruna, Ermes's wife, turns out splendid versions of *cucina casalinga modenesi* (home cooking, Modena style). Ermes recites the short list of *primi* and *secondi*, which change daily, and they arrive promptly at the table. It's no wonder this place is favored by everyone from suits to construction workers to students. *Via Ganaceto 89–91* *059/238065* *No credit cards* *Closed Sun. No dinner.*

$$$ ITALIAN **Hosteria Giusti.** The ancient stone walls here are shared with what is reputedly the world's oldest deli, the Salumeria Giusti, founded in 1605. There are only four tables and a host of antique furnishings in the tiny room, where the kitchen turns out traditional dishes like handmade tagliolini, *gnocco fritto* (fried dough) with *salumi* (cured meats) from next door, and dishes using Modena's famous balsamic vinegar. Reserve well ahead as lunch is the only meal served. Prices are high, but it's an unforgettable Modena experience. *Vicolo Squallore 46* *059/222533* *www.hosteriagiusti.it* *Reservations essential* *Closed Sun. and Mon. and Dec.–Jan. 10. No dinner.*

WHERE TO STAY

$$ **Hotel Canalgrande.** Once a ducal palace, the Canalgrande today has a lobby so gilded it's over the top. **Pros:** significant discounts for solo travelers; cheaper rates if booking online. **Cons:** caters to business travelers; feels somewhat impersonal. **TripAdvisor:** "public space is spectacular," "staff was friendly and helpful," "small, plain rooms." *Corso Canalgrande 6* *059/217160* *www.canalgrandehotel.it* *62 rooms, 2 suites* *In-room: Internet (some). In-hotel: restaurant, bar, business center, parking, some pets allowed* *Breakfast.*

9

BOLOGNA

Bologna, a city rich with cultural jewels, has long been one of the best-kept secrets in northern Italy. Tourists in the know can bask in the shadow of its leaning medieval towers and devour the city's wonderful food.

The charm of the centro storico, with its red-arcaded passageways and sidewalks, can be attributed to wise city counselors who, at the beginning of the 13th century, decreed that roads could not be built without *portici* (porticoes). Were these counselors to return to town eight centuries later, they would marvel at how little has changed.

The feeling of a university town permeates the air in Bologna. Its population is about 373,000, and it feels young and lively in a way that many other Italian cities do not. It also feels full of Italians in a way that many other towns, thronged with tourists, do not. Bolognesi come out at aperitivo time, and you might be struck by the fact that it's not just youngsters who are out doing the passeggiata, or having a glass of wine with affetati misti—the pleasure is shared by all Bolognesi.

Known as "Bologna the Fat" from as early as the Middle Ages, the town's agricultural prosperity led to a well-fed population, one that survives into the 21st century. Bolognese food is, arguably, the best in Italy. With its sublime food, lively spirit, and largely undiscovered art, Bologna is well worth a visit.

GETTING HERE

Frequent train service from Florence to Bologna makes getting here easy. *Frecciarossa* (high-speed trains) run several times an hour, and take forty minutes; *frecciabianca* (slightly less-high-speed trains) run regularly as well, and take a little over an hour; otherwise, you're left with the regionali (regional) trains, which putter along and get you to Bologna in just over two hours. The historic center is an easy and interesting walk from the station. If you're driving from Florence, take the A1, exiting onto the A14 and then catching the RA1 to Uscita 7–Bologna Centrale. The trip takes about an hour. From Milan, take the A1, exiting to the A14 as you near the city; from there, take the A13 and exit at Bologna, then follow the RA1 to Uscita 7–Bologna Centrale. The trip is just under three hours.

VISITOR INFORMATION

Bologna tourism offices (✉ *Stazione Centrale* ☎ *051/239660* ✉ *Piazza Maggiore 1* ☎ *051/239660* 🌐 *www.bolognaturismo.info*).

EXPLORING BOLOGNA

Piazza Maggiore and the adjacent Piazza del Nettuno are the historic centers of the city. Arranged around these two squares are the imposing Basilica di San Petronio, the massive Palazzo Comunale, the Palazzo del Podestà, the Palazzo Re Enzo, and the Fontana del Nettuno—one of the most visually harmonious groupings of public buildings in the country. From here, sights that aren't on one of the piazzas are but a short walk away, along delightful narrow cobbled streets or under the ubiquitous arcades that double as municipal umbrellas. Take at least a full day to explore Bologna; it's compact and lends itself to easy exploration, but there's plenty to see.

TOP ATTRACTIONS

Basilica di San Petronio. Construction on this cathedral began in 1390, and work is still in progress on this vast building some 600 years later. It's not finished yet, as you can see: the wings of the transept are missing and the facade is only partially decorated, lacking most of the marble facade originally intended to adorn it. The main doorway was carved in 1425 by the great Sienese master Jacopo della Quercia. Above the center of the door is a Madonna and Child flanked by saints Ambrose and Petronius, the city's patrons. Michelangelo, Giulio Romano, and Andrea Palladio (among others) submitted designs for the facade, which were all eventually rejected.

The interior of the basilica is huge: the Bolognesi had planned an even bigger church—you can still see the columns erected to support the larger church outside the east end—but had to tone down construction when the university seat was established next door in 1561. The **Museo di San Petronio** contains models showing how the church was

Basilica di San Petronio **2**
Le Due Torri **6**
Museo Internazionale della Musica **8**
Palazzo Comunale **3**
Palazzo del Podestà **4**
Palazzo Re Enzo **5**
Pinacoteca Nazionale **10**
San Domenico **1**
Santo Stefano **7**
Università di Bologna **9**

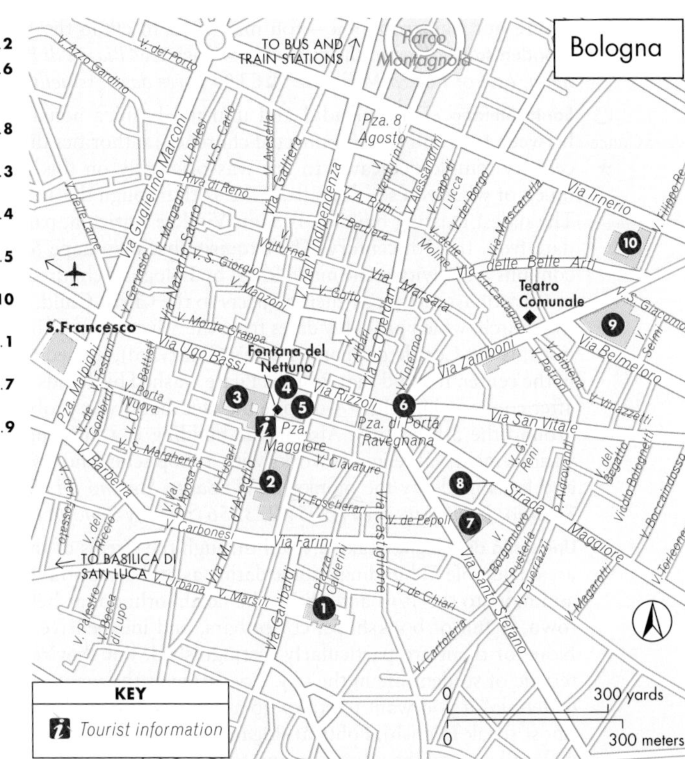

originally intended to look. The most important art in the church is in the fourth chapel on the left; these frescoes by Giovanni di Modena date from 1410–15. ✉ *Piazza Maggiore* ☎ *051/22544* 🎫 *Free* ⏲ *Church: Apr.–Sept., daily 7:45–12:30 and 3:30–6; Oct.–Mar., daily 7:30–1 and 2:30–6. Museum: Weekdays 9:30–12:30 and 3–5:30, Sat. 9:30–12:30 and 3–4:30, Sun. 3–5:30.*

Fontana del Nettuno. Sculptor Giambologna's elaborate 1563–66 baroque fountain and monument to Neptune occupying Piazza Nettuno has been aptly nicknamed *Il Gigante* ("The Giant"). Its exuberantly sensual mermaids and undraped God of the sea drew fire when it was constructed, but not enough, apparently, to dissuade the populace from using the fountain as a public washing stall for centuries. ✉ *Piazza Nettuno, next to Palazzo Re Enzo, Piazza Maggiore area.*

★ **Le Due Torri.** Two landmark towers, mentioned by Dante in *The Inferno*, stand side by side in the compact Piazza di Porta Ravegnana. Every family of importance had a tower as a symbol of prestige and power, and as a potential fortress; only 60 remain out of more than 200 that once presided over the city. **Torre Garisenda** (from the late 11th century), which tilts 10 feet off perpendicular, was shortened to 165 feet in the 1300s and is now closed to visitors. **Torre degli Asinelli** (circa 1109) is 320 feet tall and leans 7½ feet. If you're up to a serious physical challenge—and you're not claustrophobic—you may want to climb the 500 narrow, wooden steps to get to the view over Bologna. ✉ *Piazza di Porta Ravegnana, east of Piazza Maggiore* 🎫 *€3* ⏲ *Torre degli Asinelli: daily 9–5.*

Fodor's Choice ★ **Santo Stefano.** This splendid and unusual basilica actually contains between four and seven connected churches (authorities differ). A 4th-century temple dedicated to Isis was originally on this site, though much of what you see dates from the 10th through the 12th centuries. The oldest existing building is **Santi Vitale e Agricola,** parts of which date from the 5th century. The exquisite beehive-shape San Sepolcro contains a Nativity scene much loved by Bologna's children, who come at Christmastime to pay their respects to the Christ Child. Just outside the church, which probably dates from the 5th century with later alterations, is the **Cortile di Pilato** (Pilate's Courtyard), named for the basin in the center. It's said that Pontius Pilate washed his hands in this basin after condemning Christ—despite the fact that it was probably crafted around the 8th century. Also in the building is a museum displaying various medieval religious works with a shop selling honey, shampoos, and jams made by the monks. ✉ *Via Santo Stefano 24, Piazza Santo Stefano, University area* ☎ *051/223256* ⏲ *Daily 9–noon and 3:30–6.*

Università di Bologna. Take a stroll through the streets of the university area, a jumble of buildings, some dating as far back as the 15th century and most to the 17th and 18th. The neighborhood, as befits a college town, is full of bookshops, coffee bars, and inexpensive restaurants. None of them are particularly distinguished, but they're all characteristic of student life in the city. Try eating at the *mensa universitaria* (cafeteria) if you want to strike up a conversation with local students (most speak English). Political slogans and sentiments are scrawled on walls all around the university and tend to be ferociously leftist, sometimes juvenile, and often entertaining. Among the university museums, the most interesting is the **Museo di Palazzo Poggi,** which displays scientific instruments and paleontological, botanical, and university-related artifacts. ✉ *Via Zamboni 33, University area* ☎ *051/2099610* 🌐 *www.museopalazzopoggi.unibo.it* 🎫 *€3* ⏲ *Tues.–Fri. 10–1 and 2–4, weekends 10:30–1:30 and 2:30–5:30.*

WORTH NOTING

Museo Internazionale della Musica. The music museum in the spectacular Palazzo Aldini Sanguinetti, with its 17th- and 18th-century frescoes, offers among its exhibits a 1606 harpsichord and a collection of beautiful music manuscripts dating from the 1500s. ✉ *Strada Maggiore 34, University area* ☎ *051/2757711* 🌐 *www.museomusicabologna.it* 🎫 *Free* ⏲ *Oct.–July, Tues.–Fri. 9:30–4, weekends 10–6:30.*

Palazzo Comunale. A mélange of building styles and constant modifications characterize this huge palace dating from the 13th to 15th centuries. When Bologna was an independent city-state, this was the seat of government, a function it still serves today. Over the door is a statue of Bologna-born Pope Gregory XIII (reigned 1572–85), most famous for reorganizing the calendar. There are good views from the upper stories of the palace. The first-floor **Sala Rossa** (Red Room) is open on advance request and during some exhibitions, while the **Sala del**

Consiglio Comunale (City Council Hall) is open to the public for a few hours in the late morning. The old stock exchange, part of the Palazzo Comunale, which you enter from Piazza Nettuno, has been turned into a library, the **Sala Borsa** (🌐 *www.bibliotecasalaborsa.it*), which has an impressive interior courtyard. Within the palazzo there are also two museums. The **Collezioni Comunali d'Arte** exhibits paintings from the Middle Ages as well as some Renaissance works by Luca Signorelli (circa 1445–1523) and Tintoretto (1518–94). The **Museo Giorgio Morandi** (🌐 *www.museomorandi.it*) is dedicated to the 20th-century still-life artist Giorgio Morandi; in addition to his paintings, there's a re-creation of his studio and living space. Underground caves and the foundations of the old cathedral can be visited by appointment made through the tourist office. ✉ *Piazza Maggiore 6* ☎ *051/203111 Palazzo; 051/2193154 Collezioni; 051/2193338 Museo* 🎫 *€6, except during special art exhibitions* ⏲ *Sala del Consiglio Comunale: Tues.–Sat. 10–1. Sala Borsa: weekdays 9–1. Collezioni and Museo: Tues.–Fri. 11–6, weekends 11–8.*

Palazzo del Podestà. This classic Renaissance palace facing the Basilica di San Petronio was erected in 1484, and attached to it is the soaring **Torre dell'Arengo.** The bells in the tower have rung whenever the city has celebrated, mourned, or called its citizens to arms. ✉ *Piazza Nettuno, Piazza Maggiore area* ☎ *051/224500* ⏲ *During exhibitions only.*

Palazzo Re Enzo. Built in 1244, this palace became home to King Enzo of Sardinia, who was imprisoned here in 1249 after he was captured during the fierce battle of Fossalta. He died here 23 years later in 1272. The palace has other macabre associations: common criminals received last rites in the tiny courtyard chapel before being executed in Piazza Maggiore. The courtyard is worth peeking into, but the palace merely houses government offices. ✉ *Piazza Re Enzo, Piazza Maggiore area* ☎ *051/224500* ⏲ *During exhibitions only.*

9

Pinacoteca Nazionale. Bologna's principal art gallery contains many works by the immortals of Italian painting spanning the 13th to the 19th centuries. Its prize possession is the famous *Ecstasy of St. Cecilia* by Raphael (1483–1520). There's also a beautiful polyptych by Giotto (1267–1337), as well as *Madonna and Child with Saints Margaret, Jerome, and Petronio* by Parmigianino; note the rapt eye contact between St. Margaret and the Christ Child. ✉ *Via delle Belle Arti 56, University area* ☎ *051/4209411* 🌐 *www.pinacotecabologna.it* 🎫 *€4* ⏲ *Tues.–Sun. 9–7.*

San Domenico. The tomb of St. Dominic, who died here in 1221, is called the **Arca di San Domenico,** and is found in this church in the sixth chapel on the right. Many artists participated in its decoration, notably Niccolò di Bari, who was so proud of his contribution that he changed his name to Niccolò dell'Arca to recall this famous work. The young Michelangelo (1475–1564) carved the angel on the right. In the right transept of the church is a tablet marking the last resting place of the hapless King Enzo, the Sardinian ruler imprisoned in the Palazzo Re Enzo. The attached museum contains religious relics. ✉ *Piazza San Domenico 13, off Via Garibaldi, south of Piazza Maggiore* ☎ *051/6400411* ⏲ *Church: daily 8–12:30 and 3:30–6:30. Museum: weekdays 10–noon and 3:30–6, Sat. 9:30–noon and 3:30–5:30, Sun. 3:30–5:30.*

OFF THE BEATEN PATH

MAMbo. The name of this museum stands for Museo d'Arte Moderna di Bologna, or Bologna's Museum of Modern Art. It houses a permanent collection of modern art (defined as post-World War II up until five minutes ago) as well as a revolving series of temporary exhibitions by cutting-edge artists. All of this is housed in a remarkable space: you might have a hard time telling that the sleek, minimalist structure was built in 1915 as the Forno del Pane, a large bakery that made bread for many of the city's residents. A bookshop and a restaurant complete the complex; the restaurant offers Sunday brunch and delicious *aperitivi* (aperitifs). ✉ *Viale Don Minzoni 14,* ☎ *051/6496611* 🌐 *www.mambo-bologna.org* 🎫 *€6* ⏲ *Tues., Wed., and Fri. 12–6, Thurs. 12–10, weekends 12–8*

WHERE TO EAT

$ EMILIAN ★ ✕ **Casa Godot.** This restaurant used to be known as Godot Wine Bar until a change in management occurred in April 2010. Renovations included spiffing up the interior to create a sleek room with white walls and black-and-white prints adorning them, white tablecloths, and black furniture. The menu makes a nod to tradition by offering tagliolini, *passatelli*, and *tortellaci* (all types of pasta) Twists occur in the stuffings and sauces: try the tagliolini with scallops and stewed shallots. Traditional *culatello* (a particularly choice cut of cured ham) pairs in a novel combination with raw, delicately dressed artichokes, and the result is beyond pleasing. Purists will thrill to their exquisite tortellini in brodo, as well as their sublime secondi and desserts. The extensive wine list leaves no bases uncovered. ✉ *Via Cartoleria 12, University area* ☎ *051/226315* ⏲ *Closed Sun. and 3 wks in Aug.*

$$ EMILIAN ★ ✕ **Da Cesari.** Just off Piazza Maggiore, this lovely one-room restaurant has white tablecloths, dark-wood paneling, and wine bottle–lined walls. Genial host Paolino Cesari has been presiding over his restaurant since 1955, and both he and his staff go out of the way to make you feel at home. The food's terrific—if you're a lover of pork products, try anything on the menu with *mora romagnola*. Paolino has direct contact with the people who raise this once nearly extinct type of porcine (referring to it as "my pig"). The meat is deep, highly flavorful, and makes divine salame, among other things. All the usual Bolognesi classics are here, as well as—in fall and winter—an inspired version of *scaloppa all Petroniano* (veal cutlet with prosciutto and fontina) that arrives at the table smothered in white truffles. ✉ *Via de' Carbonesi 8, south of Piazza Maggiore* ☎ *051/237710* ✍ *Reservations essential* ⏲ *Closed Sun., Aug., and 1 wk in Jan.*

$$ EMILIAN ✕ **Da Gianni a la Vecia Bulagna.** Locals simply call it "da Gianni," and they fill these two unadorned rooms at lunch and at dinner. Though the decor is plain and unremarkable, it doesn't much matter—this place is all about food. The usual starters such as a tasty tortellini in brodo are on hand, as are daily specials such as gnocchi made with pumpkin, then sauced with melted cheese. Bollito misto (mixed meats boiled in a rich broth) is a fine option here, and the cotechino *con purè di patate* (a deliciously oily sausage with mashed potatoes) is elevated to sublimity by the accompanying salsa verde. ✉ *Via Clavature 18, Piazza Maggiore area* ☎ *051/229434* ✍ *Reservations essential.*

CLOSE UP

Cooking alla Bolognese

A fine way to truly appreciate the appeal of Bolognese food is to learn how to make it. Barbara Bertuzzi, author of the cookbook *Bolognese Cooking Heritage*, teaches classes at **La Vecchia Scuola Bolognese** *(the Old Bolognese Cooking School)*. Her four-hour sessions focus on pasta making and are offered daily; they begin at 9:30 am and continue to lunchtime, when you can eat the fruits of your labor. Evening courses are available, and Bertuzzi also offers lunches and dinners without the lessons. The school is near the Ospedale Maggiore—take Bus 19 from Via Rizzoli near Piazza Maggiore, or a €15 taxi ride from the centro storico. If you're the only aspiring chef in your party, the rest can join after the lesson for dinner at €35 each. ✉ *Via Malvasia 49* ☎ *051/6491576* 🌐 *www.lavecchiascuola.com* 🎟 *€70 per person, €90 with meal.*

If you prefer your cooking classes in a truly regal setting, you might want to try **La Tavola della Signoria**, held in the spectacular 17th-century rooms of the Palazzo Albergati (🌐 *www.palazzoalbergati.it*). These classes are offered only four or five times per month and are more expensive than some others, but they're also longer and more serious. Class starts at 8:30 am and runs until 5:30 pm; you can choose between different modules, such as bread making, pasta making, desserts, and so on. For the true aficionados, two- and three-day fruit-and-vegetable courses are offered periodically. It's 10 km (6 mi) west of the city center; to get here take SS569, get off at the last Zona Predosa exit, and follow signs for the Palazzo Albergati. You can sign up online. ✉ *Via Masini 46* ☎ *051/6166542* 🌐 *www.tavoladellasignoria.it* 🎟 *€170–€200 per person for 1 day; up to €480 for 3 days.*

¢ ITALIAN ✕ **Divinis.** Wine bottles line the walls on both floors of this spot, testimony to its commitment to serving fine wines (by the glass and by the bottle). Terrific food accompanies the oenophilic splendor. Cheese and cured meat plates are on offer, as are superlative soups, salads, and secondi on a frequently changing menu. Special events, such as wine tastings and tango dancing, happen throughout the week. An added plus is Divinis's continuous opening hours, a rarity in Italy; you could have a coffee at 11 am or a glass of wine well after midnight. ✉ *Via Battibecco 4/c, Piazza Maggiore* ☎ *051/2961502* ✍ *Reservations essential* ⏲ *Closed Sun.*

$$ EMILIAN ✕ **Drogheria della Rosa.** Chef Emanuele Addone, who presides over his intimate little restaurant, hits the food markets every day and buys what looks good. This brings seasonality to his menu. He sauces his tortelli stuffed with *squacquerone* and *stracchino* (two creamy, fresh cow's-milk cheeses) with artichokes, zucchini flowers, or mushrooms, depending on the time of year. In order to do this place justice, you need to come with an appetite—you won't want to skip a course. Kick off the proceedings with a glass of prosecco and a plate of *affettati misti* (mixed cured meats, a local specialty). Among the secondi, the tender *filetto al balsamico* (filet mignon with balsamic vinegar sauce on top) is exquisite. So is the wine list. ✉ *Via Cartoleria 10, University area* ☎ *051/222529* 🌐 *www.drogheriadellarosa.it* ⏲ *Closed Sun.*

¢ WINE BAR **Tamburini.** Two small rooms inside, and kegs and bar stools outside make up this lively, packed little wine bar. At lunchtime, office workers swarm at the "bistrot self service" with remarkably tasty primi and secondi. After lunch, it becomes a wine bar with a vast array of selections by the glass and the bottle. The overwhelming plate of *affettati* misti is crammed with top-quality local ham products and succulent cheeses (including, sometimes, a goat Brie). An adjacent salumeria offers many wonderful things to take away. *Via Drapperie 1, Piazza Maggiore area 051/234726 No dinner.*

$ EMILIAN **Trattoria del Rosso.** The decor's nothing to write home about, with glaring yellow walls and the oddly placed ceramic plate, but the place teems with locals. The mostly young crowd chows down on delicious, basic regional fare at rock-bottom prices. The nimble staff bearing multiple plates sashay neatly between the closely spaced tables delivering such standards as *crescentine con salumi e squacquerone* (deep-fried flour puffs with cured meats and soft cheese) and tortellini in brodo. This is the kind of place where there's always a line of hungry people outside waiting to get in, but where they don't glare at you if you only order a plate of pasta. Another reason, perhaps, why it's a favorite of university students. *Via Augusto Righi 30, University area 051/236730 Closed Thurs.*

WHERE TO STAY

$ **Albergo Centrale.** It began life as a pensione in 1875, but subsequent restructurings have comfortably brought the Albergo Centrale into the 21st century. **Pros:** very good value; excellent location. **Cons:** might be too plain for some tastes; street-facing rooms can get some noise. **TripAdvisor:** "quiet surroundings," "room was clean, comfortable," "good entrance hall." *Via della Zecca 2, Piazza Maggiore 051/225114 www.albergocentralebologna.it 31 rooms, 26 rooms with bath In-room: a/c, Wi-Fi. In-hotel: parking, some pets allowed Breakfast.*

$$$ **Art Hotel Novecento.** This swank place, inspired by the 1930s Viennese Secession movement, is in a remarkably serene cul-de-sac just minutes from Piazza Maggiore. **Pros:** spacious single rooms ideal for solo travelers; friendly, capable concierge service. **Cons:** some standard doubles are small. **TripAdvisor:** "sophistication without pretension," "smartly furnished," "steps away from main piazza." *Piazza Galileo 4/3i, Piazza Maggiore area 051/7457311 www.bolognarthotels.it/novecento 24 rooms, 1 suite In-room: Wi-Fi. In-hotel: bar, business center, parking, some pets allowed Breakfast.*

$$ ★ **Art Hotel Orologio.** The location can't be beat: it's right around the corner from Piazza Maggiore, tucked in a quiet little side street. **Pros:** central location; great views; family-friendly rooms. **Cons:** some steps to elevator. **TripAdvisor:** "historical sites in every direction," "loved the shuttered windows," "bathroom was enormous." *Via IV Novembre 10, Piazza Maggiore area 051/7457411 www.bolognarthotels.it/orologio 26 rooms, 6 suites, 1 apartment In-room: Wi-Fi. In-hotel: restaurant, business center, parking, some pets allowed Breakfast.*

NIGHTLIFE AND THE ARTS

THE ARTS

Bologna's arts scene is one of the liveliest in Italy. Opera, ballet, rock concerts, and theatrical extravaganzas happen year-round, as do food festivals. The **Bologna tourism office** (☎ *051/239660* 🌐 *www.bolognaturismo.info*) has information on performances and events.

MUSIC AND OPERA

The 18th-century **Teatro Comunale** (✉ *Largo Respighi 1, University area* ☎ *051/529958* 🌐 *www.tcbo.it*) presents concerts by Italian and international orchestras throughout the year, but is dominated by the highly acclaimed opera performances November–May, so reserve seats well in advance. The ticket office is open Tuesday–Friday 12–6 and Saturday 10:30–4.

NIGHTLIFE

As a university town, Bologna has long been known for its busy nightlife. As early as 1300 it was said to have had 150 taverns. Most of the city's current 200-plus pubs and bars are frequented by Italian students, young adults, and international students, with the university district forming the hub. In addition to the university area, the pedestrians-only zone on Via del Pratello, lined with plenty of bars, is also a hopping night scene, as is Via delle Moline, with cutting-edge cafés and bars. A more upmarket, low-key evening experience can be had at one of Bologna's many wine bars, where the food is often substantial enough to constitute dinner.

BARS

If you want a night out at a trendy spot, Bologna offers a lot to choose from.

Bar Calice (✉ *Via Clavature 13/a, at Via Marchesana, Piazza Maggiore area* ☎ *051/6569296*) runs an indoor-outdoor operation year-round (with heat lamps). It's extremely popular with thirtysomethings (sometimes pushing baby carriages). At **Le Stanze** (✉ *Via del Borgo di San Pietro 1, University area* ☎ *051/228767* 🌐 *www.lestanzecafe.com* ⊗ *Closed Mon., and July and Aug.*) you can sip an *aperitivo* or a late-night drink at a modern bar. The decor includes 17th-century frescoes in what was once the private chapel of the Palazzo Bentivoglio. The adjoining cutting-edge restaurant serves Italian fusion cooking. **Mortadella and Champagne** (✉ *Via Garibaldi 7* ☎ *051/0453478*) bills itself as a bistro. It attracts young folks who choose from the many bottles of bubbly on hand; a plate of mortadella to accompany is an absolute must. The lively **Nu Bar Lounge** (✉ *Off Buca San Petronio, Via de' Musei 6, Piazza Maggiore area* ☎ *051/222532* 🌐 *www.nu-lounge.com*) draws a cocktail-loving crowd, who enjoy bartenders mixing up fun drinks like "I'm Too Sexy for This Place," which, in this case, is a combination of vodka, triple sec, apple juice, and lemon. **In Vino Veritas** (✉ *Via Garibaldi 9/f* ☎ *051/3399332*) has three little tables, a counter, and Michele pouring serious wines to pair with his seriously good cheeses and *affettati misti*.

MUSIC VENUES

It's not hard to find drinks accompanied by live music in the city. With live music staged every night, **Cantina Bentivoglio** (✉ *Via Mascarella 4/b, University area* ☎ *051/265416*) is one of Bologna's most appealing nightspots. You can enjoy light meals here as well. **Osteria Buca delle Campane** (✉ *Via Benedetto XIV 4/a, University area* ☎ *051/220918*), an underground tavern in a 13th-century building, has good, inexpensive food and a lively after-dinner scene popular with locals, including students who come to listen to live music.

SHOPPING

CLOTHING

One of the most upscale malls in Italy, the **Galleria Cavour** (✉ *Piazza Cavour, south of Piazza Maggiore*) houses many of the fashion giants, including Gucci, Versace, and the jeweler and watchmaker Bulgari. If you don't feel like paying Galleria Cavour prices, **Castel Guelfo Outlet City** (✉ *Via del Commercio 20/a, Loc. Poggio Piccolo, Castel Guelfo* ☎ *0542/670765* 🌐 *www.thestyleoutlets.it*) is about 20 minutes outside Bologna on the autostrada A14 toward Imola (take the Castel San Pietro Terme exit; 980 feet after the tollbooth, turn right onto Via San Carlo). It includes about 50 discounted stores, some from top designers such as Ferré. It's closed Monday morning.

WINE AND FOOD

Bologna is a good place to buy wine. Several shops have a bewilderingly large selection—to go straight to the top, ask the managers which wines have won the prestigious *Tre Bicchieri* (Three Glasses) award from Gambero Rosso's wine bible, *Vini d'Italia*.

Repeatedly recognized as one of the best wine stores in Italy, **Enoteca Italiana** (✉ *Via Marsala 2/b, north of Piazza Maggiore* ☎ *051/235989*) lives up to its reputation with shelves lined with excellent selections from all over Italy at reasonable prices. Their delicious sandwiches with wines by the glass also make a great light lunch. Friendly owners run the mid-size, down-to-earth **Scaramagli** (✉ *Strada Maggiore 31/d, University area* ☎ *051/227132*) wine store. **La Baita** (✉ *Via Pescherie Vecchia 3/a, Piazza Maggiore area* ☎ *051/223940*) sells fresh tagliolini, tortellini, and other Bolognese pasta delicacies, as well as sublime food to take away. Their cheese counter teems with local cheeses of superlative quality.

If you favor sweets, head to **Le Dolcezze** (✉ *Via Murr 21i, Piazza Maggiore area* ☎ *051/444582*), a top local *pasticceria* (pastry shop) whose cakes are excellent, and whose *panettone*, a sweet bread produced only around the holidays, is considered by some to be the best in town. **Paolo Atti & Figli** (✉ *Via Caprarie 7, Piazza Maggiore area* ☎ *051/220425* 🌐 *www.paoloatti.com*) has been producing some of Bologna's finest pastas, cakes, and other delicacies for over 130 years.

Roccati (✉ *Via Clavature 17/a, Piazza Maggiore area* ☎ *051/261964* 🌐 *www.roccaticioccolato.com*) has been crafting sculptural works of chocolate, as well as basic bonbons and simpler stuff since 1909. For fresh produce, meats, and other foods, head to **Via Oberdan** (✉ *Piazza Maggiore area*), the street just off Via dell'Indipendenza downtown. The

Mercato delle Erbe (✉ *Via Ugo Bassi, Piazza Maggiore area* ☎ *051/230186*) is an equally bustling food market, open Monday through Wednesday and Friday 7–1:15 and 5–7:30 (4:30–7:30 October–March), and Thursday and Saturday 7–1:15. The **Mercato di Mezzo** (✉ *Via Peschiere Vecchie, Piazza Maggiore area*), which sells specialty foods, fruits, and vegetables, is an intense barrage of sights and smells. It's open Monday through Saturday 7–1 and 4:15–7:30, with the exception of Thursday afternoon, when it's closed.

FERRARA

47 km (29 mi) northeast of Bologna, 74 km (46 mi) northwest of Ravenna.

When the legendary Ferrarese filmmaker Michelangelo Antonioni called his beloved hometown "a city that you can see only partly, while the rest disappears to be imagined," perhaps he was referring to the low-lying mist that rolls in off the Adriatic each winter and shrouds Ferrara's winding knot of medieval alleyways, turreted palaces, and ancient wine bars—once inhabited by the likes of Copernicus—in a ghostly fog. But perhaps Antonioni was also suggesting that Ferrara's striking beauty often conceals a dark and tortured past.

Though it was settled as early as the 6th century AD, Ferrara's history really begins with the arrival of the Este, who first made their appearance in the city in 1196. For more than three centuries the dynasty ruled with an iron fist; brother killed brother, son fought father, husband murdered wife. The majestic moated castle, now the architectural gem of the historic center, was originally built as a fortress to protect the ruthless Este dukes from their own citizens; deep within the castle the Este kept generations of political dissidents in dank cells. The greatest of the dukes, Ercole I (1433–1505), attempted to poison a nephew who challenged his power, and when that didn't work he beheaded him. Though the Jews were already well established in Ferrara as early at the 1380s, it's Ercole I who invited Sephardic Jews exiled from Spain to settle in Ferrara, thus giving form to one of the liveliest Jewish communities in Western Europe. The maze of twisting cobblestone streets in the ghetto witnessed the persecution of its Jews once fascist Italy was officially at war with Nazi Germany in October 1943. This tragedy was documented in Giorgio Bassani's semiautobiographical book and Vittorio De Sica's film, *The Garden of the Finzi-Continis*.

Today you are likely to be charmed by Ferrara's prosperous air and meticulous cleanliness, its excellent restaurants and coffeehouses, and its lively wine bar scene. You'll find aficionados gathering outside any of the wine bars near the Duomo even on the foggiest of weekend evenings. Though Ferrara is a UNESCO World Heritage site, the city still draws amazingly few tourists—which only adds to its appeal.

GETTING HERE

Train service is frequent from Bologna (usually three trains per hour) and takes either a half hour or 45 minutes, depending upon which train type you take. It's a two-hour ride from Florence, and trains go just about every hour. The walk from the train station is easy but not particularly interesting. If you're driving from Bologna, take the RA1 out of town, take the A13 in the direction of Padova, and exit at Ferrara Nord. Follow the SP19 directly into the center of town. The trip should take about 45 minutes.

VISITOR INFORMATION

Ferrara tourism office (✉ *Estense* ☎ *0532/299303* ✉ *Piazza Municipale 11* 🌐 *www.ferrarainfo.com*).

EXPLORING FERRARA

If you plan to explore the city fully, consider buying a Card Musei ("museum card," €17, valid for one year) at the Palazzo dei Diamanti or at any of the museums around town; it grants admission to every museum, palace, and castle in Ferrara. The first Monday of the month is free at many museums.

TOP ATTRACTIONS

★ Massive **Castello Estense**, the former seat of Este power, dominates the center of town. The building was a suitable symbol for the ruling family: cold and menacing on the outside, lavishly decorated within. The public rooms are grand, but deep in the bowels of the castle are chilling dungeons where enemies of the state were held in wretched conditions—a function these quarters served as recently as 1943, when antifascist prisoners were detained there. In particular, the **Prisons of Don Giulio, Ugo, and Parisina** have some fascinating features, like 15th-century graffiti protesting the imprisonment of lovers Ugo and Parisina, who were beheaded in 1425 because Ugo's father, Niccolò III, didn't like the fact that his son was cavorting with Niccolò's wife.

The castle was established as a fortress in 1385, but work on its luxurious ducal quarters continued into the 16th century. Representative of Este grandeur are the **Sala dei Giochi,** extravagantly painted with athletic scenes, and the **Sala dell'Aurora,** decorated to show the times of the day. The tower, the terraces of the castle, and the hanging garden—once reserved for the private use of the duchesses—have fine views of the town and the surrounding countryside. You can cross the castle's moat, traverse its drawbridge, and wander through many of its arcaded passages at any time. Do note that the entrance price is substantially higher if there's a special exhibition on. ✉ *Piazza Castello* ☎ *0532/299233* 🌐 *www.castelloestense.it* 🎫 *Castle €8, tower €2 extra* ⏲ *Castle: Tues.–Sun. 9:30–5:30. Tower: Tues.–Sun. 10–4:45. Ticket office closes at 4:45.*

QUICK BITES

Caffetteria Castello (✉ *Largo Castello* ☎ *0532/299337* ⏲ *Tues.–Sun. 9:30–5:30*) **is spectacularly situated amid centuries of history. The second floor provides a great place to break for coffee while touring the castle, or to mingle with locals enjoying the lunchtime buffet. Right next door is a small book-and-gift shop.**

★ The magnificent Gothic **Duomo**, a few steps from the Castello Estense, has a three-tier facade of slender arches and beautiful sculptures over the central door. Work began in 1135 and took more than 100 years to complete. The interior was completely remodeled in the 17th century. ✉ *Piazza Cattedrale* ☎ *0532/207449* ⏲ *Mon.–Sat. 7:30–noon and 3–6:30, Sun. 7:30–12:30 and 3:30–7:30.*

The collection of ornate religious objects in the **Museo Ebraico** *(Jewish Museum)* bears witness to the long history of the city's Jewish community. This history had its high points—1492, for example, when Ercole I invited the Jews to come over from Spain—and its lows, notably 1627, when Jews were enclosed within the **ghetto,** where they were forced to live until the advent of a united Italy in 1860. The triangular warren of narrow, cobbled streets that made up the ghetto originally extended as far as Corso Giovecca (originally Corso Giudecca, or Ghetto Street); when it was enclosed, the neighborhood was restricted to the area between Via Scienze, Via Contrari, and Via di San Romano. The museum, in the center of the ghetto, was once Ferrara's synagogue. All visits are led by a museum guide. ✉ *Via Mazzini 95* ☎ *0532/210228* 🌐 *www.comune.fe.it/museoebraico* 🎟 *€4* ⏲ *Tours: Sun. and Thurs. at 10, 11, and noon.*

The **Palazzo dei Diamanti** *(Palace of Diamonds)* is so called because of the 12,600 small, pink-and-white marble pyramids ("diamonds") that stud the facade. The building was designed to be viewed in perspective—both faces at once—from diagonally across the street. Work began in the 1490s and finished around 1504. Today the palazzo contains the **Pinacoteca Nazionale,** which has an extensive art gallery and rotating exhibits. ✉ *Corso Ercole I d'Este 19–21* ☎ *0532/244949* 🌐 *www.artecultura.fe.it* 🎟 *€4* ⏲ *Tues., Wed. and Fri.–Sat. 9–2, Thurs. 9–7, Sun. 9–1.*

The oldest and most characteristic area of Ferrara is south of the Duomo, stretching between the Corso Giovecca and the city's ramparts. Here various members of the Este family built pleasure palaces, the most famous of which is the **Palazzo Schifanoia** (*schifanoia* means "carefree" or, literally, "fleeing boredom"). Begun in the late 14th century, the palace was remodeled between 1464 and 1469. The lavishly decorated interior, particularly the **Salone dei Mesi,** with an extravagant series of frescoes showing the months of the year and their mythological attributes, is well worth visiting. ✉ *Via Scandiana 23* ☎ *0532/244949* 🌐 *www.artecultura.fe.it* 🎟 *€6* ⏲ *Tues.–Sun. 9–6, call ahead to confirm.*

9

One of the streets most characteristic of Ferrara's past, the 2-km-long (1-mi-long) **Via delle Volte** is also one of the best-preserved medieval streets in Europe. The series of ancient *volte* (arches) along the narrow cobblestone alley once joined the merchants' houses on the south side of the street to their warehouses on the north side. The street ran parallel to the banks of the Po River, which was home to Ferrara's busy port.

WORTH NOTING

One of the loveliest of the Renaissance palaces along Ferrara's old streets is the charming **Casa Romei.** Built by the wealthy banker Giovanni Romei (1402–83), it's a vast structure with a graceful courtyard. Mid-15th-century frescoes decorate rooms on the ground floor; the *piano nobile* (main floor) contains detached frescoes from local churches as well as lesser-known Renaissance sculptures. The Sala delle Sibelle has a very large, 15th-century fireplace, and beautiful wood-coffered ceilings. ✉ *Via Savonarola 30* ☎ *0532/234130* 🌐 *www.artecultura.fe.it* 🎟 *€3* ⏲ *Tues.–Sun. 8:30–7.*

Some of the original decorations of the town's main church, the former church and cloister of San Romano, reside in the **Museo della Cattedrale**, which is across the piazza from the Duomo. Inside you'll find 22 codices commissioned between 1477–1535, moving early 13th-century sculpture by the Maestro dei Mesi, a mammoth oil on canvas by Cosmé Tura from 1469, and an exquisite Jacopo della Quercia, the *Madonna della Melograno*. Though this sculpture dates from 1403–1408, the playful expression on the Christ child seems very 21st century. ✉ *Via San Romano 1* ☎ *0532/244949* 🌐 *www.artecultura.fe.it* 🎫 *€5* ⏲ *Tues.–Sun. 9–1 and 3–6.*

On the busy Corso Giovecca is the **Palazzina di Marfisa d'Este**, a grandiose 16th-century palace that belonged to a great patron of the arts. It has painted ceilings, fine 16th-century furniture, and a garden containing a grotto and an outdoor theater. ✉ *Corso Giovecca 170* ☎ *0532/207450* 🌐 *www.artecultura.fe.it* 🎫 *€4* ⏲ *Tues.–Sun. 9–1 and 3–6.*

WHERE TO EAT

$$$ MODERN ITALIAN ★ ✕ **Il Don Giovanni.** Just down the street from Castello Estense, this warm and inviting restaurant is inside a lovely 17th-century palace and has but a handful of tables. Chef Pier Luigi Di Diego and partner Marco Merighi pay strict attention to what's seasonal, and the menu reflects this. Here tortellini are stuffed with guinea fowl and sauced with *zabaione (custard)*, Parmesan, and *prosciutto crocante* (fried prosciutto). Equally inventive is the delicate *tegame di pernice rossa ai frutti di bosco* (partridge in a fruit sauce), which delights the palate. Next door, the same proprietors run the less expensive, crowded, and trendy **La Borsa** wine bar, which has excellent cured meats, cheeses, lovely primi and secondi, as well as a fantastic wine-by-the-glass list. (The wine bar is open for lunch, but the restaurant isn't.) ✉ *Corso Ercole I d'Este 1* ☎ *0532/243363* 🌐 *www.ildongiovanni.com* ✍ *Reservations essential* ⏲ *Closed Mon. No lunch.*

$$ EMILIAN Fodor's Choice ★ ✕ **L'Oca Giuliva.** Food, service, and ambience unite in blissful harmony at this casual yet elegant restaurant minutes from Piazza Repubblica. You enter through a tiny wine bar, where you could enjoy a glass of wine and a snack or proceed directly into the restaurant. Two well-appointed rooms in a 12th-century building provide the backdrop for exquisitely prepared local foods. The chef has a deft hand with local specialties and executes them either in *tradizionale* (traditional) or *rivisitata* (updated) style. Particularly impressive are the primi, especially the *cappellacci di zucca al ragù* (pumpkin-stuffed pasta). It might be the best version in town. Meat-and-potatoes folk can opt for the *salama da sugo* (a salty, garlicky boiled sausage served over mashed potatoes), and adventurous sorts might try the *trancio di anguilla* (roasted eel) with polenta on the side. The amazing wine list is complemented by a terrific cheese plate. ✉ *Via Boccanale di Santo Stefano 38* ☎ *0532/207628* ⏲ *Closed Mon. No lunch Tues.*

¢ WINE BAR ★ ✕ **Osteria al Brindisi.** Ferrara is a city of wine bars, beginning with this, allegedly Europe's oldest, which opened in 1435. Copernicus drank here while a student in the late 1400s, and the place still has a somewhat undergraduate aura; most of the staff and clientele are twentysomethings. Perfectly dusty wine bottles line the walls, and there are wooden

CLOSE UP

Talking Politics

Emilia-Romagna might seem staid: city after city has immaculate streets filled with smartly dressed businesspeople in impeccable shoes, covertly murmuring to each other through the winter fog over cups of coffee. But after dark, from Parma to Bologna, Piacenza to Ferrara, the middle managers are replaced on the streets by young, energetic would-be intellectuals, and the murmurs turn into impassioned political discussion—usually with a leftist slant—over jugs of table wine. If you enjoy this type of conversation, take time to stop for a drink after dinner in a student cafeteria, cozy café, or back-alley bar. Don't be afraid to join in—all ages are welcome, and divergent opinions, thoughtfully argued, are treated with respect. (Locals are usually happy to practice their English, which can often be quite good.) You'll experience another side of the region—a side that's important to understanding its culture and history.

booths in another small room for those who want to eat while they drink. A young staff pours terrific wines by the glass, and offers three different sauces (butter and sage, tomato, or ragù) with its *cappellacci di zucca*. Those in search of lighter fare might enjoy any of the salads or the grilled vegetable plate with melted pecorino. ✉ *Via degli Adelardi 11* ☎ *0532/209142* ⏲ *Closed Mon.*

$ EMILIAN ✕ **Quel Fantastico Giovedì**. It's worth taking a taxi to this off-the-beaten-path eatery (you could walk, but it's hard to find), where locals seek out a sophisticated and tasty meal. Two small rooms, one white, the other with red accents, have linen tablecloths and jazz playing softly in the background. Chef Gabriele Romagnoli uses top-notch local ingredients to create gustatory taste sensations: his *sformatino di patate* more closely resembles a French gratin, but he sauces it with *salamina e Parmesan*, thus rendering it deliciously Ferraresi. Fish also figures prominently on the menu. The wine list is divine, and the service is top-notch. ✉ *Via Castelnuovo 9* ☎ *0532/760570* *Reservations essential* ⏲ *Closed Wed. No lunch Tues.*

9

WHERE TO STAY

$$$$ **Duchessa Isabella**. An elegant 16th-century palace is now a luxurious hotel just slightly off the centro storico. **Pros:** lovely staff; garden; spared the noise from the centro storico. **Cons:** slightly removed from the centro storico. **TripAdvisor:** "some old-world charm," "very overpriced," "pink wallpaper." ✉ *Via Palestra 68/70* ☎ *0532/202121* 🌐 *www.duchessaisabella.it* *21 rooms, 6 suites* *In-room: a/c, Internet, Wi-Fi. In-hotel: restaurant, room service, bar, business center, parking, some pets allowed* ⏲ *Closed Aug.* *Breakfast.*

$$ **Hotel Ripagrande**. The courtyards, vaulted brick lobby, and breakfast room of this 15th-century noble's palazzo retain much of their lordly Renaissance flair. **Pros:** beyond-helpful staff; good choice for families. **Cons:** staff goes home at midnight. **TripAdvisor:** "elegant and architecturally attractive," "glamorous bath," "staffing decidedly limited."

✉ *Via Ripagrande 21* ☎ *0532/765250* 🌐 *www.ripagrandehotel.it* *20 rooms, 20 suites* *In-room: Wi-Fi. In-hotel: restaurant, room service, bar, business center, parking, some pets allowed* *Breakfast.*

$ ★ **Locanda Borgonuovo.** It began life as a convent in the early 18th century, which was then suppressed by Napoleon. **Pros:** phenomenal breakfast featuring local foods and terrific cakes made in-house; friendly, attentive proprietors. **Cons:** steep stairs to reception area and rooms; must reserve far in advance. **TripAdvisor:** "most gracious hostess ever," "perfect old-city location," "on a quiet street." ✉ *Via Cairoli 29* ☎ *0532/211100* 🌐 *www.borgonuovo.com* *4 rooms, 2 apartments* *In-room: kitchen (some), Wi-Fi. In-hotel: restaurant, business center, parking* *Breakfast.*

ROMAGNA

Anywhere in Emilia-Romagna, the story goes, a weary, lost traveler will be invited into a family's home and offered a drink. But the Romagnesi claim that he'll be served water in Emilia and wine in Romagna. The hilly, mostly rural, and largely undiscovered Romagna region has crumbling farmhouses dotting rolling hills, smoking chimneys, early Christian churches, and rowdy local bars dishing out rounds and rounds of *piadine* (a pita-thin bread filled with meat, cheese, vegetables, or any combination thereof, and then quickly grilled). Ravenna, the site of shimmering Byzantine mosaics, dominates the region.

Heading southeast from Bologna, Via Emilia (SS9) and the parallel A14 autostrada lead to the towns of Dozza and Faenza. From here, go north to the Adriatic Coast on the SS71 to reach Ravenna. Alternatively, the slower SS16 cuts a northwest-southeast swath through Romagna.

IMOLA

42 km (26 mi) southeast of Bologna.

GETTING HERE

Imola is an easy train ride from Bologna; local trains run frequently and take a little under a half hour. If you're coming from Milan, you can take the Eurostar to Bologna, and then transfer to the local train. Travel time from Milan is about 2½ hours, and the walk from the station to the centro storico is easy. If you're driving from Bologna, take the RA1 to the A14 (following signs for Ancona). Take the exit for Imola.

VISITOR INFORMATION

Imola tourism office (✉ *Arcade of the City Center 135* ☎ *0542/602111* 🌐 *www.comune.imola.bo.it*).

EXPLORING

Affluent Imola, with its wide and stately avenues, lies on the border between Emilia and Romagna. It was populated as early as the Bronze Age, came under Roman rule, and was eventually annexed to the Papal States in 1504. Now it's best known for its Formula One auto-racing tradition; the San Marino Grand Prix has been held here in spring of every year since 1981. Auto-racing as a serious sport in Imola dates to

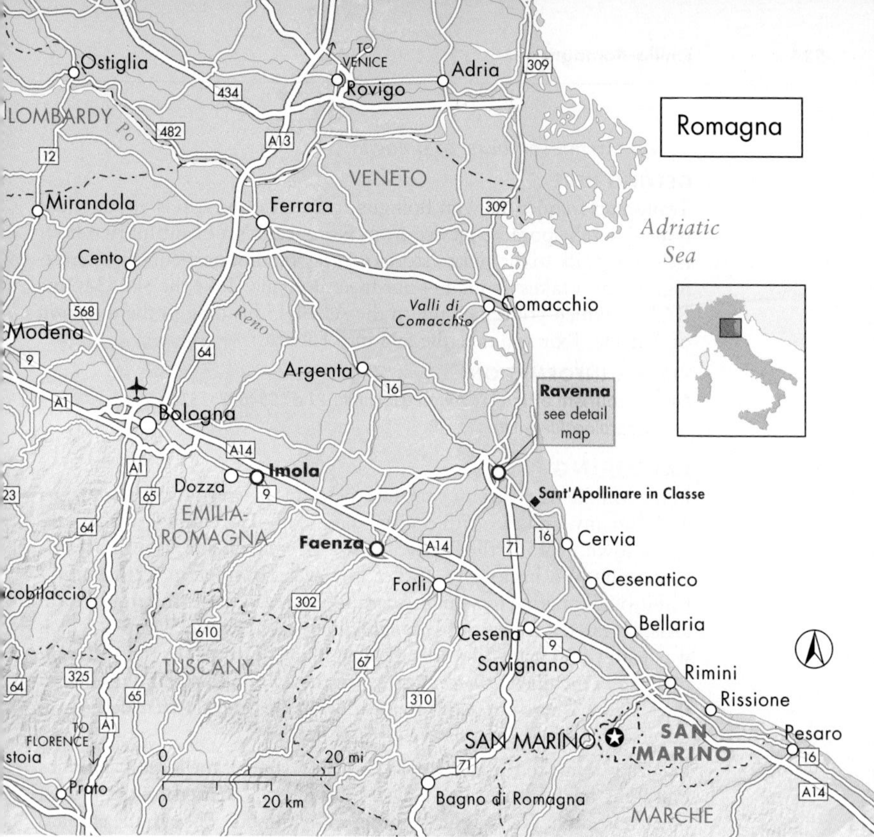

1953, when, with the support of Enzo Ferrari, the racetrack just outside the city center was inaugurated. However, unless you happen to pop into town in mid-April for the race, you'll more likely find yourself in Imola shopping for its well-known ceramics or sampling the cuisine at the town's world-famous restaurant, San Domenico.

WHERE TO EAT

$$$$ MODERN ITALIAN ★ **San Domenico.** San Domenico has defended its position as one of Italy's most refined dining destinations year after year, and heads of state, celebrities, and those with bottomless pocketbooks flock here to savor the fare. The majestic appointments complement chef Valentino Marcattilik's wondrous creations, like his memorable *uovo in raviolo San Domenico,* in which a large raviolo is stuffed with a raw egg yolk—which miraculously cooks only a little, then spills out and mixes with Parmesan cheese, *burro di malga* (butter from an Alpine dairy farm), and sensational white truffles. The impressive wine list has more than 3,000 choices. *Via G. Sacchi 1* *0542/29000* *www.sandomenico.it* *Reservations essential* *Closed Mon., Sun. June–Aug., 1 wk in Jan., and 1 wk in Aug. No lunch Sat. June–Aug. No dinner Sun. Sept.–May.*

FAENZA

49 km (30 mi) southeast of Bologna.

GETTING HERE

Trains run frequently from Bologna to Faenza; the trip is about a half hour. There's sporadic service from Florence; it's a beautiful two-hour ride. The walk to the centro storico is easy but not particularly interesting. By car it takes about an hour from Bologna. Take the SP253 to the RA1, at which point pick up on the A14/E45 heading in the direction of Ancona. Exit and take the SP8 into Faenza.

VISITOR INFORMATION

Faenza tourism office (✉ *Voltore Molinella 21* ☎ *0546/25231* 🌐 *www.prolocofaenza.it*).

EXPLORING

In the Middle Ages Faenza was the crossroads between Emilia-Romagna and Tuscany, and the 15th century saw many Florentine artists working in town. In 1509 the Papal States took control, and Faenza became something of a backwater. It did, however, continue its 12th-century tradition of making top-quality ceramic ware. In the 16th century local artists created a color called *bianchi di Faenza* ("Faenza white"), which was wildly imitated and wildly desired all over Europe. By the 16th century the Frenchified *faience,* to refer to the color and technique entered the lexicon, where it remains to this day. In the central **Piazza del Popolo,** dozens of shops sell the native ceramic wares.

Faenza is home to the **Museo delle Ceramiche**, one of the largest ceramics museums in the world. It's a well-labeled, well-lighted museum with objects from the Renaissance among its highlights. Though the emphasis is decidedly on local work, the rest of Italy is represented as well. Don't miss the 20th- and 21st-century galleries, which illustrate that decorative arts often surpass their utile limitations and become, truly, magnificently sculptural. ✉ *Viale Baccarini 19* ☎ *0546/697311* 🌐 *www.micfaenza.org* 🎫 *€6* ⏲ *Apr.–Sept., Tues.–Sat. 9:30–7; Oct.–Mar., Tues.–Thurs. 9:30–1:30, Fri.–Sun. 9:30–5:30.*

WHERE TO EAT

$ ITALIAN ✕ **Marianaza.** A large open-hearth fireplace dominates this simple trattoria, and wonderful aromas of grilled meats and garlic greet you as you walk in. Marianaza, like the town of Faenza itself, successfully blends the best of Emilian-Romagnan and Tuscan cuisine: the extraordinary primi are mostly tortellini-based, and the secondi rely heavily on the grill. Grilled garlic toasts topped with prosciutto crudo delightfully whet the appetite; and the tortellini in brodo is tasty. The mixed grill is perfect for sharing. (Note that the person at the grill is a woman: a true rarity in Italy.) ✉ *Via Torricelli 21* ☎ *0546/681461.*

RAVENNA

76 km (47 mi) east of Bologna, 93 km (58 mi) southeast of Ferrara.

A small, quiet, well-heeled city, Ravenna has brick palaces, cobbled streets, magnificent monuments, and spectacular Byzantine mosaics. The high point in the city's history occurred in the 5th century, when Pope Honorious moved his court here from Rome. Gothic kings Odoacer and Theodoric ruled the city until it was conquered by the Byzantines in AD 540. Ravenna then fell under the sway of Venice, and then, inevitably, the Papal States.

Because Ravenna spent much of its past looking to the East, its greatest art treasures show that influence. Churches and tombs with the most unassuming exteriors contain within them walls covered with sumptuous mosaics. These beautifully preserved Byzantine mosaics put great emphasis on nature, which you can see in the delicate rendering of sky, earth, and animals. Outside Ravenna, the town of Classe hides even more mosaic gems.

GETTING HERE

By car from Bologna, take the SP253 to the RA1, and then follow signs for the A14/E45 in the direction of Ancona. From here, follow signs for Ravenna, taking the A14dir Ancona-Milano-Ravenna exit. Follow signs for the SS16/E55 to the center of Ravenna. It's a more convoluted, but more interesting, drive from Ferrara: take the SS16 to the RA8 in the direction of Porto Garibaldi taking the Roma/Ravenna exit. Follow the SS309/E55 to the SS309dir/E55, taking the SS253 Bologna/Ancona exit. Follow the SS16/E55 into the center of Ravenna.

VISITOR INFORMATION

Ravenna tourism office (✉ *Via Salara 8* ☎ *0544/35404* 🌐 *www.turismo.ravenna.it*).

9

EXPLORING RAVENNA

A combination ticket (available at ticket offices of all included sights) admits you to four of Ravenna's important monuments: the Mausoleo di Galla Placidia, the Basilica di San Vitale, the Battistero Neoniano, and Sant'Apollinare Nuovo. Start out early in the morning to avoid lines (reservations are necessary for the Mausoleo and Basilica in May and June). A half day should suffice to walk the town alone; allow a half hour for the Mausoleo and the Basilica.

TOP ATTRACTIONS

Basilica di San Vitale. The octagonal church of San Vitale was built in AD 547, after the Byzantines conquered the city, and its interior shows a strong Byzantine influence. In the area behind the altar are the most famous works in the church, depicting Emperor Justinian and his retinue on one wall, and his wife, Empress Theodora, with her retinue, on the opposite wall. Notice how the mosaics seamlessly wrap around the columns and curved arches on the upper sides of the altar area. Reservations are recommended from March through mid-June. ✉ *Via San Vitale off Via Salara* ☎ *0544/541688 reservations; 800/303999 toll-free*

CLOSE UP

San Marino, a Country on a Cliff

The world's smallest and oldest republic, as San Marino dubs itself, is surrounded entirely by Italy. It consists of three ancient castles perched on sheer cliffs rising implausibly out of the flatlands of Romagna, and a tangled knot of cobblestone streets below, lined with tourist boutiques, cheesy hotels and restaurants, and gun shops. The 1½-hour drive from Faenza is easily justified, however, by the sweeping views from the castle of the countryside far below. The 3,300-foot-plus precipices will make jaws drop and acrophobes quiver.

San Marino was founded in the 4th century AD by a stonecutter named Marino who settled with a small community of Christians, escaping persecution by pagan emperor Diocletian. Over the millennia, largely because of the logistical nightmares associated with attacking a fortified rock, San Marino was more or less left alone by Italy's various conquerors, and continues to this day to be an independent country (population 26,000), supported almost entirely by its 3-million-visitors-per-year tourist industry.

San Marino's headline attractions are its **tre castelli** *(three castles)*—medieval architectural wonders that appear on every coat of arms in the city. Starting in the center of town, walk a few hundred yards past the trinket shops, along a paved cliff-top ridge, from the 10th-century **Rocca della Guaita** to the 13th-century **Rocca della Cesta** (containing a museum of ancient weapons that's worthwhile mostly for the views from its terraces and turrets), and finally to the 14th-century **Rocca Montale** (closed to the public), the most remote of the castles. Every step of the way affords spectacular views of Romagna and the Adriatic; it's said that on a clear day you can see Croatia. The walks make for a good day's exercise but are by no means arduous. Even if you arrive after visiting hours, they're supremely worthwhile. ☎ *0549/882670* 🌐 *www.museidistato.sm* 🎫 *Il Torre Guaita and il Torre Cesta €4.50* ⏲ *Mid-Sept.–mid-June, daily 9–5, mid-June–mid-Sept., daily 8–8.*

A must-see is the **Piazza della Libertà**, whose Palazzo Pubblico is guarded by soldiers in green uniforms. As you'll notice by peering into the shops along the old town's winding streets, the republic is famous for crossbows and other stuff (fireworks, firearms) that's illegal most everywhere else.

Visiting San Marino in winter—off-season—increases the appeal of the experience, as tourist establishments shut down and you more or less have the castles to yourself. In August every inch of walkway on the rock is mobbed with sightseers.

To get to San Marino by car, take highway SS72 west from Rimini. From Borgo Maggiore, at the base of the rock, a cable car will whisk you up to the town. Alternatively, you can drive up the winding road; public parking is available in the town.

Don't worry about changing money, showing passports, and the like (although the tourist office at Contrada del Collegio will stamp your passport for €2.50); San Marino is, for all practical purposes, Italy—except, that is, for its majestic perch, its gun laws, and its reported 99% national voter turnout rate.

information 🌐 *www.ravennamosaici.it* 🎫 *Combination ticket €9.50* 🕓 *Nov.–Feb., daily 9:30–4:45; Mar. and Oct., daily 9–5:15; Apr.–Sept., daily 9–6:45.*

Battistero Neoniano. The baptistery, next door to Ravenna's 18th-century cathedral, has one of the town's most important mosaics. It dates from the beginning of the 5th century AD, with work continuing through the century. In keeping with the building's role, the great mosaic in the dome shows the baptism of Christ, and beneath are the Apostles. The lowest register of mosaics contains Christian symbols, the Throne of God, and the Cross. Note the naked figure kneeling next to Christ—he is the personification of the River Jordan. ✉ *Via Battistero* ☎ *0544/541688 reservations; 800/303999 toll-free information* 🌐 *www.ravennamosaici.it* 🎫 *Combination ticket €9.50* 🕓 *Nov.–Feb., daily 10–5:45; Mar. and Oct., daily 9:30–5:15; Apr.–Sept., daily 9–6:45.*

Fodor's Choice ★ **Mausoleo di Galla Placidia.** The little tomb and the great church stand side by side, but the tomb predates the Basilica di San Vitale by at least a hundred years. These two adjacent sights are decorated with the best-known, and most elaborate, mosaics in Ravenna. Galla Placidia was the sister of the Roman emperor Honorius, who moved the imperial capital to Ravenna in AD 402. She is said to have been beautiful and strong-willed, and to have taken an active part in the governing of the crumbling empire. This mausoleum, constructed in the mid-5th century, is her memorial.

Viewed from the outside, it's a small, unassuming redbrick building; the exterior's seeming poverty of charm only serves to enhance by contrast the richness of the interior mosaics, in deep midnight blue and glittering gold. The tiny central dome is decorated with symbols of Christ, the evangelists, and striking gold stars. Over the door is a depiction of the Good Shepherd. Eight of the Apostles are represented in groups of two on the four inner walls of the dome; the other four appear singly on the walls of the two transepts. Notice the small doves at their feet, drinking from the water of faith. Also in the tiny transepts are some delightful pairs of deer (representing souls), drinking from the fountain of resurrection. There are three sarcophagi in the tomb, none of which are believed to contain the remains of Galla Placidia. She died in Rome in AD 450, and there's no record of her body's having been transported back to the place where she wished to lie. Reservations are required for the Mausoleo from March through mid-June. ✉ *Via San Vitale off Via Salara* ☎ *0544/541688 reservations; 800/303999 toll-free information* 🌐 *www.ravennamosaici.it* 🎫 *€9.50 combination ticket plus, Mar. 1–June 15, €2 supplement* 🕓 *Nov.–Feb., daily 9:30–4:45; Mar. and Oct., daily 9–5:15; Apr.–Sept., daily 9–6:45.*

Sant'Apollinare Nuovo. The mosaics displayed in this church date from the early 6th century, making them slightly older than those in San Vitale. Since the left side of the church was reserved for women, it's only fitting that the mosaics on that wall depict 22 virgins offering crowns to the Virgin Mary. On the right wall are 26 men carrying the crowns of martyrdom. They approach Christ, surrounded by angels. ✉ *Via Roma at Via Guaccimanni* ☎ *0544/219518; 0544/541688 reservations;*

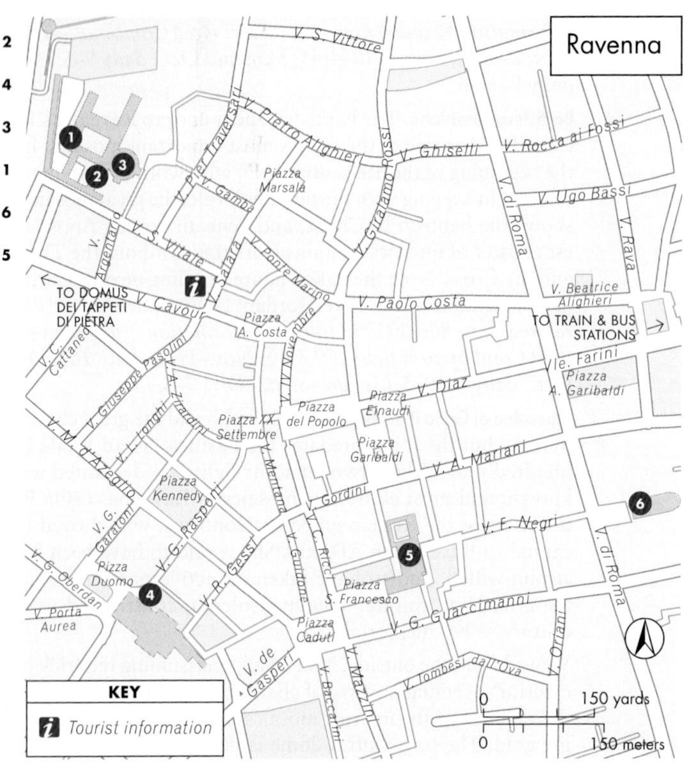

800/303999 toll-free information 🌐 *www.ravennamosaici.it* 🎫 *Combination ticket €9.50* 🕓 *Nov.–Feb., daily 10–4:45; Mar. and Oct., daily 9:30–5:15; Apr.–Sept., daily 9–6:45.*

WORTH NOTING

Domus dei Tappeti di Pietra *(Ancient Home of the Stone Carpets).* This archaeological site was uncovered in 1993 during digging for an underground parking lot near the 18th century church of Santa Eufemia. Below ground level (10 feet down) lie the remains of a Byzantine palace dating from the 5th and 6th centuries AD, in which a beautiful and well-preserved network of floor mosaics displays elaborately designed patterns, creating the effect of luxurious carpets. ✉ *Via Barbiani, enter through Sant'Eufemia* ☎ *0544/32512* 🌐 *www.domusdeitappetidipietra.it* 🎫 *€4* 🕓 *July and Aug., daily 10–6 and 8:30—10:30; Mar.–June and Sept.–Oct., daily 10–6:30; Nov.–Feb., Tues.–Fri. 10–5, weekends 10–6.*

Museo Nazionale. The National Museum of Ravenna, next to the Church of San Vitale, contains artifacts from ancient Rome, Byzantine fabrics and carvings, and pieces of early Christian art. The collection is housed in a former Benedictine monastery, and is well displayed and artfully lighted. In the delightful first cloister are marvelous Roman tomb slabs from excavations nearby; upstairs, you can see a recon-structured 18th-century pharmacy. ✉ *Via Fiandrini* ☎ *0544/543711* 🎫 *€4* ⏲ *Tues.–Sun. 8:30–7:30.*

Tomba di Dante. The tomb of Dante is in a small neoclassical building next door to the large church of St. Francis. Exiled from his native Florence, the author of *The Divine Comedy* died here in 1321. The Florentines have been trying to reclaim their famous son for hundreds of years, but the Ravennans refuse to give him up, arguing that since Florence did not welcome Dante in life it does not deserve him in death. ✉ *Via Dante Alighieri 4 and 9* ☎ *0544/30252* 🎫 *Free* ⏲ *Daily 9–noon and 2–5.*

WORD OF MOUTH

"I am not going to describe Ravenna's famous mosaics, other than to note that all are rewarding, and that the vivid greens and golds will astonish you. One other piece of advice—bring a small pair of binoculars. The detail is astounding, but will be largely lost to you without them."

—Pausanias

OFF THE BEATEN PATH

Sant'Apollinare in Classe. This church, about 5 km (3 mi) southeast of Ravenna, is landlocked now, but when it was built it stood in the center of the busy shipping port known to the ancient Romans as Classis. The arch above and the area around the high altar are rich with mosaics. Those on the arch, older than the ones behind it, are considered superior. They show Christ in Judgment and the 12 lambs of Christianity leaving the cities of Jerusalem and Bethlehem. In the apse is the figure of Sant'Apollinare himself, a bishop of Ravenna, and above him is a magnificent Transfiguration against blazing green grass, animals in odd perspective, and flowers. ✉ *Via Romea Sud, Classe* ☎ *0544/473569* 🎫 *€3* ⏲ *Daily 8:30–7.*

WHERE TO EAT

$ NORTHERN ITALIAN

✕ **Bella Venezia.** Pale yellow walls, crisp white tablecloths, and warm light provide the backdrop for some seriously good regional food. The menu offers local specialties, but also gives a major nod to Venice, Ravenna's conqueror of long ago. The flavorful and delicate *cappelleti romagnoli* (stuffed pasta in broth) is a lovely starter; *cotoletta alla Bisanzio* (a fried veal cutlet topped with cherry tomatoes and arugula), a house specialty, is a lovely follow-up. Desserts are made daily on the premises; save room for their killer tiramisu. ✉ *Via IV Novembre 16* ☎ *0544/212746* 🌐 *www.bellavenezia.it* ⏲ *Closed Sun. and 3 wks in Dec. and Jan.*

$ ITALIAN

✕ **I Battibecchi.** Simple and honest food doesn't get any tastier than the marvels at this tiny little venue (about 20 seats) with its even tinier kitchen. The short menu provides the usual local specialties, like *cappelletti* in brodo or al ragù, supplemented by an ever-changing list of daily specials. The *polpettini al lesso* (little meatballs) served in a lively tomato sauce with peas and pancetta, is one of many winning dishes that may be on offer. ✉ *Via della Tesoreria Vecchia 16* ☎ *0544/219536.*

¢ ITALIAN ✕ **La Gardèla.** The kitchen seems to operate with an otherworldly efficiency, making this bright, bustling downtown restaurant extremely popular with the local business crowd—especially at lunch (always a good sign). Avail yourself of the terrific lunchtime deal: a primo and secondo for just €15. The place is best for classics like *tagliatelle al ragù* and Adriatic fish, such as *sardoncini* (tiny sardines, breaded and fried). Don't mind the fact that the menu's written in both English and German: locals pack the place. In summer you can sit outside on a little terrace and enjoy the wonderful comfort food under the stars. ✉ *Via Ponte Marino 3* ☎ *0544/217147* ⊙ *Closed Thurs. and 10 days in Jan.*

$ NORTHERN ITALIAN ★ ✕ **Locanda del Melarancio.** This contemporary inn, in a late 16th-century palazzo in the heart of the centro storico, has an *osteria* on the ground floor and a more formal restaurant on the second. Downstairs, decor is minimalist without being stark; a long counter extends practically through the entire length of the narrow room. Here lunching locals enjoy ample plates of *affettati misti* (with carmellized figs, often), and daily specials, like the *pollo impannato alla griglia* (lightly breaded chicken breast on the grill). Upstairs a menu with a little more sophistication is served in a more sober, and pricier, setting. ✉ *Via Mentana 33* ☎ *0544/215258* 🌐 *www.locandadelmelarancio.it.*

WHERE TO STAY

$$ **Albergo Cappello.** This small pensione has been in operation since the late 19th century; in the late 20th century it was restored with marvelous results. **Pros:** good location; accommodating staff; good restaurant. **Cons:** Only seven rooms. **TripAdvisor:** "renovated former palazzo," "heart of Ravenna's historic center," "antique ceiling frescoes." ✉ *via IV novembre 41* ☎ *0544/219876* 🌐 *www.albergocappello.it* *2 rooms, 5 suites* *In-room: a/c, Wi-Fi. In-hotel: restaurant, bar, parking, some pets allowed* *No meals.*

$ **Sant'Andrea.** For a lovely little B&B on a quiet residential street a stone's throw from the Basilica of San Vitale, look no further. **Pros:** children under 12 sleep free; breakfast outdoors when it's warm; discounts for stays of three nights or more. **Cons:** can get a little noisy. **TripAdvisor:** "in the heart of the town," "room and bath both spotless," "staff were not terribly helpful." ✉ *Via Carlo Cattaneo 33* ☎ *0544/215564* 🌐 *www.santandreahotel.com* *11 rooms, 1 suite* *In-room: a/c. In-hotel: bar, parking, some pets allowed* *Breakfast.*

NIGHTLIFE AND THE ARTS

Friday nights from June to August bring **Mosaics by Night**, when the Byzantine mosaic masterpieces in town are illuminated. The event is also held on certain Tuesdays; to check, call the tourist office, which also offers guided tours. The **Ravenna Festival** is a music festival held every year in June and July. Orchestras from all over the world come to perform in Ravenna's churches and theaters.

Teatro di Tradizione Dante Alighieri (✉ *Via Mariani 2* ☎ *0544/249244* 🌐 *www.teatroalighieri.org*) stages operas and dance productions, usually on weekends, from November to March. If your Italian is up to it, you could also attend any of the theatrical productions that happen at the same theater. The season starts in late November and extends to late April.

Central Italy

WHAT'S WHERE

1 Florence. It's hard to think of a place that's more closely linked to one specific historical period than Florence. In the 15th century the city was at the center of an artistic revolution, later labeled the Renaissance, which changed the way people see the world. Five hundred years later the Renaissance remains the reason people see Florence—the abundance of treasures is mind-boggling. Present-day Florentines have a somewhat uneasy relationship with their city's past; the never-ending stream of tourists is something they seem to tolerate more often than embrace. Still, they pride themselves on living well, and that means you'll find exceptional restaurants and first-rate shopping to go with all that amazing art.

2 Tuscany. Nature outdid herself in Tuscany, the central Italian region that has Florence as its principal city. Descriptions and photographs can't do the landscape justice—the hills, draped with woods, vineyards, and olive groves, may not have the drama of mountain peaks or waves crashing on the shore, yet there's an undeniable magic about them. Aside from Florence, Tuscany has several midsize cities that are well worth visiting, but the greatest appeal lies in the smaller

towns, often perched on hilltops and not significantly altered since the Middle Ages. Despite its popularity with fellow travelers, Tuscany remains a place you can escape to.

3 Umbria and the Marches. This region is closer to the Appenines than Tuscany is, so the landscape is wilder, the valleys deeper, and the mountains higher. The greater physical isolation of Umbria's towns and, until the unification of Italy, their association with the Papal States, may have encouraged the development of a keen sense of spirituality. Several of Italy's major saints are from the region, including St. Benedict of Norcia, St. Rita of Cascia, St. Chiara of Assisi, and most famously St. Francis of Assisi. There's no city with the size or significance of Florence, but a number of the smaller towns, particularly Assisi, Perugia, Spoleto, and Orvieto, have lots to hold your interest. Umbria's Roman past is much in evidence—expect to see Roman villas, aqueducts, theaters, walls, and temples. To the east, in the region of the Marches, the main draw is the town of Urbino, where the Ducal Palace reveals more about the artistic energy of the Renaissance than a shelf of history books.

CENTRAL ITALY PLANNER

Biking and Hiking

In spring, summer, and fall, bicyclists pedaling up and down Tuscany's hills are as much a part of the landscape as the cypress trees. Many are on weeklong organized tours, but it's also possible to rent bikes for jaunts in the countryside or to join afternoon or daylong rides.

Hiking is a simpler matter: all you need is a pair of sturdy shoes. The tourist information offices in most towns can direct you on walks ranging from an hour to a full day in duration. You can also sign on for more elaborate guided tours.

Italy by Design (✉ *Via delle Lame 52, Florence* ☎ *055/6532381* 🌐 *www.italybydesign.com*) provides city walks in Florence with expert guides, and made-to-measure hiking and driving vacations throughout Italy. The Salerno-based **Genius Loci** (✉ *Via Rotondo 5, Salerno* ☎ *089/791896* 🌐 *www.genius-loci.it*) offers guided and self-guided biking and walking tours for the budget-conscious throughout Italy. **Italian Connection** (✉ *11825-11B Ave. Edmonton, AB* ☎ *800/4627911 or 780/438/5712* 🌐 *www.italian-connection.com*) conducts high-end walking and culinary trips throughout Italy.

Getting Here

Most flights to Tuscany originating in the United States stop either in Rome, London, Paris, or Frankfurt, and then connect to Florence's small **Aeroporto A. Vespucci** (commonly called **Peretola**), or to Pisa's **Aeroporto Galileo Galilei**. The only exception at this writing is Delta's New York/JFK flight going directly into Pisa.

There are several other alternatives for getting into the region. If you want to start your trip in Umbria, it works to fly into Rome's **Aeroporto Leonardo da Vinci** (commonly called Fiumicino); from Rome it's an hour by train or an hour and a half by car to reach the lovely town of Orvieto. Another option is to fly to Milan and pick up a connecting flight to Pisa, Florence, Perugia, or Ancona in the Marches.

Typical Travel Times

	HOURS BY CAR	HOURS BY TRAIN
Florence–Rome	3:00	1:35
Florence–Venice	3:30	2:05
Florence–Bologna	1:30	0:40
Florence–Pisa	1:30	1:05
Florence–Perugia	1:45	2:10
Siena–Perugia	1:30	3:00
Perugia–Assisi	0:30	0:20
Perugia–Orvieto	1:15	1:45
Assisi–Rome	2:15	2:10
Orvieto–Rome	1:30	1:10

On the Calendar: Events and Festivals

Several major events mark the calendar in Tuscany and Umbria, drawing attendees from around the world.

For the two weeks leading up to Lent, the town of Viareggio along the coast of northwest Tuscany is given over to the sometimes-bawdy revels of **Carnevale.** The festivities are second only to Venice's in size and lavishness.

Twice a year, on July 2 and August 16, Siena goes medieval with the **Palio,** a bareback horse race around its main square. It's more than a race—it's a celebration of tradition and culture dating back 1,000 years.

For two weeks in late June and early July, stars from the worlds of classical music and the performing arts make their way to the Umbria hill town of Spoleto to take part in the **Festival dei Due Mondi.** Opera fans crowd the outdoor **Puccini Festival** held in July and August at Torre del Lago, while Florence's **Maggio Musicale**, which extends through most of the year, attracts an international audience for performances of opera, classical music, and ballet.

While the big events are impressive, the calendar also overflows with smaller traditional *sagre* (festivals or fairs). You'll find them in towns of every size, January through December, with names like Sagra del Cinghiale (Wild Boar Festival), Sagra della Castagna (Chestnut Festival), and Festa del Fungo (Mushroom Festival). There's the Befanate (celebrating Italy's witchlike Santa equivalent) in Grossetto during Epiphany, the Teatro Povero (a folk theater production) in Monticchiello in July, and, throughout southern Tuscany on the night of April 30, the Canta il Maggio (Songs for Spring) are performed.

Sagre are fun, and there's often delicious traditionally prepared food to be had. You can check with the local or regional tourist information offices for the dates and times of any sagre that happen to coincide with your visit.

When to Go

Throughout Tuscany and Umbria the best times to visit are spring and fall. Days are warm, nights are cool, and though there are still tourists, the crowds are smaller. In the countryside the scenery is gorgeous, with abundant greenery and flowers in spring, and burnished leaves in autumn.

July and August are the most popular times to visit. Note, though, that the heat is often oppressive and mosquitoes are prevalent. Try to start your days early and visit major sights first to beat the crowds and the midday sun. For relief from the heat, head to the mountains of the Garfagnana, where hiking is spectacular, or hit the beach at resort towns such as Forte dei Marmi and Viareggio, along the Maremma coast, or on the island of Elba.

November through March you might wonder who invented the term "sunny Italy." The panoramas are still beautiful, even with overcast skies, frequent rain, and occasional snow. In winter, Florence benefits from shorter museum lines and less competition for restaurant tables. Outside the cities, though, many hotels and restaurants close for the season.

CENTRAL ITALY TOP ATTRACTIONS

Galleria degli Uffizi, Florence

(A) Florence has many museums, but the Uffizi is king. Walking its halls is like stepping into an art history textbook, except here you're looking at the genuine article—masterpieces by Leonardo, Michelangelo, Raphael, Botticelli, Caravaggio, and dozens of other luminaries. When planning your visit, make a point to reserve a ticket in advance. *(⇨ Chapter 10.)*

Duomo, Florence

(B) The Cathedral of Santa Maria del Fiore, commonly known as the Duomo, is Florence's most distinctive landmark, sitting at the very heart of the city and towering over the neighboring rooftops. Its massive dome is one of the world's great engineering masterpieces. For an up-close look, you can climb the 463 steps to the top—then gaze out at the city beneath you. *(⇨ Chapter 10.)*

Leaning Tower, Pisa

(C) This tower may be too famous for its own good (it's one of Italy's most popular tourist attractions), but there's something undeniably appealing about its perilous tilt, and climbing to the top is a kick. The square on which it sits, known as the Campo dei Miracoli, has a majestic beauty that no quantity of tourists can diminish. *(⇨ Chapter 11.)*

Piazza del Campo, Siena

(D) The sloping, fan-shaped square in the heart of Siena is one of the best places in Italy to engage in the distinctly Italian activity of hanging out and people-watching. The flanking Palazzo Vecchio and Torre del Mangia are first-rate sights. *(⇨ Chapter 11.)*

San Gimignano, Central Tuscany

(E) This classic Tuscan hill town has been dubbed a "medieval Manhattan" because of its numerous towers, built by noble families of the time, each striving to outdo

its neighbors. The streets fill with tour groups during the day, but if you stick around until sunset the crowds diminish and you see the town at its most beautiful. *(⇨ Chapter 11.)*

Abbazia di Sant'Antimo, Southern Tuscany

In a peaceful valley, surrounded by gently rolling hills, olive trees, and thick oak woods, Sant'Antimo is one of Italy's most beautifully situated abbeys—and a great "off the beaten path" destination. Stick around for mass and you'll hear the halls resound with Gregorian chant. *(⇨ Chapter 11.)*

Palazzo Ducale, Urbino, the Marches

(F) East of Umbria in the Marches region, Urbino is a college town in the Italian style—meaning its small but prestigious university dates to the 15th century. The highlight here is the Palazzo Ducale, a palace that exemplifies the Renaissance ideals of grace and harmony. *(⇨ Chapter 12.)*

Basilica di San Francesco, Assisi

(G) The basilica, built to honor Saint Francis, consists of two great churches: one Romanesque, fittingly solemn with its low ceilings and guttering candles; the other Gothic, with soaring arches and stained-glass windows (the first in Italy). They're both filled with some of Europe's finest frescoes. *(⇨ Chapter 12.)*

Duomo, Orvieto

(H) The facade of Orvieto's monumental Duomo contains a bas-relief masterpiece depicting the stories of the Creation and the Last Judgment (with the horrors of hell shown in striking detail). Inside, there's more glorious gore in the right transept, frescoed with Lucca Signorelli's *Stories of the Antichrist and the Last Judgment*. *(⇨ Chapter 12.)*

TOP EXPERIENCES

The View from Florence's Piazzale Michelangelo

One of the best ways to introduce yourself to Florence is by walking up to this square on the hill south of the Arno. From here you can take in the whole city, and much of the surrounding countryside, in one spectacular vista. To extend the experience, linger at one of the outdoor cafés, and for the finest view of all, time your visit to correspond with sunset.

Strolling the Ramparts of Lucca

Lucca, 80 km (50 mi) west of Florence, isn't situated on a hilltop in the way commonly associated with Tuscan towns, and it doesn't have quite the abundance of art treasures that you find in Siena or Pisa (to say nothing of Florence). Yet for many visitors, Lucca is a favorite Tuscan destination, and the source of its appeal has everything to do with its ramparts. These hulking barricades have surrounded the city center since the 17th century; built as a source of security, they now are part of an elevated, oval park, complete with walkways, picnic areas, grass, and trees. The citizens of Lucca spend much of their spare time here, strolling, biking, and lounging, oblivious to the novelty of their situation but clearly happy with it.

Taking the Waters at a Tuscan Spa

Tuscany is dotted throughout with small *terme* (thermal baths), where hot water flows from natural springs deep beneath the earth's surface. It's been believed for millennia that these waters have the power to cure whatever ails you. Although their medicinal power may be questionable, that doesn't mean a dip isn't an extremely pleasant way to spend an afternoon. In northwest Tuscany you can take the waters at Montecatini Terme (made famous as a setting for Fellini's *8½* and seemingly little has changed since then) or Bagni di Lucca (which had its heyday in the era of the 19th-century Romantic poets). To the south, Saturnia is the biggest draw, along with the more humble Chianciano Terme and Bagno Vignoni.

Wine Tasting in Chianti

The gorgeous hills of the Chianti region, between Florence and Siena, produce exceptional wines, and they never taste better than when sampled on their home turf. Many Chianti vineyards are visitor-friendly, but the logistics of a visit are different from what you may have experienced in other wine regions. If you just drop in, you're likely to get a tasting, but for a tour you usually need to make an appointment several days ahead of time. The upside is that your tour may end up being a half day of full immersion—including extended conversation with the winemakers and even a meal.

Hiking in the Footsteps of Saint Francis

Umbria, which bills itself as "Italy's Green Heart," is fantastic hiking country. Among the many options are two with a Franciscan twist. From the town of Cannara, 16 km (10 mi) south of Assisi, an easy half-hour walk leads to the fields of Pian d'Arca, where Saint Francis delivered his sermon to the birds. For a slightly more demanding walk, you can follow the saint's path from Assisi to the Eremo delle Carceri (Hermitage of Prisons), where Francis and his followers went to "imprison" themselves in prayer, and from here continue along the trails that crisscross Monte Subasio.

CENTRAL ITALY TODAY

. . . maintains its regional identities

"And what greater fortune, if in Italy there were more Tuscans and fewer Italians," writes Curzio Malaparte (Prato, 1898–Rome, 1957) in his celebrated novel *Maledetti Toscani* (*Those Cursed Tuscans*). He's being provocative and arrogant, qualities of which his fellow Tuscans, especially the Florentines, are often accused.

The Florentines, for their own part, acknowledge all this with evident pride, even using the term *toscanaccio* (nasty Tuscan) to describe themselves. Many attempts have been made to identify Italy's regional differences. In the "you are what you eat" category is Marcella Hazan's description (in the introduction to *The Classic Italian Cookbook*) of the "careful and calculating" Florentine, "a man who knows the measure of all things," whose "cooking is an austerely composed play upon essential and unadorned themes."

The end of World War II marked the beginning a large migration of Italy's rural population into the cities. In response, in the 1970s and '80s a sort of "folk revival" began, with interest developing in the festivals, food, songs, and religious events that were once a vital part of local tradition. Today the calendar overflows with resurrected sagre that derive from once-abandoned traditions. You can check with the local or regional tourist information offices for the dates and times of any sagre that coincide with your visit.

. . . tends to the left politically

Along with the Marches and Emilia-Romagna, Tuscany and Umbria form the so-called red quadrilateral of central Italy, with strong left-wing political inclinations dating back to the formation of the Italian republic at the end of World War II. Through the first decade of the 21st century a majority of Tuscan and Umbrian voters opposed Prime Minister Silvio Berlusconi's center-right rule.

. . . is feeling an economic pinch

Italy's economy has been largely stagnant since the late 1990s. The adoption of the euro in 2002 resulted in surreptitious price increases, while the average wage remained level. Cutbacks have seriously limited the number of prized state jobs, and longtime employment has been replaced by serial short-term project-based contracts with little or no job security and limited pension plans.

. is maintaining the brand

The "Made in Italy" label has come to be recognized internationally as an indication of superior quality and design (and thus a strong marketing tool). The regions of central Italy make important contributions to maintaining the good reputation. In the world of fashion, Gucci, Ferragamo, and Emilio Pucci are Florence-based, while the Della Valle family's shoe and luxury leather business, producer of the Tod's and Hogan brands, is based in Ascoli Piceno in the Marches. Fabriano, in the Marches, has since the 13th century been a center for the production of the world's highest quality artists' papers, and Deruta in Umbria has for just as long been a center for fine ceramics. On a sweet note, the chocolate makers of Tuscany's "Chocolate Valley" between Prato and Pistoia (Amedei and Catanari are two major producers), and Perugina outside Perugia, are international names nowadays.

A GREAT ITINERARY

Day 1: Florence

If you're coming in on an international flight, you'll probably settle in Florence in time for an afternoon stroll or siesta (depending on your jet-lag strategy) before dinner.

Logistics: On your flight in, read through the restaurant listings in this guide and begin anticipating the first dinner of your trip. Look for a place near your hotel, and when you arrive, reserve a table (or have your concierge do it for you). Making a meal the focus of your first day is a great way to ease into Italian life. Note that Sunday and Monday are favorite closing days for many Florence restaurants, and Monday sees most important museums closed.

Day 2: Florence

Begin your morning at the **Uffizi Gallery** (reserve your ticket in advance). The extensive collection will occupy much of your morning. Next, take in the neighboring **Piazza della Signoria,** one of Florence's impressive squares, then head a few blocks north to the **Duomo.** There, check out Ghiberti's famous bronze doors on the **Battistero** (they're high-quality copies; the originals are in the Museo dell'Opera del Duomo), and work up an appetite by climbing the 463 steps to the cupola of Brunelleschi's splendid cathedral dome, atop which you'll experience a memorable view. Spend the afternoon relaxing, shopping, and wandering Florence's medieval streets; or, if you're up for a more involved journey, head out to **Fiesole** to experience the ancient amphitheater and beautiful views of the Tuscan countryside.

Day 3: Florence

Keep the energy level up for your second full day in Florence, sticking with art and architecture for the morning, trying to see most of the following: Michelangelo's *David* at the **Galleria dell'Accademia,** the **Medici Chapels,** the **Palazzo Pitti** and **Boboli Gardens,** and the churches of **Santa Maria Novella** and **Santa Croce.** If it's a clear day, spend the afternoon on a trip to **Piazzale Michelangelo,** high on a hill, for sweeping views of idyllic Florentine countryside. Given all the walking you've been doing, tonight would be a good night to recharge by trying the famed *bistecca alla fiorentina* (a grilled T-bone steak with olive oil).

Logistics: You can get up to the Piazzale Michelangelo by taxi or by taking Bus 12 or 13 from the Lungarno. Otherwise, do your best to get around on foot; Florence is a brilliant city for walking.

Day 4: San Gimignano

Now that you've been appropriately introduced to the bewildering splendor of Renaissance Italy, it's time for a change of pace—and time for a rental car, which will enable you to see the back roads of Tuscany and Umbria. After breakfast, head on out. On a beautiful day the lazy drive from Florence to **San Gimignano,** past vineyards and typical Tuscan landscapes, is truly spectacular. The first thing that will hit you when you arrive at the hill town of San Gimignano will be its multiple towers. The medieval skyscrapers of Italy once occupied the role now played by Ferraris or Hummers: they were public displays of wealth and family power. After finding your way to a hotel in the old town, set out on foot and check out the city's turrets and alleyways, doing your best to get away from the trinket shops, and later enjoying a leisurely dinner with the light but delicious local white wine, Vernaccia di San Gimignano.

Logistics: Some hotels might be able to coordinate with some rental-car agencies so that your car can be brought to your hotel for you. The historic center of Florence is closed to nonresidents' cars (including rentals). You can drive out of the center, but must leave your license plate number with your hotel if you drive in—there's a heavy fine otherwise. Once you navigate your way out of Florence (no easy task), San Gimignano is only 57 km (35 mi) to the southwest, so it's an easy drive; you could even take a detour on the SR222 (Strada Chiantigiana), stop at one of the Chianti wine towns, and visit a winery along the way.

Day 5: Siena

In the morning, set out for nearby **Siena,** which is known worldwide for its Palio, a festival that culminates in an elaborate horse-race competition among the 17 *contrade* (medieval neighborhoods) of the city. Because of the enormous influx of tourists, especially in summer, Siena isn't everyone's cup of tea, but it's still one of Tuscany's most impressive sights. However many tourists you have to bump elbows with, it's hard not to be blown away by the city's precious medieval streets and memorable fan-shape **Piazza del Campo.** Not to be missed while in town are the spectacular **Duomo,** the **Battistero,** and the **Spedale di Santa Maria della Scala,** an old hospital and hostel that now contains an underground archaeological museum.

Logistics: It's a short and pretty drive from San Gimignano to Siena, but once there, parking can be a challenge. Look for the *stadio* (soccer stadium), where there's a parking lot that often has space. Try to avoid arriving in Siena on Wednesday morning—the town's weekly market is in full swing, and the traffic and parking can be nightmarish.

Day 6: Arezzo/Cortona

Get an early start, because there's a lot to see today. From Siena you'll first head to **Arezzo,** home to the **Basilica di San Francesco,** which contains important frescoes by Piero della Francesca. Check out the **Piazza Grande** along with its beautiful Romanesque church of **Pieve di Santa Maria.** Try to do all of this before lunch, after which you'll head straight to **Cortona.** If Arezzo didn't capture your imagination, Cortona, whose origins date to the 5th century BC, will. Olive trees and vineyards give way to a medieval hill town with views over ridiculously idyllic Tuscan countryside and Lake Trasimeno. Cortona is a town for walking and relaxing, not sightseeing, so enjoy yourself, wandering through the **Piazza della Repubblica**

and **Piazza Signorelli,** and perhaps doing a bit of shopping.

Logistics: Siena to Arezzo is 63 km (39 mi) on the E78. From Arezzo to Cortona, it's just 30 km (18 mi)—take S71.

Day 7: Assisi

Today you'll cross over into Umbria, a region just as beautiful as Tuscany but still less trodden. Yet another impossibly beautiful hill town, **Assisi,** is the home of Saint Francis and host to the many religious pilgrims that come to celebrate his legacy. Visiting here is the most treasured memory of many a traveler's visit to Italy. Upon arriving and checking into your lodging, head straight for the **Basilica di San Francesco,** which displays the tomb of Saint Francis and unbelievable frescoes. From here take Via San Francesco to **Piazza del Commune** and see the **Tempio di Minerva** before a break for lunch. After lunch, see **San Rufino,** the town cathedral, and then go back through the piazza to Corso Mazzini and see **Santa Chiara.** If you're a true Franciscan, you could instead devote the afternoon to heading out 16 km (10 mi) to **Cannara,** where Saint Francis delivered his sermon to the birds.

Logistics: From Cortona, take the S71 to the A1 autostrada toward Perugia. After about 40 km (24 mi), take the Assisi exit (E45), and it's another 14 km (8 mi) to Assisi.

Day 8: Spoleto

This morning will take you from a small Umbrian hill town to a slightly bigger one: **Spoleto,** a walled city that's home to a world-renowned arts festival each summer. But Spoleto needs no festival to be celebrated. Its **Duomo** is wonderful. Its fortress, **La Rocca,** is impressive. And the **Ponte delle Torri,** a 14th-century bridge that separates Spoleto from Monteluco, is a marvelous sight, traversing a gorge 260 feet below and built upon the foundations of a Roman aqueduct. See all these during the day, stopping for a light lunch of a panino (sandwich) or salad, saving your appetite for a serious last dinner in Italy: Umbrian cuisine is excellent everywhere, but Spoleto is a memorable culinary destination. Do your best to sample black truffles, a proud product of the region; they're delicious on pasta or meat.

Logistics: One school of thought would be to time your visit to Spoleto's world-renowned arts festival that runs from mid-June through mid-July. Another would be to do anything you can to avoid it. It all depends on your taste for big festivals and big crowds. The trip from Assisi to Spoleto is a pretty 47-km (29-mi) drive (S75 to the S3) that should take you less than an hour, a little longer if you plan a stop in the charming town of Spello on the way.

Day 9: Spoleto/Departure

It's a fair distance from Spoleto to the Florence airport, your point of departure. Depending on your comfort level with Italian driving, allow at least 2½ hours to get there.

Florence

10

WORD OF MOUTH

"The city that made me fall in love with Italy was Florence, when I visited for the first time in the mid 1990s. I have been back four times, and we have enjoyed it each and every time. Yes, it is crowded, but so are Rome and Venice. If you like history and art, there is plenty to see."

—maitaitom

WELCOME TO FLORENCE

TOP REASONS TO GO

★ **Galleria degli Uffizi:** Italian Renaissance art doesn't get much better than this vast collection bequeathed to the city by the last Medici, Anna Maria Luisa.

★ **The dome of the Duomo:** Brunelleschi's work of engineering genius is the city's undisputed centerpiece.

★ **Michelangelo's *David*:** See it in person and you'll know why this is the one of the world's most famous sculptures.

★ **The view from Piazzale Michelangelo:** From this perch the city is laid out before you. The colors at sunset heighten the experience.

★ **Piazza Santa Croce:** After you've had your fill of Renaissance masterpieces, hang out here and watch the world go by.

1 The Duomo to the Ponte Vecchio. You're in the heart of Florence here. Among the numerous highlights are the city's greatest museum (the Uffizi) and its most impressive square (Piazza della Signoria).

2 San Lorenzo to the Accademia. The blocks from the church of San Lorenzo to the Accademia museum bear the imprints of the Medici and of Michelangelo, culminating in his masterful *David.* Just to the north, the former convent of San Marco is filled with ethereal frescoes and paintings by Fra Angelico.

3 Santa Maria Novella to the Arno. This part of town includes the train station, 16th-century palaces, and the city's chicest shopping street, Via Tornabuoni.

4 Santa Croce. The district centers on its namesake basilica, which is filled with the tombs of Renaissance luminaries. The area is also known for its leather shops, some of which have been in operation for centuries.

5 The Oltrarno. Across the Arno you encounter the massive Palazzo Pitti and the narrow streets of the Santo Spirito district, which is filled with artisans' workshops and antiques stores. A climb to Piazzale Michelangelo gives you a spectacular view of the city.

GETTING ORIENTED

The historic center of Florence is flat and compact—you could walk from one end to the other in half an hour. In the middle of everything is the Duomo, with its huge dome towering over the city's terra-cotta rooftops. Radiating out from the Duomo are Renaissance-era neighborhoods identified by their central churches and piazzas. Though the majority of sights are north of the Arno River, the area to the south, known as the Oltrarno, has its charms as well.

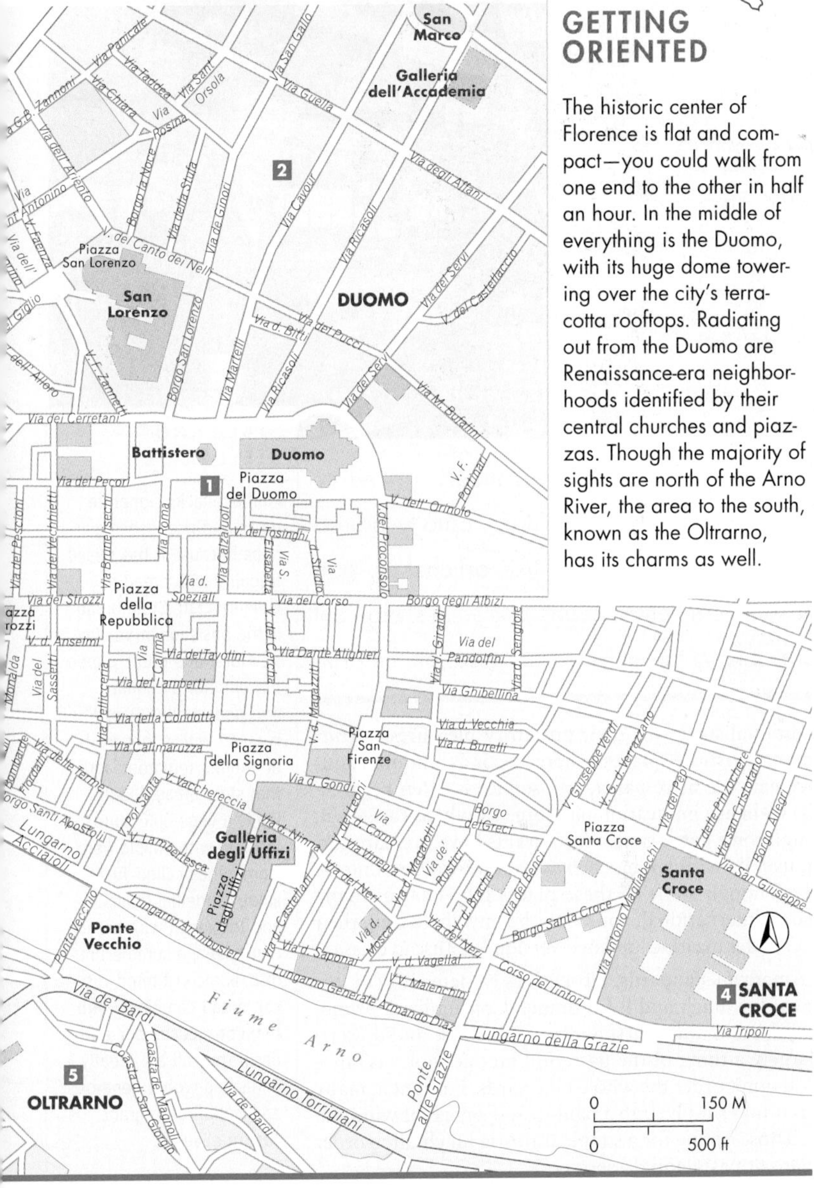

EATING AND DRINKING WELL IN FLORENCE

In Florence simply prepared meats, grilled or roasted, are the culinary stars, usually paired with seasonal vegetables like artichokes, porcini, and cannellini beans. Bistecca's big, but there's plenty more that tastes great on the grill.

Traditionalists go for their gustatory pleasures in *trattorie* and *osterie*, places where decor is unimportant, placemats are mere paper, and service is often perfunctory. Culinary innovation has come slowly to this town, though some cutting-edge restaurants have been appearing, usually with young chefs who have worked outside Italy. Though some of these places lack charm (many have an international, you-could-be-anywhere feel), their menus offer exciting, updated versions of Tuscan classics.

By American standards, Florentines eat late: 1:30 or 2 is typical for lunch and 9 for dinner. Consuming a *primo*, *secondo*, and *dolce* (first and second course and dessert) is largely a thing of the past, and no one looks askance if you don't order the whole nine yards. For lunch, many Florentines simply grab a panino and a glass of wine at a bar. Those opting for a simple trattoria lunch often order a plate of pasta and dessert.

STALE AND STELLAR

Florence lacks signature pasta and rice dishes, perhaps because it has raised frugality with bread to culinary craft. Stale bread is the basis for three classic Florentine primi: *pappa al pomodoro, ribollita,* and *panzanella.* "Pappa" is made with either fresh or canned tomatoes and that stale bread. Ribollita is a vegetable soup fortified with *cavolo nero* (sometimes called Tuscan kale), cannellini beans, and thickened with bread. Panzanella, a summertime dish, is reconstituted Tuscan bread combined with tomatoes, cucumber, and basil. They all are greatly enhanced with a generous application of fragrant Tuscan olive oil.

A CLASSIC ANTIPASTO: CROSTINI DI FEGATINI

This beloved dish consists of a chicken-liver spread, served warm or at room temperature, on toasted, garlic-rubbed bread. It can be served smooth, like a pâté, or in a rougher spread. It's made by sautéing chicken livers with finely diced carrot and onion, enlivened with the addition of wine, broth, or Marsala reductions, and mashed anchovies and capers.

A CLASSIC SECONDO: BISTECCA FIORENTINA

The town's culinary pride and joy is a thick slab of beef, resembling a T-bone steak, from large white oxen called *chianina*. The meat's slapped on the grill and served rare, sometimes with a pinch of salt.

It's always seared on both sides, and just barely cooked inside (experts say five minutes per side, and then 15 minutes with the bone sitting perpendicularly on the grill). To ask for it more well done is to incur disdain; most restaurants simply won't serve it any other way but rare.

A CLASSIC CONTORNO: CANNELLINI BEANS

Simply boiled, they provide the perfect accompaniment to bistecca. The small white beans are best when they go straight from the garden into the pot. They should be anointed with a generous outpouring of Tuscan olive oil; the

combination is oddly felicitous, and it goes a long way toward explaining why Tuscans are referred to as *mangiafagioli* (bean eaters) by other Italians.

A CLASSIC DOLCE: BISCOTTI DI PRATO

These are sometimes the only dessert on offer, and are more or less an afterthought to the glories that have preceded them. Biscotti means twice-cooked (or, in this case, twice baked). They're hard almond cookies that soften considerably when dipped languidly into *vin santo* ("holy wine"), a sweet dessert wine, or into a simple *caffè*.

A CLASSIC WINE: CHIANTI CLASSICO

This blend from the region just south of Florence relies mainly on the local, hardy Sangiovese grape; it's aged for at least one year before hitting the market. (*Riserve*—reserves—are aged at least an additional six months.)

Chianti is usually the libation of choice for Florentines, and it pairs magnificently with grilled foods and seasonal vegetables. Traditionalists opt for the younger, fruitier (and usually less expensive) versions often served in straw flasks. You can sample *Chianti classico* all over town, and buy it in local *salumerie* (delicatessens) *enoteche* (wine bars), and supermarkets.

Updated by Patricia Rucidlo

Florence, the city of the lily, gave birth to the Renaissance and changed the way we see the world. For centuries it has captured the imaginations of travelers, who have come seeking rooms with views and phenomenal art.

Florence's is a subtle beauty—its staid, unprepossessing palaces built in local stone are not showy. They take on a certain magnificence when day breaks and when the sun sets; their muted colors glow in this light. A walk along the Arno offers views that don't quit and haven't much changed in 700 years; navigating Piazza Signoria, almost always packed with tourists and locals alike, requires patience. There's a reason why everyone seems to be here, however. It's the heart of the city, and home to the Uffizi—arguably the world's finest repository of Renaissance art.

Florence was "discovered" in the 1700s by upper-class northerners making the grand tour. It became a mecca for travelers, particularly the Romantics, who were inspired by the elegance of its palazzi and its artistic wealth. Today millions of modern visitors follow in their footsteps. When the sun sets over the Arno and, as Mark Twain described it, "overwhelms Florence with tides of color that make all the sharp lines dim and faint and turn the solid city to a city of dreams," it's hard not to fall under the city's spell.

PLANNING

MAKING THE MOST OF YOUR TIME

With some planning, you can see Florence's most famous sights in a couple of days. Start off at the city's most awe-inspiring work of architecture, the **Duomo,** climbing to the top of the dome if you have the stamina. On the same piazza, check out Ghiberti's bronze doors at the **Battistero.** (They're actually high-quality copies; the Museo dell'Opera del Duomo has the originals.) Set aside the afternoon for the **Galleria degli Uffizi,** making sure to reserve tickets in advance.

On Day 2, visit Michelangelo's *David* in the **Galleria dell'Accademia**—reserve tickets here, too. Linger in **Piazza della Signoria,** Florence's central square, where a copy of *David* stands in the spot the original occupied for centuries, then head east a couple of blocks to **Santa Croce,** the city's most artistically rich church. Double back and walk across Florence's landmark bridge, the **Ponte Vecchio.**

Do all that, and you'll have seen some great art, but you've just scratched the surface. If you have more time, put the **Bargello,** the **Museo di San Marco,** and the **Cappelle Medicee** at the top of your list. When you're ready for an art break, stroll through the **Boboli Gardens** or explore Florence's lively shopping scene, from the food stalls of the **Mercato Centrale** to the chic boutiques of the **Via Tornabuoni.**

HOURS

Florence's sights keep tricky hours. Some are closed on Wednesday, some on Monday, some on every other Monday. Quite a few shut their doors each day (or on most days) by 2 in the afternoon. Things get even more confusing on weekends. Make it a general rule to check the hours closely for any place you're planning to visit; if it's someplace you have your heart set on seeing, it's worthwhile to call to confirm.

Here's a selection of major sights that might not be open when you'd expect—consult the sight listings within this chapter for the full details. And be aware that, as always, hours can and do change.

The **Uffizi** and the **Accademia** are both closed Monday. All but a few of the galleries at Palazzo Pitti are closed Monday as well.

The **Duomo** closes at 3:30 on Thursday (as opposed to 5:30 on other weekdays, 4:45 on weekends). The dome of the Duomo is closed on Sunday.

The **Battistero** is open from 12:15 until 7, Monday through Saturday, and on Sunday from 8:30 to 2.

The **Bargello** closes at 1:50 pm, and is closed entirely on alternating Sundays and Mondays.

The **Cappelle Medicee** are closed on alternating Sundays and Mondays.

Museo di San Marco closes at 1:50 on weekdays but stays open until 7 on weekends—except for alternating Sundays and Mondays, when it's closed entirely.

Palazzo Medici-Riccardi is closed Wednesday.

RESERVATIONS

At most times of day you'll see a line of people snaking around the Uffizi. They're waiting to buy tickets, and you don't want to be one of them. Instead, call ahead for a reservation (☎ 055/294883; reservationists speak English). You'll be given a reservation number and a time of admission—the further in advance you call, the more time slots you'll have to choose from. Go to the museum's reservation door at the appointed hour, give the clerk your number, pick up your ticket, and go inside. You'll pay €4 for this privilege, but it's money well spent. You can also book tickets online through the Web site 🌐 *www.polomuseale.firenze.it*; the booking process takes some patience, but it works.

Use the same reservation service to book tickets for the Galleria dell'Accademia, where lines rival those of the Uffizi. (Reservations can also be made for the Palazzo Pitti, the Bargello, and several other sights, but they usually aren't needed.) An alternative strategy is to check with your hotel—many will handle reservations.

GETTING HERE AND AROUND

AIR TRAVEL

Florence's small **Aeroporto A. Vespucci** (*10 km [6 mi] northwest of Florence* ☎ *055/30615* 🌐 *www.aeroporto.firenze.it*) commonly called **Peretola,** is just outside of town and receives flights from Milan, Rome, London, and Paris. To get into the city center from the airport by car, take the autostrada A11. A Sita bus will take you directly from the airport to the center of town. Tickets may be purchased on the bus.

Pisa's **Aeroporto Galileo Galilei** (*12 km [7 mi] south of Pisa and 80 km [50 mi] west of Florence* ☎ *050/849300* 🌐 *www.pisa-airport.com*) is the closest landing point with significant international service, including a few direct flights from New York each week on Delta. It's a straight shot down the SS67 to Florence. A train service connects Pisa's airport station with Florence's central train station, Santa Maria Novella, in roughly an hour-long trip. Trains start running at about 7 am from the airport, 6 am from Florence, and continue service every hour until about 11 pm from the airport, 10 pm from Florence.

For flight information, call the airport or **Florence Air Terminal** (✉ *Stazione Centrale di Santa Maria Novella* ☎ *055/216073*) —which, despite the misleading name, is simply an office at the Santa Maria Novella train station, around the corner from train tracks 1 and 2.

BUS TRAVEL

Long-distance buses provide inexpensive if somewhat claustrophobic service between Florence and other cities in Italy and Europe. **Lazzi Eurolines** (✉ *Via Mercadante 2, Santa Maria Novella* ☎ *055/363041* 🌐 *www.lazzi.it*) and **SITA** (✉ *Via Santa Caterina da Siena 17/r, Santa Maria Novella* ☎ *055/47821* 🌐 *www.sitabus.it*) are the major lines; they have neatly divided up their routes, so there's little overlap.

CAR TRAVEL

Florence is connected to the north and south of Italy by the Autostrada del Sole (A1). It takes about an hour and a half of driving on scenic roads to get to Bologna (although heavy truck traffic over the Apennines often makes for slower going), about three hours to Rome, and three to 3½ hours to Milan. The Tyrrhenian Coast is an hour west on the A11.

An automobile in Florence is a major liability. If your itinerary includes parts of Italy where you'll want a car (such as Tuscany), pick the vehicle up on your way out of town.

TRAIN TRAVEL

Florence is on the principal Italian train route between most European capitals and Rome, and within Italy it's served frequently from Milan, Venice, and Rome by Intercity (IC) and nonstop Eurostar trains. **Stazione Centrale di Santa Maria Novella** (☎ *892021* 🌐 *www.trenitalia.com*) is the main station and is in the center of town. Avoid trains that stop only at the Campo di Marte or Rifredi stations, which are not convenient to the city center.

VISITOR INFORMATION

The Florence tourist office, known as the **APT** (☎ *055/290832* 🌐 *www.firenze.turismo.toscana.it*), has branches next to the Palazzo Medici-Riccardi, across the street from Stazione di Santa Maria Novella (the

PUBLIC TRANSPORTATION IN FLORENCE

BUSES

Florence's flat, compact city center is made for walking, but when your feet get weary you can use the efficient bus system, which includes small electric buses making the rounds in the center. Buses also climb to Piazzale Michelangelo and San Miniato south of the Arno.

Maps and timetables for local bus service are available for a small fee at the newsagent directly outside the Santa Maria Novella train station, or for free at visitor information offices. Tickets must be bought in advance from tobacco shops, newsstands, automatic ticket machines near main stops, or ATAF booths. The ticket must be canceled in the small validation machine immediately upon boarding.

You have several ticket options, all valid for one or more rides on all lines. A €1.20 ticket is good for one hour from the time it's first canceled. A multiple ticket—four tickets, each valid for 70 minutes—costs €4.50. A 24-hour tourist ticket costs €5. Two-, three-, and seven-day passes are also available.

TAXIS

Taxis usually wait at stands throughout the city (in front of the train station and in Piazza della Repubblica, for example), or you can call for one (☎ *055/4390 or 055/4798*). The meter starts at €3.40, with extra charges at night, on Sunday, for radio dispatch, and for luggage. Women out on the town after midnight seeking taxis are entitled to a 10% discount on the fare; you must, however, request it.

main train station) and around the corner from the Basilica di Santa Croce. The offices are generally open from 9 in the morning until 7 in the evening. The multilingual staff will give you directions (but usually not free maps) and the latest on happenings in the city. It's particularly worth a stop if you're interested in finding out about performing-arts events. The APT Web site provides information in both Italian and English.

THE DUOMO TO THE PONTE VECCHIO

The heart of Florence, stretching from the Piazza del Duomo south to the Arno, is dense with artistic treasures. The churches, medieval towers, Renaissance palaces, and world-class museums and galleries contain some of the most outstanding aesthetic achievements of Western history.

Much of the *centro storico* (historic center) is closed to automobile traffic, but you still must dodge mopeds, cyclists, and masses of fellow tourists as you walk the narrow streets, especially in the area bounded by the Duomo, Piazza della Signoria, Galleria degli Uffizi, and Ponte Vecchio.

TOP ATTRACTIONS

★ **Bargello.** This building started out as the headquarters for the Capitano del Popolo (captain of the people, roughly the chief of police) during the Middle Ages and was later used as a prison. The exterior served as a "most wanted" billboard: effigies of notorious criminals and Medici enemies were painted on its walls. Today it houses the **Museo Nazionale,** home to what is probably the finest collection of Renaissance sculpture in Italy. The concentration of masterworks by Michelangelo (1475–1564), Donatello (circa 1386–1466), and Benvenuto Cellini (1500–71) is remarkable; the works are distributed among an eclectic collection of arms, ceramics, and miniature bronzes, among other things. For Renaissance art lovers, the Bargello is to sculpture what the Uffizi is to painting.

In 1401 Filippo Brunelleschi (1377–1446) and Lorenzo Ghiberti (circa 1378–1455) competed to earn the most prestigious commission of the day: the decoration of the north doors of the Baptistery in Piazza del Duomo. For the contest, each designed a bronze bas-relief panel depicting the sacrifice of Isaac; the panels are displayed together in the room devoted to the sculpture of Donatello, on the upper floor. The judges chose Ghiberti for the commission; see if you agree with their choice. ✉ *Via del Proconsolo 4, Bargello* ☎ *055/294883* 🌐 *www.polomuseale.firenze.it* 🎟 *€4* 🕒 *Daily 8:15–1:50; closed 2nd and 4th Mon. of month and 1st, 3rd, and 5th Sun. of month.*

Battistero *(Baptistery)*. The octagonal Baptistery is one of the supreme monuments of the Italian Romanesque style and one of Florence's oldest structures. Local legend has it that it was once a Roman temple dedicated to Mars; modern excavations, however, suggest that its foundations date from the 1st century AD. The round Romanesque arches on the exterior date from the 11th century. The interior dome mosaics from the beginning of the 14th century are justly renowned, but—glittering beauties though they are—they could never outshine the building's famed bronze Renaissance doors decorated with panels crafted by Lorenzo Ghiberti. The doors—or at least copies of them—on which Ghiberti worked most of his adult life (1403–52) are on the north and east sides of the Baptistery, and the Gothic panels on the south door were designed by Andrea Pisano (circa 1290–1348) in 1330. The original Ghiberti doors were removed to protect them from the effects of pollution and acid rain and have been beautifully restored; they're now on display in the Museo dell'Opera del Duomo.

Ghiberti's north doors depict scenes from the life of Christ; his later east doors (dating from 1425–52), facing the Duomo facade, render scenes from the Old Testament. Both merit close examination, for they're very different in style and illustrate the artistic changes that marked the beginning of the Renaissance. Look at the far right panel of the middle row on the earlier (1403–24) north doors (*Christ Calming the Waters*). Ghiberti here captured the chaos of a storm at sea with great skill and economy, but the artistic conventions he used are basically pre-Renaissance: Christ is the most important figure, so he is the largest; the disciples are next in size, being next in importance; and the ship on which they founder looks like a mere toy.

The exquisitely rendered panels on the east doors are larger, more expansive, more sweeping—and more convincing. The middle panel on the left-hand door tells the story of Jacob and Esau, and the various episodes of the story—the selling of the birthright, Isaac ordering Esau to go hunting, the blessing of Jacob, and so forth—have been merged into a single beautifully realized street scene. Ghiberti's use of perspective suggests depth: the background architecture looks far

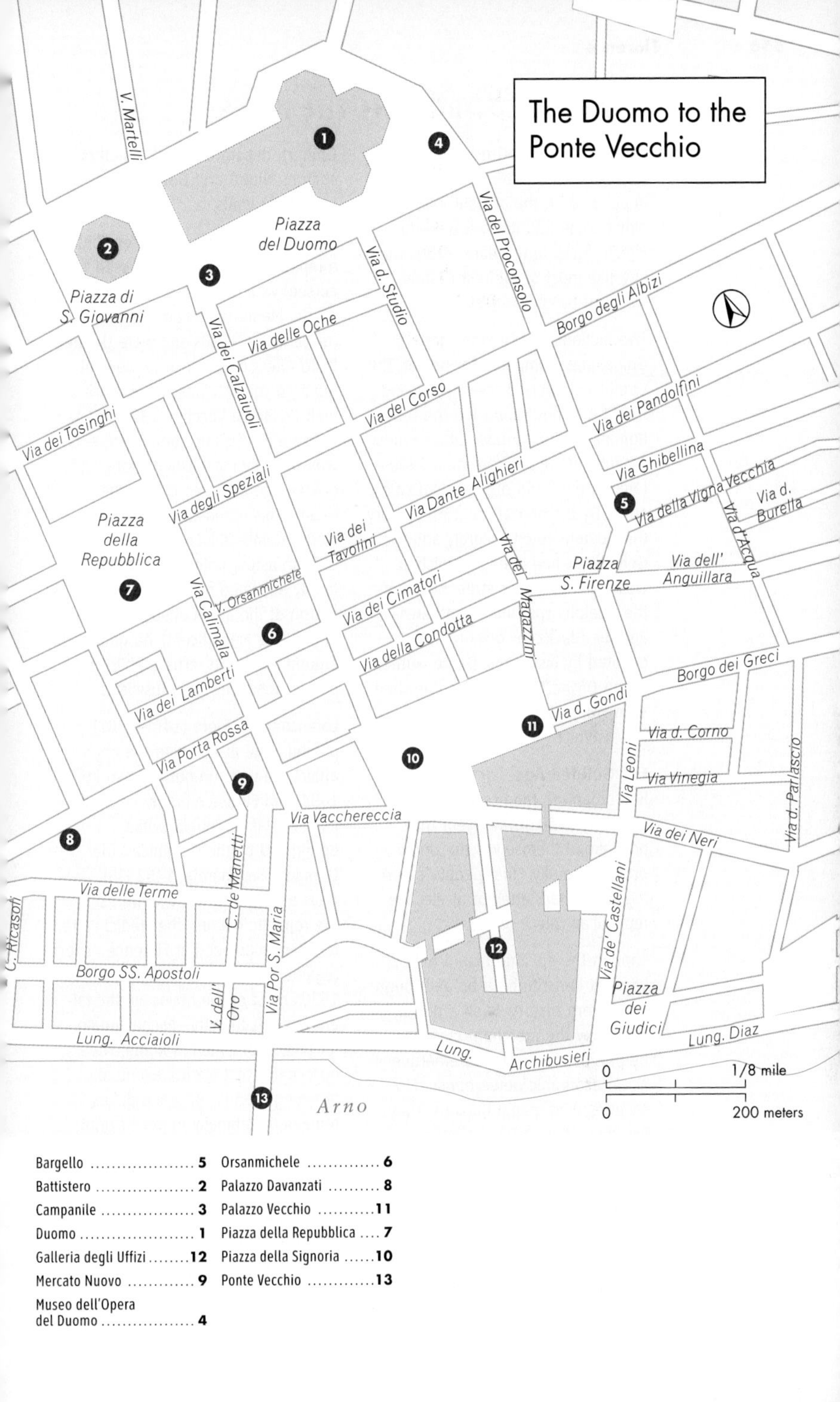

The Duomo to the Ponte Vecchio
V. Martelli
Piazza del Duomo
Piazza di S. Giovanni
Via del Proconsolo
Via d. Studio
Borgo degli Albizi
Via delle Oche
Via dei Calzaiuoli
Via del Corso
Via dei Pandolfini
Via dei Tosinghi
Via Ghibellina
Via degli Speziali
Via Dante Alighieri
Via della Vigna Vecchia
Via d. Burella
Via d'Acqua
Piazza della Repubblica
Via dei Tavolini
Via dei Magazzini
Piazza S. Firenze
Via dell' Anguillara
V. Orsanmichele
Via Calimala
Via dei Cimatori
Via della Condotta
Borgo dei Greci
Via dei Lamberti
Via d. Gondi
Via d. Corno
Via Porta Rossa
Via Leoni
Via Vinegia
Via d. Parlascio
Via Vacchereccia
Via dei Neri
C. de Manetti
Via delle Terme
Via de' Castellani
C. Ricasoli
Via Por S. Maria
Borgo SS. Apostoli
V. dell' Oro
Piazza dei Giudici
Lung. Acciaioli
Lung. Archibusieri
Lung. Diaz
Arno
0 1/8 mile
0 200 meters
Bargello 5
Battistero 2
Campanile 3
Duomo 1
Galleria degli Uffizi 12
Mercato Nuovo 9
Museo dell'Opera del Duomo 4
Orsanmichele 6
Palazzo Davanzati 8
Palazzo Vecchio 11
Piazza della Repubblica 7
Piazza della Signoria 10
Ponte Vecchio 13

FLORENCE THROUGH THE AGES

Guelph vs. Ghibelline. Though Florence can lay claim to a modest importance in the ancient world, it didn't come into its own until the Middle Ages. In the early 1200s the city, like most of the rest of Italy, was rent by civic unrest.

Two factions, the Guelphs and the Ghibellines, competed for power. The Guelphs supported the papacy, and the Ghibellines supported the Holy Roman Empire. Bloody battles—most notably one at Montaperti in 1260—tore Florence and other Italian cities apart. By the end of the 13th century the Guelphs ruled securely and the Ghibellines had been vanquished. This didn't end civic strife, however: the Guelphs split into the Whites and the Blacks for reasons still debated by historians. Dante, author of the *Divine Comedy,* was banished from Florence in 1301 because he was a White.

The Guilded Age. Local merchants had organized themselves into guilds by 1250. In that year they proclaimed themselves the *primo popolo* (literally, "first people"), making a landmark attempt at elective, republican rule.

Though the episode lasted only 10 years, it constituted a breakthrough in Western history. Such a daring stance by the merchant class was a by-product of Florence's emergence as an economic powerhouse. Florentines were papal bankers; they instituted the system of international letters of credit; and the gold florin became the international standard of currency. With this economic strength came a building boom. Palaces and basilicas were erected, enlarged, or restructured. Sculptors such as Donatello and Ghiberti decorated them; painters such as Giotto and Botticelli frescoed their walls.

Mighty Medici. Though ostensibly a republic, Florence was blessed (or cursed) with one very powerful family, the Medici, who came to prominence in the 1430s and were the de facto rulers of Florence for several hundred years. It was under patriarch Cosimo il Vecchio (1389–1464) that the Medici's position in Florence was securely established. Florence's golden age occurred during the reign of his grandson Lorenzo de' Medici (1449–92). Lorenzo was not only an astute politician but also a highly educated man and a great patron of the arts. Called "Il Magnifico" (the Magnificent), he gathered around him poets, artists, philosophers, architects, and musicians.

Lorenzo's son, Piero (1471–1503), proved inept at handling the city's affairs. He was run out of town in 1494, and Florence briefly enjoyed its status as a republic while dominated by the Dominican friar Girolamo Savonarola (1452–98). After a decade of internal unrest, the republic fell and the Medici were recalled to power, but Florence never regained its former prestige. By the 1530s most of the major artistic talent had left the city—Michelangelo, for one, had settled in Rome. The now-ineffectual Medici, eventually attaining the title of grand dukes, remained nominally in power until the line died out in 1737, after which time Florence passed from the Austrians to the French and back again until the unification of Italy (1865–70), when it briefly became the capital under King Vittorio Emanuele II.

more credible than on the north-door panels, the figures in the foreground are grouped realistically, and the naturalism and grace of the poses (look at Esau's left leg and the dog next to him) have nothing to do with the sacred message being conveyed. Although the religious content remains, the figures and their place in the natural world are given new prominence, and are portrayed with a realism not seen in art since the fall of the Roman Empire nearly a thousand years before.

WORD OF MOUTH

"Central Florence is quite small, so distances on maps are often deceiving in that things look farther apart than they actually are. That said, it's easy to get a bit lost (so many intriguing medieval streets) so give yourself a bit of leeway for that possibility!"

—sacc

As a footnote to Ghiberti's panels, one small detail of the east doors is worth a special look. To the lower left of the Jacob and Esau panel, Ghiberti placed a tiny self-portrait bust. From either side, the portrait is extremely appealing—Ghiberti looks like everyone's favorite uncle—but the bust is carefully placed so that you can make direct eye contact with the tiny head from a single spot. When that contact is made, the impression of intelligent life—of *modern* intelligent life—is astonishing. It's no wonder that these doors received one of the most famous compliments in the history of art from an artist known to be notoriously stingy with praise: Michelangelo declared them so beautiful that they could serve as the Gates of Paradise. ✉ *Piazza del Duomo* ☎ *055/2302885* 🌐 *www.operaduomo.firenze.it* 🎫 *€6* ⏲ *Mon.–Sat. 12:15–7, Sun. 8:30–2; 1st Sat. of month 8:30–2.*

Fodor's Choice ★ **Galleria degli Uffizi.** The venerable Uffizi Gallery occupies the top floor of the U-shaped **Palazzo degli Uffizi** fronting the Arno, designed by Giorgio Vasari (1511–74) in 1560 to hold the *uffizi* (administrative offices) of the Medici grand duke Cosimo I (1519–74). The Medici installed their art collections here, creating what was Europe's first modern museum, open to the public (at first only by request) since 1591.

10

Among the highlights are Paolo Uccello's *Battle of San Romano,* its brutal chaos of lances one of the finest visual metaphors for warfare ever captured in paint; the *Madonna and Child with Two Angels,* by Fra Filippo Lippi (1406–69), in which the impudent eye contact established by the angel would have been unthinkable prior to the Renaissance; the *Birth of Venus* and *Primavera* by Sandro Botticelli (1445–1510), the goddess of the former seeming to float on air and the fairy-tale charm of the latter exhibiting the painter's idiosyncratic genius at its zenith; the portraits of the Renaissance duke Federico da Montefeltro and his wife Battista Sforza, by Piero della Francesca (circa 1420–92); the *Madonna of the Goldfinch* by Raphael (1483–1520), which underwent a stunning years-long restoration, completed in 2009 (check out the brilliant blues that decorate the sky, as well as the eye contact between mother and child, both clearly anticipating the painful future; Michelangelo's *Doni Tondo*; the *Venus of Urbino* by Titian (circa 1488/90–1576); and the splendid *Bacchus* by Caravaggio (circa 1571/72–1610). In the last two works, the approaches to myth and

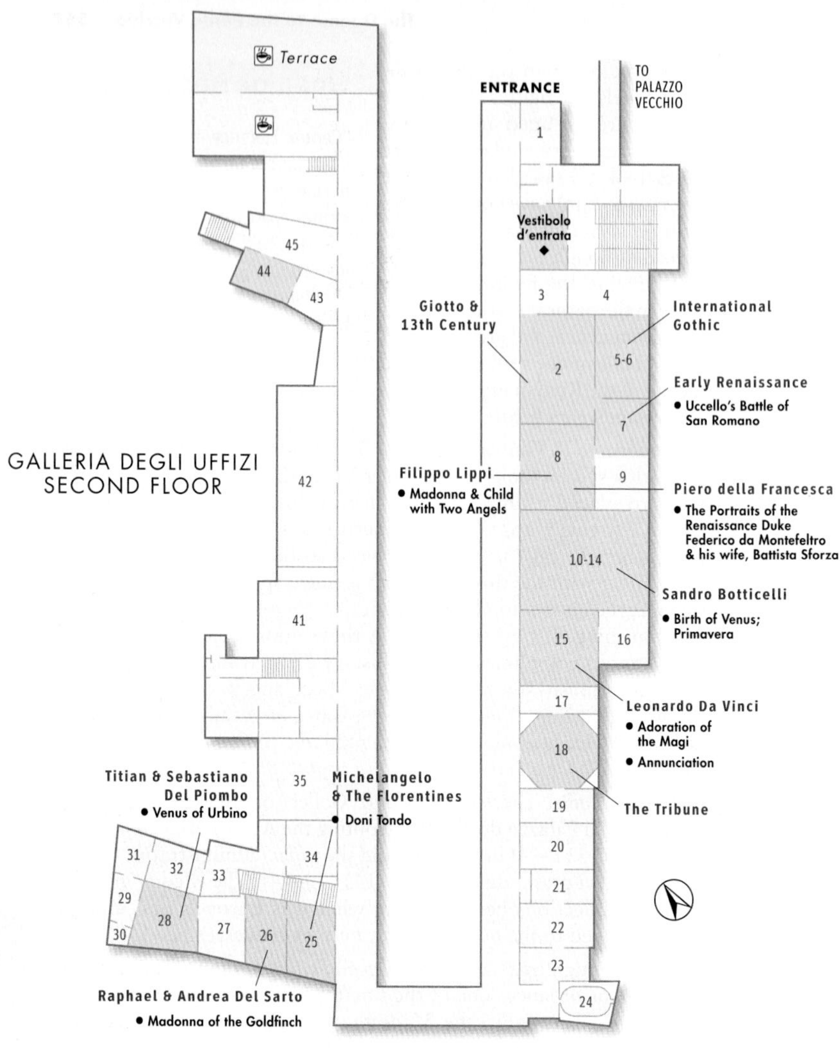

Gallery Rooms ▼

- Archaeology 1
- Giotto & Thirteenth Century 2
- Sienese Painting & Fourteenth Century 3
- Florentine Painting & Fourteenth Century 4
- International Gothic 5, 6
- Early Renaissance 7
- Filippo Lippi, Piero della Francesca 8
- Antonio & Piero del Pollaiolo 9
- Sandro Botticelli 10-14
- Leonardo da Vinci 15
- Maps 16
- Stanzino delle Matematiche 17
- The Tribune 18
- Perugino & Luca Signorelli 19
- Albrecht Dürer & German Renaissance 20
- Giovanni Bellini & Giorgione 21
- Flemish & German Renaissance 22
- Andrea Mantegna & Correggio 23
- Miniatures 24
- Michelangelo & the Florentines 25
- Raphael & Andrea del Sarto 26
- Pontormo & Rosso Fiorentino 27
- Titian & Sebastiano del Piombo 28
- Dosso Dossi & Parmigianino 29
- Emilian Painting 30
- Veronese 31
- Jacopo Bassano & Tintoretto 32
- Sixteenth Century Painting 33
- Lombard Masters 34
- Federico Barocci 35
- Rubens 41
- Niobe 42
- Seventeenth Century Painting 43
- Rembrandt 44
- Eighteenth Century 45

sexuality are diametrically opposed, to put it mildly. Late in the afternoon is the least crowded time to visit. For a €4 fee advance tickets can be reserved by phone, online, or, once in Florence, at the Uffizi reservation booth at least one day in advance of your visit. Keep the confirmation number and take it with you to the door at the museum marked "Reservations." Usually you're ushered in almost immediately. Come with cash, because credit cards aren't accepted (though you can use a credit card when booking online). When there's a special exhibit on, which is often, the base ticket price goes up to €10. ✉ *Piazzale degli Uffizi 6, Piazza della Signoria* ☎ *055/23885 advance tickets* ✉ *Consorzio ITA, Piazza Pitti 1* ☎ *055/294883* 🌐 *www.uffizi.firenze.it; reservations www.polomuseale.firenze.it* 🎫 *€6.50, €10 during special exhibitions; reservation fee €4* ⏲ *Tues.–Sun. 8:15–6:50.*

★ **Piazza della Signoria.** This is by far the most striking square in Florence. It was here, in 1497, that the famous "bonfire of the vanities" took place, when the fanatical friar Savonarola induced his followers to hurl their worldly goods into the flames; it was also here, a year later, that he was hanged as a heretic and, ironically, burned. A bronze plaque in the piazza pavement marks the exact spot of his execution.

The statues in the square and in the 14th-century **Loggia dei Lanzi** on the south side vary in quality. Cellini's famous bronze *Perseus* holding the severed head of Medusa is certainly the most important sculpture in the loggia. Other works here include *The Rape of the Sabine* and *Hercules and the Centaur,* both late-16th-century works by Giambologna (1529–1608), and along the wall, a row of sober matrons dating from Roman times.

In the square, the Neptune Fountain, created between 1550 and 1575, wins the booby prize. It was created by Bartolomeo Ammannati, who considered it a failure himself. The Florentines call it *il Biancone,* which may be translated as "the big white man" or "the big white lump." Giambologna's equestrian statue, to the left of the fountain, portrays Grand Duke Cosimo I. Occupying the steps of the Palazzo Vecchio are a copy of Donatello's proud heraldic lion of Florence, the *Marzocco* (the original is now in the Bargello), a copy of Donatello's *Judith and Holofernes* (the original is in the Palazzo Vecchio), a copy of Michelangelo's *David* (the original is in the Galleria dell'Accademia), and Baccio Bandinelli's *Hercules* (1534). The Marzocco, the Judith, and the David were symbols of Florentine civic pride—the latter two subjects had stood up to their oppressors. They provided apt metaphors for the republic-loving Florentines, who often chafed at Medici hegemony.

Ponte Vecchio *(Old Bridge).* This charmingly simple bridge was finished in 1345 to replace an earlier bridge swept away by flood. Its shops first housed butchers, then grocers, blacksmiths, and other merchants. But in 1593 the Medici grand duke Ferdinand I (1549–1609), whose private corridor linking the Medici palace (Palazzo Pitti) with the Medici offices (the Uffizi) crossed the bridge atop the shops, decided that all this plebeian commerce under his feet was unseemly. So he threw out the butchers and blacksmiths and installed 41 goldsmiths and eight jewelers. The bridge has been devoted solely to these two trades ever since.

Continued on page 565

THE DUOMO

FLORENCE'S BIGGEST MASTERPIECE

For all its monumental art and architecture, Florence has one undisputed centerpiece: the Cathedral of Santa Maria del Fiore, better known as the Duomo. Its cupola dominates the skyline, presiding over the city's rooftops like a red hen over her brood. Little wonder that when Florentines feel homesick, they say they have *"nostalgia del cupolone."*

The Duomo's construction began in 1296, following the design of Arnolfo da Cambio, Florence's greatest architect of the time. By modern standards, construction was slow and haphazard—it continued through the 14th and into the 15th century, with some dozen architects having a hand in the project.

In 1366 Neri di Fioravante created a model for the hugely ambitious cupola: it was to be the largest dome in the world, surpassing Rome's Pantheon. But when the time finally came to build the dome in 1418, no one was sure how—or even if—it could be done. Florence was faced with a 143-ft hole in the roof of its cathedral, and one of the greatest challenges in the history of architecture.

Fortunately, local genius Filippo Brunelleschi was just the man for the job. Brunelleschi won the 1418 competition to design the dome, and for the next 18 years he oversaw its construction. The enormity of his achievement can hardly be overstated. Working on such a large scale (the dome weighs 37,000 tons and uses 4 million bricks) required him to invent hoists and cranes that were engineering marvels. A "dome within a dome" design and a novel herringbone bricklaying pattern were just two of the innovations used to establish structural integrity. Perhaps most remarkably, he executed the construction without a supporting wooden framework, which had previously been thought indispensable.

Brunelleschi designed the lantern atop the dome, but he died soon after its first stone was laid in 1446; it wouldn't be completed until 1461. Another 400 years passed before the Duomo received its façade, a 19th-century neo-Gothic creation.

DUOMO TIMELINE

1296 Work begins, following design by Arnolfo di Cambio.

1302 Arnolfo dies; work continues, with sporadic interruptions.

1331 Management of construction taken over by the Wool Merchants guild.

1334 Giotto appointed project overseer, designs campanile.

1337 Giotto dies; Andrea Pisano takes leadership role.

1348 The Black Plague; all work ceases.

1366 Vaulting on nave completed; Neri di Fioravante makes model for dome.

1417 Drum for dome completed.

1418 Competition is held to design the dome.

1420 Brunelleschi begins work on the dome.

1436 Dome completed.

1446 Construction of lantern begins; Brunelleschi dies.

1461 Antonio Manetti, a student of Brunelleschi, completes lantern.

1469 Gilt copper ball and cross added by Verrocchio.

1587 Original façade is torn down by Medici court.

1871 Emilio de Fabris wins competition to design new façade.

1887 Façade completed.

WHAT TO LOOK FOR INSIDE THE DUOMO

The interior of the Duomo is a fine example of Florentine Gothic with a beautiful marble floor, but the space feels strangely barren—a result of its great size and the fact that some of the best art has been moved to the nearby **Museo dell'Opera del Duomo.**

Notable among the works that remain are two towering equestrian frescoes of famous mercenaries: *Niccolò da Tolentino* (1456), by Andrea del Castagno, and *Sir John Hawkwood* (1436), by Paolo Uccello. There's also fine terra-cotta work by Luca della Robbia. Ghiberti, Brunelleschi's great rival, is responsible for much of the stained glass, as well as a reliquary urn with gorgeous reliefs. A vast fresco of the Last Judgment, painted by Vasari and Zuccari, covers the dome's interior. Brunelleschi had wanted mosaics to go there; it's a pity he didn't get his wish.

In the crypt beneath the cathedral, you can explore excavations of a Roman wall and mosaic fragments from the late sixth century; entry is near the first pier on the right. On the way down you pass Brunelleschi's modest tomb.

1. Entrance; stained glass by Ghiberti
2. Fresco of Niccolò da Tolentino by Andrea del Castagno
3. Fresco of John Hawkwood by Paolo Uccello
4. *Dante and the Divine Comedy* by Domenico di Michelino
5. Lunette: *Ascension* by Luca della Robbia
6. Above altar: two angels by Luca della Robbia. Below the altar: reliquary of St. Zenobius by Ghiberti.
7. Lunette: *Resurrection* by Luca della Robbia
8. Entrance to dome
9. Bust of Brunelleschi by Buggiano
10. Stairs to crypt
11. Campanile

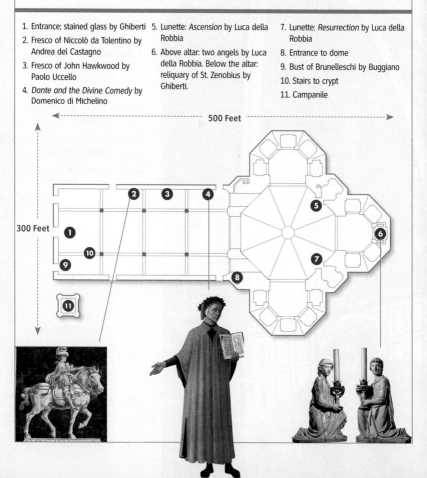

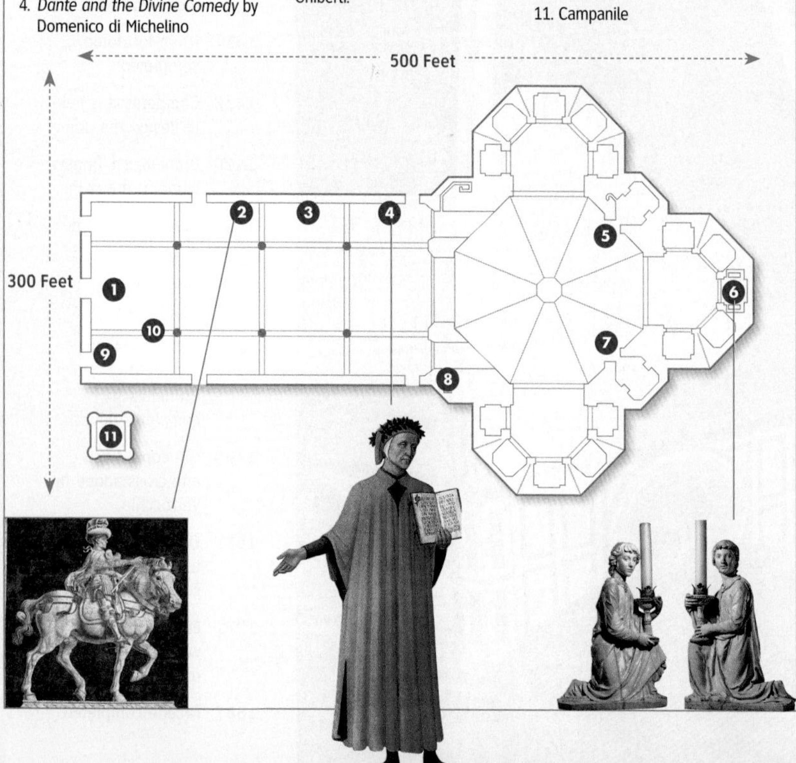

MAKING THE CLIMB

Climbing the 463 steps to the top of the dome is not for the faint of heart—or for the claustrophobic—but those who do it will be awarded a smashing view of Florence ❶. Keep in mind that the way up is also the way down, which means that while you're huffing and puffing in the ascent, people very close to you in a narrow staircase are making their way down ❷.

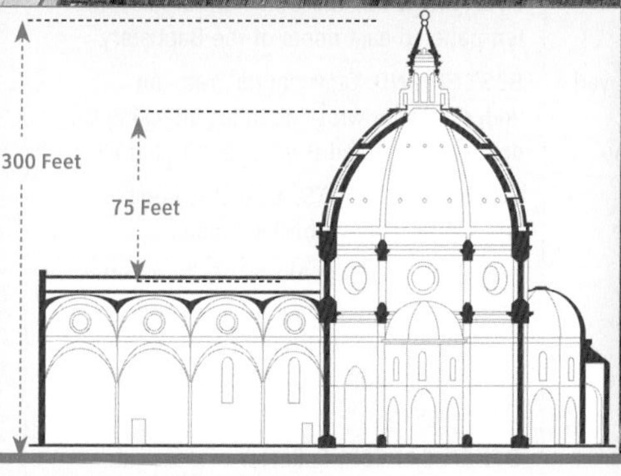

DUOMO BASICS

- Even first thing in the morning during high season (May through September), a line is likely to have formed to climb the dome. Expect an hour wait.
- For an alternative to the dome, consider climbing the less trafficked campanile, which gives you a view from on high of the dome itself.
- Dress code essentials: covered shoulders, no short shorts, and hats off upon entering.

✉ Piazza del Duomo

☎ 055/2302885

🌐 www.operaduomo.firenze.it

🎫 Free, crypt €3, cupola €6

⏲ Crypt: Mon.–Wed., Fri., Sun. 10–5; Thurs. 10–4:30; Sat. 10–5:45; first Sat. of month 10–3:30. Cupola: Weekdays 8:30–7, Sat. 8:30–5:40, 1st Sat. of month 8:30–4. Duomo: Mon.–Wed. and Fri. 10–5, Thurs. 10–4:30, Sat., 10–4:45, Sun 1:30–4:45, 1st Sat. of month 10–3:30.

BRUNELLESCHI vs. GHIBERTI
The Rivalry of Two Renaissance Geniuses

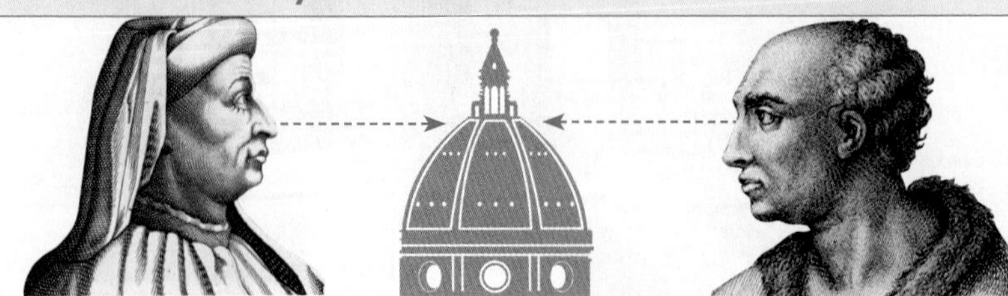

In Renaissance Florence, painters, sculptors, and architects competed for major commissions, with the winner earning the right to undertake a project that might occupy him (and keep him paid) for a decade or more. Stakes were high, and the resulting rivalries fierce—none more so than that between Filippo Brunelleschi and Lorenzo Ghiberti.

The two first clashed in 1401, for the commission to create the bronze doors of the Baptistery. When Ghiberti won, Brunelleschi took it hard, fleeing to Rome, where he would remain for 15 years. Their rematch came in 1418, over the design of the Duomo's cupola, with Brunelleschi triumphant. For the remainder of their lives, the two would miss no opportunity to belittle each other's work.

FILIPPO BRUNELLESCHI (1377–1446)

MASTERPIECE: The dome of Santa Maria del Fiore.

BEST FRIENDS: Donatello, whom he stayed with in Rome after losing the Baptistery doors competition; the Medici family, who rescued him from bankruptcy.

SIGNATURE TRAITS: Paranoid, secretive, bad tempered, practical joker, inept businessman.

SAVVIEST POLITICAL MOVE: Feigned sickness and left for Rome after his dome plans were publicly criticized by Ghiberti, who was second-in-command. The project proved too much for Ghiberti to manage on his own, and Brunelleschi returned triumphant.

MOST EMBARRASSING MOMENT: In 1434 he was imprisoned for two weeks for failure to pay a small guild fee. The humiliation might have been orchestrated by Ghiberti.

OTHER CAREER: Shipbuilder. He built a huge vessel, *Il Badalone*, to transport marble for the dome up the Arno. It sank on its first voyage.

INSPIRED: The dome of St. Peter's in Rome.

LORENZO GHIBERTI (1378–1455)

MASTERPIECE: *The Gates of Paradise*, the ten-paneled east doors of the Baptistery.

BEST FRIEND: Giovanni da Prato, an underling who wrote diatribes attacking the dome's design and Brunelleschi's character.

SIGNATURE TRAITS: Instigator, egoist, know-it-all, shrewd businessman.

SAVVIEST POLITICAL MOVE: During the Baptistery doors competition, he had an open studio and welcomed opinions on his work, while Brunelleschi labored behind closed doors.

OTHER CAREER: Collector of classical artifacts, historian.

INSPIRED: *The Gates of Hell* by Auguste Rodin.

The Gates of Paradise detail

The **Corridoio Vasariano** (✉ *Piazzale degli Uffizi 6, Piazza della Signoria* ☎ *055/23885 or 055/294883*), the private Medici corridor, was built by Vasari in 1565. Though the ostensible reason for its construction was one of security, it was more likely designed so that the Medici family wouldn't have to walk amid commoners. The corridor is notoriously fickle with its operating hours; at this writing, it's open. Even if it's closed, it can sometimes be visited by prior special arrangement. Call for the most up-to-date details. Take a moment to study the Ponte Santa Trinita, the next bridge downriver, from either the bridge or the corridor. It was designed by Bartolomeo Ammannati in 1567 (probably from sketches by Michelangelo), blown up by retreating German forces during World War II, and painstakingly reconstructed after the war. The view from Ponte Santa Trinita is beautiful, which might explain why so many young lovers seem to hang out there.

WORD OF MOUTH

"My husband and I had read *Brunelleschi's Dome* and were eager to climb to the top. We got there first thing in the morning (maybe 30 minutes after opening) and there was no line. It was definitely warm, and a bit crowded, but we *loved* the experience. Honestly, though, I don't know how anyone can do this in the middle of the day in the summer heat with crowds."

—dina4

WORTH NOTING

Campanile. The Gothic bell tower designed by Giotto (circa 1266–1337) is a soaring structure of multicolor marble originally decorated with sculptures by Donatello and reliefs by Giotto, Andrea Pisano, and others (which are now in the Museo dell'Opera del Duomo). A climb of 414 steps rewards you with a close-up of Brunelleschi's cupola on the Duomo next door and a sweeping view of the city. ✉ *Piazza del Duomo* ☎ *055/2302885* 🌐 *www.operaduomo.firenze.it* 🎫 *€6* 🕘 *Daily 8:30–7:30.*

Mercato Nuovo *(New Market)*. The open-air loggia, built in 1551, teems with souvenir stands, but the real attraction is a copy of Pietro Tacca's bronze *Porcellino* (which translates as "little pig" despite the fact the animal is, in fact, a wild boar). The *Porcellino* is Florence's equivalent of the Trevi Fountain: put a coin in his mouth, and if it falls through the grate below (according to one interpretation), it means you'll return to Florence someday. The statue dates from around 1612, but the original version, in the Museo Bardini, is an ancient Greek work. ✉ *Corner of Via Por Santa Maria and Via Porta Rossa, Piazza della Repubblica* 🕘 *Market: Tues.–Sat. 8–7, Mon. 1–7.*

Museo dell'Opera del Duomo *(Cathedral Museum)*. Ghiberti's original Baptistery door panels and the *cantorie* (choir loft) reliefs by Donatello and Luca della Robbia (1400–82) keep company with Donatello's *Mary Magdalene* and Michelangelo's *Pietà* (not to be confused with his more famous *Pietà* in St. Peter's in Rome). Renaissance sculpture is in part defined by its revolutionary realism, but in its palpable suffering Donatello's *Magdalene* goes beyond realism. Michelangelo's heart-wrenching *Pietà* was unfinished at his death; the female figure supporting the body of Christ on the left was added by Tiberio Calcagni (1532–65), and never has the difference between competence and genius been manifested so clearly. ✉ *Piazza del Duomo 9* ☎ *055/2302885* 🌐 *www.operaduomo.firenze.it* 🎫 *€6* 🕓 *Mon.–Sat. 9–7:30, Sun. 9–1:45.*

> **WORD OF MOUTH**
>
> "Palazzo Vecchio is very worthwhile. I am palace fan though. There is a hidden elevator behind the ticket desk that will save lots of steps."
>
> —charlesg

Orsanmichele. This multipurpose structure began as an 8th-century oratory and then in 1290 was turned into an open-air loggia for selling grain. Destroyed by fire in 1304, it was rebuilt as a loggia-market. Between 1367 and 1380 the arcades were closed and two stories were added above; finally, at century's end it was turned into a church. Inside is a beautifully detailed 14th-century Gothic tabernacle by Andrea Orcagna (1308–68). The exterior niches contain sculptures, now copies of the originals by Donatello and Verrocchio (1435–88), among others, dating from the early 1400s to the early 1600s and paid for by the guilds. Although it's a copy, Verrocchio's *Doubting Thomas* (circa 1470) is particularly deserving of attention. Here you see Christ, like the building's other figures, entirely framed within the niche, and St. Thomas standing on its bottom ledge, with his right foot outside the niche frame. This one detail, the positioning of a single foot, brings the whole composition to life. You can see nearly all of the original sculptures at the **Museo di Orsanmichele,** which is open Monday. The museum entrance is on Via Arte della Lana. ✉ *Via dei Calzaiuoli, Piazza della Repubblica* ☎ *055/284944* 🕓 *Museum: Mon. 10–5.*

Palazzo Davanzati. The prestigious Davanzati family owned this 14th-century palace in one of Florence's swankiest medieval neighborhoods. The place is a delight, as you can wander through the surprisingly light-filled courtyard, and climb the steep stairs to the *piano nobile* (main floor), where the family did most of its living. The beautiful *Sala dei Pappagalli* (Parrot Room) is adorned with trompe-l'oeil tapestries and gaily painted birds. Though some claim that these date from the 14th century, many art historians are much less sure. ✉ *Piazza Davanzati 13, Piazza della Repubblica* ☎ *055/2388610* 🎫 *€2* 🕓 *Daily 8:15–1:50. Closed 1st, 3rd, and 5th Sun. of month; closed 2nd and 4th Mon. of month.*

Palazzo Vecchio *(Old Palace)*. Florence's forbidding, fortresslike city hall was begun in 1299, presumably designed by Arnolfo di Cambio, and its massive bulk and towering campanile dominate Piazza della Signoria. It was built as a meeting place for the heads of the seven major guilds governing the city at the time; over the centuries it has served lesser purposes, but today it's once again City Hall. The interior courtyard is a good deal less severe, having been remodeled by Michelozzo (1396–1472) in 1453; a copy of Verrocchio's bronze *puttino* (cherub), topping the central fountain, softens the space. (The original is upstairs.)

The main attraction is on the second floor: two adjoining rooms that supply one of the most startling contrasts in Florence. The first is the vast **Sala dei Cinquecento** (Room of the Five Hundred), named for the 500-member Great Council, the people's assembly established after the death of Lorenzo the Magnificent, that met here. Giorgio Vasari and others decorated the room, around 1563–65, with gargantuan frescoes celebrating Florentine history; depictions of battles with nearby cities predominate. Continuing the martial theme, the room also contains Michelangelo's *Victory*, intended for the never-completed tomb of Pope Julius II (1443–1513), plus other sculptures of decidedly lesser quality.

The second room is the little **Studiolo,** to the right of the Sala dei Cinquecento's entrance. Here the melancholy Francesco I (1541–87), son of Cosimo I, stored his priceless treasures and conducted scientific experiments. Designed by Vasari, it was decorated by him, Giambologna, and many others. ✉ *Piazza della Signoria* ☎ *055/2768465* 🎟 *€6* ⏲ *Mon.–Wed. and Fri.–Sun. 9–7, Thurs. 9–2.*

Piazza della Repubblica. The square marks the site of the ancient forum that was the core of the original Roman settlement. The street plan around the piazza still reflects the carefully plotted Roman military encampment. The Mercato Vecchio (Old Market), which had been here since the Middle Ages, was demolished and the current piazza was constructed between 1885 and 1895 as a neoclassical showpiece. The piazza is lined with outdoor cafés, affording an excellent opportunity for people-watching.

SAN LORENZO TO THE ACCADEMIA

A sculptor, painter, architect, and a poet, Florentine native son Michelangelo was a consummate genius, and some of his finest creations remain in his hometown. A key to understanding Michelangelo's genius can be found in the magnificent Cappelle Medicee, where both his sculptural and architectural prowess can clearly be seen. Planned frescoes were never completed, sadly, for they would have shown in one space the artistic triple threat that he certainly was. The towering yet graceful *David,* his most famous work, resides in the Galleria dell'Accademia.

After visiting San Lorenzo, resist the temptation to explore the market that surrounds the church. You can always come back later, after the churches and museums have closed; the market is open until 7 pm. Note that the Museo di San Marco closes at 1:50 on weekdays.

TOP ATTRACTIONS

★ **Cappelle Medicee** *(Medici Chapels).* This magnificent complex includes the **Cappella dei Principi,** the Medici chapel and mausoleum that was begun in 1605 and kept marble workers busy for several hundred years, and the **Sagrestia Nuova** (New Sacristy), designed by Michelangelo and so called to distinguish it from Brunelleschi's Sagrestia Vecchia (Old Sacristy) in San Lorenzo.

Michelangelo received the commission for the New Sacristy in 1520 from Cardinal Giulio de' Medici (1478–1534), who later became Pope Clement VII. The cardinal wanted a new burial chapel for his cousins Giuliano, Duke of Nemours (1478–1534), and Lorenzo, Duke of Urbino (1492–1519), and he also wanted to honor his father, also named Giuliano, and his uncle, Lorenzo il Magnifico. The result was a tour de force of architecture and sculpture. Architecturally, Michelangelo was as original and inventive here as ever, but it is, quite properly, the powerfully sculpted tombs that dominate the room. The scheme is allegorical: on the tomb on the right are figures representing Day and Night, and on the tomb to the left are figures representing Dawn and Dusk; above them are idealized sculptures of the two men, usually interpreted to represent the active life and the contemplative life. But the allegorical meanings are secondary; what is most important is the intense presence of the sculptural figures and the force with which they hit the viewer. ✉ *Piazza di Madonna degli Aldobrandini, San Lorenzo* ☎ *055/294883 reservations* 🎫 *€9* ⏲ *Easter–Nov., daily 8:15–5; Dec.–Easter, daily 8:15–1:50. Closed 1st, 3rd, and 5th Mon. and 2nd and 4th Sun. of month.*

WORD OF MOUTH

"When you go to see *David* at the Accademia, go later in the afternoon (about 5 pm), the bus groups will have gone by then and the queue will be short. The gallery doesn't close until about 7 pm so you have plenty of time to see the very divine *David*."
—cathies

★ **Galleria dell'Accademia** *(Accademia Gallery)*. The collection of Florentine paintings, dating from the 13th to the 18th centuries, is largely unremarkable, but the sculptures by Michelangelo are worth the price of admission. The unfinished *Slaves*, fighting their way out of their marble prisons, were meant for the tomb of Michelangelo's overly demanding patron Pope Julius II (1443–1513). But the focal point is the original *David*, moved here from Piazza della Signoria in 1873. *David* was commissioned in 1501 by the Opera del Duomo (Cathedral Works Committee), which gave the 26-year-old sculptor a leftover block of marble that had been ruined forty years earlier by another artist. Michelangelo's success with the block was so dramatic that the city showered him with honors, and the Opera del Duomo voted to build him a house and a studio in which to live and work.

Today *David* is beset not by Goliath but by tourists, and seeing the statue at all—much less really studying it—can be a trial. Save yourself a long wait in line by reserving tickets in advance. A Plexiglas barrier surrounds the sculpture, following a 1991 attack on it by a hammer-wielding artist who, luckily, inflicted only a few minor nicks on the toes. The statue is not quite what it seems. It's so poised and graceful and alert—so miraculously alive—that it's often considered the definitive sculptural embodiment of the High Renaissance perfection. But its true place in the history of art is a bit more complicated.

As Michelangelo well knew, the Renaissance painting and sculpture that preceded his work were deeply concerned with ideal form. Perfection of proportion was the ever-sought holy grail; during the Renaissance, ideal proportion was equated with ideal beauty, and ideal beauty was equated with spiritual perfection. But *David*, despite its supremely calm and dignified pose, departs from these ideals. Michelangelo didn't give the statue perfect proportions. The head is slightly too large for the body, the arms are too large for the torso, and the hands are dramatically large for the arms. The work was originally commissioned to adorn the exterior of the Duomo and was intended to be seen from a distance and

CLOSE UP

Florence's Trial by Fire

One of the most striking figures of Renaissance Florence was Girolamo Savonarola, a Dominican friar who, for a moment, captured the conscience of the city. In 1491 he became prior of the convent of San Marco, where he adopted a life of austerity and delivered sermons condemning Florence's excesses and the immorality of his fellow clergy. Following the death of Lorenzo de' Medici, Savonarola was instrumental in the formation of the republic of Florence, ruled by a representative council with Christ enthroned as monarch. In one of his most memorable acts, he urged Florentines to toss worldly possessions—from frilly dresses to Botticelli paintings—onto a "bonfire of the vanities" in Piazza della Signoria. Savonarola's antagonism toward church hierarchy led to his undoing: he was excommunicated in 1497, and the following year was hanged and burned on charges of heresy. Today, at the Museo di San Marco, you can visit Savonarola's cell and see his arresting portrait.

on high. Michelangelo knew exactly what he was doing, calculating that the perspective of the viewer would be such that, in order for the statue to appear proportioned, the upper body, head, and arms would have to be bigger, as they're farther away from the viewer. But he also did it to express and embody, as powerfully as possible in a single figure, an entire biblical story. *David*'s hands *are* big, but so was Goliath, and these are the hands that slew him. Music lovers might want to check out the Museo degli Instrumenti Musicali contained within the Accademia; its Stradivarius is the main attraction. ✉ *Via Ricasoli 60, San Marco* ☎ *055/294883 reservations, 055/2388609 gallery* 🎫 *€10, reservation fee €4* 🕙 *Tues.–Sun. 8:15–6:50.*

★ **Museo di San Marco.** A Dominican convent adjacent to the church of San Marco now houses this museum, which contains many stunning works by Fra Angelico (circa 1400–55), the Dominican friar famous for his piety as well as for his painting. When the friars' cells were restructured between 1439 and 1444, he decorated many of them with frescoes meant to spur religious contemplation. His unostentatious paintings extol the simple beauties of the contemplative life. Fra Angelico's works are everywhere, from the friars' cells to the superb panel paintings on view in the museum. Don't miss the famous *Annunciation,* on the upper floor, and the works in the gallery off the cloister as you enter. Here you can see his beautiful *Last Judgment*; as usual, the tortures of the damned are far more inventive and interesting than the pleasures of the redeemed. ✉ *Piazza San Marco 1* ☎ *055/2388608* 🎫 *€4* 🕙 *Weekdays 8:15–1:50, weekends 8:15–6:50. Closed 1st, 3rd, and 5th Sun., and 2nd and 4th Mon. of month.*

San Lorenzo. Filippo Brunelleschi designed this basilica, as well as that of Santo Spirito in the Oltrarno, in the 15th century. He never lived to see either finished. The two interiors are similar in design and effect. San Lorenzo, however, has a grid of dark, inlaid marble lines on the floor, which considerably heightens the dramatic effect. The grid makes the

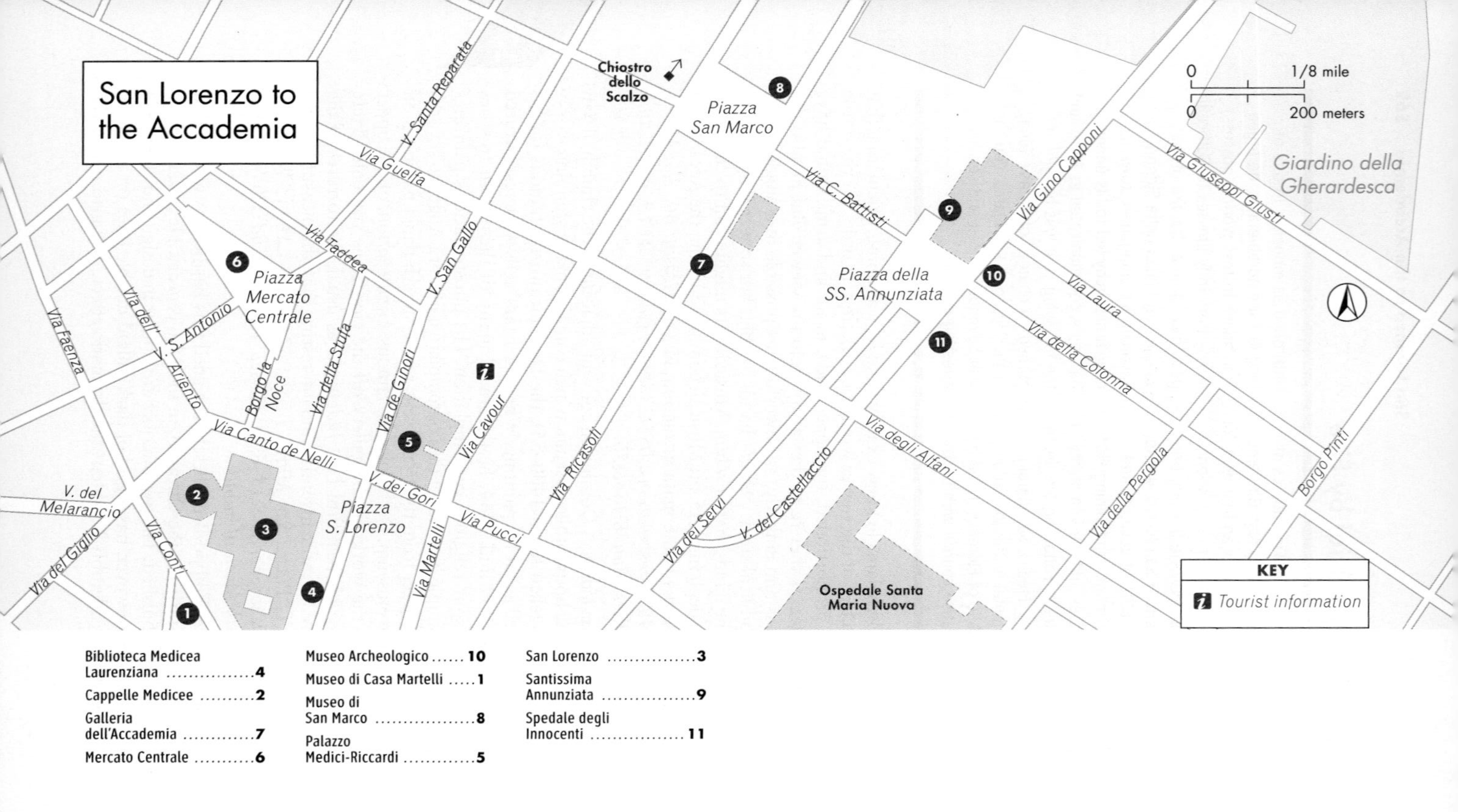
San Lorenzo to the Accademia
0
1/8 mile
0
200 meters
Giardino della Gherardesca
Chiostro dello Scalzo
Piazza San Marco
Via Giuseppi Giusti
Via Gino Capponi
Via C. Battisti
Piazza della SS. Annunziata
Via Laura
Via della Colonna
Via degli Alfani
Via della Pergola
Borgo Pinti
V. Santa Reparata
Via Guelfa
Via Taddea
V. San Gallo
Piazza Mercato Centrale
Via Faenza
Via dell'
V. S. Antonio
V. Ariento
Borgo la Noce
Via della Stufa
Via de Ginori
Via Cavour
Via Ricasoli
Via dei Servi
V. del Castellaccio
Via Canto de Nelli
V. dei Gori
Via Pucci
Via Martelli
Piazza S. Lorenzo
V. del Melarancio
Via del Giglio
Via Conti
Ospedale Santa Maria Nuova
KEY
Tourist information
Biblioteca Medicea Laurenziana 4
Cappelle Medicee 2
Galleria dell'Accademia 7
Mercato Centrale 6
Museo Archeologico 10
Museo di Casa Martelli 1
Museo di San Marco 8
Palazzo Medici-Riccardi 5
San Lorenzo 3
Santissima Annunziata 9
Spedale degli Innocenti 11

rigorous geometry of the interior immediately visible, and is an illuminating lesson on the laws of perspective. If you stand in the middle of the nave at the church entrance, on the line that stretches to the high altar, every element in the church—the grid, the nave columns, the side aisles, the coffered nave ceiling—seems to march inexorably toward a hypothetical vanishing point beyond the high altar, exactly as in a single-point-perspective painting. Brunelleschi's **Sagrestia Vecchia** (Old Sacristy) has stucco decorations by Donatello; it's at the end of the left transept. ✉ *Piazza San Lorenzo* ☎ *055/2645144* 🎫 *€3.50* ⏲ *Mon.–Sat. 10–5; Mar.–Oct., Sun. 1:30–5. Closed Sun. Nov.–Feb.*

WORTH NOTING

Biblioteca Medicea Laurenziana *(Laurentian Library)*. Michelangelo the architect was every bit as original as Michelangelo the sculptor. Unlike Brunelleschi (the architect of the Spedale degli Innocenti), however, he wasn't obsessed with proportion and perfect geometry. He was interested in experimentation, invention, and the expression of a personal vision at times highly idiosyncratic.

It was never more idiosyncratic than in the Laurentian Library, begun in 1524 and finished in 1568 by Bartolomeo Ammannati. Its famous **vestibolo,** a strangely shaped anteroom, has had scholars scratching their heads for centuries. In a space more than two stories high, why did Michelangelo limit his use of columns and pilasters to the upper two-thirds of the wall? Why didn't he rest them on strong pedestals instead of on huge, decorative curlicue scrolls, which rob them of all visual support? Why did he recess them into the wall, which makes them look weaker still? The architectural elements here don't stand firm and strong and tall, as they do inside San Lorenzo, next door; instead, they seem to be pressed into the wall as if into putty, giving the room a soft, fluid look that creates a strange effect. It's almost as if Michelangelo intentionally flouted the conventions of the High Renaissance to see what kind of bizarre, mannered effect might result. His innovations were tremendously influential, and produced a period of architectural experimentation. As his contemporary Giorgio Vasari put it, "Artisans have been infinitely and perpetually indebted to him because he broke the bonds and chains of a way of working that had become habitual by common usage."

10

The anteroom's staircase (best viewed straight on), which emerges from the library with the visual force of an unstoppable lava flow, has been exempted from the criticism, however. In its highly sculptural conception and execution, it's quite simply one of the most original and fluid staircases in the world. ✉ *Piazza San Lorenzo 9, entrance to left of San Lorenzo* ☎ *055/210760* 🌐 *www.bml.firenze.sbn.it* 🎫 *Special exhibitions €5, museum €3* ⏲ *Mon.–Sat. 9:30—1;30. Closed first Sat. of month.*

Mercato Centrale. Some of the food at this huge, two-story market hall is remarkably exotic. The ground floor contains meat and cheese stalls, as well as some very good bars serving *panini* (sandwiches), and the second floor teems with vegetable stands. ✉ *Piazza del Mercato Centrale, San Lorenzo* ☎ *No phone* ⏲ *Mon.–Sat. 7–2.*

Museo Archeologico *(Archaeological Museum).* Of the Etruscan, Egyptian, and Greco-Roman antiquities here, the Etruscan collection is particularly notable—one of the most important in Italy (the other being in Turin). The famous bronze *Chimera* was discovered (without the tail, which is a 16th-century reconstruction by Cellini). If you're traveling with kids, they might particularly enjoy the small mummy collection. Those with a fondness for gardens should visit on Saturday morning, when the tiny but eminently pleasurable garden is open for tours. ✉ *Via della Colonna 38, Santissima Annunziata* ☎ *055/294883* 🌐 *www.firenzemusei.it* 🎫 *€3* ⏲ *Mon. 2–7, Tues. and Thurs. 8:30–7, Wed. and Fri.–Sun. 8:30–2.*

WORD OF MOUTH

"For a different experience, go to the Mercato Centrale (Central Market) which is full of specialty food stalls that will just amaze you! This is only a few blocks from the Accademia where the Michelangelo *David* is."

—Charnees

Museo di Casa Martelli. The wealthy Martelli family lived from the 16th century in this palace on a quiet street near the basilica of San Lorenzo. The last Martelli died in 1986, and in October 2009 the casa-museo (house-museum) opened to the public. It's the only non-reconstructed example of such a house in all of Florence, and for that reason alone it's worth a visit. The family collected art, and while most of the stuff is B-list, a couple of gems by Beccafumi, Salvatore Rosa, and Piero di Cosimo adorn the walls. Reservations are essential, and you'll be shown the glories of this place by well-informed, English-speaking guides. ✉ *Via Zanetti 8, San Lorenzo* ☎ *055/294883* 🌐 *www.polomuseale.firenze.it* 🎫 *€3* ⏲ *Guided tours: Thurs. 2, 3:30, and 5; Sat. 9, 10:30, and noon.*

Palazzo Medici-Riccardi. The main attraction of this palace, begun in 1444 by Michelozzo for Cosimo de' Medici, is the interior chapel, the so-called **Cappella dei Magi** on the piano nobile. Painted on its walls is Benozzo Gozzoli's famous *Procession of the Magi,* finished in 1460 and celebrating both the birth of Christ and the greatness of the Medici family. Gozzoli wasn't a revolutionary painter, and today is considered by some not quite first-rate because of his technique, which was old-fashioned even for his day. ✉ *Via Cavour 1, San Lorenzo* ☎ *055/2760340* 🎫 *€7* ⏲ *Thurs.–Tues. 9–7.*

Santa Maria Maddalena dei Pazzi. One of Florence's hidden treasures, a cool and composed *Crucifixion* by Perugino (circa 1445/50–1523), is in the chapter house of the monastery below this church. Here you can see the Virgin Mary and Saint John the Evangelist with Mary Magdalene and Saints Benedict and Bernard of Clairvaux posed against a simple but haunting landscape. The figure of Christ crucified occupies the center of this brilliantly hued fresco. Perugino's colors radiate—note the juxtaposition of the yellow-green cuff against the orange tones of the Magdalene's robe. ✉ *Borgo Pinti 58, Santa Croce* ☎ *055/2478420* 🎫 *Suggested donation €1* ⏲ *Mon.–Sat. 9–noon, 5–5:20, and 6–7; Sun. 9–noon and 5–6:20.*

Santissima Annunziata. Dating from the mid-13th century, this church was restructured in 1447 by Michelozzo, who gave it an uncommon (and lovely) entrance cloister with frescoes by Andrea del Sarto (1486–1530), Pontormo (1494–1556), and Rosso Fiorentino (1494–1540). The interior is a rarity for Florence: an overwhelming example of the baroque. But it's not really a fair example, because it's merely 17th-century baroque decoration applied willy-nilly to an earlier structure—exactly the sort of violent remodeling exercise that has given the baroque a bad name. The **Cappella dell'Annunziata,** immediately inside the entrance to the left, illustrates the point. The lower half, with its stately Corinthian columns and carved frieze bearing the Medici arms, was commissioned by Piero de' Medici in 1447; the upper half, with its erupting curves and impish sculpted cherubs, was added 200 years later. Fifteenth-century-fresco enthusiasts should also note the very fine *Holy Trinity with St. Jerome* in the second chapel on the left. Andrea del Castagno (circa 1421–57) has depicted a wiry and emaciated St. Jerome with Paula and Eustochium, two of his closest followers. ✉ *Piazza di Santissima Annunziata* ☎ *055/266186* ⏲ *Daily 7–12:30 and 4–6:30.*

Spedale degli Innocenti. Begun by Brunelleschi in 1419 to serve as an orphanage, it takes the historical prize as the very first Renaissance building. Brunelleschi designed its portico with his usual rigor, building it out of the two shapes he considered mathematically (and therefore philosophically and aesthetically) perfect: the square and the circle. Below the level of the arches, the portico encloses a row of perfect cubes; above the level of the arches, the portico encloses a row of intersecting hemispheres. The entire geometric scheme is articulated with Corinthian columns, capitals, and arches borrowed directly from antiquity. At the time he designed the portico, Brunelleschi was also designing the interior of San Lorenzo, using the same basic ideas. But because the portico was finished before San Lorenzo, the Spedale degli Innocenti can claim the honor of ushering in Renaissance architecture. The 10 ceramic medallions depicting swaddled infants that decorate the portico are by Andrea della Robbia (1435–1525/28), executed in about 1487.

Within the Spedale degli Innocenti is a small museum, or **Pinacoteca** (🎟 *€4* ⏲ *Thurs.–Tues. 8:30–2*). Most of the objects are minor works by major artists, but well worth a look is Domenico Ghirlandaio's (1449–94) *Adorazione dei Magi* (*Adoration of the Magi*), executed in 1488. His use of color, and his eye for flora and fauna, shows that art from north of the Alps made a great impression on him. ✉ *Piazza di Santissima Annunziata 12* ☎ *055/20371* 🎟 *€5* ⏲ *Daily 10–7.*

SANTA MARIA NOVELLA TO THE ARNO

Piazza Santa Maria Novella, near the train station, has been restored to its former glory thanks to a years-long project completed in 2009. The streets in and around the piazza have their share of architectural treasures, including some of Florence's most tasteful palaces. Between Santa Maria Novella and the Arno is Via Tornabuoni, Florence's finest shopping street.

TOP ATTRACTIONS

Santa Maria Novella. The facade of this church looks distinctly clumsy by later Renaissance standards, and with good reason: it's an architectural hybrid. The lower half was completed mostly in the 14th century; its pointed-arch niches and decorative marble patterns reflect the Gothic style of the day. About 100 years later (around 1456), architect Leon Battista Alberti was called in to complete the job. The marble decoration of his upper story clearly defers to the already existing work below, but the architectural motifs he added evince an entirely different style. The central doorway, the four ground-floor half-columns with Corinthian capitals, the triangular pediment atop the second story, the inscribed frieze immediately below the pediment—these are borrowings from antiquity, and they reflect the new Renaissance style in architecture, born some 35 years earlier at the Spedale degli Innocenti. Alberti's most important addition, however, the S-curve scrolls that surmount the decorative circles on either side of the upper story, had no precedent in antiquity. The problem was to soften the abrupt transition between wide ground floor and narrow upper story. Alberti's solution turned out to be definitive. Once you start to look for them, you'll find scrolls such as these (or sculptural variations of them) on churches all over Italy, and every one of them derives from Alberti's example here.

The architecture of the interior is, like that of the Duomo, a dignified but somber example of Florentine Gothic. Exploration is essential, however, because the church's store of art treasures is remarkable. Highlights include the 14th-century stained-glass rose window depicting the *Coronation of the Virgin* (above the central entrance); the Cappella Filippo Strozzi (to the right of the altar), containing late-15th-century frescoes and stained glass by Filippino Lippi; the *cappella maggiore* (the area around the high altar), displaying frescoes by Ghirlandaio; and the Cappella Gondi (to the left of the altar), containing Filippo Brunelleschi's famous wood crucifix, carved around 1410 and said to have so stunned the great Donatello when he first saw it that he dropped a basket of eggs.

Of special interest for its great art-historical importance and beauty is Masaccio's *Trinity,* on the left-hand wall, almost halfway down the nave. Painted around 1426–27 (at the same time he was working on his frescoes in Santa Maria del Carmine), it unequivocally announced the arrival of the Renaissance. The realism of the figure of Christ was revolutionary in itself, but what was probably even more startling to contemporary Florentines was the barrel vault in the background. The mathematical rules for employing perspective in painting had just been discovered (probably by Brunelleschi), and this was one of the first works of art to employ them with utterly convincing success.

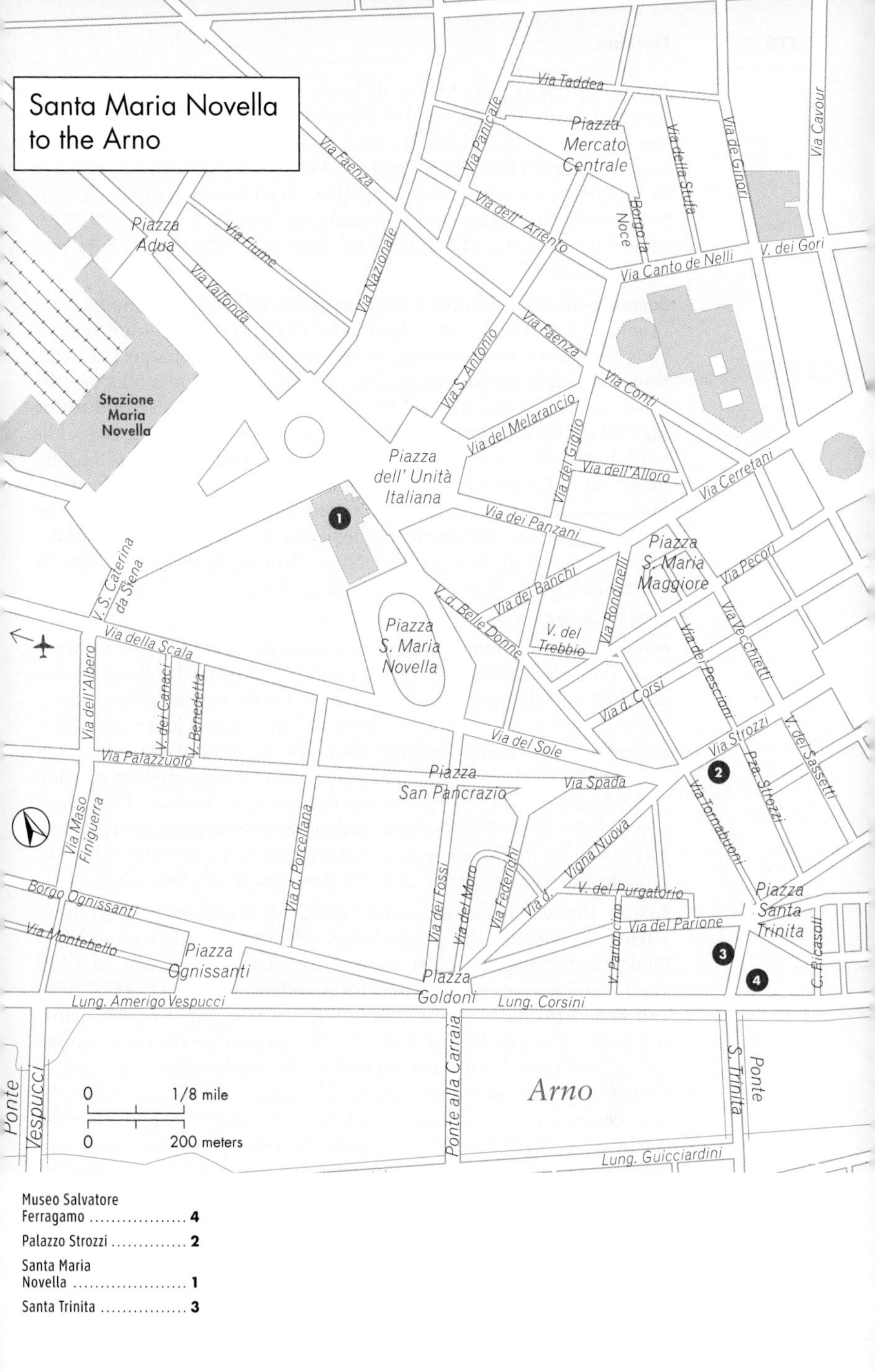

Museo Salvatore Ferragamo **4**

Palazzo Strozzi **2**

Santa Maria Novella **1**

Santa Trinita **3**

In the cloisters of the **Museo di Santa Maria Novella,** to the left of Santa Maria Novella, is a faded fresco cycle by Paolo Uccello depicting tales from Genesis, with a dramatic vision of the Deluge. Earlier and better-preserved frescoes painted in 1348–55 by Andrea da Firenze are in the chapter house, or the **Cappellone degli Spagnoli** (Spanish Chapel), off the cloister. ✉ *Piazza Santa Maria Novella 19* ☎ *055/210113, Museo 055/282187* 🎫 *Museum and chapel €2.70* ⏲ *Mon.–Thurs. and Sat. 9–5.*

Santa Trinita. Started in the 11th century by Vallombrosian monks and originally Romanesque in style, the church underwent a Gothic remodeling during the 14th century. (Remains of the Romanesque construction are visible on the interior front wall.) Its major works are the fresco cycle and altarpiece in the Cappella Sassetti, the second to the high altar's right, painted by Ghirlandaio between 1480 and 1485. His work here possesses such graceful decorative appeal as well as a proud depiction of his native city (most of the cityscapes show 15th-century Florence in all her glory). The wall frescoes illustrate scenes from the life of St. Francis, and the altarpiece, depicting the *Adoration of the Shepherds,* veritably glows. ✉ *Piazza Santa Trinita, Santa Maria Novella* ☎ *055/216912* ⏲ *Mon.–Sat. 8–noon and 4–6.*

WORTH NOTING

Museo Salvatore Ferragamo. If there's such a thing as a temple for footwear, this is it. The shoes in this dramatically displayed collection were designed by Salvatore Ferragamo (1898–1960) beginning in the early 20th century. Born in southern Italy, the late master jump-started his career in Hollywood by creating shoes for the likes of Mary Pickford and Rudolph Valentino. He then returned to Florence and set up shop in the basement of the 13th-century Palazzo Spini Ferroni. The collection includes about 16,000 shoes, and those on exhibition are frequently rotated. ✉ *Via dei Tornabuoni 2, Santa Maria Novella* ☎ *055/3360846* 🌐 *www.museoferragamo.it* 🎫 *€5* ⏲ *Mon. and Wed.–Sun. 10–6.*

Palazzo Strozzi. The Strozzi family built this imposing palazzo in an attempt to outshine the nearby Palazzo Medici. Based on a model by Giuliano da Sangallo (circa 1452–1516) dating from around 1489 and executed between 1489 and 1504 under il Cronaca (1457–1508) and Benedetto da Maiaino (1442–97), it was inspired by Michelozzo's earlier Palazzo Medici-Riccardi. The palazzo's exterior is simple, severe, and massive: it's a testament to the wealth of a 15th-century Florentine patrician family. The interior courtyard, entered from the rear of the palazzo, is another matter altogether. It's here that the classical vocabulary—columns, capitals, pilasters, arches, and cornices—is given uninhibited and powerful expression. Blockbuster art shows frequently occur here. ✉ *Via Tornabuoni, Piazza della Repubblica* ☎ *055/2776461* 🌐 *www.palazzostrozzi.org* 🎫 *Free, except during exhibitions* ⏲ *Daily 10–7.*

CLOSE UP

Meet the Medici

The Medici were the dominant family of Renaissance Florence, wielding political power and financing some of the world's greatest art. You'll see their names at every turn around the city. These are some of the clan's more notable members:

Cosimo il Vecchio (1389–1464), incredibly wealthy banker to the popes, was the first in the family line to act as de facto ruler of Florence. He was a great patron of the arts and architecture, and the moving force behind the family palace and the Dominican complex of San Marco.

Lorenzo il Magnifico (1449–92), grandson of Cosimo il Vecchio, presided over a Florence largely at peace with her neighbors. A collector of cameos, a writer of sonnets, and lover of ancient texts, he was the preeminent Renaissance man.

Leo X (1475–1521), also known as Giovanni de' Medici, became the first Medici pope, helping extend the family power base to include Rome and the Papal States. His reign was characterized by a host of problems, the biggest one being a former friar named Martin Luther.

Catherine de' Medici (1519–89), was married by her cousin Pope Clement VII to Henry of Valois, who later became Henry II of France. Wife of one king and mother of three, she was the first Medici to marry into European royalty. Lorenzo il Magnifico, her great-grandfather, would have been thrilled.

Cosimo I (1519–74), the first grand duke of Tuscany, should not be confused with his ancestor Cosimo il Vecchio.

SANTA CROCE

10

The Santa Croce quarter, on the southeast fringe of the historic center, was built up in the Middle Ages outside the second set of medieval city walls. The centerpiece of the neighborhood was the basilica of Santa Croce, which could hold great numbers of worshippers. Since the middle of the 16th century, the vast piazza served as a playing field for no-holds-barred soccer games. A center of leather working since the Middle Ages, the neighborhood is still packed with leatherworkers and leather shops.

TOP ATTRACTIONS

Piazza Santa Croce. Originally outside the city's 12th-century walls, this piazza grew with the Franciscans, who used the large square for public preaching. During the Renaissance it was used for *giostre* (jousts), including one sponsored by Lorenzo de' Medici. "Bonfires of the vanities" occurred here, as well as soccer matches, in the 16th century. Lined with many palazzi dating from the 15th century, it remains one of Florence's loveliest piazzas and is a great place to people-watch.

Fodor's Choice ★ **Santa Croce.** Like the Duomo, this church is Gothic, but, also like the Duomo, its facade dates from the 19th century. As a burial place, the church probably contains more skeletons of Renaissance celebrities than any other in Italy. The tomb of Michelangelo is on the right at the front

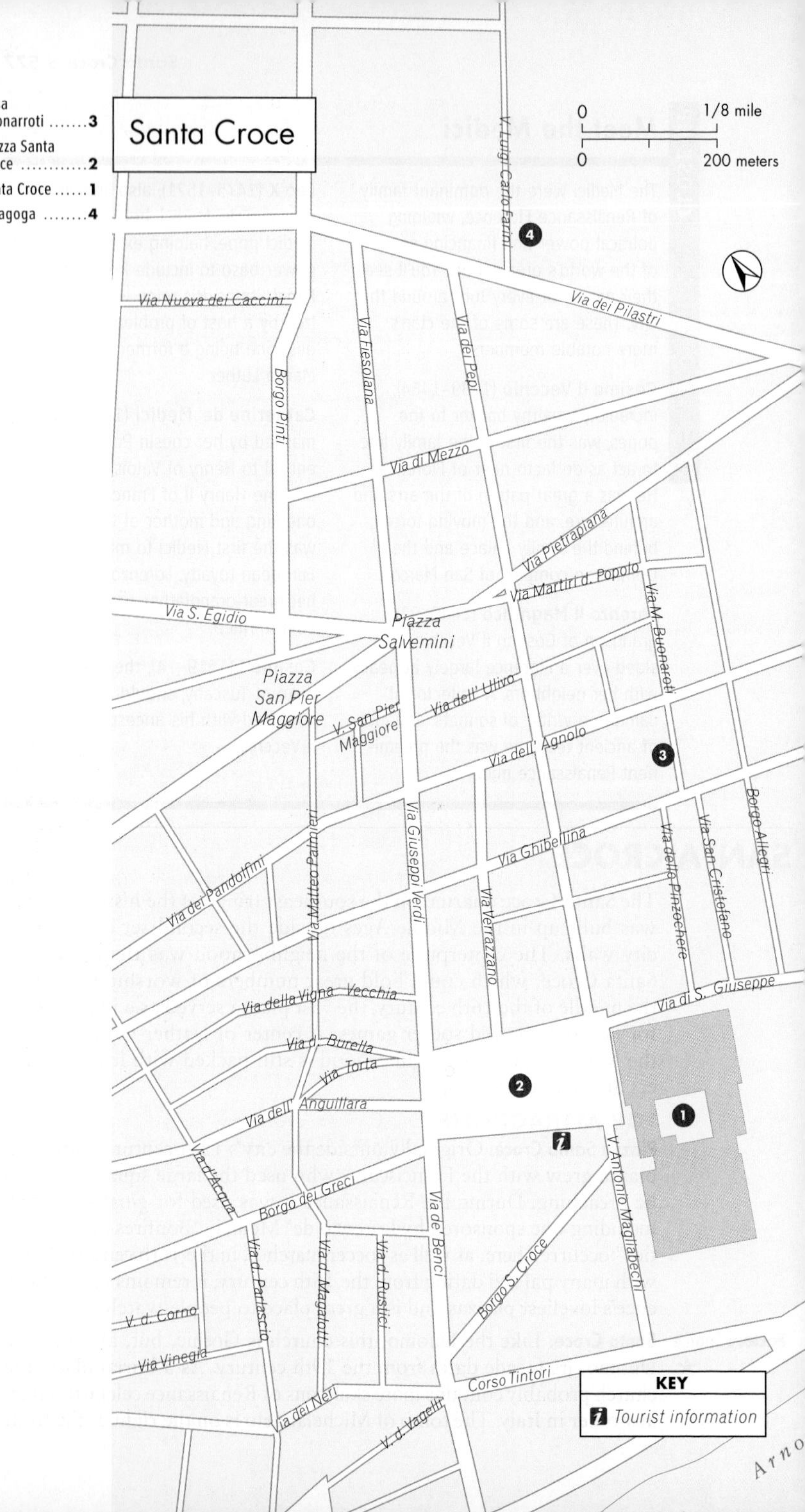

Casa Buonarroti 3
Piazza Santa Croce 2
Santa Croce 1
Sinagoga 4
Santa Croce
0 1/8 mile
0 200 meters
Via L. C. Farini
Via dei Pilastri
Via Nuova dei Caccini
Via Fiesolana
Via dei Pepi
Borgo Pinti
Via di Mezzo
Via Pietrapiana
Via Martiri d. Popolo
Via M. Buonarroti
Via S. Egidio
Piazza Salvemini
Piazza San Pier Maggiore
V. San Pier Maggiore
Via dell' Ulivo
Via dell' Agnolo
Borgo Allegri
Via San Cristofano
Via della Pinzochere
Via Ghibellina
Via Giuseppe Verdi
Via Matteo Palmieri
Via dei Pandolfini
Via Verrazzano
Via di S. Giuseppe
Via della Vigna Vecchia
Via d. Burella
Via Torta
Via dell' Anguillara
V. d. Acqua
Borgo dei Greci
V. Antonio Magliabechi
Via de' Benci
Borgo S. Croce
Via d. Parlascio
Via d. Magalotti
Via d. Rustici
V. d. Corno
Via Vinegia
Corso Tintori
Via dei Neri
V. d. Vagelli
KEY
Tourist information
Arno

of the basilica; he is said to have chosen this spot so that the first thing he would see on Judgment Day, when the graves of the dead fly open, would be Brunelleschi's dome through Santa Croce's open doors. The tomb of Galileo Galilei (1564–1642) is on the left wall; he was not granted a Christian burial until 100 years after his death because of his controversial contention that Earth is not the center of the universe. The tomb of Niccolò Machiavelli (1469–1527), the political theoretician whose pragmatic philosophy so influenced the Medici, is halfway down the nave on the right. The grave of Lorenzo Ghiberti, creator of the Baptistery doors, is halfway down the nave on the left. Composer Gioacchino Rossini (1792–1868) is buried at the end of the nave on the right. The monument to Dante Alighieri (1265–1321), Italy's greatest poet, is a memorial rather than a tomb (he's buried in Ravenna); it's on the right wall near the tomb of Michelangelo.

The collection of art within the complex is by far the most important of any church in Florence. The most famous works are probably the Giotto frescoes in the two chapels immediately to the right of the high altar. They illustrate scenes from the lives of Saint John the Evangelist and Saint John the Baptist (in the right-hand chapel) and scenes from the life of Saint Francis (in the left-hand chapel). Time has not been kind to these frescoes; through the centuries, wall tombs were placed in the middle of them, then they were whitewashed and plastered over, and in the 19th century, they suffered a clumsy restoration. But the reality that Giotto introduced into painting can still be seen. He didn't paint beautifully stylized religious icons, as the Byzantine style that preceded him prescribed; he instead painted drama—Saint Francis surrounded by grieving friars at the very moment of his death. This was a radical shift in emphasis: before Giotto, painting's role was to symbolize the attributes of God; after him, it was to imitate life. His work is indeed primitive compared with later painting, but in the early 14th century it caused a sensation that was not equaled for another 100 years. He was, for his time, the equal of both Masaccio and Michelangelo.

Among the church's other highlights are Donatello's *Annunciation,* a moving expression of surprise (on the right wall two-thirds of the way down the nave); 14th-century frescoes by Taddeo Gaddi (circa 1300–66) illustrating scenes from the life of the Virgin Mary, clearly showing the influence of Giotto (in the chapel at the end of the right transept); and Donatello's *Crucifix,* criticized by Brunelleschi for making Christ look like a peasant (in the chapel at the end of the left transept). Outside the church proper, in the **Museo dell'Opera di Santa Croce** off the cloister, is the 13th-century *Triumphal Cross* by Cimabue (circa 1240–1302), badly damaged by the flood of 1966. A model of architectural geometry, the Cappella Pazzi, at the end of the cloister, was designed by Brunelleschi, who didn't live to see it finished. ✉ *Piazza Santa Croce 16* ☎ *055/2466105* 🎫 *Church and museum €5* ⏲ *Mon.–Sat. 9:30–5:30, Sun. 1–5.*

Sinagoga. Jews were well settled in Florence by 1396, when the first money-lending operations became officially sanctioned. Medici patronage helped Jewish banking houses to flourish, but by 1570 Jews were required to live within the large "ghetto," near today's Piazza della

Repubblica, by decree of Cosimo I, who had cut a deal with Pope Pius V (1504–72): in exchange for ghettoizing the Jews, he would receive the title Grand Duke of Tuscany.

Construction of the modern Moorish-style synagogue began in 1874 as a bequest of David Levi, who wished to endow a synagogue "worthy of the city." Falcini, Micheli, and Treves designed the building on a domed Greek cross plan with galleries in the transept and a roofline bearing three distinctive copper cupolas visible from all over Florence. The exterior has alternating bands of tan travertine and pink granite, reflecting an Islamic style repeated in Giovanni Panti's ornate interior. Of particular interest are the cast-iron gates by Pasquale Franci, the eternal light by Francesco Morini, and the Murano glass mosaics by Giacomo dal Medico. The gilded doors of the Moorish ark, which fronts the pulpit and is flanked by extravagant candelabra, are decorated with symbols of the ancient Temple of Jerusalem and bear bayonet marks from vandals. The synagogue was used as a garage by the Nazis, who failed to inflict much damage in spite of an attempt to blow up the place with dynamite. Only the columns on the left side were destroyed, and even then, the Women's Balcony above did not collapse. Note the Star of David in black and yellow marble inlaid in the floor. The original capitals can be seen in the garden.

Some of the oldest and most beautiful Jewish ritual artifacts in all of Europe are displayed upstairs in the small **Museo Ebraico.** Exhibits document the Florentine Jewish community and the building of the synagogue. The donated objects all belonged to local families and date from as early as the late 16th century. Take special note of the exquisite needlework and silver pieces. A small but well-stocked gift shop is downstairs. ✉ *Via Farini 4, Santa Croce* ☎ *055/2346654* 🎫 *Synagogue and museum €5* ⏲ *Apr.–Sept., Sun.–Thurs. 10–6, Fri. 10–2; Oct.–Mar., Sun.–Thurs. 10–3.*

WORTH NOTING

Casa Buonarroti. If you're really enjoying walking in the footsteps of the great genius, you may want to complete the picture by visiting the Buonarroti family home. Michelangelo lived here from 1516 to 1525, and later gave it to his nephew, whose son, called Michelangelo il Giovane (Michelangelo the Younger) turned it into a gallery dedicated to his great uncle. The artist's descendants filled it with art treasures, some by Michelangelo himself. Two early marble works—the *Madonna of the Steps* and the *Battle of the Centaurs*—hint at the marvels to come. ✉ *Via Ghibellina 70, Santa Croce* ☎ *055/241752* 🌐 *www.casabuonarroti.it* 🎫 *€6.50* ⏲ *Wed.–Mon. 10–5.*

WHO'S WHO IN RENAISSANCE ART

Michelangelo. Leonardo da Vinci. Raphael. This heady triumvirate of the Italian Renaissance is synonymous with artistic genius. Yet they are only three of the remarkable cast of characters whose work defines the Renaissance, that extraordinary flourishing of art and culture in Italy, especially in Florence, as the Middle Ages drew to a close. The artists were visionaries, who redefined painting, sculpture, architecture, and even what it means to be an artist.

THE PIONEER. In the mid-14th century, a few artists began to move away the flat, two-dimensional painting of the Middle Ages. **Giotto**, who painted seemingly three-dimensional figures who show emotion, had a major impact on the artists of the next century.

THE GROUNDBREAKERS. The generations of **Brunelleschi** and **Botticelli** took center stage in the 15th century. **Ghiberti, Masaccio, Donatello, Uccello, Fra Angelico**, and **Filippo Lippi** were other major players. Part of the Renaissance (or "re-birth") was a renewed interest in classical sources—the texts, monuments, and sculpture of Ancient Greece and Rome. Perspective and the illusion of three-dimensional space in painting was another discovery of this era, known as the Early Renaissance. Suddenly the art appearing on the walls looked real, or more realistic than it used to.

Roman ruins were not the only thing to inspire these artists. There was an incredible exchange of ideas going on. In Santa Maria del Carmine, Filippo Lippi was inspired by the work of Masaccio, who in turn was a friend of Brunelleschi. Young artists also learned from the masters via the apprentice system. Ghiberti's workshop (*bottega* in Italian) included, at one time or another, Donatello, Masaccio, and Uccello. Botticelli was apprenticed to Filippo Lippi.

THE BIG THREE. The mathematical rationality and precision of 15th-century art gave way to what is known as the High Renaissance. **Leonardo, Michelangelo**, and **Raphael** were much more concerned with portraying the body in all its glory and with achieving harmony and grandeur in their work. Oil paint, used infrequently up until this time, became more widely employed: as a result, Leonardo's colors are deeper, more sensual, more alive. For one brief period, all three were in Florence at the same time. Michelangelo and Leonardo surely knew one another, as they were simultaneously working on frescoes (never completed) inside Palazzo Vecchio.

When Michelangelo left Florence for Rome in 1508, he began the slow drain of artistic exodus from Florence, which never really recovered her previous glory.

A RENAISSANCE TIMELINE

IN THE WORLD

Black Death in Europe kills one third of the population, 1347-50.

Joan of Arc burned at the stake, 1431.

IN FLORENCE

Dante, a native of Florence, writes *The Divine Comedy,* 1302-21.

Founding of the Medici bank, 1397.

Medici family made official papal bankers.

1434, Cosimo il Vecchio becomes de facto ruler of Florence. The Medici family will dominate the city until 1494.

1300

1400

IN ART

EARLY RENAISSANCE

GIOTTO (ca. 1267-1337)

Giotto fresoes in Santa Croce, 1320-25.

1334, 67-year-old Giotto is appointed chief architect of Santa Maria del Fiore, Florence's Duomo (below). He begins to work on the Campanile, which will be completed in 1359, after his death.

Masaccio and Masolino fresco Sant Maria del Carmine, 1424-28.

BRUNELLESCHI (1377-1446)

LORENZO GHIBERTI (ca. 1381-1455)

DONATELLO (ca. 1386-1466)

PAOLO UCCELLO (1397-1475)

FRA ANGELICO (ca. 1400-1455)

MASACCIO (1401-1428)

FILIPPO LIPPI (ca. 1406-1469)

Ghiberti wins the competition for the Baptistery doors (above) in Florence, 1401.

Donatello sculpts his bronze *David,* ca 1440.

Fra Angelico frescoes friars' cells in San Marco, 1438-45.

Uccello's *Sir John Hawkwood,* ca. 1436.

Brunelleschi wins the competition for the Duomo cupola (right), 1418.

Gutenberg Bible is printed, 1455.

Columbus discovers America, 1492.

Martin Luther posts his 95 theses on the door at Wittenberg, kicking off the Protestant Reformation, 1517.

Constantinople falls to the Turks, 1453.

Machiavelli's *Prince* appears, 1513.

Copernicus proves that the earth is not the center of the universe, 1530-43.

Lorenzo "il Magnifico" (right), the Medici patron of the arts, rules in Florence, 1449-92.

Two Medici popes Leo X (1513-21) and Clement VII (1523-34) in Rome.

Catherine de'Medici becomes Queen of France, 1547.

1450 1500 1550

HIGH RENAISSANCE

Fra Filippo Lippi's *Madonna and Child*, ca. 1452.

Botticelli paints the *Birth of Venus*, ca. 1482.

1508, Raphael begins work on the chambers in the Vatican, Rome.

1504, Michelangelo's *David* is put on display in Piazza della Signoria, where it remains until 1873.

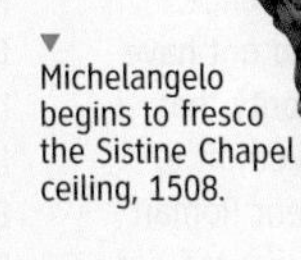

Michelangelo begins to fresco the Sistine Chapel ceiling, 1508.

Giorgio Vasari publishes his first edition of *Lives of the Artists*, 1550.

BOTTICELLI (ca. 1444-1510)

LEONARDO DA VINCI (1452-1519)

RAPHAEL (1483-1520)

MICHELANGELO (1475-1564)

Leonardo paints *The Last Supper* in Milan, 1495-98.

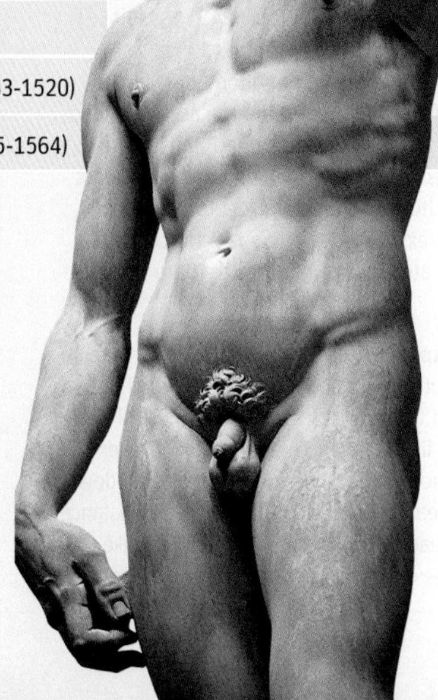

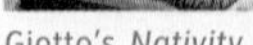

Giotto's *Nativity*

Donatello's *St. John the Baptist*

Ghiberti's *Gates of Paradise*

GIOTTO (CA. 1267-1337)

Painter/architect from a small town north of Florence.

He unequivocally set Italian painting on the course that led to the triumphs of the Renaissance masters. Unlike the rather flat, two-dimensional forms found in then prevailing Byzantine art, Giotto's figures have a fresh, life-like quality. The people in his paintings have bulk, and they show emotion, which you can see on their faces and in their gestures. This was something new in the late Middle Ages. Without Giotto, there wouldn't have been a Raphael.

In Florence: **Santa Croce; Uffizi; Campanile; Santa Maria Novella**

Elsewhere in Italy: **Scrovegni Chapel, Padua; Vatican Museums, Rome**

FILIPPO BRUNELLESCHI (1377-1446)

Architect/engineer from Florence.

If Brunelleschi had beaten Ghiberti in the Baptistery doors competition in Florence, the city's Duomo most likely would not have the striking appearance and authority that it has today. After his loss, he sulked off to Rome, where he studied the ancient Roman structures first-hand. Brunelleschi figured out how to vault the Duomo's dome, a structure unprecedented in its colossal size and great height. His Ospedale degli Innocenti employs classical elements in the creation of a stunning, new architectural statement; it is the first truly Renaissance structure.

In Florence: **Duomo; Ospedale degli Innocenti; San Lorenzo; Santo Spirito; Baptistery Doors Competition Entry, Bargello; Santa Croce**

LORENZO GHIBERTI (CA. 1381-1455)

Sculptor from Florence.

Ghiberti won a competition—besting his chief rival, Brunelleschi—to cast the gilded bronze North Doors of the Baptistery in Florence. These doors, and the East Doors that he subsequently executed, took up the next 50 years of his life. He created intricately worked figures that are more true-to-life than any since antiquity, and he was one of the first Renaissance sculptors to work in bronze. Ghiberti taught the next generation of artists; Donatello, Uccello, and Masaccio all passed through his studio.

In Florence: **Door Copies, Baptistery; Original Doors, Museo dell'Opera del Duomo; Baptistry Door Competition Entry, Bargello; Orsanmichele**

DONATELLO (CA. 1386-1466)

Sculptor from Florence.

Donatello was an innovator who, like his good friend Brunelleschi, spent most of his long life in Florence. Consumed with the science of optics, he used light and shadow to create the effects of nearness and distance. He made an essentially flat slab look like a three- dimensional scene. His bronze *David* is probably the first free-standing male nude since antiquity. Not only technically brilliant, his work is also emotionally resonant; few sculptors are as expressive.

In Florence: ***David*, Bargello; *St. Mark*, Orsanmichele; Palazzo Vecchio; Museo dell'Opera del Duomo; San Lorenzo; Santa Croce**

Elsewhere in Italy: **Padua; Prato; Venice**

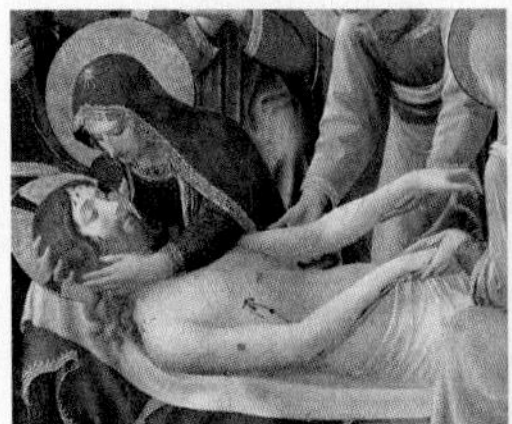
Fra Angelico's *The Deposition*

Masaccio's *Trinity*

Filippo Lippi's *Madonna and Child*

PAOLO UCCELLO (1397-1475)

Painter from Florence.

Renaissance chronicler Vasari once observed that had Uccello not been so obsessed with the mathematical problems posed by perspective, he would have been a very good painter. The struggle to master single-point perspective and to render motion in two dimensions is nowhere more apparent than in his battle scenes. His first major commission in Florence was the gargantuan fresco of the English mercenary Sir John Hawkwood (the Italians called him Giovanni Acuto) in Florence's Duomo.

In Florence: *Sir John Hawkwood*, Duomo; *Battle of San Romano*, Uffizi; Santa Maria Novella

Elsewhere in Italy: Urbino

FRA ANGELICO (CA. 1400-1455)

Painter from a small town north of Florence.

A Dominican friar, who eventually made his way to the convent of San Marco, Fra Angelico and his assistants painted frescoes for aid in prayer and meditation. He was known for his piety; Vasari wrote that Fra Angelico could never paint a crucifix without a tear running down his face. Perhaps no other painter so successfully translated the mysteries of faith and the sacred into painting. And yet his figures emote, his command of perspective is superb, and his use of color startles even today.

In Florence: Museo di San Marco; Uffizi

Elsewhere in Italy: Vatican Museums, Rome; Fiesole; Cortona; Perugia; Orvieto

MASACCIO (1401-1428)

Painter from San Giovanni Valdarno, southeast of Florence.

Masaccio and Masolino, a frequent collaborator, worked most famously together at Santa Maria del Carmine. Their frescoes of the life of St. Peter use light to mold figures in the painting by imitating the way light falls on figures in real life. Masaccio also pioneered the use of single-point perspective, masterfully rendered in his *Trinity*. His friend Brunelleschi probably introduced him to the technique, yet another step forward in rendering things the way the eye sees them. Masaccio died young and under mysterious circumstances.

In Florence: Santa Maria del Carmine; *Trinity*, Santa Maria Novella

FILIPPO LIPPI (CA. 1406-1469)

Painter from Prato.

At a young age, Filippo Lippi entered the friary of Santa Maria del Carmine, where he was highly influenced by Masaccio and Masolino's frescoes. His religious vows appear to have made less of an impact; his affair with a young nun produced a son, Filippino (Little Philip, who later apprenticed with Botticelli), and a daughter. His religious paintings often have a playful, humorous note; some of his angels are downright impish and look directly out at the viewer. Lippi links the earlier painters of the 15th century with those who follow; Botticelli apprenticed with him.

In Florence: Uffizi; Palazzo Medici Riccardi; San Lorenzo; Palazzo Pitti

Elsewhere in Italy: Prato

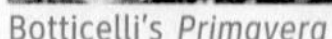
Botticelli's *Primavera*

Leonardo's *Portrait of a Young Woman*

Raphael's *Madonna on the Meadow*

BOTTICELLI (CA. 1444-1510)

Painter from Florence.

Botticelli's work is characterized by stunning, elongated blondes, cherubic angels (something he undoubtedly learned from his time with Filippo Lippi), and tender Christs. Though he did many religious paintings, he also painted monumental, nonreligious panels—his *Birth of Venus* and *Primavera* being the two most famous of these. A brief sojourn took him to Rome, where he and a number of other artists frescoed the Sistine Chapel walls.

In Florence: ***Birth of Venus, Primavera,*** **Uffizi; Palazzo Pitti**

Elsewhere in Italy: **Vatican Museums, Rome**

LEONARDO DA VINCI (1452-1519)

Painter/sculptor/engineer from Anchiano, a small town outside Vinci.

Leonardo never lingered long in any place; his restless nature and his international reputation led to commissions throughout Italy, and took him to Milan, Vigevano, Pavia, Rome, and, ultimately, France. Though he is most famous for his mysterious *Mona Lisa* (at the Louvre in Paris), he painted other penetrating, psychological portraits in addition to his scientific experiments: his design for a flying machine (never built) predates Kitty Hawk by nearly 500 years. The greatest collection of Leonardo's work in Italy can be seen on one wall in the Uffizi.

In Florence: ***Adoration of the Magi,*** **Uffizi**

Elsewhere in Italy: ***Last Supper,*** **Santa Maria delle Grazie, Milan**

RAPHAEL (1483-1520)

Painter/architect from Urbino.

Raphael spent only four highly productive years of his short life in Florence, where he turned out made-to-order panel paintings of the Madonna and Child for a hungry public; he also executed a number of portraits of Florentine aristocrats. Perhaps no other artist had such a fine command of line and color, and could render it, seemingly effortlessly, in paint. His painting acquired new authority after he came up against Michelangelo toiling away on the Sistine ceiling. Raphael worked nearly next door in the Vatican, where his figures take on an epic, Michelangelesque scale.

In Florence: **Uffizi; Palazzo Pitti**

Elsewhere in Italy: **Vatican Museums, Rome**

MICHELANGELO (1475-1564)

Painter/sculptor/architect from Caprese.

Although Florentine and proud of it (he famously signed his St. Peter's *Pietà* to avoid confusion about where he was from), he spent most of his 90 years outside his native city. He painted and sculpted the male body on an epic scale and glorified it while doing so. Though he complained throughout the proceedings that he was really a sculptor, Michelangelo's Sistine Chapel ceiling is arguably the greatest fresco cycle ever painted (and the massive figures owe no small debt to Giotto).

In Florence: ***David,*** **Galleria dell'Accademia; Uffizi; Casa Buonarroti; Bargello**

Elsewhere in Italy: **St. Peter's Basilica, Vatican Museums, and Piazza del Campidoglio in Rome**

THE OLTRARNO

A walk through the Oltrarno (literally "the other side of the Arno") takes in two very different aspects of Florence: the splendor of the Medici, manifest in the riches of the mammoth Palazzo Pitti and the gracious Giardino di Boboli; and the charm of the Oltrarno, a slightly gentrified but still fiercely proud working-class neighborhood with artisans' and antiques shops.

Farther east across the Arno, a series of ramps and stairs climbs to Piazzale Michelangelo, where the city lies before you in all its glory (skip this trip if it's a hazy day). You can avoid the long walk by taking Bus 12 or 13 at the west end of Ponte alle Grazie and getting off at Piazzale Michelangelo; you still have to climb the monumental stairs to and from San Miniato, but you can then take the bus from Piazzale Michelangelo back to the center of town. If you decide to take a bus, remember to buy your ticket before you board.

TOP ATTRACTIONS

Giardino di Boboli *(Boboli Gardens).* The main entrance to these landscaped gardens is from the right side of the courtyard of the **Palazzo Pitti.** The gardens began to take shape in 1549, when the Pitti family sold the palazzo to Eleanor of Toledo, wife of the Medici grand duke Cosimo I. The initial landscaping plans were laid out by Niccolò Tribolo (1500–50). After his death, work was continued by Ammannati, Giambologna, Bernardo Buontalenti (circa 1536–1608), and Giulio (1571–1635) and Alfonso Parigi (1606–56), among others. Italian landscaping is less formal than French, but still full of sweeping drama. A copy of the famous *Morgante,* Cosimo I's favorite dwarf astride a particularly unhappy tortoise, sits near the exit. Sculpted by Valerio Cioli (circa 1529–99), the work seems to illustrate the perils of culinary overindulgence. A visit here can be disappointing, because the gardens are somewhat underplanted and undercared-for, but it's still a great walk with some terrific views. ✉ *Enter through Palazzo Pitti* ☎ *055/294883* 🌐 *www.polomuseale.firenze.it* 🎫 *€12, combined ticket with Museo degli Argenti, Museo delle Porcellane, Villa Bardini, and Giardino Bardini* ⏲ *Jan., Feb., Nov., and Dec., daily 8:15–4:30; Mar., daily 8:15–5:30; Apr., May, Sept., and Oct., daily 8:15–6:30; June–Aug., daily 8:15–7:30. Closed 1st and last Mon. of month.*

Piazzale Michelangelo. From this lookout you have a marvelous view of Florence and the hills around it, rivaling the vista from the Forte di Belvedere. It has a copy of Michelangelo's *David* and outdoor cafés packed with tourists during the day and with Florentines in the evening. In May the **Giardino dell'Iris** (Iris Garden) off the piazza is abloom with more than 2,500 varieties of the flower. The **Giardino delle Rose** (Rose Garden) on the terraces below the piazza is also in full bloom in May and June.

Palazzo Pitti. This enormous structure is Florence's largest private family palace. The original palazzo, built for the Pitti family around 1460, comprised only the main entrance and the three windows on either side. In 1549 the property was sold to the Medici, and Bartolomeo Ammannati was called in to make substantial additions. Today the palace houses several museums: The **Museo degli Argenti** displays a vast collection of Medici treasures, including exquisite antique vases belonging to Lorenzo the Magnificent. The **Galleria del Costume** showcases fashions from the past 300 years. The **Galleria d'Arte Moderna** holds a collection of 19th- and 20th-century paintings, mostly Tuscan. The **Galleria Palatina,** the most famous of the Pitti galleries, contains a broad collection of paintings from the 15th to 17th centuries. The rooms of the Galleria Palatina remain much as the Lorena, the rulers who took over after the last Medici died in 1737, left them. The collection has its high points, including a number of portraits by Titian and an unparalleled collection of paintings by Raphael, notably the double portraits of Angelo Doni and his wife, the sullen Maddalena Strozzi. The price of admission to the Galleria Palatina also allows you to explore the former **Appartamenti Reali,** containing furnishings mostly from the 19th century. ✉ *Piazza Pitti* ☎ *055/210323* 🎫 *Galleria Palatina and Galleria d'Arte Moderna, combined ticket €12; Galleria del Costume, Giardino Bardini, Giardino di Boboli, Museo degli Argenti, and Museo Porcelleane, combined ticket €10* ⏲ *Tues.–Sun. 8:15–6:50.*

San Miniato al Monte. This church, like the Baptistery, is a fine example of Romanesque architecture and is one of the oldest churches in Florence, dating from the 11th century. A 12th-century mosaic topped by a gilt-bronze eagle, emblem of San Miniato's sponsors, the *Calimala* (cloth merchants' guild), crowns the lovely green-and-white marble facade. Inside are a 13th-century inlaid-marble floor and apse mosaic. Artist Spinello Aretino (1350–1410) covered the walls of the **Sagrestia** with frescoes depicting scenes from the life of St. Benedict. The **Cappella del Cardinale del Portogallo** (Chapel of the Portuguese Cardinal) is one of the richest 15th-century Renaissance works in Florence. It contains the tomb of a young Portuguese cardinal, Prince James of Lusitania, who died in Florence in 1459. Its glorious ceiling is by Luca della Robbia, and the sculpted tomb by Antonio Rossellino (1427–79). ✉ *Viale Galileo Galilei, Piazzale Michelangelo, Lungarno Sud* ☎ *055/2342731* ⏲ *Apr.–Oct., daily 8–7; Nov.–Mar., Mon.–Sat. 8–1 and 2:30–6, Sun. 3–5.*

Santa Maria del Carmine. The **Cappella Brancacci,** at the end of the right transept of this church, houses a masterpiece of Renaissance painting: a fresco cycle that changed the course of Western art. Fire almost destroyed the church in the 18th century; miraculously, the Brancacci Chapel survived nearly intact. The cycle is the work of three artists: Masaccio and Masolino (1383–circa 1447), who began it around 1424, and Filippino Lippi, who finished it some 50 years later, after a long interruption during which the sponsoring Brancacci family was exiled. It was Masaccio's work that opened a new frontier for painting, as he was among the first artists to employ single-point perspective; tragically, he died in 1428 at the age of 27, so he didn't live to experience the revolution his innovations caused.

Masaccio collaborated with Masolino on several of the frescoes, but his style predominates in the *Tribute Money,* on the upper-left wall; *St. Peter Baptizing,* on the upper altar wall; the *Distribution of Goods,* on the lower altar wall; and the *Expulsion of Adam and Eve,* on the chapel's upper-left entrance pier. If you look closely at the last painting and

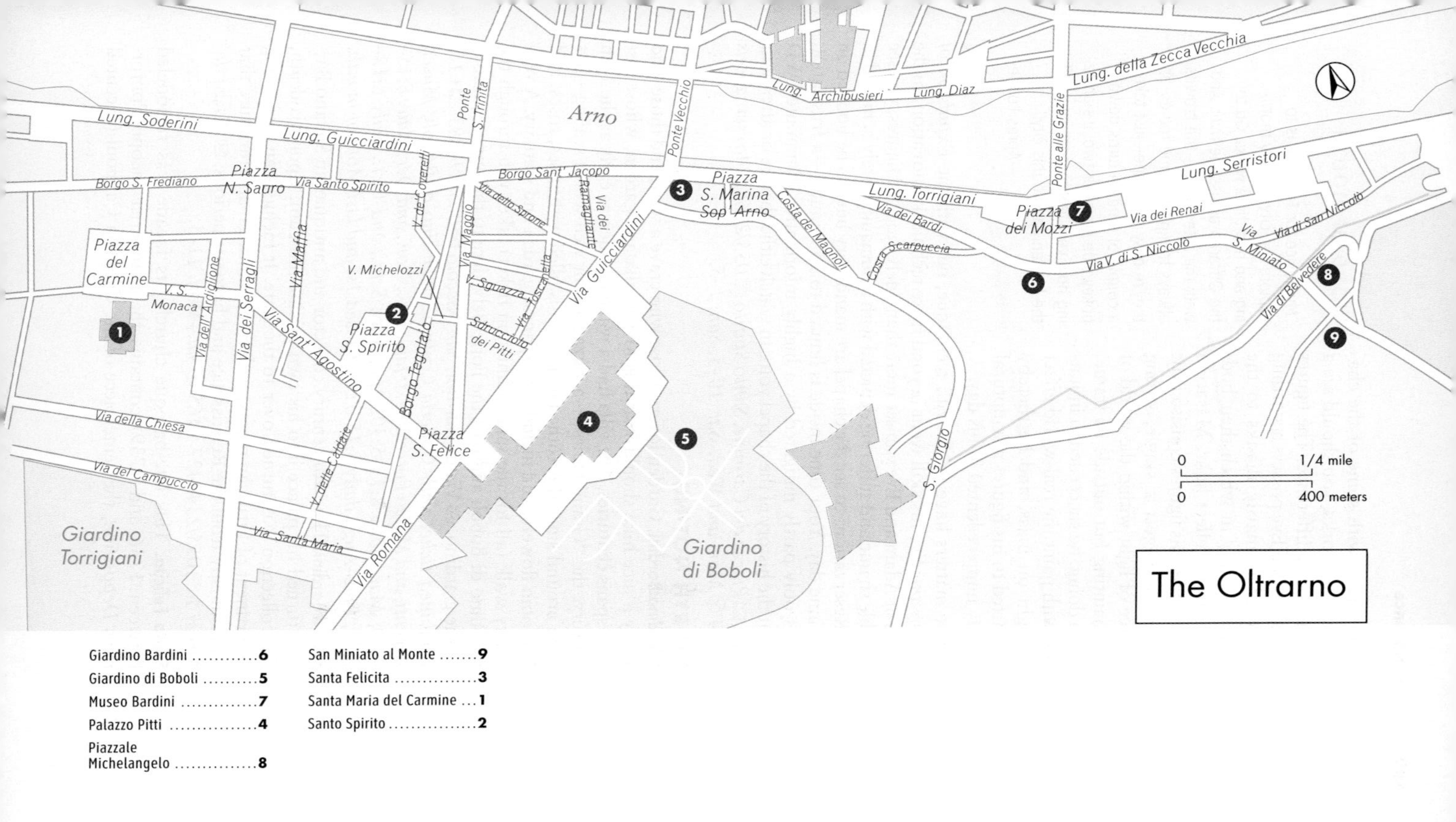
The Oltrarno
Arno
Lung. Soderini
Lung. Guicciardini
Lung. Archibusieri
Lung. Diaz
Lung. della Zecca Vecchia
Lung. Torrigiani
Lung. Serristori
Ponte S. Trinita
Ponte Vecchio
Ponte alle Grazie
Borgo S. Frediano
Piazza N. Sauro
Via Santo Spirito
V. de' Coverelli
Borgo Sant' Jacopo
Via dello Sprone
Via dei Ramagliante
Piazza S. Marina Sop' Arno
Costa dei Magnoli
Via dei Bardi
Costa Scarpuccia
Piazza dei Mozzi
Via dei Renai
Via V. di S. Niccolò
Via S. Miniato
Via di San Niccolò
Via di Belvedere
Piazza del Carmine
V. S. Monaca
Via dell' Ardiglione
Via dei Serragli
Via Maffia
Via Sant' Agostino
V. Michelozzi
Piazza S. Spirito
Borgo Tegolaio
Via Maggio
V. Sguazza
Via Toscanella
Sdrucciolo dei Pitti
Via Guicciardini
Via della Chiesa
Via del Campuccio
V. delle Caldaie
Via Santa Maria
Via Romana
Piazza S. Felice
S. Giorgio
Giardino Torrigiani
Giardino di Boboli
0 1/4 mile
0 400 meters
Giardino Bardini 6
Giardino di Boboli 5
Museo Bardini 7
Palazzo Pitti 4
Piazzale Michelangelo 8
San Miniato al Monte 9
Santa Felicita 3
Santa Maria del Carmine ...1
Santo Spirito 2

compare it with some of the chapel's other works, you should see a pronounced difference. The figures of Adam and Eve possess a startling presence primarily thanks to the dramatic way in which their bodies seem to reflect light. Masaccio here shaded his figures consistently, so as to suggest a single, strong source of light within the world of the painting but outside its frame. In so doing, he succeeded in imitating with paint the real-world effect of light on mass, and he thereby imparted to his figures a sculptural reality unprecedented in his day. These matters have to do with technique, but with the *Expulsion of Adam and Eve* his skill went beyond mere technical innovation. In the faces of Adam and Eve you see more than finely modeled figures; you see terrible shame and suffering depicted with a humanity rarely achieved in art. Reservations to see the chapel are mandatory but can be booked on the same day. Your time inside is limited to 15 minutes—a frustration that's only partly mitigated by a highly informative 40-minute DVD about the history of the chapel you can watch either before or after your visit. ✉ *Piazza del Carmine, Santo Spirito* ☎ *055/2768224 reservations* 🎫 *€4* ⏲ *Mon. and Wed.–Sat. 10–5, Sun. 1–5.*

WORD OF MOUTH

"My advice for Florence is to explore the city in early morning and nighttime walks. Go to the Oltrarno across the river. And walk the side streets—the crowds always tramp the same routes, and they're easy to escape—just take a couple of random turns down a pokey side street or two. It's amazing how very few tourists stray off the beaten path in this city."

—Apres Londee

WORTH NOTING

Giardino Bardini. Garden lovers, those who crave a view, and those who enjoy a nice hike should visit this lovely villa and garden, whose history spans centuries. The villa had a walled garden as early as the 14th century; the "Grand Stairs"—a zigzag ascent well worth scaling—has been around since the 16th. The garden is filled with irises, roses, and heirloom flowers, and includes a Japanese garden and statuary. A very pretty walk (all for the same admission ticket) takes you through the Giardino di Boboli and past the Forte Belvedere to the upper entrance to the giardino. ✉ *Via de'Bardini, San Niccolò* ☎ *005/294883* 🎫 *€10, combined ticket with Galleria Costume, Giardino di Boboli, Museo Argenti, and Museo Porcellane* ⏲ *Jan., Feb., Nov., and Dec., daily 8:15–4:30; Mar., daily 8:15–5:30; Apr., May, Sept., and Oct., daily 8:15–6:30; June–Aug., daily 8:15–7:30. Closed 1st and last Mon. of month.*

Museo Bardini. The 19th-century collector and antiquarian Stefano Bardini turned his palace into his own private museum. Upon his death, the collection was turned over to the state. It includes an interesting assortment of Etruscan pieces, sculpture, paintings, and furniture that dates mostly from the Renaissance and baroque periods. ✉ *Piazza de' Mozzi 1* ☎ *055/2342427* 🎫 *€5* ⏲ *Sat.–Mon. 11–5.*

Santa Felicita. This late-baroque church (its facade was remodeled between 1736 and 1739) contains the mannerist Jacopo Pontormo's *Deposition,* the centerpiece of the Cappella Capponi (executed

1525–28) and a masterpiece of 16th-century Florentine art. The remote figures, which transcend the realm of Renaissance classical form, are portrayed in tangled shapes and intense pastel colors (well preserved because of the low lights in the church), in a space and depth that defy reality. Note, too, the exquisitely frescoed *Annunciation,* also by Pontormo, at a right angle to the *Deposition.* The granite column in the piazza was erected in 1381 and marks a Christian cemetery. ✉ *Piazza Santa Felicita, Via Guicciardini, Palazzo Pitti* ⏲ *Mon.–Sat. 9–noon and 3–6, Sun. 9–1.*

Santo Spirito. The plain, unfinished facade gives nothing away, but the interior, although it appears chilly compared with later churches, is one of the most important examples of Renaissance architecture in Italy.

The interior is one of a pair designed in Florence by Filippo Brunelleschi in the early decades of the 15th century (the other is San Lorenzo). It was here that Brunelleschi supplied definitive solutions to the two major problems of interior Renaissance church design: how to build a cross-shaped interior using classical architectural elements borrowed from antiquity, and how to reflect in that interior the order and regularity that Renaissance scientists (among them Brunelleschi himself) were at the time discovering in the natural world around them.

Brunelleschi's solution to the first problem was brilliantly simple: turn a Greek temple inside out. While ancient Greek temples were walled buildings surrounded by classical colonnades, Brunelleschi's churches were classical arcades surrounded by walled buildings. This brilliant architectural idea overthrew the previous era's religious taboo against pagan architecture once and for all, triumphantly claiming that architecture for Christian use.

Brunelleschi's solution to the second problem—making the entire interior orderly and regular—was mathematically precise: he designed the ground plan of the church so that all its parts were proportionally related. The transepts and nave have exactly the same width; the side aisles are precisely half as wide as the nave; the little chapels off the side aisles are exactly half as deep as the side aisles; the chancel and transepts are exactly one-eighth the depth of the nave; and so on, with dizzying exactitude. For Brunelleschi, such a design technique was a matter of passionate conviction. Like most theoreticians of his day, he believed that mathematical regularity and aesthetic beauty were flip sides of the same coin, that one was not possible without the other. In the **Santo Spirito refectory** (✉ *Piazza Santo Spirito 29* ☎ *055/287043*), adjacent to the church, you can see Andrea Orcagna's highly damaged fresco of the Crucifixion. ✉ *Piazza Santo Spirito* ☎ *055/210030* 🎫 *Refectory €2.20* ⏲ *Church: Thurs.–Sat. and Mon.–Tues. 9:30–12:30 and 4–5:30; Sun. 12–5. Refectory: Apr.–Oct., Sat. 9–5; Nov.–Mar., Sat. 10:30–1:30.*

WHERE TO EAT

Florence's popularity with tourists means that, unfortunately, there's a higher percentage of mediocre restaurants here than you'll find in most Italian towns. Some restaurant owners cut corners and let standards slip, knowing that a customer today is unlikely to return tomorrow, regardless of the quality of the meal. So, if you're looking to eat well, it pays to do some research, starting with the recommendations here—we promise there's not a tourist trap in the bunch. Try to avoid places where waiters stand outside and invite you in, as well as those spots with little billboards outside showing pictures of their food. (Both practices are prevalent around San Lorenzo.)

Hours start at around 1 for lunch and 8 for dinner. Many of Florence's restaurants are small, so reservations are a must. You can sample such specialties as creamy *fegatini* (a chicken-liver spread) and ribollita (minestrone thickened with bread and beans and swirled with extra-virgin olive oil) in a bustling, convivial trattoria, where you share long wooden tables set with paper place mats, or in an upscale *ristorante* with linen tablecloths and napkins.

Those with a sense of culinary adventure should not miss the tripe sandwich, served from stands throughout town. This Florentine favorite comes with a fragrant *salsa verde* (green sauce) or a piquant red hot sauce—or both. Follow the Florentines' lead and take a break at an *enoteca* (wine bar) during the day and discover some excellent Chiantis and Super Tuscans from small producers who rarely export.

WHAT IT COSTS IN EUROS

	¢	$	$$	$$$	$$$$
At dinner	under €20	€20–€30	€30–€45	€45–€65	over €65

Prices are for a first course (primo), second course (secondo), and dessert (dolce).

THE DUOMO TO THE PONTE VECCHIO

$ MODERN ITALIAN ✕ **Coquinarius.** This rustically elegant space, which has served many purposes over the past 600 years, offers some of the tastiest food in town at great prices. It's the perfect place to come to if you aren't sure what you're hungry for, as they offer a little bit of everything: salad-lovers will have a hard time choosing from among the lengthy list (the Scozzeze, with poached chicken, avocado, and bacon, is a winner); those with a yen for pasta will face agonizing choices (the ravioli with pecorino and pears is particularly good). A revolving list of *piatti unici* (single dishes that can be ordered on their own, usually served at lunch) can also whet the whistle, as well as terrific cheese and cured meat plates. The well-culled wine list has lots of great wines by the glass, and even more by the bottle. ✉ *Via delle Oche 15/r, Piazza della Signoria* ☎ *055/2302153* 🌐 *www.coquinarius.it* ✍ *Reservations essential* ✣ *E3.*

BEST BETS FOR IN FLORENCE DINING

With hundreds of restaurants to choose from, how will you decide where to eat? Fodor's writers and editors have selected their favorite restaurants by price, cuisine, and experience in the Best Bets lists below. In the first column, Fodor's Choice properties represent the "best of the best."

Fodor's Choice ★

Cibrèo, $$$$, p. 598
Mario, ¢, p. 594
Taverna del Bronzino, $$$, p. 594

Best by Price

¢

All'Antico Vinaio, p. 601
da Nerbone, p. 594
da Rocco, p. 599
La Casalinga, p. 600
Mario, p. 594

$

Cibrèo Trattoria, p. 598
Il Santo Bevitore, p. 600
Osteria Antica Mescita San Niccolò, p. 601
Baldovino, p. 598

$$

Frescobaldi Wine Bar, p. 594
Il Latini, p. 595

$$$

La Giostra, p. 599
Ora d'Aria, p. 594
Taverna del Bronzino, p. 594

$$$$

Cibrèo, p. 598

Best Experiences

GOOD FOR KIDS

Baldovino, $, p. 598
Il Latini, $$, p. 595

ROMANTIC

Enoteca Pinchiorri, $$$$, p. 599

BISTECCA FIORENTINA (TUSCAN STEAK)

Buca Lapi, $$$$, p. 595
Il Latini, $$, p. 595
La Giostra, $$$, p. 599
Osteria de'Benci, $$, p. 599

OUTDOOR DINING

Fuori Porta, ¢, p. 600
Osteria de'Benci, $$, p. 599

WINE BARS

Casa del Vino, $, p. 601
Il Santino, ¢, p. 601
Le Volpi e l'Uva, $, p. 602

ALTA CUCINA (SOPHISTICATED CUISINE)

Enoteca Pinchiorri, $$$$, p. 599
Ora d'Aria, $$$, p. 594
Taverna del Bronzino, $$$, p. 594

CASALINGA (HOME COOKING)

La Casalinga, ¢, p. 600
Mario, ¢, p. 594

LUNCH SPOTS

Antico Noe, $$, p. 598
Cantinetta Antinori, $$$, p. 595
Frescobaldi Wine Bar, $$, p. 594

EXCEPTIONAL WINE LIST

Cantinetta Antinori, $$$, p. 595
Enoteca Pinchiorri, $$$$, p. 599
Fuori Porta, ¢, p. 600
Taverna del Bronzino, $$$, p. 594

GOOD FOR VEGETARIANS

Antico Noe, $$, p. 598
Frescobaldi Wine Bar, $$, p. 594
La Giostra, $$$, p. 599
Ora d'Aria, $$$, p. 594
Osteria de'Benci, $$, p. 599

POPULAR WITH LOCALS

La Casalinga, ¢, p. 600
La Giostra, $$$, p. 599
La Vecchia Bettola, $, p. 601
Mario, ¢, p. 594
Osteria de'Benci, $$, p. 599

GOOD FOR PEOPLE WATCHING

Borgo San Jacopo, $$$, p. 600
Cantinetta Antinori, $$$, p. 595
La Giostra, $$$, p. 599

$$ WINE BAR

✕ **Frescobaldi Wine Bar.** The Frescobaldi family has run a vineyard for more than 700 years, and this swanky establishment offers tasty and sumptuous fare to accompany the seriously fine wines. Warm terra-cotta-color walls with trompe-l'oeil tapestries provide a soothing atmosphere. The menu is typically Tuscan, but turned up a notch or two: the *faraona in umido con l'uva* (stewed guinea fowl with grapes) comes with a side of feather-light mashed potatoes. Save room for dessert, as well as one of the dessert wines. A separate wine bar called Frescobaldino has a shorter menu and a delightful barman called Primo. ✉ *Via de' Magazzini 2-4/r, Piazza della Signoria* ☎ *055/284724* ⏲ *Closed Sun. No lunch Mon.* ✥ *F3.*

$$$ MODERN ITALIAN

✕ **Ora d'Aria.** The name means "Hour of Air" and refers to the time of day when prisoners were let outside for fresh air—alluding to the fact that this gem was originally located across the street from what was once the old prison. In the kitchen, gifted young chef Marco Stabile turns out exquisite Tuscan classics as well as more fanciful dishes, which are as beautiful as they are delicious; intrepid diners will be vastly rewarded for ordering the tortellini *farciti con piccione* (stuffed with pigeon) if it's on the day's menu. At lunchtime, a delicious menu is offered in two portion sizes—full plate and tapas—that can make lunch a more economical option than dinner. ✉ *Via Georgofili 79/r, Piazza della Signoria* ☎ *055/2001699* ⏲ *Closed Sun. No lunch Mon.* ✥ *E4.*

SAN LORENZO AND BEYOND

¢ TUSCAN

✕ **da Nerbone.** The place has been around since 1872, and it's easy to see why: this tiny stall in the middle of the covered Mercato Centrale has been serving up food to Florentines who like their tripe. Tasty primi and secondi are available every day, but cognoscenti come for the panino *con il lampredotto* (tripe sandwich). Less adventurous sorts might want to sample the *panino con il bollito* (boiled beef sandwich). Ask that the bread be *bagnato* (briefly dipped in the tripe cooking liquid), and have both the salsa verde and *salsa piccante* (a spicy cayenne sauce) slathered on top. ✉ *Mercato San Lorenzo* ☎ *055/219949* ▭ *No credit cards* ⏲ *Closed Sun. No dinner* ✥ *D1.*

¢ TUSCAN Fodor's Choice ★

✕ **Mario.** Florentines flock to this narrow family-run trattoria near San Lorenzo to feast on Tuscan favorites served at simple tables under a wooden ceiling dating from 1536. A distinct cafeteria feel and genuine Florentine hospitality prevail: you'll be seated wherever there's room, which often means with strangers. Yes, there's a bit of extra oil in most dishes, which imparts calories as well as taste, but aren't you on vacation in Italy? Worth the splurge is *riso al ragù* (rice with ground beef and tomatoes); another happy marriage is the grilled lombatina (a veal T-bone) with French fries. ✉ *Via Rosina 2/r, corner of Piazza del Mercato Centrale, San Lorenzo* ☎ *055/218550* 🌐 *www.trattoriamario.com* ✍ *Reservations not accepted* ▭ *No credit cards* ⏲ *Closed Sun. and Aug. No dinner* ✥ *E1.*

$$$ TUSCAN Fodor's Choice ★

✕ **Taverna del Bronzino.** Want to have a sophisticated meal in a 16th-century Renaissance artist's studio? The former studio of Santi di Tito, a student of Bronzino's, has a simple, formal decor, with white tablecloths. The classic, dramatically presented Tuscan food is superb, and the solid, affordable wine list rounds out the menu. Start with the *antipasto toscano*, a plate of superb cured pork products, before moving on to the remarkable fare that follows, and hope that the made-in-house *mirtillo* (a blueberry-based digestive) is available. The service is outstanding. Reservations are essential if you want to eat at the wine cellar's only table. ✉ *Via delle Ruote 25/r, San Marco* ☎ *055/495220* ⊙ *Closed Sun. and 3 wks in Aug.* ✣ *G1.*

SANTA MARIA NOVELLA TO THE ARNO

$$$$ TUSCAN ✕ **Buca Lapi.** The Antinori family started selling wine from their palace's basement in the 15th century. Six hundred years later, this *buca* (hole) is now a lively, subterranean restaurant filled with Florentine aristocrats chowing down on what might be the best (and most expensive) bistecca fiorentina in town. The classical Tuscan menu has the usual suspects: crostino di *cavolo nero* (black cabbage on toasted garlic bread), and *ribollita and pappa al pomodoro* (both are bread-based soups) are among the highlights of the primi. You might want to cut directly to the chase, however, and order the bistecca, an immense slab of Chianina beef impeccably grilled on the outside, just barely warmed on the inside. (If you're not into rare meat, order something else from the grill.) Roast potatoes and cannellini beans make perfect accompaniments. ✉ *Via del Trebbio 1/r, Santa Maria Novella* ☎ *055/213768* 🌐 *www.bucalapi.com* ✍ *Reservations essential* ✣ *C3.*

$$$ ITALIAN ✕ **Cantinetta Antinori.** After a morning of shopping on Via Tornabuoni, stop for lunch in this 15th-century palazzo in the company of Florentine ladies (and men) who lunch and come to see and be seen. The panache of the food matches its clientele: expect treats such as *tramezzino con pane di campagna al tartufo* (country pâté with truffles served on bread) and the *insalata di gamberoni e gamberetti con carciofi freschi* (crayfish and prawn salad with shaved raw artichokes). The stellar wine list teems with Antinori wines; you can even order the superstar Super Tuscan Tignanello by the glass. ✉ *Piazza Antinori 3, Santa Maria Novella* ☎ *055/292234* ⊙ *Closed weekends, 20 days in Aug., and Dec. 25–Jan. 6* ✣ *D3.*

$$ TUSCAN ✕ **Il Latini.** It may be the noisiest, most crowded trattoria in Florence, but it's also one of the most fun. The genial host, Torello ("little bull") Latini, presides over his four big dining rooms, and somehow it feels as if you're dining in his home. Ample portions of ribollita prepare the palate for the hearty meat dishes that follow. Both Florentines and tourists alike tuck into the *agnello fritto* (fried lamb) with aplomb. Though reservations are advised, there's always a wait anyway. ✉ *Via dei Palchetti 6/r, Santa Maria Novella* ☎ *055/210916* ⊙ *Closed Mon. and 15 days at Christmas* ✣ *C3.*

10

$ ITALIAN ★ ✕ **La Sostanza.** It's been around since 1869, and has been serving top-notch, unpretentious food to Florentines who like their bistecca fiorentina very large and very rare. A single room with white tiles on the wall and paper mats on the tables provides the setting for delicious meals. Along with fine Tuscan classics, they have two signature dishes here: the *tortino di carciofi* (artichoke tart) and the *pollo al burro* (chicken with butter). The latter is an amazing surprise, a succulent chicken breast that has been cooked very very quickly and served as soon as it leaves the grill. Leave room for dessert, as their *torta alla Meringa* (semi-frozen dessert flecked with chocolate and topped with meringue) is scrumptious. ✉ *Via della Porcellana 25, Santa Maria Novella* ☎ *055/212691* ✍ *Reservations essential* 💳 *No credit cards* ✣ *B3.*

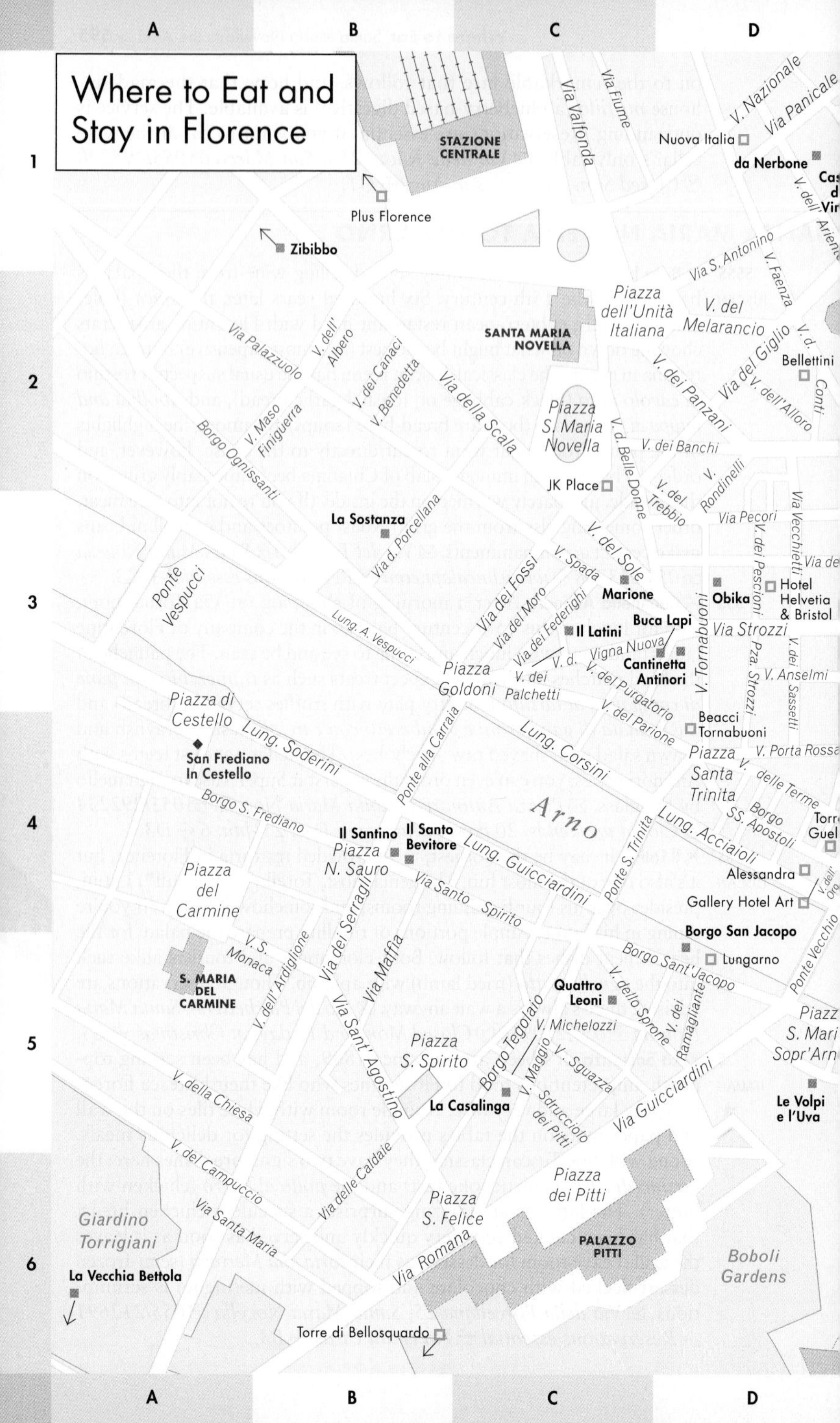
Where to Eat and Stay in Florence
A
B
C
D
1
2
3
4
5
6
STAZIONE CENTRALE
Plus Florence
Zibibbo
Via Valfonda
Via Fiume
V. Nazionale
Via Panicale
Nuova Italia
da Nerbone
V. dell' Ariento
Via S. Antonino
V. Faenza
Piazza dell'Unità Italiana
V. del Melarancio
SANTA MARIA NOVELLA
Via Palazzuolo
V. dell' Albero
V. dei Canaci
V. Benedetta
Via della Scala
Via del Giglio
V. d. Conti
Bellettini
V. dell'Alloro
V. dei Panzani
V. Maso Finiguerra
Borgo Ognissanti
Piazza S. Maria Novella
V. d. Belle Donne
V. dei Banchi
V. Rondinelli
JK Place
V. del Trebbio
Via Pecori
Via Vecchietti
La Sostanza
Via d. Porcellana
V. del Sole
V. Spada
V. dei Pescioni
Ponte Vespucci
Via dei Fossi
Via del Moro
Marione
Obika
Hotel Helvetia & Bristol
Via dei Federighi
Il Latini
Buca Lapi
Via Strozzi
Lung. A. Vespucci
Vigna Nuova
V. d.
Cantinetta Antinori
V. Tornabuoni
Pza. Strozzi
V. dei Sassetti
Piazza Goldoni
V. dei Palchetti
V. del Purgatorio
V. Anselmi
Piazza di Cestello
Lung. Soderini
V. del Parione
Beacci Tornabuoni
Ponte alla Carraia
Lung. Corsini
Piazza Santa Trinita
V. Porta Rossa
San Frediano In Cestello
V. delle Terme
Borgo S. Frediano
Arno
Borgo SS. Apostoli
Lung. Acciaioli
Ponte S. Trinita
Il Santino
Il Santo Bevitore
Piazza N. Sauro
Lung. Guicciardini
Piazza del Carmine
Via Santo Spirito
Alessandra
Gallery Hotel Art
V. dell' Oro
Ponte Vecchio
Borgo San Jacopo
V. S. Monaca
Via dei Serragli
Via Maffia
Borgo Sant'Jacopo
Lungarno
S. MARIA DEL CARMINE
V. dell' Ardiglione
Quattro Leoni
V. dello Sprone
V. dei Ramaglianti
Piazza S. Maria Sopr'Arno
Via Sant' Agostino
Borgo Tegolaio
V. Michelozzi
Piazza S. Spirito
V. Maggio
V. Sguazza
V. della Chiesa
La Casalinga
Sdrucciolo dei Pitti
Via Guicciardini
Le Volpi e l'Uva
V. del Campuccio
Via delle Caldaie
Piazza dei Pitti
Via Santa Maria
Piazza S. Felice
Giardino Torrigiani
PALAZZO PITTI
Boboli Gardens
Via Romana
La Vecchia Bettola
Torre di Bellosquardo

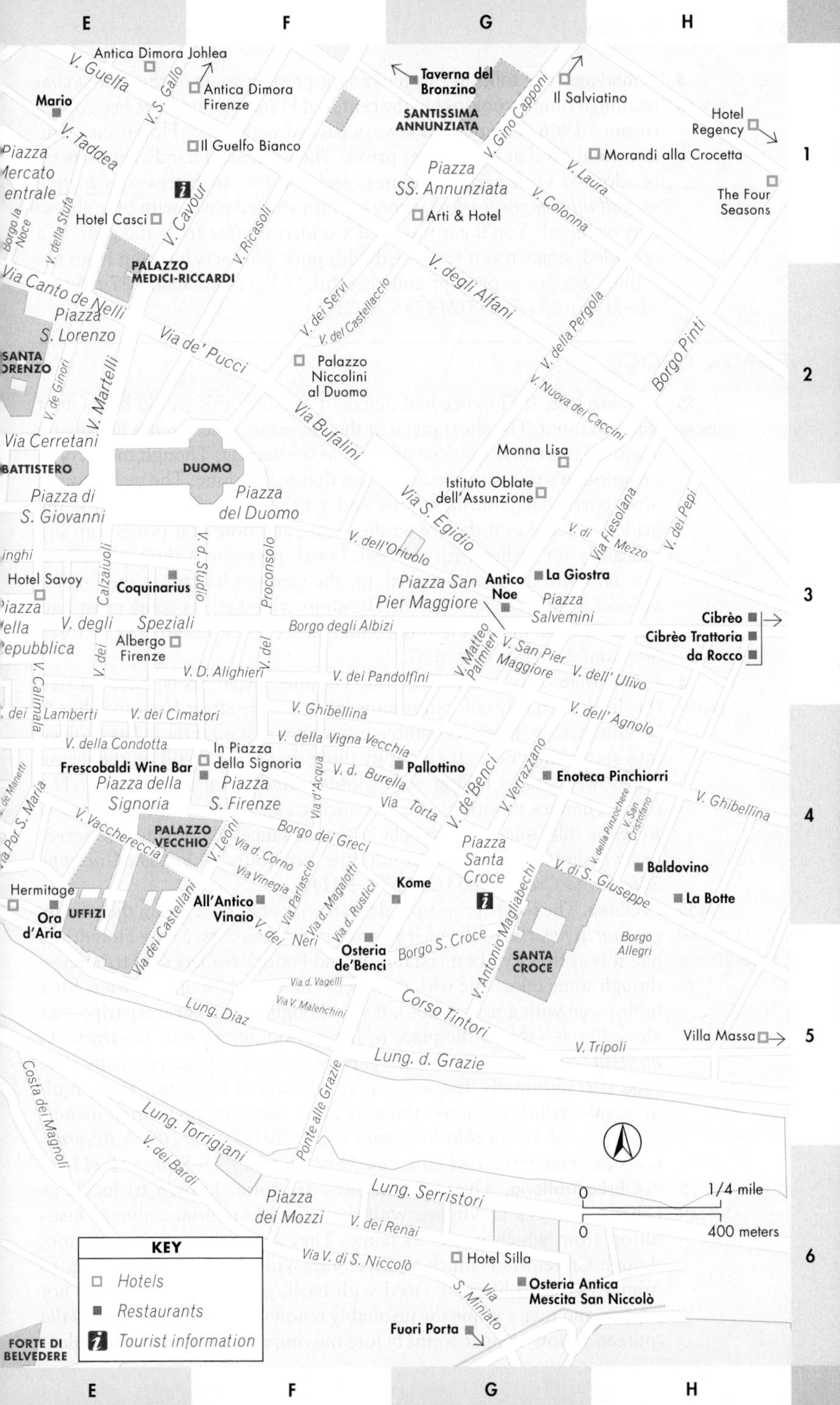

E
F
G
H
1
2
3
4
5
6
Antica Dimora Johlea
V. Guelfa
V. S. Gallo
Antica Dimora Firenze
Taverna del Bronzino
SANTISSIMA ANNUNZIATA
V. Gino Capponi
Il Salviatino
Hotel Regency
Mario
V. Taddea
Il Guelfo Bianco
Morandi alla Crocetta
Piazza SS. Annunziata
V. Laura
The Four Seasons
V. Cavour
V. della Stufa
Borgo la Noce
Hotel Casci
V. Ricasoli
Arti & Hotel
V. Colonna
PALAZZO MEDICI-RICCARDI
V. degli Alfani
Via Canto de Nelli
Piazza S. Lorenzo
V. dei Servi
V. del Castellaccio
V. della Pergola
Via de' Pucci
Borgo Pinti
V. de Ginori
V. Martelli
Palazzo Niccolini al Duomo
V. Nuova dei Caccini
Via Bufalini
Via Cerretani
Monna Lisa
BATTISTERO
DUOMO
Istituto Oblate dell'Assunzione
Piazza di S. Giovanni
Piazza del Duomo
Via S. Egidio
Via Fiesolana
V. dei Pepi
V. di Mezzo
V. dell'Oriuolo
V. d. Studio
V. del Proconsolo
Calzaiuoli
Hotel Savoy
Coquinarius
Piazza San Pier Maggiore
Antico Noe
La Giostra
Piazza Salvemini
V. degli Speziali
Borgo degli Albizi
Cibrèo
Cibrèo Trattoria da Rocco
Albergo Firenze
V. Matteo Palmieri
V. San Pier Maggiore
V. dei
V. del
V. D. Alighieri
V. dei Pandolfini
V. dell' Ulivo
V. Calimala
Lamberti
V. dei Cimatori
V. Ghibellina
V. dell' Agnolo
V. della Condotta
In Piazza della Signoria
V. della Vigna Vecchia
Frescobaldi Wine Bar
V. d. Burella
Pallottino
V. Verrazzano
Enoteca Pinchiorri
Piazza della Signoria
Piazza S. Firenze
Via d'Acqua
Via Torta
V. de' Benci
V. della Pinzochere
V. San Cristofano
V. Ghibellina
Via Por S. Maria
V. Vacchereccia
PALAZZO VECCHIO
V. Leoni
Borgo dei Greci
Piazza Santa Croce
V. d. Corno
Via Vinegia
V. di S. Giuseppe
Baldovino
Hermitage
UFFIZI
Via dei Castellani
All'Antico Vinaio
Via Parlascio
Via d. Magalotti
V. d. Rustici
Kome
V. Antonio Magliabechi
La Botte
Ora d'Aria
V. dei Neri
Osteria de'Benci
Borgo S. Croce
SANTA CROCE
Borgo Allegri
Via d. Vagelli
Via V. Malenchini
Corso Tintori
Lung. Diaz
Villa Massa
V. Tripoli
Lung. d. Grazie
Costa dei Magnoli
Ponte alle Grazie
Lung. Torrigiani
V. dei Bardi
0
1/4 mile
400 meters
Lung. Serristori
Piazza dei Mozzi
V. dei Renai
KEY
Hotels
Restaurants
Tourist information
Via V. di S. Niccolò
Hotel Silla
Via S. Miniato
Osteria Antica Mescita San Niccolò
Fuori Porta
FORTE DI BELVEDERE

$ TUSCAN ✕ **Marione.** The folks at this lively spot prepare some of the best *cucina casalinga* (home cooking) in the center of Florence, and have been doing so since 1966. The place is always packed with savvy Florentines who like good food at even better prices. The whimsical handwritten menu is adorned with cartoon figures, and features such treats as *tortelli mugellani con gorgonzola e noci* (potato-stuffed pasta with blue cheese and walnuts). You'll eat this, and wonderful meat from the grill, in a crowded, noisy room festooned with pork products hanging from the ceiling. Service is prompt and cheerful. ✉ *Via della Spada 27/r, Santa Maria Novella* ☎ *055/214756* ⊕ *C3.*

SANTA CROCE

$$ TUSCAN ✕ **Antico Noe.** If Florence had diners (it doesn't), this would be the best diner in town. The short menu at the one-room eatery relies heavily on seasonal ingredients picked up daily at the market. Though the secondi are good, it's the antipasti and primi that really shine. The menu comes alive particularly during truffle and artichoke season (don't miss the grilled artichokes if they're on the menu, and note that prices leap significantly for dishes with truffles). Locals rave about the tagliatelle *ai porcini* (with mushrooms). Ask for the menu in Italian, as the English version is much more limited. The short wine list has some great bargains. ✉ *Volta di San Piero 6/r, Santa Croce* ☎ *055/2340838* ⊗ *Closed Sun. and 2 wks in Aug.* ⊕ *G3.*

$ ITALIAN ✕ **Baldovino.** David and Catherine Gardner, expat Scots, have created this lively, brightly colored restaurant down the street from the church of Santa Croce. From its humble beginnings as a pizzeria, it has evolved into something more. It's a happy thing that pizza is still on the menu, but now it shares billing with sophisticated primi and secondi. The menu changes monthly, and has such treats as *filetto di manzo alla Bernaise* (filet mignon with light béarnaise sauce). Baldovino also serves pasta dishes and grilled meat until the wee hours. ✉ *Via San Giuseppe 22/r, Santa Croce* ☎ *055/241773* ⊕ *H4.*

$$$$ TUSCAN Fodor's Choice ★ ✕ **Cibrèo.** The food at this upscale trattoria is fantastic, from the creamy *crostini di fegatini* to the melt-in-your-mouth desserts. Many Florentines hail this as the city's best restaurant, and Fodor's readers tend to agree—though some take issue with the prices and complain of long waits for a table (even with a reservation). If you thought you'd never try tripe—let alone like it—this is the place to lay any doubts to rest: the *trippa in insalata* (cold tripe salad) with parsley and garlic is an epiphany. The food is traditionally Tuscan, impeccably served by a staff that's multilingual—which is a good thing, because there are no written menus. ✉ *Via A. del Verrocchio 8/r, Santa Croce* ☎ *055/2341100* *Reservations essential* ⊗ *Closed Sun. and Mon. and July 25–Sept. 5* ⊕ *H3.*

$ TUSCAN ✕ **Cibrèo Trattoria.** This intimate little trattoria, known to locals as Cibreino, shares its kitchen with the famed Florentine culinary institution from which it gets its name. They share the same menu, too, though Cibreino's is much shorter. Start with *il gelatina di pomodoro* (tomato gelatin) liberally laced with basil, garlic, and a pinch of hot pepper, and then sample the justifiably renowned *passato in zucca gialla* (pureed yellow-pepper soup) before moving on to any of the succulent second courses. Save room for dessert, as the pastry chef has a deft hand with chocolate tarts. To avoid sometimes agonizingly long waits, come early (7 pm) or late (after 9:30). ✉ *Via dei Macci 118, Santa Croce* ☎ *055/2341100* ✍ *Reservations not accepted* ▭ *No credit cards* ⊙ *Closed Sun. and Mon. and July 25–Sept. 5* ✥ *H3.*

¢ TUSCAN ✕ **da Rocco.** At one of Florence's biggest markets you can grab lunch to go, or you could cram yourself into one of the booths and pour from the straw-cloaked flask (wine here is *da consumo,* which means they charge you for how much you drink). Food is abundant, Tuscan, and fast; locals pack in. The menu changes daily, and the prices are great. ✉ *In Mercato Sant'Ambrogio, Piazza Ghiberti, Santa Croce* ☎ *No phone* ✍ *Reservations not accepted* ▭ *No credit cards* ⊙ *Closed Sun. No dinner* ✥ *H2.*

$$$$ ITALIAN ✕ **Enoteca Pinchiorri.** A sumptuous Renaissance palace with high frescoed ceilings and bouquets in silver vases provides the backdrop for this restaurant, one of the most expensive in Italy. Some consider it one of the best, and others consider it a non-Italian rip-off, as the kitchen is presided over by a Frenchwoman with sophisticated, yet internationalist, leanings. Prices are high (think $100 for a plate of spaghetti) and portions are small; the vast holdings of the wine cellar (undoubtedly the best in Florence), as well as stellar service, dull the pain, however, when the bill is presented. ✉ *Via Ghibellina 87, Santa Croce* ☎ *055/242777* ✍ *Reservations essential* ⊙ *Closed Sun., Mon., and Aug. No lunch Tues. or Wed.* ✥ *G4.*

$–$$ JAPANESE ★ ✕ **Kome.** If you're looking for a break from the ubiquitous ribollita, stop in at this eatery, which may be the only Japanese restaurant in the world to be housed in a 15th-century Renaissance palazzo. High, vaulted arches frame the *kaiten* sushi conveyor belt. It's Japanese food, cafeteria style: selections, priced according to the color of the plate, make their way around a bar, where diners pick whatever they find appealing. Those seeking a more substantial meal head to the second floor, where Japanese barbecue is prepared at your table. The minimalist basement provides a subtle but dramatic backdrop for a well-prepared cocktail. ✉ *Via de'Benci 41/r, Santa Croce* ☎ *055/2008009* ✥ *G4.*

10

$$$ ITALIAN ★ ✕ **La Giostra.** This clubby spot, whose name means "carousel" in Italian, was created by the late Prince Dimitri Kunz d'Asburgo Lorena, and is now expertly run by his handsome twin sons. In perfect English they'll describe favorite dishes, such as the *taglierini con tartufo bianco,* a decadently rich pasta with white truffles. (Keep in mind that the presence of truffles on the menu considerably raises the prices; it's possible to eat less expensively here as well.) The constantly changing menu has terrific vegetarian and vegan options. For dessert, this might be the only show in town with a sublime tiramisu *and* a wonderfully gooey Sacher torte. ✉ *Borgo Pinti 12/r, Santa Croce* ☎ *055/241341* ✥ *G3.*

$$–$$$ ITALIAN ★ ✕ **Osteria de'Benci.** A few minutes from Santa Croce, this charming osteria serves some of the most eclectic food in Florence. Try the spaghetti *dell' Ubriacone* ("drunkard's spaghetti" cooked in red wine). The grilled meats are justifiably famous; the *carbonata* is a succulent piece of grilled beef served rare (or, as the menu takes pains to point out, "bloody"). Save room for dessert: they have a terrific tiramisu. When it's warm,

you can dine outside with a view of the 13th-century tower belonging to the prestigious Alberti family. ✉ *Via de' Benci 11–13/r, Santa Croce* ☎ *055/2344923* ⊙ *Closed Sun. and 2 wks in Aug.* ✣ *F5.*

$ TUSCAN ✕ **Pallottino.** With its tile floor, photograph-filled walls, and wooden tables, Pallottino is the quintessential Tuscan trattoria, with hearty, heartwarming classics such as *pappa al pomodoro* and *peposa alla toscana* (beef stew laced with black pepper). The menu changes frequently to reflect what's seasonal. The staff is friendly, as are the diners who often share a table and, eventually, conversation. They also do pizza here, as well as great lunch specials. ✉ *Via Isola delle Stinche 1/r, Santa Croce* ☎ *055/289573* ⊙ *Closed Mon. and 2–3 wks in Aug.* ✣ *G4.*

THE OLTRARNO

$$$ MODERN ITALIAN ✕ **Borgo San Jacopo.** It makes perfect sense that any restaurant owned by the Ferragamo family would look sleek, elegant, and sophisticated. In the kitchen is Beatrice Segoni, one of the few female chefs in Florence. Her intimate, romantic restaurant has low lighting, white walls lined with prints, and a stunning view of the Arno. If you're lucky enough to book the terrace when it's warm, you will float over the river as you enjoy her remarkable offerings. The menu changes every three months or so, and fish is the emphasis. Before tucking in to her delicious *grigliata* (mixed grill, including sole, sea bass, and stuffed squid), start with the innovative *sformato di carciofi con petto d'anatra ai tre pepi* (an artichoke flan topped with three-peppered duck), while remembering to leave room for her amazing desserts. ✉ *Borgo San Jacopo 14, Oltrarno* ☎ *055/281661* 🌐 *www.lungarnohotels.com* ✍ *Reservations essential* ⊙ *No lunch. Closed Tues.* ✣ *D5*

¢ WINE BAR ✕ **Fuori Porta.** One of the oldest and best wine bars in Florence, this place serves cured meats and cheeses, as well as daily specials such as the sublime spaghetti *al curry.* Crostini and *crostoni*—grilled breads topped with a mélange of cheeses and meats—are the house specialty; the *verdure sott'olio* (vegetables with oil) are divine. All this can be enjoyed at rustic wooden tables, and outdoors when weather allows. One shortcoming is the staff, some of whom can be disinclined to explain the absolutely wonderful wine list. ✉ *Via Monte alle Croci 10/r, San Niccolò* ☎ *055/2342483* ✣ *G6.*

$ TUSCAN ✕ **Il Santo Bevitore.** Florentines and other lovers of good food flock to "The Holy Drinker" for tasty, well-priced dishes. Unpretentious white walls, dark-wood furniture, and paper placemats provide the simple decor. Start with the exceptional *verdure sott'olio* or the *terrina di fegatini* (a creamy chicken-liver spread) before sampling any of the divine pastas, such as the fragrant spaghetti with shrimp sauce. The extensive wine list is well priced, and the well-informed staff is happy to explain it. ✉ *Via Santo Spirito 64/66r, Santo Spirito* ☎ *055/211264* ⊙ *No lunch Sun.* ✣ *B4.*

¢ TUSCAN ✕ **La Casalinga.** *Casalinga* means "housewife," and this place has the nostalgic charm of a 1950s kitchen with Tuscan comfort food to match. If you eat ribollita anywhere in Florence, eat it here—it couldn't be more authentic. Mediocre paintings clutter the semipaneled walls, tables are set close together, and the place is usually jammed. The menu is long, portions are plentiful, and service is prompt and friendly. For dessert, the lemon sorbet perfectly caps off the meal. ✉ *Via Michelozzi 9/r, Santo Spirito* ☎ *055/218624* ⏲ *Closed Sun., 1 wk at Christmas, and 3 wks in Aug.* ✥ *C5.*

$ TUSCAN ✕ **La Vecchia Bettola.** The name doesn't exactly mean "old dive," but it comes pretty close. This lively trattoria has been around only since 1979, but it feels as if it's been a whole lot longer. Tile floors and simple wood tables and chairs provide the interior decoration, such as it is. The recipes come from "wise grandmothers" and celebrate Tuscan food in its glorious simplicity. Here prosciutto is sliced with a knife, portions of grilled meat are tender and ample, service is friendly, and the wine list is well priced and good. This place is worth a taxi ride, even though it's just outside the centro storico. ✉ *Viale Vasco Pratolini, Oltrarno* ☎ *055/224158* ▭ *No credit cards* ✥ *A6.*

$ TUSCAN ✕ **Osteria Antica Mescita San Niccolò.** It's always crowded, always good, and always cheap. The osteria is next to the church of San Niccolò, and if you sit in the lower part you'll find yourself in what was once a crypt dating from the 11th century. The subtle but dramatic background is a nice complement to the food, which is simple Tuscan at its best. The *pollo con limone* is tasty pieces of chicken in a lemon-scented broth. In winter, try the *spezzatino di cinghiale con aromi* (wild boar stew with herbs). Reservations are advised. ✉ *Via San Niccolò 60/r, San Niccolò* ☎ *055/2342836* ⏲ *Closed Sun. and Aug.* ✥ *G6.*

BEYOND THE CITY CENTER

$$$ TUSCAN ✕ **Zibibbo.** Benedetta Vitali, formerly of Florence's famed Cibrèo, has a restaurant of her very own. It's a welcome addition to the sometimes-claustrophobic Florentine dining scene—particularly as you have to drive a few minutes out of town to get here. Off a quiet piazza, it has two intimate rooms with rustic, maroon-painted wood floors and a sloped ceiling. The tagliatelle *al sugo d'anatra* (with duck sauce) is aromatic and flavorful, and *crocchette di fave con salsa di yogurt* (fava-bean croquettes with a lively yogurt sauce) are innovative and tasty. ✉ *Via di Terzollina 3/r, northwest of city center* ☎ *055/433383* ⏲ *Closed Sun.* ✥ *B1.*

WINE BARS

All'Antico Vinaio (✉ *Via de'Neri 6, Santa Croce*) sells wines by the glass, which you can often pour yourself. Though they make delicious primi, it's easier to balance your wine glass with one of their tasty crostini in the other hand; there are only about five stools and a counter.

Casa del Vino (✉ *Via dell'Ariento 16/r, San Lorenzo* ☎ *055/215609* ✥ *D1*) has lots of wines available by the glass, and because they do such a high volume of business, bottles are constantly being opened. Delicious crostini, panini, and salads can be had here, though a balancing act is required, as there's only one table.

Il Santino (✉ *Via Santo Spirito 60/r, Lungarno Sud* ☎ *055/2302820* 🌐 *www.ilsantobevitore.com* ✥ *B4*) sells wine by the glass in a tiny little room with a handful of tables; a little snack (a piece of cheese, or a slice of prosciutto, depending upon the wine chosen) accompanies each glass.

La Botte (✉ *Via San Giuseppe 18/r, Santa Croce* ☎ *055/2476420* ⊕ *www.enotecaintelligente.com* ✥ *H4*) calls itself an "intelligent enoteca," and there really is something to be said for the fact that you buy a card, and then plug it into various vats showcasing the region's best wines. You can choose the size (small, medium, large); in this way, you can have a do-it-yourself wine tasting.

Le Volpi e l'Uva (✉ *Piazza de' Rossi 1, Lungarno Sud* ☎ *055/2398132* ✥ *D5*) has an almost reverential air about it: this is a serious wine bar for those who are serious about their wines. You can have a glass of wine while nibbling on a cheese plate featuring products from France—a rarity in these parts.

CAFÉS

Cafés in Italy serve not only coffee concoctions and pastries but also drinks; some also serve light and inexpensive lunches. They open early in the morning and usually close around 8 pm.

The always-crowded **Caffè Giacosa/Roberto Cavalli** (✉ *Via della Spada 10, near Santa Maria Novella* ☎ *055/2776328*), joined at the hip with the Florentine fashion designer's shop, is open for breakfast, lunch, tea, and cocktails—except on Sunday.

Gran Caffè (✉ *Piazza San Marco 11/r* ☎ *055/215833*), around the corner from the Accademia, is a perfect stop for a marvelous panino or sweet while raving about the majesty of Michelangelo's *David*.

Classy **Procacci** (✉ *Via Tornabuoni 64/r, near Santa Maria Novella* ☎ *055/211656*) is a Florentine institution dating back to 1885; try one of the panini *tartufati* (a small roll with truffled butter) and swish it down with a glass of prosecco (a dry, sparkling white wine). It's closed Sunday.

Perhaps the best café for people-watching is **Rivoire** (✉ *Piazza della Signoria, Via Vacchereccia 4/r* ☎ *055/214412*). Stellar service, light snacks, and terrific *aperitivi* (aperitifs) are the norm.

GELATERIE AND PASTICCERIE

The convenient **Caffè delle Carrozze** (✉ *Piazza del Pesce 3–5/r, near Piazza della Signoria* ☎ *055/2396810*) is around the corner from the Uffizi; their gelato, according to some, is the best in the historic center. **Dolci e Dolcezze** (✉ *Piazza C. Beccaria 8/r, near Santa Croce* ☎ *055/2345458*), a *pasticceria* (bakery) in Borgo La Croce, probably has the prettiest and tastiest cakes, sweets, and tarts in town. It's closed Monday. **Gelateria Carabe** (✉ *Via Ricasoli 60/r, San Marco* ☎ *055/289476*) specializes in Sicilian desserts (including cannoli). Its *granità* (granular, flavored ices), made only in summer, are tart and flavorful—perfect thirst-quenchers.

Grom (✉ *Via del Campanile, Duomo* ☎ *055/216158*) a stone's throw from the Duomo, is one of the best gelaterias in town. Flavors change frequently according to the season, so expect a fragrant gelato *di cannella* (cinnamon ice cream) in the winter and lively fresh fruit flavors in the summer. **Perché No?** (✉ *Via dei Tavolini 19/r, Piazza della Signoria* ☎ *055/2398969*) is favored by many Florentines and U.S. junior-year-abroad students.

Vestri (✉ *Borgo Albizi 11/r, near Santa Croce* ☎ *055/2340374*) is devoted to chocolate in all its guises, every day but Sunday. The small but sublime selection of chocolate-based gelati includes one with hot peppers. Most visitors consider **Vivoli** (✉ *Via Isola delle Stinche 7/r, near Santa Croce* ☎ *055/292334*) the best gelateria around; Florentines find it highly overrated. It's closed Sunday.

SALUMERIE

Delicatessens and gourmet food shops (*salumerie*) specialize in cured meats and cheeses; they can be great places to assemble a picnic or purchase dinner. Most are closed Sunday.

The cheese collection at **Baroni** (✉ *Mercato Central, enter at Via Signa, San Lorenzo* ☎ *055/289576*) may be the most comprehensive in Florence. They also have high-quality truffle products, vinegars, and other delicacies. **Il Santino Gastronomia** (✉ *Via Santo Spirito 60/r, Santo Spirito* ☎ *055/211264* 🌐 *www.ilsantobevitore.com*) has top-quality cured meats, vegetables, and piatti unici (one-dish meals) to take away. **'ino** (✉ *Via dei Georgofili 3/r–7/r* ☎ *055/219208*) sells artisanal products such as olive oil, cheeses from all over Italy, top-notch chocolates, and boutique wines. It's right behind the Uffizi, making it a perfect place to grab a tasty sandwich and glass of wine before forging on to the next museum.

Looking for some cheddar cheese to pile in your panino? **Pegna** (✉ *Via dello Studio 8, Duomo* ☎ *055/282701*) has been selling both Italian and non-Italian food since 1860. It's closed Saturday afternoon in July and August, Wednesday afternoon September through June, and Sunday year-round. **Perini** (✉ *Mercato Centrale, enter at Via dell'Aretino, San Lorenzo* ☎ *055/2398306*), closed Sunday, sells prosciutto, mixed meats, sauces for pasta, and a wide assortment of antipasti. They're generous with their free samples.

WHERE TO STAY

No stranger to visitors, Florence is equipped with hotels for all budgets; for instance, you can find both budget and luxury hotels in the centro storico and along the Arno. Florence has so many famous landmarks that it's not hard to find lodging with a panoramic view. The equivalent of the genteel *pensioni* of yesteryear still exist, though they're now officially classified as hotels. Generally small and intimate, they often have a quaint appeal that usually doesn't preclude modern plumbing.

Florence's importance not only as a tourist city but as a convention center and the site of the Pitti fashion collections guarantees a variety of accommodations. The high demand also means that, except in winter, reservations are a must. If you find yourself in Florence with no reservations, go to **Consorzio ITA** (✉ *Stazione Centrale, Santa Maria Novella* ☎ *055/282893*). You must go there in person to make a booking.

Hotel reviews have been condensed for this book. Please go to Fodors.com for full reviews of each property.

	WHAT IT COSTS IN EUROS				
	¢	$	$$	$$$	$$$$
For two people	under €75	€75–€125	€125–€200	€200–€300	over €300

Prices are for a standard double room in high season, including tax and service.

THE DUOMO TO THE ARNO

$$ **Albergo Firenze.** A block from the Duomo, this hotel is on one of the oldest piazzas in Florence. **Pros:** for the location, a great bargain. **Cons:** no-frills public areas. **TripAdvisor:** "walk to just about anywhere," "affordable and accessible," "basic but clean." ✉ *Piazza Donati 4, Duomo* ☎ *055/214203* 🌐 *www.hotelfirenze-fi.it* *57 rooms* *In-hotel: parking* *Breakfast* ✣ *E3.*

$$$ **Hermitage.** A stone's throw from the Ponte Vecchio, this is a fine little hotel with an enviable location. **Pros:** views; friendly staff. **Cons:** short flight of stairs to reach elevator; some of the rooms are small. **TripAdvisor:** "heaven on the Arno," "beautiful rooftop garden," "very cool and quiet." ✉ *Vicolo Marzio 1, Piazza della Signoria* ☎ *055/287216* 🌐 *www.hermitagehotel.com* *28 rooms* *In-hotel: parking, some pets allowed* *Breakfast* ✣ *E4.*

$$$$ ★ **Hotel Helvetia and Bristol.** Painstaking care has gone into making this "urban palace" one of the prettiest, most luxurious, most intimate hotels in town. **Pros:** central location; superb staff; inviting lobby. **Cons:** rooms facing the street get some noise; breakfast costs extra. **TripAdvisor:** "distinctly Tuscan flavor," "elegant furniture," "staff is extraordinary." ✉ *Via dei Pescioni 2, Piazza della Repubblica* ☎ *055/26651* 🌐 *www.hbf.royaldemeure.com* *54 rooms, 13 suites* *In-room: Wi-Fi. In-hotel: restaurant, room service, bar, parking, some pets allowed* *No meals* ✣ *D3.*

$$$$ **Hotel Savoy.** From the outside it looks very much like the turn-of-the-19th-century building that it is. **Pros:** location; trendy clientele (if that's your thing). **Cons:** smallish rooms; trendy clientele (if that's not your thing); breakfast ought to be included at these prices. **TripAdvisor:** "very small and intimate," "elegant public spaces," "walking distance to everything." ✉ *Piazza della Repubblica 7* ☎ *055/27351* 🌐 *www.roccofortehotels.com* *88 rooms, 14 suites* *In-room: Wi-Fi. In-hotel: restaurant, room service, bar, children's programs, parking* *No meals* ✣ *E1.*

$$$ Fodor's Choice ★ **In Piazza della Signoria.** Proprietors Alessandro and Sonia Pini want you to use their house—in this case, part of a 15th-century palazzo—as if it were your own. **Pros:** marvelous staff; tasty breakfast with a view of Piazza della Signoria. **Cons:** short flight of stairs to reach elevator. **TripAdvisor:** "better than the photos," "steps from the Uffizi," "old-world charm." ✉ *Via dei Magazzini 2, near Piazza della Signoria* ☎ *055/2399546* 🌐 *www.inpiazzadellasignoria.com* *10 rooms, 3 apartments* *In-room: kitchen (some), Wi-Fi. In hotel: parking* *Breakfast* ✣ *E4.*

$$$ **Palazzo Niccolini al Duomo.** The graceful Marchesa Ginevra Niccolini di Camugliano refers to her lovingly restored hotel as her third child. **Pros:** steps away from the Duomo; amazing beds. **Cons:** street noise sometimes a problem. **TripAdvisor:** "quiet and intimate," "right beside the Duomo," "Renaissance grandeur." ✉ *Via dei Servi 2* ☎ *055/282412* 🌐 *www.niccolinidomepalace.com* *5 rooms, 5 suites* *In-room: Wi-Fi. In-hotel: parking* *Breakfast* ⊕ *F2.*

WORD OF MOUTH

"Two nights in Florence is just not long enough—but anyone could have told me this and did. It was a choice between doing a little of Florence, and a little of Venice, or more of only one. I chose the two and don't regret it, but if you can stretch your holidays do more than two nights."

—drjem

SAN LORENZO AND BEYOND

$ **Antica Dimora Firenze.** Each room in the intimate *residenza* is painted a different pastel color—peach, rose, and powder-blue. **Pros:** ample DVD library; honor bar with Antinori wines. **Cons:** staff goes home at 8; no credit cards accepted. **TripAdvisor:** "like living in your own apartment," "clean and beautifully furnished," "delicious decorations." ✉ *Via San Gallo 72, San Marco* ☎ *055/4627296* 🌐 *www.anticadimorafirenze.it* *6 rooms* *In-room: Wi-Fi* *No credit cards* *Breakfast* ⊕ *E1.*

$$ **Antica Dimora Johlea.** Lively color runs rampant at this small, cheerful hotel just minutes from San Marco. **Pros:** great staff; cheerful rooms; honor bar. **Cons:** staff goes home at 7; narrow staircase to get to roof terrace. **TripAdvisor:** "terrace has a great view," "beds draped in silk," "friendly welcome." ✉ *Via San Gallo 80, San Marco* ☎ *055/4633292* 🌐 *www.johanna.it* *6 rooms* *In-room: Internet, Wi-Fi. In hotel: business center, Wi-Fi, parking* *No credit cards* *Breakfast* ⊕ *E1.*

$$ **Arti & Hotel.** If Florence had town houses, this would be one: the entrance to the public room downstairs feels as if you're in someone's living room. **Pros:** down the street from the Duomo. **Cons:** staff goes home at 11. **TripAdvisor:** "hidden treasure," "staff is friendly and helpful," "extremely spacious room." ✉ *Via dei Servi 38/a, Santissima Annunziata* ☎ *055/2645307* 🌐 *www.hoteldellearti.it* *9 rooms* *In-room: Wi-Fi. In-hotel: some pets allowed (fee)* *Breakfast* ⊕ *G1.*

10

$$ **Bellettini.** You're in good hands at this small hotel run by Gina Naldini and Claudio, her husband. **Pros:** excellent staff. **Cons:** two rooms have shared bath (but at significantly lower rates). **TripAdvisor:** "this place was a bargain," "nearby flea market," "reception area is really nice." ✉ *Via dei Conti 7, Santa Maria Novella* ☎ *055/213561* 🌐 *www.hotelbellettini.com* *28 rooms, 26 with private bath* *In-room: Wi-Fi (some). In-hotel: bar, parking, some pets allowed* *Breakfast* ⊕ *D2.*

$$ **Hotel Casci.** In this refurbished 14th-century palace, the home of Giacchino Rossini in 1851–55, the friendly Lombardi family runs a hotel with spotless rooms. **Pros:** helpful staff; good option for families; English-language DVD collection with good selections for kids. **Cons:** bit of a college-dorm atmosphere; small elevator. **TripAdvisor:** "a few minutes from the cathedral," "facilities are spotless," "great

hospitality." ✉ *Via Cavour 13, San Marco* ☎ *055/211686* 🌐 *www.hotelcasci.com* 25 *rooms* *In-room: Wi-Fi. In-hotel: parking, some pets allowed* 🍴 *Breakfast* ✣ *E1.*

$$$ **Il Guelfo Bianco.** The 15th-century building has all modern conveniences, but its Renaissance charm still shines. **Pros:** stellar multilingual staff. **Cons:** rooms facing the street can be noisy. **TripAdvisor:** "great hotel for the price," "beds are firm, but comfy," "marvelous interior." ✉ *Via Cavour 29, San Marco* ☎ *055/288330* 🌐 *www.ilguelfobianco.it* *40 rooms, 1 apartment* *In-hotel: parking, some pets allowed* 🍴 *Breakfast* ✣ *F1.*

¢ **Plus Florence.** The name is the only odd thing about this hostel, which has been in operation since 2008. **Pros:** bargain price; multilingual staff. **Cons:** feels like a college dorm; somewhat removed from the action. **TripAdvisor:** "heaps of space," "excellent steam room and sauna," "a bit away from center." ✉ *Via Santa Caterina d'Alessandria 15, San Marco* ☎ *055/4628934* 🌐 *www.plusflorence.com* *100 rooms* *In-room: Wi-Fi. In hotel: restaurant, bar, pool, spa, laundry facilities, business center, parking* 🍴 *No meals* ✣ *B1.*

SANTA MARIA NOVELLA TO THE ARNO

$$ **Alessandra.** The location, a block from the Ponte Vecchio, and the clean, ample rooms make this a good choice. **Pros:** several rooms have views of the Arno; the spacious suite is a bargain. **Cons:** stairs to elevator; some rooms share bath. **TripAdvisor:** "clean and largish rooms," "beautiful big windows," "ancient historic building." ✉ *Borgo Santi Apostoli 17, Santa Maria Novella* ☎ *055/283438* 🌐 *www.hotelalessandra.com* *26 rooms, 19 with bath; 1 suite; 1 apartment* *In-room: Wi-Fi. In-hotel: parking* *Closed Dec. 10–26* 🍴 *Breakfast* ✣ *D4.*

$$$ **Beacci Tornabuoni.** Florentine pensioni don't get any classier than this. **Pros:** Angelo, the all-knowing concierge, who's presided here for 40 years; views from the terrace; the Honeymoon Suite with its 18th-century frescoes. **Cons:** Some rooms suffer from a bit of street noise. **TripAdvisor:** "turn-of-the-century charm," "location couldn't be better," "delightful large terrace." ✉ *Via Tornabuoni 3, Santa Maria Novella* ☎ *055/212645* 🌐 *www.tornabuonihotels.com* *37 rooms, 16 suites* *In-hotel: restaurant, bar, parking, some pets allowed* 🍴 *Breakfast* ✣ *D4.*

$$$$ ★ **Gallery Hotel Art.** Elegance doesn't miss a beat at this sleek Ferragamo hotel. **Pros:** the cool atmosphere; beautiful people; miso soup on the breakfast menu. **Cons:** might be too style-conscious for some tastes; elevator sometimes slow. **TripAdvisor:** "most magnificent room," "cool, modern and chic," "surprisingly quiet." ✉ *Vicolo dell'Oro 5, Santa Maria Novella* ☎ *055/27263* 🌐 *www.lungarnohotels.com* *65 rooms, 9 suites* *In-room: Wi-Fi. In-hotel: restaurant, room service, bar, parking* 🍴 *Breakfast* ✣ *D4.*

$$$$ Fodor's Choice ★ **JK Place.** This sumptuously appointed boutique hotel has all the comforts of a luxe home away from home. **Pros:** intimate feel; stellar staff; linen sheets; amazing lighting systems in guest rooms. **Cons:** breakfast at a shared table. **TripAdvisor:** "common spaces are elegant," "beautifully appointed rooms," "tailor-made concierge service." ✉ *Piazza Santa Maria Novella 7* ☎ *055/2645181* 🌐 *www.jkplace.com* *14*

doubles, 6 suites ♿ *In-room: Wi-Fi. In-hotel: bar, parking, some pets allowed* 🍽 *Breakfast* ⊕ *C3.*

$ **Nuova Italia.** The genial English-speaking Viti family runs this hotel near the train station and well within walking distance of the sights. **Pros:** reasonable rates. **Cons:** no elevator. **TripAdvisor:** "roomy and comfortable," "made me feel welcome," "good breakfast." ✉ *Via Faenza 26, Santa Maria Novella* ☎ *055/268430* 🌐 *www.hotel-nuovaitalia.com* *20 rooms* *In-room: Wi-Fi (some). In-hotel: parking, some pets allowed* ⏲ *Closed Dec. 8–26* 🍽 *Breakfast* ⊕ *D1.*

$$ **Torre Guelfa.** If you want a taste of medieval Florence, try this hotel hidden within a 13th-century tower. **Pros:** rooftop terrace with tremendous views; wonderful staff; some family-friendly triple rooms. **Cons:** 72 steps to get to terrace; continental breakfast is available only at 8 am. **TripAdvisor:** "quiet and exclusive feel," "panoramic view of the Duomo," "charming nooks and crannies." ✉ *Borgo Santi Apostoli 8, Santa Maria Novella* ☎ *055/2396338* 🌐 *www.hoteltorreguelfa.com* *24 rooms, 2 suites* *In-room: no TV (some). In-hotel: business center (fee), parking, some pets allowed* 🍽 *Breakfast* ⊕ *D4.*

THE OLTRARNO AND BEYOND

$$ **Hotel Silla.** The entrance to this slightly off-the-beaten-path hotel is through a 15th-century courtyard lined with potted plants and sculpture-filled niches. **Pros:** a Fodor's reader raves, "It's in the middle of everything except the crowds." **Cons:** some readers complain of street noise and too-small rooms. **TripAdvisor:** "one block off the Arno," "best in its class," "breakfasts were hot and tasty." ✉ *Via de' Renai 5, San Niccolò* ☎ *055/2342888* 🌐 *www.hotelsilla.it* *35 rooms* *In-room: Wi-Fi. In-hotel: bar, parking, some pets allowed* 🍽 *Breakfast* ⊕ *G6.*

$$$$ **Lungarno.** The river Arno is very present here, as this refined hotel is perched practically on top of it. **Pros:** upscale without being stuffy; great concierges. **Cons:** rooms without Arno views feel less special. **TripAdvisor:** "classy but not stuffy," "overlooking the Arno," "beautiful breakfast buffet." ✉ *Borgo San Jacopo 14, Lungarno Sud* ☎ *055/27261* 🌐 *www.lungarnohotels.com* *60 rooms, 13 suites* *In-room: Wi-Fi. In-hotel: restaurant, bar, parking* 🍽 *Breakfast* ⊕ *D5.*

SANTA CROCE

$$$$ **The Four Seasons.** Seven years of restoration have turned this 15th-century palazzo in Florence's center into a luxury hotel unlike any other in town. **Pros:** a unique "city meets country" experience; terrific restaurant. **Cons:** expensive breakfast; rooms facing the street get some street noise. **TripAdvisor:** "a piece of art in itself," "gardens were glorious," "service is classic." ✉ *Borgo Pinti 99, Santa Croce* ☎ *055/26261* 🌐 *www.fourseasons.com/florence* *117 rooms* *In-room: Internet. In-hotel: restaurants, room service, bars, pool, gym, spa, business center, parking* 🍽 *No meals* ⊕ *H1.*

$$$$ **Hotel Regency.** The noise and crowds of Florence seem far from this stylish hotel in a residential district near the Sinagoga, though you're not more than 10 minutes from the Accademia and Michelangelo's *David*. **Pros:**

faces one of the few green parks in the center of Florence. **Cons:** a small flight of stairs takes you to reception. **TripAdvisor:** "in a quiet residential square," "beautifully appointed rooms," "breakfasts by the gardens." *Piazza d'Azeglio 3, Santa Croce 055/245247 www.regency-hotel.com 30 rooms, 4 suites In-room: Wi-Fi. In-hotel: restaurant, room service, bar, parking, some pets allowed Breakfast H1.*

$ **Istituto Oblate dell'Assunzione.** Twelve nuns run this convent, which is minutes from the Duomo. **Pros:** bargain price; great location; quiet rooms; garden. **Cons:** curfew; no credit cards. **TripAdvisor:** "beautiful courtyard garden," "simple, clean and quiet," "short walk to the Duomo." *Borgo Pinti 15, Santa Croce 055/2480582 055/2346291 28 rooms, 22 with bath In-room: no TV. In-hotel: parking No credit cards No meals G3.*

$$ ★ **Monna Lisa.** Housed in a 15th-century palazzo, this hotel retains some of its wood-coffered ceilings from the 1500s, as well as its original staircase. **Pros:** lavish buffet breakfast; cheerful staff; garden. **Cons:** rooms in annex are much less charming than those in palazzo. **TripAdvisor:** "quiet, relaxing oasis," "room was impeccable," "stunning art." *Borgo Pinti 27, Santa Croce 055/2479751 www.monnalisa.it 45 rooms In-hotel: bar, business center (fee), parking, some pets allowed Breakfast G3.*

$$ ★ **Morandi alla Crocetta.** You're made to feel like privileged friends of the family at this charming and distinguished residence near Piazza Santissima Annunziata. **Pros:** interesting, offbeat location; terrific staff. **Cons:** extra charge for breakfast; two flights of stairs to reach reception and rooms. **TripAdvisor:** "sense of nostalgia," "furnished with original antiques," "great value." *Via Laura 50, Santissima Annunziata 055/2344747 www.hotelmorandi.it 10 rooms In-room: Wi-Fi. In-hotel: parking, some pets allowed No meals H1.*

OUTSIDE THE CITY

$$$$ ★ **Il Salviatino.** A winding drive up a cypress-studded lane brings you to this jewel of a hotel just outside Florence. **Pros:** great views; attentive staff. **Cons:** no reception area; some hall noise. **TripAdvisor:** "enchanting villa," "beautiful frescoed rooms," "unobtrusively attentive." *Via del Salviatino 21 055/9041111 www.salviatino.com 23 rooms, 22 suites In-room: a/c, Wi-Fi. In-hotel: restaurant, bar, pool, gym, spa, business center, parking, some pets allowed Breakfast G1.*

$$$ **Torre di Bellosguardo.** *Bellosguardo* means "beautiful view"; given the sweeping views of Florence and the countryside you get here, the name is fitting. **Pros:** great for escaping heat of the city in summer; a villa experience with the city just minutes away. **Cons:** taxi or a car is a necessity. **TripAdvisor:** "upon a hill overlooking Florence," "in its own terraced gardens," "dignified and grand." *Via Roti Michelozzi 2 055/2298145 www.torrebellosguardo.com 9 rooms, 7 suites In-room: no a/c (some), no TV, Internet. In-hotel: bar, pool, parking, some pets allowed Breakfast B6.*

$$$$ **Villa La Massa.** You approach this tall and imposing villa, 15 minutes out of town, via a gravel drive lined with flowers. **Pros:** pleasing mix of city and country life; sumptuous buffet breakfast; views of the Tuscan

hills; phenomenal staff. **Cons:** even with shuttle a car is a necessity; not open year-round. **TripAdvisor:** "overlooking the River Arno," "beautiful countryside setting," "perfect romantic getaway." ✉ *Via della Massa 24, Candeli* ☎ *055/62611* 🌐 *www.villalamassa.com* *19 rooms, 18 suites* *In-room: Internet. In-hotel: restaurant, bar, pool, parking, some pets allowed* ⏲ *Closed Dec.–Mar.* *Breakfast* ⊕ *H5.*

NIGHTLIFE AND THE ARTS

THE ARTS

MUSIC

The **Accademia Bartolomeo Cristofori** (✉ *Via di Camaldoli 7/r, Santo Spirito/San Frediano* ☎ *055/221646* 🌐 *www.accademiacristofori.it*), also known as the Amici del Fortepiano (Friends of the Fortepiano), sponsors fortepiano concerts throughout the year. **Amici della Musica** (🌐 *www.amicimusica.fi.it*) organizes concerts at the **Teatro della Pergola** (*Box office* ✉ *Via della Pergola 24* ☎ *055/2264353* 🌐 *www.teatrodellapergola.com*).

The **Maggio Musicale Fiorentino** (✉ *Via Alamanni 39* ☎ *055/210804*), a series of internationally acclaimed concerts and recitals, is held in the **Teatro Comunale** (✉ *Corso Italia 16, Lungarno North* ☎ *055/287222* 🌐 *www.maggiofiorentino.com*). Within Italy you can purchase tickets from late April through July directly at the box office or by phone at ☎ *055/287222*. You can also buy them online. Other events—opera, ballet, and additional concerts—occur regularly throughout the year at different venues in town.

The **Orchestra da Camera Fiorentina** (✉ *Via Monferrato 2, Piazza della Signoria* ☎ *055/783374* 🌐 *www.orcafi.it*) performs various concerts of classical music throughout the year at Orsanmichele, the grain market turned church.

The concert season of the **Orchestra della Toscana** (✉ *Via Verdi 5, Santa Croce* ☎ *055/2340710* 🌐 *www.orchestradellatoscana.it*) runs from November to June.

NIGHTLIFE

Florentines are rather proud of their nightlife options. Most bars now have some sort of happy hour, which usually lasts for many hours and often has snacks that can substitute for a light dinner. (Check, though, that the buffet is free or comes with the price of a drink.) Clubs typically don't open until very late in the evening and don't get crowded until 1 or 2 in the morning. Though the cover charges can be steep, finding free passes around town is fairly easy.

BARS

At **Colle Bereto**(✉ *Piazza della Strozzi 5* ☎ *055/283156*) you can have a light lunch after taking in a blockbuster show at Palazzo Strozzi just across the street. Or come at apertivo time when twentysomething Florentines and visitors alike swarm the bar and the piazza. One of the hottest spots in town is the bar at the Gallery Hotel Art, **Fusion Bar** (✉ *Vicolo dell'Oro 13, Santa Maria Novella* ☎ *055/27266987*). **Kitsch** (✉ *Via San Gallo 22/r, San Marco* ☎ *055/4620016*) has indoor and outdoor seating and a great list of wines by the glass. At aperitivo time €8 will buy you a truly tasty cocktail and give you access to the tremendous buffet—it's so good, you won't need dinner afterward. The oh-so-cool vibe at **La Dolce Vita** (✉ *Piazza del Carmine 6/r, Santo Spirito* ☎ *055/284595* 🌐 *www.dolcevitaflorence.com*) attracts Florentines and the occasional visiting American movie star. **Rex** (✉ *Via Fiesolana 23–25/r, Santa Croce* ☎ *055/2480331*) attracts a trendy, artsy clientele. **Sant'Ambrogio Caffè** (✉ *Piazza Sant'Ambrogio 7–8/r, Santa Croce* ☎ *055/2477277*) has outdoor summer seating with a view of an 11th-century church (Sant'Ambrogio) directly across the street.

WORD OF MOUTH

"Negronis (the cocktail) were invented in Firenze. Have one. Or two."

—zeppole

Zoe (✉ *Via de' Renai 11 3/r, San Niccolò* ☎ *055/243111*) calls itself a "caffetteria," and while coffee may indeed be served (as well as terrific salads and burgers at lunchtime), elegant youngish Florentines flock here for the fine cocktails. Here's people-watching at its very best, done while listening to the latest CDs imported from England.

SHOPPING

Window-shopping in Florence is like visiting an enormous contemporary-art gallery. Many of today's greatest Italian artists are fashion designers, and most keep shops in Florence. Discerning shoppers may find bargains in the street markets. ■ **TIP→ Don't buy any knockoff goods from any of the hawkers plying their fake Prada (or any other high-end designer) on the streets.** It's illegal, and fines are astronomical if the police happen to catch you. (The vendor doesn't pay the fine, you do.)

Shops are generally open 9 to 1 and 3:30 to 7:30 and are closed Sunday and Monday mornings most of the year. Summer (June to September) hours are usually 9 to 1 and 4 to 8, and some shops close Saturday afternoon instead of Monday morning. When looking for addresses, you'll see two color-coded numbering systems on each street. The red numbers are commercial addresses and are indicated, for example, as 31/r. The blue or black numbers are residential addresses. Most shops take major credit cards and ship purchases, but because of possible delays it's wise to take your purchases with you.

MARKETS

The **Mercato Centrale** (✉ *Piazza del Mercato Centrale, San Lorenzo*) is a huge indoor food market with a staggering selection of things edible. The clothing and leather-goods stalls of the **Mercato di San Lorenzo** in the streets next to the church of San Lorenzo have bargains for shoppers on a budget. It's possible to discover some great finds at the **Mercato di Sant'Ambrogio** (✉ *Piazza Ghiberti, off Via dei Macci, Santa Croce*), where clothing stalls abut the fruit and vegetables. Every Thursday morning from September through June the covered loggia in Piazza della Repubblica hosts a **Mercato dei Fiori** (*flower market* ✉ *Piazza della Repubblica*); it's awash in a lively riot of plants and flowers. If you're looking for cheery, inexpensive trinkets to take home, you might want to stop and roam through the stalls under the loggia of the **Mercato del Porcellino** (✉ *Via Por Santa Maria at Via Porta Rossa, Piazza della Repubblica*). You can find bargains at the **Piazza dei Ciompi flea market** (✉ *Sant'Ambrogio, Santa Croce*) Monday through Saturday and on the last Sunday of the month. The second Sunday of every month brings the **Spirito flea market.** On the third Sunday of the month, vendors at the Fierucola organic fest sell such delectables as honeys, jams, spice mixes, and fresh vegetables.

SHOPPING DISTRICTS

Florence's most fashionable shops are concentrated in the center of town. The fanciest designer shops are mainly on **Via Tornabuoni** and **Via della Vigna Nuova.** The city's largest concentrations of antiques shops are on **Borgo Ognissanti** and the Oltrarno's **Via Maggio.** The **Ponte Vecchio** houses reputable but very expensive jewelry shops, as it has since the 16th century. The area near **Santa Croce** is the heart of the leather merchants' district.

SPECIALTY STORES

BOOKS AND PAPER

Alberto Cozzi (✉ *Via del Parione 35/r, Santa Maria Novella* ☎ *055/294968*) keeps an extensive line of Florentine papers and paper products. The artisans in the shop rebind and restore books and works on paper. One of Florence's oldest paper-goods stores, **Giulio Giannini e Figlio** (✉ *Piazza Pitti 37/r* ☎ *055/212621*) is *the* place to buy the marbleized stock, which comes in many shapes and sizes, from flat sheets to boxes and even pencils. Photograph albums, frames, diaries, and other objects dressed in handmade ★ paper can be purchased at **Il Torchio** (✉ *Via dei Bardi 17, San Niccolò* ☎ *055/2342862*). The stuff is high quality, and the prices lower than usual. **La Tartaruga** (✉ *Borgo Albizzi 60/r, Santa Croce* ☎ *055/2340845*) sells brightly colored, recycled paper in lots of guises (such as calendars and stationery), as well as toys for children. **Libreria d'Arte Galleria Uffizi** (✉ *Piazzale degli Uffizi 6, near Palazzo Vecchio* ☎ *055/284508*) carries monographs on famous artists, some of whose work can be found in the Uffizi. It also carries scholarly works in both Italian and English.

Long one of Florence's best art-book shops, **Libreria Salimbeni** (✉ *Via Matteo Palmieri 14–16/r, Santa Croce* ☎ *055/2340905*) has an outstanding selection. **Pineider** (✉ *Piazza della Signoria 13/r, Piazza della Signoria* ☎ *055/284655*) has shops throughout the world, but the business began in Florence and still does all its printing here. Stationery and business cards are the mainstay, but the stores also sell fine leather desk accessories as well as a less stuffy, more lighthearted line of products.

CLOTHING

The usual fashion suspects—Prada, Gucci, Versace, to name but a few—all have shops in Florence.

Bernardo (✉ *Via Porta Rossa 87/r, Piazza della Repubblica* ☎ *055/283333*) specializes in men's trousers, cashmere sweaters, and shirts with details like mother-of-pearl buttons. **Cabó** (✉ *Via Porta Rossa 77–79/r, Piazza della Repubblica* ☎ *055/215774*) carries that sinuous Missoni knit-wear. Trendy **Diesel** (✉ *Via dei Lamberti 13/r, Piazza della Signoria* ☎ *055/2399963*) started in Vicenza; its gear is on the "must-have" list of many self-respecting Italian teens.

The aristocratic Marchese di Barsento, **Emilio Pucci** (✉ *Via Tornabuoni 20–22/r, Santa Maria Novella* ☎ *055/2658082*), became an international name in the late 1950s when the stretch ski clothes he designed for himself caught on with the dolce vita crowd. His pseudopsychedelic prints and "palazzo pajamas" have become all the rage. You can take home a custom-made suit or dress from **Giorgio Vannini** (✉ *Borgo Santi Apostoli 43/r, Santa Maria Novella* ☎ *055/293037*), who has a show-room for his prêt-à-porter designs.

The intrepid shopper might want to check out some other, lesser-known shops. **Maçel** (✉ *Via Guicciardini 128/r, Palazzo Pitti* ☎ *055/287355*) has collections by lesser-known Italian designers, many of whom use the same factories as the A-list. Florentine designer **Patrizia Pepe** (✉ *Piazza San Giovanni 12/r, Duomo* ☎ *055/2645056*) has body-conscious clothes perfect for all ages, especially for women with a tiny streak of rebelliousness. Members of the junior set desiring to look well clad, Florentine style, should consider stopping at **Piccolo Slam** (✉ *Via dei Neri 9–11/r, Santa Croce* ☎ *055/214504*).

Principe (✉ *Via del Sole 2, Santa Maria Novella* ☎ *055/292764*) is a Florentine institution with casual clothes for men, women, and children at far-from-casual prices. It also has a great housewares department. For cutting-edge fashion, the fun and funky window displays at **Spazio A** (✉ *Via Porta Rossa 109–115/r, Piazza della Repubblica* ☎ *055/212995*) merit a stop. The shop carries such well-known designers as Alberta Ferretti and Moschino, as well as lesser-known Italian, English, and French designers.

FRAGRANCES

Aromatherapy has been elevated to an art form at **Antica Officina del Farmacista Dr. Vranjes** (✉ *Via della Spada 9/r* ☎ *055/288796* ✉ *Via San Gallo 63/r* ☎ *055/494537*). Dr. Vranjes makes scents for the body and for the house.

Lorenzo Villoresi (✉ *Via de'Bardi 14, Lungarno Sud* ☎ *055/2341187* 🌐 *www.lorenzovilloresi.it*) makes one-of-a-kind fragrances, which he develops after meeting with you. Such personalized attention doesn't come cheap.

The essence of a Florentine holiday is captured in the sachets of the **Officina Profumo Farmaceutica di Santa Maria Novella** (✉ *Via della Scala 16, Santa Maria Novella* ☎ *055/216276*), an art-nouveau emporium of herbal cosmetics and soaps that are made following centuries-old recipes created by Dominican friars.

JEWELRY

Angela Caputi (✉ *Borgo Santi Apostoli 44/46* ☎ *055/292993*) wows Florentine cognoscenti with her highly creative, often outsized, plastic jewelry. A small, but equally creative, collection of women's clothing made of fine fabrics is also on offer. **Carlo Piccini** (✉ *Ponte Vecchio 31/r, Piazza della Signoria* ☎ *055/292030*) has been around for several generations, selling antique jewelry as well as making pieces to order; you can also get old jewelry reset here. **Cassetti** (✉ *Ponte Vecchio 54/r, Piazza della Signoria* ☎ *055/2396028*) combines precious and semiprecious stones and metals in contemporary settings. **Gatto Bianco** (✉ *Borgo Santi Apostoli 12/r, Santa Maria Novella* ☎ *055/282989*) has breathtakingly beautiful jewelry worked in semiprecious and precious stones. The feel is completely contemporary. **Oro Due** (✉ *Via Lambertesca 12/r, Piazza della Signoria* ☎ *055/292143*) sells gold jewelry the old-fashioned way: beauteous objects are priced according to the level of craftsmanship and the price of gold bullion that day. **Penko** (✉ *Via F. Zannetti 14/16r, Santa Maria Novella* ☎ *055/211661* 🌐 *www.penkofirenze.it*) looks back to the Renaissance masters for inspiration and creates something completely contemporary yet timeless while doing so.

One of Florence's oldest jewelers, **Tiffany** (✉ *Via Tornabuoni 25/r, Santa Maria Novella* ☎ *055/215506*) has supplied Italian (and other) royalty with finely crafted gems for centuries. Its selection of antique-looking classics has been updated with a selection of contemporary silver.

LINENS AND FABRICS

Antico Setificio Fiorentino (✉ *Via L. Bartolini 4, Santo Spirito/San Frediano* ☎ *055/213861* 🌐 *www.anticosetificiofiorentino.com*) has been providing damasks and other fine fabrics for royalty and those who aspire to it since 1786. Visits by appointment are preferred. **Loretta Caponi** (✉ *Piazza Antinori 4/r, Santa Maria Novella* ☎ *055/213668*) is synonymous with Florentine embroidery, and the luxury lace, linens, and lingerie have earned the eponymous signora worldwide renown. **Valli** (✉ *Via della Vigna Nuova 81/r, Santa Maria Novella* ☎ *055/282485* 🌐 *www.tessutialtamodavalli.it*) sells sumptuous silks, beaded fabrics, lace, wool, and tweeds.

OUTLETS

For bargains on Italian designer clothing, you need to leave the city. At **Barberino Designer Outlet** (✉ *Via Meucci snc* ☎ *055/842161* 🌐 *www.mercatoglenn.it*) you'll find Prada, Pollini, Missoni, and Bruno Magli, among others. To get here, take the A1 to the Barberino di Mugello exit, and follow signs to the mall.

One-stop bargain shopping awaits at the **Mall** (✉ *Via Europa 8* ☎ *055/8657775* 🌐 *www.themall.it*), where the stores sell goods by such names as Bottega Veneta, Giorgio Armani, Loro Piana, Sergio Rossi, and Yves St. Laurent. Cognoscenti drive 45 minutes or take the train to Montevarchi, and then taxi out of town to the **Prada Outlet** (✉ *Levanella Spacceo, Estrada Statale 69, Montevarchi* ☎ *055/91911*).

SHOES AND LEATHER ACCESSORIES

The ultimate in fine leathers is crafted into classic shapes at **Casadei** (✉ *Via Tornabuoni 33/r, Santa Maria Novella* 🌐 *www.casadei.com* ☎ *055/287240*), winding up as women's shoes and bags. **Cellerini** (✉ *Via del Sole 37/r, Santa Maria Novella* ☎ *055/282533* 🌐 *www.cellerini.it*) is an institution in a city where it seems that just about everybody wears an expensive leather jacket. The classy **Ferragamo** (✉ *Via Tornabuoni 2/r, Santa Maria Novella* ☎ *055/292123*), in a 13th-century palazzo, displays deigner clothing and accessories, but elegant footwear still underlies the Ferragamo success. **Furla** (✉ *Via Calzaiuoli 47/r, Piazza della Repubblica* ☎ *055/2382883*) makes beautiful leather bags and wallets in up-to-the-minute designs. **Giotti** (✉ *Piazza Ognissanti 3–4/r, Lungarno Nord* ☎ *055/294265*) has a full line of leather goods, including clothing. **Il Bisonte** (✉ *Via del Parione 31/r, off Via della Vigna Nuova, Santa Maria Novella* ☎ *055/215722* 🌐 *www.ilbisonte.net*) is known for its natural-looking leather goods, all stamped with the store's bison symbol. **Madova** (✉ *Via Guicciardini 1/r, Palazzo Pitti* ☎ *055/2396526*) has high-quality leather gloves in a rainbow of colors and a choice of linings (silk, cashmere, and unlined). **Paolo Carandini** (✉ *Borgo Allegri 17/r, Santa Croce* ☎ *055/245397*) crafts exquisite leather objects such as picture frames, jewelry boxes, and desk accessories.

A consortium of leatherworkers plies its trade at **Scuola del Cuoio** (✉ *Piazza Santa Croce 16* ☎ *055/244533* 🌐 *www.leatherschool.com*), in the former dormitory of the convent of Santa Croce. High-quality, fairly priced jackets, belts, and purses are sold here.

A SIDE TRIP FROM FLORENCE: FIESOLE

GETTING HERE

The simplest way to get to Fiesole from Florence is by public bus: Take the number 7, marked "Fiesole," which you can pick up at Piazza San Marco. If you decide to drive (the bus is so much easier), go to Piazza Liberta and cross the Ponte Rosso heading in the direction of the SS65/SR65. Turn right onto Via Salviati and continue onto Via Roccettini. Make a left turn to Via Vecchia Fiesolana, which will take you directly into the center of town.

There are several possible routes for a two-hour walk from central Florence to Fiesole. One route begins in a residential area of Florence called Salviatino (Via Barbacane, near Piazza Edison, on the Bus 7 route), and after a short time offers peeks over garden walls of beautiful villas, as well as the view over your shoulder at the panorama of Florence in the valley.

VISITOR INFORMATION

Fiesole tourism office (✉ *Via Portigiani 3* ☎ *055/598720* 🌐 *www.comune.fiesole.fi.it*).

EXPLORING

A half-day excursion to Fiesole, in the hills 8 km (5 mi) above Florence, gives you a pleasant respite from museums and a wonderful view of the city. From here the view of the Duomo, with Brunelleschi's powerful cupola, gives you a new appreciation for what the Renaissance accomplished. Fiesole began life as an ancient Etruscan and later Roman village that held some power until it succumbed to barbarian invasions. Eventually it gave up its independence in exchange for Florence's protection. The medieval cathedral, ancient Roman amphitheater, and lovely old villas behind garden walls are clustered on a series of hilltops. A walk around Fiesole can take from one to three hours, depending on how far you stroll from the main piazza.

The **Duomo** reveals a stark medieval interior. In the raised presbytery, the **Cappella Salutati** was frescoed by 15th-century artist Cosimo Rosselli, but it was his contemporary, sculptor Mino da Fiesole (1430–84), who put the town on the artistic map. The Madonna on the altarpiece and the tomb of Bishop Salutati are fine examples of the artist's work. ✉ *Piazza Mino da Fiesole* ☎ *055/59400* ⏲ *Nov.–Mar., daily 7:30–noon and 2–5; Apr.–Oct., daily 7:30–noon and 3–6.*

Near the Duomo, the beautifully preserved 2,000-seat **Anfiteatro Romano** *(Roman Amphitheater)* dates from the 1st century BC and is still used for summer concerts. To the right of the amphitheater are the remains of the **Terme Romani** (Roman Baths), where you can see the gymnasium, hot and cold baths, and rectangular chamber where the water was heated. A beautifully designed **Museo Archeologico,** an intricate series of levels connected by elevators, is built amid the ruins and contains objects dating from as early as 2000 BC. The nearby **Museo Bandini** contains works from the private collection of Canon Angelo Maria Bandini (1726–1803); he gathered 13th- to 15th-century Florentine paintings, terra-cotta pieces, and wood sculpture, which he later bequeathed to the Diocese of Fiesole. ✉ *Via Portigiani 1* ☎ *055/5961293* 🎫 *€10* ⏲ *Apr.–Sept., daily 9:30–7; Oct.–Mar., Wed.–Mon. 10–4:30.*

The hilltop church of **San Francesco** has a good view of Florence and the plain below from its terrace and benches. Halfway up the hill you'll see sloping steps to the right; they lead to a lovely wooded park with trails that loop out and back to the church.

If you really want to stretch your legs, walk 4 km (2½ mi) toward the center of Florence along Via Vecchia Fiesolana, a narrow lane in use since Etruscan times, to the church of **San Domenico**. Sheltered in the church is the *Madonna and Child with Saints* by Fra Angelico, who was a Dominican friar here. ✉ *Piazza San Domenico, off Via Giuseppe Mantellini* ☎ *055/59230* ⏲ *Daily 9–noon.*

From the church of San Domenico, it's a five-minute walk northwest to the **Badia Fiesolana**, which was the original cathedral of Fiesole. Dating to the 11th century, it was first the home of Camaldolese monks; later, Benedictines and Augustinians lived here. Thanks to Cosimo il Vecchio, the complex was substantially restructured. The facade, never completed due to the death of Cosimo, contains elements of its original Romanesque decoration. The attached convent once housed Cosimo's valued manuscripts;

today it's the site of the European Institute, for pre- and postdoctoral studies. Its mid-15th-century cloister is well worth a look. ✉ *Via della Badia dei Roccettini 11* ☎ *055/59155* ⏲ *Weekdays 9–6, Sat. 9:30–12:30.*

WHERE TO EAT AND STAY

$$ ITALIAN ✕ **La Reggia degli Etruschi.** If you want a breath of fresh air—literally—this lovely little eatery is worth a detour. Stamina is necessary to get here, as it's on a steep hill on the way up to the church of San Francesco. The rewards upon arrival are well worth it, in the form of inventive reworkings of Tuscan classics. The mezzaluna di pera a pecorino (little half moon pasta stuffed with pear and pecorino) is sauced with Roquefort and poppy seeds. Slivers of papaya—a rare commodity in these parts—anoints the tasty carpaccio di tonno affumicato (smoked tuna carpaccio). The wine list and the attentive service help make this a terrific place to have a meal. When it's warm, you can sit on the little terrace outside. ✉ *Via San Francesco 1850014* ☎ *055/59385* 🌐 *www.lareggiadeglietruschi.com* ⏲ *No lunch Sun. Closed Tues.*

$$ TUSCAN ✕ **Le Cave di Maiano.** If you're looking to get out of town, head to this simple trattoria in the hills just outside Florence. Italians flock here for Sunday lunch, probably because they enjoy the *buon rapporto fra qualità e prezzo* (good match of quality and price). Tuscan staples are on hand, as is a fine plate of spaghetti with truffled asparagus. They grill well here, so consider one of the meat dishes. Though the food is typical, they do it exceedingly well. ✉ *Via Cave di Maiano 16* ☎ *055/59133.*

$$ 🏨 **Villa Aurora.** This attractive hotel on the main piazza takes advantage of its hilltop spot, with beautiful views in many of the rooms, some of which are on two levels with beamed ceilings and balconies. **Pros:** pretty views, lots of fresh air. **Cons:** a little worn at the edges. **TripAdvisor:** "most sensational view," "easy bus ride in and out of Florence," "bathrooms have been expensively refurbished." ✉ *Piazza Mino da Fiesole 39* ☎ *055/59363* 🌐 *www.villaurora.net* *24 rooms* *In-hotel: restaurant, room service, bar, pool, some pets allowed* 🍴 *Breakfast.*

$$$$ 🏨 **Villa San Michele.** The cypress-lined driveway provides an elegant preamble to this incredibly gorgeous (and extremely expensive) hotel nestled in the hills of Fiesole. **Pros:** luxurious lodging; plenty of history. **Cons:** money must be no object. **TripAdvisor:** "charm and understated luxury," "staff were unbelievably attentive," "breathtaking scenery." ✉ *Via Doccia 4* ☎ *055/59451* 🌐 *www.villasanmichele.com* *21 rooms, 24 suites* *In-room: Wi-Fi. In-hotel: restaurant, room service, bar, pool, gym, business center, parking, some pets allowed* ⏲ *Closed Dec.–Easter* 🍴 *Breakfast.*

NIGHTLIFE AND THE ARTS

From June through August, **Estate Fiesolana** (✉ *Teatro Romano* ☎ *055/5961284* 🌐 *www.comune.fiesole.fi.it*), a festival of theater, music, dance, and film, takes place in Fiesole's churches and in the Roman amphitheater—demonstrating that the ancient Romans knew a thing or two about acoustics.

Tuscany

WORD OF MOUTH

"North of Montalcino was, to us, an extraordinarily beautiful, surprising landscape, that left us amazed with every new twist and turn. In the low light of day, well into autumn, it was ablaze with rich color and deep shadows."

—SuddenlyTuscany

WELCOME TO TUSCANY

TOP REASONS TO GO

★ **Piazza del Campo, Siena:** Sip a cappuccino, lick some gelato, and take in this spectacular shell-shaped piazza.

★ **Piero della Francesca's True Cross frescoes, Arezzo:** If your holy grail is great Renaissance art, seek out these 12 enigmatic scenes.

★ **San Gimignano:** Grab a spot at sunset on the steps of the Collegiata church as swallows swoop in and out of the famous medieval towers.

★ **Wine tasting in Chianti:** Sample the fruits of the region's gorgeous vineyards, at either the wineries themselves or the wine bars found in the towns.

★ **Leaning Tower of Pisa:** It may be touristy, but now that you can once again climb to the top, it's touristy fun.

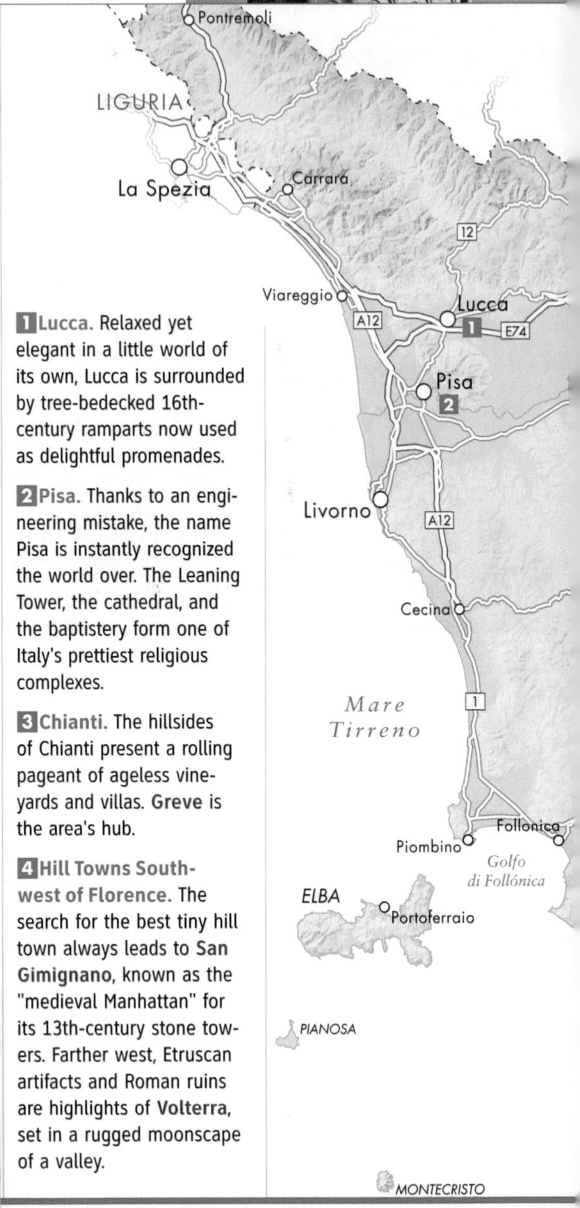

1 Lucca. Relaxed yet elegant in a little world of its own, Lucca is surrounded by tree-bedecked 16th-century ramparts now used as delightful promenades.

2 Pisa. Thanks to an engineering mistake, the name Pisa is instantly recognized the world over. The Leaning Tower, the cathedral, and the baptistery form one of Italy's prettiest religious complexes.

3 Chianti. The hillsides of Chianti present a rolling pageant of ageless vineyards and villas. **Greve** is the area's hub.

4 Hill Towns Southwest of Florence. The search for the best tiny hill town always leads to **San Gimignano**, known as the "medieval Manhattan" for its 13th-century stone towers. Farther west, Etruscan artifacts and Roman ruins are highlights of **Volterra**, set in a rugged moonscape of a valley.

Pontremoli
LIGURIA
La Spezia
Carrara
12
Viareggio
Lucca
1
A12
E74
Pisa
2
Livorno
A12
Cecina
Mare Tirreno
1
Follonica
Piombino
Golfo di Follónica
ELBA
Portoferraio
PIANOSA
MONTECRISTO

5 Siena. The privileged hilltop site that helped Siena flourish in the Middle Ages keeps it one of Italy's most enchanting medieval towns today. At its heart is il Campo, where the frenzied 700-year-old horse race, the Palio, is held every July 2 and August 16.

6 Arezzo and Cortona. These two towns south of Chianti are rewarding side trips. **Arezzo** is best known for its sublime frescoes by Piero della Francesca. **Cortona** sits high above the perfectly flat Valdichiana valley, offering great views of beautiful countryside.

7 Southern Tuscany. Among the highlights of Tuscany's southern reaches are the wine-producing centers of **Montalcino** and **Montepulciano**, and, farther south, the thermal waters of **Saturnia**.

GETTING ORIENTED

Hillsides blanketed with vineyards, silver-green olive groves, and enchanting towns are the essence of Tuscany, one of Italy's most beautiful landscapes. Little seems changed since the Renaissance: to the west of Florence, Pisa's tower still leans; to the south, Chianti's roads wind through cypress groves, taking you to Siena, with its captivating piazza.

EATING AND DRINKING WELL IN TUSCANY

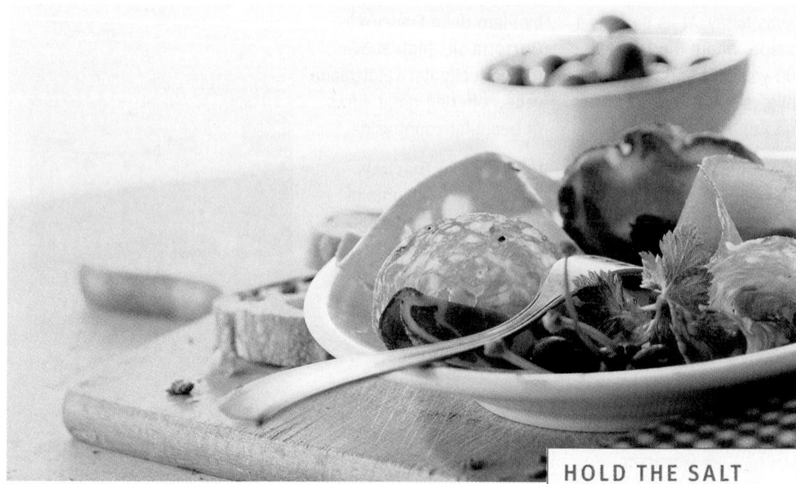

The influence of the ancient Etruscans—who favored the use of fresh herbs—is still felt in Tuscan cuisine three millennia later. Simple and earthy, Tuscan food celebrates the seasons with fresh vegetable dishes, wonderful bread-based soups, and meats perfumed with sage, rosemary, and thyme.

Throughout Tuscany there are excellent upscale restaurants that serve elaborate dishes, but to get a real taste of the flavors of the region, head for the family-run trattorias found in every town. The service and setting are often basic, but the food can be memorable.

Few places serve lighter fare at midday, so expect substantial meals at lunch and dinner, especially in out-of-the-way towns. Dining hours are fairly standard: lunch between 12:30 and 2, dinner between 7:30 and 10.

HOLD THE SALT

Tuscan bread is famous for what it's missing: it's made without salt. That's because it's intended to pick up seasoning from the food it accompanies; it's not meant to be eaten alone or dipped in a bowl of oil (which is a custom developed by American restaurants—it's not standard practice in Italian ones).

That doesn't mean Tuscans don't like to start a meal with bread, but usually it's prepared in some way. It can be grilled and drizzled with olive oil *(fettunta)*, covered with chicken liver spread *(crostino nero)*, or rubbed with garlic and topped with tomatoes (*bruschetta*).

AFFETTATI MISTI

The name, roughly translated, means "mixed cold cuts," pictured left, and it's something Tuscans do exceptionally well. A platter of cured meats, served as an antipasto, is sure to include *prosciutto crudo* (ham, cut paper thin) and *salame* (dry sausage, prepared in dozens of ways—some spicy, some sweet). The most distinctly Tuscan affettati are made from *cinta senese* (a once nearly extinct pig found only in the heart of the region) and *cinghiale* (wild boar, which roam all over central Italy). You can eat these delicious slices unadorned or layered on a piece of bread.

PASTA

Restaurants throughout Tuscany serve dishes similar to those in Florence, but they also have their own local specialties. Many recipes are from the *nonna* (grandmother) of the restaurant's owner, handed down through time but never written down.

Look in particular for pasta creations made with *pici* (a long, thick, hand-rolled spaghetti), pictured below. Pappardelle (a long, ribbon-like pasta noodle, pictured upper right) is frequently paired with sauces made with game, such as *lepre* (hare) or cinghiale. In the northwest, a specialty of Lucca is *tordelli di carne al ragù* (meat-stuffed pasta with a meat sauce).

MEAT

Bistecca fiorentina (a thick T-bone steak, grilled rare) is the classic meat dish of Tuscany, but there are other specialties as well. Many menus will include *tagliata di manzo* (thinly sliced, roasted beef, drizzled with olive oil), *arista di maiale* (roast pork with sage and rosemary), and *salsiccia e fagioli* (pork sausage and beans). In the southern part of the region, don't be surprised to find *piccione* (pigeon), which can be roasted, stuffed, or baked.

WINE

Grape cultivation here also dates from Etruscan times, and, particularly in Chianti, vineyards are abundant. The resulting medium-body red wine is a staple on most tables; however, you can select from a multitude of other varieties, including such reds as Brunello di Montalcino and Vino Nobile di Montepulciano and such whites as Vermentino and Vernaccia.

Super Tuscans (a fanciful name given to a group of wines by American journalists) now command attention as some of the best produced in Italy; they have great depth and complexity. The dessert wine *vin santo* is made throughout the region, and is often sipped with *biscotti* (twice-baked almond cookies), perfect for dunking.

Updated by Peter Blackman and Patricia Rucidlo

Midway down the Italian peninsula, Tuscany (Toscana in Italian) is distinguished by rolling hills, snowcapped mountains, dramatic cypress trees, and miles of coastline on the Tyrrhenian Sea—which all adds up to gorgeous views at practically every turn. The beauty of the landscape proves a perfect foil for the region's abundance of superlative art and architecture. It also produces some of Italy's finest wines and olive oils. The combination of unforgettable art, sumptuous landscapes, and eminently drinkable wines that pair beautifully with its simple food makes a trip to Tuscany something beyond special.

Many of Tuscany's cities and towns have retained the same fundamental character over the past 500 years. Civic rivalries that led to bloody battles centuries ago have given way to soccer rivalries. Renaissance pomp lives on in the celebration of local feast days and centuries-old traditions such as the Palio in Siena and the Giostra del Saracino (Joust of the Saracen) in Arezzo. Often, present-day Tuscans look as though they might have served as models for paintings produced hundreds of years ago. In many ways, the Renaissance still lives on in Tuscany.

PLANNING

MAKING THE MOST OF YOUR TIME

Tuscany isn't the place for a jam-packed itinerary. One of the greatest pleasures here is indulging in rustic hedonism, marked by long lunches and showstopping sunsets. Whether by car, bike, or on foot, you'll want to get out into the glorious landscape, but it's smart to keep your plans modest. Set a church or a hill town or an out-of-the-way restaurant as your destination, knowing that half the pleasure is in getting there—admiring as you go the stately palaces, the tidy geometry of row upon row of grapevines, the fields vibrant with red poppies, sunflowers, and yellow broom.

You'll need to devise a Siena strategy. The town shouldn't be missed; it's compact enough that you can see the major sights on a day trip, and that's exactly what most people do. Spend the night, and you'll get to see the town breathe a sigh and relax upon the day-trippers' departure. The flip side is, your favorite Tuscan hotel isn't likely to be in Siena.

You face similar issues with Pisa and Lucca in the northwest. Pisa's famous tower is worth seeing, but ultimately Lucca has greater charms, making it a better choice for an overnight.

GETTING AROUND

BUS TRAVEL

Buses are a reliable but time-consuming means of getting around the region because they tend to stop in every town. Trains are a better option in virtually every respect when you're headed to Pisa, Lucca, Arezzo, and other cities with good rail service. But for most smaller towns, buses are the only option. Be aware that making arrangements for bus travel, particularly for a non-Italian speaker, can be a test of patience.

There are two primary bus services: **Tra-In** (☎ *0577/204111* 🌐 *www.trainspa.it*) covers much of the territory south of Siena, including Montalcino and Montepulciano. It also has several runs a day between Rome and Siena (2½ hours). **SITA** (☎ *0577/204270* 🌐 *www.sitabus.it*) has regular service between Florence and Siena (1 hour) as well as to numerous towns in Chianti. A third line, **CPT** (☎ *050/502564* 🌐 *www.cpt.pisa.it*), has infrequent buses between Volterra and Colle di Val d'Elsa, and also connects Volterra with the nearest train station and Cecina.

CAR TRAVEL

Driving is the only way (other than hiking or biking) to get to many of Tuscany's small towns and vineyards. The cities west of Florence are easily reached by the A11, which leads to Lucca and then to the sea. The A1 takes you south from Florence to Arezzo and Chiusi (where you turn off for Montepulciano). Florence and Siena are connected by a superstrada and also the panoramic SR222, which threads through Chianti. The hill towns north and west of Siena lie along superstrade and winding local roads—all are well marked, but still you should arm yourself with a good map.

The Florence–Siena Superstrada (no number) is a four-lane, divided highway with exits onto smaller country roads. The Via Cassia (SR2) winds its way south from Florence to Siena, along the western edge of the Chianti region. The superstrada is more direct, but much less scenic, than the SR2, and it can have a lot of traffic, especially on Sunday evenings. The Strada Chiantigiana (SR222) cuts through the center of Chianti, to the east of the superstrada, in a curvaceous path past vineyards and countryside.

TRAIN TRAVEL

Trains on Italy's main north-south rail line stop in Florence as well as Prato, Arezzo, and Chiusi. Another major line connects Florence with Pisa, and the coastal line between Rome and Genoa passes through Pisa as well. There's regular, nearly hourly service from Florence to Lucca, and several trips a day between Florence and Siena. Siena's train station is 2 km (1 mi) north of the *centro storico* (historic center), but cabs and city buses are readily available.

For other parts of Tuscany—Chianti, Montalcino, and Montepulciano, for example—you're better off traveling by bus or by car. Train stations, when they exist, are far from the historic centers, and service is infrequent.

You can check online for schedules of the state railway, the **Ferrovie dello Stato** (☎ *892021 toll-free within Italy* 🌐 *www.trenitalia.com*). You can also get information and tickets at most travel agencies.

ABOUT THE HOTELS

A visit to Tuscany is a trip into the country. There are plenty of good hotels in the larger towns, but the classic experience is to stay in one of the rural accommodations—often converted private homes, sometimes working farms or vineyards (known as *agriturismi*).

Though it's tempting to think you can stumble upon a little out-of-the-way hotel at the end of the day, you're better off not testing your luck. Make reservations before you go. If you don't have a reservation, you may be able to get help finding a room from the local tourist office.

Hotel reviews have been condensed for this book. Please go to Fodors.com for full reviews of each property.

WHAT IT COSTS (IN EUROS)					
	¢	$	$$	$$$	$$$$
Restaurants	under €20	€20–€30	€30–€45	€45–€65	over €65
Hotels	under €75	€75–€125	€125–€200	€200–€300	over €300

Restaurant prices are for a first course (primo), second course (secondo), and dessert (dolce). Hotel prices are for two people in a standard double room in high season, including tax and service.

VISITOR INFORMATION

Many towns in Tuscany have tourist information offices, which can be useful resources for trip-planning advice (and sometimes maps). You'll find contact information for offices at the beginning of town listings throughout this chapter. Such offices are typically open from 8:30 to 1 and 3:30 to 6 or 7; those in smaller towns are usually closed Saturday afternoon and Sunday, and often shut down entirely from early November through Easter.

The tourist information office in Greve is particularly noteworthy as an excellent source for general information about the Chianti wine region and its hilltop towns. In Siena the centrally located tourist office, in Piazza del Campo, has information about Siena and its province. Both offices book hotel rooms for a nominal fee. Offices in smaller towns can also be a good place to check if you need last-minute accommodations.

LUCCA

Ramparts built in the 16th and 17th centuries enclose a charming town filled with churches (99 of them), terra-cotta-roof buildings, and narrow cobblestone streets, along which locals maneuver bikes to do their daily shopping. Here Caesar, Pompey, and Crassus agreed to rule Rome as a triumvirate in 60 BC. Lucca was later the first Tuscan town to accept Christianity, and it still has a mind of its own: when most of Tuscany was voting communist as a matter of course, Lucca's citizens rarely followed suit. The famous composer Giacomo Puccini (1858–1924) was born here; his work forms the nucleus of the summer Opera Theater and Music Festival, staged in open-air venues from mid-June through mid-July. The ramparts circling the center city are the perfect place to take a stroll, ride a bicycle, kick a ball, or just stand and look down upon Lucca.

WORD OF MOUTH

"For history and charm the small walled city of Lucca is, I think, absolutely magical. The food in Lucca also eclipses most all of Tuscany too!"

—hanabilly

GETTING HERE

You can reach Lucca easily by train from Florence; the historic center is a short walk from the station. If you're driving, take the A11/E76.

VISITOR INFORMATION

Lucca tourism office (✉ *Piazza Santa Maria 35* ☎ *0583/91991* 🌐 *www.luccaturismo.it*).

EXPLORING LUCCA

The walled historic center of Lucca, 51 km (31 mi) west of Florence, restricts motorized traffic. Walking and biking are the most efficient and most enjoyable ways to get around the mostly flat neighborhood. A combination ticket costing €6.50 gains you admission to both the Museo Nazionale di Villa Guinigi and the Museo Nazionale di Palazzo Mansi.

TOP ATTRACTIONS

★ **Duomo.** The blind arches on the cathedral's facade are a fine example of the rigorously ordered Pisan Romanesque style, in this case happily enlivened by an extremely varied collection of small, carved columns. Take a closer look at the decoration of the facade and that of the portico below; they make this one of the most entertaining church exteriors in Tuscany. The Gothic interior contains a moving Byzantine crucifix—called the Volto Santo, or Holy Face—brought here, according to legend, in the 8th century (though it probably dates from between the 11th and early 13th centuries). The masterpiece of the Sienese sculptor Jacopo della Quercia (circa 1371–1438) is the marble *Tomb of Ilaria del Carretto* (1407–08). ✉ *Piazza del Duomo* ☎ *0583/490530* 🌐 *www.museocattedralelucca.it* 🎫 *€4* ⏲ *Duomo: Mar. 10–Nov. 2, daily 10–8; Nov 3–Mar. 9, Mon.–Fri. 10–2, weekends 10–5.*

★ **Passeggiata delle Mura.** Any time of day when the weather is clement, you can find the citizens of Lucca cycling, jogging, strolling, or kicking a soccer ball in this green, beautiful, and very large park—neither inside nor outside the city but rather right on the ring of ramparts that defines Lucca. Sunlight streams through two rows of tall plane trees to dapple the *passeggiata delle mura* (walk on the walls), which is 4.2 km (2½ mi) in length. Ten bulwarks are topped with lawns, many with picnic tables and some with play equipment for children. Be aware at all times of where the edge is—there are no railings, and the drop to the ground outside the city is a precipitous 40 feet.

QUICK BITES

Gelateria Veneta (✉ *Via V. Veneto 74* ☎ *0583/467037*) makes outstanding gelato, sorbet, and ices (some sugar-free). They prepare their confections three times a day, using the same recipes with which the Brothers Arnoldo opened the place in 1927. The pièces de résistance are frozen fruits stuffed with creamy filling: don't miss the apricot sorbet-filled apricot. Note that they close up shop in October and reopen around Easter.

Piazza dell'Anfiteatro Romano. Here's where the ancient Roman amphitheater once stood; some of the medieval buildings built over the amphitheater retain their original oval shape and brick arches. ✉ *Off Via Fillungo, near north side of old town.*

San Frediano. The church of San Frediano, just steps from the Anfiteatro, has a 14th-century mosaic decorating its facade, and contains works by Jacopo della Quercia (circa 1371–1438) and Matteo Civitali (1436–1501), as well as the lace-clad mummy of Saint Zita (circa 1218–78), the patron saint of household servants. ✉ *Piazza San Frediano* ☎ *No phone* ⏲ *Mon.–Sat. 8:30–noon and 3–5, Sun. 10:30–5.*

San Michele in Foro. The facade here is even more fanciful than that of the Duomo. Its upper levels have nothing but air behind them (after the front of the church was built, there were no funds to raise the nave), and the winged Archangel Michael, who stands at the very top, seems precariously poised for flight. The facade, heavily restored in the 19th century, displays busts of 19th-century Italian patriots such as Garibaldi and Cavour. Check out the superb Filippino Lippi (1457/58–1504) panel painting of Saints Jerome, Sebastian, Rocco, and Helen in the right transept. ✉ *Piazza San Michele* ☎ *No phone* ⏲ *Nov.–Mar., daily 9–noon and 3–5; Apr.–Oct., daily 9–noon and 3–6.*

Torre Guinigi. The tower of the medieval Palazzo Guinigi contains one of the city's most curious sights: a grove of ilex trees has grown at the top of the tower, and their roots have pushed their way into the room below. From the top you have a magnificent view of the city and the surrounding countryside. (Only the tower is open to the public, not the palazzo.) ✉ *Palazzo Guinigi, Via Sant'Andrea* ☎ *0583/316846* 🎫 *€3.50* ⏲ *Mar. and Apr., daily 9:30–6:30; May–Sept., daily 9–7:30; Oct.–Feb., daily 10–5:30.*

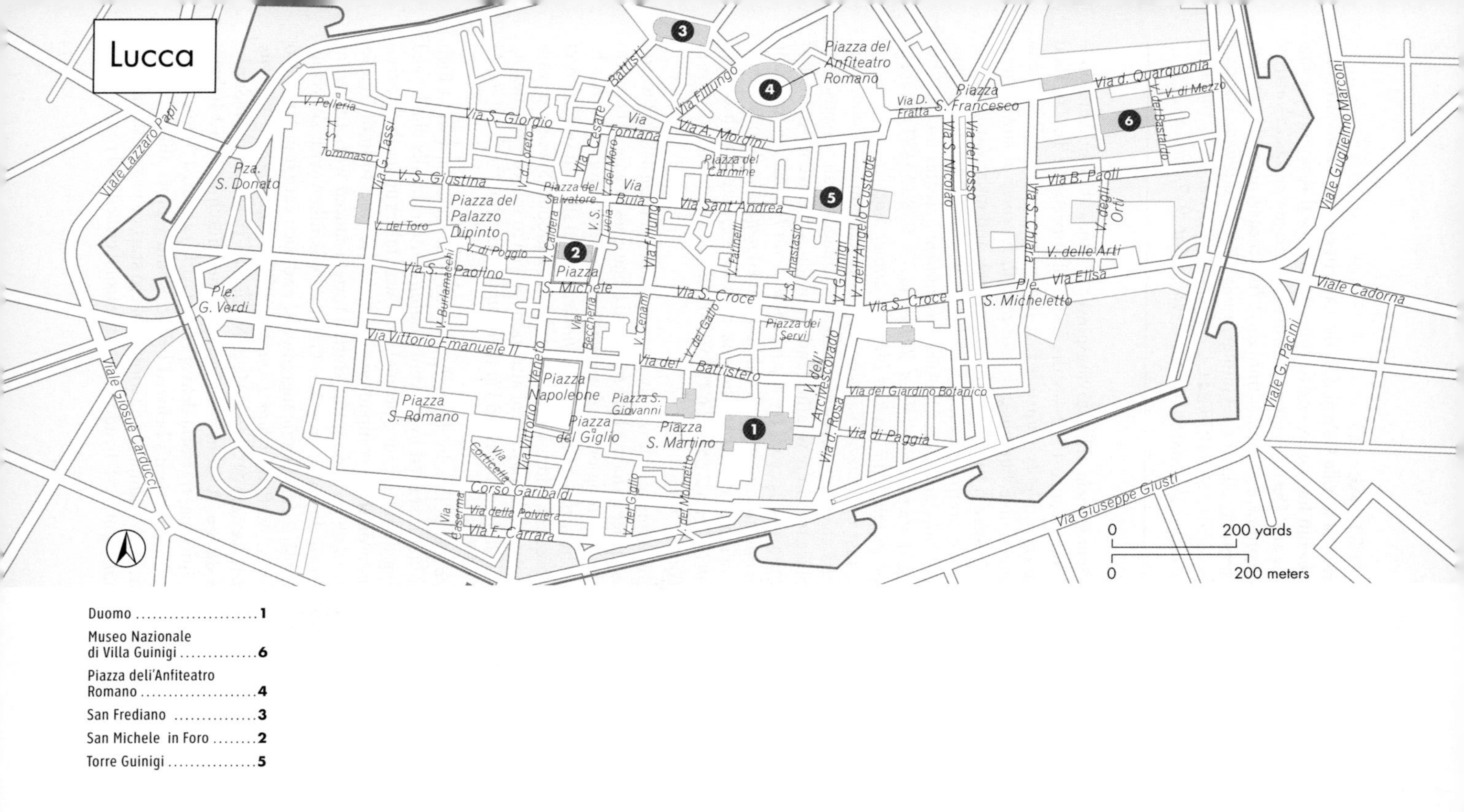
Lucca
Piazza del Anfiteatro Romano
Via d. Quarquonia
V. di Mezzo
V. del Bastardo
Piazza S. Francesco
Via D. Fratta
Via S. Giorgio
V. Pelleria
V. S. Tommaso
Via G. Tassi
Viale Lazzaro Papi
Pza. S. Donato
V. S. Giustina
Piazza del Palazzo Dipinto
V. del Toro
V. di Poggio
Via S. Paolino
V. Burlamacchi
Ple. G. Verdi
Via Vittorio Emanuele II
Via Cesare Battisti
Via Fontana
Via Fillungo
Via A. Mordini
Piazza del Carmine
Piazza del Salvatore
V. del Moro
Via Buia
V. S. Lucia
V. Caldera
V. d. Loreto
Piazza S. Michele
Via Sant'Andrea
V. Fatinelli
V. S. Anastasio
V. Guinigi
V. dell'Angelo Custode
Via S. Nicolao
Via del Fosso
Via S. Chiara
Via B. Paoli
V. degli Orti
V. delle Arti
Via Elisa
Ple. S. Micheletto
Via S. Croce
Via Beccheria
V. Cenami
V. del Gallo
Piazza dei Servi
V. dell' Arcivescovado
Via del Battistero
Via del Giardino Botanico
Piazza Napoleone
Via Vittorio Veneto
Piazza S. Giovanni
Piazza del Giglio
Piazza S. Martino
Via d. Rosa
Via di Paggia
Piazza S. Romano
Via Corticella
Corso Garibaldi
Via Caserma
Via della Polviera
Via F. Carrara
V. del Giglio
V. del Molinetto
Viale Giosuè Carducci
Via Giuseppe Giusti
Viale G. Pacini
Viale Cadorna
Viale Guglielmo Marconi
0 200 yards
0 200 meters
Duomo 1
Museo Nazionale di Villa Guinigi 6
Piazza deli'Anfiteatro Romano 4
San Frediano 3
San Michele in Foro 2
Torre Guinigi 5

WORTH NOTING

Museo Nazionale di Villa Guinigi. On the eastern end of the historic center, this museum has an extensive collection of local Romanesque and Renaissance art. The museum represents an overview of Lucca's artistic traditions from Etruscan times until the 17th century, housed in the former 15th-century villa of the Guinigi family. ✉ *Villa Guinigi, Via della Quarquonia* ☎ *0583/496033* 🎫 *€4, combination ticket €6.50 (includes Museo Nazionale di Palazzo Mansi)* 🕙 *Tues.–Sat. 9–7, Sun. 9–2.*

WHERE TO EAT

$$ TUSCAN ★ ✕ **Buca di Sant'Antonio.** The staying power of Buca di Sant'Antonio—it's been around since 1782—is the result of superlative Tuscan food brought to the table by waitstaff that doesn't miss a beat. The menu includes the simple but blissful, like *tortelli lucchesi al sugo* (meat-stuffed pasta with a tomato-and-meat sauce), and more daring dishes such as roast *capretto* (goat kid) with herbs. A white-wall interior hung with copper pots and brass musical instruments creates a classy but comfortable dining space. ✉ *Via della Cervia 3* ☎ *0583/55881* 🕙 *Closed Mon., 1 wk in Jan., and 1 wk in July. No dinner Sun.*

$–$$ TUSCAN ✕ **Il Giglio.** Just off Piazza Napoleone, this restaurant has quiet, late-19th-century charm and classic cuisine. It's a place for all seasons, with a big fireplace for chilly weather and an outdoor terrace in summer. If mushrooms are in season, try the *tacchonni con funghi,* a homemade pasta with mushrooms and a local herb called *nepitella.* A local favorite during winter is the *coniglio con olive* (rabbit stew with olives). ✉ *Piazza del Giglio 2* ☎ *0583/494508* 🕙 *Closed Wed. and 15 days in Nov. No dinner Tues.*

$$ WINE BAR ✕ **i Santi.** This intimate little wine bar, just outside the Piazza dell'Anfiteatro, is the perfect place to have a light meal and a fine glass of wine. The extensive wine list is strong on local varietals, as well as on foreign (French) selections. The *carpaccio di manzo affumicato* (thin slices of smoked beef served with celery and a young cheese) is a standout. Specials always include a pasta of the day. Great attention is given to sourcing top-quality local, seasonal ingredients. ✉ *Via dell'Anfiteatro 29/a* ☎ *0583/496124* 🕙 *Closed Wed.*

$ ITALIAN ✕ **La Pecora Nera.** This lively, gaily colored little trattoria with a high vaulted ceiling is staffed by giovani *disabili* (both mentally challenged and learning-disabled young people), who wait tables under the supervision of a non-disabled companion. The food's terrific, from the made-in-house *tordelli lucchesi* (meat-stuffed tortelli sauced with a fragrant meat ragù) to the tasty crostata. Great care is taken with sourcing, when possible, local organic ingredients, and such care translates into a lovely meal. ✉ *Piazza San Francesco 4* ☎ *0583/469738* 🌐 *www.lapecoraneralucca.it* 🕙 *Closed Mon. No dinner Tues. No lunch Sun.*

$ ITALIAN ✕ **Trattoria da Leo.** A stone's throw from the church of San Michele, this noisy, informal trattoria delivers *cucina alla casalinga* (home cooking) in the best sense; it's beloved by locals and visitors alike. Try the tasty penne with walnuts and Gorgonzola to start or just go straight to *secondi piatti* (entrées). In addition to the usual grilled and roast meats, there's excellent chicken with olives and a good cold dish of boiled meats served with a parsley and pine-nut sauce. The vegetable sides, such as the *finocchi alla Parmigiano* (fennel gratinee with Parmesan cheese) pair nicely with just about anything. Save room for a dessert, such as the rich, sweet, fig-and-walnut torte or the lemon sorbet brilliantly dotted with bits of sage, an astoundingly pleasing combination. ✉ *Via Tegrimi 1, at corner of Via degli Asili* ☎ *0583/492236* ▭ *No credit cards* ⏱ *No lunch Sun. Closed Sun., Nov.–Mar.*

WHERE TO STAY

$ **Albergo San Martino.** Down a narrow street facing a quiet, sun-sprinkled *piazzale* (small square) stands this small hotel, where the brocade bedspreads are fresh and crisp, and the proprietor friendly. **Pros:** comfortable beds; great breakfasts. **Cons:** breakfast costs €10. **TripAdvisor:** "inside the walled city," "very modern amenities," "cool bar." ✉ *Via della Dogana 9* ☎ *0583/469181* 🌐 *www.albergosanmartino.it* *6 rooms, 2 suites* *In-room: Wi-Fi. In- hotel: bar* *No meals.*

$$ **Hotel Ilaria.** The former stables of the Villa Bottini have been transformed into a modern hotel within the historic center. **Pros:** a Fodor's reader sums it up as a "nice, modern small hotel"; free bicycles. **Cons:** though in the city center, it's a little removed from main attractions. **TripAdvisor:** "walking distance of everything," "clean and comfortable," "best customer service." ✉ *Via del Fosso 26* ☎ *0583/47615* 📠 *0583/991961* 🌐 *www.hotelilaria.com* *36 rooms, 5 suites* *In-room: Wi-Fi. In-hotel: bar, business center, parking, some pets allowed (fee)* *Breakfast.*

$$ ★ **Palazzo Alexander.** This small, elegant boutique hotel is on a quiet side street a short walk from San Michele in Foro. **Pros:** intimate feel; gracious staff; bacon and eggs included in the buffet breakfast. **Cons:** some Fodor's readers complain of too-thin walls. **TripAdvisor:** "wonderful views," "nice antique furniture," "an enchanting experience." ✉ *Via S. Giustina 48* ☎ *0583/583571* 📠 *0583/583610* 🌐 *www.hotelpalazzoalexander.com* *9 rooms, 3 suites, 1 apartment* *In-room: Wi-Fi. In-hotel: bar, business center, parking* *Breakfast.*

$ **Piccolo Hotel Puccini.** Steps away from the busy square and church of San Michele, this little hotel is quiet and calm—and a great deal. **Pros:** cheery, English-speaking staff. **Cons:** breakfast costs extra; some rooms are on the dark side. **TripAdvisor:** "just off Lucca's main square," "every comfort and amenity," "a most gracious host." ✉ *Via di Poggio 9* ☎ *0583/55421* 📠 *0583/53487* 🌐 *www.hotelpuccini.com* *14 rooms* *In-room: no a/c. In-hotel: bar, some pets allowed* *No meals.*

SPORTS AND THE OUTDOORS

A splendid bike ride may be had by circling the entire historic center along the top of the bastions—affording something of a bird's-eye view. **Antonio Poli Biciclette** (✉ *Piazza Santa Maria 42* ☎ *0583/493787*) is an option for bicycle rental on the east side. Rentals cost about €15 for the day.

SHOPPING

Lucca's justly famed olive oils are available throughout the city (and exported around the world). Look for those made by Fattoria di Fubbiano and Fattoria Fabbri—two of the best. **Antica Bottega di Prospero** (✉ *Via San Lucia 13* ☎ *No phone*) sells top-quality local products, including dried porcini mushrooms, olive oil, and wine.

You can wine taste, have a light lunch, or snack at **il Cuore** (✉ *Via del Battistero 2* ☎ *0583/493196* 🌐 *www.ilcuorelucca.com*) They also have marvelous things to take away, including delicious pasta dishes, cured pork products, vegetable side dishes, and cheeses.

★ Chocoholics can get their fix at **Caniparoli** (✉ *Via S. Paolino 96, San Donato* ☎ *0583/53456*). They're so serious about their sweets here that they don't make them from June through August because of the heat.

PISA

Most people think "Leaning Tower of" when they think of Pisa. Its position as one of Italy's most famous landmarks attracts hordes of day-trippers from around the world. But even if the building doesn't captivate you, Pisa has other treasures that make a visit worthwhile. Taken as a whole, the Campo dei Miracoli—the "Field of Miracles" where the Leaning Tower, the Duomo, the Camposanto, and the Baptistery are located—is one of the most dramatic and beautiful architectural complexes in Italy.

Pisa may have been inhabited as early as the Bronze Age. It was certainly populated by the Etruscans and, in turn, became part of the Roman Empire. In the early Middle Ages it flourished as an economic powerhouse—along with Amalfi, Genoa, and Venice, it was one of the maritime republics. The city's economic and political power ebbed in the early 15th century as it fell under the domination of Florence, though it enjoyed a brief resurgence under Cosimo I in the mid-16th century. Pisa endured heavy Allied bombing—miraculously, the Duomo and Leaning Tower, along with some other grand Romanesque structures, were spared, but the Camposanto sustained heavy damage.

GETTING HERE

About 84 km (52 mi) west of Florence, Pisa is a straight shot on the Fi-Pi-Li autostrada. By train it's an easy hour-long ride. The Pisa–Lucca train runs frequently and takes about 30 minutes.

VISITOR INFORMATION

Pisa tourism office (✉ *Piazza Vittorio Emanuele II* ☎ *050/42291* 🌐 *www.pisaunicaterra.it*).

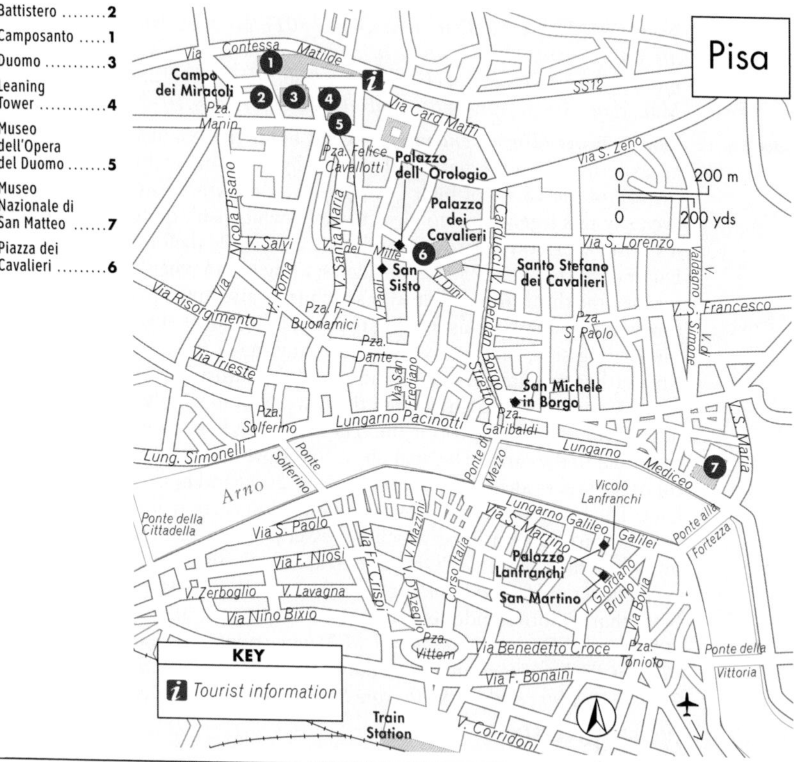

EXPLORING PISA

Pisa, like many Italian cities, is best explored on foot, and most of what you'll want to see is within walking distance. The views along the Arno River are particularly grand and shouldn't be missed—there's a feeling of spaciousness that isn't found along the Arno in Florence.

As you set out, note that there are various combination-ticket options for sights on the Piazza del Duomo.

TOP ATTRACTIONS

Battistero. This lovely Gothic baptistery (Italy's largest) is best known for the pulpit carved by Nicola Pisano (circa 1220–84; father of Giovanni Pisano) in 1260. Ask one of the ticket takers if he'll sing for you inside; the acoustics are remarkable. ✉ *Piazza del Duomo* ☎ *050/835011* 🌐 *www.opapisa.it* 🎫 *€5, discounts available if bought in combination with tickets for other monuments* ⏲ *Nov.–Feb., daily 10–5; Mar., daily 9–6; Apr.–Sept., daily 8–8; Oct., daily 8:30–7.*

Duomo. Pisa's cathedral brilliantly utilizes the horizontal marble-stripe motif (borrowed from Moorish architecture) that became common to Tuscan cathedrals. It's famous for the Romanesque panels on the transept door facing the tower that depict scenes from the life of Christ. The beautifully carved 14th-century pulpit is by Giovanni Pisano (son of

Nicola). ✉ *Piazza del Duomo* ☎ *050835011* 🌐 *www.opapisa.it* 🎫 *€2, discounts available if bought in combination with tickets for other monuments; free Nov.–Feb.* ⏲ *Nov.–Feb., daily 10–12:45 and 2–5; Mar., daily 10–6; Apr.–Sept., daily 10–8; Oct., daily 10–7.*

Fodor's Choice ★ **Leaning Tower** *(Torre Pendente)*. Legend holds that Galileo conducted an experiment on the nature of gravity by dropping metal balls from the top of the 187-foot-high Leaning Tower of Pisa. Historians, however, say this legend has no basis in fact—which isn't quite to say that it's false. Work on this tower, built as a *campanile* (bell tower) for the Duomo, started in 1173: the lopsided settling began when construction reached the third story. The tower's architects attempted to compensate through such methods as making the remaining floors slightly taller on the leaning side, but the extra weight only made the problem worse. The settling continued, and by the late 20th century it had accelerated to such a point that many feared the tower would simply topple over, despite all efforts to prop it up. The structure has since been firmly anchored to the earth. The final phase to restore the tower to its original tilt of 300 years ago was launched in early 2000 and finished two years later. The last phase removed some 100 tons of earth from beneath the foundation. Reservations, which are essential, can be made online or by calling the Museo dell'Opera del Duomo; it's also possible to arrive at the ticket office and book for later the same day if space is available. Note that children under eight years of age are not allowed to climb. ✉ *Piazza del Duomo* ☎ *050/835011* 🌐 *www.opapisa.it* 🎫 *€15 on site, €17 on Web* ⏲ *Dec. and Jan., daily 10–4:30; Nov. and Feb., daily 9:30–5:30; Mar., daily 9–5:30; Apr.–Sept., daily 8:30–8; Oct., daily 9–7.*

WORTH NOTING

Camposanto. According to legend, the cemetery—a walled structure on the western side of the Campo dei Miracoli—is filled with earth that returning Crusaders brought back from the Holy Land. Contained within are numerous frescoes, notably *The Drunkenness of Noah*, by Renaissance artist Benozzo Gozzoli (1422–97), presently under restoration; and the disturbing *Triumph of Death* (14th century; artist uncertain), whose subject matter shows what was on people's minds in a century that saw the ravages of the Black Death. ✉ *Piazza del Duomo* ☎ *050/835011* 🌐 *www.opapisa.it* 🎫 *€5, discounts available if bought in combination with tickets for other monuments* ⏲ *Nov.–Feb., daily 10–5; Mar., daily 9–6; Apr.–Sept., daily 8–8; Oct., daily 9–7.*

Museo dell'Opera del Duomo. At the southeast corner of the sprawling Campo dei Miracoli, this museum holds a wealth of medieval sculptures and the ancient Roman sarcophagi that inspired Nicola Pisano's figures. ✉ *Piazza del Duomo* ☎ *050/835011* 🌐 *www.opapisa.it* 🎫 *€5, discounts available if bought in combination with tickets for other monuments* ⏲ *Nov.–Feb., daily 10–5; Mar., daily 9–6; Apr.–Sept., daily 8–8; Oct., daily 9–7.*

Museo Nazionale di San Matteo. On the north bank of the Arno, this museum contains some incisive examples of local Romanesque and Gothic art. ✉ *Lungarno Mediceo* ☎ *050/541865* 🎫 *€5* ⏲ *Tues.–Sat. 9–7, holidays 9–2.*

Piazza dei Cavalieri. The piazza, with its fine Renaissance **Palazzo dei Cavalieri, Palazzo dell'Orologio,** and **Chiesa di Santo Stefano dei Cavalieri,** was laid out by Giorgio Vasari in about 1560. The square was the seat of the Ordine dei Cavalieri di San Stefano (Order of the Knights of St. Stephen), a military and religious institution meant to defend the coast from possible invasion by the Turks. Also in this square is the prestigious **Scuola Normale Superiore,** founded by Napoléon in 1810 on the French model. Here graduate students pursue doctorates in literature, philosophy, mathematics, and science. In front of the school is a large statue of Ferdinando I de' Medici dating from 1596. On the extreme left is the tower where the hapless Ugolino della Gherardesca (died 1289) was imprisoned with his two sons and two grandsons; legend holds that he ate them. Dante immortalized him in Canto XXXIII of his *Inferno*. Duck into the **Church of Santo Stefano** (if you're lucky enough to find it open) and check out Bronzino's splendid *Nativity of Christ* (1564–65).

WHERE TO EAT

$–$$ ITALIAN ★ **Beny.** Apricot walls hung with etchings of Pisa make this small, single-room restaurant warmly romantic. Husband and wife Damiano and Sandra Lazzerini have been running the place for two decades, and it shows in their obvious enthusiasm while talking about the menu and daily specials. Beny specializes in fish: its *ripieno di polpa di pesce a pan grattato con salsa di seppie e pomodoro* (fish-stuffed ravioli with tomato-octopus sauce) delights. Beny relies heavily on seasonal ingredients; Sandra works wonders with *tartufi estivi* (summer truffles), artichokes, and market fish of the day. ✉ *Piazza Gambacorti 22* ☎ *050/25067* ⊙ *Closed Sun. and 2 wks in mid-Aug. No lunch Sat.*

$ ITALIAN ★ **Osteria dei Cavalieri.** This charming white-wall restaurant, a few steps from Piazza dei Cavalieri, is reason enough to come to Pisa. They can do it all here—serve up exquisitely grilled fish dishes, please vegetarians, and prepare *tagliata* (thin slivers of rare beef) for meat lovers. Three set menus, from the sea, garden, and earth, are available, or you can order à la carte. For dinner there's an early seating (around 7:30) and a later one (around 9); opt for the later one if you want time to linger over your meal. You might also want to try their other restaurant, La Sosta dei Cavalieri, just down the street. ✉ *Via San Frediano 16* ☎ *050/580858* *Reservations essential* ⊙ *Closed Sun., 2 wks in Aug., and Dec. 29–Jan. 7. No lunch Sat.*

$ ITALIAN **Trattoria la Faggiola.** It's only seconds away from the Leaning Tower, which probably explains the "No Pizza" written in big, bold letters on the blackboard outside. Inside, another blackboard lists two or three primi and secondi. The amiable Carlo Silvestrini presides over this little eatery, and he cares if you don't clean your plate. That's not a problem, because everything's good, from the *pasta pasticciata con speck e carciofi* (oven-baked penne with cured ham and artichokes) to the finishing touch of *castagnaccio con crema di ricotta* (a chestnut flan topped with ricotta cream). ✉ *Via della Faggiola 1* ☎ *050/556179* *Reservations essential* *No credit cards* ⊙ *No dinner Nov.–Mar. Closed Sun.*

WHERE TO STAY

$$$ **Hotel Relais dell'Orologio.** What used to be a private family palace opened as an intimate hotel in spring of 2003. **Pros:** location—in the center of town, but on a quiet side street. **Cons:** breakfast costs extra. **TripAdvisor:** "medieval style," "amazing attention to detail," "sights are at your doorstep." *Via della Faggiola 12/14, off Campo dei Miracoli, Santa Maria 050/830361 050/551869 www.hotelrelaisorologio.com 16 rooms, 5 suites In-room: Wi-Fi. In-hotel: restaurant, room service, bar, parking, some pets allowed No meals.*

$$ **Royal Victoria.** In a pleasant palazzo facing the Arno, a 10-minute walk from the Campo dei Miracoli, this comfortably furnished hotel has been in the Piegaja family since 1837. **Pros:** friendly staff; free use of a Lancia that seats five—a great vehicle for tooling around Pisa. **Cons:** rooms vary significantly in size; all are a little worn. **TripAdvisor:** "has such character," "museum-quality decor," "loved the evening wine and olives." *Lungarno Pacinotti 12 050/940111 050/940180 www.royalvictoria.it 48 rooms, 40 with bath In-room: no a/c (some), Wi-Fi. In-hotel: room service, parking, some pets allowed Breakfast.*

CHIANTI

Chianti, directly south of Florence, is one of Italy's most famous wine-producing areas; its hill towns, olive groves, and vineyards are quintessential Tuscany. Many British and northern Europeans have relocated here, drawn by the unhurried life, balmy climate, and charming villages; there are so many Britons, in fact, that the area has been nicknamed Chiantishire. Still, it remains strongly Tuscan in character, with drop-dead views of vine-quilted hills and elegantly elongated cypress trees.

The sinuous SR222 highway, known as the Strada Chiantigiana, runs from Florence through the heart of Chianti. Its most scenic section connects Strada in Chianti, 16 km (10 mi) south of Florence, and Greve in Chianti, whose triangular central piazza is surrounded by restaurants and vintners offering *degustazioni* (wine tastings), 11 km (7 mi) farther south.

GREVE IN CHIANTI

40 km (25 mi) northeast of Colle Val d'Elsa, 27 km (17 mi) south of Florence.

GETTING HERE

Driving from Florence or Siena, Greve is easily reached via the Strada Chiantigiana (SR222). SITA buses travel frequently between Florence and Greve. Tra-In and SITA buses connect Siena with Greve, but a direct trip is virtually impossible. There's no train service to Greve.

VISITOR INFORMATION

Greve in Chianti tourism office (*Piazza Matteoti 10 055/8546299*).

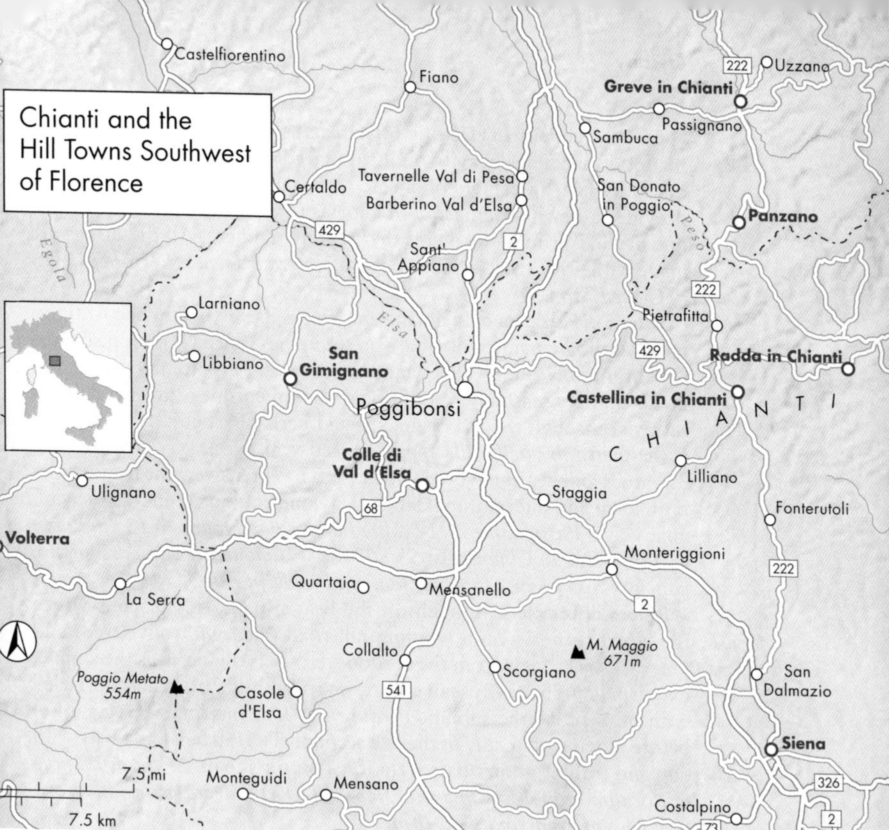

EXPLORING

If there's a capital of Chianti, it's Greve, a friendly market town with no shortage of cafés, *enoteche* (wine bars), and crafts shops lining its streets. The gently sloping, asymmetrical **Piazza Matteotti** is an attractive arcade whose center holds a statue of the discoverer of New York harbor, Giovanni da Verrazano (circa 1480–1527). Check out the lively market held here on Saturday morning.

A heavy-handed 19th-century restoration has left the medieval church of **Santa Croce** with a neoclassical facade and a rather charmless interior. Remnants of better days are evident in a triptych attributed to Bicci di Lorenzo (1373–1452) with a gold-leaf background and a small 14th-century fresco depicting the Madonna and Child. ✉ *Piazza Santa Croce 1* ☎ *055/853085* ⏲ *Daily 9–1 and 3–7.*

About 2 km (1 mi) west of Greve in Chianti is the tiny hilltop hamlet of **Montefioralle.** This is the ancestral home of Amerigo Vespucci (1454–1512), the mapmaker, navigator, and explorer who named America. (His niece Simonetta may have been the inspiration for Sandro Botticelli's *Birth of Venus*, painted sometime in the 1480s.)

WHERE TO EAT

$ TUSCAN **Enoteca Fuoripiazza.** Detour off Greve's flower-strewn main square for food that relies heavily on local ingredients (especially those produced by nearby makers of cheese and salami). The lengthy wine list provides a bewildering array of choices to pair with *affettati misti* or one of their primi—the pici is deftly prepared here. All the dishes are made with great care. *Via I Maggio 2, Piazza Trenta 055/8546313 Closed Mon.*

$$$$ ITALIAN ★ **Osteria di Passignano.** In an ancient wine cellar owned by the Antinori family (who own much of what you see in these parts) is a sophisticated restaurant ably run by chef Marcello Crini and his attentive staff. The menu changes seasonally; traditional Tuscan cuisine is given a delightful twist through the use of unexpected herbs. Particularly tantalizing is the *filetto di vitello alle spezie* (spiced veal fillet), served with roast tomatoes and beans flavored with sage. The extensive wine list includes both local and international labels. Daylong cooking courses are available. *Via Passignano 33, Località Badia a Passignano 15 km (9 mi) east of Greve in Chianti 055/8071278 www.osteriadipassignano.com Closed Sun., 3 wks in Jan., and 1 wk in Aug.*

$$$ TUSCAN ★ **Ristoro di Lamole.** Although off the beaten path, this place is worth the effort to find—up a winding hill road lined with olive trees and vineyards. The view from the outdoor terrace is divine, as is the simple, exquisitely prepared Tuscan cuisine. Start with the bruschetta drizzled with olive oil or the sublime *verdure sott'olio* (marinated vegetables) before moving on to any of the fine secondi. The kitchen has a way with *coniglio* (rabbit); don't pass it up if it's on the menu. *Via di Lamole 6, Località Lamole in Chianti 055/8547050 www.ristorodilamole.it Closed Wed. and Nov.–Apr.*

WHERE TO STAY

$ **Albergo del Chianti.** At a corner of the Piazza Matteotti, the Albergo del Chianti has rooms with views of the square or out over the tile rooftops toward the surrounding hills. **Pros:** central location; best value in Greve. **Cons:** rooms facing the piazza can be noisy; lobby is run-down; small bathrooms. **TripAdvisor:** "adjacent to the main square," "great place to relax," "wine from their own vineyards." *Piazza Matteotti 86 055/853763 www.albergodelchianti.it 16 rooms In-hotel: restaurant, bar, pool Closed Jan. Breakfast.*

$$$ Fodor's Choice ★ **Villa Bordoni.** David and Catherine Gardner, Scottish expats, have transformed a 16th-century villa into a stunning little hotel nestled in the hills above Greve. **Pros:** splendidly isolated; beautiful decor; wonderful hosts. **Cons:** on a long and bumpy dirt road. **TripAdvisor:** "like a renovated castle," "highlight of our trip," "enjoyed sitting at the bar." *Via San Cresci 31/32, Località Mezzuola 055/8547453 www.villabordoni.com 8 rooms, 3 suites In-room: Wi-Fi. In-hotel: restaurant, pool, parking Closed Feb and last 3 wks in Jan. Breakfast.*

$$ Fodor's Choice ★ **Villa Il Poggiale.** A 16th-century villa with Renaissance gardens, beautiful rooms with high ceilings and elegant furnishings, a panoramic pool, and expert staff all make a stay here memorable. **Pros:** Beautiful gardens and panoramic setting; exceptionally professional

staff. **Cons:** A little isolated; some rooms face a country road and may be noisy during the day. **TripAdvisor:** "beautiful Tuscan villa," "an enchanted garden," "very romantic." ✉ *Via Empolese 69, 20 km (12 mi) northwest of Greve, San Casciano Val di Pesa* ☎ *055/828311* 🌐 *www.villailpoggiale.it* *20 rooms, 4 suites* *In-room: Wi-Fi. In-hotel: restaurant, bar, tennis court, pool, business center* ⏲ *Closed Nov.–Easter* 🍽 *Breakfast.*

PANZANO

7 km (4½ mi) south of Greve, 29 km (18 mi) south of Florence.

GETTING HERE

From Florence or Siena, Panzano is easily reached by car along the Strada Chiantigiana (SR222). SITA buses travel frequently between Florence and Panzano. From Siena, the journey by bus is extremely difficult because SITA and Tra-In don't coordinate their schedules. There's no train service to Panzano.

EXPLORING

The magnificent views of the valleys of the Pesa and Greve rivers easily make Panzano one of the prettiest stops in Chianti. The triangular Piazza Bucciarelli is the heart of the new town. A short stroll along Via Giovanni da Verrazzano brings you up to the old town, Panzano Alto, which is still partly surrounded by medieval walls. The town's 13th-century castle is now almost completely absorbed by later buildings (its central tower is now a private home).

An ancient church even by Chianti standards, the hilltop **San Leolino** probably dates from the 10th century, but it was completely rebuilt in Romanesque style sometime in the 13th century. It has a 14th-century cloister worth seeing. The 16th-century terra-cotta tabernacles are attributed to Giovanni della Robbia, and there's also a remarkable triptych (attributed to the Master of Panzano) that was executed sometime in the mid-14th century. Opening days and hours are unpredictable; check with the tourist office in Greve in Chianti for the latest. ✢ *3 km (2 mi) south of Panzano, Località San Leolino* ☎ *No phone.*

WHERE TO EAT AND STAY

¢ ITALIAN ✕ **Dario +.** Dario Cecchini's empire of meat has extended to include a space located directly above his butcher shop. Here, you'll find only two items on the menu: the "Dario +," a half-pound burger in a crisp crumb crust, served with roast potatoes and onions; and the "Welcome," four beef and pork dishes served with fresh garden vegetables. Both are a welcome change from the conventional fare at restaurants throughout Chianti. Outdoor seating is available in summer, but get here early—it's enormously popular. Enter from the public parking area behind the restaurant. ✉ *Via XX Luglio 11,* ☎ *055/852176* 🌐 *www.dariocecchini.com* *Reservations not accepted* ⏲ *Closed Sun.*

$$ TUSCAN ✕ **Solociccia.** "Abandon all hope, ye who enter here," announces the menu, "you're in the hands of a butcher." Indeed you are, for this restaurant is the creation of Dario Cecchini, Panzano's local merchant of meat. Served at communal tables, the set meal consists of no fewer than six meat courses, chosen at Dario's discretion. They're accompanied

by seasonal vegetables, white beans with olive oil, and focaccia bread. Though Cecchini emphasizes that steak is never on the menu, this lively, crowded place is definitely not for vegetarians. The entrance is on Via XX Luglio. ✉ *Via Chiantigiana 5* ☎ *055/852727* 🌐 *www.solociccia.it* *Reservations essential* ⏲ *Closed Mon.–Wed. No dinner Sun.*

$$$ Fodor'sChoice ★ **Villa Le Barone.** Once the home of the Viviani della Robbia family, this 16th-century villa in a grove of ancient cypress trees retains many aspects of a private country dwelling. **Pros:** beautiful location; wonderful restaurant; great base for exploring the region. **Cons:** noisy air-conditioning; 20-minute walk to nearest town. **TripAdvisor:** "views of the vineyards," "lovely, serene setting," "best food we had in Italy." ✉ *Via San Leolino 19* ☎ *055/852621* 🌐 *www.villalebarone.it* *30 rooms* *In-room: no a/c (some), no TV. In-hotel: restaurant, bar, tennis court, pool, business center* ⏲ *Closed Nov.–Easter* *Breakfast.*

RADDA IN CHIANTI

26 km (15 mi) south of Panzano, 52 km (32 mi) south of Florence.

GETTING HERE

Radda can be reached by car from either Siena or Florence along the SR222 (Strada Chiantigiana), and from the A1 highway. Three Tra-In buses a day make their way from Siena to Radda. One morning SITA bus travels from Florence to Radda. There's no train service convenient to Radda.

VISITOR INFORMATION

Radda in Chianti tourism office (✉ *Piazza Ferrucci 1* ☎ *0577/738494*).

EXPLORING

Radda in Chianti sits on a hill separating two valleys, Val di Pesa and Val d'Arbia. It's one of many tiny Chianti villages that invite you to stroll their steep streets; follow the signs pointing you toward the *camminamento,* a covered medieval passageway circling part of the city inside the walls.

Palazzo del Podestà, or Palazzo Comunale, the city hall for more than four centuries, has 51 coats of arms imbedded in the facade, but apart from the tourism office, which is housed here, the building is not open to visitors. ✉ *Piazza Ferrucci 1.*

★ If you have time for only one castle, visit the stunning **Castello di Brolio.** At the end of the 12th century, when Florence conquered southern Chianti, Brolio became Florence's southernmost outpost, and it was often said, "When Brolio growls, all Siena trembles." Brolio was built about AD 1000 and owned by the monks of the Badia Fiorentina; the "new" owners, the Ricasoli family, have been in possession since 1141. Bettino Ricasoli (1809–80), the so-called Iron Baron, was one of the founders of modern Italy, and is said to have invented the original formula for Chianti wine. Brolio, one of Chianti's best-known labels, is still justifiably famous. Its cellars may be toured by appointment. The grounds are worth visiting, even though the 19th-century manor house is not open to the public. (The current baron is very much in residence.) A small museum, where the Ricasoli Collection is housed in a 12th-century tower, displays objects that relate the long history of the family and the origins of Chianti

Continued on page 645

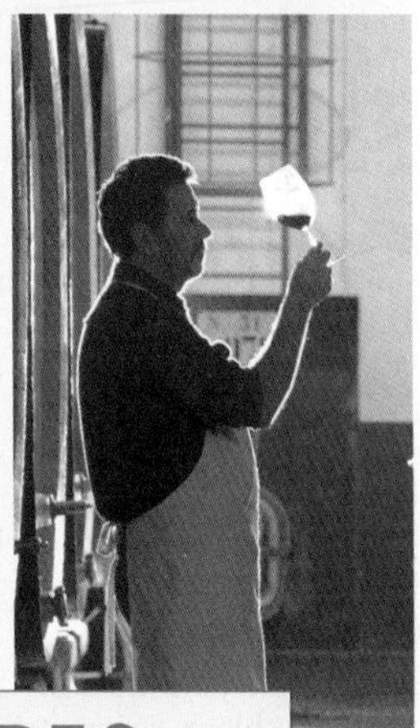

GRAPE ESCAPES

THE PLEASURES OF TUSCAN WINE

The vineyards stretching across the landscape of Tuscany may look like cinematic backdrops, but in fact they're working farms, and they produce some of Italy's best wines. No matter whether you're a wine novice or a connoisseur, there's great pleasure to be had from exploring this lush terrain, visiting the vineyards, and uncorking a bottle for yourself.

GETTING TO KNOW TUSCAN WINE

Most of the wine produced in Tuscany is red (though there are some notable whites as well), and most Tuscan reds are made primarily from one type of grape, sangiovese. That doesn't mean, however, that all wines here are the same. God (in this case Bacchus) is in the details: differences in climate, soil, and methods of production result in wines with several distinct personalities.

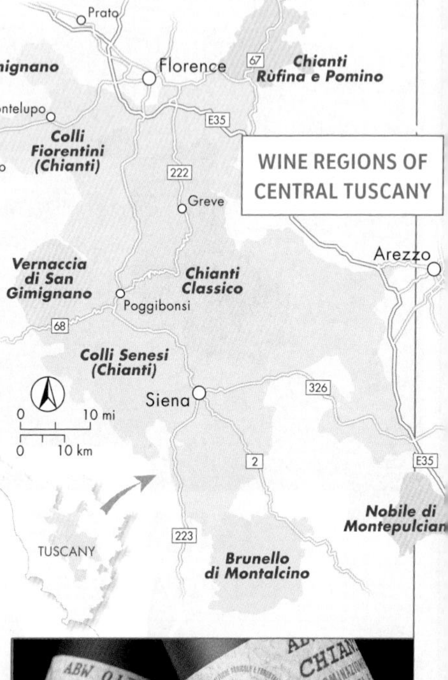

Chianti

Chianti is the most famous name in Tuscan wine, but what exactly the name means is a little tricky. It once identified wines produced in the region extending from just south of Florence to just north of Siena. In the mid-20th century, the official Chianti zone was expanded to include a large portion of central Tuscany. That area is divided into eight subregions. **Chianti Classico** is the name given to the original zone, which makes up 17,000 of the 42,000 acres of Chianti-producing vineyards.

Classico wines, which bear the *gallo nero* (black rooster) logo on their labels, are the most highly regarded Chiantis (with **Rùfina** running second), but that doesn't mean Classicos are always superior. All Chiantis are strictly regulated (they must be a minimum 75% to 80% sangiovese, with other varieties blended in to add nuance), and they share a strong, woodsy character that's well suited to Tuscan food. It's a good strategy to drink the local product—**Colli Senesi Chianti** when in Siena, for example. The most noticeable, and costly, difference comes when a Chianti is from *riserva* (reserve) stock, meaning it's been aged for at least two years.

DOC & DOCG The designations "DOC" and "DOCG"—Denominazione di Origine Controllata (e Garantita)—mean a wine comes from an established region and adheres to rigorous standards of production. Ironically, the esteemed Super Tuscans are labeled *vini da tavola* (table wines), the least prestigious designation, because they don't use traditional grape blends.

Brunello di Montalcino

The area surrounding the hill town of Montalcino, to the south of Siena, is drier and warmer than the Chianti regions, and it produces the most powerful of the sangiovese-based wines. Regulations stipulate that Brunello di Montalcino be made entirely from sangiovese grapes (no blending) and aged at least four years. **Rosso di Montalcino** is a younger, less complex, less expensive Brunello.

The Super Tuscans

Beginning in the 1970s, some winemakers, chafing at the regulations imposed on established Tuscan wine varieties, began blending and aging wines in innovative ways. Thus were born the so-called Super Tuscans. These pricey, French oak–aged wines are admired for their high quality, led by such star performers as **Sassicaia**, from the Maremma region, and **Tignanello**, produced at the Tenuta Marchesi Antinori near Badia a Passignano. Purists, however, lament the loss of local identity resulting from the Super Tuscans' use of nonnative grape varieties such as cabernet sauvignon and merlot.

Vino Nobile di Montepulciano

East of Montalcino is Montepulciano, the town at the heart of the third, and smallest, of Tuscany's top wine districts.

Blending regulations aren't as strict for Vino Nobile as for Chianti and Brunello, and as a result it has a wider range of characteristics. Broadly speaking, though, Vino Nobile is a cross between Chianti and Brunello—less acidic than the former and softer than the latter. It also has a less pricey sibling, **Rosso di Montepulciano.**

The Whites

Most whites from Tuscany are made from **trebbiano** grapes, which produce a wine that's light and refreshing but not particularly aromatic or flavorful—it may hit the spot on a hot afternoon, but it doesn't excite connoisseurs.

Golden-hewed **Vernaccia di San Gimignano** is a local variety with more limited production but greater personality—it's the star of Tuscan whites. Winemakers have also brought chardonnay and sauvignon grapes to the region, resulting in wines that, like some Super Tuscans, are pleasant to drink but short on local character.

TOURING & TASTING IN TUSCAN WINE COUNTRY

Tuscany has visitor-friendly wineries, but the way you go about visiting is a bit different here from what it is in California or France. Many wineries welcome drop-ins for a tasting, but for a tour you usually need to make an appointment a few days in advance. There are several approaches you can take, depending on how much time you have and how serious you are about wine:

PLAN 1: FULL IMMERSION. Make an appointment to tour one of the top wineries (see our recommendations on the next page), and you'll get the complete experience: half a day of strolling through vineyards, talking grape varieties, and tasting wine, often accompanied by food. Groups are small; in spring and fall, it may be just you and the winemaker. The cost is usually €10 to €15 per person, but can go up to €40 if a meal is included. Remember to specify a tour in English.

PLAN 2: SEMI-ORGANIZED. If you want to spend a few hours going from vineyard to vineyard, make your first stop one of the local tourist information offices—they're great resources for maps, tasting itineraries, and personalized advice about where to visit. The offices in **Greve**, **Montalcino**, and **Montepulciano** are the best equipped. **Enoteche** (for more about them, turn the page) can also be good places to pick up tips about where to go for tastings.

PLAN 3: SPONTANEOUS. Along Tuscany's country roads you'll see signs for wineries offering **vendita diretta** (direct sales) and **degustazioni** (tastings). For a taste of the local product with some atmosphere thrown in, a spontaneous visit is a perfectly viable approach. You may wind up in a simple shop or an elaborate tasting room; either way, there's a fair chance you'll sample something good. Expect a small fee for a three-glass tasting.

THE PICK OF THE VINEYARDS

Within the Chianti Classico region, these wineries should be at the top of your to-visit list, whether you're dropping in for a taste or making a full tour. (Tours require reservations unless otherwise indicated.)

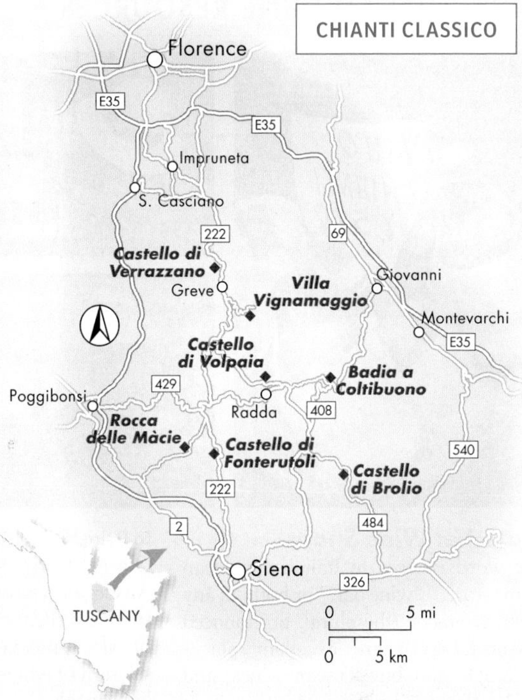

Badia a Coltibuono (✉ Gaiole in Chianti ☎ 0577/749498 🌐 www.coltibuono.com). Along with an extensive prelunch tour and tasting, there are shorter afternoon tours, no reservation required, starting on the hour from 2 to 5. (See "Radda in Chianti" in this chapter.)

Castello di Fonterutoli (✉ Castellina in Chianti ☎ 0577/73571 🌐 www.fonterutoli.it). Hour-long tours include a walk through the neighboring village.

Castello di Volpaia (✉ Radda in Chianti ☎ 0577/738066 🌐 www.volpaia.com). The winery is part of the tiny town of Volpaia, perched above Radda.

Castello di Verrazzano (✉ Via S. Martino in Valle 12, Greve in Chianti ☎ 055/854243 🌐 www.verrazzano.com). Tours here take you down to the cellars, through the gardens, and into the woods in search of wild boar.

Villa Vignamaggio (✉ Via Petriolo 5, Greve in Chianti ☎ 055/854661 🌐 www.vignamaggio.com). Along with a wine tour, you can spend the night at this villa where Mona Lisa is believed to have been born. (See "Where to Stay" under "Greve in Chianti" in this chapter.)

Rocca delle Màcie (✉ Località Le Macìe 45, Castellina in Chianti ☎ 0577/732236 🌐 www.roccadellemacie.com). A full lunch or dinner can be incorporated into your tasting here.

Castello di Brolio (✉ Gaiole in Chianti ☎ 0577/730220 🌐 www.ricasoli.it). One of Tuscany's most impressive castles also has a centuries-old winemaking tradition. (See "Radda in Chianti" in this chapter.)

REMEMBER 

Always have a designated driver when you're touring and tasting. Vineyards are usually located off narrow, curving roads. Full sobriety is a must behind the wheel.

MORE TUSCAN WINE RESOURCES

Enoteche: Wine Shops

The word *enoteca* in Italian can mean "wine store," "wine bar," or both. In any event, *enoteche* (the plural, pronounced "ay-no-*tek*-ay") are excellent places to sample and buy Tuscan wines, and they're also good sources of information about local wineries. There are scores to choose from. These are a few of the best:

Enoteca Italiana, Siena (Fortezza Medicea, Viale Maccari ☎ 0577/288497 🌐 www.enoteca-italiana.it). The only one of its kind, this *enoteca* represents all the producers of DOC and DOCG wines in Italy and stocks over 400 labels. Wine by the glass and snacks are available.

Enoteca Osticcio, Montalcino (✉ Via Matteotti 23 ☎ 0577/848271 🌐 www.osticcio.com). There are more than one thousand labels in stock. With one of the best views in Montalcino, it is also a very pleasant place to sit and meditate over a glass of Brunello.

Enoteca del Gallo Nero, Greve in Chianti (✉ Piazzetta S. Croce 8 ☎ 055/853297). This is one of the best stocked *enoteche* in the Chianti region.

La Dolce Vita, Montepulciano (Via di Voltaia nel Corso 80/82 ☎ 0578/757872). An elegantly restored monastery is home to the excellent enoteca in the upper part of Montepulciano, which has a wide selction of wines by the glass and serves light meals.

Wine on the Web

Tuscan wine country is well represented on the Internet. A good place for an overview is 🌐 www.terreditoscana.regione.toscana.it. (Click on "Le Strade del Vino"; the page that opens next will give you the option of choosing an English-language version.) This site shows 14 *strade del vino* (wine roads) that have been mapped out by consortiums representing major wine districts (unfortunately, Chianti Classico isn't included), along with recommended itineraries.

The Chianti Classico consortium's site is 🌐 www.chianticlassico.com. The Vino Nobile di Montepulciano site is 🌐 www.vinonobiledimontepulciano.it, and Brunello di Montalcino is 🌐 www.consorziobrunellodimontalcino.it. All have English versions.

wine. There are two apartments here available for rent by the week. ✉ *Località Brolio* ✣ *2 km (1 mi) southeast of Gaiole* ☎ *0577/730280* *www.ricasoli.it* 🎫 *€5* gardens, €8 gardens and museum, €10 guided tour ⏲ *Last 2 wks Mar., Mon.–Fri. 10–6:30, weekends 11–6:30; Apr.–Oct., daily 10–7. Last entrance 1 hr before closing. Guided tours: daily 3, Wed. and Fri.–Mon. 10:30, Mon. and Fri. 5; must be booked in advance.*

North of Gaiole a turnoff leads to the **Badia a Coltibuono** *(Abbey of the Good Harvest)*, which has been owned by Lorenza de' Medici's family for more than a century and a half (the family isn't closely related to the Renaissance-era Medici). Wine has been produced here since the abbey was founded by Vallombrosan monks in the 11th century. Today the family continues the tradition, making Chianti Classico and other wines, along with cold-pressed olive oil and various flavored vinegars and floral honeys. A small Romanesque church with campanile is surrounded by 2,000 acres of oak, fir, and chestnut woods threaded with walking paths—open to all—that pass two small lakes. Though the abbey itself, built between the 11th and 18th centuries, serves as the family's home, parts are open for tours (in English, German, or Italian). Visit the jasmine-draped main courtyard, the inner cloister with its antique well, the musty old aging cellars, and the Renaissance-style garden redolent of lavender, lemons, and roses. In the shop, **L'Osteria,** you can taste wine and honey, as well as pick up other items like homemade beeswax hand lotion in little ceramic dishes. The Badia is closed on public holidays. ✉ *Località Badia a Coltibuono* ✣ *4 km (2½ mi) north of Gaiole* ☎ *0577/749498 for tours, 0577/749479 for shop* 🌐 *www.coltibuono.com* 🎫 *Abbey €5* ⏲ *Tours: May–Oct., weekdays at 2, 3, 4, and 5; shop: Mar.–mid-Jan., daily 9–1 and 2–7.*

WHERE TO EAT

$ TUSCAN Fodor's Choice ★

✕ **Osteria Le Panzanelle.** Silvia Bonechi's experience in the kitchen—armed with a few precious recipes handed down from her grandmother—is one of the reasons for the success of this small restaurant. The other is the front-room hospitality of Nada Michelassi. These two *panzanelle* (women from Panzano) serve a short menu of tasty and authentic dishes at what the locals refer to as *prezzi giusti* (the right prices). Both the *pappa al pomodoro* (tomato soup) and the *peposo* (peppery beef stew) are exceptional. Whether you're eating inside or under large umbrellas on the terrace near a tiny stream, the experience is always congenial. "The best food we had in Tuscany," writes one user of fodors.com. Reservations are essential in July and August. ✉ *Località Lucarelli 29* ✣ *8 km (5 mi) northwest of Radda on road to Panzano* ☎ *0577/733511* 🌐 *www.osteria.lepanzanelle.it* ⏲ *Closed Mon. and Jan. and Feb.*

¢ 🏨 **La Bottega di Giovannino.** The name is actually that of the wine bar run by Giovannino Bernardoni and his daughter Monica, who also rent rooms in the house next door. **Pros:** great location in the center of town; close to restaurants and shops; super value. **Cons:** some rooms are small; some bathrooms are down the hall; basic decor. **TripAdvisor:** "a can't-miss experience," "view of the rolling countryside," "rates were so inexpensive." ✉ *Via Roma 6–8* ☎ *0577/738056* 🌐 *www.labottegadigiovannino.it* *10 rooms, 2 apartments* *In-room: no a/c. In-hotel: bar* *No meals.*

$$ **Palazzo San Niccolò.** A 19th-century palace conveniently located in the center of Radda has been converted into an elegant hotel. **Pros:** central location; friendly service. **Cons:** some rooms face a main street; some rooms and bathrooms are on the small side. **TripAdvisor:** "refurbished medieval palace," "gorgeous frescoes," "splendid, romantic and quiet." *Via Roma 16 0577/735666 www.hotelsanniccolo.com 17 rooms, 1 suite In-room: a/c, Internet. In-hotel: bar, business center, some pets allowed Closed Nov.–Mar. Breakfast.*

$$$ Fodor's Choice ★ **Relais Fattoria Vignale.** On the outside, it's a rather plain manor house with an annex across the street; inside, it's a refined and comfortable country house with numerous sitting rooms that have terra-cotta floors and nice stonework. **Pros:** intimate public spaces; excellent restaurant; helpful and friendly staff. **Cons:** north-facing rooms blocked by tall cypress trees; single rooms are small; annex across a busy road. **TripAdvisor:** "overlooking the hills," "large, beautiful fireplace," "beautiful pool." *Via Pianigiani 9 0577/738300 hotel, 0577/738094 restaurant, 0577/738012 enoteca www.vignale.it 37 rooms, 5 suites In-hotel: restaurant, bar, pool, business center Closed Nov.–Mar. 15 Breakfast.*

CASTELLINA IN CHIANTI

14 km (8 mi) west of Radda, 59 km (35 mi) south of Florence.

GETTING HERE

As with all the towns along the Strada Chiantigiana (SR222), Castellina is an easy drive from either Siena or Florence. From Siena, Castellina is well served by the local Tra-In bus company. However, only one bus a day travels here from Florence. The closest train station is at Castellina Scalo, some 15 km (9 mi) away.

VISITOR INFORMATION

Castellina tourism office (*Piazza del Comune 1 0577/741392*).

EXPLORING

Castellina in Chianti, or simply Castellina, is on a ridge above the Val di Pesa, Val d'Arbia, and Val d'Elsa, with beautiful panoramas in every direction. The imposing 14th-century tower in the central piazza hints at the history of this village, which was an outpost during the continuing wars between Florence and Siena. Don't miss a walk along Via delle Volte, a covered passage that follows the medieval walls on one side of the town.

WHERE TO EAT

$$$ TUSCAN **Albergaccio.** The fact that the dining room can seat only 35 guests makes a meal here an intimate experience. The ever-changing menu mixes traditional and creative dishes. In late September and October *zuppa di funghi e castagne* (mushroom and chestnut soup) is a treat, as is the *colombaccio scaloppato* (sliced pigeon in a white wine and anchovy sauce); grilled meats and seafood are on the list throughout the year. There's also an excellent wine list. When the weather is warm, the best spot to dine is on the terrace. *Via Fiorentina 25 0577/741042 www.albergacciocast.com Reservations essential No credit cards Closed Sun. No lunch Wed. and Thurs.*

$–$$ TUSCAN ✕ **Ristorante Le Tre Porte.** The specialty of the house, a thick slab of beef called *bistecca alla fiorentina,* is usually served very rare. Paired with grilled fresh porcini mushrooms when in season (in spring and fall), it's a heady dish. The main floor of the restaurant has a small dining room serving full-course meals. In the evening a second room is opened downstairs where you can order pizzas from the wood-burning oven. Reservations are essential in July and August. ✉ *Via Trento e Trieste 4* ☎ *0577/741163* ⊙ *Closed Tues.*

$–$$ TUSCAN ✕ **Sotto Le Volte.** As the name suggests, you'll find this small restaurant under the arches of Castellina's medieval walkway. The restaurant has vaulted ceilings as well, which make for a particularly romantic setting. The menu is short and eminently Tuscan, with the usual soups and pasta dishes that you find everywhere. The *costolette di agnello alle erbe* (herbed lamb chops) are especially tasty. ✉ *Via delle Volte 14-16* ☎ *0577/056530* ▭ *No credit cards* ⊙ *Closed Wed.*

WHERE TO STAY

$–$$ Fodor's Choice ★ **Palazzo Squarcialupi.** In the center of Castellina, this 15th-century palace is a tranquil place to stay, and rooms are spacious, with high ceilings, tile floors, and 18th-century furnishings; bathrooms are tiled in local stone. **Pros:** great location; elegant public spaces. **Cons:** on a street with no car access; across from a noisy restaurant. **TripAdvisor:** "common rooms are wonderful," "gorgeous Chianti countryside," "fantastic spa."✉ *Via Ferruccio 22* ☎ *0577/741186* 📠 *0577/740386* 🌐 *www.palazzosquarcialupi.com* *17 rooms* *In-hotel: bar, pool, some pets allowed* ⊙ *Closed Nov.–Mar.* 🍽 *Breakfast.*

HILL TOWNS SOUTHWEST OF FLORENCE

Submit to the draw of Tuscany's enchanting fortified cities that crown the hills west of Siena, many dating to the Etruscan period. San Gimignano, known as the "medieval Manhattan" because of its forest of stout medieval towers built by rival families, is the most heavily visited. This onetime Roman outpost, with its tilted cobbled streets and ancient buildings, can make the days of Guelph-Ghibelline conflicts palpable. Rising from a series of bleak gullied hills and valleys, Volterra has always been popular for its minerals and stones, particularly alabaster, which was used by the Etruscans for many implements. Examples are now displayed in the exceptional (and exceptionally large) Museo Etrusco Guarnacci.

VOLTERRA

48 km (30 mi) south of San Miniato, 75 km (47 mi) southwest of Florence.

GETTING HERE

By car, the best route from San Gimignano follows the SP1 south to Castel San Gimignano and then the SS68 all the way to Volterra. Coming from the west, take the SS1, a coastal road to Cecina, then follow the SS68 to Volterra. Either way, there's a long, winding climb at the end of your trip. Getting here by bus or train is complicated; avoid it if possible. From Florence or Siena, the journey is best made by bus and involves a change in Colle di Val d'Elsa.

VISITOR INFORMATION

Volterra tourism office (✉ *Piazza dei Priori 20* ☎ *0588/87257* 🌐 *www.volterratur.it*).

EXPLORING

Unlike other Tuscan hill towns rising above sprawling vineyards and rolling fields of green, Volterra is surrounded by desolate terrain marred with industry and mining equipment. D.H. Lawrence described it as "somber and chilly alone on her rock" in his *Etruscan Places*. Its fortress (now a maximum-security prison), walls, and gates still stand mightily over Le Balze, a distinctive series of gullied hills and valleys to the west that were formed by irregular erosion. But don't be put off by this gloomy introduction. Volterra is a lively and fascinating town that grows on you with each visit. There are spectacular views from the outer walls, winding narrow streets bustling with activity, and some amazing museums and archeological sites. (Even the inmates of the prison have become internationally famous for their theatrical performances!) The town has also long been known for its alabaster, which has been mined since Etruscan times; today the Volterrans use it to make ornaments and souvenirs. You'll find it sold all over town, and you may have the chance to peek into an artisan's studio to see the work in progress.

Volterra has some of Italy's best small museums. The extraordinarily large and unique collection of Etruscan artifacts at the **Museo Etrusco Guarnacci** is a treasure in the region. (Many of the other Etruscan finds from the area have been shipped off to state museums or the Vatican.) If only a curator had thought to cull the best of the 700 funerary urns rather than to display every last one of them. ✉ *Via Don Minzoni 15* ☎ *0588/86347* 🌐 *www.comune.volterra.pi.it* 🎫 *€8, includes admission to Museo Diocesano di Arte Sacra and Pinacoteca* ⏲ *Mid-Mar.–early Nov., daily 9–6:45; early Nov.–mid-Mar., daily 9–1:15.*

The **Pinacoteca e Museo Civico** houses a highly acclaimed collection of religious art, including a *Madonna and Child with Saints* by Luca Signorelli (1445/50–1523) and a *Deposition* by Rosso Fiorentino (1494–1541). These alone are reason enough to visit Volterra. ✉ *Via dei Sarti 1* ☎ *0588/87580* 🌐 *www.comune.volterra.pi.it* 🎫 *€8, includes admission to Museo Etrusco Guarnacci and Museo Diocesano di Arte Sacra* ⏲ *Mid-Mar.–early Nov., daily 9–7; early Nov.–mid-Mar., daily 9–1:45.*

Next to the altar in the town's unfinished **Duomo** is a magnificent 13th-century carved-wood *Deposition*. Note the fresco by Benozzo Gozzoli in the Cappella della Addolorata depicting the Arrival of the Magi as a backdrop to a terra-cotta nativity scene attributed to Andrea della Robbia. The gilt-wood ceiling (1580) above the nave is particularly fine. ✉ *Piazza San Giovanni* ☎ *0588/86192* ⏲ *Daily 7–7.*

Among Volterra's best-preserved ancient remains is the Etruscan **Porta all'Arco**, an arch dating from the 4th century BC, and once part of the ancient city walls. Just outside the arch, a commemorative plaque commemorates the citizens of Volterra who blocked this entrance to town to prevent its destruction by the occupying Nazi troops.

The ruins of the 1st-century BC **Teatro Romano**, a beautifully preserved Roman theater, are worth a visit. Behind the theater are the remains of the *terme* (baths) from the 4th century AD. The complex is outside the town walls to the left of Porta Fiorentina. ✉ *Viale Francesco Ferrucci* ☎ *0586/260837* €2 ⏲ *Mar.–May and Sept.–Nov., daily 10–1 and 2–4; June–Aug., daily 10–6:45; Dec.–Feb., weekends 10–1 and 2–4.*

WHERE TO EAT AND STAY

$$ TUSCAN ★ ✕ **Il Sacco Fiorentino.** Start with the *antipasti del Sacco Fiorentino*—a medley of sautéed chicken liver, porcini mushrooms, and polenta drizzled with balsamic vinegar. The meal just gets better when you move on to the tagliatelle *del Sacco Fiorentino,* a riot of curried spaghetti with chicken and roasted red peppers. The wine list is a marvel, as it's long and very well priced. White walls, tile floors, and red tablecloths create an understated tone that's unremarkable, but once the food starts arriving, it's easy to forgive the lack of decoration. ✉ *Piazza XX Settembre 18* ☎ *0588/88537* ⏲ *Closed Wed.*

$ ★ **Etruria.** Giuseppina and Lisa, owners of this simple yet tasteful hotel, go out of their way to make your visit memorable. **Pros:** on a pedestrian street; helpful staff; tranquil garden. **Cons:** rooms can be noisy during the day; steps to climb; some bathrooms old-fashioned and small. **TripAdvisor:** "felt the pull of history," "delightful rooftop garden," "staff is super-friendly."✉ *Via Matteotti 32* ☎ *0588/87377* 🌐 *www.albergoetruria.it* *21 rooms* *In-room: no a/c. In-hotel: business center* *Breakfast.*

$ **San Lino.** Within the town's medieval walls, this convent-turned-hotel has wood-beam ceilings, graceful archways, and terra-cotta floors in public spaces. **Pros:** steps away from center of town; friendly and helpful staff; convenient parking. **Cons:** a little run-down; elevators are noisy; breakfast is adequate, but nothing to write home about. **TripAdvisor:** "beautiful facade," "plenty of deck space," "just fine for the price."✉ *Via San Lino 26* ☎ *0588/85250* *0588/80620* 🌐 *www.hotelsanlino.com* *43 rooms* *In-hotel: restaurant, bar, pool, parking, some pets allowed* ⏲ *Closed Nov.–Jan.* *Breakfast.*

SAN GIMIGNANO

27 km (17 mi) east of Volterra, 57 km (35 mi) southwest of Florence.

GETTING HERE

You can reach San Gimignano by car from the Florence–Siena Superstrada. Exit at Poggibonsi Nord and follow signs for San Gimignano. Although it involves changing buses in Poggibonsi, getting to San Gimignano by bus is a relatively straightforward affair. SITA operates the service between Siena or Florence and Poggibonsi, while Tra-In takes care of the Poggibonsi to San Gimignano route. If you're traveling with luggage, be aware that there are no storage facilities available. You cannot reach San Gimignano by train.

VISITOR INFORMATION

San Gimignano tourism office (✉ *Piazza Duomo 1* ☎ *0577/940008* 🌐 *www.sangimignano.com*).

EXPLORING

When you're on a hilltop surrounded by soaring medieval towers silhouetted against the sky, it's difficult not to fall under the spell of San Gimignano. Its tall walls and narrow streets are typical of Tuscan hill towns, but it's the medieval "skyscrapers" that set the town apart from its neighbors. Today 14 towers remain, but at the height of the Guelph–Ghibelline conflict there was a forest of more than 70, and it was possible to cross the town by rooftop rather than by road. The towers were built partly for defensive purposes—they were a safe refuge and useful for pouring boiling oil on attacking enemies—and partly for bolstering the egos of their owners, who competed with deadly seriousness to build the highest tower in town.

WORD OF MOUTH

"It's nice to arrive in San Gimignano after the bus tours leave for the day. Make sure you take a walk around the walls of the town . . . it's lovely in the morning. There's a path to follow and the views are jaw dropping."
—CRAZY4TRAVEL

Today San Gimignano isn't much more than a gentrified walled city, touristy but still very much worth exploring because, despite the profusion of cheesy souvenir shops lining the main drag, there's some serious Renaissance art to be seen here. Tour groups arrive early and clog the wine-tasting rooms—San Gimignano is famous for its light white Vernaccia—and art galleries for much of the day, but most sights stay open through late afternoon, when all the tour groups have long since departed.

San Gimignano is particularly beautiful in the early morning. Take time to walk up to the rocca (castle), at the highest point of town. Here, you can enjoy 360° views of the surrounding countryside. Apart from when it's used for summer outdoor film festivals, it's always open.

The town's main church is not officially a *duomo* (cathedral) because San Gimignano has no bishop. Behind the simple facade of the Romanesque **Collegiata** lies a treasure trove of fine frescoes, covering nearly every part of the interior. Bartolo di Fredi's 14th-century fresco cycle of Old Testament scenes extends along one wall. Their distinctly medieval feel, with misshapen bodies, buckets of spurting blood, and lack of perspective, contrasts with the much more reserved scenes from the *Life of Christ* (attributed to 14th-century artist Lippo Memmi), painted on the opposite wall just 14 years later. Taddeo di Bartolo's otherworldly *Last Judgment* (late 14th century), with its distorted and suffering nudes, reveals the great influence of Dante's horrifying imagery in *The Inferno* and was surely an inspiration for later painters. Proof that the town had more than one protector, Benozzo Gozzoli's arrow-riddled *St. Sebastian* was commissioned in gratitude after the locals prayed to the saint for relief from plague. The Renaissance **Cappella di Santa Fina** is decorated with a fresco cycle by Domenico Ghirlandaio illustrating the life of Saint Fina. A small girl who suffered from a terminal disease, Fina repented for her sins—among them having accepted an orange from a boy—and in penance lived out the rest of her short life on a wooden board, tormented by rats. The scenes depict the arrival of Saint Gregory, who appeared to assure her that death was near; the flowers that miraculously grew from the wooden plank; and the miracles that accompanied her funeral, including the healing of her nurse's paralyzed hand and the restoration of a blind choirboy's vision. ✉ *Piazza Pecori 2* ☎ *0577/940316* 🎫 *€3.50; €5.50 includes the Museo d'Arte Sacra* ⏲ *Apr.–Oct., weekdays 10–7:10, Sat. 10–5:10, Sun. 12:30–7:10; Nov. 1–15, Dec. 1–Jan. 15, and Feb. 1–Mar., Mon.–Sat. 10–4:40, Sun. 12:30–4:10. Closed Nov. 16–30, and Jan. 16–31.*

★ The impressive **Museo Civico** occupies what was the "new" Palazzo del Popolo; the Torre Grossa is adjacent. Dante visited San Gimignano for only one day as a Guelph ambassador from Florence to ask the locals to join the Florentines in supporting the pope—just long enough to get the main council chamber, which now holds a 14th-century *Maestà* by Lippo Memmi, named after him. Off the stairway is a small room containing the racy frescoes by Memmo di Filippuccio (active 1288–1324) depicting the courtship, shared bath, and wedding of a young, androgynous-looking couple. That the space could have been a private room for the commune's chief magistrate may have something to do with the work's highly charged eroticism.

Upstairs, paintings by famous Renaissance artists Pinturicchio (*Madonna Enthroned*), Benozzo Gozzoli (*Madonna and Child*), and two large *tondi* (circular paintings) by Filippino Lippi (circa 1457–1504) attest to the importance and wealth of San Gimignano. Also worth seeing are Taddeo di Bartolo's *Life of San Gimignano,* with the saint holding a model of the town as it once appeared; Lorenzo di Niccolò's gruesome martyrdom scene in the *Life of St. Bartholomew* (1401); and scenes from the *Life of St. Fina* on a tabernacle that was designed to hold her head. Admission includes the steep climb to the top of the Torre Grossa, which on a clear day has spectacular views. ✉ *Piazza Duomo 2* ☎ *0577/990312* 🎫 *€5; €7.50 includes tower, archaeological museum, modern art gallery, and ornithological museum* ⏲ *Apr.–Oct., daily 9:30–7; Nov.–Mar., daily 10–5:30.*

★ Make a beeline for Benozzo Gozzoli's superlative frescoes inside the church of **Sant'Agostino**. This Romanesque-Gothic church contains Benozzo's stunning 15th-century fresco cycle depicting scenes from the life of Saint Augustine. The saint's work was essential to the early development of church doctrine. As thoroughly discussed in his autobiographical *Confessions* (an acute dialogue with God), Augustine, like many saints, sinned considerably in his youth before finding God. But unlike the lives of other saints, where the story continues through a litany of deprivations, penitence, and often martyrdom, Augustine's life and work focused on philosophy and the reconciliation of faith and thought. Benozzo's 17 scenes on the choir wall depict Augustine as a man who traveled and taught extensively in the 4th and 5th centuries. The 15th-century altarpiece by Piero del Pollaiolo (1443–96) depicts *The Coronation of the Virgin* and the various protectors of the city. On your way out of Sant'Agostino, stop at the **Cappella di San Bartolo,** with a sumptuously elaborate tomb by Benedetto da Maiano (1442–97). ✉ *Piazza Sant'Agostino, off Via San Matteo* ☎ *0577/907012* ⏲ *Apr.–Oct., daily 7–noon and 3–7; Nov. 1–23 and Dec. 16–Feb., daily 7–noon and 3–6; Nov. 24–Dec. 15, Tues.–Sun. 7–noon and 3–6;-Mar., Mon. 4–6, Tues.-Sat. 10–noon and 3–6, and Sun. 8–noon and 3–7.*

WHERE TO EAT

¢ WINE BAR ★ **Enoteca Gustavo.** The ebullient Maristella Becucci reigns supreme in this tiny wine bar (three small tables in the back, two in the bar, two bar stools) serving divine, and ample, crostini. The *crostino con carciofini e pecorino* (toasted bread with artichokes topped with semi-aged pecorino) packs a punch. The changing list of wines by the glass has about 16 reds and whites, mostly local, all good. The cheese plate is a bit more expensive than the crostini, but it's worth it. *Via San Matteo 29* *0577/940057* *Reservations not accepted* *Closed Tues. Oct.–Mar.*

$$ TUSCAN **Osteria del Carcere.** There's no shortage of places to eat in tourist-packed San Gimignano, but, despite portions that can be on the small side, Il Carroccio stands out for the quality of its fare. The menu is traditional Tuscan, with bruschetta, pappa al pomodoro, and typical pasta dishes all available. The *faraona con le castagne* (guinea fowl with chestnuts) and the *tonno del Chianti con fagioli* (pork cooked in white wine with beans) are excellent, and the desserts are all homemade. *Via del Castello 13* *0577/941905* *No credit cards* *Closed Wed. No lunch Thurs.*

WHERE TO STAY

$$$$ **La Collegiata.** After serving as a Franciscan convent and then residence of the noble Strozzi family, the Collegiata has been transformed into a fine hotel. **Pros:** gorgeous views from terrace; elegant rooms in main building. **Cons:** long walk into town; service can be impersonal; some rooms dimly lit. **TripAdvisor:** "old-world feel," "four-star modern luxury," "meticulous attention to detail." *Località Strada 27, 1 km (½ mi) north of town center* *0577/943201* *www.relaischateaux.com* *20 rooms, 1 suite* *In-hotel: restaurant, room service, bars, pool, parking, some pets allowed* *Closed Jan. 7–Mar. 12* *No meals.*

$–$$ **Pescille.** A rambling farmhouse has been transformed into a handsome hotel with understated contemporary furniture in the bedrooms and country-classic motifs such as farm implements hanging on the walls in the bar. **Pros:** splendid views; quiet atmosphere; 10-minute walk to town. **Cons:** furnishings a bit austere; there's an elevator for luggage but not for guests. **TripAdvisor:** "ideal country stay," "friendly and casual atmosphere," "pool with a spectacular view." *Strada Provinciale Castel San Gimignano, Località Pescille 4 km (2½ mi) south of San Gimignano town center* *0577/940186* *www.pescille.it* *38 rooms, 12 suites* *In-room: Wi-Fi. In-hotel: bar, tennis court, pool, gym, business center, parking* *Closed Nov.–Mar.* *Breakfast.*

$$ **Torraccia di Chiusi.** A perfect retreat for families, this tranquil hilltop *agriturismo* (farm stay) with its own restaurant and extensive grounds, is just 5 km (3 mi) from the hubbub of San Gimignano. **Pros:** tranquil haven close to San Gimignano; great walking possibilities; family-run hospitality. **Cons:** 30 minutes by car from nearest town. **TripAdvisor:** "heart of the Tuscan countryside," "peaceful and quiet," "excellent public rooms." *Località Montauto* *0577/941972* *www.torracciadichiusi.com* *8 rooms, 3 apartments* *In-room: no a/c, no safe, kitchen (some). In-hotel: restaurant, pool, sauna, some pets allowed* *Breakfast.*

COLLE DI VAL D'ELSA

15 km (9 mi) southeast of San Gimignano, 50 km (31 mi) southwest of Florence.

GETTING HERE

You can reach Colle di Val d'Elsa by car on either the SR2 from Siena or the Florence-Siena Superstrada. Bus service to and from Siena and Florence is frequent.

VISITOR INFORMATION

Colle di Val d'Elsa Tourism Office (✉ *Via Campana 43* ☎ *0577/922791*).

EXPLORING

Most people pass through on their way to and from popular tourist destinations Volterra and San Gimignano—a shame, since Colle di Val d'Elsa has a lot to offer. It's another town on the Via Francigena that benefited from trade along the pilgrimage route to Rome. Colle got an extra boost in the late 16th century when it was given a bishopric, probably related to an increase in trade when nearby San Gimignano was cut off from the well-traveled road.

The town is arranged on two levels, and from the 12th century onward the flat lower portion was given over to a flourishing paper-making industry; today the area is mostly modern, and efforts have shifted toward the production of fine glass and crystal—surprisingly, 15 percent of the world's fine crystal is made here. Colle alto (the upper town) should not be missed. It's essentially a one street affair that runs gently uphill from a panoramic terrace overlooking Colle basso (the lower town), past the house where Arnolfo di Cambio (architect of the Duomo in Florence) was born, along a road lined with 16th-century town palaces, to the upper defensive ramparts built by the Florentines. If you don't like the idea of the short climb, you can take a free public elevator linking the upper and lower sections of the town.

NEED A BREAK?

At Bar Barone (✉ *Via Gracco del Secco 32* ☎ *0577/921768*) in the upper section of Colle Alto, Mario Barone makes delicious ice cream and the best pastries for miles around. A mouth-watering selection of freshly made goodies is on display all year round.

WHERE TO EAT AND STAY

$$$$ MODERN ITALIAN Fodor's Choice ★ **Ristorante Arnolfo.** Food lovers should not miss Arnolfo, one of Tuscany's most highly regarded restaurants. Chef Gaetano Trovato sets high standards of creativity; his dishes daringly ride the line between innovation and tradition, almost always with spectacular results. The menu changes frequently and has a fixed-price option, but you're always sure to find fish and lots of fresh vegetables in the summer. You're in for a special treat if the specials include *carrè di agnello al vino rosso e sella alle olive* (rack of lamb in a red wine sauce and lamb saddle with olives). ✉ *Piazza XX Settembre 52* ☎ *0577/920549* 🌐 *www.arnolfo.com* ⏲ *Closed Tues. and Wed., last wk in Jan.–Feb., and last wk in Aug.*

$$ **Palazzo San Lorenzo.** At this hotel occupying a 17th-century palace in the historic center of Colle, rooms exude a feeling of freshness, with light-colored wooden floors, soothingly tinted fabrics, and large bright

windows. **Pros:** central location; spotless and extremely well maintained. **Cons:** caters to business groups; some of the public spaces feel rather sterile. **TripAdvisor:** "modern but tasteful," "feels new and pristine," "spa totally worth it." ✉ *Via Gracco del Secco 113* ☎ *0577/923675* 🌐 *www.palazzosanlorenzo.it* *43 rooms, 6 suites, 6 apartments* *In-room: a/c, Internet. In-hotel: restaurant, bar, pool, gym, spa, business center, parking, some pets allowed* 🍽 *Breakfast.*

SIENA

With its narrow streets and steep alleys, a stunning Gothic duomo, a bounty of early Renaissance art, and the glorious Palazzo Pubblico overlooking its magnificent Piazza del Campo (or just, "Campo"), Siena is often described as Italy's best-preserved medieval city. Victory over Florence in 1260 at Montaperti marked the beginning of Siena's golden age. During the following decades Siena erected its greatest buildings (including the Duomo); established a model city government presided over by the Council of Nine; and became a great art, textile, and trade center. Siena succumbed to Florentine rule in the mid-16th century, when a yearlong siege virtually eliminated the native population. Ironically, it was precisely this decline that, along with the steadfast pride of the Sienese, prevented further development, to which we owe the city's marvelous medieval condition today.

Although much looks as it did in the early 14th century, Siena is no museum. Walk through the streets and you can see that the medieval *contrade,* 17 neighborhoods into which the city has been historically divided, are a vibrant part of modern life. You may see symbols of the *contrada*—Tartuca (turtle), Oca (goose), Istrice (porcupine), Torre (tower)—emblazoned on banners and engraved on building walls. The Sienese still strongly identify themselves by the contrada where they were born and raised; loyalty and rivalry run deep. At no time is this more visible than during the centuries-old Palio, a twice-yearly horse race held in the Piazza del Campo. But you need not visit during the wild festival to come to know the rich culture and enchanting pleasures of Siena; those are evident at every step.

GETTING HERE

From Florence, the quickest way to Siena is via the Florence-Siena Superstrada. Otherwise, take the Via Cassia (SR2), for a scenic route. Coming from Rome, leave the A1 at Valdichiana, and follow the Siena-Bettole Superstrada. SITA provides excellent bus service between Florence and Siena. Because buses are direct and speedy, they're preferable to the train, which sometimes involves a change in Empoli.

VISITOR INFORMATION

Siena tourism office (✉ *Piazza del Campo 56* ☎ *0577/280551* 🌐 *www.terresiena.it*).

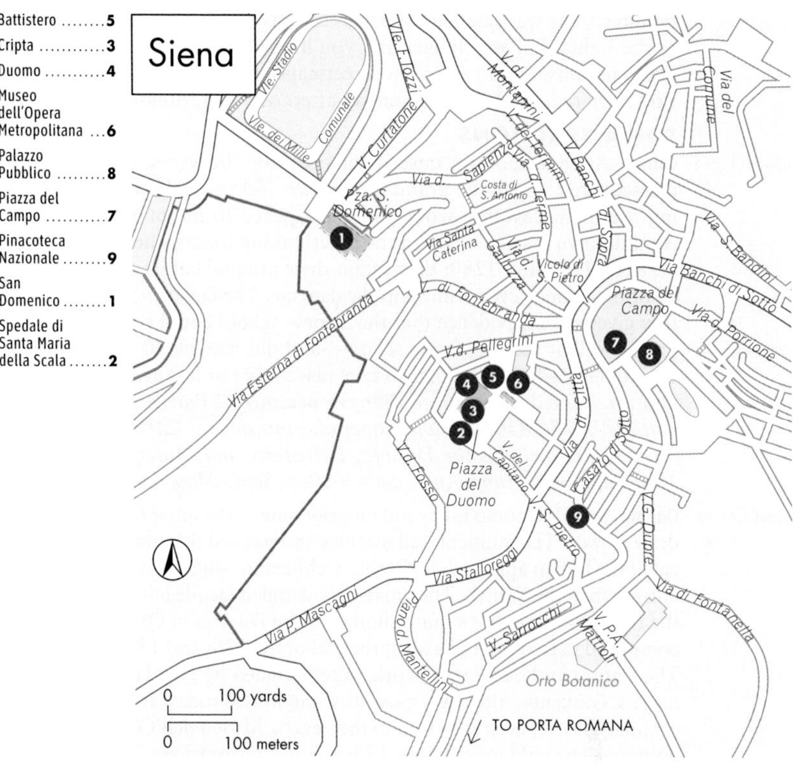

EXPLORING SIENA

If you come by car, you're better off leaving it in one of the parking lots around the perimeter of town. Driving is difficult or impossible in most parts of the city center. Practically unchanged since medieval times, Siena is laid out in a "Y" over the slopes of several hills, dividing the city into *terzi* (thirds). Although the most interesting sites are in a fairly compact area around the Campo at the center of town in the neighborhoods of Città, Camollìa, and San Martino, be sure to leave some time to wander into the narrow streets that rise and fall steeply from the main thoroughfares, giving yourself at least two days to really explore the town. At the top on the list of things to see is the Piazza del Campo, considered by many to be the finest public square in Italy. The Palazzo Pubblico sits at the lower end of the square and is well worth a visit. The Duomo is a must-see, as is the nearby Cripta.

Tra-In (☎ *0577/204111* 🌐 *www.trainspa.it*) buses also run frequently within and around Siena, including through the centro storico. Tickets cost €1 within the city and should be bought in advance at tobacconists or newsstands. Routes are marked with signposts.

TIMING It's a joy to walk in Siena—hills notwithstanding—as it's a rare opportunity to stroll through a medieval city rather than just a town. (There's quite a lot to explore, in contrast to tiny hill towns that can be crossed in minutes.) The walk can be done in as little as a day, with minimal stops at the sights. But stay longer and you'll have time to tour the church and museums, and to enjoy the streetscapes themselves. Several of the sites have reduced hours on Sunday afternoon and Monday.

TOP ATTRACTIONS

Fodor's Choice ★ **Cripta.** After it had lain unseen for possibly 700 years, a crypt was rediscovered under the grand *pavimento* (floor) of the Duomo during routine excavation work and was opened to the public in 2003. An unknown master executed the breathtaking frescoes here sometime between 1270 and 1280; they retain their original colors and pack an emotional punch even with sporadic damage. The *Deposition/Lamentation* gives strong evidence that the Sienese school could paint emotion just as well as the Florentine school—and did it some 20 years before Giotto. Guided tours in English take place more or less every half hour and are limited to no more than 35 persons. ✉ *Piazza del Duomo, Città* ☎ *0577/283048* 🌐 *www.operaduomo.siena.it* 🎫 *€6; €10 combined ticket includes the Duomo, Battistero, and Museo dell'Opera Metropolitana* ⏲ *June–Aug., daily 9:30–8; Sept.–May, daily 9:30–7.*

Fodor's Choice ★ **Duomo.** Siena's Duomo is beyond question one of the finest Gothic cathedrals in Italy. The multicolored marbles and painted decoration are typical of the Italian approach to Gothic architecture—lighter and much less austere than the French. The amazingly detailed facade has few rivals in the region, although it's quite similar to the Duomo in Orvieto. It was completed in two brief phases at the end of the 13th and 14th centuries. The statues and decorative work were designed by Nicola Pisano and his son Giovanni, although most of what we see today are copies, the originals having been removed to the nearby Museo dell'Opera Metropolitana. The gold mosaics are 18th-century restorations. The Campanile (no entry) is among central Italy's finest, the number of windows increasing with each level, a beautiful and ingenious way of reducing the weight of the structure as it climbs to the heavens.

The Duomo's interior, with its black-and-white striping throughout and finely coffered and gilded dome, is simply striking. Step in and look back up at Duccio's (circa 1255–1319) panels of stained glass that fill the circular window. Finished in 1288, it's the oldest example of stained glass in Italy. The Duomo is most famous for its unique and magnificent inlaid-marble floors, which took almost 200 years to complete; more than 40 artists contributed to the work, made up of 56 separate compositions depicting biblical scenes, allegories, religious symbols, and civic emblems. The floors are covered for most of the year for conservation purposes, but are unveiled during September and October. The Duomo's carousel pulpit, also much appreciated, was carved by Nicola Pisano (circa 1220–84) around 1265; the *Life of Christ* is depicted on the rostrum frieze. In striking contrast to all the Gothic decoration in the nave are the magnificent Renaissance frescoes in the **Biblioteca Piccolomini,** off the left aisle. Painted by Pinturicchio (circa 1454–1513) and completed in 1509, they depict events from the life of native son Aeneas Sylvius Piccolomini (1405–64), who became Pope Pius II in 1458. The frescoes are in excellent condition, and have a freshness rarely seen in work so old.

The Duomo is grand, but the medieval Sienese people had even bigger plans. They wanted to enlarge the building by using the existing church as a transept for a new church, with a new nave running toward the southeast, to make what would be the largest church in the world. But only the side wall and part of the new facade were completed when the Black Death struck in 1348, decimating Siena's population. The city fell into decline, funds dried up, and the plans were never carried out. (The dream of building the biggest church was actually doomed to failure from the start—subsequent attempts to get the project going revealed that the foundation was insufficient to bear the weight of the proposed structure.) The beginnings of the new nave, extending from the right side of the Duomo, were left unfinished, perhaps as a testament to unfulfilled dreams, and ultimately enclosed to house the adjacent **Museo dell'Opera Metropolitana.** ✉ *Piazza del Duomo, Città* ☎ *0577/283048* 🌐 *www.operaduomo.siena.it* 🎫 *€3 Nov.–Aug; €6 Sept. and Oct; €10 combined ticket includes the Cripta, Battistero, and Museo dell'Opera Metropolitana* ⏲ *Mar.–Oct., Mon.–Sat. 10:30–7:30, Sun. 1:30–6:30; Nov.–Feb., Mon.–Sat. 10:30–6:30, Sun. 1:30–5:30.*

WORTH NOTING

Battistero. The Duomo's 14th-century Gothic Baptistery was built to prop up one side of the Duomo. There are frescoes throughout, but the highlight is a large bronze 15th-century baptismal font designed by Jacopo della Quercia (1374–1438). It's adorned with bas-reliefs by various artists, including two by Renaissance masters: the *Baptism of Christ* by Lorenzo Ghiberti (1378–1455) and the *Feast of Herod* by Donatello. ✉ *Entrance on Piazza San Giovanni* ☎ *0577/283048* 🌐 *www.operaduomo.siena.it* 🎫 *€3; €10 combined ticket includes the Duomo, Cripta, and Museo dell'Opera del Duomo* ⏲ *June–Aug., daily 9:30–8; Sept.–May, daily 9:30–7.*

Museo dell'Opera Metropolitana. Part of the unfinished nave of what was to have been a new cathedral, the museum contains the Duomo's treasury and some of the original decoration from its facade and interior. The first room on the ground floor displays weather-beaten 13th-century sculptures by Giovanni Pisano (circa 1245–1318) that were brought inside for protection and replaced by copies, as was a tondo of the *Madonna and Child* (now attributed to Donatello) that once hung on the door to the south transept. The masterpiece is unquestionably Duccio's *Maestà,* one side with 26 panels depicting episodes from the Passion, the other side with a *Madonna and Child Enthroned.* Painted between 1308 and 1311 as the altarpiece for the Duomo (where it remained until 1505), its realistic elements, such as the lively depiction of the Christ child and the treatment of interior space, proved an enormous influence on later painters. The second floor is divided between the treasury, with a crucifix by Giovanni Pisano and several statues and busts of biblical characters and classical philosophers, and La Sala della Madonna degli Occhi Grossi (the Room of the Madonna with the Big Eyes), named after the namesake painting it displays by the Maestro di Tressa, who painted in the early 13th century. The work originally decorated the Duomo's high altar, before being displaced by Duccio's *Maestà.* There's a fine view from the tower inside the museum. ✉ *Piazza del Duomo 8, Città* ☎ *0577/283048* 🌐 *www.operaduomo.siena.it*

Continued on page 662

Climbing the 400 narrow steps of the **Torre del Mangia** rewards you with unparalleled views of Siena's rooftops and the countryside beyond.
The **Palazzo Pubblico**, Siena's town hall since the 14th century.
Something about the fan-shaped, sloping design of encourages people to sit and relax (except during the Palio, when they stand and scream). The communal atmosphere here is unlike that of any other Italian piazza.

PIAZZA DEL CAMPO

❼ dor'sChoice ★ The fan-shaped **Piazza del Campo,** known simply as il Campo (The Field), is one of the finest squares in Italy. Constructed toward the end of the 12th century on a market area unclaimed by any contrada, it's still the heart of town. The bricks of the Campo are patterned in nine different sections—representing each member of the medieval Government of Nine. At the top of the Campo is a copy of the **Fonte Gaia,** decorated in the early 15th century by Siena's greatest sculptor, Jacopo della Quercia, with 13 sculpted reliefs of biblical events and virtues. Those lining the rectangular fountain are 19th-century copies; the originals are in the Spedale di Santa Maria della Scala. On Palio horse race days (July 2 and August 16), the Campo and all its surrounding buildings are packed with cheering, frenzied locals and tourists craning their necks to take it all in.

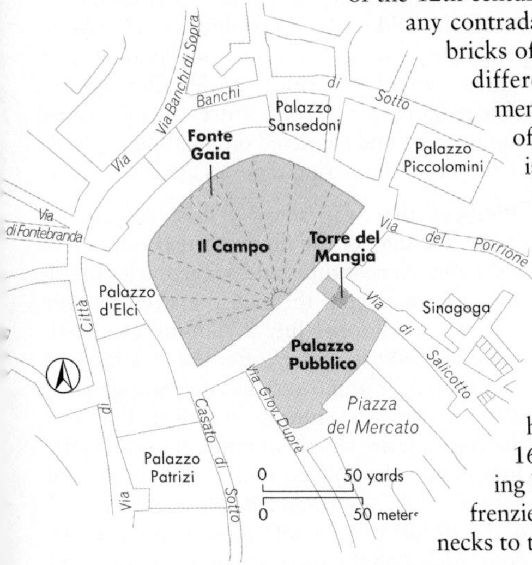

❽ The Gothic **Palazzo Pubblico,** the focal point of the Piazza del Campo, has served as Siena's town hall since the 1300s. It now also contains the **Museo Civico,** with walls covered in early Renaissance frescoes. The nine governors of Siena once met in the Sala della Pace, famous for Ambrogio Lorenzetti's frescoes called *Allegories of Good and Bad Government,* painted in the late 1330s to demonstrate the dangers of tyranny. The good government side depicts utopia, showing first the virtuous ruling council surrounded by angels and then scenes of a perfectly running city and countryside. Conversely, the bad government fresco tells a tale straight out of Dante. The evil ruler and his advisers have horns and fondle strange animals, and the town scene depicts the seven mortal sins in action. Interestingly, the bad government fresco is severely damaged, and the good government fresco is in terrific condition. The **Torre del Mangia,** the palazzo's famous bell tower, is named after one of its first bell ringers, Giovanni di Duccio (called Mangiaguadagni, or earnings eater). The climb up to the top is long and steep, but the view makes it worth every step. ✉ *Piazza del Campo 1, Città* ☎ *0577/41169* 🎫 *Museo €7, Torre €6, combined ticket €10* ⏲ *Museo Nov.–Mar. 15, daily 10–6:30; Mar. 16–Oct., daily 10–7. Torre Nov.–Mar. 15, daily 10–4; Mar. 16–Oct., daily 10–7.*

THE PALIO

The three laps around a makeshift racetrack in Piazza del Campo are over in less than two minutes, but the spirit of Siena's Palio—a horse race held every July 2 and August 16—lives all year long.

The Palio is contested between Siena's contrade, the 17 neighborhoods that have divided the city since the Middle Ages. Loyalties are fiercely felt. At any time of year you'll see on the streets contrada symbols—Tartuca (turtle), Oca (goose), Istrice (porcupine), Torre (tower)—emblazoned on banners and engraved on building walls. At Palio time, simmering rivalries come to a boil.

It's been that way since at least August 16, 1310, the date of the first recorded running of the Palio. At that time, and for centuries to follow, the race went through the streets of the city. The additional July 2 running was instituted in 1649; soon thereafter the location was moved to the Campo and the current system for selecting the race entrants established. Ten of the contrade are chosen at random to run in the July Palio. The August race is then contested between the 7 contrade left out in July, plus 3 of the 10 July participants, again chosen at random. Although the races are in theory of equal importance, Sienese will tell you that it's better to win the second and have bragging rights for the rest of the year.

The race itself has a raw and arbitrary character—it's no Kentucky Derby. There's barely room for the 10 horses on the makeshift Campo course, so falls and collisions are inevitable. Horses are chosen at random three days before the race, and jockeys (who ride bareback) are mercenaries hired from surrounding towns. Almost no tactic is considered too underhanded. Bribery, secret plots, and betrayal are commonplace—so much so that the word for "jockey," *fantino*, has come to mean "untrustworthy" in Siena. There have been incidents of drugging (the horses) and kidnapping (the jockeys); only sabotaging a horse's reins remains taboo.

Above: The tension of the starting line. Top left: The frenzy of the race. Bottom left: A solemn flag bearer follows in the footsteps of his ancestors.

17 MEDIEVAL CONTRADE

AQUILA

BRUCO

Festivities kick off three days prior to the Palio, with the selection and blessing of the horses, trial runs, ceremonial banquets, betting, and late-night celebrations. Residents don their contrada's colors and march through the streets in medieval costumes. The Campo is transformed into a racetrack lined with a thick layer of sand. On race day, each horse is brought to the church of the contrada for which it will run, where it's blessed and told, "Go little horse and return a winner." The Campo fills through the afternoon, with spectators crowding into every available space until bells ring and the piazza is sealed off. Processions of flag wavers in traditional dress march to the beat of tambourines and drums and the roar of the crowds. The *palio* itself—a banner for which the race is named, dedicated to the Virgin Mary—makes an appearance, followed by the horses and their jockeys.

The race begins when one horse, chosen to ride up from behind the rest of the field, crosses the starting line. There are always false starts, adding to the frenzied mood. Once underway, the race is over in a matter of minutes. The victorious rider is carried off through the streets of the winning contrada (where in the past tradition dictated he was entitled to the local girl of his choice), while winning and losing sides use television replay to analyze the race from every possible angle. The winning contrada will celebrate into the night, at long tables piled high with food and drink. The champion horse is guest of honor.

Reserved seating in the stands is sold out months in advance of the races; contact the Siena Tourist Office (✉ Piazza del Campo 56 ☎ 0577/280551) to find out about availability, and ask your hotel if it can procure you a seat. The entire area in the center is free and unreserved, but you need to show up early in order to get a prime spot against the barriers.

€6; €10 combined ticket includes the Duomo, Cripta, and Battistero ⏲ Mar.–May, Sept., and Oct., daily 9:30–7; June–Aug., daily 9:30 am–10 pm; Nov.–Feb., daily 10–5.

WORD OF MOUTH

"The one thing I'd do in Siena—short of attending the Palio—is stay overnight. All the tourists leave and it's very dark and medieval. It feels like you've time-traveled back 500 years."

—Mimar

Pinacoteca Nazionale. The superb collection of five centuries of local painting in Siena's national picture gallery can easily convince you that the Renaissance was by no means just a Florentine thing. Siena was arguably just as important a center of art and innovation as its rival to the north, especially in the mid-13th century. Accordingly, the most interesting section of the collection, chronologically arranged, has several important "firsts." Room 1 contains a painting of the *Stories of the True Cross* (1215) by the so-called Master of Tressa, the earliest identified work by a painter of the Sienese school, and is followed in Room 2 by late-13th-century artist Guido da Siena's *Stories from the Life of Christ,* one of the first paintings ever made on canvas (earlier painters used wood panels). Rooms 3 and 4 are dedicated to Duccio, a student of Cimabue (circa 1240–1302) and considered to be the last of the proto-Renaissance painters. Ambrogio Lorenzetti's landscapes in Room 8 are the first truly secular paintings in Western art. Among later works in the rooms on the floor above, keep an eye out for the preparatory sketches used by Domenico Beccafumi (1486–1551) for the 35 etched marble panels he made for the floor of the Duomo. ✉ *Via San Pietro 29, Città* ☎ *0577/281161* *€4* ⏲ *Mon. 9–1, Tues.–Sat. 10–6, Sun. 9–1; last entrance ¼ hr before closing.*

San Domenico. Although the Duomo is celebrated as a triumph of 13th-century Gothic architecture, this church, built at about the same time, turned out to be an oversize, hulking brick box that never merited a finishing coat in marble, let alone a graceful facade. Named for the founder of the Dominican order, the church is now more closely associated with Saint Catherine of Siena. Just to the right of the entrance is the chapel in which she received the stigmata. On the wall is the only known contemporary portrait of the saint, made in the late 14th century by Andrea Vanni (circa 1332–1414). Farther down is the famous **Cappella di Santa Caterina,** the church's official shrine. Catherine, or bits and pieces of her, was literally spread all over the country—a foot is in Venice, most of her body is in Rome, and only her head and finger are here (kept in a reliquary on the altar). She was revered throughout the country long before she was officially named a patron saint of Italy in 1939. On either side of the chapel are well-known frescoes by Sodoma (aka Giovanni Antonio Bazzi, 1477–1549) of *St. Catherine in Ecstasy.* Don't miss the view of the Duomo and town center from the apse-side terrace. ✉ *Costa di Sant'Antonio, Camollìa* ☎ *0577/280893* ⏲ *Mid-Mar.–Oct., daily 7–1 and 2:30–6:30; Nov.–mid-Mar., daily 9–1 and 3–6.*

Spedale di Santa Maria della Scala. For more than a thousand years, this complex across from the Duomo was home to Siena's hospital, but now it serves as a museum to display some terrific frescoes and other Sienese

Renaissance treasures. Restored 15th-century frescoes in the Sala del Pellegrinaio (once the emergency room) tell the history of the hospital, which was created to give refuge to passing pilgrims and to those in need, and to distribute charity to the poor. Incorporated into the complex is the church of the Santissima Annunziata, with a celebrated *Risen Christ* by Vecchietta (also known as Lorenzo di Pietro, circa 1412–80). Down in the dark Cappella di Santa Caterina della Notte is where Saint Catherine went to pray at night. The subterranean archaeological museum contained within the *ospedale* (hospital) is worth seeing even if you're not particularly taken with Etruscan objects: the interior design is sheer brilliance—it's beautifully lighted, eerily quiet, and an oasis of cool on hot summer days. The displays—including the *bucchero* (dark, reddish clay) ceramics, Roman coins, and tomb furnishings—are clearly marked and can serve as a good introduction to the history of regional excavations. Don't miss della Quercia's original sculpted reliefs from the Fonte Gaia. Although the fountain has been faithfully copied for the Campo, there's something incomparably beautiful about the real thing. ✉ *Piazza del Duomo, Città* ☎ *0577/224811* 🌐 *www.santamariadellascala.com* 🎫 *€6* ⏲ *Mid-Mar.–mid-Oct., daily 10:30–6:30; mid-Oct.–mid-Mar., daily 10:30–4:30.*

WHERE TO EAT

$$$ TUSCAN ★ ✕ **Antica Trattoria Botteganova.** Along the road that leads to Chianti is arguably the best restaurant in Siena. Chef Michele Sorrentino's cooking is all about clean flavors, balanced combinations, and inviting presentation. Look for inspiring dishes such as spaghetti *alla chitarra in salsa di astice piccante* (with a spicy lobster sauce), or ravioli *di ricotta con ragù d'agnello* (with sheep's-milk cheese and lamb sauce). The interior, with high vaulting, is relaxed yet elegant, and the service is first-rate. ✉ *Strada per Montevarchi 29* ✣ *2 km (1 mi) northeast of Siena* ☎ *0577/284230* ✍ *Reservations essential* ⏲ *Closed Sun.*

$$$ TUSCAN ✕ **Le Logge.** Bright flowers provide a dash of color at this classic Tuscan dining room, and stenciled designs on the ceilings add some whimsy. The wooden cupboards (now filled with wine bottles) lining the walls recall its past as a turn-of-the-19th-century grocery store. The menu, with four or five primi and secondi, changes regularly, but almost always includes their classic *malfatti all'osteria* (ricotta and spinach dumplings in a cream sauce). Desserts such as *coni con mousse al cioccolato e gelato allo zafferano* (two diminutive ice-cream cones with chocolate mousse and saffron ice cream) provide an inventive ending to the meal. When not vying for one of the outdoor tables, make sure to ask for one in the main downstairs room. ✉ *Via del Porrione 33, San Martino* ☎ *0577/48013* 🌐 *www.osterialelogge.it* ✍ *Reservations essential* ⏲ *Closed Sun. and 3 wks in Jan.*

¢ TUSCAN ✕ **Osteria Il Grattacielo.** Wiped out from too much sightseeing? Consider a meal at this hole-in-the-wall restaurant where locals congregate for a simple lunch over a glass of wine. There's a collection of *verdure sott'olio*, a wide selection of *affettati misti*, and various types of frittatas. All of this can be washed down with the cheap, yet eminently drinkable, house red. A couple of bench tables provide outdoor seating in summer. Don't be put off by the absence of a written menu. All the food is displayed at the counter, so you can point if you need to. ✉ *Via Pontani 8, Camollìa* ☎ *0577/289326* ▭ *No credit cards* ⏲ *Closed Sun.*

$ TUSCAN ★ ✕ **Trattoria Papei.** The menu hasn't changed for years, and why should it? The pici *al cardinale* (with a duck and bacon sauce) is wonderful, and all the other typically Sienese dishes are equally delicious. Grilled meats are the true specialty; the bistecca di vitello (grilled veal steak) is melt-in-your-mouth delicious. Tucked away behind the Palazzo Pubblico, in a square that serves as a parking lot for most of the day, the restaurant's location isn't great, but the food is. Thanks to portable heaters, there's outdoor seating all year round. ✉ *Piazza del Mercato 6, Città* ☎ *0577/280894* ⏲ *Closed Mon.*

WHERE TO STAY

$ **Antica Torre.** The cordial Landolfo family has carefully evoked a private home with their eight guest rooms inside a restored 16th-century tower. **Pros:** near the town center; charming atmosphere. **Cons:** narrow stairway up to the rooms; low ceilings; cramped bathrooms. **TripAdvisor:** "room was extremely quiet," "in the historical center," "simple country style." ✉ *Via Fieravecchia 7, San Martino* ☎ *0577/222255* 🌐 *www.anticatorresiena.it* *8 rooms* *In-hotel: business center* *Breakfast.*

$$ ★ **Borgo Pretale.** A small hamlet hidden in the hills to the south of Siena has been converted into this delightful hotel. **Pros:** bucolic location; lots of walking trails; lovely rooms. **Cons:** few restaurant options nearby; need a car to get around. **TripAdvisor:** "unique setting away from town," "views across the Tuscan hills," "room was spacious and clean." ✉ *Località Pretale* ✣ *11 km (7 mi) east of Siena Sovicille* ☎ *0577/345401* *0577/345625* 🌐 *www.borgopretale.it* *20 rooms, 7 suites* *In-hotel: restaurant, bar, tennis court, pool, gym, business center* ⏲ *Closed Nov.–Easter* *Breakfast.*

$$ ★ **Hotel Santa Caterina.** Manager Lorenza Capannelli and her fine staff are welcoming, hospitable, enthusiastic, and go out of their way to ensure a fine stay. **Pros:** friendly staff; a short walk to center of town; breakfast in the garden. **Cons:** on a busy intersection; outside city walls. **TripAdvisor:** "just outside the Porta Romana," "quiet and peaceful," "countryside was just beautiful." ✉ *Via Piccolomini 7, San Martino* ☎ *0577/221105* 🌐 *www.hscsiena.it* *22 rooms* *In-room: Internet. In-hotel: business center, parking, some pets allowed* *Breakfast.*

$$ ★ **Palazzo Ravizza.** This romantic palazzo exudes a sense of genteel shabbiness. **Pros:** 10-minute walk to the center of town; pleasant garden with a view beyond the city walls; professional staff. **Cons:** not all rooms have views; some rooms are a little cramped. **TripAdvisor:** "a real palazzo," "views are magnificent," "nice period features." ✉ *Pian dei Mantellini 34, Città* ☎ *0577/280462* 🌐 *www.palazzoravizza.it* *38 rooms, 4 suites* *In-room: Wi-Fi (some). In-hotel: restaurant, bar, business center, parking, some pets allowed* *Breakfast.*

AREZZO AND CORTONA

The hill towns of Arezzo and Cortona carry on age-old local traditions—in June and September, for example, Arezzo's Romanesque and Gothic churches are enlivened by the Giostra del Saracino, a costumed medieval joust. Arezzo has been home to important artists since ancient times, when Etruscan potters produced their fiery-red vessels here. Fine examples of the work of Luca Signorelli are preserved in Cortona, his hometown.

WORD OF MOUTH

"Arezzo holds a huge antiques fair the first weekend of each month that takes over the streets in the historical center of town. You may want to check your dates, either to avoid or take advantage of it."
—shellio

AREZZO

63 km (39 mi) northeast of Siena, 81 km (50 mi) southeast of Florence.

GETTING HERE

Arezzo is easily reached by car from the A1 (Autostrada del Sole), the main highway running between Florence and Rome. When you arrive, look for the "Pietri" parking lot, on the far side of town, and take the public escalators to the upper part of town. Direct trains connect Arezzo with Rome (2½ hours) and Florence (1 hour). Direct bus service is available from Florence, but not from Rome.

VISITOR INFORMATION

Arezzo tourism office (✉ *Piazza della Repubblica 28* ☎ *0575/377678* 🌐 *www.apt.arezzo.it*).

EXPLORING

The birthplace of the poet Petrarch (1304–74) and the Renaissance artist and art historian Giorgio Vasari (1511–74), Arezzo is today best known for the magnificent Piero della Francesca frescoes in the church of San Francesco. The city dates from pre-Etruscan times and thrived as an Etruscan capital from the 7th to the 4th century BC. During the Middle Ages it was fully embroiled in the conflict between the Ghibellines (pro–Holy Roman Emperor) and the Guelphs (pro-pope), losing its independence to Florence at the end of the 14th century after many decades of doing battle.

Urban sprawl testifies to the fact that Arezzo (population 90,000) is the third-largest city in Tuscany (after Florence and Pisa). But the old town, set on a low hill, is relatively small, and almost completely closed to traffic. Look for parking along the roads that circle the lower part of town and walk into town from there. You can explore the most interesting sights in a few hours, adding time to linger for some window-shopping at Arezzo's many antiques shops. Several scenes of Roberto Benigni's award-winning film *Life is Beautiful* were shot here; the tourist office provides a map that highlights the locations.

Fodor's Choice ★ The remarkable frescoes by Piero della Francesca (circa 1420–92) in the **Basilica di San Francesco** were painted between 1452 and 1466. They depict scenes from the *Legend of the True Cross* on three walls of the *Capella Bacci,* a chapel behind the high altar. What Sir Kenneth Clark called "the most perfect morning light in all Renaissance painting" may be seen in the lowest section of the right wall, where the troops of the emperor Maxentius fled before the sign of the cross. A 15-year project restored the works to their original brilliance. A distant but free view of the frescoes is to be had from the main body of the church. For a closer look, make reservations at the ticket office in Piazza San Francesco, two doors down from the church. ✉ *Piazza San Francesco* ☎ *0575/20630 church, 0575/352757 Capella Bacci reservations* 🌐 *www.pierodellafrancesca.it* 🎫 *Capella Bacci €6* ⏲ *Church: daily 8:30–6:30. Capella Bacci: Apr.–Oct., weekdays 9–6:30, Sat. 9–5:30, Sun. 1–5:30; Nov.–Mar., weekdays 9–5:30, Sat. 9–5, Sun. 1–5.*

Some historians maintain that Arezzo's oddly shaped, sloping **Piazza Grande** was once the site of an ancient Roman forum. Now it hosts a first-Sunday-of-the-month antiques fair as well as the **Giostra del Saracino** (Joust of the Saracen), featuring medieval costumes and competition, held here in the middle of June and on the first Sunday of September. Check out the 16th-century loggia designed by native son Giorgio Vasari, architect of the Uffizi Gallery, on the northeast side of the piazza.

The curving, tiered apse on Piazza Grande belongs to **Santa Maria della Pieve**, one of Tuscany's finest Romanesque churches, built in the 12th century. Don't miss the Portale Maggiore (great door) with its remarkably vibrant polychrome figures representing the months. ✉ *Corso Italia 7* ☎ *0575/22629* ⏲ *May–Sept., daily 8–1 and 3–7; Oct.–Apr., daily 8–noon and 3–6.*

Arezzo's medieval **Duomo** (at the top of the hill) contains a fresco of a somber *Magdalen* by Piero della Francesca; look for it next to the large marble tomb near the organ. ✉ *Piazza del Duomo 1* ☎ *0575/23991* ⏲ *Daily 6:30–12:30 and 3–6:30.*

WHERE TO EAT

$$ SOUTHERN ITALIAN ✕ **Antica Trattoria da Guido.** Owned by a southern Italian family, this small trattoria serves tasty adaptations of Calabrian dishes, such as homemade pasta served with *salsa ai pomodori secchi* (a spicy sauce of sun-dried tomatoes, capers, and red peppers). If it's on the menu, try mamma Lidia's wonderful spezzatino (beef stew). The display of homemade pastries makes decisions difficult at the end of the meal. The dining room is a pleasant mix of rustic and modern, and the service is friendly. ✉ *Via di San Francesco 1* ☎ *0575/23760* ⏲ *Closed Sun. and 2 wks in mid-Aug.*

$ ITALIAN ✕ **La Torre di Gnicche.** Wine lovers shouldn't miss this wine bar/eatery with more than 700 labels on the list, just off Piazza Grande. Seasonal dishes of traditional fare, such as *acquacotta del casentino* (porcini mushroom soup) and *baccalà in umido* (salt-cod stew), are served in the simply decorated, vaulted dining room. You can accompany your meal with one, or more, of the almost 30 wines that are available by the glass. Limited outdoor seating is available in warm weather. ✉ *Piaggia San Martino 8* ☎ *0575/352035* 🌐 *www.latorredignicche.it* ⏲ *Closed Wed., Jan., and 2 wks in July.*

Arezzo, Cortona
and Southern Tuscany
Ligurian Sea
Tyrrhenian Sea
TUSCANY
UMBRIA
THE MARCHES
LATIUM
CHIANTI
PRATOMAGNO
Florence
Pisa
Livorno
Empoli
Arno
Marina di Pisa
Tirrenia
Cascina
Pontedera
San Miniato
Castelfiorentino
Certaldo
San Gimignano
Poggibonsi
Volterra
Monteriggioni
Castiglioncello
Cécina
San Vincenzo
Piombino
Massa Marittima
Roccastrada
Abbazia di San Galgano
Siena
San Casciano in Val di Pesa
Impruneta
Bagno a Ripoli
Greve in Chianti
Castellina in Chianti
Consuma
Poppi
Bibbiena
Sansepolcro
Arezzo
Monte San Savino
Castiglion Fiorentino
Cortona
Città di Castello
Urbino
Cagli
Gubbio
Perugia
Assisi
Lake Trasimene
Abbazia di Monte Oliveto Maggiore
Montepulciano
Pienza
Montalcino
Abbazia di Sant'Antimo
Chianciano Terme
Chiusi
Sarteano
Città d. Pieve
Castel del Piano
Arcidosso
Abbadia di San Salvatore
Roccalbegna
Acquapendente
Orvieto
Todi
Saturnia
Scansano
Pitigliano
Manciano
Magliano in Toscana
Grosseto
Castiglione della Pescaia
Marina di Grosseto
Monti dell'Uccellina
Orbetello
Monte Argentario
Capalbio
Lake Bolsena
Marta
Montefiascone
Tuscania
Viterbo
Amelia
Terni
Narni
GORGONA
Scalo
CAPRAIA
Portoferraio
ELBA
Cavo
Rio Marina
Porto Azzurro
PIANOSA
GIGLIO
Giglio Porto
MONTECRISTO
0
20 miles
0
30 km
A1
A12
E78
1
2
3
3bis
68
71
73
74
75bis
146
204
222
223
312
322
323
327
329
398
408
429
436
438
439
441
448
540
541

WHERE TO STAY

$$ **Castello di Gargonza.** Enchantment reigns at this tiny 13th-century countryside hamlet, part of the fiefdom of the aristocratic Florentine Guicciardini. **Pros:** romantic, one-of-a-kind accommodation in a medieval castle; peaceful, isolated setting. **Cons:** standard rooms are extremely basic; a little out of the way for exploring the region; private transportation is a necessity. **TripAdvisor:** "inside thick stone walls," "hidden away in the forest," "comfortable, large rooms." ✉ *SR73* ✥ *28 km (17 mi) southwest of Arezzo, Monte San Savino* ☎ *0575/847021* 🖷 *0575/847054* 🌐 *www.gargonza.it* *37 rooms, 8 apartments* *In-room: no a/c, kitchen (some), no TV. In-hotel: restaurant, bar, pool, business center* ⏲ *Closed Jan. and Feb.* 🍽 *Breakfast.*

$$ **Cavaliere Palace Hotel.** On a quiet backstreet in the old town, the Cavaliere is moments away from the main sights. **Pros:** location, location, location. **Cons:** some complain of noise from nearby disco; very plain decor. **TripAdvisor:** "room not too big but comfortable," "location is great," "does not deserve 4 stars." ✉ *Via Madonna del Prato 83, Arezzo* ☎ *0575/26836* 🌐 *www.cavalierehotels.com* *27 rooms* *In-room: Wi-Fi. In-hotel: business center, parking* 🍽 *Breakfast.*

$$$$ ★ **Il Borro.** The location has been described as "heaven on earth," and a stay at Salvatore Ferragamo's estate, 20 km (12 m) northwest of Arezzo, may well evoke similar sentiments; once a luxurious hunting lodge, the main 10-bedroom villa is now rented out as a single unit, but the principle attraction is the medieval village that sits atop a low knoll also on the property. **Pros:** superlative service; great location for exploring western Tuscany; unique setting and atmosphere **Cons:** remote location makes private transport a must; not all suites have country views; ultramodern spa seems out of place. **TripAdvisor:** "magical place to stay," "beyond top-shelf service," "almost the perfect location." ✉ *Località Il Borro 1, S. Giustino Valdarno* ☎ *055/977053* 🌐 *www.ilborro.com* *16 suites, 3 villas, 7 farmhouses, 4 apartments* *In-room: safe, kitchen (some), laundry facilities (some), Internet, Wi-Fi (some). In-hotel: 2 restaurants, bar, tennis courts, pools, gym, spa, parking, some pets allowed* 🍽 *Breakfast.*

SHOPPING

Ever since Etruscan goldsmiths set up their shops here more than 2,000 years ago, Arezzo has been famous for its jewelry. Today the town lays claim to being one of the world's capitals of jewelry design and manufacture, and you can find an impressive display of big-time baubles in the town center's shops.

Arezzo is also famous, at least in Italy, for its antiques dealers. The first weekend of every month, between 8:30 and 5:30, a popular and colorful flea market selling antiques and not-so-antique items takes place in the town's main square and in the streets and parks nearby.

CORTONA

29 km (18 mi) south of Arezzo, 79 km (44 mi) east of Siena, 117 km (73 mi) southeast of Florence.

GETTING HERE

Cortona is easily reached by car from the A1 (Autostrada del Sole): take the Valdichiana exit toward Perugia, then follow signs for Cortona. Regular bus service, provided by Etruria Mobilità, is available between Arezzo and Cortona (1 hour). Train service to Cortona is made inconvenient by the location of the train station, in the valley 3 km (2 mi) steeply below the town itself. From there, you have to rely on bus or taxi service to get up to Cortona.

VISITOR INFORMATION

Cortona tourism office (✉ *Via Nazionale 42* ☎ *0575/630352* 🌐 *www.apt.arezzo.it*).

EXPLORING

With olive trees and vineyards creeping up to its walls, pretty Cortona—popularized by Frances Mayes's glowing descriptions in *Under the Tuscan Sun*—commands sweeping views over Lake Trasimeno and the plain of the Valdichiana. Its two galleries and churches are rarely visited; its delightful medieval streets are a pleasure to wander for their own sake. The heart of town is formed by Piazza della Repubblica and the adjacent Piazza Signorelli; both contain pleasant shops to browse in.

The **Museo Diocesano** *(Diocesan Museum)* houses an impressive number of large and splendid paintings by native son Luca Signorelli, as well as a stunning *Annunciation* by Fra Angelico, a delightful surprise in this small town. ✉ *Piazza Duomo 1* ☎ *0575/62830* 🎟 *€5* ⏲ *Apr.–Oct., Tues.–Sun. 10–7; Nov.–Mar., Tues.–Sun. 10–5.*

★ Legend has it that **Santa Maria del Calcinaio** was built between 1485 and 1513 after the image of the Madonna appeared on a wall of the medieval *calcinaio* (lime pit used for curing leather) that had occupied the site. The linear gray-and-white interior recalls Florence's Duomo. Sienese architect Francesco di Giorgio (1439–1502) most likely designed the sanctuary: the church is a terrific example of Renaissance architectural principles. ✉ *Località Il Calcinaio 227* ✣ *3 km (2 mi) southeast of Cortona's center on Via Guelph* ☎ *0575/604830* ⏲ *Mon.–Sat. 3:30–6, Sun. 10–12:30.*

WHERE TO EAT AND STAY

$–$$ TUSCAN ★ ✕ **Osteria del Teatro.** Photographs from theatrical productions spanning many years line the walls of this tavern off Cortona's large Piazza del Teatro. The food is simply delicious—try the *strozzapreti al ragù di cinta* (pasta with pork sauce) or the equally delicious *filetto al lardo di colonnata e prugne* (beef cooked with bacon and prunes); service is warm and friendly. ✉ *Via Maffei 2* ☎ *0575/630556* 🌐 *www.osteria-delteatro.it* ⏲ *Closed Wed. and 2 wks in Nov. and in Feb.*

$$$ ★ 🏨 **Il Falconiere.** Choose here from rooms in an 18th-century villa, suites in the *chiesetta* (chapel, or little church), or for more seclusion, Le Vigne del Falco suites at the far end of the property. **Pros:** attractive

setting in the valley beneath Cortona; excellent service; elegant, but relaxed. **Cons:** a car is a must; some find rooms in main villa a little noisy. **TripAdvisor:** "place is simply amazing," "rustic yet modern feel," "great views towards the city." ✉ *Località San Martino 370* ✣ *3 km (1½ mi) north of Cortona* ☎ *0575/612679* 📠 *0575/612927* 🌐 *www.ilfalconiere.com* *13 rooms, 7 suites* *In-room: Internet. In-hotel: restaurant, room service, bar, pools, spa, business center, parking, some pets allowed (fee)* ⏲ *No lunch in restaurant Tues. Nov.–Mar. Hotel closed last 3 wks in Jan.–mid-Feb.* 🍽 *Breakfast.*

SOUTHERN TUSCANY

Along the roads leading south from Siena, soft green olive groves give way to a blanket of oak, cypress, and reddish-brown earth. Towns are small and as old as the hills. The scruffy mountain landscapes of Monte Amiata make up some of the wildest parts of Tuscany, and once you're across the mountains the terrain is still full of cliffs. Southern Tuscany has good wine (try Brunello di Montalcino or the fruity, lesser-known Morellino di Scansano for a true treat), thermal baths at Saturnia, and Etruscan ruins.

MONTEPULCIANO

36 km (22 mi) southeast of Monte Oliveto Maggiore, 64 km (40 mi) southeast of Siena.

GETTING HERE

From Rome or Florence, take the Chiusi-Chianciano exit from the A1 highway (Autostrada del Sole). From Siena, take the SR2 south to San Quirico and then the SP146 to Montepulciano. Tra-In offers bus service from Siena to Montepulciano several times a day. Montepulciano's train station is in Montepulciano Stazione, 10 km (6 mi) away.

VISITOR INFORMATION

Montepulciano tourism office (✉ *Via di Gracciano nel Corso 59A* ☎ *0578/757341* 🌐 *www.prolocomontepulciano.it*).

EXPLORING

Perched high on a hilltop, Montepulciano is made up of a cluster of Renaissance buildings set within a circle of cypress trees. At an altitude of almost 2,000 feet, it's cool in summer and chilled in winter by biting winds that sweep the spiraling streets. Vino Nobile di Montepulciano, a robust red wine, is justifiably the town's greatest claim to fame. You can sample it in various wineshops and bars lining the twisting roads, as well as in most restaurants. The town is 13 km (8 mi) west of the Chiusi/Chianciano exit of the A1 highway.

★ Montepulciano's pièce de résistance is the beautiful **Piazza Grande**, filled with handsome buildings. On the Piazza Grande is the **Duomo**, which has an unfinished facade that doesn't measure up to the beauty of the neighboring palaces. On the inside, however, its Renaissance roots shine through. You can see fragments of the tomb of Bartolomeo Aragazzi, secretary to Pope Martin V (who reigned from 1417 to 1431);

it was created by Michelozzo between 1427 and 1436, and pieces of it have been dispersed to museums in other parts of the world. ✉ *Piazza Grande* ☎ *0578/757761* ⏲ *Daily 9–12:30.*

★ On the hillside below the town walls is the church of **San Biagio** (Saint Blaise), designed by Antonio Sangallo il Vecchio. A model of Renaissance architectural perfection, it's considered his masterpiece. Inside the church is a painting of the Madonna. According to legend, the painting was the only thing remaining in an abandoned church that two young girls entered on April 23, 1518. The girls saw the eyes of the Madonna moving, and that same afternoon so did a farmer and his cow, who knelt down in front of the painting. In 1963 the image was proclaimed the Madonna del Buon Viaggio (Madonna of the Good Journey), the protector of tourists in Italy. ✉ *Via di San Biagio* ☎ *0578/7577761* ⏲ *Daily 9–12:30 and 3:30–7:30.*

WHERE TO EAT

$$$ TUSCAN Fodor's Choice ★ ✕ **La Grotta.** You might be tempted to pass right by this restaurant's innocuous entrance across the street from San Biagio, but you'd miss some fantastic food. Try the *tagliolini con carciofi e rigatino* (thin noodles with artichokes and bacon) or tagliatelle *di grano saraceno con asparagi e zucchine* (flat, buckwheat-flour noodles with asparagus and zucchini). Their pappa al pomodoro and tagliata di carne chianina (grilled sliced Chianina beef) are equally delicious. Wash it down with the local wine, which just happens to be one of Italy's finest—Vino Nobile di Montepulciano. The desserts, such as an extravagantly rich triple-chocolate flan, are out of this world. ✉ *Via di San Biagio 16* ☎ *0578/757479* ⏲ *Closed Wed. and Jan. and Feb.*

WHERE TO STAY

$$$$ ★ **Podere Dionora.** The cypress-lined drive to this secluded country retreat hints that you've found something special. **Pros:** secluded setting; great views; attentive service. **Cons:** long walk to the nearest town; need a car to get around. **TripAdvisor:** "tranquil Tuscan retreat," "deer and pheasant abound," "attention to detail." ✉ *Via Vicinale di Poggiano* ✣ *3 km (2 mi) east of Montepulciano town center* ☎ *0578/717496* 🌐 *www.dionora.it* *6 rooms* *In-hotel: pool* ⏲ *Closed mid-Nov.–Feb.* 🍽 *Breakfast.*

$$$ Fodor's Choice ★ **Relais San Bruno.** Alberto Pavoncelli converted his family's summer home, just minutes from the town center, into a splendid inn. **Pros:** king-size beds; functioning fireplaces; relaxed but attentive service. **Cons:** cottages can be chilly; need a car to get around. **TripAdvisor:** "cottages were enchanting," "beautifully appointed," "large and tranquil pool." ✉ *Via di Pescaia 5/7* ☎ *0578/716222* 🌐 *www.sanbrunorelais.com* *7 rooms, 1 suite* *In-hotel: bar, pool, business center* 🍽 *Breakfast.*

$ ★ **San Biagio.** A five-minute walk from the church of the same name, the San Biagio makes a great base for exploring the surrounding countryside. **Pros:** heated indoor pool; family-friendly atmosphere. **Cons:** some rooms face a busy road; lots of tour groups. **TripAdvisor:** "clean and comfortable," "mellow, relaxing inn," "made us feel very welcome." ✉ *Via San Bartolomeo 2* ☎ *0578/717233* 🌐 *www.albergosanbiagio.it* *27 rooms* *In-hotel: restaurant, pool* 🍽 *Breakfast.*

PIENZA

★ *15 km (9 mi) east of Montepulciano, 52 km (32 mi) southeast of Siena.*

GETTING HERE

From Siena, drive south along the SR2 to San Quirico d'Orcia and then the SP146. The trip should take just over an hour. Tra-In shuttles passengers between Siena and Pienza. There's no train service to Pienza.

VISITOR INFORMATION

Pienza tourism office (✉ *Piazza Pio II* ☎ *0578/749071* 🌐 *www.portalepienza.it*).

EXPLORING

Pienza owes its urban design to Pope Pius II, who had grand plans to transform his home village of Corsignano—the town's former name—into a model Renaissance town. The man entrusted with the project was Bernardo Rossellino (1409–64), a protégé of the great Renaissance architectural theorist Leon Battista Alberti (1404–74). His mandate was to create a cathedral, a papal palace, and a town hall (plus miscellaneous other buildings) that adhered to the humanist pope's principles. The result was a project that expressed Renaissance ideals of art, architecture, and civilized good living in a single scheme: it stands as a fine example of the architectural canon that Alberti formulated in the 15th century and emulated in many of Italy's finest buildings and piazzas. Today the cool nobility of Pienza's center seems almost surreal in this otherwise unpretentious village, though at times it can seem overwhelmed by the tourists it attracts. Pienza's pecorino, a sheep's-milk cheese, is a superior gastronomic experience.

In 1459, Pius II commissioned Rossellino to design the perfect palazzo for his papal court. The architect took Florence's Palazzo Rucellai by Alberti as a model and designed the 100-room **Palazzo Piccolomini**. Three sides of the building fit perfectly into the urban plan around it, while the fourth, looking over the valley, has a lovely loggia uniting it with the gardens in back. Guided tours departing every 30 minutes take you to visit the papal apartments, including a beautiful library, the Sala delle Armi—with an impressive weapons collection—and the music room, with its extravagant wooden ceiling forming four letter P's, for Pope, Pius, Piccolomini, and Pienza. The last tour departs 30 minutes before closing. ✉ *Piazza Pio II 1* ☎ *0578/286300* 🌐 *www.palazzopiccolominipienza.it* 🎫 *€7* 🕑 *Mid-Mar.–mid-Oct., Tues.–Sun. 10–6:30; mid-Oct.–mid-Mar., Tues.–Sun. 10–4:30.*

The 15th-century **Duomo** was also built by the architect Rossellino under the influence of Alberti. The facade is divided in three parts with Renaissance arches under the pope's coat of arms encircled by a wreath of fruit. Inside, the cathedral is simple but richly decorated with Sienese paintings. The Duomo's perfection didn't last long—the first cracks appeared immediately after the building was completed, and its foundations have shifted slightly ever since as rain erodes the hillside behind. You can see this effect if you look closely at the base of the first column as you enter the church and compare it with the last. ✉ *Piazza Pio II* ☎ *No phone* 🕑 *Tues.–Sun. 10–1 and 3–7.*

WHERE TO EAT

$ TUSCAN **La Chiocciola.** Take the few minutes to walk from the old town for typical Pienza fare, including homemade pici with hare or wild-boar sauce. The restaurant's version of *formaggio in forno* (baked cheese) with assorted accompaniments such as fresh porcini mushrooms is reason enough to venture here. *Via dell'Acero 2* *0578/748683* *www.trattorialachiocciola.it* *Closed Wed. and 10 days in Feb.*

$ TUSCAN **La Porta.** Well worth the drive (or even the walk), lunch here is a rare treat. About 4 km (2½ mi) east of Pienza, in the hilltop town of Monticchiello, the restaurant sits astride medieval walls and offers one of the best views in the Val d'Orcia to those who eat on the terrace. The food is simple and delicious, but if there happen to be truffles on the menu, order them. *Via del Piano 1, Monticchiello* *0578/755163* *www.osterialaporta.it* *Reservations essential* *Closed Thurs. and mid-Jan.–mid-Feb.*

$$ TUSCAN ★ **Latte di Luna.** With Roberto and his wife Enrica out front and their mothers in the kitchen, this is truly a family affair, and it's enormously popular with locals and tourists alike. Highlights of the menu are the pici all'aglione (with tomato and garlic sauce) and the out-of-this-world maialino (roast suckling pig). Top it off with some of the delicious homemade hazelnut and orange ice cream. The umbrella-shaded seating in the small square out front is much sought after during the summer, so make sure to reserve well in advance. *Via San Carlo 2-4* *0578/748606* *Reservations essential* *Closed Tues.*

¢ TUSCAN **Osteria Sette di Vino.** Tasty dishes based on the region's cheeses are the specialty at this simple and inexpensive *osteria* (tavern). Try versions of pici or the starter of radicchio baked quickly to brown the edges. The local pecorino cheese appears often on the menu—the pecorino *grigliata con pancetta* (grilled with cured bacon) is divine. Can't decide? Try the pecorino tasting menu. Osteria Sette di Vino is on a quiet, pleasant square in the center of Pienza. *Piazza di Spagna 1* *0578/749092* *No credit cards* *Closed Wed., July 1–15, and Nov.*

WHERE TO STAY

$ **Hotel Corsignano.** Just outside the old city walls, Hotel Corsignano is modern and comfortable. **Pros:** steps away from center of town; helpful staff. **Cons:** modern building lacks charm; some rooms face a busy street. **TripAdvisor:** "short walk into town," "great location," "helpful and courteous." *Via della Madonnina 11* *0578/748501* *www.corsignano.it* *40 rooms* *In-hotel: restaurant, business center, parking, some pets allowed* *Breakfast.*

MONTALCINO

24 km (15 mi) west of Pienza, 41 km (25 mi) south of Siena.

GETTING HERE

By car, follow the SR2 south from Siena, then follow the SP45 to Montalcino. Several Tra-In buses travel between Siena and Montalcino daily, making a tightly scheduled day trip possible. There's no train service available.

VISITOR INFORMATION

Montalcino tourism office (✉ *Costa del Municipio 8* ☎ *0577/849331* 🌐 *www.prolocomontalcino.it*).

EXPLORING

Another medieval hill town with a special claim to fame, Montalcino is the source for Brunello di Montalcino, one of Italy's most esteemed red wines. You can sample it in wine cellars in town or visit one of the nearby wineries for a guided tour and tasting; you must call ahead for reservations—your hotel or the local tourist office can help with arrangements.

La Fortezza, a 14th-century Sienese fortress that served as their last defense against the invading Florentines in 1555, has remarkably well-preserved battlements. Climb up the narrow, spiral steps for the 360-degree view of most of southern Tuscany. There's also an enoteca for tasting wines on-site. ✉ *Via Panfilo dell'Oca* ☎ *0577/849211* 🎫 *€3* 🕒 *Nov.–Mar., Tues.–Sun. 9–6; Apr.–Oct., daily 9–8.*

The **Museo Civico e Diocesano d'Arte Sacra** is in a building that belonged in the 13th century to the Augustinian monastic order. The ticket booth is in the glorious refurbished cloister, and the sacred art collection, gathered from churches throughout the region, is displayed on two floors in former monastic quarters. Though the art here might be called "B-list," a fine altarpiece by Bartolo di Fredi (circa 1330–1410), the *Coronation of the Virgin,* makes dazzling use of gold. In addition, there's a striking 12th-century crucifix that originally adorned the high altar of the church of Sant'Antimo. Also on hand are many wood sculptures, a typical medium in these parts during the Renaissance. ✉ *Via Ricasoli 21* ☎ *0577/846014* 🎫 *€8* 🕒 *Apr.–Oct., Tues.–Sun. 10–1 and 4–5:50; Nov.–Mar., Tues.–Sun. 10–1 and 2–5:40.*

WHERE TO EAT

$ WINE BAR ★ ✕ **Enoteca Osteria Osticcio.** Tullio and Francesca Scrivano have beautifully remodeled this restaurant and wineshop. Upon entering, you descend a curving staircase to a tasting room filled with rustic wooden tables. Adjacent is a small dining area with a splendid view of the hills far below, and outside is a lovely little terrace perfect for sampling Brunello di Montalcino when the weather is warm. The menu is light and pairs nicely with the wines, which are the main draw. The *acciughe sotto pesto* (anchovies with pesto) is a particularly fine treat. ✉ *Via Matteotti 23* ☎ *0577/848271* 🕒 *Closed Sun. No dinner.*

$$$$ TUSCAN Fodor's Choice ★ ✕ **Poggio Antico.** One of Italy's renowned chefs, Roberto Minnetti, abandoned his highly successful restaurant in Rome to move to the countryside outside Montalcino. Now he and his wife Patrizia serve in a relaxed dining room with regal arches and beamed ceilings. The Tuscan cuisine is masterfully interpreted: a frequent option on the changing menu is *pappardelle al ragù di agnello* (flat, wide noodles in a lamb sauce) or venison in a sweet-and-sour sauce. ✉ *On road to Grosseto ⊕ 4 km (2½ mi) south of Montalcino, Località I Poggi* ☎ *0577/849200* 🌐 *www.poggioantico.com* ⊗ *Closed Mon. and Nov.–Mar. No dinner Sun.*

WHERE TO STAY

$$$$ **Castiglion del Bosco.** This estate, one of the largest still in private hands in Tuscany, was purchased by Massimo Ferragamo at the beginning of the century and meticulously converted into a second-to-none resort. **Pros:** exclusive and tranquil setting; top-notch service; breathtaking scenery. **Cons:** well off the beaten track; private transportation required. **TripAdvisor:** "a feast for the soul," "effortless luxury," "pampered at every turn." ✉ *Località Castiglion del Bosco* ☎ *0577/1913111* 🌐 *www.castigliondelbosco.com* *23 suites, 9 villas* *In-room: a/c, kitchen (some), Wi-Fi. In-hotel: restaurants, bars, golf course, tennis courts, pools, gym, spa, children's programs, some pets allowed* *Breakfast.*

$ **La Crociona.** A quiet and serene family-owned farm, La Crociona is in the middle of a small vineyard with glorious views. **Pros:** peaceful location; great for families. **Cons:** no air-conditioning; need a car to get around. **TripAdvisor:** "highlight of trip," "beautiful estate," "treated like family." ✉ *Località La Croce* ☎ *0577/848007* 🌐 *www.lacrociona.com* *7 apartments* *In-room: no a/c, kitchen. In-hotel: pool, laundry facilities, business center* *No meals.*

ABBAZIA DI SANT'ANTIMO

10 km (6 mi) south of Montalcino, 51 km (32 mi) south of Siena.

GETTING HERE

Abbazia di Sant'Antimo is a 15-minute drive from Montalcino. Tra-In bus service is extremely limited. The abbey cannot be reached by train.

EXPLORING

It's well worth your while to visit this 12th-century Romanesque abbey, as it's a gem of pale stone in the silvery green of an olive grove. The exterior and interior sculpture is outstanding, particularly the nave capitals, a combination of French, Lombard, and even Spanish influences. The sacristy (seldom open) forms part of the primitive Carolingian church (founded in AD 781), its entrance flanked by 9th-century pilasters. The small vaulted crypt dates from the same period. Above the nave runs a *matroneum* (women's gallery), an unusual feature once used to separate the congregation. Equally unusual is the ambulatory, for which the three radiating chapels were almost certainly copied from a French model. Stay to hear the canonical hours celebrated in Gregorian chant. On the drive that leads up toward Castelnuovo dell'Abate is a small shop that sells souvenirs and has washrooms. A 2½-hour hiking trail (signed as #2) leads to the abbey from Montalcino. Starting near Montalcino's small cemetery, the trail heads south through woods, along a ridge road to the tiny hamlet of Villa a Tolli, and then downhill to Sant'Antimo. ✉ *Località Sant'Antimo Castelnuovo dell'Abate* ☎ *0577/835659* 🌐 *www.antimo.it* ⏲ *Daily 6 am–9 pm.*

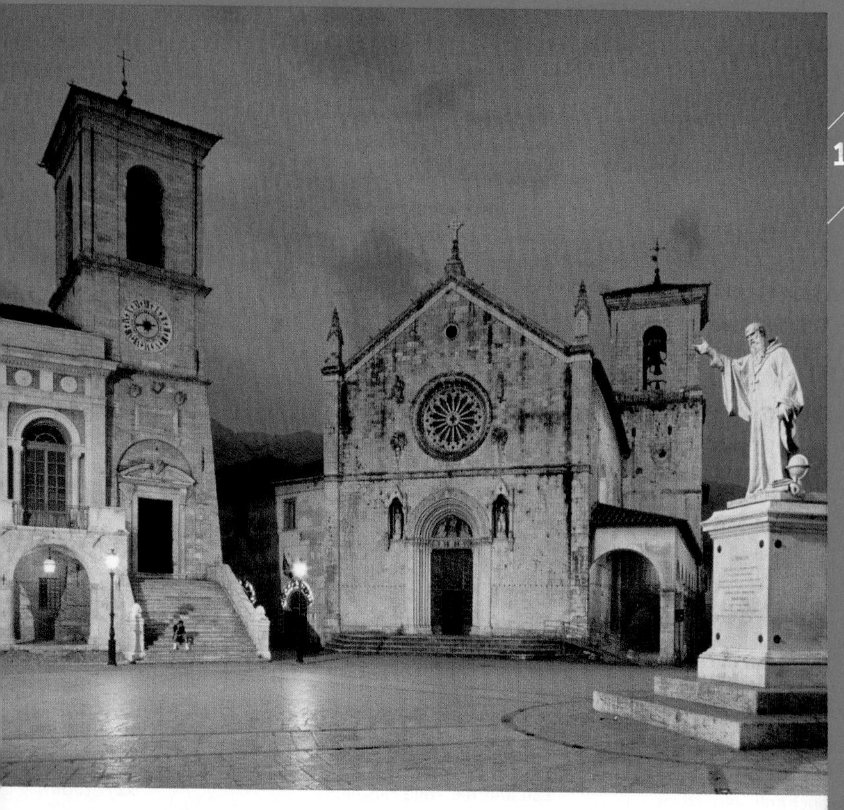

12

Umbria and the Marches

WORD OF MOUTH

"If I could only return to one town in Umbria, it would be Assisi. Loved the setting, the history, the evening ambiance. But Perugia would be a very close second choice for many of the above reasons."

—galelstorm

WELCOME TO UMBRIA AND THE MARCHES

TOP REASONS TO GO

★ **Palazzo Ducale, Urbino:** A visit here reveals more about the ideals of the Renaissance than a shelf of history books.

★ **Assisi, shrine to Saint Francis:** Recharge your soul in this rose-color hill town with a visit to the gentle saint's majestic basilica, adorned with great frescoes.

★ **Spoleto, Umbria's musical Mecca:** Crowds may descend and prices ascend here during summer's Festival dei Due Mondi, but Spoleto's hushed charm enchants year-round.

★ **Tantalizing truffles:** Are Umbria's celebrated "black diamonds" coveted for their pungent flavor, their rarity, or their power in the realm of romance?

★ **Orvieto's Duomo:** Arresting visions of heaven and hell on the facade and brilliant frescoes within make this Gothic cathedral a dazzler.

1 Perugia. Umbria's largest town is easily reached from Rome, Siena, or Florence. Home to some of Perugino's great frescoes and a hilltop *centro storico* (historic center), it's also favored by chocolate lovers, who celebrate their passion at October's Eurochocolate Festival.

2 Assisi. The city of Saint Francis is a major pilgrimage site, crowned by one of Italy's greatest churches. Despite the throngs of visitors, it still maintains its medieval hill-town character.

3 Northern Umbria. The quiet towns lying around Perugia include **Deruta**, which produces exceptional ceramics, and **Torgiano**, where you can tour the Wine Museum and taste the wines from the surrounding valley. A trip through the rugged terrain of northeast Umbria takes you to **Gubbio**, where from the Piazza della Signoria you can admire magnificent views of the countryside below.

4 Spoleto. Though it's known to the world for its annual performing-arts festival, Spoleto offers much more than Puccini in its Piazza del Duomo. There are Filippo Lippi frescoes in the cathedral, a massive castle towering over the town, and a bridge across the neighboring valley that's an engineering marvel.

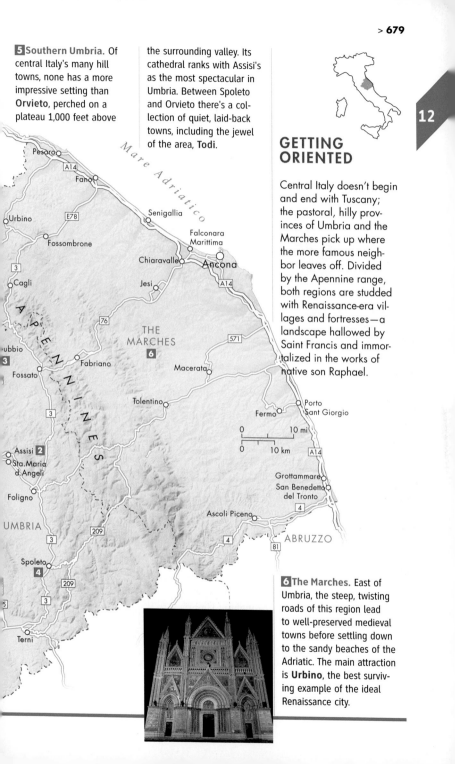

5 Southern Umbria. Of central Italy's many hill towns, none has a more impressive setting than **Orvieto**, perched on a plateau 1,000 feet above the surrounding valley. Its cathedral ranks with Assisi's as the most spectacular in Umbria. Between Spoleto and Orvieto there's a collection of quiet, laid-back towns, including the jewel of the area, **Todi**.

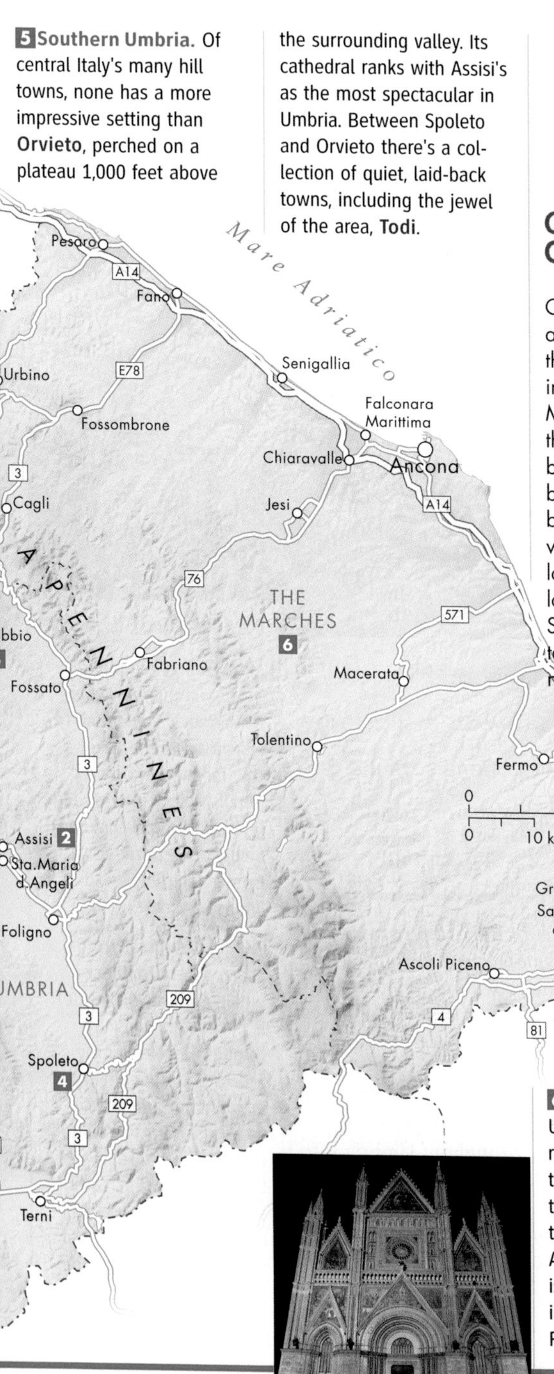

GETTING ORIENTED

Central Italy doesn't begin and end with Tuscany; the pastoral, hilly provinces of Umbria and the Marches pick up where the more famous neighbor leaves off. Divided by the Apennine range, both regions are studded with Renaissance-era villages and fortresses—a landscape hallowed by Saint Francis and immortalized in the works of native son Raphael.

6 The Marches. East of Umbria, the steep, twisting roads of this region lead to well-preserved medieval towns before settling down to the sandy beaches of the Adriatic. The main attraction is **Urbino**, the best surviving example of the ideal Renaissance city.

EATING AND DRINKING WELL IN UMBRIA AND THE MARCHES

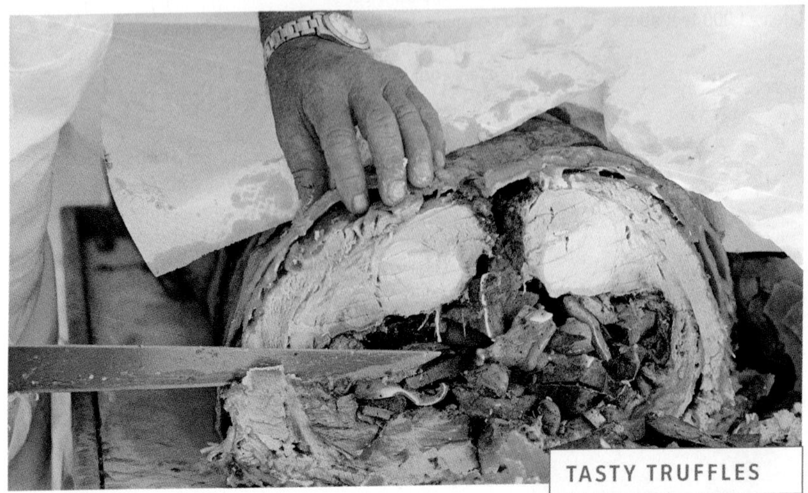

Central Italy is mountainous, and its food is hearty and straightforward, with a stick-to-the-ribs quality that sees hardworking farmers and artisans through a long day's work and helps them make the steep climb home at night.

In restaurants here, as in much of Italy, you're rewarded for seeking out the local cuisines, and you'll often find better, and cheaper food if you're willing to stray a few hundred yards from the main sights. Spoleto is noted for its good food and service, probably a result of high expectations from the international arts crowd. For gourmets, however, it's hard to beat Spello, which has both excellent restaurants and first-rate wine merchants.

A rule of thumb for eating well throughout Umbria is to order what's in season; the trick is to stroll through local markets to see what's for sale. A number of restaurants in the region offer *degustazione* (tasting) menus, which give you a chance to try different local specialties without breaking the bank.

TASTY TRUFFLES

More truffles are found in Umbria than anywhere else in Italy. Spoleto and Norcia are prime territory for the *tartufo nero* (reddish-black interior and fine white veins), pictured below right, prized for its extravagant flavor and intense aroma.

The mild summer truffle, *scorzone estivo* (black outside and beige inside), is in season from May through December. The *scorzone autunnale* (burnt brown color and visible veins inside) is found from October through December. Truffles can be shaved into omelets or over pasta, pounded into sauces, or chopped and mixed with oil.

OLIVE OIL

Nearly everywhere you look in Umbria, olive trees grace the hillsides. The soil of the Apennines allows the olives to ripen slowly, guaranteeing low acidity, a cardinal virtue of fine oil. Look for restaurants that proudly display their own oil, often a sign that they care about their food.

Umbria's finest oil is found in Trevi, where the local product is intensely green and fruity. You can sample it in the town's wine bars, which often do double duty, offering olive-oil tastings.

PORK PRODUCTS

Much of traditional Umbrian cuisine revolves around pork. It can be cooked in wood-fire stoves, sometimes basted with a rich sauce made from innards and red wine. The roasted pork known as *porchetta*, pictured at left, is grilled on a spit and flavored with fennel and herbs, leaving a crisp outer sheen.

The art of pork processing has been handed down through generations in Norcia, so much that charcuterie producers throughout Italy are often known as *norcini*. Don't miss *prosciutto di Norcia*, which is aged for two years.

LENTILS AND SOUPS

The town of Castelluccio di Norcia is particularly known for its lentils and its *farro* (an ancient grain used by the Romans, similar to wheat), and a variety of beans used in soups. Throughout

Umbria, look for *imbrecciata*, a soup of beans and grains, delicately flavored with local herbs. Other ingredients that find their way into thick Umbrian soups are wild beet, sorrel, mushrooms, spelt, chickpeas, and the elusive, fragrant saffron, grown in nearby Cascia.

WINE

Sagrantino grapes are the star in Umbria's most notable red wines. For centuries they've been used in Sagrantino *passito*, a semisweet wine made by leaving the grapes to dry for a period after picking in order to intensify their sugar content. In recent decades, the *secco* (dry) Sagrantino has occupied the front stage. Both passito and secco have a deep red-ruby color, with a full body and rich flavor.

In the past few years the phenomenon of the *enoteca* (wineshop and wine bar) has taken off, making it easier to arrange wine tastings. Many also let you sample different olive oils on toasted bread, known as *bruschetta*. Some wine information centers, such as La Strada del Sagrantino in the town of Montefalco, will help set up appointments for tastings.

Updated by Jonathan Willcocks

Birthplace of saints and home to some of the country's greatest artistic treasures, central Italy is a collection of misty green valleys and picture-perfect hill towns laden with centuries of history.

Umbria and the Marches are the Italian countryside as you've imagined it: verdant farmland, steep hillsides topped with medieval fortresses, and winding country roads. No single town here has the extravagant wealth of art and architecture of Florence, Rome, or Venice, but this works in your favor: small jewels of towns feel knowable, not overwhelming. And the cultural cupboard is far from bare. Orvieto's cathedral and Assisi's basilica are two of the most important sights in Italy, while Perugia, Todi, Gubbio, and Spoleto are rich in art and architecture.

East of Umbria, the Marches (Le Marche to Italians) stretch between the Apennines and the Adriatic Sea. It's a region of great turreted castles on high peaks defending passes and roads—a testament to the centuries of battle that have taken place here. Rising majestically in Urbino is a splendid palace, built by Federico da Montefeltro, where the humanistic ideals of the Renaissance came to their fullest flower, while the town of Ascoli Piceno can lay claim to one of the most beautiful squares in Italy. Virtually every small town in the region has a castle, church, or museum worth a visit—but even without them, you'd still be compelled to stop for the interesting streets, panoramic views, and natural beauty.

PLANNING

MAKING THE MOST OF YOUR TIME

Umbria is a nicely compact collection of character-rich hill towns; you can settle in one, then explore the others, as well as the countryside and forest in between, on day trips.

Perugia, Umbria's largest and most lively city, is a logical choice for your base, particularly if you're arriving from the north. If you want something a little quieter, virtually any other town in the region will suit your purposes; even Assisi, which overflows with bus tours during the day, is delightfully quiet in the evening and early morning. Spoleto and Orvieto are the most developed towns to the south, but they're still of modest proportions.

If you have the time to venture farther afield, consider trips to Gubbio, northeast of Perugia, and Urbino, in the Marches. Both are worth the time it takes to reach them, and both make for pleasant overnight stays. In southern Umbria, Valnerina and the Piano Grande are out-of-the-way spots with the region's best hiking.

FESTIVALS

Each summer Umbria hosts two of Italy's biggest music festivals. Spoleto's **Festival dei Due Mondi** (🌐 *www.spoletofestival.it*), from late June through early July, features classical music and also ventures into theater and the visual arts. Perugia is hopping for 10 days in July, when famous names in contemporary music perform at the **Umbria Jazz Festival** (🌐 *www.umbriajazz.com*). If you want to attend either event, you should make arrangements in advance. And if you don't want to attend, you should plan to avoid the cities during festival time, when hotel rooms and restaurant tables are at a premium. A similar caveat applies for Assisi during religious festivals at Christmas, Easter, the feast of Saint Francis (October 4), and Calendimaggio (May 1), when pilgrims arrive en masse.

If you've got a sweet tooth and you're visiting in fall, head to Perugia for the **Eurochocolate Festival** (🌐 *www.eurochocolate.perugia.it*) in the third week of October.

GETTING HERE AND AROUND

BUS TRAVEL

Perugia's bus station is in Piazza Partigiani, which you can reach by taking the escalators from the town center. Perugia is served by the **Sulga Line** (☎ *075/5009641* 🌐 *www.sulga.it*), which has daily departures to Rome's Stazione Tiburtina and to Florence's Piazza Adua. Connections between Rome, Spoleto, and the Marches are provided by the bus company **Bucci** (☎ *0721/32401* 🌐 *www.autolineebucci.com*).

Local bus services between all the major and minor towns of Umbria are good. Some of the routes in rural areas are designed to serve as many places as possible and are, therefore, quite roundabout and slow. Schedules change often, so consult with local tourist offices before setting out.

CAR TRAVEL

On the western edge of the region is the Umbrian section of the Autostrada del Sole (A1), Italy's principal north-south highway. It links Florence and Rome with Orvieto and passes near Todi and Terni. The S3 intersects with A1 and leads on to Assisi and Urbino. The Adriatica superhighway (A14) runs north-south along the coast, linking the Marches to Bologna and Venice.

The steep hills and deep valleys that make Umbria and the Marches so idyllic also make for challenging driving. Fortunately, the area has an excellent, modern road network, but be prepared for tortuous mountain roads if your explorations take you off the beaten track. Central Umbria is served by a major highway, the S75bis, which passes along the shore of Lake Trasimeno and ends in Perugia. Assisi is served by the modern highway S75; S75 connects to S3 and S3bis, which cover the heart of the region. Major inland routes connect coastal A14 to large towns in the Marches, but inland secondary roads in mountain areas can be winding and narrow. Always carry a good map, a flashlight, and, if possible, a cell phone in case of a breakdown.

TRAIN TRAVEL

Several direct daily trains run by the Italian state railway, **Ferrovia dello Stato** (☎ *892021 toll-free in Italy* 🌐 *www.trenitalia.com*), link Florence and Rome with Perugia and Assisi, and local service to the same area is available from Terontola (on the Rome–Florence line) and from Foligno (on the Rome–Ancona line). Intercity trains between Rome and Florence make stops in Orvieto, and the main Rome–Ancona line passes through Narni, Terni, Spoleto, and Foligno.

Within Umbria, a small, privately owned railway operated by **Ferrovia Centrale Umbra** (☎ *024/73000541*) runs from Città di Castello in the north to Terni in the south via Perugia. Note: train service isn't available to either Gubbio or Urbino.

ABOUT THE HOTELS

Virtually every older town, no matter how small, has some kind of hotel. A trend, particularly around Gubbio, Orvieto, and Todi, is to convert old villas, farms, and monasteries into first-class hotels. The natural splendor of the countryside more than compensates for the distance from town—provided you have a car. Hotels in town tend to be simpler than their country cousins, with a few notable exceptions in Spoleto, Gubbio, and Perugia.

Hotel reviews have been condensed for this book. Please go to Fodors.com for expanded reviews of each property.

WHAT IT COSTS (IN EUROS)

	¢	$	$$	$$$	$$$$
Restaurants	under €20	€20–€30	€30–€45	€45–€65	over €65
Hotels	under €75	€75–€125	€125–€200	€200–€300	over €300

Restaurant prices are for a first course (primo), second course (secondo), and dessert (dolce). Hotel prices are for two people in a standard double room in high season, including tax and service.

VISITOR INFORMATION

Umbria's regional tourism office (✉ *Piazza Matteotti 18* ☎ *075/5736458* 🌐 *www.regioneumbria.eu*) is in Perugia. The staff is well informed about the area and can give you a wide selection of leaflets and maps to assist you during your trip. It's open Monday to Saturday 8:30 to 1:30 and 3 to 6:30, and Sunday 8:30 to 1.

12

PERUGIA

Perugia is a majestic, handsome, wealthy city, and with its trendy boutiques, refined cafés, and grandiose architecture, it doesn't try to hide its affluence. A student population of more than 30,000 means that the city is abuzz with activity throughout the year. Umbria Jazz, one of the region's most important music festivals, attracts music lovers from around the world, and Eurochocolate, the international chocolate festival, is an irresistible draw for anyone with a sweet tooth.

GETTING HERE

The best approach to the city is by train. The area around the station doesn't attest to the rest of Perugia's elegance, but buses running from the station to Piazza d'Italia, the heart of the old town, are frequent. If you're in a hurry, take the minimetro, a one-line subway, to Stazione della Cupa. If you're driving to Perugia and your hotel doesn't have parking facilities, leave your car in one of the lots close to the center. Electronic displays indicate the location of lots and the number of spaces free. If you park in the Piazza Partigiani, take the escalators that pass through the fascinating subterranean excavations of the Roman foundations of the city and lead to the town center.

EXPLORING PERUGIA

Thanks to Perugia's hilltop position, the medieval city remains almost completely intact. It's the best-preserved hill town of its size, and few other places in Italy better illustrate the model of the self-contained city-state that so shaped the course of Italian history.

TOP ATTRACTIONS

★ **Collegio del Cambio** *(Bankers' Guild Hall)*. These elaborate rooms, on the ground floor of the **Palazzo dei Priori,** served as the meeting hall and chapel of the guild of bankers and moneychangers. Most of the frescoes were completed by the most important Perugian painter of the Renaissance, Pietro Vannucci, better known as Perugino. He included a remarkably honest self-portrait on one of the pilasters. The iconography includes common religious themes, such as the Nativity and the Transfiguration seen on the end walls. On the left wall are female figures representing the virtues, beneath them the heroes and sages of antiquity. On the right wall are figures presumed to have been painted in part by Perugino's most famous pupil, Raphael. (His hand, experts say, is most apparent in the figure of Fortitude.) The *cappella* (chapel) of San Giovanni Battista has frescoes painted by Giannicola di Paolo, another student of Perugino's. ✉ *Corso Vannucci 25* ☎ *075/5728599* 🎟 *€4.50, €5.50 with Collegio della Mercanzia* 🕘 *Mon.–Sat. 9–1 and 2:30–5:30, Sun. 9–1.*

Corso Vannucci. A string of elegantly connected *palazzi* (palaces) expresses the artistic nature of this city center, the heart of which is concentrated along Corso Vannucci. Stately and broad, this pedestrians-only street runs from Piazza d'Italia to Piazza IV Novembre. Along the way, the entrances to many of Perugia's side streets might tempt you to wander off and explore. But don't stray too far as evening falls, when Corso

Collegio del Cambio 4
Duomo 1
Galleria Nazionale dell'Umbria 3
Museo Archeologico Nazionale 5
Palazzo dei Priori 2

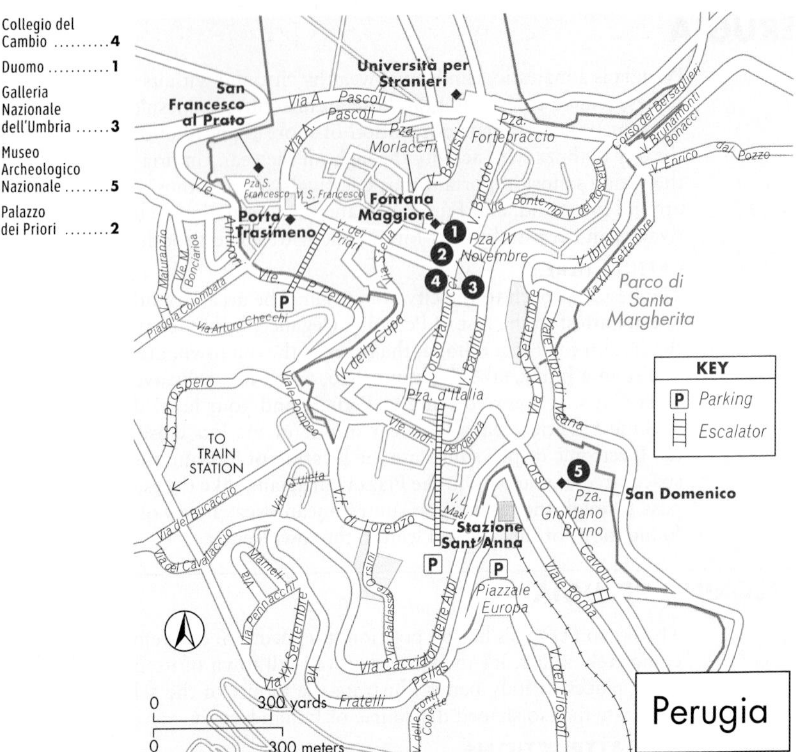

Vannucci fills with Perugians out for their evening *passeggiata,* a pleasant pre-dinner stroll that may include a pause for an aperitif at one of the many bars that line the street.

Fodor's Choice ★ **Galleria Nazionale dell'Umbria.** The region's most comprehensive art gallery is housed on the fourth floor of the **Palazzo dei Priori.** Enhanced by skillfully lit displays and computers that allow you to focus on the works' details and background information, the collection includes work by native artists—most notably Pintoricchio (1454–1513) and Perugino (circa 1450–1523)—and others of the Umbrian and Tuscan schools, among them Gentile da Fabriano (1370–1427), Duccio (circa 1255–1318), Fra Angelico (1387–1455), Fiorenzo di Lorenzo (1445–1525), and Piero della Francesca (1420–92). In addition to paintings, the gallery has frescoes, sculptures, and some superb examples of crucifixes from the 13th and 14th centuries. Some rooms are dedicated to Perugia itself, showing how the medieval city evolved. ✉ *Corso Vannucci 19, Piazza IV Novembre* ☎ *075/5721009* 🌐 *www.gallerianazionaleumbria.it* 🎫 *€6.50* ⏲ *Tues.–Sun. 8:30–7:30; last admission ½ hr before closing.*

★ **Palazzo dei Priori** *(Palace of Priors).* A series of elegant connected buildings, the palazzo serves as Perugia's city hall and houses three of the city's museums. The buildings string along Corso Vannucci and wrap around the Piazza IV Novembre, where the original entrance is located.

UMBRIA THROUGH THE AGES

The earliest inhabitants of Umbria, the Umbri, were thought by the Romans to be the most ancient inhabitants of Italy. Little is known about them; with the coming of Etruscan culture the tribe fled into the mountains in the eastern portion of the region. The Etruscans, who founded some of the great cities of Umbria, were in turn supplanted by the Romans. Unlike Tuscany and other regions of central Italy, Umbria had few powerful medieval families to exert control over the cities in the Middle Ages—its proximity to Rome ensured that it would always be more or less under papal domination.

In the center of the country, Umbria has for much of its history been a battlefield where armies from north and south clashed. Hannibal destroyed a Roman army on the shores of Lake Trasimeno, and the bloody course of the interminable Guelph-Ghibelline conflict of the Middle Ages was played out here. Dante considered Umbria the most violent place in Italy. Trophies of war still decorate the Palazzo dei Priori in Perugia, and the little town of Gubbio continues a warlike rivalry begun in the Middle Ages—every year it challenges the Tuscan town of Sansepolcro to a crossbow tournament. Today the bowmen shoot at targets, but neither side has forgotten that 500 years ago they were shooting at each other. In spite of—or perhaps because of—this bloodshed, Umbria has produced more than its share of Christian saints. The most famous is Saint Francis, the decidedly pacifist saint whose life shaped the Church of his time. His great shrine at Assisi is visited by hundreds of thousands of pilgrims each year. Saint Clare, his devoted follower, was Umbria-born, as were Saint Benedict, Saint Rita of Cascia, and the patron saint of lovers, Saint Valentine.

The steps here lead to the **Sala dei Notari** (Notaries' Hall). Other entrances lead to the **Galleria Nazionale dell'Umbria,** the **Collegio del Cambio,** and the **Collegio della Mercanzia.** The Sala dei Notari, which dates back to the 13th century and was the original meeting place of the town merchants, had become the seat of the notaries by the second half of the 15th century. Wood beams and an interesting array of frescoes attributed to Maestro di Farneto embellish the room. Coats of arms and crests line the back and right lateral walls; you can spot some famous figures from Aesop's *Fables* on the left wall. The palazzo facade is adorned with symbols of Perugia's pride and past power: the griffin is the city symbol, and the lion denotes Perugia's allegiance to the Guelph (or papal) cause. ✉ *Piazza IV Novembre* 🎫 *Free* ⏲ *June–Sept., Tues.–Sun. 9–1 and 3–7.*

Rocca Paolina. A labyrinth of little streets, alleys, and arches, this underground city was originally part of a fortress. It was built at the behest of Pope Paul III between 1540 and 1543 to confirm papal dominion over the city. Parts of it were destroyed after the end of papal rule, but much still remains. Begin your visit by taking the escalators from Piazza Italia and Via Masi. In the summer this is the coolest place in the city. 🎫 *€3.50* ⏲ *Daily 10:30–1 and 2:30–5.*

WORTH NOTING

Duomo. Severe yet mystical, the Duomo, also called the Cathedral of San Lorenzo, is most famous for being the home of the wedding ring of the Virgin Mary, stolen by the Perugians in 1488 from the nearby town of Chiusi. The ring, kept high up in a red-curtained vault in the chapel immediately to the left of the entrance, is kept under lock—15 locks, to be precise—and key most of the year. It's shown to the public on July 30 (the day it was brought to Perugia) and the second-to-last Sunday in January (Mary's wedding anniversary). The cathedral itself dates from the Middle Ages, and has many additions from the 15th and 16th centuries. The most visually interesting element is the altar to the Madonna of Grace; an elegant fresco on a column at the right of the entrance of the altar depicts *La Madonna delle Grazie* and is surrounded by prayer benches decorated with handwritten notes to the Holy Mother. Around the column are small amulets—symbols of gratitude from those whose prayers were answered. There are also elaborately carved choir stalls, executed by Giovanni Battista Bastone in 1520. The altarpiece (1484), an early masterpiece by Luca Signorelli (circa 1441–1523), shows the Madonna with Saint John the Baptist, Saint Onophrius, and Saint Lawrence. Sections of the church may be closed to visitors during religious services.

WORD OF MOUTH

"Two things you must not fail to do in Perugia are to (a) join the evening walk on the Corso Vannucci beginning at about 5 pm and (b) take the escalators that go up and down and through the historic city walls. Also: Hang out as often as you dare at Sandri's, one of Italy's most marvelous cafe/pastry shops, on the Corso Vanucci."
—nessundorma

The **Museo Capitolare** displays a large array of precious objects associated with the cathedral, including vestments, vessels, and manuscripts. Outside the Duomo is the elaborate **Fontana Maggiore,** which dates from 1278. It's adorned with zodiac figures and symbols of the seven arts. ✉ *Piazza IV Novembre* ☎ *075/5724853* 🎫 *Museum €3.50* ⏲ *Duomo: Mon.–Sat. 7–12:30 and 4–6:45, Sun. 8–12:30 and 4–6:45; museum: daily 10–1 and 2:30–5:30; last admission ½ hr before closing.*

Museo Archeologico Nazionale. The museum, next to the imposing church of San Domenico, contains an excellent collection of Etruscan artifacts from throughout the region. Perugia was a flourishing Etruscan city long before it fell under Roman domination in 310 BC. Little else remains of Perugia's mysterious ancestors, although the Arco di Augusto, in Piazza Fortebraccio, the northern entrance to the city, is of Etruscan origin. ✉ *Piazza G. Bruno 10* ☎ *075/5727141* 🌐 *www.archeopg.arti.beniculturali.it* 🎫 *€4* ⏲ *Mon. 2:30–7:30, Tues.–Sun. 8:30–7:30.*

WHERE TO EAT

$$$ UMBRIAN ✕ **Antica Trattoria San Lorenzo.** Brick vaults are not the only distinguishing feature of this small restaurant next to the Duomo, as both the food and the service are outstanding. Particular attention is paid to adapting traditional Umbrian cuisine to the modern palate. There's also a nice variety of seafood dishes on the menu. The *trenette alla farina di noce*

con pesce di mare (flat noodles made with walnut flour topped with fresh fish) is a real treat. ✉ *Piazza Danti 19-A* ☎ *075/5721956* 🌐 *www.anticatrattoriasanlorenzo.com* ⏲ *Closed Sun.*

¢ UMBRIAN ★ ✕ **Dal Mi' Cocco.** A great favorite with Perugia's university students, this place is fun, crowded, and inexpensive. You may find yourself seated at a long table with other diners, but some language help from your neighbors could come in handy—the menu is in pure Perugian dialect. The fixed-price meals change with the season, and each day of the week brings some new creation *dal cocco* (from the "coconut," or head) of the chef. ✉ *Corso Garibaldi 12* ☎ *075/5732511* ✍ *Reservations essential* ▭ *No credit cards* ⏲ *Closed late July–mid-Aug.*

$ UMBRIAN ✕ **Il Falchetto.** Exceptional food at reasonable prices makes this Perugia's best bargain. Service is smart but relaxed in the two medieval dining rooms that put the chef on view. The house specialty is *falchetti* (homemade gnocchi with spinach and ricotta cheese). ✉ *Via Bartolo 20* ☎ *075/5731775* ⏲ *Closed Mon. and last 2 wks in Jan.*

$$ ITALIAN ✕ **La Rosetta.** The restaurant, in the hotel of the same name, is a peaceful, elegant spot. In winter you dine inside under medieval vaults; in summer, in the cool courtyard. The food is simple but reliable, and flawlessly served. The restaurant caters to travelers seeking to get away from the bustle of central Perugia. The delightful courtyard is 10 meters off the Corso Vannucci. ✉ *Piazza d'Italia 19* ☎ *075/5720841* ✍ *Reservations essential.*

$$ UMBRIAN ✕ **La Taverna.** Medieval steps lead to a rustic two-story restaurant where wine bottles and artful clutter decorate the walls. Good choices from the regional menu include *caramelle al gorgonzola* (pasta rolls filled with red cabbage and mozzarella and topped with a Gorgonzola sauce) and grilled meat dishes, such as the *medaglioni di vitello al tartuffo* (grilled veal with truffles). ✉ *Via delle Streghe 8, off Corso Vannucci* ☎ *075/5724128* ⏲ *Closed Mon.*

WHERE TO STAY

$$$ **Castello dell'Oscano.** A splendid neo-Gothic castle, a late-19th-century villa, and a converted farmhouse hidden in the tranquil hills north of Perugia offer a wide range of accommodations. **Pros:** quiet elegance; fine gardens; Umbrian wine list. **Cons:** distant from Perugia; not easy to find. **TripAdvisor:** "staff very friendly," "good food," "impressive." ✉ *Strada della Forcella 32, Cenerente* ☎ *075/584371* 🌐 *www.oscano.it* *24 rooms, 8 suites, 13 apartments* *In-room: no a/c (some), Internet. In-hotel: restaurant, bar, pool, gym* *Breakfast.*

$$ **Hotel Fortuna.** The elegant decor in the large rooms of this friendly hotel complements the frescoes, which date from the 1700s. **Pros:** central but quiet; homely atmosphere. **Cons:** some small rooms; no restaurant. **TripAdvisor:** "nice roof top balcony," "roomy and stylish," "breakfast was brilliant." ✉ *Via Bonazzi 19, Corso Vannucci* ☎ *075/5722845* 🌐 *www.hotelfortunaperugia.com* *51 rooms* *In-room: a/c. In-hotel: restaurant, bar, parking* *Breakfast.*

$$ **Il Cantico della Natura.** Don't let the rustic appearance of the buildings fool you—this is one of the plushest *agriturismi* (farm stays) in Umbria. **Pros:** views of Lake Trasimeno and the surrounding countryside. **Cons:** not easy to find; road poor in winter. **TripAdvisor:** "quiet, romantic,

charming," "beautiful grounds and trails," "restored and updated beautifully." ✉ *Case Sparse 50, Montesperello di Magione* ☎ *075/841454* 🌐 *www.ilcanticodellanatura.it* ⇨ *12 rooms* *In-room: a/c. In-hotel: restaurant, gym* 🍽 *Breakfast.*

$$ **Locanda della Posta.** In the city's old district, this lodging is in an 18th-century palazzo. **Pros:** some fine views; central position. **Cons:** uninspiring lobby; some small rooms; no restaurant. **TripAdvisor:** "perfect location," "old-world charm," "staff was very friendly." ✉ *Corso Vannucci 97* ☎ *075/5728925* ⇨ *38 rooms, 1 suite* *In-room: a/c. In-hotel: bar, parking* 🍽 *Breakfast.*

NIGHTLIFE AND THE ARTS

With its large student population, the city has plenty to offer in the way of bars and clubs. The best ones are around the city center, off Corso Vanucci. *Viva Perugia* is a good source of information about nightlife. The monthly, sold at newsstands, has a section in English.

MUSIC FESTIVALS

Summer sees two music festivals in Perugia. **Umbria Jazz** (☎ *075/5732432* 🌐 *www.umbriajazz.com*) is held for 10 days in July. Tickets are available starting at the end of April. The **Sagra Musicale Umbra** (☎ *075/5721374* 🌐 *www.perugiamusicaclassica.com*), held from mid-August to mid-September, celebrates sacred music.

SHOPPING

Take a stroll down any of Perugia's main streets, including Corso Vannucci, Via dei Priori, Via Oberdan, and Via Sant'Ercolano, and you'll see many well-known designer boutiques and specialty shops.

The most typical thing to buy in Perugia is some Perugina chocolate, which you can find almost anywhere. The best-known chocolates made by Perugina are the chocolate-and-hazelnut-filled nibbles called Baci (literally, "kisses"). They're wrapped in silver paper that includes a sliver of paper, like the fortune in a fortune cookie, with multilingual romantic sentiments or sayings.

ASSISI

The small town of Assisi is one of the Christian world's most important pilgrimage sites and home of the Basilica di San Francesco—built to honor Saint Francis (1182–1226) and erected in swift order after his death. The peace and serenity of the town is a welcome respite after the hustle and bustle of some of Italy's major cities.

Like most other towns in the region, Assisi began as an Umbri settlement in the 7th century BC and was conquered by the Romans 400 years later. The town was Christianized by Saint Rufino, its patron saint, in the 3rd century, but it's the spirit of Saint Francis, a patron saint of Italy and founder of the Franciscan monastic order, that's felt throughout its narrow medieval streets. The famous 13th-century basilica was decorated by the greatest artists of the period.

GETTING HERE

Assisi lies on the Terontola–Foligno rail line, with almost hourly connections to Perugia and direct trains to Rome and Florence several times a day. The Stazione Centrale is 4 km (2½ mi) from town, with a bus service about every half hour. Assisi is easily reached from the A1 Motorway (Rome–Florence) and the S75b highway. The walled town is closed to traffic, so cars must be left in the parking lots at Porta San Pietro, near Porta Nuova, or beneath Piazza Matteotti. Pay your parking fee at the *cassa* (ticket booth) before you return to your car to get a ticket to insert in the machine that will allow you to exit. It's a short but sometimes steep walk into the center of town; frequent minibuses (buy tickets from a newsstand or tobacco shop near where you park your car) make the rounds for weary pilgrims.

VISITOR INFORMATION

Assisi tourism office (✉ *Piazza del Commune 22* ☎ *075/8138680* 🌐 *www.regioneumbria.eu*).

EXPLORING ASSISI

Assisi is pristinely medieval in architecture and appearance, owing in large part to relative neglect from the 16th century until 1926, when the celebration of the 700th anniversary of Saint Francis's death brought more than 2 million visitors. Since then, pilgrims have flocked here in droves, and today several million arrive each year to pay homage. But not even the constant flood of visitors to this town of just 3,000 residents can spoil the singular beauty of this significant religious center, the home of some of the Western tradition's most important works of art. The hill on which Assisi sits rises dramatically from the flat plain, and the town is dominated by a medieval castle at the very top.

Even though Assisi can become besieged with sightseers disgorged by tour buses, who clamor to visit the famous basilica, it's difficult not to be charmed by the tranquillity of the town and its medieval architecture. Once you've seen the basilica, stroll through the town's narrow winding streets to see beautiful vistas of the nearby hills and valleys peeking through openings between the buildings.

TOP ATTRACTIONS

Basilica di Santa Chiara. The lovely, wide piazza in front of this church is reason enough to visit. The red-and-white-striped facade of the church frames the piazza's panoramic view over the Umbrian plains. Santa Chiara is dedicated to Saint Clare, one of the earliest and most fervent of Saint Francis's followers and the founder of the order of the Poor Ladies—or Poor Clares—which was based on the Franciscan monastic order. The church contains Clare's body, and in the **Cappella del Crocifisso** (on the right) is the cross that spoke to Saint Francis. A heavily veiled nun of the Poor Clares order is usually stationed before the cross in adoration of the image. ✉ *Piazza Santa Chiara* ☎ *075/812282* ⏲ *Nov.–mid-Mar., daily 6:30–noon and 2–6; mid-Mar.–Oct., daily 6:30–noon and 2–7.*

Cattedrale di San Rufino. Saint Francis and Saint Clare were among those baptized in Assisi's Cattedrale, which was the principal church in town until the 12th century. The baptismal font has since been redecorated, but it's possible to see the crypt of Saint Rufino, the bishop who brought Christianity to Assisi and was martyred on August 11, 238 (or 236 by some accounts). Admission to the crypt includes the small **Museo Capitolare,** with its detached frescoes and artifacts. ✉ *Piazza San Rufino* ☎ *075/5816016* 🌐 *www.sistemamuseo.it* 🎟 *Crypt and Museo Capitolare €2.50* ⏲ *Cattedrale: daily 7–noon and 2–6; crypt and Museo Capitolare: mid-Mar.–mid-Oct., daily 10–1 and 3–6; mid-Oct.–mid-Mar., daily 10–1 and 2:30–5:30.*

WORTH NOTING

Santa Maria Sopra Minerva. Dating from the time of the Emperor Augustus (27 BC–AD 14), this structure was originally dedicated to the Roman goddess of wisdom, in later times used as a monastery and prison before being converted into a church in the 16th century. The expectations raised by the perfect classical facade are not met by the interior, which was subjected to a thorough baroque transformation in the 17th century. ✉ *Piazza del Comune* ☎ *075/812268* ⏲ *Mon., Wed., Thur., and weekends 8–7; Tues. and Fri. 8–2 and 5:15–7.*

OFF THE BEATEN PATH

Eremo delle Carceri. About 4 km (2½ mi) east of Assisi is a monastery set in a dense wood against Monte Subasio. The "Hermitage of Prisons" was the place where Saint Francis and his followers went to "imprison" themselves in prayer. The only site in Assisi that remains essentially unchanged since Saint Francis's time, the church and monastery are the kinds of tranquil places that Saint Francis would have appreciated. The walk out from town is very pleasant, and many trails lead from here across the wooded hillside of Monte Subasio (now a protected forest), with beautiful vistas across the Umbrian countryside. True to their Franciscan heritage, the friars here are entirely dependent on alms from visitors. ✉ *Via Santuario delle Carceri* ✥ *4 km (2½ mi) east of Assisi* ☎ *075/812301* 🌐 *www.eremocarceri.it* 🎟 *Donations accepted* ⏲ *Nov.–Mar., daily 6:30–6; Apr.–Oct., daily 6:30 am–7:15 pm.*

WHERE TO EAT

Assisi isn't a late-night town, so don't plan on any midnight snacks. What you can count on is the ubiquitous *stringozzi* (thick spaghetti), as well as the local specialty *piccione all'assisana* (roasted pigeon with olives and liver). The locals eat *torta al testo* (a dense flatbread, often stuffed with vegetables or cheese) with their meals.

$ UMBRIAN ✕ **Buca di San Francesco.** In summer, dine in a cool green garden; in winter, under the low brick arches of the restaurant's cozy cellars. The unique settings and the first-rate fare make this central restaurant Assisi's busiest. Try homemade spaghetti *alla buca,* served with a roasted mushroom sauce. ✉ *Via Eugenio Brizi 1* ☎ *075/812204* ⏲ *Closed Mon. and 10 days late July.*

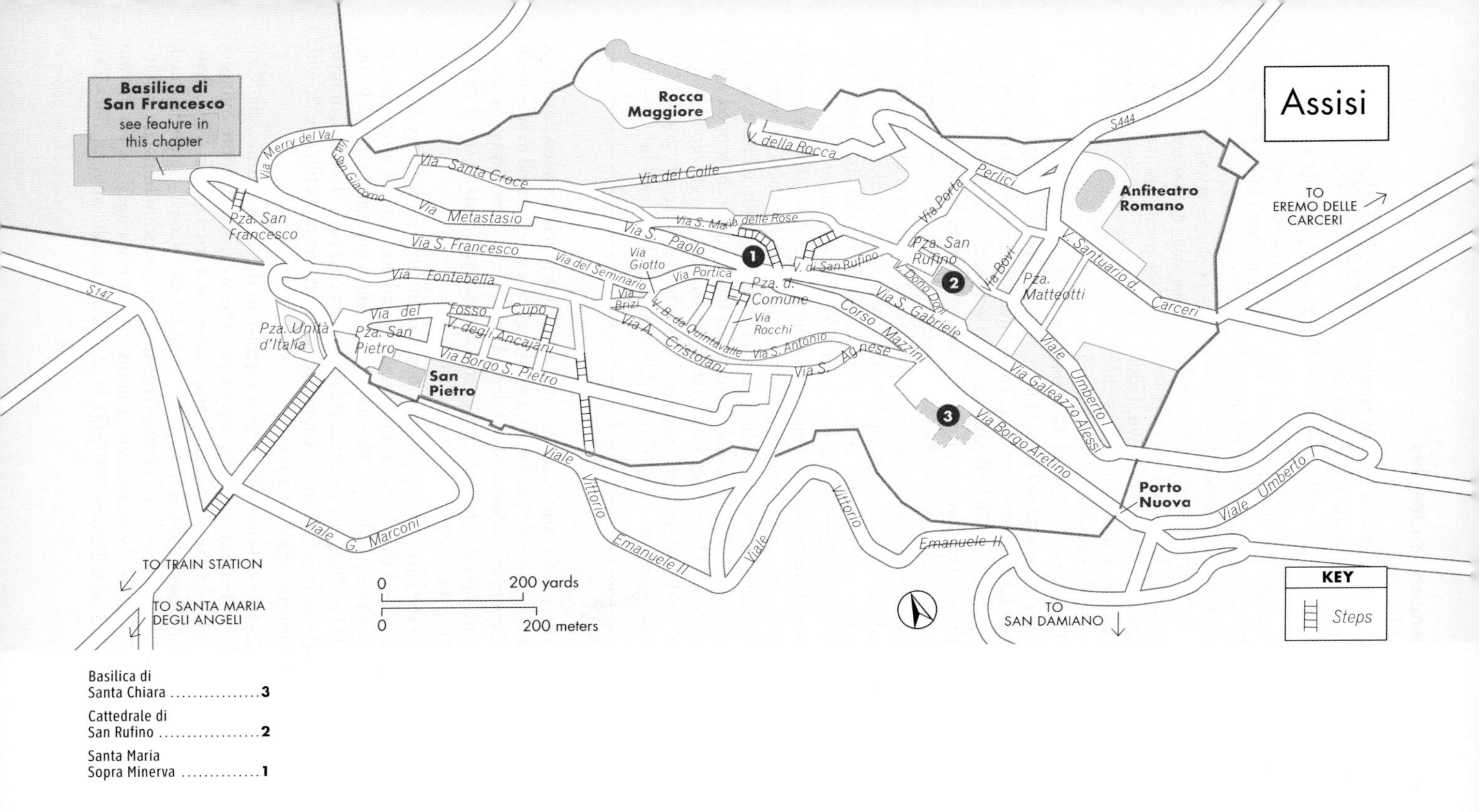
Assisi
Basilica di San Francesco
see feature in this chapter
Rocca Maggiore
Anfiteatro Romano
TO EREMO DELLE CARCERI
S444
S147
V. della Rocca
Via del Colle
Via Santa Croce
Via Merry del Val
Via San Giacomo
Via Metastasio
Pza. San Francesco
Via S. Francesco
Via S. Paolo
Via S. Maria delle Rose
Via Porta
Perlici
Pza. San Rufino
Via Bovi
Pza. Matteotti
V. Santuario d. Carceri
V. di San Rufino
V. Dono Doni
Via S. Gabriele
Corso Mazzini
Via del Seminario
Via Giotto
Via Portica
Pza. d. Comune
Via Rocchi
Via Brizi
V. B. da Quintavalle
Via A. Cristofani
Via S. Antonio
Via S. Agnese
Via Fontebella
Via del Fosso Cupo
V. degli Ancajani
Pza. Unità d'Italia
Pza. San Pietro
Via Borgo S. Pietro
San Pietro
Viale Umberto I
Via Galeazzo Alessi
Via Borgo Aretino
Porto Nuova
Viale Vittorio Emanuele II
Viale G. Marconi
TO TRAIN STATION
TO SANTA MARIA DEGLI ANGELI
0 200 yards
0 200 meters
TO SAN DAMIANO
KEY
Steps
Basilica di Santa Chiara 3
Cattedrale di San Rufino 2
Santa Maria Sopra Minerva 1

$ UMBRIAN Fodor's Choice ★ ✕ **La Pallotta.** At this homey, family-run trattoria with a crackling fireplace and stone walls, the women do the cooking and the men serve the food. Try the stringozzi *alla pallotta* (with a pesto of olives and mushrooms). Connected to the restaurant is an inn whose eight rooms have firm beds and some views across the rooftops of town. Hotel guests get a discount if they dine here. ✉ *Vicolo della Volta Pinta 3* ☎ *075/812649* ⊙ *Closed Tues. and 2 wks in Jan. or Feb.*

WORD OF MOUTH

"Assisi is surrounded by gorgeous walks. The side road from the Basilica around to the Rocca is absolutely wonderful. The same can be said for a walk out to the Eremo delle Carceri, and further into the woods past the Eremo."
—tuscanlifeedit

$$ UMBRIAN ★ ✕ **Osteria Piazzetta dell'Erba.** Hip service and sophisticated presentations attract locals to this trattoria. The owners carefully select wine at local vineyards, buy it in bulk, and then bottle it themselves, resulting in high quality and reasonable prices. Choose from the wide selection of appetizers, including smoked goose breast, and from four or five types of pasta, plus various salads and a good selection of torta al testo fillings. For dessert, try the homemade biscuits, which you dunk in sweet wine. Outdoor seating is available. ✉ *Via San Gabriele dell'Addolorata 15b* ☎ *075/815352* ⊙ *Closed Mon. and a few wks in Jan. or Feb.*

$$$ UMBRIAN ✕ **San Francesco.** An excellent view of the Basilica di San Francesco is the primary reason to come here. Locals consider this the best restaurant in town, where creative Umbrian dishes are made with aromatic locally grown herbs. The seasonal menu might include gnocchi topped with a sauce of wild herbs and *oca stufata di finocchio selvaggio* (goose stuffed with wild fennel). Appetizers and desserts are especially good. ✉ *Via di San Francesco 52* ☎ *075/812329* ⊙ *Closed Wed. and July 15–30.*

WHERE TO STAY

Advance reservations are essential at Assisi's hotels between Easter and October and over Christmas. Latecomers are often forced to stay in the modern town of Santa Maria degli Angeli, 8 km (5 mi) away. As a last-minute option, you can always inquire at restaurants to see if they're renting out rooms.

Until the early 1980s, pilgrim hostels outnumbered ordinary hotels in Assisi, and they present an intriguing and economical alternative to conventional lodgings. They're usually called *conventi* or *ostelli* ("convents" or "hostels") because they're run by convents, churches, or other Catholic organizations. Rooms are spartan but peaceful. Check with the tourist office for a list.

$ Fodor's Choice ★ **Castello di Petrata.** Built as a fortress in the 14th century, the Castello di Petrata rightfully dominates the area, with Monte Subasio, Assisi, and the distant hills and valleys of Perugia all in view. **Pros:** great views of Assisi hills, gardens, and walks. **Cons:** slightly isolated; far from Assisi town center. **TripAdvisor:** "surroundings are beautiful," "perfectly manicured grounds," "spa is a must." ✉ *Via Petrata 25, Località Petrata* ☎ *075/815451* 🌐 *www.castellopetrata.com* 16

Continued on page 699

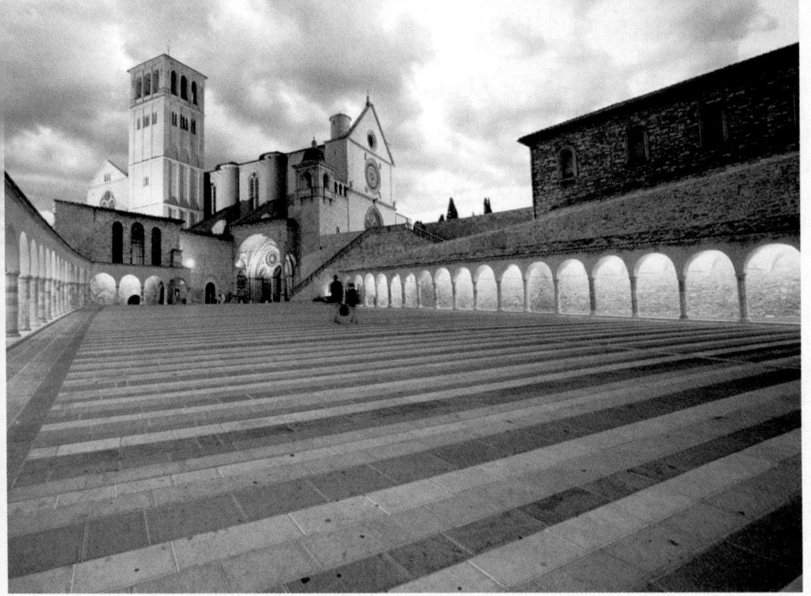

ASSISI'S BASILICA DI SAN FRANCESCO

The legacy of St. Francis, founder of the Franciscan monastic order, pervades Assisi. Each year the town hosts several million pilgrims, but the steady flow of visitors does nothing to diminish the singular beauty of one of Italy's most important religious centers. The pilgrims' ultimate destination is the massive Basilica di San Francesco, which sits halfway up Assisi's hill, supported by graceful arches.

The basilica is not one church but two. The Romanesque **Lower Church** came first; construction began in 1228, just two years after St. Francis's death, and was completed within a few years. The low ceilings and candlelit interior make an appropriately solemn setting for St. Francis's tomb, found in the crypt below the main altar. The Gothic **Upper Church**, built only half a century later, sits on top of the lower one, and is strikingly different, with soaring arches and tall stained-glass windows (the first in Italy). Inside, both churches are covered floor to ceiling with some of Europe's finest frescoes: the Lower Church is dim and full of candlelit shadows, and the Upper Church is bright and airy.

VISITING THE BASILICA

THE LOWER CHURCH

The most evocative way to experience the basilica is to begin with the dark Lower Church. As you enter, give your eyes a moment to adjust. Keep in mind that the artists at work here were conscious of the shadowy environment—they knew this was how their frescoes would be seen.

In the first chapel to the left, a superb fresco cycle by Simone Martini depicts scenes from the life of St. Martin. As you approach the main altar, the vaulting above you is decorated with the *Three Virtues of St. Francis* (poverty, chastity, and obedience) and *St. Francis's Triumph*, frescoes attributed to Giotto's followers. In the transept to your left, Pietro Lorenzetti's *Madonna and Child with St. Francis and St. John* sparkles when the sun hits it. Notice Mary's thumb; legend has it Jesus is asking which saint to bless, and Mary is pointing to Francis. Across the way in the right transept, Cimabue's *Madonna Enthroned Among Angels and St. Francis* is a famous portrait of the saint. Surrounding the portrait are painted scenes from the childhood of Christ, done by the assistants of Giotto. Nearby is a painting of the crucifixion attributed to Giotto himself.

You reach the crypt via stairs midway along the nave—on the crypt's altar, a stone coffin holds the saint's body. Steps up from the transepts lead to the cloister, where there's a gift shop, and the treasury, which contains holy objects.

THE UPPER CHURCH

The St. Francis fresco cycle is the highlight of the Upper Church. (See facing page.) Also worth special note is the 16th-century choir, with its remarkably delicate inlaid wood. When a 1997 earthquake rocked the basilica, the St. Francis cycle sustained little damage, but portions of the ceiling above the entrance and altar collapsed, reducing their frescoes (attributed to Cimabue and Giotto) to rubble. The painstaking restoration is ongoing. ⚠ **The dress code is strictly enforced—no bare shoulders or bare knees.** Piazza di San Francesco, 075/819001, Lower Church Easter–Oct., Mon.–Sat. 6 AM–6:45 PM, Sun. 6:30 AM–7:15 PM; Nov.–Easter, daily 6:30–6. Upper Church Easter–Oct., Mon.–Sat. 8:30–6:45, Sun. 8:30–7:15; Nov.–Easter, daily 8:30–6.

FRANCIS, ITALY'S PATRON SAINT

PREGANDO
ASPETTERO'
CHE TORNI

St. Francis was born in Assisi in 1181, the son of a noblewoman and a well-to-do merchant. His troubled youth included a year in prison. He planned a military career, but after a long illness Francis heard the voice of God, renounced his father's wealth, and began a life of austerity. His mystical embrace of poverty, asceticism, and the beauty of man and nature struck a responsive chord in the medieval mind; he quickly attracted a vast number of followers. Francis was the first saint to receive the stigmata (wounds in his hands, feet, and side corresponding to those of Christ on the cross). He died on October 4, 1226, in the Porziuncola, the secluded chapel in the woods where he had first preached the virtue of poverty to his disciples. St. Francis was declared patron saint of Italy in 1939, and today the Franciscans make up the largest of the Catholic orders.

THE UPPER CHURCH'S ST. FRANCIS FRESCO CYCLE

The 28 frescoes in the Upper Church depicting the life of St. Francis are the most admired works in the entire basilica. They're also the subject of one of art history's biggest controversies. For centuries they thought to be by Giotto (1267-1337), the great early Renaissance innovator, but inconsistencies in style, both within this series and in comparison to later Giotto works, have thrown their origin into question. Some scholars now say Giotto was the brains behind the cycle, but that assistants helped with the execution; others claim he couldn't have been involved at all.

Two things are certain. First, the style is revolutionary—which argues for Giotto's involvement. The tangible weight of the figures, the emotion they show, and the use of perspective all look familiar to modern eyes, but in the art of the time there was nothing like it. Second, these images have played a major part in shaping how the world sees St. Francis. In that respect, who painted them hardly matters.

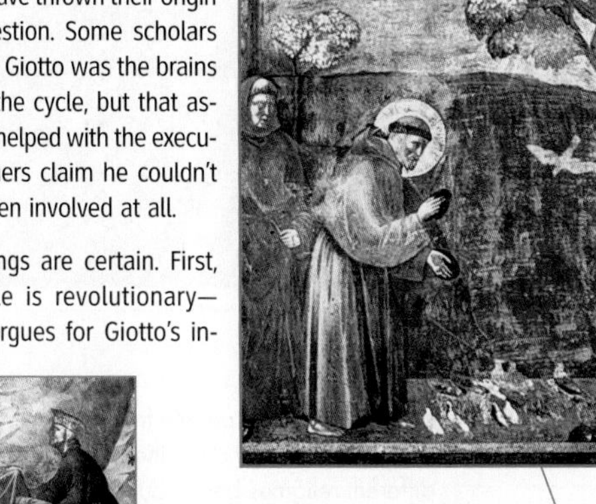

Starting in the transept, the frescoes circle the church, showing events in the saint's life (and afterlife). Some of the best are grouped near the church's entrance—look for the nativity at Greccio, the miracle of the spring, the death of the knight at Celano, and, most famously, the sermon to the birds.

The St. Francis fresco cycle

1. Homage of a simple man
2. Giving cloak to a poor man
3. Dream of the palace
4. Hearing the voice of God
5. Rejection of worldly goods
6. Dream of Innocent III
7. Confirmation of the rules
8. Vision of flaming chariot
9. Vision of celestial thrones
10. Chasing devils from Arezzo
11. Before the sultan
12. Ecstasy of St. Francis
13. Nativity at Greccio
14. Miracle of the spring
15. Sermon to the birds
16. Death of knight at Celano
17. Preaching to Honorius III
18. Apparition at Arles
19. Receiving the stigmata
20. Death of St. Francis
21. Apparition before Bishop Guido and Fra Agostino
22. Verification of the stigmata
23. Mourning of St. Clare
24. Canonization
25. Apparition before Gregory IX
26. Healing of a devotee
27. Confession of a woman
28. Repentant heretic freed

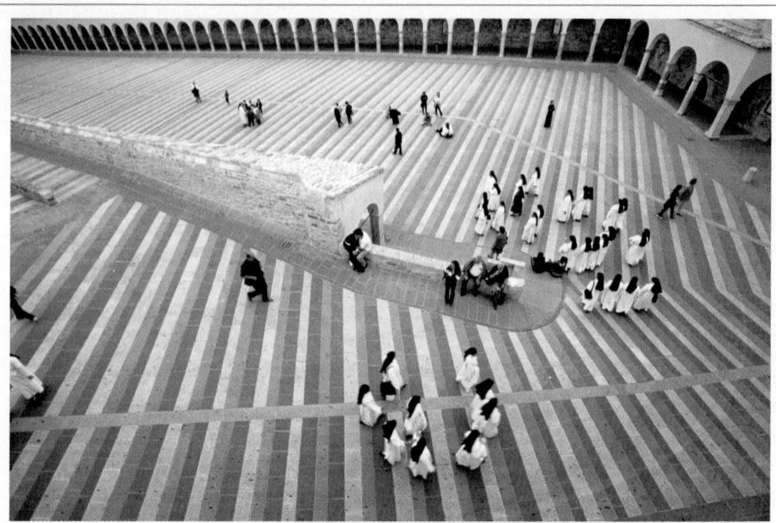

FODOR'S FIRST PERSON

Sister Marcellina,
Order of St. Bridget

Sister Marcellina of the Order of St. Bridget talks about her life in Assisi, where she and 11 other sisters live in a convent and guesthouse on the outskirts of the town:

"Before coming to Assisi, I lived in various countries. I've lived in India, and in England, and been to Holland, to Sweden, and to Finland, as well as lived in Rome. But Assisi is the place that I would never want to change for any other. I don't know, I think there is something very special about this place. I've been here 13 years now, and each year I pray that I won't be sent somewhere else. I'm very happy here.

"I like the atmosphere of Assisi, it's very friendly, and of course with St. Francis and St. Claire, but especially St. Francis, there is a simplicity to life that I like very much. Even though I'm in the Order of St. Bridget, living here I feel very much a part of Franciscan spirituality. There is also a very strong ecumenical feeling to Assisi and this is very nice. There are over 60 different religious communities, with people from all over the world. And even though they come from different religious backgrounds they still feel a part of Assisi. Living here, you don't see the people of Assisi, you see people who have come from all over the world.

"There is something you feel when you come to Assisi, something you feel in your heart that makes you want to come back. And people do return! They feel the peacefulness and tranquility. Not that there aren't other aspects, like the commercialism—but these things happen. People return for the simplicity of this place. People feel attracted to Assisi. There's always something that people feel when they come here—even the hard-hearted ones!"

Asked if she thinks Assisi is changing, Sister Marcellina answers, with laughter in her voice, "When they wanted to make all the changes in the year 2000, the Jubilee Year, our Lord said, 'I must stop everything.' They had lots of projects to build new accommodations to house the people coming for the Jubilee Year, but the Lord said, 'No!' "

rooms, 7 suites In-room: no a/c, Internet. In-hotel: restaurant, bar, pool, some pets allowed Closed Jan.–Mar. Breakfast.

$$ **Hotel Subasio.** The converted monastery close to the Basilica di San Francesco is well past its prime, when guests included celebrities like Marlene Dietrich and Charlie Chaplin. **Pros:** perfect location; views of the Assisi plain. **Cons:** lobby a bit drab; some small rooms; service can be spotty. **TripAdvisor:** "oozing with Umbrian ambiance," "short walk to cathedral," "old hotel but updated." *Via Frate Elia 2 075/812206 www.hotelsubasio.com 54 rooms, 8 suites In-room: no a/c. In-hotel: restaurant, bar, parking Breakfast.*

12

$ **Hotel Umbra.** A 16th-century town house is the setting for this charming hotel near Piazza del Comune. **Pros:** friendly welcome; pleasant small garden. **Cons:** difficult parking; some small rooms. **TripAdvisor:** "down a quiet little lane," "beautiful views of the valley," "reasonable price." *Via degli Archi 6 075/812240 www.hotelumbra.it 6 suites, 19 rooms In-room: a/c. In-hotel: restaurant, bar Closed mid-Jan.–mid-Mar. Breakfast.*

$$ **San Francesco.** You can't beat the location—the roof terrace and some of the rooms look out onto the Basilica di San Francesco, which is opposite the hotel. **Pros:** excellent location; great views. **Cons:** simple rooms; sometimes noisy in peak season. **TripAdvisor:** "in front of the basilica," "converted monastery," "rooms were small, but clean." *Via San Francesco 48 075/812281 www.hotelsanfrancescoassisi.it 44 rooms In-room: a/c, Internet. In-hotel: restaurant, bar, some pets allowed Breakfast.*

NORTHERN UMBRIA

To the north of Perugia, placid, walled Gubbio watches over green countryside, true to its nickname, City of Silence—except for its fast and furious festivals in May, as lively today as when they began more than 800 years ago. To the south, along the Tiber River valley, are the towns of Deruta and Torgiano, best known for their hand-painted ceramics and wine—as locals say, go to Deruta to buy a pitcher and to Torgiano to fill it.

GUBBIO

35 km (22 mi) southeast of Città di Castello, 39 km (24 mi) northeast of Perugia, 92 km (57 mi) east of Arezzo.

GETTING HERE

The closest train station is Fossato di Vico, about 12 mi from Gubbio. Ten daily buses connect the train station with the city, a 30-minute trip. If you're driving from Perugia, take the SS298, which rises steeply up toward the Gubbio hills. The trip will take you one hour. There are also 10 buses a day that leave from Perugia's Piazza Partigiani, the main Perugia bus terminal.

VISITOR INFORMATION

Gubbio tourism office (*Piazza Odersi 6 075/9220693*).

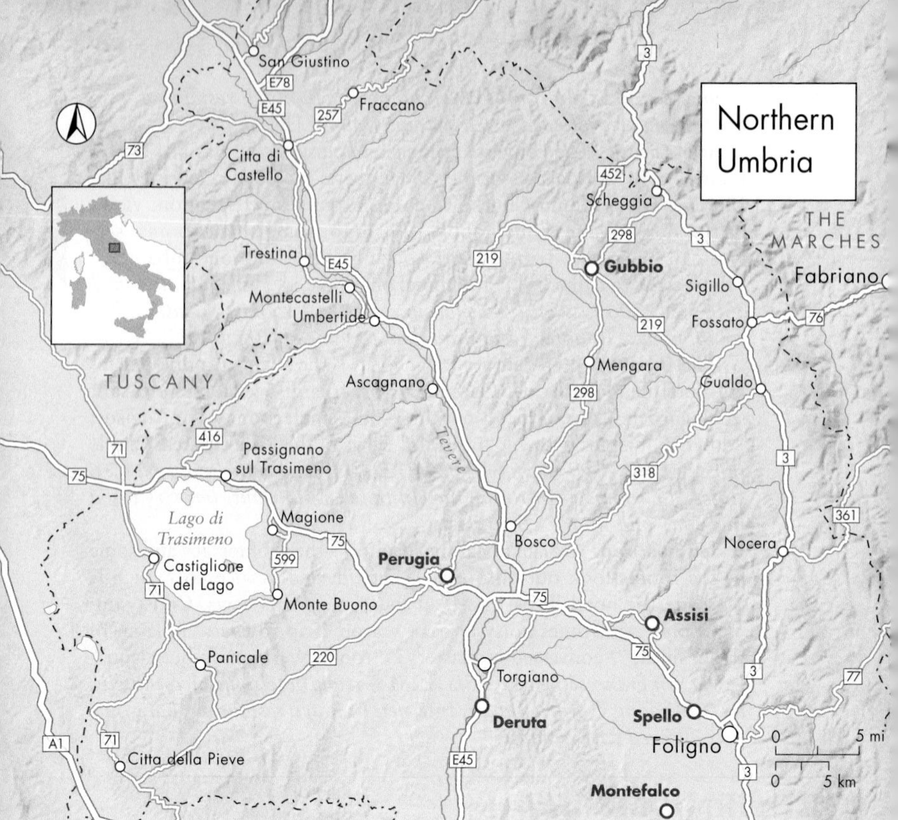

EXPLORING

There's something otherworldly about this jewel of a medieval town tucked away in a mountainous corner of Umbria. Even at the height of summer, the cool serenity and quiet of Gubbio's streets remain intact. The town is perched on the slopes of Monte Ingino, meaning the streets are dramatically steep. Gubbio's relatively isolated position has kept it free of hordes of high-season visitors, and most of the year the city lives up to its Italian nickname, *La Città del Silenzio* (City of Silence). Parking in the central Piazza dei Quaranta Martiri—named for 40 hostages murdered by the Nazis in 1944—is easy and secure, and it's wise to leave your car in the piazza and explore the narrow streets on foot.

At Christmas, kitsch is king. From December 7 to January 10, colored lights are strung down the mountainside in a shape resembling an evergreen. Why? The town is proud to be the home of the world's largest Christmas tree.

The **Duomo,** on a narrow street on the highest tier of the town, dates from the 13th century, with some baroque additions—in particular, a lavishly decorated bishop's chapel. ✉ *Via Ducale* ⏲ *Daily 8–12:45 and 3–7.*

★ The striking Piazza Grande is dominated by the medieval **Palazzo dei Consoli,** attributed to a local architect known as Gattapone, who is still much admired by today's residents. Studies have suggested that the palazzo was in fact the work of another architect, Angelo da Orvieto. In the Middle Ages the Parliament of Gubbio assembled in this palace, which has become a symbol of the town.

The Palazzo dei Consoli houses a museum, famous chiefly for the Tavole Eugubine, seven bronze tablets written in the ancient Umbrian language, employing Etruscan and Latin characters and providing the best key to understanding this obscure tongue. Also in the museum is a fascinating miscellany of rare coins and earthenware pots. The museum has exhilarating views over Gubbio's roofscape and beyond from the lofty loggia. For a few days at the beginning of May, the palace also displays the famous *ceri,* the ceremonial wooden pillars at the center of Gubbio's annual festivities. ✉ *Piazza Grande* ☎ *075/9274298* 🌐 *www.comune.gubbio.pg.it* 🎫 *€5* 🕐 *Apr.–Oct., daily 10–1 and 3–6; Nov.–Mar., daily 10–1 and 2–5.*

WORD OF MOUTH

"Gubbio has my vote for a day trip from Perugia! You *must* try out the 'birdcage' funicular that makes one feel as if they are flying up the side of the mountain without a net. Great pottery, restaurants, and the ancient Roman ruins at the bottom of the hill are beautiful."

—DonnaD44

12

The **Palazzo Ducale** is a scaled-down copy of the Palazzo Ducale in Urbino. (Gubbio was once the possession of that city's ruling family, the Montefeltro.) Gubbio's palazzo contains a small museum and a courtyard. Some of the public rooms offer magnificent views. ✉ *Via Ducale* ☎ *075/9275872* 🎫 *€5* 🕐 *Tues.–Sun. 9–7:30.*

Just outside the city walls at the eastern end of town is a **funicular** that provides a bracing ride to the top of Monte Ingino. (It's definitely not for those who suffer from vertigo.) ✉ *Follow Corso Garibaldi or Via XX Settembre to end* 🎫 *€4, €5 round-trip* 🕐 *Sept.–June, daily 10–1:15 and 2:30–6; July and Aug., daily 9–7:30.*

At the top of Monte Ingino is the **Basilica di Sant'Ubaldo,** repository of Gubbio's famous *ceri*—three 16-foot-tall pillars crowned with statues of Saints Ubaldo, George, and Anthony. The pillars are transported to the Palazzo dei Consoli on the first Sunday of May, in preparation for the Festa dei Ceri. ✉ *Monte Ingino* ☎ *075/9273872* 🕐 *Daily 8:30–noon and 4–7.*

WHERE TO EAT

$$ UMBRIAN

✕ **Grotta dell'Angelo.** The rustic trattoria sits in the lower part of the old town near the main square. The menu features simple local specialties, including *capocollo* (a type of salami), *stringozzi*, and lasagne *tartufata* (with truffles). The few outdoor tables are in high demand in the summer. The restaurant also offers a few small, basically furnished guest rooms, which should be booked in advance. ✉ *Via Gioia 47* ☎ *075/9273438* ✍ *Reservations essential* 🕐 *Closed Tues. and Jan. 7–Feb. 7.*

$$$ UMBRIAN Fodor's Choice ★

✕ **Taverna del Lupo.** One of the city's most famous taverns, this popular place gets hectic on weekends and during the high season. Lasagne made in the Gubbian fashion, with ham and truffles, is an unusual indulgence, and the *suprema di faraono* (guinea fowl in a delicately spiced sauce) is a specialty. The restaurant has two fine wine cellars and an extensive wine list. Save room for the excellent desserts. ✉ *Via Ansidei 21* ☎ *075/9274368* 🕐 *Oct.–June, closed Mon.*

$$ UMBRIAN ✕ **Ulisse e Letizia.** The building dates to the 1300s, and its original stone-and-wood structure has been kept intact. (In the 1400s the space housed an important ceramics factory.) The menu, with seasonal changes, includes traditional but creative fare: tagliatelle *al tartuffo* (in a truffle sauce), *gnochetti al finocchio selvatico* (potato dumplings with wild fennel), and *raviolini di faro con asparagi* (tiny ravioli with spelt and asparagus). ✉ *Via Mastro Giorgio 2* ☎ *075/9221970* ⏲ *Closed Mon.*

WHERE TO STAY

$ **Hotel Bosone Palace.** A former palace is now home to this elegant hotel. **Pros:** friendly welcome; excellent location. **Cons:** some noise in tourist season; simple lobby. **TripAdvisor:** "traditional Umbrian hotel," "frescoed and paneled dining room," "extremely reasonably priced." ✉ *Via XX Settembre 22* ☎ *075/9220688* 🌐 *www.bosonepalace-gubbio.com* *28 rooms, 2 suites* *In-room: no a/c. In-hotel: restaurant, bar* ⏲ *Closed 3 wks in Jan.* 🍽 *Breakfast.*

DERUTA

7 km (4½ mi) south of Torgiano, 19 km (11 mi) southeast of Perugia.

GETTING HERE

From Perugia follow the directions for Rome and the E45 highway; Deruta has its own exits. There are also trains from the smaller St. Anna train station in Perugia. Take the train in the direction of Terni, and get off at Deruta.

VISITOR INFORMATION

Deruta tourism office (✉ *Piazza dei Consoli 4* ☎ *075/9711559*).

EXPLORING

This 14th-century medieval hill town is most famous for its ceramics. A drive through the countryside to visit the ceramics workshops is a good way to spend a morning, but be sure to stop in the town itself.

The notable sights in Deruta include the **Museo Regionale della Ceramica** *(Regional Ceramics Museum)*, part of which extends into the adjacent 14th-century former convent of San Francesco. Half the museum tells the history of ceramics, with panels in Italian and English explaining artistic techniques and production processes. The museum also holds the country's largest collection of modern Italian ceramics—nearly 8,000 pieces are on display. The most notable are the Renaissance vessels using the *lustro* technique, which originated in Arab and Middle Eastern cultures some 500 years before coming into use in Italy in the late 1400s. Lustro, as the name sounds, gives the ceramics a rich finish, which is accomplished with the use of crushed precious materials such as gold and silver. ✉ *Largo San Francesco* ☎ *075/9711000* 🌐 *www.museoceramicaderuta.it* *€5, includes admission to Pinoteca Comunale* ⏲ *Apr.–June, daily 10:30–1 and 3–6; July–Sept., daily 10–1 and 3:30–7; Oct.–Mar., Wed.–Mon. 10:30–1 and 2:30–5.*

SHOPPING

Deruta is home to more than 70 ceramics shops. They offer a range of ceramics, including extra pieces from commissions for well-known British and North American tableware manufacturers. If you ask, most owners will take you to see where they actually throw, bake, and paint their wares. A drive along Via Tiberina Nord takes you past one shop after another.

SPELLO

12 km (7 mi) southeast of Assisi, 33 km (21 mi) north of Spoleto.

GETTING HERE

Spello is an easy half-hour drive from Perugia. From the E45 highway, take the exit toward Assisi and Foligno. Merge onto the SS75 and take the Spello exit. There are also regular trains on the Perugia–Assisi line. Spello is 1 km (½ mi) from the train station, and buses run every 30 minutes for Porta Consolare. From Porta Consolare continue up the steep main street that begins as Via Consolare and changes names several times as it crosses the little town, following the original Roman road. As it curves around, notice the winding medieval alleyways to the right and the more uniform Roman-era blocks to the left.

VISITOR INFORMATION

Spello tourism office (✉ *Piazza Matteotti 3* ☎ *0742/301009* 🌐 *www.prospello.it* ⏲ *Daily 9:30–12:30 and 3:30–5:30*).

EXPLORING

Spello is a gastronomic paradise, especially compared to Assisi. Only a few minutes from Assisi by car or train, this hilltop town at the edge of Monte Subasio makes an excellent strategic and culinary base for exploring nearby towns. Its hotels are well appointed and its restaurants serve some of the best cuisine and wines in the region—sophisticated in variety and of excellent quality. Spello's art scene includes first-rate frescoes by Pinturicchio and Perugino and contemporary artists who can be observed at work in studios around town. If antiquity is your passion, the town also has some intriguing Roman ruins. And the warm, rosy-beige tones of the local *pietra rossa* stone on the buildings brighten even cloudy days.

The basilica of **Santa Maria Maggiore** has vivid frescoes by Pinturicchio in the Cappella Baglioni (1501). Striking in their rich colors, finely dressed figures, and complex symbolism, the *Nativity, Christ Among the Doctors* (on the far left side is a portrait of Troilo Baglioni, the prior who commissioned the work), and the *Annunciation* (look for Pinturicchio's self-portrait in the Virgin's room) are among Pinturicchio's finest works. They were painted after the artist had already won great acclaim for his work in the Palazzi Vaticani in Rome for Borgia Pope Alexander VI. Two pillars on either side of the apse are decorated with frescoes by Perugino (circa 1450–1523), the other great Umbrian artist of the 16th century. ✉ *Piazza Matteotti 18* ☎ *0742/301792* ⏲ *Mar.–June, daily 9:30–12:30 and 3–7; July–Feb., daily 9:30–12:30 and 3–7.*

WHERE TO EAT AND STAY

$$ UMBRIAN Fodor's Choice ★ ✕ **Il Molino.** Almost a destination in itself, this former mill is one of the region's best restaurants. The types of olive oil used in the dishes and the names of the local farmers who grew the produce are noted on the menu. Appetizers are varied, and often highlight foods found only here, like the *risina,* a tiny white bean. Pasta sauces can vary from exquisitely rich to extremely delicate. The meat is first-rate, either elaborately prepared or grilled and topped with a signature sauce. The service is attentive, and the wine list has plenty of local and Italian options, including the pungent Sagrantino di Montefalco and fresh Orvieto whites. If you want something with a bit more depth, go for one of the Montepulciano wines, or even a Brunello di Montalcino, one of Italy's greatest reds. Outside seating lets you soak up the passing street scene; inside is a series of impressive 14th-century arches. ✉ *Piazza Matteotti 6/7* ☎ *0742/651305* ⏲ *Closed Tues.*

$$ ★ **Hotel Palazzo Bocci.** Quiet and elegant, this hotel is on Spello's main street. **Pros:** central location; splendid views of the valley. **Cons:** noisy in summer months; not all rooms have views. **TripAdvisor:** "Spello's best-kept secret," "large, well-appointed rooms," "wonderful outdoor terrace." ✉ *Via Cavour 17* ☎ *0742/301021* 🌐 *www.palazzobocci.com* *23 rooms* *In-room: a/c, Wi-Fi. In-hotel: restaurant, bar* *Breakfast.*

$ ★ **La Bastiglia.** This cozy hotel is in a former grain mill, but polished wood planks and handwoven rugs have replaced the rustic flooring. **Pros:** lovely terrace restaurant; cozy rooms; fine views. **Cons:** some shared balconies; breakfast is underwhelming. **TripAdvisor:** "beautiful building with great vistas," "restaurant was first-class," "unfriendly receptionist." ✉ *Via Salnitraria 15* ☎ *0742/651277* 🌐 *www.labastiglia.com* *31 rooms, 2 suites* *In-room: a/c. In-hotel: restaurant, bar, pool* ⏲ *Closed early Jan.–early Feb.* *Breakfast.*

MONTEFALCO

6 km (4 mi) southeast of Bevagna, 34 km (21 mi) south of Assisi.

GETTING HERE

If you're driving from Perugia, take the E45 toward Rome. Take the Foligno exit, then merge onto the SP445 and follow it into Montefalco. The drive takes around 50 minutes. The nearest train station is in Foligno, about 7 km (4½ mi) away. From there you can take a taxi or a bus into Montefalco.

VISITOR INFORMATION

Montefalco tourism office (✉ *Via Ringhiera Umbra* ☎ *0742/379598* 🌐 *www.regioneumbria.eu*).

EXPLORING

Nicknamed the "balcony over Umbria" for its high vantage point over the valley that runs from Perugia to Spoleto, Montefalco began as an important Roman settlement situated on the Via Flaminia. The town owes its current name—which means "Falcon's Mount"—to Emperor Frederick II (1194–1250). Obviously a greater fan of falconry than Roman architecture, he destroyed the ancient town, which was then called Coccorone, in 1249, and built in its place what would later become Montefalco. Aside from a few fragments incorporated in a private house just off Borgo Garibaldi, no traces remain of the old Roman center. However, Montefalco has more than its fair share of interesting art and architecture and is well worth the drive up the hill.

At **La Strada del Sagrantino,** the tourist office in the piazza, the staff will advise you on selecting a wine, direct you to nearby enoteche for tastings, and give you free maps with which to find your way around the Sagrantino Road and some remarkable wine territory. They can also book you a room in a hotel, at a vineyard, in a hillside apartment, or at an agriturismo. ✉ *Piazza del Comune 17* ☎ *0742/378490* 🌐 *www.stradadelsagrantino.it.*

WHERE TO EAT AND STAY

Montefalco is a good stop for sustenance: here you need go no farther than the main square to find a restaurant or bar with a hot meal, and most establishments—both simple and sophisticated—offer a splendid combination of history and small-town hospitality. Some of the wine producers, including Antonelli, have *casale,* or small apartments, near the vineyards that are usually rented by the week, but in low season are often available for a weekend. For information, contact the office of **Strada del Sagrantino** (☎ *0742/378490* 🌐 *www.stradadelsagrantino.it*).

¢ ITALIAN — ✕ **L'Alchemista.** "The Alchemist" is an apt name, as the chef's transformations are magical. Try the *fiore molle della Valnerina,* baked saffron cheese, bacon, and zucchini—served only here. In summer, cold dishes to try are *panzanella,* a local vegetable salad mixed with bread, or the barley salad tossed with vegetables. The *farro* (spelt) soup made with Sagrantino wine is a local specialty. The desserts are delicious: all are made on the premises and not too sweet. ✉ *Piazza del Comune 14* ☎ *0742/378558* ⏲ *Closed Tues. Jan.–Mar.*

$$ Fodor's Choice ★ — **Villa Pambuffetti.** If you want to be pampered in the refined atmosphere of a private villa, this is the spot. **Pros:** peaceful gardens; refined furnishings. **Cons:** outside the town center; can get crowded on weekends. **TripAdvisor:** "spectacular views over Umbria," "park-like setting," "distinctive tiled floors." ✉ *Viale della Vittoria 20* ☎ *0742/379417* 🌐 *www.villapambuffetti.com* *15 rooms, 3 suites* *In-room: a/c. In-hotel: restaurant, bar, pool* *Breakfast.*

SPOLETO

GETTING HERE

Spoleto is an hour's drive from Perugia. From the E45 highway, take the exit toward Assisi and Foligno, then merge onto the SS75 until you reach the Foligno Est exit. Merge onto the SS3, which leads to Spoleto. There are regular trains on the Perugia–Foligno line. From the train station it's a 15-minute uphill walk to the center, so you'll probably want to take a taxi.

VISITOR INFORMATION

Spoleto tourism office (✉ *Piazza della Libertà 7* ☎ *0743/238921* 🌐 *www.regioneumbria.eu*).

CLOSE UP

The Sagrantino Story

Sagrantino grapes have been used for the production of red wine for centuries. The wine began centuries ago as Sagrantino *passito,* a semisweet version in which the grapes are left to dry for a period after picking to intensify the sugar content. One theory traces the origin of Sagrantino back to ancient Rome in the works of Pliny the Elder, the author of the *Natural History,* who referred to the Itriola grape that some researchers think may be Sagrantino. Others believe that in medieval times Franciscan friars returned from Asia Minor with the grape. ("Sagrantino" perhaps derives from sacramenti, the religious ceremony in which the wine was used.)

The passito is still produced today, and is preferred by some. But the big change in Sagrantino wine production came in the past decades, when Sagrantino *secco* (dry) came onto the market. Both passito and secco have a deep ruby-red color that tends toward garnet highlights, with a full body and rich flavor.

For the dry wines, producers not to be missed are Terre di Capitani, Antonelli, Perticaia, and Caprai. Try those labels for the passito as well, in addition to Ruggeri and Scacciadiavoli. Terre di Capitani is complex, and has vegetable and mineral tones that join tastes of wild berries, cherries, and chocolate—this winemaker hand-pampers his grapes and it shows. Antonelli is elegant, refined, and rich. The Ruggeri passito is one of the best, so don't be put off by its homespun label. Caprai is bold and rich in taste, and has the largest market share, including a high percentage exported to the United States. Perticaia has a full taste with a surprising "up" finish that suggested some divine presence other than Sagrantino.

Some wineries are small and not equipped to receive visitors. Arrange your winery visits at **La Strada del Sagrantino** (✉ *Piazza del Comune 17* ☎ *0742/378490* 🌐 *www.stradadelsagrantino.it*) in Montefalco's main square. There you can pick up a map of the wine route and set up appointments, book accommodations, and then visit local enoteche. At the enoteche, ask the sommelier to guide you to some smaller producers you'll have difficulty finding elsewhere.

Sagrantino di Montefalco is celebrated twice yearly in the town of Montefalco, during September's Festa Della Vendemmia (Grape or Harvest Festival) and spring's Settimana Enologica (Wine Week), during which area grape farmers turn out for a parade through the streets and a tasting of past years' labors in the Piazza del Comune. Details can be obtained from the **Centro Agro-Alimentare dell'Umbria** (☎ *0742/349119* 🌐 *www.umbriadoc.com*) or the Strada del Sagrantino (⇨ *above*). Salute!

EXPLORING SPOLETO

The walled city is set on a slanting hillside, with the most interesting sections clustered toward the upper portion. Parking options inside the walls include Piazza Campello (just below the Rocca) on the southeast end, Via del Trivio to the north, and Piazza San Domenico on the west end. You can also park at Piazza della Vittoria farther north, just outside the walls. There are also several well-marked lots near the train station.

Casa Romana **2**
Duomo **3**
La Rocca **4**
Ponte delle Torri **5**
Teatro Romano **1**

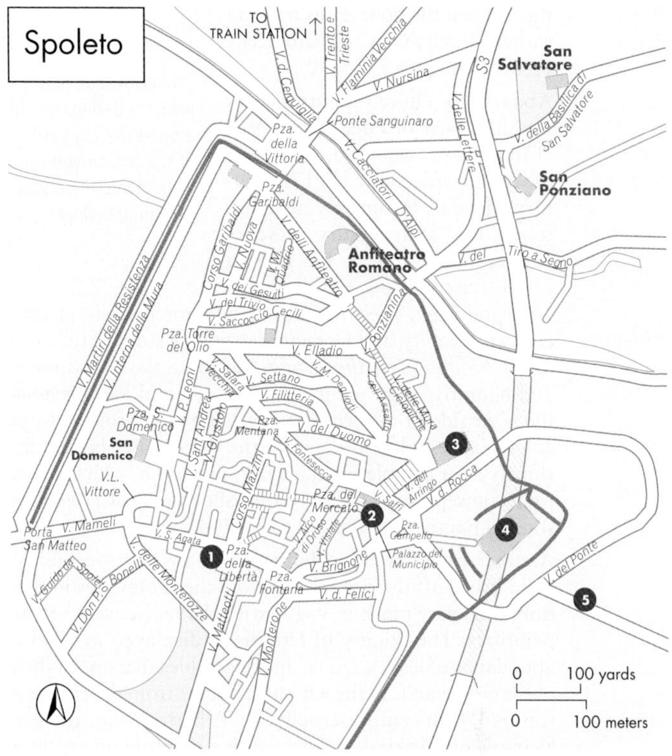

If you arrive by train, you can walk 1 km (½ mi) from the station to the entrance to the lower town. Regular bus connections are every 15 to 30 minutes. You can also use the *trenino*, as locals call the shuttle service, from the train station to Piazza della Libertà, near the upper part of the old town, where you'll find the tourist office.

Like most other towns with narrow, winding streets, Spoleto is best explored on foot. Bear in mind that much of the city is on a steep slope, so there are lots of stairs and steep inclines. The well-worn stones can be slippery even when dry; wear rubber-sole shoes for good traction. Several pedestrian walkways cut across Corso Mazzini, which zigzags up the hill. A €12 combination ticket purchased at the tourist office allows you entry to all the town's museums and galleries.

TOP ATTRACTIONS

★ **Duomo.** The cathedral's 12th-century Romanesque facade received a Renaissance face-lift with the addition of a loggia in a rosy pink stone. A stunning contrast in styles, the Duomo is one of the finest cathedrals in the region. The eight rose windows are especially dazzling in the late afternoon sun. Look under the largest rose window and you see two figures that appear to be holding up the structure; in the corners of the square surrounding the window, the four Evangelists are sculpted. Inside, the original tile floor dates from an earlier church that was destroyed by Frederick I (circa 1123–90).

Above the church's entrance is Bernini's bust of Pope Urban VIII (1568–1644), who had the rest of the church redecorated in 17th-century baroque; fortunately he didn't touch the 15th-century frescoes painted in the apse by Fra Filippo Lippi (circa 1406–69) between 1466 and 1469. These immaculately restored masterpieces—the *Annunciation, Nativity,* and *Dormition*—tell the story of the life of the Virgin. The *Coronation of the Virgin,* adorning the half dome, is the literal and figurative high point. Portraits of Lippi and his assistants are on the right side of the central panel. The Florentine artist priest "whose colors expressed God's voice" (the words inscribed on his tomb) died shortly after completing the work. His tomb, which you can see in the right transept (note the artist's brushes and tools), was designed by his son, Filippino Lippi (circa 1457–1504).

WORD OF MOUTH

"In Spoleto, be sure to take the walk up through the old city and around the big castle at the top of the hill, so you can see, and walk along, the enormous ancient Roman aqueduct."

—simpsonc510

Another fresco cycle, including work by Pinturicchio, is in the Cappella Eroli, off the right aisle. Note the grotesques in the ornamentation, then very much in vogue with the rediscovery of ancient Roman paintings. The bounty of Umbria is displayed in vivid colors in the abundance of leaves, fruits, and vegetables that adorn the center seams of the cross vault. In the left nave, not far from the entrance, is the well-restored 12th-century crucifix by Alberto Sozio, the earliest known example of this kind of work, with a painting on parchment attached to a wood cross. To the right of the presbytery is the Cappella della Santissima Icona (Chapel of the Most Holy Icon), which contains a small Byzantine painting of a Madonna given to the town by Frederick Barbarossa as a peace offering in 1185, following his destruction of the cathedral and town three decades earlier. ✉ *Piazza del Duomo* ☎ *0743/44307* ⏲ *Apr.–Oct., daily 8:30–12:30 and 3:30–7; Nov.–Mar., daily 8:30–12:30 and 3:30–5.*

★ **Ponte delle Torri** *(Bridge of the Towers).* Standing massive and graceful through the deep gorge that separates Spoleto from Monteluco, this 14th-century bridge is one of Umbria's most photographed monuments, and justifiably so. Built over the foundations of a Roman-era aqueduct, it soars 262 feet above the forested gorge—higher than the dome of St. Peter's in Rome. Sweeping views over the valley and a pleasant sense of vertigo make a walk across the bridge a must, particularly on a starry night. ✉ *Via del Ponte.*

WORTH NOTING

Casa Romana. Spoleto became a Roman colony in the 3rd century BC, but the best excavated remains date from the 1st century AD. Excavated in the late 9th century, the Casa Romana was not a typical Roman residence. According to an inscription, it belonged to Vespasia Polla, the mother of Emperor Vespasian (one of the builders of the

Colosseum and perhaps better known by the Romans for taxing them to install public toilets, later called "Vespasians"). The rooms, arranged around a large central atrium built over an *impluvium* (rain cistern), are decorated with black-and-white geometric mosaics. ✉ *Palazzo del Municipio, Via Visiale 9* ☎ *0743/234250* 🎟 *€2.50, €6 combination ticket (includes Pinacoteca Comunale and Galleria d'Arte Moderna)* ⏲ *Daily 11–5; closed last wk Dec.*

La Rocca. Built in the mid-14th century for Cardinal Egidio Albornoz, this massive fortress served as a seat for the local pontifical governors, a tangible sign of the restoration of the Church's power in the area when the pope was ruling from Avignon. Several popes spent time here, and one of them, Alexander VI, in 1499 sent his capable teenage daughter Lucrezia Borgia (1480–1519) to serve as governor for three months. The Gubbio-born architect Gattapone (14th century) used the ruins of a Roman acropolis as a foundation and took materials from many Roman-era sites, including the Teatro Romano. La Rocca's plan is long and rectangular, with six towers and two grand courtyards, an upper loggia, and inside some grand reception rooms. In the largest tower, Torre Maestà, you can visit an apartment with some interesting frescoes. A small shuttle bus gives you that last boost up the hill from the ticket booth to the entrance of the fortress. If you phone in advance, you may be able to secure an English-speaking guide. ✉ *Via del Ponte* ☎ *0743/223055* 🎟 *€6* ⏲ *Tues.–Sun. 9–5:30.*

Teatro Romano. The Romans who had colonized the city in 241 BC constructed this small theater in the 1st century AD; for centuries afterward it was used as a quarry for building materials. The most intact portion is the hallway that passes under the *cavea* (stands). The rest was heavily restored in the early 1950s and serves as a venue for Spoleto's Festival dei Due Mondi. The theater was the site of a gruesome episode in Spoleto's history: during the medieval struggle between Guelph (papal) and Ghibelline (imperial) forces, Spoleto took the side of the Holy Roman Emperor. Afterward, 400 Guelph supporters were massacred in the theater, their bodies burned in an enormous pyre. In the end, the Guelphs were triumphant, and Spoleto was incorporated into the states of the Church in 1354. Through a door in the west portico of the adjoining building is the **Museo Archeologico,** with assorted artifacts found in excavations primarily around Spoleto and Norcia. The collection contains Bronze Age and Iron Age artifacts from Umbrian and pre-Roman eras. Another section contains black-glaze vases from the Hellenistic period excavated from the necropolis of Saint Scolastica in Norcia. The highlight is the stone tablet inscribed on both sides with the Lex Spoletina (Spoleto Law). Dating from 315 BC, this legal document prohibited the desecration of the woods on the slopes of nearby Monteluco. ✉ *Piazza della Libertà* ☎ *0743/223277* 🎟 *€4* ⏲ *Daily 8:30–7:30.*

WHERE TO EAT

$$ UMBRIAN **Apollinare.** Low wooden ceilings and flickering candlelight make this monastery from the 10th and 11th centuries Spoleto's most romantic spot. The kitchen serves sophisticated, innovative variations on local dishes. Sauces of cherry tomatoes, mint, and a touch of red pepper, or of porcini mushrooms, top the long, slender strangozzi. The *caramella* (light puff-pastry cylinders filled with local cheese and served with a creamy Parmesan sauce) is popular. In warm weather you can dine under a canopy on the piazza across from the archaeological museum. *Via Sant'Agata 14 0743/223256 Closed Tues.*

$$ UMBRIAN **Il Tartufo.** As the name indicates, dishes prepared with truffles are the specialty here—don't miss the risotto al tartufo. But there are also dishes not perfumed with this expensive delicacy. Incorporating the ruins of a Roman villa, the restaurant's decor is rustic on the ground floor and more modern upstairs. In summer, tables appear outdoors and the traditional fare is spiced up to appeal to the cosmopolitan crowd attending (or performing in) the Festival dei Due Mondi. *Piazza Garibaldi 24 0743/40236 Reservations essential Closed Mon. and last 2 wks in July. No dinner Sun.*

$ UMBRIAN **Osteria del Trivio.** At this friendly trattoria everything is made on the premises. The menu changes daily, depending on what's in season. Dishes might include stuffed artichokes, pasta with local mushrooms, or chicken with artichokes. For dessert, try the homemade biscotti, made for dunking in sweet wine. There's a printed menu, but the owner can explain the dishes in a number of languages. A complete meal from appetizer to dessert with house wine is likely to cost no more than €25. *Via del Trivio 16 0743/44349 Closed Tues.*

$$ UMBRIAN ★ **Ristorante Panciolle.** In the heart of Spoleto's medieval quarter, this restaurant has one of the most appealing settings you could wish for: a small garden filled with lemon trees. Dishes change throughout the year, and may include pastas served with asparagus or mushrooms, as well as grilled meats. More expensive dishes prepared with fresh truffles are also available in season. *Via Duomo 3/5 0743/224289 Reservations essential Closed Wed.*

WHERE TO STAY

$$ ★ **Cavaliere Palace Hotel.** An arched passageway off one of the city's busy shopping streets leads to an elegant world through a quiet courtyard. **Pros:** quiet elegance; central position. **Cons:** finding parking can be a problem; crowded in summer. **TripAdvisor:** "perfect for exploring the old town," "room was very comfortable," "bathroom was gorgeous." *Corso Garibaldi 49 0743/220350 www.hotelcavaliere.eu 29 rooms, 2 suites In-room: a/c. In-hotel: restaurant, bar Breakfast.*

$ **Hotel Clitunno.** A renovated 18th-century building in the center of town houses this pleasant hotel. **Pros:** friendly staff; good restaurant. **Cons:** difficult to find a parking space; some small rooms. **TripAdvisor:** "lovely, quiet hotel," "nice outdoor area," "rooms are adequate and clean." *Piazza Sordini 6 0743/223340 www.hotelclitunno.com 45 rooms In-room: a/c. In hotel: restaurant, bar Breakfast.*

CLOSE UP

A Taste of Truffles

Umbria is rich with truffles—more are found here than anywhere else in Italy—and those not consumed fresh are processed into pastes or flavored oils. The primary truffle areas are around the tiny town of Norcia, which holds a truffle festival every February, and near Spoleto, where signs warn against unlicensed truffle hunting at the base of the Ponte delle Torri.

Although grown locally, the rare delicacy can cost a small fortune, up to $200 for a quarter pound—fortunately, a little goes a long way. At such a price there's great competition among the nearly 10,000 registered truffle hunters in the province, who use specially trained dogs to sniff them out among the roots of several types of trees, including oak and ilex. Despite a few incidents involving inferior tubers imported from China, you can be reasonably assured that the truffle shaved onto your pasta has been unearthed locally. Don't pass up the opportunity to try this delectable treat. The intense aroma of a dish perfumed with truffles is unmistakable and the flavor memorable.

$$ Fodor's Choice ★ **Hotel San Luca.** The elegant San Luca is one of Spoleto's finest hotels, thanks to its commendable attention to detail, such as the hand-painted friezes that decorate the walls of the spacious guest rooms and the generous selection of up-to-date magazines for your reading pleasure. **Pros:** very helpful staff; peaceful location. **Cons:** outside the town center; a long walk to the main sights. **TripAdvisor:** "historic building is charming," "very refined taste," "armchairs by the crackling fire." ✉ *Via Interna delle Mura 19* ☎ *0743/223399* 🌐 *www.hotelsanluca.com* *33 rooms, 2 suites* *In-room: a/c, Internet. In-hotel: restaurant, business center, parking* *Breakfast.*

THE ARTS

Fodor's Choice ★ In 1958, composer Gian Carlo Menotti chose Spoleto for the first **Festival dei Due Mondi** (*Festival of Two Worlds* ✉ *Piazza del Comune 1* ☎ *0743/221689* 🌐 *www.festivaldispoleto.com*), a gathering of artists, performers, and musicians intending to bring together the "new" and "old" worlds of America and Europe. (A corresponding festival in South Carolina is no longer connected to this festival.) The annual event, held in late June and early July, is one of the most important cultural happenings in Europe, attracting big names in all branches of the arts, particularly music, opera, and theater.

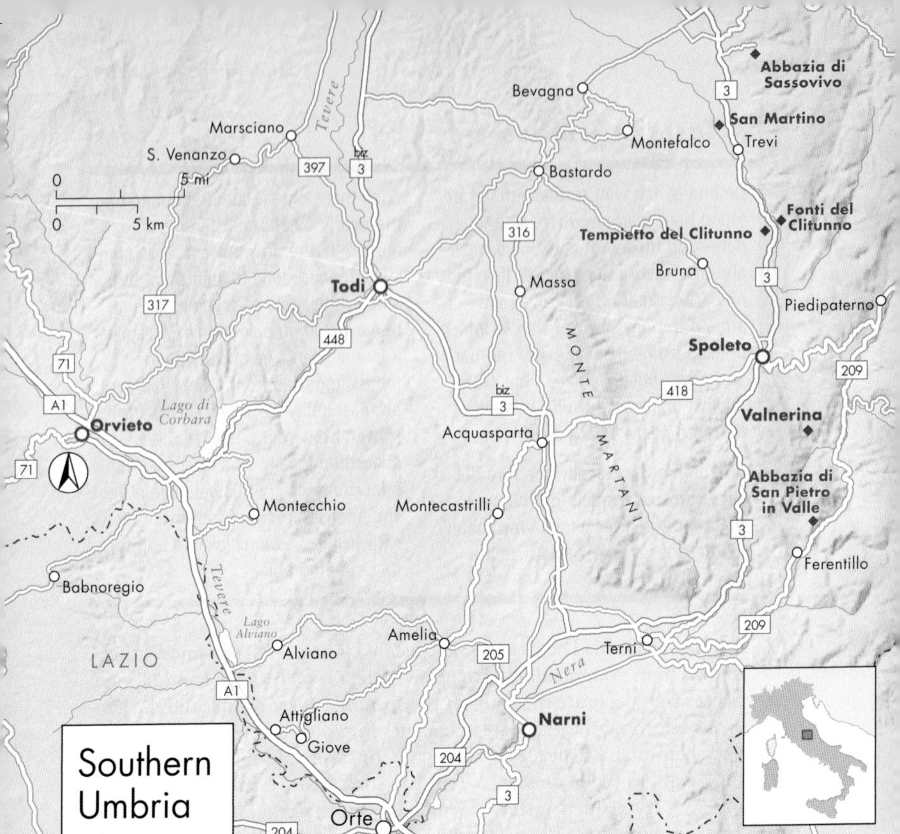

SOUTHERN UMBRIA

Orvieto, built on a tufa mount, produces one of Italy's favorite white wines and has one of the country's greatest cathedrals and most compelling fresco cycles. Nearby Narni and Todi are pleasant medieval hill towns. The former stands over a steep gorge, its Roman pedigree evident in dark alleyways and winding streets; the latter is a fairy-tale village with incomparable views and one of Italy's most perfect piazzas.

TODI

34 km (22 mi) south of Perugia, 34 km (22 mi) east of Orvieto.

GETTING HERE

Todi is best reached by car, as the town's two train stations are way down the hill and connected to the center by infrequent bus service. From Perugia, follow the E45 toward Rome. Take the Todi/Orvieto exit, then follow the SS79bis into Todi. The drive takes around 40 minutes.

VISITOR INFORMATION

Todi tourism office (✉ *Piazza del Popolo 38* ☎ *075/8942526* 🌐 *www.regioneumbria.eu*).

EXPLORING

As you stand on Piazza del Popolo, looking out onto the Tiber Valley below, it's easy to see how Todi is often described as Umbria's prettiest hill town. Legend has it that the town was founded by the Umbri, who followed an eagle who had stolen a tablecloth. They liked this lofty perch so much that they settled here for good. The eagle is now perched on the insignia of the medieval palaces in the main piazza.

Built above the Roman Forum, **Piazza del Popolo** is Todi's high point, a model of spatial harmony with stunning views onto the surrounding countryside. In the best medieval tradition, the square was conceived to house both the temporal and the spiritual centers of power.

On one end of the Piazza del Popolo is the 12th-century Romanesque-Gothic **Duomo**, which was built over the site of a Roman temple. The simple facade is enlivened by a finely carved rose window. Look up at that window as you step inside and you'll notice its peculiarity: each "petal" of the rose has a cherub's face in the stained glass. Take a close look at the capitals of the double columns with pilasters: perched between the acanthus leaves are charming medieval sculptures of saints—Peter with his keys, George and the dragon, and so on. You can see the rich brown tones of the wooden choir near the altar, but unless you have binoculars or request special permission in advance, you can't get close enough to see all the exquisite detail in this Renaissance masterpiece of woodworking (1521–30). The severe, solid mass of the Duomo is mirrored by the Palazzo dei Priori (1595–97) across the way. ✉ *Piazza del Popolo* ☎ *075/8943041* ⏲ *Daily 8–1 and 3–6*

WHERE TO EAT AND STAY

$$ UMBRIAN ✕ **Ristorante Umbria.** Todi's most popular restaurant for more than four decades, the Umbria is reliable for its sturdy country food and its wonderful view from the terrace. Since it has only 16 tables outside, make sure you reserve ahead. In winter, try legume soup, homemade pasta with truffles, or *palombaccio alla ghiotta* (roasted squab). Steaks, accompanied by a rich dark-brown wine sauce, are good as well. ✉ *Via San Bonaventura 13* ☎ *075/8942737* ⏲ *Closed Tues.*

$ **San Lorenzo 3.** Surrounded by antique furniture, paintings, and period knickknacks, you get a sense of a place more in tune with the 19th than the 21st century. **Pros:** delightful Old World atmosphere; excellent central location. **Cons:** few modern amenities; basic furnishings. **TripAdvisor:** "sweeping view of Umbria," "wall and ceiling frescoes," "spacious and well appointed." ✉ *Via San Lorenzo 3* ☎ *075/8944555* 🌐 *www.sanlorenzo3.it* *6 rooms, 3 with bath* *In-room: no a/c, no TV* *No credit cards* ⏲ *Closed Jan. and Feb.* *Breakfast.*

ORVIETO

30 km (19 mi) west of Todi, 81 km (51 mi) west of Spoleto.

GETTING HERE

Orvieto is well connected by train to Rome, Florence, and Perugia. It's also adjacent to the A1 Superstrada that runs between Florence and Rome. Parking areas in the upper town tend to be crowded. A better idea is to follow the signs for the Porta Orvetiana parking lot, then take the funicular that carries people up the hill.

VISITOR INFORMATION

Orvieto tourism office (✉ *Piazza del Duomo 24* ☎ *0763/341772* 🌐 *www.regioneumbria.eu*).

A *Carta Orvieto Unica* (single ticket) is expensive but a great deal if you want to visit everything; for €18 you get admission to the four major sights in town—Cappella di San Brizio (at the Duomo), Museo Claudio Faina, Torre del Moro, and Orvieto Underground—plus a combination bus-funicular pass or five hours of free parking.

EXPLORING

Carved out of an enormous plateau of volcanic rock high above a green valley, Orvieto has natural defenses that made the high walls seen in many Umbrian towns unnecessary. The Etruscans were the first to settle here, digging a honeycombed network of more than 1,200 wells and storage caves out of the soft stone. The Romans attacked, sacked, and destroyed the city in 283 BC; since then, it has grown up out of the rock into an enchanting maze of alleys and squares. Orvieto was solidly Guelph in the Middle Ages, and for several hundred years popes sought refuge in the city, at times needing protection from their enemies, at times seeking respite from the summer heat of Rome.

When painting his frescoes inside the Duomo, Luca Signorelli asked that part of his contract be paid in Orvietan wine, and he was neither the first nor the last to appreciate the region's popular white. In past times the caves carved underneath the town were used to ferment the Trebbiano grapes used in making Orvieto Classico; now local wine production has moved out to more traditional vineyards, but you can still while away the afternoon in tastings at any number of shops in town.

Fodor's Choice ★ **Duomo.** Orvieto's Duomo is, quite simply, stunning. The church was built to commemorate the Miracle at Bolsena. In 1263 a young priest who questioned the miracle of transubstantiation (in which the Communion bread and wine become the flesh and blood of Christ) was saying mass at nearby Lago di Bolsena. His doubts were put to rest, however, when a wafer he had just blessed suddenly started to drip blood, staining the linen covering the altar. The cloth and the host were taken to the pope, who proclaimed a miracle and a year later provided for a new religious holiday—the Feast of Corpus Domini. Thirty years later, construction began on a *duomo* to celebrate the miracle and house the stained altar cloth.

It's thought that Arnolfo di Cambio (circa 1245–1302), the famous builder of the Duomo in Florence, was given the initial commission for the Duomo, but the project was soon taken over by Lorenzo Maitani (circa 1275–1330), who consolidated the structure and designed the monumental facade. Maitani also made the bas-relief panels between the doorways, which graphically tell the story of the Creation (on the left) and the Last Judgment (on the right). The lower registers, now protected by Plexiglas, succeed in conveying the horrors of hell as few other works of art manage to do, an effect made all the more powerful by the worn gray marble. Above, gold mosaics are framed by finely detailed Gothic decoration.

Inside, the cathedral is rather vast and empty; the major works are in the transepts. To the left is the **Cappella del Corporale,** where the square linen cloth (corporale) is kept in a golden reliquary that's modeled on the cathedral and inlaid with enamel scenes of the miracle. The cloth is removed for public viewing on Easter and on Corpus Domini (the ninth Sunday after Easter). In the right transept is the **Cappella di San Brizio,** or Cappella Nuova. In this chapel is one of Italy's greatest fresco cycles, notable for its influence on Michelangelo's *Last Judgment,* as well as for the extraordinary beauty of the figuration. In these works, a few by Fra Angelico and the majority by Luca Signorelli, the damned fall to hell, demons breathe fire and blood, and Christians are martyred. Some scenes are heavily influenced by the imagery in Dante's (1265–1321) *Divine Comedy.* ✉ *Piazza del Duomo* ☎ *0763/342477* 🎟 *Cappella Nuova €5* ⏲ *Mar.–Oct., daily 9:30–7:30; Nov.–Feb., daily 9:30–1 and 2:30–5.*

WORD OF MOUTH

"Orvieto makes a nice day or overnight stop. Lots of great shoe shops. The nearby hilltop village of Civita makes a great side trip—you have to park your vehicle and walk across a suspension bridge to get there, but when you arrive, you'll find a quaint and cute village."

—DOCK

★ **Museo Archeologico Claudio Faina.** This superb private collection, beautifully arranged and presented, goes far beyond the usual museum offerings of a scattering of local remains. The collection is particularly rich in Greek- and Etruscan-era pottery, from large Attic amphorae (6th–4th century BC) to Attic black- and red-figure pieces to Etruscan *bucchero* (dark-reddish clay) vases. Other interesting pieces in the collection include a 6th-century sarcophagus and a substantial display of Roman-era coins. ✉ *Piazza del Duomo 29* ☎ *0763/341511* 🌐 *www.museofaina.it* 🎟 *€4.50* ⏲ *Apr.–Sept., daily 11–4; Oct.–Mar., Tues.–Sun. 1–3.*

Orvieto Underground. More than just about any other town, Orvieto has grown from its own foundations—if one were to remove from present-day Orvieto all the building materials that were dug up from below, there would hardly be a building left standing. The Etruscans, the Romans, and those who followed dug into the tufa (the same soft volcanic rock from which catacombs were made), and over the centuries created more than 1,000 separate cisterns, caves, secret passages, storage areas, and production areas for wine and olive oil. Some of the tufa removed was used as building blocks for the city that exists today, and some was partly ground into *pozzolana,* which was made into mortar. The most thorough **Orvieto Underground tour** (✉ *Orvieto tourism office, Piazza del Duomo 24* ☎ *0763/341772*) is run daily at 11, 12:15, 4, and 5:15. (In February tours are given only on weekends.) Admission for the hour-long English tour is €5.50. If you're short on time but still want a look at what it was like down there, head for the **Pozzo della Cava** (✉ *Via della Cava 28* ☎ *0763/342373*), an Etruscan well for spring water. It's open Tuesday through Friday from 9 to 8, and costs €3.

WHERE TO EAT

The streets around the Duomo are lined with all types of bars and restaurants where you can eat simple or elaborate food and try the wines by the glass.

$$ UMBRIAN Fodor's Choice ★ **Il Giglio D'Oro.** A great view of the Duomo is coupled with superb food. Eggplant is transformed into an elegant custard with black truffles in the *sformatino di melenzane con vellutata al tartuffo nero.* Pastas, like *ombrichelli al pesto umbro,* are traditional, but perhaps with a new twist like fresh coriander leaves instead of the usual basil. Lamb roasted in a crust of bread is delicately seasoned with a tomato cream sauce. The wine cellar includes some rare vintages. ✉ *Piazza Duomo 8* ☎ *0763/341903* ⏲ *Closed Wed.*

$$ UMBRIAN **Le Grotte del Funaro.** If you can't do the official hour-long tour of Underground Orvieto, dine here instead, inside tufa caves under central Orvieto, where the two windows have splendid views of the hilly countryside during the day. The traditional Umbrian food is average, but with good, simple grilled meats and vegetables and pizzas. Oddly, the food is outclassed by an extensive wine list, with top local and Italian labels and quite a few rare vintages. ✉ *Via Ripa Serancia 41* ☎ *0763/343276* *Reservations essential* ⏲ *Closed Mon. and 1 wk in July.*

$$ UMBRIAN ★ **Trattoria La Grotta.** The owner has been in this location for more than 20 years, and locals are still fond of him. He has attracted a steady American clientele without losing his touch with homemade pasta, perhaps with a duck or wild-boar sauce. Roast lamb, veal, and pork are all good, and the desserts are homemade. Franco knows the local wines well and has a carefully selected list, including some from smaller but excellent wineries, so ask about them. ✉ *Via Luca Signorelli 5* ☎ *0763/341348* ⏲ *Closed Tues.*

WHERE TO STAY

$$ ★ **Hotel La Badia.** One of the region's best-known country hotels occupies a 12th-century monastery. **Pros:** elegant atmosphere; fine views. **Cons:** slightly overpriced; need a car to get around. **TripAdvisor:** "like stepping back in time," "beautiful and full of charm," "grounds lovely to walk around." ✉ *Località La Badia, Orvieto Scalo* ☎ *0763/301959* 🌐 *www.labadiahotel.it* *18 rooms, 9 suites* *In-hotel: restaurant, bar, tennis courts, pool, parking* ⏲ *Closed Jan. and Feb.* *Breakfast.*

$$ **Hotel Palazzo Piccolomini.** This hotel is often preferred by local winemakers and other professionals for its updated look with inviting lobby areas and a convenient location near the church of San Giovanni. **Pros:** peaceful atmosphere; efficient staff; good location. **Cons:** unattractive building; slightly overpriced. **TripAdvisor:** "looks like a medieval castle," "nice common rooms," "surprisingly quiet." ✉ *Piazza Ranieri 36* ☎ *0763/341743* 🌐 *www.hotelpiccolomini.it* *28 rooms, 3 suites* *In-room: Internet. In-hotel: bar, parking* *Breakfast.*

CLOSE UP

Hiking the Umbrian Hills

Magnificent scenery makes the heart of Italy excellent walking, hiking, and mountaineering country. In Umbria, the area around Spoleto is particularly good; several pleasant, easy, and well-signed trails begin at the far end of the Ponte alle Torri bridge over Monteluco. From Cannara, an easy half-hour walk leads to the fields of Pian d'Arca, the site of Saint Francis's sermon to the birds. For slightly more arduous walks, you can follow the saint's path, uphill from Assisi to the Eremo delle Carceri, and then continue along the trails that crisscross Monte Subasio. At 4,250 feet, the Subasio's treeless summit affords views of Assisi, Perugia, far-off Gubbio, and the distant mountain ranges of Abruzzo.

For even more challenging hiking, the northern reaches of the Valnerina are exceptional; the mountains around Norcia should not be missed. Throughout Umbria and the Marches, you'll find that most recognized walking and hiking trails are marked with the distinctive red-and-white blazes of the Club Alpino Italiano. Tourist offices are a good source for walking and climbing itineraries to suit all ages and levels of ability, while bookstores, *tabacchi* (tobacconists), and *edicole* (newsstands) often have maps and hiking guides that detail the best routes in their area. Depending on the length and location of your walk, it can be important that you have comfortable walking shoes or boots, appropriate attire, and plenty of water to drink.

NARNI

13 km (8 mi) southwest of Terni, 46 km (29 mi) southeast of Orvieto.

GETTING HERE

From Perugia, take the E45 highway toward Rome. Merge onto the SS675, then take the exit to San Gemini and follow signs for Narni Scalo. The drive takes around 1½ hours. There are also regular trains from Perugia.

VISITOR INFORMATION

The **Terni tourism office** (✉ *Via Cassian Bon 4, Terni* ☎ *0744/423047* 🌐 *www.regioneumbria.eu*) provides information for Narni and a number of other smaller towns.

EXPLORING

Once a bustling and important town at a major crossroads on the Via Flaminia, Narni is now a quiet backwater with only the occasional tourist invading its hilltop streets. Modern development is kept out of sight in the new town of Narni Scalo, below. This means that you'll find the older neighborhood safely preserved behind, and in the case of Narni's subterranean Roman ruins, beneath, the town's sturdy walls.

You can take a unique tour of Narni's underground **Roman aqueduct**—the only one open to the public in all of Italy—but it's not for the claustrophobic. Contact Narni Sotterranea at least ten days ahead to book a visit. ✉ *Narni Sotterranea, Via San Bernardo 12* ☎ *0744/722292* 🌐 *www.narnisotterranea.it* 🎫 *€20* ⏲ *Apr.–Oct., weekends by appointment.*

WHERE TO EAT

$-$$ UMBRIAN **Il Cavallino.** Run by the third generation of the Bussetti family, this trattoria is south of Narni on the Via Flaminia. The most dependable menu selections are the grilled meats. Rabbit roasted with rosemary and sage and juicy grilled T-bone steaks are house favorites; in the winter, phone ahead to request the wild pigeon. The wine list has a limited selection of dependable local varieties. *Via Flaminia Romana 220 3 km (2 mi) south of center 0744/761020 Closed Tues. and Dec. 20–26.*

VALNERINA

Terni is 13 km (8 mi) northeast of Narni, 27 km (17 mi) southwest of Spoleto.

The Valnerina (the valley of the River Nera, to the east of Spoleto) is the most beautiful of central Italy's many well-kept secrets. The twisting roads that serve the rugged landscape are poor, but the drive is well worth the effort for its forgotten medieval villages and dramatic mountain scenery.

GETTING HERE

You can head into the area from Terni on the S209, or on the SP395bis north of Spoleto, which links the Via Flaminia (S3) with the middle reaches of the Nera Valley through a tunnel. For information on the area, contact the tourist office in Terni.

VISITOR INFORMATION

Terni tourism office (*Via Cassian Bon 4, Terni 0744/423047 www.regioneumbria.eu*).

EXPLORING

The road east of Terni (SS Valnerina) leads 10 km (6 mi) to the **Cascata delle Marmore** (Waterfalls of Marmore), which, at 541 feet, are the highest in Europe. A canal was dug by the Romans in the 3rd century BC to prevent flooding in the nearby agricultural plains. Nowadays the waters are often diverted to provide hydroelectric power for Terni, reducing the roaring falls to an unimpressive trickle, so check with the information office at the falls (there's a timetable on their Web site) or with Terni's tourist office before heading here. On summer evenings, when the falls are in full spate, the cascading water is floodlit to striking effect. The falls are usually at their most energetic at midday and at around 4 pm. This is a good place for hiking, except in December and January, when most trails may be closed. *SP79 10 km (6 mi) east of Terni 0744/62982 www.marmorefalls.it €5 May, weekends noon–1 and 4–5; June–Aug., daily 11am–10 pm; mid-Mar.–Apr. and Sept., weekends noon–9; Jan.–mid-Mar., weekends noon–4.*

Norcia, the birthplace of Saint Benedict, is better known for its Umbrian pork and truffles. Norcia exports truffles to France and hosts a truffle festival, the Sagra del Tartufo, every February. The surrounding mountains provide spectacular hiking. *67 km (42 mi) northeast of Terni.*

Piano Grande, a mountain plain 25 km (15 mi) to the northeast of the valley, is a hang glider's paradise, a wonderful place for a picnic or to fly a kite. It's also nationally famous for the quality of the lentils grown here, which are a traditional part of every Italian New Year's feast.

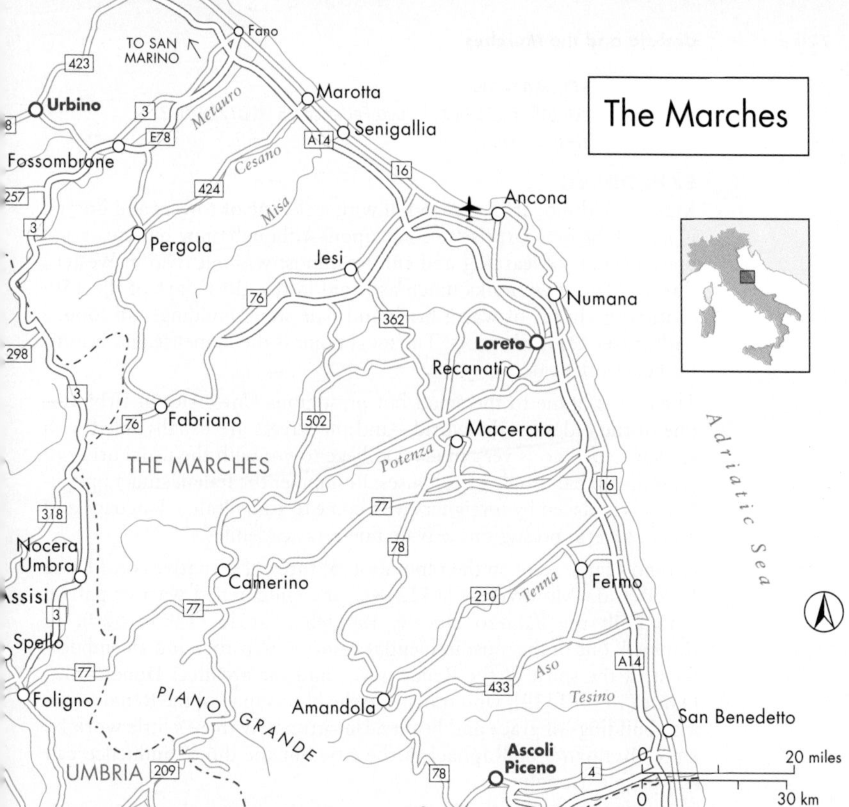

THE MARCHES

An excursion from Umbria into the Marches region allows you to see a part of Italy rarely visited by foreigners. Not as wealthy as Tuscany or Umbria, the Marches has a diverse landscape of mountains and beaches, and marvelous views. Like that of neighbors to the west, the patchwork of rolling hills of Le Marche (as it's known in Italian) is stitched with grapevines and olive trees, bearing luscious wine and olive oil.

Traveling here isn't as easy as in Umbria or Tuscany. Beyond the narrow coastal plain and away from major towns, the roads are steep and twisting. An efficient bus service connects the coastal town of Pesaro to Urbino. Train travel in the region is slow, however, and stops are limited—although you can reach Ascoli Piceno by rail.

URBINO

75 km (47 mi) north of Gubbio, 116 km (72 mi) northeast of Perugia, 230 km (143 mi) east of Florence.

GETTING HERE

Take the SS3bis from Perugia, and follow the directions for Gubbio and Cesena. Exit at Umbertide and take the SS219, then the SS452, and at Calmazzo, the SS73bis to Urbino.

VISITOR INFORMATION

Urbino tourism office (✉ *Piazza Duca Federico 35* ☎ *0722/2613* 🌐 *www.comune.urbino.ps.it*).

EXPLORING

Majestic Urbino, atop a steep hill with a skyline of towers and domes, is something of a surprise to come upon. Although quite remote, it was once a center of learning and culture almost without rival in Western Europe. The town looks much as it did in the glory days of the 15th century: a cluster of warm brick and pale stone buildings, all topped with russet-color tile roofs. The focal point is the immense and beautiful Palazzo Ducale.

The city is home to the small but prestigious Università di Urbino—one of the oldest in the world—and the streets are usually filled with students. Urbino is very much a college town, with the usual array of bookshops, bars, and coffeehouses. In summer the Italian student population is replaced by foreigners who come to study Italian language and arts at several prestigious private fine-arts academies.

Urbino's fame rests on the reputation of three of its native sons: Duke Federico da Montefeltro (1422–82), the enlightened warrior-patron who built the Palazzo Ducale; Raffaello Sanzio (1483–1520), or Raphael, one of the most influential painters in history and an embodiment of the spirit of the Renaissance; and the architect Donato Bramante (1444–1514), who translated the philosophy of the Renaissance into buildings of grace and beauty. Unfortunately there's little work by either Bramante or Raphael in the city, but the duke's influence can still be felt strongly.

The **Casa Natale di Raffaello** *(House of Raphael)* is the house in which the painter was born and where he took his first steps in painting, under the direction of his artist father. There's some debate about the fresco of the Madonna here; some say it's by Raphael, whereas others attribute it to the father—with Raphael's mother and the young painter himself standing in as models for the Madonna and Child. ✉ *Via Raffaello 57* ☎ *0722/320105* 💶 *€3* ⏲ *Mon.–Sat. 10–12:30 and 3–5:30, Sun. 10–12:30.*

Fodor's Choice ★ The **Palazzo Ducale** *(Ducal Palace)* holds a place of honor in the city. If the Renaissance was, ideally, a celebration of the nobility of man and his works, of the light and purity of the soul, then there's no place in Italy, the birthplace of the Renaissance, where these tenets are better illustrated. From the moment you enter the peaceful courtyard, you know you're in a place of grace and beauty, the harmony of the building reflecting the high ideals of the time. Today the palace houses the **Galleria Nazionale delle Marche** (National Museum of the Marches), with a superb collection of paintings, sculpture, and other objets d'art. Some works were originally the possessions of the Montefeltro family; others were brought here from churches and palaces throughout the region. Masterworks in the collection include Paolo Uccello's *Profanation of the Host,* Titian's *Resurrection* and *Last Supper,* and Piero della Francesca's *Madonna of Senigallia.* But the gallery's highlight is Piero's enigmatic work long known as *The Flagellation of Christ.* Much has been written about this painting, and few experts agree on its meaning. Legend had it that the figures in the foreground represent a murdered member of the Montefeltro family (the barefoot young man) and his two killers. However, Sir John Pope-Hennessy—the preeminent scholar of Italian Renaissance art—argues that they represent the arcane subject of the vision of Saint Lawrence. Academic debates notwithstanding, the experts agree that the work is one of the painter's masterpieces. Piero himself thought so: it's one of the few works he signed (on the lowest step supporting the throne). ✉ *Piazza Duca Federico* ☎ *0722/322625* 🌐 *www.comune.urbino.ps.it* €5 ⏲ *Mon. 8:30–2, Tues.–Sun. 8:30–7:15.*

WHERE TO EAT AND STAY

$ CENTRAL ITALIAN ✕ **Angolo Divino.** At this *osteria* (informal restaurant) in the center of Urbino, tradition reigns supreme: the menu is written in local dialect, flanked by Italian and English translations. Dishes range from the deliciously simple *spaghetti col pane grattugiato* (spaghetti with bread crumbs) to the temptingly rich *filetto al tartufo* (beef fillet with truffles). ✉ *Via S. Andrea 14* ☎ *0722/327559* ⏲ *Closed Mon. and mid-Oct.–mid-Nov. No dinner Sun.*

$ CENTRAL ITALIAN ✕ **La Vecchia Fornarina.** Locals often crowd this small, two-room trattoria near the Piazza della Repubblica. The specialty is meaty country fare, such as *coniglio* (rabbit) and *vitello alle noci* (veal cooked with walnuts) or *ai porcini* (with mushrooms). There's also a good selection of pasta dishes. ✉ *Via Mazzini 14* ☎ *0722/320007* *Reservations essential.*

$$ **Hotel Bonconte.** This classic hotel dating from the beginning of the 20th century is just inside the city walls and close to the Palazzo Ducale. **Pros:** some nice views; away from the bustle. **Cons:** slightly overpriced; service is sleepy. **TripAdvisor:** "all the modern amenities," "breathtaking view," "near the center of the town." ✉ *Via delle Mura 28* ☎ *0722/2463* 🌐 *www.viphotels.it* *23 rooms, 2 suites* *In-room: a/c, Internet. In-hotel: bar* *No meals.*

LORETO

31 km (19 mi) south of Ancona, 118 km (73 mi) southeast of Urbino.

GETTING HERE

If you're driving from Perugia, take the SS318 and then the SS76 highway to Fabriano and then on to Chiaravalle, where it merges with the A14 autostrada. The drive takes around 2½ hours. Trains also go to Loreto, but the station is about a mile outside the town center. Regular buses leave from the station to the center.

VISITOR INFORMATION

Loreto tourism office (✉ *Via Solari 3* ☎ *071/970276* 🌐 *www.turismo.marche.it*).

EXPLORING

★ Loreto is famous for one of the best-loved shrines in the world, that of the **Santuario della Santa Casa** (House of the Virgin Mary), within the **Basilica della Santa Casa.** Legend has it that angels moved the house from Nazareth, where the Virgin Mary was living at the time of the Annunciation, to this hilltop in 1295. The reason for this sudden and divinely inspired move was that Nazareth had fallen into the hands of Muslim invaders, whom the angelic hosts viewed as unsuitable keepers of this important shrine. Excavations made at the behest of the Catholic Church have shown that the house did once stand elsewhere and was brought to the hilltop—by either crusaders or a family named Angeli—around the time the angels (*angeli*) are said to have done the job.

The house itself consists of three rough stone walls contained within an elaborate marble tabernacle. Built around this centerpiece is the giant basilica of the Holy House, which dominates the town. Millions of visitors come to the site every year (particularly at Easter and on the December 10 Feast of the Holy House), and the little town of Loreto can become uncomfortably crowded with pilgrims. Many great Italian architects, including Bramante, Antonio da Sangallo the Younger (1483–1546), Giuliano da Sangallo (circa 1445–1516), and Sansovino (1467–1529), contributed to the design of the basilica. It was begun in the Gothic style in 1468 and continued in Renaissance style through the late Renaissance. The bell tower is by Luigi Vanvitelli (1700–73). Inside the church are a great many mediocre 19th- and 20th-century paintings but also some fine works by Renaissance masters such as Luca Signorelli and Melozzo da Forlì (1438–94).

If you're a nervous air traveler, you can take comfort in the fact that the Holy Virgin of Loreto is the patron saint of air travelers and that Pope John Paul II composed a prayer for a safe flight—available here in a half-dozen languages. ✉ *Piazza della Madonna* ☎ *071/970104* 🌐 *www.santuarioloreto.it* ⏲ *Apr.–Sept., daily 6 am–8 pm; Oct.–Mar., daily 6:15 am–7:30 pm. Santuario della Santa Casa closed daily 12:30–2:30.*

ASCOLI PICENO

88 km (55 mi) south of Loreto, 105 km (65 mi) south of Ancona.

GETTING HERE

From Perugia take the SS75 to Foligno, then merge onto the SS3 to Norcia. From here take the SS4 to Ascoli Piceno. There are also trains, but the journey would be quite long, taking you from Perugia to Ancona before changing for Ascoli Piceno.

VISITOR INFORMATION

Ascoli Piceno tourism office (✉ *Aringo 7* ☎ *0736/298204* 🌐 *www.comune.ascolipiceno.it*).

EXPLORING

Ascoli Piceno sits in a valley ringed by steep hills and cut by the Tronto River. In Roman times it was one of central Italy's best-known market towns, and today, with almost 60,000 residents, it's a major fruit and olive producer, making it one of the most important towns in the region. Despite growth during the Middle Ages and at other times, the streets in the town center continue to reflect the grid pattern of the ancient Roman city. You'll even find the word *rua,* from the Latin *ruga,* used for "street" instead of the Italian *via.* Now largely closed to traffic, the city center is great to explore on foot.

★ The heart of the town is the majestic **Piazza del Popolo,** dominated by the Gothic church of **San Francesco** and the **Palazzo del Popolo,** a 13th-century town hall that contains a graceful Renaissance courtyard. The square itself functions as the living room of the entire city. At dusk each evening the piazza is packed with people strolling and exchanging news and gossip—the sweetly antiquated ritual called the *passeggiata,* performed all over the country.

WHERE TO EAT AND STAY

$ ITALIAN ★ **Ristorante Tornasacco.** You won't find nouvelle cuisine here, at one of Ascoli Piceno's oldest restaurants. The owners pride themselves on meaty local specialties such as *olive ascolane* (olives stuffed with minced meat, breaded and deep-fried), *maccheroncini alla contadina* (homemade short pasta in a lamb, pork, and veal sauce), and *bistecca di toro* (bull steak). ✉ *Piazza del Popolo 36* ☎ *0736/254151* ⌚ *Closed Fri., July 15–31, and Dec. 23–28.*

$ **Il Pennile.** Look for this modern, family-run hotel in a quiet residential area outside the old city center, amid a grove of olive trees. **Pros:** peaceful; a good budget option. **Cons:** distance from town center; basic rooms. **TripAdvisor:** "clean and efficient," "a pine forest," "simple but pleasant." ✉ *Via G. Spalvieri* ☎ *0736/41645* 🌐 *www.hotelpennile.it* *33 rooms* *In-room: a/c, Internet. In-hotel: bar, gym, business center* *Breakfast.*

Southern Italy

WHAT'S WHERE

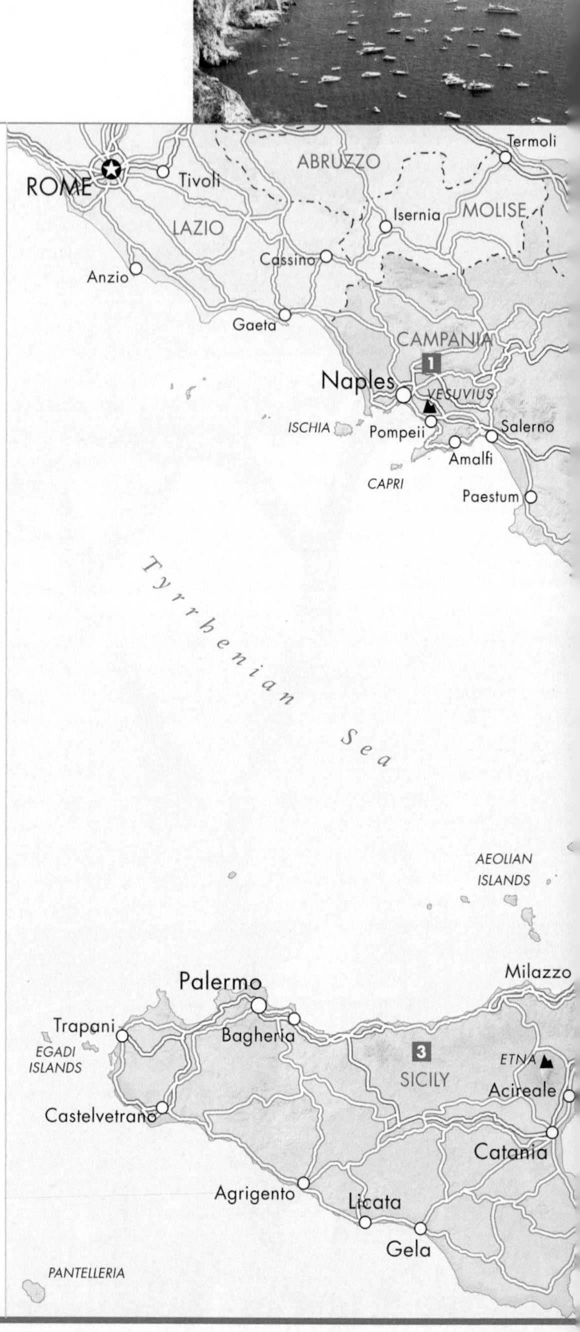

1 Naples and Campania. Campania is the gateway to southern Italy—and as far south as many travelers get. The region's happy combination of spectacular geology and rich cultural heritage makes it a popular place both to unwind—on the pint-size islands of Capri and Ischia or the resorts of the Amalfi Coast—and to explore the past—at the archaeological ruins of Pompeii, Herculaneum, and Paestum. In the middle of everything is Naples, a chaotic metropolis that people love and hate in nearly equal measure, though after a decade of urban renewal the lovers now appear to be in the majority. On a good day it's Italy's most fun and friendly large city. On a bad one it's a giant traffic jam, filled with crooked cabbies and purse-snatching kids on scooters.

2 The Southern Peninsula. The southernmost regions of the peninsula—Puglia, Basilicata, and Calabria—are known for their laid-back medieval villages, shimmering seas, and varied landscapes. The coastline of Puglia, along the heel of Italy's boot, is popular with beachgoers, but for the most part you're off the beaten path here, with all the pleasures and challenges that entails. You'll find fewer

English-speakers but more genuine warmth from the people you encounter. The most distinctive attractions are the *Sassi* (cave dwellings in the Basilicata village of Matera) and *trulli* (mysterious conical-roof dwellings found in abundance in Puglia's Valle d'Itria). Both are UNESCO World Heritage sites.

3 Sicily. The architecture of Sicily reflects the island's centuries of successive dominion by the Greeks, Romans, Byzantines, Arabs, Normans, Spaniards, and, most recently, Italians. Baroque church–hopping could be a sport in the cacophonous streets of Palermo and seafaring Siracusa. The breezes are sultry, and everyday life is without pretense, as witnessed in the workaday stalls of the fish markets in ports all along the Tyrrhenian and Ionian coasts, bursting with tuna, swordfish, and sardines. Greek ruins stand sentinel in Agrigento's Valley of the Temples, blanketed in almond, oleander, and juniper blossoms. All over the island the ins and outs of life are celebrated each day as they have been for centuries—over a morning coffee, at the family lunch table, and in the evening *passeggiata* (stroll).

SOUTHERN ITALY PLANNER

Speaking the Language

Here, as in much of Italy, when locals talk among themselves, they often revert to dialect that's unintelligible to the student of textbook Italian. Each region has a dialect of its own; Salentinu (spoken in the tip of the heel) and Barese (around Bari) are distinctive enough to be considered separate languages, though they developed in neighboring areas.

Thanks to the education system and the unifying influence of radio and television, nearly everyone speaks standard Italian as well, so you can still benefit from whatever knowledge you have of the language. English-speakers aren't as prevalent as in points north, but this is the land of creative gesticulation and other improvised nonverbal communication. Chances are, you'll be able to get your message across.

Getting Here

Located 8 km (5 mi) outside Naples, **Aeroporto Capodichino** (NAP) serves the Campania region. It handles domestic and international flights, including several flights daily between Naples and Rome (flight time 55 minutes).

The three main airports of the deep south are Bari and Brindisi, in Puglia, and Lamezia Terme, in Calabria. All three have regular flights to and from Rome and Milan. In addition, Reggio di Calabria's airport has flights to and from Rome.

Sicily can be reached from all major international cities on flights connecting through Rome, Milan, or Naples. Planes to Palermo land at **Aeroporto Falcone-Borsellino** (named in memory of two anti-Mafia judges famously assassinated in 1992) in Punta Raisi, 32 km (19 mi) west of town. Catania's Aeroporto Fontanarossa, 5 km (3 mi) south of the city center, is the main airport on Sicily's eastern side.

There are direct express trains from Milan and Rome to Palermo, Catania, and Siracusa. The Rome-Palermo and Rome-Siracusa trips take at least 11 hours. After Naples, the run is mostly along the coast, so try to book a window seat on the right if you're not on an overnight train. At Villa San Giovanni, in Calabria, the train is separated and loaded onto a ferryboat to cross the strait to Messina. Direct trains run from Milan, Rome, and Bologna to Bari and Lecce.

Typical Travel Times

	Hours by Car	Hours by Train
Naples–Rome	2:30	1:30
Naples–Bari	3:00	4:00
Bari–Lecce	1:45	1:45
Naples–Matera	3:15	6:00
Naples–Cosenza	4:00	3:45
Naples–Messina	7:00	5:30
Messina–Palermo	2:30	3:45
Messina–Siracusa	2:00	2:45
Siracusa–Palermo	3:00	4:15
Palermo–Agrigento	1:15	2:05

When to Go

Spring: In April, May, and early June southern Italy is at its best. The weather is generally pleasant, and the fields are in full bloom. Easter is a busy time for most tourist destinations—if you're traveling then, you should have lodging reserved well ahead of time. By May the seawater is warm enough for swimming by American standards, but you can often have the beach to yourself, as Italians shy away until at least June.

Summer: Temperatures can be torrid in summer, making it a less than ideal time for a visit to the south. In Campania, Naples can feel like an inferno, the archaeological sites swarm with visitors, and the islands and Amalfi Coast resorts are similarly overrun. Even the otherwise perfect villages of the interior are too dazzlingly white for easy comfort from July to early September. If you seek a beach, whether on the mainland or in Sicily, keep in mind that during August all of Italy flocks to the shores. Even relatively isolated resorts can be overrun.

Fall: Visit the south from late September through early November and you can find gentle, warm weather and acres of beach space; swimming temperatures last through October. Watch the clock, however, as the days get shorter. At most archaeological sites you're rounded up two hours before sunset—but by then most crowds have departed, so late afternoon is still an optimum time to see Pompeii, Herculaneum, or Agrigento in peace and quiet.

Winter: Early winter is relatively mild (bougainvillea and other floral displays can bloom through Christmas), but particularly later in the season, cold fronts can arrive and stay for days. In resort destinations many hotels, restaurants, and other tourist facilities close down from November until around Easter. Elsewhere, you need to reserve rooms well in advance between Christmas and Epiphany (January 6) and during Agrigento's almond festival in February and the Carnevale in Acireale and Sciacca.

On the Calendar

These are some of the top seasonal events in southern Italy:

From December through June, the **stagione operistica** (opera season) is underway at Teatro San Carlo in Naples.

In early February in Agrigento's Valley of the Temples, **Sagra del Mandorlo in Fiore** (Almond Blossom Festival, 🌐 *www.mandorloinfiore.net*) is a week of folk music and dancing, with participants from many countries.

The **Settimana Santa** (Holy Week), culminating with Easter, features parades and outdoor events in every city and most small towns. Naples and Trapani have particularly noteworthy festivities.

Twice a year, the first Sunday in May and on September 19, Naples celebrates the **Feast of San Gennaro.** In the Duomo, at 9 am, a remnant of the saint's blood miraculously liquefies, after which there's a ceremonial parade.

Maggio dei Monumenti is a cultural initiative in Naples lasting the entire month of May. Special exhibits, palaces, private collections, and churches are open to the public for free or at a discount.

Every fourth year in June, the **Regata delle Antiche Repubbliche Marinare** (Regatta of the Great Maritime Republics) sees keen boating competitions in Amalfi, Genoa, Pisa, or Venice. In 2012 Amalfi is the site for the event.

SOUTHERN ITALY TOP ATTRACTIONS

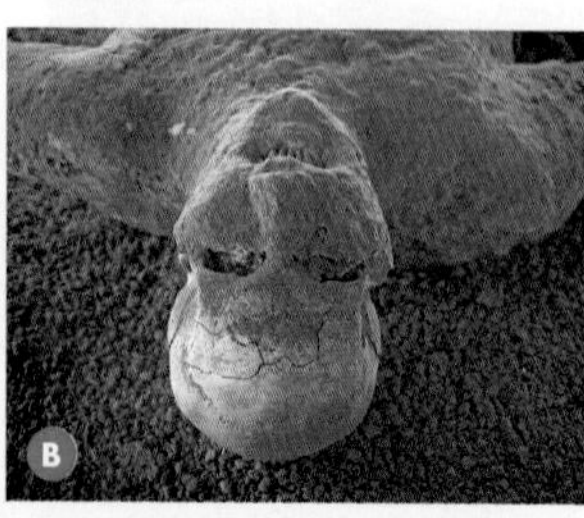

Underground Naples

(A) In Naples the locals point to the ground and say there's another city underneath. This is *Napoli Sotterranea*, a netherworld of ancient Greek quarries and aqueducts, Roman streets, and World War II bomb shelters. Parts have been cleaned up and made accessible to the public. (⇨ *Chapter 13.)*

The Ruins around Vesuvius

(B) This may be the closest you'll ever get to time travel. Thanks to Vesuvius's blowing its top in AD 79, the towns round its base were carpeted in fallout and preserved for posterity. Allow a good half-day to look around bustling Pompeii or the more compact, less busy, and better preserved Herculaneum. For the best Roman frescoes, head to the Villa Oplontis between the two ancient cities. (⇨ *Chapter 13.)*

The Amalfi Coast

(C) One moment you're gazing out at a luxury sailcraft, the next you're dodging mules on precipitous footpaths. "Comforts of the 21st century in a medieval setting" just about sums up the remarkable Amalfi Coast. (⇨ *Chapter 13.)*

Matera's Sassi

You can see why Matera is a favorite with filmmakers shooting biblical scenes. You get that time-warp feeling especially in early morning or at night among the *Sassi*—buildings seemingly gouged out of the limestone cliffs. (⇨ *Chapter 14.)*

Lecce

(D) With its much-feted baroque facades and extensive Roman remains in the city center, Lecce has a legitimate claim to being Puglia's fairest city. As an added bonus, nearby are a largely undeveloped coastline and the magical walled town of Otranto. (⇨ *Chapter 14.)*

Bronzi di Riace, Reggio di Calabria

(E) Few bronze statues have survived intact from the ancient Greek world. The presence of not one but two larger-than-life bronzes, restored to almost perfect condition, is reason enough to trek to Reggio di Calabria, on the eastern side of the Strait of Messina. *(⇨ Chapter 14.)*

Mount Etna

(F) You can take the single-gauge railway around its foothills, splurge on an SUV experience near the summit, or just stroll across old lavafields on its northern flank. Alternatively, go down into the gorge of Alcantara and see what happens when lava flow meets mountain spring water. *(⇨ Chapter 15.)*

Palermo, Monreale, and Cefalù

When it comes to medieval mosaics and Norman cathedrals, Palermo and its environs are the envy of the world. Biblical scenes in the newly restored Palatine Chapel in Palermo shimmer in ripples of gold leaf, and nearby Monreale and Cefalù's cathedrals are replete with heavenly golden mosaics. *(⇨ Chapter 15.)*

Imperial Roman Villa, Piazza Armerina

(G) "Villa" doesn't begin to describe this opulent palace from the latter years of the Roman Empire. The stunning mosaics that fill every room are perhaps the best preserved and certainly the most extensive of the ancient Roman Empire. *(⇨ Chapter 15.)*

Duomo, Siracusa

(H) Few buildings encapsulate history better than the Duomo of Siracusa. The cathedral started life as a temple dedicated to the goddess Athena sometime in the early 5th century BC, as one glance at the majestic fluted columns inside confirms. *(⇨ Chapter 15.)*

TOP EXPERIENCES

Red Red Wine

Although historically wine in the south was mass-produced (badly) for export or consumed locally to provide extra calories to overworked fieldworkers, the past decade has seen enormous strides in high-quality wine production. Reds are becoming especially prestigious, and compete well in the international market. Basilicata's Aglianico del Vulture and Campania's Taurasi are made from the aglianico grape. Both are rich, complex wines with potential for aging. Aglianico has even been dubbed "the Barolo of the South" by connoisseurs. In Puglia, the primitivo grapes (known as zinfandel in the New World) become rich, jammy, full-bodied reds. Sicily is where local varieties like Nero d'Avola are blended with international grapes like merlot and cabernet sauvignon to great effect.

Pasticceria Siciliana

Cannolo, *setteveli*, *cartoccio*, *cassata*, and diminutive *cassatina*: it sounds like the list of characters from an opera, but these ricotta-filled delights can be found in any self-respecting *pasticceria* (pastry shop) on the island of Sicily. The top performers cluster around Palermo and Catania: Massaro and Cappello, both just a short walk from the Porta Nuova, have been delighting palates for more than a century combined, while Savia's pedigree in Catania stretches even farther back. The secret lies in the freshness and simplicity of the ricotta made from the whey of ultrafresh sheep or goat's milk, and, depending on the recipe, studded with chocolate chips, liqueur, or candied fruit.

Fiery Landscapes

Volcanoes have long fascinated people on the move. The ancient Greeks—among the first sailors around the central Mediterranean—explained away Etna as the place where the god Hephaestus had his workshop. Millennia later, northern European visitors to Naples in the 18th and 19th centuries would climb the erupting Vesuvius or cross the steaming craters of the Campi Flegrei west of the city. Farther south, in the Lipari Islands northeast of Sicily, Stromboli performs a lightshow about every 20 minutes, ejecting incandescent cinder, lapilli, and lava bombs high into the air. To add to the fascination, several of the Lipari Islands rise sheer out of the Mediterranean, and beaches are black with volcanic fallout. Though stripped of their mythology by generations of geologists and deprived by local authorities of even a frisson of risk, Italy's volcanoes are still a terrific crowd-puller.

The Great Summer Performances

Exploiting its Mediterranean climate and atmospheric venues, the south of Italy lays on an impressive range of cultural events during those hot summer months.

The ancient theaters of Segesta, Siracusa, and Taormina in Sicily are used for anything from Greek plays to pop concerts, while in Campania the Greek temples at Paestum serve as a scenic backdrop for opera and symphonic music. The 18th-century villas near Herculaneum at the foot of Vesuvius have also joined the musical act in recent years. With time (and money), head across the bay to Capri for a sunset concert at Villa San Michele, high over the Mediterranean.

SOUTHERN ITALY TODAY

. . . really is different from the north

Southern Italy is slap bang in the middle of the Mediterranean, so it's no wonder that it has experienced invasions and migrations for millennia, many of which have left their mark culturally, linguistically, and architecturally.

The southerners really *are* different from Italians farther north. Under an ostensibly sociable and more expressive exterior, they're more formal when dealing with strangers and authority, often using the antiquated *voi* form for addressing them (rather than *Lei* or *tu*). They're also more likely to leave home to find work, traveling to northern Italy and to northern European countries, especially.

. . . contends with political "back-scratching"

Politics tends to be clientelistic in large swaths of the south. In this climate of mutual back-scratching and with unemployment rates (13.6%) twice the national average, the main preoccupation for many voters is *il posto fisso* (a steady job).

Votes are all too often cast for the politician who promises opportunities for career advancement—or lucrative contracts—preferably in the public sector. Over the years, this approach has insured inefficiencies, if not outright corruption.

. . . has its economic ups and downs

While the north has developed relatively rapidly in the past 50 years, the Italian entrepreneurial spirit in the south struggles to make good. Despite a pool of relatively cheap, willing labor, foreign investment across the entire south is merely one-tenth of that going to the northern region of Lombardy alone.

The discrepancy can be attributed in large part to the stifling presence of organized crime. Each major region has its own criminal association: in Naples, it's the Camorra. The system creates add-on costs at many levels, especially in retail.

It's not all bad news though. Southern Italy has woken up to its major asset, its remarkable cultural and natural heritage. UNESCO lists 14 World Heritage Sites in southern Italy alone, while the last decade has seen the creation of several national parks, marine parks, and regional nature preserves. Environmental and cultural associations have mushroomed as locals increasingly perceive the importance of preserving across the generations.

In general, the small average farm size in the south (5.8 hectares, under 15 acres) has helped preserve a pleasing mosaic of habitats in the interior. Landscape and product diversity has been aided by the promotion of traditionally grown products by the European Union and its PDO (Protected Designation of Origin) project.

. . . is attracting visitors

Tourism is on the rise in Puglia and Basilicata, while Campania—traditionally the biggest tourist region—has had some adversity, largely due to the black eye of garbage-collection problems in Naples. Sicily still pulls nature lovers and adventure seekers who cycle or hike its rugged terrain, and Calabria remains largely a beach holiday destination crowded only from mid-July through August. Religious tourism accounts for large visitor flows throughout the year—as many visitors pay their respects to the Madonna di Pompei sanctuary as they do to the archaeological site up the road. In almost every village and town in southern Italy you're likely to see the bearded statue of Capuchin priest Padre Pio.

A GREAT ITINERARY

Day 1: Naples

Fly into Naples's Aeroporto Capodichino, a scant 8 km (5 mi) from the city. Naples is rough around the edges and may be a bit jarring if you're a first-time visitor, but it's classic Italy, and most visitors end up falling in love with the city's alluring waterfront palazzi and spectacular pizza. First things first, though: recharge with a nap and, after that, a good caffè—Naples has some of the world's best. Revive in time for an evening stroll down Naples's wonderful shopping street, Via Toledo, to Piazza Plebescito, before dinner and bed.

Logistics: Under no circumstances should you rent a car for Naples. Take a taxi from the airport—it's not far, or overly expensive—and you should face few logistical obstacles on your first day in Italy.

Day 2: Naples

Start the day at the Museo Archaeologico Nazionale, budgeting at least two hours for the collection. Then take Via Santa Maria di Costantinopoli and grab a coffee at one of the outdoor cafés in Piazza Bellini. From here, head down Via dei Tribunali for a pizza at I Decumani or Di Matteo. Continue along Tribunali to Via del Duomo for a visit to the city's cathedral. From Via del Duomo, turn right onto Spaccanapoli, turning off for a brief stop at the Cappella Sansevero for a look at the pinnacle of Masonic sculpture before heading to Piazza del Gesù and the churches of Il Gesù Nuovo and Santa Chiara. Walk downhill, following the Via Monteoliveto and Via Medina to the harbor and the Castel Nuovo; then head past the Teatro San Carlo to the enormous Palazzo Reale. Walk 15 minutes south to the Castel dell'Ovo in the Santa Lucia waterfront area, one of Naples's most charming neighborhoods. Then it's back up to Via Caracciolo and the Villa Comunale, before heading back to your hotel for a short rest before dinner and perhaps a night out at one of Naples's lively bars or clubs.

Logistics: This entire day is easily done on foot. Naples is one of the best walking cities in Italy.

Day 3: Pompeii/Sorrento

After breakfast, pick up your rental car, pack in your luggage, and drive from Naples to Pompeii, one of the true archaeological gems of Europe. If it's summer, be prepared for an onslaught of sweltering heat as you make your way through the incredibly preserved ruins of a city that was devastated by the whims of Mt. Vesuvius nearly 2,000 years ago. You'll see the houses of noblemen and merchants, brothels, political graffiti, and more. From Pompeii, get back in your car and it's on to Sorrento, your first taste of the wonderful peninsula that marks the beginning of the fabled Amalfi Coast. Sorrento is touristy, but it may well be the Italian city of your imagination: cliff-hanging, cobblestone-paved, and graced with an infinite variety of fishing ports and coastal views. There, have a relaxing dinner of fish and white wine before calling it a day.

Logistics: Naples to Pompeii is all about the A3: a short 24 km (15 mi) brings you to this archaeological gem. From Pompeii it's a short ride back on the A3 until the exit for Sorrento; from the exit, you'll take the SS145 to reach Sorrento.

Day 4: Positano/Ravello

Your stay in Sorrento will be short, as there's much of the Amalfi Coast still to see: Positano, your next stop, is a must. It's one of the most-visited towns in Italy for good reason: its blue-green seas, stairs "as steep as ladders," and white

Moorish-style houses make for a truly memorable setting. Walk, gaze, and eat (lunch), before heading on to the less traveled, even-higher-up town of Ravello, your Amalfi Coast dream come true, an aerie that's "closer to the sky than the sea." Don't miss the Duomo, Villa Rufolo, or Villa Cimbrone before settling in for a dinner in the sky.

Logistics: Sorrento to Positano is a 30-km (19-mi) jaunt, but the winding roads will draw it out for the better part of an hour—a scenic hour. From Positano, Ravello is another slow 18 km (11 mi) to the east, perched high above the rest of the world. Be prepared to use low gears if you're driving a stick shift (as you almost surely will be).

Day 5: Matera

It'll take a bit of a drive to get to Basilicata from the Amalfi Coast; leaving Campania and entering Basilicata is generally a lonely experience. Little-traveled roads, wild hills, and distant farms are the hallmarks of this province, which produces deep, dark aglianico wines and has perfected the art of peasant food. You'll spend a while in your car to make it to Matera, a beautiful, ancient city full of Paleolithic Sassi (cavelike dwellings hewn out of rock)—but it's worth it. Traversing the city is like taking a voyage through time. Spend the afternoon exploring the Sassi, but take care not to miss the new part of the city, too. Then enjoy a relaxing dinner at one of Matera's excellent restaurants—just decide whether you want flavorful local beef (Le Botteghe) or a flurry of Basilicatan tapas (Lucanerie). Basilicata, you'll soon discover, is full of unrivaled values at restaurants, and with such options you'll be guaranteed to sleep well in the Sassi.

Logistics: It's a long haul from your starting point, Ravello, to Matera. It's a good thing Basilicata's landscape is so pretty. Once in Matera, if you're staying in the Sassi, get extra-detailed driving and parking instructions from your hotel beforehand—navigating through thousand-year-old alleyways can be challenging.

Day 6: Lecce

This drive will take a good 2½ hours, so get an early start. The baroque city of Lecce will mark your introduction to Puglia, the heel of Italy's boot. It's one of Italy's best-kept secrets, as you'll soon find out upon checking out the spectacular church of Santa Croce, the ornate Duomo, and the harmonious Piazza Sant'Oronzo. The shopping is great, the food is great,

and the evening passeggiata is great. Don't miss the opportunity, if you wind up at a bar or café in the evening, to chat with Lecce's friendly residents—unfazed by tourism, the welcoming Leccesi represent southern Italians at their best.

Logistics: It's not far from Matera to Lecce as the crow flies, but the trip is more involved than you might think; patience is required. The best route is via Taranto—don't make the mistake of going up through Bari.

Day 7: Bari

The trip from Lecce to Bari is a short one. Check into the pleasant Domina Hotel Bari Palace and spend the morning and afternoon wandering through Bari's *centro storico* (historic center). The wide-open doors of the town's humble houses and apartments, with bickering families and grandmothers drying their pasta in the afternoon sun, will give you a taste of the true flavor of Italy's deep south. Don't miss Bari's castle and the walk around the ridge of the ancient city walls, with views of wide-open sea at every turn. Finish the day with a good fish dinner, and celebrate your last night in Italy by checking out one of the city's multitude of lively bars—Bari boasts one of southern Italy's most hopping bar scenes.

Logistics: This is one of your most straightforward, if not quickest, drives: just take the coastal S16 for 154 km (95 mi) until you hit Bari. It's a two-lane highway, though, so don't be surprised if the trip takes two hours or more. If you get tired, beautiful Ostuni (dubbed the "città bianca," or the white city) is a perfect hilltop pit stop halfway there.

TIPS

Alitalia usually doesn't mark up open-jaw trips, but EasyJet (🌐 *www.easyjet.com*) has inexpensive domestic air service and operates Milan (Malpensa)–Naples, London (Gatwick and Stanstead)—Naples, Bari–Milan (Malpensa), and Bari–Rome (Fiumicino) routes. Blu-Express (*wwww.blu-express.com*) flies from Rome (Fiumicino) to Brindisi, Catania, and Lamezia Terme. If you can find a cheap round-trip fare from your home to Milan plus those two flights on low-cost carriers, you might save some money. Also look at low-cost carriers that shuttle passengers between London and southern Italy; you can often save the most money of all by combining two such one-way fares with a round-trip discount fare to London; however, beware of inconvenient connections in London (Luton, for example).

Day 8: Bari/Departure

Bad news: This is your wake-up-and-leave day. Bari's Aeroporto Palese is small but quite serviceable. Exploit its absence of crowds and easy access and use it as your way out of Italy. Connections through Rome or Milan are more frequent than you might think. Plan on leaving with southern Italy firmly established in your heart as the best way to see the Italy that once was—and be thankful that you were able to see it while it's still like this.

Logistics: Bari hotels offer easy airport transfers; take advantage of them. There are also regular public transport connections between the central train station and the airport. Return your rental car at the Bari airport; you won't have to arrive at the airport more than an hour or so before your flight.

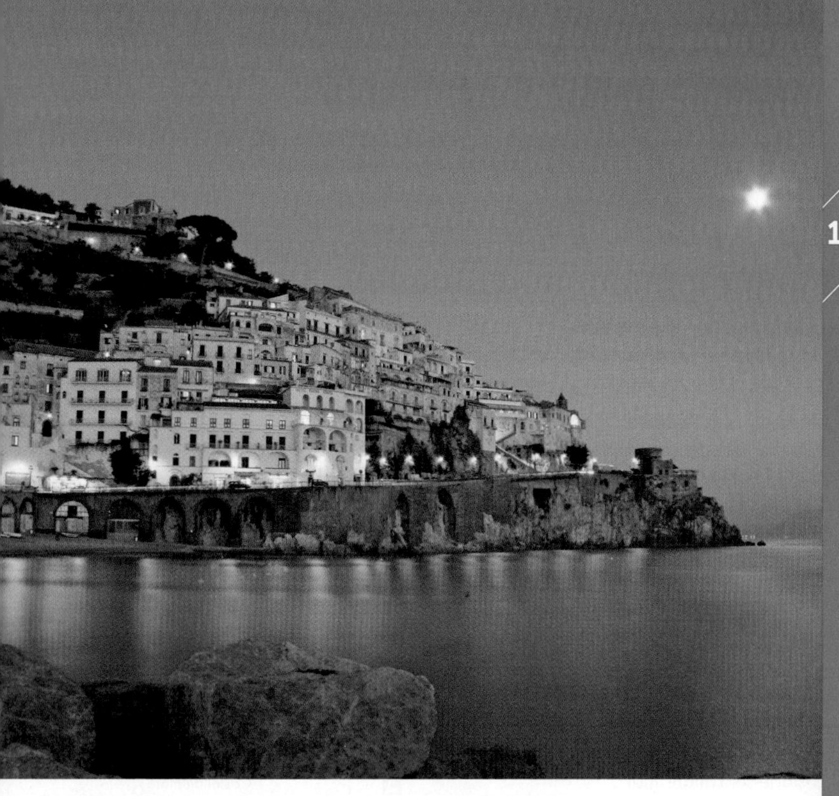

13

Naples and Campania

WORD OF MOUTH

"I much preferred Positano to Sorrento, but Sorrento is a better base for transport to Pompeii, Herculaneum (better than Pompeii in my opinion) and Naples. Definitely plan to overnight on Capri, and to get out of the two main towns."

—thursdaysd

WELCOME TO NAPLES AND CAMPANIA

TOP REASONS TO GO

★ **Walking the streets of Naples:** Its energy, chaos, and bursts of beauty make Naples the most operatic of Italian cities.

★ **Exploring Pompeii:** The excavated ruins of Pompeii are a unique and occasionally spooky glimpse into everyday life—and sudden death—in Roman times.

★ **"The Living Room of the World":** Pose oh-so-casually with the beautiful people sipping their Camparis on La Piazzetta, the central crossroads of Capri: a stage-set square that always seems ready for a gala performance.

★ **Ravishing Ravello:** High above the Amalfi Coast, two spectacular villas compete for the title of most beautiful spot in southern Italy.

★ **A world made of stairs:** Built like a vertical amphitheater piggybacked with houses, Positano may very well be the best triathlon training ground imaginable. The town's only job is to look enchanting—and it does that very well.

1 Naples. Italy's third-largest city is densely packed with people, cafés, pizzerias, and an amazing number of Norman and baroque churches.

2 Herculaneum, Vesuvius, and Pompeii. Two towns show you how ancient Romans defined the good life—until, one day in AD 79, Mount Vesuvius buried them in volcanic ash and lava.

3 Procida and Ischia. Though they lack Capri's glitz, these two sister islands in the Bay of Naples share a laid-back charm.

4 Capri. The rocky island mixes natural beauty and *dolce vita* glamour.

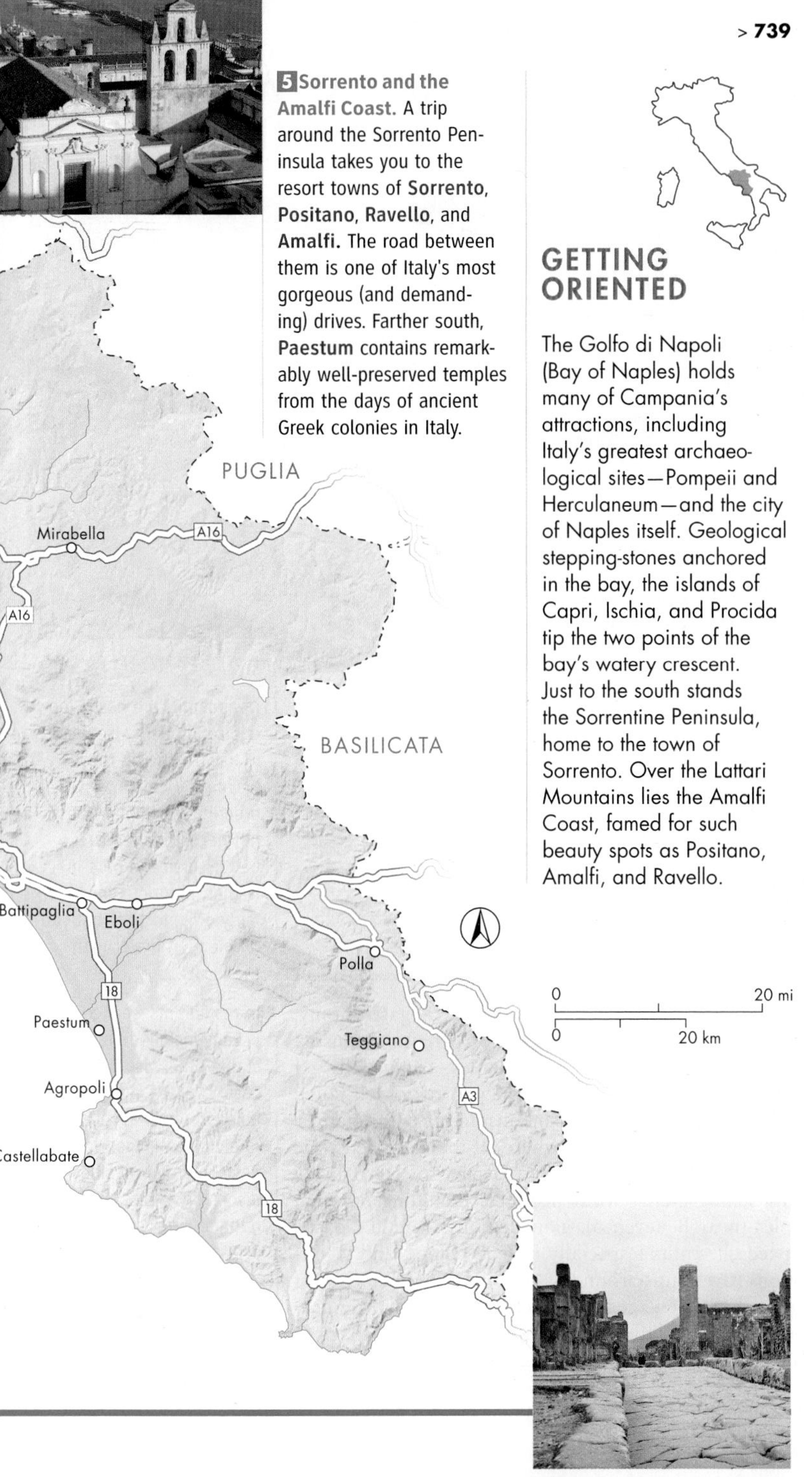

5 Sorrento and the Amalfi Coast. A trip around the Sorrento Peninsula takes you to the resort towns of **Sorrento, Positano, Ravello**, and **Amalfi.** The road between them is one of Italy's most gorgeous (and demanding) drives. Farther south, **Paestum** contains remarkably well-preserved temples from the days of ancient Greek colonies in Italy.

GETTING ORIENTED

The Golfo di Napoli (Bay of Naples) holds many of Campania's attractions, including Italy's greatest archaeological sites—Pompeii and Herculaneum—and the city of Naples itself. Geological stepping-stones anchored in the bay, the islands of Capri, Ischia, and Procida tip the two points of the bay's watery crescent. Just to the south stands the Sorrentine Peninsula, home to the town of Sorrento. Over the Lattari Mountains lies the Amalfi Coast, famed for such beauty spots as Positano, Amalfi, and Ravello.

EATING AND DRINKING WELL IN NAPLES AND CAMPANIA

Think of Neapolitan food and you conjure up pasta, pizza, and tomatoes. The stereotype barely scratches the surface of what's available in Naples, and much less in the rest of Campania, whose cuisine reflects an enormously diverse landscape.

Campania is known for its enclaves of gastronomy, notable among them the tip of the Sorrento Peninsula and the Campi Flegrei, west of Naples. You usually get better value outside Naples, and you may well come across *cucina povera,* a cuisine inspired by Campania's *contadino* (peasant) roots, where all the ingredients are sourced from a nearby garden. Expect to see roadside stalls selling stellar local produce, including *annurca* apples (near Benevento), giant lemons (Amalfi Coast), roasted chestnuts (especially near Avellino), and watermelons (the plains around Salerno). Try to get to one of the local *sagre* village feasts celebrating a *prodotto tipico* (local specialty), which could be anything from snails to wild boar to cherries to, more commonly, wine.

A TIPPING TIP

Neapolitans are easily recognized in bars elsewhere in Italy by the tip they leave on the counter when ordering. This habit does not necessarily ensure better service in bars in Naples, notorious for their fairly offhand staff, but you do blend in better with the locals.

In restaurants, service is usually included unless stated otherwise (in which case 5%–10% is reasonable). In pizzerias, tips are rarely given unless you have splurged on side dishes or sweets, or have had particularly good service.

PIZZA

Naples is the undisputed homeland of pizza, and you'll usually encounter it here in two classic forms: *margherita* and *marinara*. Given the size of standard pizzas—they virtually flop off the rim of the plate onto the tabletop—it is legitimate to ask for a *mignon* (kids' portion), or even share, divided on two plates. When pressed for time and stomach space, you can choose from take-away outlets in most town centers selling pizza by the slice, along with the usual range of fried *arancini* (rice balls) and *crocchè di patate* (potato fritters).

COFFEE

Given the same basic ingredients—coffee grounds, water, a machine—what makes *caffè* taste so much better in Naples than elsewhere remains a mystery. If you find the end product too strong, ask to have it with a dash of milk (*caffè macchiato*) or a little diluted (*caffè lungo*).

BUFFALO

Long feted for the melt-in-your-mouth mozzarella cheese (pictured at right) made from its milk, the river buffalo—related to the Asian water buffalo—is also the source of other culinary delights. Throughout the region, look for buffalo ricotta and mascarpone, as well as buffalo *provola* and *scamorza*, which may be lightly smoked (resulting in a golden crust). In Caserta look for more-mature *nero di bufala* (aged like sheep's cheese), while around Salerno you'll find smoked *caciocavallo* cheese and also *carne di bufala* (buffalo meat), which can be braised to perfection.

THE ORAL TRADITION

Locals in Campania like to bypass the restaurant menu and ask what the staff recommends. Take this approach and you'll often wind up with a daily special or house specialty. Though you're unlikely to get multilingual staff outside the larger hotels and main tourist areas, the person you talk to will spare no effort to get the message across.

WINE

Wine in Campania has an ancient pedigree: some say fancifully that Campania's undisputed king of reds, the Aglianico varietal, got its name from the word "Hellenic," and Fiano, the primary white grape, closely resembles the Roman variety Apianus. Horace, the Latin poet, extolled the virtues of drinking wine from Campania. A century later, Pliny the Elder was harsher in his judgment: wine from Pompeii would give you a hangover until noon the next day, and Sorrento wine tasted of vinegar.

In recent decades though, Campania has gained respect for its boutique reds. Due to the rugged landscape, small farms, and limited mechanization, prices can be relatively high, but the quality is high as well.

Updated by Martin Wilmot Bennett, Fergal Kavanagh, and Fiorella Squillante

A kinetic gust of garlic-and-basil aromatherapy, Campania is a destination that no one ever forgets. More travelers visit this region than any other in the south, and it's no wonder.

A region of evocative names—Capri, Sorrento, Pompeii, Positano, Amalfi—Campania conjures up visions of cliff-shaded, sapphire-hue coves, sun-dappled waters, and mighty ruins. Home to Vesuvius, the area's unique geology is responsible for Campania's photogenic landscape. A languid coastline stretches out along a deep blue sea, punctuated by rocky islands.

Through the ages, the area's temperate climate, warm sea, fertile soil, and natural beauty have attracted Greek colonists, then Roman emperors—who called the region Campania Felix ("the happy land")—and later Saracen raiders and Spanish invaders. The result has been a rich and varied history, reflected in everything from architecture to mythology. The highlights span millennia: the near-intact Roman towns of Pompeii and Herculaneum, the Greek temples in Paestum, the Norman and baroque churches in Naples, the white-dome fisherman's houses of Positano, the dolce vita resorts of Capri. Campania piles them all onto one mammoth must-see sandwich.

The region's complex identity is most intensely felt in its major metropolis, Naples. It sprawls around its bay as though attempting to embrace the island of Capri, while behind it Mount Vesuvius glowers. The most operatic city in Italy, Napoli exasperates both its critics and its defenders. Naples is lush, chaotic, scary, funny, confounding, intoxicating, and very beautiful. Few who visit remain ambivalent. You needn't participate in the mad whirl of the city, however. The best pastime in Campania is simply finding a spot with a stunning view and indulging in *"il dolce far niente"* ("the sweetness of doing nothing").

PLANNING

MAKING THE MOST OF YOUR TIME

In Campania there are three primary travel experiences: Naples, with its restless exuberance; the resorts (Capri, Sorrento, the Amalfi Coast), dedicated to leisure and indulgence; and the archaeological sights (Pompeii, Herculaneum, Paestum), where the ancient world is frozen in time. Each is wonderful in its own way. If you have a week, you can get a good taste of all three, but with less time, you're better off choosing between them rather than stretching yourself thin.

Pompeii is the simplest to plan for: it's a day trip. To get a feel for Naples, you should give it a couple of days at a minimum. The train station makes a harsh first impression, but the city grows on you as you take in the sights and interact with the locals.

That said, many people bypass Naples and head right for the resorts. These places are all about relaxing—you'll miss the point if you're in a rush. Sorrento isn't as spectacular as Positano or Capri, but it's a good base because of its central location.

THE CAMPANIA ARTECARD

The Campania Artecard is a big boon for museum lovers. This pass offers free or discounted admission to almost 50 museums and monuments over a three- or seven-consecutive-day period for the city or the whole region, as well as discounted services ranging from audio guides to theater tickets and car parks.

The benefits depend on the pass: A three-day pass gets you free admission to the first three sites you visit, then half price for the others, plus free transport—including the Alibus from the airport and the Metro del Mare around the bay. The main passes are: Naples historic center, €12 (access to all sites); Naples and Campi Flegrei, €16; Naples and Caserta, €20; Archeologia del golfo including Pompeii, Herculaneum, Caserta, and Paestum, €30; and Naples and Campi Flegrei, €20 (access to all sites); in addition, there are generous youth discounts. As sites and discounts are frequently updated, check 🌐 *www.campaniartecard.it* for the latest information. Cards are available at all the major participating museums and archaeological sites, at main city hotels, as well as at the airport and the station.

GETTING HERE AND AROUND

BUS TRAVEL

Within Campania there's an extensive network of local buses, although finding information about it can be trying. **SITA** buses (☎ *199/730749* 🌐 *www.sitabus.it*) bound for Salerno leave every 30 minutes Monday to Saturday and every two hours on Sunday from its terminal in the port near the Stazione Marittima. SITA buses also serve the Amalfi Coast, connecting Sorrento with Salerno.

CAR TRAVEL

You can get along fine without a car in Campania, and there are plenty of reasons not to have one: traffic in Naples is even worse than in Rome; you can't bring a car to Capri or Ischia (except in winter, when everything's closed); and parking in the towns of the Amalfi Coast is hard to come by and expensive.

Italy's main north–south route, the A1 (also known as the Autostrada del Sole), connects Rome with Naples and Campania. In good traffic the drive to Naples takes less than three hours. Autostrada A3, a continuation of the A1, runs south from Naples through Campania and into Calabria. Herculaneum (Ercolano) and Pompeii (Pompei) both have marked exits off the A3. For Vesuvius, take the Ercolano exit. For the Sorrento Peninsula and the Amalfi Coast, exit at Castellammare di Stabia. To get to Paestum, take the A3 to the Battipaglia exit and take the road to Capaccio Scalo–Paestum. The roads on the Sorrento Peninsula and Amalfi Coast are narrow and twisting, but they have outstanding views.

TRAIN TRAVEL

There are trains every hour between Rome and Naples. Alta Velocità, Eurostar, and Intercity, the fastest types of train service, make the trip in less than two hours. Almost all trains to Naples stop at **Stazione Centrale** (✉ *Piazza Garibaldi* ☎ *892021* 🌐 *www.trenitalia.it*).

The efficient (though run-down) suburban **Circumvesuviana** (☎ *081/7722444* 🌐 *www.vesuviana.it*) runs from Naples's Stazione Circumvesuviana and stops at Stazione Centrale before continuing to Herculaneum, Pompeii, and Sorrento. Travel time between Naples and Sorrento on the Circumvesuviana line is about 75 minutes.

For ticketing purposes, the region is divided into travel zones depending on distance from Naples. A Fascia 2 ticket (€2.10 for 120 minutes) takes you to Herculaneum, Fascia 3 (€2.80 for 140 minutes) includes Pompeii, and Fascia 5 (€4 for 180 minutes) covers trips to Sorrento. If you're traveling from Naples to anywhere else in Campania, there's no need to buy a separate ticket for your subway, tram, or bus ride to the train station. Your train ticket covers the whole journey. Buy the ticket the day before, as some of the ticket types are hard to find.

ABOUT THE HOTELS

Most parts of Campania have accommodations in all price categories, but they tend to fill up in high season, so reserve well in advance. In summer, hotels on the coast that serve meals almost always require you to take half board.

Hotel reviews have been condensed for this book. Please go to Fodors.com for full reviews of each property.

WHAT IT COSTS (IN EUROS)

	¢	$	$$	$$$	$$$$
Restaurants	under €20	€20–€30	€30–€45	€45–€65	over €65
Hotels	under €75	€75–€125	€125–€200	€200–€300	over €300

Restaurant prices are for a first course (*primo*), second course (*secondo*), and dessert (*dolce*). Hotel prices are for two people in a standard double room in high season, including tax and service.

CAMPANIA THROUGH THE AGES

Ancient History. Lying on Mediterranean trade routes plied by several pre-Hellenic civilizations, Campania was settled by the ancient Greeks from approximately 800 BC onward. Here myth and legend blend with historical fact: the town of Herculaneum is said—rather improbably—to have been established by Hercules himself, and Naples in ancient times was called Parthenope, the name attributed to one of the sirens who preyed on hapless sailors in antiquity.

Thanks to archaeological research, some of the layers of myth have been stripped away to reveal a pattern of occupation and settlement well before Rome became established. Greek civilization flourished for hundreds of years all along this coastline, but there was nothing in the way of centralized government until centuries later when the Roman Republic, uniting all Italy for the first time, absorbed the Greek colonies with little opposition. Generally, the peace of Campania was undisturbed during these centuries of Roman rule.

Foreign Influences. Naples and Campania, with the rest of Italy, decayed with the Roman Empire and collapsed into the abyss of the Middle Ages. Naples itself regained some importance under the rule of the Angevins in the latter part of the 13th century and continued its progress in the 1440s under Aragonese rule. The nobles who served under the Spanish viceroys in the 16th and 17th centuries enjoyed their pleasures, even as Spain milked the area for taxes.

After a short Austrian occupation, Naples became the capital of the Kingdom of the Two Sicilies, which the Bourbon kings established in 1738. Their rule was generally benevolent as far as Campania was concerned, and their support of papal authority in Rome was important in the development of the rest of Italy. Their rule was important artistically, too, contributing to the architecture of the region, and attracting great musicians, artists, and writers drawn by the easy life at court. Finally, Giuseppe Garibaldi launched his famous expedition, and in 1860 Naples was united with the rest of Italy.

Modern Times. Things were relatively tranquil through the years that followed—with visitors thronging to Capri, to Sorrento, to Amalfi, and, of course, to Naples—until World War II. Allied bombings did considerable damage in and around Naples. At the fall of the fascist government, the sorely tried Neapolitans rose up against Nazi occupation troops and in four days of street fighting drove them out of the city. A monument was raised to the *scugnizzo* (the typical Neapolitan street urchin), celebrating the youngsters who participated in the battle. The war ended, and artists, tourists, writers, and other lovers of beauty returned to the Campania region.

As the years passed by, some parts gained increased attention from knowing visitors, while others lost the cachet they once had. Though years of misgovernment have left their mark, the region's cultural and natural heritage is finally being revalued as local authorities and inhabitants recognize the importance the area's largest industry—tourism.

NAPLES

In the period before the Italian unification of 1860, Naples rivaled Paris as a brilliant and refined cultural capital, the ultimate destination for northern European travelers on their Grand Tour. Although a decade of farsighted city administration and a massive injection of European Union funds have put the city back on course, signs of urban malaise are still evident. Naples is a difficult place for the casual visitor to take a quick liking to: noise and air pollution levels are uncomfortably high, graffiti on urban trains and monuments are unsightly, unemployment protest marches and industrial disputes frequently disrupt public transportation and may even result in the temporary closure of major tourist attractions. Armed with the right attitude—"be prepared for the worst but hope for the best"—you will find that Napoli does not disappoint. Among other things, it's one of Italy's top *città d'arte,* with world-class museums and a staggering number of fine churches. The most important finds from Pompeii and Herculaneum are on display at the Museo Archeologico Nazionale—a cornucopia of sculpture, frescoes, and mosaics—and seeing them will add to the pleasure of trips to the ancient ruins. And Naples has a wonderful location: thanks to the backdrop of Vesuvius and the islands in the bay, it's one of those cities that are instantly recognizable.

In Naples you need a good sense of humor and a firm grip on your pocketbook and camera. Expect to do a lot of walking (take care crossing the chaotic streets); buses are crowded, and taxis often get held up in traffic. Use the funiculars or the metro Line 1 to get up and down the hills, and take the quick—but erratic—metro Line 2 (the city's older subway system) when crossing the city between Piazza Garibaldi and Pozzuoli. For Pompeii, Herculaneum, and Sorrento, take the Circumvesuviana train line, while the Cumana line from Piazza Montesanto is best for the port of Pozzuoli and Baia.

ROYAL NAPLES

Naples hasn't been a capital for 150 years, but it still prides itself on its royal heritage. Most of the modern center of the town owes its look and feel to various members of the Bourbon family, who built their palaces and castles in this area. Allow plenty of time for museum visits, especially the Palazzo Reale. The views of the bay from the Castel dell'Ovo are good at any time, but are especially fine at sunset.

TOP ATTRACTIONS

Castel dell'Ovo. Dangling over the Porto Santa Lucia on a thin promontory, this 12th-century fortress built over the ruins of an ancient Roman villa overlooks the whole harbor—proof, if you need it, that the Romans knew a premium location when they saw one. For the same reason, some of the city's top hotels share the site. Walk up onto the roof's Sala della Terrazze for a postcard-come-true view of Capri. Then, as the odd car honk drifts across from inland, use the tiled map to identify the sights of the city and maybe plot an itinerary for the rest of the day. It's a peaceful spot for strolling and enjoying the views. ✉ *Santa Lucia waterfront, Via Partenope* ☎ *081/2400055* 🎫 *Free* 🕑 *Weekdays 8–7:30; Sun. 8–2.*

13

★ **Castel Nuovo.** Known to locals as Maschio Angioino, in reference to its Angevin builders, this imposing castle is now used more for marital than military purposes—a portion of it serves as a government registry office. Its looming Angevin stonework is upstaged by a white four-tiered triumphal entrance arch, ordered by Alfonso of Aragon after his entry into the city in 1443 to seize power from the increasingly beleaguered Angevin Giovanna II. At the arch's top, as if justifying Alfonso's claim to the throne, the Archangel Gabriel slays a demon.

Across the courtyard within the castle is the Sala Grande, also known as the Sala dei Baroni, which has a stupendous vaulted ceiling 92 feet high. In 1486 local barons hatched a plot against Alfonso's son, King Ferrante, who reacted by inviting them to this hall for a wedding banquet, which turned promptly into a mass arrest. (Ferrante is also said to have kept a crocodile in the castle as his special executioner.) You can also visit the Sala dell'Armeria, where a glass floor reveals recent excavations of Roman baths from the Augustan period. In the next room on the left, the Cappella Palatina, look on the frescoed walls for Nicolo di Tomaso's painting of Robert Anjou, one of the first realistic portraits ever.

The castle's first floor holds a small gallery that includes a beautiful early Renaissance Adoration of the Magi by Marco Cardisco, with the roles of the three Magi played by the three Aragonese kings, Ferrante I, Ferrante II, and Charles V. ✉ *Piazza Municipio, Toledo* ☎ *081/7952003* 🎫 *€5* ⏲ *Mon.–Sat. 9–6* Ⓜ *Montesanto (in construction: Piazza Municipio).*

Fodor's Choice ★ **Palazzo Reale.** Dominating Piazza del Plebiscito, this huge palace—perhaps best described as overblown imperial—dates from the early 1600s. It was renovated and redecorated by successive rulers, including Napoléon's sister Caroline and her ill-fated husband, Joachim Murat (1767–1815), who reigned briefly in Naples after the French emperor sent the Bourbons packing and before they returned to reclaim their kingdom. Don't miss seeing the **royal apartments**, sumptuously furnished and full of precious paintings, tapestries, porcelains, and other objets d'art. The monumental marble staircase gives you an idea of the scale on which Neapolitan rulers lived. ✉ *Piazza del Plebiscito, Toledo* 🌐 *www.palazzorealenapoli.it* ☎ *081/400547, 848/800288 schools and guided tours* 🎫 *€4* ⏲ *Thurs.–Tues. 9–7* Ⓜ *Dante (in construction: Piazza Municipio).*

QUICK BITES

Across from the Palazzo Reale is the most famous coffeehouse in town, the Caffè Gambrinus (✉ *Piazza Trieste e Trento, near Piazza del Plebiscito* ☎ *081/417582*). Founded in 1850, this 19th-century jewel once functioned as a brilliant intellectual salon. The glory days are over, but the inside rooms, with amazing mirrored walls and gilded ceilings, make this an essential stop for any visitor to the city. To its credit, the caffè doesn't inflate prices to cash in on its fame.

★ **Palazzo Zevallos.** Tucked inside this beautifully restored palazzo, which houses the Banca Intesa San Paolo (one of Italy's major banks), is a small museum that's worth seeking out. Enter the bank through Cosimo Fanzago's gargoyled doorway and take the handsome elevator to the upper floor. The first room to the left holds the star attraction, Caravaggio's last work, *The Martyrdom of Saint Ursula*. The saint here is, for dramatic

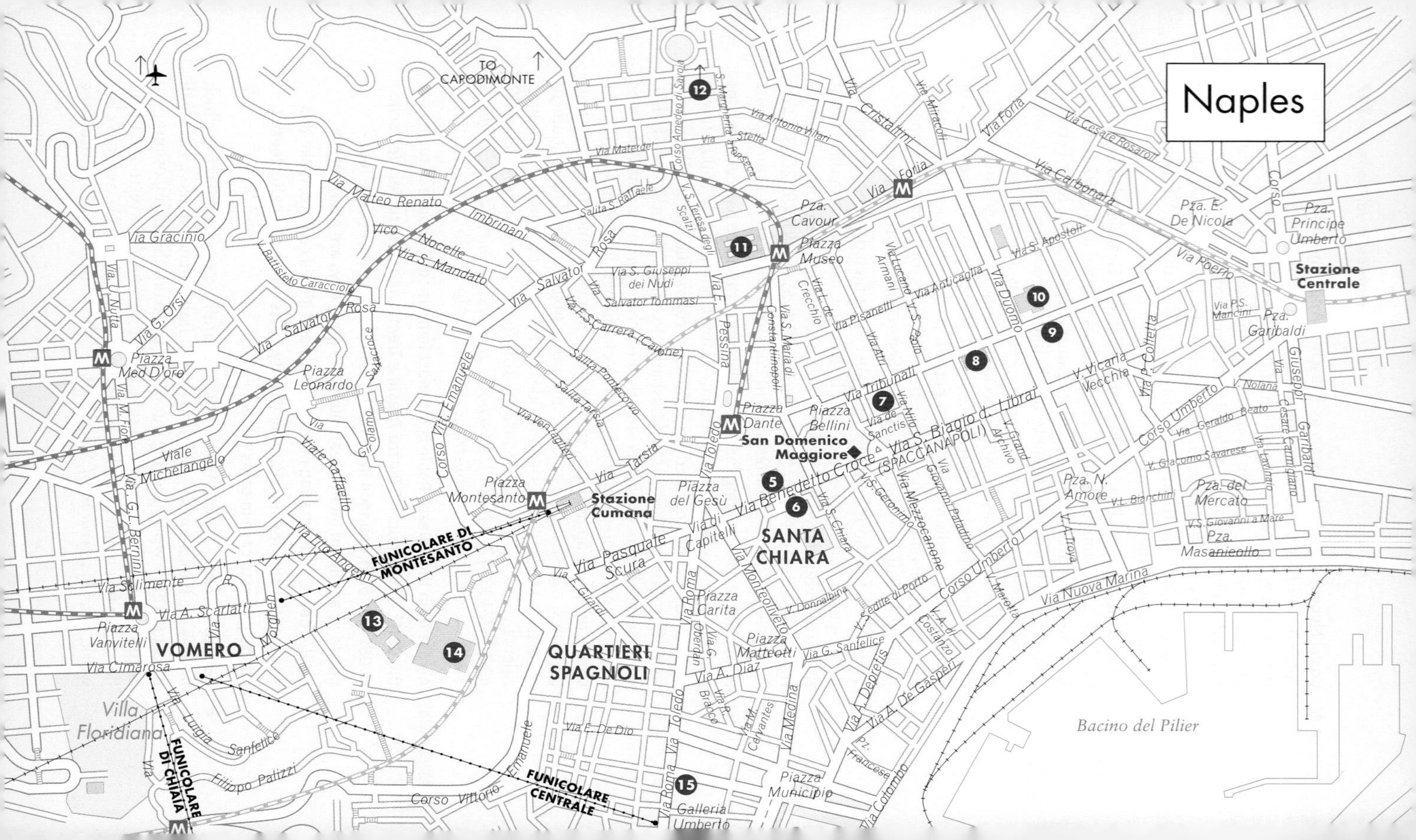
Naples
Stazione Centrale
Pza. Principe Umberto
Pza. Garibaldi
Pza. E. De Nicola
Via Carbonara
Via Foria
Via Cesare Rosaroll
Via Poerio
Via Duomo
Via Tribunali
Via S. Biagio d. Librai (SPACCANAPOLI)
Via Benedetto Croce
Corso Umberto I
Via Nuova Marina
Pza. del Mercato
Pza. Masaniello
Piazza Museo
Pza. Cavour
Piazza Dante
Piazza Bellini
San Domenico Maggiore
Piazza del Gesù
SANTA CHIARA
Via Toledo
Via Roma
Piazza Carita
Piazza Matteotti
Piazza Municipio
Galleria Umberto
QUARTIERI SPAGNOLI
Stazione Cumana
Piazza Montesanto
FUNICOLARE DI MONTESANTO
FUNICOLARE CENTRALE
FUNICOLARE DI CHIAIA
VOMERO
Piazza Vanvitelli
Villa Floridiana
Corso Vittorio Emanuele
Via Salvator Rosa
Piazza Leonardo
Piazza Med D'oro
Via Gracinio
Via Matteo Renato Imbriani
TO CAPODIMONTE
Corso Amedeo di Savoia
Via Mezzocanone
Via Medina
Via A. Depretis
Via A. De Gasperi
Via Colombo
Bacino del Pilier
5
6
7
8
9
10
11
12
13
14
15

Cappella Sansevero 7
Castel dell'Ovo 4
Castel Nuovo 1
Castel Sant'Elmo 13
Certosa di San Martino 14
Duomo 10
Gesù Nuovo 5
Museo Archeologico Nazionale 11
Museo di Capodimonte ... 12
Palazzo Reale 3
Palazzo Zevallos 15
Pio Monte della Misericordia 9
San Lorenzo Maggiore 8
Santa Chiara 6
Teatro San Carlo 2

effect, deprived of her usual retinue of a thousand followers. On the left, a face of pure spite, is the king of the Huns, who has just shot Ursula with an arrow after his proposal of marriage has been rejected. Opposite the painting is an elaborate map of the city of Caravaggio's day, not so different from now. ✉ *Via Toledo 185, Piazza Plebiscito* ☎ *00800/16052007* 🌐 *www.palazzozevallos.com* 🎫 *€3* 🕐 *Mon.–Sat. 10–6.*

Piazza Plebiscito. After spending time as a car park, this square was restored in 1994 to one of Napoli Nobilissima's most majestic spaces, with a Doric semicircle of columns resembling Saint Peter's Square in Rome. It was originally built under the Napoleonic rule. When the Napoleonic regime fell, Ferdinand, new king of the Two Sicilies, ordered the addition of the Church of San Francesco di Paola. On the left as you approach the church is a statue of Ferdinand and on the right his father, Charles III, both clad in Roman togas. Around dusk the floodlights come on, to magical effect. The square is aired by a delightful sea breeze and on Sunday one corner becomes an improvised soccer stadium where local youth emulate their heroes.

Teatro San Carlo. This large theater was built in 1737, 40 years earlier than Milan's La Scala—though it was destroyed by fire and rebuilt in 1816. You can visit the interior, decorated in the white-and-gilt stucco of the neoclassical era, as part of a 30-minute guided tour. Tours were suspended due to renovation work when we visited in early 2010, but should resume by the time this book is published. The space is made for opera on a grand scale: nearly 200 boxes are arranged on six levels, and the huge stage (12,000 square feet) permits productions with horses, camels, and elephants. A removable backdrop can be lifted to reveal the Palazzo Reale Gardens. ✉ *Via San Carlo 101–103, Toledo* ☎ *081/7972331 box office, 081/7972412* 🌐 *www.teatrosancarlo.it* Ⓜ *Piazza Municipio (in construction).*

QUICK BITES

Across from the Teatro San Carlo towers the imposing entrance to the glass-roof neoclassical Galleria Umberto (✉ *Via San Carlo, near Piazza Plebiscito*), a late-19th-century shopping arcade where you can sit at one of several cafés and watch the vivacious Neapolitans as they go about their business.

Via Toledo. Sooner or later you'll wind up at one of the busiest commercial arteries, also known as Via Roma, which is thankfully closed to through traffic—at least along the stretch leading from the Palazzo Reale. Don't avoid dipping into this parade of shops and coffee bars where plump pastries are temptingly arranged.

VOMERO

Heart-stopping views of the Bay of Naples are framed by this gentrified neighborhood on a hill served by the Montesanto, Centrale, and Chiaia funiculars. The upper stations for all three are an easy walk from Piazza Vanvitelli, a good starting point for exploring this thriving district with no shortage of smart bars and trattorias.

GETTING AROUND NAPLES

PUBLIC TRANSIT

Naples's rather old Metropolitana (subway system), also called Linea 2, provides fairly frequent service and can be the fastest way to get across the traffic-clogged city.

The other urban subway system, Metropolitana Collinare (or Linea 1), links the hill area of the Vomero and beyond with the National Archaeological Museum and Piazza Dante. Trains on both lines run from 5 am until 10:30 pm.

For standard public transportation, including the subways, buses, and funiculars, an UnicoNapoli costs €1.10 and is valid for 90 minutes as far as Pozzuoli to the west and Portici to the east; €3.10 buys a *biglietto giornaliero,* good for the whole day (€2.60 on weekends).

Bus service has become viable over the last few years, especially with the introduction of larger buses on the regular R1, R2, R3, and R4 routes. Electronic signs display wait times at many stops.

PARKING

If you come to Naples by car, find a garage, agree on the cost, and leave it there for the duration of your stay. (If you park on the street, you run the risk of theft.) **Garage Cava** (✉ *Via Mergellina 6* ☎ *081/660023*), **Grilli** (✉ *Via Ferraris 40, near Stazione Centrale* ☎ *081/264344*), and **Turistico** (✉ *Via de Gasperi 14, near port* ☎ *081/5525442*) are all centrally located, safe, and open 24 hours a day.

TAXIS

When taking a taxi in Naples, make sure that the meter is switched on at the start of your trip. Trips around the city are unlikely to cost less than €10 or more than €20. Set fares for various destinations within the city should be displayed in the taxi, as should extra charges for things like baggage and night service. For trips outside the city, negotiate your fare before getting in. Watch out for overcharging at three locations: the airport, the railway station, and the hydrofoil marina. And in peak summer weeks, don't forget that most cabs in Naples have no air-conditioning—which the city's buses and metro do have—and you can practically bake if caught in one during a half-hour traffic jam.

TOURS

Handily close to the port is the terminal for double-decker buses belonging to **City Sightseeing** (✉ *Piazza Municipio* ☎ *081/5517279* 🌐 *www.napoli.city-sightseeing.it*). For €22 you can take two or three different excursions, giving you reasonable coverage of the downtown sights and outlying attractions like the Museo di Capodimonte.

A welcome center in the old town, the **Centro di Accoglienza Turistica Museo Aperto Napoli** (✉ *Via Pietro Colletta 89* ☎ *081/5636062* 🌐 *www.museoapertonapoli.it*), offers €6 audio guides you can listen to as you wander around.

For in-depth tours of Naples, the **Comune di Napoli** (✉ *Piazza Municipio* ☎ *081/5422090* 🌐 *www.comune.napoli.it*) occasionally offers English-language guided tours. These tours are a great way to see monuments that are otherwise off-limits.

13

TOP ATTRACTIONS

Castel Sant'Elmo. Perched on the Vomero, this massive castle is almost the size of a small town. It was built by the Angevins in the 14th century to dominate the port and the old city and remodeled by the Spanish in 1537. The parapets, configured in the form of a six-pointed star, provide fabulous views: the whole bay on one side; on another, the city spread out like a map, its every dome and turret clearly visible; and to the east, slumbering Vesuvius. Once a major military outpost, the castle these days hosts occasional cultural events. Its prison, the Carcere alto di Castel Sant'Elmo, is the site of the **Museo di Novecento Napoli,** which traces Naples's 20th-century artistic output, from the Futurists through to work of the 1980s. You get in the castle free if you have a ticket to the adjoining Certosa di San Martino. ✉ *Largo San Martino, Vomero* ☎ *081/2294401* 🌐 *www.polomusealenapli.beniculturali.it* 🎫 *€3; Museo del Novecento Napoli, €5* ⏲ *Wed.–Mon. 8:30–7:30; Museo del Novecento Napoli, Wed.–Mon. 9–7* Ⓜ *Vanvitelli.*

WORD OF MOUTH

"Naples itself should not be overlooked. I particularly enjoyed walking along Spaccanapoli. The integrated bus/tram/funicular ticket is excellent value—allows you to hop on/hop off various means of transport within the city. Although there is not much to see at the castle itself, the views of Naples from the walls make the Castel Sant'Elmo one of my favorite places."

—willit

★ **Certosa di San Martino.** Atop a rocky promontory with a fabulous view of the entire city, and with majestic salons that would please any monarch, the Certosa di San Martino is a monastery that seems more like a palace. A Carthusian monastery restored in the 17th century in exuberant Neapolitan baroque style, this structure has now been transformed into a diverse museum. The gorgeous Chiostro Grande (great cloister) and the panoramic garden terraces—strangely quiet, with a view of the city sprawling below—are among the most impressive spots in the city. Popular exhibits include the *presepi* (Christmas crèches) and an anonymous painting that depicts the Naples waterfront in the 15th century and the return of the Aragonese fleet from the Battle of Ischia. Take the funicular from Piazza Montesanto to Vomero. ✉ *Piazzale San Martino 5, Vomero* ☎ *081/2294589* 🌐 *museosanmartino.campaniabeniculturali.it* 🎫 *€6 includes admission to Castel Sant'Elmo* ⏲ *Thurs.–Tues. (Sezione Presepiale, Thurs.–Mon.) 8:30–7:30. Some rooms are often closed (Quarto del Priore) depending on staffing* Ⓜ *Vanvitelli.*

SPACCANAPOLI AND CAPODIMONTE

Nowhere embodies the spirit of Naples better than the arrow-straight street informally known as Spaccanapoli (literally, "split Naples"). Gazing down it, you can sense where the name comes from—the street resembles a trench, running from the central station (near where the old city walls stood) up to the Vomero hill, retracing one of the main arteries of the ancient Greek, and later Roman, settlements. Along its western section, Spaccanapoli is officially named Via Benedetto Croce, in honor of the illustrious philosopher born here in 1866, in the building at No. 12. As it runs its course, the street changes it name seven times. No matter the name, it's a place of vibrant street culture.

Capodimonte, to the north, was open countryside until the Bourbon kings built a hunting lodge there, after which it rapidly became part of the city proper. Between the two neighborhoods is the Museo Archeologico, Naples's finest museum. It's best to visit shortly after lunchtime, when the crowds have thinned out. Two hours will be just enough to get your bearings and cover the more important collections. The museum in Capodimonte—unlike many of the churches and the archaeological museum—is well lighted and can be viewed in fading daylight, so it's best left until last.

TOP ATTRACTIONS

★ **Cappella Sansevero.** Off Vicolo Domenico Maggiore at the beginning of Via Francesco de Sanctis, this chapel/museum has one of the most intriguing sculpture collections you're likely find anywhere. The chapel was founded in 1590 by Prince Giovan Francesco di Sangro, fulfilling a vow to the Virgin after recovery from an illness. (His statue is on the second niche to the left.) Over the generations the simple chapel became a family mausoleum, with statues of the various princes lining the walls.

Most of the building work here is due to restructuring in the mid-18th century under the seventh Sangro di Sansevero prince, Raimondo—a larger-than-life figure, popularly believed to have signed a pact with the devil allowing him to plumb nature's secrets. Prince Raimondo commissioned the young sculptor Giuseppe Sammartino to create numerous works, including the chapel's centerpiece, the remarkable *Veiled Christ,* which has a seemingly transparent marble veil some say was created using a chemical formula provided by the prince. If you have the stomach for it, take a look in the crypt, where some of the anatomical experiments conducted by the prince are gruesomely displayed. ✉ *Via Francesco de Sanctis 19, Spaccanapoli* ☎ *081/5518470* 🌐 *www.museosansevero.it* 🎫 *€6* ⏲ *Mon. and Wed.–Fri. 10–5:10, weekends 10–1:10.*

Duomo di San Gennaro. Though the Duomo was established in the 1200s, the building you see was erected a century later and has since undergone radical changes, especially during the baroque period. Inside the cathedral, 110 ancient columns salvaged from pagan buildings are set into the piers that support the 350-year-old wooden ceiling. Off the left aisle you step down into the 4th-century church of **Santa Restituta,** which was incorporated into the cathedral; though Santa Restituta was redecorated in the late 1600s in the prevalent baroque style, a few very old mosaics remain in the **Battistero** (Baptistery).

On the right aisle of the cathedral, in the **Cappella di San Gennaro,** are multicolor marbles and frescoes honoring Saint Januarius, miracle-working patron saint of Naples, whose altar and relics are encased in silver. Three times a year—on September 19 (his feast day); on the Saturday preceding the first Sunday in May, which commemorates the transfer of his relics to Naples; and on December 16—his dried blood, contained in two sealed vials, is believed to liquefy during rites in his honor. On these days large numbers of devout Neapolitans offer up prayers in his memory.

The **Museo del Tesoro di San Gennaro** houses a rich collection of treasures associated with the saint. Paintings by Solimena and Luca Giordano hang alongside statues, busts, candelabras, and tabernacles in gold, silver, and marble by Cosimo Fanzago and other 18th-century baroque masters. An audio tour is included in the ticket price. *Spaccanapoli* ☎ *081/449097 Duomo, 081/294764 museum* 🌐 *www.museosangennaro.com* 🎫 *€6 (extra €1.50 for Baptistery)* ⏲ *Daily 9–6; Baptistery, 8:30–12:30, 2:30–6:30.*

WORD OF MOUTH

"The Neapolitans' joy at just being alive spills over with enthusiasm and generosity. The personal warmth one can find in Naples can't be matched in any city in the world."

—Waldo

Gesù Nuovo. The oddly faceted stone facade of this church dates to the late 16th century. It was designed as part of a palace, but plans were changed as construction progressed, and it became the front of an elaborately decorated baroque church. Be sure not to miss the votive chapel dedicated to San Ciro (Saint Cyrus) in the far left corner. Here hundreds of tiny silver ex-voto images have been hung on the walls to give thanks to the saint for his assistance in medical matters. ✉ *Piazza Gesù Nuovo, Spaccanapoli* ☎ *081/5578111* ⏲ *Daily 7–12:30 and 4–7:30.*

Fodor's Choice ★ **Museo Archeologico Nazionale** *(National Museum of Archaeology).* Those who know and love this legendary museum have the tendency upon hearing it mentioned to heave a sigh: it's famous not only for its unrivaled collections but also for its cordoned-off rooms, missing identification labels, poor lighting, billows of dust, suffocating heat in summer, and indifferent personnel—a state of affairs seen by some critics as an encapsulation of everything that's wrong with southern Italy in general.

Precisely because of this emblematic value, the National Ministry of Culture has decided to lavish attention and funds on the museum in a complete reorganization. This process has been ongoing for some time and looks as if it will continue for a while longer. Ticketing has been privatized and opening hours extended (for the center-core "masterpiece" collection, that is; other rooms are subject to staffing shortages and can be closed on a rotating basis). Some of the "newer" rooms, covering archaeological discoveries in the Greco-Roman settlements and necropolises in and around Naples, have helpful informational panels in English. A fascinating free display of the finds unearthed during digs for the Naples metro has been set up in the Museo station close to the museum entrance.

Even if some rooms may be closed, this still leaves available the core of the museum, a nucleus of world-renowned archaeological finds that puts most other museums to shame. It includes the legendary Farnese collection of ancient sculpture, together with local sculptural finds, and almost all the good stuff—the best mosaics and paintings—from Pompeii and Herculaneum. The quality of these collections is unexcelled and, as far as the mosaic, painting, and bronze sections are concerned, unique in the world. ✉ *Piazza Museo 19, Spaccanapoli* ☎ *081/440166* 🌐 *marcheo.napolibeniculturali.it* 🎫 *€6.50, €10 for special exhibits* ⏲ *Wed.–Mon. 9–7.*

QUICK BITES

Timpani e Tempura (✉ *Vico della Quercia 17, Spaccanapoli* ☎ *081/5512280*) is a tiny shrine to local culinary culture. There are only three small tables and bar-style counter, but it's worth the squeeze for the *timballi di maccheroni* (baked pasta cakes) and unique *mangiamaccheroni*, spaghetti in broth with caciocavallo cheese, butter, basil, and pepper. High-quality wines by the glass make this a spot for a swift but excellent lunch. You can also buy cheese and salami to take home with you.

★ **Museo di Capodimonte.** The grandiose 18th-century neoclassical Bourbon royal palace houses an impressive collection of fine and decorative art. Capodimonte's greatest treasure is the excellent collection of paintings well displayed in the **Galleria Nazionale,** on the palace's first and second floors. Besides the art collection, part of the royal apartments still has a complement of beautiful antique furniture, most of it on the splashy scale so dear to the Bourbons, and a staggering collection of porcelain and majolica from the various royal residences. The walls of the apartments are hung with numerous portraits, providing a close-up of the unmistakable Bourbon features, a challenge to any court painter. Most rooms have fairly comprehensive information cards in English, whereas the audio guide is overly selective and somewhat quirky. The main galleries on the first floor are devoted to work from the 13th to 18th centuries, including many pieces by Dutch and Spanish masters. On the second floor look out for stunning paintings by Simone Martini (circa 1284–1344), Titian (1488/90–1576), and Caravaggio (1573–1610). The palace is situated in the vast Bosco di Capodimonte (Capodimonte Park), which served as the royal hunting preserve and later as the site of the Capodimonte porcelain works. ✉ *Via Miano 2, Porta Piccola, Via Capodimonte, Capodimonte* ☎ *848/800288 for information and tickets for special exhibitions* 🎫 *€7.50, after 2 pm €6.50* ⏲ *Daily 8:30–7:30; ticket office closes at 6:30.*

★ **Pio Monte della Misericordia.** One of the defining landmarks of Spaccanapoli, this octagonal church was built around the corner from the Duomo for a charitable institution founded in 1601 by seven noblemen. The institution's aim was to carry out acts of Christian charity: feeding the hungry, clothing the poor, nursing the sick, sheltering pilgrims, visiting prisoners, ransoming Christian slaves, and burying the indigent dead—acts immortalized in the history of art by the famous altarpiece, painted by Caravaggio depicting the *Sette Opere della Misericordia* (*Seven Acts of Mercy*). In this haunting work the artist has brought the Virgin, borne atop the shoulders of two angels, down into the streets of Spaccanapoli (scholars have suggested a couple of plausible locations) populated by figures in whose spontaneous and passionate movements the people could see themselves. The original church was considered too small and was destroyed in 1655 to make way for a new church, designed by Antonio Picchiatti and built between 1658 and 1678. Pride of place is given to the great Caravaggio above the altar, but there are other important baroque-era paintings on view here; some hang in the church while others are in the adjoining *pinacoteca* (picture gallery). ✉ *Via Tribunali 253, Spaccanapoli* ☎ *081/446973* 🌐 *www.piomontedellamisericordia.it*

€5, including audio guide Thurs.–Tues. 9–2:30 Ⓜ Piazza Cavour (in construction: Duomo).

Santa Chiara. This monastery church is a Neapolitan landmark and the subject of a famous old song. It was built in the 1300s in Provençal Gothic style, and it's best known for the quiet charm of its cloister garden, with columns and benches sheathed in 18th-century ceramic tiles painted with delicate floral motifs and vivid landscapes. An adjoining museum traces the history of the convent; the entrance is off the courtyard at the left of the church. *Piazza Gesù Nuovo, Spaccanapoli 081/7971231 www.santachiara.info Museum and cloister €5 Church: daily 7–12:30 and 4:30–6:30. Museum and cloister: Mon.–Sat. 9:30–5:30, Sun. 10–2:30 Ⓜ Dante (in construction: Piazza Borsa-Università).*

QUICK BITES

While you're exploring the old part of town, take a break at what the Neapolitans call "the best pastry shop in Italy"—Scaturchio (*Piazza San Domenico Maggiore 19, Spaccanapoli 081/5516944*). Although the coffee is top-of-the-line and the ice cream and pastries quite good—including the specialty, the *ministeriale*, a pert chocolate cake whipped with rum-cream filling—it's the atmosphere that counts here. In the heart of Spaccanapoli, it's where nuns, punks, businesspeople, and housewives come to share the good things they all have in common.

WORTH NOTING

Quadreria dei Girolamini. Off an improbably quiet cloister enclosing a prolific forest of citrus, fig, and loquat trees, the Girolamini art museum is attached to the restored Girolamini church. Its intimate, high-quality collection of 16th- and 17th-century paintings is one of the city's best-kept secrets, well worth a half-hour visit. *Via Duomo 142, Spaccanapoli 081/294444 www.girolamini.it Free Mon.–Sat. 9–12:50 Ⓜ Piazza Cavour.*

San Lorenzo Maggiore. It's unusual to find French Gothic style in Naples, but it has survived to great effect in this church, which was built in the Middle Ages and decorated with 14th-century frescoes. Outside the 17th-century cloister is the entrance to the underground archaeological site, revealing what was once part of the Roman forum, and before that the Greek agora. You can walk among the streets, shops, and workshops of the ancient city and see a model of how the Greek Neapolis might have looked. Next door to the church is the four-story **museum**, housed in a 16th-century palazzo, displaying a wealth of archaeological finds and religious art (panels regrettably are only in Italian). *Via dei Tribunali 316, Spaccanapoli 081/2110860 www.sanlorenzomaggiore.na.it Excavations and museum €9 Museum, Mon.–Sat. 8–1 and 4–6:30, Sun. 9:30–1:30; church Mon.–Sat. 9–noon, Sun. closed to sightseers Ⓜ Dante.*

WHERE TO EAT

CHIAIA

$$ SOUTHERN ITALIAN

✕ **Amici Miei.** A place favored by meat eaters who can't take another bite of sea bass, this small, dark, and cozy den is well loved for specials such as tender carpaccio with fresh artichoke hearts, and a rice-and-arugula dish featuring duck breast. There are also excellent pasta dishes, such as *orecchiette* with chickpeas or *alla barese* (with chewy green turnips), or that extravaganza, the *carnevale lasagne,* an especially rich concoction relied on to sustain revelers in the build-up before Lent. Everyone finishes with a slice of chocolate and hazelnut *torta caprese.* ✉ *Via Monte di Dio 78, Chiaia* ☎ *081/7646063* ✍ *Reservations essential* ⏲ *Closed Mon. and July and Aug. No dinner Sun.*

$$$ NEAPOLITAN

✕ **Coco Loco.** This place has taken the Naples dining scene by storm, thanks to the innovative cuisine of master chef Diego Nuzzo, a stylish ambience, and a quiet location off Via Filangieri, a 10-minute walk from the Palazzo Reale. If possible, take a table in the more-spacious outdoor section in the square, and then be pampered with subtle dishes like *insalata di aragosta e gamberi alla catalana* (lobster and prawn salad garnished with citrus). ✉ *Piazzetta Rodinò 31, Chiaia* ☎ *081/415482* ⏲ *Closed Sun. and 3 wks in Aug. No lunch July–Sept.*

$$$ NEAPOLITAN Fodor's Choice ★

✕ **Da Dora.** Despite its location up an unpromising-looking *vicolo* (alley) off the Riviera di Chiaia, this small restaurant has achieved cult status for its seafood platters. It's remarkable what owner-chef Giovanni can produce in his tiny kitchen. Start with the pasta dish linguine *alla Dora,* laden with local seafood and fresh tomatoes, and perhaps follow up with grilled *pezzogna* (blue-spotted bream). Like many restaurants on the seafront, Dora has its own guitarist, who is often robustly accompanied by the kitchen staff. ✉ *Via Fernando Palasciano 30, Chiaia* ☎ *081/680519* ✍ *Reservations essential* ⏲ *Closed Sun., 2 wks in Dec., and 2 wks in mid-Aug.*

$ ITALIAN

✕ **L'Ebbrezza di Noè.** A small bar leads into a larger dining area decorated in the style of a very elegant farmhouse. Owner Luca has an enthusiasm for what he does that is quite moving—as you sip a recommended wine you can sense that he hopes you like it as much as he does. The attention paid to the quality of the wine carries over to the food—here you can taste delicate *carpaccio di chianina* (thinly sliced Tuscan steak), rare cheeses such as the Sicilian *ragusano di razza modicana* and the local *caciocavallo podolico,* and a daily selection of hot dishes. ✉ *Vico Vetriera a Chiaia 8b/9, Chiaia* ☎ *081/400104* ⏲ *Closed Mon. No lunch.*

$$$ NEAPOLITAN Fodor's Choice ★

✕ **Radici.** Combining low-key elegance with well-tried combinations of Mediterranean cuisine, Radici is one of Naples's best restaurants. Among a cluster of restaurants set on Naples's busy Riviera di Chiaia, it affords views of the leafy gardens of the Villa Comunale but your attention will be taken at once by the master of ceremonies, Agostino, as he steers you through the elaborate choices on offer. Dishes invariably taste as good as they sound, as this fine pasta favorite, *ravioli di ricotta di bufala profumata al limone e vongole veraci* (ravioli filled with lemon-scented buffalo ricotta, served with clams). Or should it be the delicate *riso giallo sauté ai frutti di mare e crostacei, verdurine di stagione* (rice

Continued on page 760

PIZZA: THE CLASSIC MARGHERITA

Locally grown San Marzano tomatoes are a must.

The best pizza should come out with cheese bubbling and be ever-so-slightly charred around its edges.

Only buffalo-milk mozzarella or fior di latte cheese should be used.

The dough has to use the right kind of durum wheat flour and be left to rise for at least six hours.

Be prepared: ranging from the size of a plate to that of a Hummer wheel, Neapolitan pizza is pretty different from anything you might find elsewhere in Italy—not to mention what's served up at American pizza chains. The "purest" form is the marinara, topped with only tomatoes, garlic, oregano, and olive oil.

OTHER FAVORITES ARE . . .

- **CAPRICCIOSA** (the "capricious"), made with whatever the chef has on hand.
- **SICILIANA** with mozzarella and eggplant.
- **DIAVOLA** with spicy salami.
- **QUATTRO STAGIONE** ("four seasons"), made with produce from each one.
- **SALSICCIA E FRIARIELLI** with sausage and a broccoli-like vegetable.

A PIZZA FIT FOR A QUEEN

Legend has it that during the patriotic fervor following Italian unification in the late 19th century, a Neapolitan chef decided to celebrate the arrival in the city of the new Italian queen Margherita by designing a pizza in her—and the country's—honor. He took red tomatoes, white mozzarella cheese, and a few leaves of fresh green basil—reflecting the three colors of the Italian flag—and gave birth to the modern pizza industry.

ONLY THE BEST

An association of Neapolitan pizza chefs has standardized the ingredients and methods that have to be used to make pizza certified DOC (*denominazione d'origine controllata*) or STG (*specialità tradizionale garantita*). See the illustration on the opposite page for the basic requirements.

FIRED UP!

The Neapolitan pizza must be made in a traditional wood-burning oven. Chunks of beech or maple are stacked up against the sides of the huge, tiled ovens, then shoved onto the slate base of the oven where they burn quickly at high temperatures. If you visit Pompeii, you will see how similar the old Roman bread-baking ovens are to the modern pizza oven. The *pizzaiolo* (pizza chef) then uses a long wooden paddle to put the pizza into the oven, where it cooks quickly.

PIZZERIE

There are hundreds of restaurants that specialize in pizza in Naples, and the best of these make pizza and nothing else. As befits the original fast food, *pizzerie* tend to be simple, fairly basic places, with limited menu choices, and quick, occasionally brusque service: the less complicated your order, the happier the waiters.

THE REAL THING

Naples takes its contribution to world cuisine seriously. The Associazione Verace Pizza Napoletana (www.pizzanapoletana.org) was founded in 1984 in order to share expertise, maintain quality levels, and provide courses for aspirant pizza chefs and pizza lovers. They also organize the annual Pizzafest—three days in September, dedicated to the consumption of pizza, when *maestri* from all over the region get together and cook off.

Margherita of Savoy

Buffalo-milk mozzarella

A pizzaiolo at work

Typical pizzeria in Naples

Simple, fresh toppings

garnished with sea food and fresh greens)? With all the delights on offer here, you could easily be forgiven for indecision. Dessert? You can't go wrong with the cannolo filled with a mousse of lemon-flavored ricotta cheese. ✉ *Riviera di Chiaia 268, Chiaia* ☎ *081/2481100* ⊙ *No lunch except Sat. and Sun.*

$–$$ NEAPOLITAN **Umberto.** Run by the Di Porzio family since 1916, Umberto is one of the city's classic restaurants. It combines the classiness of the Chiaia neighborhood and the friendliness of other parts of the city. Try the *tubettini 'do tre dita* ("three-finger" pasta with a mixture of seafood), which bears the nickname of the original Umberto. Owner Massimo and sister Lorella (Umberto's grandchildren) are both wine experts and oversee a fantastic cellar. Umberto is also one of the few restaurants in the city that cater to those who have a gluten allergy. ✉ *Via Alabardieri 30–31, Chiaia* ☎ *081/418555* 🌐 *www.umberto.it* ⊙ *Closed Mon. and 3 wks in Aug.*

PIAZZA GARIBALDI

¢ PIZZA Fodor's Choice ★ **Da Michele.** You have to love a place that has, for more than 130 years, offered only two types of pizza—marinara (with tomato, garlic, and oregano) and *margherita* (with tomato, mozzarella, and basil)—and a small selection of drinks, and still manages to attract long lines. The prices have something to do with it, but the pizza itself suffers no rivals, so even those waiting in line are good-humored; the boisterous, joyous atmosphere wafts out with the smell of yeast and wood smoke onto the street. So step right up to get a number at the door and then hang outside until it's called. Note: The restaurant is off Corso Umberto, between Piazza Garibaldi and Piazza Nicola Amore. ✉ *Via Sersale 1/3, Piazza Garibaldi* ☎ *081/5539204* 💳 *No credit cards* ⊙ *Closed Sun. and 2 wks in Aug.*

$$ NEAPOLITAN **Mimì alla Ferrovia.** Clients of this Neapolitan institution have included Fellini and that magnificent true-Neapolitan comic genius and aristocrat, Totò. Mimì manages to live up cheerfully to its history, proudly serving fine versions of everything from pasta *e fagioli* (with beans) to the sea bass *al presidente,* baked in a pastry crust and enjoyed by any number of Italian presidents on their visits to Naples. Not so much a place to see and be seen as a common ground where both the famous and the unknown can mingle, feast, and be of good cheer, Mimì's sober beige-and-green hues, accented with updated art deco features, pale yellow tablecloths, and retro bentwood chairs, pleasantly tone down the bustle. Given the fairly seedy neighborhood, splurge on a taxi there and back, especially at night. ✉ *Via A. D'Aragona 19/21, Piazza Garibaldi* ☎ *081/289004* 🌐 *www.mimiallaferrovia.com* ⊙ *Closed Sun. (except Dec.) and last 2 wks in Aug.*

SANTA LUCIA

$$$$ ITALIAN **La Terrazza.** The Hotel Excelsior's Terrazza attracts A-list stars visiting the area with its Pompeian-red marble floorings and brown leather furnishings (all aimed at highlighting the gold cutlery, *capisce?*). A breathtaking buffet counts as an appetizer (but would be a banquet in itself for mere mortals), while the à la carte menu creates a fusion of Italian regional culinary styles. Dress up, and expect to be impressed. ✉ *Hotel Excelsior, Via Partenope 48, Santa Lucia* ☎ *081/7640111.*

CLOSE UP

Folk Songs à la Carte

If you want to hear *canzoni napoletane*—the fabled Neapolitan folk songs—performed live, you can try to catch the city's top troupes, such as the Cantori di Posillipo and I Virtuosi di San Martino, in performances at venues like the Teatro Trianon. But an easier alternative is to head for one of the city's more traditional restaurants, such as La Bersagliera or Mimì alla Ferrovia, where most every night you can expect your meal to be interrupted by a *posteggiatore*. These singers aren't employed by the restaurants, but they're encouraged to come in, swan around the tables with a battered old guitar, and belt out classics such as "Santa Lucia," "O' Surdato Innamurate," "Torna a Surriento," and, inevitably, "Funiculi Funiculà."

These songs are the most famous of a vast repertoire that found international fame with the mass exodus of southern Italians to the United States in the early 20th century. "Funiculi Funiculà" was written by Peppino Turco and Luigi Denza in 1880 to herald the new funicular railway up Vesuvius. "O Sole Mio," by Giovanni Capurro and Eduardo di Capua, has often been mistakenly taken for the Italian national anthem. "Torna a Surriento" was composed by Ernesto di Curtis in 1903 to help remind the current Italian prime minister how wonderful he thought Sorrento was (and how many government subsidies he had promised the township).

The singers are more than happy to do requests, even inserting the name of your *innamorato* or *innamorata* into the song. When they've finished they'll stand discreetly by your table. Give them a few euros and you'll have friends for life (or at least for the night).

SPACCANAPOLI

¢ PIZZA **Gino Sorbillo.** There are three restaurants called Sorbillo along Via dei Tribunali; this is the one with the crowds waiting outside. Order the same thing the locals are here for: a basic Neapolitan pizza (try the unique pizza al pesto or the stunningly simple marinara—just tomatoes and oregano). They're cooked to perfection by the third generation of pizza makers who run the place. The pizzas are enormous, flopping over the edge of the plate onto the white marble tabletops. ✉ *Via dei Tribunali 32, Spaccanapoli* ☎ *081/446643* ⏲ *Closed Sun. (except Dec.) and 3 wks in Aug.*

¢ PIZZA **I Decumani.** Every pizzeria along Via dei Tribunali is worth the long wait (all the good ones are jammed and you'll have to wait for a table) and none more so than the Decumani, thanks to the superlative *pizzaioli* (pizza makers)—say hello to Gianni and Enzo for us—at work here. They turn out a wide array of pizzas and do them all to perfection. If you are not on a diet, try the *frittura* and you'll be pleasantly surprised with this mix of Neapolitan-style tempura: zucchini, eggplants, riceballs, and many other delicacies. ✉ *Via dei Tribunali 58, Spaccanapoli* ☎ 081/5571309 ▭ *No credit cards* ⏲ *Closed Mon. (except Dec.).*

$$$ NEAPOLITAN Fodor's Choice ★ **Palazzo Petrucci.** Nestled in a 17th-century mansion facing the grandeur of Piazza San Domenico Maggiore, Palazzo Petrucci doesn't lack for dramatic dining options. Choose between tables under the vaulted ceiling of the former stables, in the gallery where a glass partition lets

you keep an eye on the kitchen, or in the cozy room overlooking the piazza, where the famous Guglia di San Domenico marble monument soars heavenward. Fortify yourself with a complimentary glass of prosecco before making the agonizing choice between the à la carte offerings and the *menu degustazione* (€45). A popular starter is *millefeuille* of local mozzarella with raw prawns and vegetable sauce. The *paccheri all'impiedi* (large tube-shape pasta served standing up) in a rich ricotta and meat sauce is an interesting twist on an old regional favorite. The decor is elegantly minimal but the culinary delights found here are anything but. ✉ *Piazza San Domenico Maggiore 4, Spaccanapoli* ☎ *081/5524068* ✍ *Reservations essential* ⏲ *Closed 3 wks in Aug. No dinner Sun., no lunch Mon.*

TOLEDO

¢–$ NEAPOLITAN ★ ✕ **Cantina della Tofa.** Two blocks up one of the narrow alleys that lead off Via Toledo into the Quartieri Spagnoli, this small, welcoming restaurant serves traditional Neapolitan fare that goes beyond standard pasta with seafood or tomatoes. Try the *vellutata di cicerchie,* a creamy soup made from beans that are a cross between chickpeas and fava beans, or a delicious mix of *contorni* (side dishes). ✉ *Vico Tofa 71, Piazza Municipio* ☎ *081/406840* ▭ *No credit cards* ⏲ *Closed Sun. No dinner Mon.*

$$ NEAPOLITAN ★ ✕ **Trattoria San Ferdinando.** Almost the first doorway on the right as you go up Via Nardones from Piazza Trieste e Trento—ring the bell outside to get let in—this cheerful trattoria is open in the evening only from Wednesday to Friday, with the fine intention of running a restaurant for the sheer pleasure of it. Try the excellent fish or the traditional (but cooked with a lighter modern touch) pasta dishes, especially those with *verdura,* fresh leaf vegetables, or those with potatoes and smoked mozzarella, *pasta e patate con la provola.* Close to the San Carlo Theater and aptly decorated with playbills and theatrical memorabilia both ancient and modern, this is an excellent place to stop after a visit to the opera. ✉ *Via Nardones 117, Toledo* ☎ *081/421964* ⏲ *Closed Sun. No dinner Sat.–Tues.*

WHERE TO STAY

CHIAIA

$ Fodor's Choice ★ **Cappella Vecchia 11.** One of the city's outstanding budget options lies just a stone's throw from the Platinum Card square of Naples, Piazza dei Martiri, now colonized by the likes of Cartier, Ferragamo, and Versace. **Pros:** fabulous location off chic Martiri square; friendly staff. **Cons:** lack of room phones; prefers cash payment. **TripAdvisor:** "outstanding B&B," "on a nice, quiet street," "friendly and helpful." ✉ *Vicolo Santa Maria a Capella Vecchia 11, Chiaia* ☎ *081/2405117* *6 rooms* 🌐 *www.cappellavecchia11.it* *In-room: no phone. In-hotel: Internet terminal (free), Wi-Fi hotspot (paid)* 🍽 *Breakfast.*

$$ **Chiaja Hotel de Charme.** No views, but there's plenty of atmosphere in these converted first-floor apartments that occupy a spruce 18th-century palazzo. **Pros:** central location on bustling; pedestrians-only street. **Cons:** small rooms get hot in summer (a/c notwithstanding); on second floor of historic palazzo (elevator was recently renovated). **TripAdvisor:**

"location is superb," "staff were a delight," "loved the doughnuts." ✉ *Via Chiaia 216* ☎ *081/415555* 🌐 *www.hotelchiaia.it* *27 rooms* *In-room: safe, Internet. In-hotel: bar* *Breakfast* ✢ *D4.*

$$ Fodor's Choice ★ **Palazzo Alabardieri.** Just off the chic Piazza dei Martiri, Palazzo Alabardieri is the most fashionable choice among the city's growing number of smaller luxury hotels. **Pros:** impressive public salons; central yet quiet location (a rare combination); fancy Martiri boutiques a short stroll away; polite, pleasant staff. **Cons:** no sea view; difficult to reach by car. **TripAdvisor:** "very charming and discreet," "walking distance from the port," "breakfast was plentiful." ✉ *Via Alabardieri 38, Chiaia* ☎ *081/415278* 🌐 *www.palazzoalabardieri.it* *35 rooms* *In-room: a/c, safe, refrigerator, Internet. In-hotel: bar, Internet terminal, parking (free), some pets allowed* *Breakfast.*

13

$$ **Pinto Storey.** The name juxtaposes a 19th-century Englishman who fell in love with Naples and a certain Signora Pinto who together went on to establish this hotel, which overflows with warmth and charm. **Pros:** safe neighborhood; near public transportation: option of rooms without a/c with a €9-a-day reduction. **Cons:** not close to major sights; rickety elevator; only a few rooms have views. **TripAdvisor:** "views over the bay," "in the heart of the city," "air conditioning costs extra." ✉ *Via G. Martucci 72, Chiaia* ☎ *081/681260* 🌐 *www.pintostorey.it* *16 rooms* *In-room: a/c, safe, refrigerator, Internet. In-hotel: Internet terminal (paid)* *No meals.*

SANTA LUCIA

$$$–$$$$ Fodor's Choice ★ **Grand Hotel Vesuvio.** You'd never guess from the modern exterior that this is the oldest of Naples' great seafront hotels—the place where Enrico Caruso died, Oscar Wilde escaped with lover Lord Alfred Douglas, and Bill Clinton charmed the waitresses. **Pros:** luxurious atmosphere; historic setting; location directly opposite Borgo Marinaro. **Cons:** extra charge for health club and Internet use; reception staff can be snooty; not all rooms have great views. **TripAdvisor:** "gorgeous view of Castel d'Ovo," "elegant and comfortable," "pastries are particularly tasty." ✉ *Via Partenope 45, Santa Lucia* ☎ *081/7640044* 🌐 *www.vesuvio.it* *146 rooms, 17 suites* *In-room: safe, refrigerator, Internet. In-hotel: restaurant, bar, gym, spa, Internet terminal, parking (paid)* *Breakfast.*

$$$$ **Hotel Santa Lucia.** Neopolitan enchantment can be yours if you stay here, for right outside your window will be the port immortalized in the song "Santa Lucia," bobbing with hundreds of boats, lined with seafood restaurants, and backed by the medieval Castel dell'Ovo. **Pros:** great views; close to the main port, so convenient for trips to the islands and along the coast. **Cons:** rooms disappointingly boxy; the entrance is on the busy Via Partenope. **TripAdvisor:** "view is a treat for the eyes," "old-world charm," "spotlessly clean." ✉ *Via Partenope 46, Santa Lucia* ☎ *081/7640666* 🌐 *www.santalucia.it* *95 rooms* *In-room: Wi-Fi. In-hotel: restaurant, bar* *Breakfast.*

$$$ **Parteno.** Undoubtedly proud of their premier address—"No. 1" on Naples's main waterfront street—welcoming owner Alex Ponzi has installed an exclusive and elegant bed-and-breakfast near the Villa Comunale, five minutes from Castel dell'Ovo and 15 from the hydrofoils to the bay islands. **Pros:** in the five-star neighborhood, without

the five-star price; friendly, helpful staff. **Cons:** except for the "Azalea" room (with a twin balcony onto the bay and islands beyond), rooms are neither large nor light. **TripAdvisor:** "feel of an upper-class home," "overlooking the Bay of Naples," "quiet and comfortable." ✉ *Via Partenope 1, Santa Lucia* ☎ *081/2452095* 🌐 *www.parteno.it* *6 rooms* *In-hotel: room service, Wi-Fi hotspot* *Breakfast.*

$ Fodor's Choice ★ **Transatlantico Napoli.** Enjoying perhaps the most enchanting setting in all of Naples, this new modestly priced hotel recently opened and has promptly zoomed to the top of most travelers' dream list of places to stay. **Pros:** fabulous location; gentle prices. **Cons:** rather cheap and ugly hotel furniture. **TripAdvisor:** "modern and functional," "360 degree view," "breakfast on the beach." ✉ *Via Luculliana 15, Santa Lucia* ☎ *081/768842* 🌐 *www.transatlanticonapoli.com* *8 rooms* *In-room: a/c, safe, refrigerator, Internet. In-hotel: restaurant, bar, Internet terminal* *Breakfast.*

SPACCANAPOLI

$$$ Fodor's Choice ★ **Costantinopoli 104.** An oasis of what Italians call *Stile Liberty* (Art Nouveau style), with impressive colorful glass fittings, this calm and elegant hotel is well placed between the Museo Archeologico Nazionale and Spaccanapoli. **Pros:** swimming pool (a rarity in Neapolitan hotels) and garden; pleasant service. **Cons:** can be difficult to find from street (look for the sign saying Villa Spinelli, the name of the original building). **TripAdvisor:** "treast all guests like VIPs," "public spaces are classy," "charming garden." ✉ *Via Costantinopoli 104, Spaccanapoli* ☎ *081/5571035* 🌐 *www.costantinopoli104.com* *19 rooms* *In-room: safe, refrigerator, Internet. In-hotel: bar, pool, laundry service, parking (paid)* *Breakfast.*

$$–$$$ Fodor's Choice ★ **Hotel Palazzo Decumani.** Opened in 2008, the Decumani is a welcome addition to the small list of higher-end hotels in Spaccanapoli. **Pros:** well located for both transportation links and sightseeing; large rooms and bathrooms; soundproofed windows. **Cons:** the location on a side street can be hard to find—follow signs from Corso Umberto. **TripAdvisor:** "top-notch in every respect," "service was impeccable," "quiet and tranquil." ✉ *Piazzetta Fortunato Giustino 8, Spaccanapoli* ☎ *081/4201379* 🌐 *www.palazzodecumani.com* *28 rooms* *In-room: Wi-Fi. In-hotel: restaurant, bar* *Breakfast.*

TOLEDO

$$ **Il Convento.** In a 17th-century palazzo tucked away in the (sometimes dicey) Quartieri Spagnoli, Il Convento is close to Via Toledo. **Pros:** close to cafés and shops; free Internet access; warm Neapolitan reception and pleasantly personal touch. **Cons:** church bells may wake you in the morning; on a busy street; tiny lobby. **TripAdvisor:** "tasteful historical ambience," "room was spacious," "woken by the bells at 7 am." ✉ *Via Speranzella 137/A, Toledo* ☎ *081/403977* 🌐 *www.hotelilconvento.com* *12 rooms, 2 suites* *In-room: refrigerator. In-hotel: bar, Internet terminal* *Breakfast.*

$$ **Palazzo Turchini.** Adjacent to the impressive *fontana di Nettuno*, just a few minutes' walk from the Castel Nuovo, Palazzo Turchini is one of the more-attractive smaller hotels in the city center. **Pros:** good

location for centro storico and the port; more intimate than neighboring business hotels. **Cons:** fee for Internet in room, but free Wi-Fi and Internet area. **TripAdvisor:** "heart of the tourist district," "down narrow cobbled streets," "very friendly staff." ✉ *Via Medina 21, Toledo* ☎ *081/5510606* 🌐 *www.palazzoturchini.it* *27 rooms* *In-room: safe, Internet. In-hotel: bar, Internet terminal (free), Wi-Fi hotspot* *Breakfast.*

VOMERO

$$$–$$$$ Fodor's Choice ★ **Grand Hotel Parker's.** Set midway up the Vomero hill, this landmark hotel (whose doors first opened in 1870) continues to serve up a supremely elegant dose of old-style atmosphere. **Pros:** the excellent restaurant; fabulous views. **Cons:** a very long walk or taxi ride from city center and seafront; not quite as grand as it once was. **TripAdvisor:** "fantastic views over the bay," "magnificent room," "breakfast was very good." ✉ *Corso Vittorio Emanuele 135, Vomero* ☎ *081/7612474* 🌐 *www.grandhotelparkers.com* *83 rooms* *In-room: a/c, refrigerator, safe, Wi-Fi. In-hotel: restaurant, bar, parking (paid)* *Breakfast.*

NIGHTLIFE AND THE ARTS

OPERA

Opera is a serious business in Naples—not in terms of the music so much as the costumes, the stage design, the players, and the politics. What's happening on stage can be secondary to the news of who's there, who they're with, and what they're wearing. Given the circumstances, it's hardly surprising that the city's famous San Carlo Company doesn't offer a particularly innovative repertoire. Nonetheless, the company is usually of very high quality—and if they're not in form the audience lets them know it. Performances take place in the historic **Teatro San Carlo** (✉ *Via San Carlo 101–103, Piazza Municipio* ☎ *081/7972412 box office, 081/7972331* 🌐 *www.teatrosancarlo.it*), the luxury liner of opera houses in southern Italy. In 2008 the concert hall underwent a massive renovation, with everything from the seats to the gold inlay on the ceiling frescoes replaced, and the statue of the mermaid Parthenope (missing since 1969) restored to its place on the building's facade.

NIGHTLIFE

Bars and clubs are found in many areas around Naples. The sophisticated crowd heads to Posillipo and the Vomero, Via Partenope along the seafront, and the Chiaia area (between Piazza dei Martiri and Via dei Mille). A more bohemian crowd makes for the centro storico and the area around Piazza Bellini. The scene is relatively relaxed—you might even be able to sit down at a proper table. Keep in mind that clubs, and their clientele, can change rapidly, so do some investigating before you hit the town.

Caffè Intramoenia (✉ *Piazza Bellini 70, Spaccanapoli* ☎ *081/290988* 🌐 *www.intramoenia.it*) is the granddaddy of all the bars in Piazza Bellini; it was set up as a bookshop in the late 1980s and still has its own small publishing house with a variety of attractive titles. Seats in the heated veranda are at a premium in winter, though many sit outside all year round. **Bere Vino** (✉ *62 Via San Sebastiano, Spaccanapoli* ☎ *081/29313*) looks like a shop from the outside, but inside you can find long wooden tables and shelves of wine from all over Italy that are consumed on the premises. Peppery *taralli* biscuits, olives, and selections of cheeses and smoked meats can be used to *appoggiare* ("prop up") whatever you're drinking. Look for recommended wines by the glass on the chalkboard or spend ages perusing the encyclopedic list. **Aret' 'a Palm** (✉ *Piazza S. Maria La Nova 14, Spaccanapoli* ☎ *339/8486949*) is Neapolitan for "behind the palm tree," and that's exactly where you can find this agreeably dark bar on Piazza Santa Maria La Nova. Its long marble bar and mirrored walls suggest Paris more than Naples. The **Enoteca Belledonne** (✉ *Vico Belledonne a Chiaia 18, Chiaia* ☎ *081/403162* 🌐 *www.enotecabelledonne.com*) is something of an institution among inhabitants of the more upscale Chiaia area. Between 8 and 9 in the evening it seems like the whole neighborhood has descended into the tiny space for an *aperitivo* (cocktail). The small tables and low stools are notably uncomfortable, but the cozy atmosphere and the pleasure of being surrounded by glass-front cabinets full of wine bottles with beautiful labels more than makes up for it. Excellent local wines are available by the glass at great prices. A particularly quiet and refined option in Chiaia is **L'ebbrezza di Noè** (✉ *Vico Vetriera a Chaia 9, Chiaia* ☎ *081/400104* 🌐 *www.lebbrezzadinoe.com*), which is both a stand-up bar and a sit-down eatery.

SHOPPING

Leather goods, jewelry, and cameos are some of the best items to buy in Campania. In Naples you can generally find good deals on handbags, shoes, and clothing. Most boutiques and department stores are open Monday 4:30–8 and Tuesday–Saturday 9:15–1 and 4:30–8. The larger chains now open on Sunday.

SHOPPING DISTRICTS

Most of the luxury shops in Naples are along a crescent that descends the Via Toledo to Piazza Trieste e Trento and then continues along Via Chiaia to Via Filangieri and on to Piazza Amedeo, as well as continuing south toward Piazza dei Martiri and the Riviera di Chiaia. Within this area, the Via Chiaia probably has the greatest concentration and variety of shops (and caffè–pastry shop Cimmino, on the corner of Via Filangieri and Via Chiaia, makes for an excellent rest stop along this route). The area around Piazza Vanvitelli, and Via Scarlatti in particular, in the Vomero also has a nice selection of shops outside the tourist zone. This area can be conveniently reached by funiculars from Piazza Amedeo, Via Toledo, or Montesanto. Secondhand book dealers tend to collect in the area between Piazza Dante, Via Port'Alba, and Via Santa Maria di Constantinopoli. Antique shops can also be found in the latter. The charming shops specializing in Presepi (Nativity scenes) are in Spaccanapoli, on the Via San Gregorio Armeno. Via San Sebastiano, close to the Conservatory, is the kingdom of musical instruments.

SPECIALTY STORES

Since 1865 **Tramontano** (✉ *Via Chiaia 143, Chiaia* ☎ *081/414837*) has crafted some of the finest leather luggage, bags, shoes, belts, and wallets. Shops selling Nativity scenes cluster along the Via San Gregorio Armeno in Spaccanapoli, and they're all worth a glance, but the most famous is **Ferrigno** (✉ *Via San Gregorio Armeno 10, Spaccanapoli* ☎ *081/5523148*) Maestro Giuseppe Ferrigno died in 2008, but the family business continues, still faithfully using 18th-century techniques. **Nel Regno di Pulcinella** (✉ *Vico San Domenico Maggiore 9, Spaccanapoli* ☎ *081/5514171*) is the workshop of Lello Esposito, renowned Neapolitan artist, famous for his renderings of a famous puppet named Pulcinella.

The **Ospedale delle Bambole** (✉ *Via San Biagio dei Librai 81, Spaccanapoli* ☎ *081/203067*), a tiny storefront operation, is a world-famous "hospital" for dolls. It's a wonderful place to take kids.

HERCULANEUM, VESUVIUS, AND POMPEII

Volcanic ash and mud preserved the Roman towns of Herculaneum and Pompeii almost exactly as they were on the day Mount Vesuvius erupted in AD 79, leaving them not just archaeological ruins but museums of daily life in the ancient world. The two cities and the volcano that buried them can be visited from either Naples or Sorrento, thanks to the Circumvesuviana, the suburban railway that provides fast, frequent, and economical service.

HERCULANEUM

★ *10 km (6 mi) southeast of Naples.*

GETTING HERE

Take a train on the Circumvesuviana to Ercolano. From the station, walk across at the nearest roundabout and head down Via 4 Novembre for 10 minutes. If driving from Naples, take the Ercolano exit from the Napoli-Salerno autostrada. Follow signs for Scavi di Ercolano.

VISITOR INFORMATION

The **Ufficio Turistico** (✉ *Via IV Novembre 82, Ercolano* ☎ *081/7881243*) is open 9–2, closed Sunday.

EXPLORING

Herculaneum ruins. Lying more than 60 feet below the present-day town of Ercolano, the ruins of Herculaneum are set among the acres of greenhouses that make this area one of Europe's principal flower-growing centers. About 5,000 people lived here when it was destroyed; many of them were fishermen, craftsmen, and artists. In AD 79 the gigantic eruption of Vesuvius (which also destroyed Pompeii) buried the town under a tide of volcanic mud. The semiliquid mass seeped into the crevices and niches of every building, covering household objects and enveloping textiles and wood—sealing all in a compact, airtight tomb.

Casual excavation—and haphazard looting—began in the 18th century, but systematic digs were not initiated until the 1920s. Today less than half of Herculaneum has been excavated; with present-day

Ercolano and the unlovely Resina Quarter (famous among bargain hunters for its secondhand-clothing market) sitting on top of the site, progress is limited. From the ramp leading down to Herculaneum's well-preserved edifices, you get a good overall view of the site, as well as an idea of the amount of volcanic debris that had to be removed to bring it to light.

Though Herculaneum had only one-fourth the population of Pompeii and has been only partially excavated, what has been found is generally better preserved. In some cases you can even see the original wooden beams, staircases, and furniture. Much excitement is presently focused on one excavation in a corner of the site, the Villa dei Papiri, built by Julius Caesar's father-in-law. The building is named for the 1,800 carbonized papyrus scrolls dug up here in the 18th century, leading scholars to believe that this may have been a study center or library. Given the right funds and political support, it is hoped that the villa can be properly excavated and ultimately opened to the public.

Make sure to stock up on refreshments beforehand, as there is no food at the archaeological site. At the entrance, pick up a map showing the gridlike layout of the dig. Splurge on an audio guide (€6.50 for one, €10 for two) and head down the tunnel to start the tour at the old shoreline. Though many of the houses are closed and some are in dire need of restoration, a fair cross section of domestic, commercial, and civic buildings is still accessible. Decorations are especially delicate in the **Casa del Nettuno ed Anfitrite** (House of Neptune and Amphitrite), named for the subjects of a still-bright mosaic on the wall of the *nymphaeum* (a recessed grotto with a fountain), and in the **Terme Femminili** (Women's Baths), where several delicate black-and-white mosaics embellished the rooms. Annexed to the former house is a remarkably preserved wine shop, where amphorae still rest on carbonized wooden shelves. On the other side of the house is the **Casa del Bel Cortile** (House of the Beautiful Courtyard). In one of its inner rooms is the temporary display of a cast taken of two skeletons found in the storerooms down at the old seafront, where almost 300 inhabitants sought refuge from the eruption and were ultimately encapsulated for posterity. The **Casa dei Cervi** (House of the Stags), with an elegant garden open to the sea breezes, is evocative of a lively and luxurious way of life. The sumptuously decorated **Terme Suburbane** (Suburban Baths) was closed at the time of this writing, but is well worth a visit if it is open. ✉ *Corso Resina 6, Ercolano* ☎ *081/8575347* 🌐 *www.pompeiisites.org* 🎫 *€11 for Herculaneum only; €20 for biglietto cumulativo ticket to 5 sites (Pompeii, Herculaneum, Boscoreale, Oplontis, and Stabiae) valid for 3 days* ⏲ *Nov.–Mar., daily 8:30–5, ticket office closes at 3:30; Apr.–Oct., daily 8:30–7:30, ticket office closes at 6.*

Fodor's Choice ★ Spectacular "virtual" re-creations of Herculaneum's streets and squares, computerized re-creations of the House of the Faun, even a vaporized steam bath standing in for the "burning cloud" of 79 AD: it is all here, in Herculaneum's 1st-century-meets-the-21st-century museum extravaganza, the **Museo Archeologico Virtuale (MAV)**. You first stop off at the ticket office for the headset audio tour and then descend, as in an excavation, to a floor below. Passing ancient faces that have

Bay of Naples
Marina di Lago di Pátria
Qualiano
Casavatore
Marano di Nápoli
Miano
Casória
Marina di Varcature
Capodimonte
Volla
Cumae
Naples
see detail map
Pomigliano
Somma
S Anastasia
Cércola
Ottaviano
Vesuvius
Parco del Vesúvio
Terzigno
S Giuseppe
Palma
Nola
Parco Regionale del Partenio
Monteforte
Sarno
Pogglomarino
Pompeii
see detail map
Pagani
Nocera
Boscoreale
Boscotrecase
Torre del Greco
Oplontis
Torre Annunziata
Circumvesuviana Rail Line
S António
Pórtici
Herculaneum
Solfatara
Pozzuoli
Mergellina
Agnano Terme
Marechiaro
Baia
Bacoli
Golfo di Pozzuoli
Ísola di Nisida
Miseno
Capo Miseno
Procida Porto
Procida
Ísola di Prócida
Punta Solchiaro
Golfo di Napoli
Punta Cornácchia
Lacco Ameno
Íschia Porto
Ischia
Forio
Spiaggia di Citord
Barano D'Ischia
Sant' Angelo
Ísola d'Íschia
Punta Sant'Angelo
Tyrrhenian Sea
Sorrento & Amalfi Coast
see detail map
Castellammare di Stábia
Gragnana
Vico Equense
Marina di Équa
Alimuri
Piano di Sorrento
Meta
Sorrento
Marina di Puolo
Massa Lubrense
Sant'Agata sui Due Golfi
Metrano
Términi
Punta Campanella
Bocca Piccola
SORRENTINE PENINSULA
Positano
Praiano
Amalfi
Ravello
Maiori
Cetara
THE AMALFI COAST
Capri
see detail map
Ísola di Capri
Grotta Azzurra
Punta dell'Arcera
Anacapri
Marina Grande
Capri
Marina Piccola
A1
A16
A30
A3
18
145
0
10 mi
0
10 km

CLOSE UP

Pompeii Prep

Pompeii is impressive under any circumstances, but it comes alive if you do some preparation before your visit.

First, read up—there are piles of good books on the subject, including these engaging, jargon-free histories: *Pompeii: The Day a City Died* by Robert Etienne, *Pompeii: Public and Private Life* by Paul Zanker, and *The Lost World of Pompeii* by Colin Amery. For accurate historical information woven into the pages of a thriller, pick up *Pompeii: A Novel* by Robert Harris.

Second, be sure to visit the Museo Archeologico Nazionale in Naples, where most of the finest art from Pompeii now resides. The museum is a remarkable treasure trove—it's a rewarding place to visit even if Pompeii isn't in your plans.

now been given a name, the "percorso" path inserts you inside a re-creation of Herculaneum's first dig, replete with voices echoing from large terra-cotta vases.

Then get ready to experience, complete with mephitic effects, Herculaneum's Villa dei Papiri before and—even more dramatically—during the eruption. Then enter, courtesy of vaporized water, "the burning cloud" of 79 AD and finally emerge, at least virtually speaking, inside Pompeii's House of the Faun, both as it is now and, depending on a mere movement of your feet, as it was for two centuries BC. The next re-creation—complete with rippling grass and moving cart and oxen—is, again, Ercolano's Villa dei Papirii. Then comes a magical pre- and post-flooding view of Baia's "Nymphaeum," the now displaced statues arrayed as they were in days of Emperor Claudius who commissioned them. Another screen displays Capri's more-town-than-a-palace of the Villa Jovis that was Tiberius's residence atop the island.

Most spectacular of all, take a front-row seat for "Day and Night in the Forum of Pompeii," with soldiers, litter-bearing slaves, and toga-clad figures moving spectrally to complete the spell. Down a corridor at the back you can make a vicarious visit to the "Lupari," brothels, their various pleasures illustrated in virtual and graphic frescoes along the walls. There are also holograms of jewelry of the earthquake fugitives and a touch-and-browse section of the Papyrii's 1,800 scrolls. "Wonder is the beginning of knowledge," said somebody and this museum does yeoman work in joining the two to impressive effect. ✉ *Via IV Novembre 44, Ercolano* ☎ *081/19806511/2* 🌐 *www.museomav.com* 🎫 *€7.50* ⏲ *Closed Mon.*

ANCIENT POMPEII
TOMB OF A CIVILIZATION

The site of Pompeii, petrified memorial to Vesuvius's eruption on the morning of August 24, AD 79, is the largest, most accessible, and probably most famous of excavations anywhere.

A busy commercial center with a population of 10,000–20,000, ancient Pompeii covered about 160 acres on the seaward end of the fertile Sarno Plain. Today Pompeii is choked with both the dust of 25 centuries and more than 2 million visitors every year; only by escaping the hordes and lingering along its silent streets can you truly fall under the site's spell. On a quiet backstreet, all you need is a little imagination to sense the shadows palpably filling the dark corners, to hear the ancient pipe's falsetto and the tinny clash of cymbals, to envision a rain of rose petals gently covering a Roman senator's dinner guests. Come in the late afternoon when the site is nearly deserted and you will understand that the true pleasure of Pompeii is not in the seeing but in the feeling.

A FUNNY THING HAPPENS ON THE WAY TO THE FORUM

as you walk through Pompeii. Covered with dust and decay as it is, the city seems to come alive. Perhaps it's the familiar signs of life observed along the ancient streets: bakeries with large ovens just like those for making pizzas, tracks of cart wheels cut into the road surface, graffiti etched onto the plastered surfaces of street walls. Coming upon a *thermopolium* (snack bar), you imagine natives calling out, "Let's move on to the am-phitheater." But a glance up at Vesuvius, still brooding over the scene like an enormous headstone, reminds you that these folks—whether

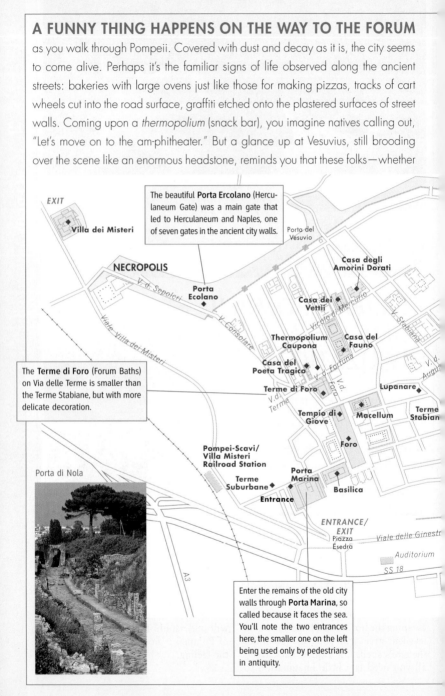

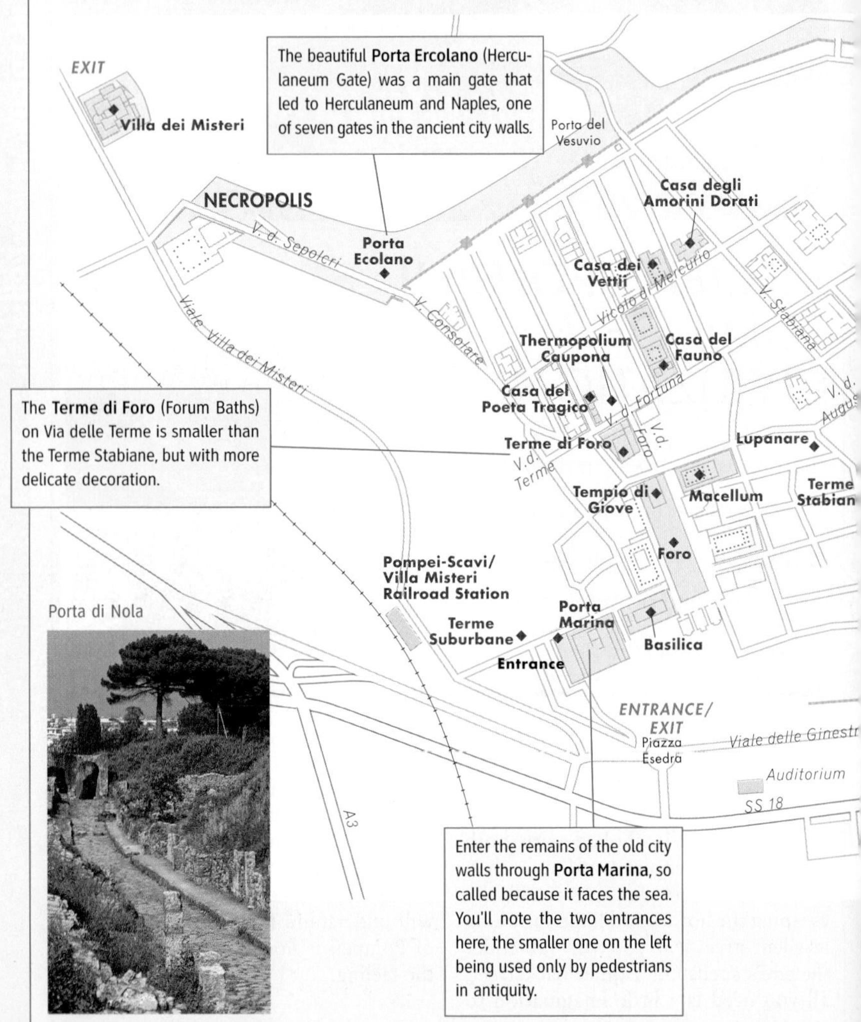

Via dell'Abbondanza

imagined in your head or actually wearing a mantle of lava dust—have not taken a breath for centuries. The town was laid out in a grid pattern, with two main intersecting streets. The wealthiest took a whole block for themselves; those less fortunate built a house and rented out the front rooms, facing the street, as shops. There were good numbers of *tabernae* (taverns) and *thermopolia* on almost every corner, and frequent shows at the amphitheater.

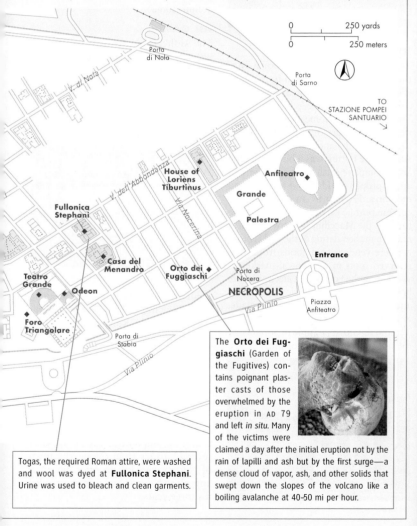

0 250 yards
0 250 meters
Porta di Nola
V. di Nola
Porta di Sarno
TO STAZIONE POMPEI SANTUARIO
House of Loriens Tiburtinus
V. dell'Abbondanza
Anfiteatro
Grande Palestra
Via Nocerina
Fullonica Stephani
Casa del Menandro
Orto dei Fuggiaschi
Entrance
Porta di Nocera
Teatro Grande
Odeon
NECROPOLIS
Via Plinio
Piazza Anfiteatro
Foro Triangolare
Porta di Stabia
Via Plinio

The **Orto dei Fuggiaschi** (Garden of the Fugitives) contains poignant plaster casts of those overwhelmed by the eruption in AD 79 and left *in situ.* Many of the victims were claimed a day after the initial eruption not by the rain of lapilli and ash but by the first surge—a dense cloud of vapor, ash, and other solids that swept down the slopes of the volcano like a boiling avalanche at 40–50 mi per hour.

Togas, the required Roman attire, were washed and wool was dyed at **Fullonica Stephani**. Urine was used to bleach and clean garments.

PUBLIC LIFE IN ANCIENT POMPEII

Forum

THE CITY CENTER

As you enter the ruins at Porta Marina, make your way uphill to the **Foro** (Forum), which served as Pompeii's cultural, political, and religious center. You can still see some of the two stories of colonnades that used to line the square. Like the ancient Greek *agora* in Athens, the Forum was a busy shopping area, complete with public officials to apply proper standards of weights and measures. Fronted by an elegant three-column portico on the eastern side of the forum is the **Macellum**, the covered meat and fish market dating to the 2nd century BC; here vendors sold goods from their reserved spots in the central market. It was also in the Forum that elections were held, politicians let rhetoric fly, speeches and official announcements were made, and worshippers crowded around the **Tempio di Giove** (Temple of Jupiter), at the northern end of the forum.

Basilica

On the southwestern corner is the **Basilica**, the city's law court and the economic center. These rectangular aisled halls were the model for early Christian churches, which had a nave (central aisle) and two side aisles separated by rows of columns. Standing in the Basilica, you can recognize the continuity between Roman and Christian architecture.

THE GAMES

The **Anfiteatro** (Amphitheater) was the ultimate in entertainment for Pompeians and offered a gamut of experiences, but essentially this was for gladiators rather than wild animals. By Roman standards, Pompeii's amphitheater was quite small (seating 20,000). Built in about 80 BC, making it the oldest permanent amphitheater in the Roman world, it was oval and divided into four seating areas. There were two main entrances—at the north and south ends—and a narrow passage on the west called the Porta Libitinensis, through which the dead were probably dragged out. A wall painting found in a house near the theater (now in the Naples Museum) depicts the riot in the amphitheater in AD 59 when several citizens from the nearby town of Nocera were killed. After Nocerian appeals to Nero, shows were suspended for three years.

Amphitheater

Fresco of Pyramus and Thisbe in the House of Loreius Tiburtinus

BATHS AND BROTHELS

In its day, Pompeii was celebrated as the Côte d'Azur, the seaside Brighton, the Fire Island of the ancient Roman empire. Evidence of a Sybaritic bent is everywhere—in the town's grandest villas, in its baths, and especially in its rowdiest *lupanaria* (brothels), murals still reveal a worship of hedonism. Satyrs, bacchantes, hermaphrodites, and acrobatic couples are pictured indulging in hanky-panky.

The first buildings to the left past the ticket turnstiles are the **Terme Suburbane** (Suburban Baths), built—by all accounts without permission—right up against the city walls. The baths have eyebrow-raising frescoes in the *apodyterium* (changing room) that strongly suggest that more than just bathing and massaging went on here. Reservations are required for entry.

On the walls of **Lupanare** (brothel) are scenes of erotic games in which clients could engage. The **Terme Stabiane** (Stabian Baths) had underground furnaces, the heat from which circulated beneath the floor, rose through flues in the walls, and escaped through chimneys. The water temperature could be set for cold, lukewarm, or hot. Bathers took a lukewarm bath to prepare themselves for the hot room. A tepid bath came next, and then a plunge into cold water to tone up the skin. A vigorous massage with oil was followed by rest, reading, horseplay, and conversation.

GRAFFITI

Thanks to those deep layers of pyroclastic deposits from Vesuvius that protected the site from natural wear and tear over the centuries, graffiti found in Pompeii provide unique insights into the sort of things that the locals found important 2,000 years ago. A good many were personal and lend a human dimension to the disaster that not even the sights can equal.

At the baths:**"What is the use of having a Venus if she's made of marble?"**At the entrance to the front lavatory at a private house:**"May I always and everywhere be as potent with women as I was here."**

On the Viale ai Teatri:**"A copper pot went missing from my shop. Anyone who returns it to me will be given 65 bronze coins."**In the Basilica:**"A small problem gets larger if you ignore it."**

PRIVATE LIFE IN ANCIENT POMPEII

The facades of houses in Pompeii were relatively plain and seldom hinted at the care and attention lavished on the private rooms within. When visitors arrived they passed the shops and entered an open peristyle, from which the occupants received air, sunlight, and rainwater, the latter caught by the *impluvium*, a rectangular-shaped receptacle under the sloped roof. In the back was a receiving room, the *tablinum,* and behind was another open area, the atrium. Life revolved around this uncovered inner courtyard, with rows of columns and perhaps a garden with a fountain. Only good friends ever saw this part of the house, which was surrounded by *cubicula* (bedrooms) and the *triclinium* (dining area). Interior floors and walls usually were covered with colorful marble tiles, mosaics, and frescoes.

House of Paquius Proculus

Several homes were captured in various states by the eruption of Vesuvius, each representing a different slice of Pompeiian life.

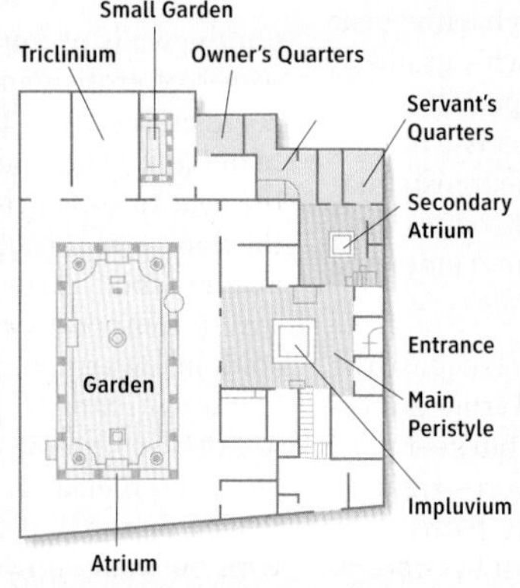

The **Casa del Fauno** (House of the Faun) displayed wonderful mosaics, now at the Museo Archeologico Nazionale in Naples. The **Casa del Poeta Tragico** (House of the Tragic Poet) is a typical middle-class house. On the floor is a mosaic of a chained dog and the inscription *cave canem* ("Beware of the dog"). The **Casa degli Amorini Dorati** (House of the Gilded Cupids) is an elegant, well-preserved home with original marble decorations in the garden. Many paintings and mosaics were executed at **Casa del Menandro** (House of Menander), a patrician's villa named for a fresco of the Greek playwright. Two blocks beyond the Stabian Baths you'll notice on the left the current digs at the **Casa dei Casti Amanti** (House of the Chaste Lovers). A team of plasterers and painters were at work here when Vesuvius erupted, redecorating one of the rooms and patching up the cracks in the bread oven near the entrance—possibly caused by tremors a matter of days before.

CASA DEI VETTII

The **House of the Vettii** is the best example of a house owned by wealthy *mercatores* (merchants). It contains vivid murals—a magnificent *pinacoteca* (picture gallery) within the very heart of Pompeii. The scenes here—except for those in the two wings off the atrium—were all painted after the earthquake of AD 62. Once inside, cast an admiring glance at the delicate frieze around the wall of the *triclinium* (on the right of the peristyle garden as you enter from the atrium), depicting cupids engaged in various activities, such as selling oils and perfumes, working as goldsmiths and metalworkers, acting as wine merchants, or performing in chariot races. Another of the main attractions in the Casa dei Vettii is the small cubicle beyond the kitchen area (to the right of the atrium) with its faded erotic frescoes now protected by Perspex screens.

UNLOCKING THE VILLA DEI MISTERI

Villa dei Misteri

There is no more astounding, magnificently memorable evidence of Pompeii's devotion to the pleasures of the flesh than the frescoes on view at the **Villa dei Misteri** (Villa of the Mysteries), a palatial abode 400 yards outside the city gates, northwest of Porta Ercolano. Unearthed in 1909, this villa had more than 60 rooms painted with frescoes; the finest are in the *triclinium*. Painted in the most glowing Pompeiian reds and oranges, the panels relate the saga of a young bride (Ariadne) and her initiation into the mysteries of the cult of Dionysus, who was a god imported to Italy from Greece and then given the Latin name of Bacchus. The god of wine and debauchery also represented the triumph of the irrational—of all those mysterious forces that no official state religion could fully suppress.

Pompeii's best frescoes, painted in glowing reds and oranges, retain an amazing vibrancy.

The Villa of the Mysteries frescoes were painted circa 50 BC, most art historians believe, and represent the peak of the Second Style of Pompeiian wall painting. The triclinium frescoes are thought to have been painted by a local artist, although the theme may well have been copied from an earlier cycle of paintings from the Hellenistic period. In all there are 10 scenes, depicting children and matrons, musicians and satyrs, phalluses and gods. There are no inscriptions (such as are found on Greek vases), and after 2,000 years historians remain puzzled by many aspects of the triclinium cycle. Scholars endlessly debate the meaning of these frescoes, but anyone can tell they are the most beautiful paintings left to us by antiquity. In several ways, the eruption of Vesuvius was a blessing in disguise, for without it, these masterworks of art would have perished long ago.

PLANNING FOR YOUR DAY IN POMPEII

GETTING THERE

The archaeological site of Pompeii has its own stop (Pompei–Villa dei Misteri) on the Circumvesuviana line to Sorrento, close to the main entrance at the Porta Marina, which is the best place from which to start a tour. If, like many visitors every year, you get the wrong train from Naples (stopping at the other station "Pompei"), all is not lost. There's another entrance to the excavations at the far end of the site, just a seven-minute walk to the Amphitheater.

ADMISSION

Single tickets cost €11 and are valid for one full day. The site is open Apr.–Oct., daily 8:30–7:30 (last admission at 6), and Nov.–Mar., daily 8:30–5 (last admission at 3:30). For more information, call 081/8575347 or visit www.pompeiisites.org.

WHAT TO BRING

The only restaurant inside the site is both overpriced and busy, so it makes sense to bring along water and snacks. If you come so equipped, there are some shady, underused picnic tables outside the Porta di Nola, to the northeast of the site.

MAKING THE MOST OF YOUR TIME

Visiting Pompeii does have its frustrating aspects: many buildings are blocked off by locked gates, and enormous group tours tend to clog up more popular attractions. But the site is so big that it's easy to lose yourself amid the quiet side streets. To really see the site, you'll need four or five hours.

Three buildings within Pompeii—Terme Suburbane, Casa del Menandro, and Casa degli Amorini Dorati—are open for restricted viewing. Reservations must be made on-line at www.arethusa.net, where you can find information on opening times.

TOURS

To get the most out of Pompeii, rent an audio guide (€6.50 for one, €10 for two; you'll need to leave an ID card) and opt for one of the three itineraries (2 hours, 4 hours, or 6 hours). If hiring a guide, make sure the guide is registered for an English tour and standing inside the gate; agree beforehand on the length of the tour and the price, and prepare yourself for soundbites of English mixed with dollops of hearsay. For a higher quality (but more expensive) full-day tour, try Context Travel (🌐 www.contexttravel.com).

MODERN POMPEI

Caught between the hammer and anvil of cultural and religious tourism, the modern town of Pompei (to use the modern-day Italian spelling, not the ancient Latin) is now endeavoring to polish up its act. In attempts to ease congestion and improve air quality at street level, parts of the town have been pedestrianized and parking restrictions tightened. Several hotels have filled the sizable niche in the market for excellent deals at affordable prices. As for recommendable restaurants, if you deviate from the archaeological site and make for the center of town, you will be spoiled for choice.

IF YOU LIKE POMPEII

If you intend to visit other archaeological sites nearby during your trip, you should buy the *biglietto cumulativo* pass, a combination ticket with access to four area sites (Herculaneum, Pompeii, Oplontis, Boscoreale). It costs €20 and is valid for three days. Unlike many archaeological sites in the Mediterranean region, those around Naples are almost all well served by public transport; ask about transportation options at the helpful Porta Marina information kiosk.

VESUVIUS

8 km (5 mi) northeast of Herculaneum, 16 km (10 mi) east of Naples.

> **WORD OF MOUTH**
>
> "You can't beat the views from the top of Vesuvius, and it is pretty cool to watch the volcano smolder and smoke. You get a good overview of the region and can see the entire gulf all the way from Naples to Sorrento and out to Capri."
>
> —nnolen

13

GETTING HERE

To arrive by car, take the A3 Napoli–Salerno highway exit "Torre del Greco" and follow Via E. De Nicola from the tollbooth. Follow signs for the Parco Nazionale del Vesuvio.

There's regular bus service up Vesuvius operated by **Vesuviana Mobilitá** (☎ *081/9634420* 🌐 *www.vesuvianamobilita.it*) (€10.60 return from Pompeii Piazza Anfiteatro, €9.60 from Ercolano Circumvesuviana station), although it's far quicker to take the trips up Vesuvius on minibuses run by **Vesuvio Express** (☎ *081/7393666* 🌐 *www.vesuvioexpress.it*) (€10 return from Ercolano Circumvesuviana station). Both services will take you up to the car park and the starting point of the path up to the cone's top.

EXPLORING

Vesuvius. As you tour the cities that it destroyed, you may be overwhelmed by the urge to explore Vesuvius. In summer especially, the prospect of rising above the sticky heat of Naples is a heady one. The view when the air is clear is magnificent, with the curve of the coast and the tiny white houses among the orange and lemon blossoms. If the summit is lost in mist you'll be lucky to see your hand in front of your face. When you see the summit clearing—it tends to be clearer in the afternoon—head for it. If possible, see Vesuvius after you've toured the ruins of buried Herculaneum to appreciate the magnitude of the volcano's power.

From Ercolano train station, riding a 10-seat minibus run by Vesuvio Express (☎ *081/7393666* 🌐 *www.vesuvioexpress.it*) is a quick, painless, and relatively cheap way of getting to the top. The vehicles thread their way rapidly up on back roads, reaching the top in 20 minutes. Allow at least 2½ hours for the journey, including a 30-minute walk to the crater on a soft cinder track. The cost is €16.50, including admission to the crater. The fee includes a compulsory guide service, usually young geologists with a smattering of English. At the bottom you'll be offered a stout walking stick (a small tip is appreciated on return). The climb can be tiring if you're not used to steep hikes. Because of the volcanic stone you should wear athletic shoes, not sandals. ✉ ☎ *081/7775720* 🎫 *€6.50* ⏲ *Daily 9 am–2 hrs before sunset.*

You can visit **Osservatorio Vesuviano** *(Vesuvius Observatory)*—2,000 feet up—and view instruments used to study the volcano, some dating to the mid-19th century. ✉ *Via Osservatorio, Ercolano* ☎ *081/6108483 or 081/7777149* 🌐 *www.ov.ingv.it* 🎫 *Free* ⏲ *Weekends 10–2.*

ISCHIA AND PROCIDA

Though Capri gets star billing among the islands that line the bay of Naples, Ischia and Procida also have their own, lower-key appeal. Ischia is a popular destination on account of its spas, beaches, and hot springs. Procida, long the poor relation of the three and the closest to Naples, is starting to capitalize on its chief natural asset, the unspoiled isle of Vivara. The pastel colors of Procida will be familiar to anyone who has seen the widely acclaimed film *Il Postino*.

PROCIDA

35 mins by hydrofoil, 1 hr by car ferry from Naples.

GETTING HERE

Procida's ferry timetable caters to the many daily commuters who live on the island and work in Naples or Pozzuoli. The most frequent—and cheapest—connections are from the Port of Pozzuoli. After stopping at Procida's main port, Marina Grande (also called Sancio Cattolico), many ferries and hydrofoils continue on to Ischia, for which Procida is considered a halfway house.

VISITOR INFORMATION

Procida tourism office (✉ *Via Vittorio Emanuele 173* ☎ *081/8969628* 🌐 *www.procida.net*).

EXPLORING

Lying barely 3 km (2 mi) from the mainland and 10 km (6 mi) from the nearest port of Pozzuoli, Procida is an island of enormous contrasts. It is the most densely populated island in Europe—just over 10,000 people crammed into less than 3½ square km (less than 1½ square mi)—and yet there are oases such as Marina Corricella and Vivara that seem to have been bypassed by modern civilization. It's no surprise that picturesque Procida has strong artistic traditions and is widely considered a painters' paradise.

The sleepy fishing village of **Corricella,** used as the setting for the waterfront scenes in the Oscar-winning film *Il Postino,* has been relatively immune to life in the limelight. Apart from the opening of an extra restaurant and bar, there have been few changes. This is the type of place where even those with failing grades in art class feel like reaching for a paintbrush to record the delicate pink and yellow facades. The **Graziella** bar at the far end of the seafront offers the island's famous lemons squeezed over crushed ice to make an excellent granita.

WHERE TO EAT

$$ SOUTHERN ITALIAN ★ **La Conchiglia.** A dinner at this beachfront spot really lets you appreciate the magic of Procida. Beyond the lapping of the waves, Capri twinkles in the distance. The seafood is divinely fresh, the pasta dishes usually soul-warming. Access here is either on foot down the steps from Via Pizzaco or by boat from the Corricella harborfront—phone owner Gianni if you want the boat to pick you up (free for diners). ✉ *Via Pizzaco 10* ☎ *081/8967602* 🌐 *www.laconchigliaristorante.com* ⏲ *Closed mid-Nov.–Mar.*

ISCHIA

45 mins by hydrofoil, 90 mins by car ferry from Naples, 60 mins by ferry from Pozzuoli.

GETTING HERE

Ischia is well connected with the mainland in all seasons. The last boats leave for Naples and Pozzuoli at about 8 pm (though in the very high season there is a midnight sailing), and you should allow plenty of time for getting to the port and buying a ticket. Ischia has three ports—Ischia Porto, Casamicciola, and Forio (hydrofoils only)—so you should choose your ferry or hydrofoil according to your destination. Non-Italians can bring cars to the island relatively freely.

VISITOR INFORMATION

Housed in the historic municipal bath building, **Azienda Autonoma di Cura, Soggiorno e Turismo** (✉ *Ufficio Informazioni, Banchina Porto Salvo, Ischia Porto* ☎ *081/5074231* 📠 *081/5074230* 🌐 *www.infoischiaprocida.it*) in Ischia Porto is open Monday–Saturday 9 am–2 pm and 3–8.

EXPLORING

Whereas Capri wows you with its charm and beauty, Ischia takes time to cast its spell. In fact, an overnight stay is probably not long enough for the island to get into your blood. It does have its share of vine-growing villages beneath the lush volcanic slopes of Monte Epomeo, and unlike Capri it enjoys a life of its own that survives when the tourists head home. But there are few signs of antiquity here, the architecture is unremarkable, the traffic can be overwhelming, and hoteliers have yet to achieve a balanced mix of clientele—most are either German (off-season) or Italian (in-season). But should you want to plunk down in the sun for a few days and tune out the world, this is an ideal spot; just don't expect an unspoiled, undiscovered Capri. When Augustus gave the Neapolitans Ischia for Capri, he knew what he was doing.

Ischia is volcanic in origin. From its hidden reservoir of seething molten matter come the thermal springs said to cure whatever ails you. As early as 1580 a doctor named Lasolino published a book about the mineral wells at Ischia. "If your eyebrows fall off," he wrote, "go and try the baths at Piaggia Romano. If you know anyone who is getting bald, anyone who suffers from elephantiasis, or another whose wife yearns for a child, take the three of them immediately to the Bagno di Vitara; they will bless you." Today the island is covered with thermal baths, often surrounded by tropical gardens.

A good 35-km (22-mi) road makes a circuit of the island; the ride takes most of a day if you stop along the way to enjoy the views and perhaps have lunch. You can book a boat tour around the island at the booths in various ports along the coast; there's a one-hour stop at Sant'Angelo. The information office is at the harbor. You may drive on Ischia year-round. There's also fairly good bus service, and you'll find plenty of taxis.

Ischia Porto is the largest town on the island and the usual point of debarkation. It's no workaday port, however, but a lively resort with plenty of hotels, the island's best shopping area, and low, flat-roof houses on terraced hillsides overlooking the water. Its narrow streets often

GETTING TO CAPRI, ISCHIA, AND PROCIDA

Several companies offer a variety of fast craft and passenger and car ferries connecting the islands of Capri, Ischia, and Procida with Naples and Pozzuoli year-round. Hydrofoils and other fast craft leave from Naples's Molo Beverello, adjacent to Piazza Municipio, and also from Mergellina, about 1½ km (1 mi) west of Piazza Municipio. Slower car ferries leave from the more inaccessible berths at Calata Porta di Massa, a 10-minute walk east of Molo Beverello.

Information on departures is published every day in the local paper, *Il Mattino*. Alternatively, ask at the tourist office or at the port, or contact the companies—**Alilauro** (☎ *081/7614909* 🌐 *www.alilauro.it*), **Caremar** (☎ *081/5513882* 🌐 *www.caremar.it*), **Coop Sant'Andrea** (☎ *089/873190* 🌐 *www.coopsantandrea.it*), **Navigazione Libera del Golfo** (*NLG* ☎ *089/5520763* 🌐 *www.navlib.it*), and **SNAV** (☎ *081/7612348* 🌐 *www.snavali.com*) —directly. Always double-check schedules in stormy weather.

become flights of steps that scale the hill, and its villas and gardens are framed by pines.

Most of the hotels are along the beach in the part of town called **Ischia Ponte,** which gets its name from the *ponte* (bridge) built by Alfonso of Aragon in 1438 to link the picturesque castle on a small islet offshore with the town and port. For a while the castle was the home of Vittoria Colonna, poetess, granddaughter of Renaissance Duke Federico da Montefeltro (1422–82), and platonic soul mate of Michelangelo, with whom she carried on a lengthy correspondence. You'll find a typical resort atmosphere: countless cafés, shops, and restaurants, and a 1-km (½-mi) stretch of fine-sand beach.

Casamicciola, a popular beach resort, is 5 km (3 mi) west of Ischia Porto.

Chic and upscale **Lacco Ameno,** next to Casamicciola, is distinguished by a mushroom-shape rock offshore and some of the island's best hotels. Here, too, you can enjoy the benefits of Ischia's therapeutic waters.

The far-western and southern coasts of Ischia are more rugged and attractive. **Forio,** at the extreme west, has a waterfront church and is a good spot for lunch or dinner.

The sybaritic hot pools of the **Giardini Poseidon Terme** *(Poseidon Gardens Spa)* are on Citara Beach, south of Forio. You can sit like a Roman senator on a stone chair recessed in the rock and let the hot water cascade over you—all very campy, and fun.

Sant'Angelo, on the southern coast, is a charming village; the road doesn't reach all the way into town, so it's free of traffic. It's a five-minute boat ride from the beach of Maronti, at the foot of cliffs.

The inland town of Fontana is the base for excursions to the top of **Monte Epomeo,** the long-dormant volcano that dominates the island landscape. You can reach its 2,585-foot peak in less than 1½ hours of relatively easy walking.

13

WHERE TO EAT

$ SOUTHERN ITALIAN

Ristorante Calise Capriccio. The town's most centrally located restaurant is run by Caffè Calise, which has been in the business since 1925. Bang in the middle of the square, this one-time nightclub has a terrace overlooking the busy road and the boats of the tourist marina. Presided over by Giuseppe Marra (with an impressive international CV), the menu is based on the day's catch with an experimental twist. Starters include fried *calamaretti* (squid) with onion and swordfish with capers. Local wine accompanies *paccheri con cozze e pecorino*, a bold combination of pasta with mussels sprinkled with cheese. Leave space for the glorious deserts, all from the renowned Calise *pasticceria*—try the yummy Valentina cake (strawberries and cream on a sponge base). ✉ *Piazza Marina* ☎ *081/994724* ⏲ *Closed Nov.–Mar.*

$$ SOUTHERN ITALIAN

Da Gennaro. The oldest restaurant on the island, this has been a favorite of the stars, including Tom Cruise and Sophia Loren. Family-run, it opened on the seafront overlooking the boats in 1965 and continues to serve excellent fish in a convivial atmosphere. Specialties include *risotto alla pescatore* (rice with shellfish) and linguine *all'aragosta* (with lobster). In perfect English, friendly owner Gennaro will happily take you through the celebrity-laden wall of photos. ✉ *Via Porto 59* ☎ *081/992917* ⏲ *Closed Nov.–mid-Mar.*

$$$ MODERN ITALIAN

Il Melograno. One of the island's finest restaurants is tucked away on the road leading to Citara Beach. Try the *crudo italiana* (an Italian take on sushi) to start and then just indulge in food that tastes as good as it looks. New dishes with a twist are regularly introduced—the fried anchovies stuffed with provola cheese and homemade tomato bread was one year's winner. Another specialty is the *beccaccia,* a rabbit dish. Those on a higher budget and with a healthy appetite should treat themselves to the featured special menu, particulary the *Mano Libera,* the chef's choice, replete with local fish and vegetables given a nouvelle twist. Popular as this place is, be sure to reserve for summer dinners. ✉ *Via G. Mazzella 110* ☎ *081/998450* 🌐 *www.ilmelogranoischia.it* ⏲ *Closed Jan.–mid-Mar., Mon. and Wed. Nov.–Dec.*

WHERE TO STAY

$–$$ Fodor's Choice ★

Albergo Il Monastero. Within the Castello Aragonese at Ischia Ponte, with rustic rooms that peer down into the Mediterranean hundreds of feet below, this is the ultimate in ambience combined with the peace and quiet of a traffic-free area. **Pros:** stunning views; how often do you get to stay in a real castle? **Cons:** rather difficult to negotiate the steps before reaching the elevator; some consider this too far away from the town's action. **TripAdvisor:** "just magical," "huge patio overlooking Ischia," "homemade cakes and cookies." ✉ *Castello Aragonese 3* ☎ *081/992435* 🌐 *www.albergoilmonastero.it* *21 rooms* *In-room: no a/c, no TV, Internet. In-hotel: restaurant* ⏲ *Closed Nov.–Mar.* *Breakfast.*

$$$$ Fodor's Choice ★

Mezzatorre Resort & Spa. Far from the madding, sunburned crowds that swamp Ischia, this luxurious getaway perches in splendid isolation on the extreme promontory of Punta Cornacchia. **Pros:** the ideal getaway location; wonderful views. **Cons:** very isolated. **TripAdvisor:** "relaxing, private respite," "great spa facilities," "wonderful heated pool." ✉ *Via Mezzatorre 13, Forio d'Ischia* ☎ *081/986111* 🌐 *www.*

mezzatorre.it *57 rooms* *In-room: a/c, safe, refrigerator. In-hotel: restaurant, tennis court, pools, spa, Wi-Fi hotspot, parking* *Closed Nov.–Apr.* *Breakfast.*

$ ★ **Villa Antonio.** Blessed with a stunning perch over the Bay of Cartaromana, with the Castello Aragonese posing front and center in a panoramic vista, the Antonio offers a quiet haven five minutes from the crowds. **Pros:** no better view of the castle; seaside location. **Cons:** many steps to negotiate before elevator; guest rooms' small windows don't do justice to the view. **TripAdvisor:** "wonderful private beach," "simple but clean," "relaxed and cheap." ✉ *Via S. Giuseppe della Croce* ☎ *081/982660* *www.villantonio.it* *18 rooms* *In-room: a/c, safe, refrigerator. In-hotel: bar* *No credit cards* *Closed Nov.–mid-Mar.* *Breakfast.*

CAPRI

GETTING HERE

Capri is well connected with the mainland in all seasons, though there are more sailings between April and October. However, you can't return to Naples after about 10:20 pm in high season (in low season often 8 pm or even earlier). Hydrofoils, Seacats, and similar vessels leave from Molo Beverello (below Piazza Municipio) in Naples, while ferries leave from Calata Porta di Massa, 1,000 yards to the east, and *aliscafi* (hydrofoils) also sail from the small marina of Mergellina, a short distance west of the Villa Comunale in Naples.

VISITOR INFORMATION

Azienda Autonoma di Cura, Soggiorno e Turismo (✉ *Banchina del Porto, Marina Grande* ☎ *081/8370634* ✉ *Piazza Umberto I, Capri Town* ☎ *081/8370686* ✉ *Via G. Orlandi 59, Anacapri* ☎ *081/8371524* *www.capritourism.com*) offices in Capri, Capri Town, and Anacapri are open daily 8:30–8:30 in high season (9–3 on Sunday), and 8:30–2:30 in winter. Their excellent Web site has an English-language version.

EXPLORING

Once a pleasure dome to Roman emperors and now Italy's most glamorous seaside getaway, Capri (pronounced with an accent on the first syllable) is a craggy island at the southern end to the bay, 75 minutes by boat, 40 minutes by hydrofoil from Naples. The boom in cruises to the Naples area (almost 1 million passengers annually) means that Capri is inundated with day-trippers, making seemingly simple trips (like the funicular ride up from Marina Grande) a nerve-fraying experience. Yet even the crowds are not enough to destroy Capri's special charm. The town is a Moorish opera set of shiny white houses, tiny squares, and narrow medieval alleyways hung with flowers. It rests on top of rugged limestone cliffs hundreds of feet above the sea, and on which herds of *capre* (goats) once used to roam (giving the name to the island). Unlike the other islands in the Bay of Naples, Capri is not of volcanic origin; it may be a continuation of the limestone Sorrentine Peninsula.

Limestone caves on Capri have yielded rich prehistoric and Neolithic finds. The island is thought to have been settled by Greeks from Cumae in the 6th century BC and later by other Greeks from Neapolis, but it was the Romans in the early Imperial period who really left their mark. Emperor Augustus vacationed here; Tiberius built a dozen villas around the island, and, in later years, he refused to return to Rome, even when he was near death. Capri was one of the strongholds of the 16th-century pirate Barbarossa, who first sacked it and then made it a fortress. In 1806 the British wanted to turn the island into another Gibraltar and were beginning to build fortifications until the French took it away from them in 1808. Over the next century, from the opening of its first hotel in 1826, Capri saw an influx of visitors that reads like a Who's Who of literature and politics, especially in the early decades of the 20th century.

WORD OF MOUTH

"We spent 3 nights on Capri in May, and had a wonderful time. We did a lot of hiking, and I mean a lot. One must really walk to see this beautiful island. We found most food to be costly, but that didn't stop us from enjoying our time there."

—tuscanlifeedit

Like much else about Capri, the island's rare and delicious white wine is sensuous and intoxicating. Note that most of the wine passed off as "local" on Capri comes from the much-more-extensive vineyards of Ischia.

On arrival at the port, pick up the excellent map of the island at the tourist office (€1). You may have to wait in line for the funicular railway (€1.40 oneway) to **Capri Town,** perched some 450 feet above the harbor. This might be the time to splurge on an open-top taxi—it could save you an hour in line for the funicular. From the upper station, walk out into Piazza Umberto I, much better known as the Piazzetta, the island's social hub.

You can window-shop in expensive boutiques and browse in souvenir shops along Via Vittorio Emanuele, which leads south toward the many-domed **Certosa di San Giacomo.** You will be able to visit the church and cloister of this much-restored monastery and also pause long enough to enjoy the breathtaking view of Punta Tragara and the Faraglioni, three towering crags, from the viewing point at the edge of the cliff. ✉ *Via Certosa* ☎ *081/8376218* ⏲ *Tues., Wed., Fri.–Sun. 9–2, Thurs. 3–7.*

OFF THE BEATEN PATH

Villa Jovis. From Capri Town, the 45-minute hike east to Villa Jovis, the grandest of those built by Tiberius, is strenuous but rewarding. Follow the signs for Villa Jovis, taking Via Le Botteghe from the Piazzetta, then continuing along Via Croce and Via Tiberio. At the end of a lane that climbs the steep hill, with pretty views all the way, you come to the precipice over which the emperor reputedly disposed of the victims of his perverse attentions. From a natural terrace above, near a chapel, are spectacular views of the entire Bay of Naples and, on clear days, part of the Gulf of Salerno. Here starts the footpath around the somewhat neglected ruins of Tiberius's palace. Allow 45 minutes each way for the walk alone. ✉ *Via A. Maiuri* ☎ *081/8374549* 🎫 *€2* ⏲ *Feb.–Oct., daily 9–1 hr before sunset; Nov.–Jan., daily 9–3:15.*

From the terraces of **Giardini di Augusto** *(Gardens of Augustus)*, a beautifully planted public garden with excellent views, you can see the village of Marina Piccola below—restaurants, cabanas, and swimming platforms huddle among the shoals—and admire the steep and winding Via Krupp, actually a staircase cut into the rock. Friedrich Krupp, the German arms manufacturer, loved Capri and became one of the island's most generous benefactors. You can reach the beach by taking a bus from the Via Roma terminus down to Marina Piccola. ✉ *Via Matteotti beyond monastery of San Giacomo* ⏲ *Daily dawn–dusk.*

A tortuous road leads up to **Anacapri,** the island's "second city," about 3 km (2 mi) from Capri Town. To get here you can take a bus either from Via Roma in Capri Town or from Marina Grande (both €1.40), or a taxi (about €25 one-way; agree on the fare before starting out). Crowds are thick down Via Capodimonte leading to Villa San Michele and around the square, Piazza Vittoria, which is the starting point of the chairlift to the top of Monte Solaro. Elsewhere, Anacapri is quietly appealing. It's a good starting point for walks, such as the 80-minute round-trip journey to the **Migliara Belvedere,** on the island's southern coast.

An impressive limestone formation and the highest point on Capri (1,932 feet), **Monte Solaro** affords gasp-inducing views toward the bays of both Naples and Salerno. A 12-minute chairlift ride will take you right to the top (refreshments available at the bar), which is a starting point for a number of scenic trails on the western side of the island. Picnickers should note that even in summer it can get windy at this height, and there are few trees to provide shade or refuge. ✉ *Piazza Vittoria, Anacapri* ☎ *081/8371428* 🎫 *€7 one-way, €9 round-trip* ⏲ *Daily 9:30–5. Closed in adverse weather conditions.*

In the heart of Anacapri, the octagonal baroque church of **San Michele,** finished in 1719, is best known for its exquisite majolica pavement designed by Solimena and executed by the *mastro-riggiolaro* (master tiler) Chiaiese from Abruzzo. A walkway skirts the depiction of Adam and a duly contrite Eve being expelled from the Garden of Eden, but you can get a fine overview from the organ loft, reached by a winding staircase near the ticket booth (a privileged perch you have to pay for). Outside the church is the Via Finestrale, which leads to Anacapri's noted **Le Boffe quarter.** This section of town, centered on the Piazza Ficacciate, owes its name to the distinctive domestic architecture prevalent here, which uses vaults and sculpted groins instead of crossbeams. ✉ *Piazza San Nicola, Anacapri* ☎ *081/8372396* 🌐 *www.chiesa-san-michele.com* 🎫 *€2* ⏲ *Apr.–Oct., daily 9–7; Nov and Mar., daily 10–2.*

★ From Anacapri's Piazza Vittoria, picturesque Via Capodimonte leads to **Villa San Michele,** the charming former home of Swedish doctor and philanthropist Axel Munthe (1857–1949) that Henry James called "the most fantastic beauty, poetry, and inutility that one had ever seen clustered together." At the ancient entranceway to Anacapri at the top of the Scala Fenicia, the villa is set around Roman-style courtyards, marble walkways, and atria. Rooms display the doctor's varied collections, which range from bric-a-brac to antiquities. Medieval choir stalls, Renaissance lecterns, and gilded statues of saints are all part of

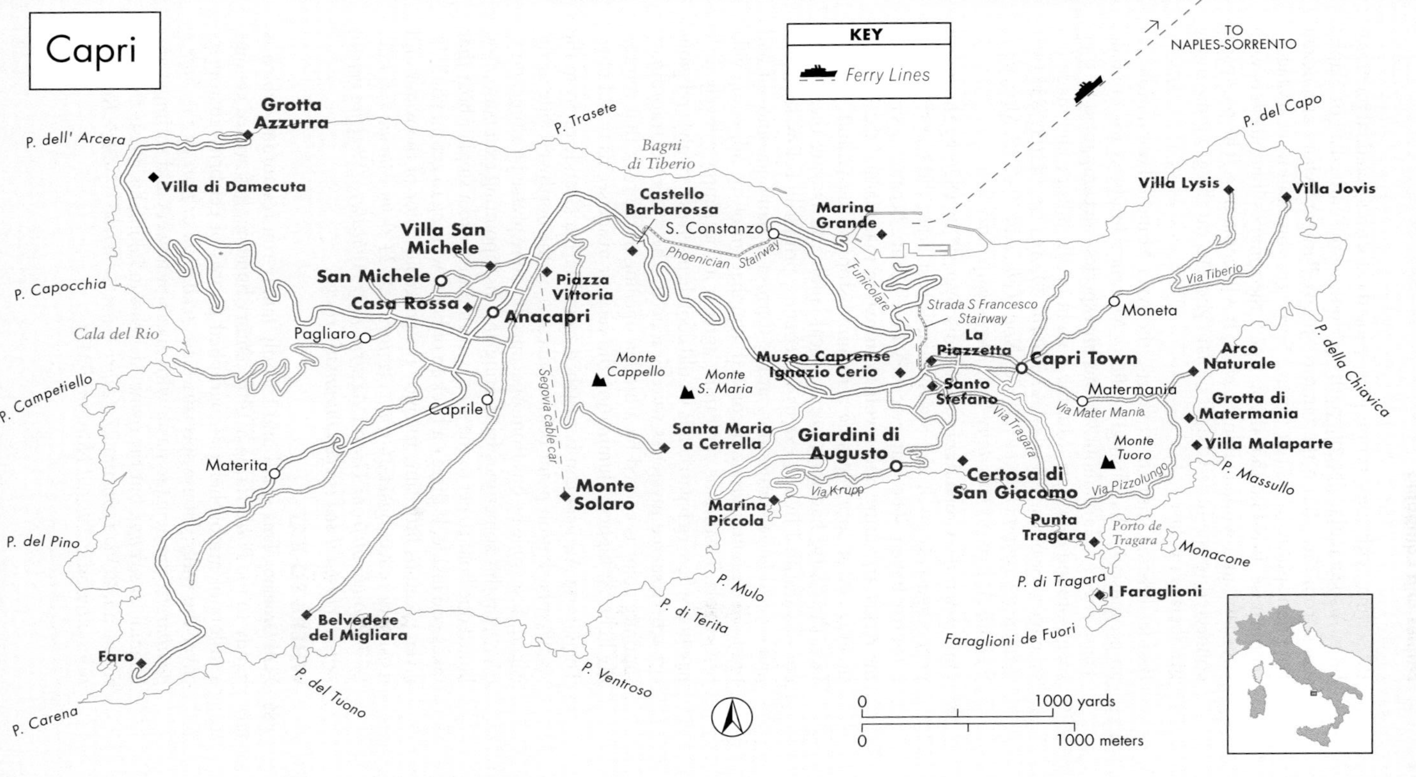
Capri
KEY
Ferry Lines
TO NAPLES-SORRENTO
Grotta Azzurra
P. dell' Arcera
Villa di Damecuta
P. Trasete
Bagni di Tiberio
Castello Barbarossa
S. Constanzo
Phoenician Stairway
Marina Grande
Funicolare
Villa San Michele
San Michele
Casa Rossa
Anacapri
Piazza Vittoria
P. Capocchia
Cala del Rio
Pagliaro
P. Campetiello
Caprile
Materita
Segovia cable car
Monte Cappello
Monte S. Maria
Monte Solaro
Santa Maria a Cetrella
Museo Caprense Ignazio Cerio
Strada S Francesco Stairway
La Piazzetta
Santo Stefano
Capri Town
Moneta
Via Tiberio
Villa Lysis
Villa Jovis
P. del Capo
P. della Chiavica
Arco Naturale
Matermania
Via Mater Mania
Grotta di Matermania
Villa Malaparte
Monte Tuoro
Via Tragara
Via Pizzolungo
P. Massullo
Giardini di Augusto
Via Krupp
Certosa di San Giacomo
Marina Piccola
Punta Tragara
Porto de Tragara
Monacone
P. di Tragara
I Faraglioni
Faraglioni de Fuori
P. del Pino
P. Mulo
P. di Terita
Belvedere del Migliara
Faro
P. Carena
P. del Tuono
P. Ventroso
0
1000 yards
0
1000 meters

the setting, with some rooms preserving the doctor's personal memorabilia. A spectacular pergola path overlooking the entire Bay of Naples leads from the villa to the famous Sphinx Parapet, where an ancient Egyptian sphinx looks out toward Sorrento; you cannot see its face—on purpose. It is said that if you touch the sphinx's hindquarters with your left hand while making a wish, it will come true. The parapet is connected to the little Chapel of San Michele, on the grounds of one of Tiberius's villas.

Besides hosting summer concerts, the Axel Munthe Foundation has an ecomuseum that fittingly reflects Munthe's fondness for animals. There you can learn about various bird species—accompanied by their songs—found on Capri. Munthe bought up the hillside and made it a sanctuary for birds. ✉ *Viale Axel Munthe 34, Anacapri* ☎ *081/8371401* 🌐 *www.villasanmichele.eu* 🎫 *€6* ⏲ *Nov.–Feb., daily 9–3:30; Mar., daily 9–4:30; Apr. and Oct., daily 9–5; May–Sept., daily 9–6.*

★ Only when the **Grotta Azzurra** was "discovered" in 1826 by the Polish poet August Kopisch and Swiss artist Ernest Fries, did Capri become a tourist haven. The watery cave's blue beauty became a symbol of the return to nature and revolt from reason that marked the Romantic era, and it soon became a required stop on the Grand Tour. In fact, the grotto had long been a local landmark. During the Roman era—as testified by the extensive remains, primarily below sea level, and several large statues now at the Certosa di San Giacomo—it had been the elegant, mosaic-decorated nymphaeum of the adjoining villa of Gradola. Historians can't quite agree if it was simply a lovely little pavilion where rich patricians would cool themselves or truly a religious site where sacred mysteries were practiced. The water's extraordinary sapphire color is caused by a hidden opening in the rock that refracts the light. At highest illumination the very air inside seems tinted blue.

The Grotta Azzurra can be reached from Marina Grande or from the small embarkation point below Anacapri on the northwest side of the island, accessible by bus from Anacapri. If you're pressed for time, however, skip this sometimes frustrating and disappointing excursion. You board one boat to get to the grotto, then transfer to a smaller boat that takes you inside. If there's a backup of boats waiting to get in, you'll be given precious little time to enjoy the gorgeous color of the water and its silvery reflections. ✉ *Grotta Azzurra* 🎫 *€21 from Marina Grande, €7 by rowboat from Grotta Azzurra near Anacapri* ⏲ *9–1 hr before sunset, closed if sea is even minimally rough.*

WHERE TO EAT

$$ SOUTHERN ITALIAN

✕ **Al Grottino.** This small and friendly family-run restaurant, which is handy to the Piazzetta, in a 14th-century building, has arched ceilings and lots of atmosphere; autographed photos of celebrity customers cover the walls. House specialties are *scialatielli ai fiori di zucchine e gambaretti* (homemade pasta with zucchini flowers and shrimps) and linguine *ai scampi*, but the owner delights in taking his guests through the menu. ✉ *Via Longano 27, Capri Town* ☎ *081/8370584* ✍ *Reservations advised* ⏲ *Closed Nov.–mid-Mar.*

$$$$ SOUTHERN ITALIAN

✕ **Aurora.** Though often frequented by celebrities—photographs of famous guests adorn the walls inside and out—this restaurant offers courtesy and *simpatia* irrespective of your persona. Although the oldest restaurant on the island (it used to be set high on the hill), now in its third generation, its decor is sleekly minimalist. If you want to see and be seen, reserve a table outside on one of Capri's chicest thoroughfares; otherwise go for extra privacy and ambience within. The cognoscenti start by sharing a pizza all'Acqua, a thin pizza with mozzarella and a sprinkling of *peperoncino* (chili). If tiring of pasta, try the *sformatino alla Franco* (rice pie in prawn sauce) but leave room for the homemade sweets. The place fills up quickly, so be sure to reserve. ✉ *Via Fuorlovado 18/22, Capri Town* ☎ *081/8370181* 🌐 *www.auroracapri.com* ✍ *Reservations essential* ⏲ *Closed Jan.–mid-Mar.*

$ PIZZA

✕ **Barbarossa.** This ristorante-pizzeria is the first you'll see if you arrive in Anacapri by bus. Its panoramic covered terrace takes in views of the Barbarossa castle on the hill as well as the sea. The no-frills ambience belies the quality of the *cucina*: besides *pizze* they specialize in local dishes—be sure to try the *risotto con gamberi a limone* (shrimp with lemon). Barbarossa is open all year. ✉ *Piazza Vittoria 1, Anacapri* ☎ *081/8371483.*

$$ SOUTHERN ITALIAN ★

✕ **Da Gelsomina.** Set amid its own terraced vineyards with inspiring views to the island of Ischia and beyond, this is much more than just a well-reputed restaurant. The owner's mother was a friend of Axel Munthe and encouraged her to open a kiosk serving hot food, which evolved into Da Gelsomina. It has an immaculately kept swimming pool, which is open to the public for a small fee—a buffet is served as you lounge here. Located close to one of the island's finer walks as well as the Philosophy Park, it's an excellent base for a whole day or longer. There's also a five-room pensione, with free transfer service by request from Anacapri center. ✉ *Via Migliara 72, Anacapri* ☎ *081/8371499* 🌐 *www.dagelsomina.com* ⏲ *Closed Jan.–mid-Feb. and Tues. in winter. No dinner in winter.*

$$$ SOUTHERN ITALIAN ★

✕ **La Canzone del Mare.** Although it's not primarily a restaurant, luncheon in the covered pavilion of this legendary bathing lido of the Marina Piccola is Capri at its most picture-perfect. With two seawater pools as well as rocky beach, and I Faraglioni in the distance, this was the erstwhile haunt of Gracie Fields, Emilio Pucci, Noël Coward, and any number of 1950s and '60s glitterati. The VIPs may have departed for more private beaches, but this setting is as magical as ever. You need to pay a fee (€20) to actually use this bathing *stabilimento* (club) but why not make a day of it? There are also five suites available if a day is not enough. Boats also depart from here for Da Luigi, the lido/restaurant at the base of I Fariglioni. ✉ *Via Marina Piccola 93, Capri Town* ☎ *081/8370104* 🌐 *www.lacanzonedelmare.com* ⏲ *Closed Oct.–Mar. No dinner.*

$$$ SOUTHERN ITALIAN ★

✕ **La Capannina.** For decades one of Capri's most celebrity-haunted restaurants, La Capannina is a few steps from the busy social hub of the Piazzetta. The walls are covered with photos of celebrities enjoying their meal here, and the discreet covered veranda, with its hanging baskets, is ideal for dining by candlelight in a florid garden setting, all pink, green, and white. Another alternative to avoid the stuffy indoor rooms is to join the regulars in the outdoor courtyard. The specialties, aside from an authentic Capri wine with the house label, are homemade *ravioli capresi* and *linguine con lo scorfano* (flat spaghetti with scorpion fish), the squid stuffed with caciotta cheese and marjoram, and the "Pezzogna," an exquisite sea bream cooked whole in a copper casserole and garnished with a layer of baked potatoes. The small bar across the side alleyway is run by the same owners. ✉ *Via Le Botteghe 12b, Capri Town* ☎ *081/8370732* 🌐 *www.capannina-capri.com* *Reservations essential* ⏲ *Closed Nov.–mid-Mar. and Wed. in Mar. and Oct.*

$$ SOUTHERN ITALIAN ★ ✕ **La Fontelina.** Lying just below Punta Tragara at the base of Capri's impressive offshore rocks (the Faraglioni), this is the place to enjoy a delightfully comatose day on the island. Given its position right on the water's edge, seafood is almost de rigueur. For a slightly different starter, try the *polpette di melanzane* (eggplant fritters), and then dip into the vegetable buffet. Highly recommendable is the house sangria, a blissful mix of white wine and fresh fruit. La Fontelina also functions as a lido, with steps and ladders affording access to fathoms-deep blue water. Access is by boat from Marina Piccola or on foot from Punta Tragara (10 minutes). Only lunch is served. Across the way is the archrival lido-restaurant, Da Luigi, with a more evocative setting but now a bit too famous for its own good. ✉ *I Faraglioni, at end of Via Tragara, Capri Town* ☎ *081/8370845* ⏲ *Closed mid-Oct.–Easter. No dinner.*

$$$ SOUTHERN ITALIAN ★ ✕ **Le Grottelle.** Enjoying one of Capri's most distinctive settings, this extremely informal trattoria is built up against the limestone rocks not far from the Arco Naturale—a cave at the back doubles as the kitchen and wine cellar. Whether you stumble over this place or make it your destination after an island hike, Le Grottelle will prove memorable, thanks to that ambience and sea view taking in the Amalfi Coast's Li Galli islands. The food? Oh, that . . . the menu includes ravioli and local rabbit, but go for the seafood, with *linguine con gamberetti e rucola* (pasta with shrimp and arugula) one of the more interesting specialties. ✉ *Via Arco Naturale 13* ☎ *081/8375719* *Reservations essential* ⏲ *Closed Nov.–mid-Mar.*

WHERE TO STAY

$$ **Biancamaria.** This tastefully refurbished hotel with its pleasing facade and whitewashed spreading arches lies in a traffic-free zone close to the heart of Anacapri. **Pros:** friendly staff; Anacapri literally at your doorstep. **Cons:** on the main pedestrian road; no gardens. **TripAdvisor:** "in the center of Anacapri," "extremely comfortable," "nice place and price." ✉ *Via G. Orlandi 54, Anacapri* ☎ *081/8371000* 🌐 *www.hotelbiancamaria.com* *25 rooms* *In-room: a/c, refrigerator. In-hotel: bar, pool* ⏲ *Closed mid-Oct.–Mar.* *Breakfast.*

$$$$ Fodor's Choice ★ **J. K. Place.** The most supremely stylish hotel in southern Italy, this luxurious Xanadu has almost made every other accommodation on Capri seem dowdy and dull since it opened in 2007. **Pros:** gorgeous decor; exquisite pool; very close to chic Tiberio beach; free shuttle to town. **Cons:** only for high rollers; many guests clear out for Capri nightspots. **TripAdvisor:** "out of your dreams," "style meets sophistication," "idyllic, luxurious, and romantic." ✉ *Via Provinciale Marina Grande 225, Marina Grande* ☎ *081/8384001* 🌐 *www.jkcapri.com* *22 rooms*

In-room: a/c, safe, refrigerator, Wi-Fi. In-hotel: pool, gym, spa, Wi-Fi hotspot ⏲ *Closed mid-Oct.–mid-Apr.*

$$ ★ **La Tosca.** Although it's hard to find in the warren of side streets in Capri Town, La Tosca is worth all the trouble. **Pros:** in the heart of things; pleasant owner. **Cons:** skimpy facilities; not all rooms have good views. **TripAdvisor:** "light-filled and beautiful," "modern and stylish," "excellent value and service." ✉ *Via Birago 5, Capri Town* ☎ *081/8370989* 🌐 *www.latoscahotel.com* *10* rooms *In-room: Wi-Fi* ⏲ *Closed Nov.–Feb.*

13

$$$$ Fodor's Choice ★ **Punta Tragara.** The most beautiful hotel on Capri, this has a hold-your-breath perch directly over the famed rocks of I Faraglioni. **Pros:** a taste of the good life; the view of I Faraglioni. **Cons:** a 10-minute walk from the center; some find the decor dated but others find that a plus. **TripAdvisor:** "truly spectacular views," "pool and sun area was great," "incredibly glamorous." ✉ *Via Tragara 57, Capri Town* ☎ *081/8370844* 🌐 *www.hoteltragara.com* *44 rooms* *In-room: a/c, safe, refrigerator. In-hotel: restaurant, bar, pools, Internet terminal, Wi-Fi hotspot* ⏲ *Closed mid-Oct.–mid-Apr.* *Breakfast.*

$$$$ ★ **Quisisana.** Some people say there are really three villages on Capri: Capri Town, Anacapri, and this celebrated landmark, which looms large in the island's mythology. **Pros:** luxe atmosphere on a large scale. **Cons:** the food isn't all star quality (steer clear of the pizza); convention-size and far from cozy. **TripAdvisor:** "truly was magnificent," "how the rich and famous travel," "comes with an attitude." ✉ *Via Camerelle 2, Capri Town* ☎ *081/8370788* 🌐 *www.quisisana.com* *148 rooms* *In-room: a/c, safe, refrigerator, Wi-Fi. In-hotel: restaurant, bar, tennis court, pools, gym, Internet terminal, Wi-Fi hotspot* ⏲ *Closed Nov.–mid-Mar.* *Breakfast.*

$$ **Villa Krupp.** Occupying a beautiful house overlooking the idyllic Gardens of Augustus, this historic hostelry was once the home of Maxim Gorky, whose guests included Lenin. **Pros:** direct access to the Gardens of Augustus. **Cons:** a lot of steps to be negotiated; rooms are simple. **TripAdvisor:** "fabulous view from the terrace," "amazing tiled floors," "pretty terraced gardens." ✉ *Viale Matteotti 12, Capri Town* ☎ *081/8370362* 🌐 *www.villakrupp.it* *12 rooms* *In-room: no TV. In-hotel: restaurant, bar, tennis court, pools, gym, Wi-Fi hotspot* ⏲ *Closed Nov.–Mar.* *Breakfast.*

$$$ Fodor's Choice ★ **Villa Sarah.** Few hotels offer such a quintessentially Caprese spirit as this villa jewel. **Pros:** gorgeous pool; wonderful gardens. **Cons:** a steep and long climb back from the Piazzetta; no elevator. **TripAdvisor:** "pure Italian hospitality," "away from the thick crowds," "staff are a pleasure." ✉ *Via Tiberio 3/a, Capri Town* ☎ *081/8377817* 🌐 *www.villasarah.it* *19 rooms* *In-room: a/c, refrigerator. In-hotel: hotel: bar, pool* ⏲ *Closed Nov.–Mar.* *Breakfast.*

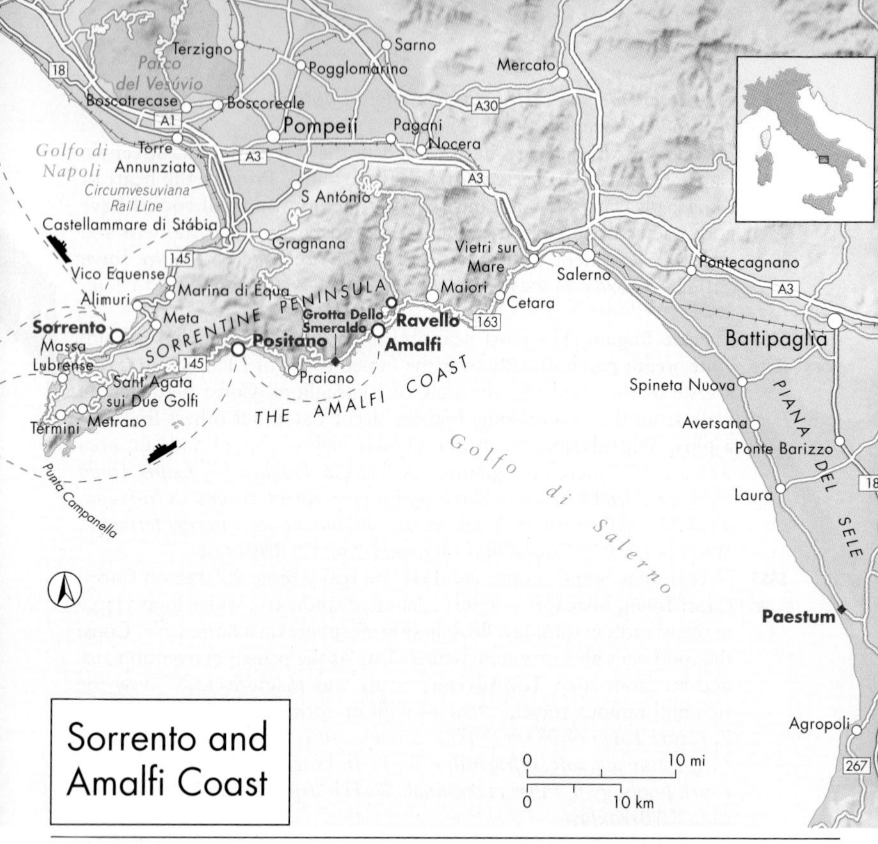

SORRENTO AND THE AMALFI COAST

As you journey down the fabled Amalfi Coast, your route takes you past rocky cliffs plunging into the sea and small boats lying in sandy coves like brightly colored fish. Erosion has contorted the rocks into shapes resembling figures from mythology and hollowed out fairy grottoes, where the air is turquoise and the water an icy blue. In winter, Nativity scenes of moss and stone are created in the rocks. White villages dripping with flowers nestle in coves or climb like vines up the steep, terraced hills. Lemon trees abound, loaded with blossoms (and netting in winter to protect the fruit—locals joke that they look after their lemons better than their children). The road must have a thousand turns, each with a different view, on its dizzying 69-km (43-mi) journey from Sorrento to Salerno.

SORRENTO

50 km (31 mi) south of Naples, 50 km (31 mi) west of Salerno.

GETTING HERE

From downtown Naples, take a Circumvesuviana train from Stazione Centrale (Piazza Garibaldi), SITA bus from in front of the station, or hydrofoil from Molo Beverello. If you're coming directly from the airport in Naples, pick up a direct bus to Sorrento. By car, take the A3

Naples–Salerno highway, exiting at Castellammare, and then following signs for Penisola Sorrentina, then for Sorrento.

VISITOR INFORMATION

In Sorrento the office of the **Azienda Autonoma di Soggiorno Sorrento-Sant'Agnello** (✉ *Via L. De Maio 35, Sorrento* ☎ *081/8074033* 🌐 *www.sorrentotourism.com*) is open weekdays 8:30–4:15. Besides dispensing a wealth of information, they also have a useful booking service for hotels, B&Bs, and holiday flats throughout the peninsula.

EXPLORING

Sorrento is across the Bay of Naples from Naples itself, on the SS145 road accessed from autostrada A3. The Circumvesuviana railway, which stops at Herculaneum and Pompeii, provides another connection. The coast between Naples and Castellammare, where road and railway turn onto the Sorrento Peninsula, seems at times depressingly overbuilt and industrialized. Yet Vesuvius looms to the left, you can make out the 3,000-foot-high mass of Monte Faito ahead, and on a clear day you can see Capri off the tip of the peninsula. The scenery improves considerably as you near Sorrento, where the coastal plain is carved into russet cliffs of compacted volcanic ash rising perpendicularly from the sea. This is the Sorrento (north) side of the peninsula; on the other side is the more dramatically scenic Amalfi Coast. But Sorrento has at least two advantages over Amalfi: the Circumvesuviana railway terminal and a fairly flat terrain. A stroll around town is a pleasure—you'll encounter narrow alleyways and interesting churches, and the views of the Bay of Naples from the Villa Comunale and the Museo Correale are priceless.

Until the mid-20th century Sorrento was a small, genteel resort favored by central European princes, English aristocrats, and American literati. Now the town has grown and spread out along the crest of its famous cliffs, and apartments stand where citrus groves once bloomed. Like most resorts, Sorrento is best off-season, in spring, autumn, or even winter, when Campania's mild climate can make a stay pleasant anywhere along the coast.

A highlight of Sorrento is **Museo Correale di Terranova,** an 18th-century villa with a lovely garden on land given to the patrician Correale family by Queen Joan of Aragon in 1428. It has an eclectic private collection amassed by the count of Terranova and his brother. The building itself is fairly charmless, with few period rooms, but the garden offers an allée of palm trees, citrus groves, floral nurseries, and an esplanade with a panoramic view of the Sorrento coast. The collection itself is one of the finest devoted to Neapolitan paintings, decorative arts, and porcelains, so for connoisseurs of the *seicento* (Italian 17th century), this museum is a must. Magnificent 18th-century inlaid tables by Giuseppe Gargiulo, Capodimonte porcelains, and rococo portrait miniatures are reminders of the age when pleasure and delight were all. Also on view are regional Greek and Roman archaeological finds, medieval marble work, glasswork, old-master paintings, 17th-century majolicas—even the poet Tasso's death mask. ✉ *Via Correale 50* ☎ *081/8781846* 🌐 *www.museocorreale.it* 🎫 €6 ⏲ *Wed.–Mon. 9:30–1:30.*

The largest public park in Sorrento, the **Villa Comunale** sits on a cliff top overlooking the entire Bay of Naples and offers benches, flowers, palms, and people-watching, plus a seamless vista that stretches from Capri to Vesuvius. From here steps lead down to Sorrento's main harbor, the Marina Piccola. ✉ *Adjoining church of San Francesco.*

Near the Villa Comunale gardens and sharing its vista over the Bay of Naples, **Convento di San Francesco** is celebrated for its 14th-century cloister. Filled with greenery and flowers, the Moorish-style cloister has interlaced pointed arches of tufa rock, alternating with octagonal columns topped by elegant capitals, supporting smaller arches, and makes a suitably evocative setting for summer concerts and theatrical presentations—make this a must if you can catch an event. The church portal is particularly impressive, with the original 16th-century door featuring intarsia (inlaid) work. The interior's 17th-century decoration includes an altarpiece depicting St. Francis receiving the stigmata, by a student of Francesco Solimena. The convent is now an art school, where students' works are often exhibited. ✉ *Piazza S. Francesco* ☎ *081/8781269* *Free* ⏲ *Daily 8–8.*

Enchanting showpiece of the Largo Dominova—the little square that is the heart of Sorrento's historic quarter—the **Sedile Dominova** is a picturesque open loggia with expansive arches, balustrades, and a green-and-yellow-tile cupola, originally constructed in the 16th century. The open-air structure is frescoed with 18th-century trompe-l'oeil columns and the family coats of arms, which once belonged to the *sedile* (seat), the town council where nobles met to discuss civic problems as early as the Angevin period. Today Sorrentines still like to congregate around the umbrella-topped tables near the tiny square. ✉ *Largo Dominova, at Via S. Cesareo and Via P.R. Giuliani.*

Via Marina Grande turns into a pedestrian lane, then a stairway leading to Sorrento's only real beach at **Marina Grande**, where fishermen pull up their boats and there are some good seafood restaurants. A frequent bus also plies this route; tickets are sold at the *tabacchi* (tobacconist).

WHERE TO EAT

$$ SOUTHERN ITALIAN Fodor's Choice ★

✕ **Antico Francischiello da Peppino.** Overlooking rows of olive trees that seem to run into the sea, this eatery is away from the throng, halfway between Sorrento and Massa Lubrense. Two huge, beamed dining rooms with brick archways, old chandeliers, antique mirrored sideboards, hundreds of mounted plates, and tangerine tablecloths make for quite a sight. Specialties at this fourth-generation establishment include ravioli filled with sea bass and baked bream in a potato crust with lemon. The towering dessert trolley is full of goodies, and you can taste as many as you like. ✉ *Via Partenope 27, halfway between Sant'Agata and Massa Lubrense* ☎ *081/5339780* 🌐 *www.francischiello.com* ⏲ *Closed Wed. Nov.–Mar.*

$$$$ SOUTHERN ITALIAN ★

✕ **Don Alfonso 1890.** The most heralded restaurant in Campania is the domain of Alfonso Iaccarino; *haute*-hungry pilgrims come here to feast on culinary rarities, often centuries-old recipes given a unique spin. The braciola of lamb with pine nuts and raisins is a recipe that dates to the Renaissance, and the cannoli stuffed with foie gras pays homage to the Neapolitan Bourbon court. Nearly everything is homegrown, and the wine cellar is one of the finest in Europe. Those who want to make a night of it can stay in one of five apartments above the restaurant. ✉ *Corso Sant'Agata 13* ☎ *081/8780026* 🌐 *www.donalfonso.com* ⏲ *June–Sept., no lunch and closed Mon.; Apr., May, and Oct. closed Mon. and Tues.; closed Nov.–Mar.*

$ SOUTHERN ITALIAN ✕ **La Basilica.** Opened by the same owner as the **Ristorante Museo Caruso**, this is a budget alternative to its famous brother. No cover, no service charge, but the same extensive wine list (about 1,700 different labels) plus a bountiful choice of hearty Italian dishes. In a tiny alley between piazzas Tasso and St. Antonino, its main salon is decorated with modern paintings of an erupting Vesuvius. You can watch the *pizzaiolo* baking pizza or bread for you in the wood oven, but if you want a romantic dinner, choose the smaller room on the opposite side of the road. Here—vertigo permitting!—you can dine on a tiny balcony overlooking the tortuous road leading to the harbor. There is also outside seating for the less adventurous. Choose the *strozzapreti* (priest-chokers) pasta with scampi and cherry tomatoes or go for the fabulous rice cake on zucchini sauce. ✉ *Via S. Antonino 28* ☎ *081/8774790* 🌐 *www.ristorantelabasilica.com.*

13

$$ SOUTHERN ITALIAN Fodor's Choice ★ ✕ **La Favorita–'O Parrucchiano.** This restaurant is in a sprawling, multilevel, high-ceiling greenhouse and orchard, with tables and chairs amid enough tropical greenery to fill a Victorian conservatory—the effect is enchantingly 19th century. Opened in 1868 by an ex-priest ('o Parrucchiano means "the priest's place" in the local dialect), La Favorita continues to serve classic Sorrentine cuisine. The shrimp baked in lemon leaves, cannelloni, homemade Sorrentine pasta, chocolate and hazelnut cake, and lemon profiteroles are all excellent, but they can't compete with the unique decor. ✉ *Corso Italia 71* ☎ *081/8781321* 🌐 *www.parrucchiano.it* ⏲ *Closed Wed. only mid-Nov.–mid-Mar.*

$$$ SOUTHERN ITALIAN Fodor's Choice ★ ✕ **Ristorante Museo Caruso.** A classic international and operatic theme is carried out from *preludio* appetizers, such as shrimp in a limoncello dressing, to the *rapsodia delicatesse* desserts, including crêpes suzette. Sorrentine favorites are tweaked creatively as well, including ravioli with broccoli sauce and squid with almonds. The staff is warm and helpful, the singer on the sound system is the long-departed "fourth tenor" himself, and the operatic memorabilia with posters and old photos of Caruso is viewed in a flattering blush-pink light. This elegant restaurant deserves its longtime popularity. It is open from noon to midnight to cater for hunger pangs at any time of day. There are five-course tasting menus from €50. ✉ *Via S. Antonino 12* ☎ *081/8073156* 🌐 *www.ristorantemuseocaruso.com.*

WHERE TO STAY

$$$$ Fodor's Choice ★ **Bellevue Syrene.** In the late 19th century, Empress Eugénie of France came here for a week and wound up staying three months. **Pros:** spectacular views; impeccable design elements; elegantly furnished common areas; half board available. **Cons:** very expensive (parking alone costs €25 a day). **TripAdvisor:** "lived up to the hype," "puts you in the holiday mood," "beautiful and romantic." ✉ *Piazza della Vittoria 5* ☎ *081/8781024* 🌐 *www.bellevue.it* *49 rooms* *In-room: a/c, safe, refrigerator, Internet, Wi-Fi. In-hotel: 4 restaurants, bar, gym, beachfront, Internet terminal, Wi-Fi hotspot, some pets allowed* ⏲ *Closed Jan.–Mar.* *Breakfast.*

$$$$ Fodor's Choice ★ **Excelsior Vittoria.** Overlooking the Bay of Naples, this Belle Epoque dream offers gilded salons worthy of a Proust heroine; gardens and orange groves; and an impossibly romantic terrace where musicians sometimes lull guests with equal doses of Cole Porter and Puccini. **Pros:** unbeatable location in the center of town; gardens buffer city noise. **Cons:** not all rooms have sea views; some rooms are on the small side; front desk can be cold. **TripAdvisor:** "Victorian-era treasure," "pool area is calm and relaxing," "away from the hustle." ✉ *Piazza Tasso 34* ☎ *081/8071044, 800/980053 in Italy only* 🌐 *www.exvitt.it* *98 rooms* *In-room: a/c, safe, refrigerator, Wi-Fi. In-hotel: 2 restaurants, bars, pool, gym, spa, Internet terminal, Wi-Fi hotspot, parking (free), some pets allowed* *Breakfast.*

$$$–$$$$ ★ **La Favorita.** Sorrento is home to some of the most gorgeous and sumptuous hotels in Italy, but they all now have to make room for this newborn, a striking beauty that can hold its own against some great hotel names. **Pros:** central location; beautiful terrace; idyllic garden. **Cons:** no views from the guest rooms. **TripAdvisor:** "place was gorgeous," "real hidden gem," "rooms are simply fantastic." ✉ *Via T. Tasso 61* ☎ *081/8782031* 🌐 *www.hotellafavorita.com* *85 rooms* *In-room: safe, Wi-Fi. In-hotel: restaurant, 2 bars, pool, parking, some pets allowed* *Closed Nov. and Jan.–Mar.* *Breakfast.*

¢–$ **Relais Palazzo Starace.** There may be no elevator, no lobby, and no view, but this place does boast a gentle price tag in a central part of town, and that's a winning combo for sizzling, summertime Sorrento. **Pros:** great location; competitive prices; discounted parking at nearby garage. **Cons:** no elevator; no views; room with the air conditioner on balcony is noisy. **TripAdvisor:** "very close to everything," "lots of steps," "skimpiest breakfast." ✉ *Via Santa Maria della Pietà 9* ☎ *081/8784031* 🌐 *www.palazzostarace.com* *5 rooms* *In-room: a/c, safe, refrigerator* *Closed Jan. and Feb.*

POSITANO

★ *14 km (9 mi) east of Sorrento, 57 km (34 mi) south of Naples.*

GETTING HERE

Local buses leave from the Circumvesuviana train station in Sorrento. In summer, buses also run from Rome and Naples. From June to September your best option is the ferry from Sorrento, Salerno, or Naples.

VISITOR INFORMATION

In Positano the **Azienda Autonoma Soggiorno e Turismo** (✉ *Via del Saracino 4, Positano* ☎ *089/875067* 🌐 *www.aziendaturismopositano.it*) is open weekdays 8:30–2:30, and June to September it remains open until 8 pm, as well as Sunday mornings.

EXPLORING

When John Steinbeck lived here in 1953, he wrote that it was difficult to consider tourism an industry because "there are not enough *tourists.*" It's safe to say that Positano, a village of white Moorish-style houses clinging to slopes around a small sheltered bay, has since been discovered. Another Steinbeck observation still applies, however: "Positano bites deep. It is a dream place that isn't quite real when you are there and becomes beckoningly real after you have gone. . . . The small curving bay of unbelievably blue and green water laps gently on a beach of small pebbles. There is only one narrow street, and it does not come down to the water. Everything else is stairs, some of them as steep as ladders. You do not walk to visit a friend, you either climb or slide."

In the 10th century Positano was part of Amalfi's maritime republic, which rivaled Venice as an important mercantile power. Its heyday was in the 16th and 17th centuries, when its ships traded in the Near and Middle East carrying spices, silks, and precious woods. The coming of the steamship in the mid-19th century led to the town's decline; some three-fourths of its 8,000 citizens emigrated to America.

What had been reduced to a forgotten fishing village is now the number-one attraction on the coast. From here you can take hydrofoils to Capri in summer, escorted bus rides to Ravello, and tours of the Grotta dello Smeraldo. If you're staying in Positano, check whether your hotel has a parking area. If not, you will have to pay for space in a parking lot, which is almost impossible to find during the high season, from Easter to September. The best bet for day-trippers is to arrive by bus—there is a regular, if crowded, service from Sorrento—or else get to Positano early enough to find an overpriced parking space.

No matter how much time you spend in Positano, make sure you have some comfortable walking shoes (no heels) and that your back and legs are strong enough to negotiate those daunting *scalinatelle* (little stairways). Alternatively, you can ride the municipal bus, which frequently plies along the one-and-only-one-way Via Pasitea, a hairpin road running from Positano's central Piazza dei Mulini to the mountains and back, making a loop through the town every half hour. Heading down from the Sponda bus stop toward the beach, you pass Le Sirenuse, the hotel where John Steinbeck stayed in 1953. Its stepped terraces offer vistas over the town, so you might splurge on lunch or a drink here on the pool terrace, a favorite gathering place for Modigliani-sleek jet-setters.

QUICK BITES

If you want to catch your breath after a bus ride to Positano, take a quick time-out for an espresso, a slice of *Positanese* (a chocolate cake as delectable as its namesake), or a fresh-fruit iced granita; check out Bar-Pasticceria La Zagara (✉ *Via dei Mulini 8* ☎ *089/875964*). Deservedly famous for its lemon profiteroles as much as for its tree-lined terrace, suspended on a wooden platform above the Lower Town, Zagara is ideal for morning coffee, predinner aperitivo, or postdinner digestivo.

Past a bevy of resort boutiques, head to Via dei Mulini 23 to view the prettiest garden in Positano—the 18th-century courtyard of the **Palazzo Murat,** named for Joachim Murat, who sensibly chose the palazzo as his summer residence. This was where Murat, designated by his brother-in-law Napoléon as King of Naples in 1808, came to forget the demands of power and lead the simple life. Since Murat was one of Europe's leading style setters, it couldn't be *too* simple; he built this grand abode (now a hotel) just steps from the main beach. ✉ *Via dei Mulini 23* ☎ *089/875177* 🌐 *www.palazzomurat.it.*

Beyond the Palazzo Murat is the Chiesa Madre, or parish church of **Santa Maria Assunta,** its green-and-yellow majolica dome topped by a perky cupola visible from just about anywhere in town. Built on the site of the former Benedictine abbey of Saint Vito, the 13th-century Romanesque structure was almost completely rebuilt in 1700. The last piece of the ancient mosaic floor can be seen under glass behind the altar. Note the carved wooden Christ, a masterpiece of devotional religious art, with its bathetic face and bloodied knees, on view before the altar. At the altar is a Byzantine 13th-century painting on wood of Madonna with Child, known popularly as the Black Virgin, carried to the beach every August 15 to celebrate the Feast of the Assumption. Legend claims that the painting was once stolen by Saracen pirates, who, fleeing in a raging storm, heard from a voice on high saying, "*Posa, posa*"—"Put it down, put it down." When they placed the image on the beach near the church, the storm calmed, as did the Saracens. Embedded over the doorway of the church's bell tower, set across the tiny piazza, is a medieval bas-relief of fishes, a fox, and a pistrice, the mythical half-dragon, half-dog sea monster. This is one of the few relics of the medieval abbey of Saint Vito. The Oratorio houses historic statues from the Sacristy, while renovations to the Crypt have unearthed ancient (1st century) Roman columns. ✉ *Piazza Flavio Gioia* ☎ *089/875480* 🌐 *www.chiesapositano.com* 🎟 *€2, Crypt* ⏲ *Church daily 8–noon, 4–9, Crypt daily 9:30–1, 4:30–8.*

The walkway from the Piazza Flavio Gioia leads down to the **Spiaggia Grande,** or main beach, bordered by an esplanade and some of Positano's best—and priciest—restaurants. Head over to the stone pier to the far right of the beach as you face the water.

A staircase leads to the **Via Positanesi d'America,** a lovely seaside walkway. Halfway up the path you can find the Torre Trasìta, the most distinctive of Positano's three coastline defense towers, which, in various states of repair, define the edges of Positano. The Trasìta—now a residence available for summer rental—was one of the defense towers used to warn of pirate raids. Continuing along the Via Positanesi d'America you pass tiny inlets and emerald coves until the large beach, Spiaggia di Fornillo, comes into view.

WHERE TO EAT

$ SOUTHERN ITALIAN

✕ **Da Adolfo.** Several coves away from the Spiaggia Grande, on a little beach where pirates used to build and launch their boats, this laid-back trattoria has been a favorite Positano landmark for more than 40 years. The pirates are long gone, but their descendants now ferry you free to the private cove, round-trip from Positano (look for the boat with the red fish on the mast named for the restaurant— it leaves every half hour in the morning; you can also make a steep descent from the main coastal road off the hamlet of Laurito). Sit under a straw canopy on a wooden terrace to enjoy *totani con patate* (squid and potatoes with garlic and oil), then sip white wine with peaches until sundown. Some diners even swim here—so bathing suits are just fine. It gets busy here, so it may be best to ask your hotel to reserve, since personal reservations are often not honored. ✉ *Spiaggia di Laurito* ☎ *089/875022* 🌐 *www.daadolfo.com* ✍ *Reservations essential* ⏲ *Closed Oct.–Apr.*

CLOSE UP

Above It All: Montepertuso and Nocelle

Thousands of travelers head to Positano every summer for some escapist entertainment, but how do *you* escape *them*? The answer lies way up in the Lattari Mountains, where two adorable villages perch on rocky spurs 1,700 feet above Positano's coastline. It's hard to believe two such different settlements share the same air space as their jet-set neighbor while managing, for the most part, to escape the glare of discovery.

Take Positano's local bus 3 km (2 mi) to the village of **Montepertuso** (Pierced Mountain). This sky-high village is where Emperor Frederick II of Sicily bred and trained hawks; some feathery descendants—mainly kestrels and peregrine falcons—still nest on seemingly precarious ledges around the area.

The dramatic hole in the arched rock (*arco naturale*) below Monte Sant'Angelo a Tre Pizzi is one of only three in the world that both the sun's and the moon's rays can penetrate (April to July); the other two are in India. Try to see it in the morning, when the sun shines through.

Legend says the hole was created when the devil challenged the Madonna to a contest: whoever pierced the rock would own the village. In 10 attempts, the devil could only scratch the limestone, but when the Madonna touched the rock, it crumbled, the sky appeared, and she walked right through, sinking the devil into the hole. On July 2, a holy performance, games, and fireworks commemorate the Virgin's success.

Another popular village festival is the Sagra del Fagiolo, held in the first week of September, which celebrates the humble bean. The town is lined with numerous stalls full of beans and other fare, and waiters dress in traditional folkloric garb.

The Positano bus continues from Montepertuso to just above the "lost" mountainside village of **Nocelle**, but many skip the ride and choose to hike instead. Along a well-paved road, then a curving, tree-shaded pathway, you skirt bottomless crevasses, hike under towering cliffs, and climb stairways that are relatively easy going. Finally, Nocelle appears and, in two minutes, the hamlet fully reveals itself: a stone alley, a scattering of houses and stairways, a pint-size piazza, a church.

Oh, yes, and a "panaromantic" view—the kind that resets your inner clock. Sheep bleat, children giggle, birds call melodiously, and the rustling wind congratulates you on being far from the madding crowd.

13

$$ SOUTHERN ITALIAN ✕ **La Pergola.** Occupying a prime piece of real estate near dead center on the Spaggia Grande beach, this arbor-covered seating area offers a truly idyllic (though festive, due to the happy crowds) setting. Often confused with the equally good Buca di Bacco upstairs, until the 1970s it functioned as a dance club. Dining here is just as seductive, with seafood unsurprisingly being the main fare—be sure to try the *scialatielli ai frutti di mare* or sea bass in *acqua pazza*—while pizza is also served. The chicken breast with fries is another great way to carb up for an afternoon under the beach umbrella. Open until midnight, there's plenty of time to digest before trying their *dolci* (desserts) and ice cream made

in their own *pasticceria,* Il Vicoletto on Via Sariceno. ✉ *Via del Brigantino 35* ☎ *089/811461* 🌐 *www.bucapositano.it* ⏲ *Closed Jan. 7–Feb.*

$$ SOUTHERN ITALIAN ★ ✕ **La Tagliata.** If your enthusiasm for overpriced seafood dishes is waning, La Tagliata has the answer: great antipasti, homemade pastas with rich tomato sauce, and meats grilled before your eyes in the dining room. (Ask for a *piccola porzione* unless you are ravenous.) All this comes with endless views of the Amalfi Coast. The prices are reasonable, and include a jug of red wine. (Aficionados will do better choosing their own bottle, however.) Though it lies between Montepertuso and Nocelle, the restaurant will arrange a shuttle to pick you up from your hotel in Positano. ✉ *Via Tagliata 22* ☎ *089/875872* ✍ *Reservations essential* ⏲ *Closed weekdays, Dec.–Feb.*

$–$$ SOUTHERN ITALIAN Fodor's Choice ★ ✕ **Lo Guarracino.** Enjoy a setting to make you fall in love, or rekindle it (be careful who you sit with)—this partly arbor-covered, perched-on-a-cleft aerie is about the most idyllic place to enjoy your lemon pasta and glass of vino as you watch the yachts come and go. Set a few steps above Positano's prettiest seaside path, the terrace vista takes in the cliffs, the sea, Li Galli islands, Spiaggia Fornillo, and Torre Clavel. The supercharming backroom arbor, covered with thick, twining vines and set with little tables covered in cloths that match the tint of the bay, is the place to sit. Fine fish specialties are top delights on the menu. In fact, the day's catch is often cooked, with potatoes, in the wood-fired pizza oven (adorned with an icon of Saint Francesco di Paola, patron saint of bakers, renamed here Saint Pizza), giving it a distinct flavor. ✉ *Via Positanesi d'America 12* ☎ *089/875794* 🌐 *www.loguarracino.net* ⏲ *Closed Jan.–Mar.*

$$ SOUTHERN ITALIAN ★ ✕ **O' Capurale.** Even though *o' capurale* ("the corporal") himself no longer runs the place, his eponymous restaurant is still a great find in the crowded center of Positano. Positano is about easy-come elegance, and this dining spot sums it all up. Graced with a coved ceiling adorned with a colorful Fauvist-style fresco, the dining room is filled with happy, stylish diners, literally unwinding before your eyes, thanks to the delicious, serious food (veal cutlet in white wine, fresh pasta with mussels and pumpkin, or rockfish *all'acqua pazza* with a few tomatoes and garlic are favorites) and lovely setting. Alfresco diners walk downstairs to choose the tables on the backstreet with a charmingly framed view of the beach. ✉ *Via Saracino 7* ☎ *089/875374* 🌐 *www.ocapuralepositano.it* ⏲ *Closed Nov.–Feb.*

WHERE TO STAY

$$ Fodor's Choice ★ **La Fenice.** This tiny and unpretentious hotel on the outskirts of Positano beckons with bougainvillea-laden vistas, castaway cottages, and a turquoise seawater pool, all perched over a private beach (250 steps away), just across a cove from Franco Zeffirelli's famous villa (now a superluxury hotel). **Pros:** paradise; private beach. **Cons:** some rooms overlook noisy road; a 10-minute walk to town. **TripAdvisor:** "heaven in Positano," "the most breathtaking views," "treated us as family." ✉ *Via G. Marconi 4* ☎ *089/875513* 🌐 *www.lafenicepositano.com* *14 rooms* *In-room: no a/c, no TV. In-hotel: pool* 💳 *No credit cards* 🍽 *Breakfast.*

$$$$ ★ **Le Sirenuse.** As legendary as its namesake sirens, this exquisite, in-town 18th-century palazzo has long set the standard for superluxury in Italian hotels. **Pros:** unrivalled views; pure luxury; close to the bus

stop. **Cons:** a bit of a climb from the town center; the restaurant is astoundingly expensive. **TripAdvisor:** "views to die for," "charming and magical," "breakfast was a true feast." ✉ *Via Cristoforo Colombo 30* ☎ *089/875066* 🌐 *www.sirenuse.it* *63 rooms* *In-room: a/c, safe, Wi-Fi. In-hotel: 2 restaurants, bars, pool, spa, Internet terminal, Wi-Fi hotspot, parking (paid)* *Breakfast.*

$$$ ★ **Palazzo Murat.** With a perfect location in the heart of town above the beachside church of Santa Maria Assunta, and an even more perfect entrance through a bougainvillea-draped patio and garden, the Murat is one of Positano's winners. **Pros:** one-time home of a king; stunning surroundings. **Cons:** only five rooms with seaside views; a constant stream of curious day-trippers. **TripAdvisor:** "really number one," "oasis of calm and charm," "courtyard is truly magical." ✉ *Via dei Mulini 23* ☎ *089/875177* 🌐 *www.palazzomurat.it* *31 rooms* *In-room: a/c, safe, refrigerator. In-hotel: restaurant, bar, parking (paid)* *Closed Nov.–Mar.* *Breakfast.*

$$ ★ **Villa Flavio Gioia.** For longer stays this is the ideal option, with a super location overlooking Piazza Flavio Gioia and the town's landmark parish church, and a hop, skip, and a jump to the Spiaggia Grande. **Pros:** prime location; ideal for longer stays. **Cons:** short stays are discouraged; no pool. **TripAdvisor:** "very romantic location," "rooms are big and airy," "nearby beach is great." ✉ *Piazza Flavio Gioia 2* ☎ *089/875222* 🌐 *www.villaflaviogioia.it* *13 rooms* *In-room: a/c, safe, kitchen. In-hotel: parking (paid)* *Closed Feb.*

GROTTA DELLO SMERALDO

13 km (8 mi) east of Positano, 27 km (17 mi) east of Sorrento.

GETTING HERE

A peculiar green light that casts an eerie emerald glow over impressive formations of stalagmites and stalactites, many of them under water, inspired the name of the Grotta dello Smeraldo (Emerald Grotto). You can park at the signposts for the grotto along the coast road and take an elevator down, or you can drive to Amalfi and take a return trip to the grotto by more romantic means—via boat (€10 return from Amalfi, excluding entrance to grotto). ✉ *Beyond Punta Acquafetente by boat, or off Amalfi Dr.* ☎ *089/871107 Amalfi tourist board* *€5* *Daily 9–4:30.*

AMALFI

17 km (11 mi) east of Positano, 35 km (22 mi) east of Sorrento.

GETTING HERE

From April to October the best way to get to Amalfi is by ferry from Salerno. From June to September you can also get here from Naples by fast craft. For the rest of the year, buses from Sorrento and Salerno are the only option.

VISITOR INFORMATION

Amalfi tourism office (✉ *Corso delle Repubbliche Marinare 27* ☎ *089/871107* 🌐 *www.amalfitouristoffice.it*).

EXPLORING

> **WORD OF MOUTH**
>
> "I love Amalfi so much, we stayed in a beautiful apartment there for two weeks. At night the town is just for the locals and the stay-overs, which makes it so pleasant. I think we tried almost all the restaurants in town, some of them hidden away in the covered alleys." —SeaUrchin

"The sun—the moon—the stars—and Amalfi," Amalfitans used to say. During the Middle Ages Amalfi was an independent maritime state with a population of 50,000. The republic also brought the art of papermaking to Europe from Arabia. Before World War II there were 13 mills making paper by hand in the Valle Molini, but now only two remain. The town is romantically situated at the mouth of a deep gorge and has some good hotels and restaurants. It's also a convenient base for excursions to Capri, Positano, and the Grotta dello Smeraldo. The parking problem here is as bad as that in Positano. The small lot in the center of town fills quickly; if you're willing to pay the steep prices, make a lunch reservation at one of the hotel restaurants and have your car parked for you.

★ Amalfi's main historic sight is its **Duomo di Sant' Andrea**, which shows an interesting mix of Moorish and early Gothic influences. You're channeled first into the adjoining **Chiostro del Paradiso** (Paradise Cloister), built around 1266 as a burial ground for Amalfi's elite and one of the architectural treasures of southern Italy. Its flower-and-palm-filled quadrangle has a series of exceptionally delicate intertwining arches on slender double columns in a combination of Byzantine and Arabian styles. Next stop is the 9th-century basilica, a museum housing sarcophagi, sculpture, Neapolitan gold artifacts, and other treasures from the cathedral complex.

Steps from the basilica lead down into the **Cripta di Sant'Andrea** (Crypt of Saint Andrew). The cathedral above was built in the 13th century to house the saint's bones, which came from Constantinople and supposedly exuded a miraculous liquid believers call the "manna of Saint Andrew." Following the one-way traffic up to the cathedral itself, you finally get to admire the elaborate polychrome marbles and painted, coffered ceilings from its 18th-century restoration; art historians shake their heads over this renovation, as the original decoration of the apse must have been one of the wonders of the Middle Ages. ✉ *Piazza Duomo* ☎ *089/871324* 🎫 *€3* ⏲ *Daily: Mar., Sept., 9:30–5:30; Apr.–June and Oct., 9–6:45; July and Aug., 9–7:45; Nov.–mid-Jan. 10–3:30, closed mid-Jan.–Feb. (daily services excepted).*

The **Valle dei Mulini** *(Valley of the Mills)*, uphill from town, was for centuries Amalfi's center for papermaking, an ancient trade learned from the Arabs (who learned it from the Chinese). Beginning in the 12th century, former flour mills in the town were converted to produce paper made from cotton and linen, being among the first in Europe to do so. In 1211 Frederick II of Sicily prohibited this lighter, more readable paper for use in the preparation of official documents, favoring traditional sheepskin parchment, but by 1811 more than a dozen mills here, with more along the coast, were humming. Natural waterpower ensured that the

CLOSE UP

Amalfi's Luscious Lemons

Lemons as big as oranges (and oranges as big as grapefruits) are cultivated on the seemingly endless net-covered pergolas of the Amalfi Coast. From linguine with lemon at trattorias to lemon soufflés at fancy restaurants, the yellow citrus is everywhere, and all parts are used, as can be seen from the delicious habit of baking raisins, figs, or pieces of cheese wrapped in lemon leaves, bound up with thin red thread.

Not only are lemons a main component of meals and drinks, but they are used as a remedy for everything from flu to bunions. But the most renowned end product is that local digestif known as limoncello, which captures in a bottle the color, fragrance, and taste of those tart-sweet lemons. Drink it cold in a tiny, frosty glass or after a shot of hot espresso—a golden memory quenched with each sip.

handmade paper was cost-effective, but catastrophic flooding in 1954 closed most of the mills for good, and many of them have now been converted into private housing. The **Museo della Carta** (Museum of Paper) opened in 1971 in a 15th-century mill; paper samples, tools of the trade, old machinery, and the audiovisual presentation are all enlightening. ✉ *Via delle Cartiere 23* ☎ *089/8304561* 🎫 *€4* 🌐 *www.museodellacarta.it* 🕓 *Mar.–Oct., daily 10–6:30; Nov.–Feb., Tues.–Sun. 10–3:30.*

WHERE TO EAT

$$ SOUTHERN ITALIAN ✕ **Al Teatro.** Once a children's theater, this informal white-stucco restaurant in the medieval quarter is 50 steps above the main drag and most charming. A house specialty is grilled squid and calamari with mint sauce, reflecting the position of the place—suspended between sea and mountains. Try also the *Scialatielli al Teatro*, with tomatoes and eggplant. The pizzas, from their wood oven, are terrific. ✉ *Via E. Marini 19* ☎ *089/872473* 🕓 *Closed Wed. and Jan.–mid-Feb.*

$$ SOUTHERN ITALIAN ✕ **Il Tari.** Locals highly recommend this little *ristorante* named after the ancient coin of the Amalfi Republic and a few minutes' walk north of the Duomo. This used to be a stable, and the space has changed little since those equine days, but appealing local art, blue-and-white check tablecloths, old photos, and tile floors make this cozy enough, not to mention the vast menu, where winners include the wood-oven-baked thin-crust pizza with fresh sauces, and the *scialatielli alla Saracena,* long spaghetti-style pasta seemingly laden with everything you can imagine from the sea. ✉ *Via P. Capuano 9–11* ☎ *089/871832* 🌐 *www.amalfiristorantetari.it* 🕓 *Closed Tues.*

$$$$ SOUTHERN ITALIAN Fodor's Choice ★ ✕ **La Caravella.** With tables adorned with lace tablecloths, *ciucciù* (donkey) ceramics, tall candles, and fresh floral bouquets, salons coved with frescoes and marble floors, it is little wonder this is considered the most romantic restaurant in Amalfi. Opened in 1959, it became the first restaurant in Southern Italy to earn a Michelin star (1966), and once drew the most gilded guest list in town, including such fans as Andy Warhol, Agnelli, and Federico Fellini. Now in its third generation, the menu maintains dishes favored fifty years ago, including slices of fish grilled in lemon leaves and marinated with an almond and wild fennel

sauce. A tasting menu is available, but don't miss out on the antipasti—especially the *panzerottini neri* (ravioli stuffed with ricotta cheese and squid) or the fish *vellutata di limone* (dressed with lemon sauce). There is also an art gallery in the side alley displaying ceramics from Vietri sul Mare. ✉ *Via Matteo Camera 12, near Arsenale* ☎ *089/871029* 🌐 *www.ristorantelacaravella.it* *Reservations essential* ⏲ *Closed Nov. and Dec. and Tues.*

WHERE TO STAY

$ Fodor's Choice ★ **Albergo Sant'Andrea.** With everyone gazing at the magnificent steps leading to Amalfi's cathedral, few turn around to notice that this tiny, family-run pensione occupies one of the top spots in town. **Pros:** on the main square; best views of Duomo; delightful staff. **Cons:** steep flight of steps to entrance; rooms very simple. **TripAdvisor:** "quite nice and charming," "very cheap for Amalfi," "bells are quite loud." ✉ *Piazza Duomo* ☎ *089/871145* 🌐 *www.albergosantandrea.it* *8 rooms* *In-room: a/c* *No meals.*

$$$$ Fodor's Choice ★ **Grand Hotel Convento di Amalfi.** Under the moniker Hotel Cappuccini Convento this fabled medieval monastery was the most richly atmospheric hotel on the Amalfi Coast, if not in all of Italy. **Pros:** a slice of paradise; iconic Amalfi. **Cons:** traditionalists will miss its old-world charm; a 10-minute walk to town. **TripAdvisor:** "treated like royalty," "totally flawless," "truly beautiful building." ✉ *Via Annunziatella 46* ☎ *089/8736711* 🌐 *www.ghconventodiamalfi.com* *53 rooms* *In-room: a/c, refrigerator, Wi-Fi. In-hotel: restaurant, bar, pool, Internet terminal, Wi-Fi hotspot, parking (paid)* ⏲ *Closed Nov.–Mar.* *Breakfast.*

RAVELLO

Fodor's Choice ★ *5 km (3 mi) northeast of Amalfi, 40 km (25 mi) east of Sorrento.*

GETTING HERE

Buses from Amalfi make the 20-minute trip along white-knuckle roads. From Naples, take the Naples-Salerno motorway, then exit at Angri and follow signs for Ravello. The journey takes about 75 minutes. Save yourself the trouble of driving by hiring a car and driver.

VISITOR INFORMATION

In Ravello, the **Azienda Autonoma Soggiorno e Turismo** is open daily 9 to 6, and 9 to 1, 2 to 6 November through March. ✉ *Via Roma 18b, Ravello* ☎ *089/857096* 📠 *089/877977* 🌐 *www.ravellotime.it.*

EXPLORING

Perched on a ridge high above Amalfi and the neighboring town of Atrani, the enchanting village of Ravello has stupendous views, quiet lanes, two important Romanesque churches, and several irresistibly romantic gardens. Set "closer to the sky than the sea," according to André Gide, the town has been the ultimate aerie ever since it was founded as a smart suburb for the richest families of Amalfi's 12th-century maritime republic. Rediscovered by English aristocrats a century ago, the town now hosts one of Italy's most famous music festivals.

Crowning Via della Repubblica and the hillside which overlooks the spectacular vista of the Bay of Salerno, **Auditorium Niemeyer** is a startling piece of modernist architecture. Designed with a dramatically curved, all-white roof by Brazilian architect Oscar Niemeyer (creator of Brasília), it was conceived as an alternative indoor venue for concerts (including those of the famed town music festival). The subject of much controversy since its first conception back in 2000, it raised the wrath of some locals who denounced such an ambitious modernist building in medieval Ravello. They need not have worried, as the result is a design masterpiece—a huge, overhanging canopied roof suspended over a 400-seat concert area, with a giant eye-shaped window allowing spectators to contemplate the extraordinary bay vista during performances. Although it was inaugurated in January 2010, the doors were immediately closed and, at this writing, the contoversy rages on, with authorities battling over who will run the structure. ✉ *Via della Repubblica* 🌐 *www.auditoriumoscarniemeyer.it.*

The **Duomo,** dedicated to patron saint Pantaleone, was founded in 1086 by Orso Papiro, the town's first bishop. Rebuilt in the 12th and 17th centuries, it retains traces of medieval frescoes in the transept, an original mullioned window, a marble portal, and a three-story 13th-century bell tower playfully interwoven with mullioned windows and arches. The 12th-century bronze door has 54 embossed panels depicting Christ's life, and saints, prophets, plants, and animals, all narrating biblical lore. The nave's three aisles are divided by ancient columns, and treasures include sarcophagi from Roman times and paintings by southern Renaissance artist Andrea da Salerno. Most impressive are the two medieval pulpits: the earlier one (on your left as you face the altar), used for reading the Epistles, is inset with a mosaic scene of Jonah and the whale, symbolizing death and redemption. The more famous one opposite, used for reading the Gospels, was commissioned by Nicola Rufolo in 1272 and created by Niccolò di Bartolomeo da Foggia. It seems almost Tuscan in style, with exquisite mosaic work and bas-reliefs and six twisting columns sitting on lion pedestals. An eagle grandly tops the inlaid marble lectern.

A chapel to the left of the apse is dedicated to Saint Pantaleone, a physician who was beheaded in the 3rd century in Nicomedia. Every July 27 devout believers gather in hope of witnessing a miracle (similar to that of San Gennaro in Naples), in which the saint's blood, collected in a vial and set out on an inlaid marble altar, appears to liquefy and come to a boil; it hasn't happened in recent years. In the crypt is the **Museo del Duomo,** which displays treasures from about the 13th century, during the reign of Frederick II of Sicily. ✉ *Museo del Duomo, Piazza del Duomo* ☎ *089/858311* 🌐 *www.chiesaravello.com* 🎫 *€2* ⏲ *Sept.–May, daily 9–7; June–Aug., daily 9–9:30; between noon and 5:30 access to church is through museum, to right of steps.*

Directly off Ravello's main piazza is the **Villa Rufolo,** which—if the master storyteller Boccaccio is to be believed—was built in the 13th century by Landolfo Rufolo, whose immense fortune stemmed from trade with Moors and Saracens. Within is a scene from the earliest days of the Crusades. Norman and Arab architecture mingle in profusion in a welter of color-filled gardens so lush that composer Richard Wagner used them as his inspiration for the home of the Flower Maidens in his opera *Parsifal.* Beyond the Arab-Sicilian cloister and the Norman tower lie the two spectacular terrace gardens, with the lower one, the "Wagner Terrace," often the site for concerts, with the orchestra perched on a precarious-looking platform constructed over the precipice. ✉ *Piazza Duomo* ☎ *089/857866* 🌐 *www.villarufolo.it* 🎟 *€5, concerts extra charge* ⏲ *Daily 9–8; closes earlier when concert rehearsals are taking place; winter 9–6.*

From Ravello's main piazza, head west along Via San Francesco and Via Santa Chiara to the **Villa Cimbrone**, a medieval-style fantasy that sits 1,500 feet above the sea. Created in 1905 by England's Lord Grimthorpe and made world famous when Greta Garbo stayed here in 1937, the Gothic castle is set in fragrant rose gardens that lead to the **Belvedere dell'Infinità** (Belvedere of Infinity), a grand stone parapet that overlooks the impossibly blue Gulf of Salerno and frames a panorama that former Ravello resident Gore Vidal has called "the most beautiful in the world." The villa itself is now a hotel. ✉ *Via S. Chiara 26* ☎ *089/857459* 🌐 *www.villacimbrone.it* 🎟 *€6* ⏲ *Daily 9–half hr before sunset.*

WHERE TO EAT

$$$ SOUTHERN ITALIAN ★ ✕ **Cumpa' Cosimo.** Lustier-looking than most Ravello spots, Cumpa' Cosimo is run devotedly by Netta Bottone, who tours the tables to ensure her clients are content. Her family has owned this *cantina* for 75 of its 300-plus years, and she has been cooking under the arched ceiling for around 60 of them. You can't miss here with any of the dishes featuring classic Ravellian cuisine. A favorite (share it—it's huge) is a *misto* of fettuccine, fusilli, tortellini, and whatever other homemade pasta inspires her, served with a fresh, fragrant pesto. Meats are generally excellent—after all, they are supplied by the butcher shop next door, also run by Netta. The *funghi porcini* mushroom starter and the house cheesecake are so delicious you'll drop your fork. Local wines ease it all down gently, and homemade gelato is a luscious ending. ✉ *Via Roma 46* ☎ *089/857156* ✍ *Reservations essential* ⏲ *Sometimes closed Mon. in winter.*

$$ PIZZA ★ ✕ **Vittoria.** Between the Duomo and the church of San Francesco, this is a good place for a return to reality and an informal bite. Vittoria's thin-crust pizza with loads of fresh toppings is the star attraction, and locals praise it *molto*—it was a favorite of Gore Vidal. But also try the pasta, maybe fusilli with tomatoes, zucchini, and mozzarella. Vittoria is pretty, too, with arches and tile floors. All this adds up to crowds, so try to get here on the early side. ✉ *Via dei Rufolo 3* ☎ *089/857947* 🌐 *www.ristorantepizzeriavittoria.it* ⏲ *Closed Nov.–Mar.*

WHERE TO STAY

$$$$ Fodor's Choice ★ 🏨 **Palumbo.** This is the real deal—the only great hotel left in Ravello that is still a monument to the Grand Tour sensibility that first put the town on the map. **Pros:** impossibly romantic; wonderful coastal retreat. **Cons:** with all this finery it can be difficult to relax; great restaurant closed in winter. **TripAdvisor:** "old-school elegance," "spectacular destination," "narrow staircases." ✉ *Via S. Giovanni del Toro 16* ☎ *089/857244* 🌐 *www.hotelpalumbo.it* 🛏 *17 rooms* 👍 *In-room: a/c, safe, refrigerator, Internet, Wi-Fi. In-hotel: restaurant, bar, parking (paid)* 🍽 *Some meals.*

13

$$ **Parsifal.** In 1288 this diminutive property was a convent housing an order of Augustinian friars; today the intact cloister hosts travelers simply intent on enjoying themselves mightily. **Pros:** staying in a convent in Ravello; friendly staff. **Cons:** slightly removed from the main town; tiny rooms. **TripAdvisor:** "charming architecture and decor," "renowned for its great views," "staff were wonderful." *Viale Gioacchino d'Anna 5 089/857144 www.hotelparsifal.com 17 rooms In-room: a/c, safe, refrigerator, Internet, Wi-Fi. In-hotel: restaurant, bar, parking (paid), some pets allowed All meals.*

$ **Villa Amore.** A 10-minute walk from the Piazza Duomo, this charmingly secluded hotel with a garden is family-run and shares the same exhilarating view of the Bay of Salerno as Ravello's most expensive hotels. **Pros:** charmingly secluded; wonderful views. **Cons:** rather far from the main drag; modest rooms. **TripAdvisor:** "good value budget hotel," "warm, caring service," "steps, steps, and more steps." *Via del Fusco 5 089/857135 www.villaamore.it 10 rooms In-room: a/c, safe, refrigerator, Internet, Wi-Fi. In-hotel: restaurant, bar, some pets allowed All meals.*

$$$$ Fodor's Choice ★ **Villa Cimbrone.** Suspended over the azure sea and set amid rose-laden gardens, this magical place was once the home of Lord Grimthorpe and the holiday hideaway of Greta Garbo. **Pros:** the gardens are all yours after closing time; stay where Garbo chose to "be alone." **Cons:** a longish hike from town center; daily arrival of respectful day-trippers. **TripAdvisor:** "ultimate in luxury," "gardens are the best around," "beautiful and romantic." *Via Santa Chiara 26 089/857459 www.villacimbrone.com 19 rooms In-room: a/c, safe, refrigerator, Internet, Wi-Fi. In-hotel: restaurant, bar, pool, gym, spa, Internet terminal, Wi-Fi hotspot, some pets allowed, parking (paid) Closed Nov.–Mar. Breakfast.*

PAESTUM

★ *99 km (62 mi) southeast of Naples.*

GETTING HERE

By car, take the A3 motorway south from Salerno, take the Battipaglia exit to SS 18. Exit at Capaccio Scala. Trains to Paestum depart from Stazione Centrale in Naples every hour. The archaeological site is a 10-minute walk from the station.

VISITOR INFORMATION

Paestum tourism office (*Via Magna Grecia 887 0828/811016 www.infopaestum.it*).

EXPLORING

One of Italy's most majestic sights lies on the edge of a flat coastal plain: the remarkably well-preserved **Greek temples** of Paestum. This is the site of the ancient city of Poseidonia, founded by Greek colonists probably in the 6th century BC. When the Romans took over the colony in 273 BC and the name was latinized to Paestum, they changed the layout of the settlement, adding an amphitheater and a forum. Much of the archaeological material found on the site is displayed in the well-labeled

Museo Nazionale, and several rooms are devoted to the unique tomb paintings discovered in the area, rare examples of Greek and pre-Roman pictorial art.

At the northern end of the site opposite the ticket barrier is the **Tempio di Cerere** (Temple of Ceres). Built in about 500 BC, it's now thought to have been originally dedicated to the goddess Athena. Follow the road south past the **Foro Romano** (Roman Forum) to the **Tempio di Nettuno** (Temple of Poseidon), a magnificent Doric edifice with 36 fluted columns and an extraordinarily well-preserved entablature (area above the capitals) that rivals those of the finest temples in Greece. Beyond is the so-called **Basilica,** the earliest of Paestum's standing edifices; it dates from early in the 6th century BC. The name is an 18th-century misnomer, for the structure was in fact a temple to Hera, the wife of Zeus. Try to see the temples in the late afternoon, when the light enhances the deep gold of the limestone and tourists have left them almost deserted. ✉ *Via Magna Grecia* ☎ *0828/722654* 🎫 *Site €4, museum €4, combination ticket €6.50* ⏲ *Excavations daily 8:45–2 hrs before sunset, 8:45–4 in winter; museum daily 8:30–6:45; museum closed 1st and 3rd Mon. of month.*

WHERE TO STAY

$ **Azienda Agrituristica Seliano.** This working-farm-with-a-difference is about 3 km (2 mi) from the temples and consists of a cluster of 19th-century baronial buildings. **Pros:** a great taste of a working farm; a banquet every evening. **Cons:** confusing to find; not for non–dog fans. **TripAdvisor:** "pool was delightful," "wonderful old building," "rustic, but relatively spacious." ✉ *Via Seliano, about 1 km (½ mi) down dirt track west off main road from Capaccio Scalo to Paestum, Paestum* ☎ *0828/723634* 🌐 *www.agriturismoseliano.it* *14 rooms* *In-hotel: restaurant, pool, bicycles, some pets allowed* ⏲ *Closed Nov.–Mar., will open for bookings* 🍽 *All meals.*

14

Puglia, Basilicata, and Calabria

WORD OF MOUTH

"The real eye-poppers in Lecce are the churches, whose exteriors are a riot of figurative carving: saints, devils, plants and animals, supplementing an already profuse embellishment of decorative devices. Their interiors are likewise riotously elaborate—for example, with side chapels framed with twisted stone pillars decorated from top to bottom with carved figures."

—tedgale

WELCOME TO PUGLIA, BASILICATA, AND CALABRIA

TOP REASONS TO GO

★ **A wander through Matera's Sassi:** A complex network of ancient cave dwellings partially hewn from rock, some of which now house chic bars and restaurants, endow this simple Basilicata town with one of the most unusual landscapes in Europe.

★ **A trip to peasant-food heaven:** Dine on Puglia's famous puree of fava beans with chicory and olive oil in a humble country restaurant, and you'll be transported back to a simpler culinary era.

★ **Lecce and its baroque splendors:** The beautiful, friendly city of Lecce might be known for its peculiar brand of fanciful baroque architecture, but it's not yet famous enough to have lost even an ounce of its Pugliese charm.

★ **The *trulli* of the Valle d'Itria:** Strange, conical homes—many of them still in use—dot the rolling countryside of Puglia, centering around Alberobello, a town still composed almost entirely of these trulli. They must be seen to be believed.

1 Bari. Puglia's biggest city is a lively, quirky, and sometimes seamy port on the Adriatic Coast. It's also home to the region's principal airport.

2 Gargano Promontory. Jutting into the Adriatic like a spur, this region is full of summertime beaches, wooded campgrounds, and cliff-hanging hotels.

3 The Trulli District. Named for its mysterious conical houses, the Trulli District is centered on the town of **Alberobello**.

4 Salento and Ports of the Heel. The ports of Puglia include Casbah-like fishing villages such as **Gallipoli** and the gritty shipping centers of **Taranto** and **Brindisi**. Italy's heel finally smooths out and terminates in a region of Puglia known as **Salento**, home to the youthful nerve center of **Lecce**, famous for its ornate baroque architecture.

5 Basilicata. One of Italy's least-visited and most secluded regions, Basilicata is home to the unique town of **Matera**, whose Sassi cave dwellings make the city feel like a Nativity scene.

6 Calabria. The region that makes up Italy's "toe" is a land of dusty hill towns, rows of olive trees, and spicy food. **Cosenza** mixes turn-of-the-20th-century cafés with fascist-era architecture, and Tropea is an enticing seaside getaway.

CAMPANIA
Naples
Salerno
Sorrento
Capri

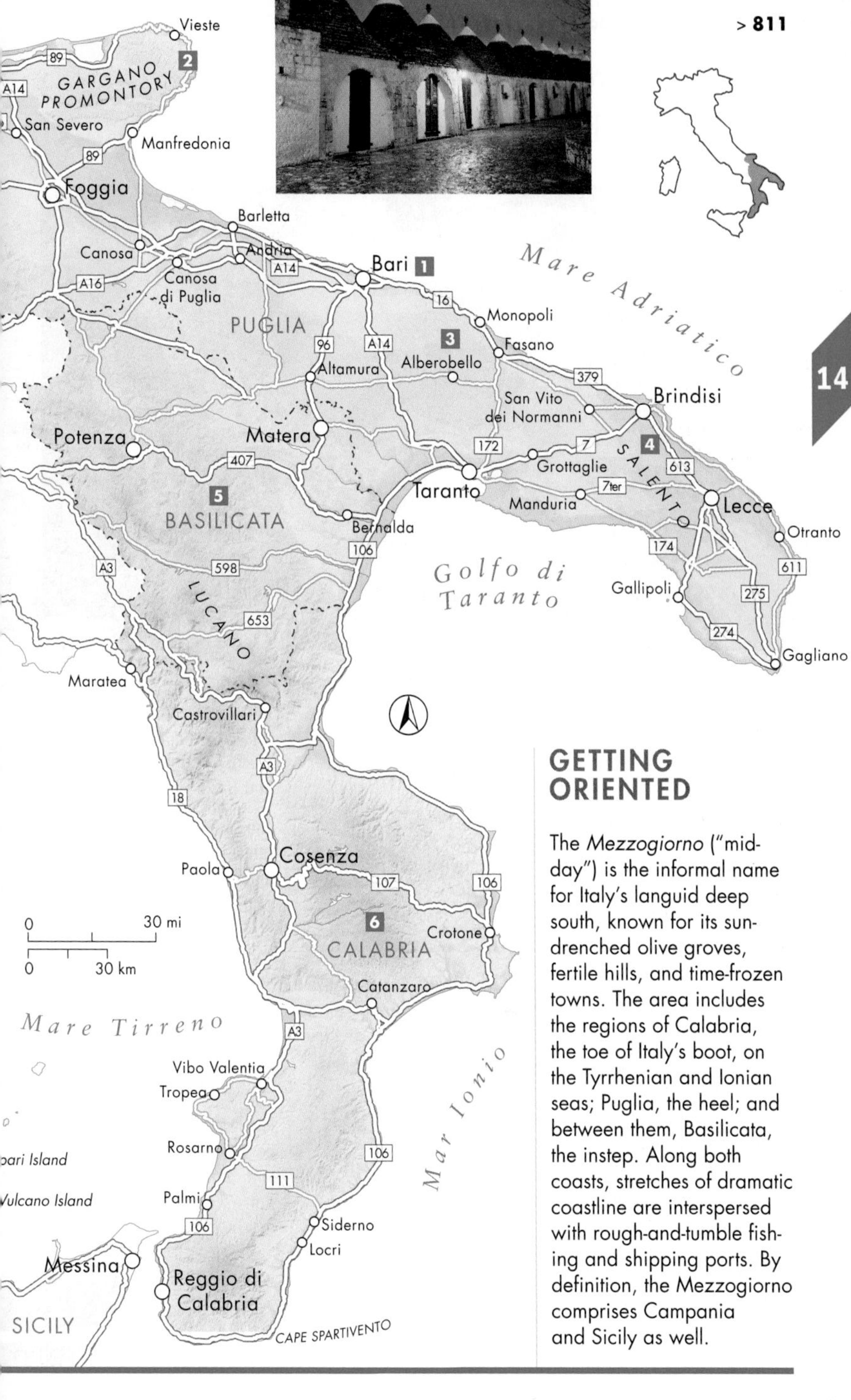

GETTING ORIENTED

The *Mezzogiorno* ("mid-day") is the informal name for Italy's languid deep south, known for its sun-drenched olive groves, fertile hills, and time-frozen towns. The area includes the regions of Calabria, the toe of Italy's boot, on the Tyrrhenian and Ionian seas; Puglia, the heel; and between them, Basilicata, the instep. Along both coasts, stretches of dramatic coastline are interspersed with rough-and-tumble fishing and shipping ports. By definition, the Mezzogiorno comprises Campania and Sicily as well.

EATING AND DRINKING WELL IN THE SOUTH

Southern Italian cuisine is rustic and healthful, featuring homemade pasta and cheese, fresh vegetables, seafood, and olive oil. A defining principle of Italian cooking is to take excellent ingredients and prepare them simply. That philosophy reaches its purest expression here.

The best—and cheapest—meals are often found at a rustic family-run trattoria (sometimes referred to as a *casalinga*), commonly located in the countryside or city outskirts. These bare-bones places often dispense with printed menus, but they manage to create flavors rivaling those of any high-brow restaurant. Assent to the waiter's suggestions with a simple *va bene* (that's fine) or *faccia Lei* (you decide) and leave yourself in the chef's hands.

More-upscale establishments turn authentic local ingredients into deliciously inventive dishes. Fish, unsurprisingly, is the star attraction on the coast. Many such restaurants are set in breathtaking locations, yet prices remain relative bargains compared to similar places farther north.

FABULOUS FAVA

Puré di fave e cicorielle, a puree of dried fava beans topped with sautéed chicory, is unique to Puglia and Basilicata.

The simple recipe has been prepared here for centuries and continues to be a staple of the local diet. The dried favas are soaked overnight, cooked with potatoes, seasoned with salt and olive oil, and served warm with wild green chicory, often with a side of cracked cayenne pepper.

Mix it together before eating and wash it down with a glass of Primitivo or Aglianico.

PASTA

Puglia is the home of orecchiette, pictured at right, with *cime di rapa* (broccoli rabe) and olive oil, a melodious preparation that's wondrous in its simplicity. Try also *cavatelli* (rolled up orecchiette) and *strascenate* (rectangles of pasta with one rough side and one smooth side).

MEAT

With cattle grazing on the plains and pigs fed only natural foods, the south is a meat eater's paradise. As well as its excellent beef, Basilicata is known for its *salsicce lucane* (sausages), seasoned with salt, cayenne pepper, and fennel seeds. Enormous grills are a feature of many of the region's restaurants, infusing the dining area with the aroma of freshly cooked meat. Adventurous eaters in Puglia should look for *turcinieddhri* (a blend of lamb's innards) and *pezzetti di cavallo* (braised horse meat).

PEPPERS

Calabria is known for hot peppers—try *peperonata,* a stew of peppers and capers. They also pop up in *nduja* (creamy spicy salami), *sopressata* (dried spicy salami), and *salsiccia piccante* (hot sausage), pictured at left, often sold by street vendors on a roll with peppers, onions, french fries, and mayonnaise. Pasta dishes are often seasoned with dried *peperoncini* or *olio piccante* (spicy olive oil). The delicious *peperoni cruschi* or *senesi* are grown in Basilicata—they're used both fresh and dried, and are often powdered for seasoning cheeses and cured meats.

SEAFOOD

With so much coastline, seafood is an essential element of Southern Italian cuisine. Fish can be grilled (*alla griglia*), baked (*al forno*), roasted (*arrosto*), or steamed (*in umido*). Among the highlights are delicate *orata* (sea bream), pictured below, *branzino* (sea bass), *gamberi rossi* (sweet red shrimp), and calamari, while Puglia is the home of *cozze pelose* (an indigenous mussel). The *frutti di mare* (shellfish) can be enjoyed as an antipasto, in a *zuppa* (soup), or with homemade linguine.

WINES

Puglia produces around 17% of Italy's wine, more than the whole of Australia. For years, most of it was *vino sfuso* (jug wine), but since the mid-1990s quality has risen. The ancient primitivo grape (an ancestor of California's zinfandel) yields strong, heady wines like Primitivo di Manduria. The Negroamaro grape is transformed into palatable *rosato* (rosé), as well as the robust Salice Salentino. Pair a dessert with the sweet red Aleatico di Puglia or Moscato di Trani.

In Basilicata, producers use the aglianico grape variety to outstanding effect in the prestigious Aglianico del Vulture. In Calabria, they've worked wonders with the gaglioppo variety.

Updated by Mark Walters

Making up the heel and toe of Italy's boot, the Puglia, Basilicata, and Calabria regions are the largest part of what is known informally as the *Mezzogiorno,* a name that translates literally as "midday." It's a curiously telling nickname, because midday is when it's quietest here. While the blazing sun bears down, cities, fishing ports, and sleepy hillside villages turn into ghost towns, as residents retreat to their homes for three or more hours.

This is Italy's deep south, where whitewashed buildings stand silently over three turquoise seas, castles guard medieval alleyways, and grandmothers dry their handmade orecchiette, the most Puglian of pastas, in the mid-afternoon heat. The city-states of Magna Graecia (Greek colonies) once ruled here, and ancient names, such as Lucania, are still commonly used.

At every turn, these three regions boast unspoiled scenery, a wonderful country food tradition, and an openness to outsiders that's unequaled elsewhere on the boot. It's here that the Italian language is at its lilting, hand-gesturing best, and it's here that a local you've met only minutes before is most likely to whisk you away to show you the delights of the region.

Italians and foreign visitors alike return summer after summer to the beaches of the south, where the relative lack of industry has preserved mile after mile of largely unpolluted coastline. One of southern Italy's most popular vacation destinations is the Gargano Promontory, where safe, sandy shores and secluded coves are nestled between whitewashed coastal towns and craggy limestone cliffs. Elsewhere the beach scene is more laid-back. You won't find impeccably manicured sand lined with regiments of sunbathers, but you can pick and choose strands at whim and spread out.

There are cultural gems everywhere, from Valle d'Itria's fairy-tale trulli (curious conical structures, some dating from the 15th century) to Matera's *Sassi* (a network of ancient dwellings carved out of rock) to the baroque churches in vibrant Lecce, the town that's the jewel of the south. Beyond the cities, seaside resorts, and the few major sights, there's a sparsely populated, sun-baked countryside where road signs are rare and expanses of silvery olive trees, vineyards of primitivo and aglianico grapes, and giant prickly-pear cacti fight their way through the rocky soil in defiance of the relentless summer heat. Farmhouses, country trattorias, and weary low-lying factories sit among eternally half-built structures that tell a hard-luck story of economic stagnation. Year after year, even as tourism grows in the region—especially in Salento—economic woes persist. In any case, the region still doesn't make it onto the itineraries of most visitors to Italy. This translates into an unusual opportunity to engage with a rich culture and landscape virtually untouched by international tourism.

PLANNING

MAKING THE MOST OF YOUR TIME

If your priority is relaxing on the beach, plan on a few days in the Gargano Promontory's seaside fishing villages-cum-resorts, such as Peschici, Rodi Garganico, and Vieste, and perhaps a further stay at one of the Calabrian coastal resorts, such as Diamante or Tropea, or Maratea in Basilicata.

Otherwise, choose a base like Polignano a Mare or Trani, especially if you land or dock in Bari. Take day trips out to the Valle d'Itria and its conical trulli, or to the remarkable octagonal Castel del Monte. Then head east along the Adriatic route (SS16), stopping to see the idyllic hilltop Ostuni before continuing on to Lecce, where you'll want to spend at least two to three nights exploring the city's baroque wonders and taking a day trip down to Otranto and Gallipoli.

Next, take regional roads and Via Appia (SS7) to reach Matera, whose Sassi cave dwellings are a Southern Italian highlight; allow at least two nights here. Then it's back out to the SS106 to Calabria, along the coast dotted with ancient Greek settlements, as far as Crotone. At this point, cut inland on the SS107 across the Sila Massif to the hill resort of Camigliatello or carry on to the more vibrant lowland Cosenza. Reggio di Calabria is worthwhile only if you're an archaeology buff and must see its museum.

GETTING AROUND

BUS TRAVEL

Direct, if not always frequent, connections operate between most destinations within Calabria, Puglia, and Basilicata. In many cases bus service is the backup when problems with train service arise. Matera is linked with Bari by frequent **Ferrovie Appulo-Lucane** (☎ *080/5725229* 🌐 *www.fal-srl.it*) buses and with Taranto by **SITA** (☎ *0835/385007* 🌐 *www.sitabus.it*). In Calabria various companies make the north-south run with stops along both coasts. **Ferrovie della Calabria** (☎ *0961/896111* 🌐 *www.ferroviedellacalabria.it*) operates many of the local routes.

CAR TRAVEL

Though roads are generally good in the south and major cities are linked by fast autostrade or four-lane highways, driving here is a major test of navigation skills. Junctions are poorly signposted—especially in Puglia—and cutting straight through town centers can add considerably to travel time. Seemingly under eternal construction, the toll-free A3 Autostrada del Sole links Salerno with Reggio Calabria, with major exits at Sicignano (for the interior of Basilicata and Matera), Cosenza (the Sila Massif and Crotone), and Pizzo (for Tropea). Parts of the A3 in northern Calabria cross uplands over 3,000 feet high, so snow chains may be required during winter months. In the summer and during holiday weekends, this is the main north-south route for Italy's sun-seekers, so factor in plenty of time for delays and avoid peak travel times. Take the SS18 for coastal destinations—or for a better view—on the Tyrrhenian side, and likewise the SS106 (which is uncongested and fast) for the Ionian. Given state-of-the-art speed detectors and driver tracking technology, stick to speed limits: You may become unpopular with the traffic behind but you'll be spared an unwelcome ticket when you get home.

Entering the centers of many towns requires a very small car, folding side-view mirrors, and a bit of nerve; tentative drivers should park outside the center and venture in on foot. If you're squeamish about getting lost, don't plan on night driving in the countryside—roads can be confusing without the aid of landmarks or large towns. Bari, Brindisi, and Reggio di Calabria are notorious for car thefts and break-ins. In these cities, don't leave valuables in the car, and find a guarded parking space if possible.

TRAIN TRAVEL

Within Puglia, the Italian national railway **Trenitalia** (☎ *892021* 🌐 *www.trenitalia.com*) links Bari to Brindisi, Lecce, and Taranto, but smaller destinations can often be reached only by completing the trip by bus. The private **Ferrovie Sud-Est** (☎ *080/5462111 in Bari; 0832/668111 in Lecce* 🌐 *www.fseonline.it*) connects Martina Franca with Bari and Taranto, and the fishing port of Gallipoli with Lecce. **Ferrovie Appulo-Lucane** (☎ *080/5725229* 🌐 *www.fal-srl.it*) links Matera to Altamura in Puglia (for connections to Bari) and to Ferrandina (for connections to Potenza). Trenitalia trains run to Calabria, either following the Ionian Coast as far as Reggio Calabria or swerving inland to Cosenza and the Tyrrhenian Coast.

HOTELS

Hotels in the region range from grand, if slightly faded, high-class resorts to family-run rural *agriturismi* (country inns, often part of farms), which compensate for a lack of amenities with their famous southern hospitality. *Fattorie* and *masserie* (small farms and grander farm estates) offering accommodation are listed at local tourist offices.

In beach areas such as the Gargano Promontory and Salento, campgrounds and bungalow lodgings are ubiquitous and popular with families and young budget travelers alike. Note that many seaside hotels open up just for the summer season, when they often require several-day stays with full or half board. And do remember that in a region like this—blazingly hot in summer and chilly in winter—air-conditioning and central heating can be important.

Hotel reivews have been condensed for this book. Please go to Fodors.com for expanded reviews of each property.

WHAT IT COSTS (IN EUROS)					
	¢	$	$$	$$$	$$$$
Restaurants	under €20	€20–€30	€30–€45	€45–€65	over €65
Hotels	under €75	€75–€125	€125–€200	€200–€300	over €300

Restaurant prices are for a first course (primo), second course (secondo), and dessert (dolce). Hotel prices are for two people in a standard double room in high season, including tax and service.

BARI AND THE ADRIATIC COAST

The coast of Puglia has a strong flavor of the Norman presence in the south, embodied in the distinctive Apulian-Romanesque churches, the most atmospheric being in Trani. The busy commercial port of Bari offers architectural nuggets in its compact, labyrinthine old quarter abutting the sea, while Polignano a Mare combines accessibility to the major centers with the charm of a medieval town. For a unique excursion, drive inland to the imposing Castel del Monte, an enigmatic 13th-century octagonal fortification.

BARI

260 km (162 mi) southeast of Naples, 450 km (281 mi) southeast of Rome.

GETTING HERE

By car, take the Bari-Nord exit from the A14 motorway. Bari's train station is a hub for Puglia-bound trains. Alitalia, Air One, and easyJet fly to Bari Airport from Rome and Milan.

VISITOR INFORMATION

Bari tourism office (✉ *Piazza Moro 33/a* ☎ *080/9909341* 🌐 *www.viaggiareinpuglia.it/apt-bari*).

EXPLORING

The biggest city in the region, Bari is a major port and a transit point for travelers catching ferries across the Adriatic to Greece, Croatia, and Albania. It's also a cosmopolitan city with one of the most interesting historic centers in the region. Most of Bari is set out in a logical 19th-century grid, following the designs of Joachim Murat (1767–1815), Napoléon's brother-in-law and King of the Two Sicilies. The heart of the modern town is **Piazza della Libertà,** but just beyond it, across Corso Vittorio Emanuele, is the *città vecchia* (old town), a maze of narrow streets on the promontory that juts out between Bari's old and new ports, circumscribed by Via Venezia, offering elevated views of the Adriatic in every direction.

PUGLIA, PAST AND PRESENT

Puglia has long been inhabited, conquered, and visited. On sea voyages to their colonies and trading posts in the west, the ancient Greeks invariably headed for Puglia first—it was the shortest crossing—before filtering southward into Sicily and westward to the Tyrrhenian coast. In turn, the Romans—often bound in the opposite direction—were quick to recognize the strategic importance of the peninsula. Later centuries were to see a procession of other empires raiding or colonizing Puglia: Byzantines, Saracens, Normans, Swabians, Turks, and Spaniards all swept through, each group leaving its mark. Romanesque churches and the powerful castles built by 13th-century Holy Roman Emperor Frederick II (who also served as king of Sicily and Jerusalem) are among the most impressive of the buildings in the region. Frederick II, dubbed *Stupor Mundi* (Wonder of the World) for his wide-ranging interests in literature, science, mathematics, and nature, was one of the foremost personalities of the Middle Ages.

The last 10 years have brought a huge economic revival after the decades of neglect following World War II. Having benefited from EU funding, state incentive programs, and subsidies for irrigation, Puglia is now Italy's biggest producer of wine, with most of the rest of the land devoted to olives, citrus fruits, and vegetables. The main ports of Bari, Brindisi, and Taranto are thriving centers, though there remain serious problems of unemployment and poverty. However, the much-publicized arrival of thousands of asylum seekers from Eastern Europe and beyond has not significantly destabilized these cities, as had been feared, and the economic and political refugees have dispersed throughout Italy. Today a strong air of prosperity wafts through the streets of Lecce, Trani, and other towns.

By day, explore the old town's winding alleyways, where Bari's open-door policy offers a glimpse into the daily routine of southern Italy—matrons hand-rolling pasta with their grandchildren home from school for the midday meal, and handymen perched on rickety ladders, patching up centuries-old arches and doorways. Back in the new town, join the evening *passeggiata* (stroll) on pedestrians-only **Via Sparano**, then, when night falls, saunter amid the exploding scene of outdoor bars and restaurants in Piazza Mercantile, past Piazza Ferrarese at the end of Corso Vittorio Emanuele.

★ In the città vecchia, overlooking the sea and just off Via Venezia, is the **Basilica di San Nicola**, built in the 11th century to house the bones of Saint Nicholas, also known as Saint Nick, or Santa Claus. His remains, buried in the crypt, are said to have been stolen by Bari sailors from Myra, where Saint Nicholas was bishop, in what is now Turkey. The basilica, of solid and powerful construction, was the only building to survive the otherwise wholesale destruction of Bari by the Normans in 1152. ✉ *Piazza San Nicola* ☎ *080/5737111* 🌐 *www.basilicasannicola.it* ⏲ *Daily 7 am–8 pm.*

Looming over Bari's cathedral is the huge **Castello Svevo**. The current building dates from the time of Holy Roman Emperor Frederick II

(1194–1250), who rebuilt an existing Norman-Byzantine castle to his own exacting specifications. Designed more for power than beauty, it looks out beyond the cathedral to the small Porto Vecchio (Old Port). Inside, a haphazard collection of medieval Puglian art is frequently enlivened by changing exhibitions featuring local, national, and international artists. ✉ *Piazza Federico II di Svevia* ☎ *080/5286262* 🎫 *€2* ⏲ *Thurs.–Tues. 8:30–7:30. Last entrance at 7.*

Bari's 12th-century **Cattedrale di San Sabino** is the seat of the local bishop and was the scene of many significant political marriages between important families in the Middle Ages. The cathedral's solid architecture reflects the Romanesque style favored by the Normans of that period. ✉ *Piazza dell'Odegitria* ☎ *080/5210605* ⏲ *Mon.–Sat. 8–12 and 4–8, Sun. 8–12:30 and 4–10.*

14

WHERE TO EAT AND STAY

$$ SOUTHERN ITALIAN ✕ **Ristorante al Pescatore.** This is one of Bari's best seafood restaurants, in the old town opposite the castle and just around the corner from the cathedral. In summer the fish is grilled outdoors, so you can enjoy the delicious aroma as you sit amid a cheerful clamor of quaffing and dining. Try a whole fish accompanied by a crisp salad and a carafe of invigorating local wine. Reservations are essential in July and August. Beware of bag snatchers if you sit outside. ✉ *Piazza Federico II di Svevia 6/8* ☎ *080/5237039* ⏲ *Closed Mon. and 2 wks mid-Jan.*

$$ **Palace Hotel.** This downtown landmark is steps away from Corso Vittorio Emanuele in the New City, but is also extremely convenient to the medieval center. **Pros:** convenient location. **Cons:** often very busy; staff can be brusque. **TripAdvisor:** "quite ornate," "room was lovely," "in the heart of downtown." ✉ *Via Lombardi 13* ☎ *080/5216551* 🌐 *www.palacehotelbari.it* *196 rooms, 6 suites* *In-room: a/c, Wi-Fi. In-hotel: restaurant, room service, bars, gym, parking* *Some meals.*

TRANI

43 km (27 mi) northwest of Bari.

GETTING HERE

By car, take the Trani exit from the A14 motorway. Frequent trains run from Bari.

VISITOR INFORMATION

Trani tourism office (✉ *Piazza Trieste 10* ☎ *0883/588830* 🌐 *www.viaggiareinpuglia.it*).

EXPLORING

Smaller than the other ports along this coast, Trani has a harbor filled with fishing boats and a quaint old town with polished stone streets and medieval churches. Trani is also justly famous for its sweet dessert wine, Moscato di Trani.

The boxy, well-preserved **Castello** (✉ *Piazza Manfredi 16* ☎ *0883/506603* 🌐 *www.castelloditrani.beniculturali.it* 🎫 *€2* ⏲ *Daily 8:30–7:30*) was built by Frederick II in 1233.

Puglia

0 — 50 miles
0 — 75 km

Adriatic Sea

Golfo di Taranto

Golfo di Manfredonia

Golfo di Salerno

KEY
Ferry lines

ISOLE TREMITI
I Cameroni
ISOLE S. DOMINO
Peschici
Vieste
Rodi Garganico
Lago di Varano
← TO TERMOLI
Foresta Umbra
GARGANO PROMONTORY
Mattinata
Monte Sant'Angelo
Manfredonia
San Giovanni Rotondo
L' Annunziata
San Severo
Zapponeta
Lucera
Foggia
Barletta
Trani
Molfetta
Bari
Cerignola
Andria
Corato
PUGLIA
Castel del Monte
Polignano a Mare
Grotte di Castellana
Fasano
TRULLI DISTRICT
Ostuni
Brindisi
Alberobello
Locorotondo
Martina Franca
Ceglie Messapica
Via Appia
Mesagne
CAMPANIA
Melfi
Spinazzola
Gravina in Puglia
Santeramo in Colle
Gioia del Colle
Altamura
Matera
Massafra
Grottaglie
Francavilla Fontana
Campi
Lecce
S. Angelo dei Lombardi
Taranto
Mare Grande
Mare Piccolo
Manduria
SALENTO
Otranto
Potenza
Castellaneta Marina
Lido di Metaponto
Nardo
Maglie
Santa Cesarea Terme
BASILICATA
Gallipoli
Castro
← TO NAPLES
Eboli
Auletta
LUCANO
Scanzano
Salerno
Battipaglia
Leuca
Capo Santa Maria di Leuca

89, 528, 272, 16, A14, 160, 17, 159, 90, 655, A16, 170, 96, 271, 97, 168, 91, 164, 7, 407, 100, 611, 101, 174, 106, 598, 92, 653, 166, A3, 18, 275, 274

The stunning, pinkish-white-hue 11th-century **Cattedrale** (✉ *Piazza Duomo* ☎ *0883/494210* ⏲ *Daily 9–noon and 3.30–6*), considered one of the finest in Puglia, is built on a spit of land jutting into the sea.

A Jewish community flourished here in medieval times, and on **Via Sinagoga** *(Synagogue Street)* two of the four synagogues still stand. **Santa Maria Scolanova** and **Santa Anna,** both built in the 13th century, are now churches; the latter still bears a Hebrew inscription.

WHERE TO STAY

$$ **La Regia.** This small hotel-restaurant occupies a 17th-century palazzo superbly positioned in front of the Duomo, on a swath of land jutting out into the sea. **Pros:** great restaurant; hospitable staff; most rooms have sea views. **Cons:** no parking outside hotel; area can be very busy on weekends. **TripAdvisor:** "terrace looking at the sea," "pleased with the staff," "beautiful palace." ✉ *Piazza Mons. Addazi 2* ☎ *0883/584444* 🌐 *www.hotelregia.it* *10 rooms* *In-room: a/c, Wi-Fi. In-hotel: restaurant, bar, business center* ⏲ *Restaurant closed Mon.* *Breakfast.*

$ **Hotel Trani.** This centrally located hotel isn't a showplace, but the rooms are clean and it's efficiently and courteously run. **Pros:** close to the railway station; within walking distance of the old town; off-street parking at low prices. **Cons:** uninspiring 1960s architecture; basic rooms. ✉ *Corso Imbriani 137* ☎ *0883/588010* 🌐 *www.hoteltrani.it* *46 rooms* *In-room: a/c. In-hotel: restaurant, bar, business center, parking* ⏲ *Restaurant closed Sun.*

POLIGNANO A MARE

35 km (22 mi) southeast of Bari, 14 km (9 mi) north of Castellana.

GETTING HERE

From Bari, take the Polignano exit from the SS16. Frequent trains run from Bari.

EXPLORING

With a well-preserved whitewashed old town perched on limestone cliffs overlooking the Adriatic, Polignano a Mare makes an atmospheric base for exploring the surrounding area. The town is virtually lifeless all winter, but becomes something of a weekend hot spot for city dwellers in summer.

WHERE TO STAY

$$ ★ **Grotta Palazzese.** Carved out of a cliff opening onto the Adriatic, the Grotta Palazzese inhabits a stunning group of rocks and grottoes that have wowed onlookers from time immemorial. **Pros:** romantic restaurant; great location. **Cons:** a long climb down to the sea. **TripAdvisor:** "wonderful setting," "small but charming," "disappointed with the service." ✉ *Via Narciso 59* ☎ *080/4240677* 🌐 *www.grottapalazzese.it* *23 rooms* *In-room: a/c, Wi-Fi (some). In-hotel: restaurants, bar, beach, parking* ⏲ *Outdoor restaurant closed Nov.–Apr.* *Breakfast.*

CASTEL DEL MONTE

56 km (35 mi) southwest of Bari.

GETTING HERE

Take the Andria-Barletta exit from the A14 motorway, then follow the SS170d to Castel del Monte. From April through October there's minibus service from Piazza Bersaglieri d'Italia in Andria.

VISITOR INFORMATION

Castel del Monte tourism office (✉ *Via Vespucci 114Andria* ☎ *0883/592283* 🌐 *www.casteldelmonte.beniculturali.it*).

Fodor's Choice ★ **Castel del Monte.** Built by Frederick II in the first half of the 13th century, Castel del Monte is an imposing octagonal castle with eight austere towers. Little is known about the structure on an isolated hill, since virtually no records exist. The ground-floor gift shop (closed in winter months) has many books that explore its mysterious past and posit fascinating theories based on its dimensions and Federico II's love of mathematics. It has none of the usual defense features associated with medieval castles, so it probably had little military significance. Some theories suggest it might have been built as a hunting lodge or may have served as an astronomical observatory, or even a stop for pilgrims on their quest for the Holy Grail. Most of the helpful information panels in the castle are translated into English. Note that if coming by car from April to September you have to park in designated areas about a mile away and then get a shuttle bus. ✉ *On signposted minor road 18 km (11 mi) south of Andria* ☎ *0883/569997; 0883/592283 tour reservations* 🌐 *www.casteldelmonte.beniculturali.it* 🎫 *€3* 🕑 *Mar.–Sept., daily 10:15–7:15; Oct.–Feb., daily 9–6. Last entrance ½ hr before closing.*

THE GARGANO PROMONTORY

Forming the spur of Italy's boot, the Gargano Promontory (Promontorio del Gargano) is a striking contrast to the Adriatic's flatter coastline. This is a land of whitewashed coastal towns, wide sandy beaches interspersed with secluded coves, and craggy limestone cliffs topped by deep-green pine and lush Mediterranean maquis. Not surprisingly, it pulls in the crowds in July and August, driving up the prices considerably. Camping is almost always an option, as plentiful and pretty campgrounds dot the Gargano's curvy, cliff-hugging roads. For the kids, the beaches and the Foresta Umbra national park are great places to let off steam.

MATTINATA

138 km (86 mi) northwest of Bari.

GETTING HERE

From Foggia (the chief city in Puglia's northernmost province), take the winding SS89. Regular buses leave from Foggia's train station.

VISITOR INFORMATION

Mattinata tourism office (✉ *Corso Mattino 68* ☎ *0884/559169* 🌐 *www.viaggiareinpuglia.it*).

EXPLORING

The town of Mattinata itself is an unlovely urban sprawl halfway up the hillside. Most visitors stay down at sea level, where there's a fine sandy beach.

Pilgrims have flocked to the nearby town of Monte Sant'Angelo for nearly 1,500 years—among them Saint Francis of Assisi and crusaders setting off for the Holy Land from the then-flourishing port of Manfredonia. Monte Sant'Angelo is centered on the **Santuario di San Michele** (☎ *0884/561150* ⏲ *June–Sept., Mon.–Sat. 7:30–7, Sun. 6:30 am–7:30 pm; Oct.–May, Mon.–Sat. 7:30–12.30 and 2:30–5, Sun. 7–1 and 2.30–7*), built over the grotto where the archangel Michael is believed to have appeared before shepherds in the year 490. Walk down a long series of steps to get to the grotto itself; on its walls you can see the hand tracings left by pilgrims.

14

WHERE TO EAT AND STAY

$$ SOUTHERN ITALIAN **Trattoria dalla Nonna.** The waves lap at the shore just inches from your table at this elegant but unpretentious coastal restaurant. The memorable assorted raw seafood antipasto includes some shellfish you might not find anywhere else. *Cozze pelose* (an indigenous Puglian mussel), hiding inside spiked-hair shells, are briny and buttery; tiny *noci* shellfish have a wonderful sweetness; and big, rich local oysters are all about texture. Try sweet grilled scampi with oil and lemon, and wash it all down with one of the great white wines on the extensive list. If you find it hard to leave, you can stay the night in their simple, inexpensive rooms ($). ✉ *Contrada Funni al Lido, Località Funni* ☎ *0884/559205* 🌐 *www.dallanonna.it* ⏲ *Closed Jan., 1st 2 wks of Feb., and Tues. Oct.–Apr.*

$$ **Baia delle Zagare.** This secluded cluster of bungalows, on the shore road between Mattinata and Vieste, overlooks an inlet and stands of 500-year-old olive trees. **Pros:** incredible location. **Cons:** impossible to get to without a car; rooms a bit drab. **TripAdvisor:** "view is stunning," "two beautiful beaches," "rooms aren't terribly special." ✉ *Litoranea Mattinata-Vieste, 17 km (10 mi) northeast of Mattinata* ☎ *0884/550155* 🌐 *www.hotelbaiadellezagare.it* *150 rooms* *In-room: a/c. In-hotel: restaurant, tennis court, bars, pool, beach, business center, parking* ⏲ *Closed mid-Sept.–May* *Some meals.*

VIESTE

93 km (58 mi) northeast of Foggia, 179 km (111 mi) northwest of Bari.

GETTING HERE

If you're driving from Foggia, take the winding SS89. Regular buses leave from Foggia's train station.

VISITOR INFORMATION

Vieste tourism office (✉ *Piazza Kennedy* ☎ *0884/708806* 🌐 *www.viaggiareinpuglia.it*).

EXPLORING

This large, whitewashed town jutting off the tip of the spur of Italy's boot is an attractive place to wander around. Though curvy mountain roads render it slightly less accessible from the autostrada and mainline rail stations than, say, Peschici and Mattinata, the range of accommodations (including camping) makes it a useful base for exploring Gargano. The resort attracts legions of tourists in summer, some bound for the Isole Tremiti, a tiny archipelago connected to Vieste by regular ferries.

While in Vieste, take a look at the **Castello Svevo**. Originally built by Frederick II, it was enlarged by the Spanish to defend against attacks from the Turks. Today it's occupied by the Italian navy, and the interior isn't open to the public. ✉ *Via Duomo* ☎ *0884/712232*.

WHERE TO EAT AND STAY

$$ SOUTHERN ITALIAN Fodor's Choice ★ ✕ **Al Dragone**. Dine on exquisite Gargano fare at this charmingly intimate eatery in the shadow of the cathedral. The menu is dominated by locally caught fish. While dishes draw on traditional recipes, expect occasional innovations like cuttlefish, shrimp, and zucchini soufflé. Such desserts as *millefoglie*, layers of puff pastry and chantilly cream, make it worth the visit. The wine list is an exhaustive who's who of great Pugliese producers. ✉ *Via Duomo 8* ☎ *0884/701212* 🌐 *www.aldragone.it* ⏲ *Closed Nov.–Mar. and Tues. in Apr., May, Sept., and Oct.*

$ 🏨 **Punta San Francesco**. After starting its life as an olive-oil factory, this hotel was tastefully refurbished in the mid-1990s. **Pros:** quiet location; hospitable staff. **Cons:** parking can be difficult; rooms are basic. **TripAdvisor:** "overlooks the sea," "clean and well appointed," "friendly and helpful." ✉ *Via San Francesco 2* ☎ *0884/701422* 🌐 *www.hotelpuntasanfrancesco.it* *14 rooms* *In-room: a/c. In-hotel: restaurant, bar, parking* 🍽 *Breakfast.*

PESCHICI

22 km (14 mi) northwest of Vieste, 199 km (124 mi) northwest of Bari.

GETTING HERE

From Foggia, take the winding S89 road. Regular buses leave from Foggia's train station. Seasonal ferry service leaves from the Trémiti archipelago between June and September.

VISITOR INFORMATION

Peschici tourism office (✉ *Via Magenta 3* ☎ *0884/915362* 🌐 *www.viaggiareinpuglia.it*).

EXPLORING

Peschici is a pleasant resort on Gargano's north shore, a cascade of whitewashed houses and streets with a beautiful view over a sweeping cove. Some surrounding areas are particularly popular with campers from northern Europe. Development has not wreaked too much havoc on the town: the mazelike center retains its characteristic low houses topped with little Byzantine cupolas.

★ In the middle of the Gargano Promontory is the majestic **Foresta Umbra** (Shady Forest), a dense growth of beech, maple, and oak generally found in more northerly climates, thriving here because of the altitude, 3,200 feet above sea level. Between the trees in this national park are occasional dramatic vistas opening out over the Golfo di Manfredonia.

THE TRULLI DISTRICT

The inland area to the southeast of Bari is one of Italy's oddest enclaves, mostly flat terrain given over to olive cultivation and interspersed with the idiosyncratic habitations that have lent their names to the district. The origins of the beehive-shape trulli go back to the 15th century and maybe further. The trulli, found nowhere else in the world, are built of local limestone, without mortar, and with a hole in the top for escaping smoke. Some are painted with mystical or religious symbols, some are isolated, and others are joined together with common roofs. Legends of varying credibility surround the trulli (for example, that they were originally built so that residents could quickly take apart their homes when the tax collectors came by). The center of trulli country is Alberobello in the enchanting Valle d'Itria: it has the greatest concentration of buildings. You'll spot them all over this region, some in the middle of desolate fields, and many in disrepair, but always adding a quirky charm to the landscape.

ALBEROBELLO

59 km (37 mi) southeast of Bari, 45 km (28 mi) north of Taranto.

GETTING HERE

By car, take the Monopoli exit from the SS16, follow the SP237 to Putignano, then SS172 to Alberobello. Trains run hourly from Bari.

VISITOR INFORMATION

Alberobello tourism office (✉ *Via Monte Nero 3* ☎ *080/4324419*).

EXPLORING

Although Alberobello is something of a tourist trap, the amalgamation of more than 1,000 trulli huddled together along steep, narrow streets is nonetheless a striking phenomenon that has been designated a UNESCO World Heritage Site. As one of the most popular destinations in Puglia, Alberobello has spawned some excellent restaurants (and some not-so-excellent trinket shops).

Alberobello's largest trullo, the **Trullo Sovrano**, is up the hill through the trulli zone (head up Corso Vittorio Emanuele past the obelisk and the basilica). Though you can go inside, where you can find a fairly conventional domestic dwelling, the real interest is the structure itself.

The trulli in Alberobello itself are impressive, but the most beautiful concentration of conical trulli is along a stretch of about 15 km (9 mi) on the **Alberobello–Martina Franca road**. Amid expanses of vineyards, you can see delightfully amusing examples of trulli put to use in every which way—including as wineries.

WHERE TO EAT AND STAY

$$$ SOUTHERN ITALIAN ✕ **Il Poeta Contadino.** Proprietor Leonardo Marco serves creative regional cooking in this upscale country restaurant in the heart of the attractive trulli zone. The refined, understated dining room features candles casting shadows on the ancient stone walls. Dishes might include *triglie con vinaigrette alla menta* (red mullet with a mint vinaigrette) or *coda di rospo in crosta di patate* (monkfish in a potato crust). In season, try

anything with white truffles. ✉ *Via Indipendenza 21* ☎ *080/4321917* *Reservations essential* ⊗ *Closed Mon. and 3 wks in Jan. No dinner Sun. Sept.–June.*

$$ SOUTHERN ITALIAN Fodor's Choice ★ ✕ **L'Aratro**. This welcoming rustic restaurant set inside adjoining trulli has dark-wood beams, whitewashed walls, and an outdoor patio for summer dining. The *antipasti misti* could stand as a meal in itself, but leave room for country-style dishes using lamb and veal. Among the seasonal specialties are *cavatellucci di terra madre* (tomatoes, onions, and *capocollo*—a cured meat—on a bed of fava beans) and roast lamb with *lampasciuni* (a type of wild onion). ✉ *Via Monte S. Michele 25–29* ☎ *080/4322789* 🌐 *www.ristorantearatro.it* *Reservations essential.*

$ **Hotel Lanzillotta**. This modern structure in Alberobello's main piazza is near one of the two trulli districts. **Pros:** convenient location; helpful staff. **Cons:** lacks charm; lackluster restaurant. **TripAdvisor:** "perfect base for touring," "fantastic view of Alberobello," "very accommodating." ✉ *Piazza Fernando IV 33* ☎ *080/4321511* 🌐 *www.hotellanzillotta.it* *30 rooms* *In-room: a/c, Internet. In-hotel: restaurant, bar, parking* *Breakfast.*

OSTUNI

50 km (30 mi) west of Brindisi, 85 km (53 mi) southeast of Bari.

GETTING HERE

By car, take the Ostuni exit from the SS16. The Ferrovie dello Stato (FS, the national railway) runs frequent trains from Bari.

VISITOR INFORMATION

Ostuni tourism office (✉ *Corso Mazzini 8* ☎ *0831/301268* 🌐 *www.viaggiareinpuglia.it*).

EXPLORING

This sun-bleached, medieval town lies on three hills not far from the coast. From a distance, Ostuni is a jumble of blazingly white houses and churches spilling over a hilltop and overlooking the sea—thus earning it the nickname *la Città Bianca* (the White City).

The **old town**, on the highest of the hills, has steep cobbled lanes, wrought-iron lanterns, some good local restaurants, and stupendous views out over the coast and the surrounding plain.

Piazza Libertà, the city's main square, divides the new town to the west and the old town to the east.

WHERE TO EAT

$$ SOUTHERN ITALIAN ✕ **Osteria del Tempo Perso**. Buried in the side streets of the old town, this laid-back restaurant has rough-hewn stone interiors, with intriguing objects adorning the walls. Service is friendly and preparations focus on local cuisine such as delectable eggplant Parmesan and homemade orecchiette *con cime di rapa* (with bitter greens and fried breadcrumbs). ✉ *Via G. Tanzarella Vitale 47* ☎ *0831/304819* 🌐 *www.osteriadeltempoperso.com* ⊗ *Closed Mon. and 2 wks in Jan. No lunch weekdays Apr.–Oct.*

CEGLIE MESSAPICA

11 km (7 mi) southwest of Ostuni, 18 km (11 mi) southwest of Martina Franca.

GETTING HERE

By car, take the Ostuni exit from the SS16, and follow SP22 to Ceglie Messapica. Ferrovie del Sud-Est runs frequent trains from Bari.

VISITOR INFORMATION

Ceglie Messapica tourism office (✉ *Via G. Elia 16* ☎ *0831/371003*).

EXPLORING

With its 14th-century Piazza Vecchia, tattered baroque balconies, and lordly medieval castles, the little whitewashed town of Ceglie Messapica is a jewel. The town, at the center of the triangle formed by Taranto, Brindisi, and Fasano, was once the military capital of the region, and often defended itself against invasions from the Taranto city-state, which wanted to clear a route to the Adriatic. Nowadays, more and more visitors come to Ceglie Messapica for its restaurants alone.

14

WHERE TO EAT

$$–$$$ SOUTHERN ITALIAN Fodor's Choice ★

✕ **Al Fornello Da Ricci.** Any respectable culinary tour of Puglia must pass through this elegant dining room in the whitewashed town of Ceglie Messapica, 11 km (7 mi) southwest of Ostuni. The distinguished kitchen sends out antipasti in a long succession, all inspired by ancient Pugliese traditions—meats, cheeses, perhaps fried zucchini flowers stuffed with fresh goat's milk ricotta. Then come delicate pasta dishes and ambitious meat preparations. It's an haute Pugliese experience not to be missed. ✉ *Contrada Montevicoli* ☎ *0831/377104* 🌐 *www.riccirístor.com* *Reservations essential* ⏲ *Closed Tues., 10 days in Feb., and Sept. 10–30. No dinner Sun. Nov.–Feb. or Mon.*

$$ SOUTHERN ITALIAN

✕ **Cibus.** Amid the vaulted stone archways of this humble but elegant *osteria* (tavernlike restaurant) in the old city sit rows of bottles and books devoted to the worship of food and wine. It's no wonder, then, that the food is so good: after an *antipasto del territorio* (sampling of local meats, cheeses, and other delights) comes lasagne *di pasta fresca con cime di rape* (with bitter greens), and then perhaps an *arrosto misto di capretto, capocollo, e salsiccia* (a mixture of roast meats including baby goat and sausage). For the more adventurous: braised horse meat in *ragù* (a tomato-based meat sauce). ✉ *Via Chianche di Scarano* ☎ *0831/388980* 🌐 *www.ristorantecibus.it* ⏲ *Closed Tues. and 2 wks in late June.*

MARTINA FRANCA

29 km (18 mi) west of Ostuni, 36 km (22 mi) north of Taranto.

GETTING HERE

By car, take the Fasano exit from the SS16, then follow the SS172. The Ferrovie Sud-Est runs frequent trains from Bari and Taranto.

VISITOR INFORMATION

Martina Franca tourism office (✉ *Piazza XX Settembre 3* ☎ *080/4805702* 🌐 *www.martinafrancatour.it*).

EXPLORING

Martina Franca is a beguiling town with a dazzling mixture of medieval and baroque architecture in the light-color local stone. Ornate balconies hang above the twisting, narrow streets, with little alleys leading off into the hills. Martina Franca was developed as a military stronghold in the 14th century, when a surrounding wall with 24 towers was built, but now all that remains of the wall are the four gates that had once been the only entrances to the town. Each July and August, the town holds the Valle D'Itria music festival (🌐 *www.festivaldellavalleditria.it*).

WORD OF MOUTH

"We fell in love with Puglia. The Adriatic is so beautiful, the people so friendly (and curious, as there aren't a lot of Americans that travel there), and it is unspoiled. It has a very different 'look' than other parts of Italy we have seen because they have been invaded so many times. The people are taller and more angular, and while I have never been to Greece, it is a bit of what I imagine Greece would be like."

—travel52

WHERE TO EAT AND STAY

$ SOUTHERN ITALIAN ✕ **Ristorante Sagittario.** This restaurant just outside the historical center in Martina Franca's new town is a favorite for locals. The homemade pastas and pizzas are delicious, but it's the excellent grilled meats (lamb chops and pork shoulder are first-rate) that keep people coming back for more. The atmosphere is warm and convivial. ✉ *Via Quarto 15* ☎ *080/4858982.*

$ 🏨 **Park Hotel San Michele.** This garden hotel makes a pleasant base in the warm months, thanks to its pool. **Pros:** pretty pool area; shuttle service to Bari airport. **Cons:** old-fashioned hand-held showers. **TripAdvisor:** "quick stroll into town," "gardens are quite pretty," "breakfast buffet was excellent." ✉ *Viale Carella 9* ☎ *080/4807053* 🌐 *www.parkhotelsanmichele.it* *85 rooms* *In-room: a/c, Wi-Fi. In-hotel: restaurant, bar, pool* 🍽 *Breakfast.*

SALENTO AND PORTS OF THE HEEL

This far south, the mountains run out of steam and the land is uniformly flat. The monotony of endless olive trees is redeemed by the region's most dramatic coastline, with sandstone cliffs falling fast toward the sea. Here you can find a handful of small, alluring fishing towns, such as Otranto and Gallipoli. Taranto and Brindisi don't quite fit this description: both are big ports where historical importance is obscured by unsightly heavy industry. Nonetheless, Taranto has its archaeological museum, and Brindisi, an important ferry jumping-off point, marks the end of the Appian Way (the "Queen of Roads" built by the Romans). Farther south, Salento (the Salentine Peninsula) is the local name for the part of Puglia that forms the end of the heel. Lecce is an unexpected oasis of grace and sophistication, and its swirling architecture will melt even the most uncompromising critic of the baroque.

TARANTO

100 km (62 mi) southeast of Bari, 40 km (25 mi) south of Martina Franca.

GETTING HERE

By car, the A14 motorway takes you almost directly to Taranto. Trenitalia runs frequent trains from Bari and Brindisi.

VISITOR INFORMATION

Taranto tourism office (✉ *Corso Umberto 113* ☎ *099/4532397* 🌐 *www.viaggiareinpuglia.it*).

EXPLORING

Taranto (the stress is on the first syllable) was an important port even in Greek times. It lies toward the back of the instep of the boot on the broad Mare Grande bay, which is connected to a small internal Mare Piccolo basin by two narrow channels, one artificial and one natural. The old town is a series of old palazzi in varying states of decay and narrow cobblestone streets on an island between the larger and smaller bodies of water, linked by causeways; the modern city stretches inward along the mainland. Circumnavigate the old town and take in a dramatic panorama to the north, revealing Italy's shipping industry at its busiest: steelworks, dockyards, a bay dotted with fishing boats, and a fish market teeming with pungent activity along the old town's western edge.

Little remains of Taranto's past except the 14th-century church of **San Domenico** (✉ *Via Duomo 33* ☎ *No phone* ⏲ *Daily 8:30–noon and 4–7*) jutting into the sea at one end of the island, and its famous naval academy.

★ Taranto's **Museo Nazionale** has a large collection of prehistoric, Greek, and Roman artifacts discovered mainly in the immediate vicinity, including Puglian tombs dating from before 1000 BC. Just over the bridge from the old town, the museum is a testament to the importance of this ancient port, which has always taken full advantage of its unique trading position at the end of the Italian peninsula. Only part of the museum (ten rooms on the second floor) is open to the public. ✉ *Via Cavour 10* ☎ *099/4532112* 🌐 *www.museotaranto.org* 🎫 *€5* ⏲ *Daily 8:30–7:30; last entrance at 7.*

LECCE

Fodor's Choice ★

40 km (25 mi) southeast of Brindisi, 87 km (54 mi) east of Taranto.

GETTING HERE

By car from Bari, take the main toll-free coast road via Brindisi and continue along the SS613 to Lecce. Frequent trains run along the coast from Bari and beyond. The closest airport is in Brindisi.

VISITOR INFORMATION

Lecce tourism office (✉ *Corso Vittorio Emanuele 24* ☎ *0832/332463* 🌐 *www.viaggiareinpuglia.it*).

EXPLORING

Lecce is the crown jewel of the Mezzogiorno. The city is affectionately referred to as "the Florence of the south," but that sobriquet doesn't do justice to Lecce's uniqueness in the Italian landscape. Though its pretty boutiques, lively bars, and the impossibly intricate baroque architecture draw comparisons to the cultural capitals of the north, Lecce's bustling streets, laid-back student cafés, and magical evening passeggiata are distinctively southern. The city is a cosmopolitan oasis two steps from the idyllic Otranto–Brindisi coastline and a hop from the olive-grove countryside of Puglia. Relatively undiscovered by foreign tourists, Lecce exudes an optimism and youthful joie de vivre unparalleled in any other baroque showcase. There's no Lecce of the north.

Summer is a great time to visit. In July, courtyards and piazzas throughout the city are the settings for dramatic productions. Autumn has its charms as well. A baroque music festival is held in churches throughout the city in September and October.

★ Although Lecce was founded before the time of the ancient Greeks, it's often associated with the term *Barocco leccese,* the result of a citywide impulse in the 17th century to redo the town in an exuberant fashion. But this was baroque with a difference. Such architecture is often heavy and monumental, but here it took on a lighter, more fanciful air. Just look at the church of **Santa Croce** and the adjoining **Palazzo della Prefettura.** Although every column, window, pediment, and balcony is given a curling baroque touch—and then an extra one for good measure—the overall effect is lighthearted. The buildings' proportions are unintimidating, and the local stone is a glowing honey color: it couldn't look menacing if it tried. ✉ *Via Umberto I 3* ☎ *0832/241957* 🌐 *www.basilicasantacroce.eu* 🕐 *Daily 9–noon and 5–8.*

Lecce's ornate **Duomo**, first built in 1114 but reconstructed in baroque style from 1659 to 1670, is uncharacteristically set in a solitary lateral square off a main street, rather than at a crossroads of pedestrian traffic. To the left of the Duomo, the more austere **bell tower,** reconstructed by master baroque architect Giuseppe Zimbalo in the 17th century, takes on a surreal golden hue at dusk. The facades of the adjoining 18th-century **Palazzo Vescovile** (Bishops' Palace), farther past the right side of the Duomo, and the **Seminario** on the piazza's right edge complement the rich ornamentation of the Duomo to create an effect almost as splendid as that of Santa Croce. The Seminario's tranquil **cloister** is also worth a visit. ✉ *Piazza Duomo off Corso Vittorio Emanuele* ☎ *0832/308557* 🕐 *Daily 7–noon and 5–7:30.*

In the middle of **Piazza Sant'Oronzo**, the city's putative center, surrounded by cafés, pastry shops, and newsstands, is a Roman column that once stood at the end of the Appian Way in Brindisi. This war trophy, carried off in 1660, is imaginatively surmounted by an 18th-century statue of the city's patron saint, Orontius. Next to the column, the shallow rows of seats in the **Anfiteatro Romano** suggest Verona's arena or a small-scale Roman Colosseum.

WHERE TO EAT AND STAY

$ SOUTHERN ITALIAN ✕ **Alle Due Corti.** Rosalba De Carlo, a local character, runs this traditional trattoria. The menu is printed in the Leccese dialect; the adventurous can try country dishes like *pezzetti te cavallu* (spicy horse meat in tomato sauce) or *turcineddhi* (roasted baby goat entrails)—a crisp, gamy, fully flavored delight. The white-wall decor is stark, but character comes from the red-and-white checked tablecloths and the gregarious local families and groups of friends that inevitably fill the place. ✉ *Corte dei Giugni 1* ☎ *0832/242223* 🌐 *www.alleduecorti.com* ⏲ *Closed Sun.*

$ SOUTHERN ITALIAN **Corte dei Pandolfi.** Here you can choose from a vast list of Salento's best wines and feast on an unparalleled spread of artisanal *salumi* (cured meats) and local cheeses, accompanied by delicious local honey and *mostarda* (preserved fruit). Traditional *primi* (first courses) and *secondi* (second courses) are also served, as well as vegetarian specialties. The location is on a little piazza just off Via degli Ammirati, which starts at the back of the Duomo. ✉ *Piazzetta Orsini* ☎ *0832/332309* 🌐 *www.cortedeipandolfi.com* ⏲ *No lunch Mon.–Thurs. Closed 1 wk in Nov.*

WORD OF MOUTH

"Puglia is a world in itself; we stayed for 6 weeks in the same villa rental each time we were there. I would suggest you stay in Lecce and in the centro. There's quite a bit to do in town and driving to other areas for day trips is very easy, nowhere near the traffic of Tuscany etc. Day trips to Locorotondo, Alberobello, Ostuni, Gallipoli (great seafood shops and restaurants), etc."

—oakboatkey

14

$ SOUTHERN ITALIAN Fodor's Choice ★ **Le Zie.** This is an excellent place to try traditional Pugliese cooking in a warm, casual setting of white walls and loud chatter. Don't expect a menu; choose from the daily specials, which might include homemade whole-wheat pasta served with a delicate sauce of tomato and sharp, aged ricotta *scante.* The rustic *purè di fave e cicoria* is topped with local olive oil and hot peppers; mix it together before eating. Service is informal and welcoming. ✉ *Via Costadura 19* ☎ *0832/245178* ⏲ *Closed Mon., 1 wk at Easter, last wk in Aug., 1st wk in Sept., last wk in Dec., and 1st wk in Jan. No dinner Sun.*

$$ ★ **Patria Palace.** It's a nice coincidence that the best hotel in Lecce happens to be in one of the best possible locations: a few steps from all the action. **Pros:** luxurious rooms; ideal location. **Cons:** not all rooms have great views. **TripAdvisor:** "facing magnificent cathedral," "roof terrace is lovely," "staff helpful and friendly." ✉ *Piazzetta Riccardi 13* ☎ *0832/245111* 🌐 *www.patriapalacelecce.com* *67 rooms* *In-room: a/c, Wi-Fi. In-hotel: restaurant, bar, parking* *Breakfast.*

$$ **President.** Rub elbows with visiting dignitaries at this business hotel near Piazza Mazzini. **Pros:** comfortable rooms; convenient location; low-season bargains. **Cons:** more for business than pleasure; a bit dated. **TripAdvisor:** "rooms are very spacious," "accommodating and helpful," "good value for money." ✉ *Via Salandra 6* ☎ *0832/456111* 🌐 *www.hotelpresidentlecce.it* *150 rooms, 3 suites* *In-room: a/c, Wi-Fi. In-hotel: restaurant, bar, parking* *Breakfast.*

OTRANTO

36 km (22 mi) southeast of Lecce, 188 km (117 mi) southeast of Bari.

GETTING HERE

By car from Lecce, take the southbound SS16 and exit at Maglie. To follow the coast, take the SS543 from Lecce, then follow SS611 south. There's regular train service from Lecce on Ferrovia del Sud-Est.

VISITOR INFORMATION

Otranto tourism office (✉ *Piazza Castello* ☎ *0836/801436* 🌐 *www.comune.otranto.le.it*).

EXPLORING

In one of the first great Gothic novels, Horace Walpole's 1764 *The Castle of Otranto*, the English writer immortalized this city and its mysterious medieval fortress. Otranto (the stress is on the first syllable) has likewise had more than its share of dark thrills. As the easternmost point in Italy—and therefore closest to the Balkan Peninsula—it has often borne the brunt of foreign invasions during its checkered history. A flourishing port from ancient Greek times, Otranto (Hydruntum to the Romans) has a history like most of southern Italy: after the fall of the western Roman Empire, centuries of Byzantine rule interspersed with Saracen incursions, followed by the arrival of the Normans. Modern Otranto's dank cobblestone alleyways alternatively reveal dusty, forgotten doorways and modern Italian fashion chains, and the spooky castle still looms above, between city and sea. On a clear day you can see across to Albania.

The historic city center nestles within impressive city walls and bastions, dominated by the famous **Castello Aragonese**, which is attributed to the Spanish of the 16th century. ✉ *Piazza Castello* ☎ *334/8863111* 🌐 *www.castelloaragoneseotranto.it* 🎫 €4 ⏲ *Jan.–May and Oct.–Dec., daily 10–1 and 3–7; June and Sept., daily 10–1 and 3–11; July and August, daily 10–1 and 3–midnight.*

The real jewel in Otranto is the **Cattedrale**, originally begun by the Normans and conserving an extraordinary 12th-century mosaic pavement in the nave and aisles. ✉ *Piazza Basilica* ☎ *0836/802720* ⏲ *Daily 8–noon and 3–7.*

WHERE TO STAY

$$$ Fodor's Choice ★

🏨 **Masseria Montelauro**. This *masseria*—a working farmhouse for communal living, quite common in these parts—has had many incarnations since it was built in 1878: monastery, herbal pharmacy, discotheque, and restaurant. **Pros:** interesting building; lovely decor; great food. **Cons:** car is absolutely necessary; food is pricey. **TripAdvisor:** "true Italian panache," "airy and spacious," "quiet and elegant." ✉ *S.P. Otranto–Uggiano, Località Montelauro* ☎ *0836/806203* 🌐 *www.masseriamontelauro.it* 🛏 *27 rooms, 3 suites* 👍 *In-room: a/c (some). In-hotel: restaurant, pool, parking, some pets allowed* ⏲ *Closed Nov.–Mar.* 🍽 *Breakfast.*

GALLIPOLI

37 km (23 mi) south of Lecce, 190 km (118 mi) southeast of Bari.

GETTING HERE

From Lecce, take the SS101. From Taranto, follow the coastal SS174. Frequent trains run from Lecce.

VISITOR INFORMATION

Gallipoli tourism office (✉ *Piazza Imbriani 9* ☎ *0833/262529*).

EXPLORING

The fishing port of Gallipoli, on the eastern tip of the Golfo di Taranto, is divided between a new town, on the mainland, and a beautiful fortified town, across a 17th-century bridge, crowded onto its own small island in the gulf. The Greeks called it Kallipolis, the Romans Anxa. Like the infamous Turkish town of the same name on the Dardanelles, the Italian Gallipoli occupies a strategic location and thus was repeatedly attacked through the centuries—by the Normans in 1071, the Venetians in 1484, and the British in 1809. Today life in Gallipoli revolves around its fishing trade. Fishing boats in primary colors breeze in and out of the bay during the day, and Gallipoli's fish market, below the bridge, throbs with activity all morning.

14

Gallipoli's historic quarter, a mix of narrow alleys and squares, is guarded by the **Castello Aragonese**, a massive fortification that grew out of an earlier Byzantine fortress you can still see at the southeast corner.

Gallipoli's **Duomo** (✉ *Via Antonietta de Pace* ☎ *0833/261987* 🌐 *www.cattedralegallipoli.it*), open daily 8–noon and 3–7, is a notable baroque church.

The church of **La Purità** (✉ *Riviera Nazario Sauro* ☎ *0833/261699*) has a stuccoed interior as elaborate as a wedding cake, with an especially noteworthy tile floor. The church is currently under restoration, and due to reopen in October 2012.

WHERE TO EAT AND STAY

$$ SOUTHERN ITALIAN ✕ **Marechiaro.** Unless you arrive by boat—as many do—you have to cross a little bridge to reach this simple waterfront restaurant, not far from the town's historic center. It's built out onto the sea, replete with wood paneling, flowers, and terraces, with panoramic coastal views. Try the renowned *zuppa di pesce alla gallipolina* (a stew of fish, local red shrimp, clams, and mussels) and linguine with seafood. ✉ *Lungomare Marcon* ☎ *0833/266143.*

$$$$ **Costa Brada.** The rooms all have terraces with sea views at this classic Mediterranean beach hotel. **Pros:** lovely views; stunning location. **Cons:** meal plans required in summer. **TripAdvisor:** "by its own private beach," "suite was stunning," "greeted warmly." ✉ *Baia Verde, Litoranea Santa Maria di Leuca* ☎ *0833/202551* 🌐 *www.grandhotelcostabrada.it* *80 rooms* *In-room: a/c, Wi-Fi. In-hotel: restaurants, pools, gym, spa, beach, parking* *Some meals.*

BEACHES

Ample swimming, water sports, and clean, fine sand make Gallipoli's **beaches** a good choice for families. The 5-km (3-mi) expanse of sand sweeping south from town has both public and private beaches, the latter equipped with changing rooms, sun beds, and umbrellas. Water-sports equipment can be bought or rented at the waterfront shops in town.

BASILICATA

Occupying the instep of Italy's boot, Basilicata formed part of Magna Graecia, the loose collection of colonies founded along the coast of southern Italy whose wealth and military prowess rivaled those of the city states of Greece itself. More recently it was made famous by Carlo Levi (1902–75) in his *Christ Stopped at Eboli,* a book that underscored the poverty of the region. Basilicata is no longer so desolate, as it draws travelers in search of bucolic settings, great food, and archaeological treasures. The city of Matera, the region's true highlight, is built on the side of an impressive ravine that's honeycombed with Sassi, rock-hewn dwellings, some of them still occupied, forming a separate enclave that contrasts vividly with the attractive baroque town above.

MATERA

62 km (39 mi) south of Bari.

GETTING HERE

From Bari, take the SS96 to Altamura, then the SS99 to Matera. Roughly one train per hour (Ferrovie Appulo Lucane) leaves Bari Centrale for Matera.

VISITOR INFORMATION

Matera tourism office (✉ *Via De Viti De Marco 9* ☎ *0835/331983* 🌐 *www.aptbasilicata.it*). **Sassi tourism office** (✉ *Via Lucana 238* ☎ *0835/319458*).

EXPLORING

Matera is one of southern Italy's most unusual towns. On their own, the elegant baroque churches, palazzi, and broad piazzas—filled to bursting during the evening passeggiata, when the locals turn out to stroll the streets—would make Matera stand out in Basilicata's rugged landscape. But what really sets this town apart are the Sassi.

Fodor's Choice ★ Matera's **Sassi** are rock-hewn dwellings piled chaotically atop one another, strewn across the sides of a steep ravine. Some date from Paleolithic times, when they were truly cave homes. In the years that followed, the grottoes were slowly adapted as houses only slightly more modern, with their exterior walls closed off and canals regulating rainwater and sewage. Until relatively recently, these troglodytic abodes presented a Dante-esque vision of squalor and poverty, graphically described in Carlo Levi's *Christ Stopped at Eboli,* but in the 1960s most of them were emptied of their inhabitants, who were largely consigned to the ugly block structures seen on the way into town. Today, having been designated a World Heritage Site, the area has been cleaned up and is gradually being populated once again—and even gentrified, as evidenced by the bars and restaurants that

Basilicata and Calabria
Adriatic Sea
Bari
Andria
Polignano a Mare
PUGLIA
Fasano
Ostuni
Spinazzola
Altamura
Gioia del Colle
Gravina in Puglia
Matera
Francavilla Fontana
Massafra
CAMPANIA
Potenza
Grassano
Via Appia
Taranto
TO NAPLES
Eboli
Ferrandina
Auletta
Metaponto
Battipaglia
BASILICATA
Pisticci
Lido di Metaponto
Sala Consilina
Aliano
gropoli
Colobraro
CILENTO
LUCANO
Parco Nazionale del Pollino
Francaville in Sinni
Lagonegro
Acquafredda
San Severino Lucano
Terranova di Pollino
Golfo di Taranto
Marina di Camerota
Maratea
Rotonda
Amendolara
Marina di Maratea
Cerchiara di Calabria
Sibari
Praia a Mare
Morano Calabro
Castrovillari
Scalea
Cirella
Diamante
Rossano
Parco Nazionale della Calabria
POINT ALICE
CALABRIA
La Fossiata
Cetraro
Lago di Cecita
Camigliatello
Paola
SILA GRANDE
San Giovanni in Fiore
Rende
Cosenza
Lorica
Crotone
Tyrrhenian Sea
SILA MASSIF
Amantea
Capo Rizzuto
CAPO COLONNA
CAPO RIZZUTO
Falerna
0
30 miles
Lamezia Terme
0
50 km
Catanzaro
Pizzo
Soverato
STROMBOLI
Briatico
Tropea
CAPO VATICANO
PANAREA
AEOLIAN ISLANDS
Nicotera
Marina di Monasterace
SALINA
Rosarno
Stilo
ASPROMONTE
Aspromonte
FILICUDI
LIPARI
Palmi
Lipari
Gerace
Ionian Sea
Bagnara Calabra
VULCANO
Locri
Villa San Giovanni
Scilla
Bovalino
Milazzo
Messina
Gambárie
Barcellona
Reggio Calabria
Gallico
Parco Nazionale della Calabria
SICILY
Melito di Porto Salvo
KEY
Ferry lines
A14
16
100
172
93
7
165
407
97
A3
166
598
653
18
105
106
107
280
522
111
A18
183
185

have moved in. (The filming here of Mel Gibson's controversial film *The Passion of the Christ* also raised the area's profile.) The wide Strada Panoramica leads you safely through this desolate region, which still retains its eerie atmosphere and panoramic views.

There are two areas of Sassi, the **Sasso Caveoso** and the **Sasso Barisano,** and both can be seen from vantage points in the upper town. Follow the Strada Panoramica down into the Sassi and feel free to ramble among the strange structures, which, in the words of H. V. Morton in his *A Traveller in Southern Italy,* "resemble the work of termites rather than of man." Among them you can find several *chiese rupestri,* or rock-hewn churches, some of which have medieval frescoes, notably **Santa Maria de Idris,** right on the edge of the Sasso Caveoso, near the ravine. ✉ *Sasso Caveoso* ☎ *0835/319458* 🎫 *€2.50* ⏲ *Apr.–Oct., daily 9–1 and 3–7; Nov.–Mar., daily 9:30–1:30 and 2:30–4:30.*

The **Duomo** in Matera was built in the late 13th century and occupies a prominent position between the two Sassi. It has a pungent Apulian-Romanesque flavor; inside, there's a recovered fresco, probably painted in the 14th century, showing scenes from the *Last Judgment.* On the Duomo's facade the figures of Saints Peter and Paul stand on either side of a sculpture of Matera's patron, the Madonna della Bruna. ✉ *Piazza Duomo* ☎ *0835/332908.*

In town you can find the 13th-century Romanesque church of **San Giovanni Battista,** restored to its pre-baroque simplicity in 1926. As you go in through a side door—the original end door and facade were incorporated into later buildings—note the interesting sculpted decorations in the porch. The interior still maintains its original cross vaulting, ogival arches, and curious capitals. ✉ *Via San Biagio* ☎ *0835/334182* ⏲ *Daily 7:30–12:30 and 3:30–7:30.*

Matera's archaeological **Museo Archaeologico Nazionale Domenico Ridola** is housed in the former monastery of Santa Chiara. Illustrating the history of the area, the museum includes an extensive selection of prehistoric and classical finds, notably Bronze Age weaponry and beautifully decorated red-figure pottery from Greece. ✉ *Via Ridola 24* ☎ *0835/310058* 🎫 *€2.50* ⏲ *Mon. 2–8, Tues.–Sun. 9–8.*

WHERE TO EAT AND STAY

$$ SOUTHERN ITALIAN

✕ **Le Botteghe.** This stylish restaurant occupies a pleasingly restored building in the Sassi. Carnivores will delight in the charcoal-grilled steak, especially selected by a local butcher. Cooked wonderfully rare, this is one of the finest pieces of meat in the region. It's best washed down with local Aglianico del Vulture red wine. Solid renditions of local pasta dishes are also available. ✉ *Piazza San Pietro Barisano 22* ☎ *0835/344072* ⏲ *No lunch Tues.–Fri. Oct.–Mar.*

$$ SOUTHERN ITALIAN Fodor's Choice ★

✕ **Lucanerie.** On the edge of Sasso Barisano, this restaurant's menu is based on seasonal ingredients from around Matera, some of which are gathered by the owner himself. The *cavatelli con peperoni cruschi* is dusted with breadcrumbs and full of flavor. The grilled *bistecca* (steak) is from the Podolico, a native breed of cow that grazes below the Sassi and has a tenderness all its own. Top off your meal with a slice of homemade goat cheesecake. ✉ *Via Santo Stefano 61* ☎ *0835/332133* ⏲ *Closed Sun.*

$$$ ★ **Hotel Sant'Angelo.** Looking across a piazza to the church of San Pietro Caveoso, this unusual hotel has an ideal view of the Sasso Caveoso. **Pros:** unrivaled views; atmospheric rooms. **Cons:** no elevator and many steps to climb. **TripAdvisor:** "Italian chic at its finest," "rooms are unique," "spectacular view." ✉ *Piazza San Pietro Caveoso* ☎ *0835/314010* 🌐 *www.hotelsantangelosassi.it* *23 rooms* *In-room: a/c, Wi-Fi. In-hotel: restaurant, bar* *Breakfast.*

$ Fodor's Choice ★ **Locanda di San Martino.** Combining good taste, an agreeable ambience, and excellent value, the Locanda is a prime place to stay among Matera's Sassi. **Pros:** convenient location; comfortable rooms; no traffic noise. **Cons:** rooms are reached via outdoor walkway; limited parking nearby. **TripAdvisor:** "close to the main piazza," "staff are super-friendly," "breakfast here is delightful." ✉ *Via Fiorentini 71* ☎ *0835/256600* 🌐 *www.locandadisanmartino.it* *21 rooms, 11 suites* *In-room: a/c, Wi-Fi. In-hotel: bar, pool, spa, parking* *Breakfast.*

14

MARATEA

217 km (135 mi) south of Naples.

GETTING HERE

By car, take the Lagonegro exit from the A3 motorway and continue along the SS585. Intercity and regional trains from Reggio Calabria and Naples stop at Maratea. In the summer months there's a bus linking the train station to the upper town 4 km (2½ mi) away.

VISITOR INFORMATION

Maratea tourism office (✉ *Piazza del Gesù 32, Località Fiumicello* ☎ *0973/876908* 🌐 *www.aptbasilicata.it*).

EXPLORING

When encountering Maratea for the first time, you can be forgiven for thinking you've somehow arrived at the French Riviera. The high, twisty road resembles nothing so much as a corniche, complete with glimpses of a turquoise sea below and is divided by the craggy rocks into various separate localities—Maratea, Maratea Porto, Marina di Maratea, Fiumicello, and Cersuta. Maratea is the name given to this cluster of towns, as well as to the main inland village, a tumble of cobblestone streets where the ruins of a much older settlement (Maratea Antica) can be seen. At the summit of the hill stands the giagantic Christo Redentore, a massive statue of Christ reminiscent of the one in Rio de Janeiro. There's no shortage of secluded sandy strips in between the rocky headlands, which can get crowded in August. A summer minibus service connects all the different points once or twice an hour.

WHERE TO EAT AND STAY

$$ SOUTHERN ITALIAN ★ ✕ **Da Cesare.** With an open kitchen so you can watch the chef and a veranda overlooking the azure waters of the Golfo di Policastro, this family-run seafood restaurant serves some of the freshest catch in town. The only drawback may be that the portions are very large, so you might not want every course from antipasto to dolce. Try the linguine *al nero di seppie* (with cuttlefish ink) and *grigliata mista* (mixed grilled fish and seafood). ✉ *Strada Statale 18, Località Cersuta* ☎ *0973/871840* ⊗ *Closed Thurs. Nov.–Mar.*

$$ **Villa Cheta Elite.** Immersed in Mediterranean greenery, this historic villa is in the seaside village of Acquafredda, just north of Maratea. **Pros:** surrounded by lush vegetation; beautiful views of the coast and mountains; lovely art deco building. **Cons:** on a busy road; no pool; steps to climb. **TripAdvisor:** "beautiful spot along the coast," "good old-fashioned qualities," "service was impeccable." ✉ *Via Timpone 46, Località Acquafredda* ☎ *0973/878134* 🌐 *www.villacheta.it* *23 rooms* *In-room: Wi-Fi. In-hotel: restaurant, bar, parking* *Closed Nov.–Mar.* *Some meals.*

CALABRIA

Italy's southernmost mainland region may be poor, but it also claims more than its share of fantastic scenery and great beaches. The accent here is on the landscape, the sea, and the constantly changing dialogue between the two. Don't expect much in the way of sophistication in this least trodden of regions, but do remain open to the simple pleasures to be found—the country food, the friendliness, the disarming hospitality of the people. Aside from coast and culture, there are also some destinations worth going out of your way for, from the vividly colored murals of Diamante to the hiking trails of the Pollino and Sila national parks.

The drive on the southbound A3 highway alone is a breathtaking experience, the more so as you approach Sicily, whose image grows tantalizingly nearer as the road wraps around the coastline once challenged by Odysseus. The road has been under reconstruction since his time, with little sign of completion.

DIAMANTE

51 km (32 mi) south of Maratea, 225 km (140 mi) south of Naples.

GETTING HERE

Driving from Maratea, take the SS18; from Cosenza, take the SS107 to Paola, then the SS18. Regional trains leave from Naples and Paola six times a day.

VISITOR INFORMATION

Diamante tourism office (✉ *Discesa Corvino Superiore* ☎ *0985/876046*).

EXPLORING

One of the most fashionable of the string of small resorts lining Calabria's north Tyrrhenian Coast, Diamante makes a good stop for its whitewashed maze of narrow alleys, brightly adorned with a startling variety of large-scale murals. The work of local and international artists, the murals—which range from cartoons to poems to serious portraits, and from tasteful to downright ugly—give a sense of wandering through a huge open-air art gallery. Flanking the broad, palm-lined seaside promenade are sparkling beaches to the north and south.

WHERE TO STAY

$$$ **Grand Hotel San Michele.** A survivor from a vanishing age, the San Michele, operated by the illustrious Claudia Siniscalchi and her marine biologist son, Andrea, occupies a belle epoque–style villa. **Pros:** lovely views; nice gardens; comfortable accommodations. **Cons:** a bit pricey. **TripAdvisor:** "grounds are absolutely beautiful," "very friendly and helpful," "perfect wedding venue." ✉ *Località Bosco 8/9, Cetraro* ☎ *0982/91012* 🌐 *www.sanmichele.it* *80 rooms, 6 suites, 20 apartments* *In-room: a/c, Internet. In-hotel: golf course, restaurant, tennis court, bar, beach, parking* *Closed Nov.–Mar.* *Breakfast.*

CASTROVILLARI

14

68 km (43 mi) east of Diamante, 75 km (48 mi) north of Cosenza.

GETTING HERE

By car, take the A3 motorway and exit at Frascineto-Castrovillari. Ferrovie della Calabria runs buses from Cosenza, but service is irregular.

VISITOR INFORMATION

Castrovillari tourism office (✉ *Corso Garibaldi 160* ☎ *0981/209595* 🌐 *www.prolococastrovillari.it*).

EXPLORING

Accent the first "i" when you pronounce the name of this provincial Calabrian city, notable for its Aragonese castle, synagogue, and 16th-century San Giuliano church. It's also a great jumping-off point for the Parco Nazionale Pollino. Castrovillari's world-class restaurant-inn, La Locanda di Alia, has made the city something of an out-of-the-way gastronomical destination in Calabria.

WHERE TO EAT

$$ MODERN ITALIAN Fodor's Choice ★ **La Locanda di Alia.** It's hard to say what's more surprising about this inn and gastronomical temple: its improbable location in Castrovillari, or the fact that it's been here since 1952. At the restaurant, chef Gaetano Alia's menu swerves from the unique (beef with a delicious strawberry-and-onion sauce) to the dangerously spicy (*candele,* like rigatoni without the ridges, in a pecorino cheese sauce). If you like it so much you want to stay, more than a dozen guest rooms are surrounded by plenty of greenery. They're decorated in bright colors with frescoes from local artists. ✉ *Via Ietticelli 55* ☎ *0981/46370* 🌐 *www.alia.it* *Reservations essential* *Closed Sun.*

COSENZA

75 km (48 mi) south of Diamante, 185 km (115 mi) north of Reggio Calabria.

GETTING HERE

By car, take the Cosenza exit from the A3 motorway. By train, change at Paola on the main Rome–Reggio Calabria line. Regional trains run from Naples. Ferrovie della Calabria runs buses from Spezzano della Sila, Castrovillari, and Camigliatello.

VISITOR INFORMATION

Cosenza tourism office (✉ *Piazza Bruzi* ☎ *0984/813217* 🌐 *www.regionecalabria.it*).

EXPLORING

Cosenza has a steep, stair-filled centro storico that truly hails from another age. Wrought-iron balconies overlook narrow alleyways with old-fashioned storefronts and bars that have barely been touched by centuries of development. Flung haphazardly—and beautifully—across the top and side of a steep hill ringed by mountains, and watched over by a great, crumbling medieval castle, Cosenza also provides the best gateway for the Sila, whose steep walls rear up to the town's eastern side. Though Cosenza's outskirts are largely modern and ugly, culinary gems and picturesque views await in the rolling farmland nearby and the mountains to the east.

Crowning the Pancrazio hill above the old city, with views across to the Sila mountains, **Castello Svevo** is largely in ruins, having suffered successive earthquakes and a lightning strike that ignited gunpowder stored within. The castle takes its name from the great Swabian emperor Frederick II (1194–1250), who added two octagonal towers, though it dates originally to the Normans, who fortified the hill against their Saracen foes. Occasional exhibitions and concerts are staged here in summer, and any time of year it's fun to check out the old ramparts and take in the views of the old and new cities—a shocking study in contrast. It's currently undergoing extensive restorations. ✉ *Colle Pancrazio* ☎ *No phone* 🎫 *Free* ⏲ *Daily 8–8.*

Cosenza's original **Duomo** was probably built in the middle of the 11th century but was destroyed by the earthquake of 1184. A new cathedral was consecrated in the presence of Emperor Frederick II in 1222. After many baroque additions, later alterations have restored some of the Provençal Gothic style. Inside, look for the lovely monument to Isabella of Aragon, who died after falling from her horse en route to France in 1271. ✉ *Piazza del Duomo 1* ☎ *0984/77864* ⏲ *May–Oct., daily 8–noon and 4:30–8; Nov.–Apr., daily 8–noon and 3:30–7.*

Cosenza's noblest square, **Piazza XV Marzo** (commonly called Piazza della Prefettura), houses government buildings as well as the elegant **Teatro Rendano.** From the square, the **Villa Comunale** (public garden) provides plenty of shaded benches for a rest.

WHERE TO EAT AND STAY

$$ SOUTHERN ITALIAN **Osteria dell'Arenella.** On the banks of the river, this grilled-meat specialist caters to the local bourgeoisie with a comfortable, friendly set of rooms under old archways. The place is for carnivores; go for the grigliata mista and enjoy the wonderful meatiness of local grass-fed beef—but be sure to ask for it all *al sangue* (rare). The wine list, too, is excellent. The local wine made with the gaglioppo grape pairs nicely with meat, sausage, and aged cheeses. *Via Arenella 12* *0984/76573* *Closed Mon. Oct.–May. No lunch Tues.–Sat.*

$ **Royal Hotel.** Decent accommodations are hard to come by in Cosenza, which makes this hotel in the new center quite a find. **Pros:** one of the town's best lodgings. **Cons:** not in the best part of the city. **TripAdvisor:** "very old-world," "personnel was very friendly," "clean and comfortable." *Via Molinella 24/e* *0984/412165* *www.hotelroyalsas.it* *80 rooms* *In-room: a/c, Wi-Fi. In-hotel: restaurant, bar* *Breakfast.*

14

RENDE

13 km (8 mi) northwest of Cosenza.

GETTING HERE

By car, take the A3 motorway and exit at Cosenza-Rende. Local buses make the trip from nearby Cosenza.

EXPLORING

Rende is a pleasing stop on the way to or from Cosenza. Leave your car in the parking lot at the base of a long and bizarre series of escalators and staircases, which will whisk you off to this pristine, cobblestoned hilltop town, whose winding streets and turrets preside over idyllic countryside views.

WHERE TO EAT

$$ SOUTHERN ITALIAN **Pantagruel.** You're completely in the hands of the chef at this prix-fixe–only temple to seafood. They're good hands indeed, which is why Pantagruel is one of the most respected restaurants in Calabria. The set menu depends on the day's catch, but you'll surely encounter something memorable: for instance, a salad of octopus so thinly sliced and delicate that it's reminiscent of carpaccio, or a tender whole *orata* (sea bream) with fava beans. Pantagruel is set in an elegant old house with sweeping views of hills dotted with little towns. *Via Pittore Santanna 2* *0984/443508* *www.pantagruelilristorante.it* *Closed Sun., 1 wk in late Dec., and 1 wk in Sept.*

CAMIGLIATELLO

30 km (19 mi) east of Cosenza.

GETTING HERE

By car, take the Cosenza Nord exit from the A3, then follow the SS107.

VISITOR INFORMATION

Camigliatello tourism office (*Via Roma 5* *0984/578159*).

EXPLORING

Lined with chalets, Camigliatello is one of the Sila Massif's major resort towns. Most of the Sila isn't mountainous at all; it is, rather, an extensive, sparsely populated plateau with areas of thick forest. Unfortunately, there has been considerable deforestation. However, since 1968, when the area was designated a national park called Parco Nazionale della Sila, strict rules have limited the felling of timber, and forests are now regenerating. There are well-marked trails through pine and beech woods, and ample opportunities for horseback riding. Fall and winter see droves of locals hunting mushrooms and gathering chestnuts, while ski slopes near Camigliatello draw crowds.

> **WORD OF MOUTH**
>
> "In America one of your most famous trips is 'coast to coast.' Well, also in Calabria, it is possible the coast to coast trip: from Tyrrhenian sea to the Ionian sea. One of the little differences is the distance: 6,600 kilometers in USA and 100 kilometers in Calabria!!! That's my suggestion, take a coast to coast trip in Cosenza province." —vincenzod

A couple of miles east of town, Lago Cecita makes a good starting point for exploring **La Fossiata**, a lovely wooded conservation area within the park. The forestry commission office in nearby Cupone can provide maps and arrange guides. ✉ *Cupone Frazione Spezzano della Sila* ☎ *0984/579757* 🌐 *www.parcosila.it.*

WHERE TO STAY

$ **Tasso.** On the edge of Camigliatello, less than 1 km (½ mi) from the ski slopes, this hotel is in a peaceful, picturesque location. **Pros:** beautiful surroundings; nice views, lively atmosphere. **Cons:** dated architecture; two-night minimum. ✉ *Via degli Impianti Sportivi, Spezzano della Sila* ☎ *0984/578113* 🌐 *www.hoteltasso.it* *82 rooms* *In-room: no a/c. In-hotel: restaurant, bar, parking* *Closed Apr.–May and Nov.* *Breakfast.*

TROPEA

★ *120 km (75 mi) south of Cosenza, 107 km (66 mi) north of Reggio.*

GETTING HERE

By car, exit the A3 motorway at Pizzo and follow the southbound SP6/SS522. Eight trains depart daily from Lamezia Terme.

VISITOR INFORMATION

Tropea tourism office (✉ *Piazza Ercole* ☎ *0963/61475* 🌐 *www.prolocotropea.eu*).

EXPLORING

Ringed by cliffs and wonderful sandy beaches, the Tropea Promontory is still mostly undiscovered by foreign tourists. The main town of Tropea, its old palazzi built in simple golden stone, easily wins the contest for prettiest town on Calabria's Tyrrhenian coast. On a clear day the seaward views from the waterfront promenade take in Stromboli's cone and at least four of the other Aeolians. You can visit the islands by motorboats that depart daily in summer. Accommodations are good, and beach addicts won't be disappointed by the choice of magnificent sandy bays within easy reach. Two of the best are south at Capo Vaticano and north at Briatico.

In Tropea's harmonious warren of lanes, seek out the old Norman **Cattedrale**, whose interior displays a couple of unexploded U.S. bombs from World War II, with a grateful prayer to the Madonna attached to each. ✉ *Largo Duomo* ☎ *0963/61034* ⏲ *Daily 7:30–noon and 4–7.*

From the belvedere at the bottom of the main square, Piazza Ercole, the church and Benedictine monastery of **Santa Maria dell'Isola** glisten on a rocky promontory above an aquamarine sea. The path out to the church is lined with fishermen's caves. Dating to medieval times, the church was remodeled in the Gothic style, then given another face-lift after an earthquake in 1905. The interior has an 18th-century Nativity and fragments of medieval tombs. At this writing, the monastery was closed for reconstruction. ✉ *Lungomare A Sorrentino* ☎ *0963/61475.*

14

WHERE TO EAT AND STAY

$$–$$$ SOUTHERN ITALIAN ✕ **Pimm's.** Since its glory days in the 1960s, this underground restaurant in Tropea's historic center has offered the town's top dining experience. Seafood is the best choice, with such specialties as pasta with sea urchins, smoked swordfish, and stuffed squid. The splendid sea views are an extra enticement. ✉ *Corso Vittorio Emanuele 2* ☎ *0963/666105* ⏲ *Closed Mon. Oct.–May.*

$$$ **Rocca Nettuno.** Perched on the cliffs south of the town center, this large complex has reasonably spacious rooms, almost all with balconies. **Pros:** family-friendly environment; 10-minute stroll from town. **Cons:** not the place for a quiet getaway. **TripAdvisor:** "definitely a good choice," "excellent quality of service," "lovely gardens." ✉ *Via Annunziata* ☎ *0963/998111* 🌐 *www.roccanettuno.com* *276 rooms* *In-room: a/c. In-hotel: restaurants, tennis court, bars, children's programs, pool, gym, spa, beach, business center* ⏲ *Closed Nov.–Mar.* *Some meals.*

REGGIO CALABRIA

115 km (71 mi) south of Tropea, 499 km (311 mi) south of Naples.

GETTING HERE

The A3 motorway runs directly to Reggio Calabria. Five trains depart from Naples and Rome daily. There are daily flights from Rome, Milan, Turin, and Bologna.

VISITOR INFORMATION

Reggio Calabria tourism office (✉ *Via Venezia 1a* ☎ *0965/21010* 🌐 *www.prolocoreggiocalabria.it*).

EXPLORING

Reggio Calabria, on the tip of Italy's toe, is departure point for Sicily-bound ferries. It was laid low by the same catastrophic earthquake that struck Messina in 1908. This raw city is one of Italy's busiest ports, where you can find every type of container ship and smokestack.

★ Reggio has one of southern Italy's most important archaeological museums, the **Museo Nazionale della Magna Grecia**. Prize exhibits here are two statues, known as the **Bronzi di Riace,** that were discovered by an amateur deep-sea diver off Calabria's Ionian Coast in 1972. Flaunting physiques gym enthusiasts would die for, the pair is thought to date from the 5th century BC and have been attributed to both Pheidias and Polykleitos. It's possible they were taken by the Romans as trophies from the site of Delphi and then shipwrecked on the trip to Italy. After a lengthy restoration the museum was due to reopen in 2011. If making a special trip, call the tourist office just to check the bronzes and other exhibits are back in place. ✉ *Piazza De Nava 26* ☎ *0965/812255* 🌐 *www.museonazionalerc.it* 🎫 *€8* ⏲ *Tues.–Sun. 9–7.*

WHERE TO STAY

$$ **E'Hotel.** A gently curving facade adds a bit of drama to this sleek modern hotel. **Pros:** great location; unbeatable views; luxurious rooms. **Cons:** can be busy during conferences. **TripAdvisor:** "beautiful views," "quiet, clean, excellent staff," "at the heart of Reggio Calabria seafront." ✉ *Via Giunchi 6* ☎ *0965/893000* 🌐 *www.ehotelreggiocalabria.it* *52 rooms, 4 suites* *In-room: a/c, Wi-Fi. In-hotel: restaurant, room service, bar, pool, parking* 🍽 *Breakfast.*

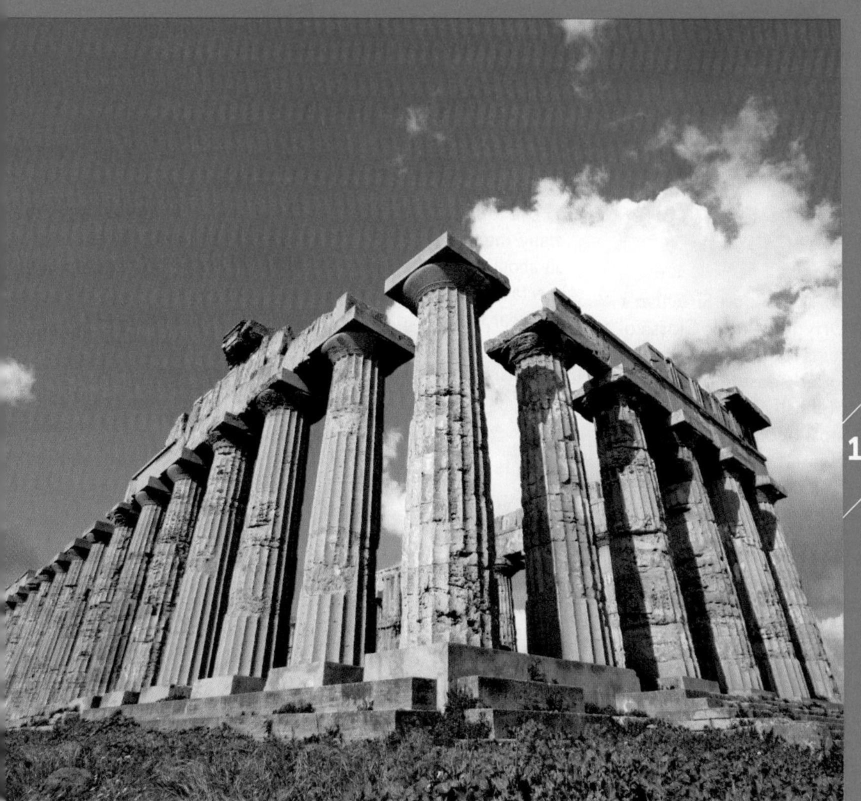

15

Sicily

WORD OF MOUTH

"If you want to see a bit of many things, I think Sicily is your best bet. There are beaches of all kinds, from white sand to black sand to cliff beaches. You can go to the Aeolians and pretend you're in the Greek islands. You can see a sunrise on the water, then a sunset on the water. Climb a few volcanoes too."

—TravMimi

WELCOME TO SICILY

TOP REASONS TO GO

★ **A walk on Siracusa's Ortygia Island:** Classical ruins rub elbows with faded seaside palaces and fish markets in Sicily's most beautiful port city, whose Duomo is literally built on the columns of an ancient Greek temple.

★ **The palaces, churches, and crypts of Palermo:** Virtually every great European empire ruled Sicily's strategically positioned capital at some point, and it shows most of all in the diverse architecture, from Roman to Byzantine to Arab-Norman.

★ **The Valley of the Temples, Agrigento:** This stunning set of ruins is proudly perched above the sea in a grove full of almond trees; not even in Athens will you find Greek temples this finely preserved.

★ **Taormina's Teatro Greco:** Watch a Greek tragedy in the very amphitheater where it was performed two millennia ago—in the shadow of smoking Mount Etna.

1 The Ionian Coast. For many, the Ionian Coast is all about touristy **Taormina**, spectacularly perched on a cliff near **Mount Etna**; but don't overlook lively **Catania**, Sicily's modern nerve center.

2 Siracusa. This was one of the great powers of the classical world. Today, full of fresh fish and remarkable ruins, it's content to be one of Italy's most charming cities.

3 The Interior. In hill towns such as **Enna**, the interior of Sicily exhibits a slower pace of life than in the frenetic coastal cities. **Piazza Armerina** features the Villa Casale and its ancient Roman mosaics.

4 Western Sicily. Following the island's northern edge west of Palermo, the western coast meanders past **Monreale** and its mosaics, **Segesta** with its temple, and the fairy-tale town of **Erice**. Greek ruins stand sentinel in **Agrigento** at the **Valley of the Temples**, blanketed in almond and juniper blossoms. Nearly as impressive is **Selinunte**, rising above rubble and overlooking the sea.

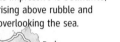

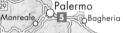

5 Palermo. Sicily's capital and one of Italy's most hectic cities, Palermo conceals notes of extraordinary beauty amid the uncontained chaos of fish markets and impossible traffic.

6 Tyrrhenian Coast. Filled with summer beachgoers, the **Tyrrhenian Coast** also has several quaint villages, including **Cefalù**, with its famous cathedral.

7 Aeolian Islands. You may know these tranquil islands, windswept from the *Odyssey*, and some of them seem to have changed little since Homer.

GETTING ORIENTED

This splendid island is known as *Trinacria* for its three corners. At the northeastern corner is Messina, connected by car and train ferry to the mainland. The eastern edge of Sicily is its Ionian Coast, which continues south to Catania, Siracusa, and the island's southeastern corner. Sicily's northern edge is the Tyrrhenian Coast, which includes Palermo and extends out to the island's third (western) corner.

EATING AND DRINKING WELL IN SICILY

Sicilian cuisine is one of the oldest in existence, with records of cooking competitions dating to 600 BC. Food in Sicily today reflects the island's unique cultural mix, imaginatively combining fish, fruits, vegetables, and nuts with Italian pastas and Arab and North African elements.

It's hard to eat badly in Sicily. From the lowliest of trattorias to the most highfalutin' *ristorante*, you'll find the classic dishes that have been the staples of the family dinner table for years—basically pasta and seafood. A more sophisticated place may introduce a few adventurous items onto the menu, but the main difference between the cheapest and the most expensive restaurants will be the level of service and the accoutrements: in more formal places you'll find greater attention to detail and a more respectful atmosphere, while less pretentious trattorias tend to be family-run affairs, often without even a menu to guide you. However, in this most gregarious of regions in the most convivial of countries, you can expect a lively dining experience wherever you choose to eat.

SICILIAN MARKETS

Sicily's natural fecundity is evident wherever you look, from the prickly pears sprouting on roadsides to the slopes of vine and citrus groves covering the inland to the ranks of fishing boats moored in every harbor.

You can come face-to-face with this bounty in the clamorous street markets of Palermo *(pictured above)* and Catania. Here, you'll encounter teetering piles of olives and oranges, enticing displays of cheeses and meats, and pastries and sweets of every description. The effect is heady and sensuous. Immerse yourself in the hustle and bustle of the Sicilian souk, and you'll emerge enriched.

DELICIOUS FISH

In Sicily, naturally, you can find some of the freshest seafood in all of Italy. Pasta *con le sarde,* an emblematic dish that goes back to the Saracen conquerors, with fresh sardines (pictured at right), olive oil, raisins, pine nuts, and wild fennel, gets a different treatment at every restaurant. Grilled *tonno* (tuna) and *orata* (daurade) are coastal staples, while delicate *ricci* (sea urchin) is a specialty. King, however, is *pesce spada* (swordfish), best enjoyed *marinato* (marinated), *affumicato* (smoked), or as the traditional *involtini di pesce spada* (roulades).

SNACKS

Sicily offers a profusion of toothsome snacks, two prime examples being *arancini* ("little oranges"—rice croquettes with a cheese or meat filling; *pictured below*), and *panelle* (seasoned chickpea flour boiled to a paste, cooled, sliced, and fried), normally bought from street vendors. Other tidbits to look out for include special foods associated with festivals, often pastries and sweets, such as the ominously named *ossa dei morti* ("dead men's bones," rolled almond cookies). But the most eye-catching of all are the *frutta martorana,* also known as *pasta reale*—sweet marzipan confections shaped to resemble fruits, temptingly arrayed in bars and *pasticcerie* (pastry shops).

LOCAL SPECIALTIES

Many ingredients and recipes are unique to particular Sicilian towns and regions. In Catania, for example, you'll be offered *caserecci alla Norma* (a short pasta with a sauce of tomato, eggplant, ricotta, and basil), named after an opera by Bellini (a Catania native). The *mandorla* (bitter almond), the pride of Agrigento, plays into everything from risotto *alle mandorle* (with almonds, butter, Grana cheese, and parsley) to incomparable almond granita—an absolute must in summer. Pistachios produced around Bronte, on the lower slopes of Etna, go into pasta sauces as well as ice cream and granita, while capers from the Aeolian Islands add zest to salads and fish sauces.

WINES

Sicily produces more wine than all of Australia, but until recent years most of it was unimpressive. Today Sicilian wines are up-and-coming but still among Italy's best bargains. The earthy Nero d'Avola grape bolsters many of Sicily's traditionally sunny, expansive reds, but now it's often softened with cabernet or merlot. Sicily also produces crisp white varieties such as Catarratto Biano, Inzoli, and Grillo that marry delightfully with the island's seafood. Lipari and Pantelleria produce sweet, golden Malvasia, but Marsala remains Sicily's most famous dessert wine.

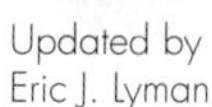
Updated by
Eric J. Lyman

Sicily has beckoned seafaring wanderers since the trials of Odysseus were first sung in Homer's *Odyssey*—perhaps the world's first travel guide. Strategically poised between Europe and Africa, this mystical land of three corners and a fiery volcano once hosted two of the most enlightened capitals of the West—one Greek, in Siracusa, and one Arab-Norman, in Palermo. The island has been a melting pot of every great civilization on the Mediterranean: Greek and Roman; then Arab and Norman; and finally French, Spanish, and Italian. Today the ancient ports of call peacefully fuse the remains of sackings past: graceful Byzantine mosaics stand adjacent to Greek temples, Roman amphitheaters, Romanesque cathedrals, and baroque flights of fancy.

The invaders through the ages weren't just attracted by the strategic location; they recognized a paradise in Sicily's deep blue skies and temperate climate, its lush vegetation, and rich marine life—all of which prevail to this day. Factor in Sicily's unique cuisine—another harmony of elements, mingling Arab and Greek spices, Spanish and French techniques, and some of the world's finest seafood, all accompanied by big, fruity wines—and you can understand why visitors continue to be drawn here, and often find it hard to leave.

In modern times the traditional graciousness and nobility of the Sicilian people have survived side by side with the destructive influences of the Mafia under Sicily's semiautonomous government. Alongside some of the most exquisite architecture in the world lie the shabby, half-built results of some of the worst speculation imaginable. In recent years coastal Sicily, like much of the Mediterranean Coast, has experienced a surge in condominium development and tourism. The island has emerged as something of an international travel hot spot, drawing increasing numbers of visitors. Astronomical prices in northern Italy have contributed to the boom in Sicily, where tourism doesn't seem to be leveling off as it has elsewhere in the country. Brits and Germans flock in ever-growing numbers to Agrigento and Siracusa, and in high season Japanese tour groups seem to outnumber the locals in Taormina. And yet, in Sicily's windswept heartland, a region that tourists have barely begun to explore, vineyards, olive groves, and lovingly kept dirt roads leading to family farmhouses still tie Sicilians to the land and to tradition, forming a happy connectedness that can't be defined by economic measures.

PLANNING

MAKING THE MOST OF YOUR TIME

You should plan a visit to Sicily around Palermo, Taormina, Siracusa, and Agrigento, four don't-miss destinations. The best way to see them all is to travel in a circle. Start your circuit in the northeast in Taormina, worth at least a night or two. If you have time, stay also in Catania, a lively, fascinating city that's often overlooked. From there, connect to the regional, two-lane SS114 toward the spectacular ancient Greek port of Siracusa, which merits at least two nights.

Next, backtrack north on the SS114, and take the A19 toward Palermo. Piazza Armerina's impressive mosaics and Enna, a sleepy mountaintop city, are worthwhile stops in the interior. Take the SS640 to the Greek temples of Agrigento. Stay here for a night before driving west along the coastal SS115, checking out Selinunte's ruins before reaching magical Erice, a good base for one night. You're now near some of Sicily's best beaches at San Vito Lo Capo. Take the A19 to Palermo, the chaotic and wonderful capital city, to wrap up your Sicilian experience. Give yourself at least two days here—or, ideally, four or five.

GETTING AROUND

BUS TRAVEL

Air-conditioned coaches connect major and minor cities and are often faster and more convenient than local trains, but are also slightly more expensive. Various companies serve the different routes. SAIS runs frequently between Palermo and Catania, Messina, and Siracusa, in each case arriving at and departing from near the train stations. **Cuffaro** (☎ *091/6161510* 🌐 *www.cuffaro.info*) runs between Palermo and Agrigento. On the south and east coasts and in the interior, **SAIS** (☎ *800/211020 toll-free* 🌐 *www.saisautolinee.it*) connects the main centers, including Catania, Agrigento, Enna, Taormina, and Siracusa. **Interbus/Etna Trasporti** (☎ *0935/42525* 🌐 *www.interbus.it*) operates between Catania, Caltagirone, Piazza Armerina, Taormina, Messina, and Siracusa.

CAR TRAVEL

This is the ideal way to explore Sicily. Modern highways circle and bisect the island, making all main cities easily reachable. A20 connects Messina and Palermo; Messina and Catania are linked by A18; running through the interior, from Catania to west of Cefalù, is A19; threading west from Palermo, A29 runs to Trapani and the airport, with a leg stretching down to Mazara del Vallo. The *superstrada* (highway) SS115 runs along the southern coast, and connecting superstrade lace the island.

You'll likely hear stories about the dangers of driving in Sicily. Some are true, and others less so. In the big cities—especially Palermo, Catania, and Messina—streets are a honking mess, with lane markings and traffic lights taken as mere suggestions; you can avoid the chaos by leaving your car in a garage. However, once outside the urban areas and resort towns, the highways and regional state roads are a driving enthusiast's dream—they're winding, sparsely populated, and well maintained, and around most bends there's a striking new view.

TRAIN TRAVEL

There are direct express trains from Milan and Rome to Palermo, Catania, and Siracusa. The Rome-Palermo and Rome-Siracusa trips take at least 10 hours. After Naples, the run is mostly along the coast, so try to book a window seat on the right if you're not on an overnight train. At Villa San Giovanni, in Calabria, the train is separated and loaded onto a ferryboat to cross the strait to Messina.

Within Sicily, main lines connect Messina, Taormina, Siracusa, and Palermo. Secondary lines are generally very slow and unreliable. The Messina-Palermo run, along the northern coast, is especially scenic. For schedules, check the Web site of the Italian state railway, **FS** (☎ *892021* 🌐 *www.trenitalia.com*).

ABOUT THE HOTELS

The high-quality hotels tend to be limited to the major cities and resorts of Palermo, Catania, Taormina, Siracusa, and Agrigento, along with the odd beach resort.

However, there has recently been an explosion in the development of *agriturismo* lodgings (rural bed-and-breakfasts), many of them quite basic but others providing the same facilities found in hotels. These country houses also offer all-inclusive, inexpensive full-board plans that can make for some of Sicily's most memorable meals.

Hotel reviews have been condensed for this book. Please go to Fodors.com for expanded reviews of each property.

WHAT IT COSTS (IN EUROS)					
	¢	$	$$	$$$	$$$$
Restaurants	under €20	€20–€30	€30–€45	€45–€65	over €65
Hotels	under €75	€75–€125	€125–€200	€200–€300	over €300

Restaurant prices are for a first course (primo), second course (secondo), and dessert (dolce). Hotel prices are for two people in a standard double room in high season, including tax and service.

THE IONIAN COAST

On the northern stretch of Sicily's eastern coast, Messina commands an unparalleled position across the Ionian Sea from Calabria, the mountainous tip of mainland Italy's boot. Halfway down the coast, Catania has the vivacity of Palermo, if not the artistic wealth; the city makes a good base for exploring lofty Mount Etna, as does Taormina.

MESSINA

8 km (5 mi) by ferry from Villa San Giovanni, 94 km (59 mi) northeast of Catania, 237 km (149 mi) east of Palermo.

GETTING HERE

Frequent hydrofoils and ferries carry passengers across the Straits of Messina. There are many more daily departures from Villa San Giovanni than from Reggio di Calabria. Trains are ferried here from Villa San Giovanni.

VISITOR INFORMATION

Messina tourism office (✉ *Via dei Mille 270* ☎ *090/2935292*).

EXPLORING

Messina's ancient history lists a series of disasters, but the city nevertheless managed to develop a fine university and a thriving cultural environment. At 5:20 am on December 28, 1908, Messina changed from a flourishing metropolis of 120,000 to a heap of rubble, shaken to pieces by an earthquake that turned into a tidal wave and left 80,000 dead and the city almost completely leveled. As you approach the city by ferry, you won't notice any outward indication of the disaster, except for the modern countenance of a 3,000-year-old city. The somewhat flat look is a precaution of seismic planning: tall buildings are not permitted.

The reconstruction of Messina's Norman and Romanesque **Duomo**, originally built by the Norman king Roger II and consecrated in 1197, has retained much of the original plan, including a handsome crown of Norman battlements, an enormous apse, and a splendid wood-beam ceiling. The adjoining bell tower contains one of the largest and most complex mechanical clocks in the world, constructed in 1933 with a host of gilded automatons, including a roaring lion, that spring into action every day at the stroke of noon. ✉ *Piazza del Duomo* ☎ *090/774895* ⏲ *Weekdays 7–7, weekends 7–12:30 and 3:30–7.*

WHERE TO EAT AND STAY

$ SICILIAN ✕ **Al Padrino.** The jovial owner of this stripped-down trattoria keeps everything running smoothly. Meat and fish dishes are served with equal verve in the white-wall dining room. Start with antipasti like eggplant stuffed with ricotta, then move on to supremely Sicilian dishes such as pasta with chickpeas or *polpette di alalunga* (albacore croquettes). ✉ *Via Santa Cecilia 54* ☎ *090/2921000* ⏲ *Closed Sun. and Aug. No dinner Sat.*

$$ **Grand Hotel Liberty.** Across from the train station, this hotel is a haven from the hustle and bustle of the surrounding streets. **Pros:** close to bus and train stations; plush public rooms. **Cons:** carpets a bit threadbare; poor views from most rooms. **TripAdvisor:** "old-world elegance," "near the harbor," "always warmly greeted." ✉ *Via I Settembre 15*

Eastern Sicily and the Aeolian Islands
TO NAPLES
TO NAPLES
TO TROPEA
AEOLIAN ISLANDS
Stromboli
Panarea
Alicudi
Filicudi
Salina
Lipari
Vulcano
Tyrrhenian Sea
Golfo di Gioia
Mortelle
Milazzo
Villa San Giovanni
Messina
CAPO D'ORLANDO
St Agata di Militello
Patti
Reggio di Calabria
Cefalù
Caldura
TYRRHENIAN COAST
Pizzo Carbonara
Randazzo
Castelmola
Taormina
Bronte
Giardini-Naxos
Riposto
Giarre
Mt. Etna
Nicosia
Adrano
Nicolosi
Biancavilla
Acireale
Enna
Paterno
Aci Castello
Aci Trezza
Caltanisetta
Catania
Golfo di Catania
Piazza Armerina
Casale
Agnone
Mazzarino
Palagonia
Caltagirone
Augusta
Vizzini
Ionian Sea
Euryalus
Gela
Palazzolo Acreide
Siracusa see detail map
Golfo di Gela
Vittoria
Comiso
Ragusa
Noto
Avola
Modica
Golfo di Noto
TO MALTA
Pachino
CAPO PASSERO
0
20 mi
0
20 km
KEY
Ferry lines
Ski Area
A20
113
116
117
120
121
185
114
A18
106
A19
192
288
191
417
626
117b
385
194
124
115
19

☎ *090/6409436* 🌐 *www.nh-hotels.com* ⇆ *48 rooms, 3 junior suites* ♁ *In-hotel: bar, business center* 🍽 *Breakfast* ⏲ *Closed 2 wks in Dec. and 6 wks in summer.*

TAORMINA

43 km (27 mi) southwest of Messina.

GETTING HERE

Buses from Messina or Catania arrive near the center of Taormina, while trains from these towns pull in at the station at the bottom of the hill. Local buses bring you the rest of the way. A cable car takes passengers up the hill from a parking lot about 2 km (1 mi) north of the train station.

VISITOR INFORMATION

Taormina tourism office (✉ *Palazzo Corvaja, Piazza Santa Caterina* ☎ *0942/23243* 🌐 *www.gate2taormina.com*).

15

EXPLORING

The medieval cliff-hanging town of Taormina is overrun with tourists, but its natural beauty is still hard to dispute. The view of the sea and Mount Etna from its jagged cactus-covered cliffs is as close to perfection as a panorama can get, especially on clear days, when the snowcapped volcano's white puffs of smoke rise against the blue sky. Writers have extolled Taormina's beauty almost since its founding in the 6th century BC by Greeks from Naples; Goethe and D. H. Lawrence were among its well-known enthusiasts. The town's boutique-lined main streets get old pretty quickly, but don't overlook the many hiking paths that wind through the beautiful hills surrounding Taormina. Nor should you miss the trip up to stunning Castelmola—whether on foot or by car.

Below the main city of Taormina is **Taormina Mare**, where beachgoers jostle for space on the minuscule pebble beach in summer. Taormina Mare is accessible by a **funivia** (✉ *Down hill from town center* ☎ *0942/23906* 🎟 *€2 one-way, €3.50 round-trip* ⏲ *Daily 8–8*), or suspended cable car, that glides past incredible views on its way down. It departs every 15 minutes. In June, July, and August, the normal hours are extended until midnight or later.

The Greeks put a premium on finding impressive locations to stage their dramas, such as Taormina's hillside **Teatro Greco**. Beyond the columns you can see the town's rooftops spilling down the hillside, the arc of the coastline, and Mount Etna in the distance. The theater was built during the 3rd century BC and rebuilt by the Romans during the 2nd century AD. Its acoustics are exceptional: even today a stage whisper can be heard in the last rows. In summer Taormina hosts an arts festival of music and dance events and a film festival; many performances are held in the Teatro Greco. ✉ *Via Teatro Greco* ☎ *0942/620198* 🎟 *€6* ⏲ *Daily 9–1 hr before sunset.*

Many of Taormina's 14th- and 15th-century palaces have been carefully preserved. Especially beautiful is the **Palazzo Corvaja**, with characteristic black-lava and white-limestone inlays. Today it houses the tourist office and the **Museo di Arte e Storia Popolare,** which has a collection of puppets and folk art, carts, and crèches. ✉ *Largo Santa Caterina* ☎ *0942/23243* 🎟 *Museum €2.60* ⏲ *Museum Tues.–Sun. 9–1 and 4–8.*

QUICK BITES

A marzipan devotee should not leave Taormina without trying one of the almond sweets—maybe in the guise of the ubiquitous *fico d'India* (prickly pear) or in more unusual frutta martorana varieties—at Pasticceria Etna (✉ *Corso Umberto 112* ☎ *0942/24735*). A block of almond paste makes a good souvenir—you can bring it home to make an almond latte or granita. It's closed Monday.

★ Stroll down Via Bagnoli Croce from the main Corso Umberto to the **Villa Comunale.** Also known as the Parco Duca di Cesarò, the lovely public gardens were designed by Florence Trevelyan Cacciola, a Scottish lady "invited" to leave England following a romantic liaison with the future Edward VII (1841–1910). Arriving in Taormina in 1889, she married a local professor and devoted herself to the gardens, filling them with Mediterranean plants, ornamental pavilions (known as the beehives), and fountains. Stop by the panoramic bar, which has stunning views. ⏲ *Daily 9 am–sunset.*

A 20-minute walk along the Via Crucis footpath takes you to the medieval **Castello Saraceno**, perched on an adjoining cliff above town. (You can also drive, of course.) The gate is often locked, but it's worth the climb just for the panoramic views. ✉ *Monte Tauro* ☎ *No phone.*

WHERE TO EAT

¢ SICILIAN ✕ **Bella Blu.** If you fancy a meal with a view but don't want to spend a lot, it would be hard to do much better than to come here for the decent €18 three-course prix-fixe meal. Seafood is the specialty; try the spaghetti with fresh clams and mussels. Through giant picture windows you can watch the gondola fly up and down from the beach, with the coastline in the distance. A pianist performs Saturday night in winter. ✉ *Via Pirandello 28* ☎ *0942/24239* 🌐 *www.bellablu.it.*

$$$$ SICILIAN ✕ **La Giara.** This restaurant, named after a giant vase unearthed under the bar, is famous for being one of Taormina's oldest restaurants. The food's not bad, either. The kitchen blends upscale modern techniques with the simple flavors of traditional specialties. The restaurant specializes in everything fish: one spectacular dish is the fish *cartoccio* (wrapped in paper and baked). You can extend your evening at the popular, if touristy, piano bar, or at the dance club that operates here on Saturday night (and every night in August). There's also a terrace with stunning views. ✉ *Vico La Floresta 1* ☎ *0942/23360* 🌐 *www.lagiara-taormina.com* ⏲ *Closed Sun. Apr.–Oct. and Sun.–Fri. Nov.–Mar. No lunch.*

$$ SICILIAN ✕ **L'Arco dei Cappuccini.** Just off Via Costantino Patricio lies this diminutive restaurant. Outdoor seating and an upstairs kitchen help make room for a few extra tables—a necessity, as locals are well aware that neither the price nor the quality is equaled elsewhere in town. Indulge in the spaghetti with sea urchin, fresh pasta with swordfish and fennel, or hand-made fetuccini with red mullet and fava beans. Reservations are usually essential for more than two people. ✉ *Via Cappuccini 5A, off Via Costantino Patricio* ☎ *0942/24893* ⏲ *Closed Wed., Feb., and 1 wk in Nov.*

¢ PIZZA ★ ✕ **Vecchia Taormina.** Warm, inviting, and unassuming, Taormina's best pizzeria produces deliciously seared crusts topped with fresh, well-balanced ingredients. Try the pizza *alla Norma,* featuring the classic

Sicilian combination of eggplant and ricotta—here, in the province of Messina, it's made with ricotta *al forno* (cooked ricotta), while in the province of Catania, it's made with ricotta *salata* (uncooked, salted ricotta). The restaurant also offers fresh fish in summer, and there's a good list of Sicilian wines. Choose between small tables on two levels or on a terrace. ✉ *Vico Ebrei 3* ☎ *0942/625589.*

WHERE TO STAY

$$$$ Fodor's Choice ★ **Grand Hotel Timeo.** The deluxe Timeo—on a princely perch overlooking the town—wears a graceful patina that suggests la dolce vita. **Pros:** feeling of indulgence; central location; quiet setting. **Cons:** very expensive; some rooms are small; staff can be scarce. **TripAdvisor:** "wonderful views over the bay," "good value for money," "breakfast was superb." ✉ *Via Teatro Greco 59* ☎ *0942/23801* 🌐 *www.grandhoteltimeo.com* *70 rooms, 13 suites* *In-room: Wi-Fi. In-hotel: restaurant, room service, bar, pool, gym, spa* *Some meals.*

$$ **Hotel Villa Paradiso.** On the edge of the old quarter, overlooking the lovely public gardens and facing the sea, this smaller hotel is not as well known as some of its neighbors. **Pros:** friendly service; good value; great rooftop views. **Cons:** only three free parking spaces; not all rooms have views; disappointing food. **TripAdvisor:** "breathtaking, to say the least," "old-world charm," "view from large terrace." ✉ *Via Roma 2* ☎ *0942/23921* 🌐 *www.hotelvillaparadisotaormina.com* *20 rooms, 17 junior suites* *In-hotel: restaurant, room service, bar, beach, business center* *Breakfast.*

$$$$ **San Domenico Palace.** Sweeping views from this converted 15th-century Dominican monastery linger in your mind: the sensuous gardens—full of red trumpet flowers, bougainvillea, and lemon trees—afford a dramatic vista of the castle, the sea, and Mount Etna. **Pros:** overflowing with character; attentive service; quiet and restful. **Cons:** very expensive; dull corridors; some small rooms. **TripAdvisor:** "original monastery," "gardens are still intact," "tranquil oasis." ✉ *Piazza San Domenico 5* ☎ *0942/613111* 🌐 *www.amthotels.it/sandomenico* *87 rooms, 15 suites* *In-room: Wi-Fi. In-hotel: restaurants, room service, bar, pool, gym, spa, business center* *Breakfast.*

$$$ **Villa Ducale.** The former summer residence of a local aristocrat has been converted into a luxurious hotel. **Pros:** away from the hubbub; fantastic views. **Cons:** long walk to the center. **TripAdvisor:** "large, historic villa," "Sicilian atmosphere," "best food in the area." ✉ *Via Leonardo da Vinci 60* ☎ *0942/28153* 🌐 *www.villaducale.com* *12 suites* *In-room: Wi-Fi. In-hotel: bar, parking* *Closed 1 month in winter (exact dates vary)* *Breakfast.*

$–$$ **Villa Fiorita.** This converted private home near the cable-car station has excellent north-coast views from nearly every room. **Pros:** good rates; pretty rooms. **Cons:** service can be slack; lots of stairs to climb. **TripAdvisor:** "has a lot of character," "enjoyed sitting on the terrace," "near the historical city center." ✉ *Via Pirandello 39* ☎ *0942/24122* 🌐 *www.villafioritahotel.com* *24 rooms, 2 suites* *In-hotel: room service, bar, pool* *Breakfast.*

15

NIGHTLIFE AND THE ARTS

The Teatro Greco and the Palazzo dei Congressi, near the entrance to the theater, are the main venues for the summer festival dubbed **Taoarte** (☎ *0942/21142* 🌐 *www.taormina-arte.com*), held each year between June and August. Performances encompass classical music, ballet, and theater. The famous **Taormina Film Festival** (🌐 *www.taorminafilmfest.it*) takes place in June. The **Teatro dei Due Mari** (✉ *Via Teatro Greco* ☎ *0941/240912* 🌐 *www.teatrodeiduemari.net*) stages Greek tragedy at the Teatro Greco, usually in May.

EN ROUTE The 50-km (30-mi) stretch of road between Taormina and Messina is flanked by lush vegetation and seascapes. Inlets are punctuated by gigantic, oddly shaped rocks.

CASTELMOLA

5 km (3 mi) west of Taormina.

GETTING HERE

Regular buses bound for Castelmola leave from two locations in Taormina: the bus station on Via Pirandello and Piazza San Pancrazio.

EXPLORING

Although many believe that Taormina has the most spectacular views, tiny Castelmola, floating 1,800 feet above sea level, takes the word "scenic" to a whole new level. Along the cobblestone streets within the ancient walls the 360-degree panoramas of mountain, sea, and sky are so ubiquitous that you almost get used to them (but not quite). Collect yourself with a sip of the sweet almond wine (best served cold) made in the local bars, or with lunch at one of the humble pizzerias or *panino* (sandwich) shops.

A 10-minute drive on a winding but well-paved road leads from Taormina to Castelmola; you must park in one of the public lots on the hillside below and climb a series of staircases to reach the center. On a nice day hikers are in for a treat if they walk instead of drive. It's a serious uphill climb, but the 1½-km (¾-mi) path is extremely well maintained and not too challenging. You'll begin at Porta Catania in Taormina, with a walk along Via Apollo Arcageta past the Chiesa di San Francesco di Paola on the left. The Strada Comunale della Chiusa then leads past Piazza Andromaco, revealing good views of the jagged promontory of Cocolanazzo di Mola to the north. Allow around an hour on the way up, a half hour down. There's another, slightly longer—2-km (1-mi)—path that heads up from Porta Messina past the Roman aqueduct, Convento dei Cappuccini, and the northeastern side of Monte Tauro. You could take one path up and the other down. In any case, avoid the midday sun, wear comfortable shoes, and carry plenty of water with you.

Fodor's Choice ★ The best place to take in Castelmola's views is from the ruins of **Castello Normanno**, reached by a set of steep staircases rising out of the town center. In all of Sicily there may be no spot more scenic than atop the castle ruins, where you can gaze upon two coastlines, smoking Mount Etna, and the town spilling down the mountainside. You can visit anytime, but come during daylight hours for the view.

WHERE TO EAT AND STAY

$$ SICILIAN **Il Vicolo.** This is one of the simpler dining choices in town, and also one of the better ones. It might not boast the views you'll find elsewhere, but a pleasant rustic ambience and a great selection of handmade pasta and, in the evening, *forno a legna* (wood-fired-oven) pizzas make up for that shortcoming (in winter, pizzas are served weekends only). Friendly staff serves the food in a pleasant little room along a side street. *Via Pio IX 26 0942/28481 or 331/9094077 www.trattoriailvicolo.com Closed Tues. Sept.–June and 2 wks late Jan.–early Feb.*

$ ITALIAN **Ristorante Pizzichella.** On the road heading down to Taormina stands this three-level terrace restaurant. The food—seafood dishes like mixed shellfish risotto, grilled prawns or swordfish, and pizzas from a wood-burning oven—is eclipsed by the memorable views from almost every table on the terraces. *Via Madonna della Scala 1 0942/28831 www.pizzichella.it Closed Wed. Oct.–Apr. and occasionally on other days in winter.*

$$ **Villa Sonia.** All the rooms at Castelmola's best hotel have private terraces with spectacular views. **Pros:** far from the madding crowds; stupendous views. **Cons:** not much to do in the evening; a bit old-fashioned. **TripAdvisor:** "flowers everywhere," "spacious and well-appointed," "worth every penny." *Via Porta Mola 9 0942/28082 www.hotelvillasonia.com 42 rooms, 2 suites In-room: Wi-Fi. In-hotel: restaurant, bar, pool, gym, parking Closed Dec.–Feb. Breakfast.*

15

NIGHTLIFE

The famous **Bar Turrisi** (*Piazza del Duomo 19 0942/28181 www.turrisibar.it*) is truly one of the most unusual places to have a drink in all of Italy. The cozy nooks and crannies of its three levels are decked out with phallus images of every size, shape, and color imaginable, from bathroom wall murals inspired by the brothels of ancient Greece to giant wooden carvings honoring Dionysus. The roof terrace has extraordinary views of Taormina and the coast.

★ The **Bar San Giorgio** (*Piazza Sant'Antonino 0942/28228*) has lorded over Castelmola's town square since 1907. The interior of the bar is filled with knickknacks that tell a fascinating history of the tiny town.

MOUNT ETNA

64 km (40 mi) southwest of Taormina, 30 km (19 mi) north of Catania.

GETTING HERE

Reaching the lower slopes of Mount Etna is easy, either by driving yourself or taking a bus from Catania. Getting to the more interesting higher levels requires taking one of the stout four-wheel-drive minibuses that leave from Piano Provenzana on the north side and Rifugio Sapienza on the south side. A cable car from Rifugio Sapienza takes you part of the way.

VISITOR INFORMATION

Nicolosi tourism office (*Piazza Vittorio Emanuele 32/33, Nicolosi 095/914488 www.aast-nicolosi.it*). **Funivia dell'Etna** (*Rifugio Sapienza, 095/914141 or 095/914142 www.funiviaetna.com*).

EXPLORING

Fodor's Choice ★ **Mount Etna** is one of the world's major active volcanoes and is the largest and highest in Europe—the cone of the crater rises to 10,902 feet above sea level. Plato sailed in just to catch a glimpse in 387 BC; in the 9th century AD the oldest gelato of all was shaved off its snowy slopes; and in the 21st century the volcano still claims annual headlines. Etna has erupted a dozen times in the past 30 or so years, most spectacularly in 1971, 1983, 2001, 2002, and 2005; there were a pair of medium-size eruptions in 2008 and one in 2009. Travel in the proximity of the crater depends on Mount Etna's temperament, but you can walk up and down the enormous lava dunes and wander over its moonlike surface of dead craters. The rings of vegetation change markedly as you rise, with vineyards and pine trees gradually giving way to growths of broom and lichen.

Club Alpino Italiano in Catania is a great resource for Mount Etna climbing and hiking guides. If you have some experience and don't like a lot of hand-holding, these are the guides for you. ✉ *Via Messina 593/a, Catania* ☎ *095/7153515* 🌐 *www.caicatania.it.*

If you're a beginning climber, call the **Gruppo Guide Etna Nord** to arrange for a guide. Their service is a little more personalized—and expensive—than others. Reserve ahead. ✉ *Via Roma 93, Linguaglossa* ☎ *095/7774502 or 348/0125167* 🌐 *www.guidetnanord.com.*

Instead of climbing up Mount Etna, you can circle it on the **Circumetnea**, which runs near the volcano's base. The private railway almost circles the volcano, running 114 km (71 mi) between Catania and Riposto—the towns are 30 km (19 mi) apart by the coast road. The line is small, slow, and only single-track, but has some dramatic vistas of the volcano and goes through lava fields. The trip takes about four hours; there are about 10 departures a day. After you've made the trip one way, you can get back to where you started from on the much quicker, but less scenic, conventional state railway line between Catania and Riposto. ✉ *Via Caronda 352, Catania* ☎ *095/541250* 🌐 *www.circumetnea.it* 🎫 *€6.85 round-trip* ⏲ *Mon.–Sat. 6 am–9 pm.*

OFF THE BEATEN PATH

The villages that surround Mount Etna offer much more than pretty views of the smoldering giant. They're charming and full of character in their own right, and make good bases for visiting nearby cities such as Catania, Acireale, and Taormina. **Zafferana Etnea** is famous for its orange-blossom honey; **Nicolosi**, at nearly 3,000 feet, is known as La Porta dell'Etna (The Door to Etna); **Trecastagni** (The Three Chestnut Trees) has one of Sicily's most beautiful Renaissance churches; **Randazzo**, the largest of the surrounding towns, is the site of a popular Sunday-morning wood, textile, and metalwork market; and **Bronte** is Italy's center of pistachio cultivation. The bars there offer various pistachio delicacies such as nougat, *colomba* (Easter sponge cake), *panettone* (Christmas fruitcake), and ice cream.

WHERE TO STAY

$$ **Hotel Villa Paradiso dell'Etna**. This 1920s hotel 10 km (6 mi) northeast of Catania was a haunt for artists before General Rommel took over during World War II. **Pros:** beautiful furnishings; delightful gardens; excellent food. **Cons:** difficult to find; not much to do in the area. **TripAdvisor:**

"great base for our trips," "grounds were nice," "well-run and friendly." ✉ *Via per Viagrande 37, San Giovanni La Punta; exit A18 ME-CT toward San Gregorio, or A19 PA-CT toward Paesi Etnei* ☎ *095/7512409* 🌐 *www.paradisoetna.it* *29 rooms, 4 suites* *In-room: Wi-Fi. In-hotel: restaurant, room service, bar, pool, gym, spa, parking* *Breakfast.*

ACIREALE

40 km (25 mi) south of Taormina, 16 km (10 mi) north of Catania.

GETTING HERE

Buses arrive frequently from Taormina and Catania. Acireale is on the main coastal train route, though the station is a long walk south of the center. Local buses pass every 20 minutes or so.

VISITOR INFORMATION

Acireale tourism office (✉ *Via Oreste Scionti 15* ☎ *095/891999* 🌐 *www.acirealeturismo.it*).

EXPLORING

Acireale sits amid a clutter of rocky pinnacles and lush lemon groves. The craggy coast is known as the Riviera dei Ciclopi, after the legend narrated in the *Odyssey* in which the blinded Cyclops Polyphemus hurled boulders at the retreating Ulysses, thus creating spires of rock, or *faraglioni* (pillars of rock rising dramatically out of the sea). Tourism has barely taken off here, so it's a good destination if you feel the need to put some distance between yourself and the busloads of tourists in Taormina. And though the beaches are rocky, there's good swimming here, too.

The Carnival celebrations, held the two weeks before Lent, are considered the best in Sicily. The streets are jammed with thousands of revelers. Acireale is an easy day trip from Catania.

Begin your visit to Acireale with a stroll down to the public gardens, **Villa Belvedere**, at the end of the main Corso Umberto, for superb coastal views.

With its cupola and twin turrets, Acireale's **Duomo** is an extravagant baroque construction dating to the 17th century. In the chapel to the right of the altar, look for the 17th-century silver statue of Santa Venera, patron saint of Acireale, made by Mario D'Angelo, and the early-18th-century frescoes by Antonio Filocamo. ✉ *Piazza del Duomo* ☎ *095/601797* *Daily 8–noon and 4–7:30.*

QUICK BITES

El Dorado (✉ *Corso Umberto 5* ☎ *095/601464*) serves delicious ice creams, and the granita *di mandorla* (almond granita), available in summer, invites a firsthand acquaintance. It's closed Tuesday between October and March.

Lord Byron (1788–1824) visited the **Belvedere di Santa Caterina** to look out over the Ionian Sea during his Italian wanderings. The viewing point is south of the old town, near the Terme di Acireale, off SS114.

WHERE TO EAT

$$ SICILIAN **✕ La Grotta.** This rustic trattoria above the harbor of Santa Maria La Scala hides a dining room within a cave, with part of the cave wall exposed. Try the *insalata di mare* (a selection of delicately boiled fish served with lemon and olive oil), pasta with clams or cuttlefish ink, or

CLOSE UP

Sweet Sicily

Sicily is famous for its desserts, none more than the wonderful cannoli (*cannolo* is the singular), whose delicate pastry shell and just-sweet-enough ricotta barely resemble their foreign impostors. They come in all sizes, from pinkie-size bites to holiday cannoli the size of a coffee table. Even your everyday bar will display a window piled high with dozens of varieties of ricotta-based desserts, including delicious fried balls of dough. The traditional cake of Sicily is the *cassata siciliana*, a rich chilled sponge cake with sheep's-milk ricotta and candied fruit. Often brightly colored, it's the most popular dessert at many Sicilian restaurants, and you shouldn't miss it. From behind bakery windows and glass cases beam tiny marzipan sweets fashioned into brightly colored apples, cherries, and even hamburgers and prosciutto.

If it's summer, do as the locals do and dip your morning brioche—the best in Italy—into a cup of brilliantly refreshing coffee- or almond-flavored granita. The world's first ice cream is said to have been made by the Romans from the snow on the slopes of Mount Etna. Top-quality gelato is also prevalent throughout the island.

fish grilled over charcoal. Chef Rosario Strano's menu is small, but there isn't a dud among the selections. ✉ *Via Scalo Grande 46* ☎ *095/7648153* ✍ *Reservations essential* ⊗ *Closed Tues. and mid-Oct.–mid-Nov.*

NIGHTLIFE AND THE ARTS

Although it has died out in most other parts of the island, the puppet-theater tradition carries on in Acireale. The **Teatro dell'Opera dei Pupi** (✉ *Via Alessi 11* ☎ *095/606272* 🌐 *www.teatropupimacri.it*) has a puppet exhibit and puppet shows every Sunday.

SHOPPING

Acireale is renowned in Sicily for its marzipan, made into fruit shapes and delicious biscuits available at many pasticcerie around town. A unique creation at **Belvedere** (✉ *Corso Savoia 109* ☎ *095/601547*) is the "nucatole," a large cookie made with heaping quantities of chocolate, Nutella, nuts, and other wholesome ingredients. Open since 1953, **Castorina** (✉ *Piazza del Duomo 20* ☎ *095/601546*) sells marzipan candies (and cute gift boxes for them).

At **Bottega d'Arte** (✉ *Via Vittorio Emanuele 88* ☎ *095/601987* ⊗ *Closed Sun.*) you can see the local artist Salvatore Chiarenza at work carving wood statues and traditional carts, as his father and grandfather did before him. He also makes brass and wooden puppets.

EN ROUTE

Aci Castello and Aci Trezza. These two gems of the coastline between Acireale and Catania—the Riviera dei Ciclopi (Cyclops Riviera)—fill with city dwellers in the summer months, but even in colder weather their beauty is hard to fault. Heading south from Acireale on the *litoranea* (coastal) road, you'll first reach Aci Trezza, said to be the land of the blind Cyclops in Homer's *Odyssey.* Legend has it that when the Cyclops threw boulders at Odysseus they became the faraglioni offshore. It should be easy to satisfy your literal (rather than literary) hunger at Aci Trezza's Trattoria da Federico (✉ *Via Provinciale 115, Aci Trezza* ☎ *095/276364* ⏲ *Closed Mon.*), which lays out a sprawling antipasto buffet featuring delectable marinated anchovies and eggplant parmigiana. Less developed than Aci Trezza, Aci Castello has its own fish houses plus the imposing Castello Normanno (Norman Castle), which sits right on the water. The castle was built in the 11th century with volcanic rock from Mount Etna—the same rock that forms the coastal cliffs.

CATANIA

16 km (10 mi) south of Acireale, 94 km (59 mi) south of Messina, 60 km (37 mi) north of Siracusa.

GETTING HERE

Catania is well connected by bus and train with Messina, Taormina, Siracusa, Enna, and Palermo.

VISITOR INFORMATION

Catania tourism office (✉ *Via Vittorio Emanuele 172* ☎ *800/841042 or 095/7425573* 🌐 *www.comune.catania.it*).

15

EXPLORING

The chief wonder of Catania, Sicily's second city, is that it's there at all. Its successive populations were deported by one Greek tyrant, sold into slavery by another, and driven out by the Carthaginians. Every time the city got back on its feet it was struck by a new calamity: plague decimated the population in the Middle Ages, a mile-wide stream of lava from Mount Etna swallowed part of the city in 1669, and 25 years later a disastrous earthquake forced the Catanese to begin again.

Today Catania is completing yet another resurrection—this time from crime, filth, and urban decay. Although the city remains loud and full of traffic, signs of gentrification are everywhere. The elimination of vehicles from the Piazza del Duomo and the main artery of Via Etnea, and the scrubbing of many of the historic buildings has added to Catania's newfound charm. Home to what is arguably Sicily's best university, Catania is full of exuberant youth, and it shows in the chic *osterie* (taverns) that serve wine, designer bistros, and trendy ethnic boutiques that have popped up all over town. Even more impressive is the vibrant cultural life.

Each February 3–5, the **Festa di Sant'Agata** honors Catania's patron saint with one of Italy's biggest religious festivals. A staggering number of people crowd the streets and piazzas for several processions and music, dancing, art, theater, and all-out street partying. Many of the town's buildings are constructed from three-centuries-old lava; the black buildings combine with baroque architecture to give the city a singular appearance. Nowhere is this clearer than in the **centro storico** (historic center). Don't miss the stunning **Piazza Università,** a nerve center made interesting by the facade of a majestic old university building, and the nearby Castello Ursino.

At the heart of **Piazza del Duomo**, which is closed to traffic, stands an elephant carved out of lava, balancing an Egyptian obelisk—the city's informal mascot, called "u Liotru," the Sicilian pronunciation of Heliodorus, an 8th-century sorcerer tied by legend to the origins of the statue. The piazza shines from a 21st-century renovation. From here you can look way down the long, straight Via Garibaldi to see a black-and-white-striped fortress and entrance to the city, the Porta Garibaldi.

The Giovanni Vaccarini–designed facade of the **Cattedrale di Sant'Agata (Duomo)** dominates the Piazza del Duomo. Inside the church, composer Vincenzo Bellini is buried. Also of note are the three apses of lava that survive from the original Norman structure and a fresco from 1675 in the sacristy that portrays Catania's submission to Etna's attack. A guided tour of the museum is available with a reservation. Across from the Cattedrale are underground ruins of Greco-Roman baths. ✉ *Piazza del Duomo, bottom end of Via Etnea* ☎ *095/281635* 🌐 *www.museodiocesicatania.it* 🎫 *€7, €10 with baths* ⏲ *Daily 7–noon and 4–7.*

Via Etnea is host to one of Sicily's most enthusiastic *passeggiate* (early-evening strolls), in which Catanese of all ages take part. Closed to automobile traffic until 10 pm during the week and all day on weekends, the street is lined with cafés and jewelry, clothing, and shoe stores.

QUICK BITES

The lively Pasticceria Savia (✉ *Via Etnea 302/304 and Via Umberto 2 near Villa Bellini* ☎ *095/322335* 🌐 *www.savia.it*) makes superlative arancini with *ragù* (a slow-cooked, tomato-based meat sauce). Or you could choose cannoli or other snacks to munch on while you rest. It's closed Monday.

Catania's greatest native son was the composer Vincenzo Bellini (1801–35), whose operas have thrilled audiences since their premieres in Naples and Milan. His home, now the **Museo Belliniano**, preserves memorabilia of the man and his work. ✉ *Piazza San Francesco 3* ☎ *095/7150535* 🎫 *Free* ⏲ *Mon.–Sat. 9–1.*

An underground river, the Amenano, flows through much of Catania. You can glimpse it at the Fontana dell'Amenano, but the best place to experience the river is at the bar-restaurant of the **Agorà Youth Hostel**. Here you can sit at an underground table as swirls of water rush by. If you're not there when the bar is open, someone at the reception desk can let you in. ✉ *Piazza Currò 6* ☎ *095/7233010* 🌐 *www.agorahostel.com.*

WHERE TO EAT

$$$ SICILIAN ✕ **Ambasciata del Mare.** When a seafood restaurant sits next door to a fish market, it bodes well for the food's freshness. Choose swordfish or *gamberoni* (large shrimp) from a display case in the front of the restaurant, then enjoy it simply grilled with oil and lemon. This simple, bright, and cozy place could not be friendlier or more easily accessed—it's right on the corner of Piazza del Duomo by the fountain. Book early. ✉ *Piazza del Duomo 6/7* ☎ *095/341003* 🌐 *www.ambasciatadelmare.it* ⏲ *Closed Mon.*

$$ SICILIAN ★ ✕ **La Siciliana.** Salvo La Rosa and sons serve memorable seafood and meat dishes, exquisite homemade desserts, and a choice of more than 220 wines. The restaurant specializes in the ancient dish *ripiddu nivicatu* (risotto with cuttlefish ink and fresh ricotta cheese), as well as *sarde a beccafico* (stuffed sardines) and calamari *ripieni alla griglia* (stuffed and

grilled squid). A meal at this fine eatery more than justifies the short taxi ride 3 km (2 mi) north of the city center. ✉ *Viale Marco Polo 52a* ☎ *095/376400* 🌐 *www.lasiciliana.it* ⏲ *Closed Mon. No dinner Sun.*

WORD OF MOUTH

"I've never had a sweet tooth, but I don't really think of cannoli as sweet. On Sicily the shells were much lighter, and the ricotta much creamier, than those I've had at home. I wouldn't waste any opportunity to indulge."

—thrusdaysd

¢ PIZZA ★ ✕ **Ristorante-Pizzeria Vico Santa Filomena.** This typical forno a legna pizzeria, on a narrow side street off Via Umberto, is one of the most respected in the city for its outstanding "apizza," as the locals call it. Enjoy it as Catanians do: only at night, and with a beer or soda—never wine. The pizzas are named after saints or Sicilian cities. The antipasti spreads are delicious, as are the meat and seafood dishes. The setting is simple, with brick arches and a few agricultural tools displayed on the exposed stone walls. Expect a long wait on weekend evenings. ✉ *Vico Santa Filomena 35* ☎ *095/316761* ⏲ *Closed Mon.*

$–$$ SICILIAN ✕ **Sicilia in Bocca alla Marina.** This bright, bustling seafood restaurant near the marina is a Catania institution, favored by locals for its faithful renditions of traditional cusine. The well-thought-out wine list includes more than 200 Sicilian wines. ✉ *Via Dusmet 35* ☎ *095/315472* 🌐 *www.siciliainbocca.it* ⏲ *No lunch Mon.*

15

WHERE TO STAY

$$$ **Excelsior Grand Hotel.** This large, modern hotel sits in a quiet part of downtown Catania. **Pros:** efficient staff; modern facilities; clean rooms. **Cons:** chain hotel lacking personality; a longish walk from the main sights. **TripAdvisor:** "authentic furniture," "updated amenities," "exceptional service." ✉ *Piazza Verga 39* ☎ *095/7476111* 🌐 *www.hotelexcelsiorcatania.it* *176 rooms* *In-room: Wi-Fi (some). In-hotel: restaurant, room service, bar, gym, spa* *Breakfast.*

$$ Fodor's Choice ★ **Residence Angiolucci.** This renovated 19th-century palazzo is stunning—not just for the impressive detail of the restoration work, but even more for the elegance of the modern apartments inside. **Pros:** friendly service; elegant building; nice kitchens. **Cons:** rooms a little sterile; limited parking. **TripAdvisor:** "glorious hotel," "location is great," "spacious rooms." ✉ *Via E. Pantano 1B* ☎ *095/3529420* 🌐 *www.angiolucciresidence.com* *30 apartments* *In-room: kitchen, Internet. In-hotel: room service, parking* *No meals.*

SHOPPING

Catania is justly famous for its sweets and bar snacks. Sample the hustle and bustle of Catania at **Café del Duomo** (✉ *Piazza Duomo 11–13* ☎ *095/7150556*), which has handmade cookies and cakes and a great local atmosphere.

The selection of almond-based delights from **I Dolci di Nonna Vincenza** (✉ *Palazzo Biscari, Piazza San Placido 7* ☎ *095/7151844* 🌐 *www.dolcinonnavincenza.it* ✉ *Aeroporto Fontanarossa* ☎ *095/7234522* ✉ *Stazione Marittima main* ☎ *095/281097*) may be small, but everything is fresh and phenomenally good. International shipping is available.

The **outdoor fish and food market**, which begins on Via Zappala Gemelli and emanates in every direction from Piazza di Benedetto, is one of Italy's most memorable markets. It's a feast for the senses: thousands of impeccably fresh fish, some still wriggling, plus endless varieties of meats, ricotta, and fresh produce, and a symphony of vendor shouts to fill the ears. Open Monday–Saturday, the market is at its best in the early morning.

SIRACUSA

Siracusa, known to English speakers as Syracuse, is a wonder to behold. One of the great ancient capitals of Western civilization, the city was founded in 734 BC by Greek colonists from Corinth and soon grew to rival, and even surpass, Athens in splendor and power. Siracusa became the largest, wealthiest city-state in the West and a bulwark of Greek civilization. Although the city lived under tyranny, rulers such as Dionysus filled their courts with Greeks of the highest artistic stature—among them Pindar, Aeschylus, and Archimedes. The Athenians didn't welcome the rise of Siracusa and set out to conquer Sicily, but the natives outsmarted them in what was one of the greatest naval battles of ancient history (413 BC). Siracusa continued to prosper until it was conquered two centuries later by the Romans.

Siracusa still has some of the finest examples of baroque art and architecture; dramatic Greek and Roman ruins; and a Duomo that's the stuff of legend—a microcosm of the city's entire history in one building. The modern city also has a wonderful lively baroque old town worthy of extensive exploration, pleasant piazzas, outdoor cafés and bars, and a wide assortment of excellent seafood. There are essentially two areas to explore in Siracusa: the Parco Archeologico, on the mainland; and the island of Ortygia, the ancient city first inhabited by the Greeks, which juts out into the Ionian Sea and is connected to the mainland by two small bridges. Ortygia is becoming increasingly popular with tourists, and is starting to lose its old-fashioned charm in favor of modern boutiques.

Siracusa's old nucleus of Ortygia is a compact area, a pleasure to amble around without getting unduly tired. In contrast, mainland Siracusa is a grid of wider avenues. At the northern end of Corso Gelone, above Viale Paolo Orsi, the orderly grid gives way to the ancient quarter of Neapolis, where the sprawling Parco Archeologico is accessible from Viale Teracati (an extension of Corso Gelone). East of Viale Teracati, about a 10-minute walk from the Parco Archeologico, the district of Tyche holds the archaeological museum and the church and catacombs of San Giovanni, both off Viale Teocrito (drive or take a taxi or city bus from Ortygia). Coming from the train station, it's a 15-minute trudge to Ortygia along Via Francesco Crispi and Corso Umberto. If you're not up for that, take one of the free electric buses leaving every 10 minutes from the bus station around the corner.

GETTING HERE

On the main train line from Messina and Catania, Siracusa is also linked to Catania by frequent buses.

VISITOR INFORMATION
Siracusa tourism office (✉ *Via Maestranza 33, Ortygia* ☎ *0931/464255* 🌐 *www.regione.sicilia.it/turismo*).

ARCHAEOLOGICAL ZONE

TOP ATTRACTIONS

Parco Archeologico. Siracusa is most famous for its dramatic set of Greek and Roman ruins. Though the various ruins can be visited separately, see them all, along with the Museo Archeologico. If the park is closed, go up Viale G. Rizzo from Viale Teracati to the belvedere overlooking the ruins, which are floodlighted at night. The last tickets are sold one hour before closing.

Before the park's ticket booth is the gigantic **Ara di Ierone** (Altar of Hieron), which was once used by the Greeks for spectacular sacrifices involving hundreds of animals. The first attraction in the park is the **Latomia del Paradiso** (Quarry of Paradise), a lush tropical garden full of palm and citrus trees. This series of quarries served as prisons for the defeated Athenians, who were enslaved; the quarries once rang with the sound of their chisels and hammers. At one end is the famous **Orecchio di Dionisio** (Ear of Dionysus), with an ear-shape entrance and unusual acoustics inside, as you'll hear if you clap your hands. The legend is that Dionysus used to listen in at the top of the quarry to hear what the slaves were plotting below.

15

★ The Teatro Greco *(Greek Theater)* is the chief monument in the Archaeological Park—and indeed one of Sicily's greatest classical sites and the most complete Greek theater surviving from antiquity. Climb to the top of the seating area (which could accommodate 15,000) for a fine view: all the seats converge upon a single point—the stage—which has the natural scenery and the sky as its background. Hewn out of the hillside rock in the 5th century BC, the theater saw the premieres of the plays of Aeschylus. Greek tragedies are still performed here every year in May and June. Above and behind the theater runs the Via dei Sepulcri, in which streams of running water flow through a series of Greek sepulchres.

The well-preserved and striking **Anfiteatro Romano** (Roman Amphitheater) reveals much about the differences between the Greek and Roman personalities. Where drama in the Greek theater was a kind of religious ritual, the Roman amphitheater emphasized the spectacle of combative sports and the circus. This arena is one of the largest of its kind and was built around the 2nd century AD. The corridor where gladiators and beasts entered the ring is still intact, and the seats, some of which still bear the occupants' names, were hauled in and constructed on the site from huge slabs of limestone. ✉ *Viale Teocrito (entrance on Via Agnello), Archaeological Zone* ☎ *0931/65068* 🎫 *€10* ⏲ *Apr.–mid-Sept., daily 9–7; mid-Sept.–mid-Oct., daily 9–3:45; mid-Oct.–Feb., Mon.–Sat. 9–5, Sun. 9–1; Mar., daily 9–6.*

QUICK BITES

For some great Sicilian cakes and ice cream on your way to the Archaeological Park, visit Leonardi (✉ *Viale Teocrito 123, Archaeological Zone* ☎ *0931/61411*), a bar-cum-pasticceria. It's popular with the locals, so you may have to line up for your cakes during holiday times. It's closed Wednesday.

WORTH NOTING

Catacomba di San Giovanni. Not far from the Archaeological Park, off Viale Teocrito, the catacombs below the church of San Giovanni are one of the earliest-known Christian sites in the city. Inside the crypt of San Marciano is an altar where Saint Paul preached on his way through Sicily to Rome. The frescoes in this small chapel are mostly bright and fresh, though some dating from the 4th century AD show their age. Opening hours may be extended in summer. ✉ *Piazza San Giovanni, Tyche* ☎ *0931/64694* 🎫 *€6* ⏲ *Daily 9:30–12:30 and 2:30–5:30; last entry at 4:30. Closed Mon. in winter.*

Museo Archeologico. The impressive collection of Siracusa's splendid archaeological museum is organized by region around a central atrium and ranges from Neolithic pottery to fine Greek statues and vases. Compare the *Landolina Venus*—a headless goddess of love who rises out of the sea in measured modesty (a 1st-century AD Roman copy of the Greek original)—with the much earlier (300 BC) elegant Greek statue of Hercules in Section C. Of a completely different style is a marvelous fanged Gorgon, its tongue sticking out, that once adorned the cornice of the Temple of Athena to ward off evildoers. ✉ *Viale Teocrito 66, Tyche* ☎ *0931/464022* 🎫 *€8* ⏲ *Tues.–Sat. 9–7, Sun. 9–2; last entry 1 hr before closing.*

Museo del Papiro. Close to Siracusa's Museo Archeologico, the Papyrus Museum demonstrates how papyri are prepared from reeds and then painted—an ancient tradition in the city. Siracusa, it seems, has the only climate outside the Nile Valley in which the papyrus plant—from which the word "paper" comes—thrives. ✉ *Viale Teocrito 66, Tyche* ☎ *0931/61616* 🎫 *Free* ⏲ *Tues.–Sun. 9–2; last entry 1 hr before closing.*

ORTYGIA ISLAND

TOP ATTRACTIONS

Fodor's Choice ★ **Duomo.** Siracusa's Duomo is an archive of island history: the bottommost excavations have unearthed remnants of Sicily's distant past, when the Siculi inhabitants worshipped their deities here. During the 5th century BC (the same time as Agrigento's Temple of Concord was built), the Greeks built a temple to Athena over it, and in the 7th century Siracusa's first Christian cathedral was built on top of the Greek structure. The massive columns of the original Greek temple were incorporated into the present structure and are clearly visible, embedded in the exterior wall along Via Minerva. The Greek columns were also used to dramatic advantage inside, where on one side they form chapels connected by elegant wrought-iron gates. The baroque facade, added in 1700, displays a harmonious rhythm of concaves and convexes. In front, the piazza is encircled by pink and white oleanders and elegant buildings ornamented with filigree grillwork. ✉ *Piazza del Duomo, Ortygia* ☎ *0931/65328* ⏲ *Daily 8–7.*

Fonte Aretusa. A freshwater spring, the Fountain of Arethus, sits next to the sea, studded with Egyptian papyrus that's reportedly natural. This anomaly is explained by a Greek legend that tells how the nymph Arethusa was changed into a fountain by the goddess Artemis (Diana) when she tried to escape the advances of the river god Alpheus. She fled from Greece, into the sea, with Alpheus in close pursuit, and emerged in Sicily at this spring. It's said if you throw a cup into the Alpheus River in Greece it'll emerge here at this fountain, which is home to a few tired ducks and some faded carp—but no cups. If you want to stand right by the fountain, you need to gain admission through the aquarium; otherwise look down on it from Largo Aretusa. ✉ *Off promenade along harbor, Ortygia.*

15

Piazza Archimede. The center of this piazza has a baroque fountain, the *Fontana di Diana,* festooned with fainting sea nymphs and dancing jets of water. Look for the Chiaramonte-style **Palazzo Montalto,** an arched-window gem just off the piazza on Via Montalto.

Piazza del Duomo. In the heart of Ortygia, this ranks as one of Italy's most beautiful piazzas, its elongated space lined with Sicilian baroque treasures and outdoor cafés.

Tempio di Apollo. Scattered through the piazza just across the bridge to Ortygia are the ruins of a temple dedicated to Apollo, a model of which is in the Museo Archeologico. In fact, little of this noble Doric temple remains except for some crumbled walls and shattered columns; the window in the south wall belongs to a Norman church that was built much later on the same spot. ✉ *Piazza Pancali, Ortygia.*

WORTH NOTING

Castello Maniace. The southern tip of Ortygia island is occupied by a castle built by Frederick II (1194–1250), now an army barracks, from which there are fine views of the sea.

Museo Bellomo. Siracusa's principal museum of art is inside Palazzo Bellomo, a lovely Catalan Gothic building with mullioned windows and an elegant exterior staircase. Among the paintings and sculptures are a *Santa Lucia* by Caravaggio (1573–1610) and a damaged but still brilliant *Annunciation* by Antonello da Messina. There are also exhibits of Sicilian nativity figures, silver, furniture, ceramics, and religious vestments. ✉ *Via Capodieci 14, Ortygia* ☎ *0931/69511* 🎫 *€8* ⏲ *Tues.– Sat. 9– 6:30, Sun. 9–2; last entry 30 mins before closing.*

Palazzo Beneventano del Bosco. At one end of Piazza del Duomo, this elegant palazzo is a private residence, but you can take a peek at the impressive interior courtyard with its central staircase. ✉ *Piazza del Duomo, Ortygia.*

WHERE TO EAT

¢ PIZZA ✕ **Archimede.** Considered the best pizzeria in Ortygia, this place offers pizzas with classical names: for example, the Polifema, with sliced tomatoes, mozzarella, speck, and corn; and the Teocrite, topped with fresh tomato, mozzarella, garlic, onion, and basil. For those who can't face

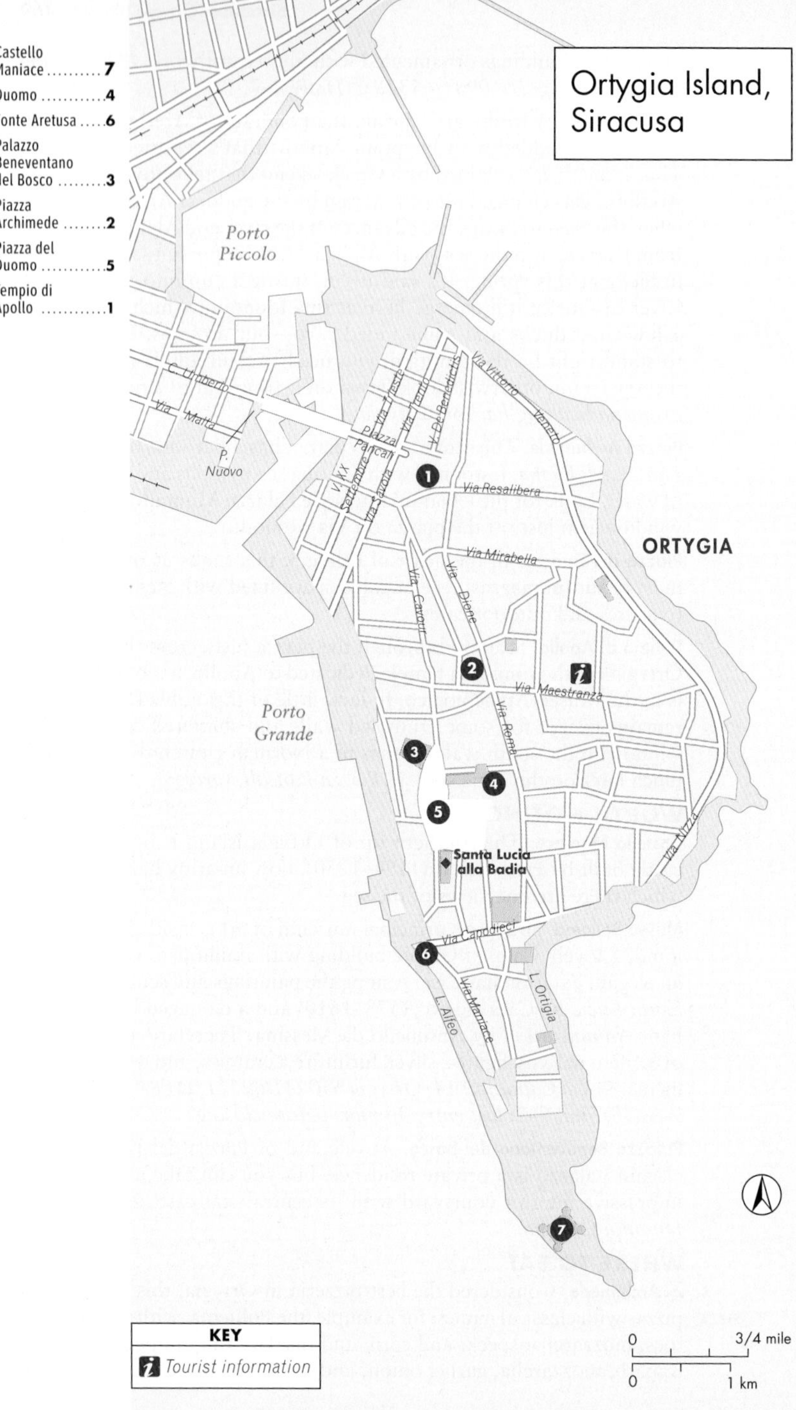

Ortygia Island, Siracusa
Castello Maniace 7
Duomo 4
Fonte Aretusa 6
Palazzo Beneventano del Bosco 3
Piazza Archimede 2
Piazza del Duomo 5
Tempio di Apollo 1
Porto Piccolo
Porto Grande
ORTYGIA
C. Umberto
Via Malta
P. Nuovo
Piazza Pancali
V. XX Settembre
Via Trieste
Via Trento
V. De Benedictis
Via Vittorio Veneto
Via Savoia
Via Resalibera
Via Mirabella
Via Cavour
Via Dione
Via Maestranza
Via Roma
Via Nizza
Santa Lucia alla Badia
Via Capodieci
Via Maniace
L. Alfeo
L. Ortigia
KEY
Tourist information
0
3/4 mile
0
1 km

the full-size offerings, mini pizzas are also available. The calzone *del ciclope* (literally "of the Cyclops") is stuffed with tomato, mozzarella, ham, and egg. Wash it all down with a good selection of beers. ✉ *Via Gemmellaro 8, Ortygia* ☎ *0931/69701* ⏲ *Closed Sun. Sept.–May.*

$$$ SICILIAN Fodor's Choice ★ ✕ **Don Camillo.** A gracious series of delicately arched rooms, lined with wine bottles and sepia-tone images of Old Siracusa, overflows with locals in the know. Preparations bring together fresh seafood and inspired creativity: taste, for instance, the sublime spaghetti *delle Sirene* (with sea urchin and shrimp in butter); a delicate *zuppa di mucco* (tiny fish floating in a broth with cherry tomatoes, olive oil, and egg); or gamberoni prepared, unexpectedly (and wonderfully), in pork fat. The wine list is, in a word, extraordinary. ✉ *Via Maestranza 96, Ortygia* ☎ *0931/67133* ⏲ *Closed Sun.*

$$ SICILIAN ✕ **Il Fermento.** "Hip" and "family-run" aren't normally terms you'll find paired together, but they accurately describe this Ortygia eatery. It's a lovely place, graced with a wonderful vaulted ceiling in the dining area. The menu revolves around seafood, including some of the freshest fish around. Leave room for the luscious homemade desserts. Two-course set-price menus (starting at €20) provide a good sampler of the delights on offer. ✉ *Via Crocifisso 44/46, Ortygia* ☎ *0931/64422* ⏲ *Closed Tues. No lunch Oct.–May.*

15

$$ SICILIAN ✕ **Ionico.** Enjoy seaside dining in the coastal Santa Lucia district. The Ionico has a terrace and veranda for alfresco meals, and the interior is plastered with diverse historical relics and has a cheerful open hearth for winter. Chef-proprietor Roberto Giudice cooks meals to order or will suggest a specialty from a selection of market-fresh ingredients. Try the farfalle with ricotta and prawns. ✉ *Riviera Dionisio il Grande 194, Santa Lucia* ☎ *0931/65540* ⏲ *Closed Tues. Sept.–May.*

$$ MODERN ITALIAN ✕ **Oinos.** This restaurant–wine bar's ambitious food represents the most modern face of Siracusa. The dining rooms are stark but inviting, carefully balancing style consciousness with restrained refinement. Surrender to the sensational antipasto *sformatino di patate, cavolo capuccio, scamorza e braduro,* a molded potato tart with cabbage and rich, creamy cheeses. In season, special dishes spotlight white truffles from Alba priced by the gram (as is customary) and worth every penny. ✉ *Via della Giudecca 69/75, Ortygia* ☎ *0931/464900* ⏲ *Closed Mon. No dinner Sun. in winter.*

WHERE TO STAY

¢–$ **Airone.** In a pretty old palazzo, this bare-bones inn caters mostly to backpackers and those who have the stamina to brave the four-story climb. **Pros:** good value; full of character. **Cons:** breakfast is not always served on the premises; some rooms are poorly furnished; stairs to climb. ✉ *Via Maestranza 111, Ortygia* ☎ *0931/69475* *9 rooms, 5 with bath* *Breakfast.*

$$ **Domus Mariae.** You can see the sea at the end of the corridor as you enter this hotel on Ortygia's eastern shore. **Pros:** nice breakfast room; gorgeous sea views; enthusiastic staff. **Cons:** stairs to climb. **TripAdvisor:** "very calm and peaceful," "large, airy and clean," "receptionists are very polite." ✉ *Via Vittorio Veneto 76, Ortygia* ☎ *0931/24854 or 0931/24858* 🌐 *www.domusmariae1.it* *12 rooms* *In-hotel: bar, gym, parking* *Breakfast.*

$$$ **Grand Hotel Ortigia.** An elegant, fantasy-inspired design prevails at this venerable institution, which has enjoyed a prime position on the Porto Grande at the base of Ortygia since 1898. **Pros:** wonderful views from the rooftop restaurant; attentive service. **Cons:** back rooms have no view; small bathrooms; Wi-Fi weak in some rooms. **TripAdvisor:** "overlooking the marina," "breakfast was great," "signs of age peak through." ✉ *Viale Mazzini 12, Ortygia* ☎ *0931/464600* 🌐 *www.grandhotelortigia.it* *41 rooms, 17 suites* *In-room: Wi-Fi. In-hotel: restaurant, bar, beach, parking* *Breakfast.*

$$$ ★ **Hotel des Étrangers et Miramare.** This stylish hotel is one of the city's top addresses for visiting dignitaries and luxury tourists. **Pros:** well-maintained facility; attentive service; central location. **Cons:** some bathrooms are poorly designed; no parking. **TripAdvisor:** "classic yet tastefully hip," "location is awesome," "felt we were in the '70s." ✉ *Passeggio Adorno 10/12, Ortygia* ☎ *0931/319100* 🌐 *www.hotel-desetrangers.it* *65 rooms, 11 suites* *In-room: Wi-Fi. In-hotel: restaurant, room service, bars, pool, gym, spa* *Breakfast.*

NIGHTLIFE AND THE ARTS

The feast of the city's patron, Santa Lucia, is held on December 13 and 20 at **Santa Lucia alla Badia** (✉ *Piazza del Duomo near Catacombs of San Giovanni, Ortygia*). A splendid silver statue of the saint is carried from the church to the Duomo: a torchlight procession and band music accompany the bearers, while local families watch from their balconies.

From mid-May to late June, Siracusa's **Teatro Greco** (✉ *Parco Archeologico, Archaeological Zone* ☎ *0931/487200; 800/542644 toll-free in Italy* 🌐 *www.indafondazione.org*) stages performances of classical drama and comedy. Tickets run €30 to €60, with a small discount if you buy the ticket in person.

THE INTERIOR

Sicily's interior is for the most part untrammeled, though the Imperial Roman Villa at Casale, outside Piazza Armerina, gives precious evidence from an epoch gone by. Don't miss windy mountaintop Enna, called the Navel of Sicily, or Caltagirone, a ceramics center of renown.

RAGUSA

90 km (56 mi) southwest of Siracusa.

GETTING HERE

Trains and buses leave from Siracusa four or five times daily.

VISITOR INFORMATION

Ragusa tourism office (✉ *Piazza San Giovanni* ☎ *0932/684780* 🌐 *www.comune.ragusa.it*).

EXPLORING

Ragusa and Modica are the two chief cities in Sicily's smallest and sleepiest province, and the centers of a region known as Iblea. The dry, rocky, gentle countryside filled with canyons and grassy knolls is a unique landscape in Sicily. Iblea's trademark squat walls divide swaths of land in a manner reminiscent of the high English countryside—but summers are decidedly Sicilian, with dry heat so intense that life grinds to a standstill for several hours each day. This remote province hums along to its own tune, clinging to local customs, cuisines, and traditions in aloof disregard even for the rest of Sicily.

WORD OF MOUTH

"If you like hand painted pottery, Caltigarone is worth a few hours, just for the amazing tiled stairs and pistachio pesto!"
—swalter518

★ Ragusa is known for some great local red wines and its wonderful cheese, a creamy, doughy, flavorful version of *caciocavallo*, made by hand every step of the way. It's a modern city with a beautiful old town called **Ibla**, which was completely rebuilt after the devastating earthquake of 1693. A tumble of buildings perched on a hilltop and suspended between a deep ravine and a sloping valley, Ibla's tiny squares and narrow lanes make for pleasant meandering.

The **Basilica di San Giorgio**, designed by Rosario Gagliardi in 1738, is a fine example of Sicilian baroque.

CALTAGIRONE

66 km (41 mi) northwest of Ragusa.

GETTING HERE

Buses and trains from Catania stop in the lower town, a pleasant stroll from the center and also well connected by local buses and taxis. Connections with Ragusa, Enna, and Piazza Armerina are less frequent.

VISITOR INFORMATION

Caltagirone tourism office (✉ *Galleria Luigi Sturzo, Piazza Municipio10* ☎ *0933/41365* 🌐 *www.comune.caltagirone.ct.it*).

EXPLORING

Built over three hills, this charming baroque town is a center of Sicily's ceramics industry. Here you can find majolica balustrades, tile-decorated windowsills, and the monumental Scala Santa Maria del Monte.

The **Scala Santa Maria del Monte** tile staircase of 142 steps—each decorated with a different pattern—leads up to the neglected Santa Maria del Monte church. On the feast of San Giacomo (July 24), the city's patron saint, the staircase is illuminated with candles that form a tapestry design over the steps. It's the result of months of work preparing the 4,000 *coppi,* or cylinders of colored paper that hold oil lamps. At 9:30 pm on the nights of July 24, July 25, August 14, and August 15 a squad of hundreds of youngsters (tourists are welcome to participate) springs into action to light the lamps, so that the staircase flares up all at once. ✉ *Begins at Piazza Municipio (main town square).*

Caltagirone was declared a UNESCO Heritage Site for its ceramics as well as for its numerous baroque churches, and it has a worthwhile **Ceramics Museum.** ✉ *Via Roma s/n (inside Giardini Pubblici)* ☎ *0933/58418 or 0933/58423* 🎫 *€4* 🕒 *Daily 9–6:30.*

CLOSE UP

Prizzi's Honor

Buried in the heart of Mafia country (22 km [14 mi] west of Lercara Friddi, which gave the world the mobster Lucky Luciano), Prizzi, population 6,000, is a fairy-tale aerie, a floating apparition of twisting stone alleyways and brown rooftops gently dusting the peak of a 3,267-foot mountain. Its medieval layout and architecture—surreally frozen in another age—and dreamy views of the surrounding countryside, perhaps best seen at sunset, make it well worth a stop along the way between Palermo and Agrigento. Prizzi was founded by the Greeks in about 480 BC, and was alternately conquered by the Byzantines (8th century AD) and Saracens (9th century AD). The latter built three lofty castles and created a "cult of water" with an elaborate network of drinking troughs. Christian conquest came in the 11th century.

The name "Prizzi" became known to the outside world through 1985's wryly comic mobster movie *Prizzi's Honor*, but the town feels as far removed as imaginable from Hollywood glamour and glitz. There's little in the way of significant art or monuments, and the secrets of the Mafia presence lie out of reach to visitors, buried in inaccessible crevices of local culture. But you can spend hours wandering in and out of the maze of steeply sloped alleyways, with tiny, still-inhabited houses built into the rock, eventually giving way to the remains of the three castles and the mountain's dazzling peak, from which, on a clear day, you can view the sea of Sciacca to one side and the cone of Mount Etna to the other.

Coming from Palermo, follow the signs to Sciacca; both Prizzi and Corleone—another name familiar to moviegoers—are on the way.

PIAZZA ARMERINA

30 km (18 mi) northwest of Caltagirone.

GETTING HERE

Piazza Armerina is linked to Caltagirone, Catania, Enna, and Palermo by regular buses. There's no train station.

VISITOR INFORMATION

Piazza Armerina tourism office (✉ *Via Generale Muscará 47a* ☎ *0935/680201* 🌐 *www.comune.piazzaarmerina.en.it*).

EXPLORING

A quick look around the fanciful town of Piazza Armerina is rewarding—it has a provincial warmth, and the crumbling yellow-stone architecture with Sicily's trademark bulbous balconies creates quite an effect. The greatest draw, however, lies just down the road.

Fodor's Choice ★ The exceptionally well-preserved **Imperial Roman Villa** is thought to have been a hunting lodge of the emperor Maximianus Heraclius (4th century AD). The excavations were not begun until 1950, and the wall decorations and vaulting have been lost. However, some of the best mosaics of the Roman world cover more than 12,000 square feet under a shelter that hints at the layout of the original buildings. The mosaics were probably made by North African artisans; they're similar to those in the Tunis Bardo Museum, in Tunisia. The entrance was through a triumphal arch that led into an atrium surrounded by a portico of columns, after which the *thermae,* or bathhouse, is reached. It's colorfully decorated with mosaic nymphs, a Neptune, and slaves massaging bathers. The peristyle leads to the main villa, where in the Salone del Circo you look down on mosaics illustrating Roman circus sports. Room 38 even reveals a touch of eroticism—surely only scratching the surface of the bacchanalian festivities that Maximianus conjured up. The villa was partially renovated in 2009, and that part is now open to the public, but the remainder is expected to remain closed for several years. Entry prices have been lowered accordingly. ✉ *SP15, Contrada Casale, 4 km (2½ mi) southwest of Piazza Armerina* ☎ *0935/680036* 🌐 *www.villaromanadelcasale.it* 🎫 *€5* ⏲ *Daily 9–1 hr before sunset.*

WHERE TO EAT

$$$ MODERN ITALIAN Fodor's Choice ★

Al Fogher. A beacon of culinary light shines in Sicily's interior, a region generally filled with good, but simple, places to eat. Ambitious—and successful—dishes here combine traditional ingredients with the creative flair of chef Angelo Treno. Try the tuna tartare with orange essence, or the fillet of baby pig served with a sauce made from *bottarga* (cured tuna roe) and green olives. The wine list includes nearly 500 labels, and there's even a water list featuring more than a dozen kinds of mineral water. The dining-room decor is simple and elegant, but the terrace is the place to be in summer. From town, follow Viale Ciancio and Viale Gaeta about 1 km (½ mi) north of Piazza Cascino. ✉ *Contrada Bellia, near SS117bis, Aidone exit* ☎ *0935/684123* 🌐 *www.alfogher.net* ⏲ *Closed Mon. No dinner Sun.*

15

ENNA

33 km (20 mi) northwest of Piazza Armerina, 136 km (85 mi) southeast of Palermo.

GETTING HERE

Just off the A19 autostrada, Enna is easily accessible by car. With the train station 5 km (3 mi) below the upper town, the most practical public transport is by bus from Palermo or Catania.

VISITOR INFORMATION

Enna tourism office (✉ *Piazza Napoleone Colajanni 6* ☎ *0935/50087* 🌐 *www.ennaturismo.info*).

EXPLORING

Deep in Sicily's interior, the fortress city of Enna (altitude 2,844 feet) commands exceptional views of the surrounding rolling plains, and, in the distance, Mount Etna. It's the highest provincial capital in Italy and, thanks to its central location, it's known as the "Navel of Sicily." Virtually unknown by tourists and relatively untouched by industrialization, this sleepy town charms and prospers in a distinctly old-fashioned, provincial, and Sicilian way. Enna makes a good stopover for the night or just for lunch, as it's right along the autostrada between Palermo and Catania (and thus Siracusa).

The narrow, winding streets are dominated at one end by the impressive cliff-hanging **Castello di Lombardia**, built by Frederick II, and easily visible as you approach town. Inside the castle, you can climb up the tower for great views from the dead center of the island; on a very clear day, you can see to all three coasts. ✉ *Piazza di Castello di Lombardia* 🎫 *Free* 🕑 *Daily 8–8.*

★ The Greek cult of Demeter, goddess of the harvest, was said to have centered on Enna. It's not hard to see why its adherents would have worshipped at the **Rocca di Cerere** *(Rock of Demeter)*, protruding out on one end of town next to the Castello di Lombardia. The spot enjoys spectacular views of the expansive countryside and windswept Sicilian interior. From here you can see Lake Pergusa, where mythology asserts that Persephone was abducted by Hades. While a prisoner in his underworld realm she ate six pomegranate seeds, and therefore was doomed to spend half of each year there. Because of its sulfur content, Lake Pergusa turns red once a year, a phenomenon that some say represents the blood of Persephone, and others believe represents the pomegranate seeds.

In town, head straight for Via Roma, which leads to **Piazza Vittorio Emanuele**, the center of Enna's shopping scene and evening passeggiata. The attached **Piazza Crispi,** dominated by the shell of the grand old Hotel Belvedere, affords breathtaking panoramas of the hillside and smoking Etna looming in the distance. The bronze fountain at the center of the piazza is a reproduction of Gian Lorenzo Bernini's famous 17th-century sculpture *The Rape of Persephone*, a depiction of Hades abducting Persephone.

The mysterious **Torre di Federico II** stands above the lower part of town. This octagonal tower, of unknown purpose, has been celebrated for millennia as marking the exact geometric center of the island—thus the tower's, and city's, nickname, Umbilicus Siciliae (Navel of Sicily). The interior is not open to the public, but the surrounding park is.

Follow Via Libertá toward Via Panoramica Monte to reach **SS. Crocifisso di Papardura**, a sanctuary built near a cave where some of the earliest evidence of Christianity in Sicily was discovered in 1659.

WHERE TO EAT AND STAY

¢ SICILIAN ✕ **Centrale**. Housed in an old palazzo, this casual place has served meals since 1889. One entire wall is covered with a vast mirror, the others are adorned with Sicilian pottery. An outdoor terrace soothes diners in summer. The seasonal menu includes local preparations such as *coppole di cacchio* (peppers stuffed with spaghetti, potato, and basil), grilled pork chops, and a 15th century specialty called *controfiletto di vitello all'annese*—a veal filet with onions, artichokes, pig jowel, and white wine. Choose from a decent selection of Sicilian wines to accompany your meal. ✉ *Piazza VI Dicembre 9* ☎ *0935/500963* 🌐 *www.ristorantecentrale.net* 🕑 *No lunch Sat. (with some exceptions).*

$ 🏨 **Hotel Sicilia**. Sicily's interior has few decent accommodations, and of Enna's two hotels, this one has more character. **Pros:** central location; friendly staff; good breakfast. **Cons:** a bit dated; some rooms can be noisy. **TripAdvisor:** "stunning views," "old-fashioned service," "pleasant breakfast." ✉ *Piazza Napoleone Colajanni 7* ☎ *0935/500850* 🌐 *www.hotelsiciliaenna.it* 🛏 *65 rooms* *In-room: Wi-Fi (some). In-hotel: room service, bar, parking* 🍴 *Breakfast.*

AGRIGENTO AND WESTERN SICILY

The crowning glory of western Sicily is the concentration of Greek temples at Agrigento, on a height between the modern city and the sea. The mark of ancient Greek culture also lingers in the cluster of ruined cliff-side temples at Selinunte and at the splendidly isolated site of Segesta. Traces of the North African culture that for centuries exerted a strong influence on this end of the island are most tangible in the coastal towns of Trapani and Marsala, and on the outlying island of Pantelleria, nearer to the Tunisian coast than the Sicilian. In contrast, the cobbled streets of hilltop Erice, outside Trapani, retain a strong medieval complexion, giving the quiet town the air of a last outpost on the edge of the Mediterranean. On the northern coast, not far outside Palermo, Monreale's cathedral glitters with mosaics that are among the finest in Italy.

15

AGRIGENTO

60 km (37 mi) southwest of Caltanissetta.

GETTING HERE

You can reach Agrigento by bus from Palermo, Caltanissetta, and Catania, and by train from Palermo, Caltanissetta, and Catania, usually with a stop in Enna. Both bus and train stations are centrally located. By car, the town is easily accessed by the coastal SS115, by the SS189 from Palermo, and by the SS640 from Caltanissetta.

VISITOR INFORMATION

Agrigento tourism office (✉ *Via Empedocle 73* ☎ *0922/20391*).

EXPLORING

Agrigento owes its fame almost exclusively to its ancient Greek temples—though it was also the birthplace of playwright Luigi Pirandello (1867–1936).

There are a few other things to do and see in the area. Along the coast around 8 km (5 mi) to the east of Agrigento is the Scala dei Turchi (Stairs of the Turks), natural white cliffs eroded into unusual shapes, and the coast closest to the temples, in the village of San Leone di Agrigento, is popular with sunbathers. Among the reasons to go up the hill from Valle dei Templi to the modern city is the opportunity to eat a more local, less overpriced meal or to stay at an inexpensive hotel; another is to ring the doorbell at the **Monastero di Santo Spirito** and try the *kus-kus* (sweet cake), made of pistachio nuts, almonds, and chocolate, that the nuns prepare. The courtyard to the church is open to the public. ✉ *Salita di Santo Spirito off Via Porcello, cortile Santo Spirito 8* ☎ *No phone* ⏱ *Mon.–Sat., hrs irregular.*

Continued on page 882

VALLE DEI TEMPLI

Built on a broad open field that slopes gently to the sun-simmered Mediterranean, Akragas (ancient Agrigento's Greek name) was a showpiece of temples erected to flaunt a victory over Carthage. Despite a later sack by the Carthaginians, mishandling by the Romans, and neglect by the Christians and Muslims, the eight or so monuments in the Valle dei Templi are considered to be, along with the Acropolis in Athens, the finest Greek ruins in all the world.

TIMING TIP

The temples are at their very best in May, when the weather is warm but the summer tourist crowds haven't yet arrived.

Whether you first come upon the Valle dei Templi in the early morning light, or bathed by golden floodlights at night, it's easy to see why Akragas was celebrated by the Greek poet Pindar as "the most beautiful city built by mortal men."

MAKING THE MOST OF YOUR VISIT

GETTING AROUND

Though getting to, from, and around the dusty ruins of the Valle dei Templi is no great hassle, this important archaeological zone deserves several hours. The site, which opens at 8:30 AM, is divided into western and eastern sections. For instant aesthetic gratification, walk through the eastern zone; for a more comprehensive tour, start way out at the western end and work your way back uphill.

The temples are a bit spread out, but the valley is all completely walkable and generally toured on foot. However, note that there is only one hotel (Villa Athena) that is close enough to walk to the ruins, so you will most likely have to drive to reach the site; parking is at the entrance to the temple area.

WHAT TO BRING

It's a good idea to pack your own snacks and drinks. There are two snack shops with limited selections within the site, and the handful of high-priced bars around the site cater to tourists.

In summer the site can get extremely hot, so wear light clothing, a hat, and sun protection if possible.

A BRIEF HISTORY OF AGRIGENTO

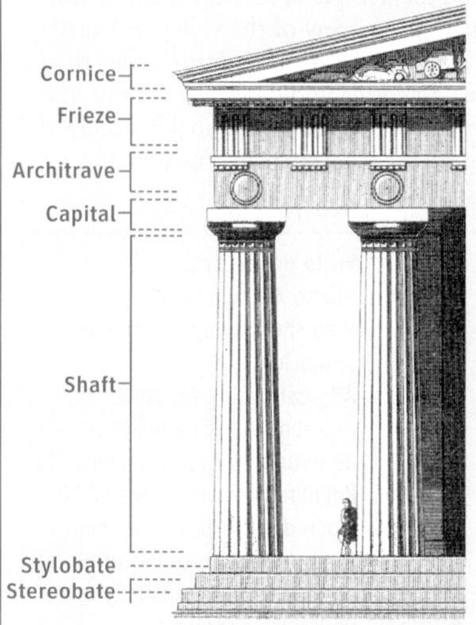

KEY DATES	
750 BC	Greek city-states begin to colonize Sicily and southern Italy.
734 BC	Neighboring Siracusa founded.
582 BC	Akragas settled. The city grows wealthy through trade with Carthage, just across the Mediterranean.
ca. 450 BC–350 BC	Temples at Akragas erected over a period of about 100 years to celebrate the city's propserity.
413 BC	Battle of Siracusa vs. Athens.
406 BC	Fire from Carthaginian attack destroys much of Akragas. Despite this and future attacks, the city and its temples survive through the Roman era, the Middle Ages, and into the modern age.

The natural defenses of ancient Akragas depended on its secure and quite lovely position between two rivers on a floodplain a short distance from the sea. In Agrigento you will be treated to what many experts consider the world's best-preserved remains of classical Greece. All of the temples in the Valle dei Templi are examples of Doric architecture, the earliest and simplest of the Greek architectural orders (the others are Ionic and Corinthian). Some retain capitals in addition to their columns, while others are reduced to nothing more than fragments of stylobate.

THE TEMPLES

TEMPIO DI ERCOLE

The eight pillars of the **Temple of Hercules**, down the hill from the Temple of Concord, make up Agrigento's oldest temple complex (dating from the 6th century BC), dedicated to the favorite god of the often-warring citizens of Akragas. Partially reconstructed in 1922, it reveals the remains of a large Doric temple that originally had 38 columns. Like all the area temples, it faces east. The nearby Museo Archeologico Regionale contains some of the marble warrior figures that once decorated the temple's pediment.

Tempio di Ercole

TEMPIO DELLA CONCORDIA

The beautiful **Temple of Concord** is perhaps *the* best-preserved Greek temple in existence. The structure dates from about 430 BC, and owes its exceptional state of preservation to the fact that it was converted into a Christian church in the 6th century and was extensively restored in the 18th century. Thirty-two Doric columns surround its large interior, and everything but the roof and treasury are still standing. For preservation, this temple is blocked off to the public, but you can still get close enough to appreciate how well it's withstood the past 2,400 years.

TEMPIO DI GIUNONE

The **Temple of Juno**, east on the Via Sacra from the Temple of Concord, commands an exquisite view of the valley, especially at sunset. It's similar to but smaller than the Concordia and dates from about 450 BC. Traces of a fire that probably occurred during the Carthaginian attack in 406 BC,

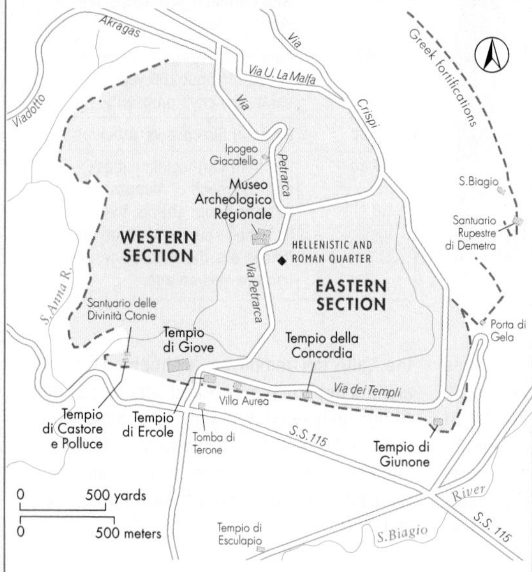

Valle dei Templi
Phone: 0922/621611
Web site: www.parcovalledetempli.it
Admission: Site €8, with museum €10. One ticket covers all temples except Giardini della Kolimbetra (which costs €2.50).
Open daily 8:30–7; Nov.–Mar., western section closes at 5; the eastern section is usually open until late in summer.

Museo Archeologico Regionale
Contrada San Nicola, 12
Phone: 0922/401565
Admission: €8, with temples site €10
Open Tues.–Sat. 9–7, Sun.–Mon. 9–1.

which destroyed the ancient town, can be seen on the walls of the cellar. Thirty of the original 34 columns still stand, of which 16 have retained their capitals.

TEMPIO DI GIOVE

Though never completed, the **Temple of Jupiter** was considered the eighth wonder of the world. With a length of more than 330 feet, it was once the biggest of the Akragas temples and one of the largest temples in the Greek world. The temple was probably built in gratitude for victory over Carthage and was constructed by prisoners captured in that war. Basically Doric in style, it did not have the usual colonnade of freestanding columns but rather a series of half columns attached to a solid wall. This design is unique among known Doric temples—alas, only the stereobate was left behind. Inside the excavation you can see a cast (not the original) of one of the 38 colossal Atlas-like figures, or telamones, that supported the temple's massive roof.

Tempio di Giove

TEMPIO DI CASTORE E POLLUCE

The **Temple of Castor and Pollux** is a troublesome reconstruction of a 5th-century BC temple. It was pieced together by some enthusiastic if misguided 19th-century romantics who, in 1836, haphazardly put together elements from diverse buildings. Ironically, the four gently crumbling columns supporting part of an entablature of the temple have become emblematic of Agrigento.

OTHER SITES OF INTEREST

To the left of the Temple of Concord is a Paleochristian **necropolis**. Early Christian tombs were both cut into the rock and dug into underground catacombs.

Right opposite the Temple of Castor and Pollux, facing north, the **Santuario delle Divinità Ctonie** (Sanctuary of the Chthonic Divinities) has cultic altars and eight small temples dedicated to Demeter, Persephone, and other Underworld deities. In the vicinity are two columns of a temple dedicated to Hephaestus (Vulcan).

At the end of Via dei Templi, where it turns left and becomes Via Petrarca, stands the **Museo Archeologico Regionale**. An impressive collection of antiquities from the site includes vases, votives, everyday objects, weapons, statues (including one of the surviving original telamones from the Temple of Jupiter), and models of the temples.

The **Hellenistic and Roman Quarter**, across the road from the archaeological museum, consists of four parallel streets, running north–south, that have been uncovered, along with the foundations of some houses from the Roman settlement (2nd century BC). Some of these streets still have their original mosaic pavements, and the complex system of sidewalks and gutters is easy to make out—reminding you that the ancient world wasn't all temples and togas.

WHERE TO EAT

$$ SICILIAN ✕ **Leon d'Oro**. In the community of San Leone di Agrigento, lying between the temples and the seaside, sits Leon d'Oro, run by local food and wine personality Totó Collura. Making adventurous use of traditional ingredients, the seasonal menu is full of pleasant surprises. Try the pasta with sardines, made with traditional Agrigento spices. The wine list is playful, organized with an opera theme and featuring frowning faces when a certain label is temporarily out of stock. ✉ *Viale Emporium 102, San Leone di Agrigento* ☎ *0922/414400* ⏲ *Closed Mon.*

$$ SICILIAN Fodor's Choice ★ ✕ **Trattoria dei Templi**. Along a road on the way up to Agrigento proper from the temple area, this simple family-run vaulted restaurant serves up some of the best food in the area. The menu includes five different homemade pastas each day and plenty of fresh fish dishes, all prepared with a Sicilian flare. The antipasti, such as the carpaccio of *cernia* (grouper), are exceptional, and the ample wine list has many Sicilian choices. The best bet is to ask for the advice of brothers Giuseppe and Simone. Reservations are recommended in the high season, as things get busy after it becomes too dark for temple exploring. ✉ *Via Panoramica dei Templi 15* ☎ *0922/403110* 🌐 *www.trattoriadeitempli.com* ⏲ *Closed 2 wks in late June–early July. No lunch in summer Fri. and Sun.*

WHERE TO STAY

$$–$$$ **Foresteria Baglio della Luna**. Fiery sunsets and moonlight cast a glow over a tower dating from the 8th century, which is central to this farmhouse-hotel complex. **Pros:** quiet location; serene environment. **Cons:** difficult to reach from the temples and the city (buses run hourly); service can be slipshod; restaurant is overpriced. **TripAdvisor:** "quiet, blissful spot," "lovely enclosed courtyard," "decor maybe a little tired." ✉ *Contrada Maddalusa, Via Serafino Amabile Guastella 1* ☎ *0922/511061* 🌐 *www.bagliodellaluna.com* *21 rooms, 2 suites* *In-room: Wi-Fi. In-hotel: restaurant, bar, some pets allowed* *Breakfast.*

$ **Tre Torri**. Stay here if you're an outdoors enthusiast bent on exploring the countryside around Agrigento. **Pros:** good facilities; sociable atmosphere; multilingual staff. **Cons:** a bit run-down; some rooms are small; busy with tour groups; a bit far from the temples and the city. **TripAdvisor:** "pool is very pleasant," "fine for the price," "bit far from everything." ✉ *Viale Cannatelo 7, Villagio Mosè* ☎ *0922/606733* 🌐 *www.hoteltretorri.eu* *118 rooms* *In-room: Wi-Fi. In-hotel: restaurant, bars, pools, gym, spa* *Breakfast.*

NIGHTLIFE AND THE ARTS

During the first half of February, Agrigento hosts a **Festa delle Mandorle** *(Almond Blossom Festival)*, with international folk dances, a costumed parade, and the sale of marzipan and other sweets made from almonds.

SELINUNTE

100 km (62 mi) northwest of Agrigento, 114 km (71 mi) south of Palermo.

GETTING HERE

You can get here by bus or car via the town of Castelvetrano, 11 km (7 mi) north, which is itself accessible from Palermo by car on the A29 autostrada, as well as by bus and train.

VISITOR INFORMATION

Selinunte tourism office (✉ *Piazzale Bovio Marconi s/n* ☎ *0924/46251*); the office is open from June 1 to September 15.

EXPLORING

★ Near the town of Castelvetrano, numerous **Greek temple ruins** perch on a plateau overlooking an expanse of the Mediterranean at Selinunte (or Selinus). The city was one of the most superb colonies of ancient Greece. Founded in the 7th century BC, Selinunte became the rich and prosperous rival of Segesta, which in 409 BC turned to the Carthaginians for help. The Carthaginians sent an army commanded by Hannibal to destroy the city. The temples were demolished, the city was razed, and 16,000 of Selinunte's inhabitants were slaughtered. The remains of Selinunte are in many ways unchanged from the day of its sacking—burn marks still scar the Greek columns, and much of the site still lies in rubble at its exact position of collapse at the hands of the Carthaginian attack. The original complex held seven temples scattered over two sites separated by a harbor. Of the seven, only one—reconstructed in 1958—is whole. This is a large archaeological site, so you might make use of the *navetta* (shuttle) to save a bit of walking.

15

Selinunte is named after a local variety of wild parsley (*Apium graveolens* or *petroselinum*) that in spring grows in profusion among the ruined columns and overturned capitals. Although there are a few places to stay right around Selinunte, many people see it as an easy stop along the road to or from Agrigento. It takes only an hour or two to see—a richly rewarding stopover. ✉ *SS115, 13 km (8 mi) southeast of Castelvetrano* ☎ *0924/46277* 🎫 *€9* ⏲ *Apr.–Oct., Tues.–Sat. 9–6; Nov.–Mar., daily 9–4.*

MARSALA

88 km (55 mi) northwest of Selinunte.

GETTING HERE

Buses and trains from Palermo, Trapani, and Castelvetrano stop in Marsala. Drivers can take the coastal SS115.

VISITOR INFORMATION

Marsala tourism office (✉ *Via XI Maggio 100* ☎ *0923/714097* 🌐 *www.comune.marsala.tp.it*).

EXPLORING

The quiet seaside town of Marsala was once the main Carthaginian base in Sicily, from which Carthage fought for supremacy over the island against Greece and Rome. Nowadays it's more readily associated with the world-famous, richly colored sweet wine named after the town.

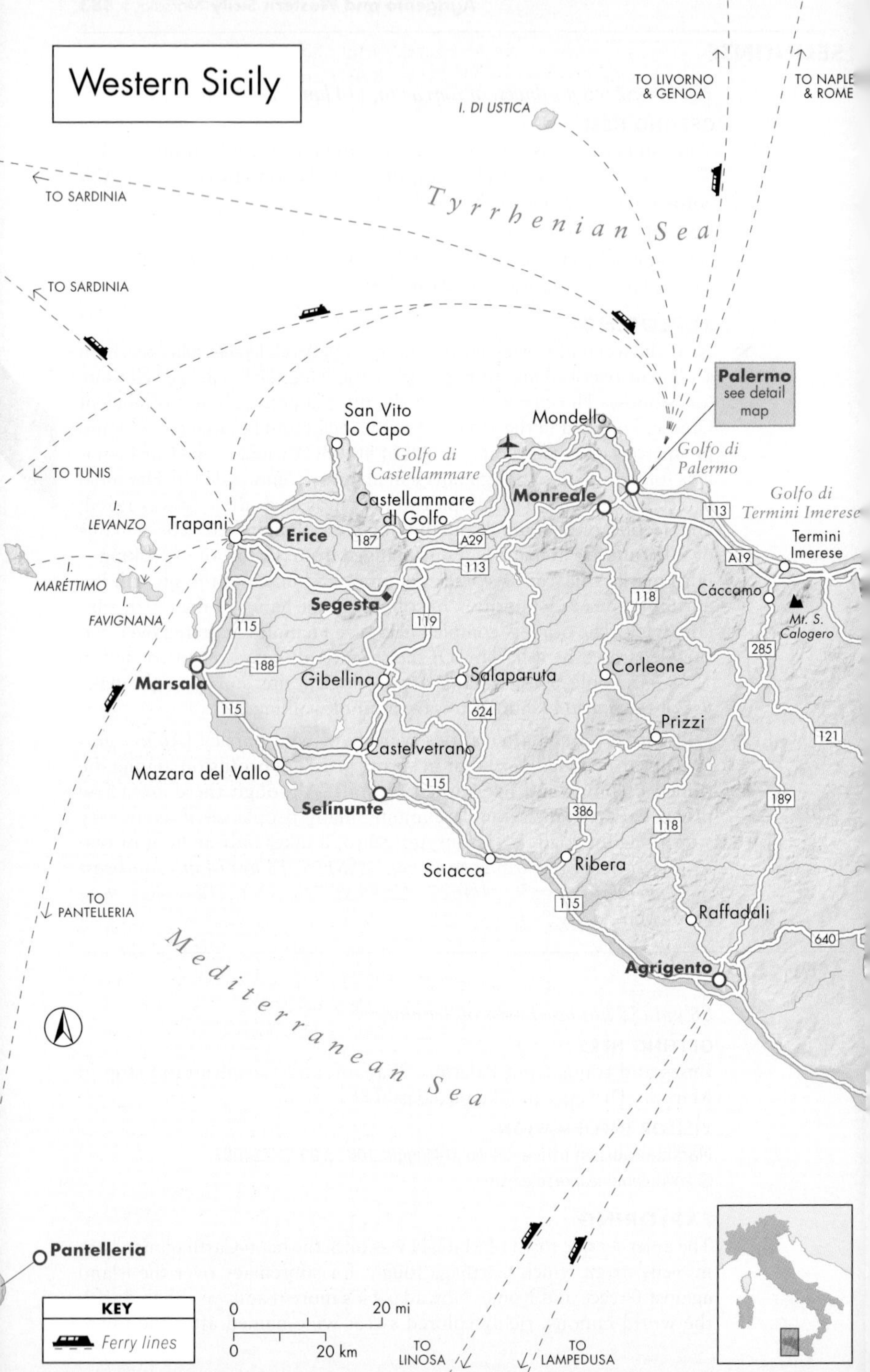

Western Sicily
TO LIVORNO & GENOA
TO NAPLE & ROME
I. DI USTICA
TO SARDINIA
Tyrrhenian Sea
TO SARDINIA
Palermo
see detail map
San Vito lo Capo
Mondello
Golfo di Castellammare
Golfo di Palermo
TO TUNIS
Castellammare dl Golfo
Monreale
Golfo di Termini Imerese
I. LEVANZO
Trapani
Erice
187
A29
113
Termini Imerese
A19
I. MARÉTTIMO
113
118
Cáccamo
I. FAVIGNANA
Segesta
115
119
Mt. S. Calogero
285
Marsala
188
Gibellina
Salaparuta
Corleone
115
624
Prizzi
121
Castelvetrano
Mazara del Vallo
115
Selinunte
189
386
118
Sciacca
Ribera
TO PANTELLERIA
115
Raffadali
640
Mediterranean Sea
Agrigento
Pantelleria
KEY
Ferry lines
0
20 mi
0
20 km
TO LINOSA
TO LAMPEDUSA

In 1773 a British merchant named John Woodhouse happened upon Marsala and discovered that the wine here was as good as the port the British had long imported from Portugal. Two other wine merchants, Whitaker and Ingram, rushed in, and by 1800 Marsala was exporting its wine all over the British Empire.

A sense of Marsala's past as a Carthaginian stronghold is captured by the well-preserved Punic warship displayed in the town's **Museo Archeologico Baglio Anselmi**, along with some of the amphoras and other artifacts recovered from the wreck. The vessel, which was probably sunk during the great sea battle that ended the First Punic War in 241 BC, was dredged up from the mud near the Egadi Islands in the 1970s. There's also a good display of maritime and archaeological finds. ✉ *Lungomare Boéo 2* ☎ *0923/952535* 🎫 *€4* 🕘 *Mon. 9–1:30, Tues.–Sun. 9–7.*

One of Sicily's foremost wine producers, the 150-year-old **Donnafugata Winery,** is open for tours of its *cantina* (wine cellar); reservations are required. It's an interesting look at the winemaking process in Sicily, and it ends with a tasting of several whites and reds and a chance to buy; don't miss the delicious, full-bodied red Mille e Una Notte, and the famous Ben Ryè Passito di Pantelleria, a sweet dessert wine made from dried grapes. ✉ *Via Lipari 18* ☎ *0923/724245* 🌐 *www.donnafugata.it* 🎫 *Free* 🕘 *Weekdays 9–1 and 3–6:30.*

15

ERICE

15 km (9 mi) northeast of Trapani.

GETTING HERE

A *funivia* (suspended cable car) runs from the outskirts of Trapani to Erice Monday 2 pm to 8:30 pm, Tuesday to Friday 7:30 am to 8:30 pm, and weekends 9:45 am to midnight. Going by car or bus from Trapani takes around 40 minutes.

VISITOR INFORMATION

Erice tourism office (✉ *Via Tommaso Guarrasi 1* ☎ *0923/869388*).

EXPLORING

Perched 2,450 feet above sea level, Erice is an enchanting medieval mountaintop aerie of palaces, fountains, and cobblestone streets. Shaped like an equilateral triangle, the town was the ancient landmark Eryx, dedicated to Aphrodite (Venus). When the Normans arrived they built a castle on Monte San Giuliano, where today there's a lovely public park with benches and belvederes from which there are striking views of Trapani, the Egadi Islands offshore, and, on a *very* clear day, Cape Bon and the Tunisian coast. Because of Erice's elevation, clouds conceal much of the view for most of winter. Sturdy shoes (for the cobbles) and something warm to wear are recommended.

Fans of Sicilian sweets make a beeline for **Pasticceria Grammatico** (✉ *Via Vittorio Emanuele 14* ☎ *0923/869390*). The place is run by Maria Grammatico, a former nun who gained international fame with *Bitter Almonds,* her life story cowritten with Mary Taylor Simeti. Her almond-paste creations are works of art, molded into striking shapes, including dolls and animals. There are a few tables and a tiny balcony with wonderful views.

At **Pasticceria del Convento** (✉ *Via Guarnotti 1* ☎ *0923/869777*), Maria Grammatico's sister sells similar delectable treats. The shop is open from March through November.

Capo San Vito, 40 km (25 mi) north of Erice, is a cape with a long sandy beach on a promontory overlooking a bay in the Gulf of Castellammare. The town here, San Vito Lo Capo, is famous for its North African couscous, made with fish instead of meat. In late September it hosts the five-day **Cous Cous Fest,** a serious international couscous competition and festival with live music and plenty of free tastings.

WHERE TO EAT AND STAY

$–$$ SICILIAN ✕ **Monte San Giuliano.** At this traditional restaurant, you can sit out on the tree-lined patio or in the white-wall room and munch on the free *panelle* (chickpea fritters), which are delicate, judiciously seasoned, and addictive. Next come the citrusy *sarde a beccafico* and exemplary ravioli in cuttlefish ink. Or try the seafood couscous, served with a bowl of fish broth on the side so you can add as much as you wish. The restaurant, near the main piazza, is hidden within the labyrinth of lanes that makes up Erice. ✉ *Vicolo San Rocco 7* ☎ *0923/869595* ⊙ *Closed Mon., 2 wks in mid-Jan., and 1st 2 wks in Nov.*

$ **Moderno.** This delightful hotel has a creaky old feel to it, but that's part of the charm. **Pros:** central location; great rooftop terrace. **Cons:** very modest rooms; street-facing rooms can be noisy. **TripAdvisor:** "great views," "lovely terrace," "clean, quiet and nice." ✉ *Via Vittorio Emanuele 67* ☎ *0923/869300* 🌐 *www.hotelmodernoerice.it* *40 rooms* *In-hotel: restaurant, bar, business center* *Breakfast.*

SEGESTA

35 km (22 mi) east of Erice, 85 km (53 mi) southwest of Palermo.

GETTING HERE

Three or four daily buses travel from Trapani to Segesta. About as many trains from Palermo and Trapani stop at Segesta-Tempio station, a 20-minute uphill walk from Segesta. The site is easily reached via the A29dir autostrada.

★ Segesta is the site of the **Tempio Dorico** *(Doric Temple)*, one of Sicily's most impressive, constructed on the side of a windswept barren hill overlooking a valley of wild fennel. Virtually intact today, the temple is considered by some to be finer in its proportions and setting than any other Doric temple left standing. The temple was actually started in the 5th century BC by the Elymian people, who some believe were refugees from Troy. At the very least, evidence—they often sided with the Carthaginians, for example—indicates that they were non-Greeks. However, the style is in many ways Greek. The temple was never finished; the walls and roof never materialized, and the columns were never fluted. A little more than 1 km (½ mi) away, near the top of the hill, are the remains of a fine **amphitheater** with impressive views, especially at sunset, of the sea and the nearby town of Monte Erice.

Concerts and plays are staged here in summer. ✉ *Calatafimi-Segesta* ☎ *0924/952356* €9 ⏲ *May–Sept., daily 9–7; Oct.–Apr., daily 9–5; last entry 1 hr before closing.*

MONREALE

59 km (37 mi) northeast of Segesta, 10 km (6 mi) southwest of Palermo.

GETTING HERE

You can reach Monreale on the frequent buses that depart from Palermo's Piazza dell'Indipendenza. From Palermo, drivers can follow Corso Calatafimi west, though the going can be slow.

EXPLORING

Fodor's Choice ★ Monreale's splendid **Duomo** is lavishly executed with mosaics depicting events from the Old and New Testaments. After the Norman conquest of Sicily the new princes showcased their ambitions through monumental building projects. William II (1154–89) built the church complex with a cloister and palace between 1174 and 1185, employing Byzantine craftsmen. The result was a glorious fusion of Eastern and Western influences, widely regarded as the finest example of Norman architecture in Sicily.

The major attraction is the 68,220 square feet of glittering gold mosaics decorating the cathedral interior. *Christ Pantocrator* dominates the apse area; the nave contains narratives of the Creation; and scenes from the life of Christ adorn the walls of the aisles and the transept. The painted wooden ceiling dates from 1816–37. The roof commands a great view (a reward for climbing 172 stairs).

Bonnano Pisano's bronze doors, completed in 1186, depict 42 biblical scenes and are considered among the most important of medieval artifacts. Barisano da Trani's 42 panels on the north door, dating from 1179, present saints and evangelists. ✉ *Piazza del Duomo* ☎ *091/6404413* ⏲ *Mid-Apr.–mid-Oct., daily 8:30–1 and 2:30–6:30; mid-Oct.–mid-Apr., daily 8–12:30 and 2:30–6:30.*

The lovely **cloister** of the abbey adjacent to the Duomo was built at the same time as the church but enlarged in the 14th century. The beautiful enclosure is surrounded by 216 intricately carved double columns, every other one decorated in a unique glass mosaic pattern. Afterward, don't forget to walk behind the cloister to the belvedere, with stunning panoramic views over the Conca d'Oro (Golden Conch) valley toward Palermo. ✉ *Piazza del Duomo* ☎ *091/6404403* €6 ⏲ *Tues.–Sun. 9–6:30; last entry ½ hr before closing.*

WHERE TO EAT

$$ SICILIAN ✕ **La Botte 1962.** It's worth the short drive or inexpensive taxi fare from Monreale to reach this restaurant, which is famous for well-prepared local specialties. Dine alfresco on seafood dishes such as *bavette don Carmelo,* a narrow version of tagliatelle with a sauce of swordfish, squid, shrimp, and pine nuts. Other regular favorites include *involtini alla siciliana,* meat roulades stuffed with salami and cheese. Local wines are a good accompaniment. The restaurant is open only on Saturday for lunch and dinner and on Sunday for lunch, or by

reservation. ✉ *Contrada Lenzitti 20, SS186 Km 10* ☎ *091/414051* 🌐 *www.mauriziocascino.it* ✍ *Reservations essential* ⏲ *Closed weekdays except by reservation, and July–mid-Sept. No dinner Sun.*

PALERMO

Once the intellectual capital of southern Europe, Palermo has always been at the crossroads of civilization. Favorably situated on a crescent bay at the foot of Monte Pellegrino, it has attracted almost every culture touching the Mediterranean world. To Palermo's credit, it has absorbed these diverse cultures into a unique personality that's at once Arab and Christian, Byzantine and Roman, Norman and Italian. The city's heritage encompasses all of Sicily's varied ages, but its distinctive aspect is its Arab-Norman identity, an improbable marriage that, mixed in with Byzantine and Jewish elements, created some resplendent works of art. These are most notable in the churches, from small jewels such as San Giovanni degli Eremiti to larger-scale works such as the cathedral. No less noteworthy than the architecture is Palermo's chaotic vitality, on display at some of Italy's most vibrant outdoor markets, public squares, street bazaars, and food vendors, and above all in its grand, discordant symphony of motorists, motor bikers, and pedestrians that triumphantly climaxes in the new town center each evening with Italy's most spectacular passeggiata.

GETTING HERE

Palermo is well connected by road and rail; its airport links it to other cities in Italy, as well as around Europe.

VISITOR INFORMATION

Palermo tourism office (✉ *Piazza Castelnuovo 34* ☎ *091/6058351* ✉ *Aeroporto Falcone-Borsellino* ☎ *091/591698* 🌐 *www.palermotourism.com*).

EXPLORING

Sicily's capital is a multilayered, vigorous metropolis; approach with an open mind when exploring the enriching city with a strong historical profile. You're likely to encounter some frustrating instances of inefficiency and, depending on the season, stifling heat. If you have a car, park it in a garage as soon as you can, and don't take it out until you're ready to depart.

Palermo is easily explored on foot, though you may choose to spend a morning taking a bus tour to help you get oriented. The Quattro Canti, or Four Corners, is the hub that separates the four sections of the old city: La Kalsa (the old Arab section) to the southeast, Albergheria to the southwest, Capo to the northwest, and Vucciria to the northeast. Each of these is a tumult of activity during the day, though at night the narrow alleys empty out and are best avoided in favor of the more-animated avenues of the new city north of Teatro Massimo. Sights to see by day are scattered along three major streets: Corso Vittorio Emanuele, Via Maqueda, and Via Roma. The tourist information office in Piazza Castelnuovo will give you a map and a valuable handout that lists opening and closing times, which sometimes change with the seasons.

WORD OF MOUTH

"If you plan to visit the western part of the island anyway, Palermo would be a very worthwhile visit. The mosaics are incredible . . . the restaurants are amazing and full of real local people. . . . Since it's a real city it can be more challenging than a small town, but if you're relatively fit you can practically walk across the entire tourist area. If anything frightened me about the place it was the tremendous density of things to see!"

—abbydog

15

TOP ATTRACTIONS

★ **Cattedrale.** This church is a lesson in Palermitan eclecticism—originally Norman (1182), then Catalan Gothic (14th to 15th century), then fitted out with a baroque and neoclassical interior (18th century). Its turrets, towers, dome, and arches come together in the kind of meeting of diverse elements that King Roger II (1095–1154), whose tomb is inside along with that of Frederick II, fostered during his reign. The back of the apse is gracefully decorated with interlacing Arab arches inlaid with limestone and black volcanic tufa. ✉ *Corso Vittorio Emanuele, Capo* ☎ *3293977513* 🌐 *www.cattedrale.palermo.it* 🎫 *€3* ⏲ *Mar.–Oct., Mon.–Sat. 9:30–5:30; Nov.–Feb., Mon.–Sat. 9:30–1:30.*

La Martorana. Distinguished by an elegant Norman campanile, this church was erected in 1143 but had its interior altered considerably during the baroque period. High along the western wall, however, is some of the oldest and best-preserved mosaic artwork of the Norman period. Near the entrance is an interesting mosaic of King Roger II being crowned by Christ. In it Roger is dressed in a bejeweled Byzantine stole, reflecting the Norman court's penchant for all things Byzantine. Archangels along the ceiling wear the same stole wrapped around their shoulders and arms. The much plainer San Cataldo is next door. ✉ *Piazza Bellini 3, Quattro Canti* ☎ *091/6161692* ⏲ *Mon.–Sat. 9:15–1 and 3:30–6:30, Sun. 8:30–1.*

Museo Archeologico Regionale Salinas *(Salinas Regional Museum of Archaeology).* Especially interesting pieces in this small but excellent collection are the examples of prehistoric cave drawings and a marvelously reconstructed Doric frieze from the Greek temple at Selinunte. The frieze reveals the high level of artistic culture attained by the Greek colonists in Sicily some 2,500 years ago. (To enter, use the door around the corner on Via Roma.) ✉ *Piazza Olivella 24, Via Roma, Olivella* ☎ *091/6116806* 🎫 *€4* ⏲ *Tues.–Fri. 8:30–1:30 and 2:30–6:30, weekends 8:30–1; last entry ½ hr before closing.*

Palazzo Reale *(Royal Palace).* This historic palace, also called Palazzo dei Normanni (Norman Palace), was for centuries the seat of Sicily's semiautonomous rulers. The building is a fascinating mesh of abutting 10th-century Norman and 17th-century Spanish structures. Because it now houses the Sicilian Parliament, little is accessible to the public. The **Cappella Palatina** (Palatine Chapel) remains open. Built by Roger II in 1132, it's a dazzling example of the harmony of artistic elements produced under the Normans. Here the skill of French and Sicilian

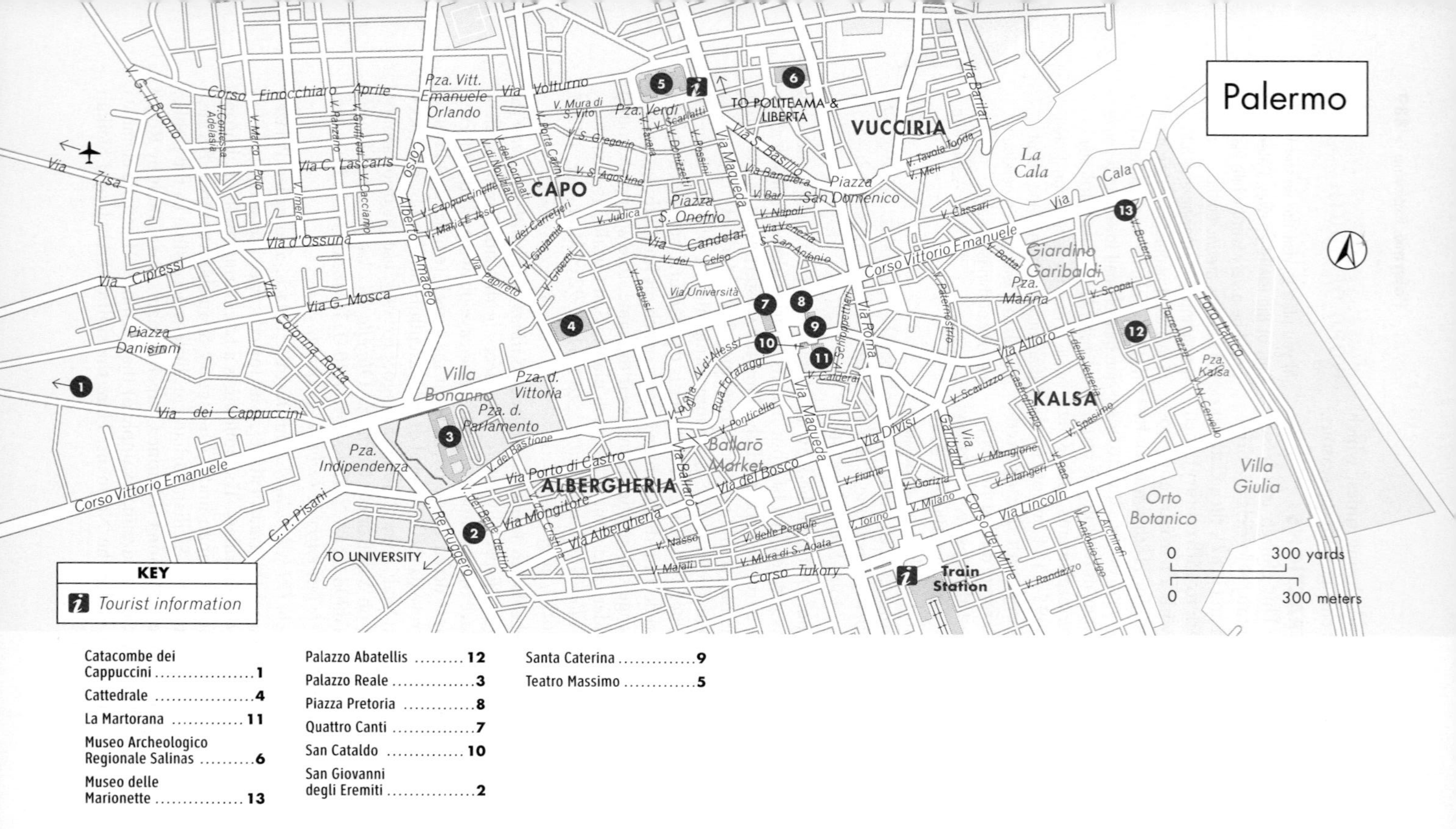

Palermo
VUCCIRIA
CAPO
KALSA
ALBERGHERIA
La Cala
Giardino Garibaldi
Villa Giulia
Orto Botanico
Villa Bonanno
Ballarò Market
Train Station
TO POLITEAMA & LIBERTÀ
TO UNIVERSITY
Corso Vittorio Emanuele
Via Maqueda
Via Roma
Corso Alberto Amedeo
Via dei Cappuccini
Foro Italico
Via Lincoln
Corso dei Mille
Corso Tukory
Pza. Verdi
Piazza San Domenico
Pza. d. Parlamento
Pza. d. Vittoria
Pza. Indipendenza
Pza. Vitt. Emanuele Orlando
Piazza Danisinni
Pza. Marina
Pza. Kalsa
0 300 yards
0 300 meters
KEY
Tourist information
Catacombe dei Cappuccini 1
Cattedrale 4
La Martorana 11
Museo Archeologico Regionale Salinas 6
Museo delle Marionette 13
Palazzo Abatellis 12
Palazzo Reale 3
Piazza Pretoria 8
Quattro Canti 7
San Cataldo 10
San Giovanni degli Eremiti 2
Santa Caterina 9
Teatro Massimo 5

masons was brought to bear on the decorative purity of Arab ornamentation and the splendor of 11th-century Greek Byzantine mosaics. The interior is covered with glittering mosaics and capped by a splendid 10th-century Arab honeycomb stalactite wooden ceiling. Biblical stories blend happily with scenes of Arab life—look for one showing a picnic in a harem—and Norman court pageantry.

Upstairs are the royal apartments, including the **Sala di Re Ruggero** (King Roger's Hall), decorated with medieval murals of hunting scenes—an earlier (1120) secular counterpoint to the religious themes seen elsewhere. To see this area of the palace, ask one of the tour guides (free) to escort you around the halls once used by one of the most splendid courts in Europe (call in advance if you want to be sure a guide is available). French, Latin, and Arabic were spoken here, and Arab astronomers and poets exchanged ideas with Latin and Greek scholars in one of the most interesting marriages of culture in the Western world. The Sala is always included with entry to the palace or chapel. ✉ *Piazza Indipendenza, Albergheria* ☎ *091/16262833* 🎫 *Palazzo Reale or Cappella Palatina €7, entry to both €8.50* 🕓 *Palazzo Reale: Mon. and Fri. 8:15–5, Sun. 8:15–12:30. Cappella Palatina: Mon.–Sat. 8:15–5, Sun. 8:15–12:30. Last entry ½ hr before closing.*

15

★ **San Cataldo.** Three striking Saracenic scarlet domes mark this church, built in 1154 during the Norman occupation of Palermo. The church now belongs to the Knights of the Holy Sepulchre, and has a spare but intense stone interior. If closed, inquire next door at La Martorana. ✉ *Piazza Bellini 3, Kalsa* ☎ *3483394617* 🎫 *€1* 🕓 *Mar.–Oct., Mon.–Sat. 9–2 and 3:30–7, Sun. 9–2; Nov.–Feb., daily 9–2.*

San Giovanni degli Eremiti. Distinguished by its five reddish-orange domes and stripped-clean interior, this 12th-century church was built by the Normans on the site of an earlier mosque—one of 200 that once stood in Palermo. The emirs ruled Palermo for nearly two centuries and brought to it their passion for lush gardens and fountains. One is reminded of this while sitting in San Giovanni's delightful cloister of twin half columns, surrounded by palm trees, jasmine, oleander, and citrus trees. ✉ *Via dei Benedettini 14, Albergheria* ☎ *091/6515019* 🎫 *€6* 🕓 *Tues.–Sat. 9–6:30; last entry ½ hr before closing.*

Teatro Massimo. Construction of this formidable neoclassical theater, the largest in Italy, was started in 1875 by Giovanni Battista Basile and completed by his son Ernesto in 1897. A reconstruction project started in 1974 ran into gross delays, and the facility remained closed until just before its centenary in 1997. Its interior is as glorious as ever. *The Godfather: Part III* ended with a famous shooting scene on the theater's steps. Visits, by 25-minute guided tour only, are available in six languages, including English. ✉ *Piazza Verdi 9, at top of Via Maqueda, Olivella* ☎ *091/6053521* 🌐 *www.teatromassimo.it* 🎫 *€7* 🕓 *Tues.–Sun. 10–3.*

WORTH NOTING

Catacombe dei Cappuccini. The spookiest sight in all of Sicily, this 16th-century catacomb houses nearly 9,000 corpses of men, women, and young children, some in tombs but many mummified and preserved, hanging in rows on the walls, divided by social caste, age, or gender; most wear signs indicating their names and the years they lived. The Capuchins were founders and proprietors of the bizarre establishment (many of the corpses are Capuchin friars) from 1599 to 1911, and it's still under the auspices of the nearby Capuchin church. It was closed when an adjacent cemetery was opened, making the catacombs redundant. It's memorable, but is not for the faint of heart; children might be frightened or disturbed. ✉ *Piazza Cappuccini1, off Via Cappuccini, near Palazzo Reale* ☎ *091/6524156* 🎟 *€3* ⏲ *Daily 9–1 and 3–6.*

Museo delle Marionette. The traditional Sicilian *pupi* (puppets), with their glittering armor and fierce expressions, have become a symbol of Norman Sicily. Plots of the weekly performances center on the chivalric legends of the troubadours, who, before the puppet theater, kept alive tales of Norman heroes in Sicily such as William the Bad (1120–66). The museum can be hard to find: look for the small alley just off Piazzetta Antonio Pasqualino 5. ✉ *Piazzetta Niscemi 5, at Via Butera, Kalsa* ☎ *091/328060* 🌐 *www.museomarionettepalermo.it* 🎟 *€5* ⏲ *Mon.–Sat. 9–1 and 2:30–6:30, Sun. 10–1.*

Palazzo Abatellis. Housed in this late-15th-century Catalan Gothic palace with Renaissance elements is the **Galleria Regionale.** Among its treasures are the *Annunciation* (1474), a painting by Sicily's prominent Renaissance master Antonello da Messina (1430–79), and an arresting fresco by an unknown painter, titled *The Triumph of Death,* a macabre depiction of the plague years. Two new rooms were opened in early 2010 after years of work. ✉ *Via Alloro 4, Kalsa* ☎ *091/6230011* 🎟 *€8* ⏲ *Tues.–Fri. 9–5:30, weekends 9–1.*

Piazza Pretoria. The square's centerpiece, a lavishly decorated fountain with 500 separate pieces of sculpture and an abundance of nude figures, so shocked some Palermitans when it was unveiled in 1575 that it got the nickname "Fountain of Shame." It's even more of a sight when illuminated at night.

Quattro Canti. The Four Corners is the intersection of Corso Vittorio Emanuele and Via Maqueda. Four rather exhaust-blackened baroque palaces from Spanish rule meet at concave corners, each with its own fountain and representations of a Spanish ruler, patron saint, and one of the four seasons.

Santa Caterina. The walls of this splendid baroque church (1596) in Piazza Bellini are covered with decorative 17th-century inlays of precious marble. ✉ *Piazza Bellini, Quattro Canti* ☎ *3384512011* ⏲ *Apr.–Sept., daily 9:30–1:30 and 3–7; Oct.–Mar., daily 9:30–1:30.*

PALERMO'S MULTICULTURAL PEDIGREE

Palermo was first colonized by Phoenician traders in the 6th century BC, but it was their descendants, the Carthaginians, who built the important fortress here that caught the covetous eye of the Romans. After the First Punic War the Romans took control of the city in the 3rd century BC. Following several invasions by the Vandals, Sicily was settled by Arabs, who made the country an emirate and established Palermo as a showpiece capital that rivaled both Córdoba and Cairo in the splendor of its architecture. Nestled in the fertile Conca d'Oro (Golden Conch) plain, full of orange, lemon, and carob groves and enclosed by limestone hills, Palermo became a magical world of palaces and mosques, minarets and palm trees.

It was so attractive and sophisticated a city that the Norman ruler Roger de Hauteville (1031–1101) decided to conquer it and make it his capital (1072). The Norman occupation of Sicily resulted in Palermo's golden age (1072–1194), a remarkable period of enlightenment and learning in which the arts flourished. The city of Palermo, which in the 11th century counted more than 300,000 inhabitants, became the European center for the Norman court and one of the most important ports for trade between East and West. Eventually the Normans were replaced by the Swabian ruler Frederick II (1194–1250), the Holy Roman Emperor, and incorporated into the Kingdom of the Two Sicilies. You'll also see plenty of evidence in Palermo of the baroque art and architecture of the long Spanish rule. The Aragonese viceroys also brought the Spanish Inquisition to Palermo, which some historians believe helped foster the protective secret societies that evolved into today's Mafia.

WHERE TO EAT

¢ SICILIAN ★ ✕ **Antica Focacceria San Francesco.** Turn-of-the-20th-century wooden cabinets, marble-top tables, and cast-iron ovens characterize this neighborhood bakery. Come here for the locally beloved snacks that can be combined to make an inexpensive meal. The big pot on the counter holds the delicious regional specialty *pani ca meusa* (boiled calf's spleen with caciocavallo cheese and salt). The squeamish can opt for some chickpea fritters, an enormous arancino, or the outstanding cannoli. ✉ *Via Paternostro 58, Kalsa* ☎ *091/320264* ⏲ *Closed Tues. Oct.–May and 2 wks mid-Jan.*

$$ SICILIAN ✕ **Casa del Brodo.** On the edge of the Vucciria is a restaurant that dates to 1890, one of Palermo's oldest. In winter, tortellini *in brodo* (in beef broth), the restaurant's namesake, is the specialty of the house. There's an extensive antipasto buffet, and you can't go wrong with the *fritella di fave, piselli, carciofi, e ricotta* (fried fava beans, peas, artichokes, and ricotta). Most days they offer a fixed-price meat menu (€16) and a fish menu (€18). A mix of tourists and locals crowds the two small rooms. ✉ *Corso Vittorio Emanuele 175, Vucciria* ☎ *091/321655* 🌐 *www.casadelbrodo.it* ⏲ *Closed Tues. Nov.–Apr. and Sun. May–Oct.*

$$$ MODERN ITALIAN ✕ **Il Ristorantino.** Pippo Anastasio, one of the true personalities of Sicilian cooking, has created one of the most modern restaurants on the island. Here pesce spada reaches its loftiest heights, served simply marinated

with olive oil, lemon, herb butter, and toast; meanwhile, Pippo's flights of fancy include *astice* (lobster) tortellini with cherry tomatoes, bottarga, and hot pepper, and *mille foglie di melanzane* (puff pastry with eggplant). Dark wood contrasts with recessed lighting and stylized wall panels to create a design fusion that echoes the creativity of the menu. The suburban restaurant is an easy taxi ride from the center. ✉ *Piazzale Papa Giovanni Paolo II, Resuttana* ☎ *091/512861* ⏲ *Closed Mon. and 2 wks in Aug.*

$$$ SICILIAN ★ ✕ **Osteria dei Vespri.** A foodie paradise occupies a cozy-but-elegant space on an unheralded piazza in the historic city center. Try the superb antipasto *cinque variazioni di crudo dal mare* (five variations of raw delicacies from the sea) and the ravioli *pieni di ricotta al forno con aroma di cedro* (ricotta ravioli smoked in cedar). Sheep's-milk cheese ravioli with basil, fresh tomato, eggplant, and crispy onions adds creative depth to traditional preparation. Local fish is the specialty. The wine list is one of the best in Palermo; each day the sommelier and chef collaborate to make a special tasting menu (€75) built around Sicilian wines. ✉ *Piazza Croce dei Vespri 6, Kalsa* ☎ *091/6171631* 🌐 *www.osteriadeivespri.it* ⏲ *Closed Sun.*

¢ SICILIAN ✕ **Pani Ca Meusa.** This supremely local institution facing Palermo's old fishing port has had only one item on the menu—and one legendary manager–cum–sandwich maker—for more than 50 years. Calf's spleen sandwich, the joint's namesake, is sprinkled with a bit of salt and some lemon and served with or without cheese to a buzzing crowd of Palermo's well-weathered elders. In our book, their sandwich beats the Antica Focacceria San Francesco's for the title of best in town. There's no seating, though—only counters—and the overall menu is better at San Francesco. ✉ *Porta Carbone, Via Cala 62, Kalsa* ☎ *No phone* ✍ *Reservations not accepted* ▬ *No credit cards* ⏲ *Closed Sun. and Mon., and unpredictable hrs on other days.*

$$$ SICILIAN Fodor's Choice ★ ✕ **Piccolo Napoli.** Founded in 1951, Piccolo Napoli is one of Old Palermo's most esteemed seafood restaurants. Locals come at midday to feast on the freshest of fish. You can begin with a memorable buffet featuring baby octopus, raw *neonata* (tiny fish resembling sardines but with a milder flavor), and chickpea fritters. Continue with spaghetti with sea urchin or *casarecce* (partially rolled pasta) with swordfish and mint, and finally, the glorious fresh fish or shellfish, roasted or grilled. Depending on the fish you select, the bill can creep up on you, but it's worth every cent. Dinner is served only Friday and Saturday nights between October and June. ✉ *Piazzetta Mulino a Vento 4, Borgo Vecchio* ☎ *091/320431* ⏲ *Closed Sun. and last 2 wks in Aug. No dinner July–Sept. and Mon.–Thurs. Oct.–June.*

¢ PIZZA ✕ **Pizzeria Ai Comparucci.** One of Palermo's best pizzerias doubles as a modern art gallery. The colorful paintings give the place a fun, casual vibe. Better yet are the delicious Neapolitan pizzas coming out of the big oven in the open kitchen. The genius is in the crust, which is seared in the oven in a matter of seconds, and the owners make their money on a quick turnover (so don't expect a long, leisurely meal). But the pizza is delicious, and the place often serves until midnight—later than almost any other restaurant in the neighborhood. ✉ *Via Garzilli 1, Libertà* ☎ *091/6090467* ⏲ *Closed Mon.*

$ SICILIAN ★ ✕ **Trattoria Altri Tempi.** This "olden-days" restaurant is a favorite among locals searching for the rustic dishes served by their ancestors. Knickknacks fill the walls of the small, friendly dining room. A meal begins when the server plunks down a carafe of the house red and a superb spread of traditional antipasti on your table. Dishes have old-fashioned names: *fave a cunigghiu* is fava beans prepared with olive oil, garlic, and remarkably flavorful oregano, and *vampaciucia c'anciova* is a lasagna-like dish with a concentrated sauce of tomatoes, anchovies, and grapes. The meal ends well, too, with free house-made herb or fruit liquors and excellent cannoli. ✉ *Via Sammartino 65/67, Libertà* ☎ *091/323480* ⏲ *Closed mid-Aug.–mid-Sept. and Sun. June–Aug. No dinner Sun.*

$$ SICILIAN ✕ **Trattoria Biondo.** It would be hard to argue that the *lasagne al forno* at this traditional local restaurant, on a convenient block near Politeama, is anything less than the best in Sicily. The baked lasagna is made with perfectly al dente noodles, a wonderfully seasoned ragù, a silky béchamel, and ham for good measure. The other traditional pasta specialties are also excellent, as are fish dishes. None of the dining rooms is bigger than an oversize pantry, making for a cozy atmosphere. ✉ *Via Giosué Carducci 15, Libertà* ☎ *091/583662* ⏲ *Closed Wed. and Aug.*

15

WHERE TO STAY

$$–$$$ **Centrale Palace Hotel.** A stone's throw from Palermo's main historic sites, the Centrale Palace is the only hotel in the heart of the centro storico that was once a stately private palace. Built in 1717, the hotel weaves old-world charm with modern comfort like few establishments on the island. The "classic" rooms have antiques and well-chosen reproductions, while the slightly pricier "neoclassic" rooms are done in a more-modern style. The young, welcoming staff provides professional service. The rooftop restaurant serves creative Sicilian cuisine. **Pros:** sparkling clean; good bathrooms; convenient garage parking. **Cons:** traffic noise; some rooms have no view. **TripAdvisor:** "stately and well maintained," "public areas look very grand," "stuck in a tiny room." ✉ *Corso Vittorio Emanuele 327, Vucciria* ☎ *091/336666* 🌐 *www.centralepalacehotel.it* *88 rooms, 16 suites* *In-room: Internet. In-hotel: restaurant, bar, parking* *Breakfast.*

$$ ★ **Grande Albergo Sole.** Here's an unusual and exciting concept: reopen a faded century-old lodging in the gritty old center as a gleaming, ultramodern hotel. **Pros:** great rooftop bar and restaurant; very central location; multilingual staff. **Cons:** no views from many rooms; stark decor. **TripAdvisor:** "terrace has wonderful views," "room was spacious enough," "receptionist was very abrupt." ✉ *Corso Vittorio Emanuele 291, Kalsa* ☎ *091/6041111* 🌐 *www.angalahotels.it* *113 rooms* *In-hotel: restaurants, bar, parking* *Breakfast.*

$$$–$$$$ **Hilton Villa Igiea.** This grand dame, a local landmark for a century, hasn't changed much since becoming a Hilton. **Pros:** secluded setting; historic building; lots of style. **Cons:** noise and fumes from nearby marina; service is hit or miss. **TripAdvisor:** "looks out over the marina,"

"very nice gardens," "oozes charm." *Salita Belmonte 42, Acquasanta, 3 km (2 mi) north of Palermo 091/6312111 www.hilton.com 110 rooms, 6 suites In-room: Internet. In-hotel: restaurant, room service, tennis court, bar, pool, gym, parking Breakfast.*

$$$ **Hotel Principe di Villafranca.** Fine Sicilian antiques, imperial striped silks, creamy marble floors, and vaulted ceilings evoke a luxurious private home in the heart of Palermo's glitzy shopping district. **Pros:** helpful staff; well-maintained building; safe neighborhood. **Cons:** breakable knickknacks make it unsuitable for small children; bathrooms are on the small side. **TripAdvisor:** "elegant and comfortable," "breakfast was very good," "good value." *Via G. Turrisi Colonna 4, Libertà 091/6118523 www.principedivillafranca.it 29 rooms, 3 junior suites In-room: Wi-Fi. In-hotel: restaurant, bar, gym, parking Breakfast.*

$ **Le Terrazze.** Though just steps from the bustling streets around the Cattedrale, complete calm envelops this small, beautifully restored B&B. **Pros:** convenient location; glorious views from terraces. **Cons:** parking can be difficult; books up quickly. *Via Pietro Novelli 14, Capo 091/6520866 or 320/4328567 www.leterrazzebb.it 2 rooms No credit cards Closed Nov. and Feb. Breakfast.*

$$–$$$ **Massimo Plaza Hotel.** This hotel has one of Palermo's best locations—opposite the renovated Teatro Massimo, on the border of the old and new towns. **Pros:** central location; modern bathrooms. **Cons:** plain decor; some noisy rooms; breakfast choices are limited. **TripAdvisor:** "location is great," "service is friendly," "overpriced." *Via Maqueda 437, Vucciria 091/325657 www.massimoplazahotel.com 15 rooms In-room: Wi-Fi. In-hotel: bar, parking Breakfast.*

NIGHTLIFE AND THE ARTS

THE ARTS

CONCERTS AND OPERA

Teatro Massimo (*Piazza Verdi at top of Via Maqueda, Capo 091/6053111 www.teatromassimo.it*), modeled after the Pantheon in Rome, is truly larger than life—it's the biggest theater in Italy. Concerts and operas are presented throughout the year, though in summer concerts are usually held outdoors. An opera at the Massimo is an unforgettable Sicilian experience. The box office is open Tuesday to Sunday 10 to 3. Ticket prices vary but generally start around €10. The shamelessly grandiose neoclassical **Teatro Politeama Garibaldi** (*Piazza Ruggero Settimo, Libertà 091/588001*) stages a season of opera and orchestral works from November through May.

PUPPET SHOWS

Palermo's tradition of puppet theater holds an appeal for children and adults alike. Street artists often perform outside the Teatro Massimo in summer. The **Figli d'Arte Cuticchio Association** (*Via Bara all'Olivella 95, Kalsa 091/323400 www.figlidartecuticchio.com €8*) hosts performances September to July on most weekends at 6:30 pm.

NIGHTLIFE

Each night between 6 and 9, Palermo's youth gather to shop, socialize, flirt, and plan the evening's affairs in an epic passeggiata along Via Ruggero Settimo (a northern extension of Via Maqueda) and filling Piazza Ruggero Settimo in front of Teatro Politeama. Some trendy bars also line Via Principe del Belmonte, intersecting with Via Roma and Via Ruggero Settimo.

BARS AND CAFÉS

Kursaal Kalhesa (✉ *Foro Umberto I 21, Kalsa* ☎ *091/6162111* 🌐 *www.kursaalkalhesa.it*) is one of the most fascinating places to drink or socialize down by the port and the Porta Felice. An energetic, eclectic crowd of Palermitan youth takes in lively jazz, coffee, and drinks inside an ancient city wall with spectacular 100-foot ceilings and an idyllic courtyard—it's truly representative of the New Palermo. Interesting, if pricey, Sicilian food with an Arab touch is served in the adjacent restaurant. Kursaal Kalhesa is closed Monday.

Parco Letterario Giuseppe Tomasi di Lampedusa (✉ *Vicolo della Neve all'Alloro 2/5, near Piazza Marina, Kalsa* ☎ *389/9941599* 🌐 *www.parcotomasi.it*) is a bar, café, language school, and tour operator. The center sponsors concerts, readings, and art shows. The little library (and just about everything else) focuses not just on Palermitan history but on the life and times of the center's namesake, Lampedusa, author of the canonical *Il Gattopardo* (*The Leopard*).

Santa Monica (✉ *Via E. Parisi 7, Libertà* ☎ *091/324735*) is a pub that's immensely popular with the twenty- and thirtysomething crowd, who belly up to the bar for pizza, bruschetta, and, of course, excellent German-style draft beer. It's also a good place to watch soccer.

Tinto (✉ *Via XX Settembre 56/A, at Via Messina, Libertà* ☎ *091/582137* 🌐 *www.tinto.it*) is a sleek establishment serving double duty as a Sicily-centric wine bar and restaurant. The room achieves a sense of effortless grace, with dark furniture and greenery. Come around aperitivo time and you'll be treated to free snacks. It's closed at lunchtime on Sunday.

SHOPPING

North of Piazza Castelnuovo, Via della Libertà and the surrounding streets represent the luxury end of the shopping scale. A second nerve center for shoppers is the pair of parallel streets connecting modern Palermo with the train station, Via Roma, and Via Maqueda, where boutiques and shoe shops become increasingly upmarket as you move from the Quattro Canti past Teatro Massimo to Via Ruggero Settimo.

Most shops are open 9–1 and 4 or 4:30–7:30 or 8 and closed Sunday and on Monday morning; in addition, most food shops close Wednesday afternoon.

FOOD AND WINE

Enoteca Picone (✉ *Via Marconi 36, Libertà* ☎ *091/331300* ✉ *Viale Strasburgo 235, Resuttana* ☎ *091/6880357* 🌐 *www.enotecapicone.it*) is the best wine shop in town, with a fantastic selection of Sicilian and national wines. Though the service can be curt, you can taste a selection of wines by the glass in the front of the store. There are tables in the back, where meats and cheeses are also served. The branch on Viale

Strasburgo offers full meals. Both branches are closed Sunday. With a name that means "Mamma Andrea's small sins," the charming **I Peccatucci di Mamma Andrea** (✉ *Via Principe di Scordia 67, near Piazza Florio, Vucciria* ☎ *091/334835* 🌐 *www.mammaandrea.it*) sells a plethora of mouthwatering original creations, including jams, preserves, and Sicilian treats like the superb marzipan *frutta di Martorana.*

Pasticceria Alba (✉ *Piazza Don Bosco 7/C, off Via della Libertà near La Favorita Park, Libertà* ☎ *091/309016* 🌐 *www.pasticeriaalba.it*), one of the most famous sweets shops in Italy, is the place to find favorite pastries such as cannoli and cassata siciliana.

MARKETS

If you're interested in truly connecting with local life while searching for souvenirs, a visit to one of Palermo's many bustling markets is essential. Between Via Roma and Via Maqueda, the many **bancherelle** *(market stalls)* on Via Bandiera sell everything from socks to imitation designer handbags.

★ It's easy to see how the **Vucciria Market** got its name (*vucciria* translates to "voices" or "hubbub"): Palermo's most established outdoor market in the heart of the centro storico is a maze of side streets around Piazza San Domenico, where hawkers deliver incessant chants from behind stands brimming with mounds of olives, blood oranges, wild fennel, and long-stem artichokes. One hawker will be going at the trunk of a swordfish with a cleaver while across the way another holds up a giant squid or dangles an octopus. Morning is the best time to see the market in full swing.

Wind your way through the Albergheria district and the historic **Ballarò Market**, where the Saracens did their shopping in the 11th century—joined by the Normans in the 12th. The market remains faithful to seasonal change as well as the original Arab commerce of fruit, vegetables, and grain. Go early; the action dies out by 4 pm most days.

THE TYRRHENIAN COAST

Sicily's northern shore, the Tyrrhenian Coast, is mostly a succession of small holiday towns interspersed with stretches of sand. It's often difficult to find a calm spot among the thousands of tourists and locals in high summer, though the scene quiets down considerably after August. The biggest attraction is the old town of Cefalù, with one of Sicily's most remarkable medieval cathedrals, encrusted with mosaics. The coast on either side is dotted with ancient archaeological remains and Arab-Norman buildings.

A couple of miles south of Cefalù, Pizzo Carbonara (6,500 feet) is the highest peak in Sicily after Mount Etna. Piano della Battaglia has a fully equipped ski resort with lifts. The area has a very un-Sicilian aspect, with Swiss-type chalets, hiking paths, and even Alpine churches.

CEFALÙ

★ *70 km (43 mi) east of Palermo, 161 km (100 mi) west of Messina.*

GETTING HERE

Trains and buses run between Palermo and Messina. Drivers can take the A20 autostrada.

VISITOR INFORMATION

Cefalù tourism office (✉ *Corso Ruggero 77* ☎ *0921/421050*).

EXPLORING

The coast between Palermo and Messina is spotted with charming villages. Tindari (which dates back to the early Christian era) and Laghetti di Maranello are two that are worth a stop, but it's Cefalù, a classically appealing Sicilian old town built on a spur jutting out into the sea, that's the jewel of the coast.

Cefalù is dominated by a massive rock—*la rocca*—and a 12th-century Romanesque **Duomo**, one of the finest Norman cathedrals in Italy. Ruggero II began the church in 1131 as an offering of thanks for having been saved here from a shipwreck. Its mosaics rival those of Monreale; whereas Monreale's Byzantine Christ figure is an austere and powerful image, emphasizing Christ's divinity, the Cefalù Christ is softer, more compassionate, and more human. The traffic going in and out of Cefalù town can be heavy in summer; you may want to take the 50-minute train ride from Palermo instead of driving. At the Duomo you must be suitably attired—no shorts or beachwear are permitted. ✉ *Piazza Duomo* ☎ *0921/922021* ⏲ *Oct.–Apr., daily 8–noon and 3:30–5; May–Sept., daily 8–7:30.*

15

WHERE TO EAT

$$–$$$ SICILIAN ✕ **Al Porticciolo.** Nicola Mendolia's restaurant is comfortable, casual, and faithfully focused on food. You might start with the *calamaretti piccoli fritti* (fried baby squid and octopus) and then follow with one of the chef's specials, which change weekly. Regardless, a refreshing *sgroppino* (whipped lemon sorbet with spumante) should end the meal. Dark, heavy, wooden tables create a comfortable environment filled with a mix of jovial locals and businesspeople. ✉ *Via C. Ortolani di Bordonaro 66* ☎ *0921/921981* ⏲ *Closed Feb. and Wed. Nov.–Apr.*

THE AEOLIAN ISLANDS

Off Sicily's northeast coast lies an archipelago of seven spectacular islands of volcanic origin. The Isole Eolie (Aeolian Islands), also known as the Isole Lipari (Lipari Islands), were named after Aeolus, the Greek god of the winds, who is said to keep all the Earth's winds stuffed in a bag in his cave here.

The Aeolians are a world of grottoes and clear-water caves carved by waves through the centuries. Superb snorkeling and scuba diving abound in the clearest and cleanest of Italy's waters. The beautiful people of high society discovered the archipelago years ago—here Roberto Rossellini courted his future wife, Ingrid Bergman, in 1950. So you shouldn't expect complete isolation, at least on the main islands.

August, in particular, can get unpleasantly overcrowded, and lodging and travel should always be booked as early as possible.

Lipari provides the widest range of accommodations and is a good jumping-off point for day trips to the other islands. Most exclusive are Vulcano and Panarea, the former noted for its black sands and stupendous sunsets, as well as the acrid smell of its sulfur emissions, whereas the latter is, according to some, the prettiest. Most remarkable is Stromboli (pronounced with the accent on the first syllable) with its constant eruptions, and remotest are Filicudi and Alicudi, where electricity was introduced only in the 1980s.

Access to the islands is via ferry and hydrofoil from Milazzo (on Sicily) or from Naples. The bars in the Aeolian Islands, and especially those on Lipari, are known for their granitas of fresh strawberries, melon, peaches, and other fruits. Many Sicilians on the Aeolians (and in Messina, Taormina, and Catania) begin the hot summer days with a granita *di caffè* (a coffee ice topped with whipped cream), into which they dunk their breakfast rolls. You can get one any time of day. The other islands are Salina, known as the greenest island, and Alicudi, the most distant and least developed.

LIPARI

2 hrs and 10 mins from Milazzo by ferry, 1 hr by hydrofoil; 60–75 mins from Reggio di Calabria and Messina by ferry.

GETTING HERE

Ferries and hydrofoils from Milazzo, which is 41 km (25 mi) west of Messina, stop here. There's also ferry service from Reggio di Calabria and Messina.

VISITOR INFORMATION

Lipari tourism office (✉ *Corso Vittorio Emanuele 202* ☎ *090/9880095* 🌐 *www.aasteolie.191.it*).

EXPLORING

The largest and most developed of the Aeolians, Lipari welcomes you with distinctive pastel-color houses. Fields of spiky agaves dot the northernmost tip of the island, Acquacalda, indented with pumice and obsidian quarries. In the west is San Calogero, where you can explore hot springs and mud baths. From the red-lava base of the island rises a plateau crowned with a 16th-century castle and a 17th-century cathedral.

★ The vast, multibuilding **Museo Archeologico Eoliano** is a terrific museum, with an intelligently arranged collection of prehistoric finds—some dating as far back as 4000 BC—from various sites in the archipelago. ✉ *Via Castello 2* ☎ *090/9880174* 🎟 *€6* ⏲ *Daily. 9–1 and 3–7; last entry 1 hr before closing.*

WHERE TO EAT AND STAY

$$–$$$ SICILIAN ★ ✕ **Filippino.** The views from the flower-strewn outdoor terrace of this restaurant in the upper town are a fitting complement to the superb fare. Founded in 1910, the restaurant is rightly rated one of the archipelago's best. Top choice is seafood: the *zuppa di pesce* (fish soup) and

the antipasto platter of smoked and marinated fish are absolute musts. Leave some room for the local version of cassata siciliana, accompanied by sweet Malvasia wine from Salina. ✉ *Piazza Mazzini Lipari* ☎ *090/9811002* 🌐 *www.bernardigroup.it* ⏲ *Closed mid-Nov.–late Dec. and Mon. Oct.–Mar.*

$$$ **Gattopardo Park Hotel.** Bright bougainvillea and fiery hibiscus set the tone at this grand villa, and its restaurant has sweeping views of the sea. **Pros:** friendly staff; good recreational facilities; large pool. **Cons:** a bit removed from the port; staff doesn't speak English. **TripAdvisor:** "flowers everywhere," "absolutely gorgeous," "huge pool." ✉ *Viale Diana* ☎ *090/9811035* 🌐 *www.gattopardoparkhotel.it* *47 rooms* *In-hotel: restaurant, bar, pool* ⏲ *Closed Nov.–Mar.* *Some meals.*

VULCANO

25 mins from Lipari by ferry, 10 mins by hydrofoil; 90 mins from Milazzo by ferry.

15

GETTING HERE

Frequent ferries and hydrofoils arrive here from Milazzo (41 km [25 mi] west of Messina), and Lipari *(⇨ above)*.

EXPLORING

True to its name—and the origin of the term—Vulcano has a profusion of fumaroles sending up jets of hot vapor, but the volcano here has long been dormant. Many come to soak in the strong-smelling sulfur springs: when the wind is right, the odors greet you long before you disembark. The island has some of the archipelago's best beaches, though the volcanic black sand can be off-putting at first. You can ascend to the crater (1,266 feet above sea level) on muleback for a wonderful view or take boat rides into the grottoes around the base. From Capo Grillo there's a view of all the Aeolians.

WHERE TO STAY

$$–$$$ ★ **Les Sables Noirs.** Named for the black sands of the beach in front, this luxury hotel is superbly sited on the beautiful Porto di Ponente. **Pros:** stunning beachfront location; nice restaurant. **Cons:** not as clean as it should be; pesky mosquitoes. **TripAdvisor:** "it all looks amazing," "staff were very courteous," "a few imperfections." ✉ *Porto di Ponente* ☎ *090/9850* 🌐 *www.framonhotels.com* *45 rooms, 3 suites* *In-hotel: restaurant, bar, pool, beach* ⏲ *Closed mid-Oct.–Apr.* *Breakfast.*

PANAREA

2 hrs from Lipari by ferry, 25–50 mins by hydrofoil; 7–9 hrs from Naples by ferry.

GETTING HERE

Ferries and hydrofoils arrive here from Lipari and Naples.

EXPLORING

Panarea has some of the most dramatic scenery of the islands: wild caves carved out of the rock and dazzling flora. The exceptionally clear water and the richness of life on the sea floor make Panarea especially suitable for underwater exploration, though there's little in the way of beaches. The outlying rocks and islets make a gorgeous sight, and you can enjoy the panorama on an easy excursion to the small Bronze Age village at Capo Milazzese.

WHERE TO STAY

$$$$ **Il Raya.** This discreet, expensive hotel is perfectly in keeping with the elite style of Panarea, most exclusive of the Aeolian Islands. **Pros:** great views of Stromboli; fashionable ambience; well-known dance club on the premises. **Cons:** snooty staff; uphill trudge to rooms; mediocre food; dance club means noise after dark. **TripAdvisor:** "we think it's magical," "beautiful, unique rooms," "rate was incredibly high." *San Pietro 090/983013 www.hotelraya.it 36 rooms In-hotel: bar, pool Closed mid-Oct.–mid-Apr. Breakfast.*

STROMBOLI

3 hrs and 45 mins from Lipari by ferry, 65–90 mins by hydrofoil; 9 hrs from Naples by ferry.

GETTING HERE

Ferries and hydrofoils arrive here from Lipari and Naples.

EXPLORING

This northernmost of the Aeolians consists entirely of the cone of an active volcano. The view from the sea—especially at night, as an endless stream of glowing red-hot lava flows into the water—is unforgettable. Stromboli is in a constant state of mild dissatisfaction, and every now and then its anger flares up, so authorities insist that you climb to the top (about 3,031 feet above sea level) only with a guide. The round-trip—climb, pause, and descent—usually starting around 6 pm, takes about six hours; the lava is much more impressive after dark. Some choose to camp overnight atop the volcano—again, a guide is essential. The main town has a small selection of reasonably priced hotels and restaurants and a choice of lively clubs and cafés for the younger set. In addition to the island tour, excursions might include boat trips around the naturally battlemented isle of Strombolicchio.

Numerous tour operators have guides that can lead you up Stromboli, among them **Pippo Navigazione** (*090/986135 or 338/9857883*). Rates are around €20 per person for three hours. A €15 night tour explores where the lava reaches the sea.

FILICUDI

30–60 mins from Salina and Lipari by hydrofoil; 2 hrs from Cefalù and Palermo, 2 hrs from Milazzo, and 4½–6½ hrs from Naples by ferry.

GETTING HERE

Ferries and hydrofoils arrive throughout the year from Salina and Lipari, and also in summer from Palermo, Cefalù, Milazzo, and Naples.

EXPLORING

Just a dot in the sea, Filicudi is famous for its unusual volcanic rock formations and the enchanting Grotta del Bue Marino (Grotto of the Sea Ox). The crumbled remains of a prehistoric village are at Capo Graziano. The island, which is spectacular for walking and hiking and is still a truly undiscovered, restful haven, has a handful of hotels and pensions, and some families put up guests. Car ferries are available only in summer.

WORD OF MOUTH

"Stromboli is just the most fabulous place. No cars (just electric golf buggies) and utter beauty. I used to take my shoes off the day I arrived and not put them back on until I got back on the ferry. It's all so laid back."

—sardiniasarena

WHERE TO STAY

$$ ★ **La Canna.** Set above the tiny port, this hotel commands fabulous views of sky and sea from its flower-filled terrace. **Pros:** relaxed setting; family-friendly atmosphere; great views. **Cons:** an uphill climb from the port. **TripAdvisor:** "great views across to Salina," "terrace overlooking the sea," "comfortable room." ✉ *Via Rosa 43* ☎ *090/9889956* 🌐 *www.lacannahotel.it* *14 rooms* *In-hotel: restaurant, bar, pool* *Some meals.*

15

ITALIAN VOCABULARY

BASICS

ENGLISH	ITALIAN	PRONOUNCIATION
Yes/no	Sí/no	see/no
Please	Per favore	pear fa-**vo**-ray
Yes, please	Sí grazie	see **grah**-tsee-ay
Thank you	Grazie	**grah**-tsee-ay
You're welcome	Prego	**pray**-go
Excuse me, sorry	Scusi	**skoo**-zee
Sorry!	Mi dispiace!	mee dis-spee-**ah**-chay
Good morning/ afternoon	Buongiorno	bwohn-**jor**-no
Good evening	Buona sera	**bwoh**-na **say**-ra
Good-bye	Arrivederci	a-ree-vah-**dare**-chee
Mr. (Sir)	Signore	see-**nyo**-ray
Mrs. (Ma'am)	Signora	see-**nyo**-ra
Miss	Signorina	see-nyo-**ree**-na
Pleased to meet you	Piacere	pee-ah-**chair**-ray
How are you?	Come sta?	**ko**-may **stah**
Very well, thanks	Bene, grazie	**ben**-ay **grah**-tsee-ay
Hello (phone)	Pronto?	**proan**-to

NUMBERS

ENGLISH	ITALIAN	PRONOUNCIATION
one	uno	**oo**-no
two	due	**doo**-ay
three	tre	tray
four	quattro	**kwah**-tro
five	cinque	**cheen**-kway
six	sei	say
seven	sette	**set**-ay
eight	otto	**oh**-to
nine	nove	**no**-vay
ten	dieci	dee-**eh**-chee
eleven	undici	**oon**-dee-chee
twelve	dodici	**doe**-dee-cee

thirteen	tredici	**tray**-dee-chee
fourteen	quattordici	kwa-**tore**-dee-chee
fifteen	quindici	**kwin**-dee-chee
sixteen	sedici	**say**-dee-chee
seventeen	diciassete	dee-cha-**set**-ay
eighteen	diciotto	dee-**cho**-to
nineteen	diciannove	dee-cha-**no**-vay
twenty	venti	**vain**-tee
twenty-one	ventuno	vain-**too**-no
twenty-two	ventidue	vain-tee-**doo**-ay
thirty	trenta	**train**-ta
forty	quaranta	kwa-**rahn**-ta
fifty	cinquanta	cheen-**kwahn**-ta
sixty	sessanta	seh-**sahn**-ta
seventy	settanta	seh-**tahn**-ta
eighty	ottanta	o-**tahn**-ta
ninety	novanta	no-**vahn**-ta
one hundred	cento	**chen**-to
one thousand	mille	**mee**-lay
ten thousand	diecimila	dee-eh-chee-**mee**-la

USEFUL PHRASES

Do you speak English?	Parla inglese?	**par**-la een-**glay**-zay
I don't speak Italian	Non parlo italiano	non **par**-lo ee-tal-**yah**-no
I don't understand	Non capisco	non ka-**peess**-ko
Can you please repeat?	Può ripetere?	pwo ree-**pet**-ay-ray
Slowly!	Lentamente!	**len**-ta-men-tay
I don't know	Non lo so	non lo **so**
I'm American	Sono americano(a)	**so**-no a-may-ree-**kah**-no(a)
I'm British	Sono inglese	so-no een-**glay**-zay
What's your name?	Come si chiama?	**ko**-may see kee-**ah**-ma

My name is . . .	Mi chiamo . . .	mee kee-**ah**-mo
What time is it?	Che ore sono?	kay **o**-ray **so**-no
How?	Come?	**ko**-may
When?	Quando?	**kwan**-doe
Yesterday/ today/tomorrow	Ieri/oggi/domani	**yer**-ee/**o**-jee/do-**mah**-nee
This morning	Stamattina	sta-ma-**tee**-na
This afternoon	Oggi pomeriggio	**o**-jee po-mer-**ee**-jo
Tonight	Stasera	sta-**ser**-a
What?	Che cosa?	kay **ko**-za
What is it?	Chee cos'é?	kay ko-**zay**
Why?	Perché?	pear-**kay**
Who?	Chi?	kee
Where is . . . the bus stop? the train station? the subway the terminal? the post office? the bank? the . . . hotel? the store? the cashier? the . . . museum? the hospital? the first-aid station? the elevator? a telephone? the restrooms?	Dov'è . . . la fermata dell'autobus? la stazione? la metropolitana? il terminale? l'ufficio postale? la banca? l'hotel . . .? il negozio? la cassa? il museo . . .? l'ospedale? il pronto soccorso? l'ascensore? un telefono? il bagno?	doe-**veh** la fer-**mah**-tadel ow-toe-**booss** la sta-tsee-**oh**-nay la may-tro-po-lee-**tah**-na eel ter-mee-**nah**-lay loo-**fee**-cho po-**stah**-lay la **bahn**-ka lo-**tel** eel nay-**go**-tsee-o la **kah**-sa eel moo-**zay**-o lo-spay-**dah**-lay Eel **pron**-to so-**kor**-so la-shen-**so**-ray oon tay-**lay**-fo-no eel **bahn**-yo
Here/there	Qui/là	kwee/la
Left/right	A sinistra/a destra	a see-**neess**-tra/a **des**-tra
Straight ahead	Avanti dritto	a-**vahn**-tee **dree**-to
Is it near/far?	È vicino/lontano?	ay vee-**chee**-no/ lon-**tah**-no
I'd like . . . a room the key a newspaper a stamp	Vorrei . . . una camera la chiave un giornale un francobollo	vo-**ray** **oo**-na **kah**-may-ra la kee-**ah**-vay oon jor-**nah**-lay oon frahn-ko-**bo**-lo

I'd like to buy . . .	Vorrei comprare . . .	vo-**ray** kom-**prah**-ray
How much is it?	Quanto costa?	**kwahn**-toe **coast**-a
It's expensive/cheap	È caro/economico	ay **car**-o/ay-ko-**no**-mee-ko
A little/a lot	Poco/tanto	**po**-ko/**tahn**-to
More/less	Più/meno	pee-**oo**/**may**-no
Enough/too (much)	Abbastanza/troppo	a-bas-**tahn**-sa/**tro**-po
I am sick	Sto male	sto **mah**-lay
Call a doctor	Chiama un dottore	kee-**ah**-mah oon doe-**toe**-ray
Help!	Aiuto!	a-**yoo**-toe
Stop!	Alt!	ahlt
Fire!	Al fuoco!	ahl **fwo**-ko
Caution/Look out!	Attenzione!	a-ten-**syon**-ay

DINING OUT

A bottle of . . .	Una bottiglia di . . .	**oo**-na bo-**tee**-lee-ahdee
A cup of . . .	Una tazza di . . .	**oo**-na **tah**-tsa dee
A glass of . . .	Un bicchiere di . . .	oon bee-key-**air**-ay dee
Bill/check	Il conto	eel **cone**-toe
Bread	Il pane	eel **pah**-nay
Breakfast ko-la-**tsee**-oh-nay	La prima colazione	la **pree**-ma
Cocktail/aperitif	L'aperitivo	la-pay-ree-**tee**-vo
Dinner	La cena	la **chen**-a
Fixed-price menu	Menù a prezzo fisso	may-**noo** a **pret**-so **fee**-so
Fork	La forchetta	la for-**ket**-a
I am diabetic	Ho il diabete	o eel dee-a-**bay**-tay
I am vegetarian	Sono vegetariano/a	**so**-no vay-jay-ta-ree -**ah**-no/a
I'd like . . .	Vorrei . . .	vo-**ray**
I'd like to order	Vorrei ordinare	vo-**ray** or-dee-**nah**-ray
Is service included?	Il servizio è incluso?	eel ser-**vee**-tzee-o ay een-**kloo**-zo
It's good/bad	È buono/cattivo	ay **bwo**-no/ka-**tee**-vo

It's hot/cold	È caldo/freddo	ay **kahl**-doe/**fred**-o
Knife	Il coltello	eel kol-**tel**-o
Lunch	Il pranzo	eel **prahnt**-so
Menu	Il menù	eel may-**noo**
Napkin	Il tovagliolo	eel toe-va-lee-**oh**-lo
Please give me . . .	Mi dia . . .	mee **dee**-a
Salt	Il sale	eel **sah**-lay
Spoon	Il cucchiaio	eel koo-kee-**ah**-yo
Sugar	Lo zucchero	lo **tsoo**-ker-o
Waiter/waitress	Cameriere/cameriera	ka-mare-**yer**-ay/ ka-mare-**yer**-a
Wine list	La lista dei vini	la **lee**-sta **day**-ee **vee**-nee

Travel Smart Italy

WORD OF MOUTH

"Note to Rental-Car Newbies: The rental agency will never ask for the International Driver's License that they tell you is required to rent. They don't care about it. The IDL is for the cops in case you get into an accident, so don't think that you wasted $15 and precious time going to AAA to get it, just be thankful that no one ever had to ask you for it."

—marigross

www.fodors.com/community

GETTING HERE AND AROUND

AIR TRAVEL

Air travel to Italy is frequent and virtually problem-free, except for airport- or airline-related union strikes that may cause delays. Although most nonstop flights are to Rome and Milan, many travelers find it more convenient to connect through a European hub to Florence, Pisa, Venice, Bologna, or another smaller airport. The airport in Venice also caters to international carriers with direct flights.

Flying time to Milan or Rome is approximately 8–8½ hours from New York, 10–11 hours from Chicago, and 11½ hours from Los Angeles.

Labor strikes are frequent and can affect not only air travel, but also local transit that serves airports (private transit isn't affected by strikes, however). Confirm flights within Italy the day before travel. Your airline will have information about strikes directly affecting its flight schedule. If you're taking a train to the airport, check with the local tourist agency or rail station about upcoming strikes. Be aware that it's not unusual for strikes to be canceled at the last minute.

Airline Security Issues Transportation Security Administration (*www.tsa.gov*) has answers for almost every question that might come up.

Contact A helpful Web site for information (location, phone numbers, local transportation, etc.) about all of the airports in Italy is *www.travel-library.com*.

AIRPORTS

The major gateways to Italy include Rome's Aeroporto Leonardo da Vinci (FCO), better known as Fiumicino, and Milan's Aeroporto Malpensa (MPX). Most flights to Venice, Florence, and Pisa make connections at Fiumicino and Malpensa or another European airport hub. You can take the FS airport train to Rome's Termini station, or an express motorcoach to Milan's central train station (Centrale) and catch a train to any other location in Italy. It'll take about 30 minutes to get from Fiumicino to Roma Termini, about an hour to Milano Centrale.

Many carriers fly into the smaller airports. Venice is served by Aeroporto Marco Polo (VCE), Naples by Aeroporto Capodichino (NAP), and Palermo by Aeroporto Punta Raisi (PMO). Florence is serviced by Aeroporto A. Vespucci (FLR), which is also called Peretola, and by Aeroporto Galileo Galilei (PSA), which is about 2 km (1 mi) outside the center of Pisa and about one hour from Florence. The train to Florence stops within 100 feet of the entrance to the Pisa airport terminal. Bologna's airport (BLQ) is a 20-minute direct Aerobus-ride away from Bologna Centrale, which is less than 30 minutes from Florence by high-speed train.

Italy's major airports aren't generally known for being new, fun, or efficient—though the Venice airport is in fact new, and Peretola, Fiumicino, and Malpensa have undergone renovations in recent years. They have been ramping up security measures, which include random baggage inspection and bomb-detection dogs. All airports have restaurants and snack bars and Wi-Fi Internet access. Each airport has at least one nearby hotel. In the case of Florence, Pisa, and Bologna, the city centers are less than a 15-minute taxi or bus ride away—so if you encounter a long delay, spend it in town.

When you take a connecting flight from an European airline hub (Frankfurt or Paris, for example) to a local Italian airport (Florence or Venice), be aware that your luggage might not make it onto the second plane with you. The airlines' lost-luggage service is efficient, however, and your delayed luggage is usually delivered to your hotel or holiday rental within 12 to 24 hours.

Airport Information Aeroporto A. Vespucci (*FLR, also called Peretola ✈ 6 km [4 mi] northwest of Florence ☎ 055/3061300 🌐 www.aeroporto.firenze.it*). **Aeroporto di Bologna** (*BLQ also called Guglielmo Marconi ✈ 6 km [4 mi] northwest of Bologna ☎ 051/6479615 🌐 www.bologna-airport.it*). **Aeroporto di Venezia** (*VCE, also called Marco Polo ✈ 6 km [4 mi] north of Venice ☎ 041/2609260 🌐 www.veniceairport.com*). **Aeroporto Galileo Galilei** (*PSA ✈ 2 km [1 mi] south of Pisa, 80 km [50 mi] west of Florence ☎ 050/849300 🌐 www.pisa-airport.com*). **Aeroporto Leonardo da Vinci** (*FCO, also called Fiumicino ✈ 35 km [20 mi] southwest of Rome ☎ 06/65951 🌐 www.adr.it*). **Aeroporto Malpensa** (*MPX ✈ 45 km [28 mi] north of Milan ☎ 02/74852200 🌐 www.sea-aeroportimilano.it*). **Naples International Airport** (*NAP, also called Capodichino ✈ 7 km [4 mi] northeast of Naples ☎ 081/7896111 🌐 www.naples-airport.com*). **Palermo International Airport** (*PMO, also called Punta Raisi ✈ 32 km [19 mi] northwest of Palermo ☎ 091/7020272 🌐 www.gesap.it*).

FLIGHTS

On flights from the United States, Alitalia and Delta Air Lines serve Rome, Milan, Pisa, and Venice. The major international hubs in Italy, Milan, and Rome are also served by Continental Airlines and American Airlines, and US Airways serves Rome. From April through October, the Italy-based Meridiana EuroFly has nonstop flights from New York to Naples and Palermo.

Alitalia and British Airways have direct flights from London to Milan, Venice, Rome, and 10 other locations in Italy. Smaller, no-frills airlines also provide service between Great Britain and Italy. EasyJet connects Gatwick with Milan, Venice, Rome, and Bologna. British Midland connects Heathrow and Milan (Linate), Naples, and Venice. Ryanair, departing from London's Stansted airport, flies to Milan, Rome, Pisa, and Venice. Meridiana has flights between Gatwick and Olbia on Sardinia in summer, and flights to Rome and Florence throughout the year.

Tickets for flights within Italy, on Alitalia and small carriers, such as EuroFly, Meridiana, and Air One, cost less when purchased from agents within Italy. Tickets are frequently sold at discounted prices, so check the cost of flights, even one-way, as an alternative to train travel.

Airline Contacts Alitalia (*☎ 800/223-5730 in U.S., 06/2222 in Rome, 800/650055 elsewhere in Italy 🌐 www.alitalia.it*). **American Airlines** (*☎ 800/433-7300, 02/69682464 in Milan 🌐 www.aa.com*). **British Airways** (*☎ 800/247-9297 in U.S., 119/712266 in Italy 🌐 www.britishairways.com*). **British Midland** (*☎ 0807/6070-555 for U.K. reservations, 1332/64-8181 callers outside U.K. 🌐 www.flybmi.com*). **Continental Airlines** (*☎ 800/523-3273 for U.S. reservations, 800/231-0856 for international reservations, 02/69633256 in Milan, 800/555580000 elsewhere in Italy 🌐 www.continental.com*). **Delta Air Lines** (*☎ 800/221-1212 for U.S. reservations, 800/241-4141 for international reservations, 848/780376 in Italy 🌐 www.delta.com*). **EasyJet** (*☎ 0905/821-0905 in U.K., 899/234589 in Italy 🌐 www.easyjet.com*). **Northwest Airlines** (*☎ 800/225-2525 🌐 www.nwa.com*). **Ryanair** (*☎ 08701/24-60000 in U.K., 899/678910 in Italy 🌐 www.ryanair.com*). **United Airlines** (*☎ 800/864-8331 for U.S. reservations, 800/538-2929 for international reservations 🌐 www.united.com*). **US Airways** (*☎ 800/428-4322 for U.S. reservations, 800/622-1015 for international reservations, 848/8813177 in Italy 🌐 www.usairways.com*).

Domestic Carriers Air One (*☎ 06/48880069 in Rome, 800/650055 elsewhere in Italy 🌐 www.flyairone.it*). **Meridiana EuroFly** (*☎ 866/387-6359 in U.S., 892928 in Italy. 🌐 www.euroflyusa.com*).

BUS TRAVEL

Italy's regional bus network, often operated by private companies with motorcoach fleets, is extensive, although not as attractive an option as in other European countries, partly due to convenient train travel. Schedules are often drawn up with commuters and students in mind and may be sketchy on weekends. Regional bus companies often provide the only means (not including car travel) of getting to out-of-the-way places. Even when this isn't the case, buses can be faster and more direct than local trains, so it's a good idea to compare bus and train schedules; check at local tourist offices. SITA operates throughout Italy; Lazzi Eurolines operates in Tuscany and central Italy. Dolomiti Bus serves the Dolomites.

All major cities in Italy have urban bus service. It's inexpensive, and tickets may be purchased in blocks or as passes. Buses can become jammed during busy travel periods and rush hours.

Smoking isn't permitted, and both public and private buses offer only one class of service. Cleanliness and comfort levels are high on private motorcoaches, which have plenty of legroom, comfortable seats, and luggage storage, but no toilets. Private bus lines usually have a ticket office in town or allow you to pay when you board. When traveling on city buses, you must buy your ticket from a machine, newsstand, or tobacco shop and stamp it on board (although some city buses have ticket machines on board).

Bus Information ATAC (✉ *Rome* ☎ *800/431784 or 06/46952027* 🌐 *www.atac.roma.it*). **ATAF** (✉ *Stazione Centrale di Santa Maria Novella, Florence* ☎ *800/424500* 🌐 *www.ataf.net*). **Dolomiti Bus** (✉ *Via Col da Ren 14, Belluno* ☎ *0437/217111* 🌐 *www.dolomitibus.it*). **Lazzi Eurolines** (✉ *Via Mercadante 2, Florence* ☎ *055/363041* 🌐 *www.lazzi.it*). **SITA** (✉ *Via Santa Caterina da Siena 17/r, Florence* ☎ *055/47821* 🌐 *www.sitabus.it*).

CAR TRAVEL

Italy has an extensive network of autostrade (toll highways), complemented by equally well maintained but free *superstrade* (expressways). Save the ticket you're issued at an autostrada entrance, as you need it to exit; on some shorter autostrade, you pay the toll when you enter. Viacards, on sale for €25 and up at many autostrada locations, allow you to pay for tolls in advance, exiting at special lanes where you simply slip the card into a designated slot.

An *uscita* is an "exit." A *raccordo annulare* is a ring road surrounding a city, while a *tangenziale* bypasses a city entirely. *Strade statale, strade regionale* and *strade provinciale* (regional and provincial highways, denoted by *S, SS, SR,* or *SP* numbers) may be two-lane roads, as are all secondary roads; directions and turnoffs aren't always clearly marked.

GASOLINE

Gas stations are along the main highways. Those on autostrade are open 24 hours. Otherwise, gas stations generally are open Monday–Saturday 7–7, with a break at lunchtime. At self-service gas stations the pumps are operated by a central machine for payment, which doesn't take credit cards; it accepts only bills in denominations of 5, 10, 20, and 50 euros, and doesn't give change. Those with attendants accept cash and credit cards. It's not customary to tip the attendant.

At this writing, gasoline (*benzina*) costs about €1.46 per liter and is available in unleaded (*verde*) and superunleaded (*super*). Many rental cars in Italy use diesel (*gasolio*), which costs about €1.34 per liter (ask about the fuel type for your rental car before you leave the agency).

DRIVING IN HISTORIC CENTERS

To avoid hefty fines added (which you may not be notified of until months after your departure from Italy), make sure you know the rules governing where you can and can't drive in historic city centers. You must have a permit to enter many towns, and Florence, for example, is very strict in enforcement. Check with your lodging and car-rental company to find out about acquiring permits for access.

PARKING

Parking is at a premium in most towns, especially in the *centri storici* (historic centers). Fines for parking violations are high, and towing is common. Don't think about tearing up a ticket, as car-rental companies can use your credit card to be reimbursed for any fines you incur. It's a good idea to park in a designated (and preferably attended) lot. And don't leave valuables in your car, as thieves often target rental cars.

In congested cities indoor parking costs €25–€30 for 12–24 hours; outdoor parking costs about €10–€20. Parking in an area signposted *zona disco* (disk zone) is allowed for short periods (from 30 minutes to two hours or more—the time is posted); if you don't have a cardboard disk (check in the glove box of your rental car) to show what time you parked, you can use a piece of paper. In most metropolitan areas you can find the curbside *parcometro:* once you insert change, it prints a ticket that you then leave on your dashboard.

RENTALS

Fiats, Fords, and Alfa Romeos in a variety of sizes are the most typical rental cars. Note that most Italian cars have standard transmission, so if you need to rent an automatic, be specific when you reserve the car. Significantly higher rates will apply.

Most American chains have affiliates in Italy, but the rates are usually lower if you book a car before you leave home. A company's rates are standard throughout the country: rates are the same for airport and city pickup; airport offices are open later. An auto broker such as AutoEurope.com can allow you to compare rates among companies while guaranteeing lowest rates.

Most rental companies will not rent to someone under age 21 and also refuse to rent any car larger than an economy or subcompact car to anyone under age 23, and, further, require customers under age 23 to pay by credit card. Additional drivers must be identified in the contract and must qualify with the age limits. There's likely a supplementary daily fee for additional drivers. Upon rental, all companies require credit cards as a warranty; to rent bigger cars (2,000 cc or more), you must often show two credit cards. There are no special restrictions on senior citizen drivers. Book car seats, required for children under age three, in advance (the cost is generally about €36 for the duration of the rental).

Hiring a car with a driver can come in handy, particularly if you plan to do some wine tasting or drive along the Amalfi Coast. Search online (the travel forums at fodors.com are a good resource) or ask at your hotel for recommended drivers. Drivers are paid by the day, and are usually rewarded with a tip of about 15% upon completion of the journey.

All rental agencies operating in Italy require that you buy a collision-damage waiver (CDW) and a theft-protection policy, but those costs will already be included in the rates you're quoted. Be aware that coverage may be denied if the named driver on the rental contract isn't the driver at the time of the incident. In Sicily there are some roads for which rental agencies deny coverage; ask in advance if you plan to travel in remote regions. Also ask your rental company about other included coverage when you reserve the car and/or pick it up.

ROAD CONDITIONS

Autostrade are well maintained, as are most interregional highways. Most autostrade have two lanes in both directions; the left lane is used only for passing. Italians drive fast and are impatient with those who don't, so tailgating (and flashing with bright beams to signal an intent to pass) is the norm if you dawdle in the left lane; the only way to avoid it is to stay to the right.

The condition of provincial (county) roads varies, but road maintenance at this level is generally good in Italy. In many small hill towns the streets are winding and extremely narrow; consider parking at the edge of town and exploring on foot.

Driving on the back roads of Italy isn't difficult as long as you're on the alert for bicycles and passing cars. In addition, street and road signs are often missing or placed in awkward spots, so a good map or GPS and lots of patience are essential. If you feel pressure from a string of cars in your rearview mirror but don't feel comfortable speeding up, put your right blinker on, pull off to the right, and let them pass.

Be aware that some maps may not use the SR or SP (strade regionale and strade provinciale) highway designations, which took the place of the old SS designations in 2004. They may use the old SS designation or no numbering at all.

ROADSIDE EMERGENCIES

Automobile Club Italiano offers 24-hour road service; English-speaking operators are available. Your rental-car company may also have an emergency tow service with a toll-free call; keep that number handy. Be prepared to report which road you're on, the *verso* (direction) you're headed, and your *targa* (license plate number). Also, in an emergency, call the police (113).

When you're on the road, always carry a good road map and a flashlight; a cell phone is highly recommended. There are also emergency phones on the autostrade and superstrade; to locate them, look on the pavement for painted arrows and the term "SOS."

Emergency Services Automobile Club Italiano (*ACI ☎ 803/116 emergency service 🌐 www.aci.it*).

RULES OF THE ROAD

Driving is on the right. Speed limits are 130 kph (80 mph) on autostrade, reduced to 110 kph (70 mph) when it rains, and 90 kph (55 mph) on state and provincial roads, unless otherwise marked. In towns the speed limit is 50 kph (30 mph), which may drop as low as 10 kph (6 mph) near schools, hospitals, and other designated areas. Note that right turns on red lights are forbidden. Headlights are required to be on while driving on all roads (large or small) outside of municipalities. You must wear seat belts and strap young children into car seats at all times. Using handheld mobile phones while driving is illegal; fines can exceed €100. In most Italian towns the use of the horn is forbidden in many areas; a large sign, *zona di silenzio*, indicates a no-honking zone.

In Italy you must be 18 years old to drive a car. A U.S. driver's license is acceptable to rent a car, but by law Italy requires non-Europeans also to carry an International Driver's Permit (IDP), which essentially translates your license into Italian (and a dozen other languages). In practice, it depends on the police officer who pulls you over whether you'll be penalized for not carrying the IDP. Obtaining an IDP is simple and costs only $15; check the AAA Web site for more information.

The blood-alcohol content limit for driving is 0.5 gr (stricter than U.S. limits) with fines up to €5,000 for surpassing the limit and the possibility of six months' imprisonment. Although enforcement of laws varies depending on the region, fines for speeding are uniformly stiff: 10 kph over the speed limit can warrant a fine of up to €500; greater than 10 kph, and your license could be taken away from you. The police have the power to levy on-the-spot fines.

TRAIN TRAVEL

In Italy, traveling by train is simple and efficient. Service between major cities is frequent, and trains usually arrive on schedule. The fastest trains on the Ferrovie dello Stato (FS), the Italian State Railways, are the Eurostar express trains, and the fastest Eurostar lines are designated as Alta Velocità; they run between all major cities from Venice, Milan, and Turin down through Florence and Rome to Naples. Seat reservations are mandatory on all Eurostar trains. You'll be assigned a specific seat in a specific coach; to avoid having to squeeze through narrow aisles, board only at your designated coach (the number on your ticket matches the one near the door of each coach). Reservations are also required for the next-fastest, and less-frequent Intercity (IC) trains, tickets for which are about half the price of Eurostar. If you miss your reserved train, go to the ticket counter within the hour and you'll be able to move your reservation to a later train (check these rules at booking).

Reservations are available but not required on Interregionale trains, which are slower and make more stops, and are less expensive still. Regionale and Espresso trains make the most stops and are the most economical; many serve commuters. There are refreshments on long-distance trains, purchased from a mobile cart or a dining car, but not on the commuter trains.

All but commuter trains have first and second classes. On local trains a first-class fare ensures you a little more space and a likely emptier coach. On long-distance trains you also get wider seats (three across as opposed to four) and a bit more legroom, but the difference is minimal. At peak travel times a first-class fare may be worth the additional cost, as the coaches may be less crowded. In Italian, *prima classe* is first class; second is *seconda classe*.

Many cities—Milan, Turin, Genoa, Naples, Florence, Rome, and even Verona included—have more than one train station, **so be sure you get off at the right place.** When buying train tickets be particularly aware that in Rome and Florence some trains don't stop at all of the cities' train stations and may not stop at the main, central station. This is a common occurrence with regional and some Intercity trains. When scheduling train travel on the Internet or through a travel agent, be sure to request to arrive at the station closest to your destination in Rome and Florence.

Except for Pisa, Milan, and Rome, none of the major cities have trains that go directly to the airports, but there are always commuter (frequently direct) bus lines connecting train stations and airports.

You can pay for your train tickets in cash or with a major credit card such as MasterCard, Visa, American Express, and Diners Club at travel agencies, and at the train station ticket counters and automatic ticketing machines. If you'd like to board a train and don't have a ticket, seek out the conductor prior to boarding; he or she will tell you whether you may board and what the surcharge will be (usually €8). If you board a train without a ticket you'll be fined €50 plus the price of the ticket. Trains can be crowded, so it's always a good idea to make a reservation when that's possible. You can review schedules at the FS Web site and reserve seats up to three months in advance at the train station or at an Italian travel agency displaying the FS emblem. You'll need to reserve seats even if you're using a rail pass.

Even though it's not required for high-speed travel, for other trains **you must validate your ticket before boarding** by punching it at a yellow box in the waiting area of smaller train stations or at the end of the track in larger stations. If you forget, tell the conductor immediately to avoid a hefty fine.

Train strikes of various kinds are common, so it's a good idea to make sure your train is running. During a strike,

Travel Times by Train

TO AUSTRIA & GERMANY
BRENNERO
TO AUSTRIA & EAST EUROPE
TARVISIO
TO SWITZERLAND
DOMODOSSOLA
CHIASSO
TO SLOVENIA & CROATIA
MODANE
TO FRANCE
VENTIMIGLIA
TO FRANCE & CÔTE D'AZUR

Bolzano/Bozen
< 2hrs >
Trento
Sondrio
Belluno
Udine
Lecco
Aosta
Bergamo
Treviso
< 2hr
40mn >
Trieste
Novara
< 1hr 20mn >
Milano
< 1hr
Brescia
30mn >
Verona
Vicenza
< 1hr 45mn >
Venezia
Vercelli
Torino
Pavia
Piacenza
Mantova
Padova
Asti
< 1hr 30mn >
Alessandria
< 1hr 30mn >
< 1hr 30mn >
< 1hr 45mn >
Ferrara
< 1hr 40mn >
Parma
Modena
Cuneo
Savona
Genova
Bologna
Imperia
La Spezia
Forlì
< 2hrs >
< 1hr >
Rimini
< 1hr 45mn >
Lucca
Pistoia
Firenze
Pisa
Livorno
Arezzo
Ancona
Perugia
15mn >
Siena
< 1hr 45mn >
< 3hrs >
< 3hrs 20mn >
Grosseto
Viterbo
Terni
Ascoli
Teramo
L'Aquila
< 1hr 20mn >
Pescara

VENEZIA - POLA, CROATIA 3HRS
TO GREECE
ANCONA - ZADAR, CROATIA 4HRS
TO GREECE
PESCARA - SPLIT, CROATIA 5HRS
TO GREECE
GENOVA - POTTO TORRES 13HRS
GENOVA - PALERMO 20HRS
5HRS
10 HRS

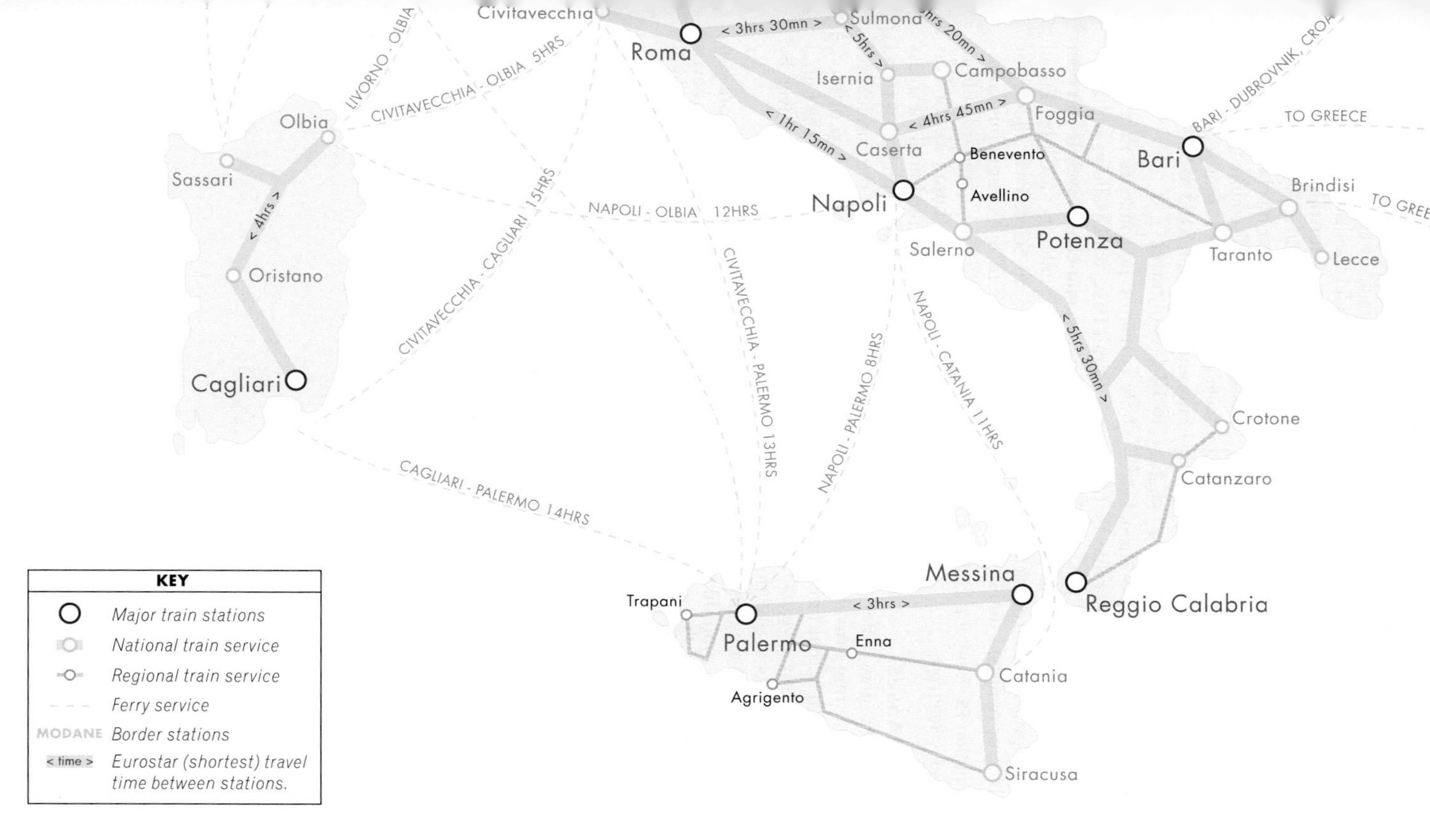

Civitavecchia
Roma
< 3hrs 30mn >
Sulmona
< 5hrs >
Isernia
Campobasso
< 4hrs 45mn >
Foggia
< 1hr 15mn >
Caserta
Benevento
Avellino
Napoli
Salerno
Potenza
Bari
BARI - DUBROVNIK, CRO
TO GREECE
Brindisi
TO GREECE
Taranto
Lecce
< 5hrs 30mn >
Crotone
Catanzaro
Reggio Calabria
LIVORNO - OLBIA
CIVITAVECCHIA - OLBIA 5HRS
Olbia
Sassari
< 4hrs >
Oristano
Cagliari
CIVITAVECCHIA - CAGLIARI 15HRS
NAPOLI - OLBIA 12HRS
CIVITAVECCHIA - PALERMO 13HRS
NAPOLI - PALERMO 8HRS
NAPOLI - CATANIA 11HRS
CAGLIARI - PALERMO 14HRS
Messina
Trapani
< 3hrs >
Palermo
Enna
Agrigento
Catania
Siracusa
KEY
Major train stations
National train service
Regional train service
Ferry service
MODANE Border stations
< time > Eurostar (shortest) travel time between stations.

minimum service is guaranteed, but what exactly that service consists of is difficult to predict.

Traveling by night can be a good deal (if somewhat of an adventure), as you'll pass a night without having to have a hotel room. More comfortable trains run on the longer routes (Sicily–Rome, Sicily–Milan, Sicily–Venice, Rome–Turin, Lecce–Milan); ask for the good-value T3 (three single beds), Intercity Notte, and Carrozza Comfort. The Vagone Letto Excelsior has private bathrooms and single-, double-, or twin-bed suites.

Information FS–Trenitalia (☎ *892021 in Italy* 🌐 *www.trenitalia.com*).

TRAIN PASSES

Rail passes may offer the possibility to save on train travel. Compare rail pass cost with actual fares to determine whether you truly save, as fares can vary considerably. Generally, the more often you plan to travel long distances on high-speed trains, the more likely a rail pass would make sense.

A Eurail Italy Pass allows a certain number of travel days within Italy over the course of two months. Three to 10 days of travel cost from $277 to $510 (first class) or $225 to $413 (second class). If you're in a group of from two to five people, consider the discounted **Eurail Italy Pass Saver:** a pass for three to ten travel days costs from $236 to $434 (first class) or $192 to $351 (second class); children's passes are further discounted. **Eurail Italy Youth** (for those under 26) is second-class only and costs from $183 to $337 for one to 10 days of travel.

Italy is one of 17 countries that accept the Eurail Pass, which allows unlimited first- and second-class travel. If you plan to rack up the miles, get a Global Eurail Pass. The Eurail Select Pass allows for travel in three to five contiguous countries. In addition to standard Eurail Passes, there are the Eurail Youth Pass (for those under 26), the Eurail Flexipass (which allows a certain number of travel days within a set period), the Eurail Saver (which gives a discount for two or more people traveling together), and the Eurail Drive Pass (which combines travel by train and rental car).

All passes must be purchased before you leave for Europe. Keep in mind that even with a rail pass you still need to reserve seats on the trains you plan to take.

Contacts Rail Europe (☎ *800/622-8600* 🌐 *www.raileurope.com*). **Europe on Rail** (☎ *866/858-6854* 🌐 *www.europeonrail.com*). **RailPass** (☎ *877/724-5727* 🌐 *www.railpass.com*).

ESSENTIALS

ACCOMMODATIONS

Italy has a varied and abundant number of hotels, bed-and-breakfasts, *agriturismi (farm stays),* and rental properties. Throughout the cities and the countryside you can find sophisticated, luxurious palaces and villas as well as rustic farmhouses and small hotels. Six-hundred-year-old palazzi and converted monasteries have been restored as luxurious hotels, while retaining the original atmosphere. At the other end of the spectrum, boutique hotels inhabit historic buildings using chic Italian design for the interiors. Increasingly, the famed Italian wineries are creating rooms and apartments for three-day to weeklong stays.

The lodgings we list are the cream of the crop in each price category. We always list the facilities that are available, but we don't specify whether they cost extra; when pricing accommodations, always ask what's included and what costs extra. Properties are assigned price categories based on the range between their least and most expensive standard double room at high season (excluding holidays).

APARTMENT AND HOUSE RENTALS

More and more travelers are turning away from the three-countries-in-two-weeks style of touring and choosing to spend a week in one city or a month in the countryside. Renting an apartment, a farmhouse, or a villa can be economical depending on the number of people in your group and your budget. All are readily available throughout Italy. Most are owned by individuals and managed by rental agents who advertise available properties on the Internet. Many properties are represented by more than one rental agent, and thus the same property is frequently renamed ("Chianti Bella Vista," "Tuscan Sun Home," and "Casa Toscana Sole" are all names of the same farmhouse) on the various Internet rental sites. The rental agent may meet you at the property for the initial check-in or the owner may be present, while the rental agent handles only the online reservation and financial arrangements.

Issues to keep in mind when renting an apartment in a city or town are the neighborhood (street noise and ambience), the availability of an elevator or number of stairs, the furnishings (including pots and pans and linens), what's supplied on arrival (dishwashing liquid, coffee or tea), and the cost of utilities (are they included in the rental rate?). Inquiries about countryside properties should also include how isolated the property is. (Do you have to drive 45 minutes to reach the nearest town?) If you're arriving too late in the day to grocery shop, request that provisions for the next day's breakfast be supplied.

Contacts At Home Abroad (☎ *212/421–9165* 🌐 *www.athomeabroadinc.com*). **Barclay International Group** (☎ *800/845–6636 or 516/364–0064* 🌐 *www.barclayweb.com*). **Drawbridge to Europe** (☎ *888/268–1148 or 541/482–7778* 🌐 *www.drawbridgetoeurope.com*). **Hosted Villas** (☎ *800/374–6637 or 416/920–1873* 🌐 *www.hostedvillas.com*). **Italy Rents** (☎ *202/821–4273* 🌐 *www.italyrents.com*). **Rent A Villa** (☎ *877/250–4366 or 206/417–3444* 🌐 *www.rentavilla.com*). **Suzanne B. Cohen & Associates** (☎ *207/622–0743*🌐 *www.villaeurope.com*). **Tuscan House** (☎ *800/844–6939* 🌐 *www.tuscanhouse.com*). **Villas & Apartments Abroad** (☎ *212/213–6435* 🌐 *www.vaanyc.com*). **Villas International** (☎ *800/221–2260 or 415/499–9490* 🌐 *www.villasintl.com*). **Villas of Distinction** (☎ *800/289–0900* 🌐 *www.villasofdistinction.com*). **Wimco** (☎ *866/850–6140* 🌐 *www.wimco.com*).

CONVENTS AND MONASTERIES

Throughout Italy, tourists can find reasonably priced lodging at convents, monasteries, and religious houses. Religious orders usually charge from €30 to €60 per person per night for rooms that are clean, comfortable, and convenient. Many have private bathrooms; spacious lounge areas and secluded gardens or terraces are standard features. A continental breakfast ordinarily comes with the room, but be sure to ask. Sometimes, for an extra fee, family-style lunches and dinners are available.

Be aware of three issues when considering a convent or monastery stay: most have a curfew of 11 pm or midnight; you need to book in advance, because they fill up quickly; and your best means of booking is usually email or fax—the person answering the phone may not speak English.

Contact Hospites.it (*www.hospites.it*) has listings of convents throughout Italy.

FARM HOLIDAYS AND AGRITOURISM

Rural accommodations in the agriturismo category are increasingly popular with both Italians and visitors to Italy; you stay on a working farm or vineyard. Accommodations vary in size, and range from luxury apartments, farmhouses, and villas to basic facilities. Agriturist has compiled *Agriturism,* which is available only in Italian, but includes more than 1,600 farms in Italy; pictures and the use of international symbols to describe facilities make the guide a good tool. Local APT tourist offices also have information.

Information Agriturismo.net *www.agriturismo.net*). **Agriturist** (*06/6852342* *www.agriturist.it*). **Italy Tourist: Farm Holiday** (*www.italytourist.it*).

HOME EXCHANGES

With a direct home exchange you stay in someone else's home while they stay in yours. Some outfits also deal with vacation homes, so you're not actually staying in someone's full-time residence, just their vacant weekend place.

Italians have historically not been as enthusiastic about home exchanges as others have been; however, there are many great villas and apartments in Italy owned by foreigners, such as Americans, who use the home-exchange services.

Exchange Clubs Home Exchange.com (*800/877-8723* *www.homeexchange.com*); membership is $9.95 monthly or $15.95 for three months. **HomeLink International** (*800/638-3841* *www.homelink.org*); $115 for one year, $118 for two. Additional listings, $18 each. **Intervac U.S.** (*800/756-4663* *www.intervacus.com*); $99 for one-year membership.

COMMUNICATIONS

INTERNET

Getting online in Italian cities isn't difficult: public Internet stations and Internet cafés, some open 24 hours, are common. Prices differ from place to place, so spend some time to find the best deal. Chains like Internet Train can be handy if you're moving about the country, as you can simply prepay your time, and then use the nearest location to connect without staff intervention. You can even use your own laptop if you prefer.

Wi-Fi hot spots can be found in lodgings from high-end hotels to B&Bs, major airports and train stations, cafés, and shopping centers, but are rarely free. Broadband and Wi-Fi connections are becoming increasingly common in lodgings, including smaller hotels and B&Bs. Some hotels have in-room modem lines, but, as with phones, using the hotel's line is relatively expensive. Always check modem rates before plugging in. You may need a plug adapter for your computer for the European-style electric socket (a converter will likely not be necessary). If you're traveling with a laptop, carry a spare battery and an adapter. Never plug your computer into any socket before asking about surge protection. IBM sells a tiny modem tester that plugs into a telephone jack to check whether the line is safe to use.

LOCAL DO'S AND TABOOS

GREETINGS

Upon meeting and leave-taking, both friends and strangers wish each other good day or good evening (*buongiorno, buona sera*); *ciao* isn't used between strangers. Italians who are friends greet each other with a kiss, usually first on the left cheek, then on the right. When you meet a new person, shake hands.

SIGHTSEEING

Italy is full of churches, and many of them contain significant works of art. They're also places of worship, however, so be sure to dress appropriately.

Shorts, tank tops, and sleeveless garments are taboo in most churches throughout the country. In summer carry a sweater or other item of clothing to wrap around your bare shoulders to avoid being denied entrance.

You should never bring food into a church, and don't sip from your water bottle while inside. If you have a cell phone, turn it off before entering. Ask whether photographs are allowed; never use flash. And never enter a church when a service is in progress, especially if it's a private affair such as a wedding or baptism.

OUT ON THE TOWN

Table manners in Italy are formal; rarely do Italians share food from their plates. In a restaurant, be formal and polite with your waiter—no calling across the room for attention.

When you've finished your meal and are ready to go, ask for the check (*il conto*); unless it's well past closing time, no waiter will put a bill on your table until you've requested it.

Italians don't have a culture of sipping cocktails or chugging pitchers of beer. Wine, beer, and other alcoholic drinks are almost always consumed as part of a meal. Public drunkenness is abhorred.

Smoking has been banned in all public establishments, much as in the United States.

Flowers, chocolates, or a bottle of wine are appropriate hostess gifts when invited to dinner at the home of an Italian.

DOING BUSINESS

Showing up on time for business appointments is the norm and expected in Italy. There are more business lunches than business dinners, and even business lunches aren't common, as Italians view mealtimes as periods of pleasure and relaxation.

Business cards (*biglietto da visita*) are used throughout Italy, and business attire is the norm for both men and women. To be on the safe side, it's best not to use first names or a familiar form of address until invited to do so.

Business gifts aren't the norm, but if one is given it's usually small and symbolic of your home location or type of business.

LANGUAGE

One of the best ways to connect with Italians is to learn a little of the local language. You need not strive for fluency; just mastering a few basic words and terms is bound to make interactions more rewarding.

"Please" is *per favore*, "thank you" is *grazie*, "you're welcome" is *prego*, and "excuse me" is *scusi*.

In larger cities such as Venice, Rome, and Florence, language isn't a big problem. Most hotels have English-speakers at their reception desks, and if not, they can always find someone who speaks at least a little English. You may have trouble communicating in the countryside, but a phrase book and expressive gestures will go a long way. A phrase book and language-tape set can help get you started before you go. *Fodor's Italian for Travelers* (available at bookstores everywhere) is excellent.

Contact Jiwire (*www.jiwire.com*) has a fairly complete, comprehensible list of Italian Wi-Fi locations, including maps. **Internet Cafes in Italy** (*cafe.ecs.net*) has an extensive list of Italian Internet cafés. The best resource, though, is likely your lodging host.

PHONES

The good news is that you can now make a direct-dial telephone call from virtually any point on Earth. The bad news? You can't always do so cheaply. Calling from a hotel is almost always the most expensive option; hotels usually add huge surcharges to all calls, particularly international ones. Calling cards can keep costs to a minimum, but only if you purchase them locally. And then there are mobile phones; as expensive as mobile phone calls can be, they're still usually a much cheaper option than calling from your hotel. With a little effort, you can manage to reduce the call expense, though.

CALL ITALY FROM ABROAD

When calling Italy from North America, dial 011 (which gets you an international line), followed by Italy's country code, 39, and the phone number, including any leading 0. Note that Italian cell numbers have 10 digits and always begin with a 3; Italian landline numbers will contain from 4 to 10 digits, and will always begin with a 0. So for example, when calling Rome, whose numbers begin with 06, you dial 011 + 39 + 06 + phone number; for a cell phone, dial 011 + 39 + cell number.

CALLING WITHIN ITALY

With the advent of mobile phones, public pay phones are becoming increasingly scarce, although they can be found at train and subway stations, main post offices, and in some bars. In rural areas, town squares usually have a pay phone. Pay phones require a *scheda telefonica* (phone card ⇨ *below*).

For all calls within Italy, whether local or long-distance, you'll dial the entire phone number that starts with 0, or 3 for cell phone numbers. Rates from landlines vary according to the time of day; it's cheaper to call before 9 am and after 7 or 8 pm; calling a cell phone will cost significantly more. Italy uses the prefix "800" for toll-free or numero verde (green) numbers.

MAKING INTERNATIONAL CALLS

Because of the high rates charged by most hotels for long-distance and international calls, you're better off making such calls from public phones or your mobile phone (⇨ *below*), using an international calling card (⇨ *below*). If you prefer to use the hotel phone to make an international call, you can still save money by using an international calling card.

Although not advised because of the exorbitant cost, you can place international calls or collect calls through an operator by dialing 170. Rates to the United States are lowest on Sunday around the clock and between 10 pm and 8 am (Italian time) on weekdays and Saturday. You can also place a direct call to the United States using your U.S. phone calling-card number. You automatically reach a U.S. operator and thereby avoid all language difficulties.

The country code for the United States and Canada is 1 (dial 00 + 1 + area code and number).

Access Codes AT&T Direct (☎ *800/172–444*). **MCI WorldPhone** (☎ *800/905–825*). **Sprint International Access** (☎ *800/172–405*).

CALLING CARDS

Prepaid *schede telefoniche* (phone cards) are available throughout Italy and are best for calls within the country. Cards in different denominations are sold at post offices, newsstands, tobacco shops, and some bars. When using with pay phones, tear off the corner of the card and insert it into the phone's slot. When you dial, the card's value appears in a display window. After you hang up, the card is returned (so don't walk off without it).

International calling cards are different; you call a toll-free number from any phone, entering the code found on the back of the card followed by the destination number. The best card for calling

North America and elsewhere in Europe is the Europa card, which comes in two denominations, €5 for 180 minutes and €10 for 360 minutes, available at tobacco shops. Just ask for a card for calling the United States (or the country you prefer).

MOBILE PHONES

If you have a multiband phone (Europe and North America use different calling frequencies) and your service provider uses the world-standard GSM network (as do T-Mobile, AT&T, and Verizon), you can probably use your own phone and provider abroad. Roaming fees can be steep, however: 99¢ a minute is considered reasonable. And overseas you normally pay the toll charges for incoming calls. It's almost always cheaper to send a text message than to make a call, since text messages have a low set fee (often less than 15¢).

To further reduce calling expenses, consider buying an Italian SIM card (making sure your service provider first unlocks your phone for use with a different SIM) and a prepaid service plan once at your destination. You then have a local number and can make calls at local rates (which also means you pay only for calls made, not received).

■ **TIP→** If you travel internationally frequently, save one of your old mobile phones (ask your cell phone company to unlock it for you) or buy an unlocked, multiband phone online; take it with you as a travel phone, buying a new SIM card with pay-as-you-go service in each destination.

The cost of cell phones is dropping; you can purchase a dual band (Europe only) cell phone with a prepaid call credit (no monthly service plan) in Italy for less than €40, then top off the credit as you go if necessary. This plan will not allow you to call the United States, but using an international calling card with the cell phone solves that problem in an inexpensive manner. Most medium to large towns have stores dedicated to selling cell phones. The purchase of a multiband phone means it'll also function once you return home, European phones aren't "locked" to their provider's SIM (which is also why they cost more). You'll need to present your passport to purchase any SIM card.

Rental cell phones are available online prior to departure (⇨ *below*) and in Italy in cities and larger towns. Many Internet cafés offer them, but shop around for the best deal. Most rental contracts require a refundable deposit that covers the cost of the cell phone (€75–€150) and then set up a monthly service plan that's automatically charged to your credit card. Frequently, rental cell phones will be triple band with a plan that allows you to call North America. Be sure to check the rate schedule to avoid a nasty surprise when you receive your credit-card bill two or three months later. Often the prepaid option will be the more cost-effective one.

■ **TIP→** Beware of cell phone (and PDA) thieves. Keep your phone or PDA in a secure pocket or purse. Don't lay it on the bar when you stop for an espresso. Don't zip it into the outside pocket of your backpack in crowded cities. Don't leave it in your hotel room. Notify your provider immediately if it's lost or stolen; providers can block your SIM and give you a new one, copying the original's contents.

Contacts Cellular Abroad (☎ *800/287–5072* 🌐 *www.cellularabroad.com*) rents and sells GMS phones and sells SIM cards that work in many countries. **Mobal** (☎ *888/888–9162* 🌐 *www.mobal.com*) rents mobiles and sells GSM phones (starting at $49) that will operate in 140 countries. Per-call rates vary throughout the world. **Planet Fone** (☎ *888/988–4777* 🌐 *www.planetfone.com*) rents cell phones, but the per-minute rates are expensive.

CUSTOMS AND DUTIES

You're always allowed to bring goods of a certain value back home without having to pay any duty or import tax. But there's a limit on the amount of tobacco and liquor you can bring back duty-free, and some countries have separate limits for perfumes; for exact figures, check with your customs department. The values of so-called duty-free goods are included in these amounts. When you shop abroad, save all your receipts, as customs inspectors may ask to see them as well as the items you purchased. If the total value of your goods is more than the duty-free limit, you'll have to pay a tax (most often a flat percentage) on the value of everything beyond that limit.

Travelers from the United States should experience little difficulty clearing customs at any airport in Italy.

Italy requires documentation of the background of all antiques and antiquities before the item is taken out of the country. Under Italian law, all antiquities found on Italian soil are considered state property, and there are other restrictions on antique artwork. Even if purchased from a business in Italy, legal ownership of such artifacts may be in question if brought into the United States. Therefore, although they don't necessarily confer ownership, documents such as export permits and receipts are required when importing such items into the United States.

When returning to the United States, clearing customs is sometimes more difficult. U.S. residents are normally entitled to a duty-free exemption of $800 on items accompanying them. Although there's no problem with aged cheese (vacuum-sealed works best), you cannot bring back any of that delicious prosciutto, salami, or any other meat product. Fresh mushrooms, truffles, or fresh fruits and vegetables are also forbidden. There are also restrictions on the amount of alcohol allowed in duty-free. Generally, you're allowed to bring in one liter of wine, beer, or other alcohol without paying a customs duty.

Information in Italy Dogana Sezione Viaggiatori (☎ *06/65954343* 🌐 *www.agenziadogane.it*). **Ministero delle Finanze, Direzione Centrale dei Servizi Doganali, Divisione I** (☎ *06/50242117* 🌐 *www.finanze.it*).

U.S. Information U.S. Customs and Border Protection (🌐 *www.cbp.gov*).

EATING OUT

Italian cuisine is still largely regional. Ask what the local specialties are: by all means, have spaghetti *alla carbonara* (with bacon and egg) in Rome, pizza in Rome or Naples, *bistecca alla fiorentina* (steak) in Florence, *cinghiale* (wild boar) in Tuscany, truffles in Piedmont, and risotto *alla milanese* in Milan. Although most restaurants in Italy serve traditional local cuisine, you can find Asian and Middle Eastern alternatives in Rome, Venice, and other cities. The restaurants we list are the cream of the crop in each price category.

MEALS AND MEALTIMES

What's the difference between a ristorante and a trattoria? Can you order food at an *enoteca* (wine bar)? Can you go to a restaurant just for a snack, or order just a salad at a pizzeria? The following definitions should help.

Not too long ago, *ristoranti* tended to be more elegant and expensive than trattorie and *osterie,* which serve traditional, home-style fare in an atmosphere to match. But the distinction has blurred considerably, and an osteria in the center of town might be far fancier (and pricier) than a ristorante across the street. In any sit-down establishment, be it a ristorante, osteria, or trattoria, you're generally expected to order at least a two-course meal, such as: a *primo* (first course) and a *secondo* (main course) or a *contorno* (vegetable side dish); an *antipasto* (starter) followed by either a primo or secondo; or a secondo and a *dolce* (dessert).

In an enoteca (wine bar) or pizzeria it's common to order just one dish. An enoteca menu is often limited to a selection of cheese, cured meats, salads, and desserts, but if there's a kitchen you can also find soups, pastas, and main courses. The typical pizzeria fare includes *affettati misti* (a selection of cured pork), simple salads, various kinds of bruschetta, *crostini* (similar to bruschetta, with a variety of toppings) and, in Rome, *fritti* (deep-fried finger food) such as *olive ascolane* (green olives with a meat stuffing) and *supplì* (rice balls stuffed with mozzarella).

The handiest and least expensive places for a quick snack between sights are probably bars, cafés, and pizza *al taglio* (by the slice) spots. Pizza al taglio shops are easy to negotiate but few have seats. They sell pizza by weight: just point out which kind you want and how much. Note that it's considered rude to walk and eat.

Bars in Italy resemble what we think of as cafés, and are primarily places to get a coffee and a bite to eat, rather than drinking establishments. Most bars have a selection of panini warmed up on the griddle (*piastra*) and *tramezzini* (sandwiches made of untoasted white bread triangles). In larger cities, bars also serve vegetable and fruit salads, cold pasta dishes, and gelato. Most bars offer beer and a variety of alcohol as well as wines by the glass (sometimes good but more often mediocre). A café is like a bar but usually with more tables. Pizza at a café should be avoided—it's usually heated in a microwave.

If you place your order at the counter, ask whether you can sit down: some places charge for table service (especially in tourist centers); others don't. In self-service bars and cafés it's good manners to clean your table before you leave. Note that in some places (such as train stations and stops along the highway) you first pay a cashier, then show your *scontrino* (receipt) at the counter to place your order. Menus are posted outside most restaurants (in English in tourist areas); if not, you might step inside and ask to take a look at the menu (but don't ask for a table unless you intend to stay).

Italians take their food as it's listed on the menu, seldom if ever making special requests such as "dressing on the side" or "hold the olive oil." If you have special dietary needs, however, make them known; they can usually be accommodated. Although mineral water makes its way to almost every table, you can order a carafe of tap water (*acqua di rubinetto* or *acqua semplice*) instead, but keep in mind that such water can be highly chlorinated.

An Italian would never ask for olive oil to dip bread in, and don't be surprised if there's no butter to spread on your bread. Wiping your bowl clean with a (small) piece of bread is usually considered a sign of appreciation, not bad manners. Spaghetti should be eaten with a fork only, although a little help from a spoon won't horrify locals the way cutting spaghetti into little pieces might. Order your caffè (Italians drink cappuccino only in the morning) after dessert, not with it. Don't ask for a doggy bag.

Breakfast (*la colazione*) is usually served from 7 to 10:30, lunch (*il pranzo*) from 12:30 to 2:30, and dinner (*la cena*) from 7:30 to 10; outside those hours, best head for a bar. Peak times are usually 1:30 for lunch and 9 for dinner. Enoteche and Venetian *bàcari* (wine bars) are open also in the morning and late afternoon for a snack at the counter. Most pizzerias open at 8 pm and close around midnight—later in summer and on weekends. Most bars and cafés are open from 7 am until 8 or 9 pm; a few stay open until midnight.

Unless otherwise noted, the restaurants listed in this guide are open daily for lunch and dinner.

PAYING

Most restaurants have a cover charge per person, usually listed at the top of the check as *coperto* or *pane e coperto*. It should be a modest charge (€1–€2.50 per person) except at the most expensive restaurants. Whenever in doubt, ask before you order to avoid unpleasant discussions later. It's customary to leave a small tip (around 10%) in appreciation of good service. If *servizio* is included at the bottom of the check, no tip is necessary. Tips are always given in cash.

The price of fish dishes is often given by weight (before cooking), so the price you see on the menu is for 100 grams of fish, not for the whole dish. (An average fish portion is about 350 grams.) In Tuscany, *bistecca alla fiorentina* (Florentine steak) is also often priced by weight (€4 for 100 grams or €40 for 1 kilogram [2.2 pounds]).

Major credit cards are widely accepted in Italy, though cash is always preferred. More restaurants take Visa and MasterCard than American Express.

When you leave a dining establishment, take your meal bill or receipt with you; although not a common experience, the Italian finance (tax) police can approach you within 100 yards of the establishment at which you've eaten and ask for a receipt. If you don't have one, they can fine you and will fine the business owner for not providing the receipt. The measure is intended to prevent tax evasion; it's not necessary to show receipts when leaving Italy.

RESERVATIONS AND DRESS

Regardless of where you are, it's a good idea to make a reservation for dinner. We only mention them specifically when reservations are essential (there's no other way you'll ever get a table) or when they're not accepted. For popular restaurants, book as far ahead as you can (often 30 days), and reconfirm as soon as you arrive. (Large parties should always call ahead to check the reservations policy.) If you change your mind, be sure to cancel, even at the last minute.

We mention dress only when men are required to wear a jacket or a jacket and tie. But unless they're dining outside or at an oceanfront resort, Italian men never wear shorts or running shoes in a restaurant. The same applies to women: no casual shorts, running shoes, or plastic sandals when going out to dinner. Shorts are acceptable in pizzerias and cafés.

WINES, BEER, AND SPIRITS

The grape has been cultivated in Italy since the time of the Etruscans, and Italians justifiably take pride in their local varieties, which are numerous. Though almost every region produces good-quality wine, Tuscany, Piedmont, the Veneto, Puglia, Calabria, and Sicily are some of the more renowned areas, with Marches and Umbria getting recognition as well. Wine in Italy is less expensive than almost anywhere else, so it's often affordable to order a bottle of wine at a restaurant rather than to stick with the house wine (which will be simple but often quite good). Many bars have their own *aperitivo della casa* (house aperitif); Italians are imaginative with their mixed drinks, so you may want to try one.

You can purchase beer, wine, and spirits in any bar, grocery store, or enoteca, any day of the week, any time of the day. Italian and German beer is readily available, but it can be more expensive than wine. Microbreweries are beginning to dot the Italian beer horizon; ask if there's a local brew available to sample.

There's no minimum drinking age in Italy. Italian children begin drinking wine mixed with water at mealtimes when they're teens (or thereabouts). Italians are rarely seen drunk in public, and public drinking, except in a bar or eating establishment, isn't considered acceptable behavior. Bars usually close by 9 pm; hotel and restaurant bars stay open until midnight. Brewpubs and discos serve until about 2 am.

ELECTRICITY

The electrical current in Italy is 220 volts, 50 cycles alternating current (AC); wall outlets take continental-type plugs, with two or three round prongs.

Consider the purchase of a universal adapter, which has several types of plugs in one lightweight, compact unit, available at travel specialty stores and online. You can pick up plug adapters in Italy in any electric supply store for about €2 each. You'll likely not need a converter, however: most portable devices are dual voltage (i.e., they operate equally well on 110 and 220 volts), so require only an adapter; just check label specifications and manufacturer instructions to be sure. Don't use 110-volt outlets marked "for shavers only" for high-wattage appliances such as hair dryers.

Contacts Steve Kropla's Help for World Travelers (*www.kropla.com*) has information on electrical and telephone plugs around the world. **Walkabout Travel Gear** (*www.walkabouttravelgear.com*) has a good coverage of electricity under "adapters."

EMERGENCIES

No matter where you are in Italy, you can dial 113 in case of emergency: the call will be directed to the local police. Not all 113 operators speak English, so you may want to ask a local person to place the call. Asking the operator for *"pronto soccorso"* (first aid and also the emergency room of a hospital) should get you an *ambulanza* (ambulance). If you just need a doctor, ask for *"un medico."*

Italy has the *carabinieri* (national police force, their emergency number is 112 from anywhere in Italy) as well as the *polizia* (local police force). Both are armed and have the power to arrest and investigate crimes. Always report the loss of your passport to the caribinieri as well as to your embassy. When reporting a crime, you'll be asked to fill out *una denuncia* (official report); keep a copy for your insurance company. You should also contact the police any time you have a car accident of any sort.

Local traffic officers, known as *vigili,* are responsible for, among other things, giving out parking tickets. They wear white (in summer) or black uniforms. Should you find yourself involved in a minor car accident in town, contact the vigili.

Pharmacies are generally open weekdays 8:30–1 and 4–8, and Saturday 9–1. Local pharmacies rotate covering the off-hours in shifts: on the door of every pharmacy is a list of which pharmacies in the vicinity will be open late.

Foreign Embassies U.S. Consulate Florence (*Via Lungarno Vespucci 38, Florence 055/266951*). **U.S. Consulate Milan** (*Via Principe Amedeo 2/10, Milan 02/290351*). **U.S. Consulate Naples** (*Piazza della Repubblica, Naples 081/5838111*). **U.S. Embassy** (*Via Veneto 119/A, Rome 06/46741 www.usembassy.it*).

General Emergency Contacts Emergencies (*113*). **National police** (*112*).

HOURS OF OPERATION

Religious and civic holidays are frequent in Italy. Depending on the holiday's local importance, businesses may close for the day. Businesses don't close Friday or Monday when the holiday falls on the weekend.

Banks are open weekdays 8:30–1:30 and for one or two hours in the afternoon, depending on the bank. Most post offices are open Monday–Saturday 9–12:30; central post offices are open 9–6:30 weekdays, 9–12:30 or 9–6:30 on Saturday. On the last day of the month all post offices close at midday.

Most churches are open from early morning until noon or 12:30, when they close for three hours or more; they open again in the afternoon, closing at about 6 pm. A few major churches, such as St. Peter's in Rome and San Marco in Venice, remain open all day. Walking around during services is discouraged. Many museums are closed one day a week, often Monday. During low season, museums often close early; during high season, many stay open until late at night.

Most shops are open Monday–Saturday 9–1 and 3:30 or 4–7:30. Clothing shops are generally closed Monday mornings.

Barbers and hairdressers, with some exceptions, are closed Sunday and Monday. Some bookstores and fashion and tourist-oriented shops in places such as Rome and Venice are open all day, as well as Sunday. Large chain supermarkets such as Standa, COOP, and Esselunga don't close for lunch and are usually open Sunday; smaller *alimentari* (delicatessens) and other food shops are usually closed one evening during the week (it varies according to the town) and are almost always closed Sunday.

HOLIDAYS

Traveling through Italy in August can be an odd experience. Although there are some deals to be had, the heat can be oppressive, and much of the population is on vacation. Most cities are deserted (except for foreign tourists) and privately run restaurants and shops are closed. The national holidays in 2012 include January 1 (New Year's Day); January 6 (Epiphany); April 8 and April 9 (Easter Sunday and Monday); April 25 (Liberation Day); May 1 (Labor Day or May Day); June 2 (Festival of the Republic); August 15 (Ferragosto); November 1 (All Saints' Day); December 8 (Immaculate Conception); and December 25 and 26 (Christmas Day and the feast of Saint Stephen).

In addition, feast days of patron saints are observed locally. Many businesses and shops may be closed in Florence, Genoa, and Turin on June 24 (Saint John the Baptist); in Rome on June 29 (Saints Peter and Paul); in Palermo on July 15 (Santa Rosalia); in Naples on September 19 (San Gennaro); in Bologna on October 4 (San Petronio); in Trieste on November 3 (San Giusto); and in Milan on December 7 (Saint Ambrose). Venice's feast of Saint Mark is April 25, the same as Liberation Day, so the Madonna della Salute on November 21 makes up for the lost holiday.

MAIL

The Italian mail system has a bad reputation but has become noticeably more efficient in recent times with some privatization. Allow from 7 to 15 days for mail to get to the United States. Receiving mail in Italy, especially packages, can take weeks, usually due to customs (not postal) delays.

Most post offices are open Monday–Saturday 9–12:30; central post offices are open weekdays 9–6:30, Saturday 9–12:30 (some until 6:30). On the last day of the month post offices close at midday. You can buy stamps at tobacco shops as well as post offices.

Posta Prioritaria (for regular letters and packages) is the name for standard postage. It guarantees delivery within Italy in three to five business days and abroad in five to six working days. The more expensive express delivery, *Postacelere* (for larger letters and packages), guarantees one-day delivery to most places in Italy and three- to five-day delivery abroad. Note that the postal service has no control over customs, however, which makes international delivery estimates meaningless.

Mail sent as Posta Prioritaria to the United States costs €0.85 for up to 20 grams, €1.50 for 21–50 grams, and €1.85 for 51–100 grams. Mail sent as Postacelere to the United States costs €43–€50 for up to 500 grams.

Other package services to check are Quick Pack Europe, for delivery within Europe; and EMS Express Mail Service, a global three- to five-day service for letters and packages that can be less expensive than Postacelere.

Two-day mail is generally available during the week in all major cities and at popular resorts via UPS and Federal Express. Service is reliable; a Federal Express letter to the United States costs about €35—but again, customs delays can slow down "express" service. If your hotel can't assist you with shipping, try an Internet café, many of which also offer two-day mail services using major carriers.

SHIPPING PACKAGES

You can ship parcels only via air, which takes about two weeks. If you have purchased antiques, ceramics, or other objects, ask if the vendor will do the shipping for you; in most cases this is a possibility, and preferable, because they have experience with these kinds of shipments. If so, ask whether the article will be insured against breakage. When shipping a package out of Italy, it's virtually impossible to find an overnight delivery option—the fastest delivery time is 48 to 72 hours, though once again this will not include any time your shipment might spend in customs.

MONEY

Prices vary from region to region and are substantially lower in the country than in the cities. Of Italy's major cities, Venice and Milan are by far the most expensive. Resorts such as Portofino and Cortina d'Ampezzo cater to wealthy people and charge top prices. Good values can be had in the scenic Trentino–Alto Adige region of the Dolomites and in Umbria and the Marches. With a few exceptions, southern Italy and Sicily also offer bargains for those who do their homework before they leave home.

Prices throughout this guide are given for adults. Substantially reduced fees are almost always available for children, students, and senior citizens from the EU; citizens of non-EU countries rarely get discounts, but be sure to inquire before you purchase your tickets, because this situation is constantly changing.

TIP→ U.S. banks never have every foreign currency on hand, and it may take as long as a week to order. If you're planning to exchange funds before leaving home, don't wait until the last minute.

ATMS AND BANKS

An ATM (*bancomat* in Italian) is the easiest way to get euros in Italy. There are numerous ATMs in large cities and small towns, as well as in airports and train stations. They're not common in places such as grocery stores. Be sure to **memorize your PIN in numbers,** as ATM keypads in Italy don't usually display letters. Check with your bank to confirm that you have an international PIN (*codice segreto*) that will be recognized in the countries you're visiting, to raise your maximum daily withdrawal allowance, and to learn what your bank's fee is for withdrawing money. (Italian banks don't charge withdrawal fees.) **TIP→** Be aware that PINs beginning with a 0 (zero) tend to be rejected in Italy.

Your own bank may charge a fee for using ATMs abroad or charge for the cost of conversion from euros to dollars. Nevertheless, you can usually get a better rate of exchange at an ATM than you will at a currency-exchange office or even when changing money inside a bank with a teller. Extracting funds as you need them is a safer option than carrying around a large amount of cash. Finally, it's a good idea to obtain more than one card that can be used for cash withdrawal, in case something happens to your main one.

CREDIT CARDS

It's a good idea to **inform your credit-card company before you travel,** especially if you're going abroad and don't travel internationally often. Otherwise, the credit-card company might put a hold on your card owing to unusual activity—not a good thing halfway through your trip. Record all your credit-card numbers—as well as the phone numbers to call if your cards are lost or stolen—in a safe place, so you're prepared should something go wrong. MasterCard and Visa have general numbers you can call (collect if you're abroad) if your card is lost, but you're better off calling the number of your issuing bank, because MasterCard and Visa generally just transfer you to your bank; your bank's number is usually printed on your card.

Although it's usually cheaper (and safer) to use a credit card abroad for large purchases (so you can cancel payments or be reimbursed if there's a problem), note that some credit-card companies *and* the banks that issue them add substantial percentages to all foreign transactions, whether they're in a foreign currency or not. Check on these fees before leaving home, so there won't be any surprises when you get the bill. Because of the exorbitant fees, avoid using your credit card for ATM withdrawals or cash advances (use a debit or cash card instead).

TIP→ Before you charge something, ask the merchant whether or not he or she plans to do a dynamic currency conversion (DCC). In such a transaction the credit-card processor (shop, restaurant, or hotel, not Visa or MasterCard) converts the currency and charges you in dollars. In most cases you'll pay the merchant a 3% fee for this service in addition to any credit-card company and issuing-bank foreign-transaction surcharges.

Dynamic currency conversion programs are becoming increasingly widespread. Merchants who participate in them are supposed to ask whether you want to be charged in dollars or the local currency, but they don't always do so. And even if they do offer you a choice, they may well avoid mentioning the additional surcharges. The good news is that you *do* have a choice. And if this practice really gets your goat, you can avoid it entirely thanks to American Express; with its cards, DCC simply isn't an option.

MasterCard and Visa are preferred by Italian merchants, but American Express is usually accepted in popular tourist destinations. Credit cards aren't accepted everywhere, though; if you want to pay with a credit card in a small shop, hotel, or restaurant, it's a good idea to make your intentions known early on.

Reporting Lost Cards American Express (☎ *800/268–9824 in U.S., 336/393–1111 collect from abroad* 🌐 *www.americanexpress.com*). **Diners Club** (☎ *800/234–6377 in U.S., 303/799–1504 collect from abroad* 🌐 *www.dinersclub.com*). **MasterCard** (☎ *800/627–8372 in U.S., 636/722–7111 collect from abroad* 🌐 *www.mastercard.com*). **Visa** (☎ *800/847–2911 in U.S., 410/581–9994 collect from abroad, 800/819014 in Italy* 🌐 *www.visa.com*).

CURRENCY AND EXCHANGE

The euro is the main unit of currency in Italy, as well as in 12 other European countries. Under the euro system there are 100 *centesimi* (cents) to the euro. There are coins valued at 1, 2, 5, 10, 20, and 50 centesimi as well as 1 and 2 euros. There are seven notes: 5, 10, 20, 50, 100, 200, and 500 euros.

At this writing, 1 euro was worth was about 1.33 U.S. dollars.

Post offices exchange currency at good rates, but you'll rarely find an employee who speaks English, so be prepared. (Writing your request can help in these cases.)

TIP→ Even if a currency-exchange booth has a sign promising no commission, rest assured that there's some kind of huge, hidden fee. You're almost always better off getting foreign currency at an ATM or exchanging money at a bank.

PASSPORTS AND VISAS

U.S. citizens need only a valid passport to enter Italy for stays of up to 90 days.

PASSPORTS

Although somewhat costly, a U.S. passport is relatively simple to obtain and is valid for 10 years. You must apply in person if you're getting a passport for the first time; if your previous passport was lost, stolen, or damaged; or if your previous passport has expired and was issued more than 15 years ago or when you were under 16. All children under 18 must appear in person to apply for or renew a passport. Both parents must accompany any child under 14 (or send a notarized statement with their permission) and provide proof of their relationship to the child.

There are 13 regional passport offices, as well as 7,000 passport acceptance facilities in post offices, public libraries, and other governmental offices. If you're renewing a passport, you can do so by mail. Forms are available at passport acceptance facilities and online.

The cost to apply for a new passport is $100 for adults, $85 for children under 16; renewals are $75. Allow six weeks for processing, both for first-time passports and renewals. For an expediting fee of $60 you can reduce this time to about two weeks. If your trip is less than two weeks away, you can get a passport even more rapidly by going to a passport office with the necessary documentation. Private expediters can get things done in as little as 48 hours, but charge hefty fees for their services.

TIP→ Before your trip, make two copies of your passport's data page (one for someone at home and another for you to carry separately). Or scan the page and email it to someone at home and/or yourself.

VISAS

When staying for 90 days or less, U.S. citizens aren't required to obtain a visa prior to traveling to Italy. If you plan to travel or live in Italy or the European Union for longer than 90 days, you must acquire a valid visa from the Italian consulate serving your state *before you leave the United States.* Plan ahead, because the process of obtaining a visa will take at least 30 days, and the Italian government doesn't accept visa applications submitted by visa expediters.

U.S. Passport Information U.S. Department of State (*877/487–2778 www.travel.state.gov/passport*).

U.S. Passport Expediters A. Briggs Passport & Visa Expeditors (*800/806–0581 or 202/338–0111 www.abriggs.com*). **American Passport Express** (*800/455–5166 www.americanpassport.com*). **Passport Express** (*800/362–8196 www.passportexpress.com*). **Travel Document Systems** (*800/874–5100 or 202/638–3800 [additional offices in New York and San Francisco] www.traveldocs.com*). **Travel the World Visas** (*866/886–8472 or 202/223–8822 www.world-visa.com*).

TAXES

A 10% V.A.T. (value-added tax) is included in the rate at all hotels except those at the upper end of the range.

No tax is added to the bill in restaurants. A service charge of approximately 10%–15% is often added to your check; in some cases a service charge is included in the prices.

The V.A.T. is 20% on clothing, wine, and luxury goods. On consumer goods it's already included in the amount shown on the price tag (look for the phrase "IVA inclusa"), whereas on services it may not be; feel free to confirm. Because you're not a European citizen, if your purchases in a single transaction total more than €155, you may be entitled to a refund of the V.A.T.

When making a purchase, ask whether the merchant gives refunds—not all stores do, nor are they required to. If they do, they'll help you fill out the V.A.T. refund form, which you'll submit to a company that will issue you the refund in the form of cash, check, or credit-card adjustment.

As you leave the country (or, if you're visiting several European Union countries, on leaving the EU), present your merchandise and the form to customs officials, who will stamp it. After you're through passport control, take the stamped form to a refund-service counter for an on-the-spot refund (the quickest and easiest option). You may also mail it to the address on the form (or on the envelope with it) after you arrive home, but processing time can be long, especially if you request a credit-card adjustment. Note that in larger cities the cash refund can be obtained at in-town offices prior to departure; just ask the merchant or check the envelope for local office addresses.

Global Refund is the largest V.A.T.-refund service with 225,000 affiliated stores and more than 700 refund counters at major airports and border crossings. Its refund form, called a Tax Free Check, is the most common across the European continent. Premier Tax Free is another company that represents more than 70,000 merchants worldwide. In some cities you may obtain the refund immediately from local offices. Look for their logos in store windows.

V.A.T. Refunds Global Refund (☎ *800/566–9828* 🌐 *www.globalrefund.com*). **Premier Tax Free** (☎ *905/542–1710* 🌐 *www.premiertaxfree.com*).

TIME

Italy is in the Central European Time Zone (CET). From March to October it institutes Daylight Saving Time. Italy is 6 hours ahead of U.S. Eastern Standard Time, 1 hour ahead of Great Britain, 10 hours behind Sydney, and 12 hours behind Auckland. Like the rest of Europe, Italy uses the 24-hour (or "military") clock, which means that after noon you continue counting forward: 13:00 is 1 pm, 23:30 is 11:30 pm.

TIPPING

In restaurants a service charge of 10% to 15% may appear on your check. If so, it's not necessary to leave an additional tip. If service isn't included, leave a tip of up to 10%. Always leave your tip in cash, even if there's a line item on your credit-card slip for a tip (otherwise the server will never see it). Tip checkroom attendants €1 per person and restroom attendants €0.50 (more in expensive hotels and restaurants). In major cities, tip €0.50 or more for table service in cafés. At a hotel bar, tip €1 and up for a round or two of drinks.

Italians rarely tip taxi drivers, which isn't to say that you shouldn't. A euro or two is appreciated, particularly if the driver helps with luggage. Service-station attendants are tipped only for special services; give them €1 for checking your tires. Railway and airport porters charge a fixed rate per bag. Tip an additional €0.25 per person, more if the porter is helpful. Give a barber €1–€1.50 and a hairdresser's assistant €1.50–€4 for a shampoo or cut, depending on the type of establishment.

On sightseeing tours, tip guides about €1.50 per person for a half-day group tour, more if they're especially knowledgeable. In monasteries and other sights where admission is free, a contribution (€0.50–€1) is expected.

In hotels, give the *portiere* (concierge) about 10% of the bill for services, or €2.50–€5 for help with dinner reservations and such. Leave the chambermaid about €0.75 per day, or about €4.50–€5 a week in a moderately priced hotel; tip a minimum of €1 for valet or room service. In an expensive hotel, double these amounts; tip doormen €0.50 for calling a cab and €1.50 for carrying bags to the check-in desk and bellhops €1.50–€2.50 for carrying your bags to the room.

TOURS

Guided tours are a good option when you don't want to do it all yourself. You travel along with a group (sometimes large, sometimes small), stay in prebooked hotels, eat with your fellow travelers (the cost of meals may or may not be included in the price of your tour), and follow a schedule. Not all guided tours are an if-it's-Tuesday-this-must-be-Belgium experience, however. A knowledgeable guide can take you places that you might never discover on your own, and you may be pushed to see more than you would have otherwise. Tours aren't for everyone, but they can be just the thing for trips to places where making travel arrangements is difficult or time-consuming, particularly when you don't speak the language.

Whenever you book a guided tour, find out what's included and what isn't. A "land-only" tour includes all your travel (by bus, in most cases) in the destination, but not necessarily your flights to and from or even within it. Also, in most cases prices in tour brochures don't include fees and taxes. You'll also want to review how much free as opposed to organized time you'll have, and see if that meets with your personal preferences. Remember, too, that you'll be expected to tip your guide (in cash) at the end of the tour.

Even when planning independent travel, keep in mind that every province and city in Italy has tour guides licensed by the government. Some are eminently qualified in relevant fields such as architecture and art history and are a pleasure to spend time with; others have simply managed to pass the test and have weaker interpersonal skills. Lots of private guides have Web sites: check online and in travel forums for recommendations. Best to book before you leave home, especially for major destinations, as popular guides and tours are in demand. Tourist offices and hotel concierges can also provide the names of knowledgeable local guides and the rates for certain services. When hiring on the spot, ask about their background and qualifications and make sure you can understand each other. Tipping is always appreciated, but never obligatory, for local guides.

Recommended Generalists
Abercrombie & Kent (*800/554–7016* *www.abercrombiekent.com*). **CIE Tours International** (*800/243–8687 +353 1/703 0888, in Ireland* *www.cietours.com*). **Maupin Tour** (*800/255–4266* *www.maupintour.com*). **Perillo Tours** (*800/431–1515* *www.perillotours.com*). **Travcoa** (*800/992–2005* *www.travcoa.com*).

Biking and Hiking Tour Contacts
Backroads (*800/462–2848* *www.backroads.com*). **Butterfield & Robinson** (*866/551–9090* *www.butterfield.com*). **Ciclismo Classico** (*800/866–7314* *www.ciclismoclassico.com*). **Genius Loci Travel** (*+39 089 791 896* *www.genius-loci.it*). **Italian Connection** (*800/462–7911* *www.italian-connection.com*).

Culinary Tour Contact Epiculinary (*888/380–9010* *www.epiculinary.com*).

Volunteer Programs Road Scholar (*800/454–5768* *www.roadscholar.org*).

Wine Tour Contacts Cellar Tours (*310/4368061* *www.cellartours.com*). **Food & Wine Trails** (*800/367–5348* *www.foodandwinetrails.com*).

TRIP INSURANCE

Comprehensive trip insurance is valuable if you're booking an expensive or complicated trip (particularly to an isolated region) or if you're booking far in advance. Comprehensive policies typically cover trip cancellation and interruption, letting you cancel or cut your trip short because of illness (yours or someone back home), or, in some cases, acts of terrorism in your destination. Such policies usually also cover evacuation and medical care. (For trips abroad you should have at least medical and medical evacuation coverage. With a few exceptions, Medicare doesn't provide coverage abroad, nor does regular health insurance.) Some also cover you for trip delays because of bad weather or mechanical problems as well as for lost or delayed luggage.

Another type of coverage to consider is financial default—that is, when your trip is disrupted because a tour operator, airline, or cruise line goes out of business. Generally you must buy this when you book your trip or shortly thereafter, and it's available to you only if your operator isn't on a list of excluded companies.

Many travel insurance policies have exclusions for preexisting conditions as a cause for cancellation. Most companies waive those exclusions, however, if you take out your policy within a short period (which varies by company) after the first payment toward your trip.

Always read the fine print of your policy to make sure that you're covered for the risks that most concern you. Compare several policies to be sure you're getting the best price and range of coverage available.

Insurance Comparison Info Insure My Trip (☎ *800/487–4722* ⊕ *www.insuremytrip.com*). **Square Mouth** (☎ *800/240–0369 or 727/564–9203* ⊕ *www.squaremouth.com*).

Comprehensive Insurers Access America (☎ *800/284–8300* ⊕ *www.accessamerica.com*). **CSA Travel Protection** (☎ *877/243–4135* ⊕ *www.csatravelprotection.com*). **HTH Worldwide** (☎ *610/254–8700* ⊕ *www.hthworldwide.com*). **Travel Guard** (☎ *800/826–4919* ⊕ *www.travelguard.com*). **Travelex Insurance** (☎ *800/228–9792* ⊕ *www.travelex-insurance.com*). **Travel Insured International** (☎ *800/243–3174* ⊕ *www.travelinsured.com*).

INDEX

D

H

I

J

U

V

PHOTO CREDITS

1, Paul D'Innocenzo. 2-3, PCL/Alamy. 5, Javier Larrea/age footstock. Experience Italy: 10-11, Paul D'Innocenzo. 12, Thomas Barrat/Shutterstock. 13 (left and right), Ackab Photography/Shutterstock. 14 (top), Peter Clark/Shutterstock. 14 (bottom), Alfio Ferlito/Shutterstock. 15, Olav Wildermann/Shutterstock. 16, Ant Clausen/Shutterstock. 18, Albo/Shutterstock. 19 (left), Antonio Petrone/Shutterstock. 19 (right), vario images GmbH & Co.KG / Alamy. 20 (left), Ronald Sumners/Shutterstock. 20 (top center), Victoria German/Shutterstock. 20(top right), Knud Nielsen/Shutterstock. 20(bottom right), pxlar8/Shutterstock. 21(left), Casper Voogt/Shutterstock, 21 (top center), John Lumb/Shutterstock. 21 (top right), Ivonne Wierink/Shutterstock. 21 (bottom right), Alfio Ferlito/Shutterstock. 22, italianestro/Shutterstock. 23 (left), Thomas M Perkins/Shutterstock. 23 (right), Yanta/Shutterstock. 24, Eric Gevaert/Shutterstock. 25, Stefano Cellai/age fotostock. 26, Gina Sanders/Shutterstock. Part I: Rome and Environs: 30-31, SIME s.a.s / eStock Photo. 32, Paul D'Innocenzo. 33 (left), Angelo Campus. 33 (right), Paul D'Innocenzo. 36 (left), Angelo Campus. 36 (top center), Paul D'Innocenzo. 36 (top right), Angelo Campus. 36(bottom right), Angelo Campus. 37 (top left), Paul D'Innocenzo. 37 (right), Public Domain. 37 (bottom left), Angelo Campus. 38, Angelo Campus. 39 (left), Angelo Campus. 39 (right), Paul D'Innocenzo. 41 (left and right), Angelo Campus. 42, Angelo Campus. 43 (left and right), Angelo Campus. 44, Jono Pandolfi. 45 (top), Angelo Campus. 45 (bottom), Jono Pandolfi. 46, Paul D'Innocenzo. Chapter 1: Rome: 47, Angelo Campus. 48, Paul D'Innocenzo. 51 (left), Justin D. Paola. 51 (right), Edis Jurcys/age fotostock. 52-53 (bottom), Justin D. Paola. 53 (top left and right), Joe Viesti/viestiphoto.com. 54-55 (bottom), Justin D. Paola. 55 (top left), Rome Tourist Board. 55 (top right), Atlantide S.N.C./age fotostock. 57 (left), Chie Ushio. 57 (right), Joe Viesti/viestiphoto.com. 59 (left), Chie Ushio. 59 (right), Corbis. 80-81, SuperStock. 80 (bottom), Public Domain. 82, Russell Mountford/age fotostock. 84-87, Dave Drapak. Chapter 2: Side Trips from Rome:131, dave tonkin/iStockPhoto. 132 (top), Maurizio Farnetti/Shutterstock. 132 (bottom), Vito Arcomano/Fototeca ENIT. 134, avatra images/Alamy. Part II: Northern Italy. 154-155, Peter Adams/Agency Jon Arnold Images/age fotostock. 156, Steven Lee/Shutterstock. 157 (left), silvano audisio/Shutterstock. 157 (right), Patricia Hofmeester/Shutterstock. 160 (left), Paul Reid/Shutterstock. 160 (top center), Thomas M Perkins/Shutterstock. 160 (right), Public Domain. 160 (bottom), Rostislav Glinsky/Shutterstock. 161 (left), Public Domain. 161

(top center), Giovanni/Shutterstock. 161(right), Public Domain. 161(bottom), RookCreations/Shutterstock. 162, Izmael/Shutterstock. 163, Alfonso 'Agostino/Shutterstock. 164, Ljupco Smokovski/Shutterstock.166, Seet/Shutterstock. Chapter 3: Venice: 167, Paul D'Innocenzo. 168 (top), Nicole Vogels, Fodors.com member 168 (bottom), John Fasciani, Fodors.com member. 169, J.J. Burns, Fodors.com member. 170, Paul D'Innocenzo. 171 (top), Bon Appetit / Alamy. 171 (bottom), Robert Milek/Shutterstock. 172, S. Greg Panosian/iStockphoto. 177, Walter Bibikow/viestiphoto.com. 178, Alexey Arkhipov/Shutterstock. 179 (left), M. Spancer/viestiphoto.com. 179 (right), Paul D'Innocenzo. 180, Javier Larrea/age fotostock. 181 (left), Steve Allen/Brand X Pictures. 181 (right), Doug Scott/age fotostock. 182, Bruno Morandi/age fotostock. 183 (left), Corbis. 183 (right), Sergio Pitamitz/age fotostock. Chapter 4: The Venetian Arc: 241, Wojtek Buss/age fotostock. 242 (top), wikipedia.org. 242 (bottom) and 243, Vito Arcomano/Fototeca ENIT. 244, Francesco Majo/age footstock. 245 (bottom), Michele Bella/age fotostock. 245 (top), Danilo Donadoni/age fotostock. 246, vesilvio/iStockphoto. 261 and 262 (top), from Quattro Libri by Andrea Palladio. 262 (bottom), Classic Vision/age fotostock 263, Erich Lessing / Art Resource. 264 (left), Vito Arcomano/Fototeca ENIT. 264 (right), Wojtek Buss/age fotostock 265, Wojtek Buss/age fotostock. Chapter 5: The Dolomites: 293, Angelani/fototeca Trentino. 294 (top), gpatchet, Fodors.com member. 294 (bottom), Angelani/fototeca Trentino 295 (top and bottom), Vito Arcomano/Fototeca ENIT. 296, Danilo Donadoni/age fotostock. 297 (bottom), CuboImages srl / Alamy. 297 (top), franco pizzochero/age fotostock. 298, MartinDry/Shutterstock. 322, APT Dolomiti di Brenta/Fototeca ENIT. Chapter 6: Milan, Lombardy, and the Lakes: 329, Worldscapes/age fotostock. 330 (top), Corbis. 330 (bottom), APT del Comasco. 331, RookCreations/Shutterstock. 332, Danilo Donadoni/age fotostock. 333 (top), ubik/age fotostock. 333 (bottom), g.lancia/Shutterstock. 334, Public domain. 358-60, Antonio Dalle Rive/Anyway Group. 361 (top), Alan Copson/age fotostock. 361 (bottom left), Antonio Dalle Rive/Anyway Group. 361 (bottom right), Javier Larrea/age fotostock. Chapter 7: Piedmont and Valle d'Aosta:393, Paroli Galpertii/viestiphoto.com. 394 (top), Krom/Shutterstock. 394 (bottom), Giuseppe Bressi/Fototeca ENIT. 395 (top), Roberto Borgo/Turismo Torino. 395 (bottom), Vito Arcomano/Fototeca ENIT. 396, CuboImages srl / Alamy. 397 (bottom), Piga & Catalano/age fotostock. 397 (top), Danilo Donadoni/age fotostock. 398, Dario Egidi/Stockphoto. 419 (top), Targa/age fotostock 419 (bottom), R&D Valterza/viestiphoto.com. 420, Michele Bella/viestiphoto.com. 421 (top and bottom), Targa/age fotostock. Chapter 8: The Italian Riviera: 435, silvano audisio/Shutterstock. 436 (left), Vincent Thompson, Fodors.com member. 436 (right), Kelli Glaser, Fodors.com member. 437 (top), luri/Shutterstock. 437 (bottom Left), skyfish/Shutterstock. 437 (bottom right), Tifonimages/Shutterstock. 438, PCL / Alamy. 439 (top), ubik/age fotostock. 439 (bottom), Bon Appetit / Alamy. 440, laura rizzi/Stockphoto. 449, Walter Bibikow/viestiphoto.com. 450 (top left), Peter Phipp/age fotostock. 450 (top center), Walter Bibikow/viestiphoto.com 450 (top right), Loren Irving/age fotostock. 450 (bottom), Carson Ganci/age fotostock. 451 (left), Angelo Cavalli/age fotostock., 451 (center), Cornelia Doerr/age fotostock. 451 (bottom), Bruno Morandi/age fotostock. 453 (top), Adriano Bacchella/viestiphoto.com. 453 (bottom), Walter Bibikow/viestiphoto.com. 454 (top), José Fuste Raga/age fotostock. 454 (center), Walter Bibikow/viestiphoto.com. 454 (bottom), Vito Arcomano/Fototeca ENIT. 455 (top and bottom), Angelo Cavalli/age fotostock. 456, Atlantide S.N.C./age fotostock. Chapter 9: Emilia–Romagna: 485, Atlantide S.N.C./age fotostock. 486 (top), Atlantide S.N.C./age fotostock. 486 (bottom), Javier Larrea/age fotostock. 487 (top), FSG/age fotostock. 487 (bottom), Angelo Tondini/viestiphoto.com. 488 and 489 (top), Matz Sjöberg/age fotostock. 489 (bottom), franco pizzochero/age fotostock. 490, maria luisa berti/iStockphoto/Thinkstock. 501, John A. Rizzo/age fotostock. 502 (top two), Federico Meneghetti/viestiphoto.com. 502 (center), Consorzio del Prosciutto di Parma. 502 (center bottom), Federico Meneghetti/viestiphoto.com. 502 (bottom), Angelo Tondini/viestiphoto.com. 503 (top two), Consorzio del Formaggio Parmigiano-Reggiano. 503 (center), Federico Meneghetti/viestiphoto.com. 503 (center bottom), Federico Meneghetti/viestiphoto.com. 503 (bottom), Vito Arcomano/Fototeca ENIT. 504 (top), Adriano Bacchella/viestiphoto.com. 504 (bottom), Federico Meneghetti/viestiphoto.com. 505 (top two), John A. Rizzo/age fotostock. 505 (center), Atlantide S.N.C./age fotostock. 505 (center bottom), Archivio Fotografico Di Bologna Turismo. 505, (bottom), Artemisia/viestiphoto.com. Part III: Central Italy: 532-33, SIME s.a.s / eStock Photo. 534, Susan Hurlburt, Fodors.com member. 535 (left), Patrick S. Golden, Fodors.com member. 535 (right), esamberg50, Fodors.com member. 537, JAX9000, Fodors.com member. 538 (left), Gijs van Ouwerkerk/Shutterstock. 538 (top center), Anja Peternelj/Shutterstock. 538 (top right), Knud Nielsen/Shutterstock. 538 (bottom right), Paul Merrett/Shutterstock. 539 (left), Danilo Ascione/Shutterstock. 539 (top center), Franco Deriu/iStockPhoto. 539 (top right), Ivonne Wierink/Shutterstock. 539 (bottom right), John Henshall/Alamy. 540, Jeremy R. Smith Sr./Shutterstock. 541, Tamara Kenyon Photography, Fodors.com member. 542, fpmassa, Fodors.com member. 544, bruno pagnanelli/Shutterstock Chapter 10: Florence: 545, alysta/Shutterstock. 546 (top), Ronald Sumners/Shutterstock. 546 (bottom), PhotoDisc. 547,

Bertrand Collet/Shutterstock. 548, CuboImages srl / Alamy. 549 (top), Paolo Gallo / Alamy. 549 (bottom), Sue Wilson / Alamy. 550, Luboslav Tiles/Shutterstock. 560-61, Wojtek Buss/age fotostock. 562 (all), Public domain 563 (top), eye35.com/Alamy. 563 (inset), Alfio Giannotti/viestiphoto.com. 563 (bottom), Rough Guides / Alamy. 564 (top left), Mary Evans Picture Library / Alamy. 564 (top right), Library of Congress Prints and Photographs Division (LC-USZ62-105343). 564 (bottom), Bruno Morandi/age fotostock. 581 (left), Classic Vision/age fotostock. 581 (center), SuperStock/Super Stock/age fotostock. 581 (right), Classic Vision/age fotostock. 582 (left) Chie Ushio. 582 (right), Planet Art 583 (top), Classic Vision/age fotostock. 583 (center), SuperStock/Super Stock/age fotostock. 583 (bottom right), Corbis. 583 (bottom left), Wojtek Buss/age fotostock. 584 (left), Public Domain. 584 (center), SuperStock/age fotostock. 584 (right), Bruno Morandi/age fotostock. 585 (left), SuperStock/age fotostock. 585 (center), Sandro Vannini/viestiphoto.com. 585 (right), PTE/age fotostock. 586 (all), Planet Art. Chapter 11: Tuscany: 617, Cornelia Doerr/age fotostock. 618 (top), CarlB9090, Fodors.com member. 618 (bottom), Maugli/Shutterstock. 619, Julius Honnor. 620, Bon Appetit / Alamy. 621 (top), marco scataglini/age fotostock. 621 (bottom), nico tondini/age fotostock. 622, javarman/Shutterstock. 639 (left), Black Rooster Consortium. 639 (top right), Cephas Picture Library / Alamy. 639 (center right), Adriano Bacchella/viestiphoto.com. 639 (bottom right), Cephas Picture Library / Alamy. 640, Cephas Picture Library / Alamy. 641 (left), Chuck Pefley / Alamy. 641 (right), Jon Arnold Images / Alamy. 642 (top left), CuboImages srl / Alamy. 642 (right), Cephas Picture Library / Alamy. 642 (bottom left), Black Rooster Consortium. 644 (left), Steve Dunwell/age fotostock. 644 (top right), IML Image Group Ltd / Alamy. 644 (bottom right), www.stradavinonobile.it. 658, Javier Larrea/age fotostock. 658 (inset), Photodisc. 660(top and center), Vittorio Sciosia/viestiphoto.com. 660 (bottom), Bruno Morandi/age fotostock. Chapter 12: Umbria and the Marches: 677, Atlantide S.N.C./age fotostock. 678, magicinfoto/Shutterstock 679, sano7/Shutterstock. 680, B&Y Photography/Alamy. 681 (top), MEHMET OZCAN/iStockphoto 681 (bottom), Doco Dalfiano/age fotostock. 682, Ale_s/Shutterstock. 695, Atlantide S.N.C./age fotostock. 696, Picture Finders/age fotostock 697 (all), Fototeca ENIT. 698, Atlantide S.N.C./age fotostock. Part IV: Southern Italy 724-25, Chris Sargent/Shutterstock. 726, Yanta/Shutterstock. 727(left), cristina ferrari/Shutterstock. 727 (right), Bensliman/Shutterstock. 728, ollirg/Shutterstock., 729, Ivan Cholakov/Shutterstock. 730 (left), Valeria73/Shutterstock. 730 (top center), John Lumb/Shutterstock. 730 (top right), wikipedia.org. 730 (bottom right), Alfio Ferlito/Shutterstock. 731 (left), Ventura/Shutterstock. 731 (top center), wikipedia.org. 731 (top right), Danilo Donadoni/age fotostock. 731 (bottom right), ollirg/Shutterstock. 732, akva/Shutterstock. 733, flabobcat, Fodors.com member. 734, Danilo Ascione/Shutterstock. 736, Mario Savoia/Shutterstock Chapter 13: Naples and Campania: 737, Stephen Miller, Fodors.com member. 738, Paola Ghirotti/Fototeca ENIT. 739 (top), Vacclav/Shutterstock. 739 (bottom), Katie Hamlin. 740, LOOK Die Bildagentur der Fotografen GmbH / Alamy. 741 (top), CuboImages srl / Alamy. 741 (bottom), Bon Appetit / Alamy. 742, tony french/Almy. 758, Campania Tourism. 759 (top), Mary Evans Picture Library / Alamy. 759 (top center), CuboImages srl / Alamy. 759 (center), Cephas Picture Library / Alamy. 759 (bottom center), Peter Horree / Alamy. 759 (bottom), Alvaro Leiva/age fotostock. 771 (top), Vincent Leblic/PHOTONONSTOP. 771 (bottom), Robert Frerck/Odyssey Productions, Inc. 772, Joe Viesti/viestiphoto.com. 773 (top), Demetrio Carrasco/Agency Jon Arnold Images/age fotostock. 773 (bottom), Peter Phipp/age fotostock. 774 (top), Vito Arcomano/Fototeca ENIT. 774 (center), Demetrio Carrasco/Agency Jon Arnold Images/age fotostock 774 (bottom), Joe Malone/Agency Jon Arnold Images/age fotostock. 775, Doug Scott/age fotostock. 776, Katie Hamlin. 777, Demetrio Carrasco/Agency Jon Arnold Images/age fotostock. Chapter 14: Puglia, Basilicata, and Calabria: 809, José Fuste Raga/age fotostock. 810, Vito Arcomano/Fototeca ENIT, 811, velefante/Shutterstock. 812, CuboImages srl / Alamy 813 (top), davide cerati/age fotostock. 813 (bottom), Tim Hill / Alamy. 814, Mi. Ti./Shutterstock. Chapter 15: Sicily: 845, Peeter Viisimaa/iStockphoto. 846 (top), Vito Arcomano/Fototeca ENIT. 846 (bottom), VIZE/Shutterstock. 847, Corbis RF. 848, Yadid Levy/age fotostock. 849 (top), Yadid Levy/age fotostock. 849 (bottom), JTB Photo Communications, Inc. / Alamy. 850, Angelo Giampiccolo/Shutterstock. 878, Alvaro Leiva/age fotostock. 880, Corbis. 881, Joe Viesti/viestiphoto.com.

ABOUT OUR WRITERS

After her first Italian coffee and her first Italian *bacio* in 1999, **Nicole Arriaga** headed to the Eternal City to work on her master's degree at Rome's La Sapienza University, write for *The American*, and work for American Study Abroad. She helped to update our Rome coverage.

Martin Wilmot Bennett's vast background in Italian art and civilization made him a natural to update our Naples Exploring section. A graduate of Cambridge University, he teaches at Rome's University of Tor Vergata.

After completing his master's degree in art history, **Peter Blackman,** updater of the Tuscany and Piedmont chapters, settled permanently in Italy in 1986. Since then he's worked as a biking and walking tour guide. When he's not leading a trip, you'll find Peter at home in Florence.

Specializing in the Neapolitan art of *arrangiarsi* (getting by), Campania updater **Fergal Kavanagh** has dabbled in teacher training, DJ-ing, writing guidebooks, translating, and organizing cultural exchanges. He currently teaches at the University of Naples and through his Web site (www.tuneintoenglish.com) demonstrates how pop music can help students learn English.

Bruce Leimsidor studied Renaissance literature and art history at Swarthmore College and Princeton University, and in addition to his scholarly works he has published articles on political and social issues in the *International Herald Tribune* and the *Frankfurter Allgemeine Zeitung*. He lives in Venice, where he teaches at the university, works for the municipality, collects 17th- and 18th-century drawings, and is rumored to make the best *pasta e fagioli* in town. He updated the Venice Exploring section and the Veneto and Friuli–Venezia Giulia chapter.

Eric J. Lyman, updater of our Sicily chapter, is a former chef and avid traveler who's been a freelance journalist based in Rome for the last decade. His work has appeared in *The Wall Street Journal*, *USA Today*, *Time*, and dozens of other publications. For more information, visit www.ericjlyman.com.

After a dozen trips to and a two-decade-long love affair with Liguria, Italian Riviera updater **Megan McCaffrey-Guerrera** moved to the seaside village of Lerici in 2004. Soon after, she started a personal travel concierge service. When not organizing tailor-made vacations of the area, Megan can be found hiking the trails of the Cinque Terre, sailing the Gulf of Poets, or searching for the freshest anchovies in the Mediterranean.

Nan McElroy is the author of the palm-size, purely practical *Italy: Instructions for Use*. (The series also includes France and Greece.) She traveled throughout Italy before relocating to Venice in 2004, where she writes www.livingveniceblog.com and publishes the Vap Map downloadable vaporetto guide. Nan is also an AIS sommelier who conducts wine tastings and an avid practitioner of the *voga alla veneta*—traditional Venetian rowing. She updated the Venice dining, lodging, arts, and shopping coverage.

Katie Parla, updater of the Rome Exploring and Where to Eat sections, is a travel writer and private guide with a degree in art history from Yale and a master's in food and wine history from the University of Rome Tor Vergata. She has lived in Rome since 2003 and spends as much time as she can traveling to Puglia, Naples, and Sicily. You can live vicariously through her travel and food experiences at her blog, www.ParlaFood.com.

Writer, photographer, and digital strategist **Sara Rosso** moved to Italy in July 2003 and has lived in Rome and Pavia as well as her current home, Milan. In her blog www.msadventuresinitaly.com she writes about cooking and her travels in Italy and beyond (24 countries and counting). She udpated the Milan, Lombardy, and the Lakes chapter.

Florence updater **Patricia Rucidlo** holds master's degrees in Italian Renaissance history and art history, and after a year of arduous study earned her license to be a tour guide in Florence. When she's not extolling the virtues of a Pontormo masterpiece or angrily defending the Medici, she's leading tours and catering private dinner parties.

A specialist in Neapolitan culture and art history, Campania updater **Fiorella Squillante** leads visits to the stately homes and private collections of Naples. Along with her laurea (bachelor's degree) in modern languages and her license as a tour guide in Campania, she also works for the education departments of the major museums of the city.

During her four decades in Rome, **Margaret Stenhouse** was correspondent for Scotland's leading daily, *The Herald,* and a contributor to the *International Herald Triune* and the monthly *Italy Italy.* She now lives in the Castelli Romani hills south of Rome and serves as updater of our Rome Side Trips chapter.

An editor, travel writer, and naturalist, **Mark Walters** first settled in Naples as a British Council lecturer in the 1980s. He spends several months a year leading tours around the Mediterranean. For this edition of the guide he updated the chapter covering Puglia, Basilicata, and Calabria

Jonathan Willcocks, a Brit by birth with degrees in French and English literature from the Sorbonne, teaches language, literature, and translation at the university in Perugia. He updated the Umbria chapter.